Street by Street

CHESHIRE

PLUS ALTRINCHAM, BRAMHALL, HAZEL GROVE, STOCKPORT, WHITCHURCH

Enlarged Areas Chester, Crewe, Ellesmere Port, Macclesfield, Nantwich, Northwich, Runcorn, Warrington, Widnes

Ist edition May 2001

© Automobile Association Developments Limited 2001

This product includes map data licensed from Ordnance Survey® with the permission of the Controller of Her Majesty's Stationery Office. © Crown copyright 2000. All rights reserved. Licence No: 399221.

Published by AA Publishing (a trading name of Automobile Association Developments Limited, whose registered office is Norfolk House, Priestley Road, Basingstoke, Hampshire, RG24 9NY. Registered number 1878835).

Mapping produced by the Cartographic Department of The Automobile Association.

A CIP Catalogue record for this book is available from the British Library.

Printed by G. Canale & C. s.p.a., Torino, Italy

The contents of this atlas are believed to be correct at the time of the latest revision. However, the publishers cannot be held responsible for loss occasioned to any person acting or refraining from action as a result of any material in this atlas, nor for any errors, omissions or changes in such material. The publishers would welcome information to correct any errors or omissions and to keep this atlas up to date. Please write to Publishing, The Automobile Association, Fanum House, Basing View, Basingstoke, Hampshire, RG21 4EA.

Ref: MX082

Key to map pages	ii-iii
Key to map symbols	iv-1
Enlarged scale pages	2-21
Street by Street	22-275
Index – towns & villages	276-277
Index – streets	278-316
Index – featured places	316-322

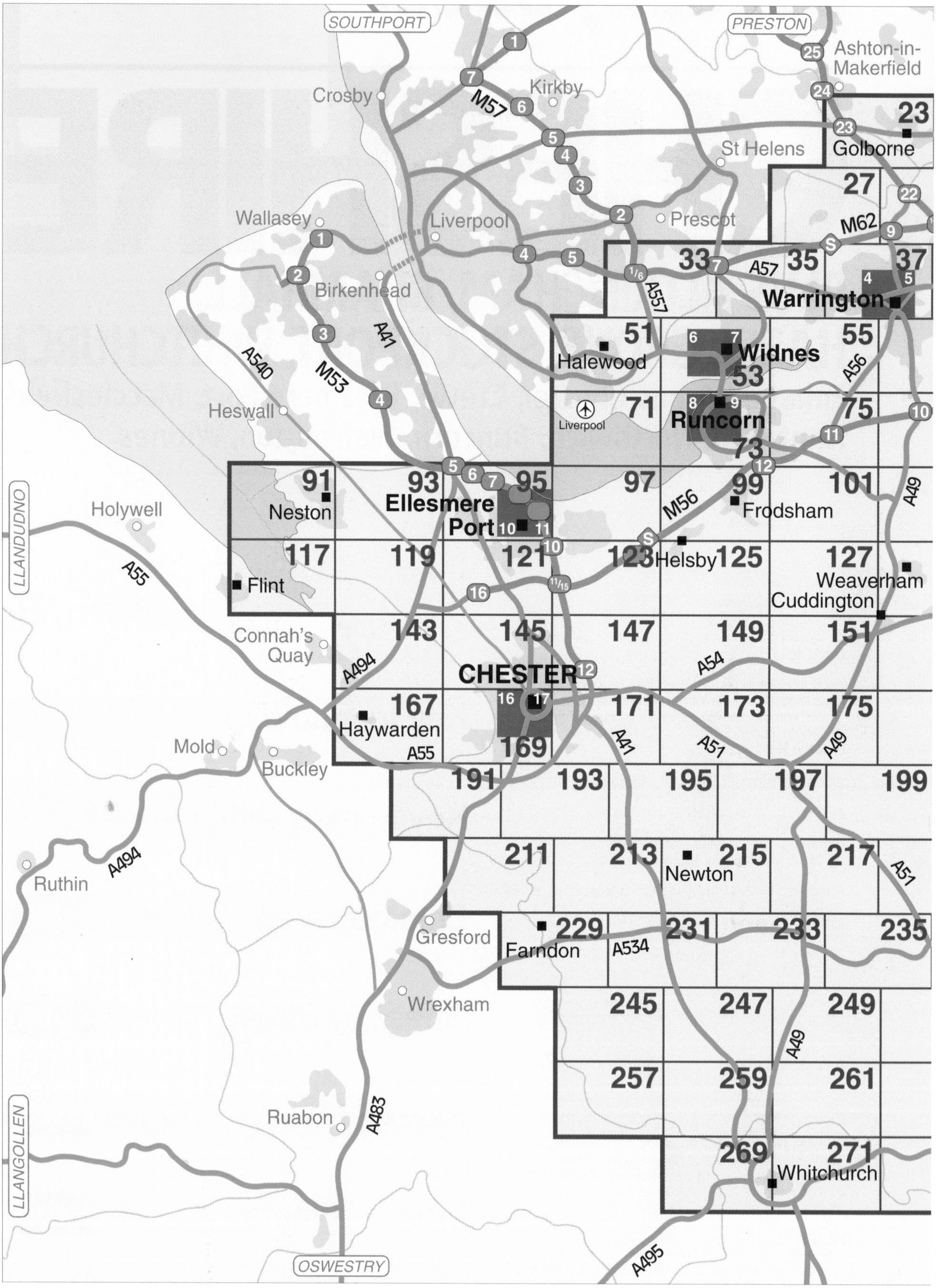

ii

SOUTHPORT

PRESTON

Ashton-in-Makerfield
25
24
23 Golborne
23

Crosby

7
M57
6

Kirkby

5
4

St Helens

27

22
M62
9

3

Wallasey

2

Prescot

Liverpool

33 7
A57
35

S

37

1

2

A41

Birkenhead

4

5

1/6
A557

4 5

Warrington

51

6 7

Widnes

55

A56

Halewood

53

M53

A540

3

Heswall

4

Liverpool

71

8 9

Runcorn

73

12

75

11

10

91
Neston

93

5 6 7

95
Ellesmere
Port

97

M56

99
Frodsham

101

A49

Holywell

10 11

10

LLANDUDNO

A55

117
Flint

119

121

11/15

123
Helsby

125

127
Weaverham
Cuddington

16

Connah's
Quay

143

145

147

149

151

A494

CHESTER

12

A54

Mold

167
Haywarden
A55

16 17

169

171
A41

173
A51

175
A49

Buckley

191

193

195

197

199

A494

Ruthin

211

213

215
Newton

217

A51

Gresford
Farndon

229
A534

231

233

235

Wrexham

245

247

249

A49

257

259

261

LLANGOLLEN

Ruabon

A483

269

271
Whitchurch

OSWESTRY

A495

Enlarged scale pages   **1:10,000**   **6.3 inches to 1 mile**

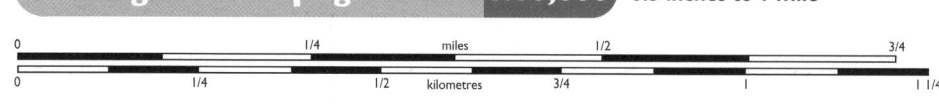

0   1/4   miles   1/2   3/4

0   1/4   1/2   kilometres   3/4   1   1 1/4

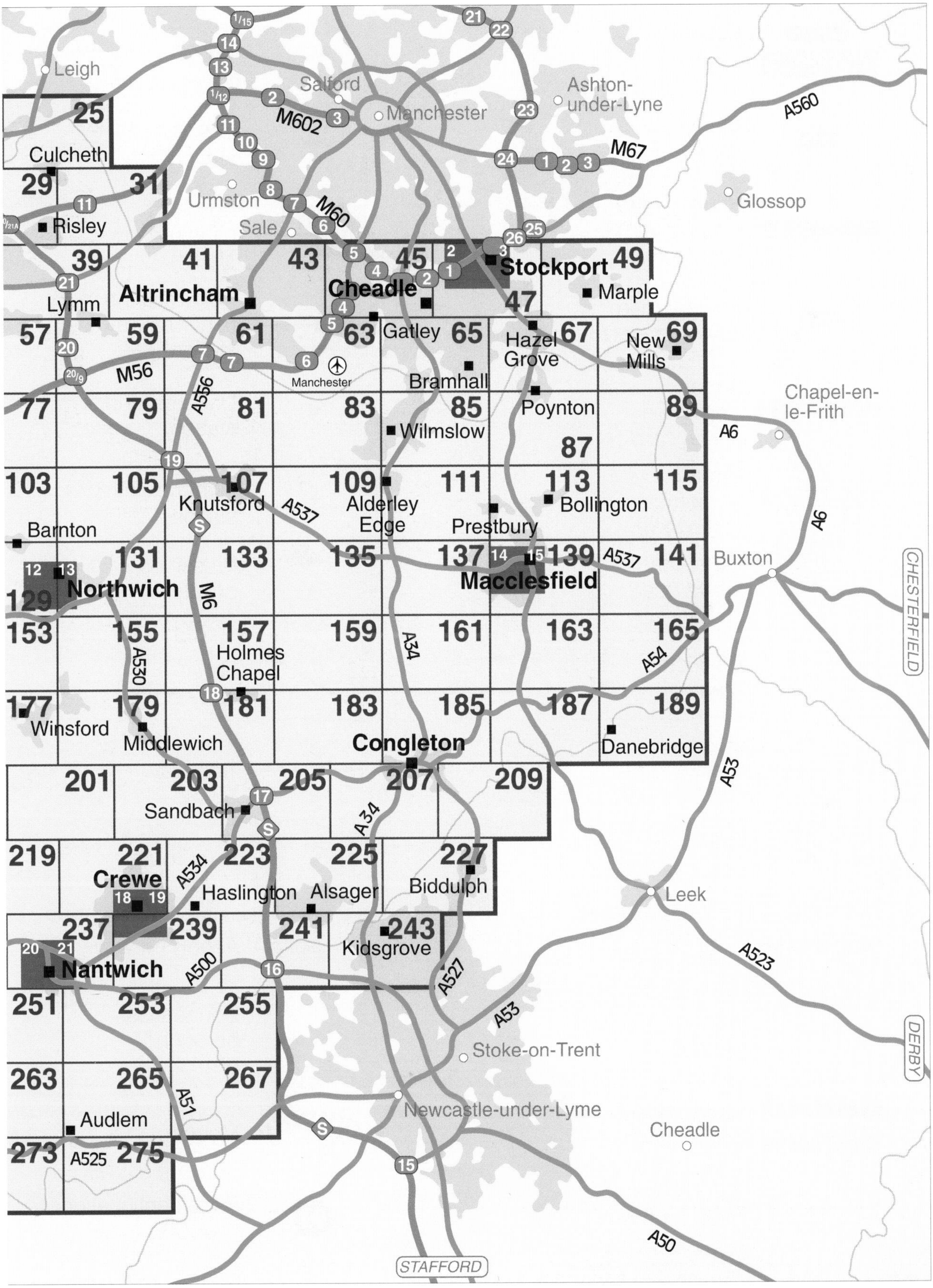

Leigh

25

Culcheth

1/15
14
13
1/12
11
10
9
8
7
6

Salford

M602
3

Manchester

21
22

Ashton-under-Lyne

23

A560

M67
24
1 2 3

Glossop

29 **31**

11

Risley

Urmston

Sale

26 25

1/21A

39

21

Lymm

41

Altrincham

43

M60

5
4

Cheadle

45
2
1

3

Stockport

49

Marple

57

20

20/9

M56

59

7
7

A556

61

6

Manchester

63

Gatley

65

Bramhall

Hazel Grove

67

New Mills

69

Chapel-en-le-Frith

77

79

19

81

83

Wilmslow

85

87

Poynton

89

A6

A6

CHESTERFIELD

103

Barnton

105

Knutsford

S

107

A537

109

Alderley Edge

111

Prestbury

113

Bollington

115

131

12 13

Northwich

M6

133

135

137

14 15

Macclesfield

139

A537

141

Buxton

129

153

155

A530

157

Holmes Chapel

159

A34

161

163

A54

165

177

Winsford

179

Middlewich

18

181

183

185

187

Danebridge

189

A53

201

Sandbach

203

17

S

205

207

A34

209

Leek

219

221

Crewe

18 19

A534

223

Haslington

Alsager

225

227

Biddulph

A523

237

20 21

Nantwich

239

A500

241

16

243

Kidsgrove

A527

A53

251

253

255

Stoke-on-Trent

263

265

A51

267

S

Newcastle-under-Lyme

Cheadle

DERBY

273

A525

275

STAFFORD

A50

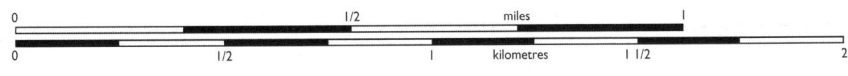

0   1/2   miles   1

0   1/2   1   kilometres   1 1/2   2

Junction 9	Motorway & junction
Services	Motorway service area
	Primary road single/dual carriageway
Services	Primary road service area
	A road single/dual carriageway
	B road single/dual carriageway
	Other road single/dual carriageway
	Restricted road
	Private road
← ←	One way street
	Pedestrian street
	Track/ footpath
	Road under construction
	Road tunnel
P	Parking

P+	Park & Ride
	Bus/coach station
	Railway & main railway station
	Railway & minor railway station
⊖	Underground station
⊖	Light railway & station
++++++++++	Preserved private railway
LC	Level crossing
•—•—•—•—•	Tramway
--------------	Ferry route
....	Airport runway
-·-·-·-·-	Boundaries- borough/ district
▼▼▼▼▼▼▼	Mounds
93	Page continuation 1:17,500
7	Page continuation to enlarged scale 1:10,000

River/canal lake, pier

Aqueduct lock, weir

465
▲
Winter Hill
Peak (with height in metres)

Beach

Coniferous woodland

Broadleaved woodland

Mixed woodland

Park

Cemetery

Built-up area

Featured building

City wall

A&E   Accident & Emergency hospital

Toilet

&   Toilet with disabled facilities

Petrol station

PH   Public house

PO   Post Office

Public library

i   Tourist Information Centre

Castle

Historic house/ building

Wakehurst Place NT   National Trust property

M   Museum/ art gallery

†   Church/chapel

Country park

Theatre/ performing arts

Cinema

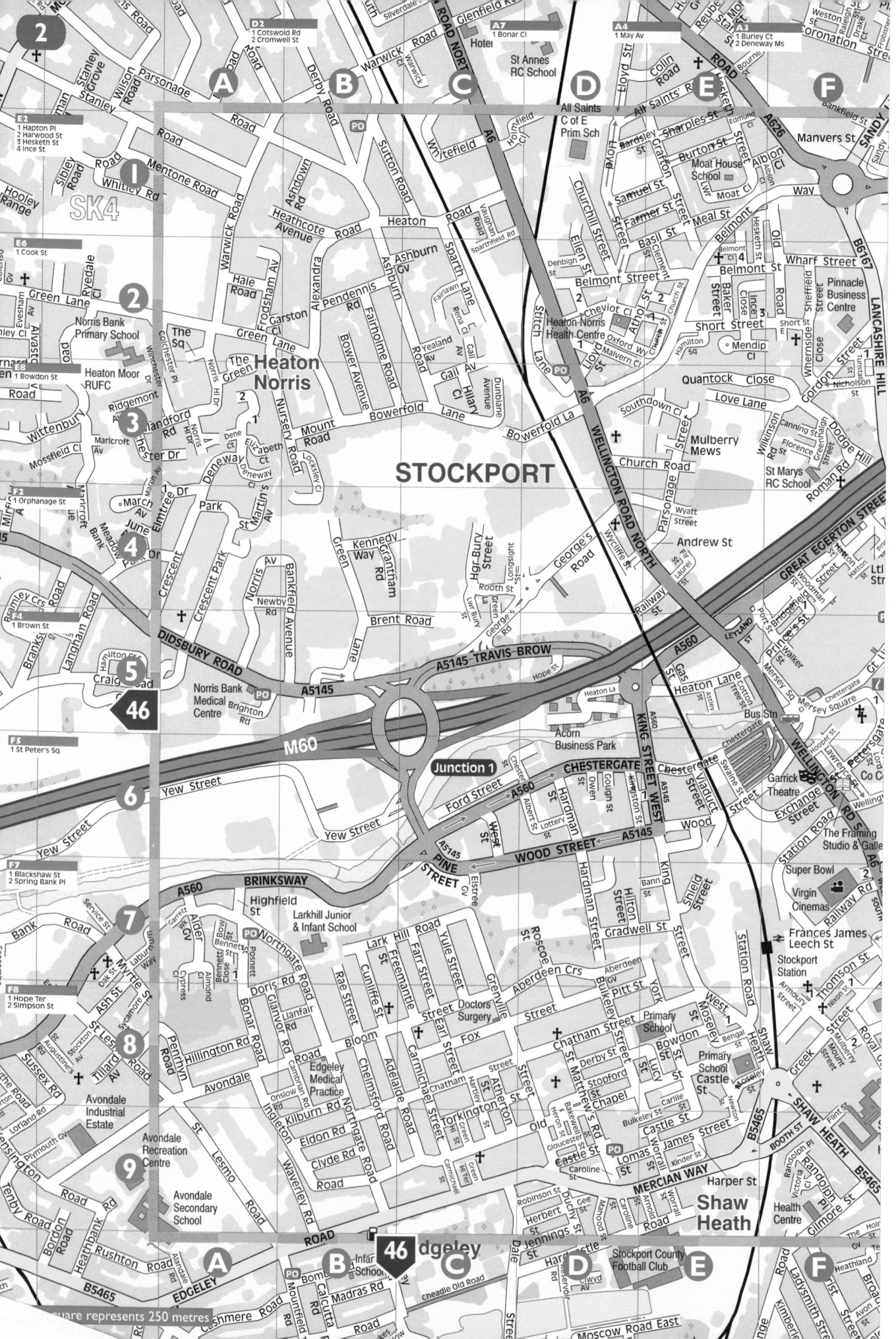

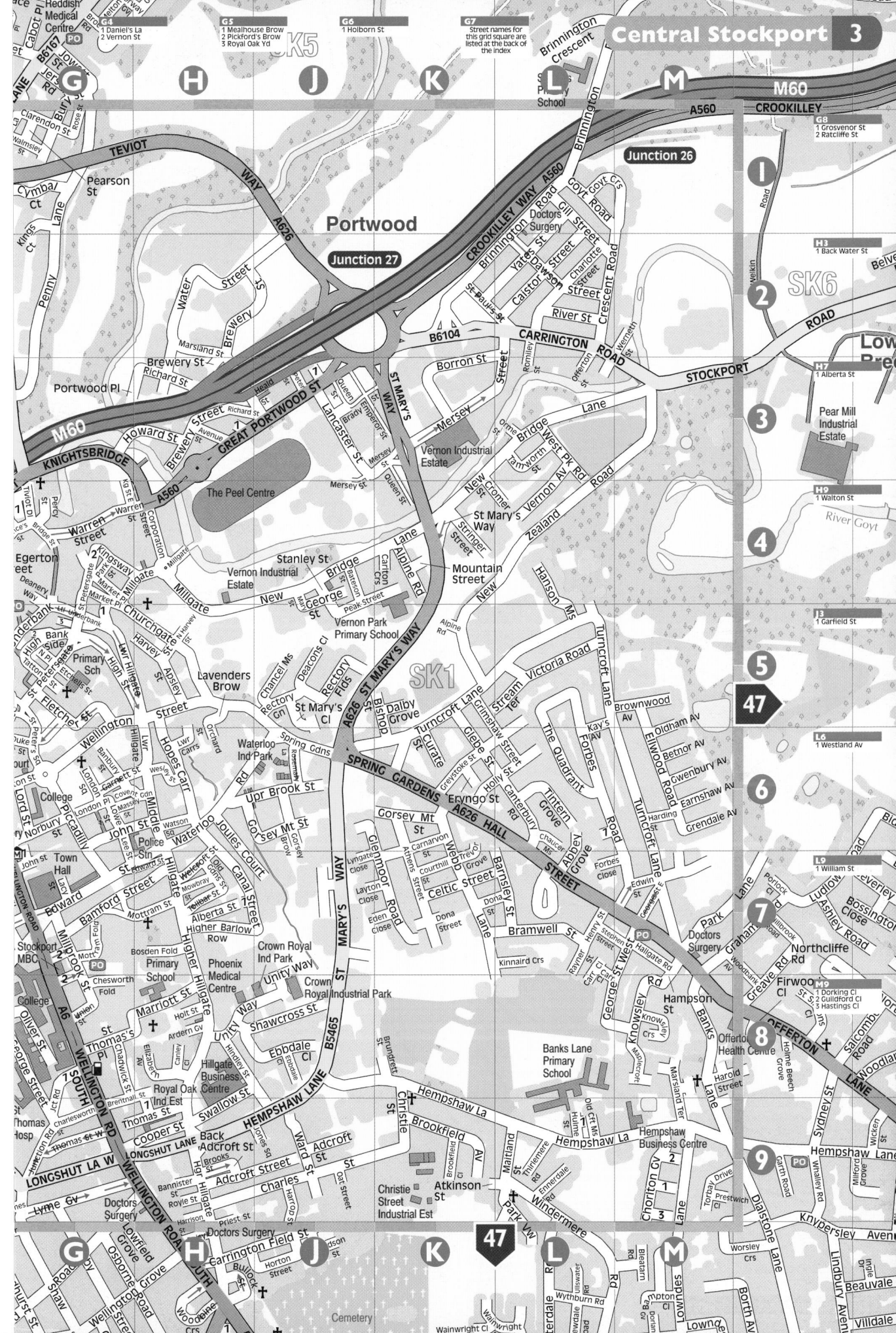

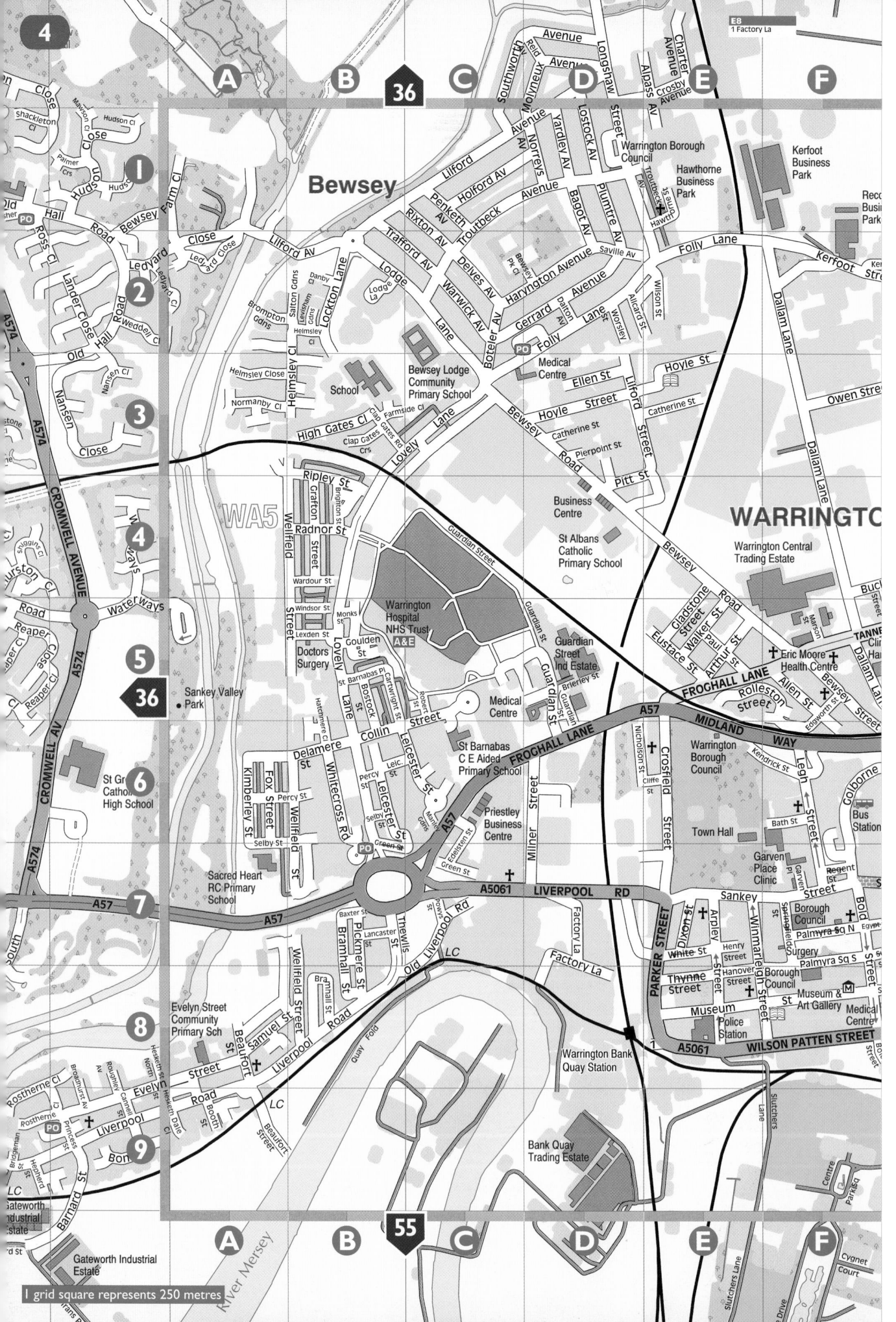

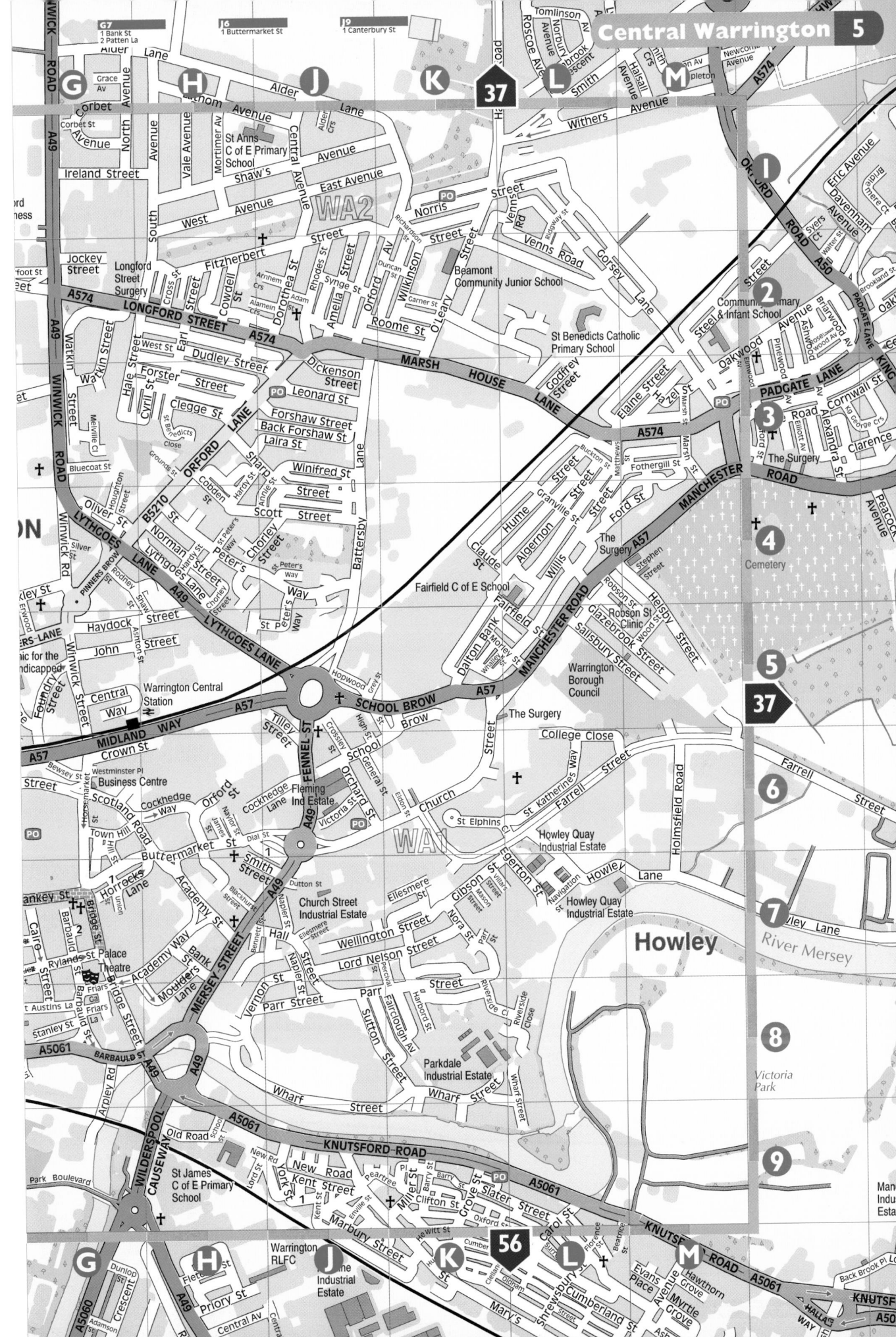

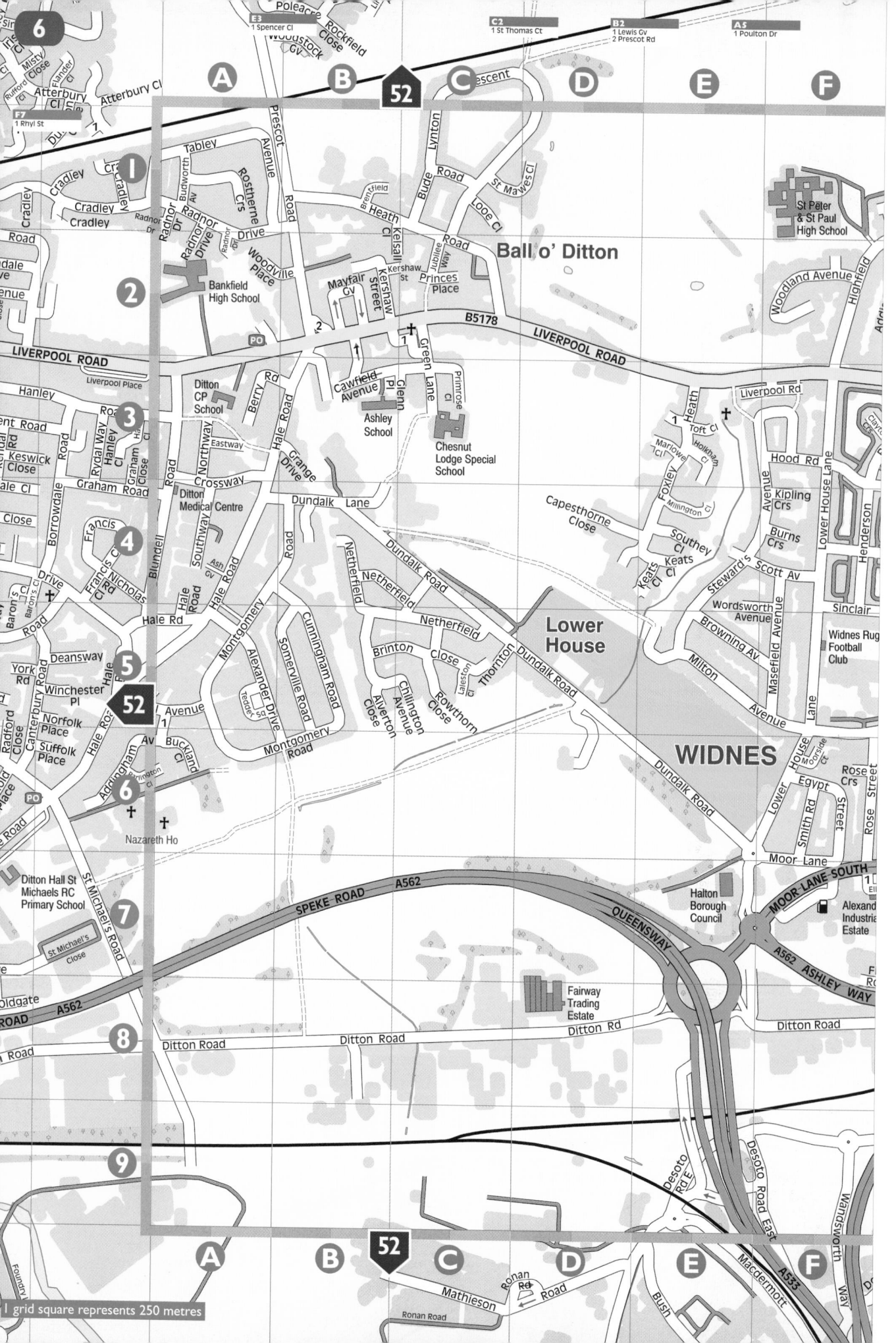

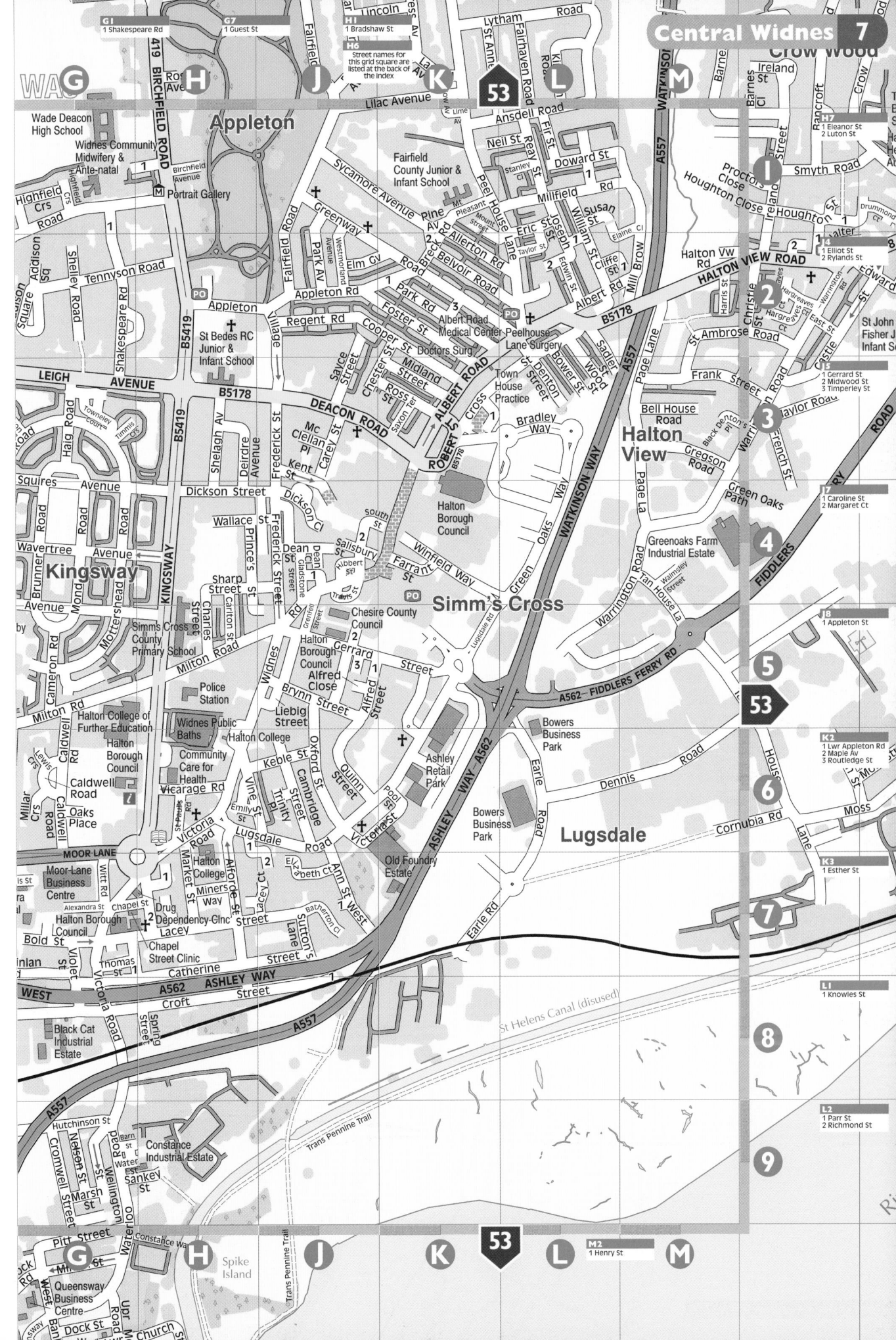

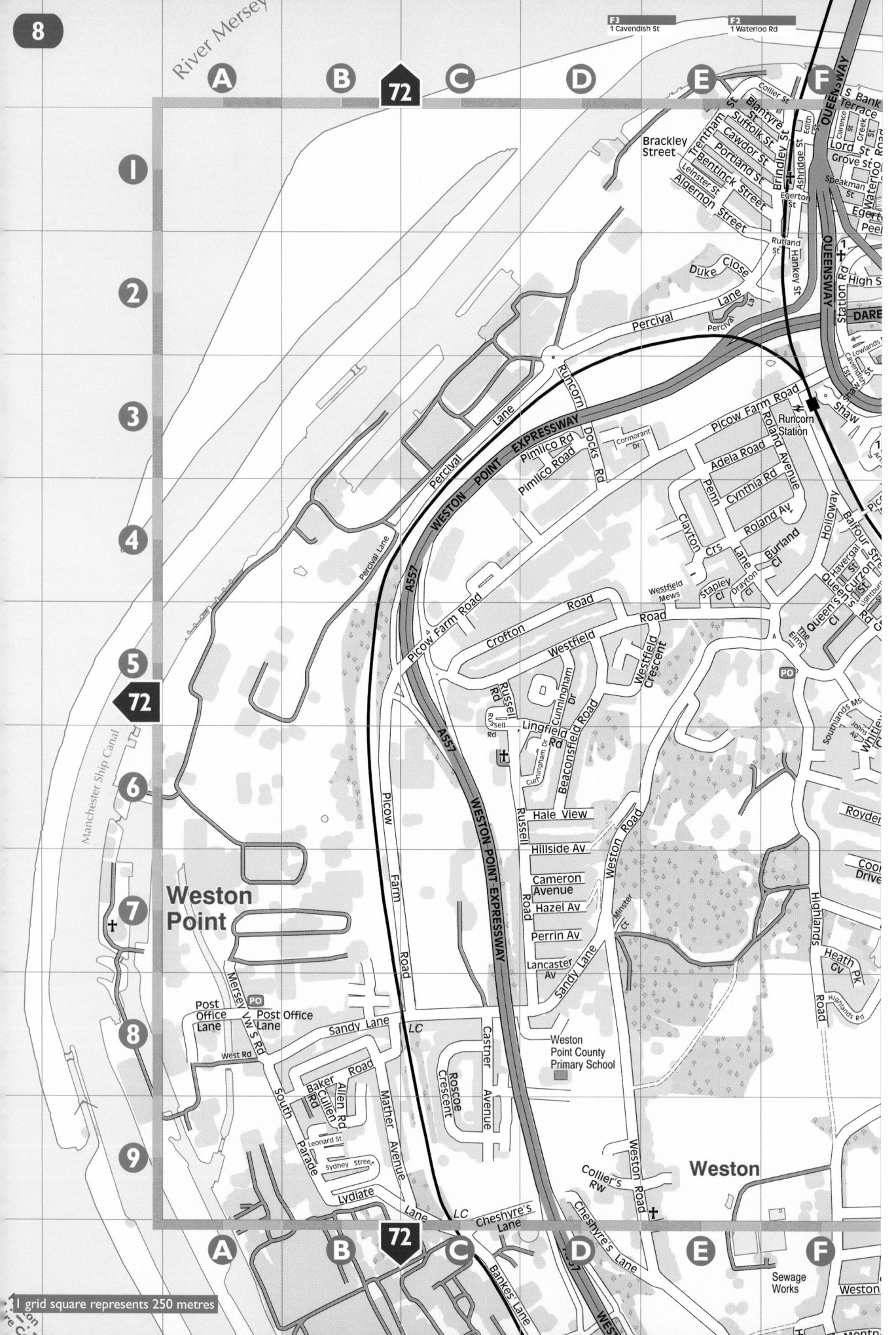

River Mersey

F3 1 Cavendish St
F2 1 Waterloo Rd

A B 72 C D E F

I

2

3

4

5 72

6

7

8

9

A B 72 C D E F

S Bank Terrace

Collier St

Blantyre St
Suffolk St
Cawdor St
Brindley St
Ashridge St
Edith St
Clarence St
Creek St
Lord St
Grove st
S Ol

Brackley Street

Bentinck St
Portland Street
Leinster St

Algernon Street

Speakman st

Egerton St

High St

Rutland st
Hankey St

Duke Close

Lane

Percival
La

Percival

DARE

QUEENSWAY

Percival

Lane

Runcorn

WESTON POINT EXPRESSWAY

Docks Rd
Pimlico Rd
Pimlico Road

Cormorant Dr

Picow Farm Road

Runcorn Avenue

Picow Station

Shaw

Adela Road

Penn

Cynthia Rd

Roland Av

Clayton

Roland Avenue

Lane

Burland Cl

Holloway

Balfour st

Picow

A557

Westfield Mews

Road

Road

Stapley Cl
Drayton Cl

Queen's

Curzon

The Elms

Queen's Cl
Rd

PO

Crofton

Westfield

Westfield Crescent

Russell Rd
Rd Russell

Cunningham Dr

Beaconsfield Road

Cunningham Dr

Lingfield Rd

A557

Russell

Highlands Ms

Whitle

Royden

Cook
Drive

Manchester Ship Canal

Hale View

Hillside Av

Cameron Avenue

Hazel Av

Perrin Av

Lancaster Av

Weston Road

Minster Ct

Sandy Lane

Highlands

Heath Gv

Highlands Rd

Road

Weston Point

Post Office Lane

PO

Mersey Vw S Rd

Post Office Lane

Sandy Lane

West Rd

LC

Baker Road

Cullen Rd
Allen Rd

South Parade

Leonard St

Sydney Street

Lydiate

Mather Avenue

Castner Avenue

Roscoe Crescent

LC

Weston Point County Primary School

Weston Road

Collier's Rw

Weston

Bankes Lane

Cheshyre's Lane

Cheshyre's Lane

WEST

Sewage Works

Weston

Montr

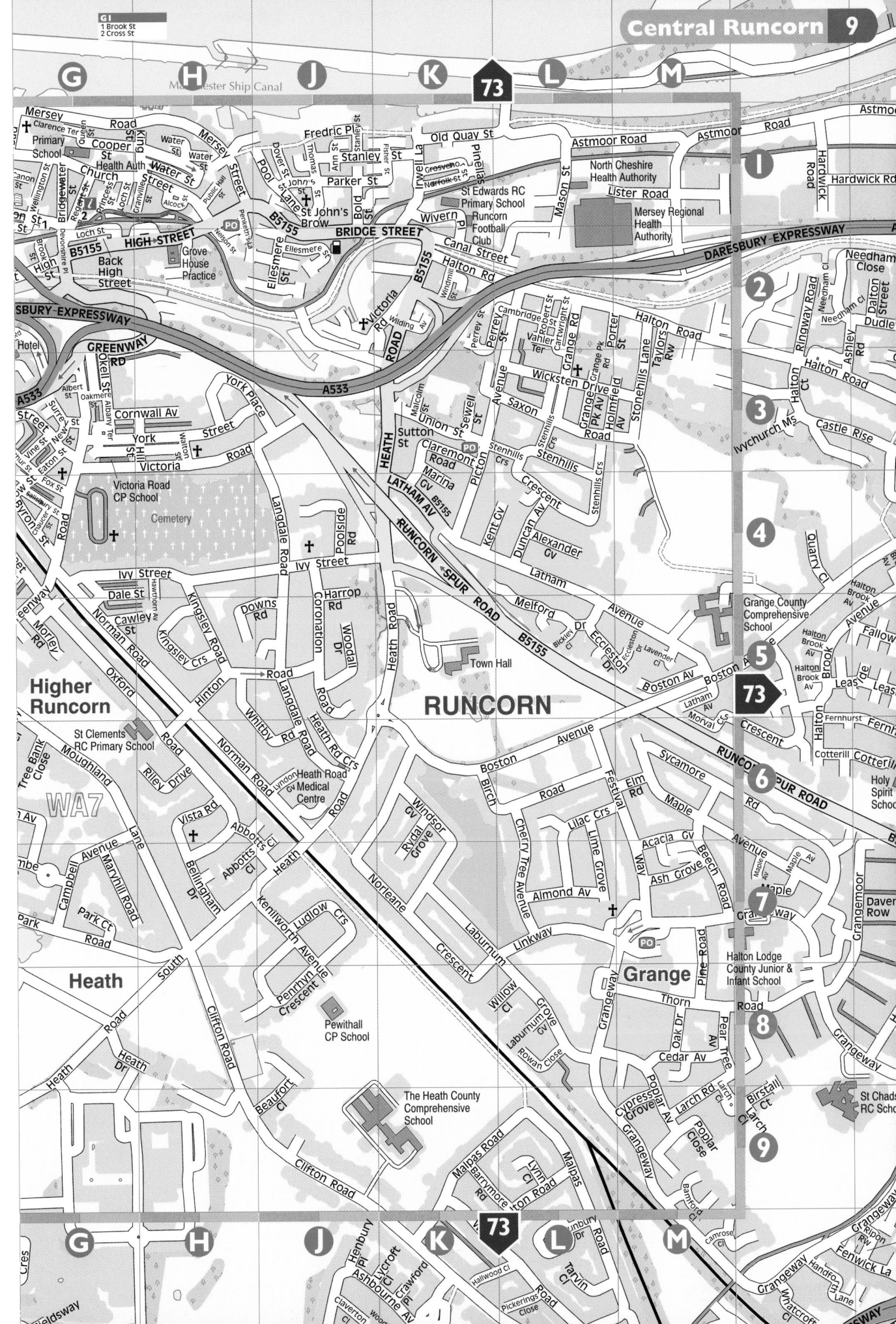

G1
1 Brook St
2 Cross St

G H J K 73 L M

Manchester Ship Canal

I 1

Mersey Road
Clarence Ter
Cooper St
Mersey
Primary
School
King St
Water St
Water St
Mersey Road
Fredric Pl
Stanley St
Thomas St
Ann St
Fisher St
Old Quay St
Pinellas
Astmoor Road
Astmoor Road
Astmoor
Road
Astmoor
Hardwick Road
Hardwick Road

Church St
Health Auth
Water Street
Dover St
John's St
Parker St
Bold St
Irwell La
Grosvenor St
Norfolk St
North Cheshire
Health Authority
Lister Road

2

Bridgewater
Canon
St
Wellington St
Devonshire Pl
Brook St
High St
Regent St
Princes St
Loch St
Alcock St
St John's
Brow
St Edwards RC
Primary School
Runcorn
Football
Club
Mersey Regional
Health
Authority
DARESBURY EXPRESSWAY

HIGH STREET
B5155
Back
High
Street
Grove House
Practice
Nelson Rd
Penketh Sq
Ellesmere St
Ellesmere St
BRIDGE STREET
B5155
Wivern
Canal Street
Halton Rd
B5155

B5155

Needham
Close
Needham Cl
Ringway Road
Needham Cl
Dalton
Street
Dudle

HESBURY EXPRESSWAY
A533
Hotel
GREENWAY RD
Okell St
Albert St
Oakmere St
A533
Victoria Rd
Wilding Av
Perrey St
Cambridge Rd
Robert St
Robert St
Cartwright St
Grange Rd
Porter St
Halton Road
Halton Road
Halton Road
Ashley Rd
Halton Rd
Ct

3
Ivychurch Ms
Castle Rise

Surrey St
Vine St
New St
Eaton St
Fox St
York Place
York
Street
Victoria
Road
Cornwall Av
Watson St
Hill St
Heath St
Sutton St
Union St
Sewell St
Avenue
Wicksten Drive
Grange Pk Av
Grange Rd
Holmfield
Grange
Pk Rd
Saxon Road
Stonehills Lane
Taylors Rw
Quarry Cl
Halton Brook Av
Fallow

Salisbury St
Byron St
Chaucer St
Victoria
Road
CP School
Cemetery
Heath Road
Claremont Road
Picton Av
Kent Gv
Stenhills Crs
Marina
Gv B5155
Stenhills
Crescent
Stenhills
Stenhills Crs
Grange County
Comprehensive
School
Halton
Brook Av

4
Halton Brook Av
Quarry Cl

Langdale Road
Poolside Rd
Ivy Street
LATHAM AV
RUNCORN SPUR ROAD
B5155
Duncan Av
Alexander Gv
Latham
Melford
Latham
Avenue
Boston Av
Halton Brook Av
Halton
Brook Av

5
73
Crescent
Fernhurst
Fernh
Leas
Leas

Ivy Street
Dale St
Hawthorn Av
Kingsley Road
Kingsley Crs
Downs Rd
Harrop Rd
Coronation Dr
Woodall Dr
Heath Road
Town Hall
RUNCORN
Bickley Cl
Eccleston Dr
Eccleston Dr
Lavender Cl
Boston Av
Boston Av
Latham
Ls
Morval Cs
RUNCORN SPUR ROAD
Cotterill
Cotterill
Holy Spirit School

6

Greenway
Morley Rd
Norman Road
Oxford Road
Cawley St
Whitby Rd
Langdale Road
Hinton Road
Road
Heath Rd Crs
Boston
Avenue
Birch Road
Festival Way
Sycamore Rd
Elm Rd
Maple Rd
Acacia Gv
Beech Road
Maple Av
Maple Av
Maple Av

7
Grangeway
Daver Row

Higher
Runcorn
St Clements
RC Primary School
Moughland
Tree Bank Close
Riley Drive
Vista Rd
Abbotts Cl
Heath Road
Lyndon Gv
Heath Road
Medical Centre
Windsor Gv
Rydal Grove
Cherry Tree Avenue
Lilac Crs
Lime Grove
Ash Grove
Almond Av
Grangeway
Avenue
Halton Lodge
County Junior &
Infant School
Road

8

WA7
Campbell Avenue
Maryhill Road
Park Ct Road
Bellingham Dr
Abbotts Cl
Kenilworth Avenue
Ludlow Crs
Penrhyn Crescent Cle
Norleane Crescent
Laburnum Crescent
Grove
Almond Av
Linkway
Thorn Rd
Oak Dr
Pine Road
Pear Tree Av
Cedar Av
Grange
PO
Poplar Av
Grangemoor
Grangeway
Grangeway

Heath
Combe
Park
South Road
Heath Road
Clifton Road
Pewithall
CP School
Willow Cl
Laburnum Gv
Rowan Close
Grove
Grangeway
Cypress Gv
Larch Rd
Poplar Close
Larch Rd
Larch Cl
Birstall Ct
St Chad's
RC Schol

9

Heath Rd
Heath Dr
Beaufort Cl
Clifton Road
The Heath County
Comprehensive
School
Malpas Road
Barrymore Rd
Lynn Cl
Lynton Road
Malpas
Malpas Road
Lunbury Dr
Tarvin Rd
Bamford
Camrose
Grangeway
Grangeway
Ripon
Handforth
Fenwick La

Fieldsway
Cres
Henbury Pl
Lycroft Cl
Ashbourne Av
Crawford
Claverton Cl
Woodfr
Hallwood Cl
Pickerings Close
Road
ESSWAY
Whitcroft

G H J 73 K L M

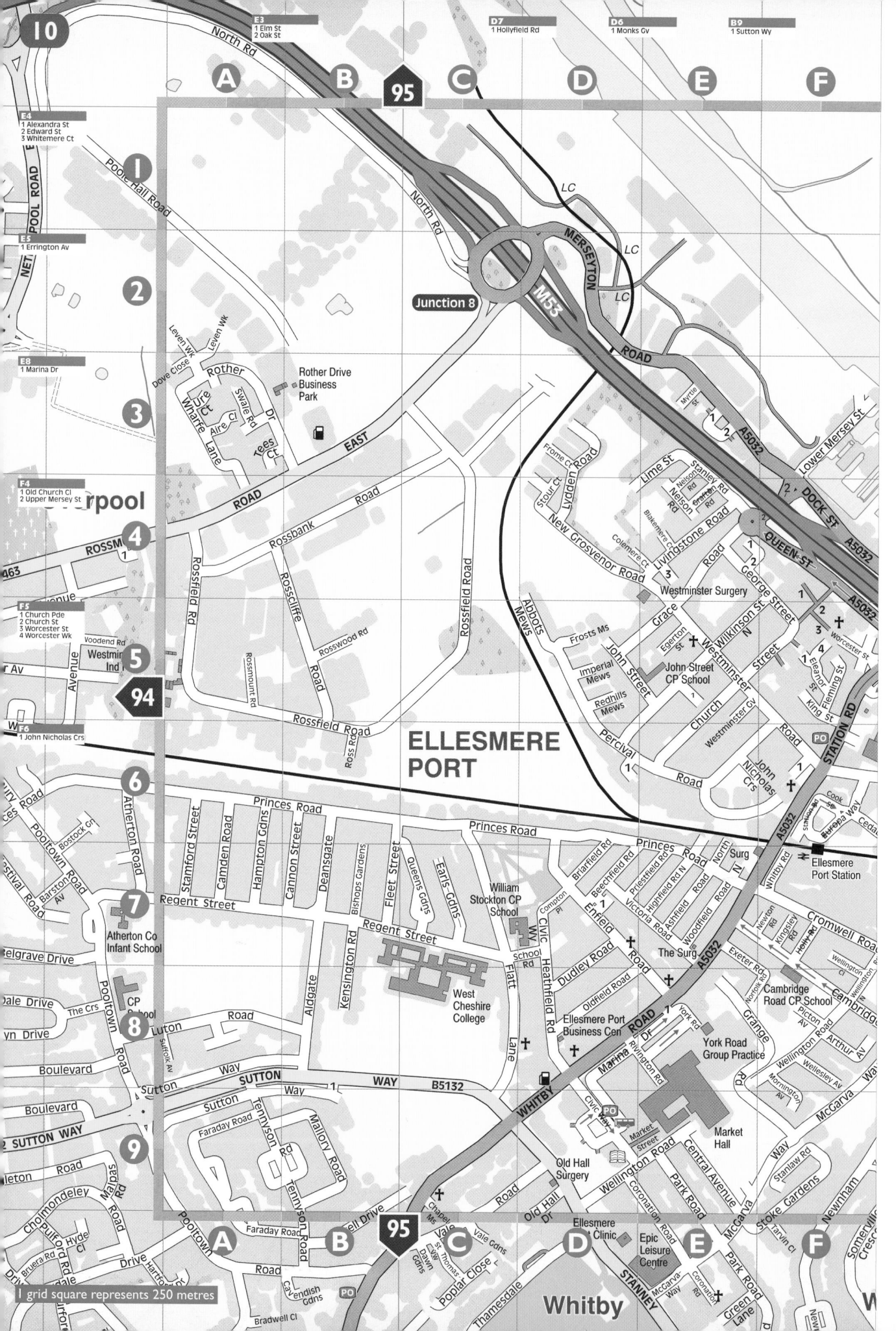

G5
1 John Nicholas Crs

G   **H**   **J**   **K**   95   **L**   **M**

River Mersey

1

2

3

South Pier Road

Boat Museum

4

Canalside Industrial Estate

Manchester Ship Canal

Junction 9

Oil Sites Road

Canalside

Yard Road

CH65

5

96

Westminster Retail Park

Crescent Road

Meadow Lane

DOCK

Meadow Lane

6

M53

1

Oil Sites Road

Oil Sites Road

7

Bridges Road

Cromwell Road

Bridges Road

Bridges Road

8

M53

Lees Lane

South Road

9

Drive

Girton Cl

Lancing Road

Girton Road

Cambridge Road

Marciwiel Rd

Milton

Eton Road

Lees Lane

Repton Road

Burnell Rd

New Bridge Road

G   **H**   **J**   **K**   95   **L**   **M**

Wolverham

PO

Manchester Av

Thornton

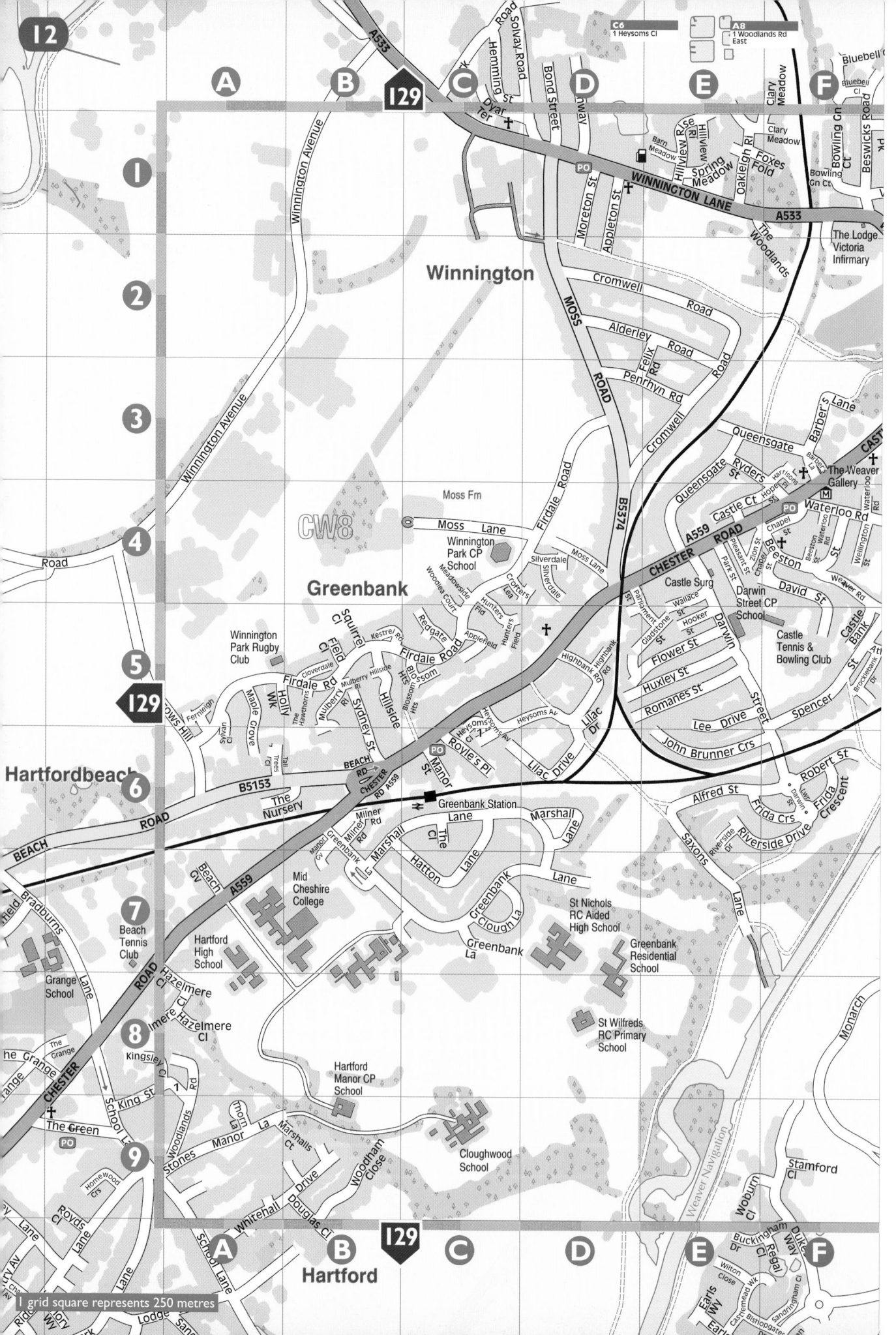

Winnington

Greenbank

CW8

Hartfordbeach

Hartford

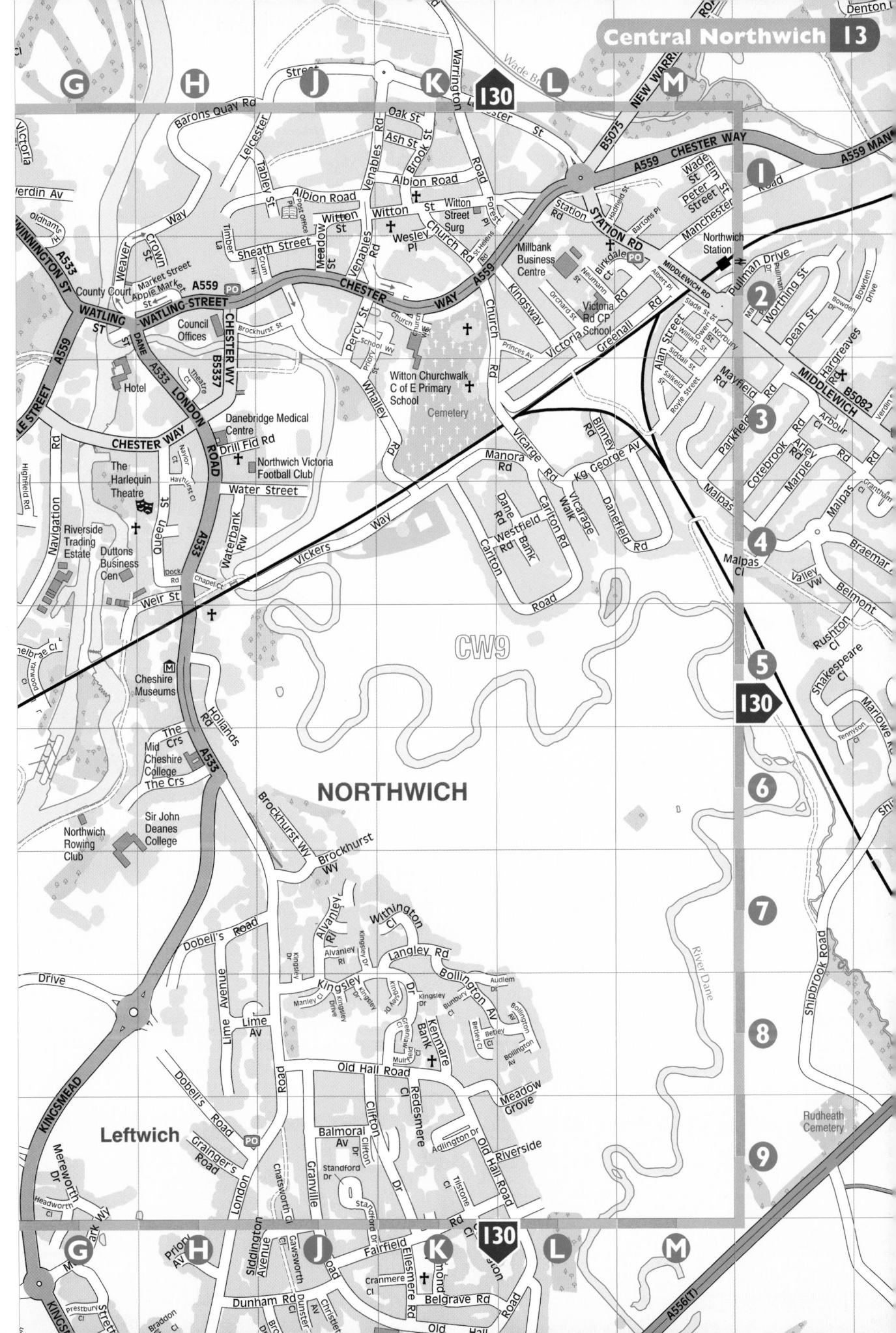

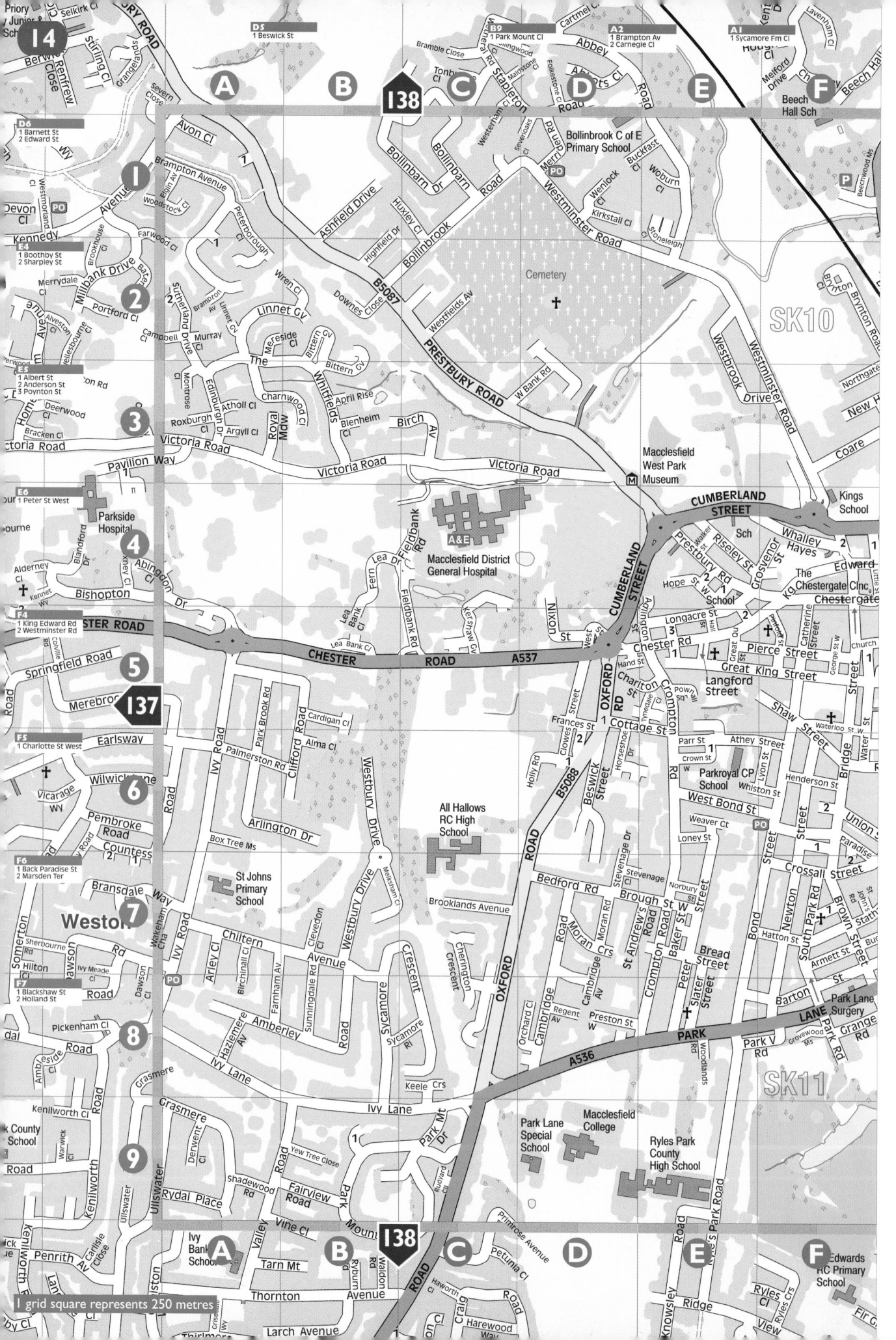

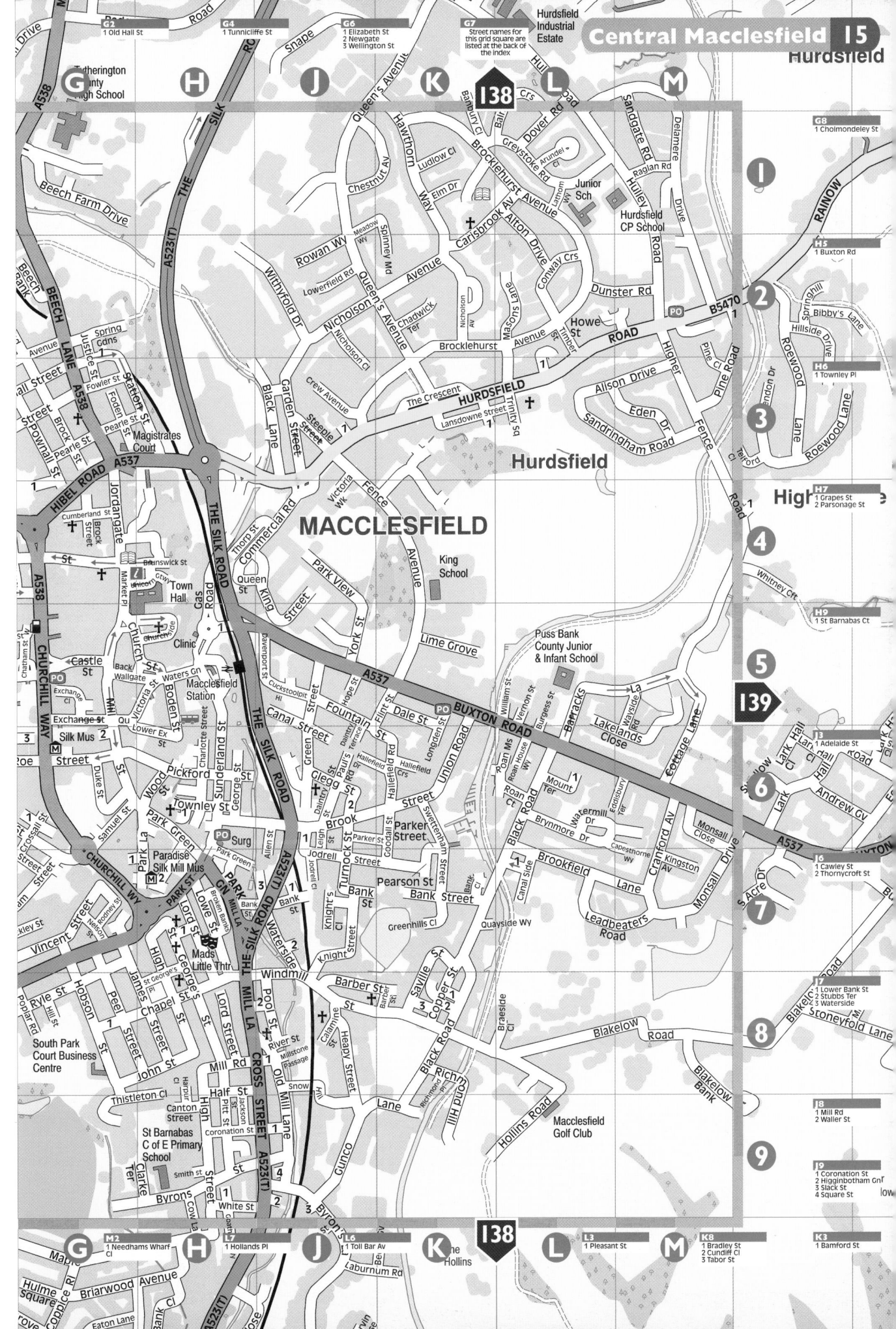

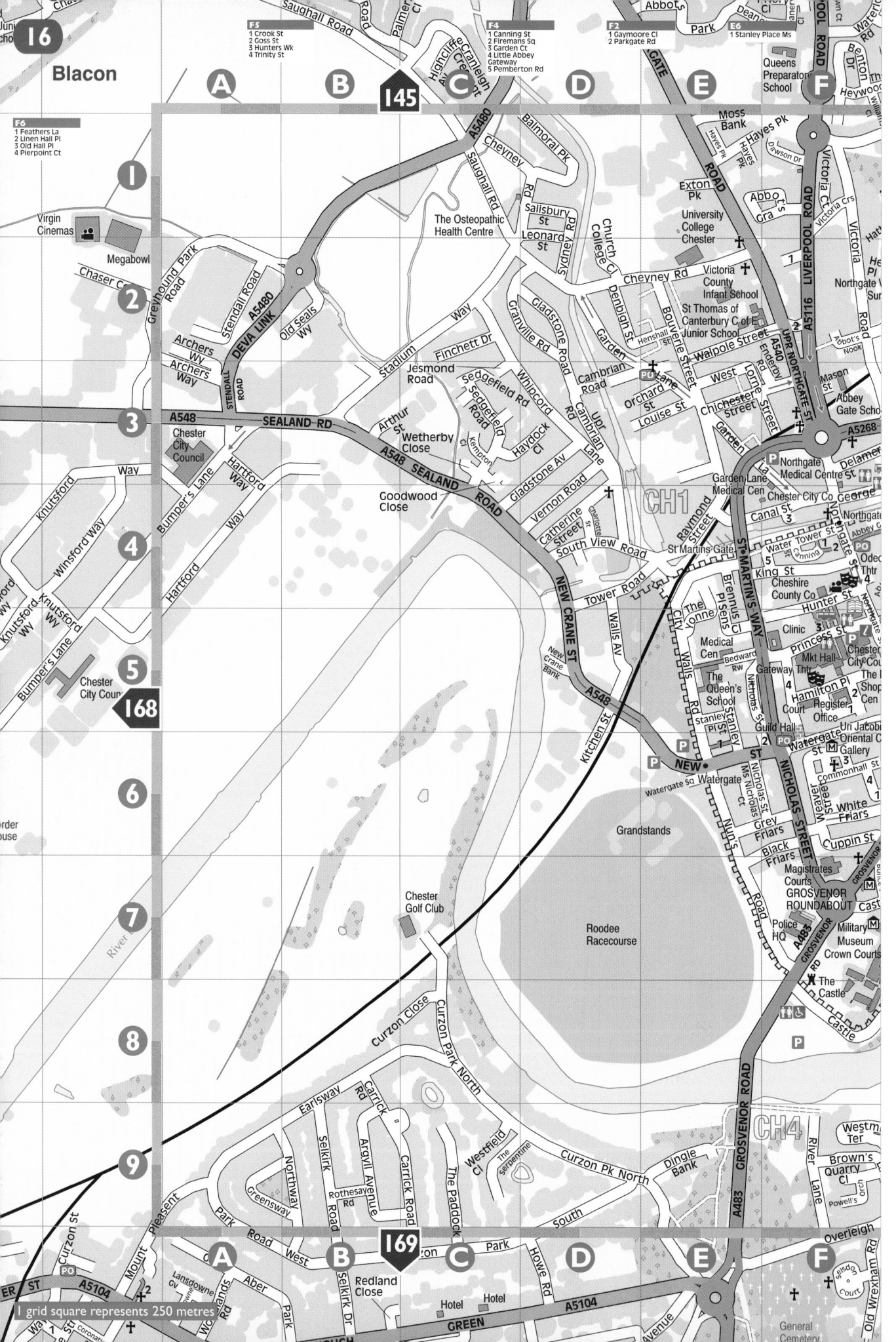

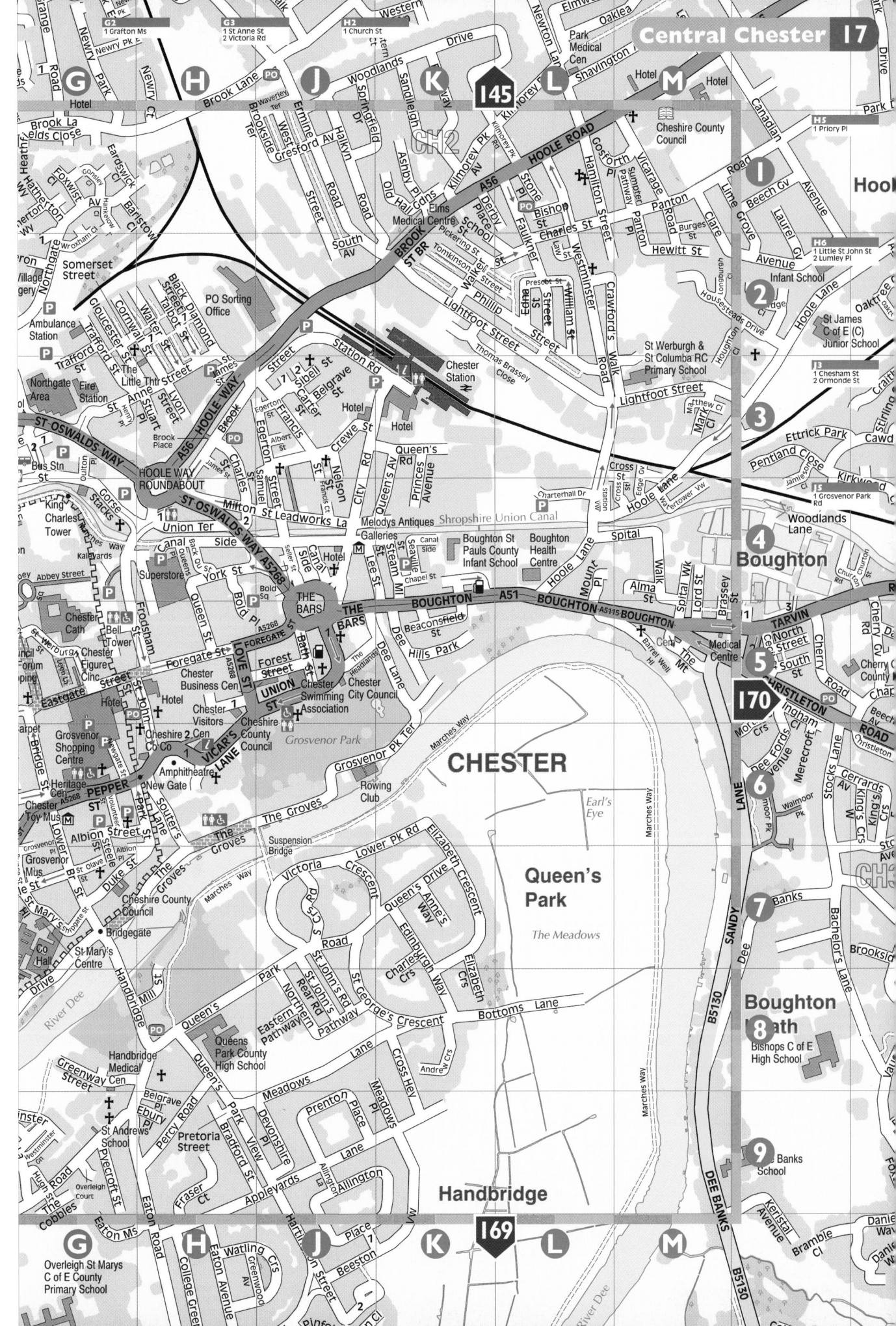

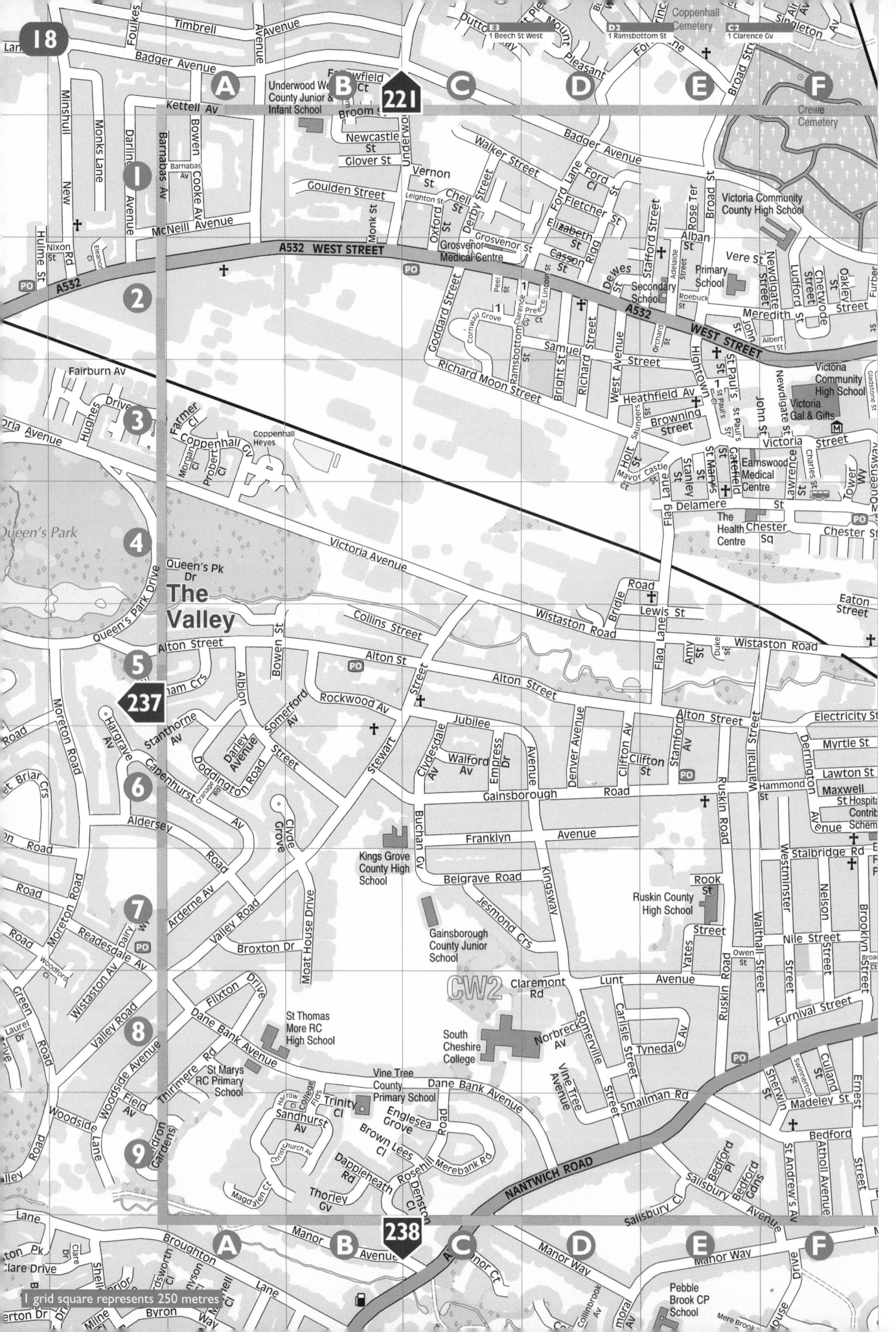

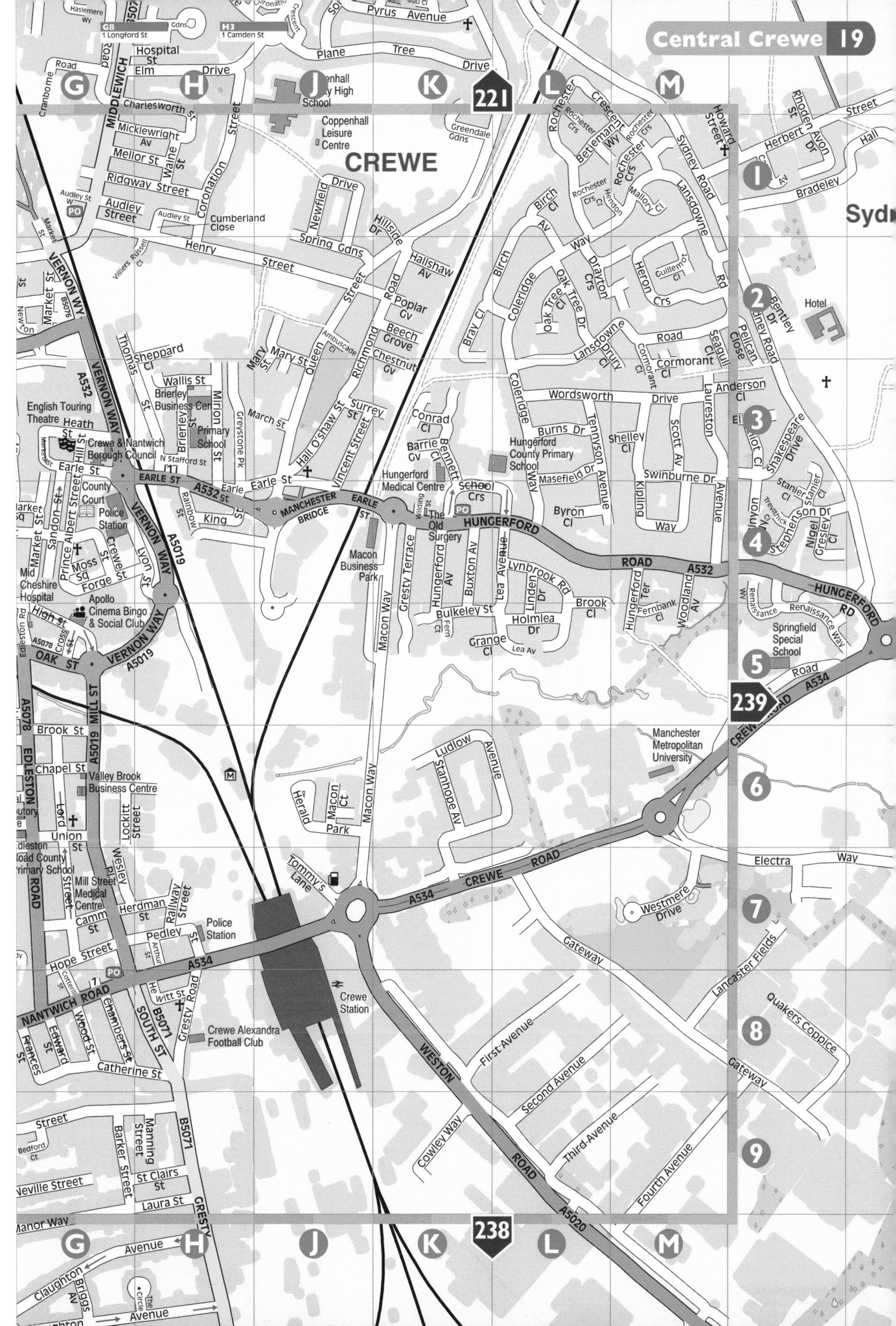

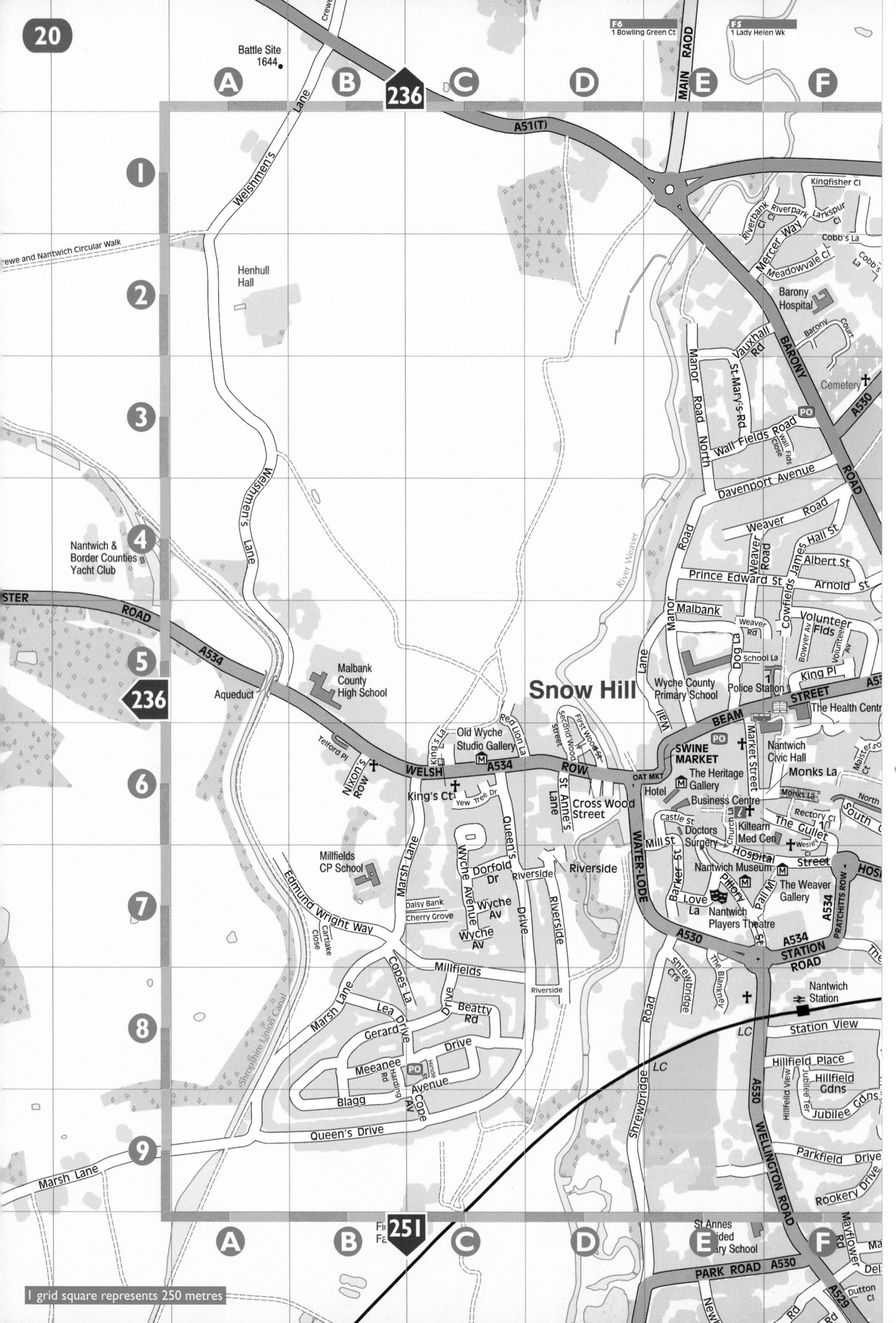

GOLBORNE

Lowton

Lowton Heath

Town of Lowton

Lane Head

24

28

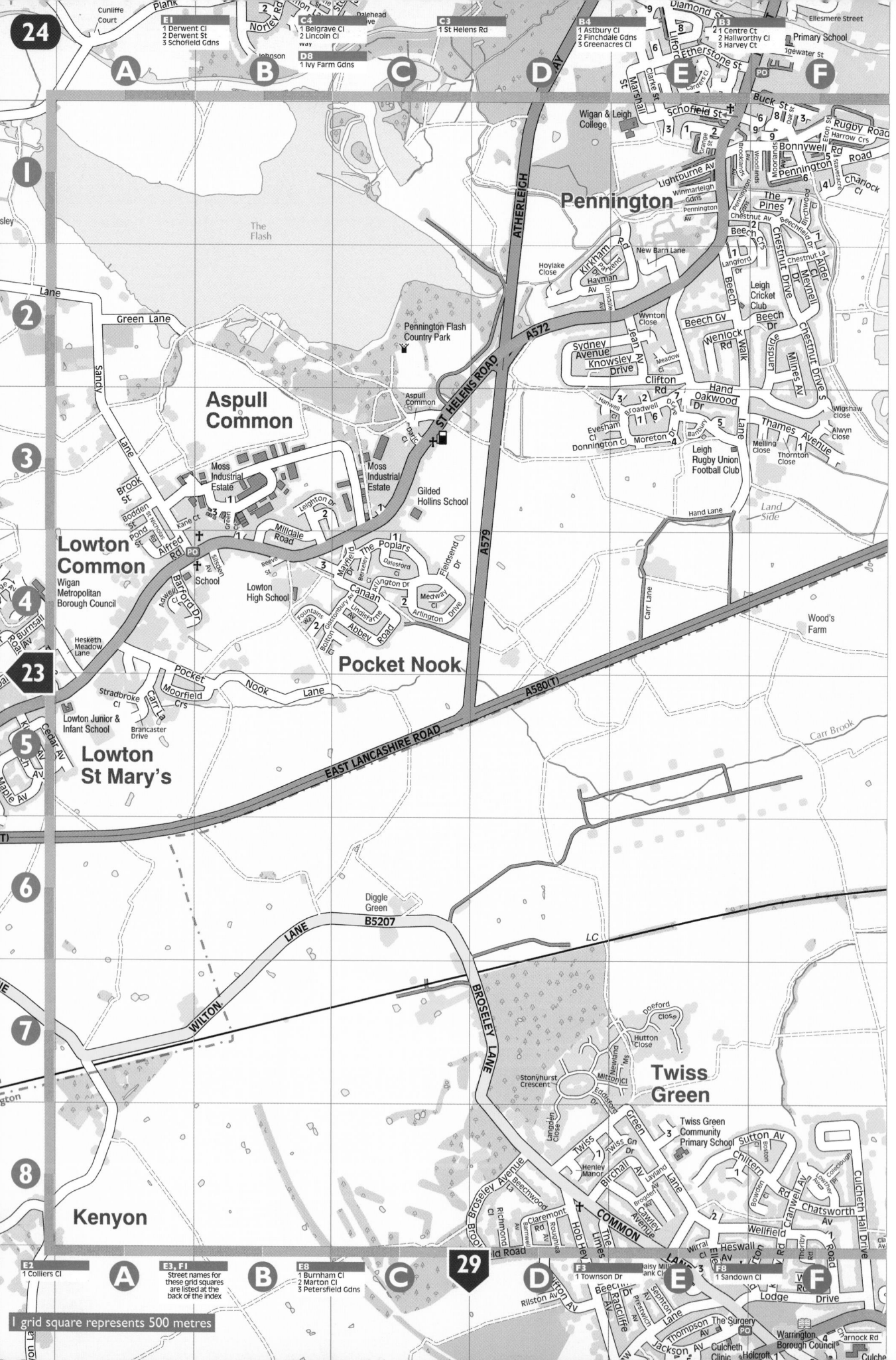

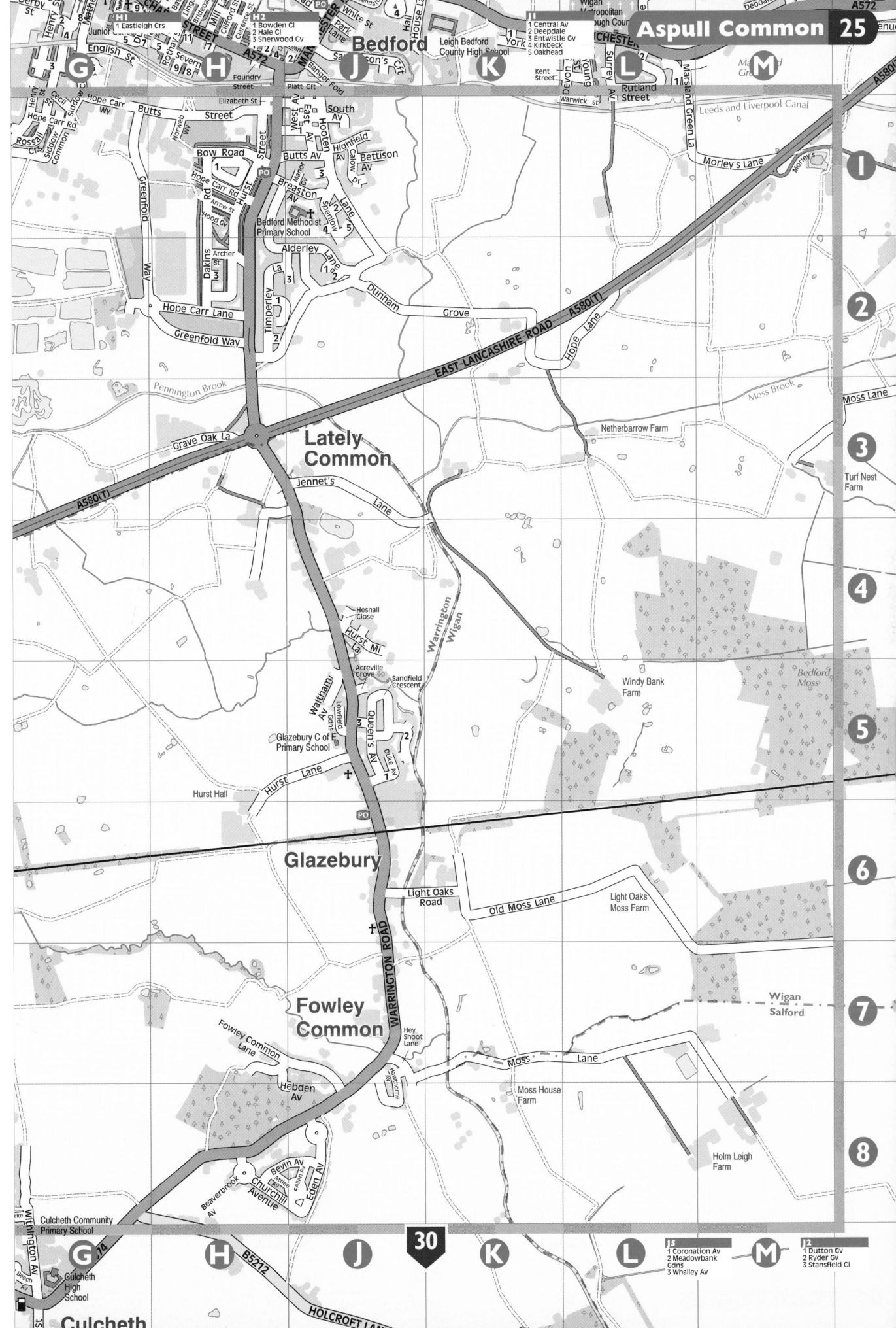

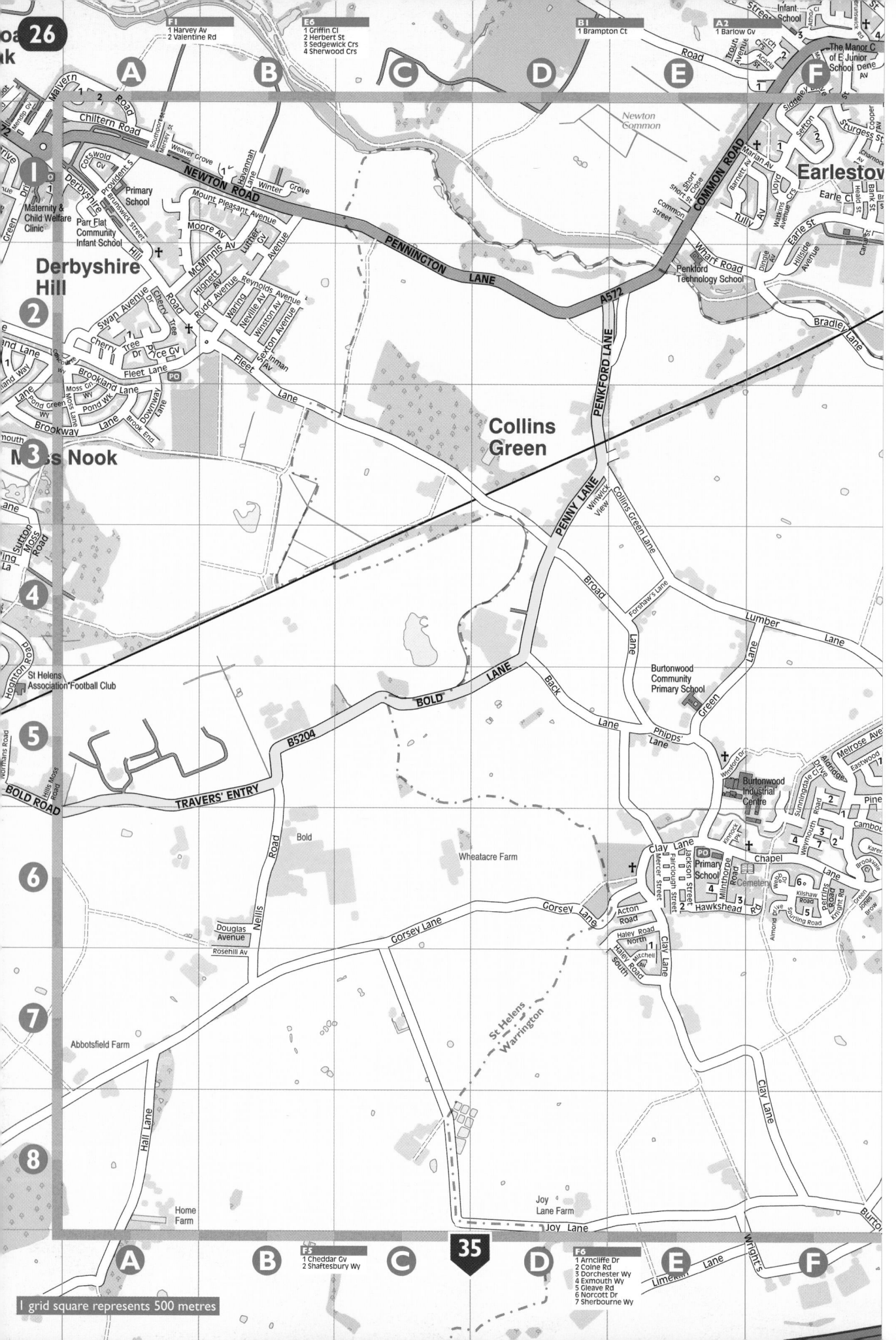

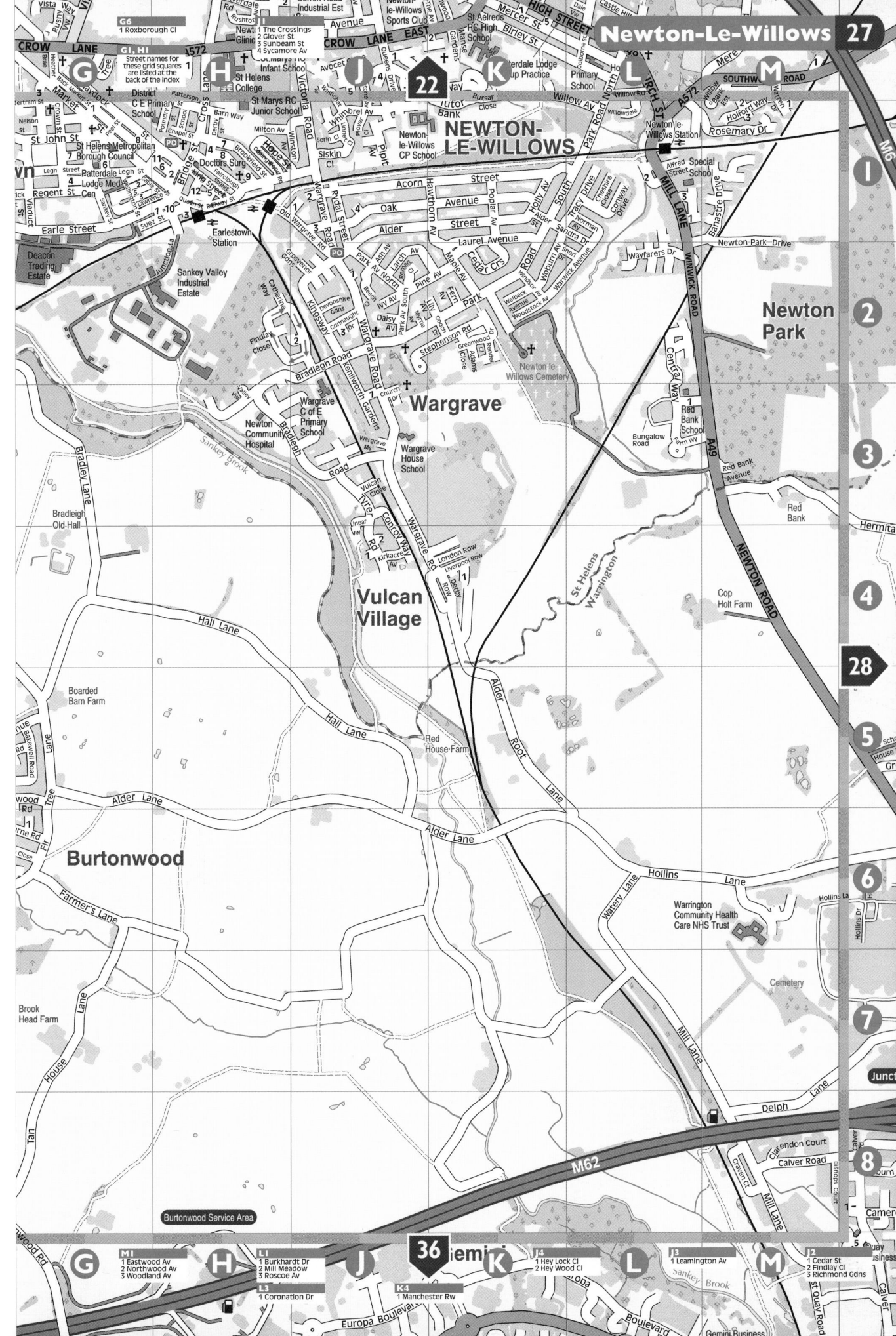

NEWTON-LE-WILLOWS

Newton Park

Wargrave

Vulcan Village

Burtonwood

Sankey Valley Industrial Estate

Deacon Trading Estate

Bradleigh Old Hall

Newton Community Hospital

Boarded Barn Farm

Brook Head Farm

Red House Farm

Cop Holt Farm

Red Bank

Warrington Community Health Care NHS Trust

Cemetery

Newton-le-Willows Cemetery

Burtonwood Service Area

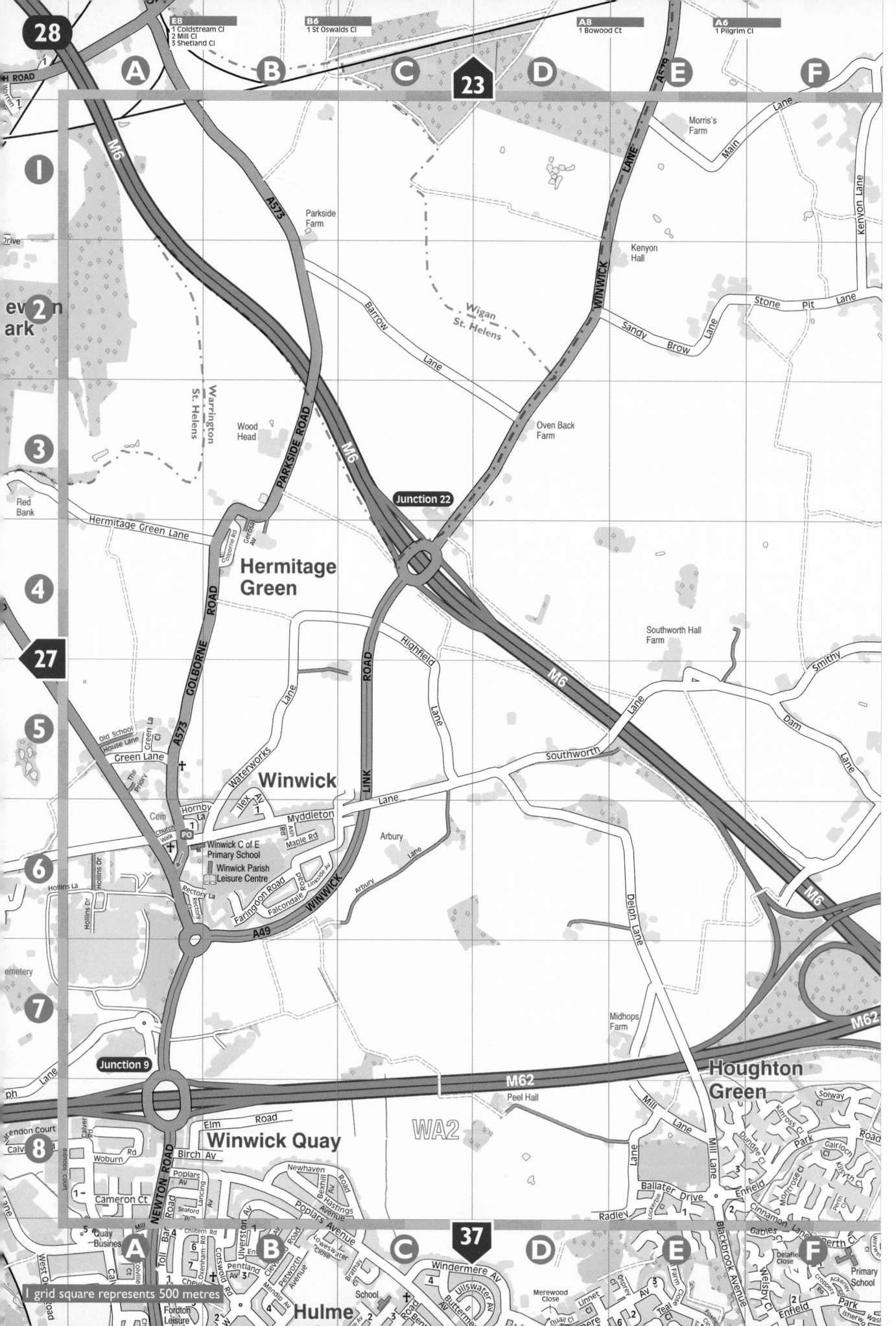

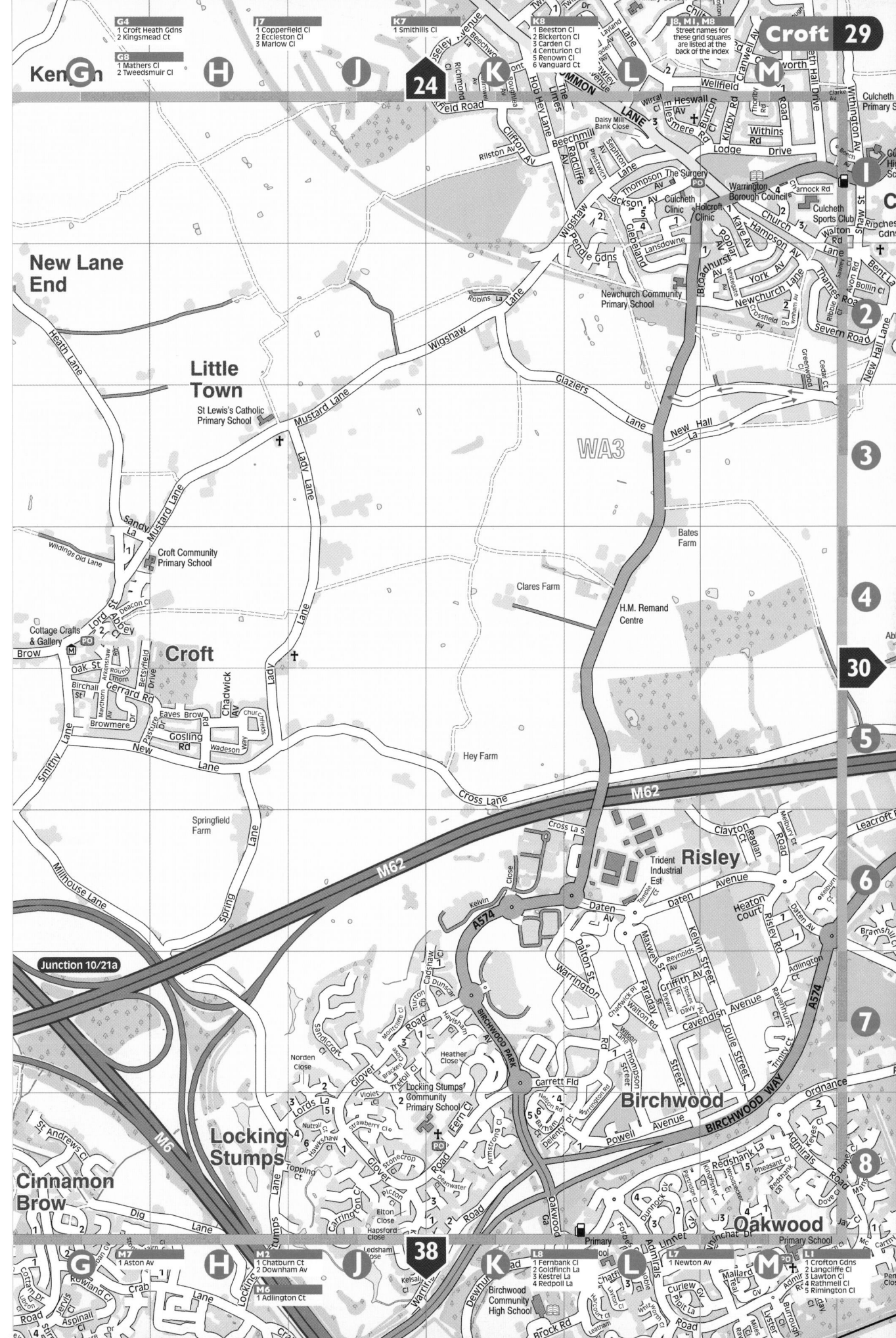

A8
1 Colebrook Cl

A7
1 Flaxley Cl
2 Rossendale Dr
3 Westhay Crs
4 Whitlewood Cl
5 Wigmore Cl

A6
1 Applecross Cl
2 Culbin Cl
3 Dunley Cl
4 Rangemoor Cl

A2
1 Derwent Cl
2 Weaver Rd

Leigh
Farm

A **B** **C** **25** **D** **E** **F**

Culcheth Community
Primary School

Culcheth High
School

Culcheth

Culcheth
Sports Club

1

HOLCROFT LANE

Salford
Warrington

Glaze Brook

2

Ribchester
Gdns

Medway Rd

Howard Road

Ratcliffe House
Farm

Little Woolden
Hall

3

Franks Farm

HOLCROFT LANE

4

Abbey Farm

Moss Side
Farm

29

5

Silver Lane

M62

Holcroft
Moss

M62

Silver
Lane

Junction 11

Leacroft Road

**Gorse
Covert**

6

Covert

Road

Glazebrook
Moss

Hoyles Moss
Farm

Fisherfield Drive

Primary
School

PO

7

Gorse Covert Rd

Gorse

Covert

Moss Gate

School Lane

Moss Lane

Ordnance Avenue

Killingworth
Lane

Omrod Farm

Hollingreave
Farm

8

Risley Moss
Nature Park

A **B** **B6** **C** **39** **D** **B7** **E** **F**

B6
1 Inglewood Cl

B7
1 Bowland Cl
2 Charnwood Cl

Prospect
Farm

Prospect Lane

Primary School

PO

1 grid square represents 500 metres

G H J K L M

K6
1 Somerset Cl

K7
1 Bankfield Av
2 Banklands Cl
3 Chester Cl
4 Hawthorn Dr

K8
1 Keswick Cl
2 Woodbine Av

L4
1 Astley Ct

Little Woolden Moss

Larkhill

Twelve Yards Road

Raspberry Lane

Astley Road

Woodstock Farm

Moss Road

M62

Cutnook La
Parksto
Quail Av
Meadow
Platts
Sandy
Newlands
Farndale
Balshaw
Doodson
Queensway
Chapel La
Vicar La
Springfield Lane
Stuart Rd
Lindon Rd
St John st

Cranford Drive

Brooklands Cl

I

2

Ratcliffe

Dimberley

M44
Worsley View Farm

IRLAM

Irlam County Primary School

Irlam Swimming Pool

3

Roscoe Road

Rose Avenue
Rose Crs
Baines Rd
Francis Av
Victoria
Greenside Drive

Conway Av
Amable
Lines Rd

LIVERPOOL ROAD

FF HILLS

4

Ring Pit Farm

M62

Woolden Road

Rosebank Farm

Astley Rd
Caroline St
Dixon Street
Boomehouse Av
Zinnia Drive
Orchid Cl
Macdonald Road Medical Cen
Salford City Council
PO
Woods Rd
Deihi Rd
Woodrow W

Fairhill Industrial Estate

Great Woolden Hall

B5212

New Farm

Moss Road

High School
Clarendon Rd
Macdonald Rd
Preston Rd
Tramway Rd
Richfield Cl
Bradburn Road
B5320

Cromwell Rd
Station

Huntsman Drive
Excalibur Way
Frank Perkins Way
Sorby

5

GLAZEBROOK

LANE
Glazebrook Station
Bank Street
Vetch
Lane
Head
Car Wash Way
PO
Norfolk
Hilton
Fairfield Road
Lord's
Pulley Cl
Berkshire Drive
Melville
Kent
Derby Rd
Cumberland Av

Glazebrook

Irlam Industrial Estate
Irlam Station

Heather Cl
Brentwood Av
High Bank
Rowson Dr
Brackley
Lynthorpe
Oxford Cv
Pembroke
Durham
Hertford Cl
Flint
Sussex Rd
Bedford
Fir Street
Buckingham
Enticott
Kenmore
Poplar Gv
Dale
Allotment
Junior School
Nelson Rd
Prospect
Dean
Drake Av
Albert
Penny
Nuttall St
Magenta
Kings Rd
Milton Av
Henley Av
Ashfield Grove
Brereton
Gilchrist Road
Bessemer Rd
Darby

A57
Irlam Rd

6

Lancaster Road
Berkshire Drive
Warwick Rd
York Rd
Belgrave Av
Laburnum
Chestnut
Dorset
Ash Av
Fir Street
Birch Av
Oak Av
Crangle
School La
Cornwall
Grange
MOSS
Meadow
Prospect
St Mary's Cof E Primary School
John St
Siemens Rd
Martens Rd
Anglers Rest
Atherton La
A57
PO

BRINELL DRIVE

7

Dam Lane

Street

Cadishead Recreation Centre
Salford City Council
The Gallery
Green La
Harriet St
Frances St
PO
Bowness

Cadishead

Lincoln Av
Essex Gdns
Hamilton Road
Dudley Road
Lytherton
Hamilton Rd

Derwent Close

Scroggins Lane
Orchard Avenue
Hallcroft
River La
8

Victory Rd
Kitchener Av
Haig Av
Byng
Allenby Rd
Graham
LIVERPOOL
Rosebank
Vale Vista
Rooks La

Manchester Ship Canal

Thirlmere Road
Elizabeth
Penrith Rd
Coniston Rd
Buckloww
Davies
MANCHESTER NEW ROAD
Hallcroft

M8
1 Manchester Rd

M6
1 Ferrous Wy

40

M4
1 Alexandra Gv
2 Lathom Rd
3 Royden Av

M3
1 Howarth Dr
2 Leader Williams Rd
3 Walker Rd

L6
1 Alfred St
2 Charles St
3 Jellicoe Av
4 Monarch Cl
5 Openshaw La
6 Sienna Cl

G H J K L M

A57 Road
Lock Lane
Buttermere Rd
Our Lady of Lourdes RC
Willows
Police Stn
Borough Council
School

Hollinfare

I grid square represents 500 metres

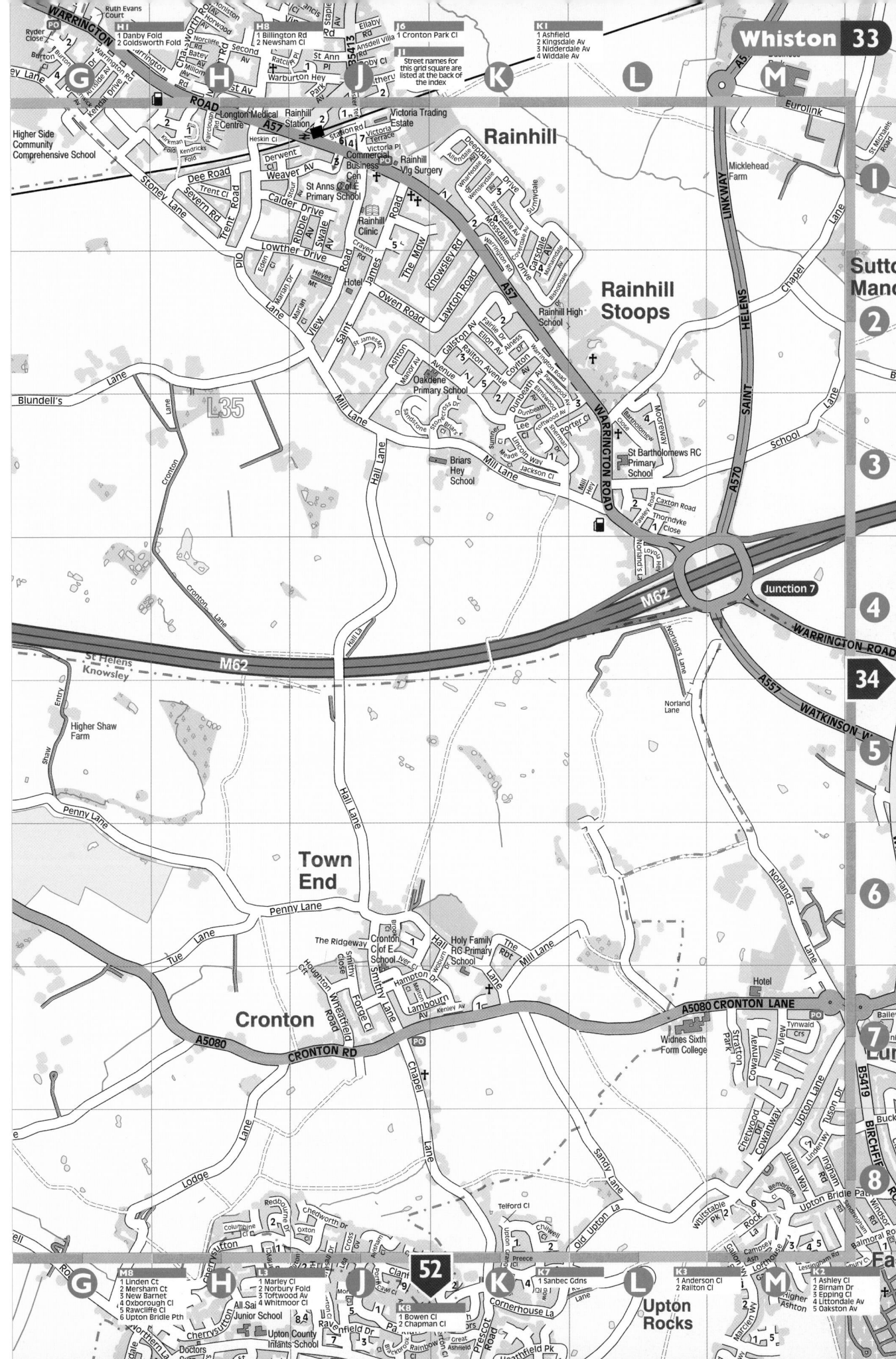

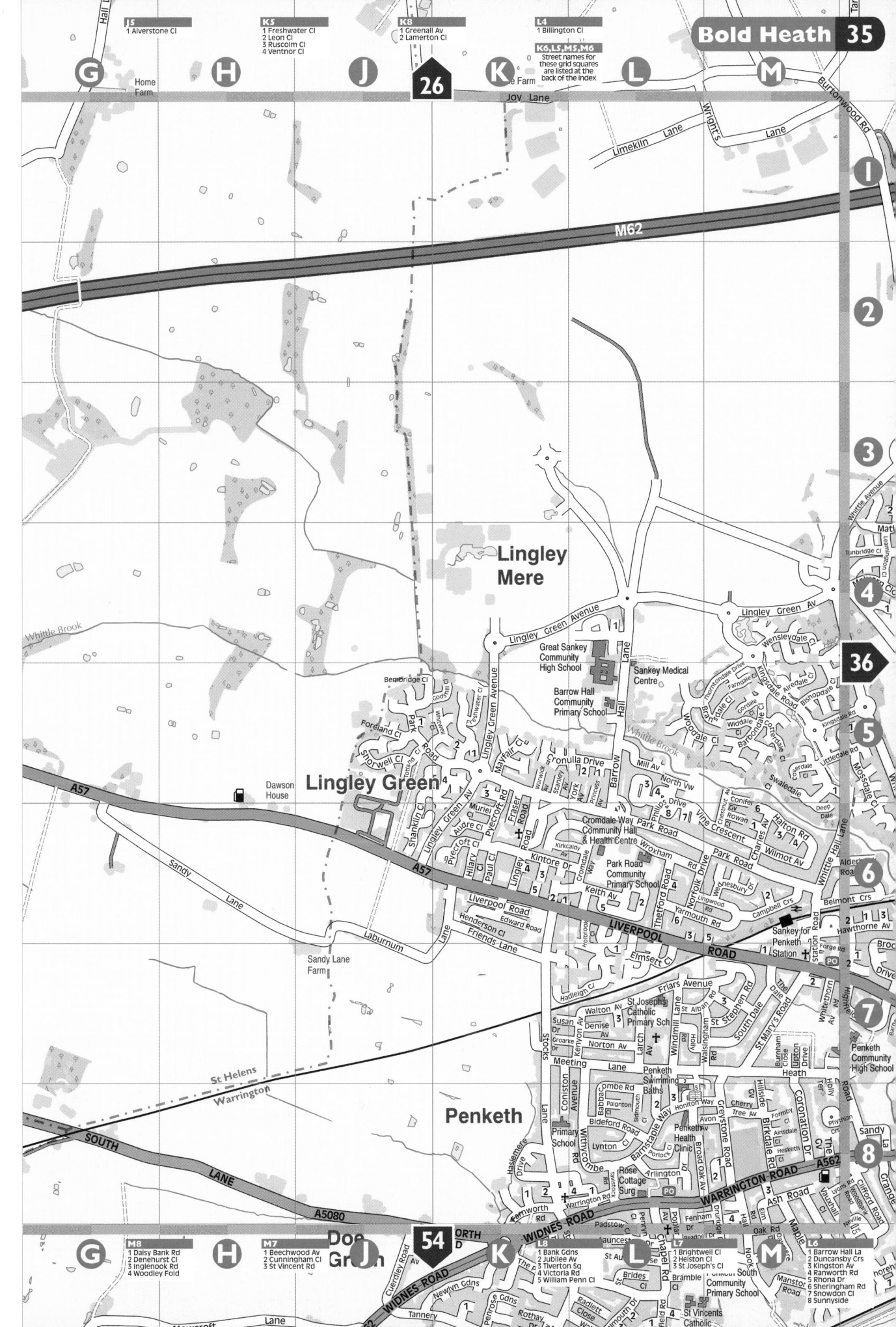

26

36

54

Lingley
Mere

Lingley Green

Penketh

Doe Grn

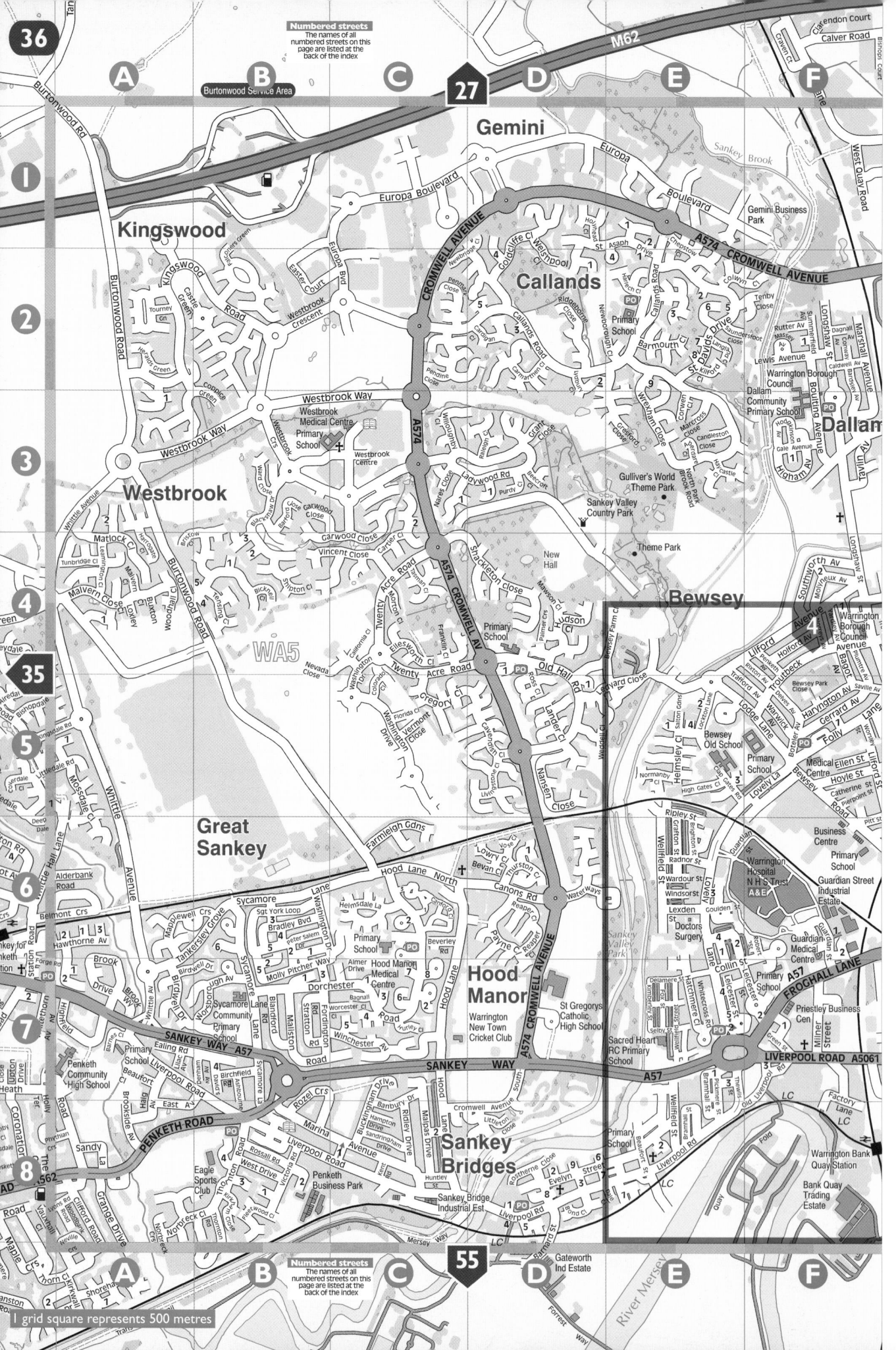

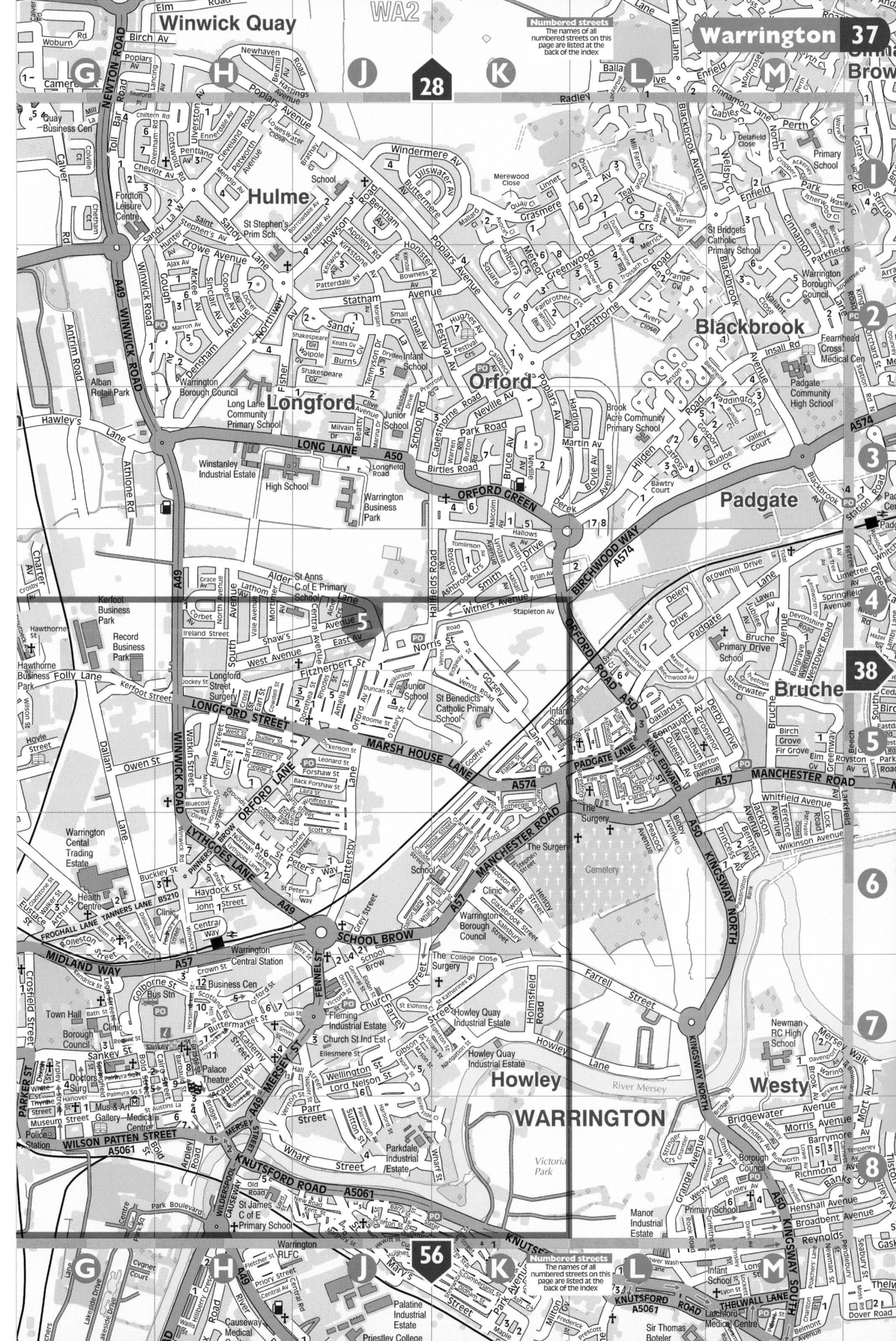

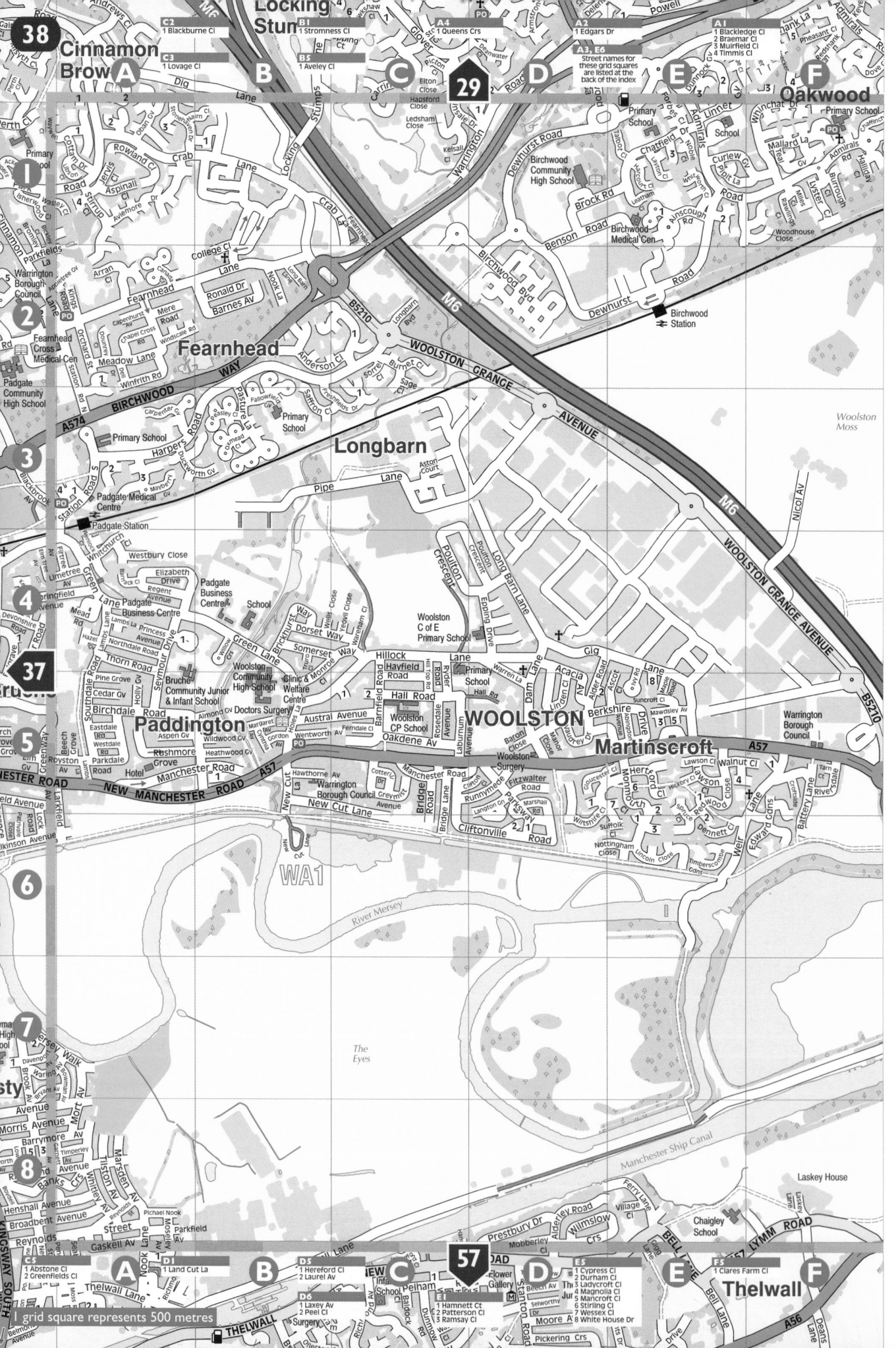

G5
1 Manchester Rd

K8
1 Albany Crs
2 Northway
3 The Poplars

M8
1 Grasmere Rd

G H J K L M

30

Prospect
Farm

Prospect Lane

Rixton
Moss

Woodend Lane

Moss Side Lane

Rixton

Moat Lane

Claydon
Gardens

Chapel Lane

MANCHESTER A57

Rixton

2

3

Marshall's Farm

Holly Bush Lane

Green Alley
Farm

A57

Rixton Old
Hall

4

40

Warrington
Trafford

5

BROOK

Juniper Lane

Lane

M6

Manchester
Road

MANCHESTER ROAD A57

Brookside
Farm

Junction 21

River Mersey

Bollin
Point

6

7

Reddish Lane

Golf Course

Thelwall
Viaduct

Rushgreen

Statham Lane

Pool Lane

Brookside

Pool Lane

Oldfield
Road

Whitbarrow
Rd

PO

Statham

Whitbarrow Road

Lymm

Reddish Crs

Reddish
Drive

Bollin
Drive

Whitbarrow Road

Brook Rd

Yew Tree
Close

Reddish Lane

8

A6144

RUSHGREEN

M6

Warrington Road

Statham
Community
Primary
School

Star Lane

Whitesands
Rd

Turnberry

Jubilee

Heath Dr

Albany

Avenue

Statham Close

Maitmans Road

Whitbarrow Road

Brooklyn
Dr

Willow
Close

Danebank

Lymm Lane

Reddish Lane

New Road

Brookfield
Surgery

Danebank
Road
East

THE CROSS

A6144

Rush Gardens

PO

Fletchers La

Mardale

Thirlmere Dr

Cross
Clinic

Rose Bank

Pepper Street

Orchard

Fairfield

Primary
School

G H J K L M

58

Lymmington Av

CAMSLEY LANE

EAGLE BROW

Thornley Rd

John Rd

David Rd

Daisy Bank

Dingle

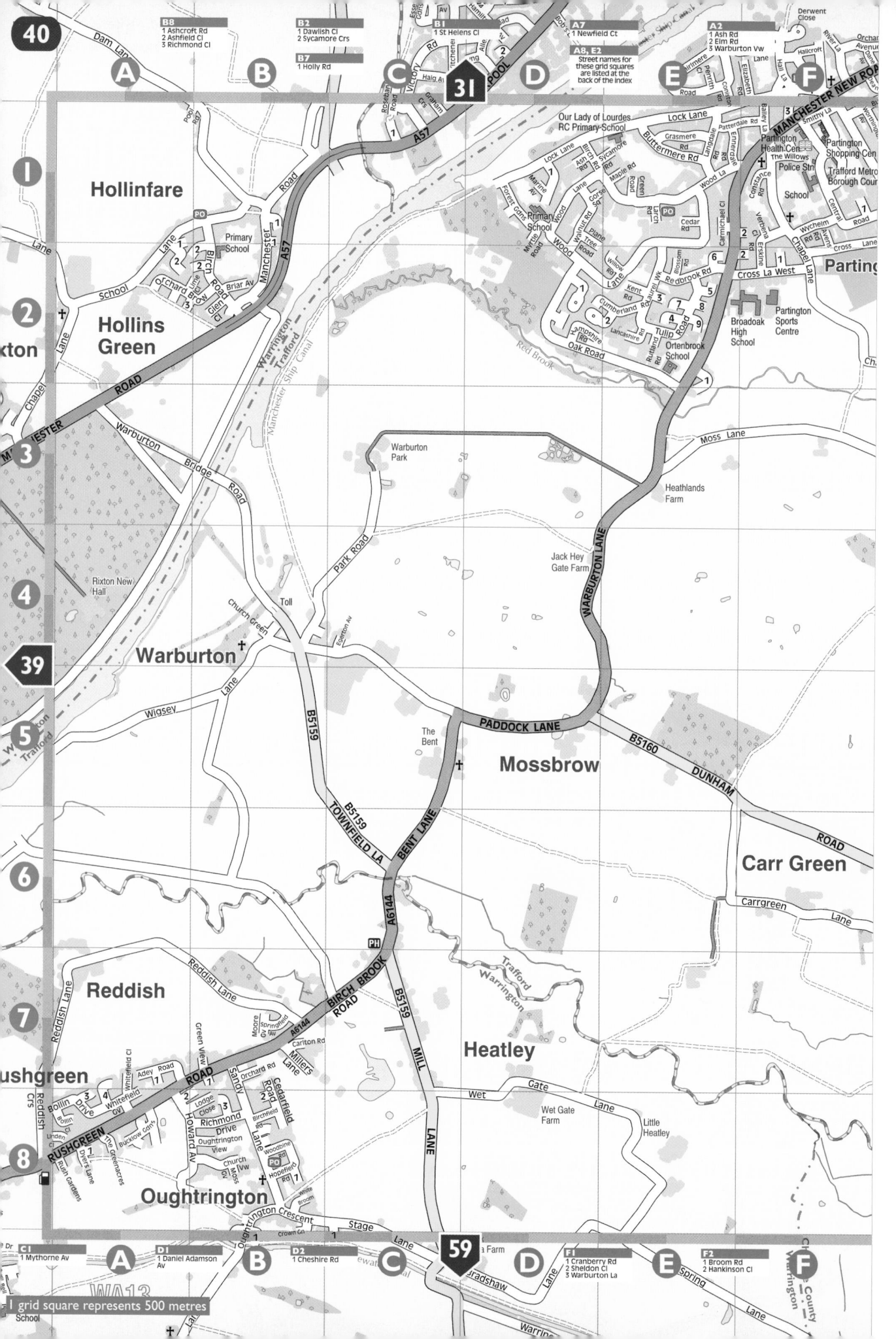

B8
1 Ashcroft Rd
2 Ashfield Cl
3 Richmond Cl

B2
1 Dawlish Cl
2 Sycamore Crs

B7
1 Holly Rd

B1
1 St Helens Cl

A7
1 Newfield Ct

A8, E2
Street names for
these grid squares
are listed at the
back of the index

A2
1 Ash Rd
2 Elm Rd
3 Warburton Vw

31

Hollinfare

Hollins Green

Our Lady of Lourdes
RC Primary School

Partington
Health Cen
The Willows
Police Stn
Trafford Metro
Borough Court
School

Partington Shopping Cen

Partington

Cross La West

Broadoak High School

Partington Sports Centre

Primary School

Manchester Trafford Ship Canal

Warburton Trafford

Red Brook

Oak Road

Warburton Park

Moss Lane

Heathlands Farm

Warburton Bridge Road

Rixton New Hall

Park Road

Jack Hey Gate Farm

Warburton Lane

Toll

Church Green

39

Warburton

Wigsey Lane

B5159

Lane

Paddock Lane

B5160 Dunham

Mossbrow

The Bent

Road

Carr Green

Carrgreen Lane

B5159 Townfield La

Bent Lane

A6144

Reddish Lane

Reddish

Birch Brook Road

B5159 Mill Lane

Heatley

Trafford Warrington

PH

Rushgreen

Reddish Lane

A6144 Road

Springfield

Carlton Rd

Moore

Green View

Millers Lane

Orchard Rd

Wet Gate Lane

Wet Gate Farm

Little Heatley

Bollin Drive

Whitefield

Adey Road

Sandy

Lodge Close

Richmond Drive

Cedarfield Road

Howard Av

Oughtrington View

Woodbine

PO

Church Moss

Hopefield Rd

Rushgreen

The Greenacres

Diver Lane

Rush Gardens

Linden Cl

Oughtrington

Oughtrington Crescent

Crown Gn

Stage Lane

59

Bradshaw

Spring

A
C1
1 Mythorne Av

D1
1 Daniel Adamson
Av

B

D2
1 Cheshire Rd

C

59

D

F
1 Cranberry Rd
2 Sheldon Cl
3 Warburton La

E

F
1 Broom Rd
2 Hankinson Cl

WA13

1 grid square represents 500 metres

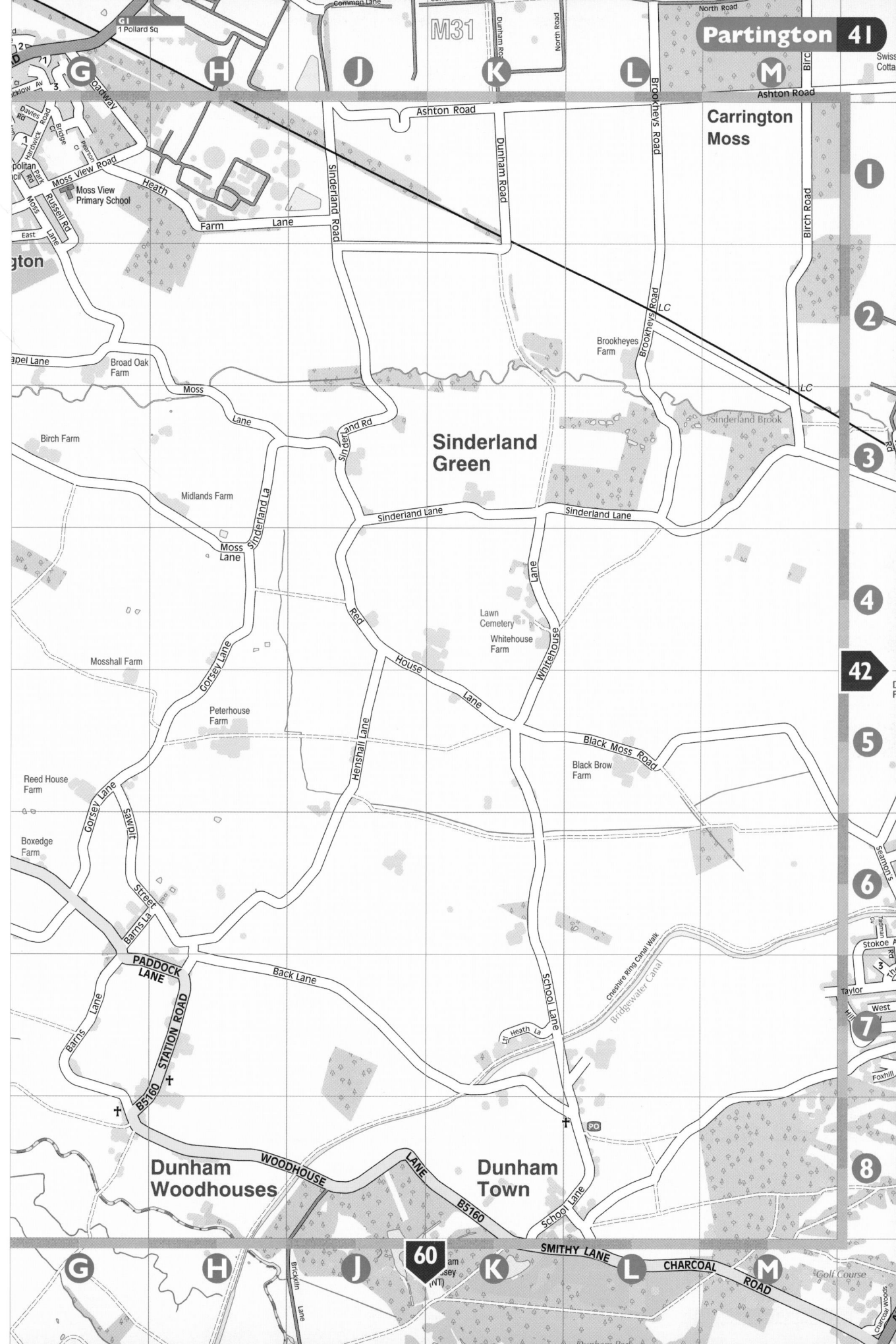

Carrington
Moss

Swiss Cottage

Ashton Road

North Road

Common Lane

M31

Dunham Rd

North Road

Birch

1 Pollard Sq

Roadway

Moss View Road

Moss View Primary School

Heath

Farm

Lane

Russell Rd

Davies

Hardwick Road

Bridge

Pearson

Park

Brocklow Av

Metropolitan Council

Chapel Lane

Broad Oak Farm

Moss

Lane

Sinderland Road

Dunham Road

Brookheys Road

Ashton Road

Birch Road

LC

Brookheys Farm

Sinderland Brook

LC

Rd

Birch Farm

Midlands Farm

Sinderland La

Sinderland Rd

Sinderland Green

Sinderland Lane

Sinderland Lane

Moss Lane

Mosshall Farm

Gorsey Lane

Red

House

Lane

Henshall Lane

Lane

Whitehouse

Lawn Cemetery

Whitehouse Farm

Peterhouse Farm

Black Moss Road

42

Reed House Farm

Gorsey Lane

Sawpit

Black Brow Farm

Stokoe Av

Seamon's

Boxedge Farm

Street

Barns La

Taylor

Hill

West

PADDOCK LANE

Back Lane

School Lane

Cheshire Ring Canal Walk

Bridgewater Canal

Foxhill

Barns Lane

B5160 STATION ROAD

Heath La

PO

Dunham Woodhouses

WOODHOUSE

LANE

B5160

Dunham Town

School Lane

Charcoal Woods

Bricklin Lane

60

SMITHY LANE

CHARCOAL ROAD

Golf Course

Dunham Park

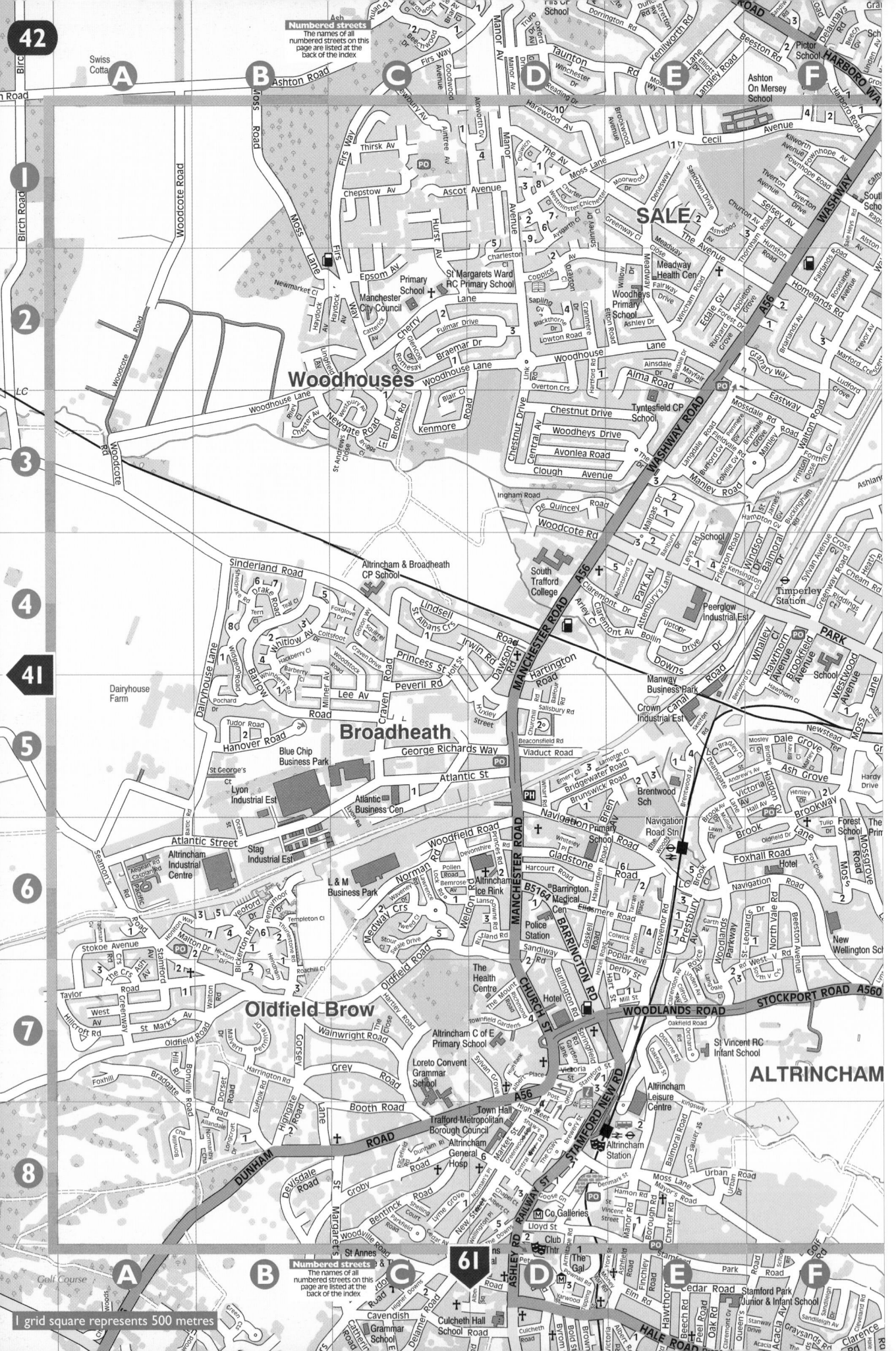

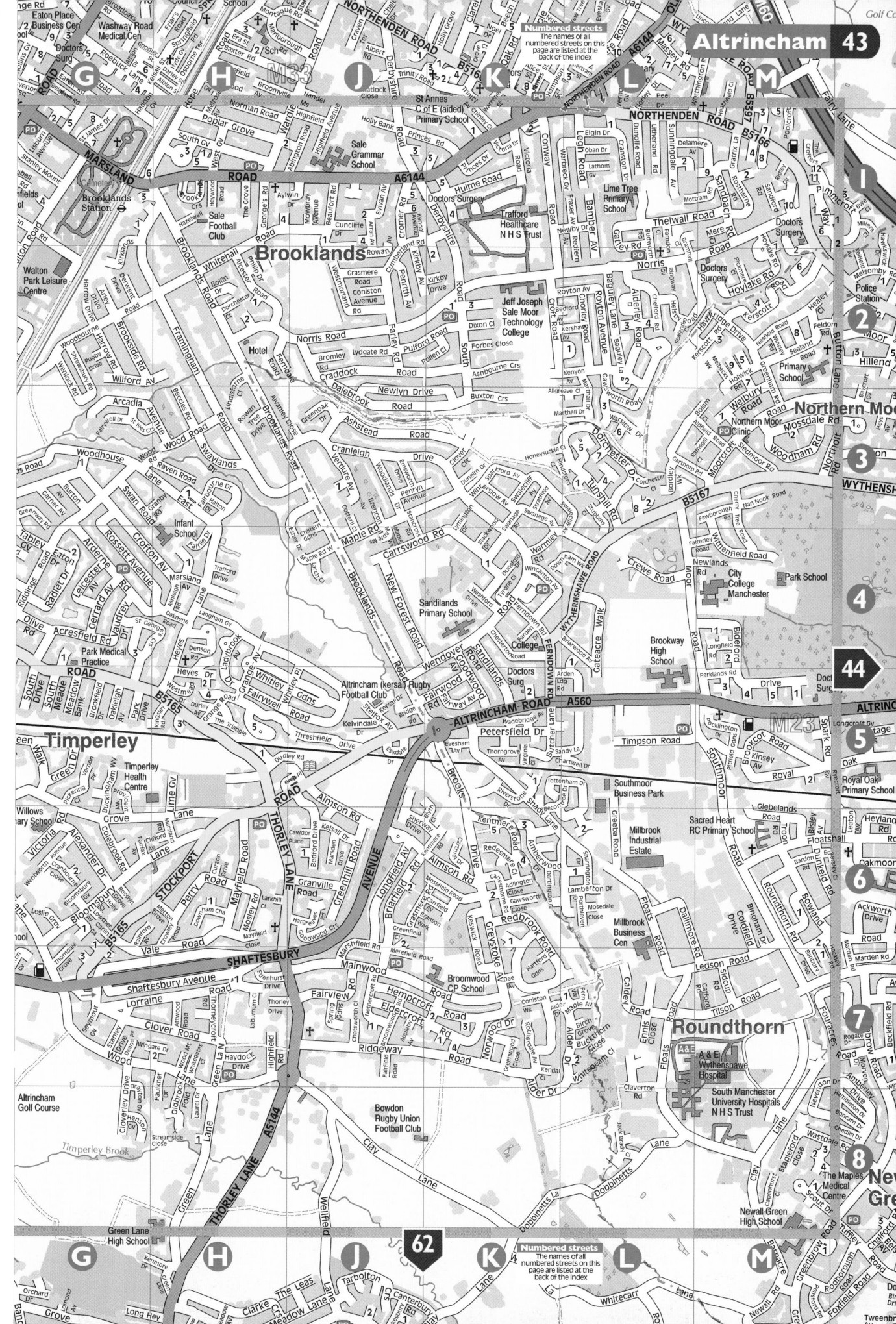

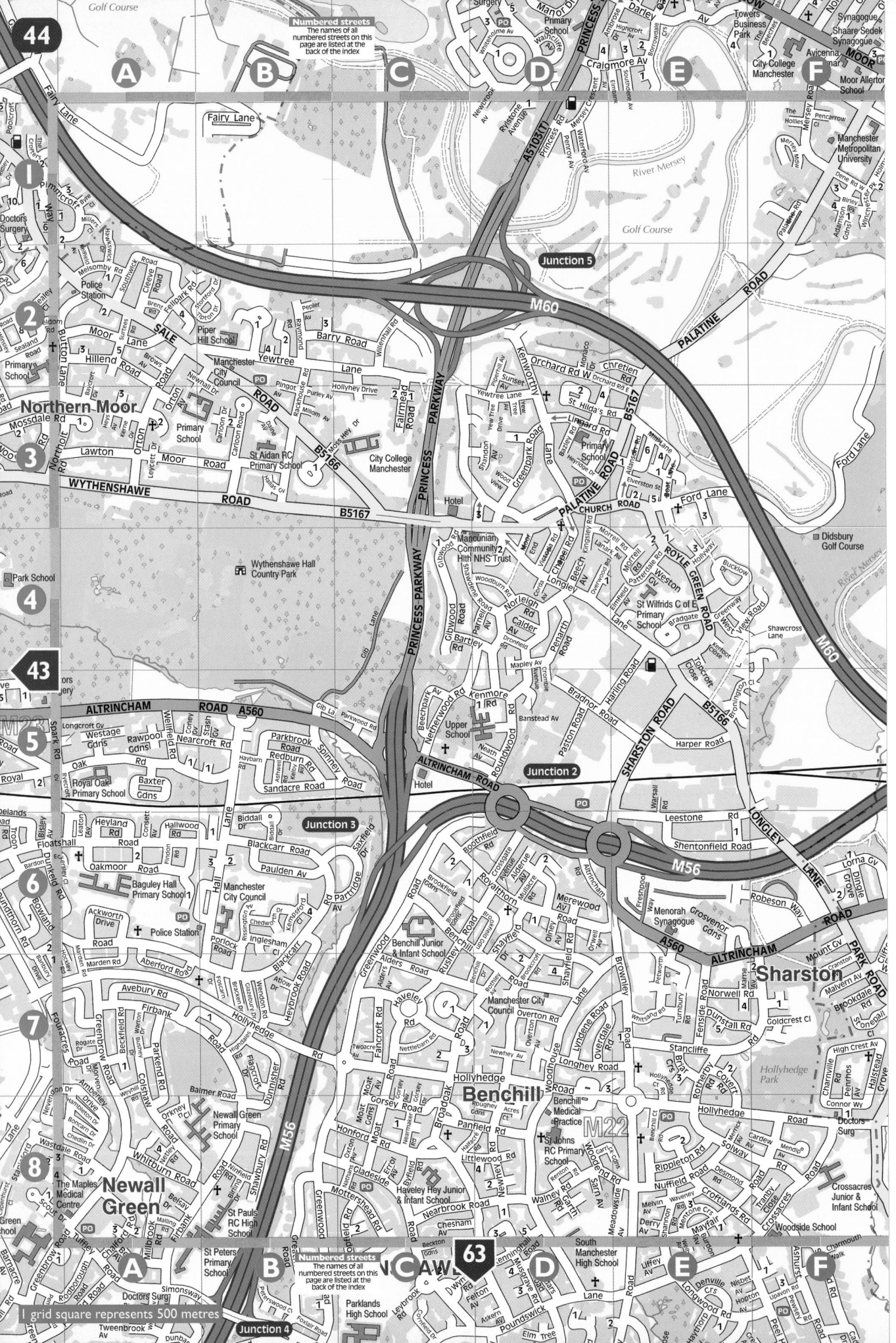

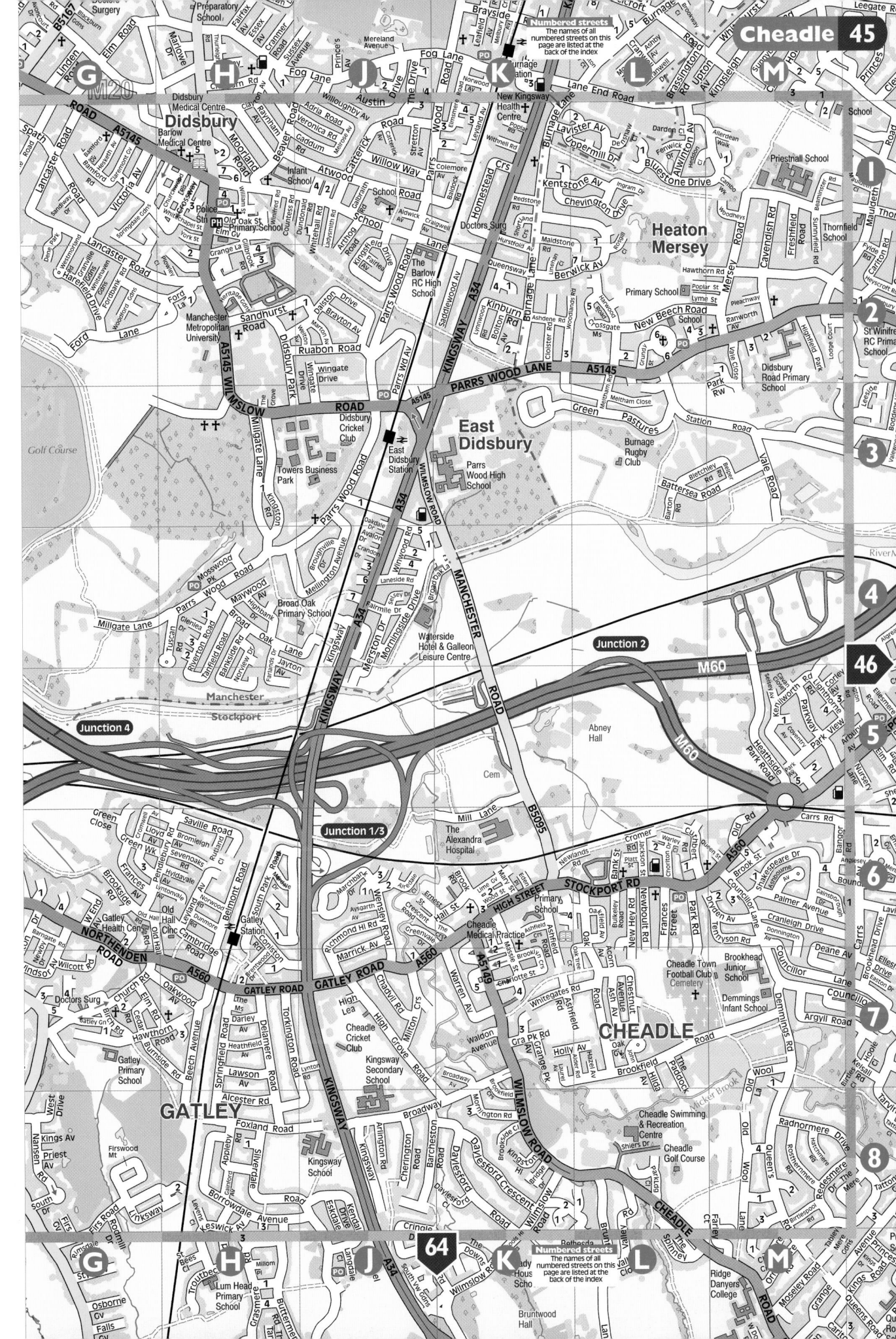

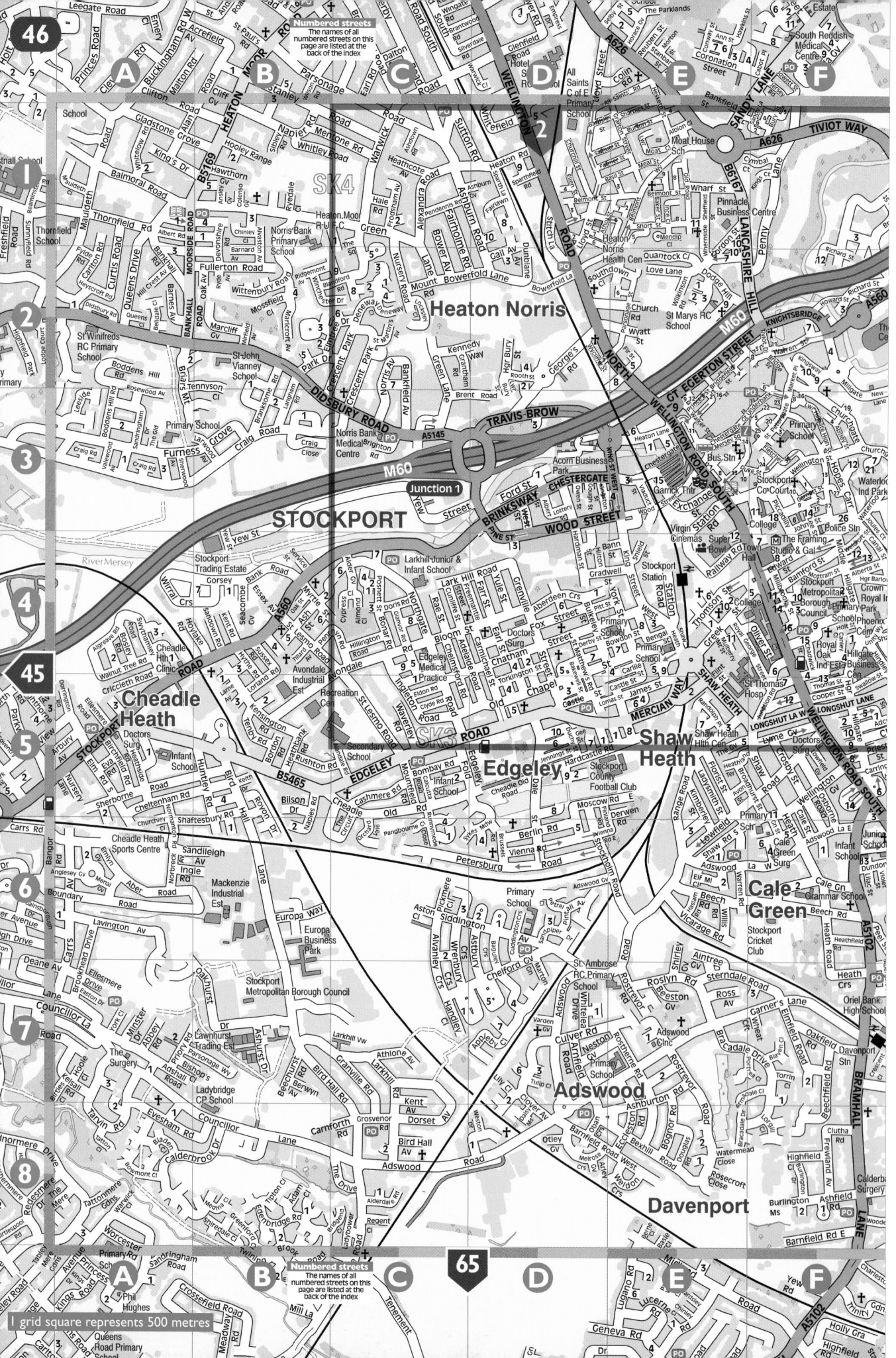

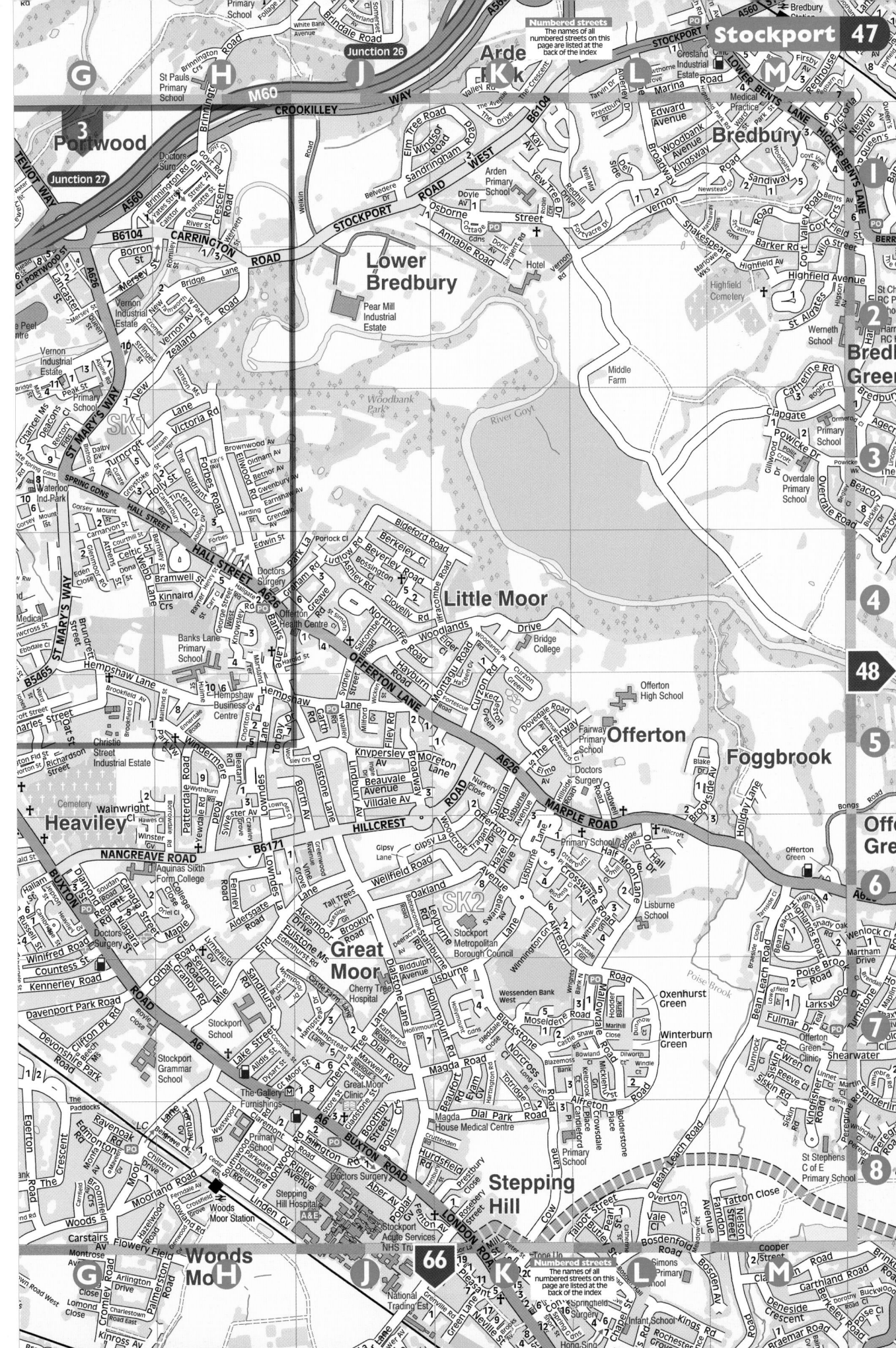

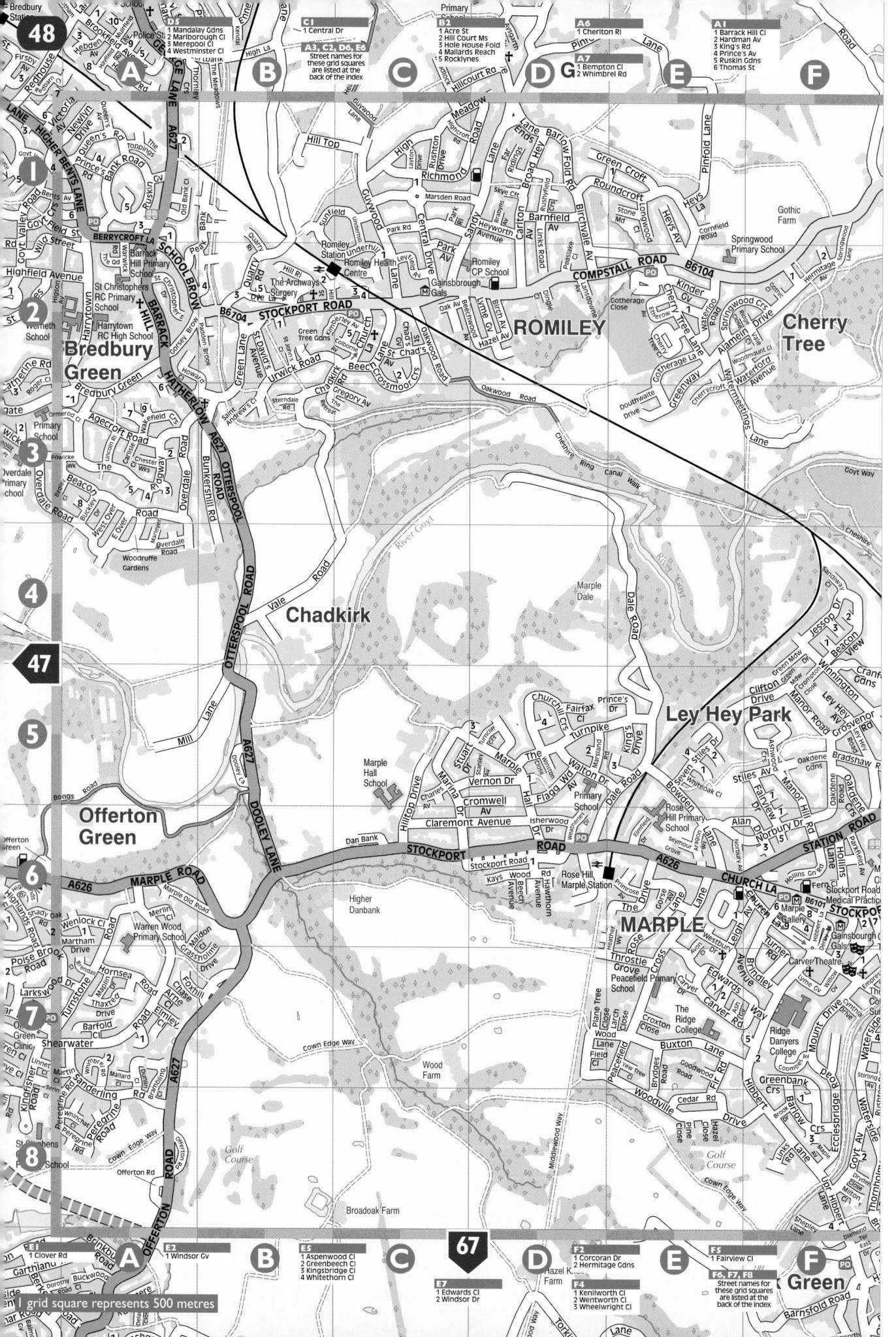

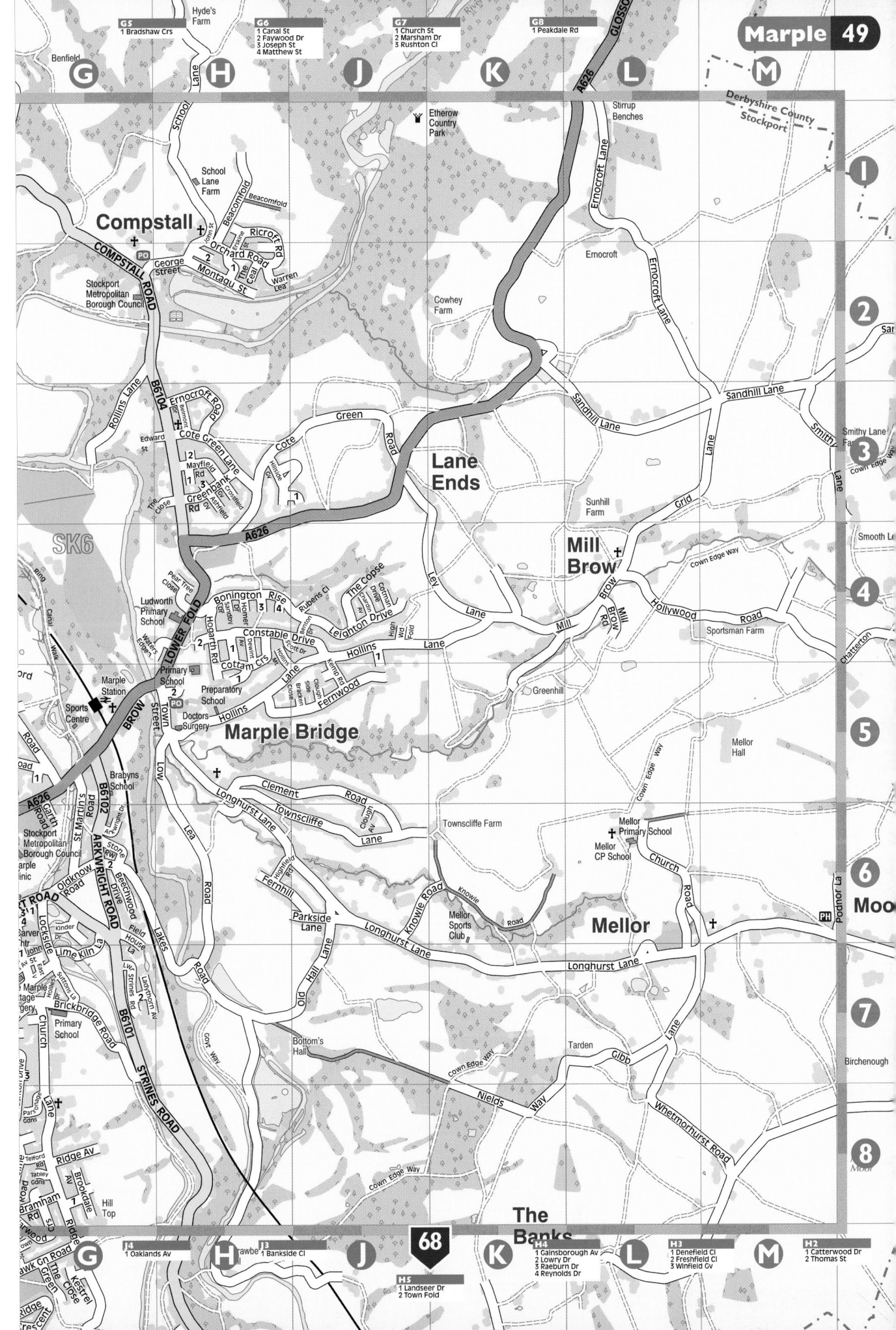

G5
1 Bradshaw Crs

G6
1 Canal St
2 Faywood Dr
3 Joseph St
4 Matthew St

G7
1 Church St
2 Marsham Dr
3 Rushton Cl

G8
1 Peakdale Rd

G H J K L M

I

2

3

4

5

6

7

8

Compstall
Benfield
School Lane Farm
Beacomfold
Ricroft Rd
Orchard Road
George Street
Montagu St
Stockport Metropolitan Borough Council
COMPSTALL ROAD
PO
B6104
Rollins Lane
Edward St
Ernocroft Road
Cote Green Lane
Mayfield Rd
Greenbank Rd
The Close
Green Road
A626

Etherow Country Park
Cowhey Farm
Lane Ends
Sandhill Lane
Sunhill Farm
Grid
Mill Brow
Cown Edge Way

Ernocroft Lane
Ernocroft
Stirrup Benches
Derbyshire County Stockport
Smithy Lane
Cown Edge Rd
Smooth Le

SK6
Pear Tree Close
Ludworth Primary School
Bonington Rise
LOWER FOLD
Hogarth Rd
Constable Drive
Cottam Crs
Leighton Drive
The Copse
Rubens Cl
Hollins
Fernwood
Preparatory School
Primary School
Marple Station
Sports Centre
PO
Doctors Surgery
Hollins
BROW
Town Street
Low
Marple Bridge
Lev
Lane
Hollins Lane
Greenhill
Mill Brow
Hollywood Road
Sportsman Farm
Mellor Hall
Chatterton

Brabyns School
B6102
St Martin's Rd
Carr Road
Stockport Metropolitan Borough Council
Marple Clinic
ARKWRIGHT ROAD
Oldknow Road
Beechwood Drive
Field House
Lea Road
Clement Road
Townscliffe
Longhurst Lane
Clough Av
Townscliffe Farm
Knowle Road
Mellor Sports Club
Knowle Road
Mellor Primary School
Mellor CP School
Church Road
Mellor
Cown Edge Way
Moo
PH
Podnor La

A626
Church Road
Primary School
Brickbridge Road
B6101
STRINES ROAD
Lime Kiln
Strines Av
Old Hall Lane
Parkside Lane
Fernhill
Longhurst Lane
Bottom's Hall
Govt Way
Longhurst Lane
Tarden
Gibb
Whetmorhurst Road
Birchenough

Ridge Av
Brookdale Av
Bramhall Rd
Hill Top
Cown Edge Way
Nields Way
The Banks

G H J K L M

68

J4
1 Oaklands Av

H
awbe
J3
1 Bankside Cl

K
H4
1 Gainsborough Av
2 Lowry Dr
3 Raeburn Dr
4 Reynolds Dr

L
H3
1 Denefield Cl
2 Freshfield Cl
3 Winfield Gv

M
H2
1 Catterwood Dr
2 Thomas St

H5
1 Landseer Dr
2 Town Fold

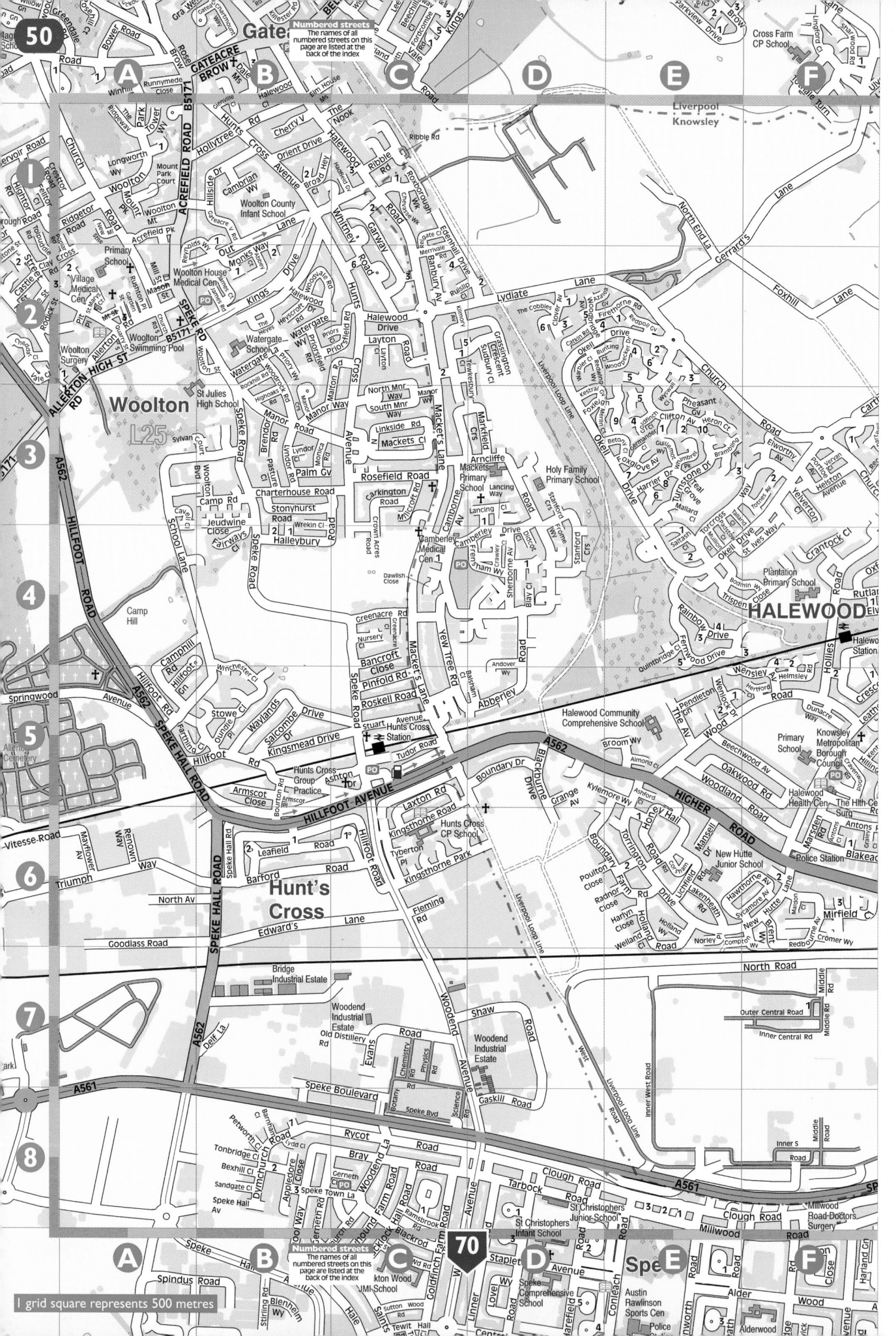

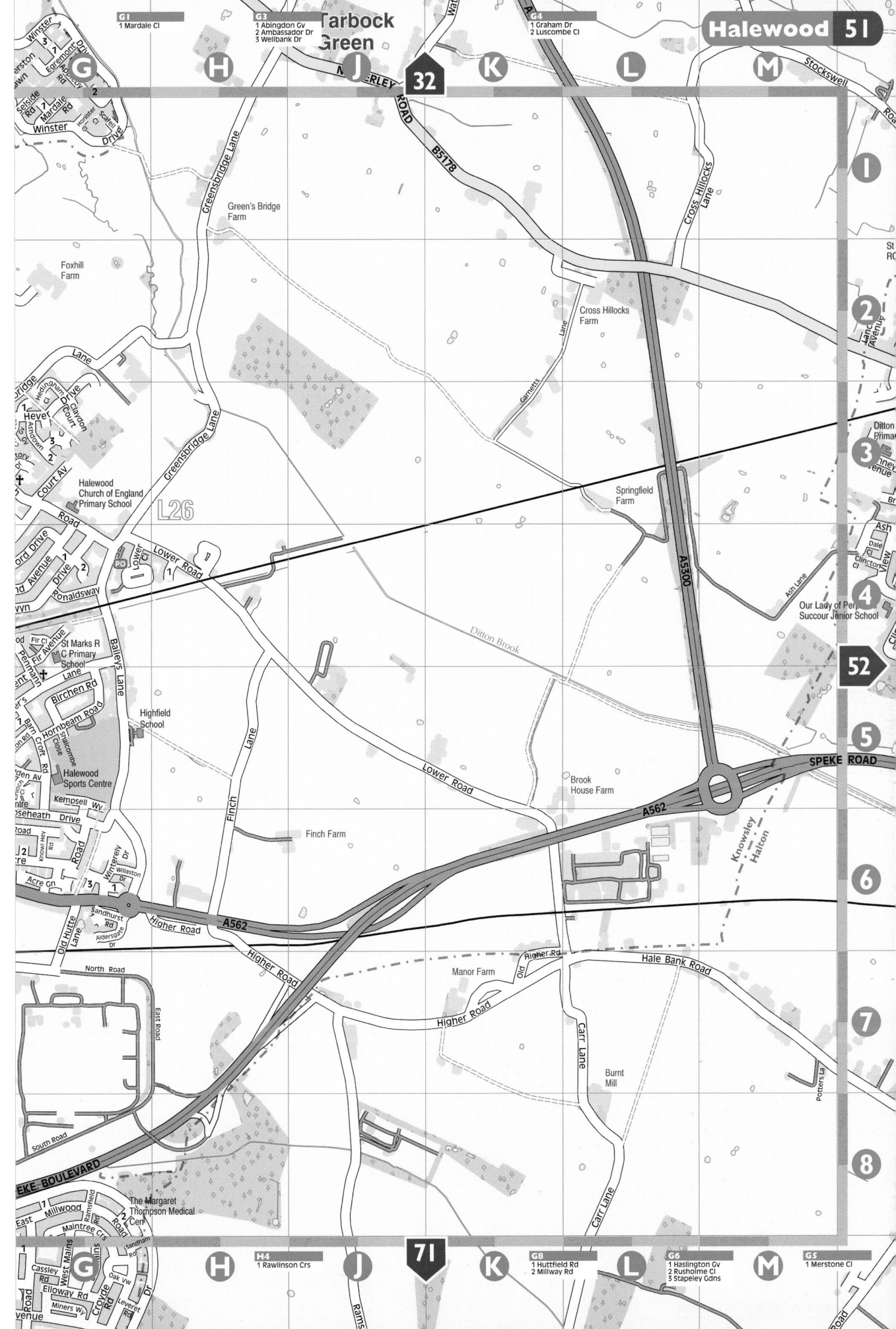

G1
1 Mardale Cl

G3
1 Abingdon Gv
2 Ambassador Dr
3 Wellbank Dr

G4
1 Graham Dr
2 Luscombe Cl

Tarbock Green

G **H** **J** **32** **K** **L** **M**

Stockswell Rd

1

2

3

4

52

5

6

7

8

Winster

Egremont Cl
Selside Rd
Mardale Rd
Winster

Hever

Claydon Court
Heddingham Court
Ashdown

Court Av

Halewood Church of England Primary School

L26

Lower Road

PO

St Marks R C Primary School

Birchen Rd

Highfield School

Hornbeam Road
Chalcombe Close

Halewood Sports Centre

Kempsell Wy

Roseheath Drive

Acre Gn

Winterley Dr
Willaston Dr

Baileys Lane

Finch Lane

Finch Farm

Lower Road

Greensbridge Lane

Green's Bridge Farm

Foxhill Farm

Cross Hillocks Lane

Cross Hillocks Farm

Garnetts

Springfield Farm

A5300

Ditton Brook

Brook House Farm

A562

SPEKE ROAD

Knowsley Halton

Ditton Prima

Ash Lane

Our Lady of Per Succour Junior School

Ash dale
Clincton View

Sandhurst Rd
Aldersgate Dr

Old Hutte Lane

Higher Road A562

North Road

East Road

South Road

SPEKE BOULEVARD

Millwood

The Margaret Thompson Medical Cen

Maintree Crs
Ramsfield Rd

Cassley Rd
West Mains
Elloway Rd
Oak Vw
Miners Wy

Higher Road

Manor Farm

Old Higher Rd

Carr Lane

Hale Bank Road

Burnt Mill

Potters La

G **H** **J** **71** **K** **L** **M**

H4
1 Rawlinson Crs

G8
1 Huttfield Rd
2 Millway Rd

G6
1 Haslington Gv
2 Rusholme Cl
3 Stapeley Gdns

G5
1 Merstone Cl

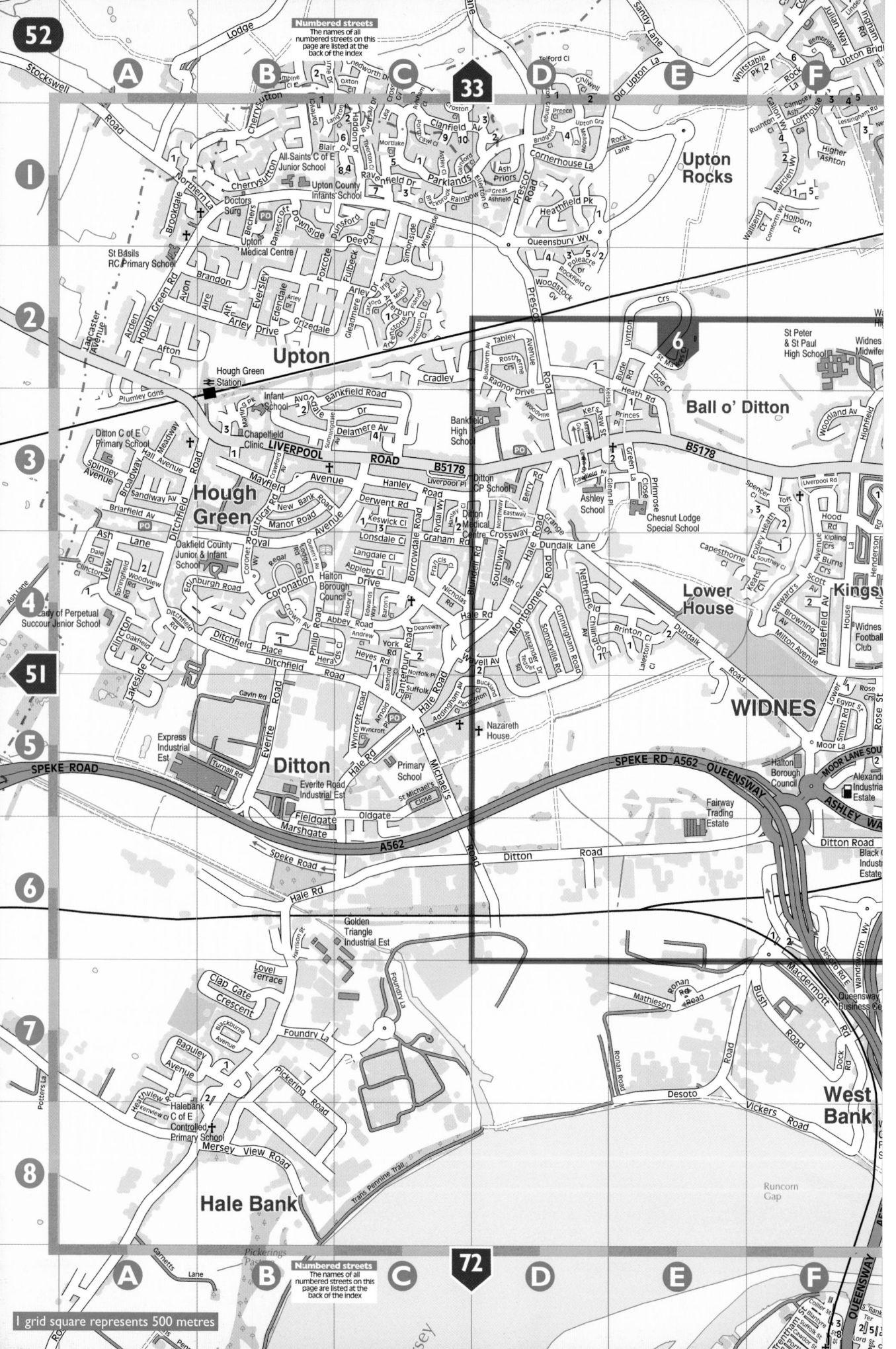

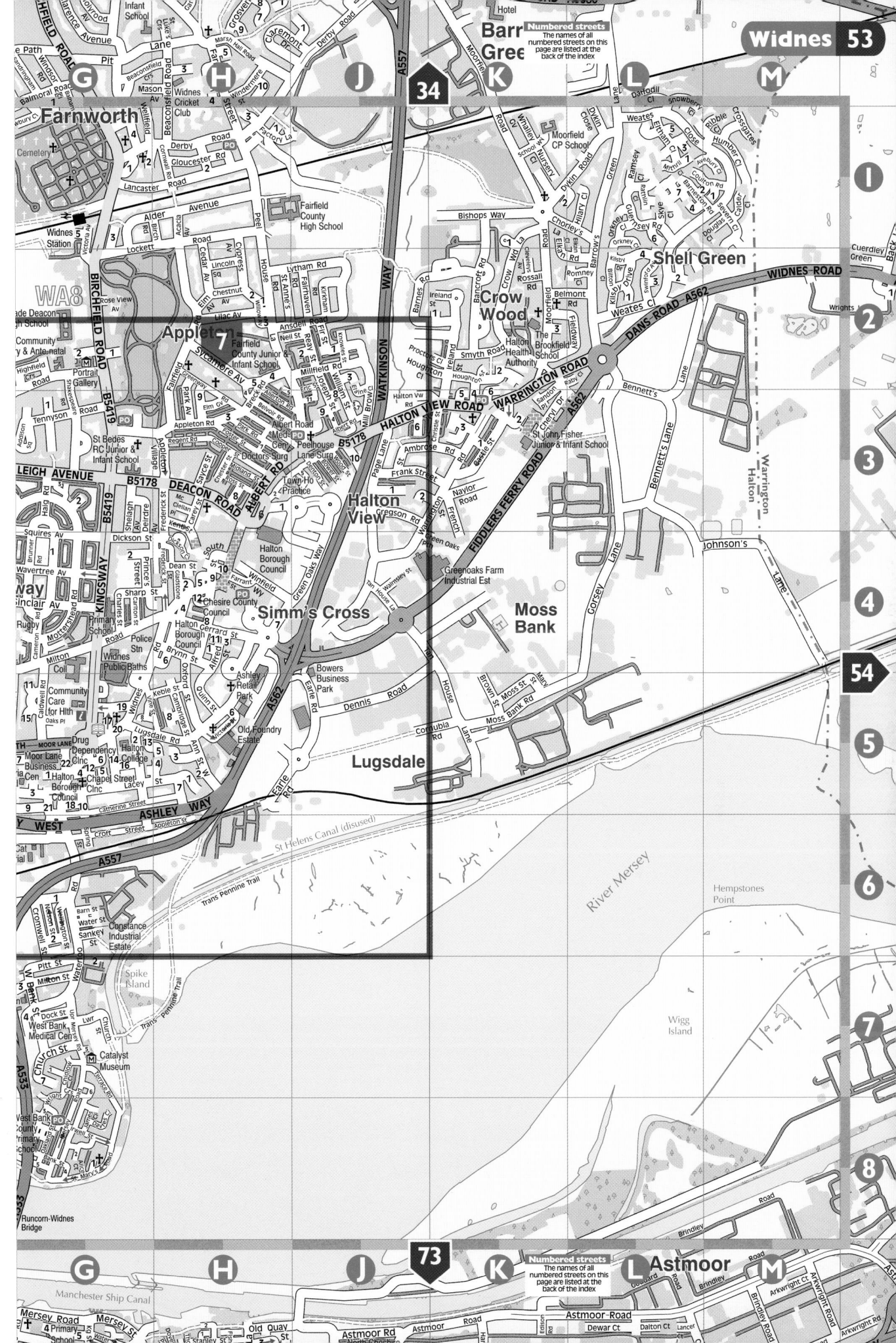

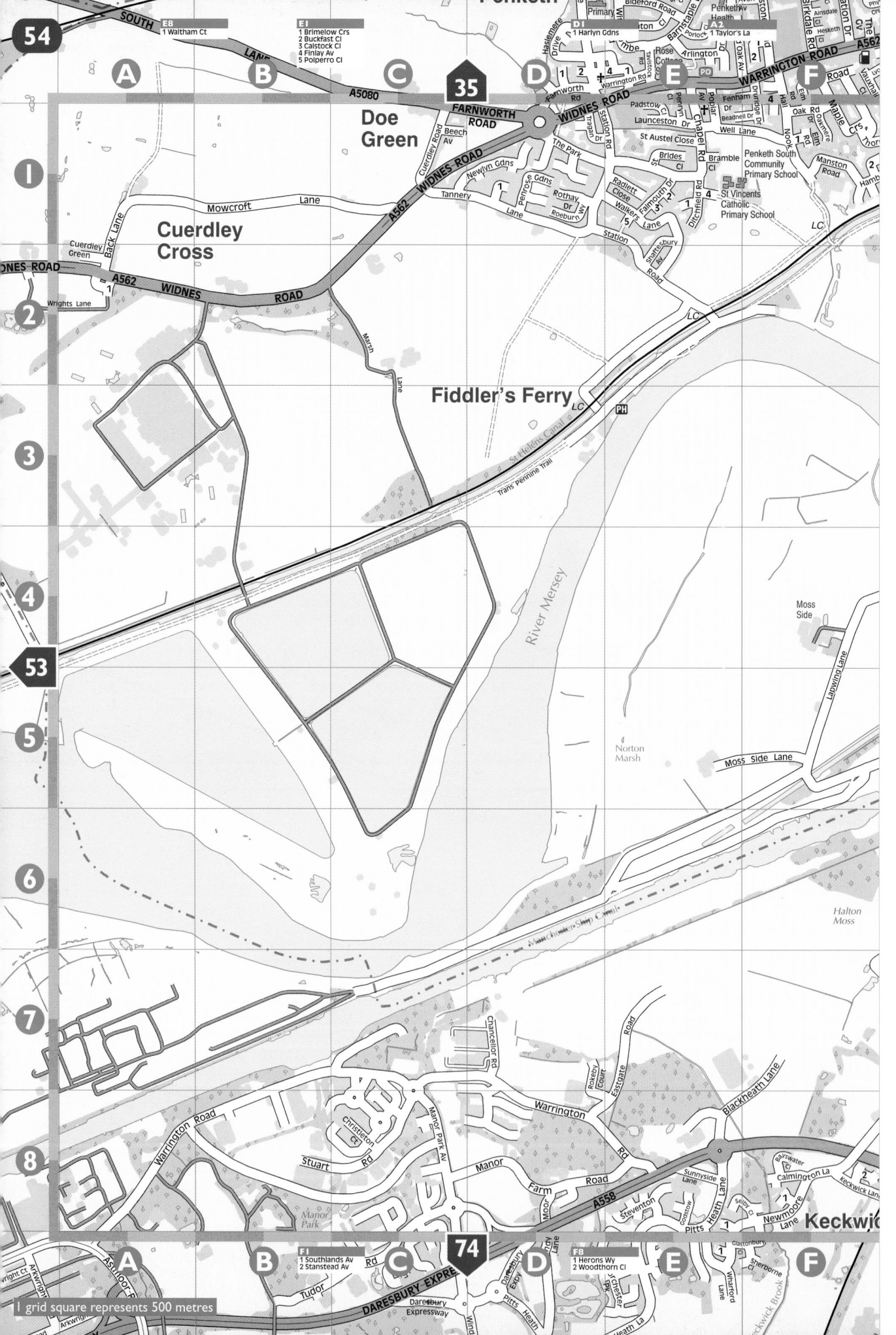

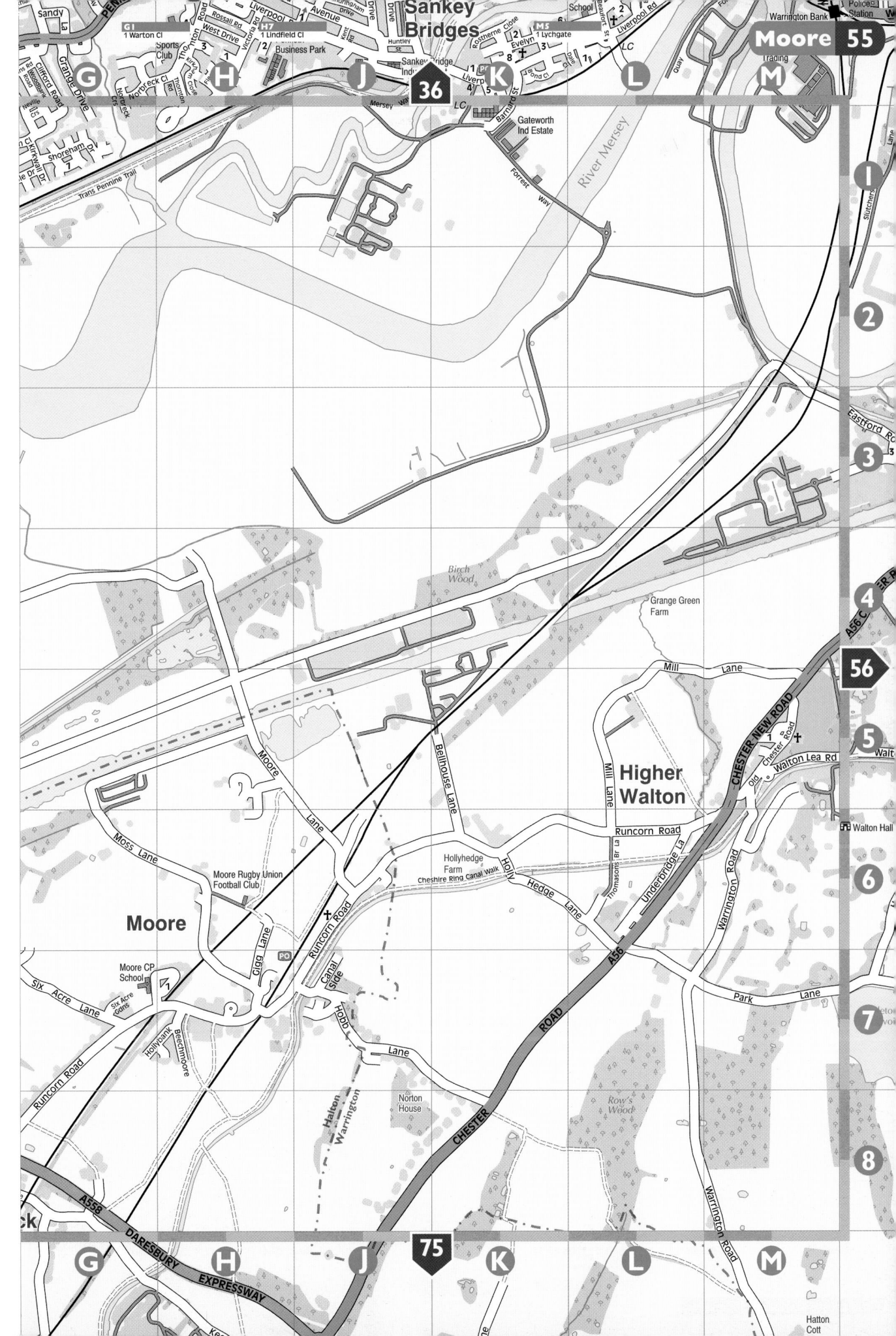

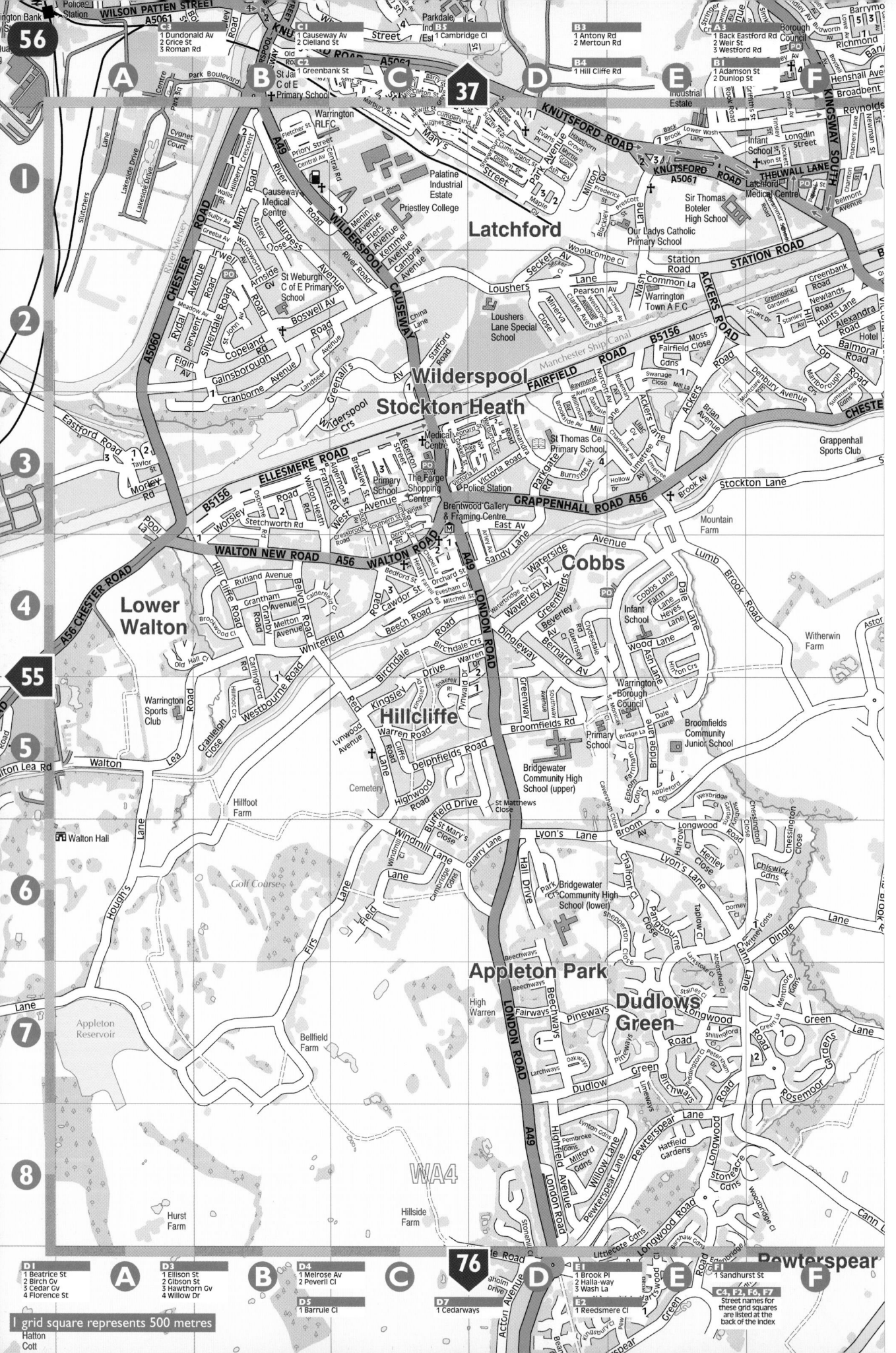

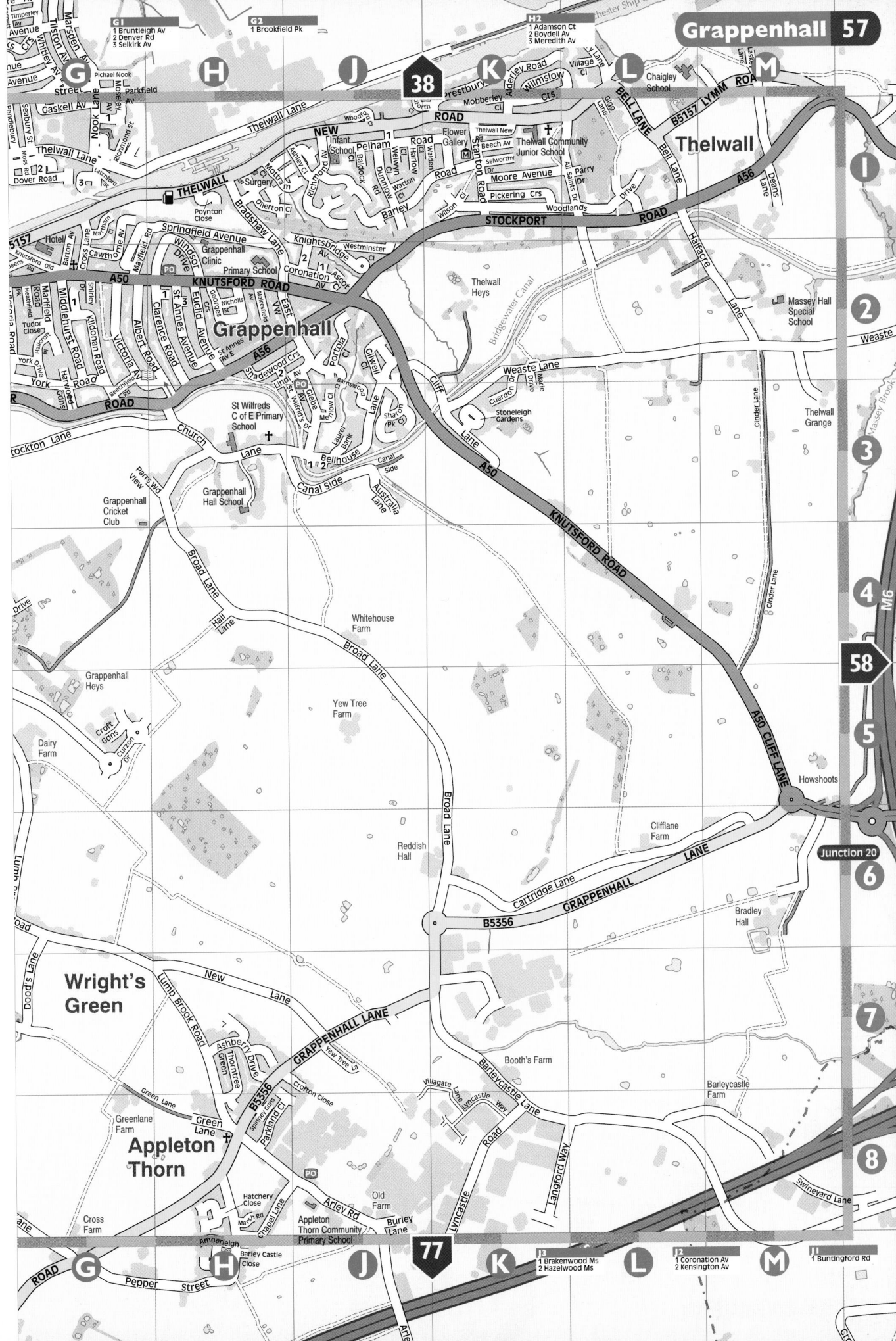

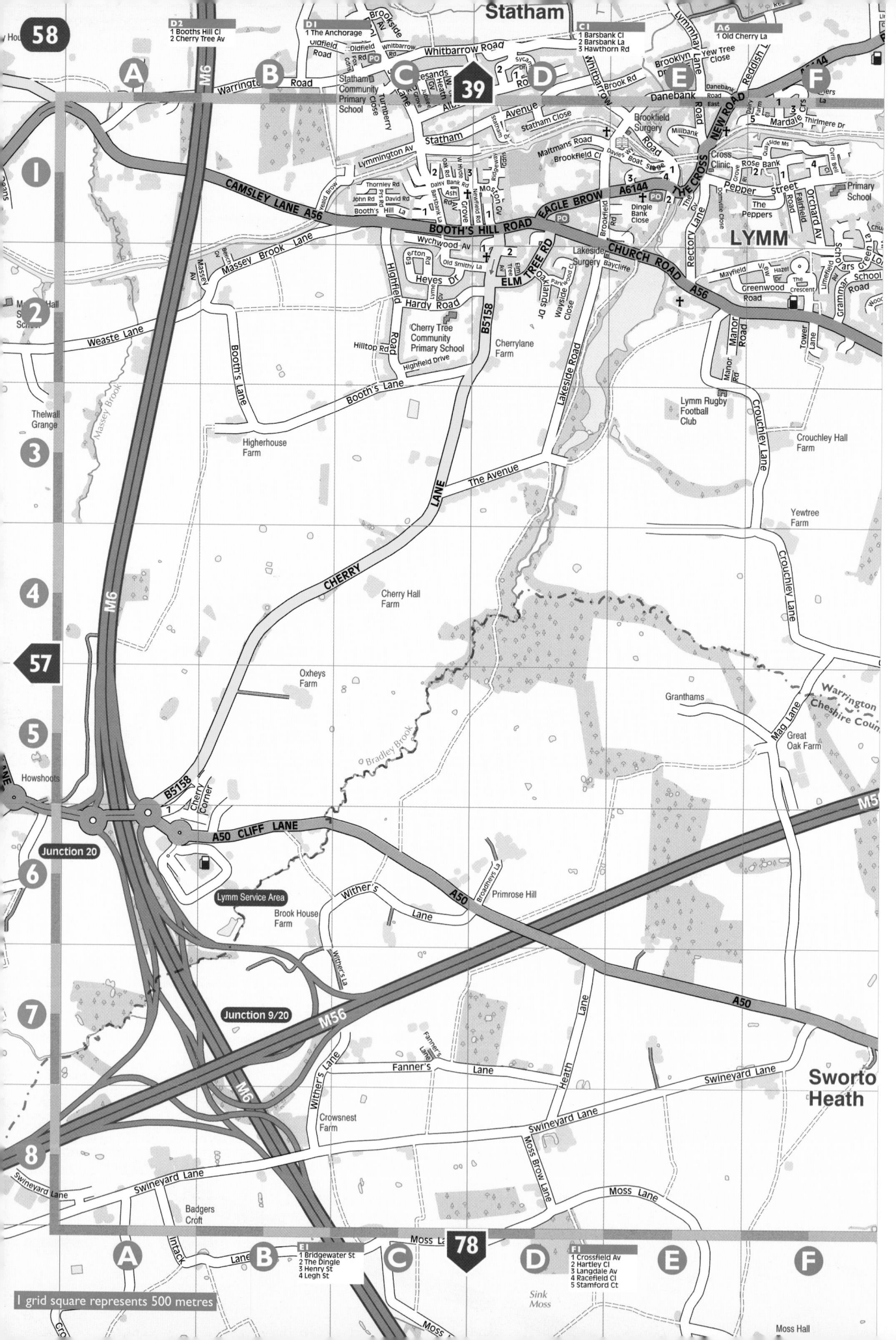

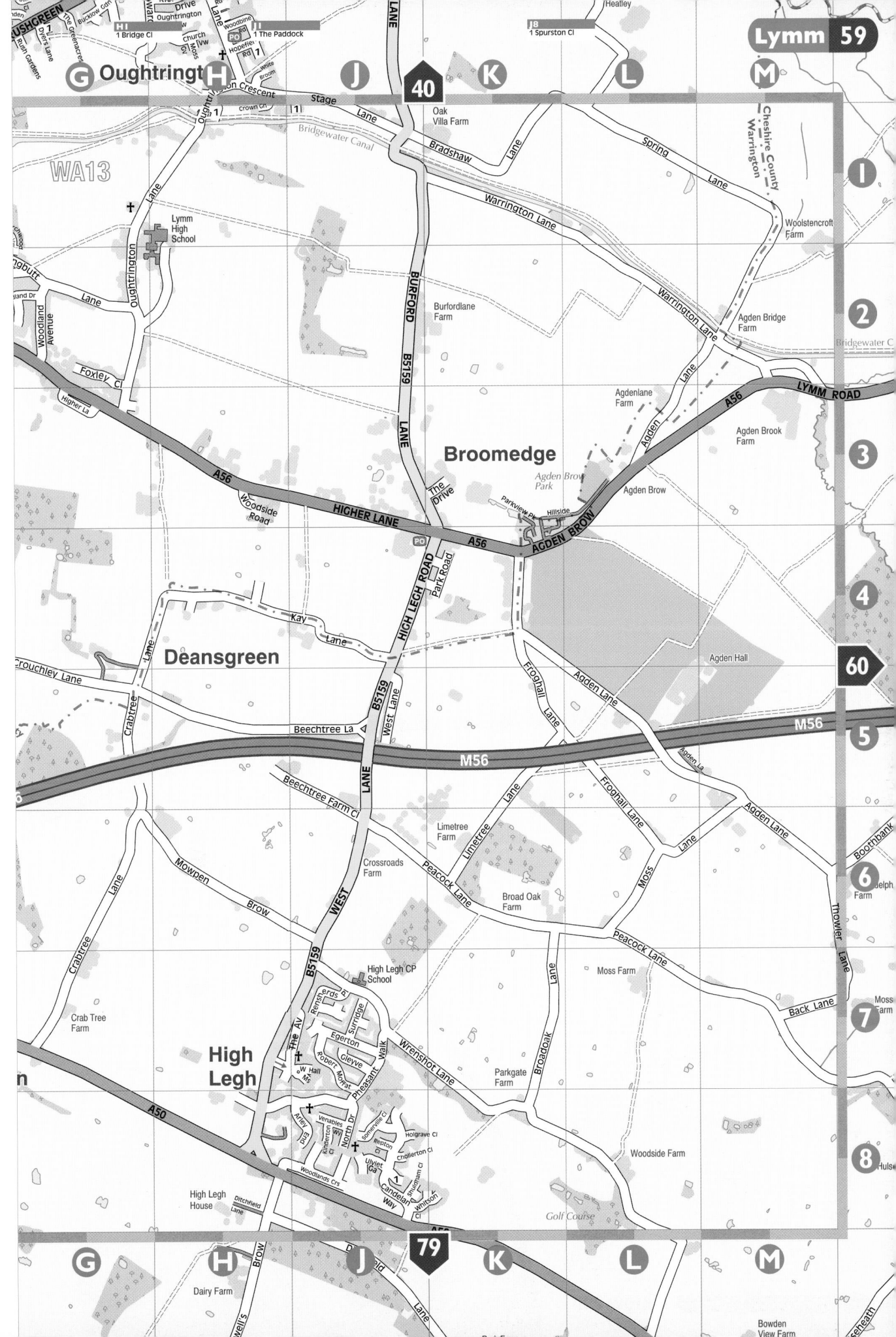

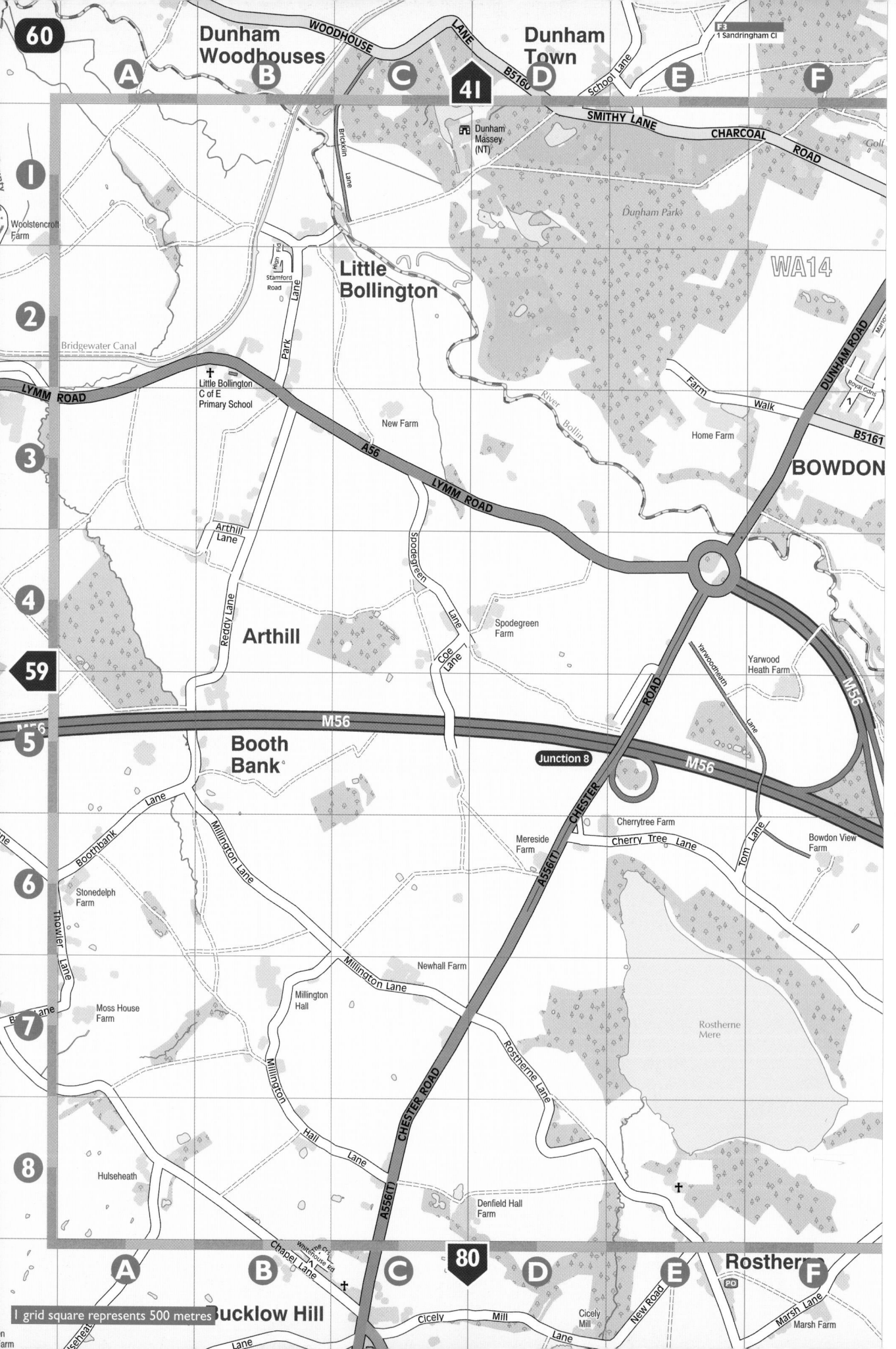

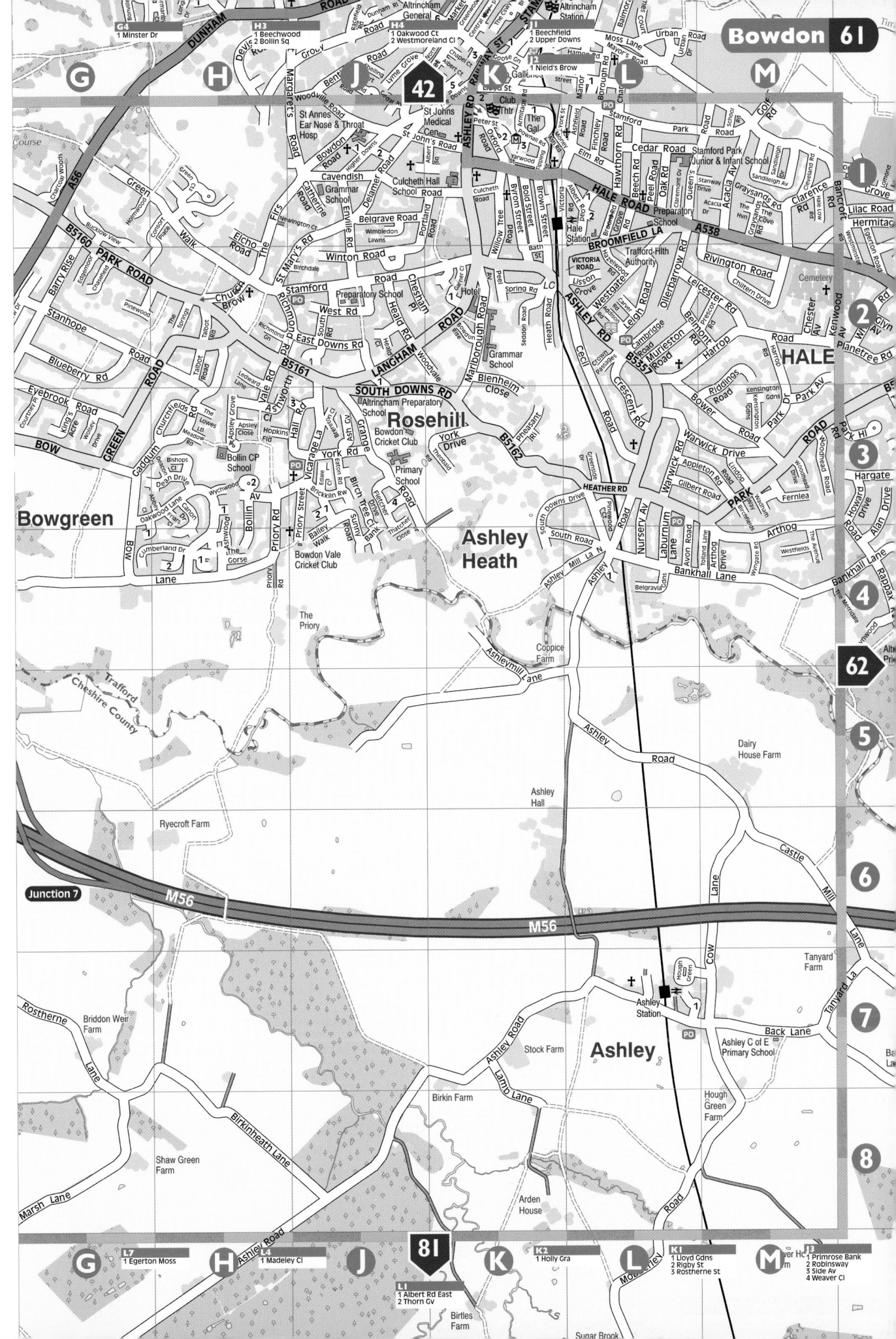

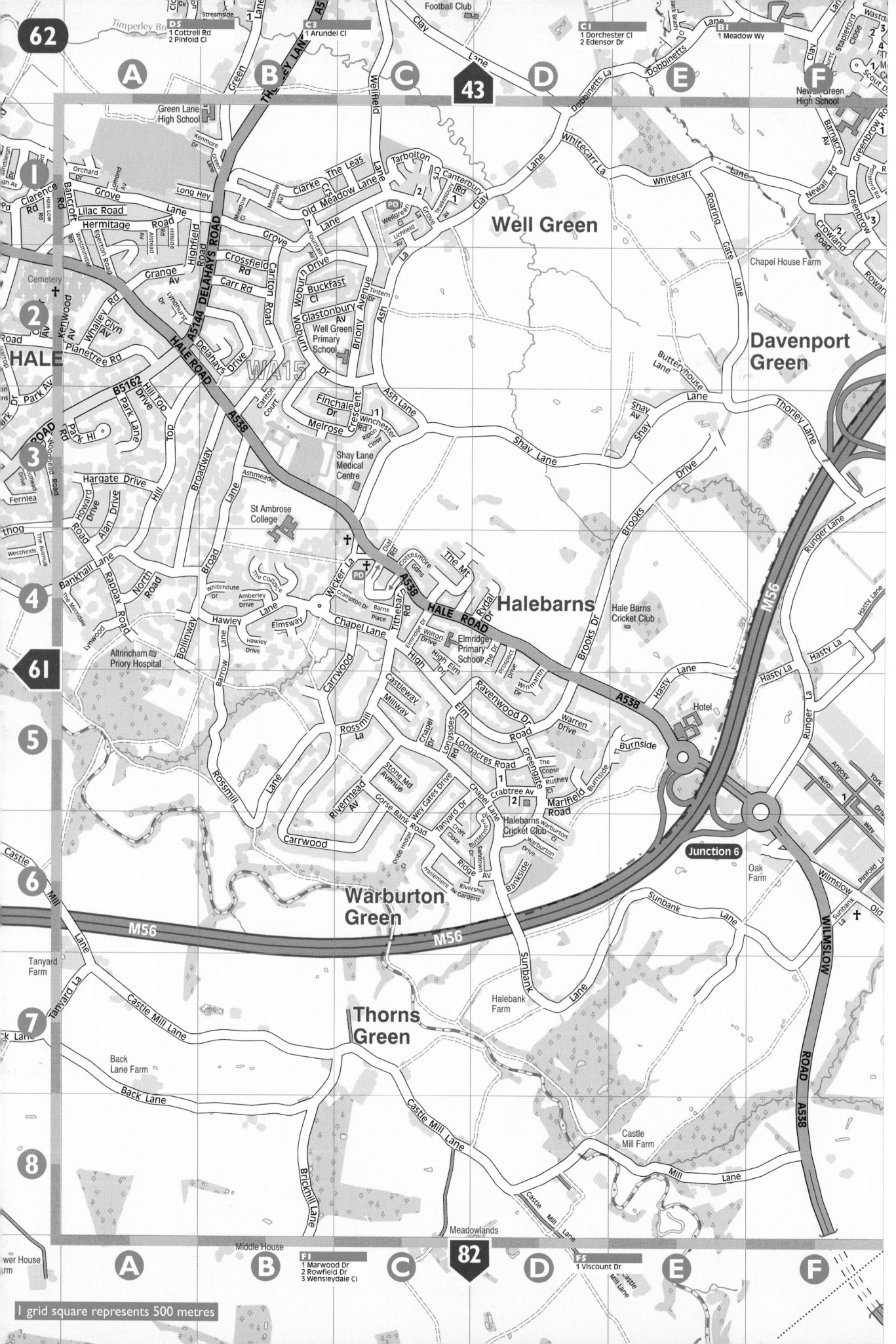

I grid square represents 500 metres

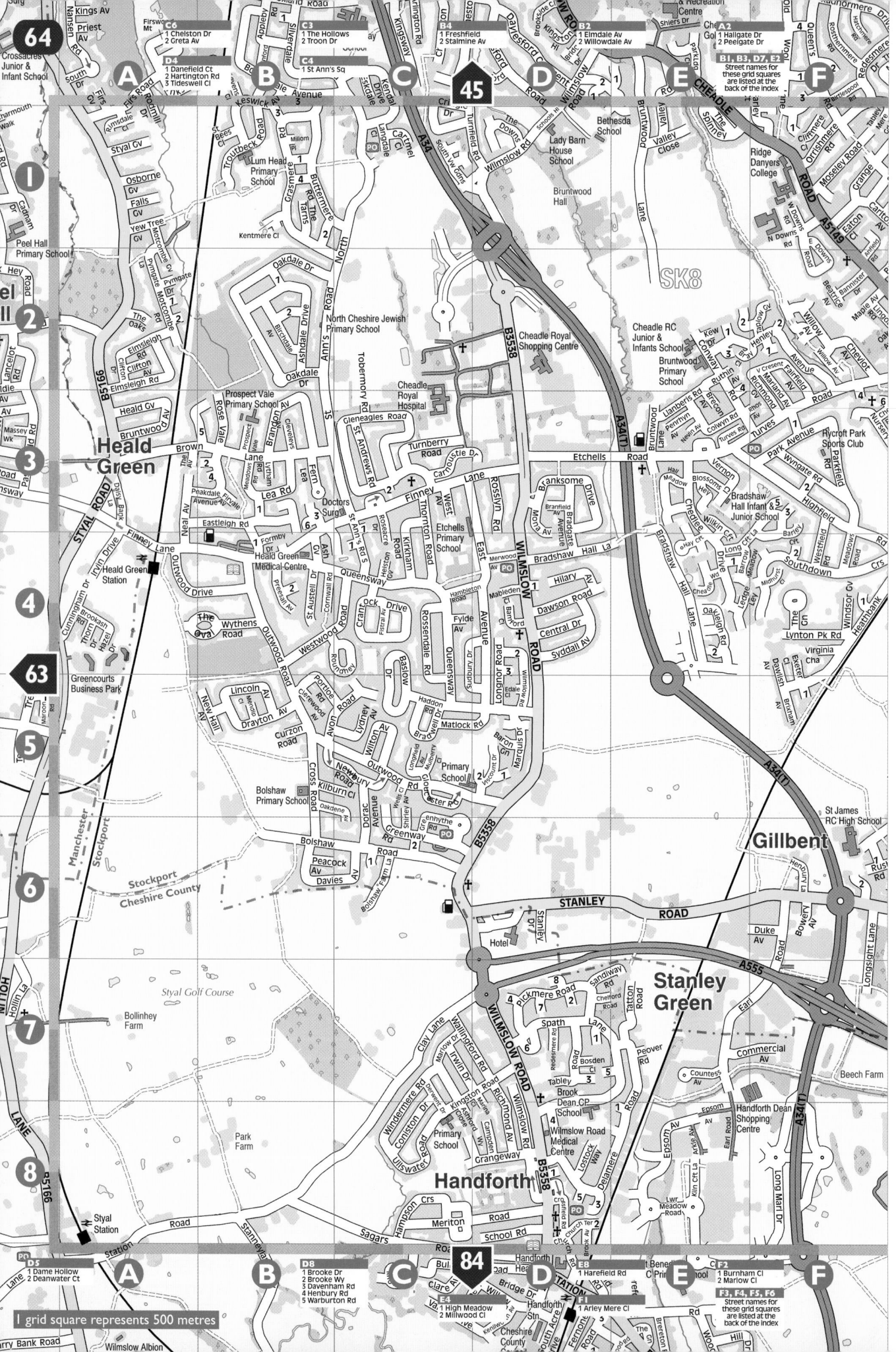

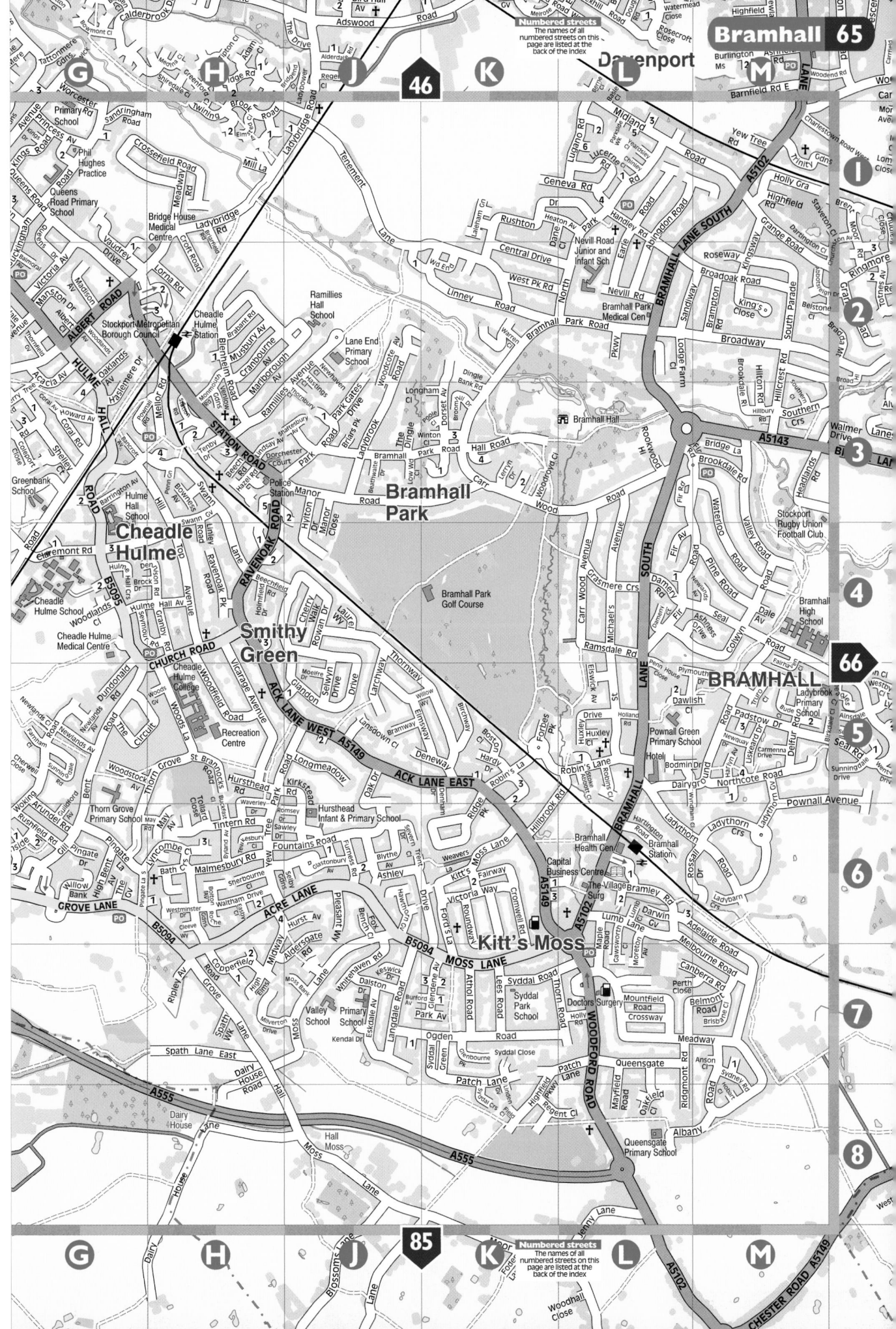

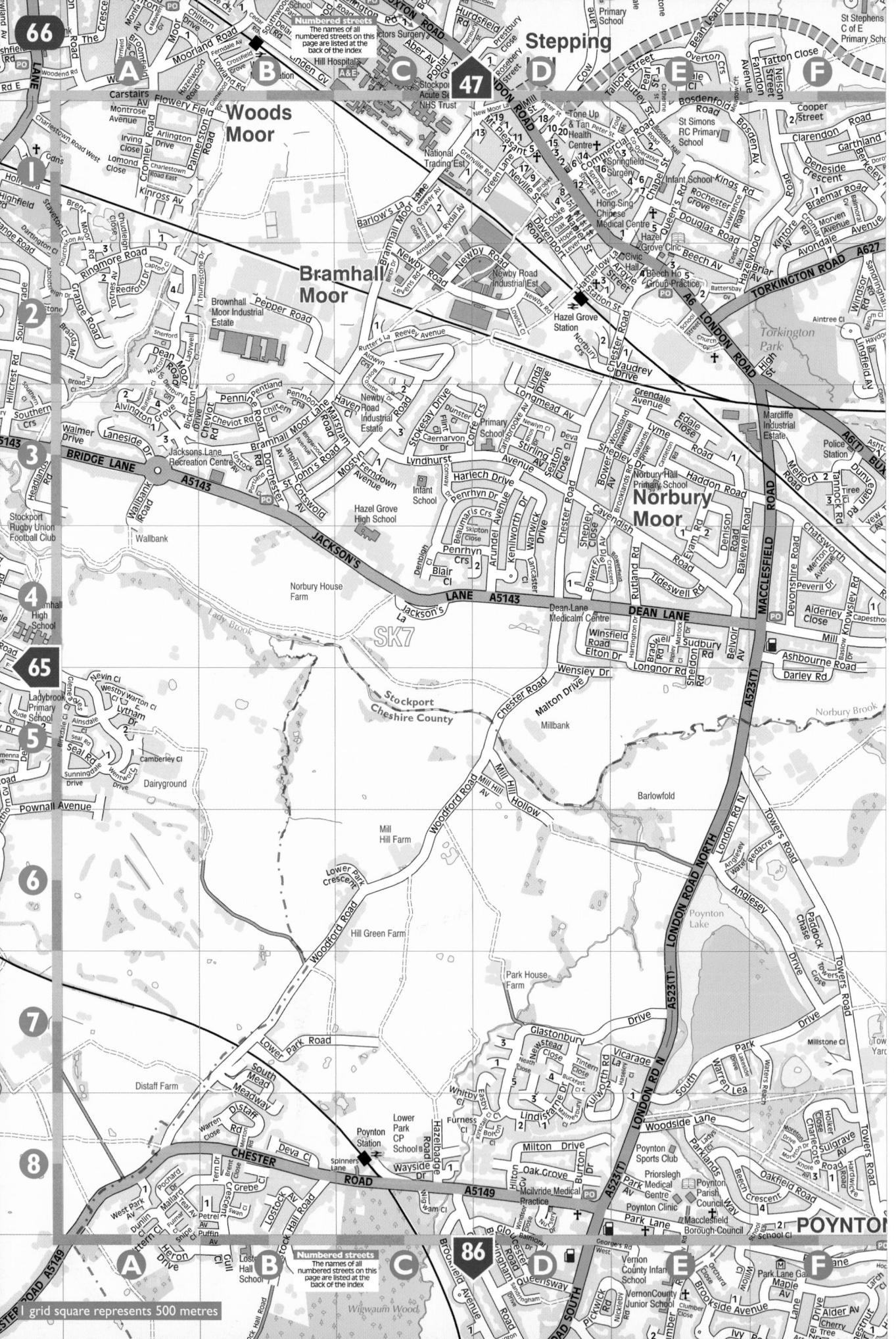

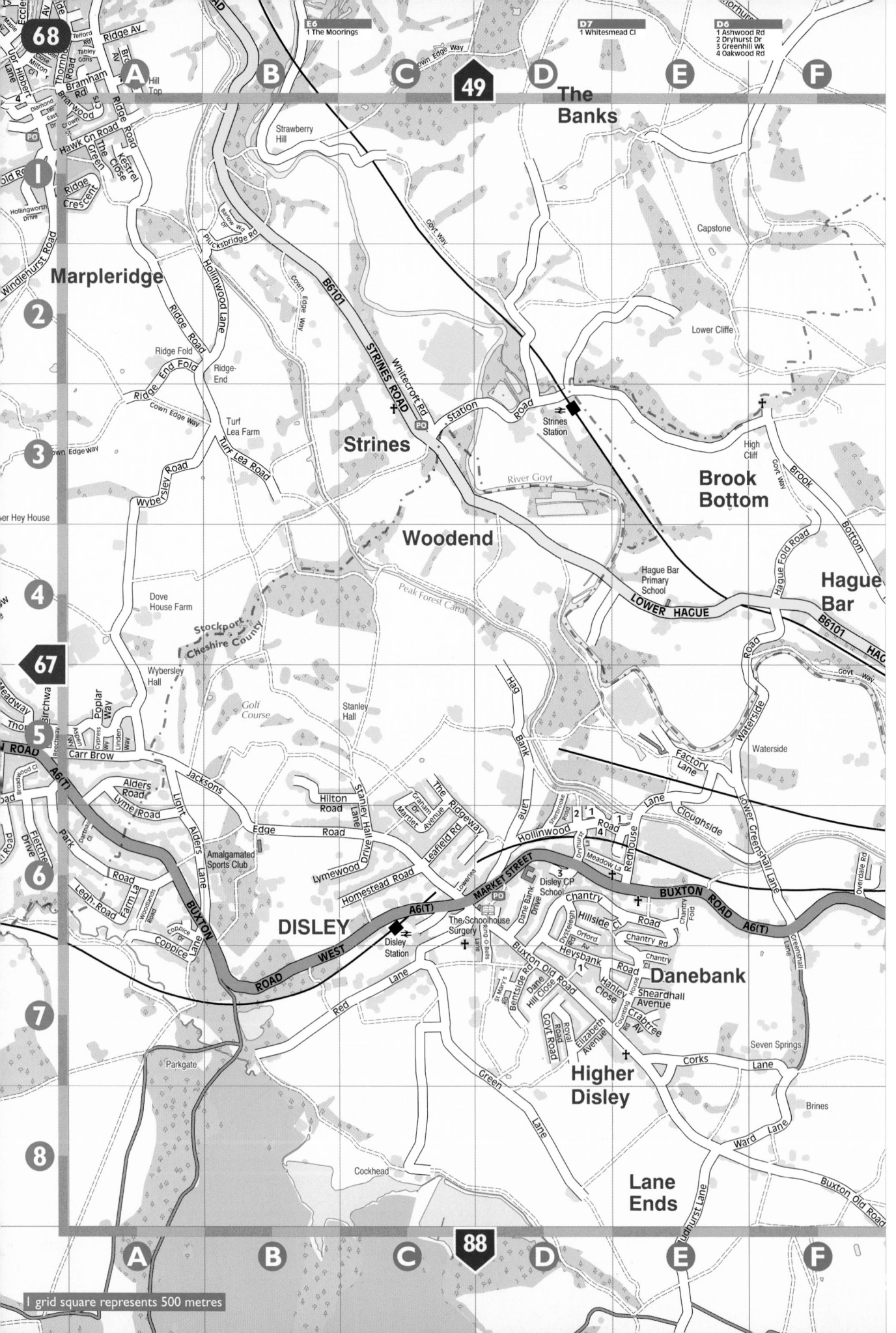

A B C **49** D E F

The Banks

E6
1 The Moorings

D7
1 Whitesmead Cl

D6
1 Ashwood Rd
2 Dryhurst Dr
3 Greenhill Wk
4 Oakwood Rd

Hill Top

Strawberry Hill

Capstone

Lower Cliffe

1

Hollingworth Drive

Marpleridge

Windlehurst Road

Pucksbridge Rd

Barlow Wd Dr

Cown Edge Way

Ridge End Fold

Ridge Fold

Ridge-End

Hollinwood Lane

Ridge Road

Cown Edge Way

Ridge End Fold

Turf Lea Farm

Turf Lea Road

Wybersley Road

2

3

Whitecroft Rd

B6101

STRINES ROAD

PO

Strines

Station Road

Goyt Way

Strines Station

High Cliff

Brook Bottom

Goyt Way

Brook Bottom

River Goyt

Woodend

Peak Forest Canal

Hague Bar Primary School

LOWER HAGUE

Hague Fold Road

Hague Bar

B6101

4

Dove House Farm

Stockport Cheshire County

Wybersley Hall

Golf Course

Stanley Hall

Hag Bank Lane

Factory Lane

Waterside

Waterside

Lower Greenshall Lane

5

Treadway

Birchwa

Beechway

A6(T) ROAD

Thor

BroadWood Cl

Poplar Way

Cypress Wy

Linden

Yew

Carr Brow

Jacksons

Light Alders Lane

Alders Road

Lyme Road

Hilton Road

Edge Road

Stanley Hall Lane

Graham Avenue

Martlet

The Ridgeway

Leafield Rd

Hollinwood

Sherdcote

Redhouse

Road

Cloughside

Meadow La

6

Fletcher Drive

Park Road

Leigh Road

Farm La

Woodlands

Dartmoor

Coppice Br

Coppice

BUXTON ROAD

Lymewood

Homestead Road

A6(T)

DISLEY

WEST

ROAD

Disley Station

Market Street

PO

Lowerlea

The Schoolhouse Surgery

Long-o-Bents

Disley CP School

Chantry

Dane Bank Drive

Buxton Old Road

Disleigh

Orford

Hillside Cl

Chantry Fold

Road

Chantry Rd

Chantry

BUXTON ROAD A6(T)

Overdale Rd

Greenshall Lane

Danebank

Heysbank Road

Hanley Close

Sheardhall Avenue

Crabtree Av

7

Parkgate

Red Lane

St Mary's

Bentside Rd

Dane Hill Close

Royal Road

Govt Road

Elizabeth Avenue

Country House

Higher Disley

Corks Lane

Seven Springs

Brines

8

Green Lane

Cockhead

Lane Ends

Tudhurst Lane

Ward Lane

Buxton Old Road

A B **88** C D E F

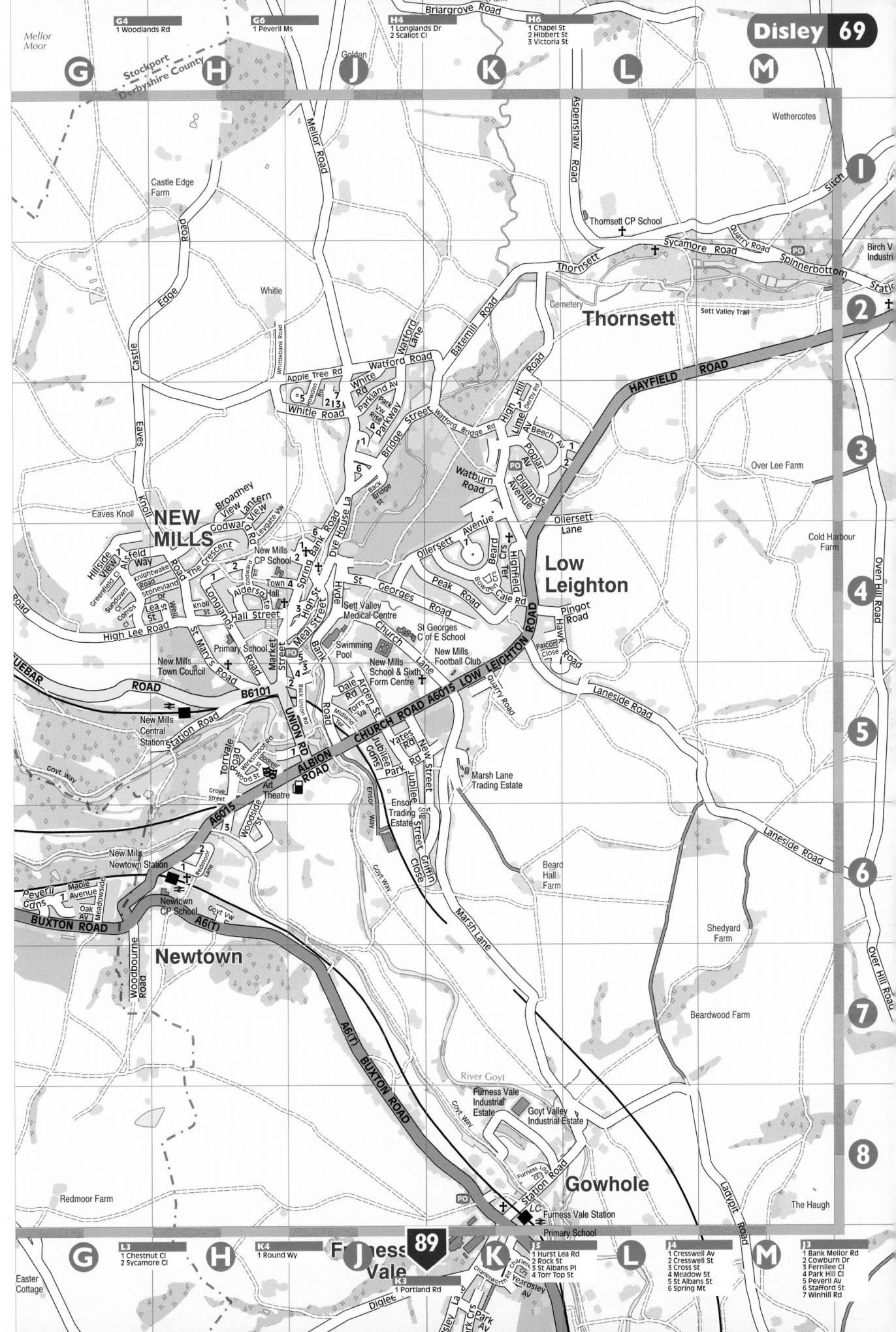

A B C **50** D E F

E2
1 Bramhall Cl
2 Ganworth Cl
3 Southern Rd

E1
1 Prenton Gn
2 Upton Cl
3 Upton Gn

D2
1 Fenton Gn
2 Marton Cl
3 Marton Gn

D1
1 Fenton Cl
2 Harefield Gn
3 Wellbrook Gn
4 Welton Cl
5 Welton Gn

Rycot Road

North Cr Road

bridge Cl church Road

Lyde

Appledore

Sandgate Cl

Speke Town La

Speke Hall Av

School Way

Gerneth Rd

Speke Church Rd

Greyhound

All Saints

Blacklock Hall

Blackrod

Stockton Wd Rd

Stockton Wood JMI School

Goldfinch Farm

Woodend La

Ramsbrook Rd

Western

Road

Road

Clough

Road

A561

Clough Road

Road-Doctors Surgery

St Christophers Junior School

St Christophers Infant School

Speke

Austin Rawlinson Sports Cen

Police Station

Hlth Authority

North Parade

Speke Family Health Clinic

South Parade

I

Spindus Road

Speke Hall Avenue

Hale Road

Blenheim Wy

Stirling Rd

Owen Dr

Tewit Hall Cl

Sutton Wood Rd

Tewit Hall Rd

Linner Road

Central

Lovel Wy

Lovel Road

Speke Comprehensive School

Harefield Road

Conleach Road

Millwood Road

Alder Wood

Heaton Close

Harland Rd

Catford Gn

Withington Rd

Ardwick Rd

Oldbridge Rd

Alderwood CP School

Little Heath Road

Ganworth Road

Burnage Cl

Eastern Avenue

AlvainEast

East

Central Way

2

The Walk

nk's

Speke Hall (NT)

Dunlop Road

Dunlop Rd

Dam Wood Road

Speke Community Comprehensive School

Holland Rd

Ganworth Rd

Dam Wood Road

Hale Drive

Oglet Lane

Liverpool Airport

L24

Hale Road

Liverpool Halton

Dungeon Lane

3

4

Mersey Way

Oglet

Oglet Lane

Mersey Way

5

6

River Mersey

7

Liverpool Cheshire County

8

A B **96** C D E F

Hale

G1
1 Harland Gn
2 Ringsfield Rd

G2
1 Almeda Rd
2 Daneswell Rd

K2
1 Bandon Cl
2 Greenore Dr

L2
1 Assheton Wk
2 Wellington Ga

SPEKE BOULEVARD

South Road

East Milliwd

Maintree Cr

Cassley Rd
Elloway Rd
Croyde Rd
West Mains
E Mains
Oak Vw
Miners Wy
Leveret Rd
Sandham Rd

Greenway Rd

Critchley Rd
Alderfield

St Ambrose Primary School

Heathgate Av
Church Rd
Church Way

Dam

The Margaret Thompson Medical Cen

Hale Road

Lane

Bailey's

Mersey Way

Brook Farm

Ramsbrook Lane

Carlow Cl
Arklow Drive
Wexford Av
Aran Cl
Langford
Langford Fld
Pheasant Fld
Kilgare Cl
Main Cl
Emls
Cockade
Pepper St La
Town La
High Street
Holly Cl

Morcott Lane

Police Station

Hale Primary School

PO

Church End

Vicarage Close

Church Road

Ertwood Cl
Gardener Wy
Heworth Road
Hoganton Rd

Town Lane

Ivy Farm
Court Doctors
School
Ireland Road
Sure

Within Way

Carr Lane

Carr Lane

Hale Gate Road

Halegate Farm

Mersey Way

Lighthouse Road

Hale Head

Mersey Way

Halton
Cheshire County

G H J K L M

I
2
3
4
72
5
6
7
8

51

97

A **B** **C** **52** **D** **E** **F**

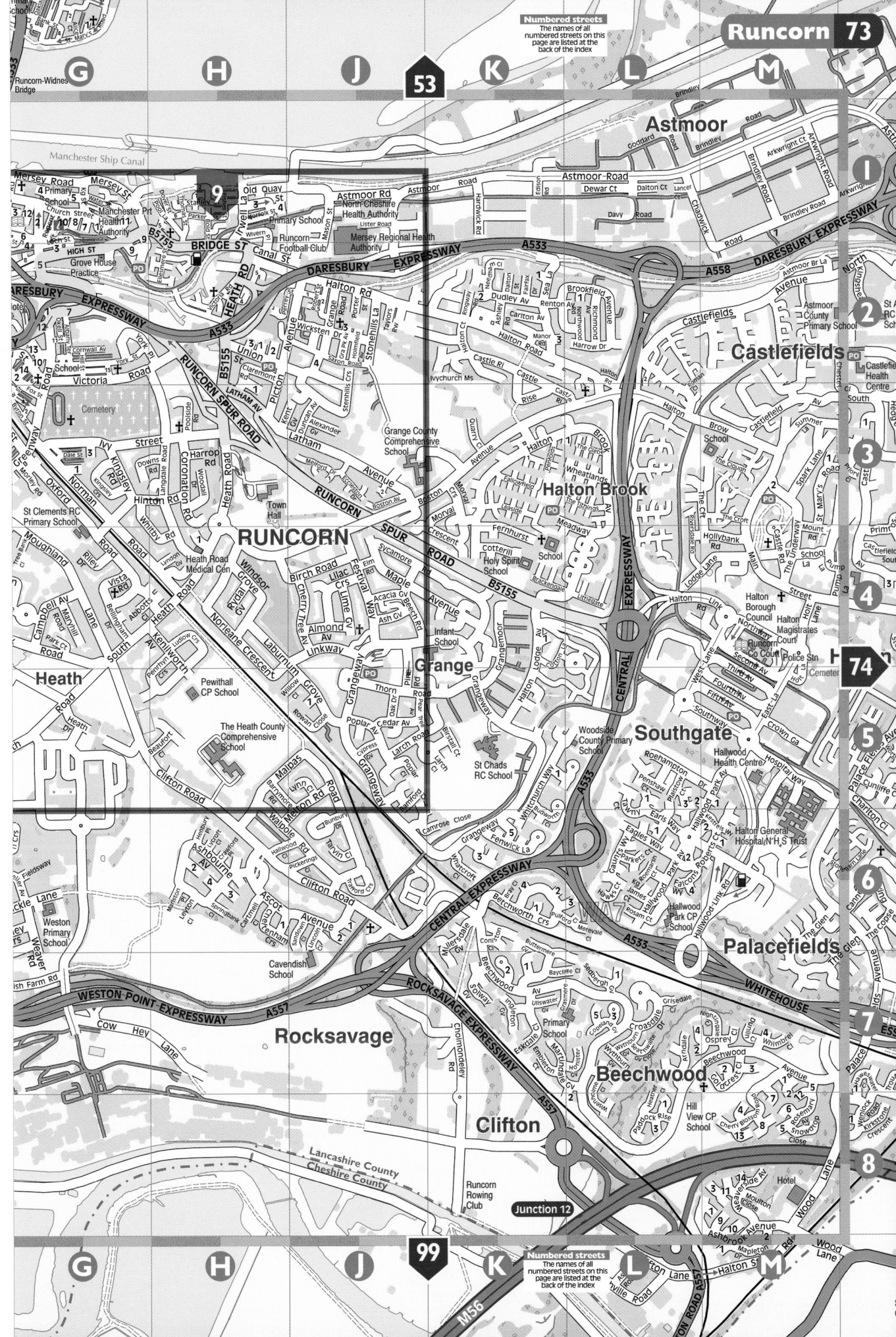

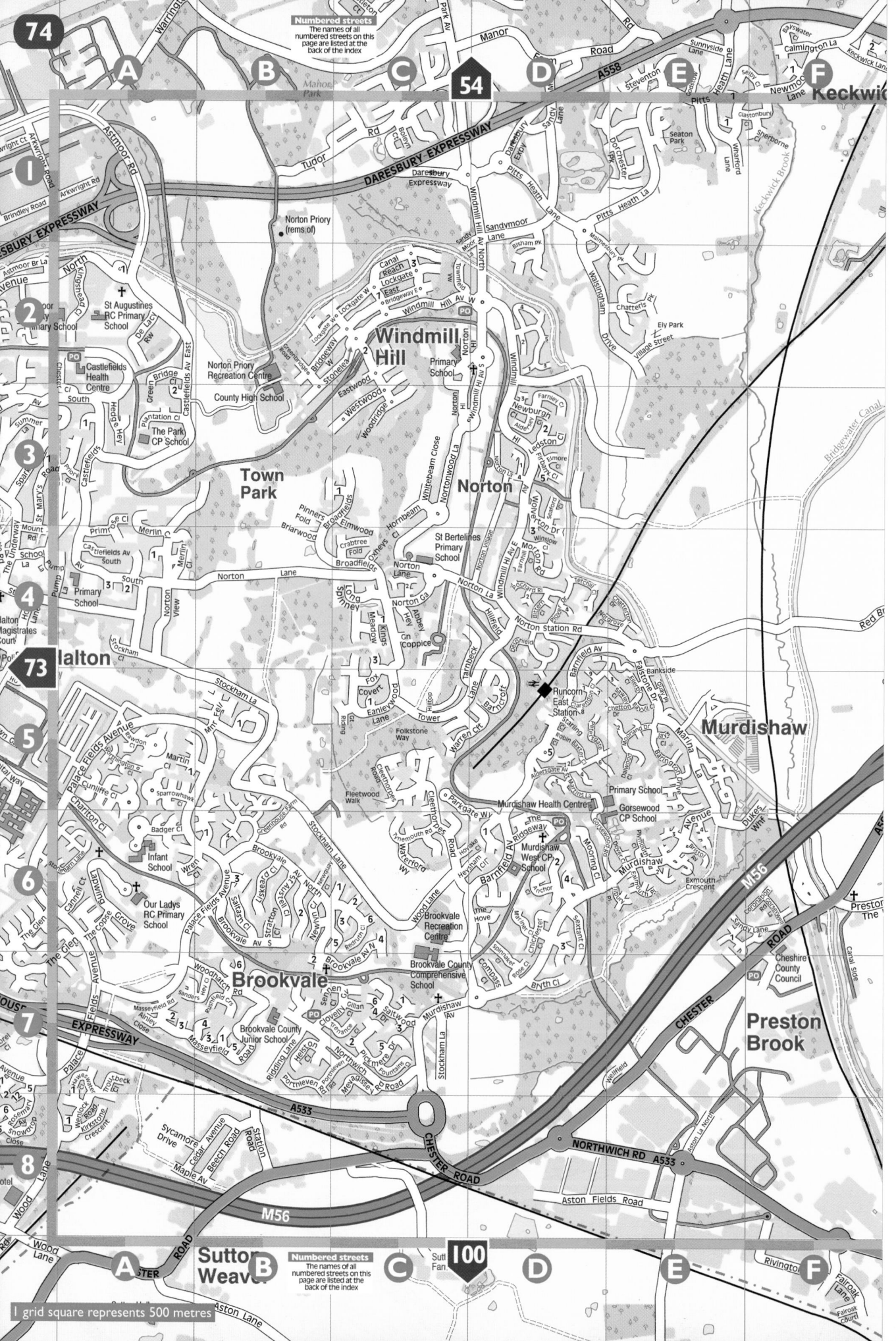

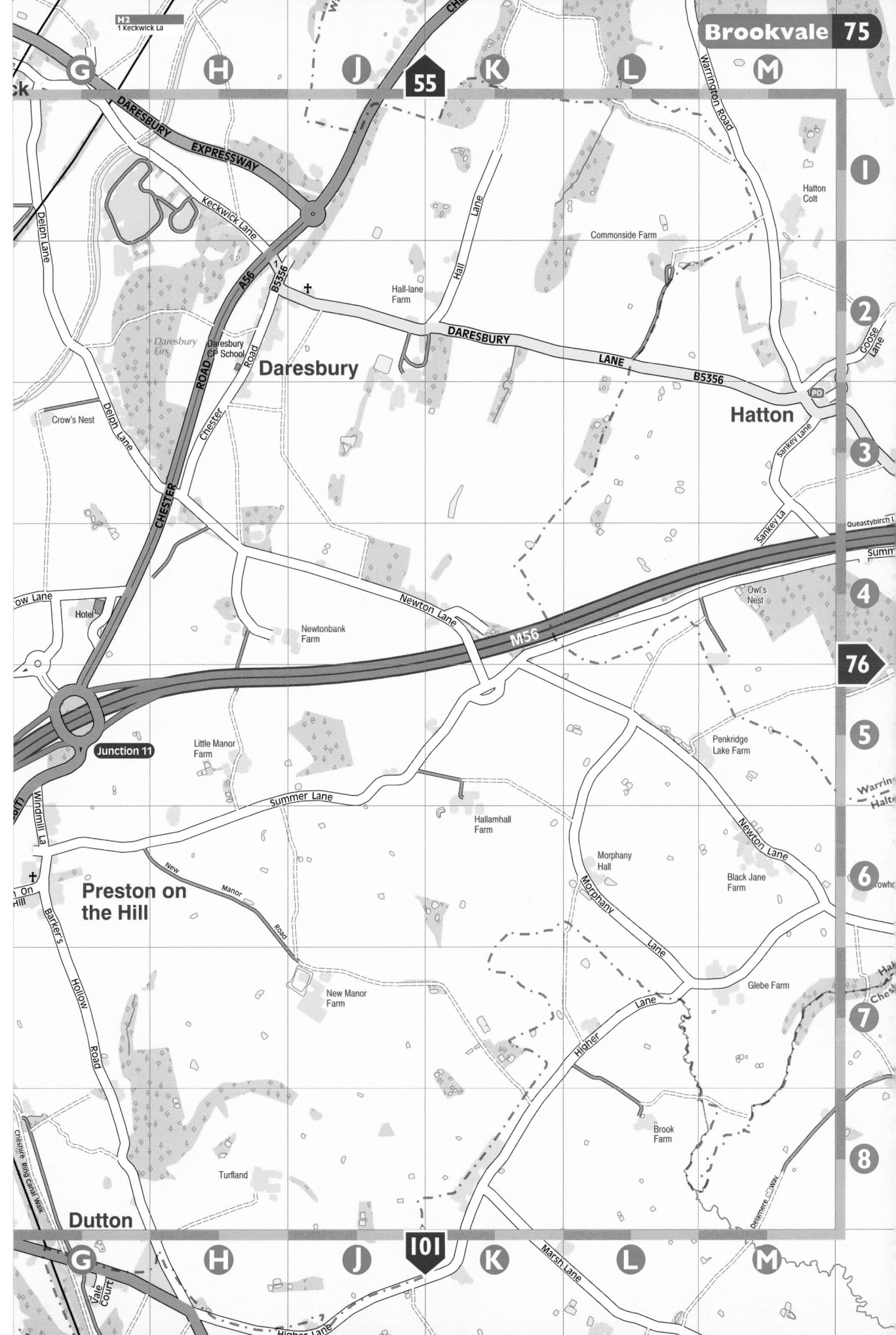

H2
1 Keckwick La

G · H · J · 55 · K · L · M

I

DARESBURY EXPRESSWAY

Keckwick Lane

A56

B5556

Chester Road

Delph Lane

Daresbury Firs

Daresbury CP School

Daresbury

Hall-lane Farm

Hall Lane

DARESBURY LANE B5356

Commonside Farm

Hatton Cott

Coose Lane

2

PO

Hatton

3

Sankey Lane

Queastybirch L

Summ

Crow's Nest

Chester Road

Newton Lane

M56

Owl's Nest

4

76

Crow Lane

Hotel

Newtonbank Farm

Penkridge Lake Farm

5

Junction 11

Little Manor Farm

Summer Lane

Hallamhall Farm

Morphany Hall

Newton Lane

Black Jane Farm

Warring
Halt

owho

6

Windmill La

Barker's Hollow Road

New Manor Road

Preston on the Hill

On Hill

Morphany Lane

Glebe Farm

Higher Lane

7

New Manor Farm

Cheshire Ring Canal Walk

Turfland

Brook Farm

Delamere Way

8

Dutton

G · H · J · 101 · K · Marsh Lane · L · M

Vale Court

Higher Lane

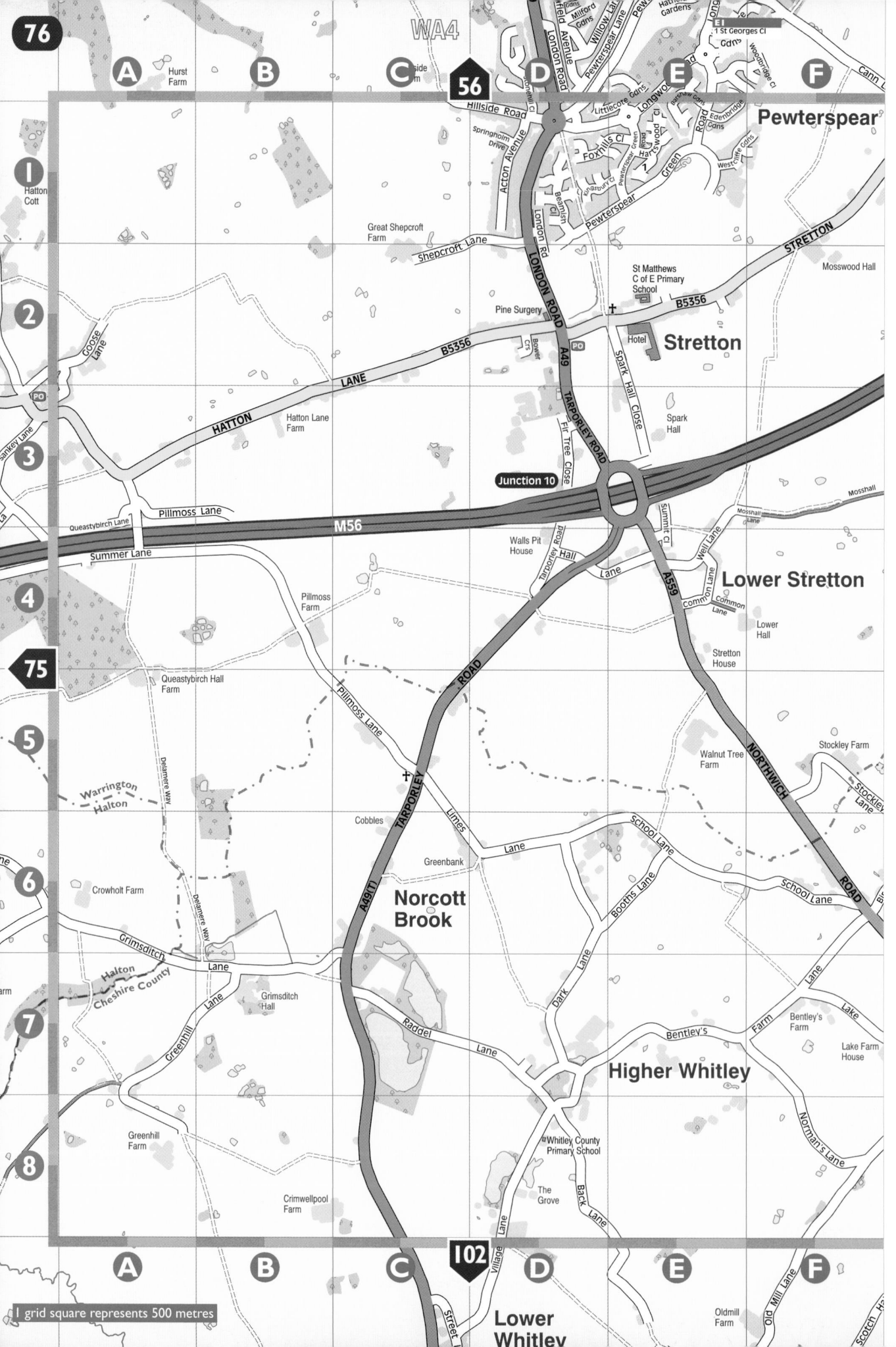

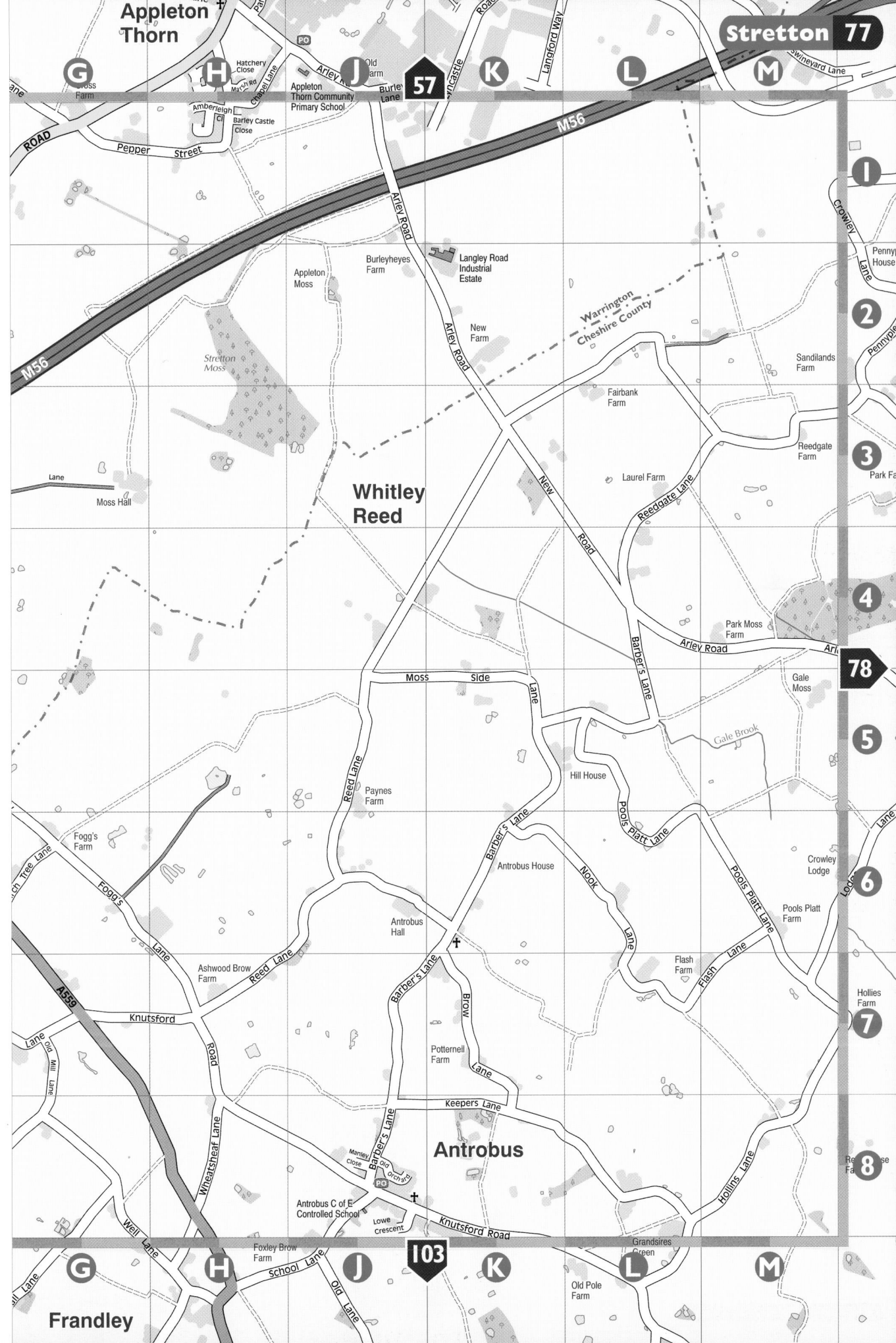

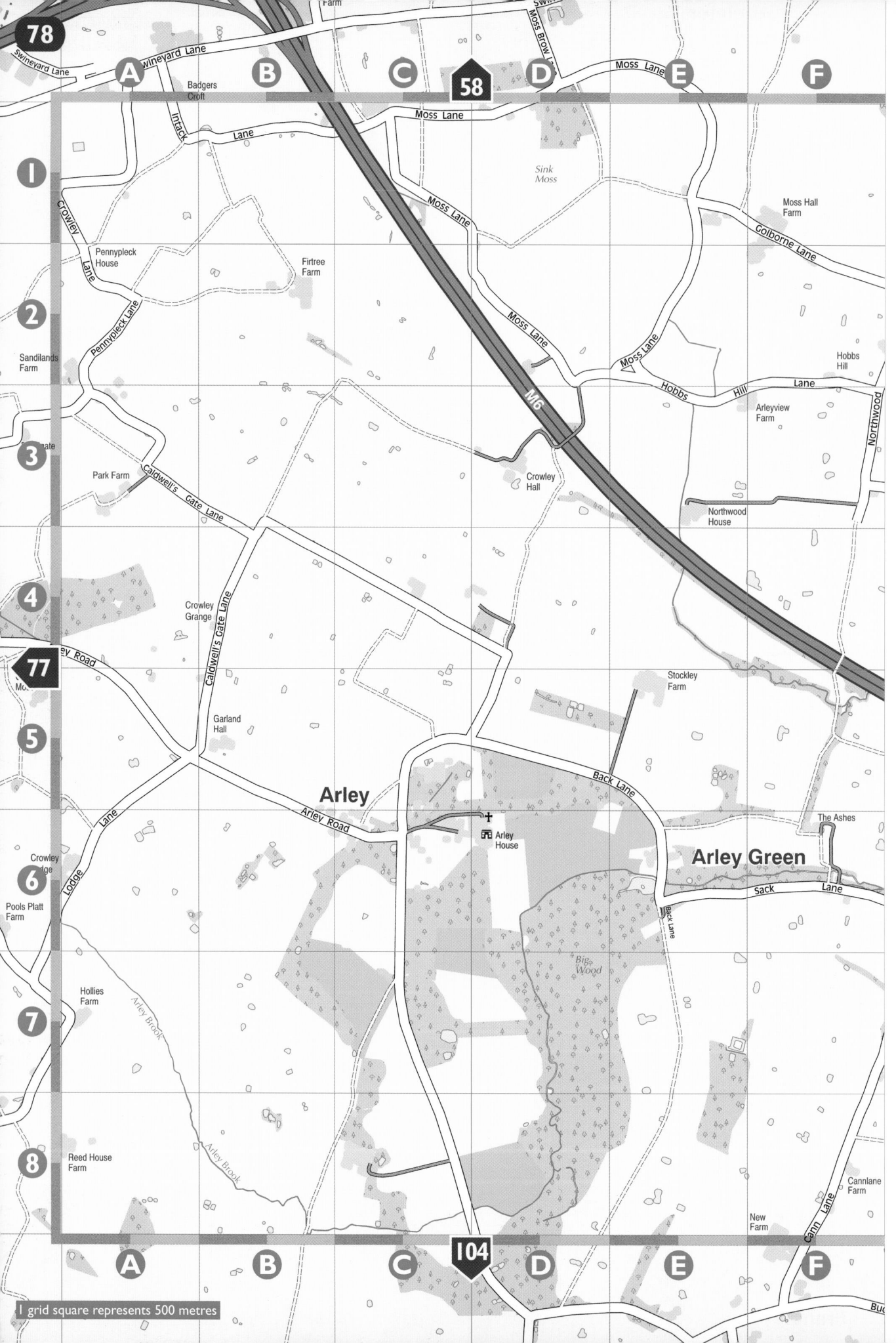

78

58

77

104

A B C D E F

I
2
3
4
5
6
7
8

Swineyard Lane

Swineyard Lane

Badgers Croft

Intack Lane

Moss Brow Lane

Moss Lane

Moss Lane

Moss Lane

Moss Hall Farm

Golborne Lane

Sink Moss

Crowley Lane

Pennypleck House

Firtree Farm

Pennypleck Lane

Sandilands Farm

Moss Lane

Hobbs Hill

Hobbs Hill Lane

Northwood

M6

Park Farm

Caldwell's Gate Lane

Arleyview Farm

Crowley Hall

Northwood House

Crowley Grange

Caldwell's Gate Lane

Moss

ey Road

Stockley Farm

Garland Hall

Back Lane

Arley

Arley Road

Arley House

Arley Green

The Ashes

Crowley Lodge Lane

Sack Lane

Back Lane

Crowley

Pools Platt Farm

Big Wood

Hollies Farm

Arley Brook

Reed House Farm

Arley Brook

New Farm

Cann Lane

Cannlane Farm

Bucl

I grid square represents 500 metres

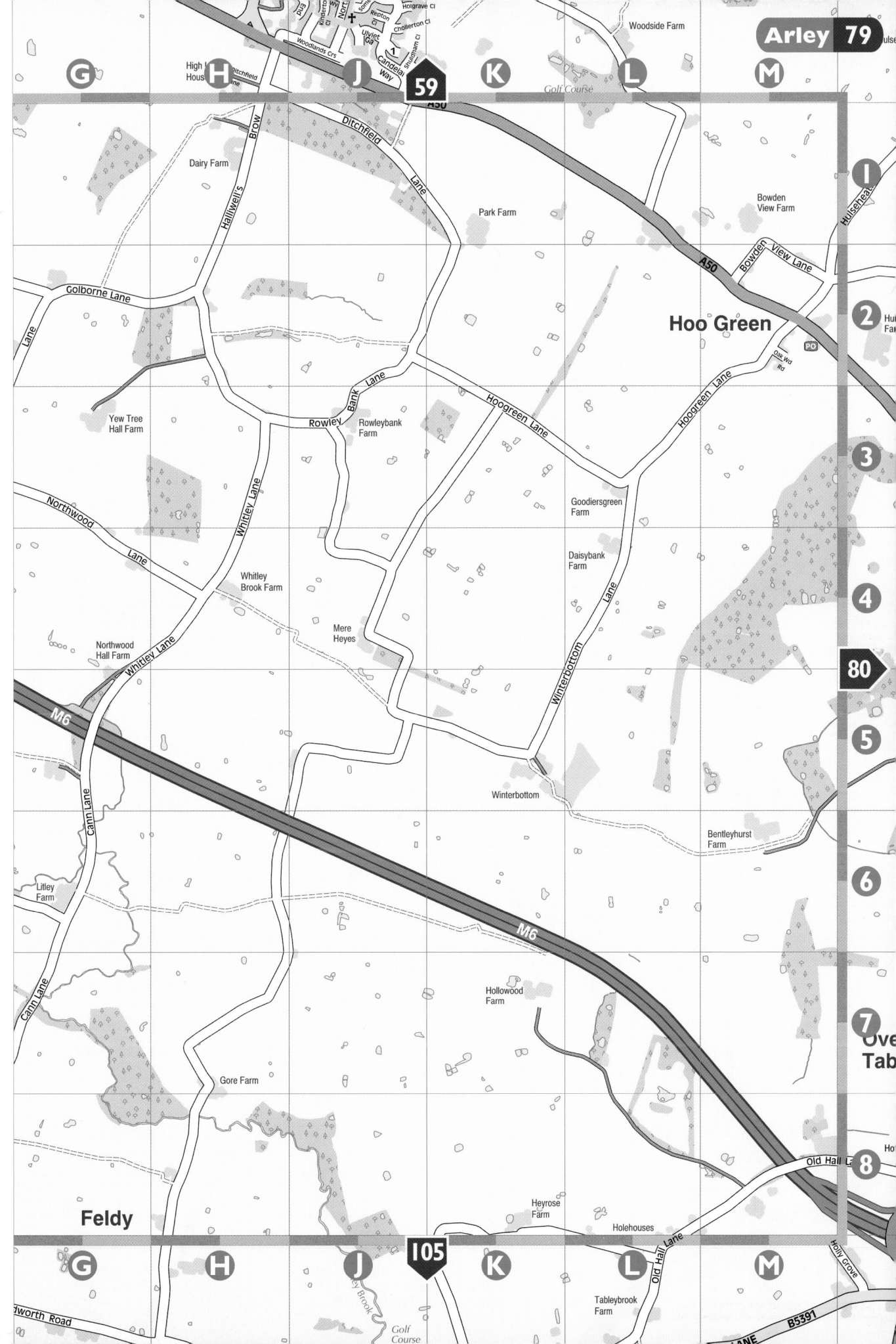

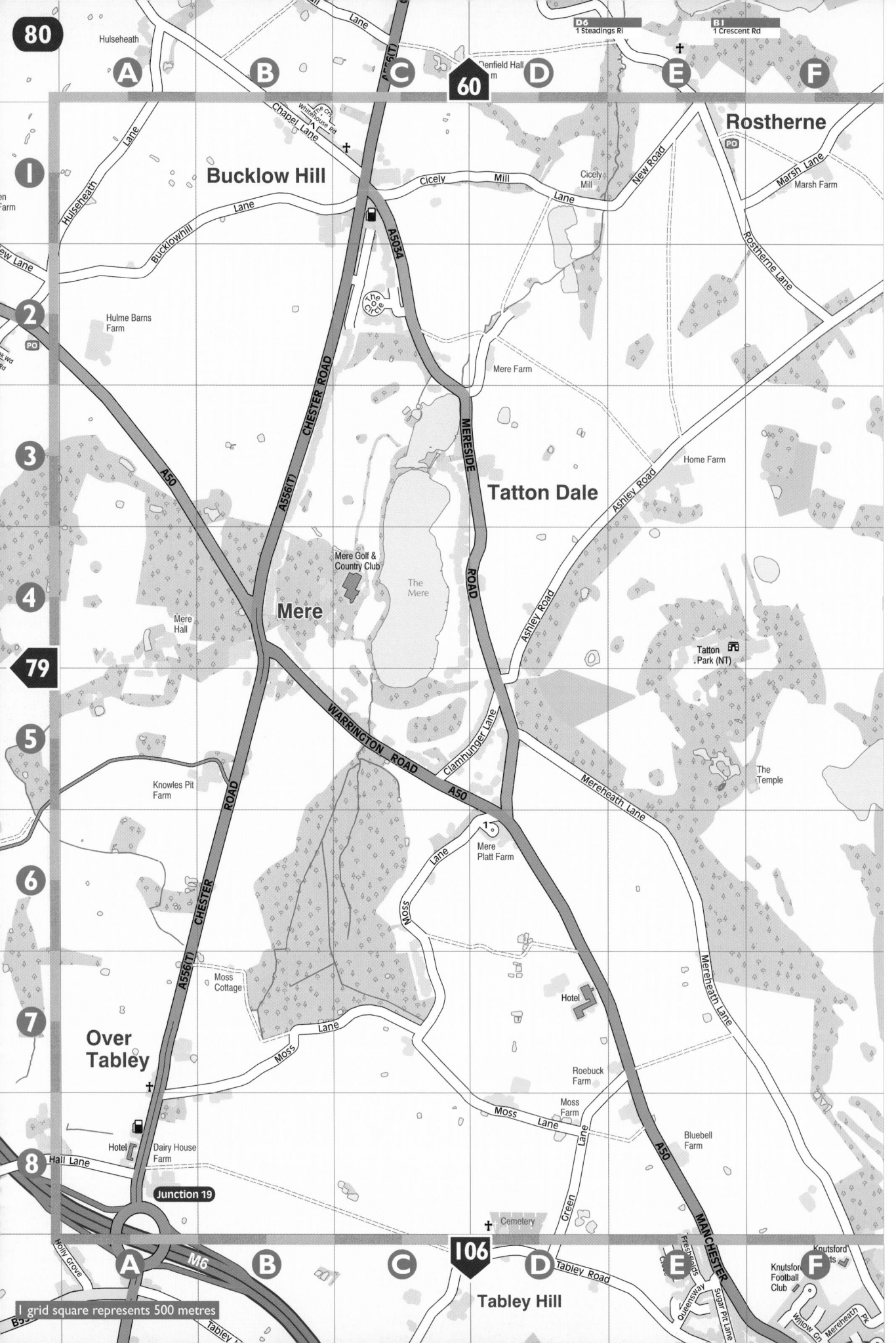

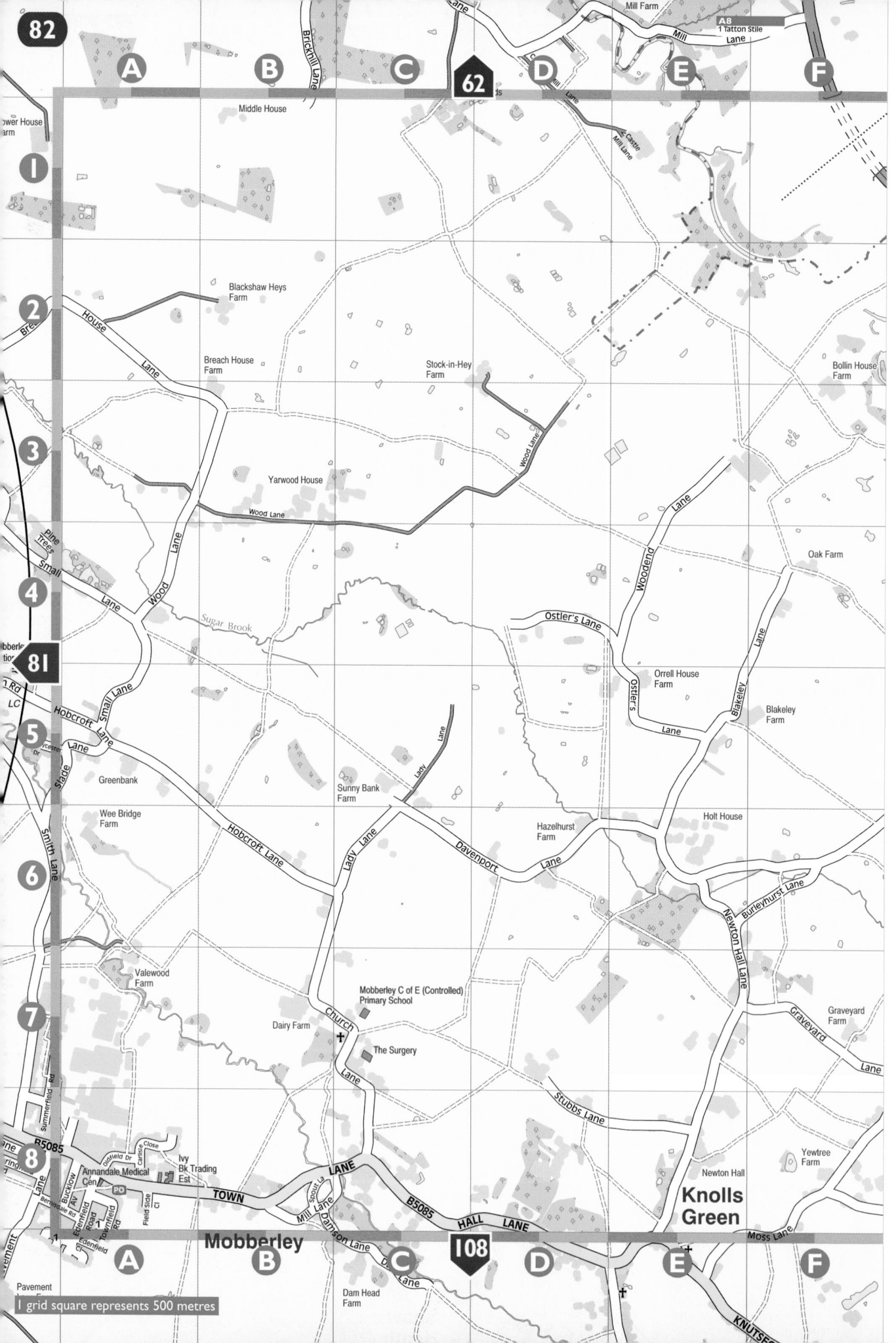

A   B   C   62   D   E   F

I

2

3

4

81

5

6

7

8

A   B   108   D   E   F

Mill Farm

A8
1 Tatton Stile
Lane

Middle House

Brickhill Lane

Castle Mill Lane

Blackshaw Heys Farm

Breach House Farm

Breach House Lane

Stock-in-Hey Farm

Bollin House Farm

Wood Lane

Woodend Lane

Yarwood House

Wood Lane

Oak Farm

Pine Trees

Small Lane

Wood Lane

Sugar Brook

Ostler's Lane

Blakeley Lane

Ostler's

Orrell House Farm

Blakeley Farm

bberle tion

Rd

LC

Hobcroft Lane

Small Lane

Slade Lane

ycerrter Dr

Greenbank

Sunny Bank Farm

Lady Lane

Hazelhurst Farm

Holt House

Smith Lane

Wee Bridge Farm

Hobcroft Lane

Lady Lane

Davenport Lane

Newton Hall Lane

Burleyhurst Lane

Valewood Farm

Mobberley C of E (Controlled) Primary School

Church Lane

Dairy Farm

The Surgery

Graveyard Farm

Stubbs Lane

Summerfield Rd

B5085

Annandale Medical Cen

Ivy Bk Trading Est

Bucklow Av

Edenfield Rd

Carlisle Close

Oddfield Dr

PO

Field Side Cl

Berneslane

Townfield Rd

Edenfield Road

TOWN LANE

Mill Lane

Damson Lane

B5085

HALL LANE

Knolls Green

Yewtree Farm

Newton Hall

Moss Lane

Pavement

Mobberley

Dam Head Farm

Dee Lane

108

KNUTSF

Styal

G H J 63 K L M

1 Lyndhurst Cl
K7

Manchester
L7
1 Winchester Cl

L8
1 The Coppins
2 Shenhurst Cl

Altrincham Road

Styal Station

Oversley Farm

Altrincham Road

Norcliffe Hall

Styal Primary School

Styal Country Park (NT)

Holt's Lane

Quarry Bank Road

Wilm Foo

I

Hotel

ALTRINCHAM ROAD

A538

Quarry Bank Mill (NT)

STYAL

2

Green Road

Dooley's La

Morley

Nantsmoss Lane

Wilmslow Rugby Club

Woodlands Road

3

Wood Farm

Morley Green

Morley Lane

Mobberley Road

Sandy Lane

Vale Rd

Pownall Hall School

Pownall Road

Carrwood

Pownall Park

The Carr

4

Eccups Lane

Greaves Road

King's Drive

Friar's Close

Manor Cl
Manor Rd
College Close
Corsey Road

Broad Road

Alton Road

Wall

Burleyhurst Farm

Greaves

ALTRINCHAM ROAD

Priory Road

Greaves Rd

Gorsey Bank CP School

84

Burleyhurst Lane

Lindow Moss

Lindow Common

A538

Park Road

5

Daven

B & J
Leisure C

Newgate Road

Lindow La

Racecourse Road

Cambridge Av

Westward Rd

Windsor Av

Alma La

Beech Gv

Beech Lane

Hawthorn

Wilms Centr

Hollingee

Oakwood Av

Wingfield Av
Wingfield Dr

Strawberry Lane

Northward Rd

Oak Cl
Oak Lane
Woodacres

Buckingham Rd
South Close
Eastward
Clifford Road

Bourne Street

Chapel Lane

PO

Birch Av
Fulshaw Av

Lane

Beechway

Fulshaw
Ms

Curzon

6

Coppock House Farm

Moor Lane

Burford Crs
Arlington Crs

Eden Cl

Sylvan Av
Granville Rd

Oak Lane

Acacia Av
Orchard Cl

Albany Road
Princess Ct

Nursery Lane

Fulshaw C of E CP School

Regent Close

Chapel La

KNUTSFORD ROAD

B5086

7

Barlow House Farm

Rotherwood Road

Springfield Drive

Moor Lane

The Circuit

Moorfield Cl

New Street

Grove

Alderdale

Beechfield Av

Gravel

Ashdene CP Sch

Thoresway Road

Stoney Lane

Ashdene Rd

Ashcroft

Fulshaw Pk S

Corner Croft

Silverdale

Fulshaw Heath

Lea Av West

Lindow Farm

Clay Lane

Leigh Road

Lindow Fold

Bramley Close

Sunny Bank

Cumber Drive

Cumber Close

Cumber Lane

Chatsworth

Mayfield Cl

Haistone Avenue

Croft Road

Capesthorne Rd

Rostherne Rd

Meadow Close

Meadow Way

Fairbourne Drive

Fairfax Drive

Wilcott Drive

Stockton Rd

Fulshaw Pk S

8

IvyHouse Farm

Davenport Avenue

Tennis Club

Gravel Lane

Clifton Drive

Ravenswood Drive

Welton Drive

Cheltenham Way
Chesham Close
Weston Close

Ashcroft

Paddockhill

Green Villa

Green Park

PO

Church Road

Links Road

B5086

G H J 109 K L M

Gore

Besw

Lindow CP School

1 Cobbett's Wy
2 Fairbourne Av
3 Fairbourne Cl
M8

B5086

Dingle Avenue

The Berrisford Gallery

Alderley Golf Club

1 Hartford Av
2 Regency Pk
M7

B5085

Daven Green

1 Crofters Gn
2 Racecourse Pk
3 Simpson St
M6

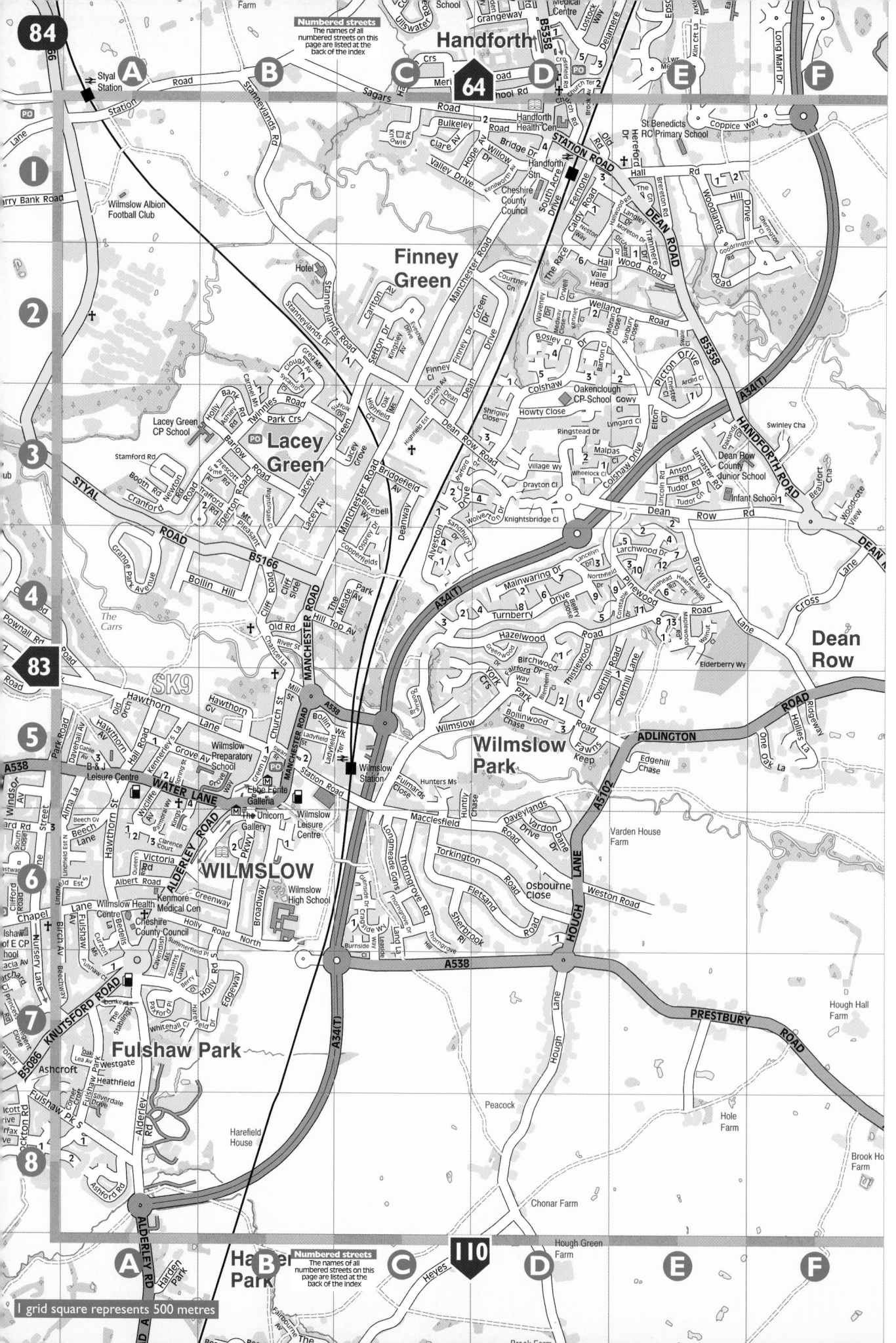

Handforth

Finney Green

Lacey Green

Dean Row

SK9

Wilmslow Park

WILMSLOW

Fulshaw Park

Handforth Park

I grid square represents 500 metres

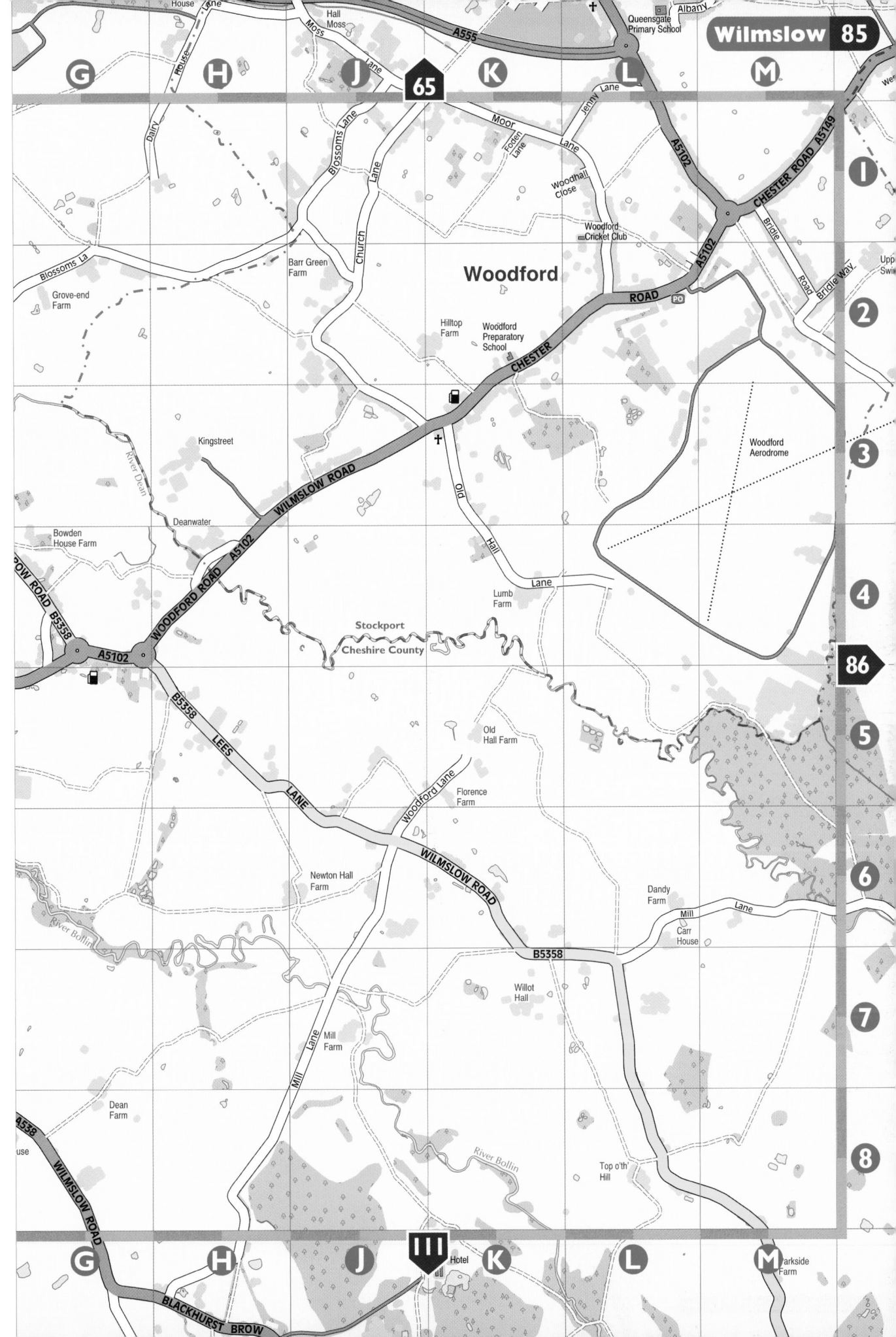

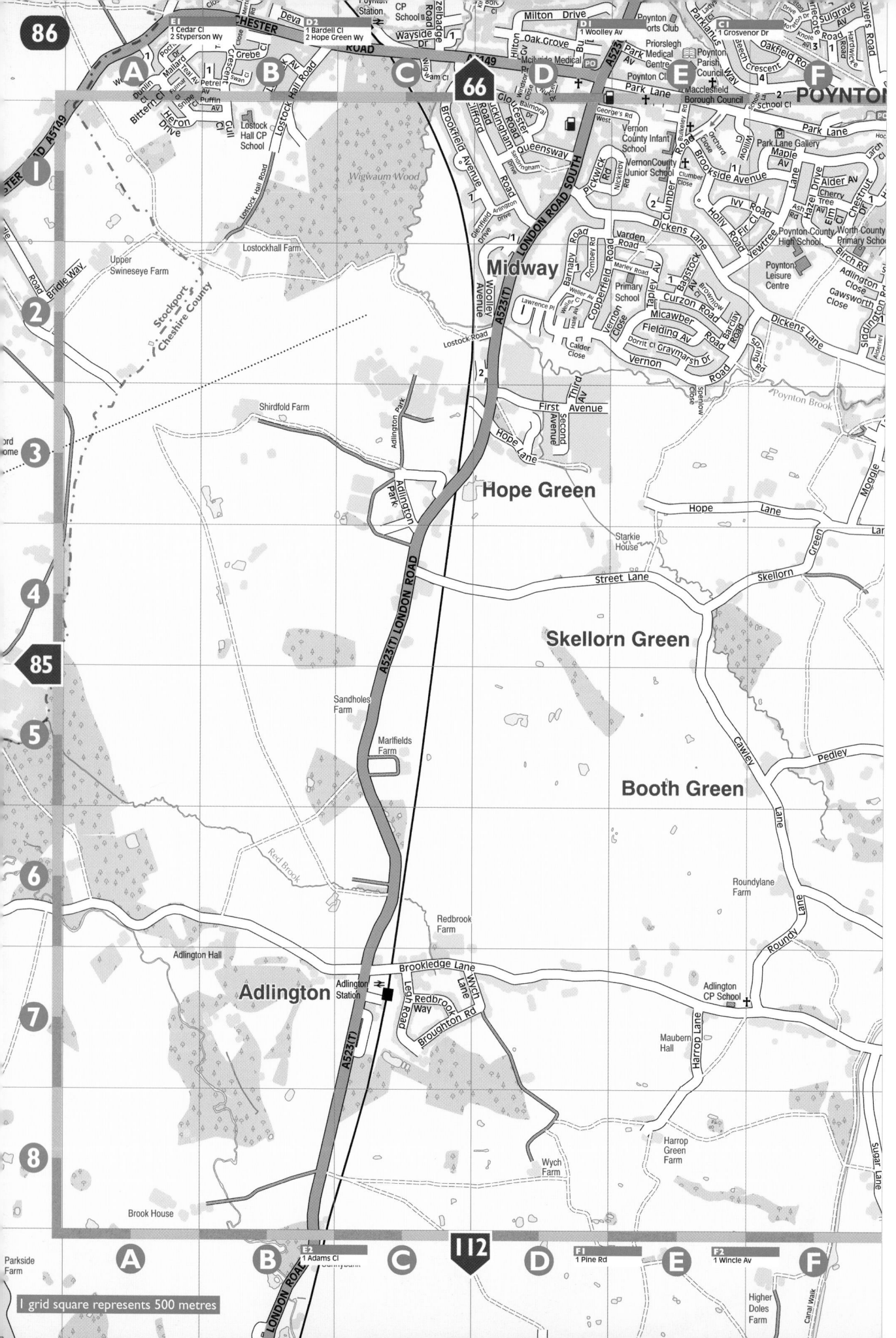

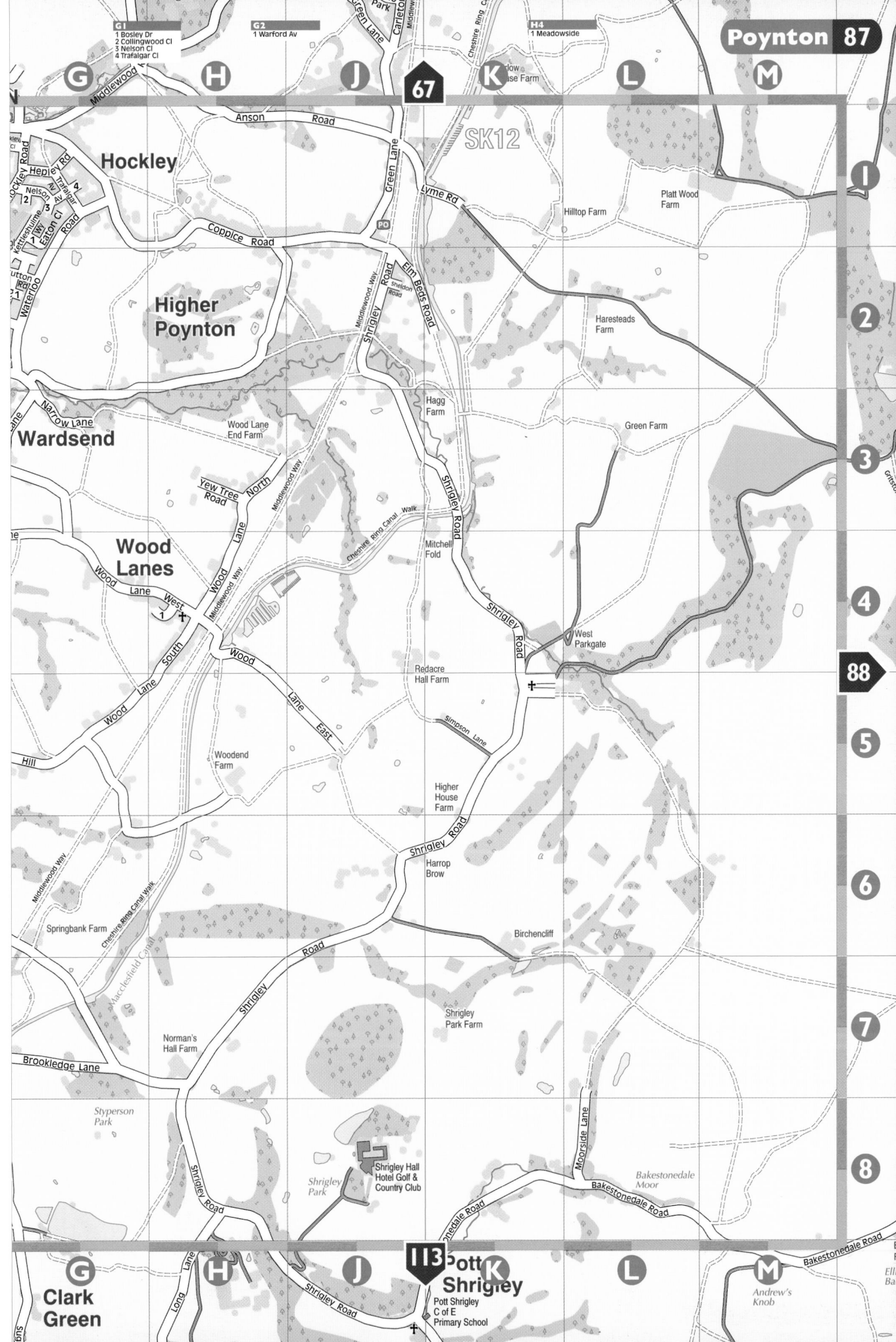

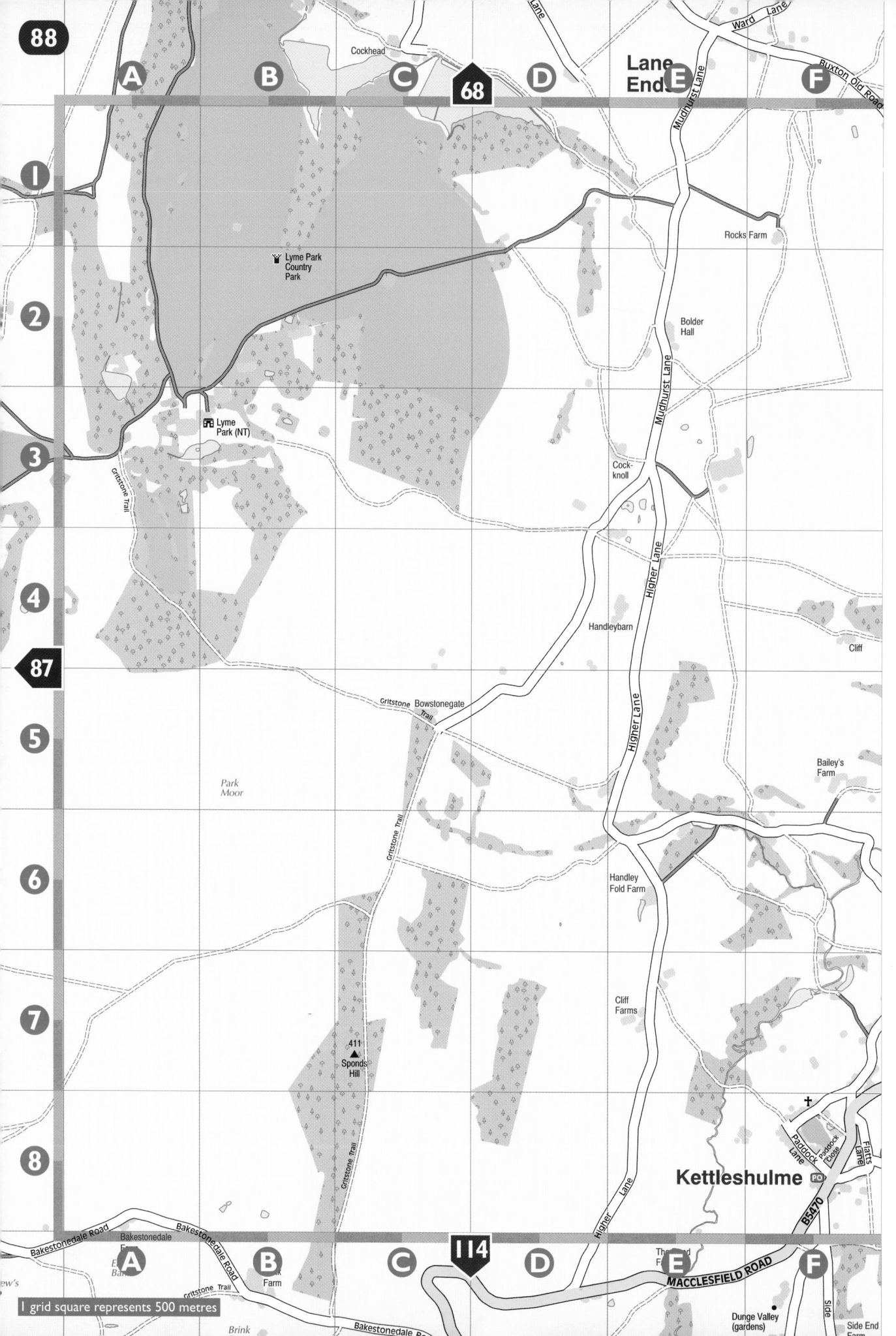

A B C 68 D Lane Ends E F

Ward Lane

Buxton Old Road

Cockhead

1

Rocks Farm

Lyme Park Country Park

Bolder Hall

2

Mudhurst Lane

Lyme Park (NT)

Cock-knoll

Gritstone Trail

3

Higher Lane

Handleybarn

Cliff

4

Gritstone Trail Bowstonegate

Higher Lane

5

Park Moor

Bailey's Farm

6

Handley Fold Farm

Gritstone Trail

7

Cliff Farms

411 Sponds Hill

Gritstone Trail

8

Kettleshulme

Paddock Lane

Flatts Lane

Bakestonedale Road

Bakestonedale Road

Bakestonedale Farm

A B C 114 D E F

Gritstone Trail

Brink

Bakestonedale Road

Macclesfield Road

B5470

Paddock Cross

The Fold

Dunge Valley (gardens)

Side End Farm

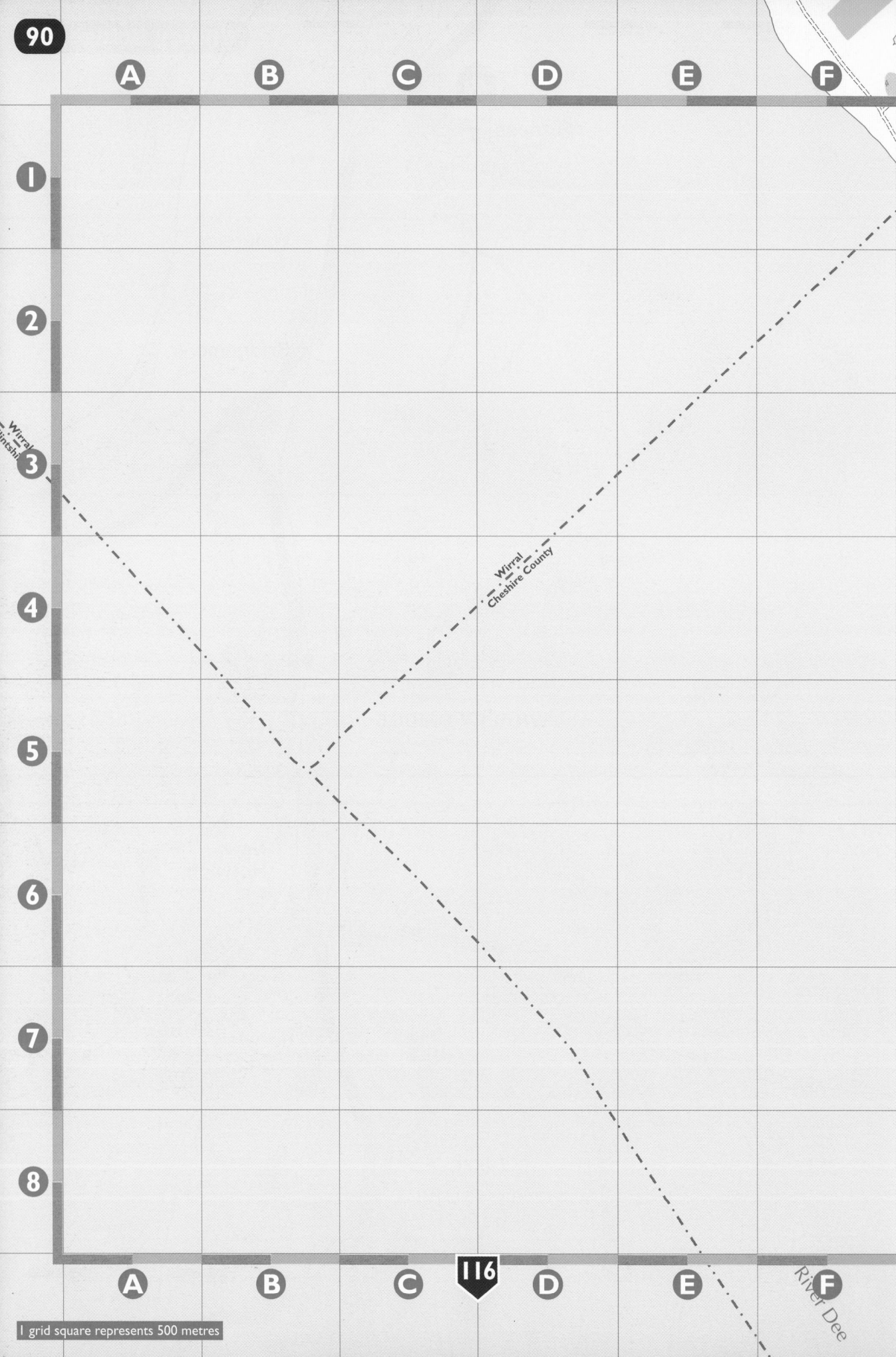

1 grid square represents 500 metres

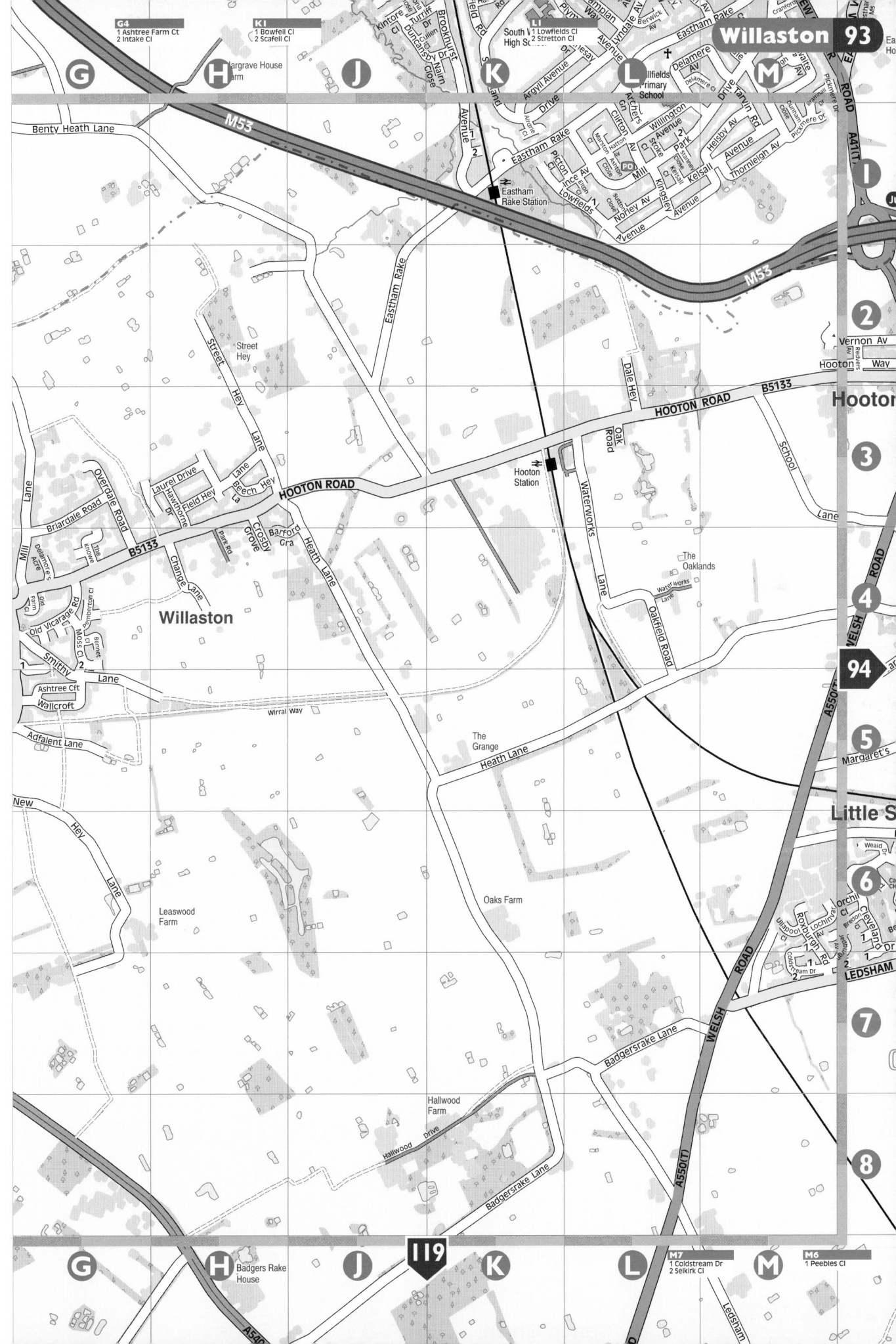

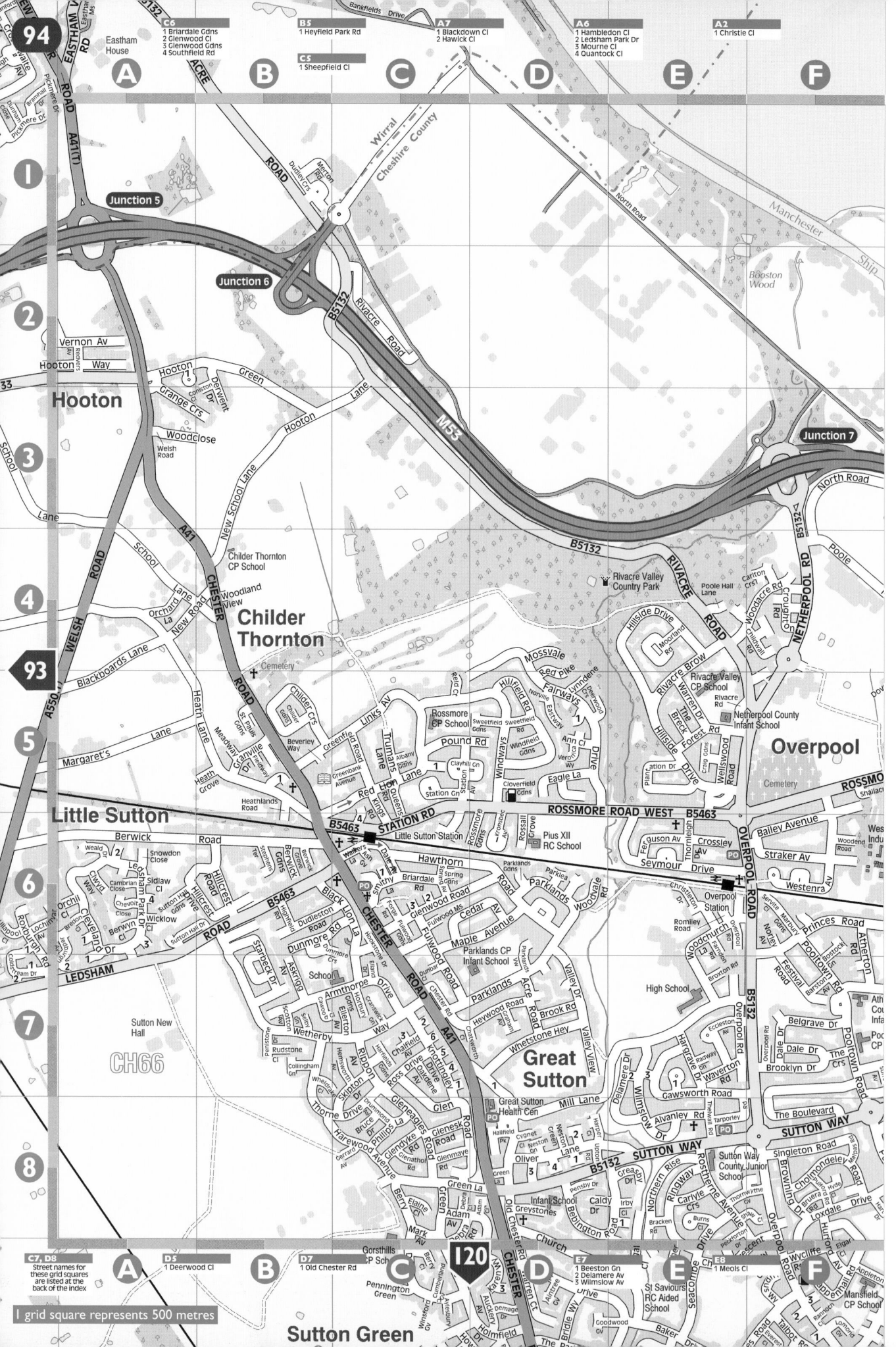

A **B** **C** **D** **E** **F**

Eastham House

EASTHAM VILLAGE RD

ACRE

WIRRAL ROAD

Wirral Cheshire County

Bankfields Drive

North Road

Manchester Ship

Booston Wood

1

Junction 5

Junction 6

B5132

RIVACRE ROAD

M53

Junction 7

North Road

B5132

NETHERPOOL RD

Poole

2

Vernon Av

Hooton Way

Rochers

33

Hooton

Hooton Green

Derwent Dr

Conison Dr

Grange Crs

Woodclose

Welsh Road

New School Lane

Hooton Lane

Lane

3

WELSH ROAD

A41

CHESTER ROAD

School Lane

School Lane

Childer Thornton CP School

Woodland View

Orchard La

New Road

Heath Lane

Rivacre Valley Country Park

Poole Hall Lane

Carlton Rd

RIVACRE ROAD

Woodacre Rd

Croughton Rd

Chidwall Rd

4

93

Childer Thornton

Cemetery

Childer Crs

St Pauls Gdns

Childer Crs

Beverley Way

Greenfield Road

Links Av

Trumans Lane

Mossvale

Red Pike

Hillfield Rd

Fairways

Lynndene

Narville

Deepwood

Eastway

Hillside Drive

Moorland Rd

Rivacre Valley CP School

Warren Dr

The Breck

Rivacre Brow

Rivacre Rd

Netherpool County Infant School

Overpool

5

A550

Blackboards Lane

Lane

Heath Lane

Granville Parkway

Meadway

Heath Grove

Heathlands Road

Greenbank Avenue

Red Hon Lane

Kings

Queens

Station Gn

Rossmore CP School

Sweetfield Gdns

Sweetfield Rd

Pound Rd

Windows

Clayhill Cn

Station

Windfield Gdns

Cloverfield Gdns

Ann Cl

Vero Wy

Eagle La

Plant Station Dr

Craig Gdns

Forest Rd

Wellswood

Hillside Road

Cemetery

ROSSMORE

Shallacres

Little Sutton

Berwick Road

Snowdon Close

Sidlaw Cl

B5463

St Margaret's

Weald

Ledsham Gdns

Stephens

Berwick Gdns

Berwick

Dale

B5463

STATION RD

Walkers

Little Sutton Station

Hawthorn

Briardale Rd

Smithy La

Rossmore Gdns

Ironstone

Rossall Grove

ROSSMORE ROAD WEST

Pius XII RC School

Ferguson Av

Thornleigh

Crossley Av

Seymour Drive

Bailey Avenue

Woodend Road

Straker Av

Westenra Av

B5463

West Indu

6

Orchil Cl

Lochinvar Cl

Roxburgh

Wirpool Rd

Cleveland Dr

Cambrian Close

Cheviot Close

Wicklow

Berwyn Av

Sutton Hall Ave

Hillcrest

Hillcrest Gdns

Sutton Hall Dr

Highfield Rd

Dudleston Rd

Black Lion La

B5463

Dunmore Rd

Dunmore Crs

Hookstone Dr

CHESTER ROAD

Fowler La

Glenwood Road

Fulwood Rd

Cedar Av

Maple Avenue

Parkands Gdns

Parklands

Parklea

Woodvale

Parklands CP Infant School

Christleton

Romiley Road

Woodchurch La

Overpool Station

Overpool

Princes Road

Pooltown Rd

Festival Road

Barston Rd

Atherton Rd

Bostock Rd

Atl Cou Inf

7

Roxburgh Rd

Cricklewood Dr

LEDSHAM ROAD

Starbeck Dr

Armthorpe Dr

Askrigg Av

Scotton Av

Ellerton Av

Wetherby

Collingham Cl

Rudstone Cl

Sutton New Hall

CH66

Chalfield Av

Riddon Dr

Ross Drive

Oakdene Av

Dunbar Av

Acre Wy

Heywood Road

Whetstone Hey

Brook Rd

Valley Dr

Valley View

High School

Delamere Dr

Wilmslow Dr

Alvanley Av

Thelwall Rd

Tarporley Rd

Eccleston Av

Radway

Overpool Rd

Hargrave Av

Waverton Rd

Gawsworth Road

Brooklyn Dr

Dale Dr

B5132

The Crs

Pooltown Rd

Belgrave Dr

Poo

8

Thorne Drive

Harewood Avenue

Skipton Dr

Bruce Av

Philips La

Gerrard Rd

Glendyke Rd

Glenathol Rd

Glenmaye

Gleneagles Road

Glen

Green La

Elaine Av

Mark Av

Adam Av

Great Sutton Health Cen

Hallfield

Cygnet

Neston Lane

Caldy Dr

Irby

Mill Lane

Northern Rise

Bebington

Greystones

Beeston Gn

Oliver

B5132

Pensby Dr

Burns Av

Great Sutton

Rostherne Avenue

Ringway

Carlyle Crs

Bruera Av

Hyde

Bracken Dr

SUTTON WAY

Sutton Way County Junior School

Singleton Road

Cholmondeley Rd

The Boulevard

SUTTON WAY

Browning Dr

Loxdale Drive

Mansfield Rd

Gorsthills CP Sch

Pennington Green

Winsford Rd

Auckery Av

demage Cl

Holmfield

Church Rd

Old Chester Rd

WARREN CT

CHESTER RD

Bridle Wy

Goodwood Gv

Baker

St Saviours RC Aided School

Seacombe Ch

Goodwood

Talbot Rd

Wycliffe

Gorstills CP School

Sutton Green

I grid square represents 500 metres

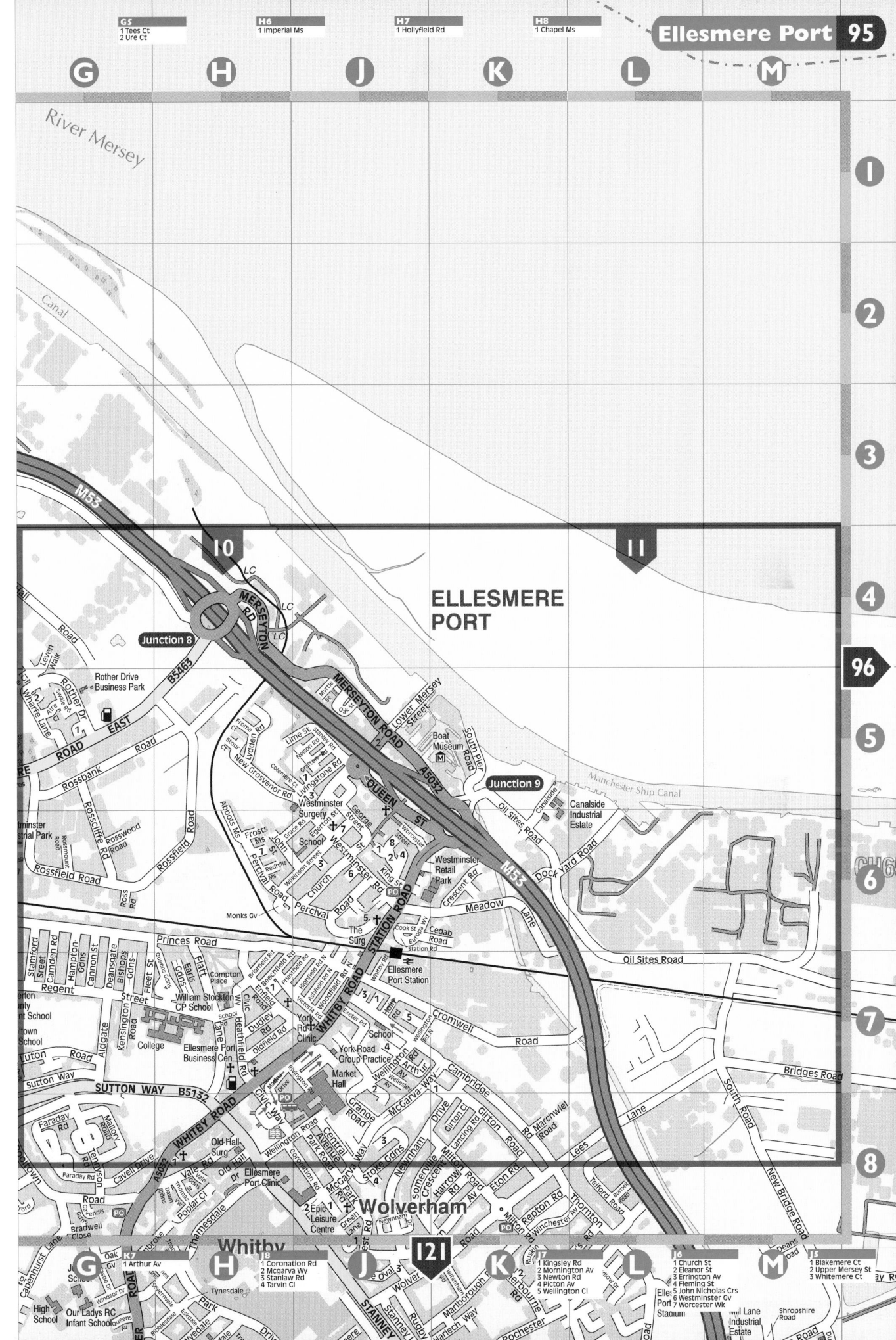

G5
1 Tees Ct
2 Ure Ct

H6
1 Imperial Ms

H7
1 Hollyfield Rd

H8
1 Chapel Ms

G H J K L M

1
2
3
4
96
5
6
7
8

10
11

ELLESMERE
PORT

River Mersey

Canal

M53

Junction 8

Rother Drive
Business Park

B5463

EAST
ROAD

Leven Walk

Rother Dr

Swale Rd
Fens Rd

Wharfe Lane

Rossbank
Road

Rossfield
Road

Rosscliffe Rd
Rosswood Rd

Rossfield Road

Rossmount
Rd

Ross Rd

minster
strial Park

MERSEYTON RD

LC
LC
LC

Myrtle St
Frome Rd

Stanley Rd

Nelson St

Lime St

Livingstone Rd

Egerton Rd

Redhills

Stour
Esk Rd
Colerane Cl

New Grosvenor Rd

Abbots Ms

MERSEYTON ROAD

A5032

Lower Mersey Street

Boat
Museum
M

South Pier Road

Westminster
Surgery
School

Grace Rd

Egerton St

George
Street

QUEEN ST

Worcester
8
7
2
3
4
6
5

Church

Westminster Rd

John St
Percival Rd

Wilkinson Street

Frosts
Ms

Westminster
Retail
Park

Junction 9

Canalside

Canalside
Industrial
Estate

Oil Sites Road

M53

Dock Yard Road

King St
PO

Crescent Rd

Manchester Ship Canal

Meadow
Lane

Monks Gv

Percival Road

Princes Road

Stamford St
Camden Rd
Hampton Gdns
Cannon St
Deansgate
Bishops Gdns
Fleet St
Earls
Gdns

Regent
Street

Kensington Rd

Aldgate

Luton
Road

Sutton Way

William Stockton
CP School

College

Ellesmere Port
Business Cen

SUTTON WAY B5132

Faraday Rd

Mallory Road

Pendle
Fendis

Bradwell
Close

Faraday Road

Queens Gdns

Compton
Place

Heathfield Rd

Dudley Rd
Oldfield Rd

Brierfield Rd
Beechfield Rd
Priestfield Rd
Highfield Rd
Enfield Rd

WHITBY ROAD

Victoria Rd
Woodfield Rd

York
Rd
Clinic

School

York Road
Group Practice

Rivington Rd

Market
Hall

CIVIC WAY

PO

Wellington Road

Central
Avenue

Grange
Road

Whitby Rd
Eccleston
Station Rd N

STATION ROAD

Exeter Rd

The
Surg

Cook St
Esq

Cedab
Road

Ellesmere
Port Station

3
5

Wellington
Arthur
Wellesley
AV

Cromwell
Road

Cambridge

McGarva Way
Girton Cl
Lancing Rd
Girton Rd

Drive

Marchwiel
Road

Lees

Lane

South Road

Oil Sites Road

Bridges Road

New Bridge Road

Faraday
Road

Caxton Road

Vale
Gdns

A5032

WHITBY ROAD

Old Hall
Surg

Old
Dr

Ellesmere
Port Clinic

Poplar Cl

Thamesdale

Coronation Rd

McCann
Park

Stoke Gdns

Green
Lane

Newnham

McCarva
Way

Somerville
Crescent

Milton
Harrow
Rd

Eton Rd

Repton Rd
Winchester Rd

Thornton
Road

Burrell
Road

Epic
Leisure
Centre

Wolverham

Newnham
Dr

PO

Deans
Road

Shropshire
Road

Whitby

Tynesdale

STANNEY

Marlborough Road

Melbourne St
Kelburne Way

Rusholme

Harlech Way

Rochester

I21

G
1 Arthur Av

H
1 Coronation Rd
2 Mcgarva Wy
3 Stanlaw Rd
4 Tarvin Cl

J

K
1 Kingsley Rd
2 Mornington Av
3 Newton Rd
4 Picton Av
5 Wellington Cl

L
1 Church St
2 Eleanor St
3 Errington Av
4 Fleming St
5 John Nicholas Crs
6 Westminster Gv
7 Worcester Wk

M
1 Blakemere Ct
2 Upper Mersey St
3 Whitemere Ct

Ellesmere
Port
Stadium

High
School

Our Ladys RC
Infant School

A B C **70** D E F

1
2
3
4
95
5

Stanlow
Point

CH65

Manchester Ship Canal

Corridor Road

6

Kinsey's Lane

Pool Lane

Oil Sites Road

7

Bridges Road

Stanlow

Stanlow & Thornton
Station

8

Fage Road

eans
Road

Shellway Road

A B C **122** D E F

Oil Refinery

nroad
oad

Road

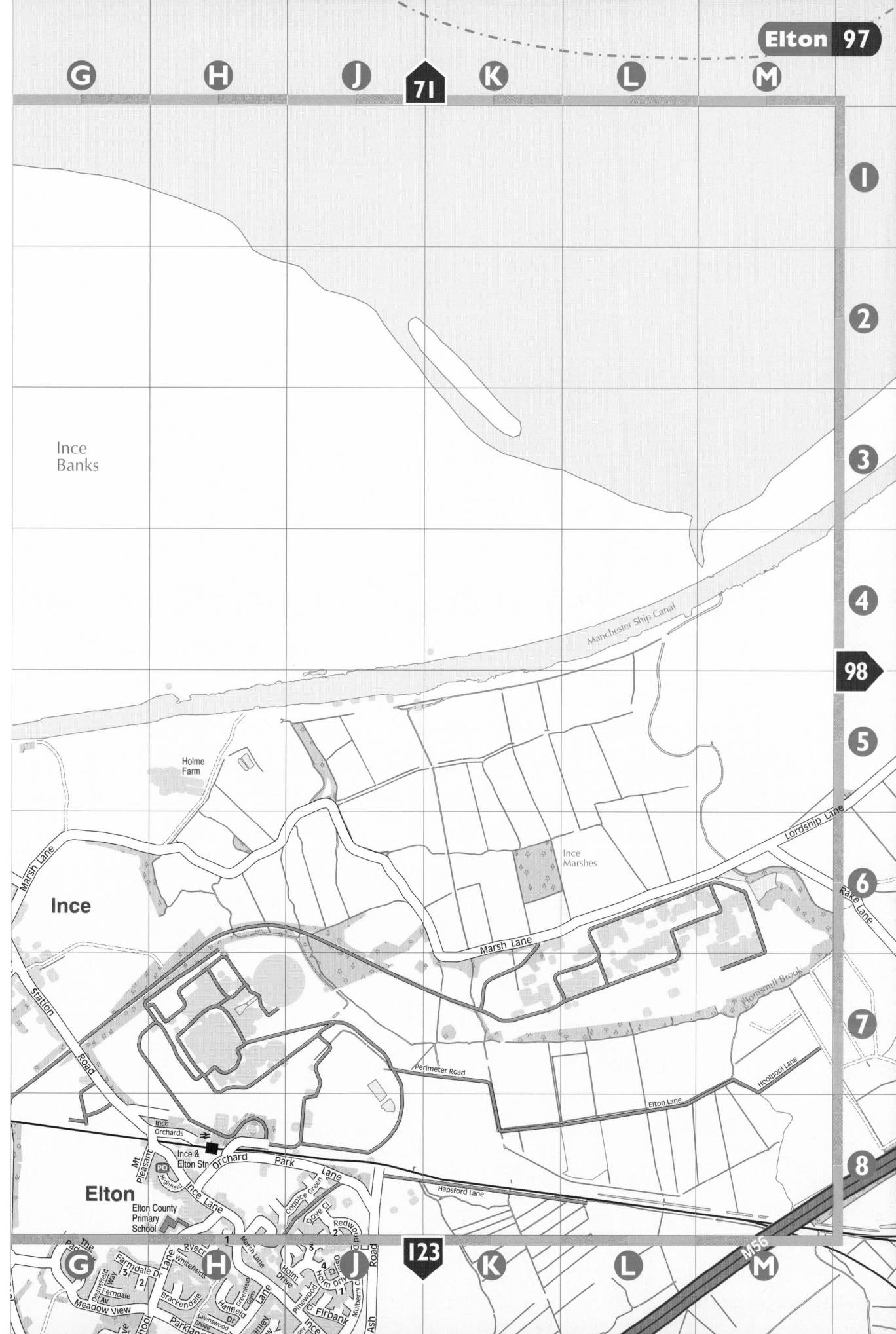

G **H** **J** **71** **K** **L** **M**

1
2
3
4
98
5
6
7
8

Ince Banks

Manchester Ship Canal

Holme Farm

Ince Marshes

Lordship Lane

Ince

Marsh Lane

Marsh Lane

Rake Lane

Station Road

Hornsmill Brook

Perimeter Road

Hoolpool Lane

Elton Lane

Ince Orchards

Ince & Elton Stn

Orchard Park Lane

Hapsford Lane

Mt Pleasant

PO

Highfield

Ince Lane

Elton

Elton County Primary School

Coppice Green

Dove Cl

Redwood Cl

The Park

Ferndale Way

Dransfield Av

Farmdale Dr

Whitefields

Ryecroft Lane

Brackendale

Meadow View

Hallfield

Greenfield Gdns

Marsh Lane

Holm Drive

Pinewood

Lawnswood grove

Swanley Lane

Parkland

Mulberry Cl

Firbank

Ash Road

Ince Lane

M56

G **H** **123** **J** **K** **L** **M**

A B C D E F

72

1
2
3

97

4
5
6
7
8

Frodsham Marsh Farm

Alder Lane

Alder Lane

Brook Furlong

Frodsham Marsh

Moorditch Lane

Tadgers Lane

Moorditch Lane

M56

Moorditch Lane

Cross Lane

Hare's Lane

Lordship Lane

Straight Length

Hatley Lane

Ma Gr

Elton Lordship Lane

Godscroft Lane

Godscroft Hall

Lordship Lane

Rake Lane

Hill View Farm

M56

CHESTER R

Helsby Marsh

Helsby County High School

Woodhouses

Smithy Lane

Holly Ct

Plovers Lane

Cem

Bank House Rd

Hallastone Rd

Barn Ct

School

Hunters Ct

Landscape Dene

Foxhill Gv

Proffitts Lane

Lower Rake Lane

Vale Gdns

The Beeches

High View

Conery

Hale View Road

Cambridge Gdns

Old Chester Road

Bates Lane

TARVIN

Covertside

Foxhill

Helsby Station

Station Av

Red Stone

Copford Cl

Birmingham Rd

Vicarage Lane

Rake La

CHELSBY

124

Lodge Hollow

Mountain View

King Dr

Queens Drive

Crescent Drive

Old Chester Road

Parkfield Dr

Robin Hood Lane

PO

A393

1 grid square represents 500 metres

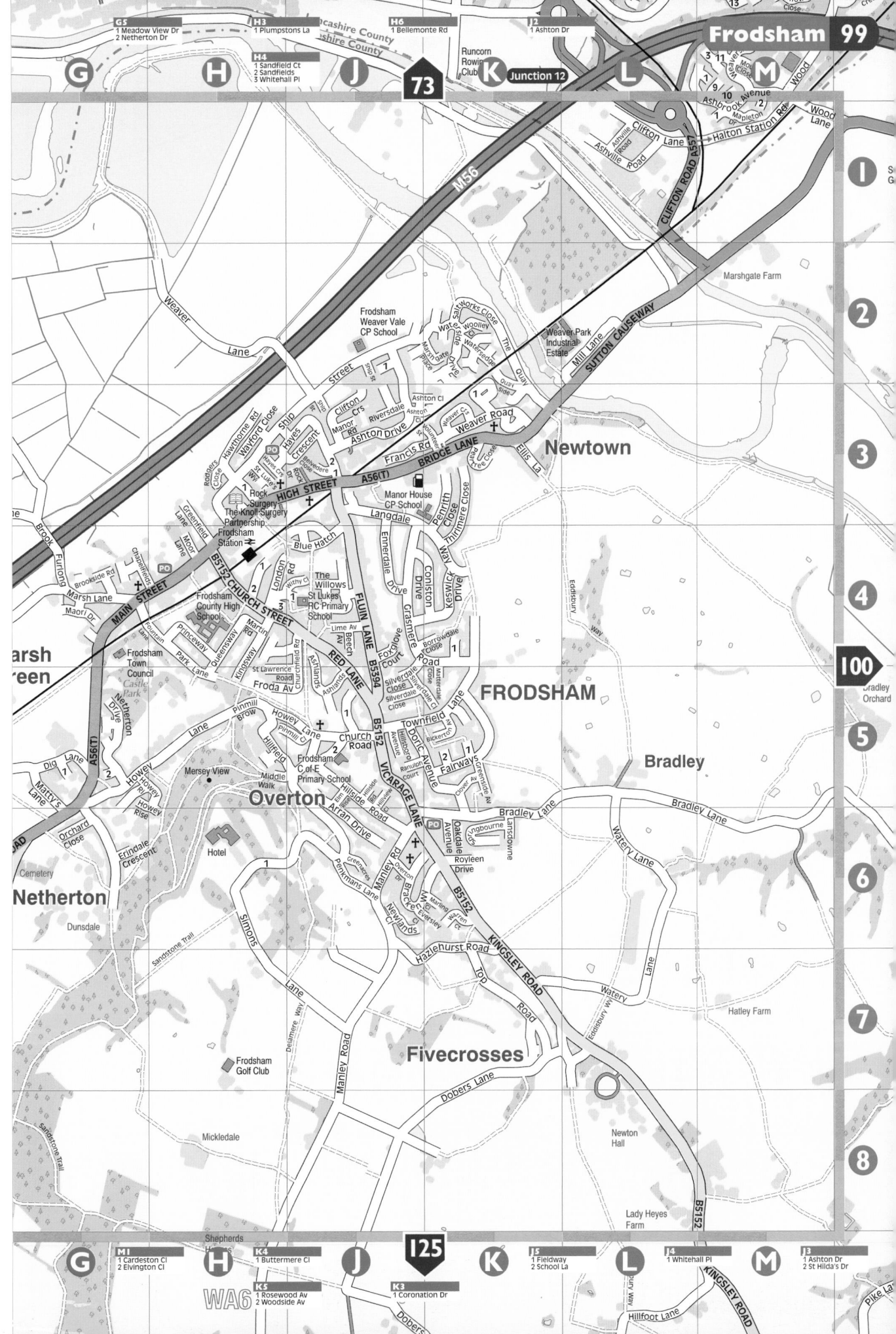

G 1 Meadow View Dr 2 Netherton Dr
H3 1 Plumpstons La
H6 1 Bellemonte Rd
J2 1 Ashton Dr
H4 1 Sandfield Ct 2 Sandfields 3 Whitehall Pl

Lancashire County
Cheshire County

G   H   J   73   K Junction 12   L   M

Runcorn Rowing Club

Marshgate Farm

Frodsham Weaver Vale CP School

Weaver Park Industrial Estate

SUTTON CAUSEWAY

Newtown

Manor House CP School

Langdale

HIGH STREET

The Knoll Surgery Partnership
Rock Surgery

Frodsham Station

BRIDGE LANE

A56(T)

Blue Hatch

FRODSHAM

Bradley Orchard

Frodsham County High School

Frodsham Town Council

Castle Park

The Willows St Lukes RC Primary School

B5152 CHURCH STREET

MAIN STREET

Marsh Green

Marsh Lane

RED LANE B5394

FLUIN LANE

Bradley

Bradley Lane

Bradley Lane

Watery Lane

Frodsham C of E Primary School

Overton

Mersey View

Hotel

VICARAGE LANE

Church Road B5152

Townfield

Fairways

Hatley Farm

Netherton

Dunsdale

Cemetery

Hazlehurst Road

KINGSLEY ROAD

Fivecrosses

Frodsham Golf Club

Dobers Lane

Mickledale

Newton Hall

Lady Heyes Farm

B5152

Shepherds

WA6

G 1 Cardeston Cl 2 Elvington Cl
K4 1 Buttermere Cl
K5 1 Rosewood Av 2 Woodside Av
K3 1 Coronation Dr
J5 1 Fieldway 2 School La
J4 1 Whitehall Pl
M1 1 Ashton Dr 2 St Hilda's Dr

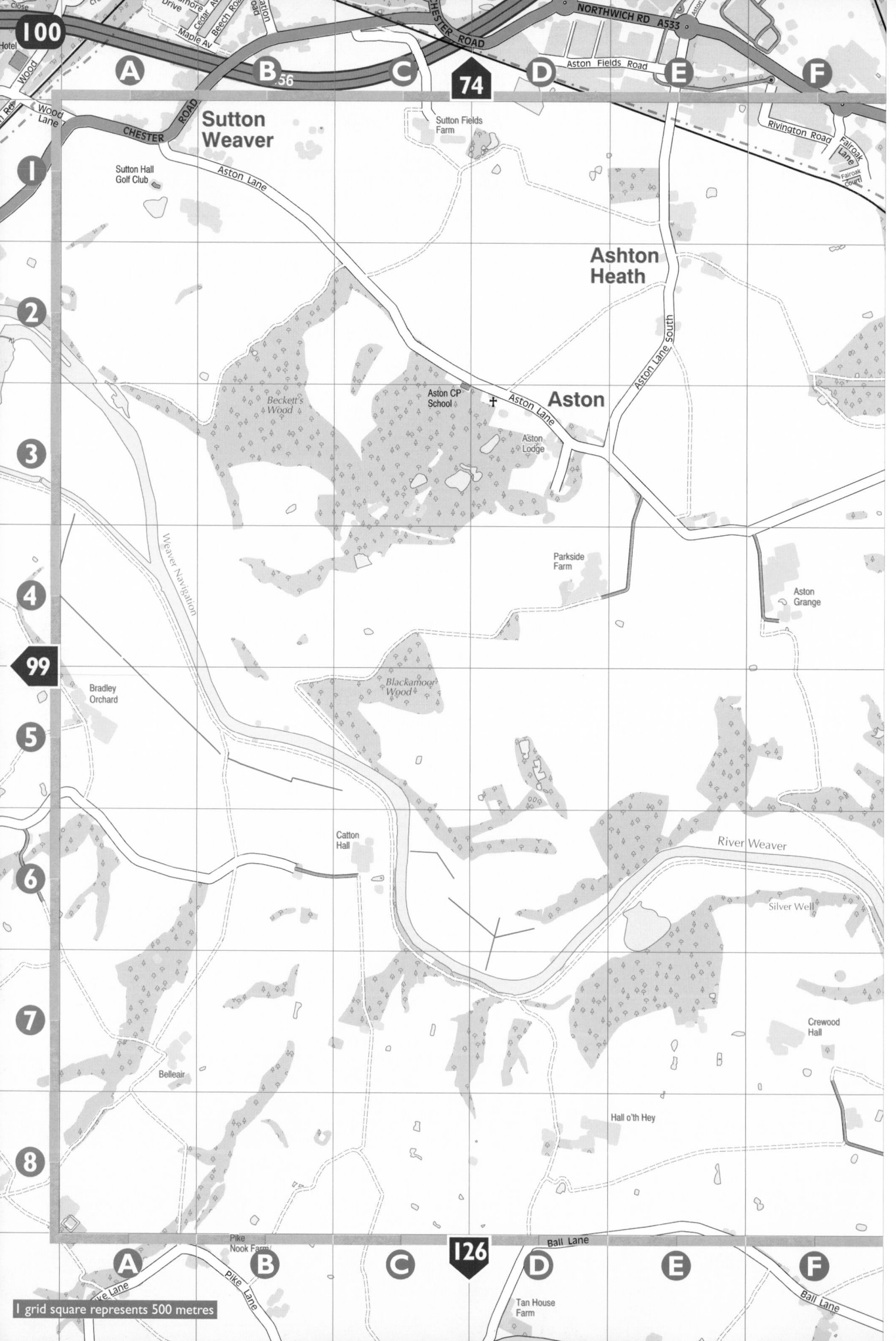

100

A   B 56   C   74   D   E   F

Wood Lane

CHESTER ROAD

Sutton Weaver

Sutton Fields Farm

NORTHWICH RD A533

Aston Fields Road

Rivington Road

Fairoak Lane

Fairoak Court

1

Sutton Hall Golf Club

Aston Lane

Ashton Heath

2

Beckett's Wood

Aston CP School

Aston Lane

Aston

Aston Lane South

3

Weaver Navigation

Aston Lodge

4

Parkside Farm

Aston Grange

99

Bradley Orchard

Blackamoor Wood

5

6

Catton Hall

River Weaver

Silver Well

7

Belleair

Crewood Hall

8

Hall o'th Hey

A   B   C   126   D   E   F

Pike Lane

Pike Nook Farm

Ball Lane

Ball Lane

Tan House Farm

I grid square represents 500 metres

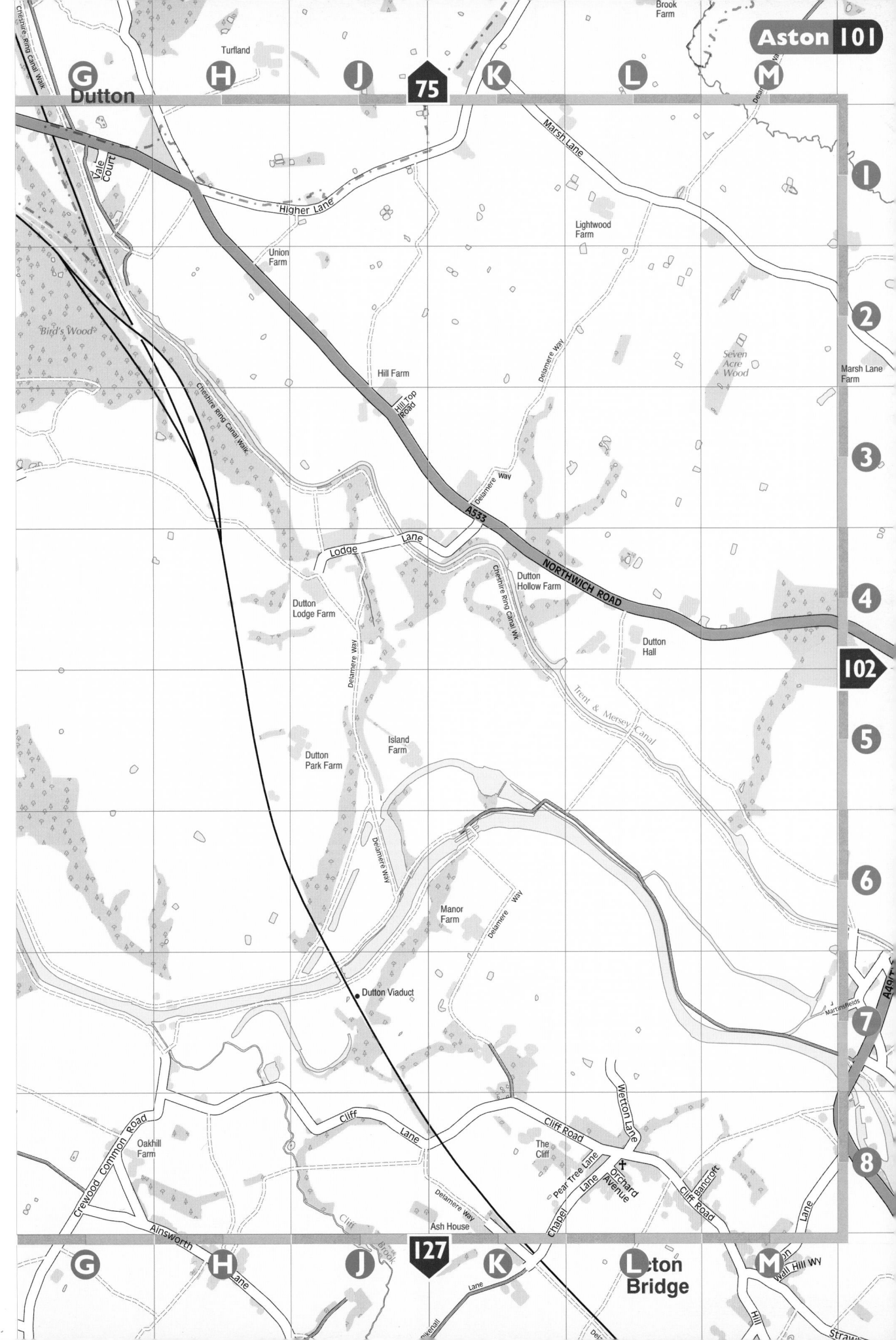

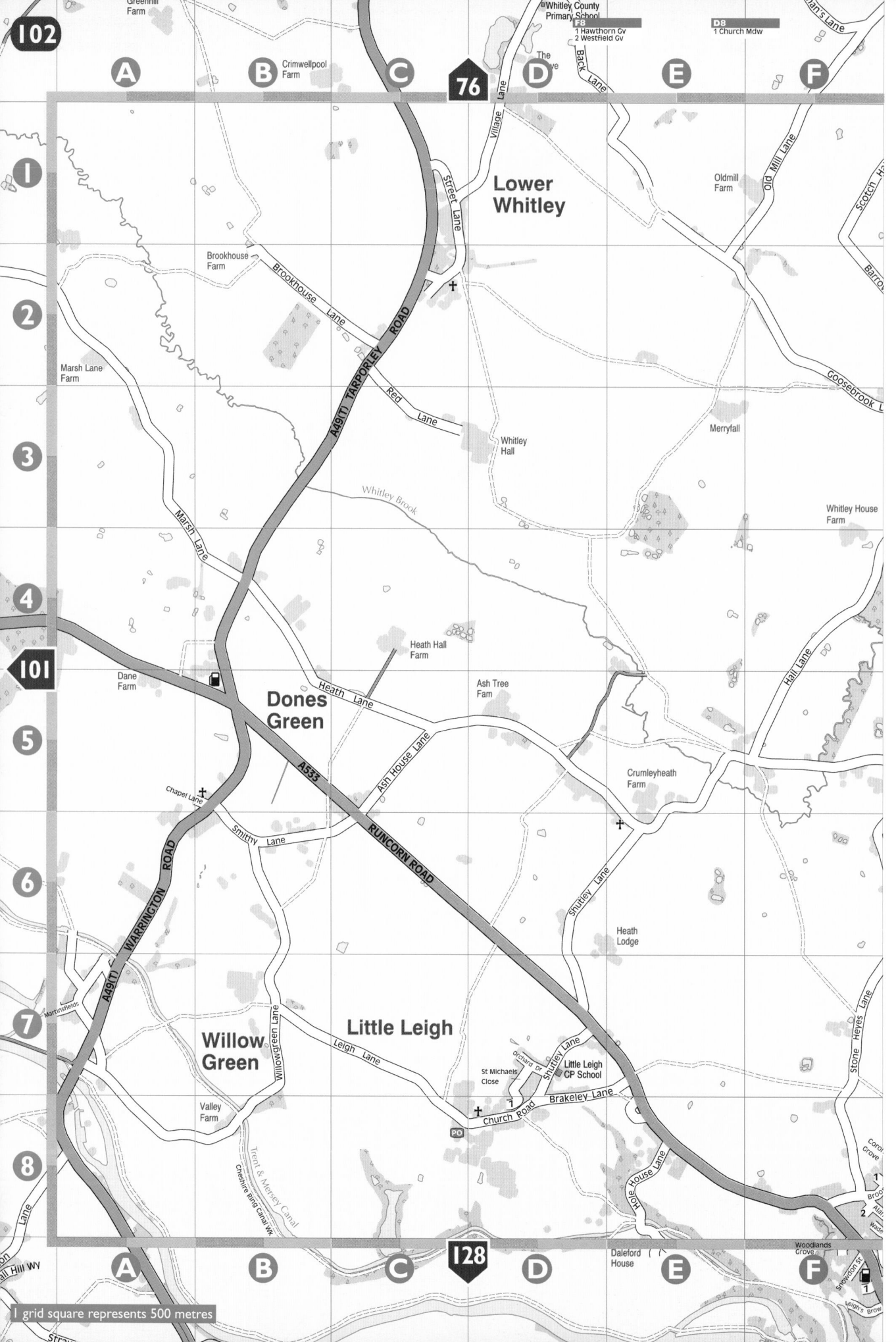

A B C 76 D E F

Greenhill Farm

Whitley County Primary School
FB
1 Hawthorn Gv
2 Westfield Gv

D8
1 Church Mdw

Jan's Lane

I

Crimwellpool Farm

Lower Whitley

The Ve

Back Lane

Oldmill Farm

Old Mill Lane

Scotch H

Brookhouse Farm

Brookhouse Lane

Village Lane

Street Lane

2

Marsh Lane Farm

A49(T) TARPORLEY ROAD

Red Lane

Whitley Hall

Merryfall

Goosebrook L

Barro

3

Marsh Lane

Whitley Brook

Whitley House Farm

4

101

Dane Farm

Heath Hall Farm

Heath Lane

Ash Tree Fam

Hall Lane

Dones Green

A533

Ash House Lane

Crumleyheath Farm

5

Chapel Lane

Smithy Lane

RUNCORN ROAD

Shutley Lane

6

WARRINGTON ROAD

A49(T)

Heath Lodge

Martinsfields

7

Willow Green

Willowgreen Lane

Leigh Lane

Little Leigh

St Michaels Close

Orchard Dr

Shutley Lane

Little Leigh CP School

Brakeley Lane

Stone Heyes Lane

Valley Farm

Church Road

PO

Hole House Lane

Corol Grove

8

Trent & Mersey Canal

Cheshire Ring Canal Wk

Daleford House

Woodlands Grove

Snowdon St

all Hill Wy

A B C 128 D E F

Stra

Leigh's Brow

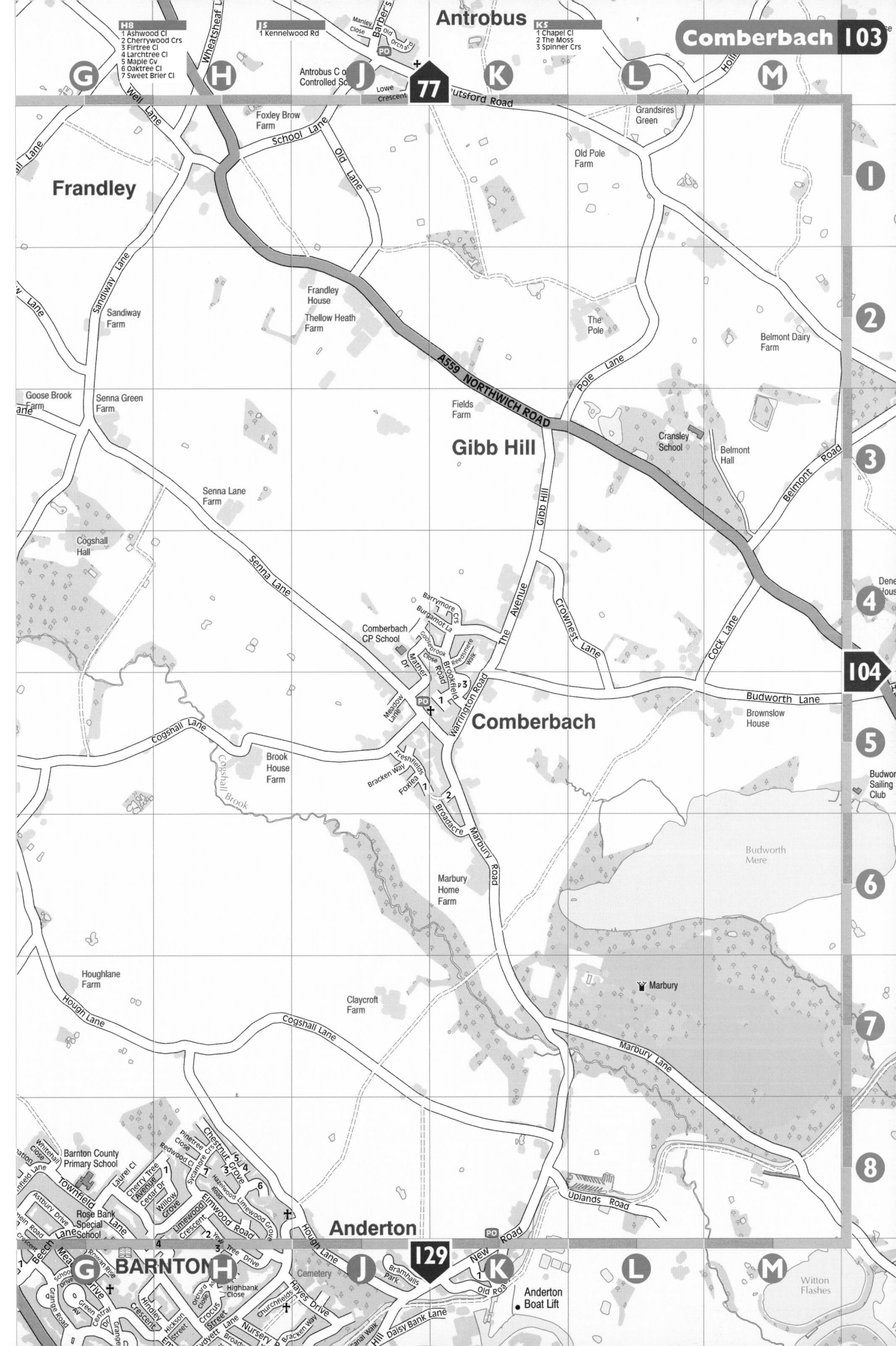

Antrobus

Frandley

Gibb Hill

Comberbach

Anderton

BARNTON

Budworth
Mere

Witton
Flashes

H8
1 Ashwood Cl
2 Cherrywood Crs
3 Firtree Cl
4 Larchtree Cl
5 Maple Gv
6 Oaktree Cl
7 Sweet Brier Cl

K5
1 Chapel Cl
2 The Moss
3 Spinner Crs

J5
1 Kennelwood Rd

Manley
Close

Barber's
Old
Orchard

Antrobus C of
Controlled Sch

Lowe
Crescent

77

Wheatsheaf La

Wall Lane

Foxley Brow
Farm

School Lane

Old Lane

Grandsires
Green

Old Pole
Farm

The
Pole

Belmont Dairy
Farm

Holl

Knutsford Road

Sandiway Lane

Sandiway
Farm

Frandley
House

Thellow Heath
Farm

A559 NORTHWICH ROAD

Pole Lane

Belmont Road

Goose Brook
Farm

Senna Green
Farm

Fields
Farm

Cransley
School

Belmont
Hall

Senna Lane
Farm

Senna Lane

Cogshall
Hall

Gibb Hill

The Avenue

Crownest Lane

Cock Lane

Dene
Hous

104

Barrymore
Crs

Burgamot La

Goosebrook
Close

Reedmere
Walk

Brookfield
Road

Comberbach CP School

Mather
Dr

Meadow
Lane

PO

Warrington Road

Budworth Lane

Brownslow
House

Cogshall Lane

Cogshall Brook

Brook
House
Farm

Freshfields

Bracken Way

Foxter

1

3

2

Broadacre

Marbury Road

Budwor
Sailing
Club

Houghlane
Farm

Claycroft
Farm

Cogshall Lane

Marbury
Home
Farm

Marbury

Marbury Lane

Hough Lane

Barnton County
Primary School

Townfield

Whitehall
Close

Chestnut Grove

Pinetree
Close

Cherry Tree
Avenue

Redwood
Close

Cedar Dr

Laurel Cl

Willow
Grove

Sycamore
Close

Limewood
Crescent

Elmwood
Road

Hazelwood
Close

Limewood Grove

6

Rose Bank
Special School

Beech
Mea

Astbury Drive

Hindley

Hickson

Crocus
Street

Churchfields

Hough Lane

Cemetery

Bramhalls
Park

Highbank
Close

Hayes Drive

Nursery
Lane

129

New Road

Daisy Bank Lane

Old Road

1

Anderton
Boat Lift

Uplands Road

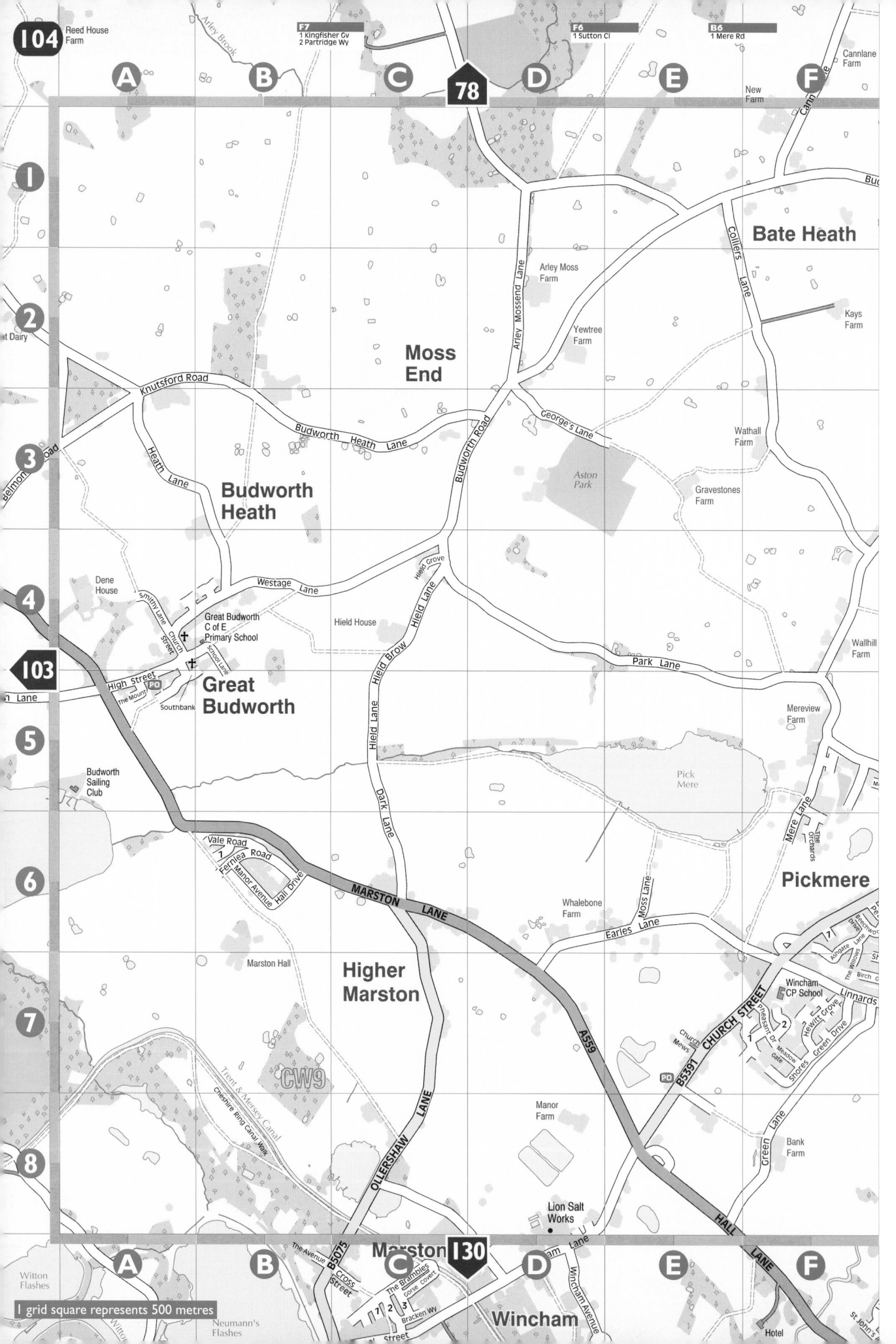

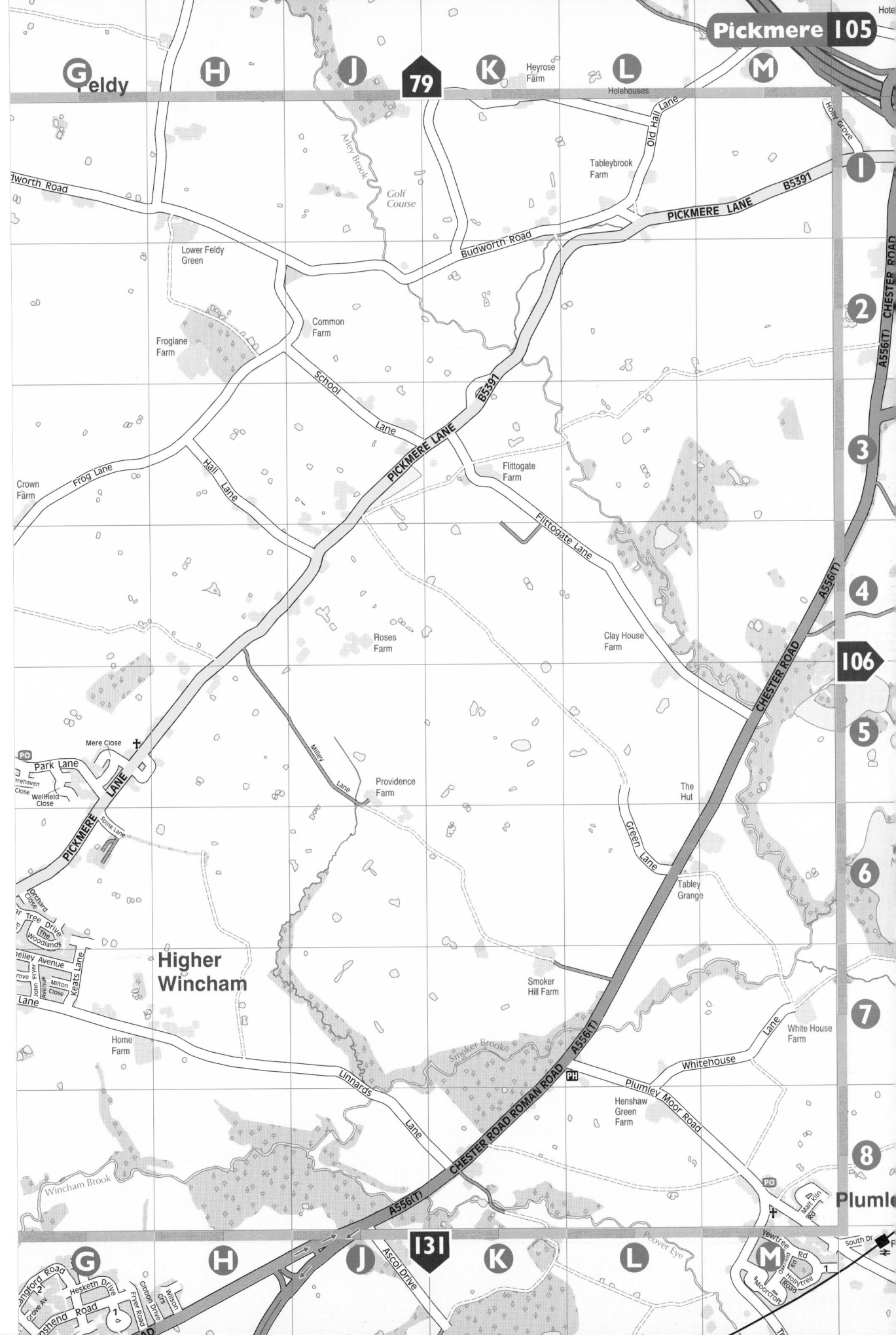

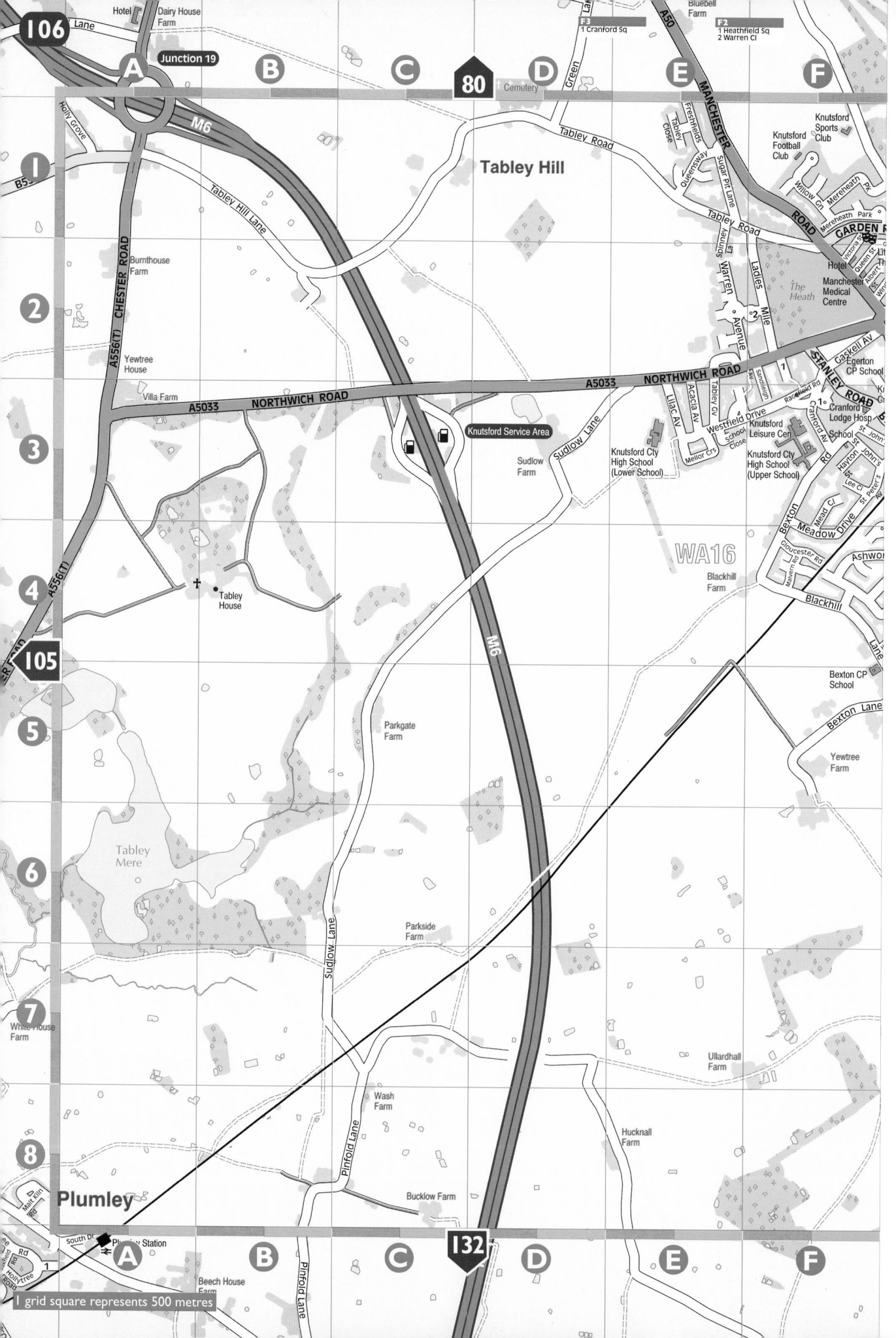

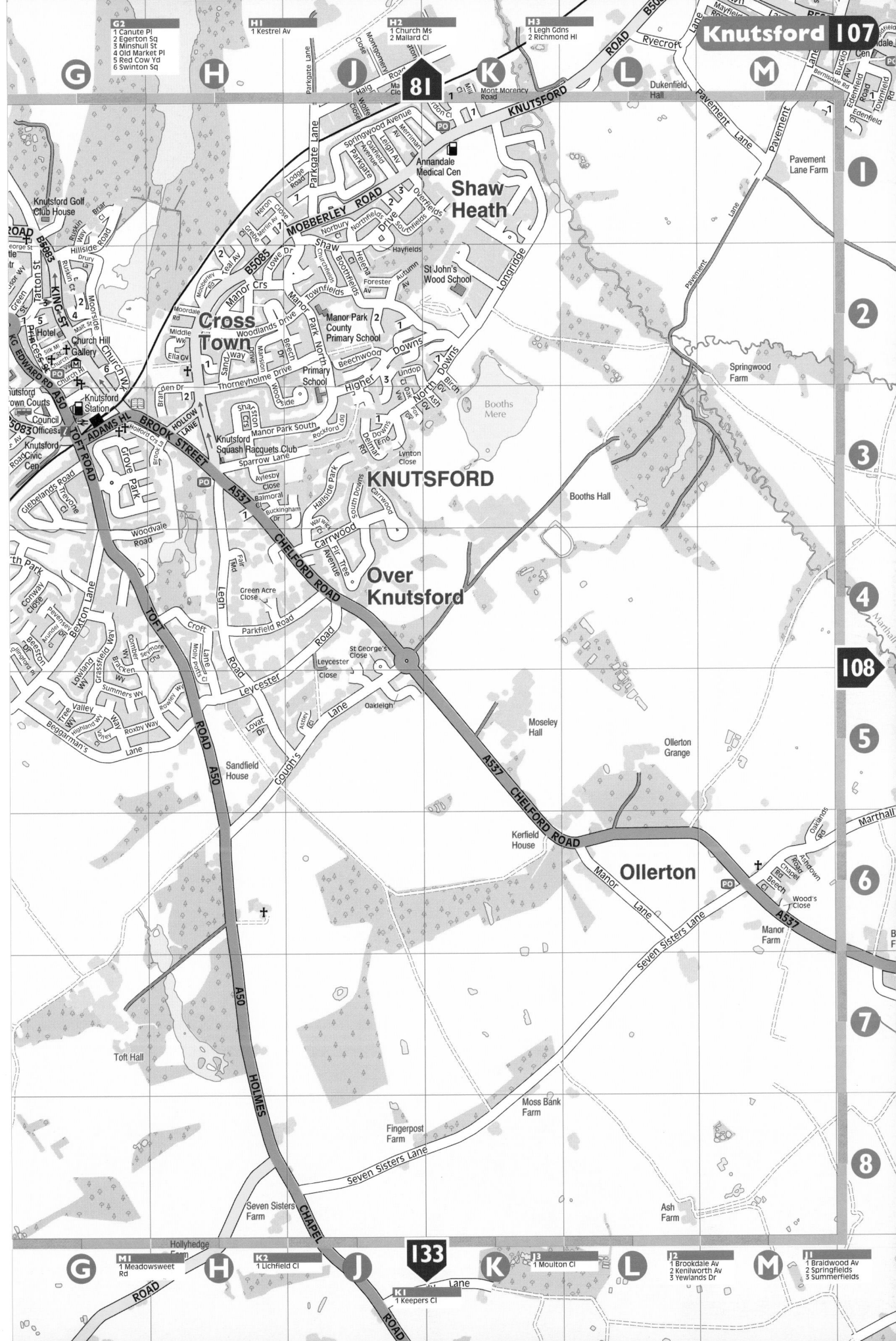

G2
1 Canute Pl
2 Egerton Sq
3 Minshull St
4 Old Market Pl
5 Red Cow Yd
6 Swinton Sq

G
H
J
K
L
M

81

1

Shaw
Heath

Annandale
Medical Cen

2

Cross
Town

KNUTSFORD

3

Over
Knutsford

108

4

5

Ollerton

6

7

8

133

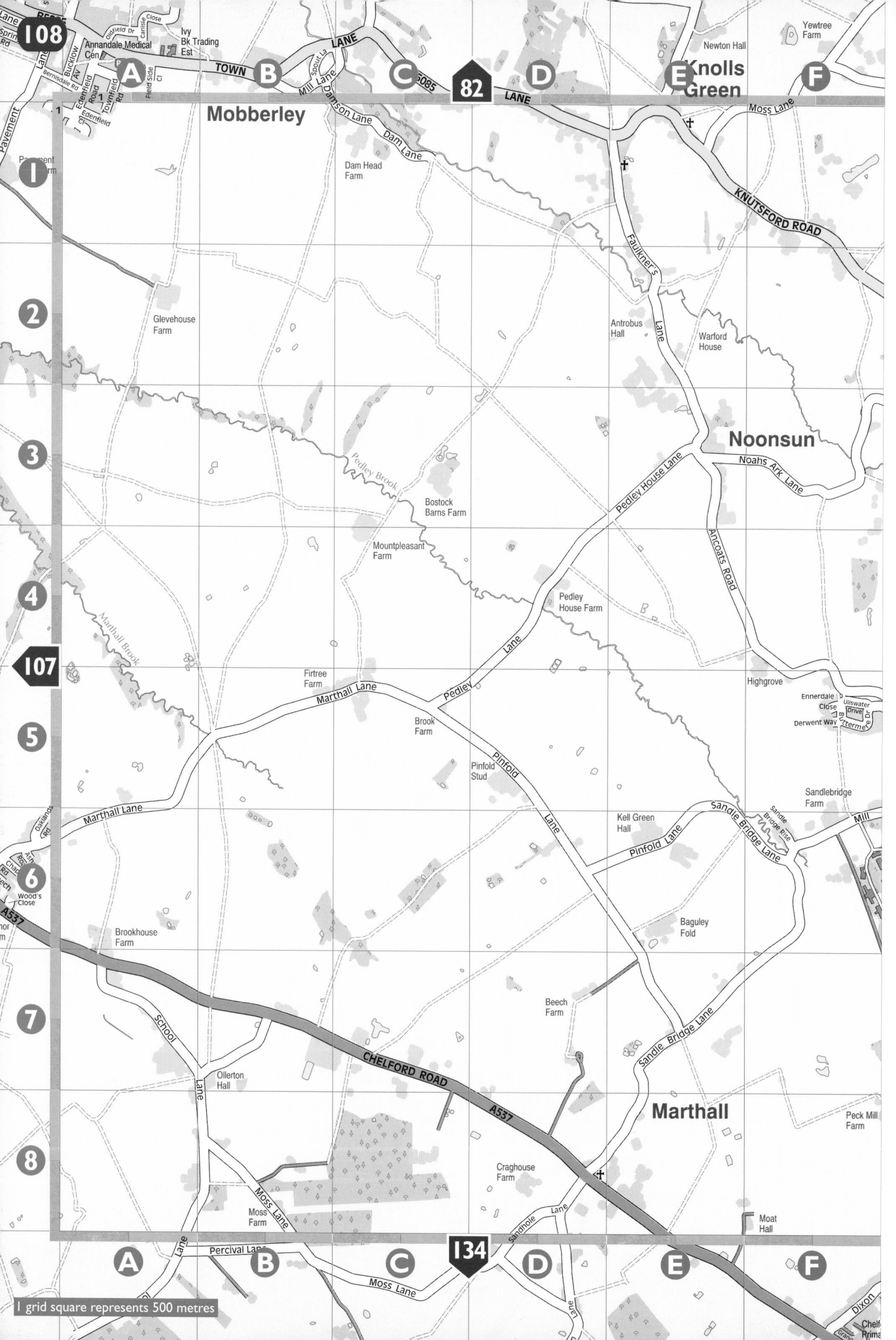

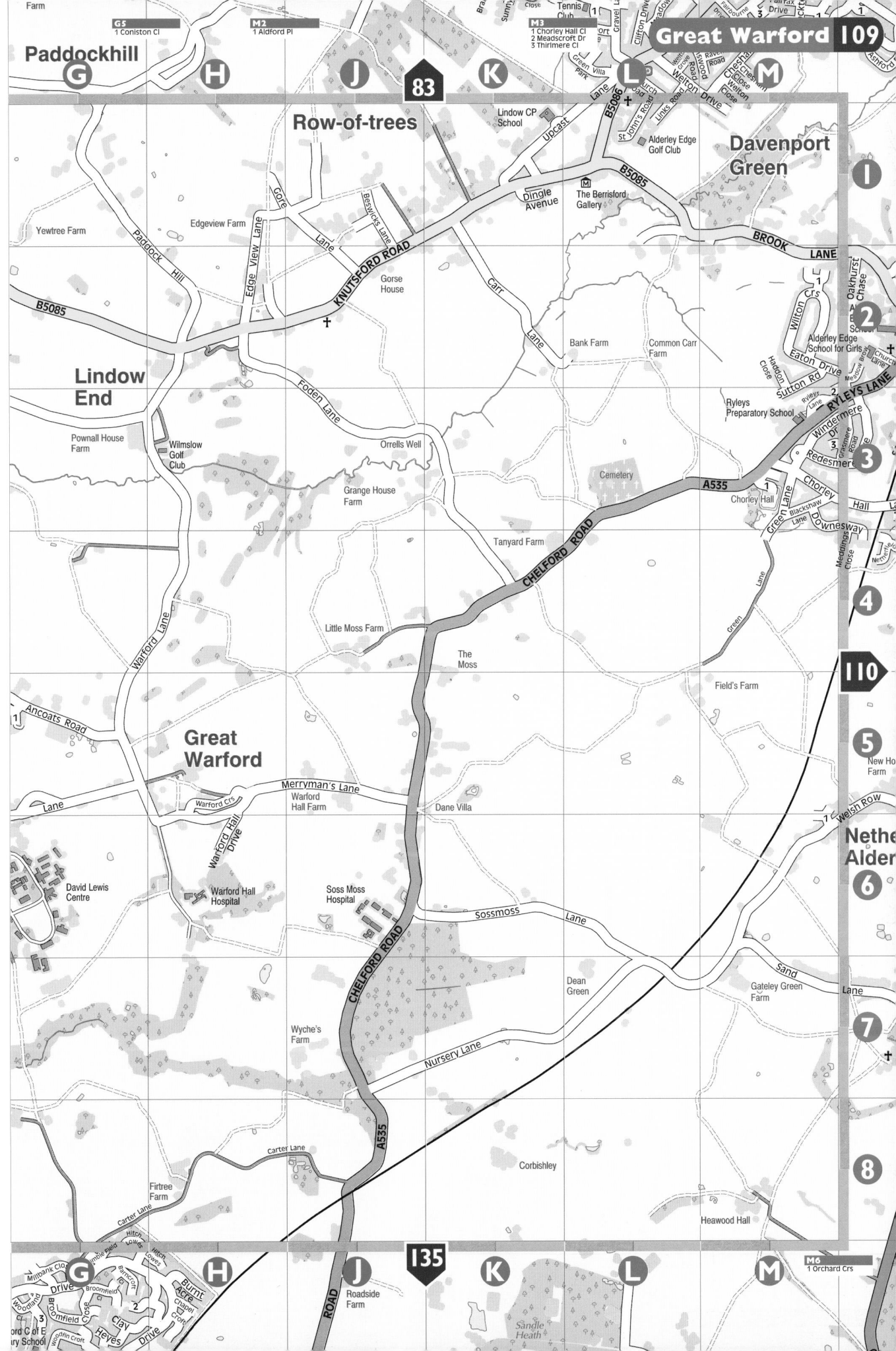

Paddockhill

G **H** **J** 83 **K** **L** **M** 1

Row-of-trees

Davenport
Green

Lindow
End

Wilmslow
Golf
Club

Pownall House
Farm

Yewtree Farm

Edgeview Farm

Gorse House

Bank Farm

Common Carr
Farm

Lindow CP
School

Dingle
Avenue

The Berrisford
Gallery

Alderley Edge
Golf Club

Tennis
Club

Oakhurst
Chase

Alderley Edge
School for Girls

Eaton Drive

Ryleys
Preparatory School

Redesmere

Chorley Hall

Cemetery

Orrells Well

Grange House
Farm

Tanyard Farm

Little Moss Farm

The
Moss

Field's Farm

New Ho
Farm

Great
Warford

Ancoats Road

David Lewis
Centre

Warford Hall
Hospital

Warford Crs

Merryman's Lane

Warford
Hall Farm

Dane Villa

Soss Moss
Hospital

Sossmoss Lane

Nethe
Alder

Welsh Row

Dean
Green

Gateley Green
Farm

Sand Lane

Wyche's
Farm

Nursery Lane

Corbishley

Heawood Hall

Firtree
Farm

Carter Lane

Roadside
Farm

Sandle
Heath

G **H** **J** 135 **K** **L** **M**

B5085

Knutsford Road

Carr Lane

Foden Lane

Warford Lane

Chelford Road

A535

Chelford Road

Brook Lane

Ryleys Lane

Downesway

Green Lane

Chorley Hall Lane

A535

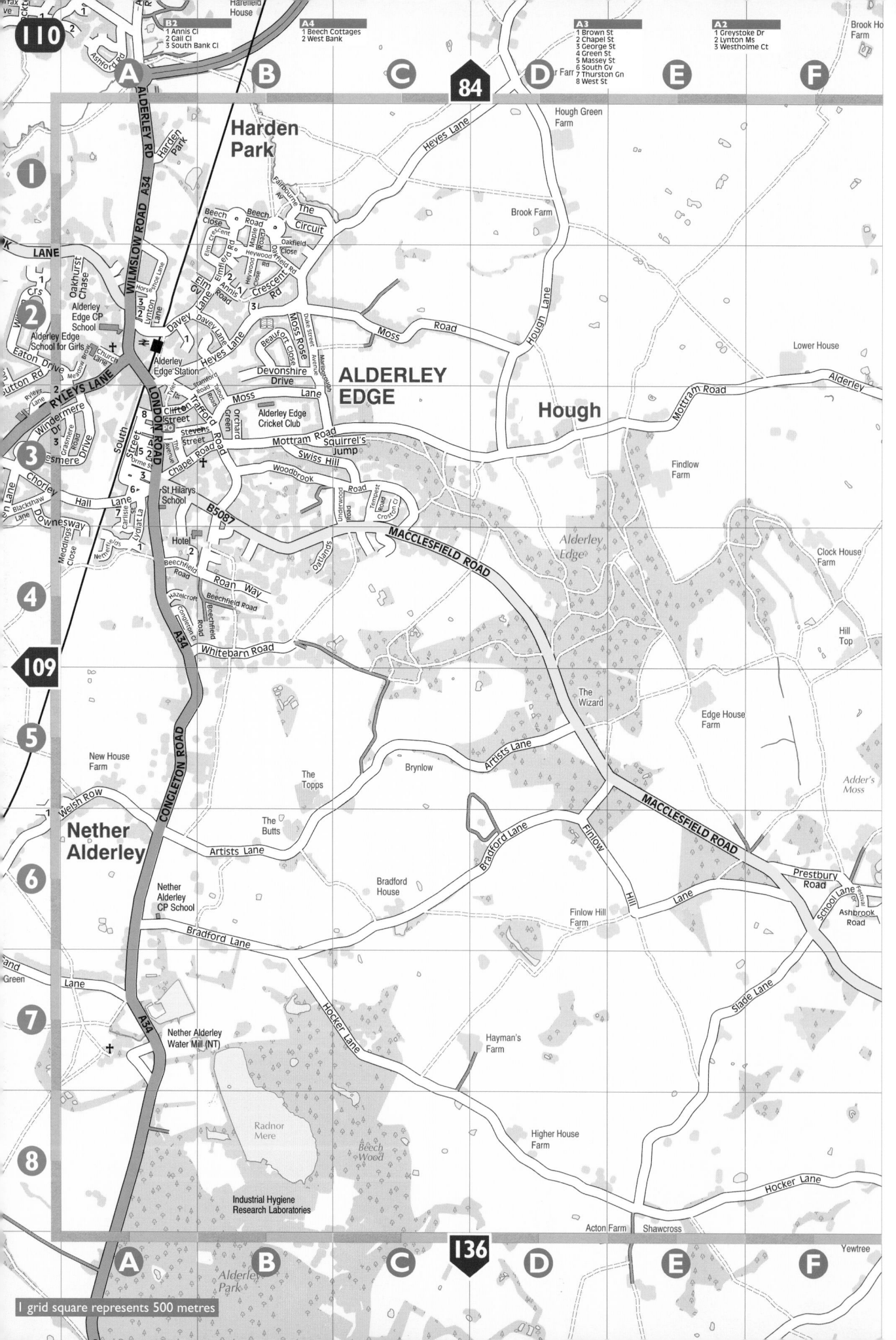

84

A   B   C   D   E   F

B2
1 Annis Cl
2 Gail Cl
3 South Bank Cl

A4
1 Beech Cottages
2 West Bank

A3
1 Brown St
2 Chapel St
3 George St
4 Green St
5 Massey St
6 South Gv
7 Thurston Gn
8 West St

A2
1 Greystoke Dr
2 Lynton Ms
3 Westholme Ct

Brook Ho
Farm

Harefield
House

I

Hough Green
Farm

LANE

Harden
Park

Harden
Park

**Harden
Park**

The
Circuit

Heves Lane

Brook Farm

K

Beech
Close

Beech
Road

Oakfield
Close

Elm
Crescent

ALDERLEY ROAD

Lower House

Oakhurst
Chase

Crs

Alderley
Edge CP
School

Alderley Edge
School for Girls

2

WILMSLOW ROAD A34

Elm
Gv

Annis
Road

Crescent
Rd

Maple
Road

Oakfield Rd

Heywood Rd

Moss
Rose

Duke Street

Moss   Road

Hough Lane

Eaton drive

Sutton Rd

RYLEYS LANE

Church
Lane

Davey

davey Lane

Heves Lane

Mottram Road

Alderley

Alderley
Edge Station

Stamford
Road

Devonshire
Drive

**ALDERLEY
EDGE**

Hough

3

Windermere
Dr

Grasmere
Road

LONDON ROAD

Clifton
Street

Trafford Road

Moss
Lane

orchard
green

Alderley Edge
Cricket Club

Squirrel's
Jump

Findlow
Farm

Esmere

Stevens
Street

Orme St

Mottram Road

Swiss Hill

Chorley

Hall   Lane

Blackshaw
Lane

South
Street

Chapel

St Hilary's
School

Woodbrook

Underwood
Road

Tempest
Road

Croston Cl

*Alderley
Edge*

Clock House
Farm

4

Downesway

Meddings
Close

Nemerle

Carlisle

Lydiat La

B5087

Hotel

Beechfield
Road

Hazelcroft

Congleton Rd

Roan Way

Beechfield Road

Beechfield
Road

Oatlands

MACCLESFIELD ROAD

Hill
Top

109

Whitebarn Road

The
Wizard

Edge House
Farm

5

New House
Farm

The
Topps

Brynlow

Artists Lane

*Adder's
Moss*

CONGLETON ROAD

Welsh Row

The
Butts

Bradford Lane

Finlow

MACCLESFIELD ROAD

6

**Nether
Alderley**

A34

Nether
Alderley
CP School

Artists Lane

Bradford
House

Finlow Hill
Farm

Hill

Lane

Prestbury
Road

School Lane

Ashbrook
Road

Bradford Lane

7

and

Green Lane

Nether Alderley
Water Mill (NT)

Hocker Lane

Hayman's
Farm

Slade Lane

8

*Radnor
Mere*

*Beech
Wood*

Higher House
Farm

Hocker Lane

Industrial Hygiene
Research Laboratories

Acton Farm   Shawcross

Yewtree

A   B   **136**   C   D   E   F

*Alderley
Park*

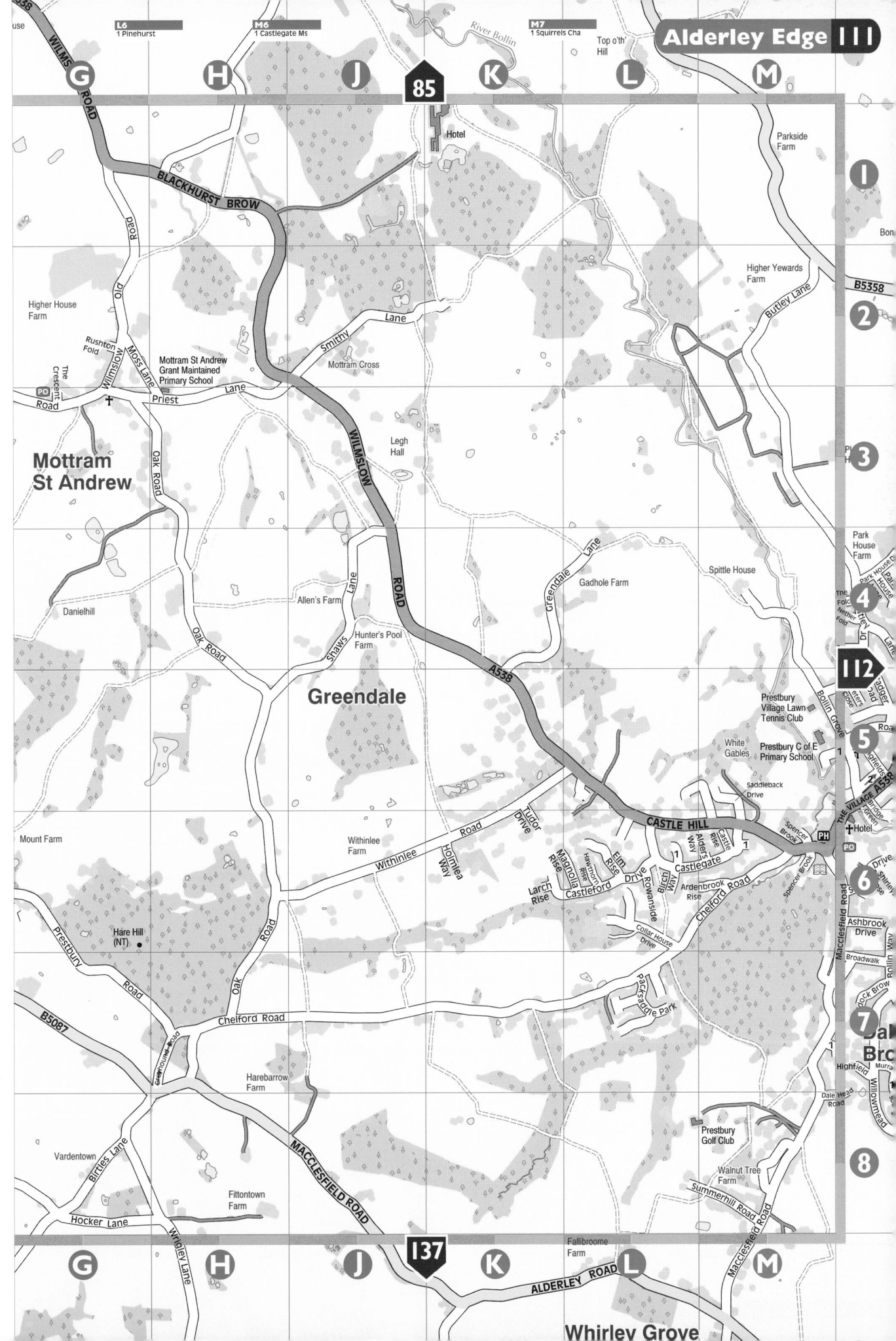

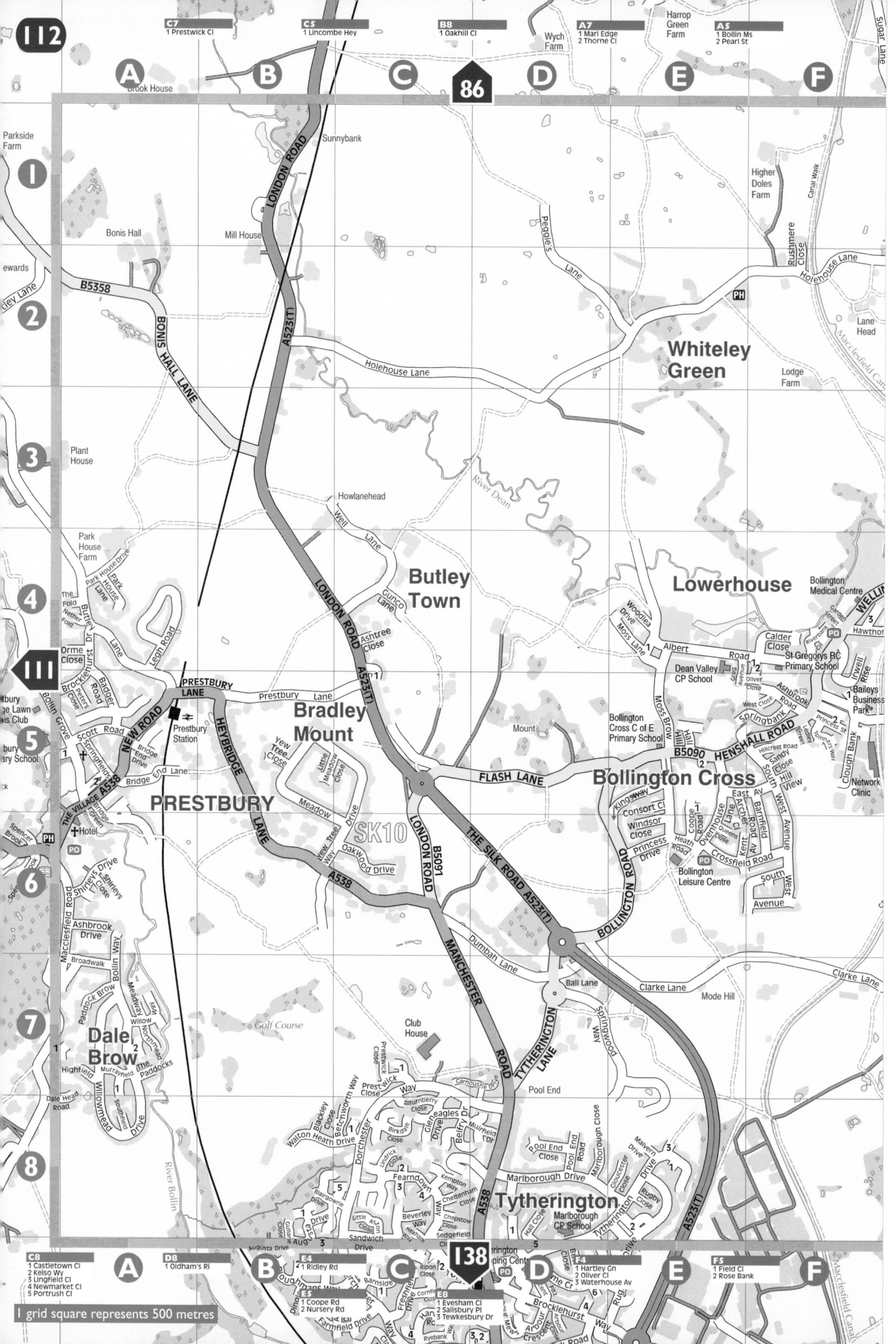

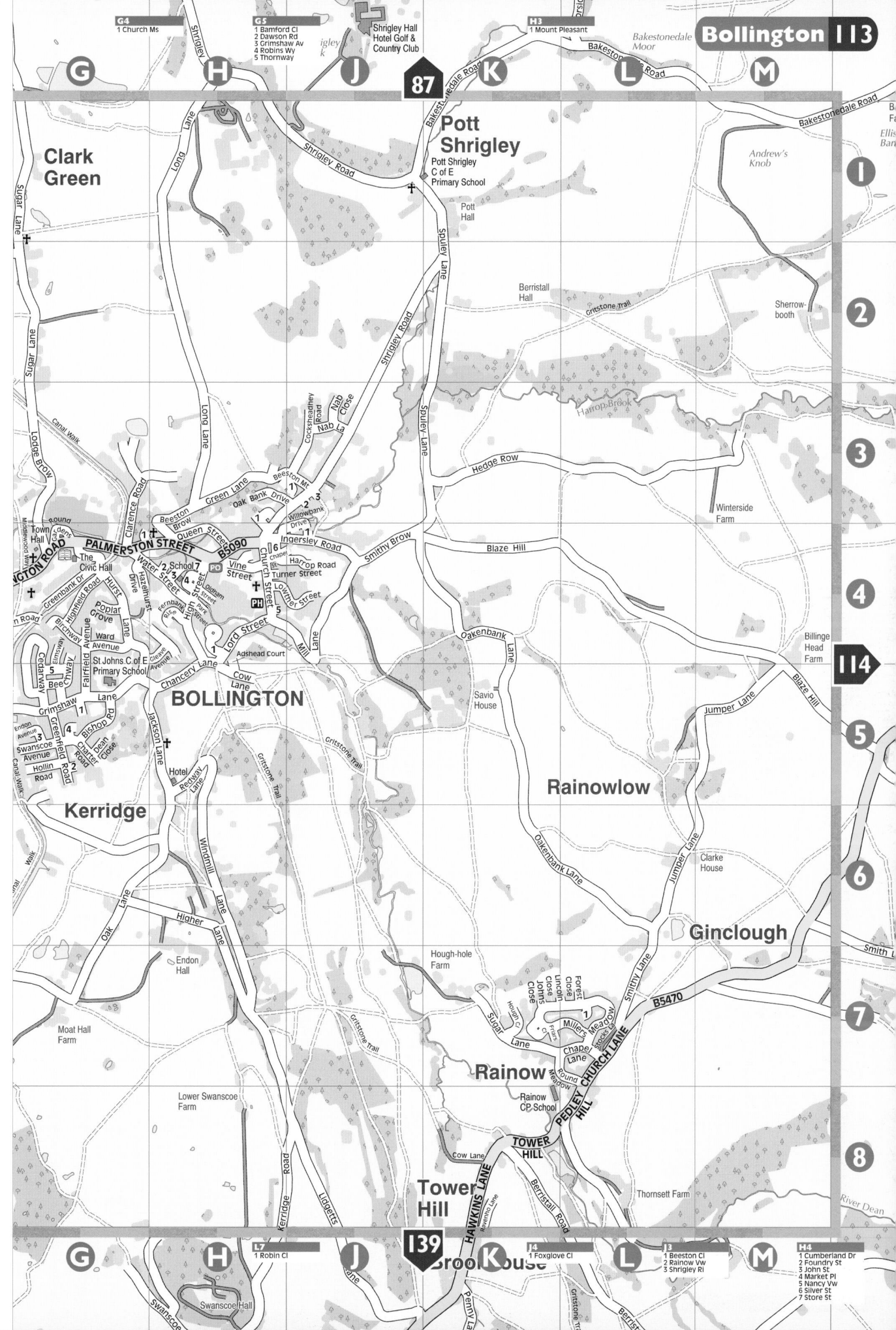

G4
1 Church Ms

G5
1 Bamford Cl
2 Dawson Rd
3 Grimshaw Av
4 Robins Wy
5 Thornway

H3
1 Mount Pleasant

87

G H J K L M

Shrigley Hall
Hotel Golf &
Country Club

Bakestonedale
Moor

Clark
Green

Pott
Shrigley

Pott Shrigley
C of E
Primary School

Andrew's
Knob

1

Pott
Hall

Berristall
Hall

Gritstone Trail

Sherrow-
booth

2

Harrop Brook

3

Winterside
Farm

Hedge Row

Nab Close
Nab La
Cocksheadhey Road

Beeston Mt
Green Lane
Oak Bank Drive
Willowpank Drive

Ingersley Road
Blaze Hill

Beeston Brow
Queen Street
Clarence Road
B5090
Chapel
Vine Street
Turner Street
Harrop Road
Smithy Brow

Billinge
Head
Farm

114

Town Hall
PALMERSTON STREET
The Civic Hall
School
PO
Church Street
Lowther Street
Oakenbank Lane
Savio House

Jumper Lane

5

PH
Lord Street
Mill Lane
Adshead Court

Rainowlow

Greenbank Dr
Highfield Road
Hurst Drive
Hazelhurst
Peter Street
Oldham Street
Park Street
Fernbank

Hinton Road
Poplar Grove
Ward Avenue
St Johns C of E
Primary School
Cow Lane
Chancery Lane
Gritstone Trail

Jackson Lane

BOLLINGTON

Clarke
House

6

Birchway
Fairfield Avenue
Elmway
Cleave Avenue
Cedarway
Bee

Grimshaw
Lane
Bishop Rd

Oakenbank Lane
Ginclough

Smith L

Endon Avenue
Swanscoe Avenue
Greenfield Road
Charter Road
Dean Close
Hollin Road

Kerridge

Renway Lane
Windmill Lane

Gritstone Trail

Jumper Lane

B5470

7

Canal Walk

Oak Lane
Higher Lane

Forest Close
Lincoln Close
Johns Close

Smithy Lane

Endon
Hall

Hough-hole
Farm

Miller's Meadow
Chapel Lane

CHURCH LANE

Moat Hall
Farm

Sugar Lane
Hough Cl
Friars

Rainow

Rainow
CP School

PEDLEY HILL
Round Meadow

Lower Swanscoe
Farm

Gritstone Trail

River Dean

8

TOWER HILL

Tower
Hill

Cow Lane
HAWKINS LANE
Berristall Road

Thornsett Farm

Swanscoe Hall

139

Brook House

G H J K L M

L7
1 Robin Cl

J4
1 Foxglove Cl

L
1 Beeston Cl
2 Rainow Vw
3 Shrigley Rl

H4
1 Cumberland Dr
2 Foundry St
3 John St
4 Market Pl
5 Nancy Vw
6 Silver St
7 Store St

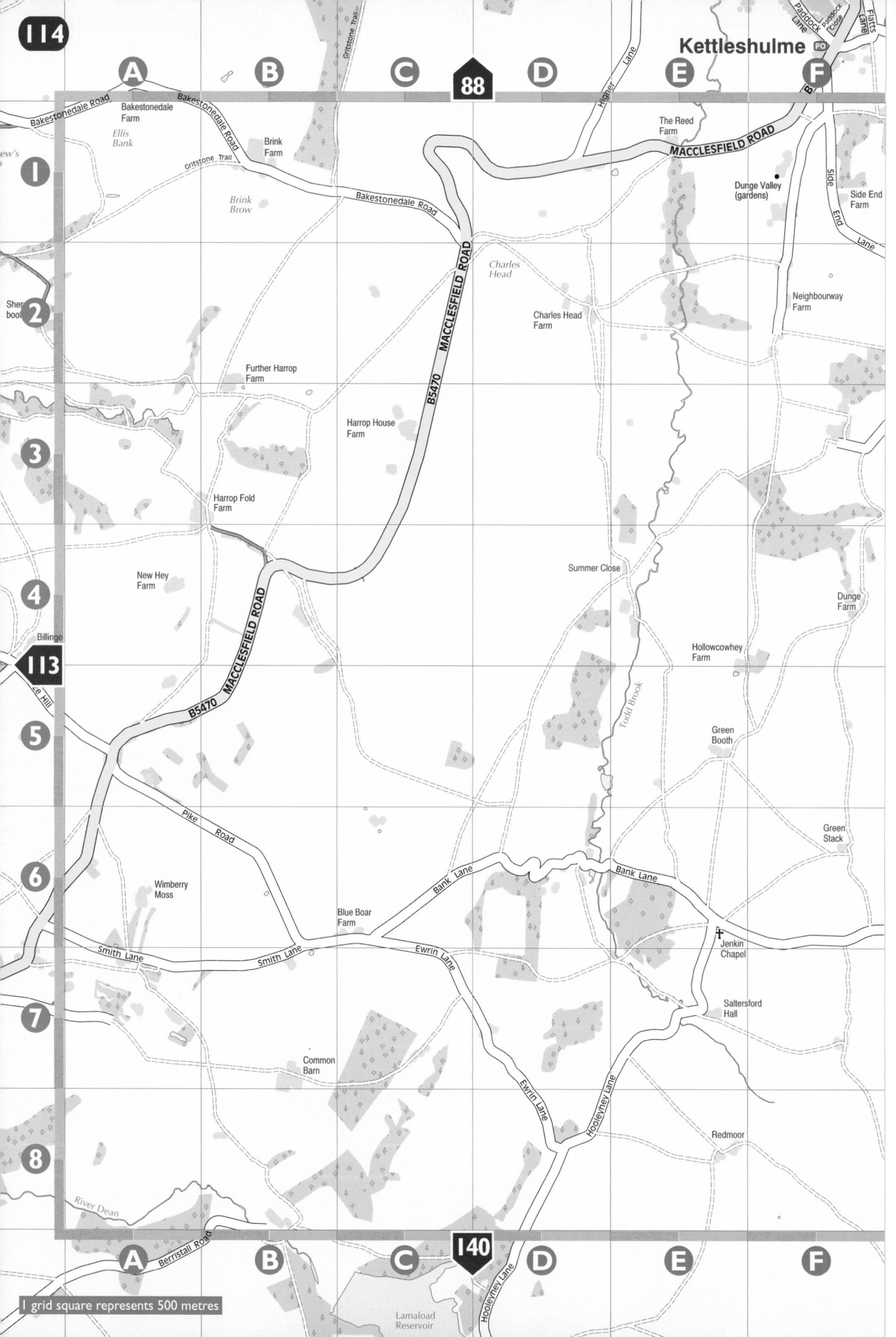

A   B   C   88   D   E   F

Kettleshulme

Bakestonedale Road
Bakestonedale Farm
Ellis Bank
Gritstone Trail
Brink Farm
Brink Brow
Bakestonedale Road
MACCLESFIELD ROAD
The Reed Farm
Dunge Valley (gardens)
Side End Farm
Side End Lane
Paddock Lane
Paddock Close
Flatts Lane

I

Sher boo
Charles Head
Charles Head Farm
Neighbourway Farm

2

Further Harrop Farm
Harrop House Farm

B5470 MACCLESFIELD ROAD

3

Harrop Fold Farm

Summer Close
Dunge Farm

New Hey Farm

4

Billinge
MACCLESFIELD ROAD

e Hill
B5470 MACCLESFIELD ROAD
Todd Brook
Hollowcowhey Farm
Green Booth

5

Pike Road
Green Stack

Wimberry Moss
Bank Lane
Bank Lane

6

Blue Boar Farm
Ewrin Lane
Jenkin Chapel

Smith Lane
Smith Lane

Saltersford Hall

7

Common Barn
Ewrin Lane
Hooleyhey Lane
Redmoor

8

River Dean

A   Berristall Road   B   C   140   D   E   F

Hooleyhey Lane

Lamaload Reservoir

90

A B C D E F

1 2 3 4 5 6 7 8

River Dee

Cheshire County
Flintshire

Flint Marsh

Ashmount Industrial Centre

Ashmount Industrial Centre

Rugby Union Football Club

HOLLYWELL ROAD

Town Hall & Mayors Parlour

Flintshire Retail Park

Flint Leisure Centre

Happy Feet Health Centre

Flint Football Club

Marsh Lane

Evans St
Castle St
Castle St
Castle Dyke St

Corporation St

Flint St

Castle Road

Henry Taylor St

FLINT

Flintshire County Council

CHESTER STREET

Flint Community Hospital

Church St
Duke St

Eyton Place Practice

Park Avenue

Flint Child Health Clinic

Borough Gv

County Primary School

HEOL YR EGLWYS

Prince Drive

Gwynedd CP Junior School

Cemetery

Rectory Cl

Trelawny Av

Woodfield Avenue

Queens Avenue

Maes-y-Dre

Maes Wales

Kings Av

Maes Gwyn

Albert Av

Bryn Siriol

BRYN ROAD

First Av

Second Av

Third Avenue

Fourth Av

Sixth Av

Kg Edward Dr

Princes Drive

Edwin Dr

Ffordd Glynawr

Ffordd Llewelyn

St Marys School

St Richard Gwyn High School

Englefield Drive

Deva Cl

Caesar Av

Mill Croft

Chester Road

A548

LC

Mount Pleasant

County Secondary School

A5119

Fifth Avenue

Tudor Av

Marian

Maes Teg

Bron Llwyn

Min Awel

Coed Onn Road

Oakenholt

Leadbrook

Paper Lane

1 grid square represents 500 metres

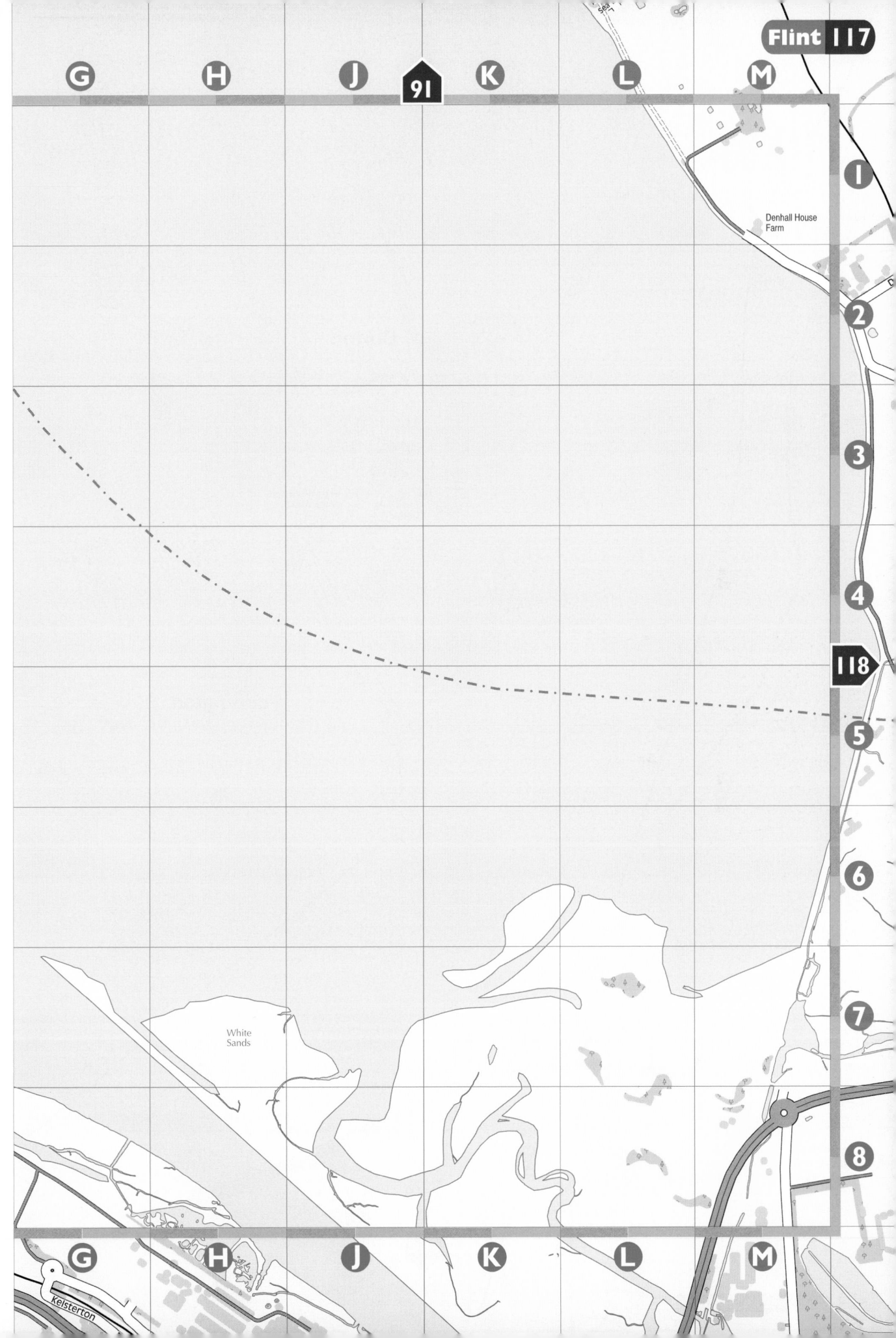

G H J **91** K L M

1

Denhall House
Farm

2

3

4

118

5

6

7

White
Sands

8

G H J K L M

Kelsterton

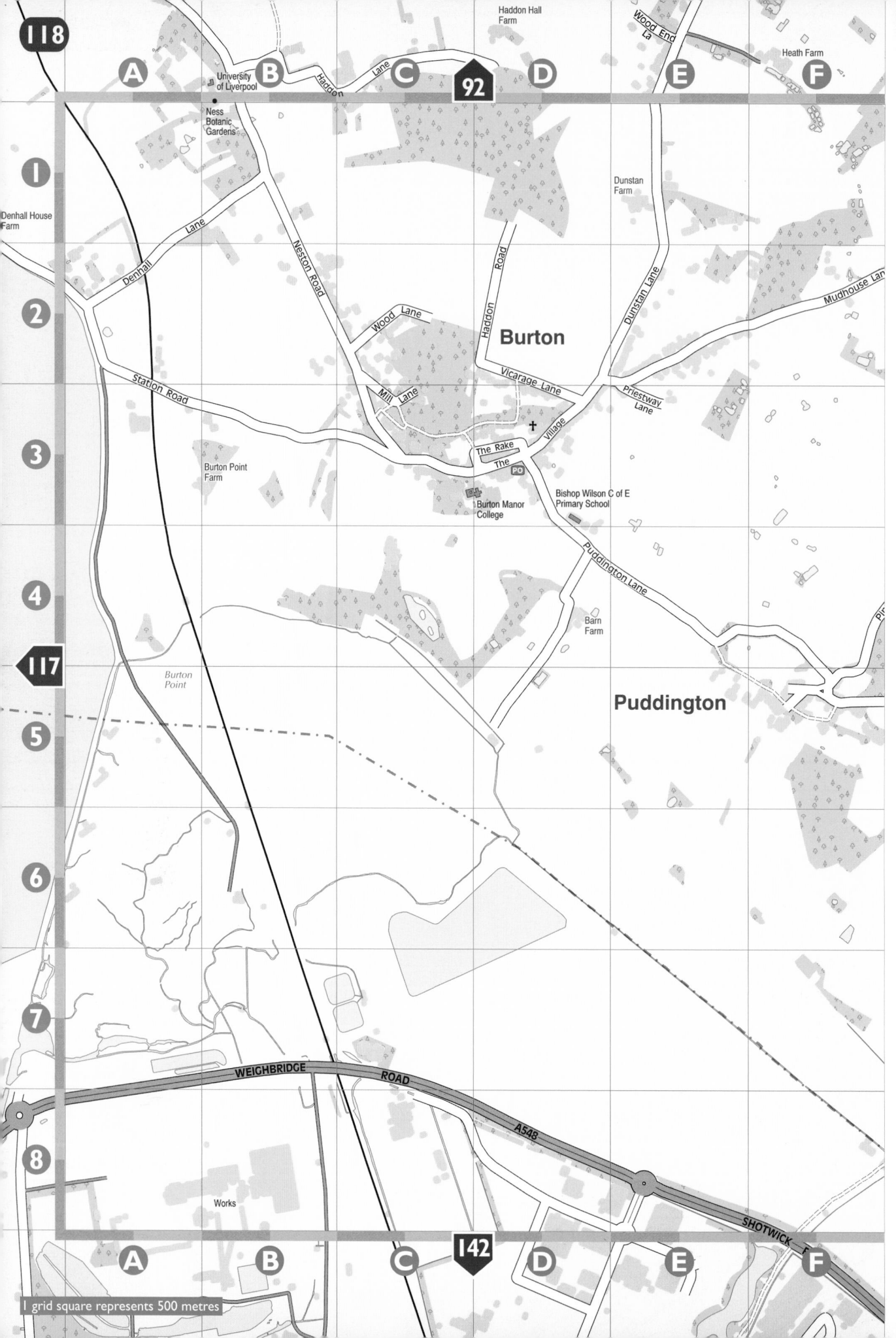

118

A   B   C   92   D   E   F

I   Denhall House Farm

Haddon Hall Farm
Wood End La
Heath Farm

University of Liverpool
Ness Botanic Gardens
Haddon Lane

Dunstan Farm
Mudhouse Lane

2   Denhall Lane

Neston Road
Wood Lane
Haddon Road
Burton
Vicarage Lane
Dunstan Lane
Priestway Lane

Station Road

3   Burton Point Farm
Mill Lane
The Rake
The Village
PO
Bishop Wilson C of E Primary School
Burton Manor College

Puddington Lane

4   Barn Farm

117   Burton Point
Puddington

5

6

7   WEIGHBRIDGE ROAD

A548

8   Works
SHOTWICK

A   B   142   C   D   E   F

1 grid square represents 500 metres

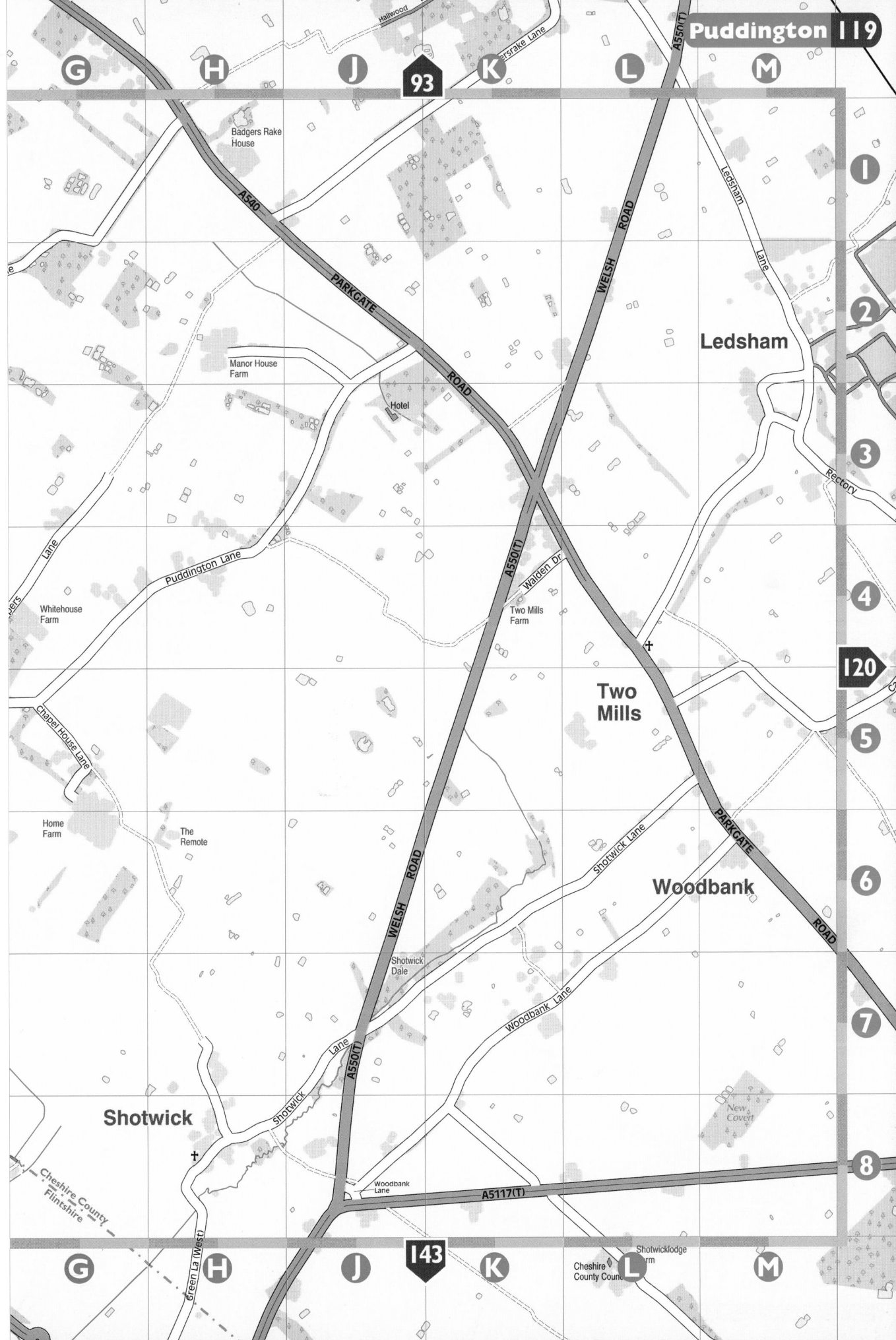

G H J K L M

93

I

Badgers Rake House

KERSRAKE LANE

HALLWOOD DR

A540

PARKGATE

ROAD

WELSH

ROAD

Ledsham

Ledsham Lane

2

3

Rectory

Manor House Farm

Hotel

Puddington Lane

Lane

A550(T)

Walden Dr

Two Mills Farm

4

120

Whitehouse Farm

ers

Two
Mills

5

Chapel House Lane

Home Farm

The Remote

PARKGATE

Shotwick Lane

6

Woodbank

ROAD

WELSH

ROAD

Shotwick Dale

Woodbank Lane

7

Shotwick

Lane

A550(T)

Shotwick

New Covert

Cheshire County
Flintshire

Woodbank Lane

A5117(T)

8

Green La (West)

A550(T)

Shotwicklodge Farm

Cheshire County Council

G H J K L M

143

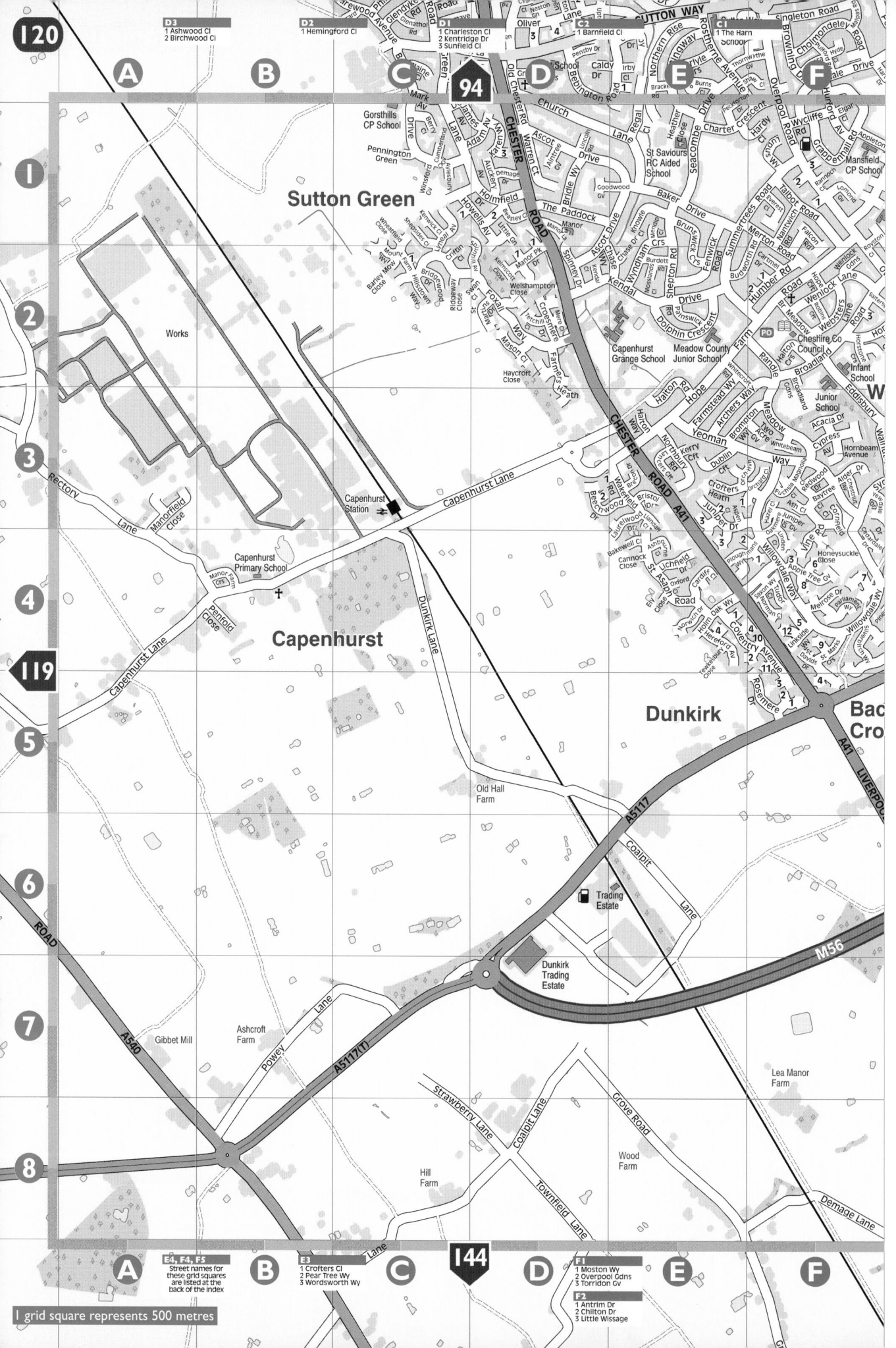

A   B   C   94   D   E   F

D3
1 Ashwood Cl
2 Birchwood Cl

D2
1 Hemingford Cl

D1
1 Charleston Cl
2 Kentridge Dr
3 Sunfield Cl

C2
1 Barnfield Cl

C1
1 The Harn School

SUTTON WAY

Gorsthills CP School

Pennington Green

Sutton Green

St Saviours RC Aided School

Mansfield CP School

1

Works

2

Capenhurst Grange School

Meadow County Junior School

Cheshire Co Council

Infant School

Capenhurst Station

Capenhurst Lane

CHESTER ROAD A41

3

Capenhurst Primary School

Rectory Lane

Manorfield Close

Penfold Close

Capenhurst Lane

Capenhurst

Dunkirk Lane

4

Dunkirk

Bac Cro

5

Old Hall Farm

A5117

Coalpit Lane

A41 LIVERPOO

6

ROAD

A540

Trading Estate

Dunkirk Trading Estate

M56

7

Gibbet Mill

Ashcroft Farm

Powey Lane

A5117(T)

Lea Manor Farm

Strawberry Lane

Grove Road

8

Hill Farm

Coalpit Lane

Townfield Lane

Wood Farm

Demage Lane

E4, F4, F5
Street names for these grid squares are listed at the back of the index

E3
1 Crofters Cl
2 Pear Tree Wy
3 Wordsworth Wy

F1
1 Moston Wy
2 Overpool Gdns
3 Torridon Gv

F2
1 Antrim Dr
2 Chilton Dr
3 Little Wissage

A   B   C   144   D   E   F

1 grid square represents 500 metres

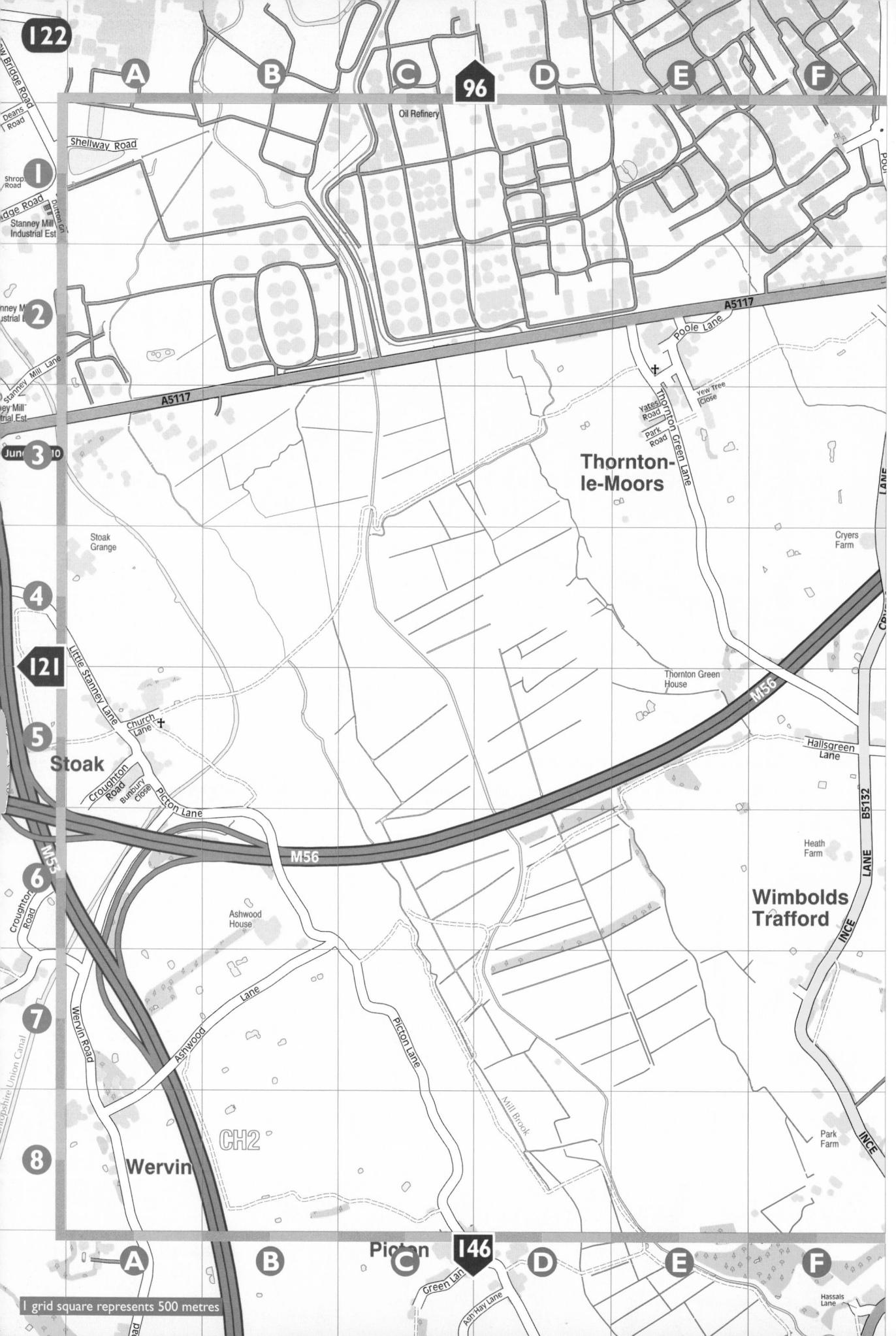

A   B   C   96   D   E   F

Oil Refinery

Shellway Road

Shrop
Road

Stanney Mill
Industrial Est

1

2

Junc 10

3

A5117

A5117

Poole Lane

Yew Tree
Close

Yates
Road

Thornton Green Lane

Park
Road

**Thornton-
le-Moors**

Cryers
Farm

Stoak
Grange

4

121

Thornton Green
House

M56

5

Church
Lane

Stoak

Croughton
Road

Bunbury
Close

Picton Lane

Hallsgreen
Lane

B5132

M56

M53

6

Croughton
Road

Ashwood
House

Heath
Farm

**Wimbolds
Trafford**

INCE LANE

7

Wervin Road

Ashwood Lane

Picton Lane

Mill Brook

INCE

Park
Farm

Shropshire Union Canal

8

CH2

Wervin

A   B   Picton 146   D   E   F

Green Lan

Ash Hay Lane

Hassals
Lane

Deans
Road

Bridge Road

Little Stanney Lane

Stanney Mill Lane

I grid square represents 500 metres

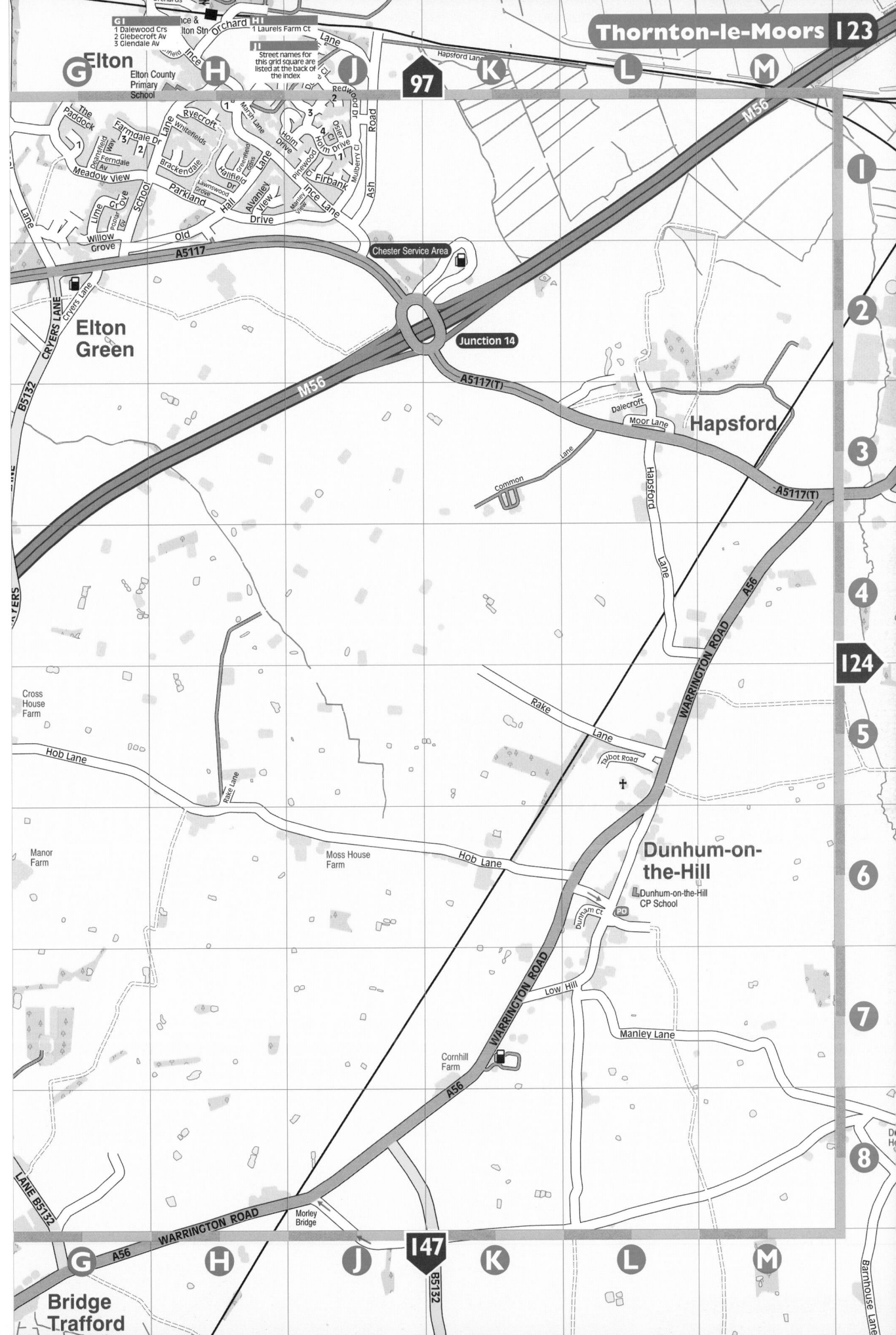

Elton

G

1 Dalewood Crs
2 Glebecroft Av
3 Glendale Av

Elton County
Primary
School

H

1 Laurels Farm Ct

Street names for
this grid square are
listed at the back of
the index

J

97

K

L

M

I

The
Paddock

Cryers Lane

Meadow View

Willow
Grove

School Lane

Parkland Drive

Old

Farndale Dr

Whitefields

Holm Drive

Marsh Lane

Brackendale Dr

Halfield

Alvanley View

Pinewood Grove

Firbank

Ince Lane

Redwood

Mulberry Cl

Osier Drive

Ash Road

B5132

Elton
Green

Cryers Lane

A5117

Chester Service Area

Junction 14

M56

A5117(T)

Dalecroft

Moor Lane

Hapsford

Common Lane

Hapsford Lane

A5117(T)

2

3

4

124

Cross
House
Farm

Hob Lane

Rake Lane

Rake Lane

Warrington Road

A56

Talbot Road

✝

5

Manor
Farm

Moss House
Farm

Hob Lane

**Dunhum-on-
the-Hill**

Dunham Ct

PO

Dunhum-on-the-Hill
CP School

6

Warrington Road

Low Hill

Manley Lane

7

Cornhill
Farm

A56

8

LANE B5132

WARRINGTON ROAD

A56

Morley
Bridge

147

B5132

Barnhouse Lane

G

H

J

K

L

M

**Bridge
Trafford**

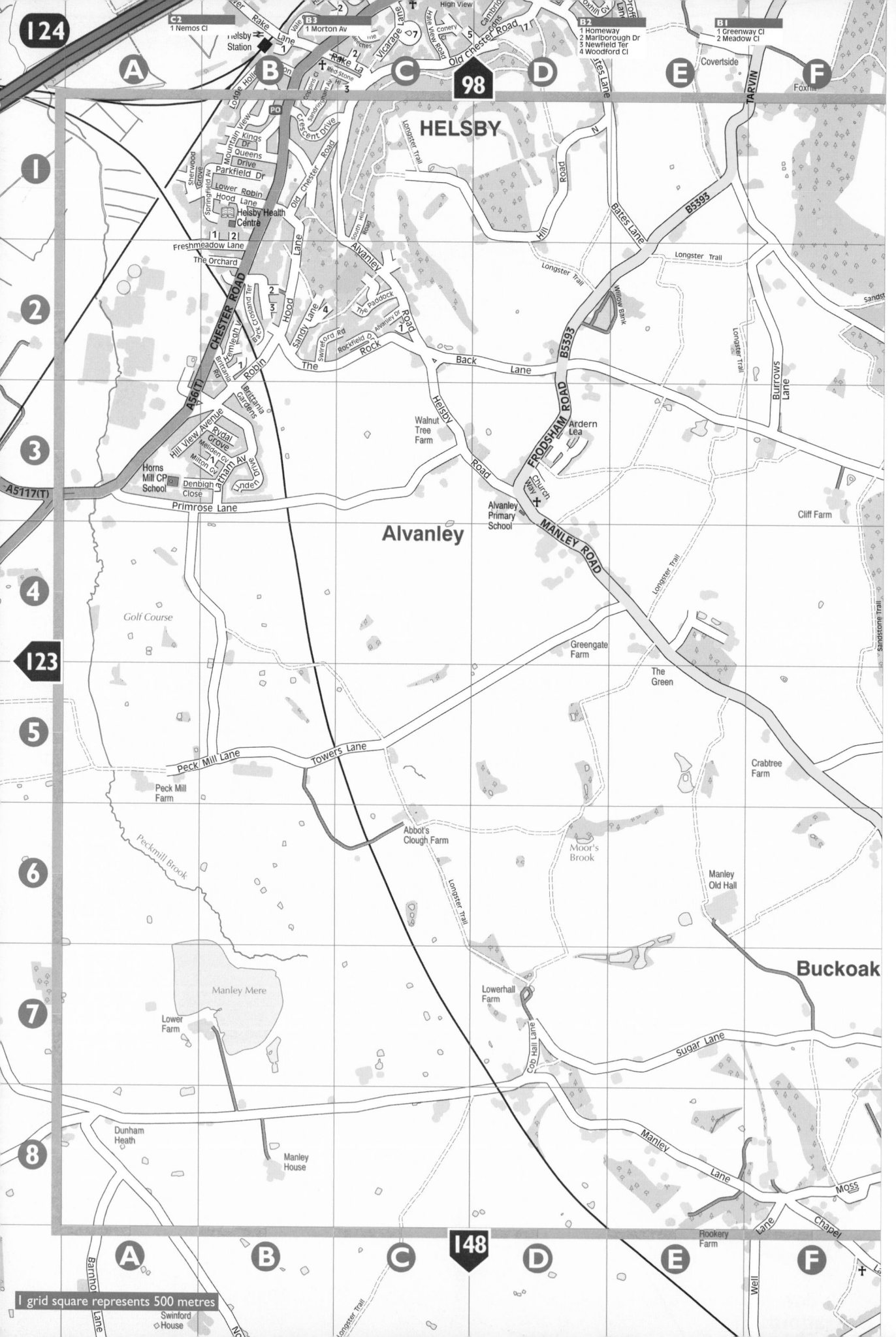

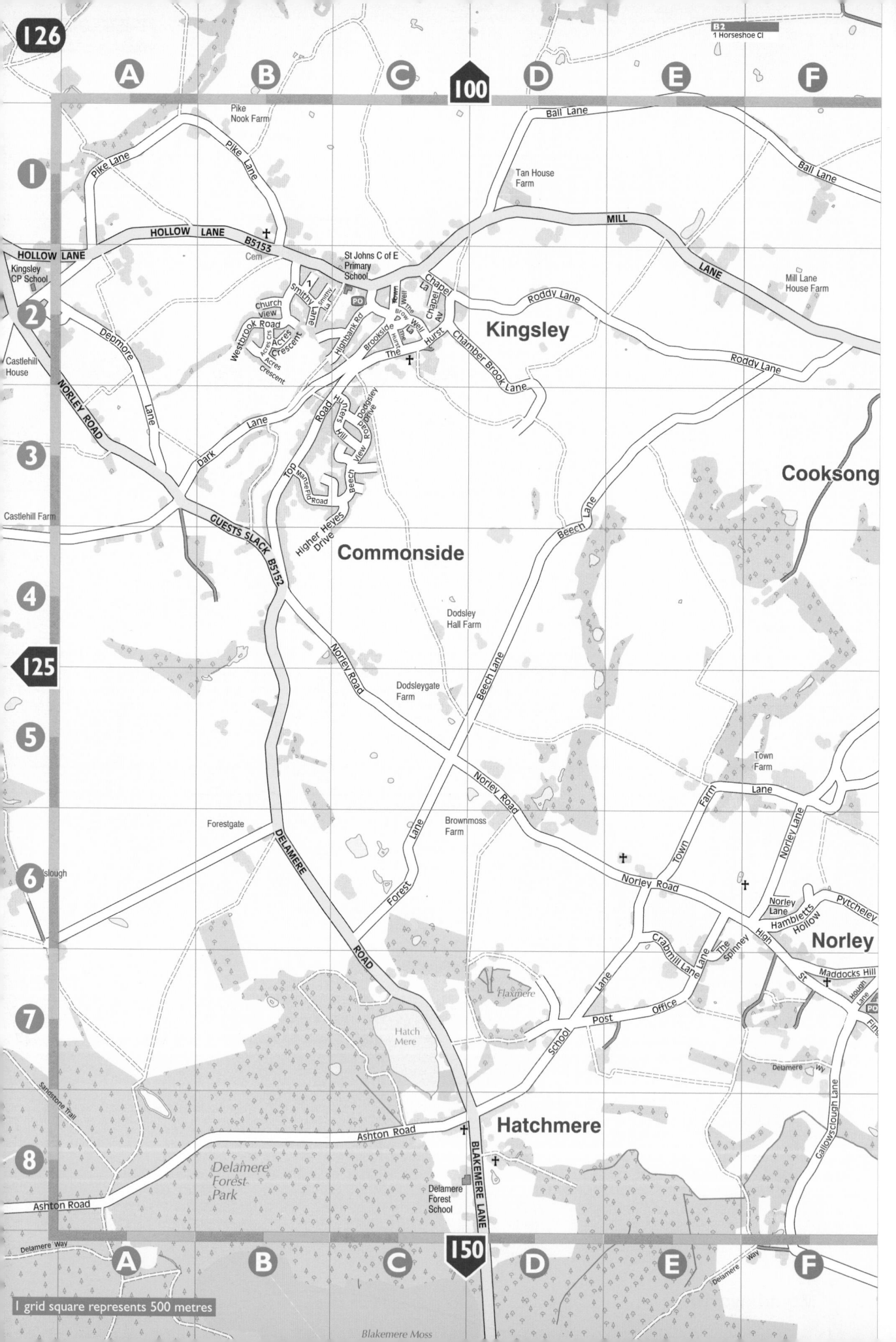

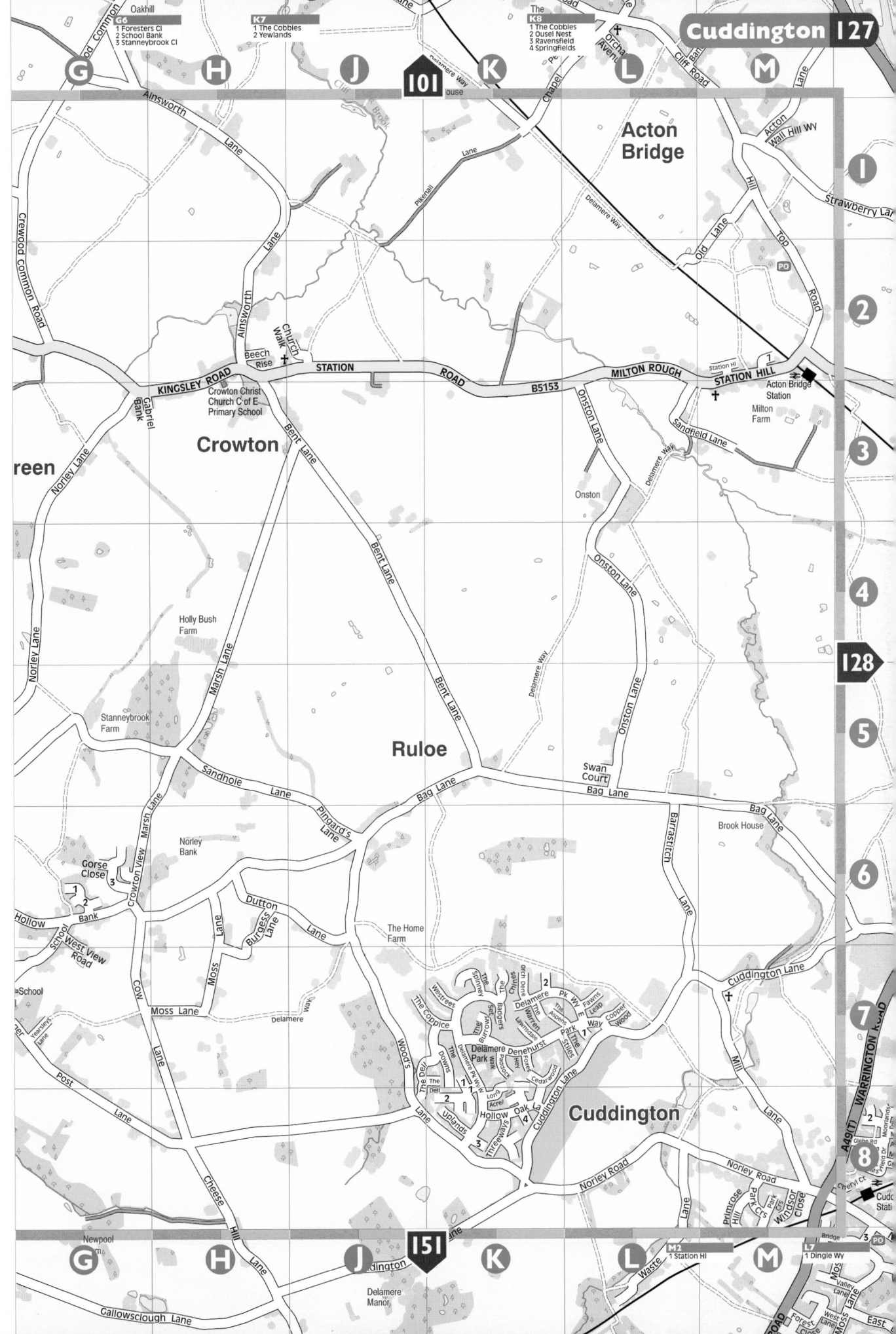

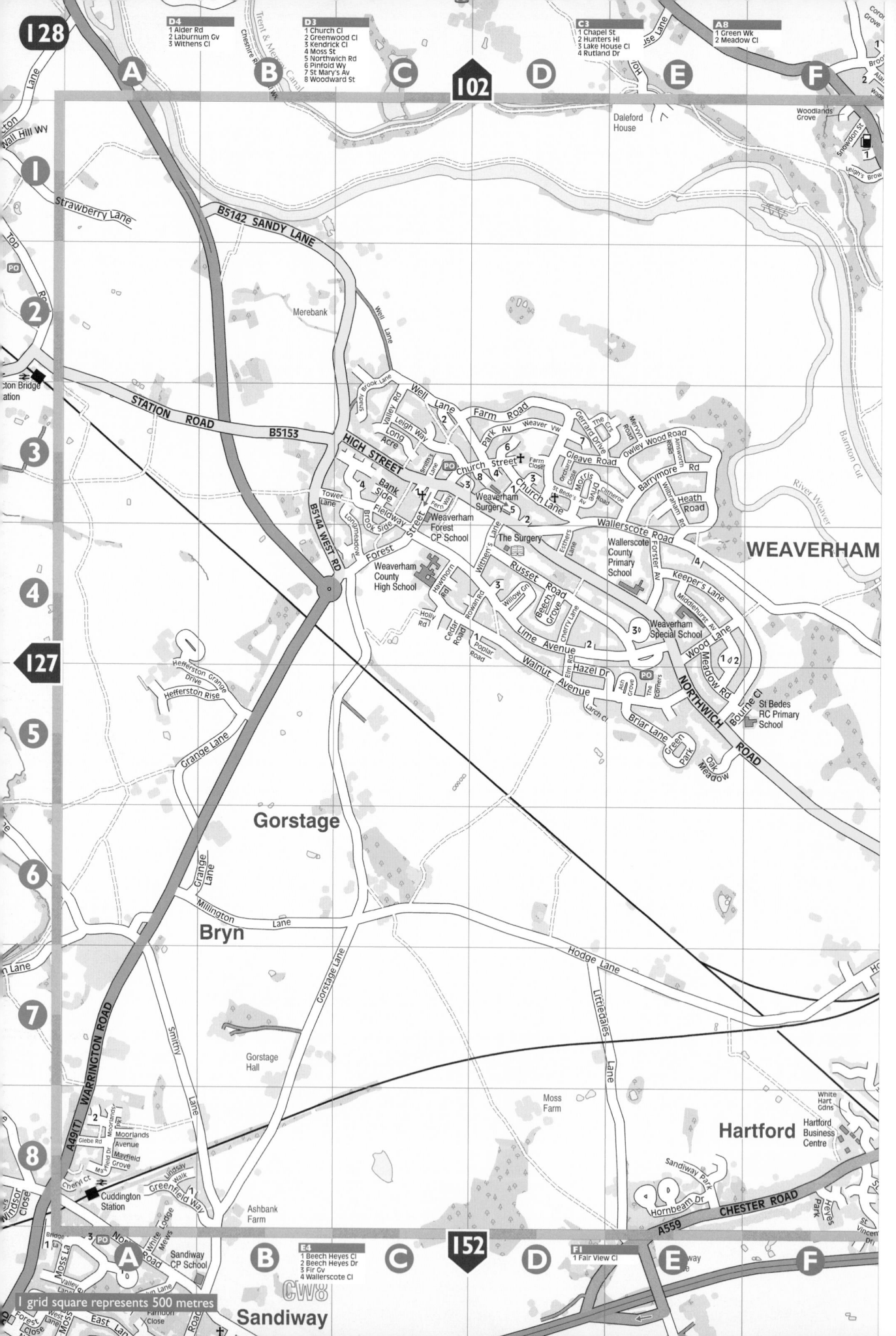

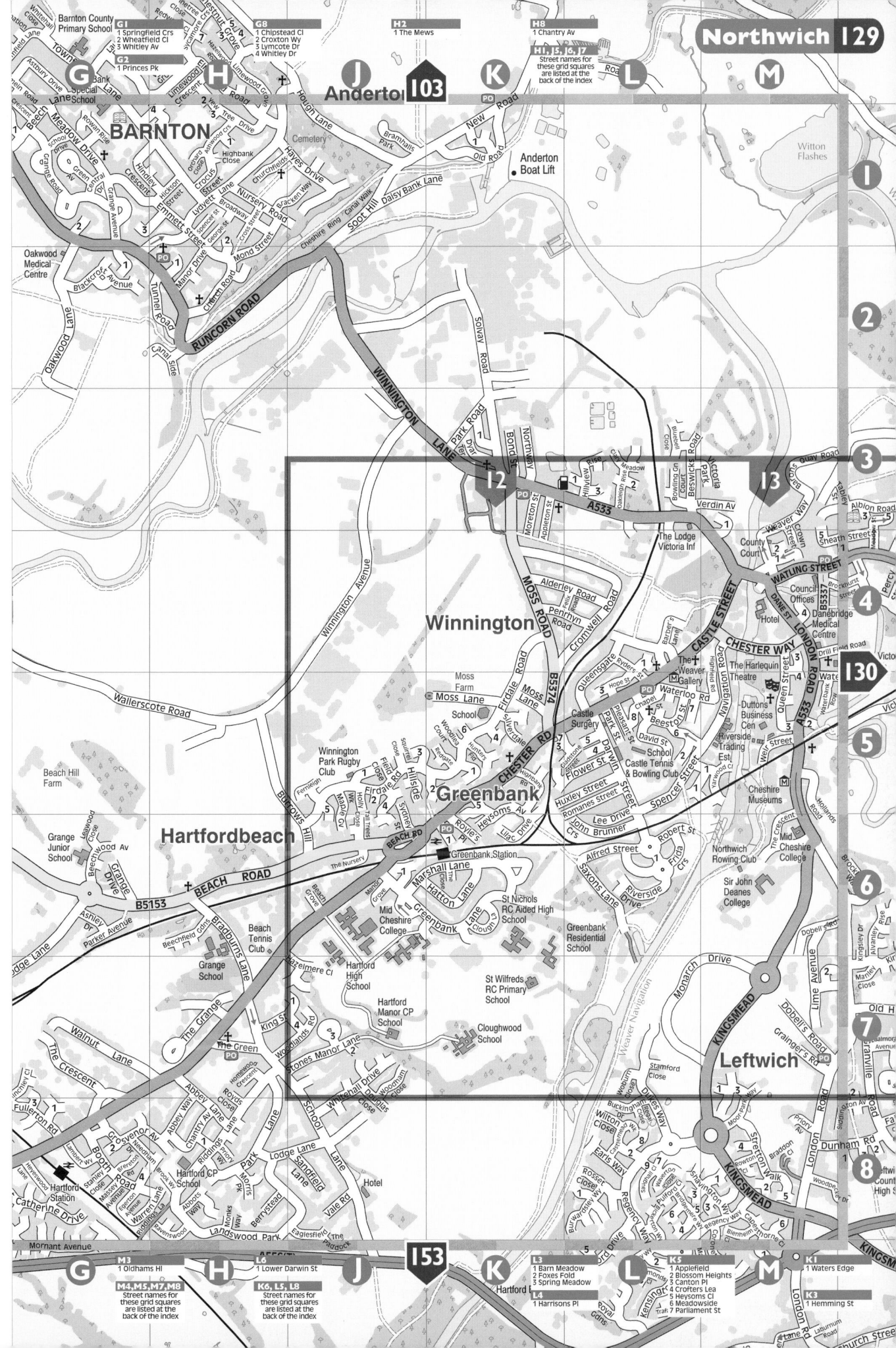

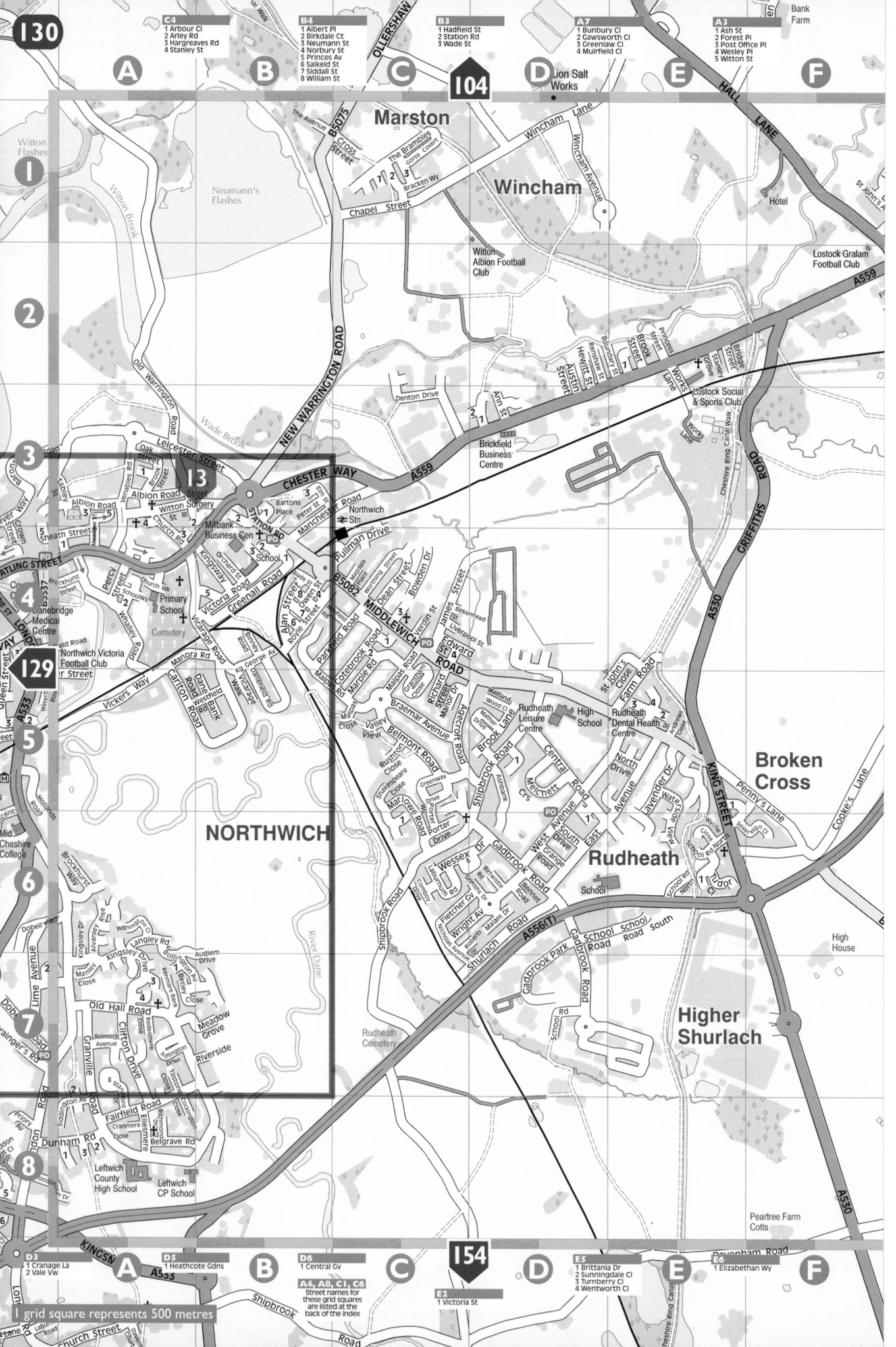

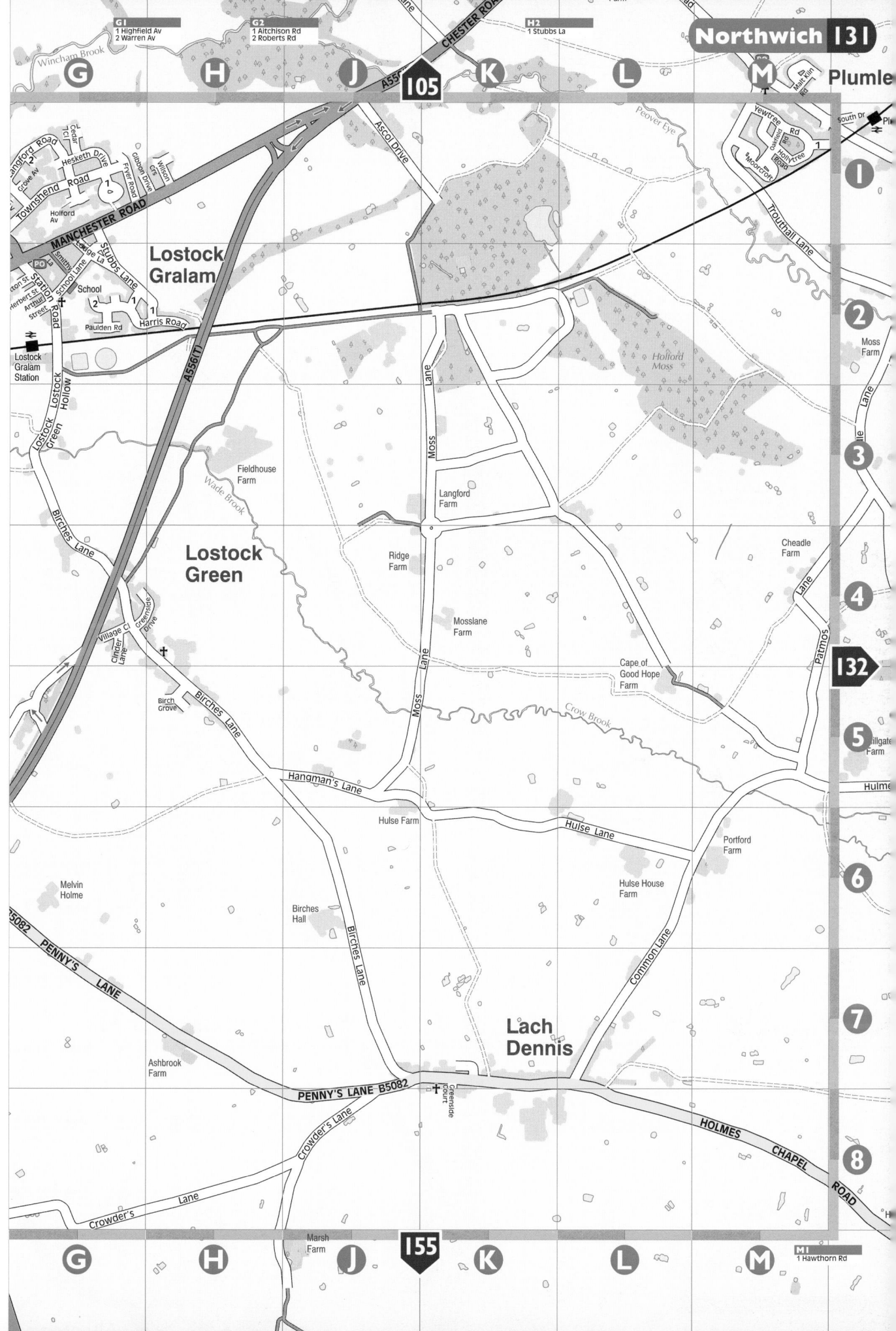

G1
1 Highfield Av
2 Warren Av

G2
1 Aitchison Rd
2 Roberts Rd

H2
1 Stubbs La

G H J 105 K L M

105

CHESTER ROAD

Wincham Brook

Ascol Drive

I

South Dr

Yewtree Rd

Moorcroft

Oakfield Rd

Holly Tree Road

Mattkin Rd

Langford Road

Cedar Crove Av

Hesketh Drive

Townshend Road

Crowe Av

Gibbon Drive

Fryer Road

Wilson Crs

Holford Av

Stubbs Lane

Lodge La

School Lane

MANCHESTER ROAD

PO

Smithy

Buxton St

Herbert St

Arthur street

School

Paulden Rd

Harris Road

Lostock Gralam

Lostock Gralam Station

Lostock Hollow

Lostock Green

Peover Eye

2

Moss Farm

3

Holford Moss

Trouthall Lane

Birches Lane

Fieldhouse Farm

Wade Brook

Langford Farm

Moss Lane

Cheadle Farm

4

Patmos Lane

132

Lostock Green

Village Cl

Greenside Drive

Cinder Lane

Ridge Farm

Mosslane Farm

Cape of Good Hope Farm

5

illgate Farm

Birch Grove

Birches Lane

Crow Brook

Hulme

Hangman's Lane

Hulse Lane

Hulse Farm

Portford Farm

6

Melvin Holme

Birches Hall

Birches Lane

Hulse House Farm

Common Lane

7

5082

PENNY'S LANE

Ashbrook Farm

PENNY'S LANE B5082

Crowder's Lane

Greenside Court

Lach Dennis

HOLMES CHAPEL ROAD

8

Crowder's Lane

Marsh Farm

M1
1 Hawthorn Rd

G H J 155 K L M

155

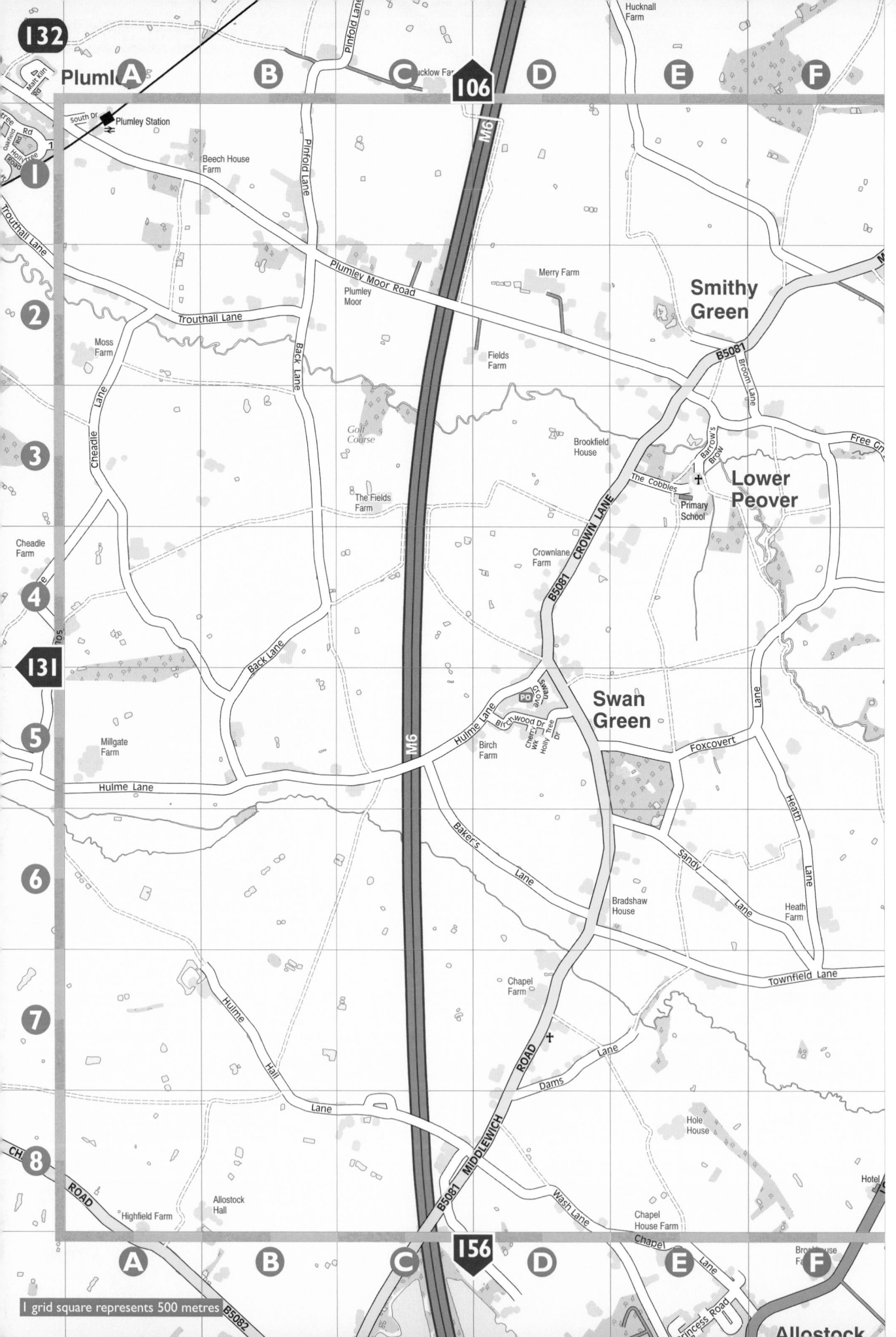

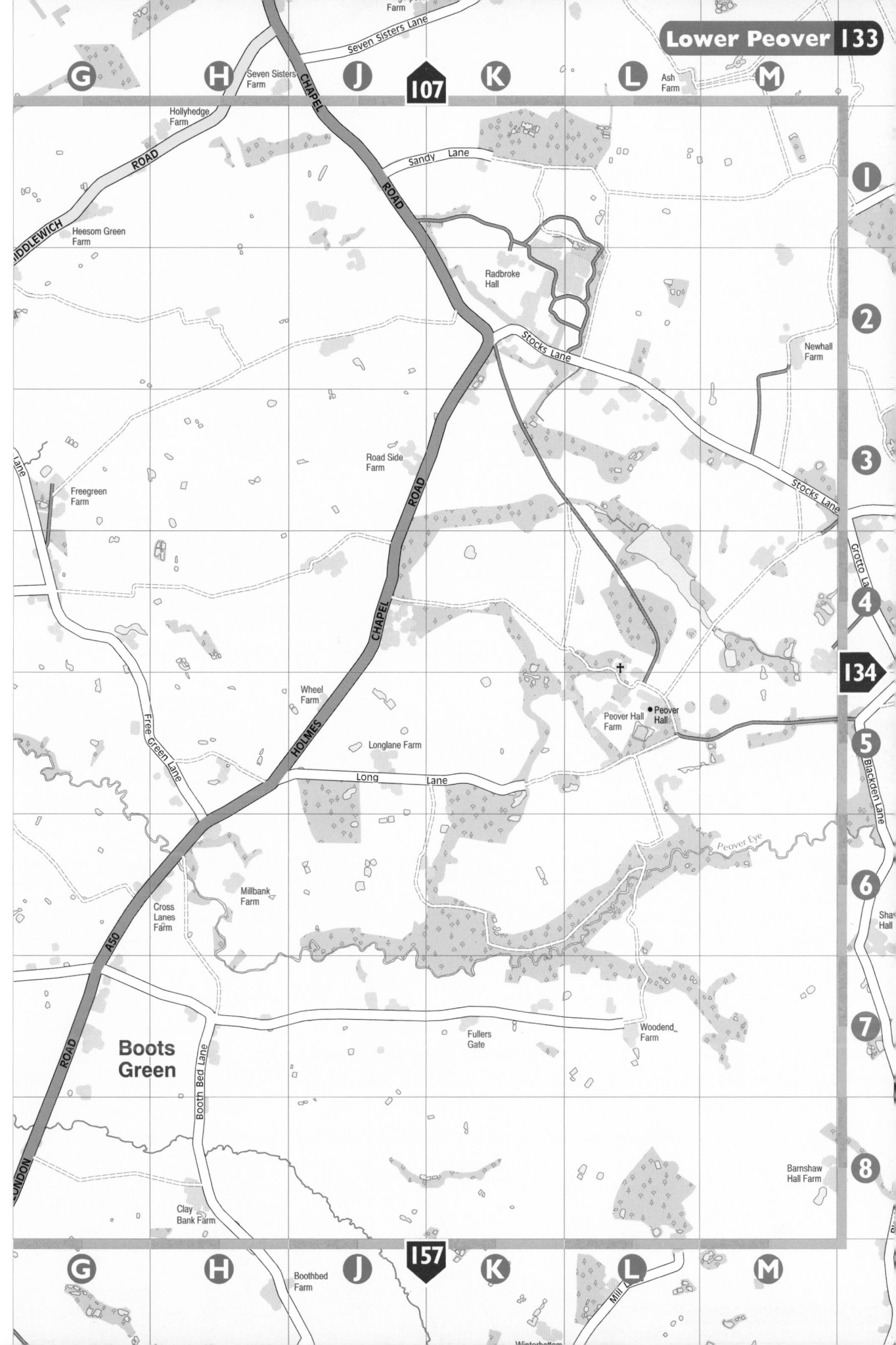

G   H   J   **107**   K   L   M

I

2

3

4

134

5

6

7

8

G   H   J   **157**   K   L   M

Seven Sisters Lane

Farm

Seven Sisters
Farm

CHAPEL

Hollyhedge
Farm

ROAD

MIDDLEWICH

Heesom Green
Farm

ROAD

Sandy   Lane

Radbroke
Hall

Stocks Lane

Ash
Farm

Newhall
Farm

Stocks Lane

Grotto La

Freegreen
Farm

Lane

Road Side
Farm

CHAPEL

ROAD

†

Blackden Lane

Wheel
Farm

HOLMES

Peover Hall
Farm

● Peover
Hall

Longlane Farm

Free Green Lane

Long   Lane

Peover Eye

Sha
Hall

Millbank
Farm

Cross
Lanes
Farm

A50

**Boots
Green**

Booth Bed Lane

ROAD

LONDON

Fullers
Gate

Woodend
Farm

7

Clay
Bank Farm

Boothbed
Farm

Barnshaw
Hall Farm

Mill

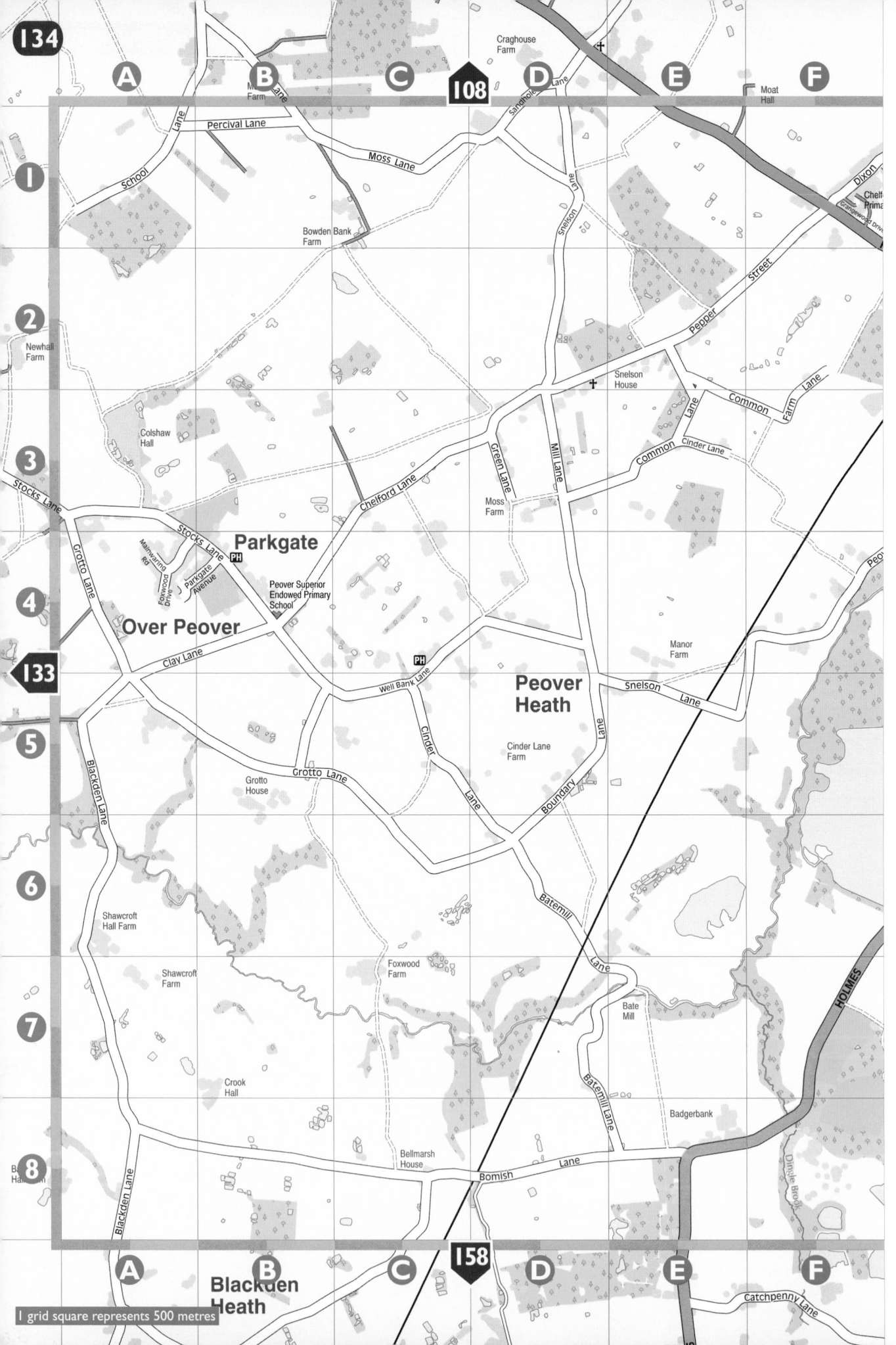

A B C 108 D E F

1

School Lane
Percival Lane
Moss Lane
Craghouse Farm
Sandhole Lane
Moat Hall
Dixon
Chelfo
Primar
Grangewood drive

Bowden Bank Farm

Snelson Lane

Pepper Street

2

Newhall Farm

Snelson House

Common Lane

Common Farm Lane
Cinder Lane

3

Stocks Lane
Colshaw Hall
Chelford Lane
Green Lane
Moss Farm
Mill Lane
Common

Stocks Lane
Parkgate
PH
Mainwaring Rd
Foxwood Drive
Parkgate Avenue
Peover Superior Endowed Primary School

4

Grotto Lane
Over Peover
Manor Farm

Clay Lane
PH
Well Bank Lane
Peover Heath
Snelson Lane
Peov

133

5

Blackden Lane
Grotto House
Grotto Lane
Cinder Lane
Cinder Lane Farm
Lane
Boundary

6

Shawcroft Hall Farm
Batemill Lane

Shawcroft Farm
Foxwood Farm

7

Bate Mill

Crook Hall
Batemill Lane
Badgerbank
HOLMES

8

B. Hall Farm
Bellmarsh House
Bomish Lane
Dimle Brook

A B C 158 D E F

Blackden Heath
Catchpenny Lane

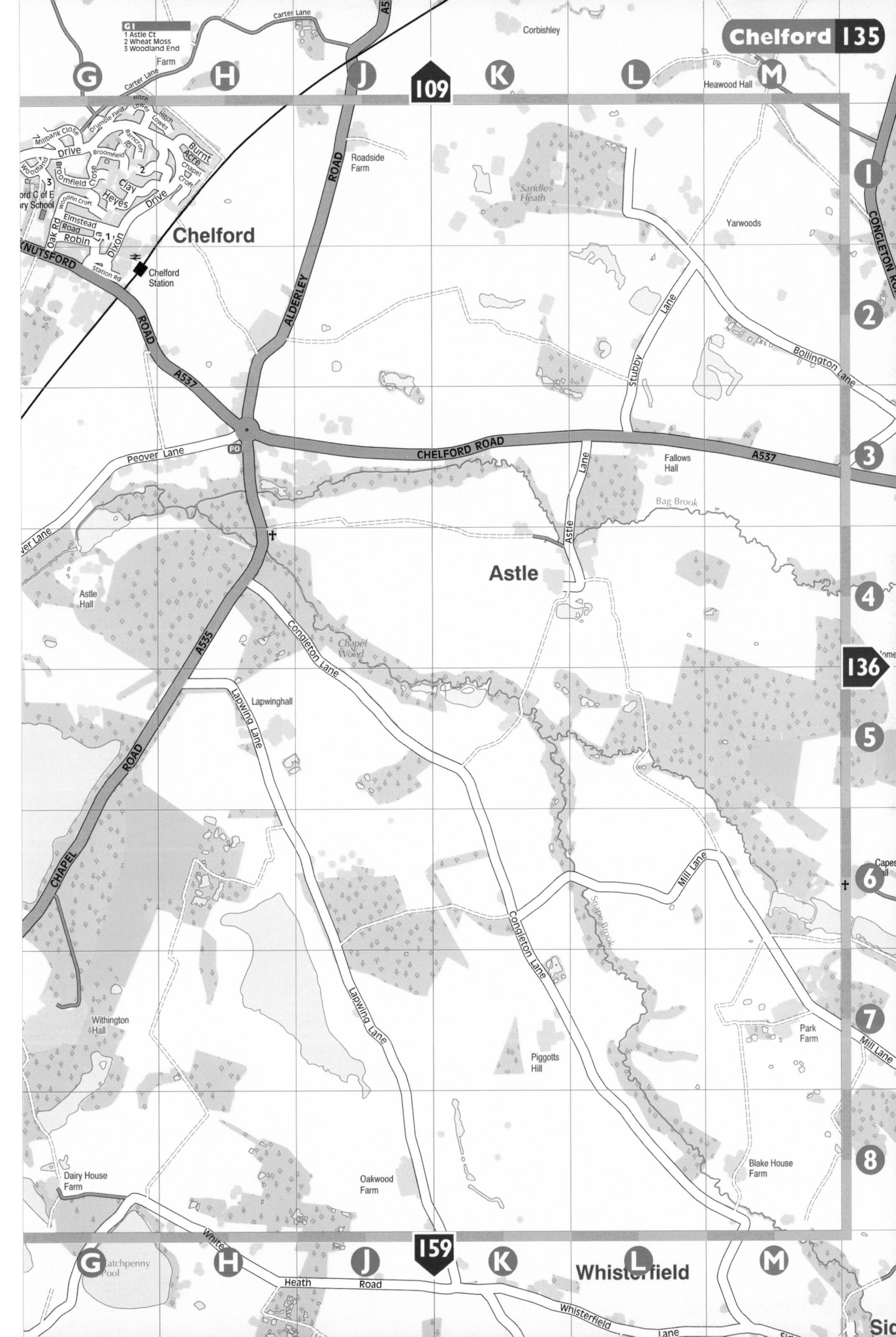

G1
1 Astle Ct
2 Wheat Moss
3 Woodland End

G **H** **J** ◆ **109** **K** **L** **M**

Corbishley

Heawood Hall

I

CONGLETON RD

Carter Lane

A5

Carter Lane

Sandle Heath

Yarwoods

Astle Ct Farm

Millbank Close

Drumble Field

Lowes

Hitch

Lowes

Woodland Drive

Broomfield

Barncroft

BURNT ACRE

Broomfield Close

CLAY HEYES

Chapel Croft

Chelford C of E Primary School

Coffin Croft

Elmstead Road

Oak Rd

Dixon Rd

Robin

Chelford

2

Stubby Lane

Bollington Lane

KNUTSFORD

Station Rd

Chelford Station

A537

ROAD

ALDERLEY ROAD

Roadside Farm

3

Peover Lane

PO

CHELFORD ROAD

Astle Lane

Fallows Hall

A537

Bag Brook

Peover Lane

†

Astle Hall

Astle

Astle Lane

4

A535

Congleton Lane

Chapel Wood

136

5

Womer...

Lapwinghall

Lapwing Lane

Mill Lane

Capes... ...all

†

6

CHAPEL ROAD

Congleton Lane

Snape Brook

Withington Hall

Park Farm

7

Mill Lane

Lapwing Lane

Piggotts Hill

Dairy House Farm

Oakwood Farm

Blake House Farm

8

Catchpenny Pool

White...

Heath Road

Whisterfield

Whisterfield Lane

Si...

G **H** **J** ◆ **159** **K** **L** **M**

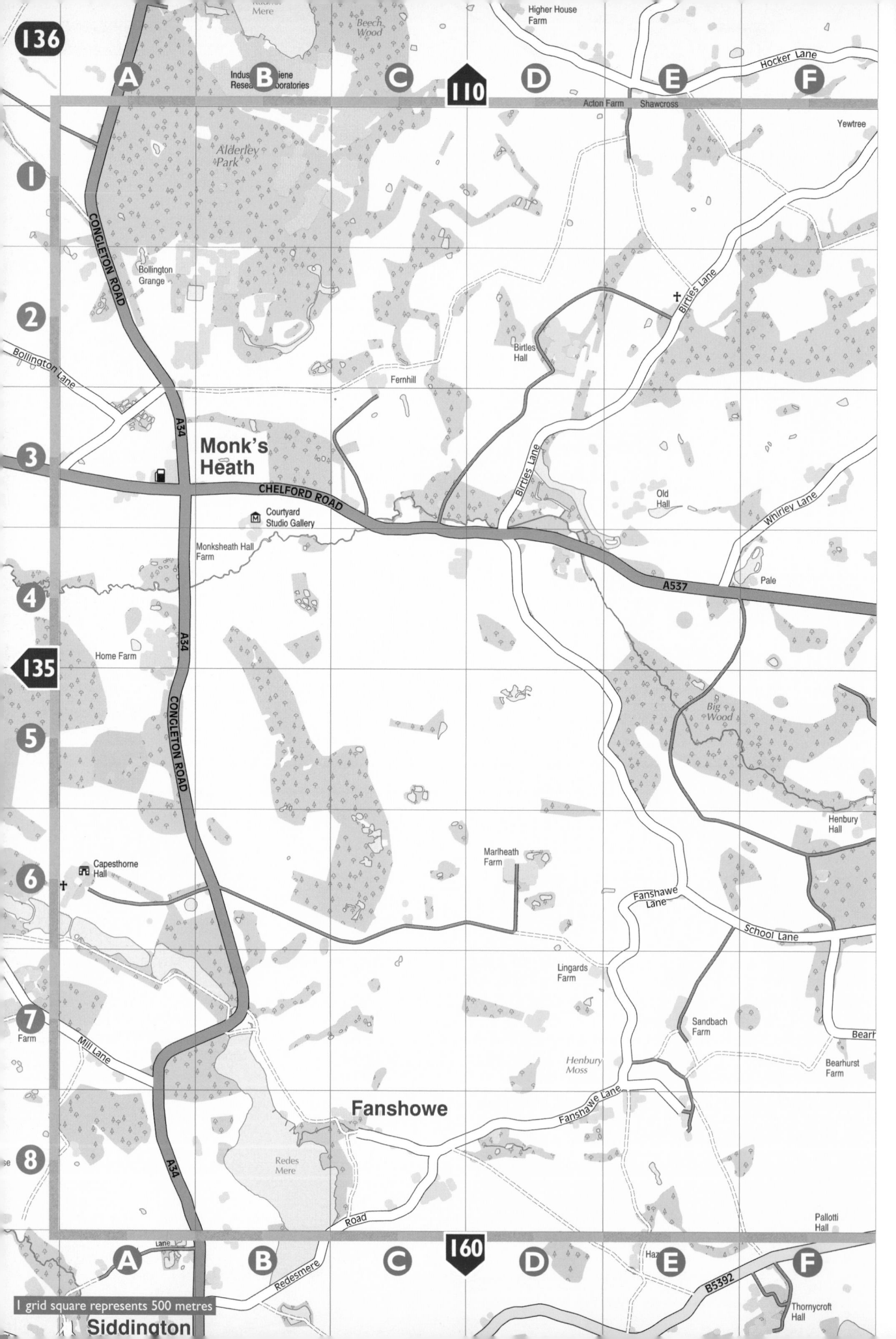

A   B   C   110   D   E   F

Higher House Farm

Hocker Lane

Yewtree

Acton Farm   Shawcross

1

Alderley Park

Beech Wood

Bollington Grange

Birtles Lane

Birtles Hall

2

Bollington Lane

Fernhill

Birtles Lane

3

Monk's Heath

CHELFORD ROAD

Courtyard Studio Gallery

Old Hall

Whirley Lane

A537

Pale

Monksheath Hall Farm

4

135

Home Farm

A34

Big Wood

5

CONGLETON ROAD

6

Capesthorne Hall

Marlheath Farm

Fanshawe Lane

School Lane

Henbury Hall

Lingards Farm

Sandbach Farm

Bearh

7

Farm

Mill Lane

Henbury Moss

Fanshawe Lane

Bearhurst Farm

Fanshowe

8

Redes Mere

A34

Road

Pallotti Hall

A   B   160   C   D   E   F

Redesmere   Lane

B5392

Haz

Thornycroft Hall

I grid square represents 500 metres

Siddington

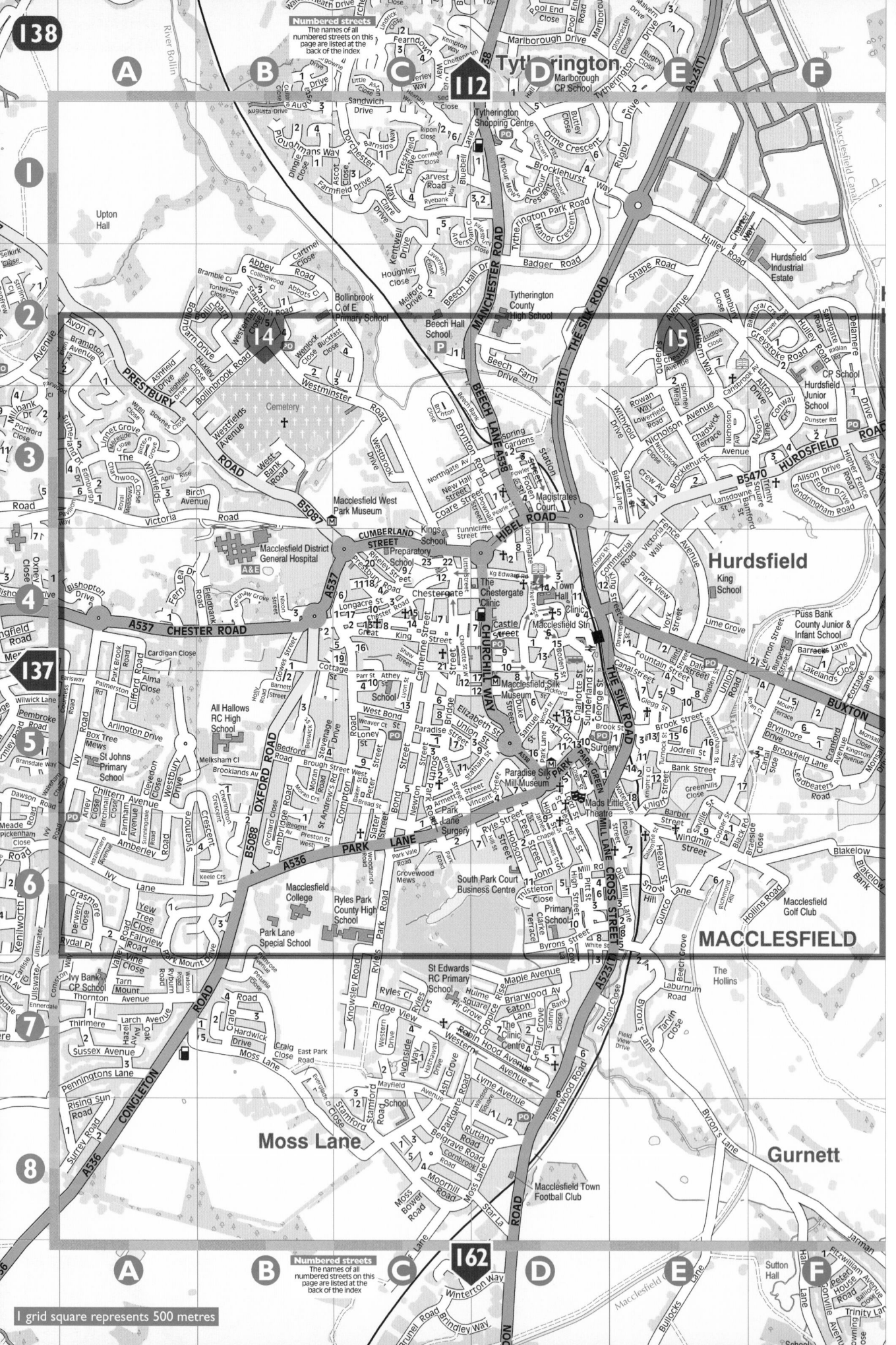

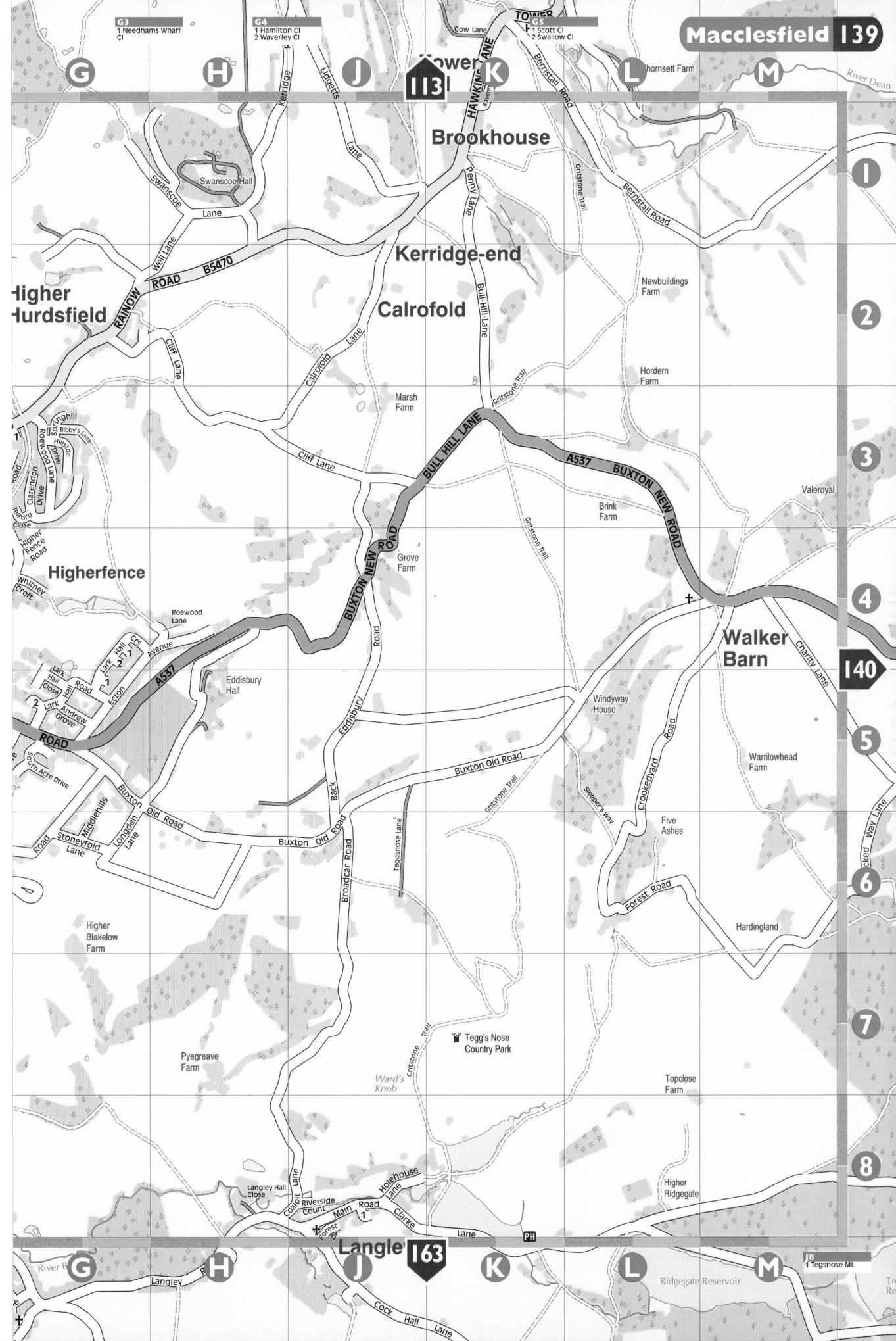

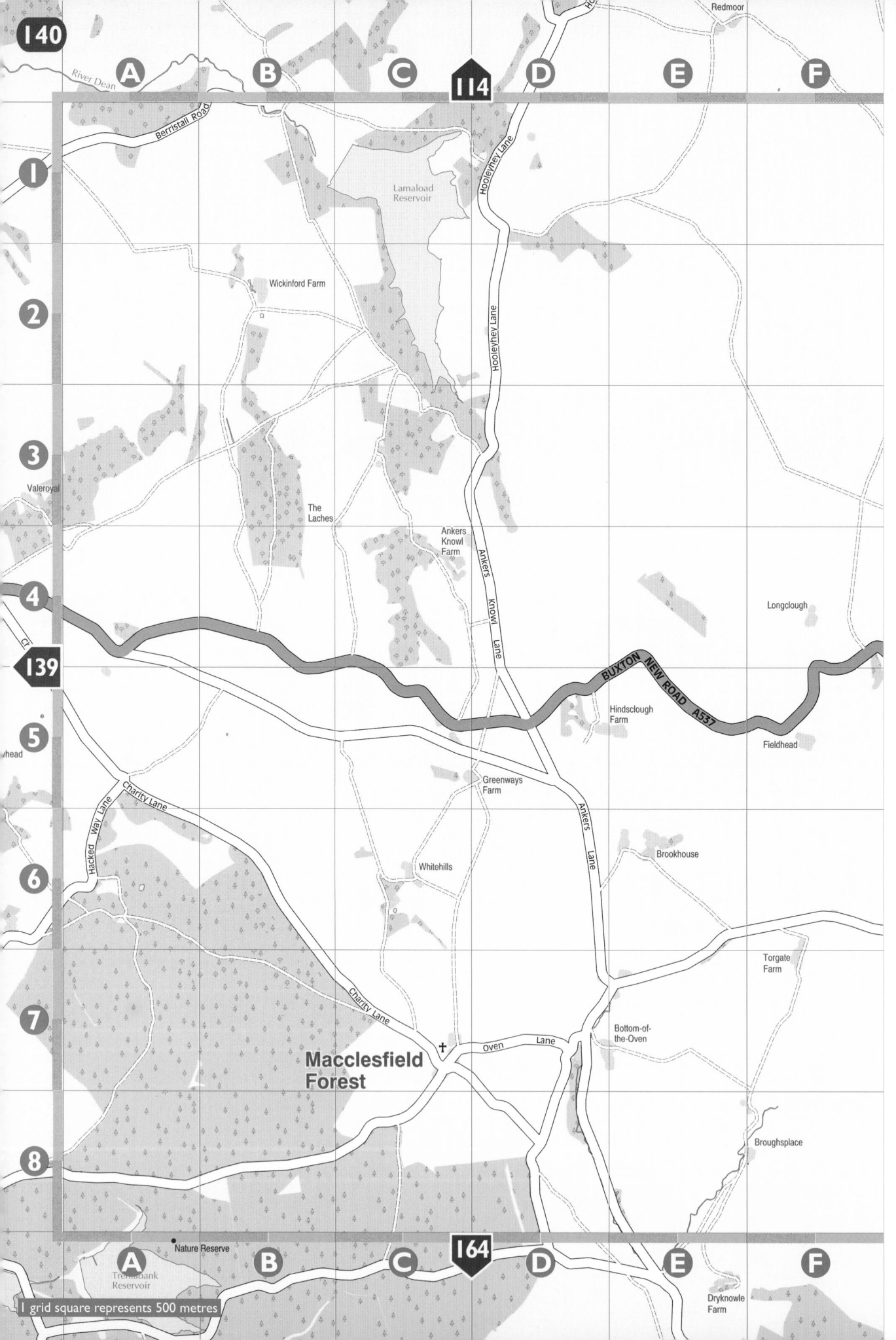

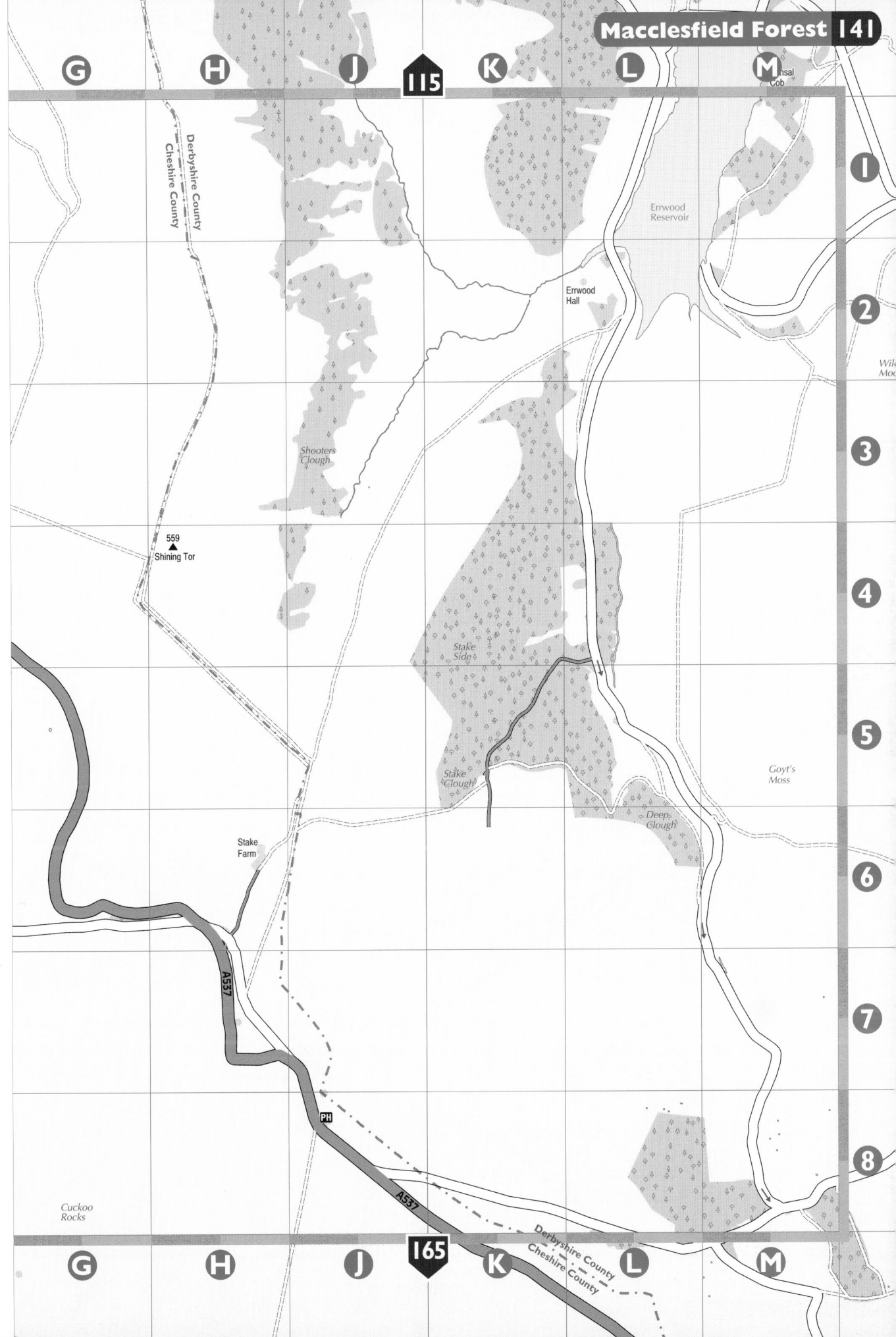

G H J **115** K L M

I

2

3

4

5

6

7

8

G H J **165** K L M

Errwood
Reservoir

Errwood
Hall

Derbyshire County
Cheshire County

Shooters
Clough

559
▲
Shining Tor

Stake
Side

Goyt's
Moss

Stake
Clough

Deep
Clough

Stake
Farm

A537

PH

A537

Cuckoo
Rocks

Derbyshire County
Cheshire County

Wil
Moo

nsal
Cob

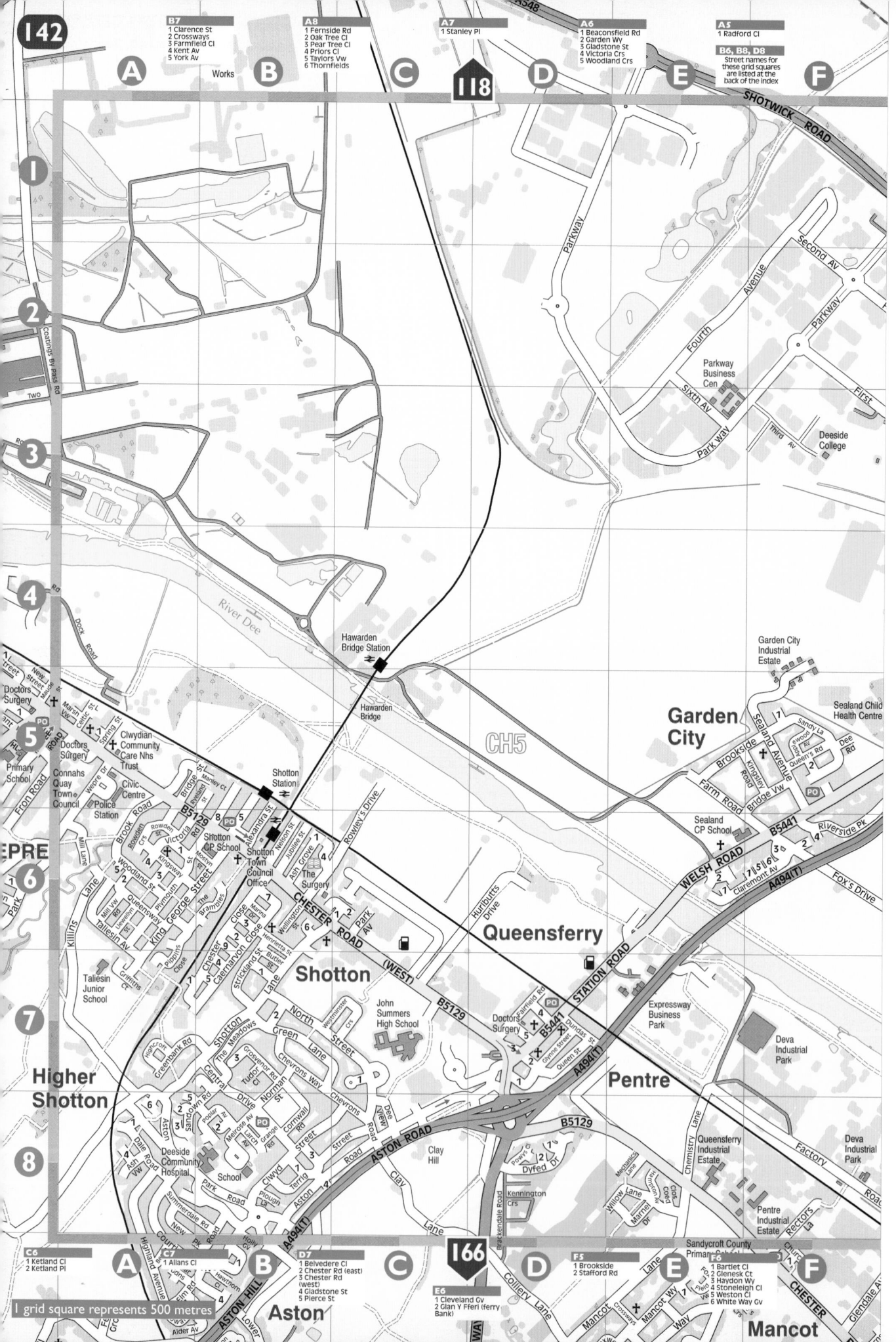

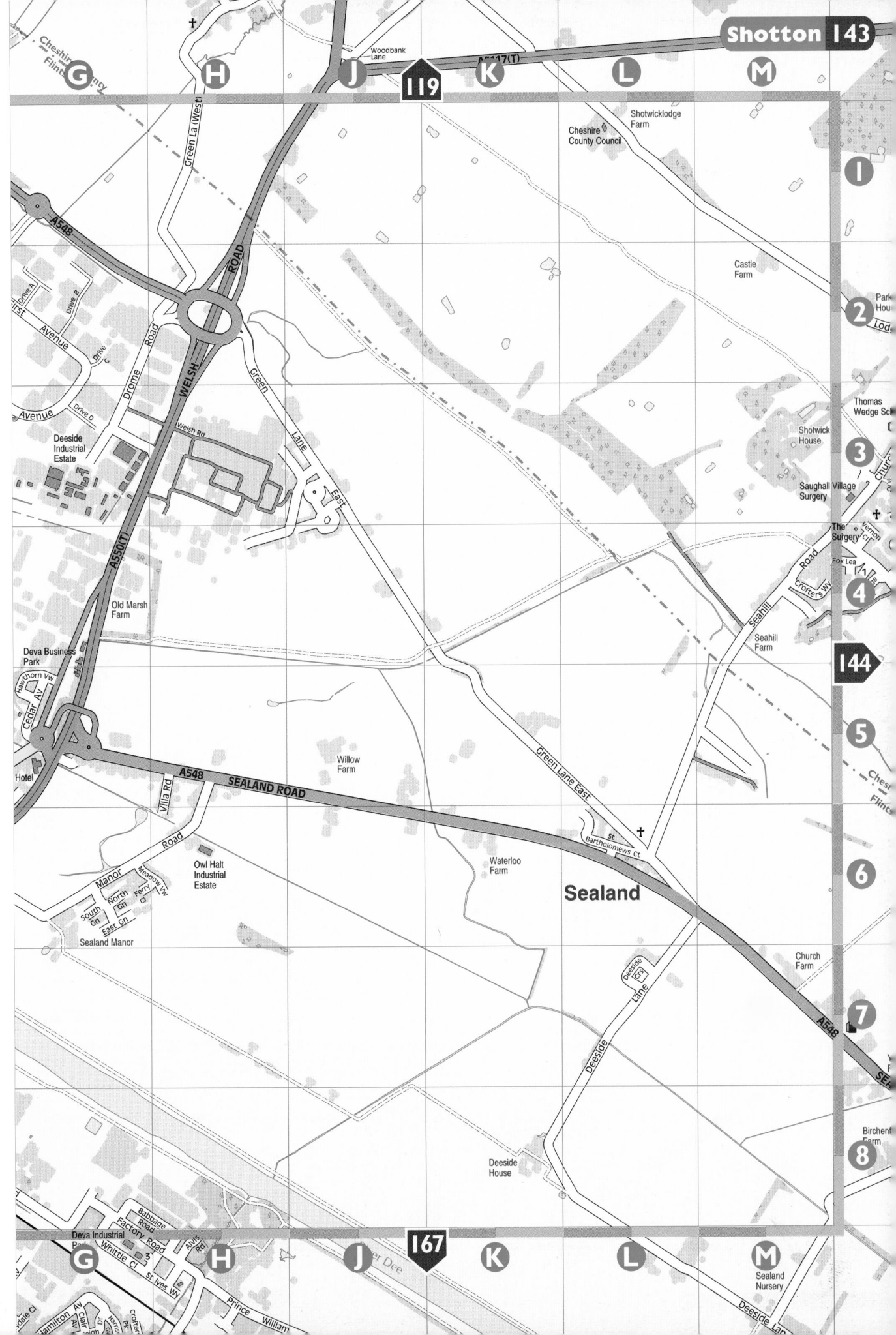

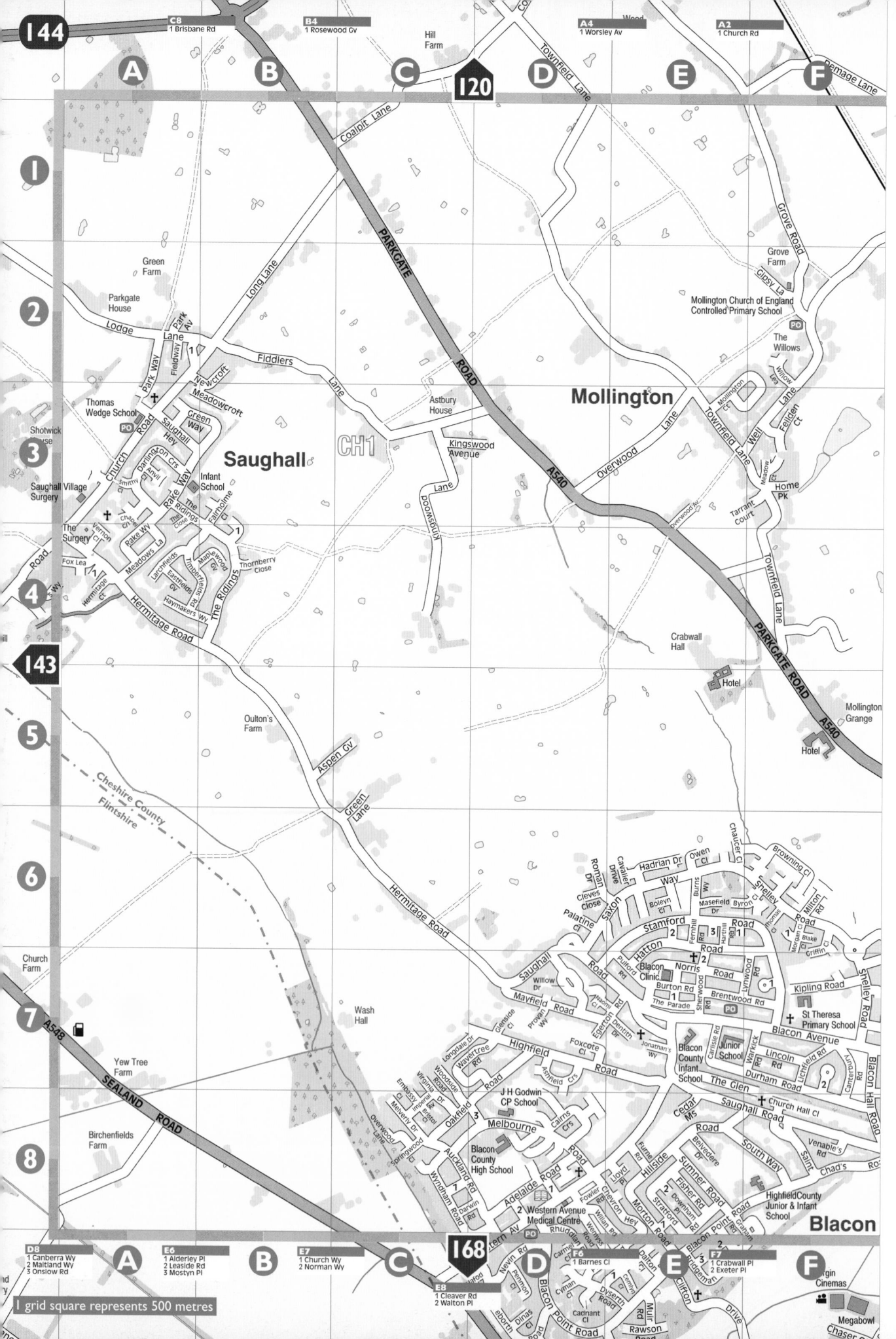

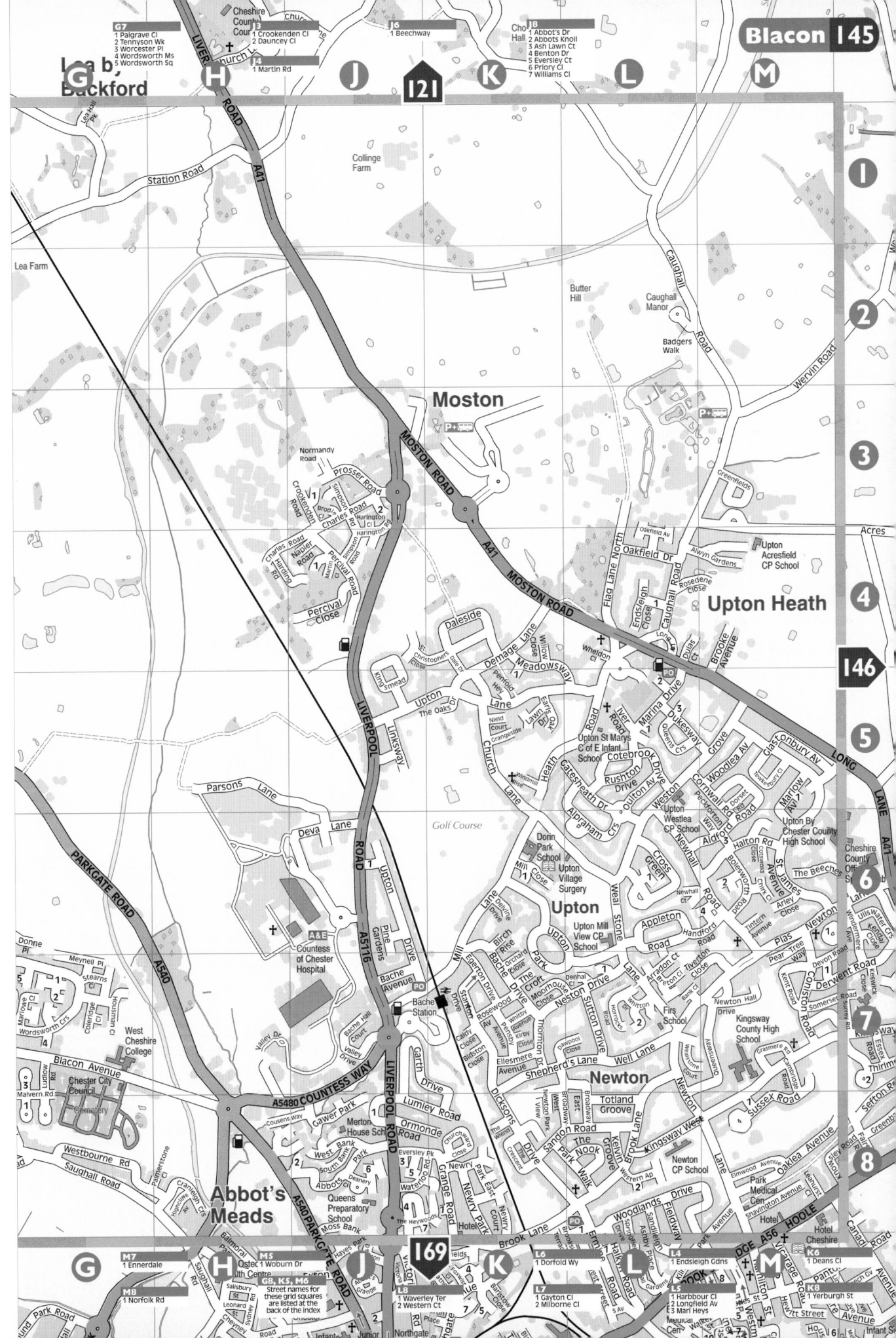

Lea b, Backford

G7
1 Palgrave Cl
2 Tennyson Wk
3 Worcester Pl
4 Wordsworth Ms
5 Wordsworth Sq

H4
1 Martin Rd

J3
1 Crookenden Cl
2 Dauncey Cl

J6
1 Beechway

K8
1 Abbot's Dr
2 Abbots Knoll
3 Ash Lawn Ct
4 Benton Dr
5 Eversley Ct
6 Priory Cl
7 Williams Cl

121

146

169

Moston

Collinge Farm

Normandy Road

Butter Hill

Caughall Manor

Badgers Walk

Greenfields

Upton Heath

Upton

Golf Course

Countess of Chester Hospital

West Cheshire College

Chester City Council Cemetery

Abbot's Meads

Newton

Queens Preparatory School

G
1 Ostec
1 Woburn Dr
Health Centre

M7
1 Ennerdale

M8
1 Norfolk Rd

H
J5, K5, M6
Street names for these grid squares are listed at the back of the index

J
L8
1 Waverley Ter
2 Western Ct

K
L5
1 Dorfold Wy
L6
1 Endsleigh Gdns
L7
1 Gayton Cl
2 Milborne Cl

L
1 Harbbour Cl
2 Longfield Av
3 Marl Heys

K6
1 Deans Cl

K8
1 Yerburgh St

M

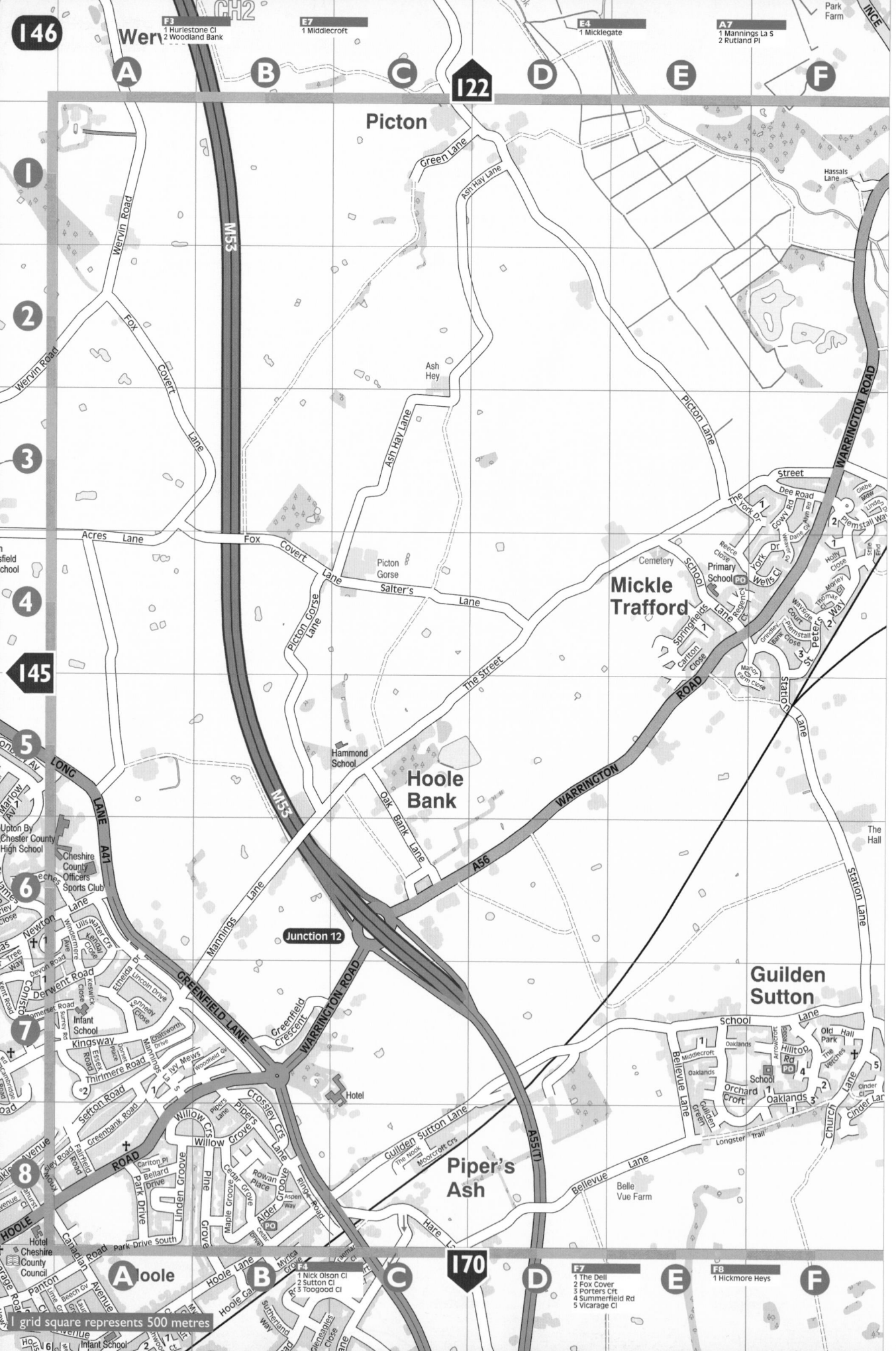

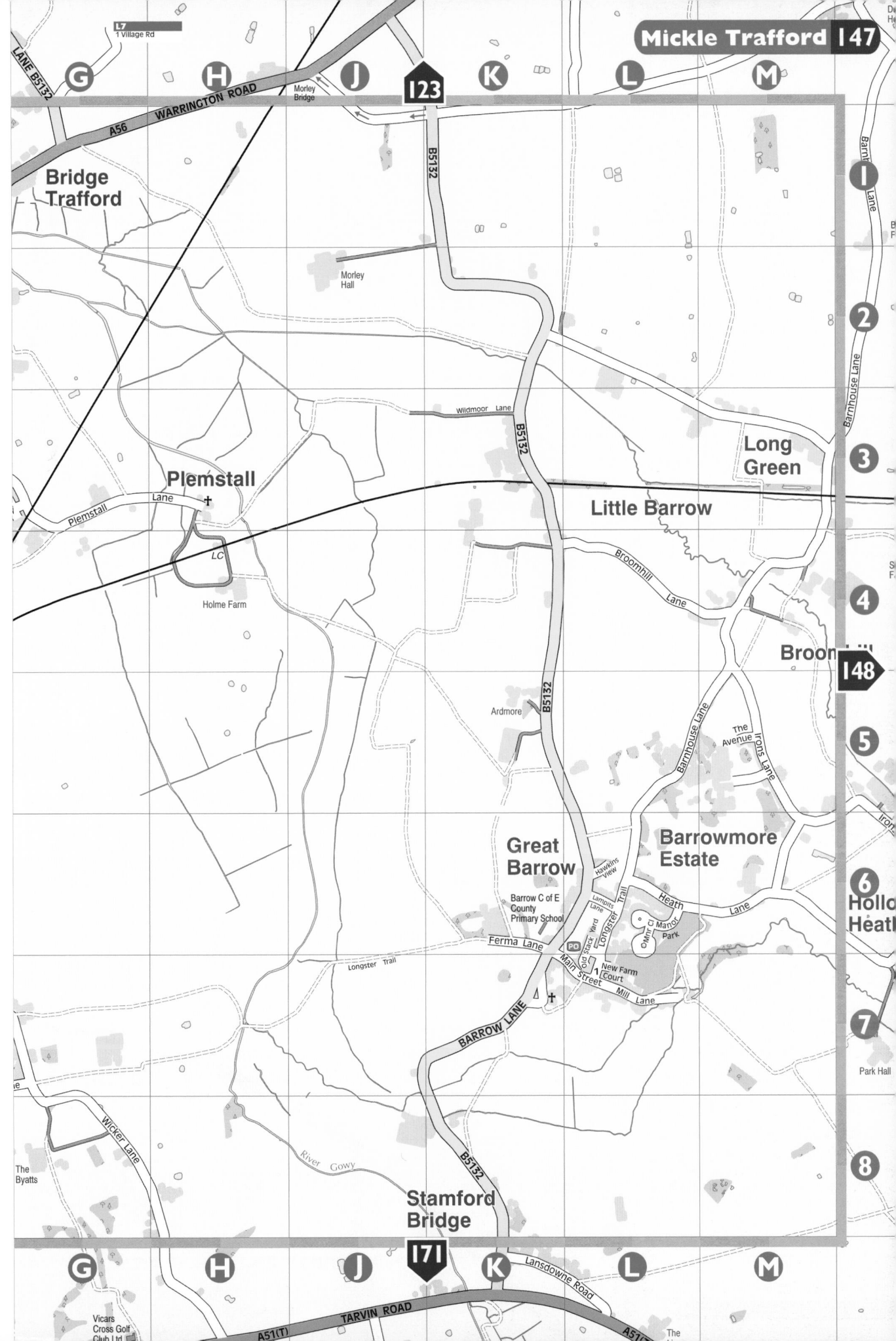

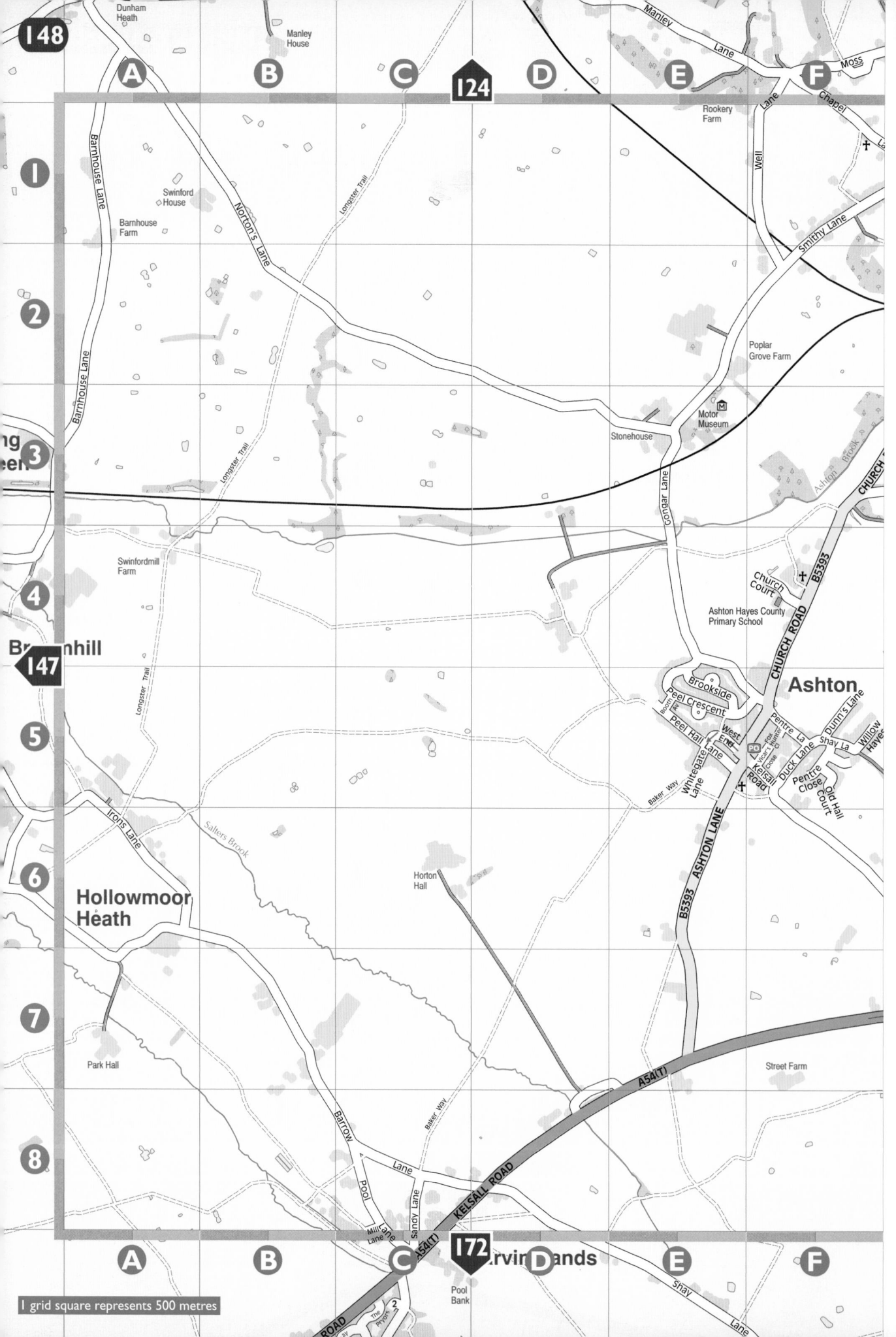

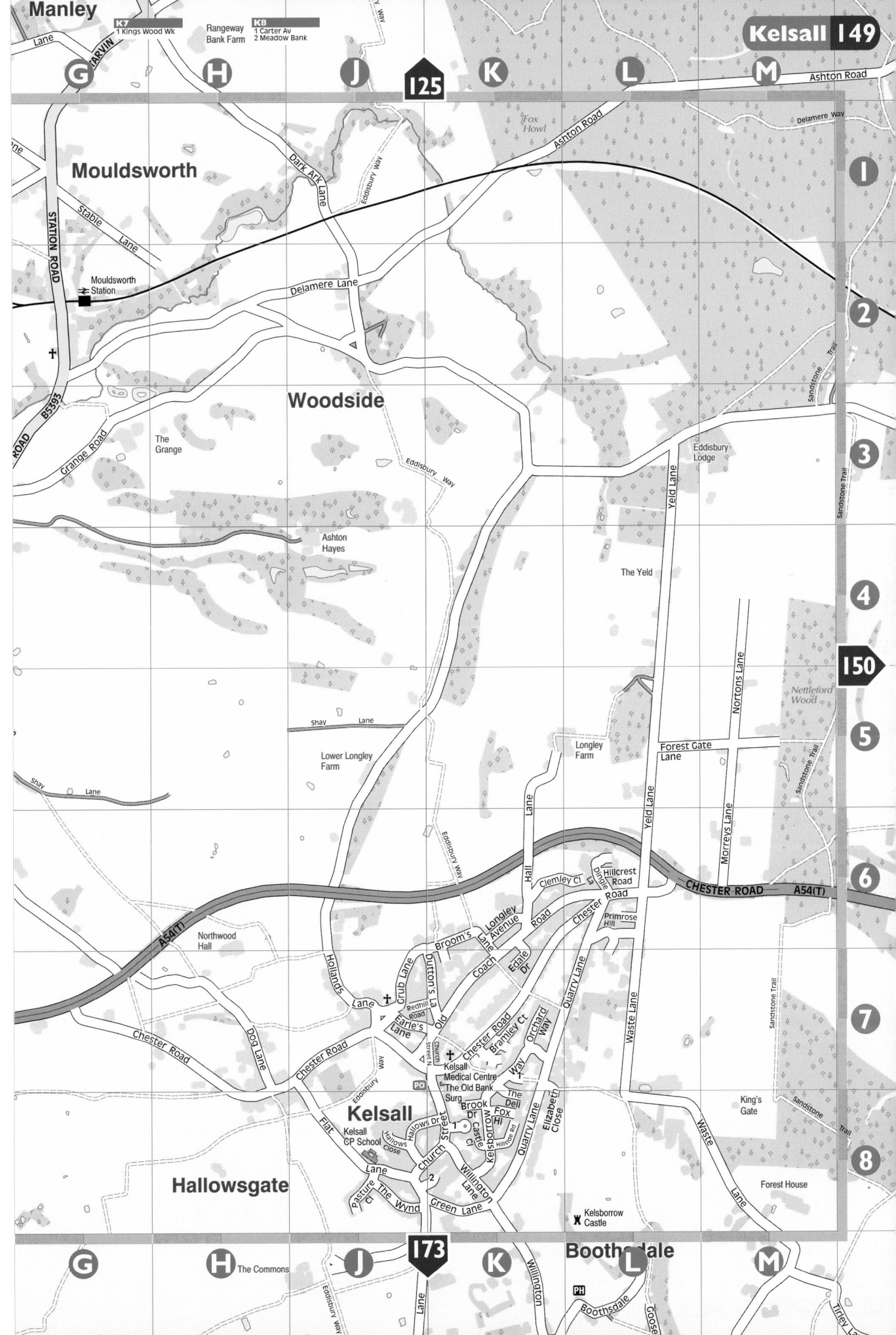

Manley

K7 1 Kings Wood Wk

Rangeway Bank Farm

K8 1 Carter Av
2 Meadow Bank

G   H   J   125   K   L   M   Ashton Road

Mouldsworth

Delamere Way

Fox Howl

Ashton Road

I

Garvin Lane

Stable Lane

STATION ROAD

Dark Ark Lane

Eddisbury Way

Mouldsworth Station

Delamere Lane

2

Sandstone Trail

B5393

Woodside

Grange Road

The Grange

Eddisbury Way

Eddisbury Lodge

3

Sandstone Trail

Yeld Lane

Ashton Hayes

The Yeld

4

Nortons Lane

150

Nettleford Wood

shay   Lane

Lower Longley Farm

Longley Farm

Forest Gate Lane

5

shay   Lane

Eddisbury Way

Longley Farm

Morreys Lane

Sandstone Trail

CHESTER ROAD   A54(T)

6

A54(T)

Northwood Hall

Hollands Lane

Broom's Lane

Hall Lane

Clemley Ct

Hillcrest Road

Dingle

Chester Road

Yeld Lane

Primrose Hill

Grub Lane

Dutton's La

Coach Lane

Longley Avenue

Edale Dr

Chester Road

Sandstone Trail

7

Chester Road

Dog Lane

Rednill Road

Earle's Lane

Old Street N

Chester Road

Bramley Ct

Orchard Way

Quarry Lane

Waste Lane

King's Gate

Sandstone Trail

Eddisbury Way

PO

Kelsall Medical Centre

The Old Bank

Surg

Brook Dr

The Deli

Fox

Way

Elizabeth Close

Quarry Lane

Kelsall

Flat Lane

Kelsall CP School

Hallows Close

Hallows Dr

Church Street

Castle Ct

Kelsborrow

Hillside Rd

Waste Lane

Forest House

8

Hallowsgate

Pasture Cl

The Wynd

Church Street

Willington Lane

Green Lane

Kelsborrow Castle

G   H   The Commons   J   173   K   L   M   Boothsdale

Eddisbury Way

Lane

Willington

PH

Boothsdale

Tirley Lane

Gooseberry

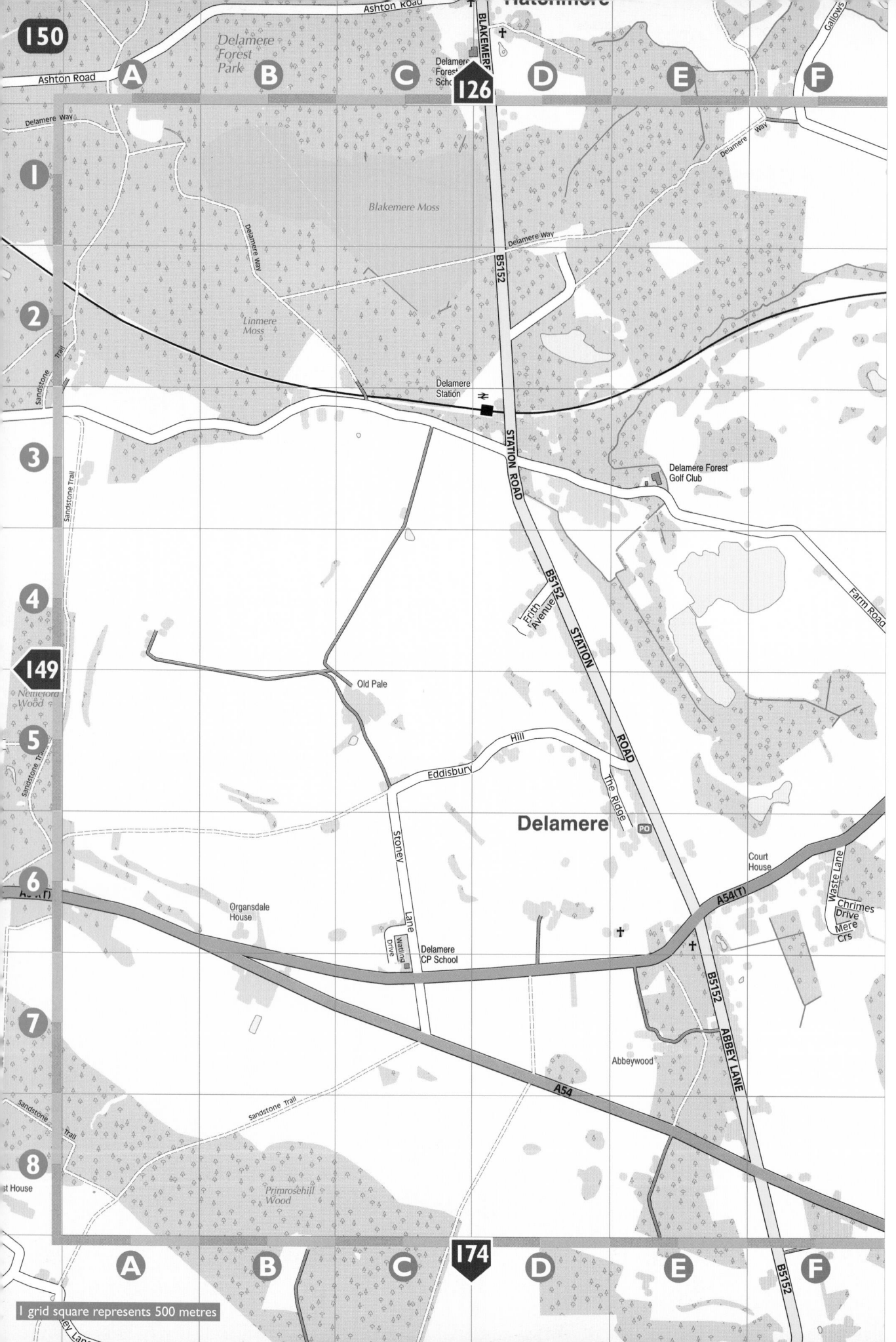

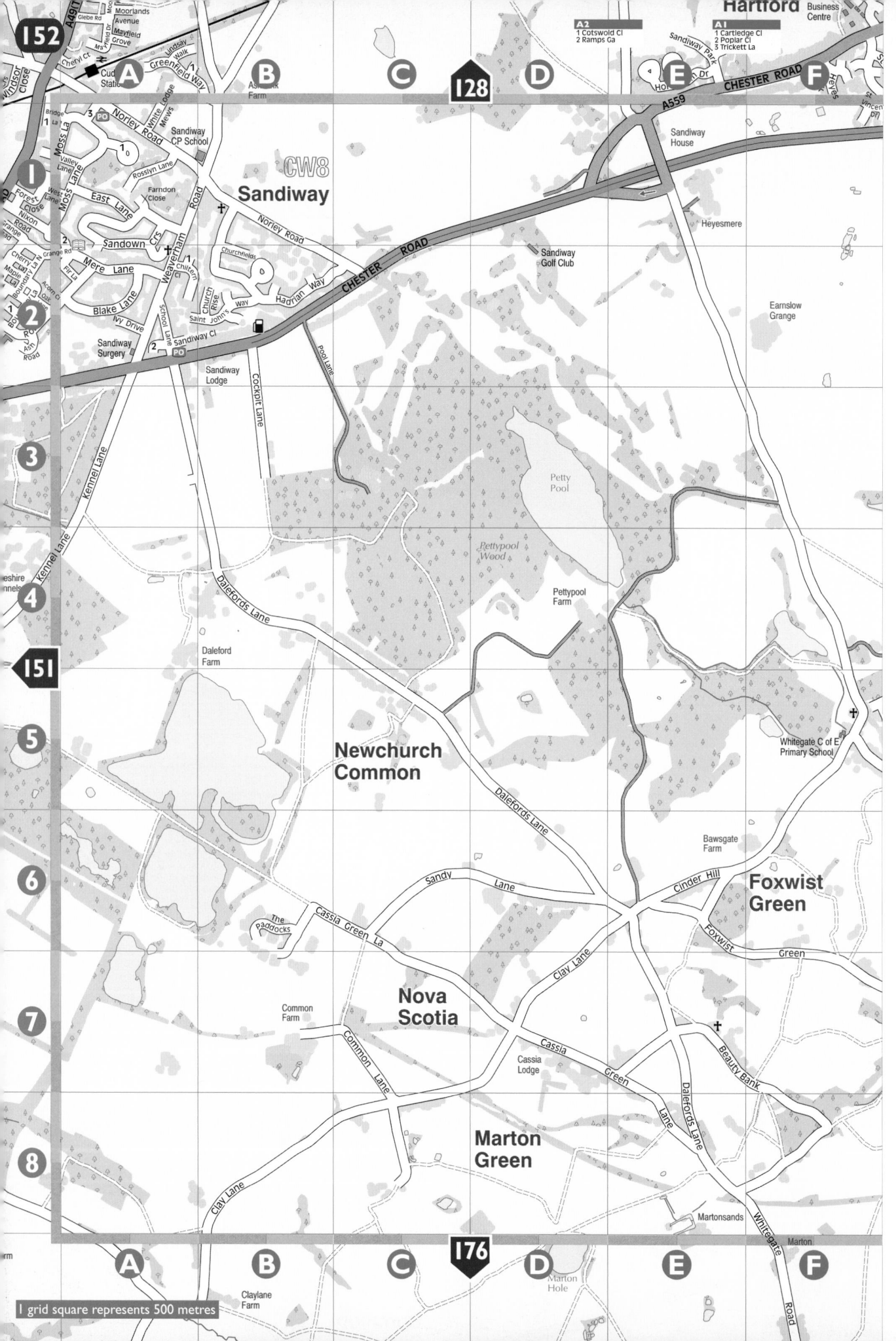

G H J K L M

L1
1 Ashley Gra
2 Harrow Wy
3 Kelsborrow Cl
4 Knightsbridge Av
5 Moreville Cl

L2
1 The Pavilions

L4
1 The Hollies
2 Lawrence Av

Hartford Station
Catherine Dr
Mornant Avenue
Hartford CP School
Berrystead
Eaglesfield
The Paddock
Landswood Park
Hotel
Vale Rd

129

A556(T)

Hartford Bridge

Earls Way

KINGSME

Green Avenue
London Rd
Church Street

PO

I

Dav

Hartford Road
Prospect Drive
Eaton Lane
Pritchard Drive
Eaton Crescent
Firth Fields Close
Firth Fields
Charles Av
Allen Drive
Grovemount
Davenham C of E Aided Primary School
Davenham Cricket Club
Mount Pleasant Rd
Fountain Lane
Whittington Gdns

2

Eaton House

Eaton Hall Farm

3

Mere Heath

Rookery Pool

Vale Royal Abbey Golf Club
St Marys Drive
Vale Royal Dr
Monk's Well

Eaton Vw
Weaver Grange
Chapel St
Orchard Rd
Chapel La
School La
Moulton CP School
Barnside Wy
Harness Ct
Summerfield Dr
Jack Lane
Rayleigh

4

St Marys drive
Vale Royal Drive
Sutton Fld
Abbey Cl

Whitegate

Main Road
Beechfield
Willow Lane
Regent St
Meadow La
Poplar
Park La
Beehive

154

Moult

5

Grange Lane
Mill Lane
Bark House
Bradford Mill
Bradford Road
Smokehall Lane

Wilson Drive
Wilson Road
Barlow Rd
Niddries Lane
Niddries Court
Hillside Farm

Valeroyal Cut

6

Bradford Wood Farm

Weaver Navigation

7

Brook House

Meadow Cv
PO
School Road

Meadowbank

Deakin's Rd
Collingtree
Upton Cl
Alderton

8

Bradford Wood House
Catsclough
Shaws Lane
Valley Road
A5018

M3
1 Lodge Dr
2 Verdin Cl

M4
1 Church St

M5
1 Hillside La

M1
1 Claremont Cl

Retail

177

G H J K L ha M n

Saltenborough
Marlborough
Wades Lane
Willow Close
Wharton
Sterling
Lyndale

Salterswall

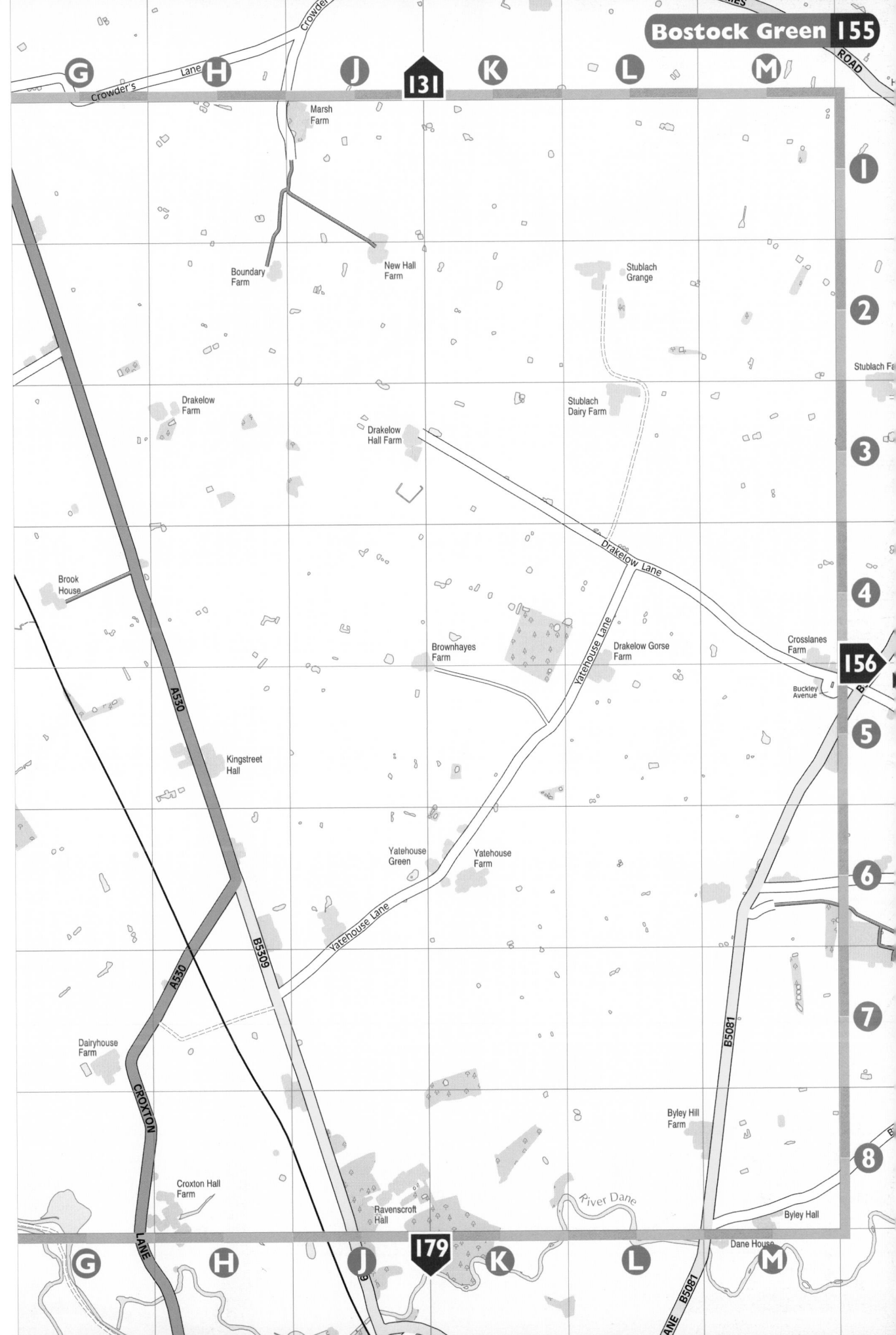

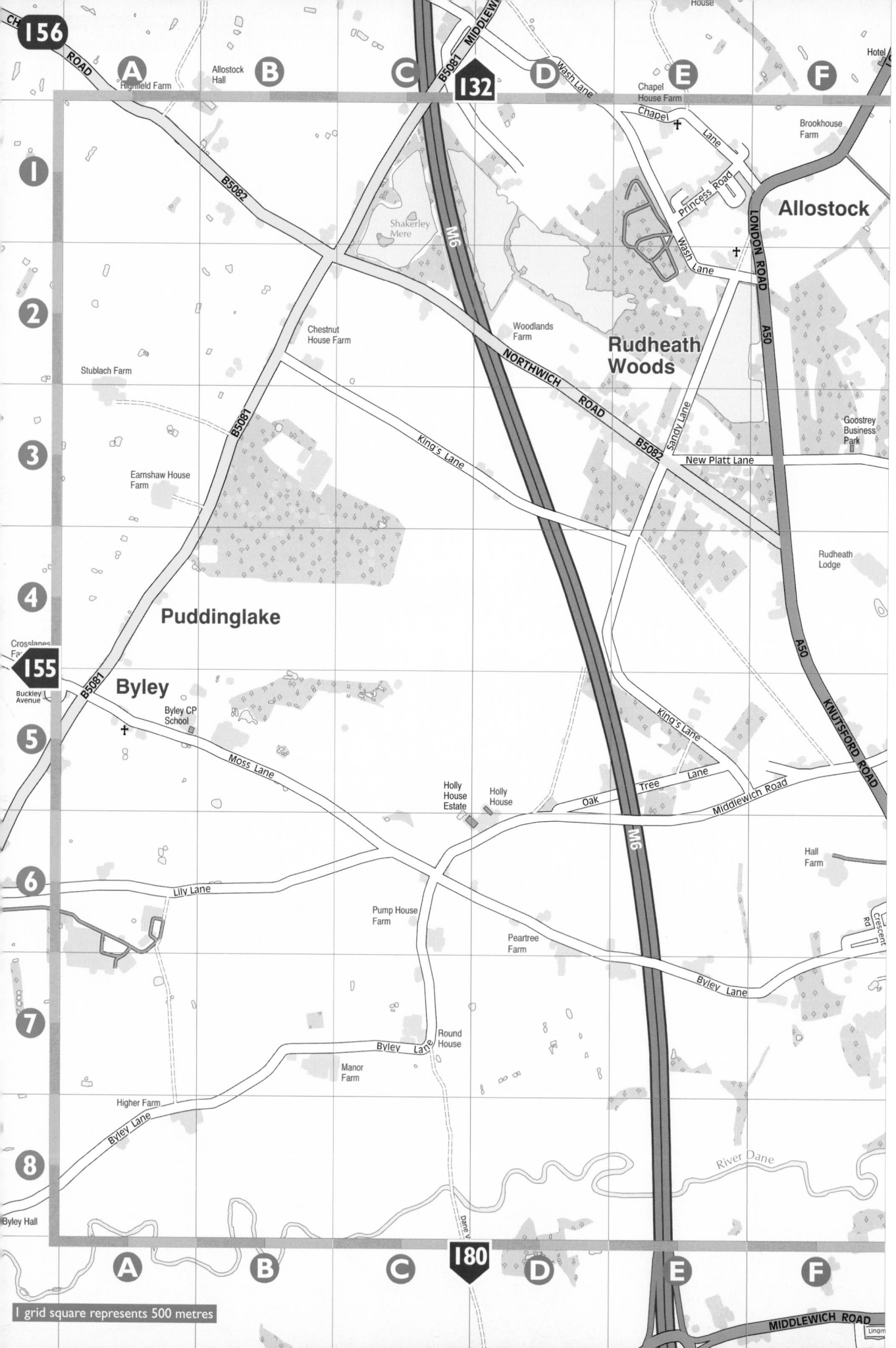

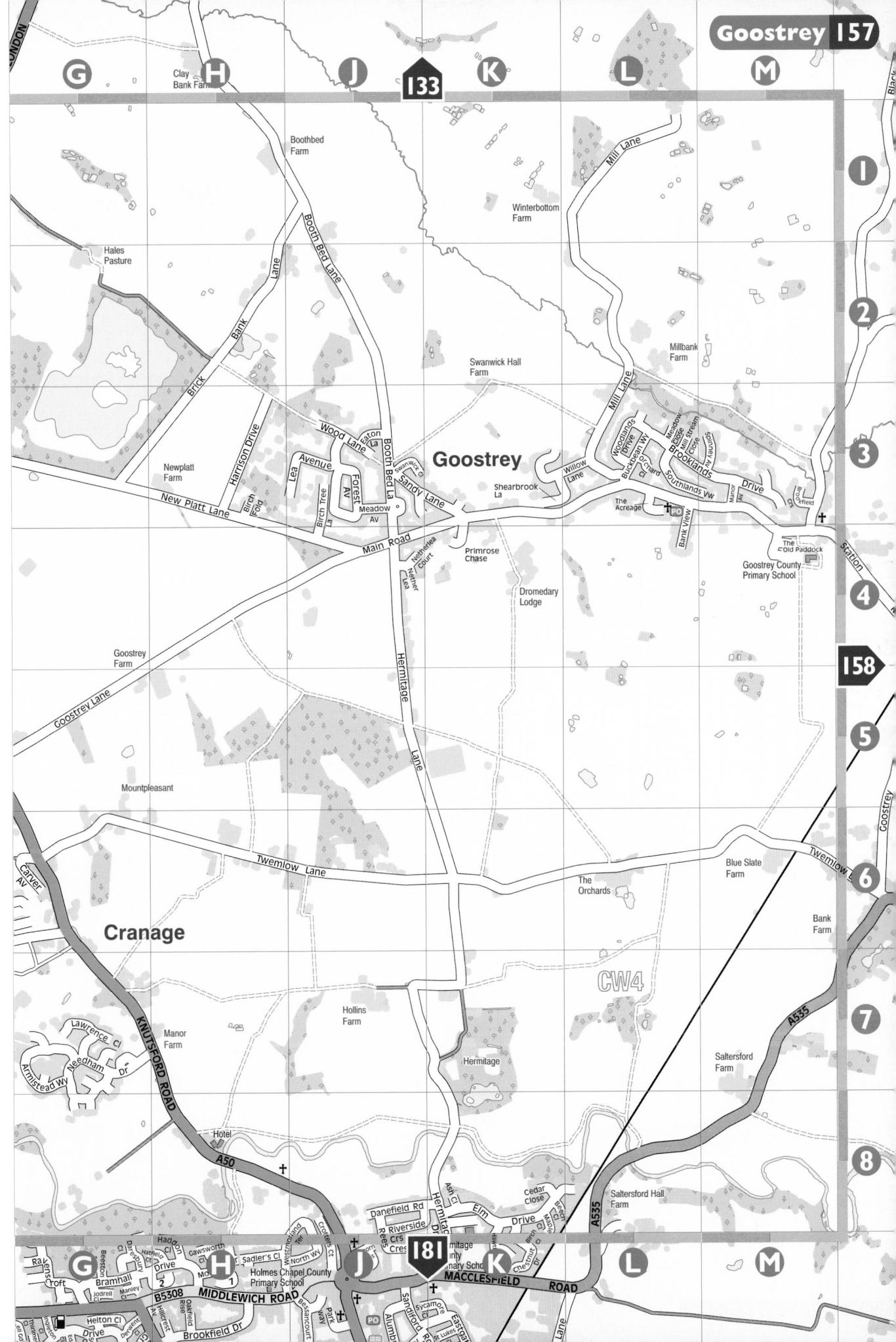

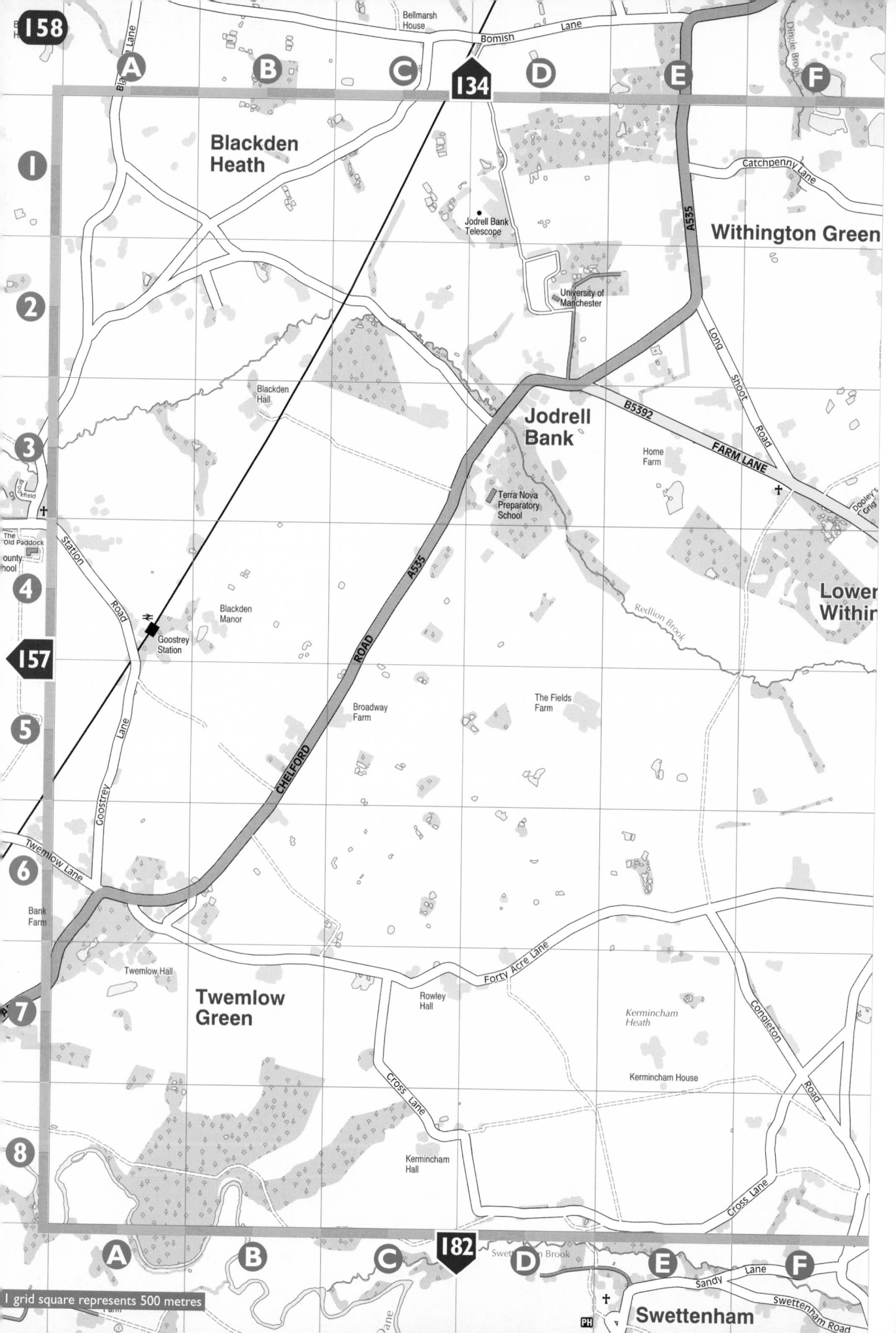

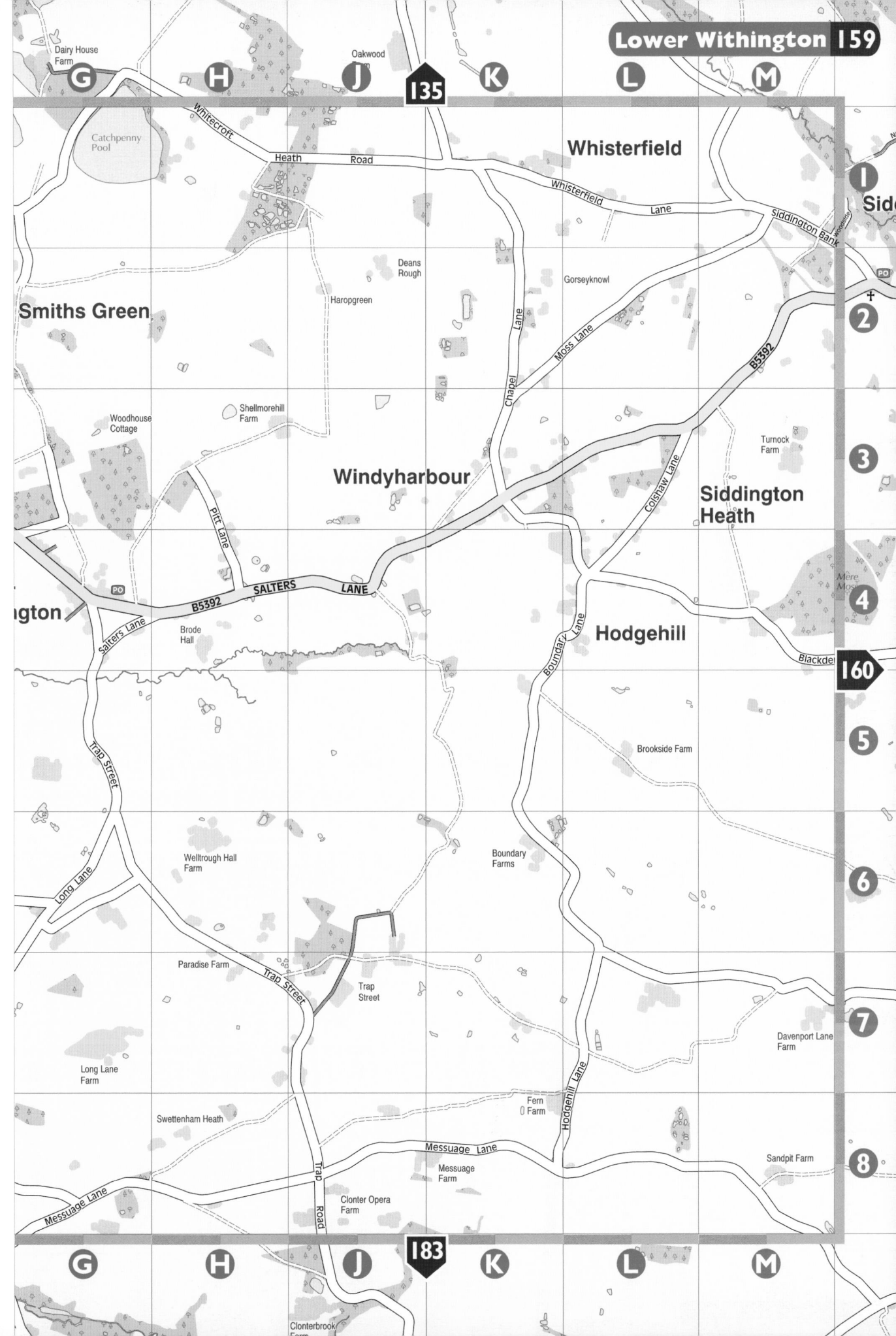

135

G H J K L M

Whitecroft

Catchpenny
Pool

Heath Road

Whisterfield

Whisterfield Lane

Siddington Bank

Oakwood

I

Sid

PO

†

2

Smiths Green

Deans
Rough

Haropgreen

Gorseyknowl

B5392

Chapel Lane

Moss Lane

Woodhouse
Cottage

Shellmorehill
Farm

Windyharbour

Turnock
Farm

3

Colshaw Lane

Siddington
Heath

Mere
Moss

4

Pitt Lane

PO

B5392 SALTERS LANE

Salters Lane

Brode
Hall

Boundary Lane

Hodgehill

Blackden

160

5

Trap Street

Brookside Farm

Long Lane

Welltrough Hall
Farm

Boundary
Farms

6

Paradise Farm

Trap Street

Trap
Street

7

Davenport Lane
Farm

Long Lane
Farm

Hodgehill Lane

Swettenham Heath

Fern
Farm

Sandpit Farm

8

Messuage Lane

Messuage
Farm

Messuage Lane

Trap Road

Clonter Opera
Farm

G H J K L M

183

Clonterbrook
Farm

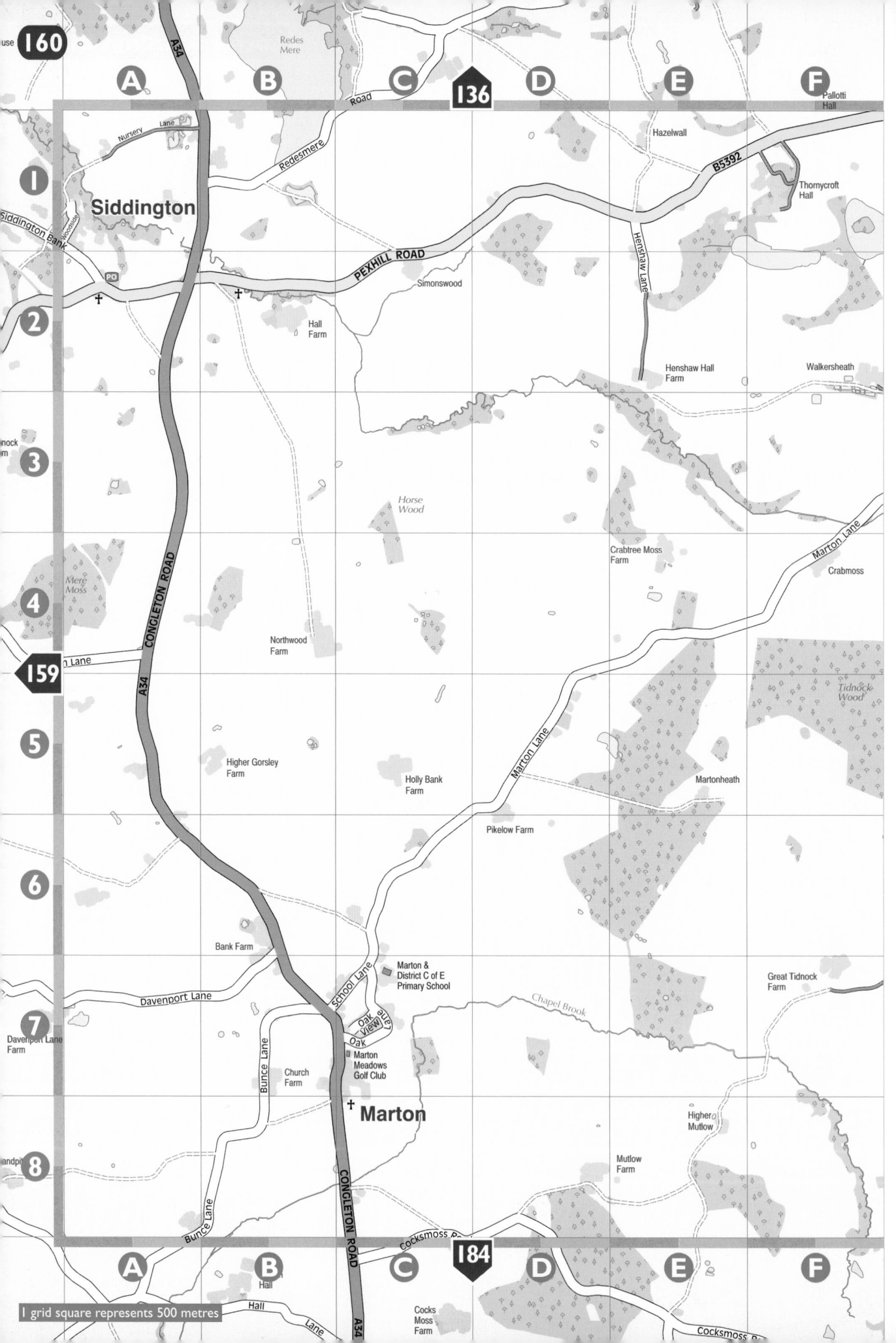

A   B   C   136   D   E   F

1

Siddington

2   PEXHILL ROAD

3

4   159

5

6

7   Marton

8

A   B   C   184   D   E   F

Redes Mere

Road

Nursery Lane

Siddington Bank

PO

Redesmere

Hall Farm

Simonswood

Hazelwall

B5392

Thornycroft Hall

Henshaw Hall Farm

Walkersheath

Horse Wood

Crabtree Moss Farm

Crabmoss

Marton Lane

Henshaw Lane

CONGLETON ROAD

A34

Mere Moss

Northwood Farm

Tidnock Wood

Higher Gorsley Farm

Holly Bank Farm

Marton Lane

Martonheath

Pikelow Farm

Davenport Lane

Bank Farm

School Lane

Marton & District C of E Primary School

Chapel Brook

Great Tidnock Farm

Davenport Lane Farm

Bunce Lane

Oak View Lane

Oak

Marton Meadows Golf Club

Church Farm

Higher Mutlow

Mutlow Farm

CONGLETON ROAD

Bunce Lane

Hall

Cocksmoss

A34

Cocks Moss Farm

Cocksmoss

Pallotti Hall

Davenport Lane

I grid square represents 500 metres

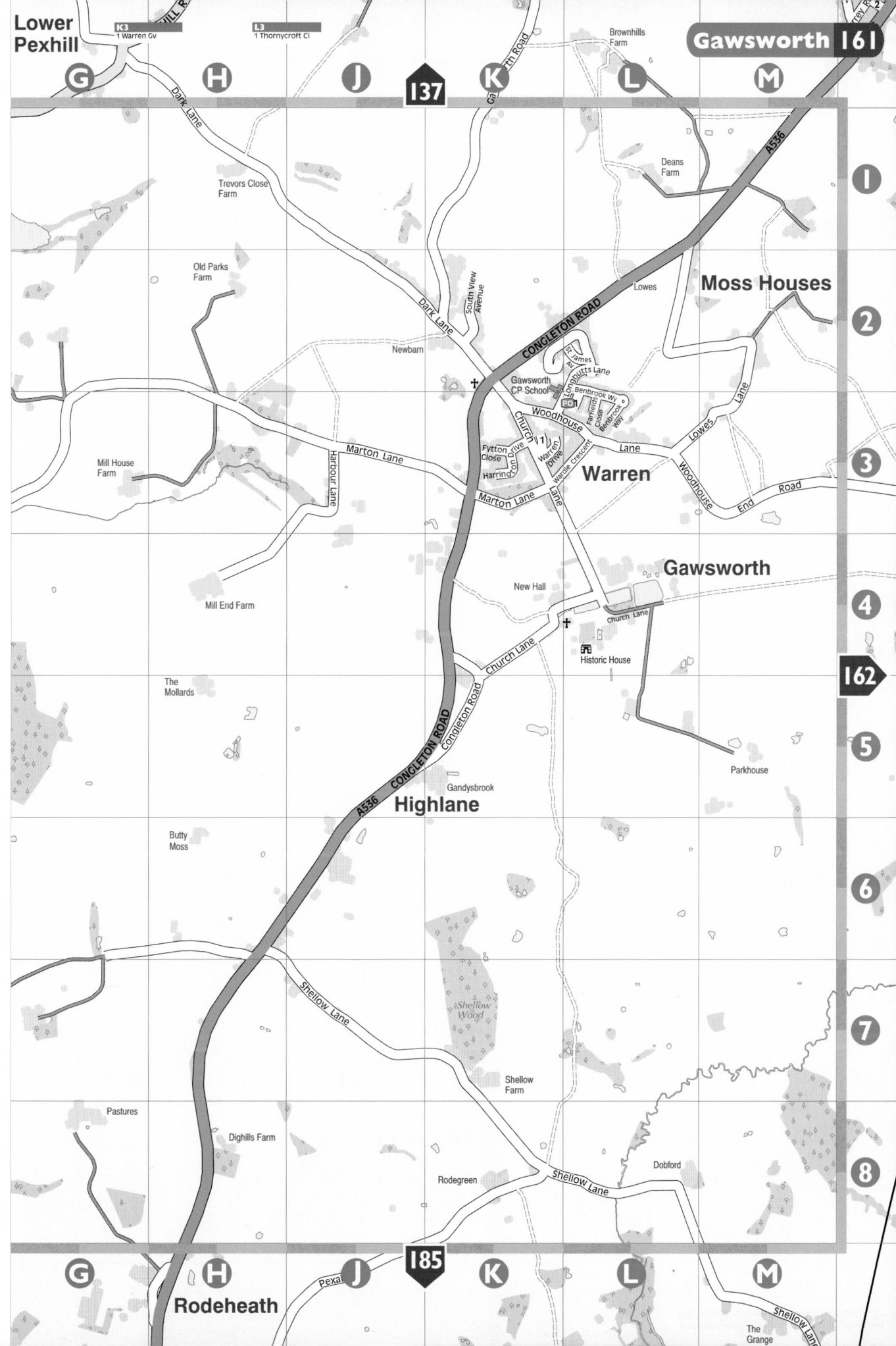

Lower Pexhill

G **H** **J** 137 **K** **L** **M**

K3
1 Warren Gv

L3
1 Thornycroft Cl

Brownhills Farm

Deans Farm

Trevors Close Farm

I

Old Parks Farm

Dark Lane

Newbarn

South View Avenue

CONGLETON ROAD

Lowes

Moss Houses

2

St James Lane

Longbutts Lane

Gawsworth CP School

PO

Benbrook Wy
Fairfields Close
Benbrook Way

Woodhouse

Lowes Lane

3

Mill House Farm

Marton Lane

Harbour Lane

Church Lane

Fytton Close

Harrington Drive

Warren Drive

Wardle Crescent

Warren

Lane

Woodhouse End Road

Marton Lane

Mill End Farm

New Hall

Gawsworth

4

The Mollards

Church Lane

Church Lane

Historic House

162

Parkhouse

5

CONGLETON ROAD

A536

Gandysbrook

Highlane

Butty Moss

6

Shellow Lane

Shellow Wood

7

Pastures

Dighills Farm

Shellow Farm

Rodegreen

Shellow Lane

Dobford

8

G **H** **J** 185 **K** **L** **M**

Pexa

Rodeheath

Shellow Lane

The Grange

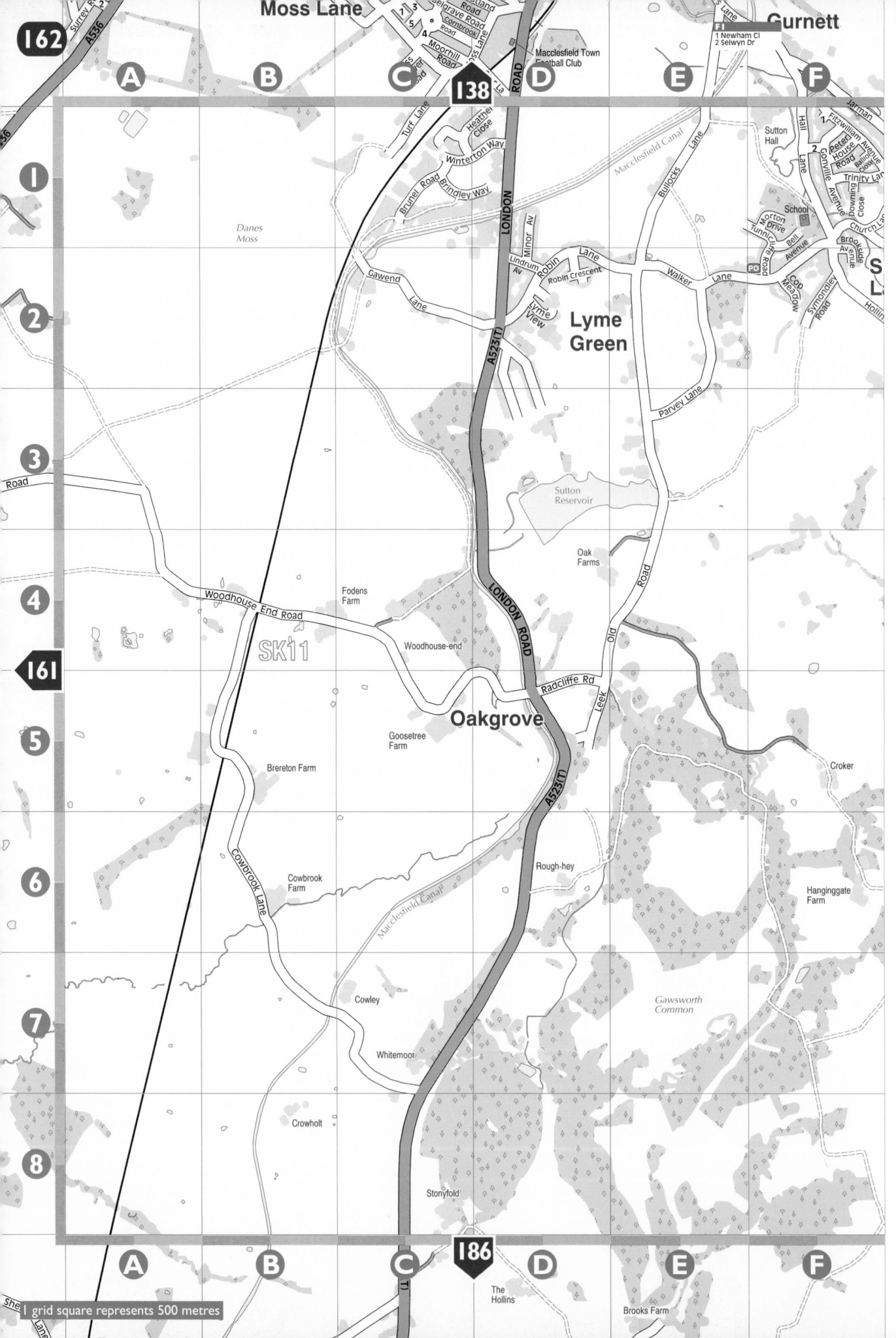

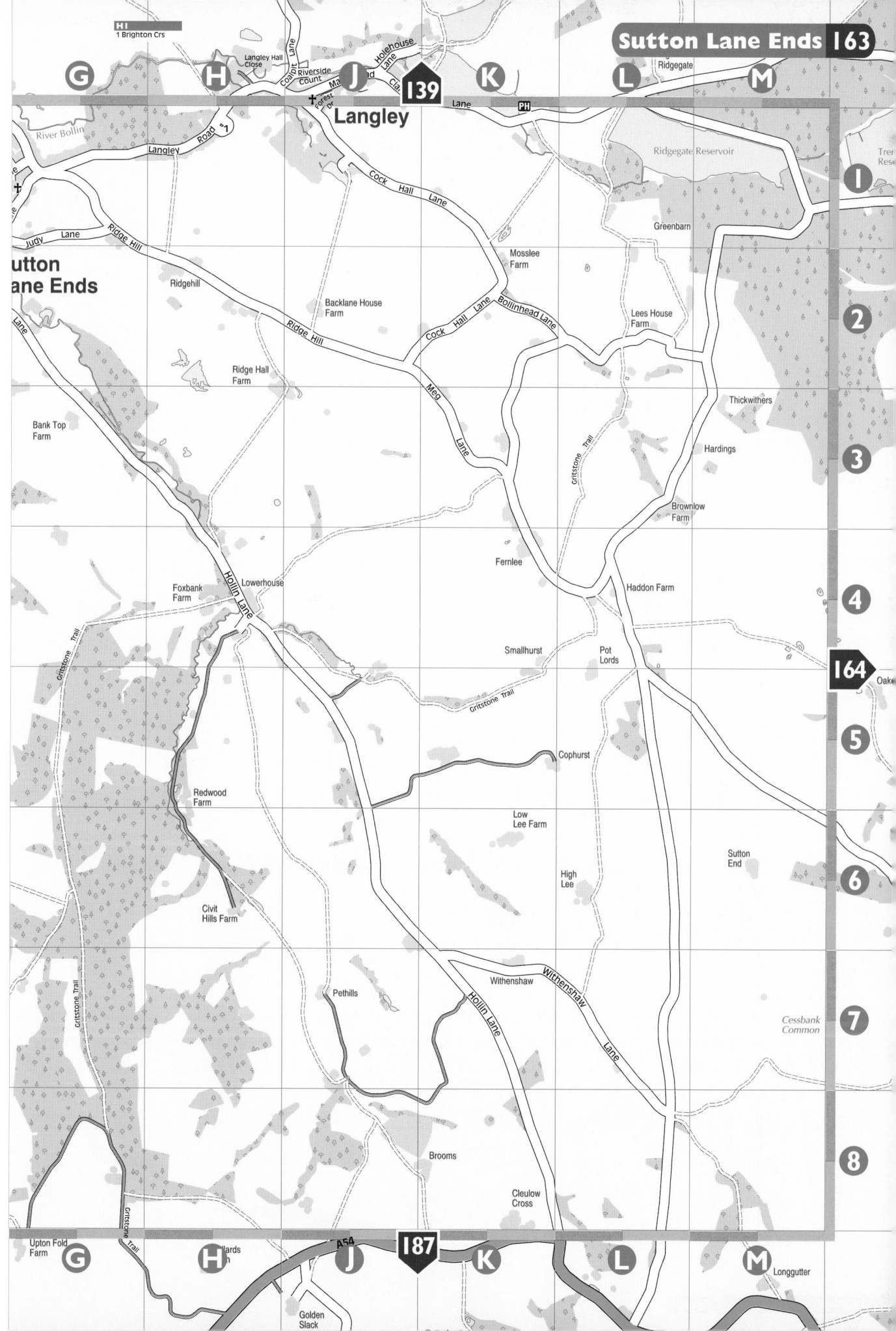

H1
1 Brighton Crs

G H J K L M

139

Langley

PH

Ridgegate

I

River Bollin

Langley Road

Ridgate Reservoir

Trent Rese

Langley Road

Cock Hall Lane

Greenbarn

Judy Lane

Ridge Hill

Mosslee Farm

2

Sutton
Lane Ends

Ridgehill

Backlane House Farm

Cock Hall Lane

Bollinhead Lane

Lees House Farm

Lane

Ridge Hill

Thickwithers

Ridge Hall Farm

Meg Lane

Gritstone Trail

Hardings

3

Bank Top Farm

Brownlow Farm

Fernlee

Foxbank Farm

Lowerhouse

Haddon Farm

4

Hollin Lane

Smallhurst

Pot Lords

164

Oak

Gritstone Trail

Gritstone Trail

Cophurst

5

Redwood Farm

Low Lee Farm

Sutton End

6

Civit Hills Farm

High Lee

Gritstone Trail

Pethills

Withenshaw

Hollin Lane

Withenshaw Lane

Cessbank Common

7

Gritstone Trail

Brooms

8

Upton Fold Farm

Gritstone Trail

Cleulow Cross

A54

187

Longgutter

G H J K L M

Golden Slack

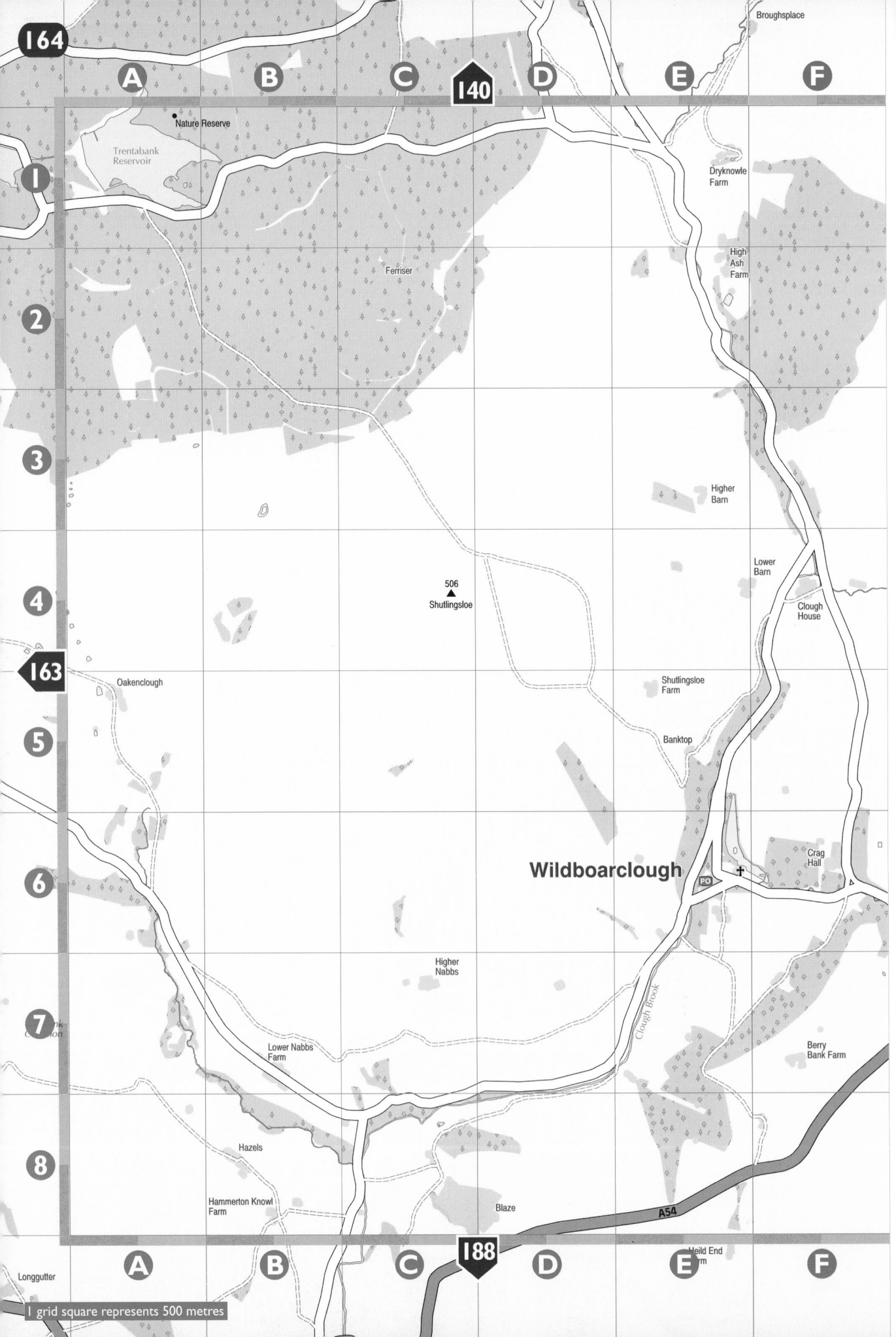

A
B
C
140
D
E
F

Broughsplace

1

Trentabank
Reservoir

Nature Reserve

Dryknowle
Farm

High
Ash
Farm

Ferriser

2

3

Higher
Barn

506
Shutlingsloe

4

Lower
Barn

Clough
House

163

Oakenclough

Shutlingsloe
Farm

5

Banktop

Crag
Hall

6

Wildboarclough

PO

Higher
Nabbs

7

Clough Brook

Lower Nabbs
Farm

Berry
Bank Farm

8

Hazels

Hammerton Knowl
Farm

Blaze

A54

Heild End
Farm

A
B
C
188
D
E
F

Longgutter

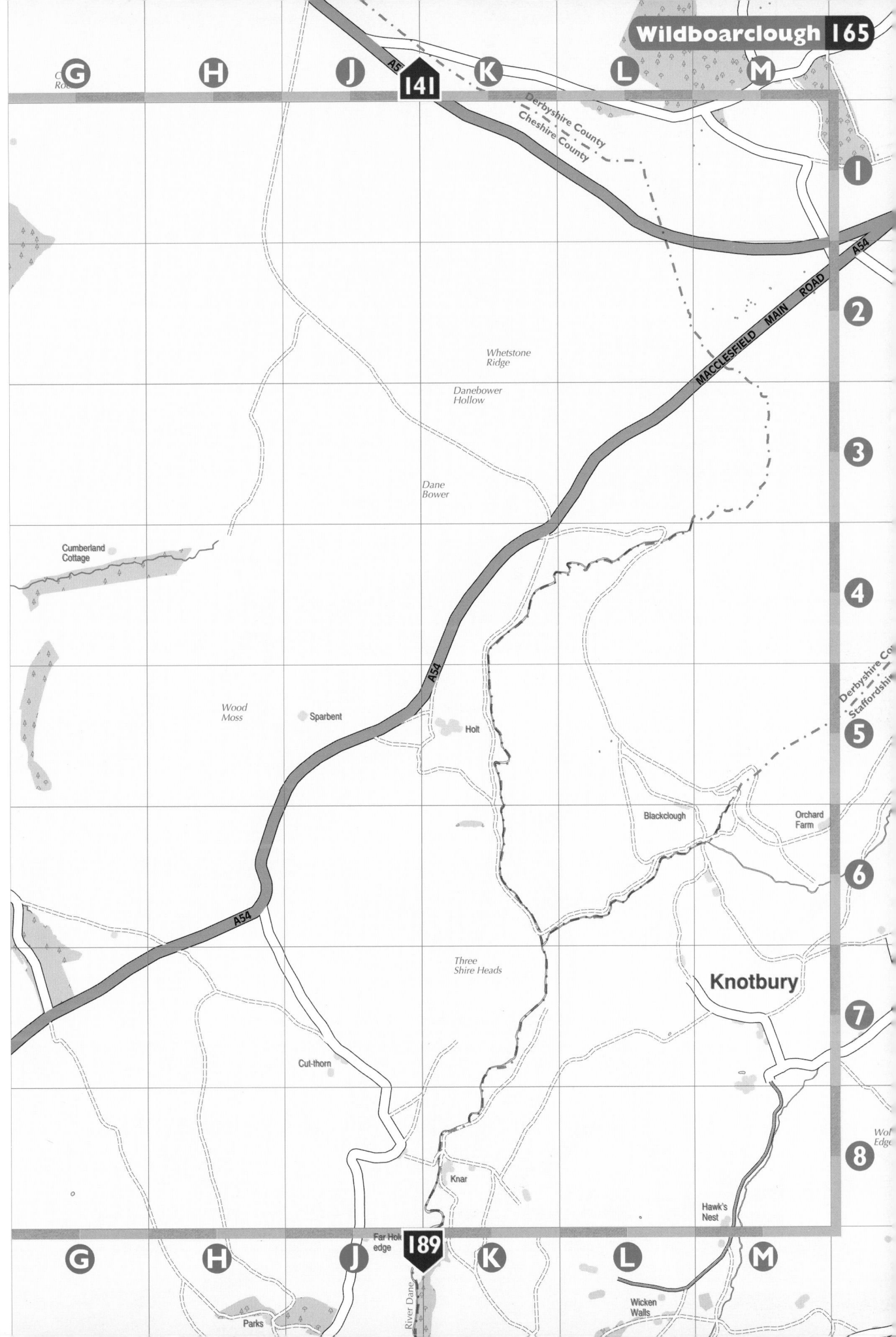

G   GH   J   A5   141   K   L   M

I

Derbyshire County
Cheshire County

MACCLESFIELD MAIN ROAD   A54

2

*Whetstone
Ridge*

3

*Danebower
Hollow*

*Dane
Bower*

Derbyshire Co
Staffordshi

Cumberland
Cottage

4

A54

5

*Wood
Moss*   Sparbent   Holt

Blackclough   Orchard
Farm

6

A54

*Three
Shire Heads*

Knotbury

7

Cut-thorn

Wol
Edge

8

Knar

Hawk's
Nest

G   H   J   189   K   L   M

Far Hole
edge

River Dane

Parks

Wicken
Walls

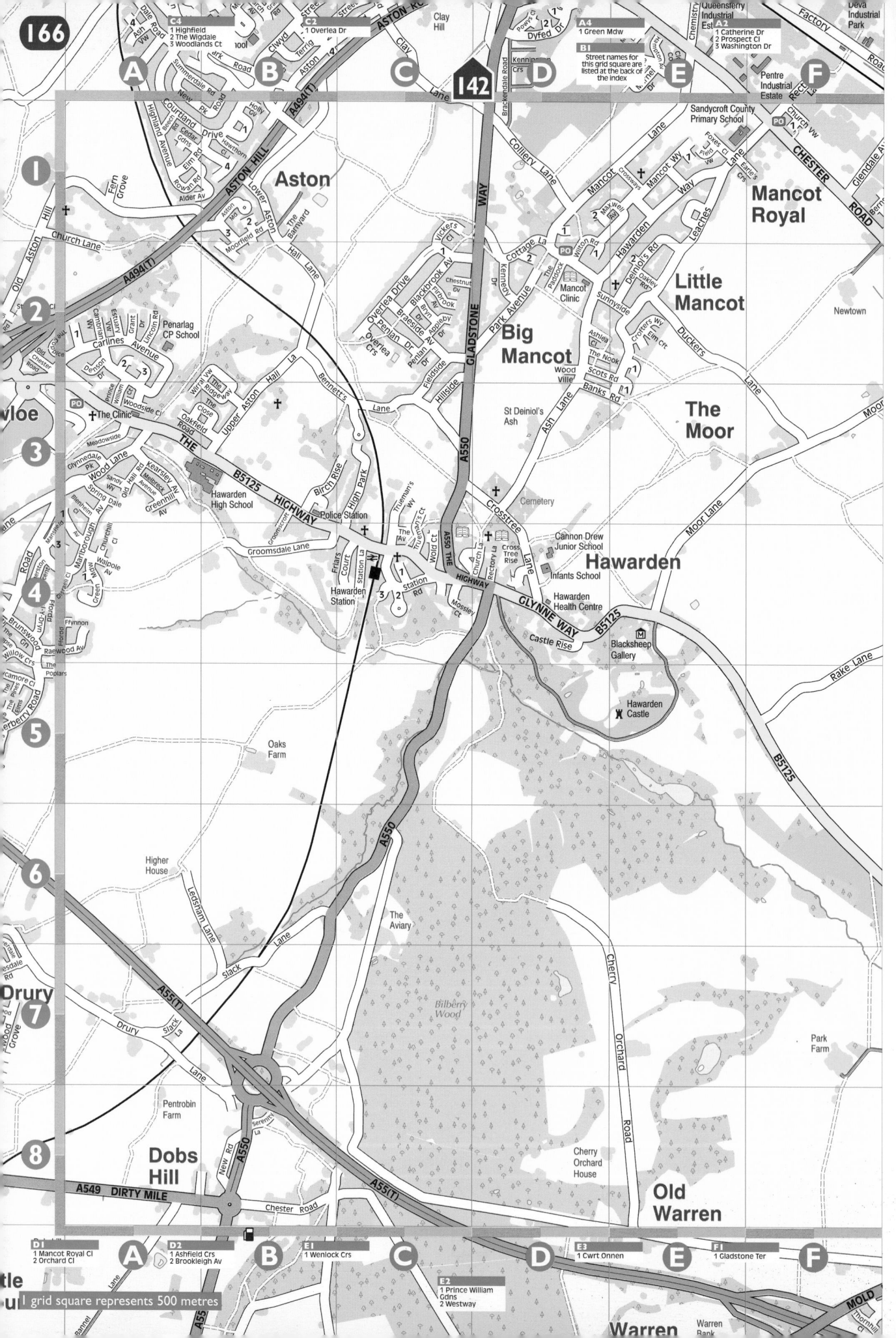

142

C4
1 Highfield
2 The Wigdale
3 Woodlands Ct

C2
1 Overlea Dr

A4
1 Green Mdw

B1
Street names for
this grid square are
listed on the back of
the index

A2
1 Catherine Dr
2 Prospect Cl
3 Washington Dr

Aston

Queensferry Industrial Est

Deva Industrial Park

Pentre Industrial Estate

Sandycroft County Primary School

Mancot Royal

Little Mancot

Newtown

Big Mancot

St Deiniol's Ash

The Moor

Mancot Clinic

Bwloe

The Clinic

Penarlag CP School

Hawarden High School

Police Station

Hawarden Station

Cemetery

Cannon Drew Junior School

Infants School

Hawarden

Hawarden Health Centre

Blacksheep Gallery

Hawarden Castle

Rake Lane

Oaks Farm

Higher House

The Aviary

Bilberry Wood

Drury

Cherry Orchard House

Park Farm

Old Warren

Dobs Hill

Pentrobin Farm

A549 DIRTY MILE

A55(T)

Chester Road

MOLD

Warren Bank

Warren

D1
1 Mancot Royal Cl
2 Orchard Cl

D2
1 Ashfield Crs
2 Brookleigh Av

E1
1 Wenlock Crs

D1
1 Cwrt Onnen

F1
1 Gladstone Ter

E2
1 Prince William Gdns
2 Westway

1 grid square represents 500 metres

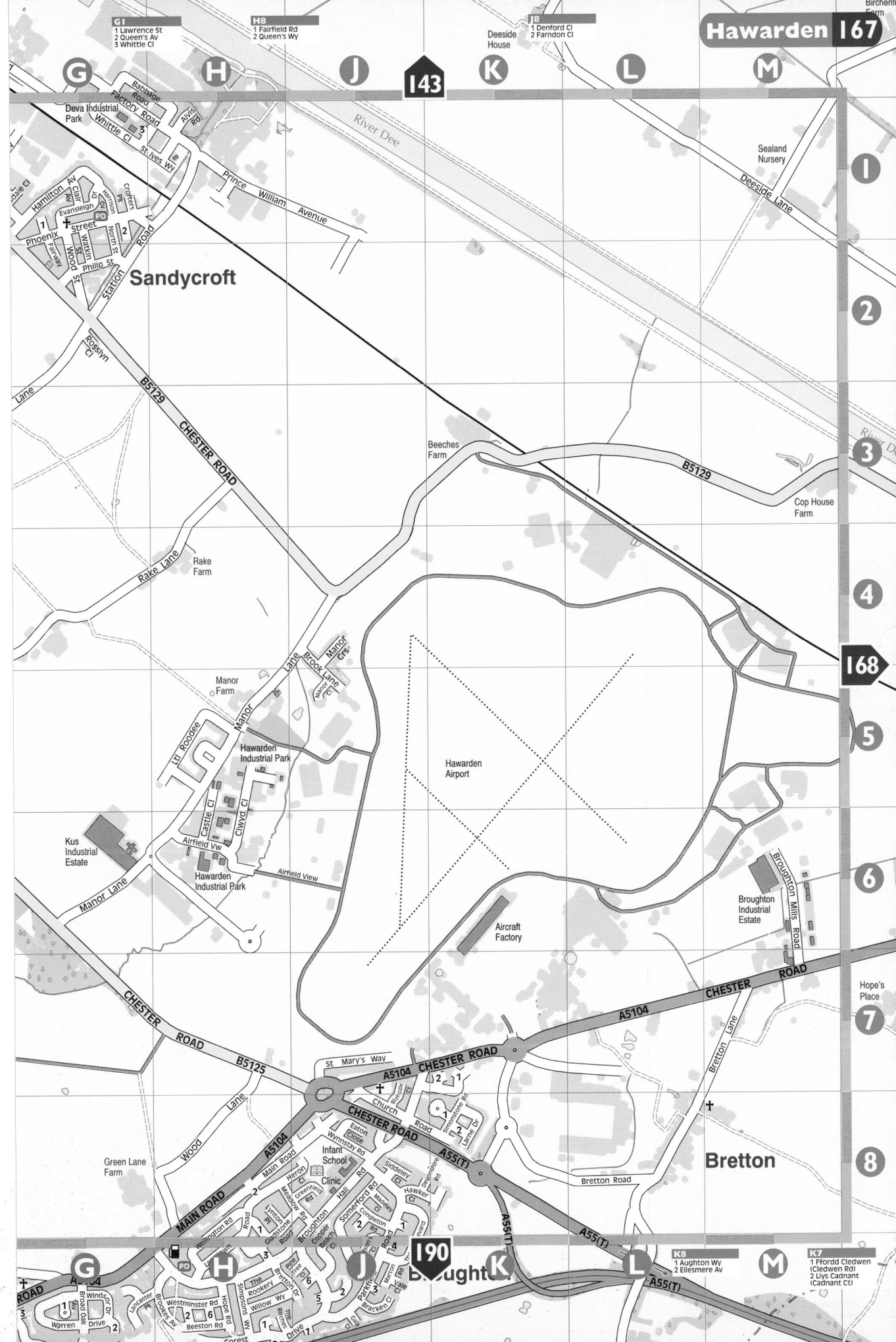

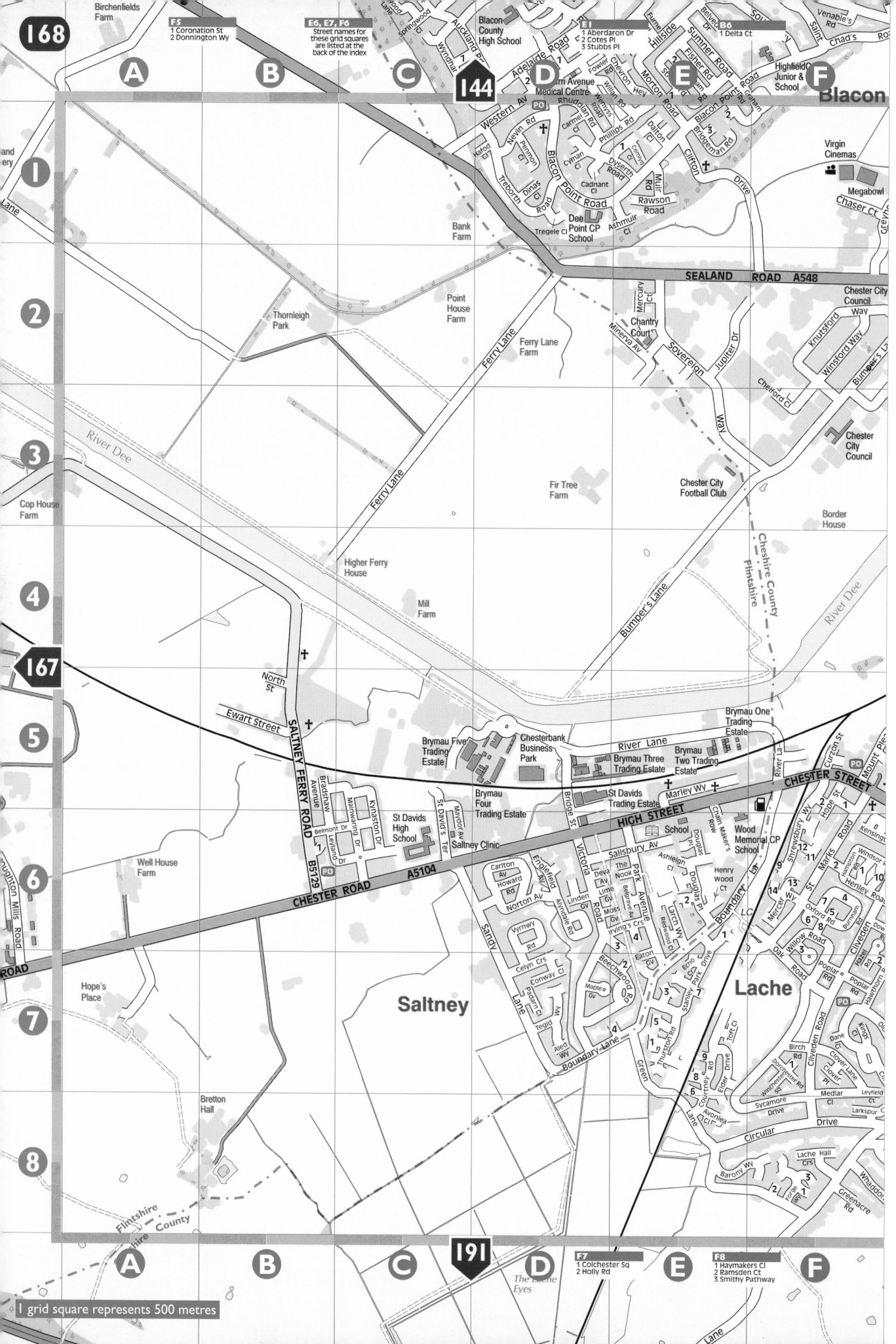

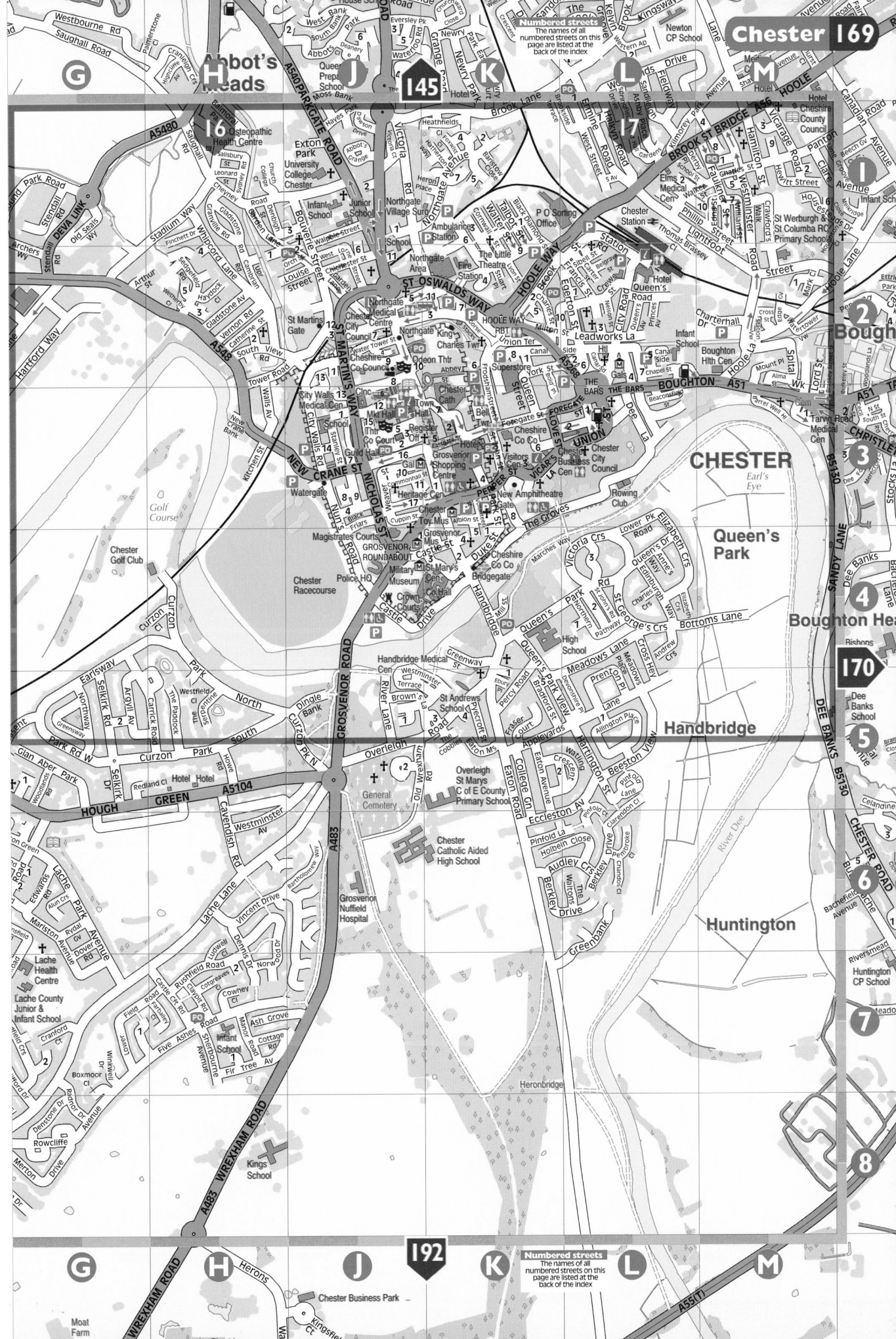

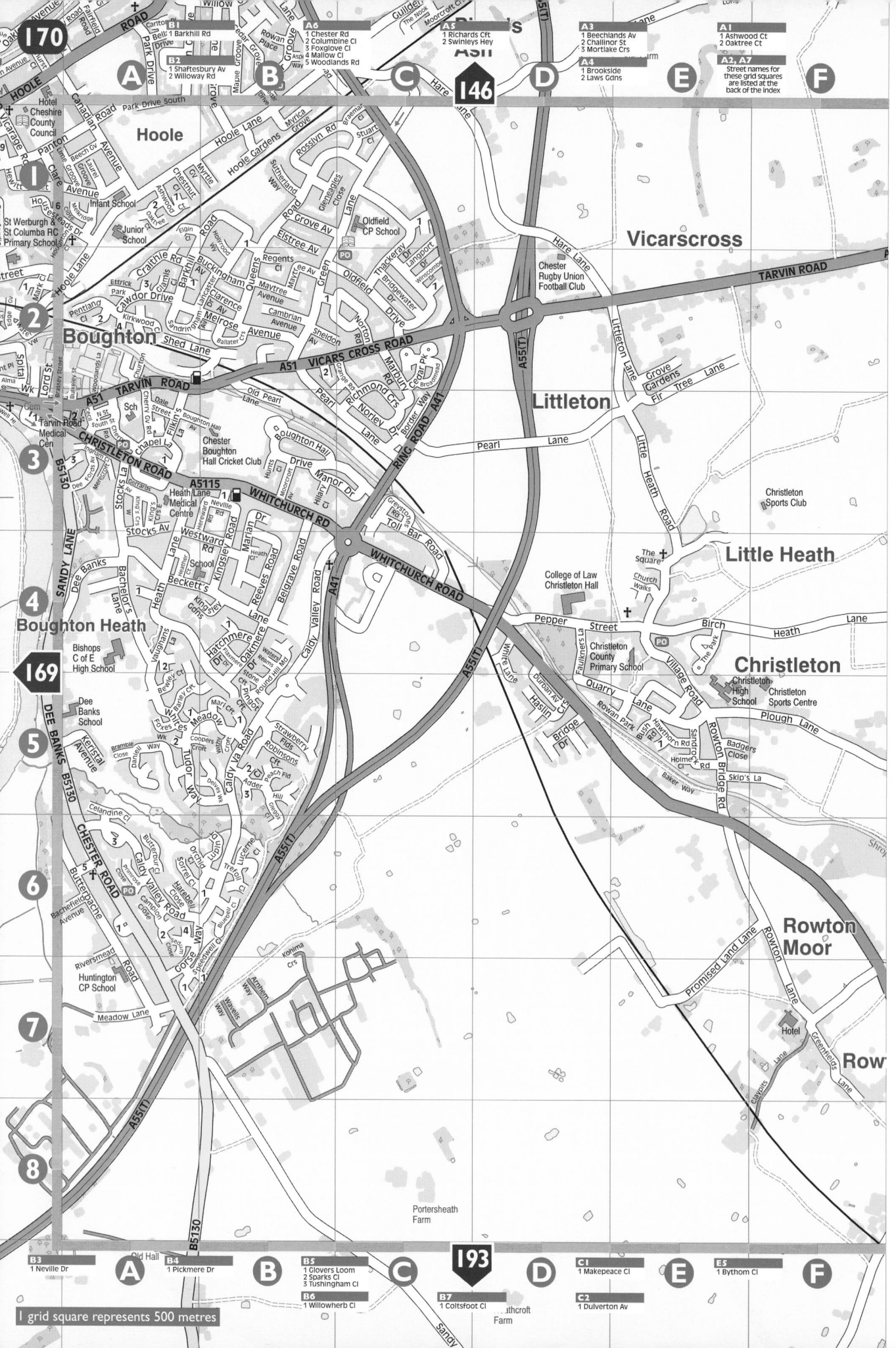

Hoole

Vicarscross

Chester Rugby Union Football Club

TARVIN ROAD

Littleton

A51 VICARS CROSS ROAD

Boughton

TARVIN ROAD A51

CHRISTLETON ROAD B5130

Chester Boughton Hall Cricket Club

RING ROAD A41

Pearl Lane

Grove Gardens

Fir Tree Lane

Christleton Sports Club

Little Heath

A5115 WHITCHURCH RD

WHITCHURCH ROAD

College of Law Christleton Hall

The square

Church Walks

Birch Heath Lane

Boughton Heath

Bishops C of E High School

169

Dee Banks School

Pepper Street

Christleton County Primary School

Christleton

Christleton High School

Christleton Sports Centre

Plough Lane

DEE BANKS B5130

SANDY LANE

CHESTER ROAD

Huntington CP School

Meadow Lane

Quarry Lane

Promised Land Lane

Rowton Moor

Portersheath Farm

Rowt

Greenfields Lane

Old Hall

I grid square represents 500 metres

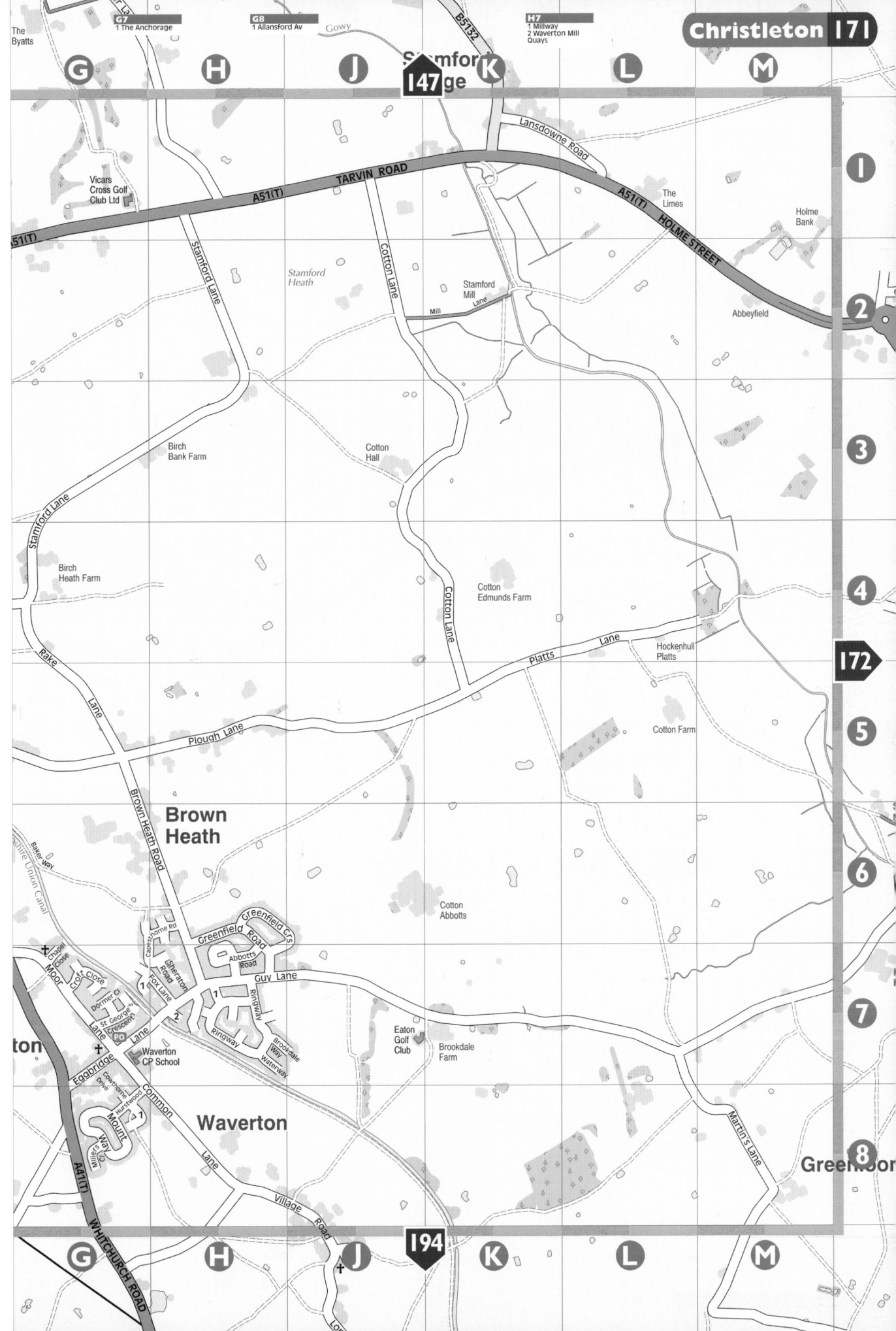

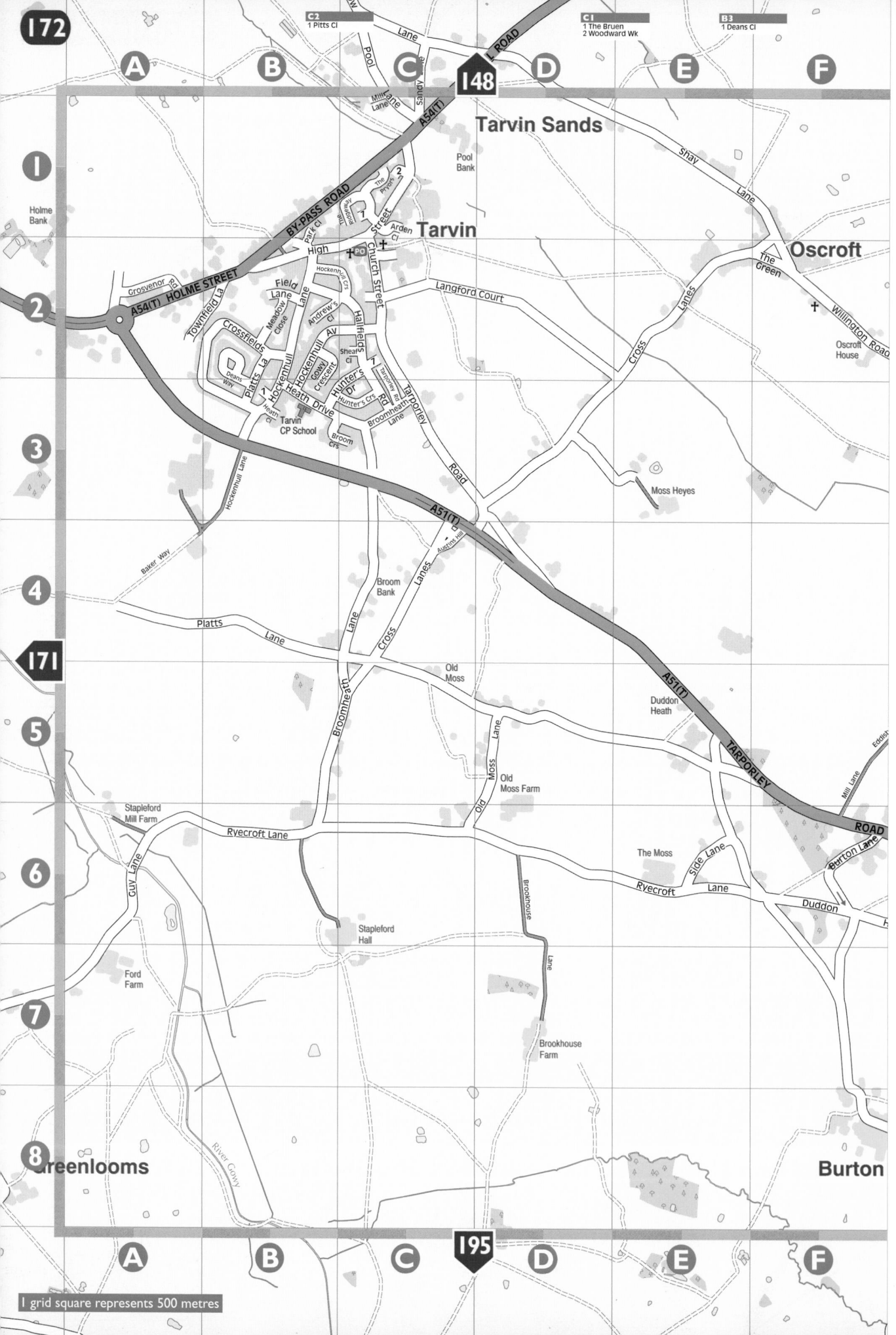

172

I

2

3

171

4

5

6

7

8

A   B   C   148   D   E   F

C2
1 Pitts Cl

C1
1 The Bruen
2 Woodward Wk

B3
1 Deans Cl

Tarvin Sands

Holme
Bank

Shay
Lane

Oscroft

The
Green

Willington Road

Oscroft
House

A54(T) HOLME STREET

Grosvenor Rd

Townfield La

Crossfields

Platts La

Deans
Way

Meadow
Close

Field
Lane

Hockennull
Lane

Hockennull
Heath Cl

Hockennull
Heath Drive

Andrew's
Cl

Coney
Crescent

Hunter's
Dr

Hunter's Crs

Broom
Crs

Tarvin
CP School

Park Cl

The
Priory

The
Ridgeway

High
Street

Church Street

Arden
Cl

PO

Av

Shears
Cl

Hallfields

Tarporley Rd

Broomheath
Lane

Tarporley

Langford Court

Moss Heyes

Cross

Lanes

BY-PASS ROAD

A54(T)

Pool
Bank

Sandy
Lane

Pool
Lane

Mill
Lane

Lane

I ROAD

Tarvin

Road

A51(T)

Austins Hill

Cross

Lanes

Broom
Bank

Platts
Lane

Baker Way

Hockennull Lane

Broomheath

Lane

Old
Moss

Old
Moss
Lane

Old
Moss Farm

Duddon
Heath

A51(T)

TARPORLEY

ROAD

Mill Lane

Eddish

Burton Lane

The Moss

Side Lane

Ryecroft

Lane

Duddon

Stapleford
Mill Farm

Ryecroft Lane

Guy Lane

Ford
Farm

Stapleford
Hall

Brookhouse

Lane

Brookhouse
Farm

River Gowy

Greenlooms

Burton

A   B   C   195   D   E   F

1 grid square represents 500 metres

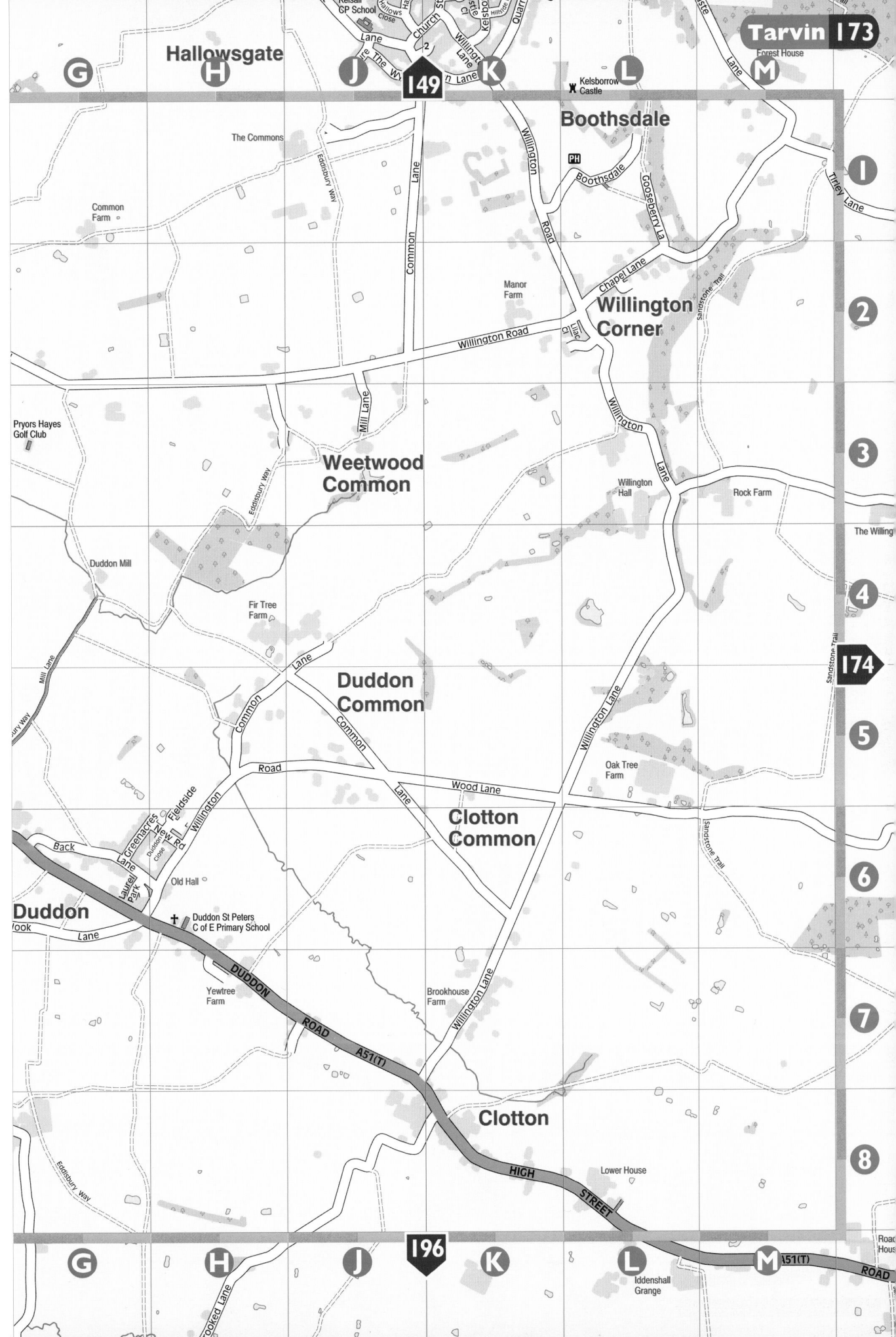

Hallowsgate

G **H** **J** **149** **K** **L** **M**

Kelsall CP School

Church Lane

Kelsborrow Castle

Boothsdale

1

The Commons

Common Farm

Eddisbury Way

Common Lane

Willington Road

Boothsdale

PH

Gooseberry La

Chapel Lane

Manor Farm

Willington Corner

Sandstone Trail

Tilney Lane

Forest House

2

Mill Lane

Willington Road

Willington Lane

3

Pryors Hayes Golf Club

Eddisbury Way

Weetwood Common

Willington Hall

Rock Farm

The Willing

Duddon Mill

Fir Tree Farm

4

Mill Lane

Common Lane

Duddon Common

Common Lane

Willington Lane

Sandstone Trail

174

5

Eddisbury Way

Willington Road

Road

Fieldside

Greenacres

Duddon View Rd

Wood Lane

Oak Tree Farm

Clotton Common

6

Back Lane

Laurel Park

Old Hall

Duddon St Peters C of E Primary School

Sandstone Trail

Duddon

Brook Lane

DUDDON ROAD A51(T)

Yewtree Farm

Brookhouse Farm

Willington Lane

7

Eddisbury Way

Clotton

8

G **H** **J** **196** **K** **L** Iddenshall Grange **M** **A51(T)**

Lower House

HIGH STREET

Road House

ROAD

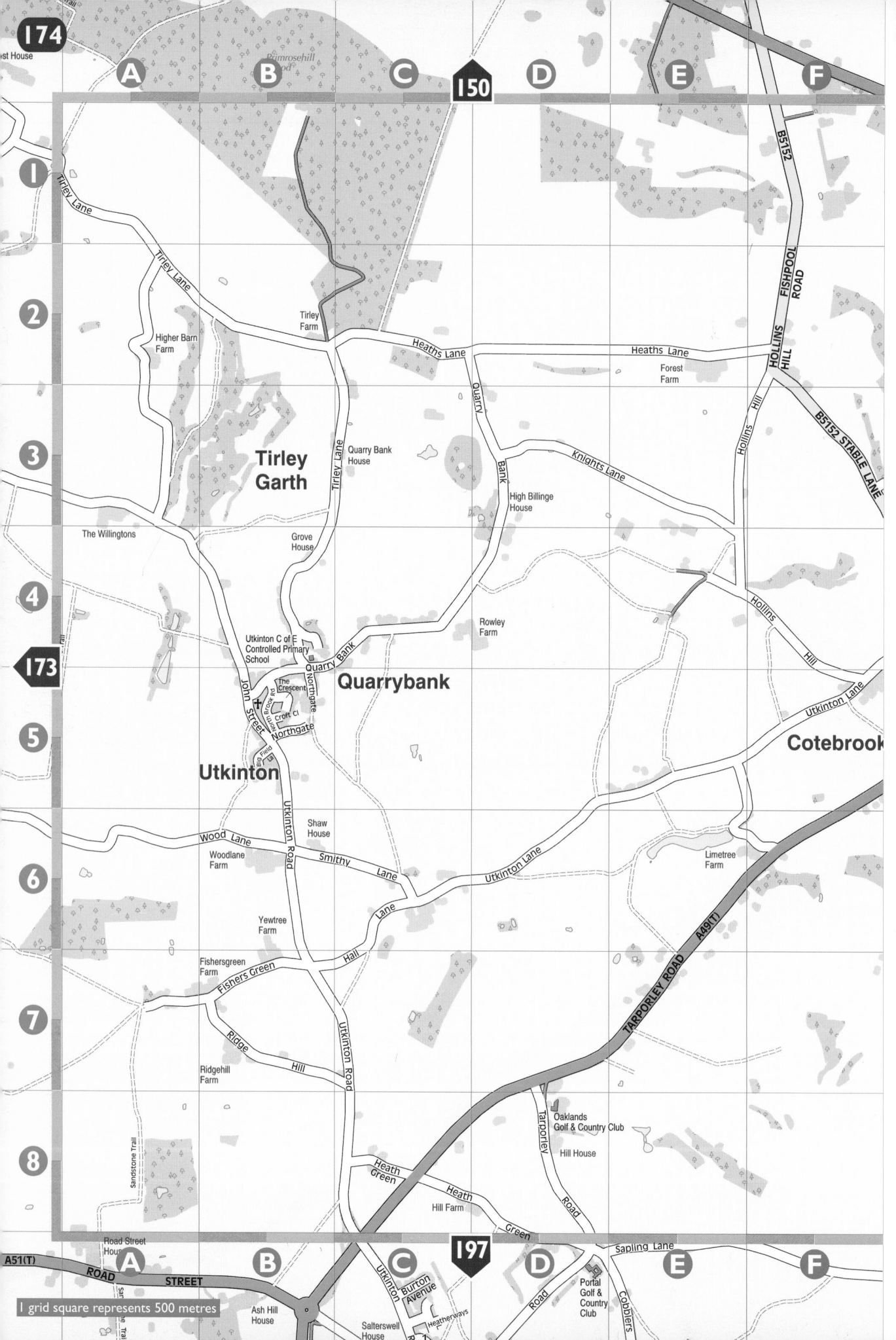

174

A B C 150 D E F

1

Tirley Lane

2

Tirley Lane

Higher Barn Farm

Tirley Farm

Heaths Lane

Heaths Lane

Forest Farm

B5152

FISHPOOL ROAD

Hollins Hill

3

Tirley Garth

Tirley Lane

Quarry Bank House

Quarry Bank

Knights Lane

High Billinge House

Hollins Hill

B5152 STABLE LANE

The Willingtons

Grove House

4

Utkinton C of E Controlled Primary School

Quarry Bank

Rowley Farm

Hollins Hill

173

The Crescent

Northgate

Croft Cl

Quarrybank

Utkinton Lane

5

John Street

Black Brook

Big Field

Northgate

Utkinton

Cotebrook

Wood Lane

Woodlane Farm

Utkinton Road

Shaw House

Smithy Lane

Lane

Utkinton Lane

Limetree Farm

6

Yewtree Farm

Hall

Lane

A49(T)

TARPORLEY ROAD

Fishersgreen Farm

Fishers Green

7

Ridge Hill

Ridgehill Farm

Utkinton Road

Oaklands Golf & Country Club

Hill House

Tarporley Road

Sandstone Trail

8

Heath Green

Heath Hill Farm

Heath Green Road

Sapling Lane

A51(T)

ROAD A STREET B Utkinton Burton Avenue 197 C D Road Cobblers E F

Road Street House

Ash Hill House

Salterswell House

Heatherways

Portal Golf & Country Club

1 grid square represents 500 metres

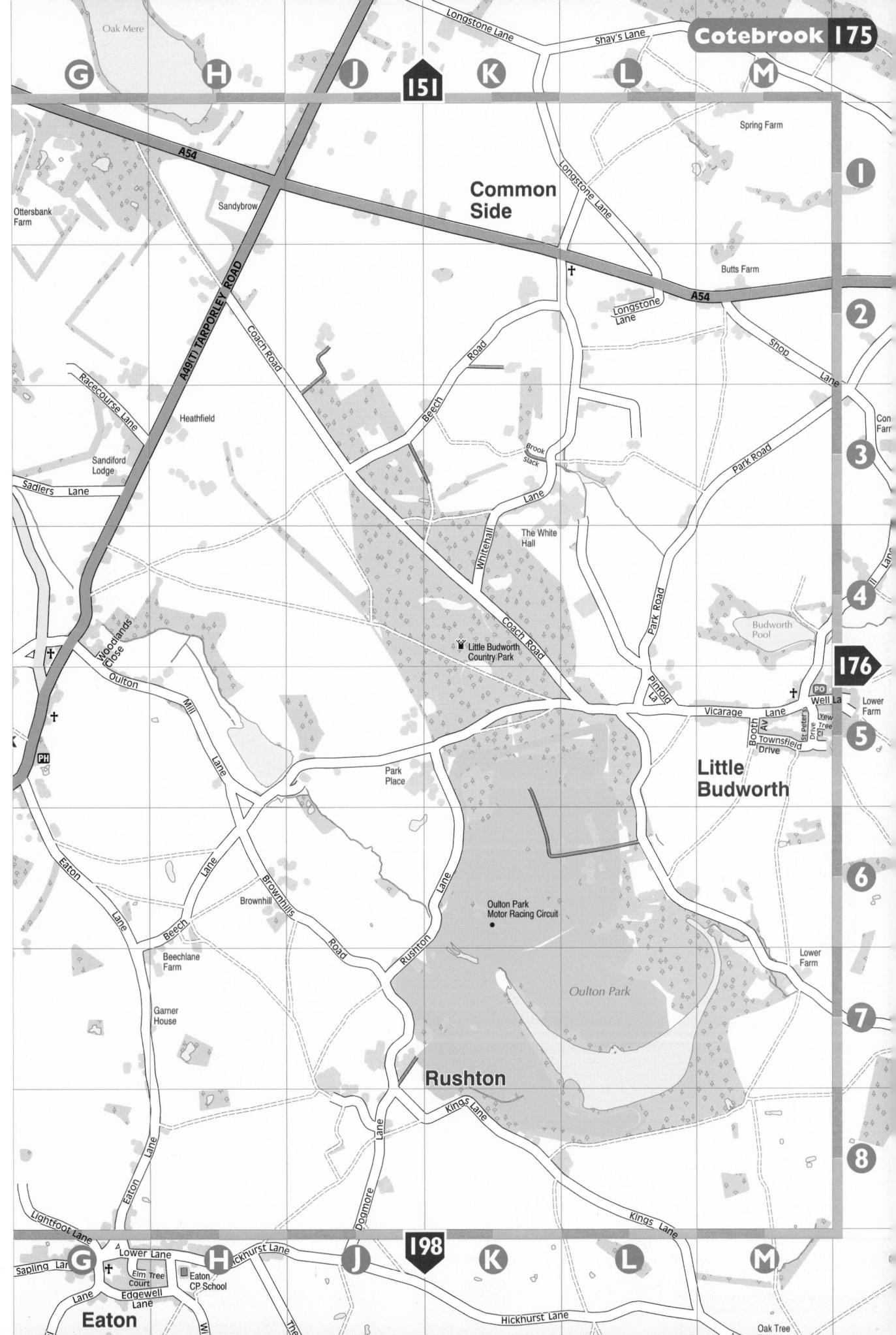

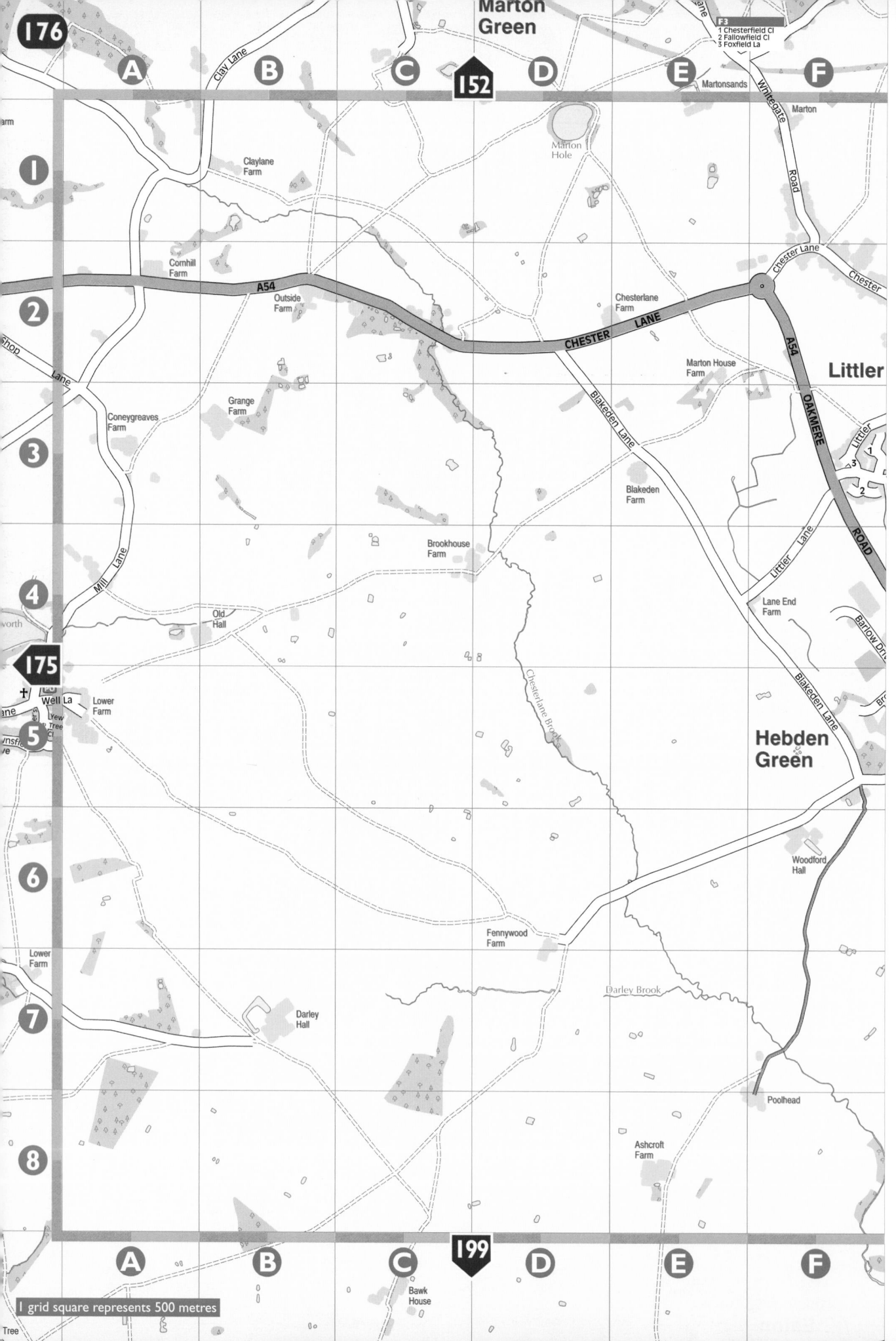

176

A B C D E F

Marton Green

152

F3
1 Chesterfield Cl
2 Fallowfield Cl
3 Foxfield La

Martonsands

Marton

I

Claylane Farm

Chester Lane

Chester

2

Cornhill Farm

A54

Outside Farm

Chesterlane Farm

CHESTER LANE

Marton House Farm

Littler

Bishop Lane

Coneygreaves Farm

Blakeden Lane

A54 OAKMERE

Littler

3

Grange Farm

Blakeden Farm

Littler Lane

4

Mill Lane

Old Hall

Brookhouse Farm

Lane End Farm

Barlow Dr

175

worth

Well La

Lower Farm

Yew Tree Cl

Chesterlane Brook

Blakeden Lane

Hebden Green

5

Woodford Hall

6

Lower Farm

Fennywood Farm

7

Darley Hall

Darley Brook

Poolhead

8

Ashcroft Farm

A B C D E F

199

Bawk House

Tree

1 grid square represents 500 metres

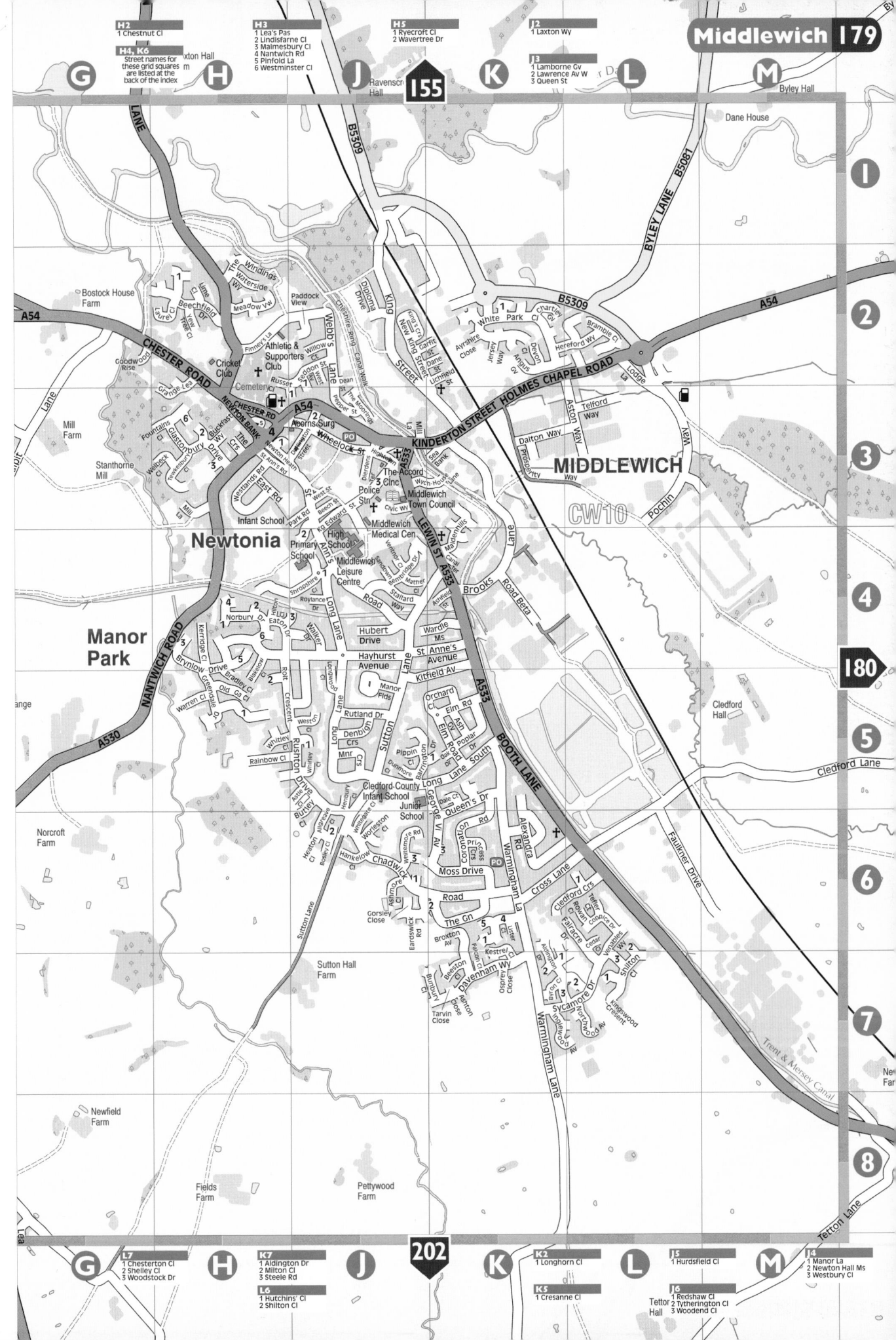

155

MIDDLEWICH

CW10

180

Newtonia

**Manor
Park**

202

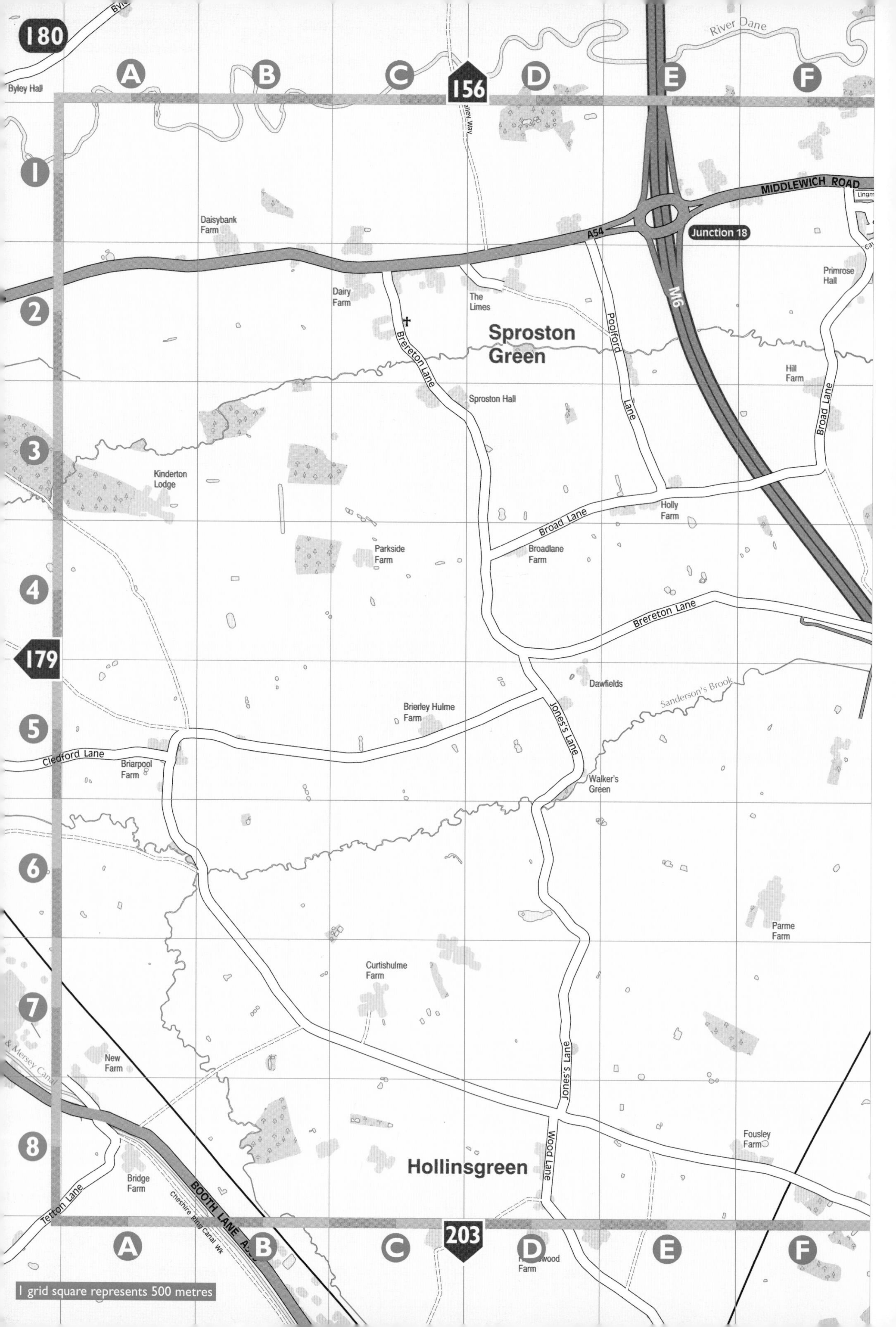
180
156
179
203
A
B
C
D
E
F
1
2
3
4
5
6
7
8
River Dane
Byley Hall
MIDDLEWICH ROAD
A54
Junction 18
M6
Daisybank Farm
Dairy Farm
The Limes
Primrose Hall
Sproston Green
Brereton Lane
Poolford Lane
Hill Farm
Broad Lane
Sproston Hall
Kinderton Lodge
Holly Farm
Broadlane Farm
Parkside Farm
Brereton Lane
Dawfields
Sanderson's Brook
Brierley Hulme Farm
Jones's Lane
Cledford Lane
Briarpool Farm
Walker's Green
Parme Farm
Curtishulme Farm
New Farm
& Mersey Canal
Jones's Lane
Wood Lane
Fousley Farm
Hollinsgreen
Bridge Farm
Tetton Lane
BOOTH LANE
Cheshire Ring Canal Wk
Farm
1 grid square represents 500 metres

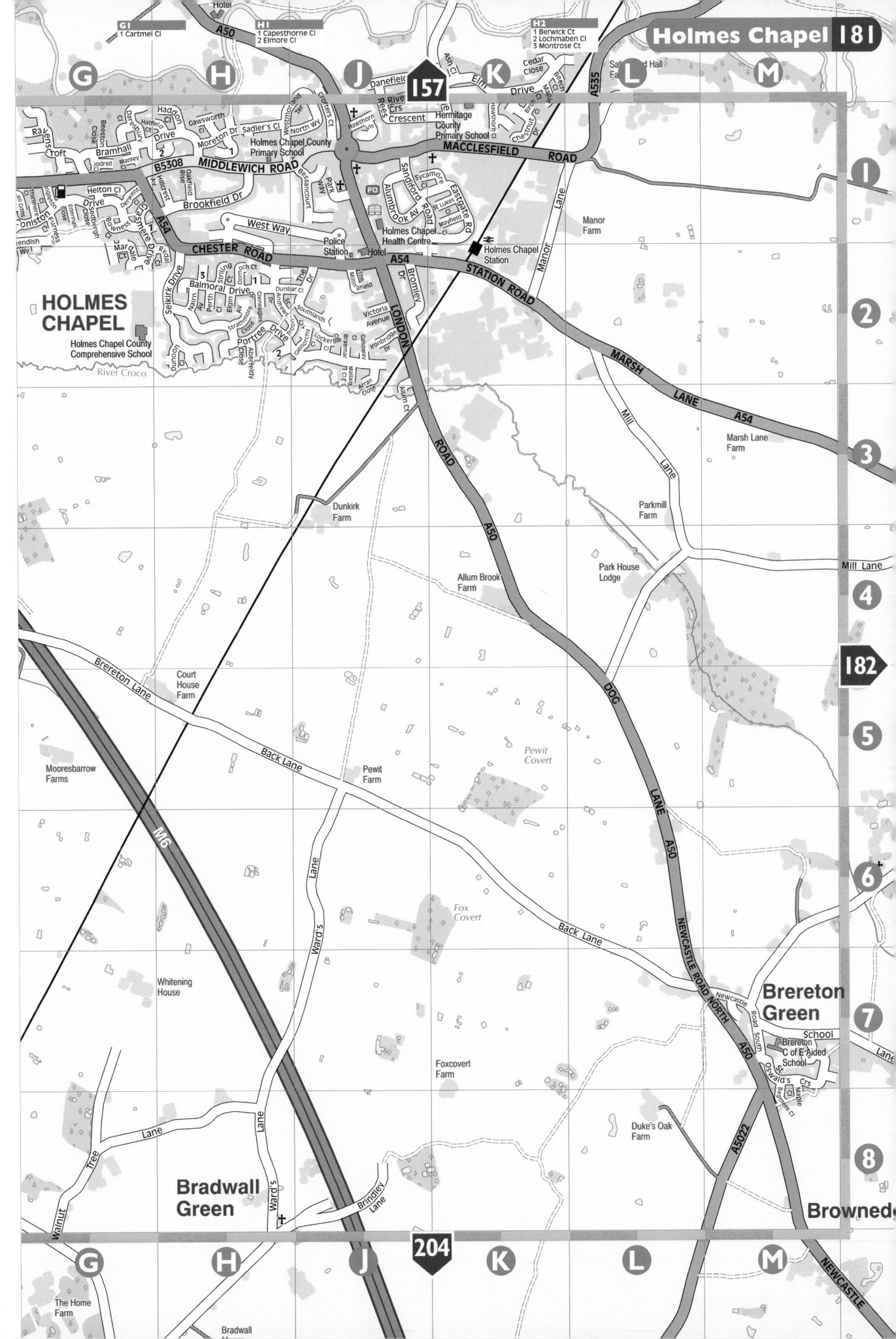

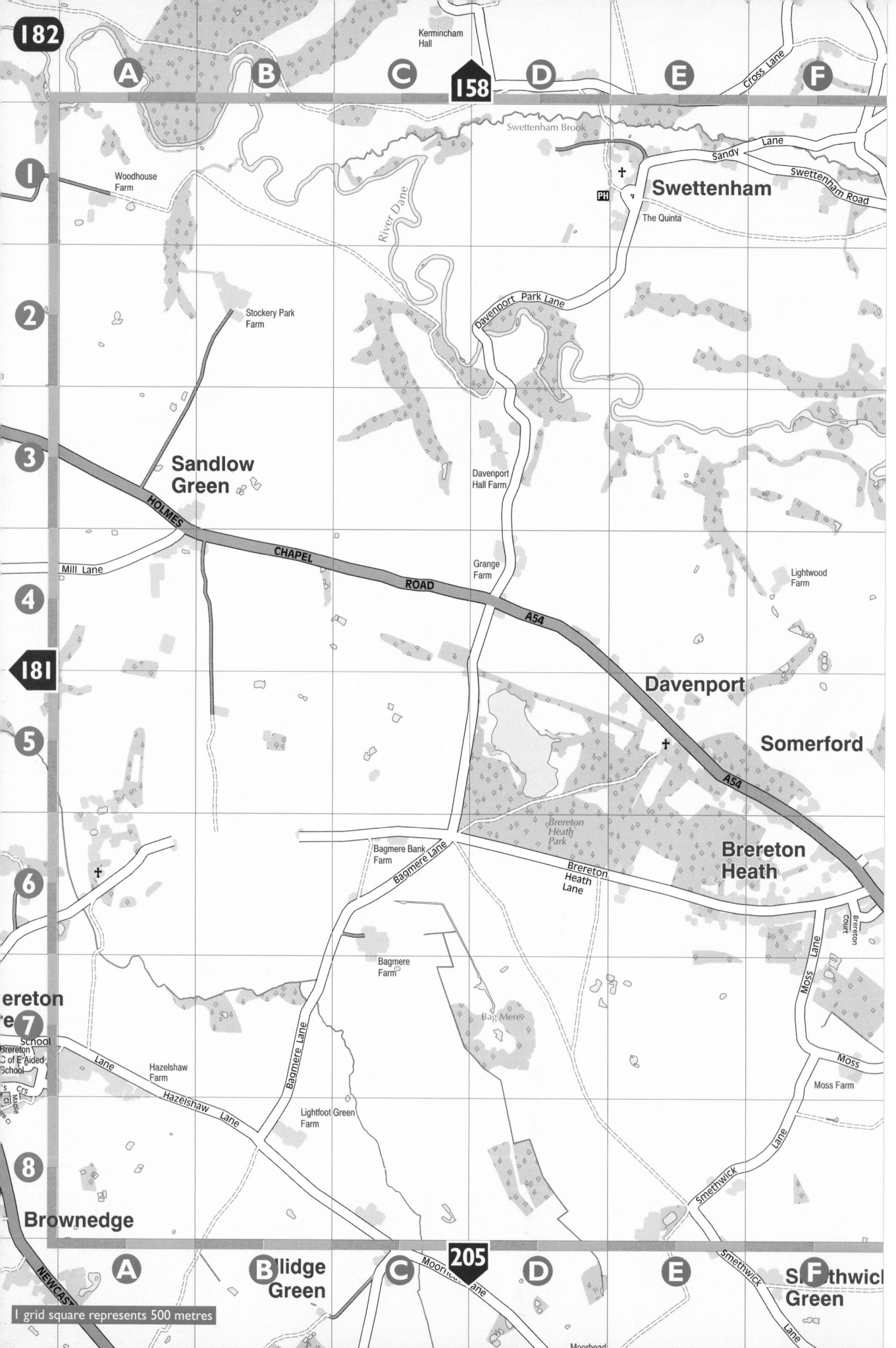

A   B   C   158   D   E   Cross Lane   F

1   Woodhouse Farm

Swettenham Brook

Sandy Lane

Swettenham Road

PH   ✝   Swettenham

The Quinta

2   Stockery Park Farm

River Dane

Davenport Park Lane

3   Sandlow Green

HOLMES

Davenport Hall Farm

CHAPEL

Mill Lane

Grange Farm

Lightwood Farm

4   ROAD

A54

181

Davenport

5   ✝   Somerford

Brereton Heath Park

A54

Bagmere Bank Farm

Bagmere Lane

Brereton Heath Lane

Brereton Heath

6   ✝   Moss Lane   Brereton Court

Bagmere Farm

Moss Lane

ereton e   7   School   Brereton C of E Aided School   Crs Mobile   Lane   Hazelshaw Farm   Hazelshaw Lane   Bagmere Lane   Lightfoot Green Farm   Bag Mere   Moss Moss Farm

8   NEWCAST   Brownedge   Smethwick Lane   Smethwick Lane

A   B   llidge Green   C   205   Moorfield ne   D   E   S thwick Green   F

Moorhead

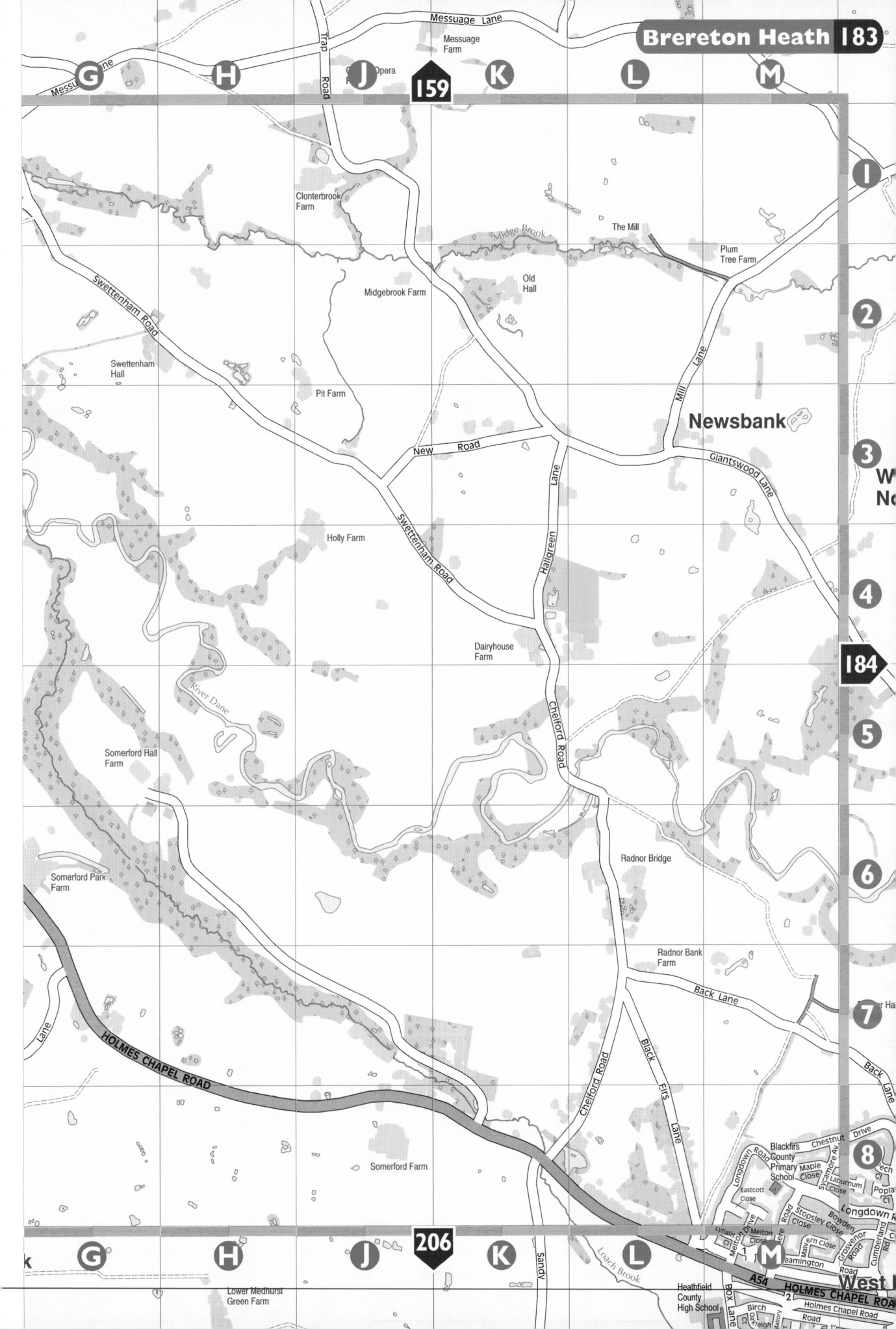

G H J **159** K L M

Messuage Lane

Messuage Lane

Messuage Farm

Trap Road

Opera

I

Clonterbrook Farm

Midge Brook

The Mill

Plum Tree Farm

2

Swettenham Road

Midgebrook Farm

Old Hall

Swettenham Hall

Pit Farm

Mill Lane

Newsbank

3

W
No

Giantswood Lane

New Road

Hallgreen Lane

Swettenham Road

Holly Farm

4

Dairyhouse Farm

184

Chelford Road

5

River Dane

Somerford Hall Farm

Radnor Bridge

6

Somerford Park Farm

Radnor Bank Farm

Back Lane

7

Lane

HOLMES CHAPEL ROAD

Chelford Road

Black

Firs Lane

Back Lane

Blackfirs County Primary School

Chestnut Drive

Longdown Road

Maple Close

Sycamore Av

Laburnum Cl

ech

Poplar

Longdown Road

8

Eastcott Close

Bowden

Grosvenor Road

Cumberland Road

Somerford Farm

Lynairs Close

Melton Close

Stopsley Close

Leamington

Holmes Chapel Road

G H J **206** K Sandy L M **West**

Lower Medhurst Green Farm

Loach Brook

Heathfield County High School

Box Lane

A54 HOLMES CHAPEL ROAD

Holmes Chapel Road

Birch

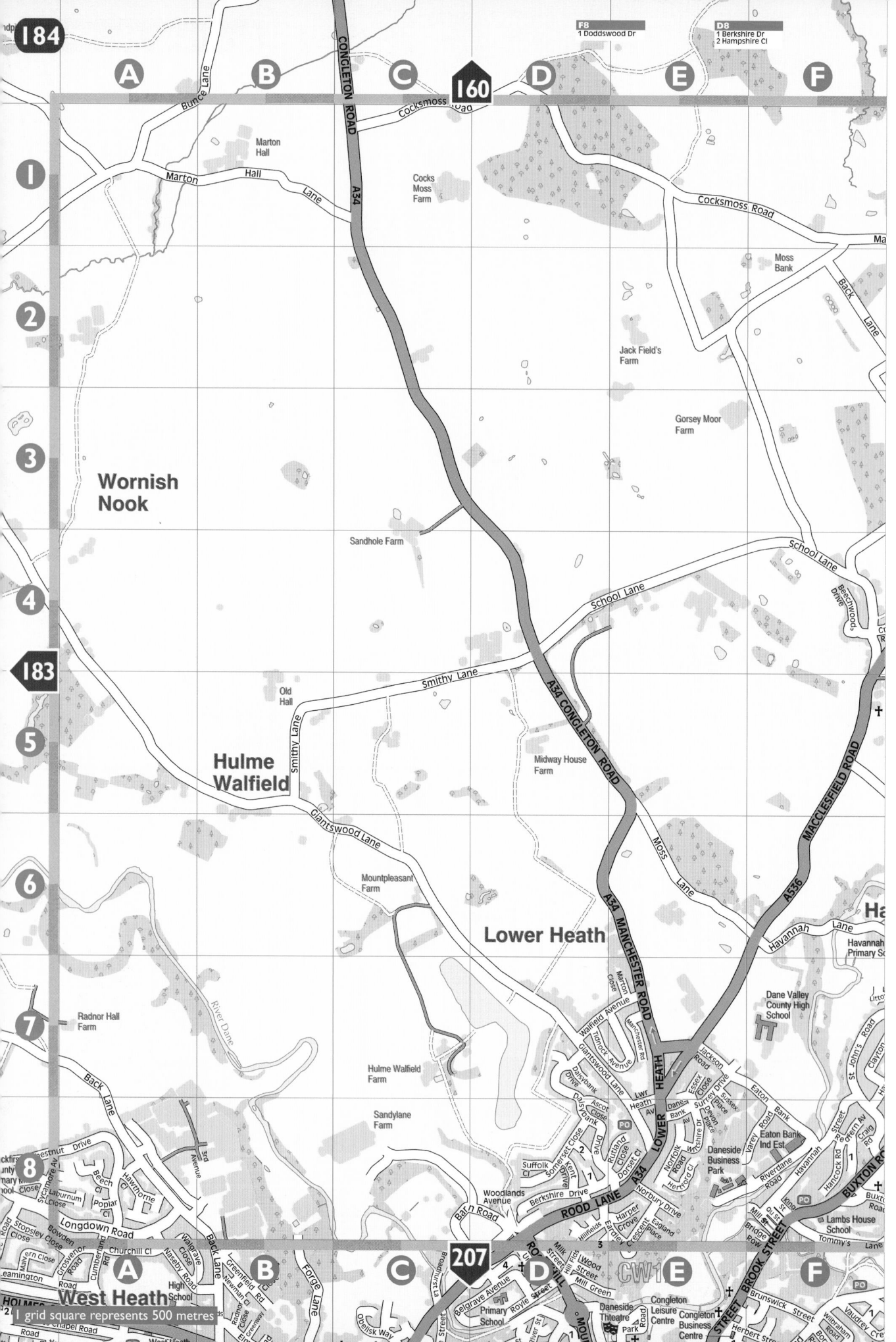

A B C D E F

160

F8
1 Doddswood Dr

D8
1 Berkshire Dr
2 Hampshire Cl

1

Bunce Lane

Marton Hall

Marton   Hall   Lane

CONGLETON ROAD

A34

Cocksmoss Road

Cocks Moss Farm

Cocksmoss Road

Moss Bank

Back Lane

2

Jack Field's Farm

Gorsey Moor Farm

3

Wornish Nook

Sandhole Farm

School Lane

School Lane

Beechwoods Drive

4

183

Old Hall

Smithy Lane

A34 CONGLETON ROAD

MACCLESFIELD ROAD

5

Hulme Walfield

Smithy Lane

Midway House Farm

Moss Lane

A536

Giantswood Lane

6

Mountpleasant Farm

Lower Heath

Havannah Lane

Havannah Primary Sc

Ha

River Dane

7

Radnor Hall Farm

Back Lane

Hulme Walfield Farm

Dane Valley County High School

A34 MANCHESTER ROAD

Jackson Road

Essex Close

Surrey Drive

Sussex

Eaton Bank

Eaton Bank Ind Est

Riverdane Road

Havannah

Walfield Avenue

Tranock Avenue

Giantswood Lane

Daisybank Drive

Ascot Drive

Manchester Rd

Marton Close

BUXTON RO

8

West Heath

Chestnut Drive

3rd Avenue

Hawthorne

Beech

Poplar

Sandylane Farm

Woodlands Avenue

Suffolk Close

Somerset Close

Kent Drive

Rutland Close

Dorset Cl

PO

Norfolk Close

Hertford Cl

Daneside Business Park

Hancock Rd

Green Av

Craig Cl

Longdown Road

Churchill Cl

Cumberland Road

Naredly Road

Walgrave

Close

Greenfield Rd

Newnham

High School

Forge Lane

Radnor C

Greenway

Barn Road

Berkshire Drive

Belgrave Avenue

Primary School

Royle

Street

Norbury Drive

ROOD LANE

A34

ROO

Milk Street

Fire

Wood Street

Mill Green

Harper Grove

Hillfields

Eardley

Eagland

Crescent

Daneside Theatre

Congleton Leisure Centre

Congleton Business Centre

Varley Road

Mill

Bridge Row

Lambs House School

Tommy's

Buxton

STREET BROOK STREET

Brunswick Street

Herbert Street

Vaudrey

Willramson Road

PO

CW1

207

A B C D E F

West Heath

HOLMES

1 grid square represents 500 metres

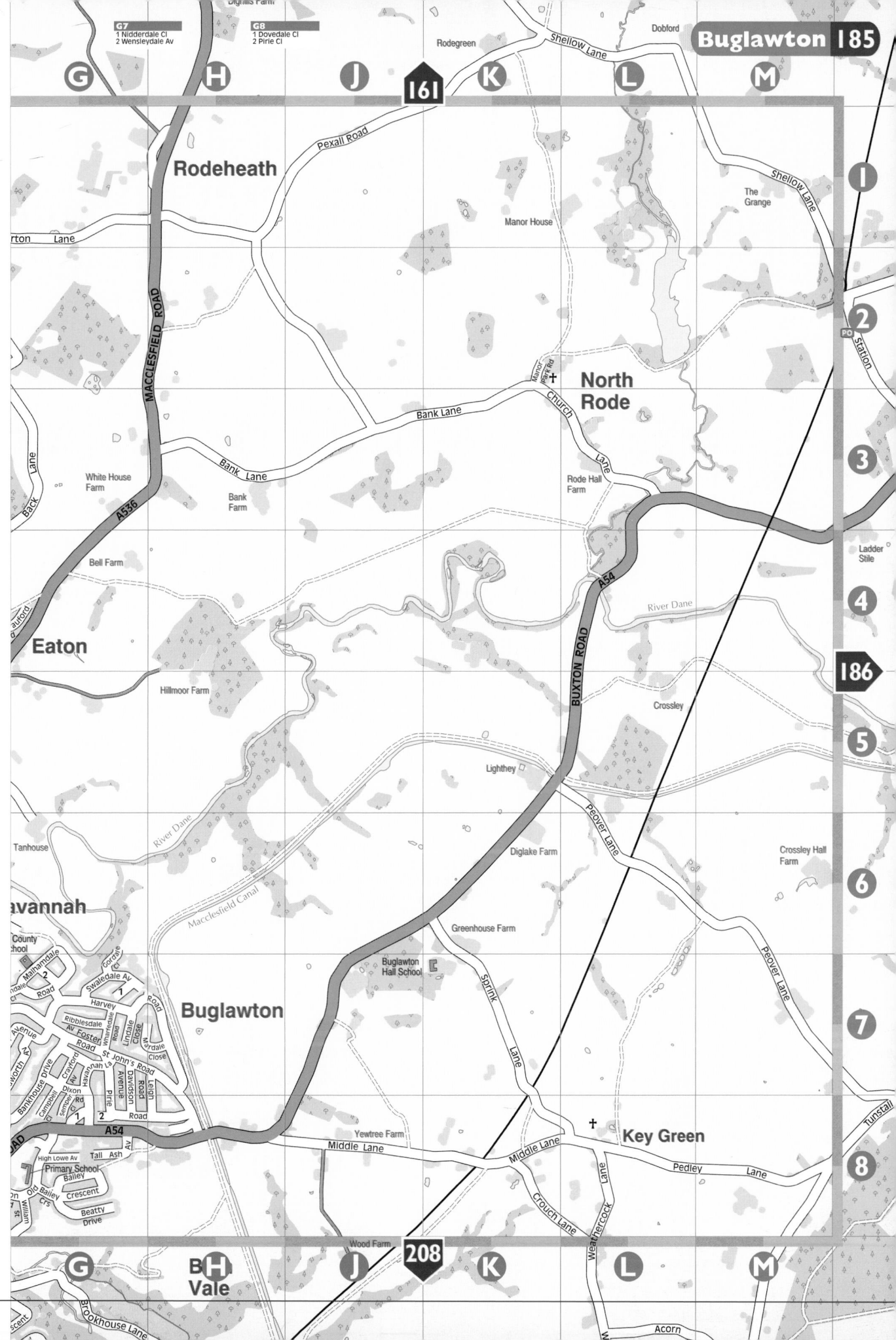

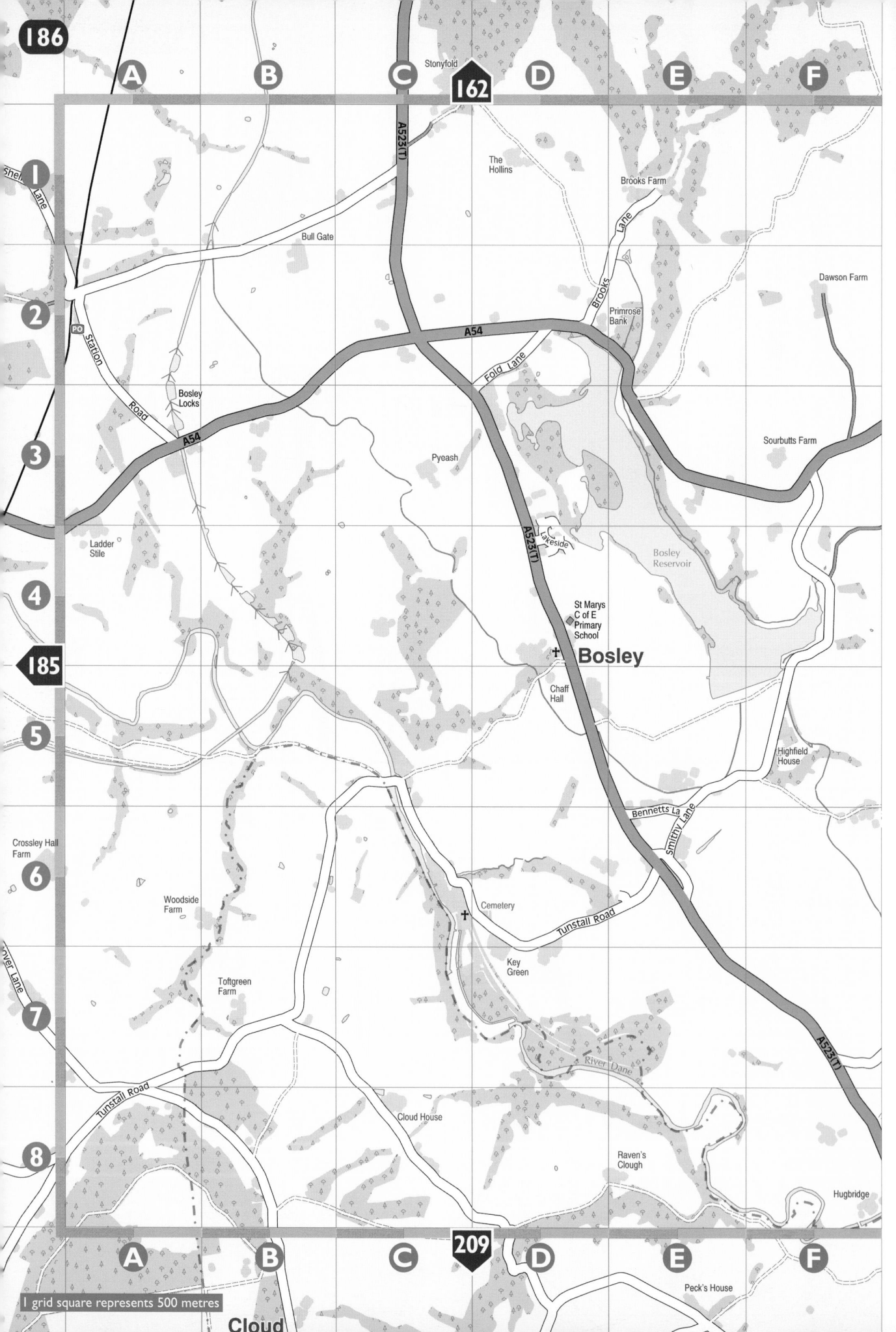

162

185

209

A   B   C   D   E   F

I 2 3 4 5 6 7 8

Stonyfold

The Hollins

Brooks Farm

Dawson Farm

Brooks Lane

Primrose Bank

A54

Fold Lane

Sourbutts Farm

Bull Gate

Shel... Lane

PO

Station Road

Bosley Locks

A54

Pyeash

Bosley Reservoir

Lakeside

A523(T)

St Marys C of E Primary School

Bosley

Chaff Hall

Ladder Stile

Highfield House

Crossley Hall Farm

Bennetts La

Smithy Lane

Woodside Farm

Cemetery

Tunstall Road

Key Green

...ver Lane

Toftgreen Farm

River Dane

A523(T)

Tunstall Road

Cloud House

Raven's Clough

Hugbridge

Peck's House

Cloud

I grid square represents 500 metres

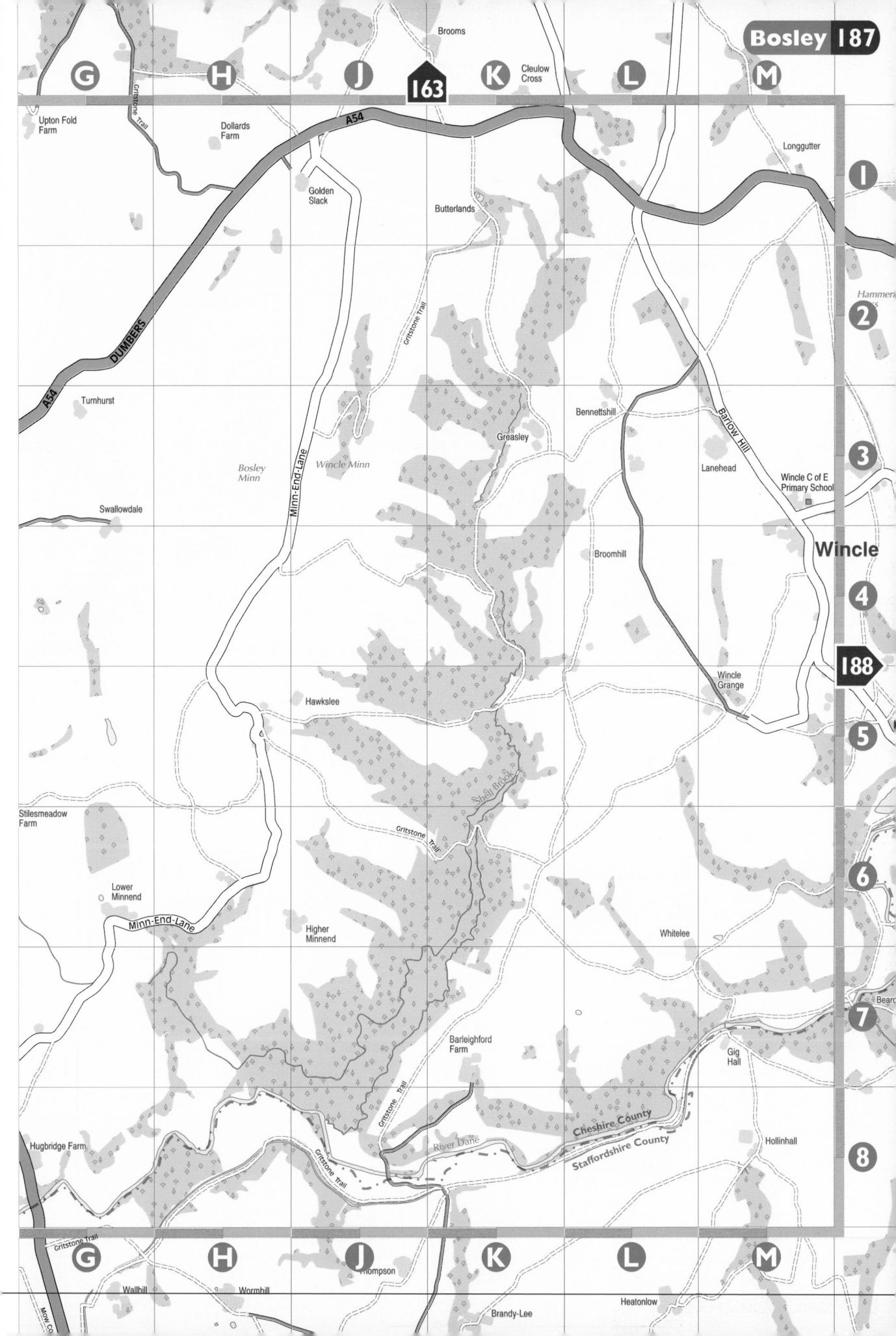

Brooms

163
Cleulow
Cross

Upton Fold
Farm

Gritstone Trail

Dollards
Farm

A54

Longgutter

1

Golden
Slack

Butterlands

Hammeri
s

2

DUMBERS

A54

Turnhurst

Gritstone Trail

Bennettshill

Barlow Hill

Greasley

Lanehead

Wincle C of E
Primary School

3

Bosley
Minn

Wincle Minn

Minn-End-Lane

Swallowdale

Broomhill

Wincle

4

188

Hawkslee

Wincle
Grange

5

Shell Brook

Stilesmeadow
Farm

Gritstone Trail

6

Lower
Minnend

Minn-End-Lane

Higher
Minnend

Whitelee

Beard

7

Barleighford
Farm

Gig
Hall

Hugbridge Farm

Gritstone Trail

Cheshire County

Staffordshire County

Hollinhall

8

River Dane

Thompson

Gritstone Trail

Wallhill

Wormhill

Brandy-Lee

Heatonlow

Mow Co

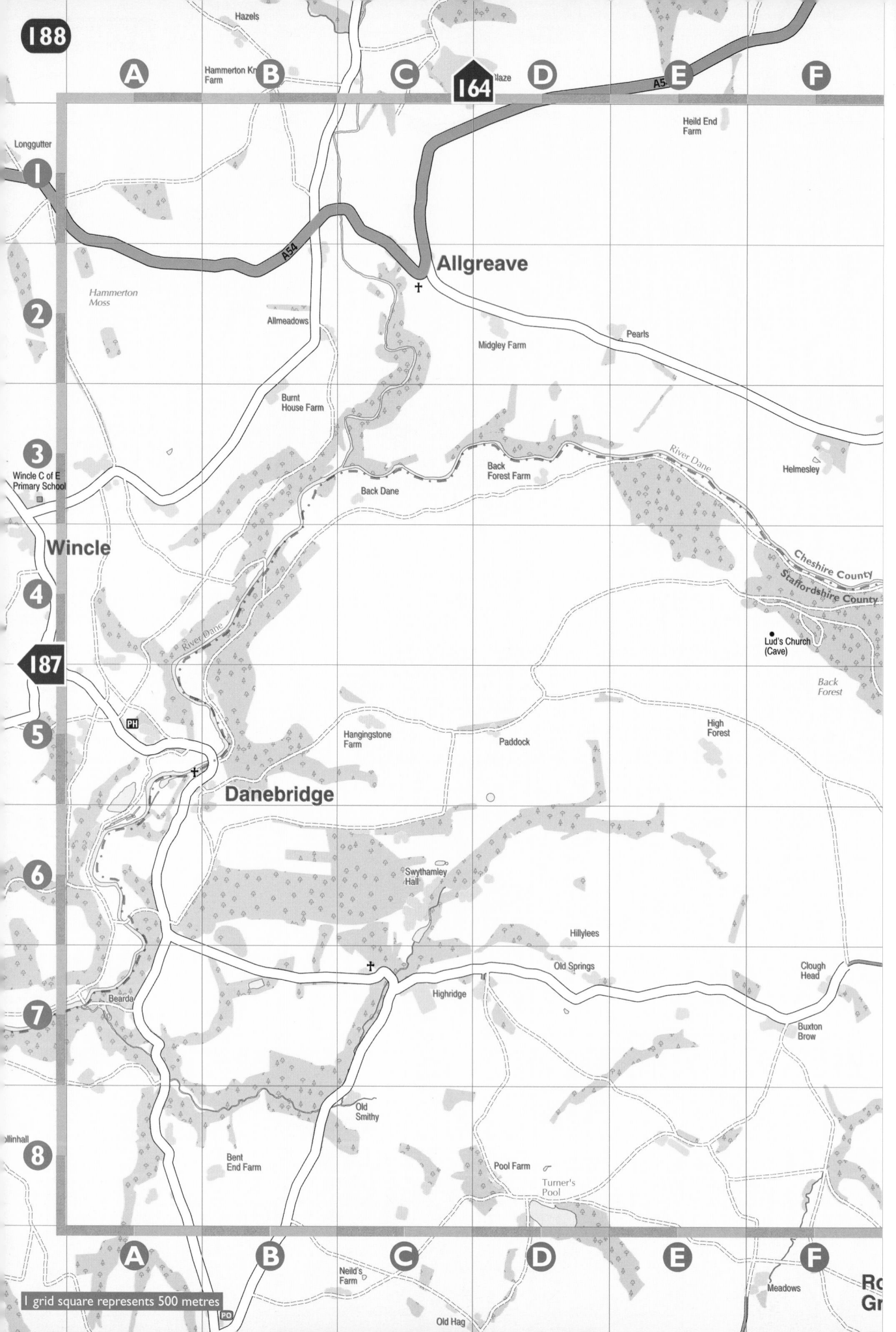

A   B   C   D   E   F

164

A5

Hazels

Hammerton Kn
Farm

Blaze

Heild End
Farm

Longgutter

1

A54

Allgreave

✝

Hammerton
Moss

2

Pearls

Allmeadows

Midgley Farm

Burnt
House Farm

River Dane

3

Wincle C of E
Primary School

Back
Forest Farm

Helmesley

Back Dane

Wincle

Cheshire County

Staffordshire County

4

River Dane

187

Lud's Church
(Cave)

Back
Forest

5

PH

Hangingstone
Farm

Paddock

High
Forest

✝

Danebridge

6

Swythamley
Hall

Hillylees

✝

Old Springs

Clough
Head

7

Bearda

Highridge

Buxton
Brow

ollinhall

8

Old
Smithy

Pool Farm

Turner's
Pool

Bent
End Farm

A   B   C   D   E   F

Neild's
Farm

Old Hag

Meadows

Ro
Gr

PO

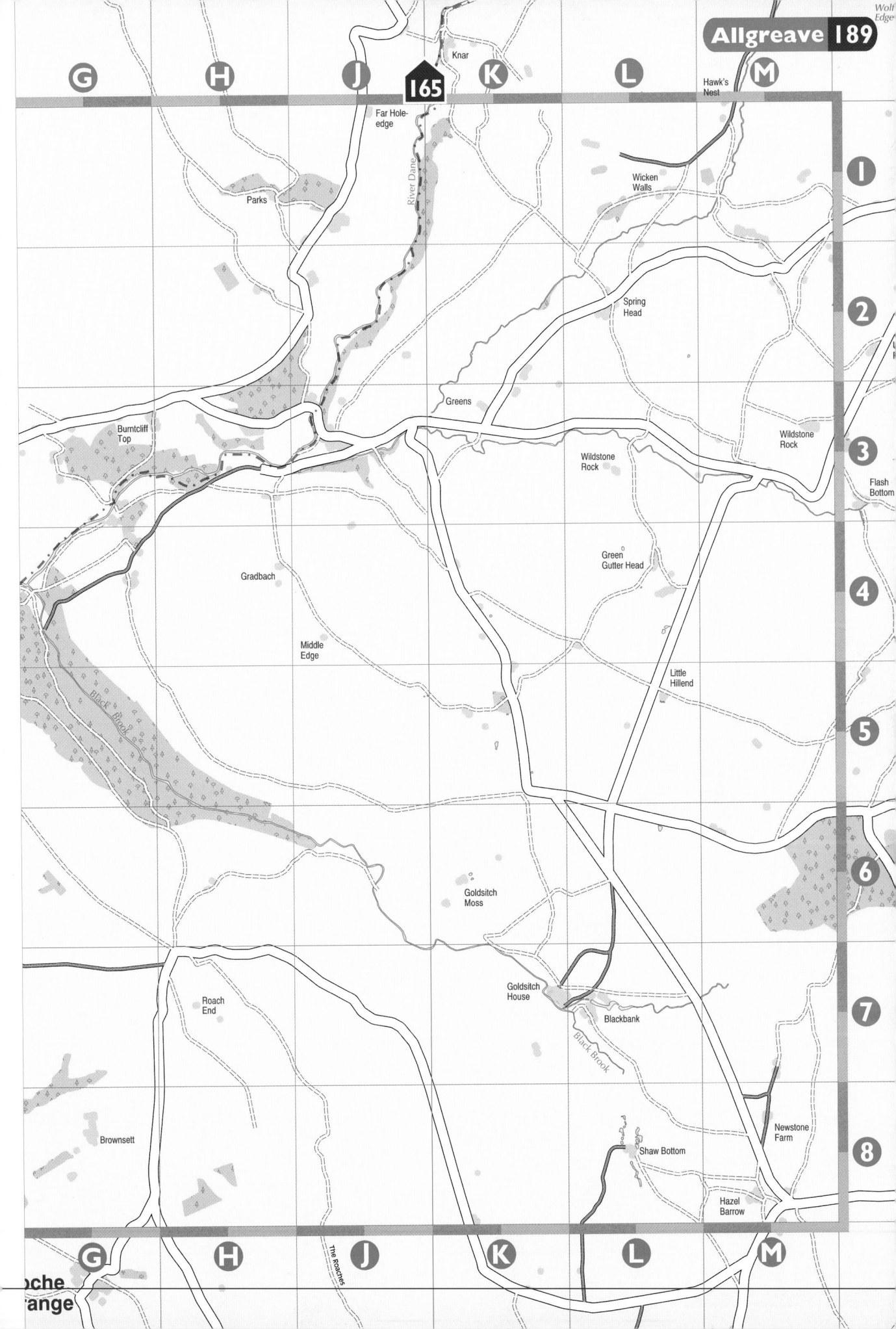

Wolf
Edge

G   H   J   K   L   M

165

Knar

Far Hole-
edge

Hawk's
Nest

1

River Dane

Wicken
Walls

Parks

Spring
Head

2

Greens

Burntcliff
Top

Wildstone
Rock

Wildstone
Rock

3

Flash
Bottom

Gradbach

Green
Gutter Head

4

Middle
Edge

Little
Hillend

Black Brook

5

6

Goldsitch
Moss

Roach
End

Goldsitch
House

7

Blackbank

Black Brook

Brownsett

Newstone
Farm

8

Shaw Bottom

Hazel
Barrow

The Roaches

oche
range

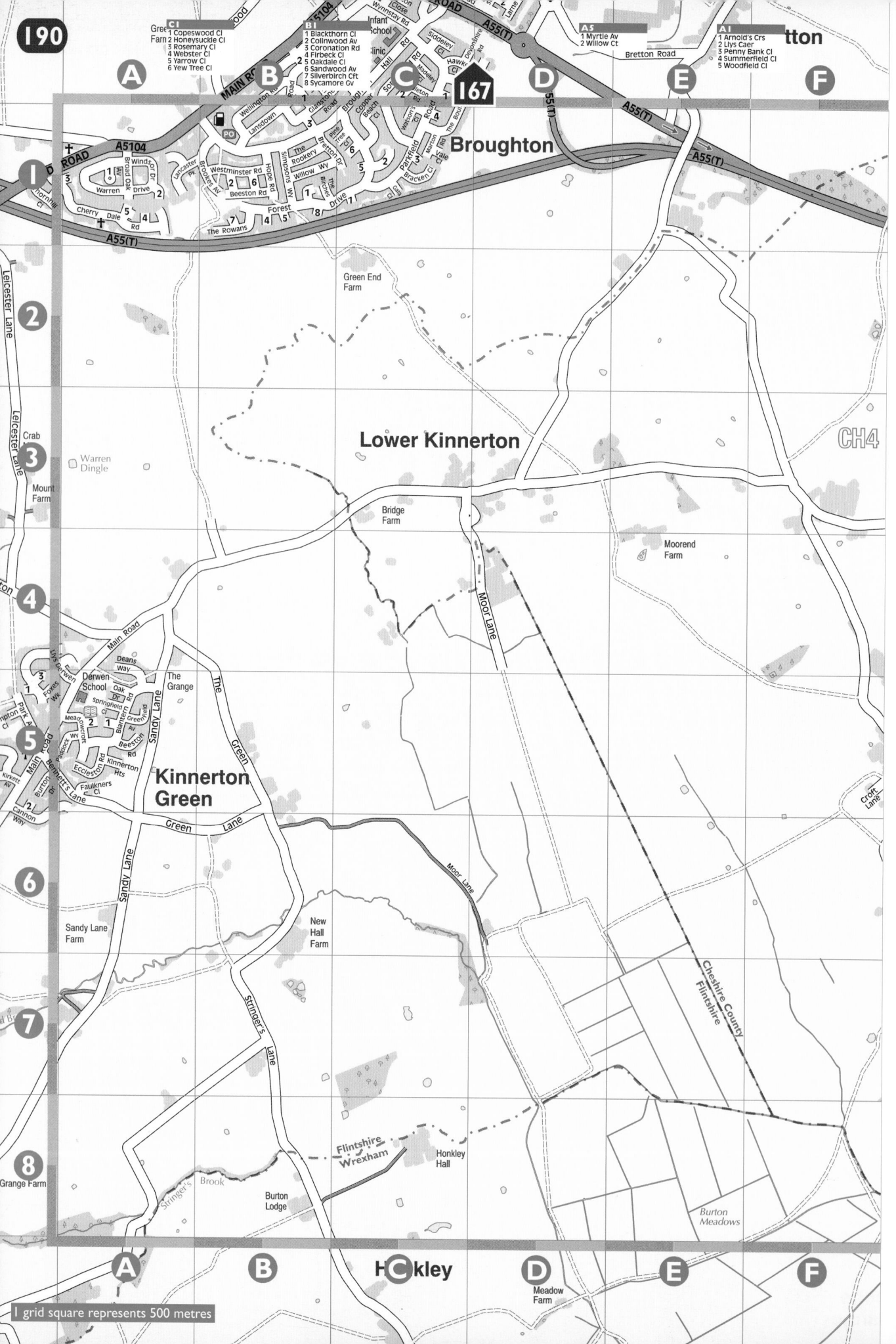

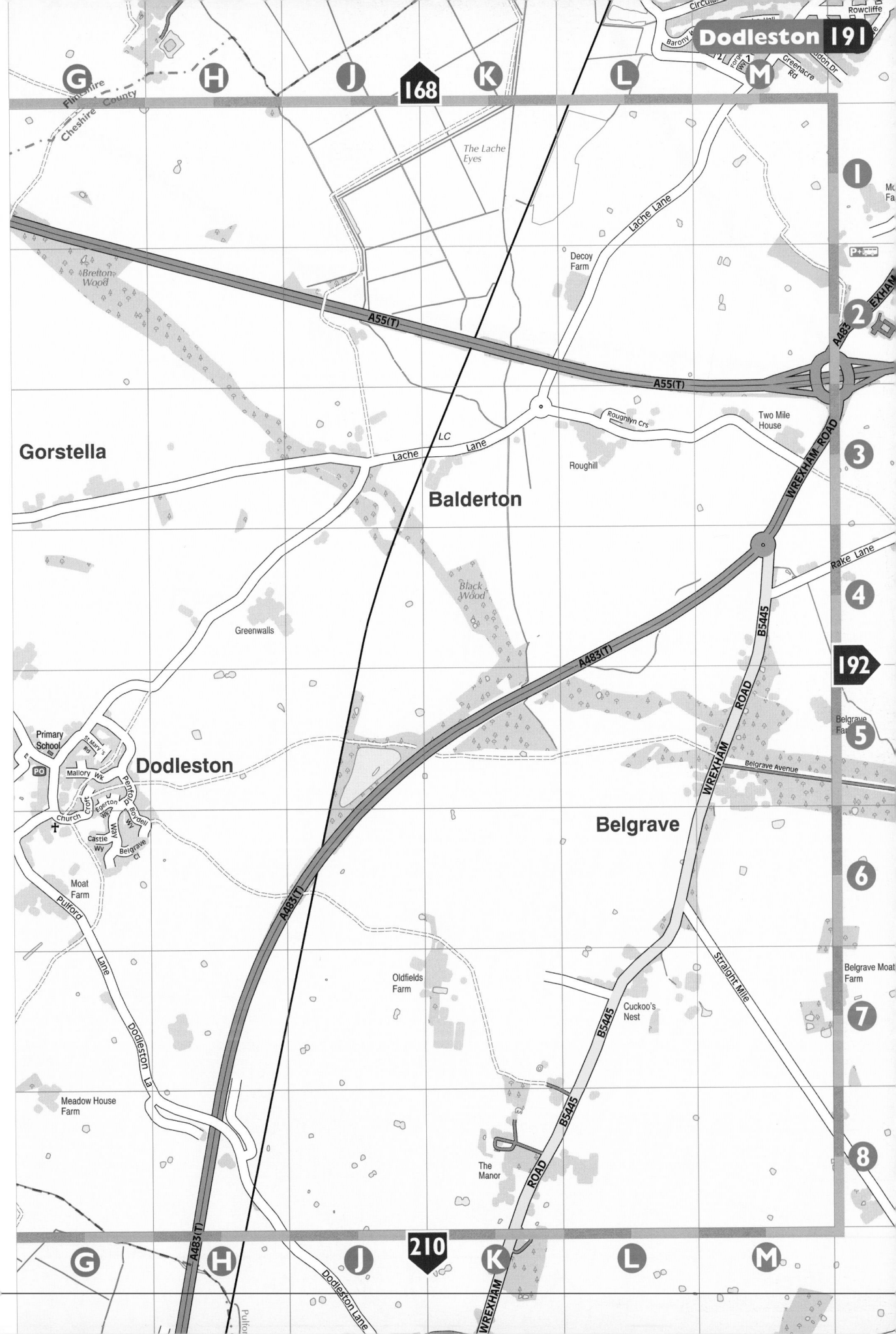

G   H   J   168   K   L   M

The Lache Eyes

Lache Lane

Decoy Farm

A55(T)

A55(T)

Gorstella

LC   Lache   Lane

Roughlyn Crs

Two Mile House

Roughill

Balderton

WREXHAM ROAD

Black Wood

Greenwalls

Rake Lane

B5A45

192

Belgrave Far

Primary School

St. Mary's Rd

Mallory Wk

PO

Dodleston

Pentre Brodell

Egerton Wy

Croft

Church

Castle Wy   Belgrave Cl

Way

Moat Farm

Pulford

A483(T)

Belgrave Avenue

WREXHAM ROAD

Belgrave

Straight Mile

Belgrave Moat Farm

Dodleston La

Oldfields Farm

B5A45

Cuckoo's Nest

Meadow House Farm

B5A45 ROAD

The Manor

WREXHAM ROAD

G   H   A483(T)   J   210   K   L   M

Dodleston Lane

Pulfor

I

P+

2   EXHAM

A483

3

4

5

6

7

8

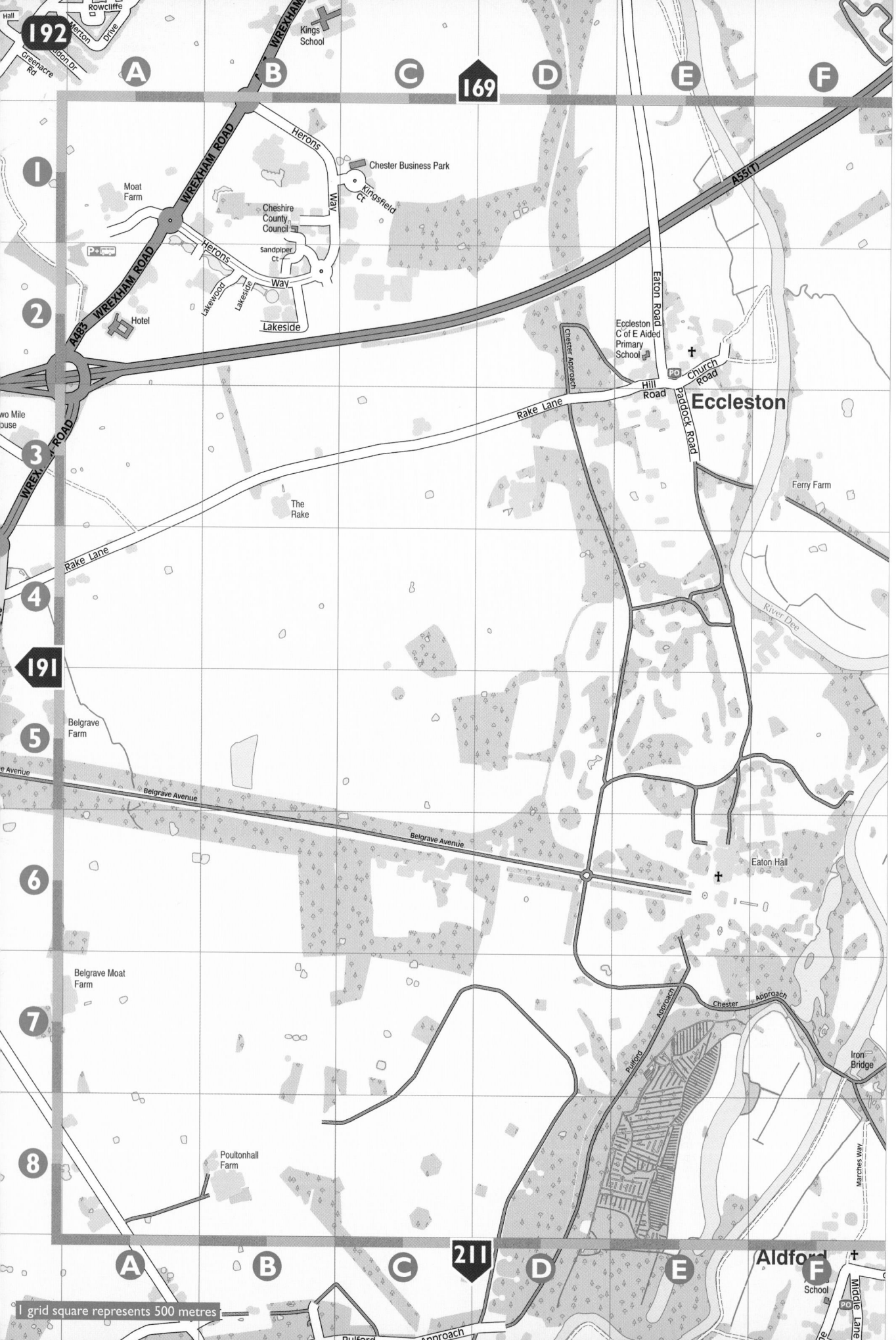

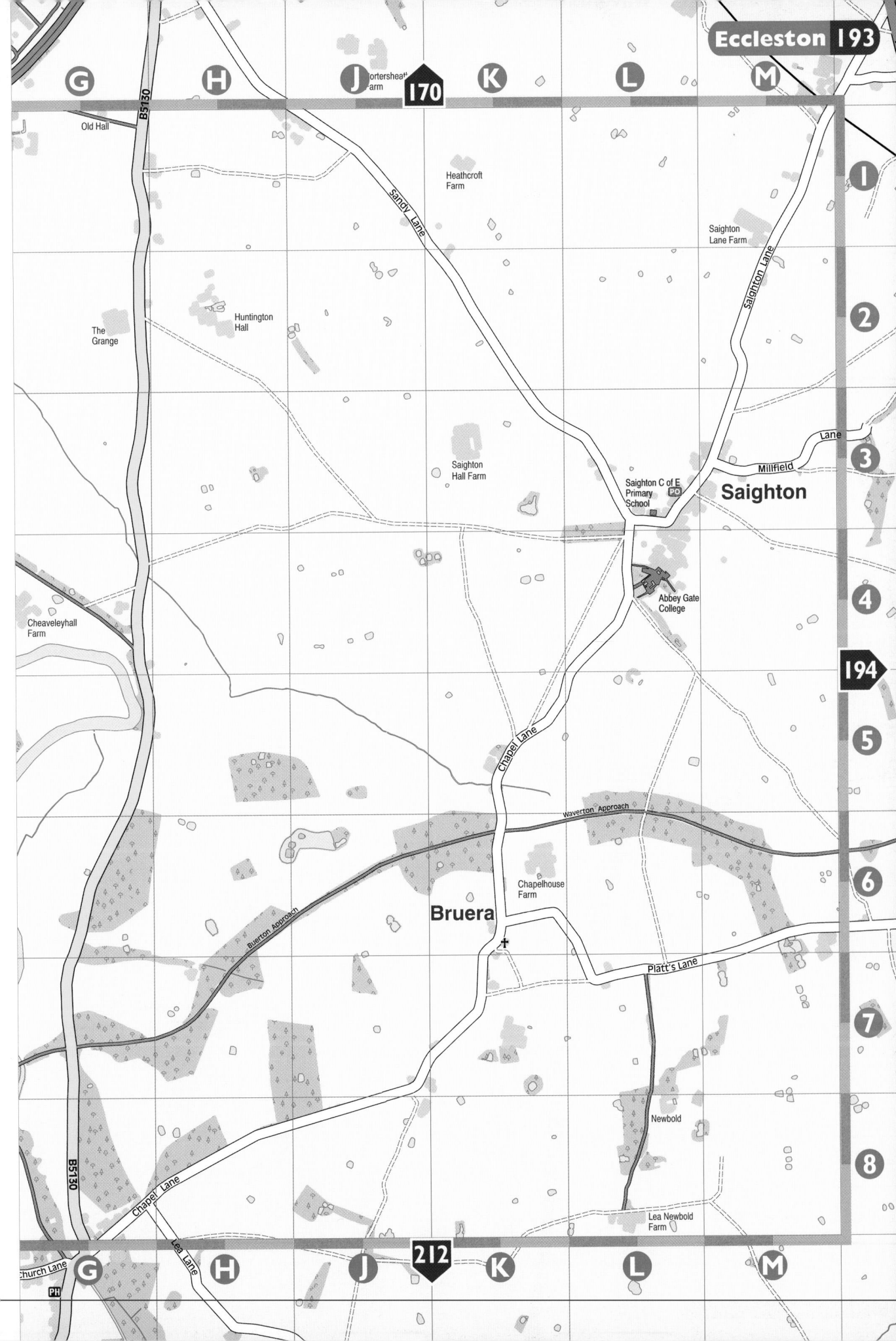

G
H
J   ortershea   170
Farm
K
L
M

Old Hall   B5130

Sandy Lane

Heathcroft
Farm

I

Saighton
Lane Farm

2

The
Grange

Huntington
Hall

Saighton Lane

3
Lane
Millfield   Saighton

Saighton
Hall Farm

Saighton C of E
Primary
School   PO

4

Cheaveleyhall
Farm

Abbey Gate
College

194

5

Chapel Lane

Waverton Approach

6

Chapelhouse
Farm

Bruera

Buerton Approach

Platt's Lane

7

B5130

Newbold

8

Chapel Lane

Lea Lane

Lea Newbold
Farm

Church Lane   G   H   J   212   K   L   M

PH

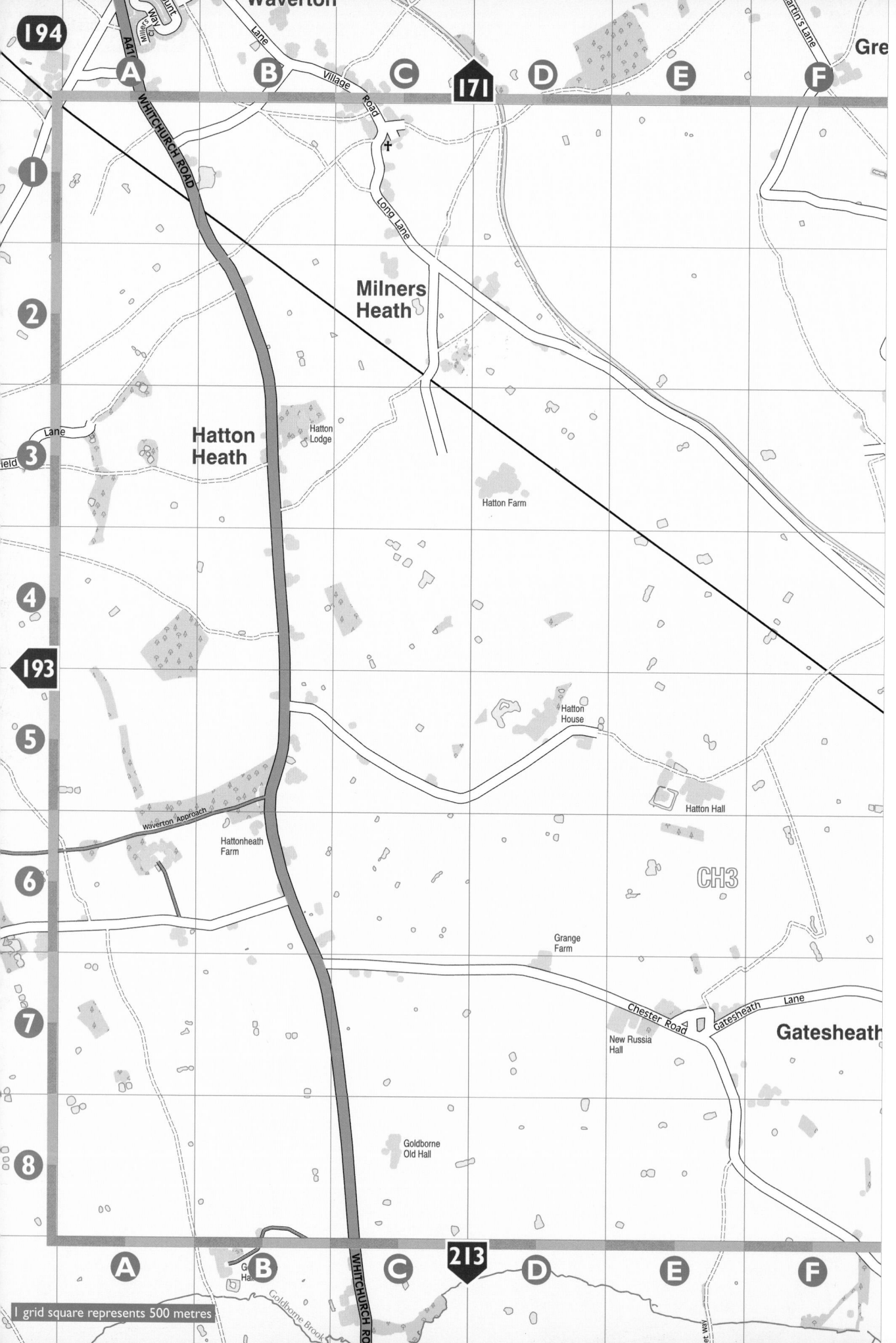

A   B   C   171   D   E   F

Waverton

Gre

Martin's Lane

Village Road

Long Lane

Milners
Heath

1

2

193

3

4

5

6

7

8

Hatton
Heath

Hatton
Lodge

Hatton Farm

Hatton
House

Hatton Hall

CH3

Waverton Approach

Hattonheath
Farm

Grange
Farm

Chester Road

Gatesheath   Lane

Gatesheath

New Russia
Hall

Goldborne
Old Hall

A   B   C   213   D   E   F

WHITCHURCH ROAD

A41

Lane

ield

Goldborne Brook

1 grid square represents 500 metres

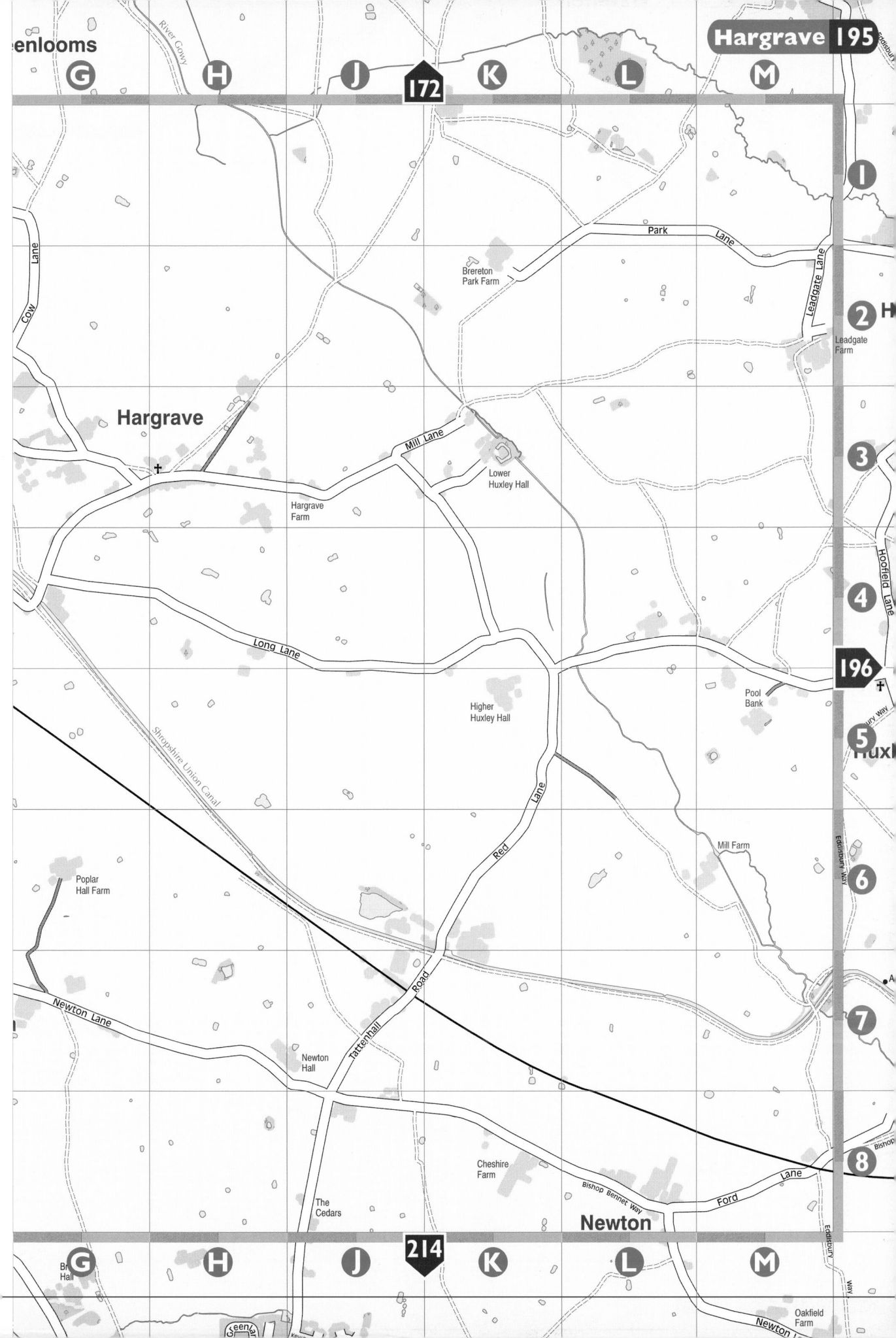

enlooms

G H J 172 K L M

I

Park Lane

Brereton
Park Farm

Leadgate Lane

2 H

Leadgate
Farm

Cow Lane

River Gowy

Hargrave

✝

Mill Lane

Lower
Huxley Hall

3

Hargrave
Farm

Hoofield Lane

4

Long Lane

196

✝

Higher
Huxley Hall

Pool
Bank

5 Hux

bury Way

Shropshire Union Canal

Red Lane

Mill Farm

Eddisbury Way

6

Poplar
Hall Farm

Road

Tattenhall

Newton Lane

7

• A

Newton
Hall

Cheshire
Farm

Bishop Bennet Way

Ford Lane

Bishop

8

The
Cedars

Newton

Oakfield
Farm

Eddisbury Way

G H J 214 K L M

Br
Hall

Green

Newton

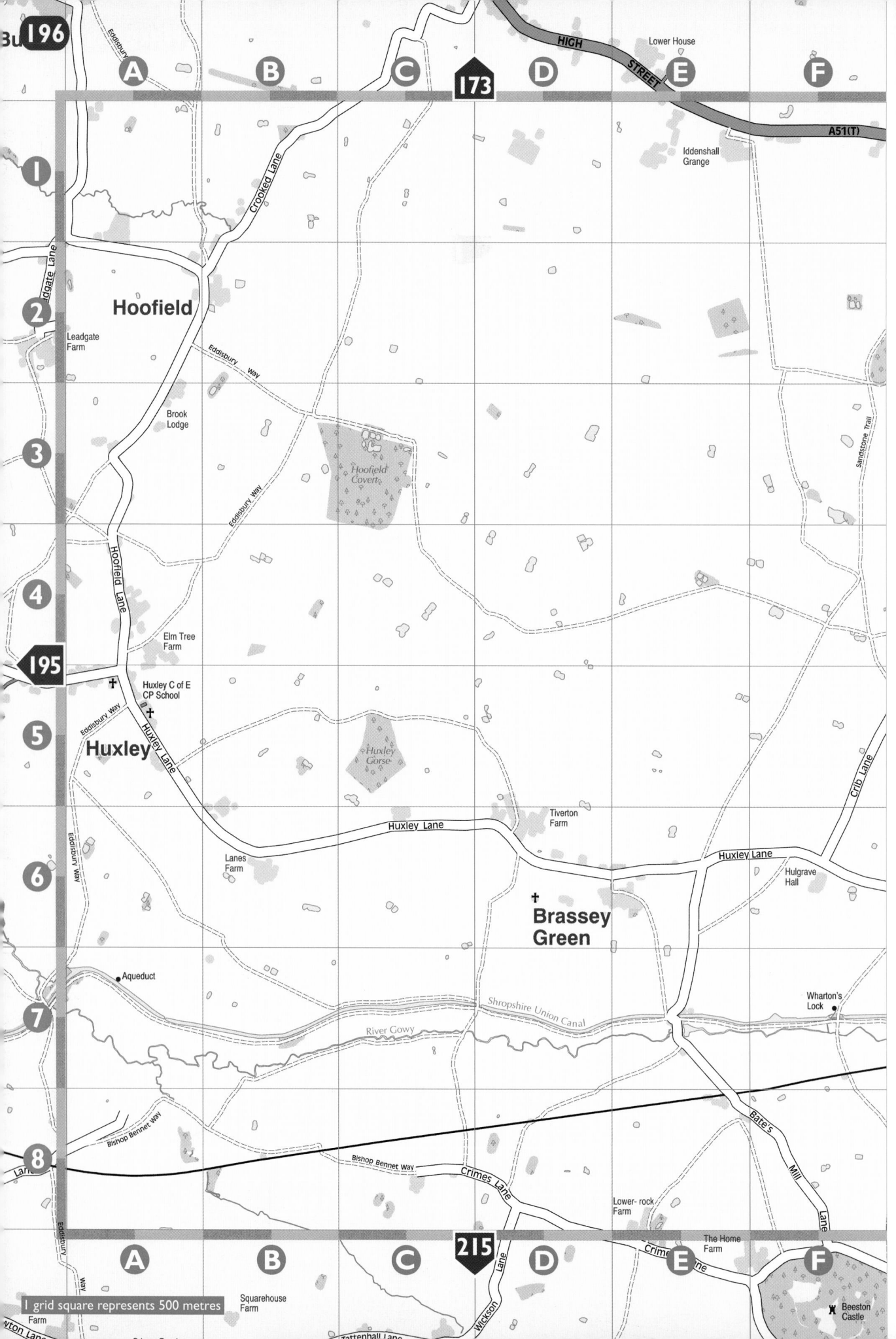

A **B** **C** 173 **D** **E** **F**

HIGH STREET
A51(T)

1

Lower House

Iddenshall Grange

2
Hoofield

Leadgate Farm

Eddisbury Way

Sandstone Trail

Brook Lodge

3

Eddisbury Way

Hoofield Covert

Hoofield Lane

4

Elm Tree Farm

195

Huxley C of E CP School

Eddisbury Way

5
Huxley

Huxley Lane

Huxley Gorse

Crib Lane

Huxley Lane

Tiverton Farm

Huxley Lane

Hulgrave Hall

6

Lanes Farm

Brassey Green

Aqueduct

Shropshire Union Canal

Wharton's Lock

7

River Gowy

Bishop Bennet Way

Bates Mill Lane

8

Lane

Bishop Bennet Way

Crimes Lane

Lower-rock Farm

Crimes Lane

The Home Farm

A **B** **C** 215 **D** **E** **F**

Eddisbury Way

Squarehouse Farm

Wickson Lane

Tattenhall Lane

Beeston Castle

I grid square represents 500 metres

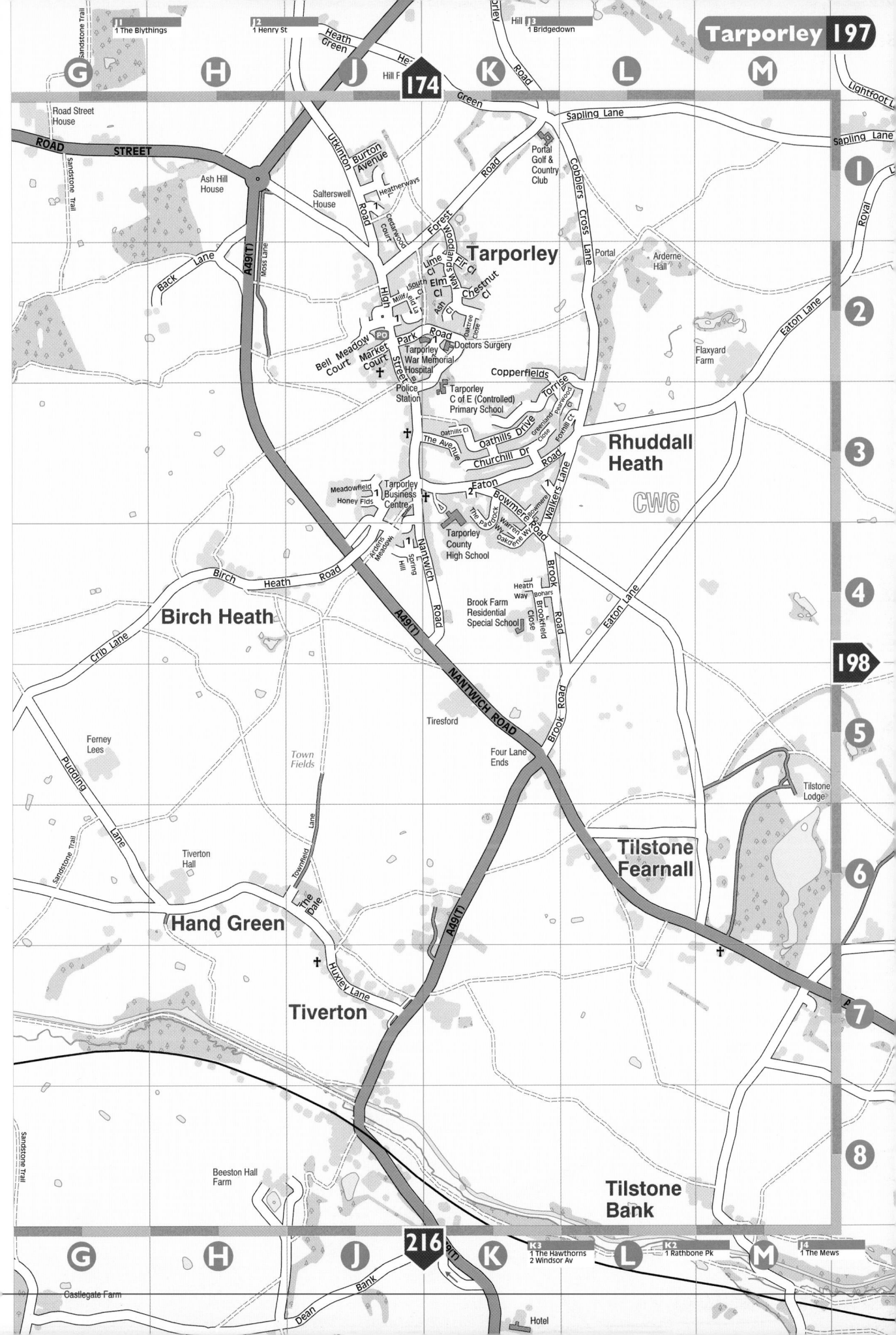

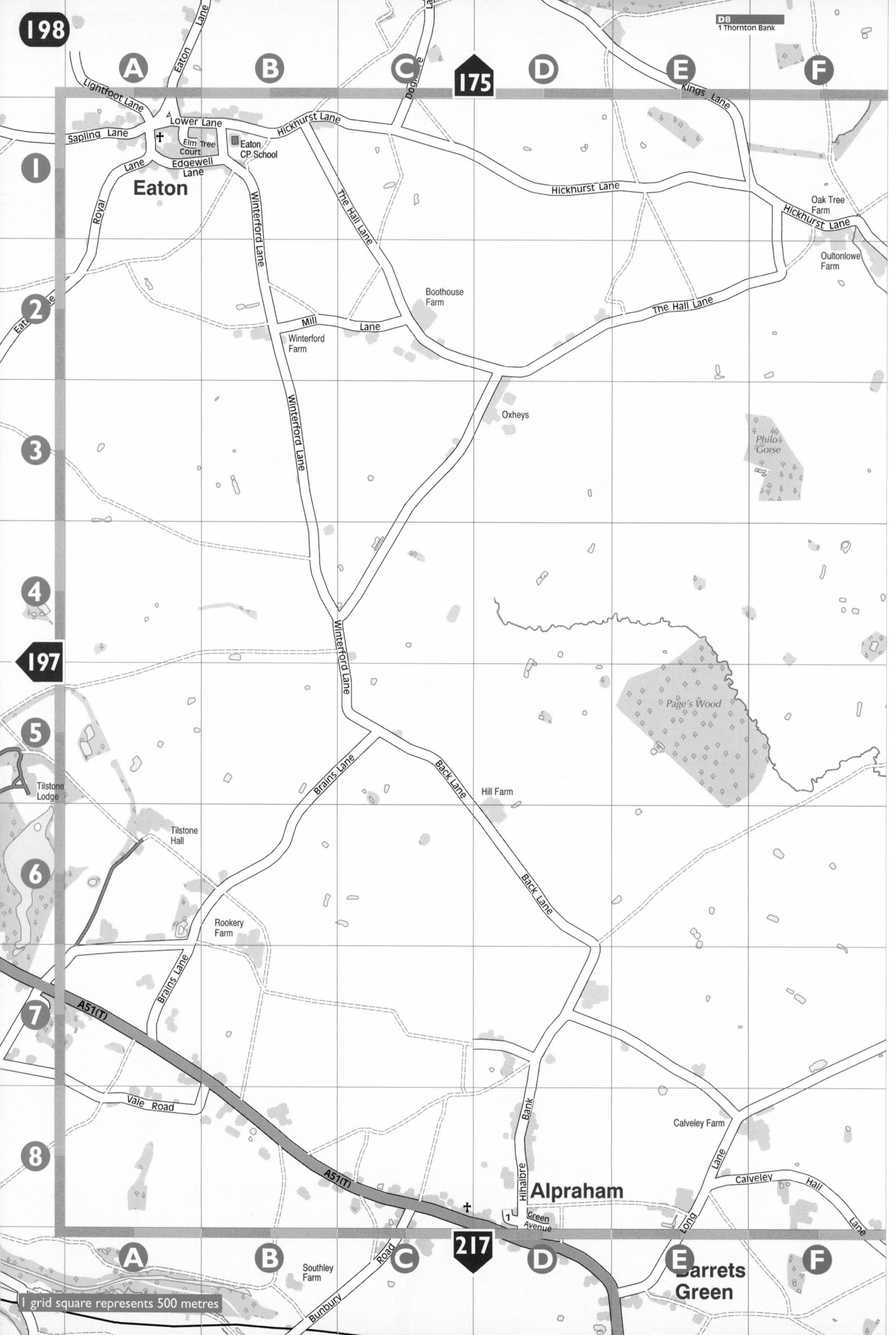

D8
1 Thornton Bank

175

197

217

A B C D E F

1

2

3

4

5

6

7

8

Lightfoot Lane

Sapling Lane

Eaton Lane

Lower Lane

Elm Tree Court

Edgewell Lane

Eaton

Royal Lane

Winterford Lane

Eaton CP School

Hickhurst Lane

The Hall Lane

Dogla... Lane

Kings Lane

Oak Tree Farm

Hickhurst Lane

Hickhurst Lane

Oultonlowe Farm

Boothouse Farm

Mill Lane

Winterford Farm

The Hall Lane

Oxheys

Philo's Gorse

Winterford Lane

Page's Wood

Brains Lane

Back Lane

Hill Farm

Tilstone Lodge

Tilstone Hall

Back Lane

Rookery Farm

Brains Lane

A51(T)

Vale Road

A51(T)

Bunbury Road

Bank

Hihalbre

Alpraham

Green Avenue

Calveley Farm

Long Lane

Calveley Hall Lane

Barrets Green

Southley Farm

1 grid square represents 500 metres

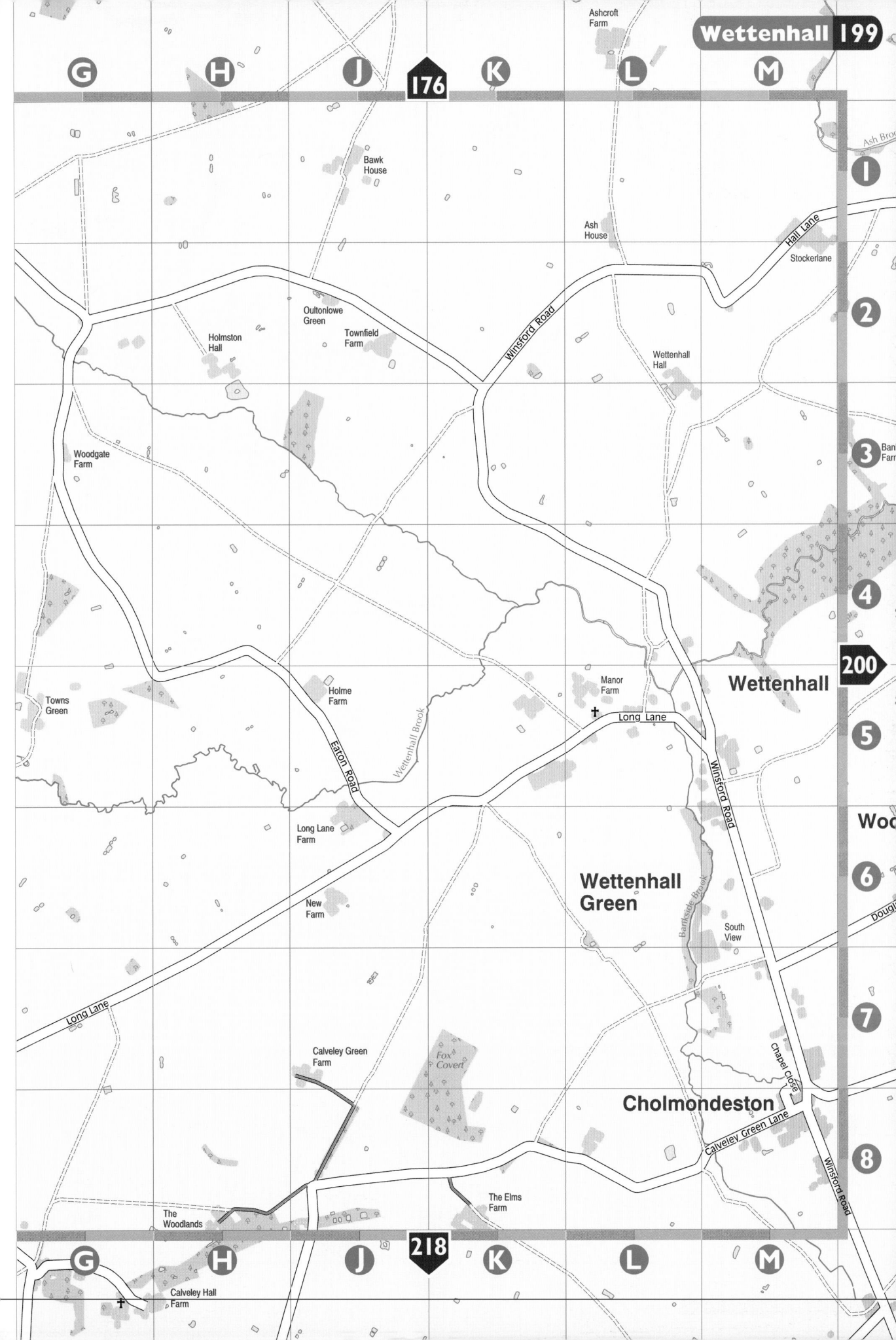

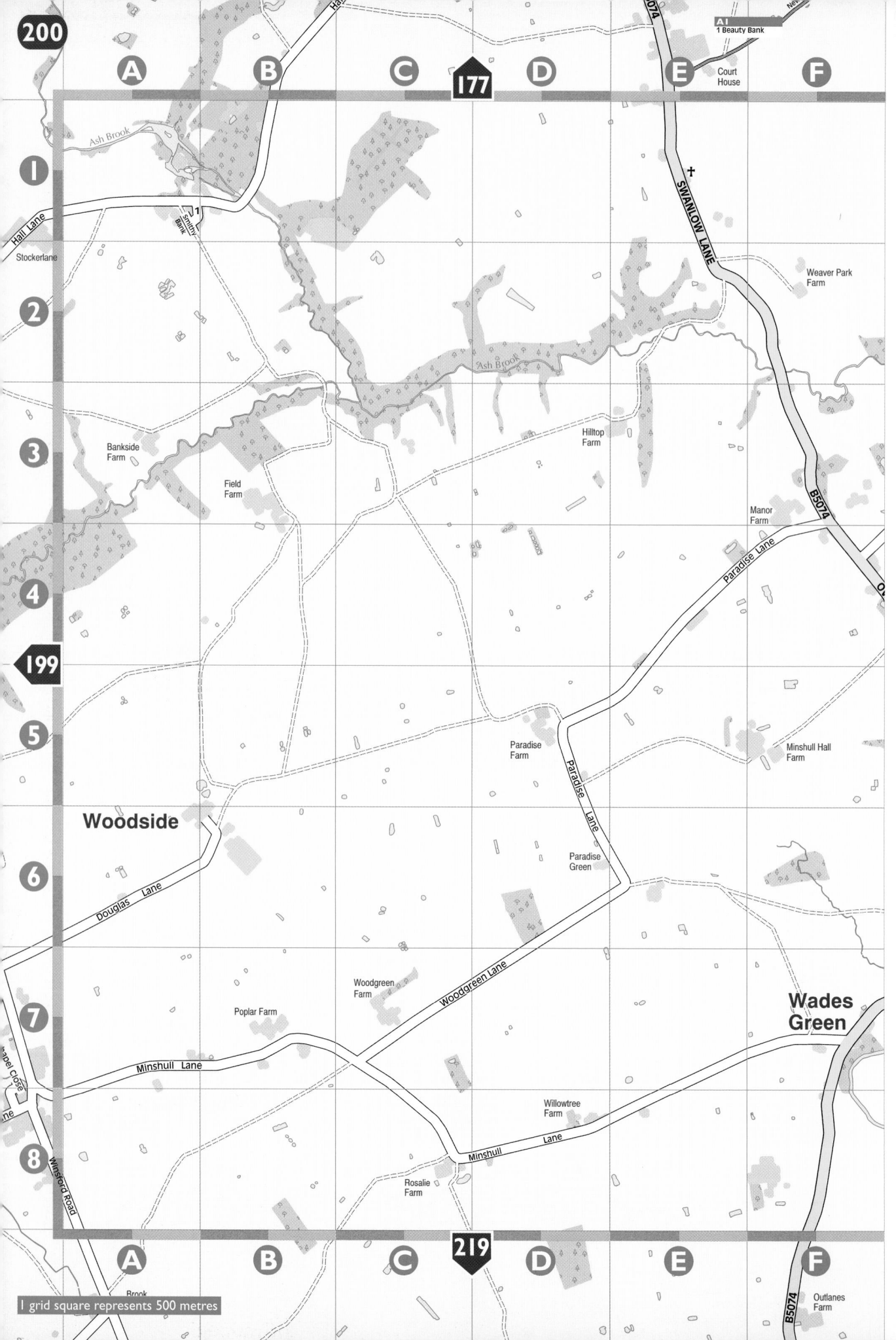

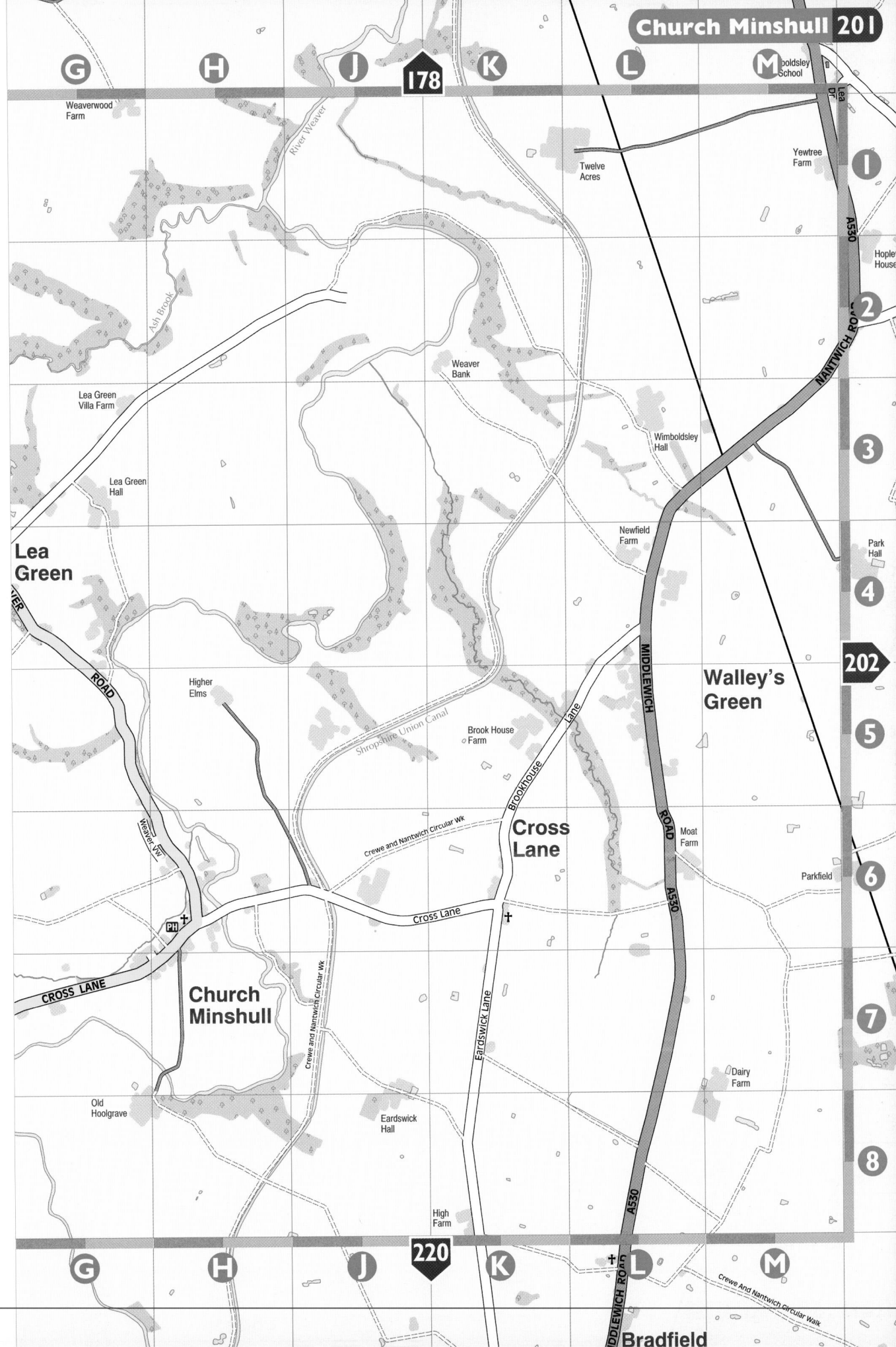

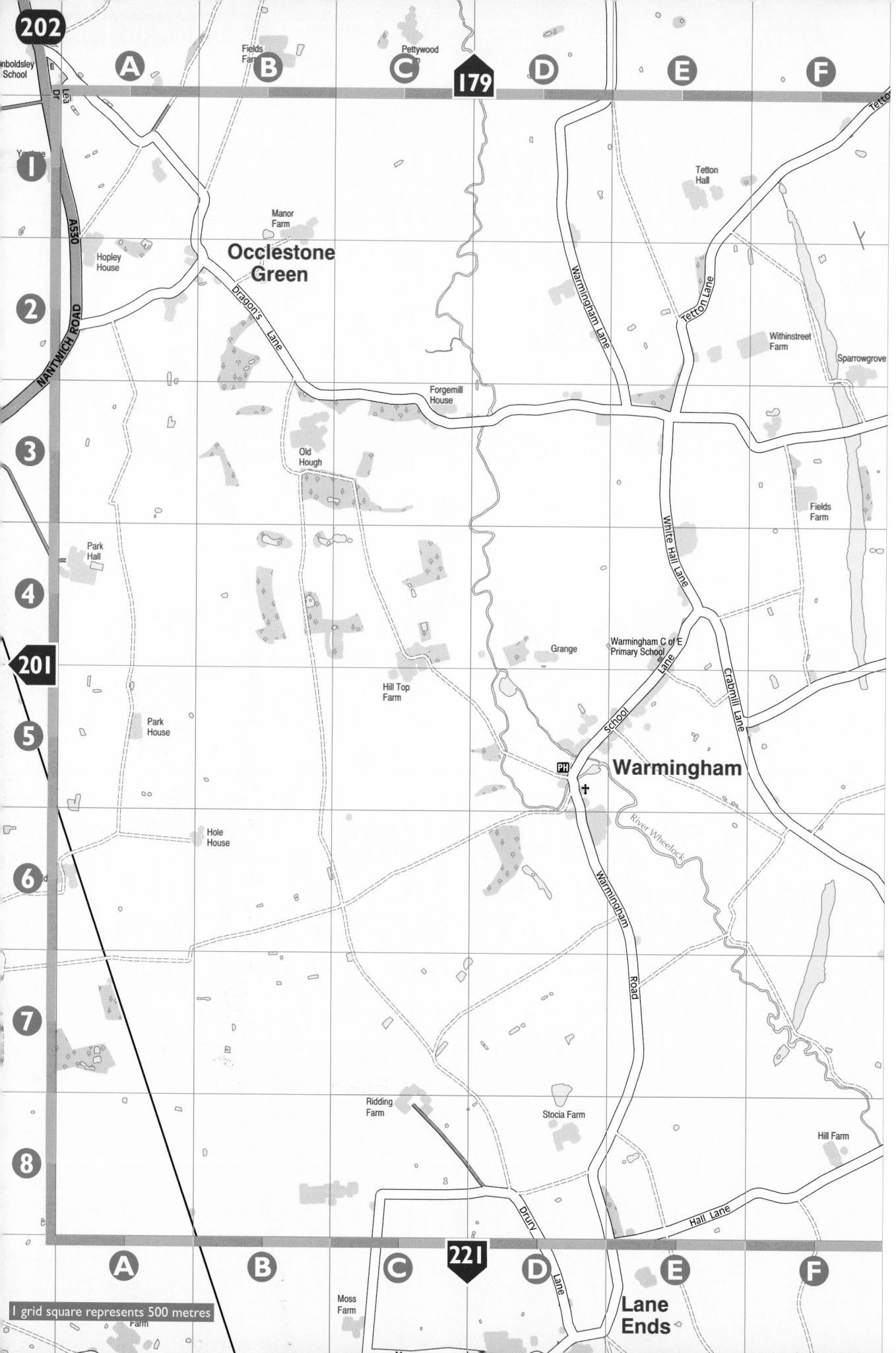

202

A B C D E F

179

I

Tetton
Hall

Tetton Lane

nboldsley
School

Lea Dr

Fields
Farm

Pettywood

Warmingham Lane

Withinstreet
Farm

Sparrowgrove

2

NANTWICH ROAD

A530

Occlestone
Green

Manor
Farm

Hopley
House

Dragons Lane

Forgemill
House

Tetton Lane

3

Old
Hough

Fields
Farm

White Hall Lane

4

Park
Hall

Warmingham C of E
Primary School

Grange

School Lane

Crabmill Lane

201

5

Park
House

Hill Top
Farm

PH

Warmingham

River Wheelock

6

Hole
House

Warmingham Road

7

Ridding
Farm

Stocia Farm

Hill Farm

8

Hall Lane

Drury Lane

A B C 221 D E F

Moss
Farm

Lane
Ends

1 grid square represents 500 metres

Farm

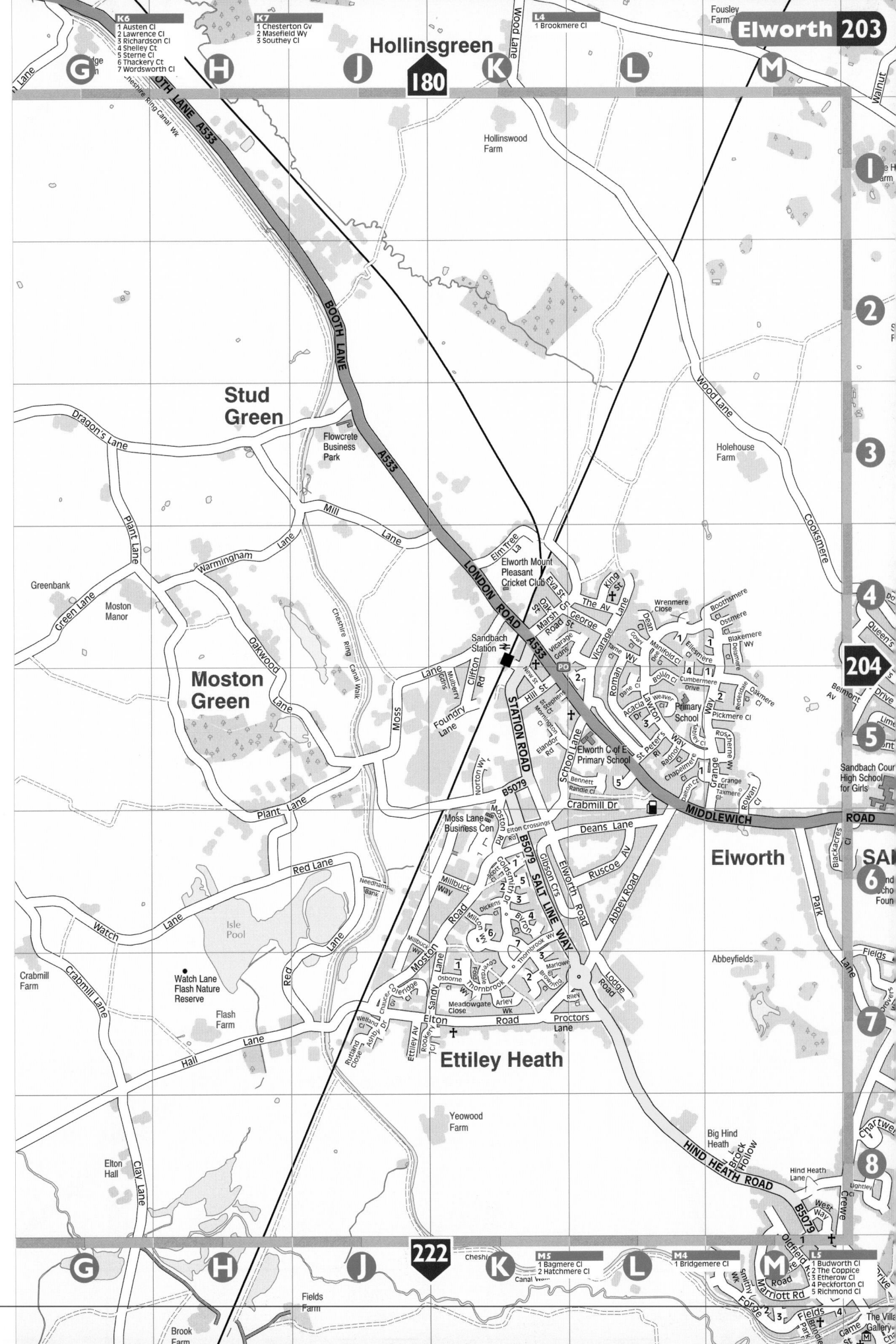

Hollinsgreen

180

G **H** **J** **K** **L** **M**

Fousley Farm

Walnut

I

2

3

BOOTH LANE A533

Cheshire Ring Canal Wk

Hollinswood Farm

Wood Lane

Stud Green

A533

Flowcrete Business Park

Mill Lane

Dragon's Lane

Plant Lane

Warmingham Lane

Greenbank

Green Lane

Moston Manor

Oakwood Lane

Cheshire Ring Canal Walk

Moston Green

Moss Lane

Foundry Lane

Clifton Rd

Mulberry Gdns

Elm Tree La

Elworth Mount Pleasant Cricket Club

Sandbach Station

LONDON ROAD A533

Eva St

Clk St

Marsh St

Vicarage Gdns

George St

King St

The Av

Vicarage Lane

Dean St

Roman

Wrenmere Close

Cumbermere Drive

Primary School

Boothmere Ct

Ossmere

Blakemere Wy

Delamere

Oakmere

Pickmere Cl

Roseherne Wy

Wood Lane

Cooksmere

Holehouse Farm

4

204

Queen's Drive

Belmont Av

Lime

5

Sandbach Court High School for Girls

New St

Hill St

St Woolington Ct

Elandor Rd

Norton Wy

Acacia Dr

Lawton

Weaver

Elworth C of E Primary School

Bennett

Randle Ct

St Peter's Rd

Redror

Chapelmere

Patton Ct

Grange

Taxmere

Grange

Rowan

STATION ROAD

B5079

Crabmill Dr

MIDDLEWICH ROAD

Elworth

Park Lane

SAN

6

Blackacres

Abbeyfields

Fields

Plant Lane

Red Lane

Watch Lane

Needhams Bank

Isle Pool

Moss Lane Business Cen

Elton Crossings

Millbuck Way

Moston Road

B5079

SALT LINE WAY

Gibson Crs

Goldsmith's

Dickens

Byron

Deans Lane

Ruscoe Av

Elworth Road

Abbey Road

Lodge Road

7

Crabmill Farm

Crabmill Lane

Watch Lane

Red Lane

Watch Lane Flash Nature Reserve

Flash Farm

Millbuck Wy

Moston Road

Sandy Lane

Coleridge Cl

Chaucer Cl

Osborne Wy

Miller Cl

Thornbrook

Fairford

Thornbrook

Meadowgate Close

Arley Wk

Marlowe

Brook

Riley

Proctors Lane

Welland Cl

Ashby Dr

Rutland Close

Ettiley Av

Rooker

Elton Road

Ettiley Heath

Yeowood Farm

Big Hind Heath

Brook Hollow

HIND HEATH ROAD

Hind Heath Lane

Chartwe

8

Elton Hall

Clay Lane

Hall Lane

B5079

Crewe

Oldfield

West Wy

Oaktley

Marriott Rd

Forge Wk

Smithy

Fields Park

The Ville Gallery

G **H** **J** **K** **L** **M**

222

Cheshi

Canal W

Fields Farm

Brook Farm

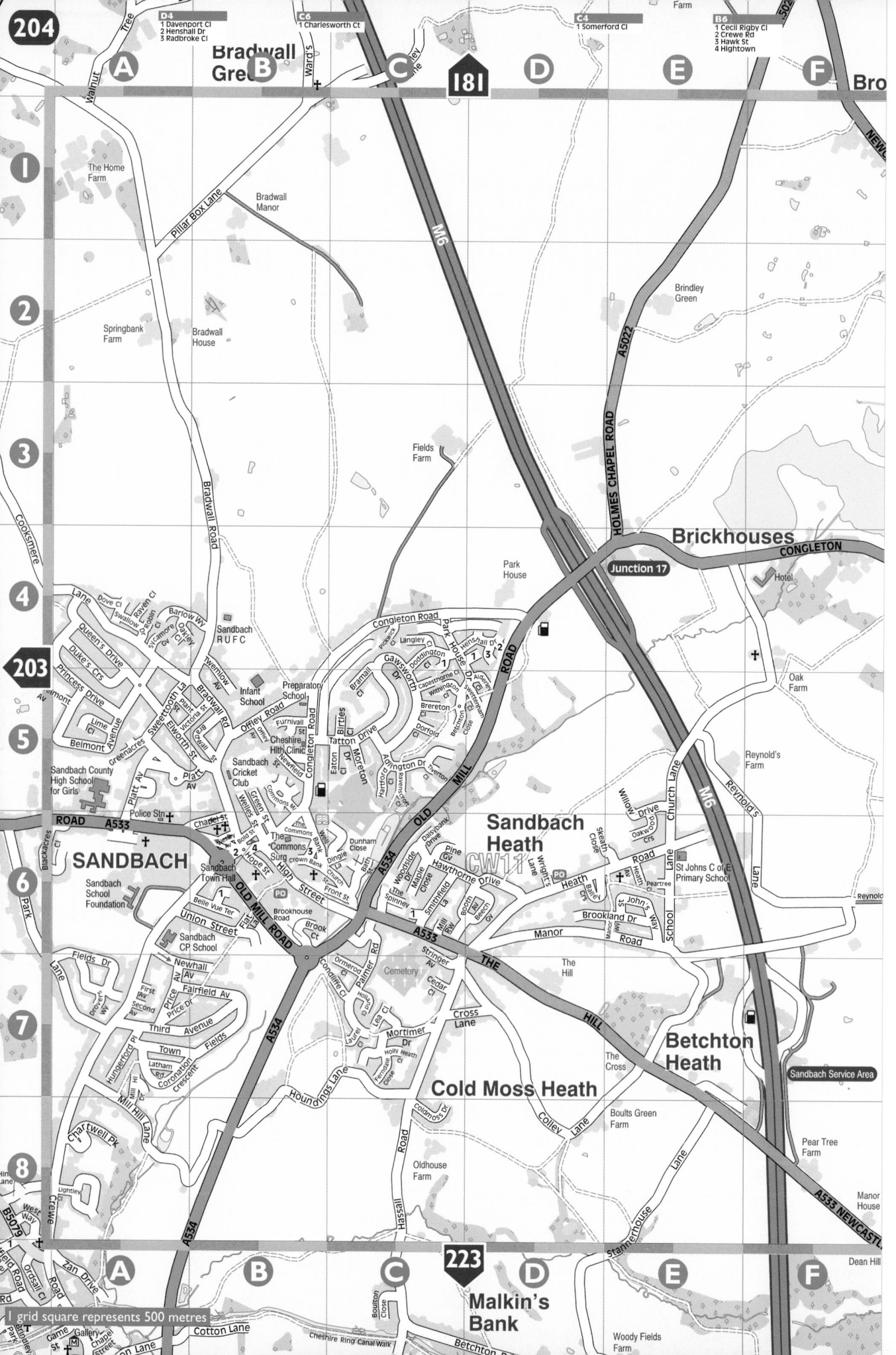

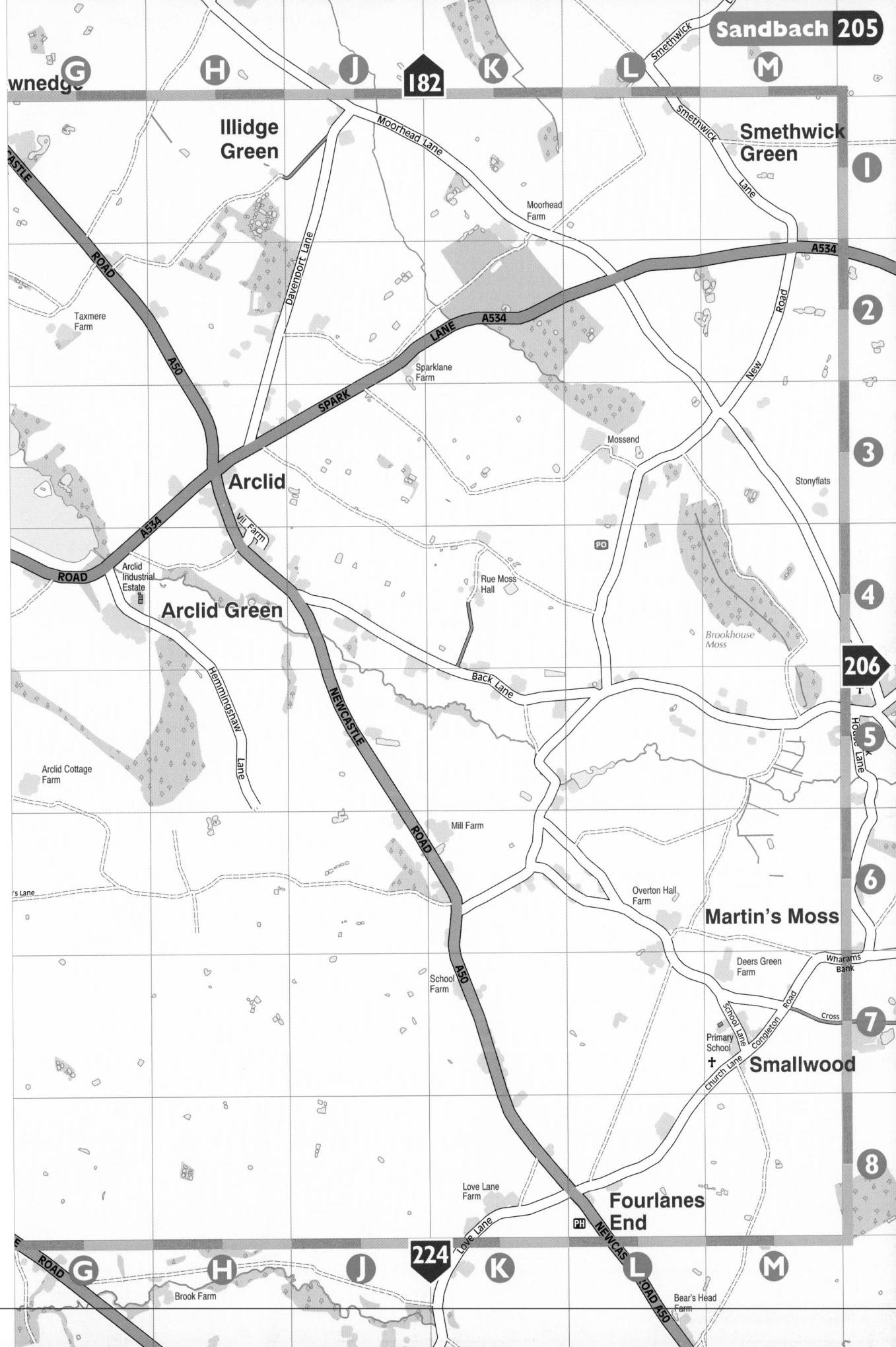

wnedge

G   H   J   182   K   L   M

Illidge
Green

Moorhead Lane

Moorhead
Farm

Smethwick
Green

Smethwick Lane

1

A534

2

Taxmere
Farm

Davenport Lane

SPARK LANE A534

Sparklane
Farm

New Road

Mossend

PO

Stonyflats

3

Arclid

Vil Farm

Arclid
Industrial
Estate

ROAD

Rue Moss
Hall

Brookhouse
Moss

4

206

Arclid Green

Hemmingshaw Lane

Back Lane

5

Arclid Cottage
Farm

NEWCASTLE ROAD

Mill Farm

6

Martin's Moss

Overton Hall
Farm

Deers Green
Farm

Wharams
Bank

's Lane

A50

School
Farm

School Lane

Congleton Road

Cross

7

Primary
School

Church Lane

Smallwood

8

Love Lane
Farm

Love Lane

Fourlanes
End

PH

NEWCAS ROAD A50

Bear's Head
Farm

G   H   J   224   K   L   M

Brook Farm

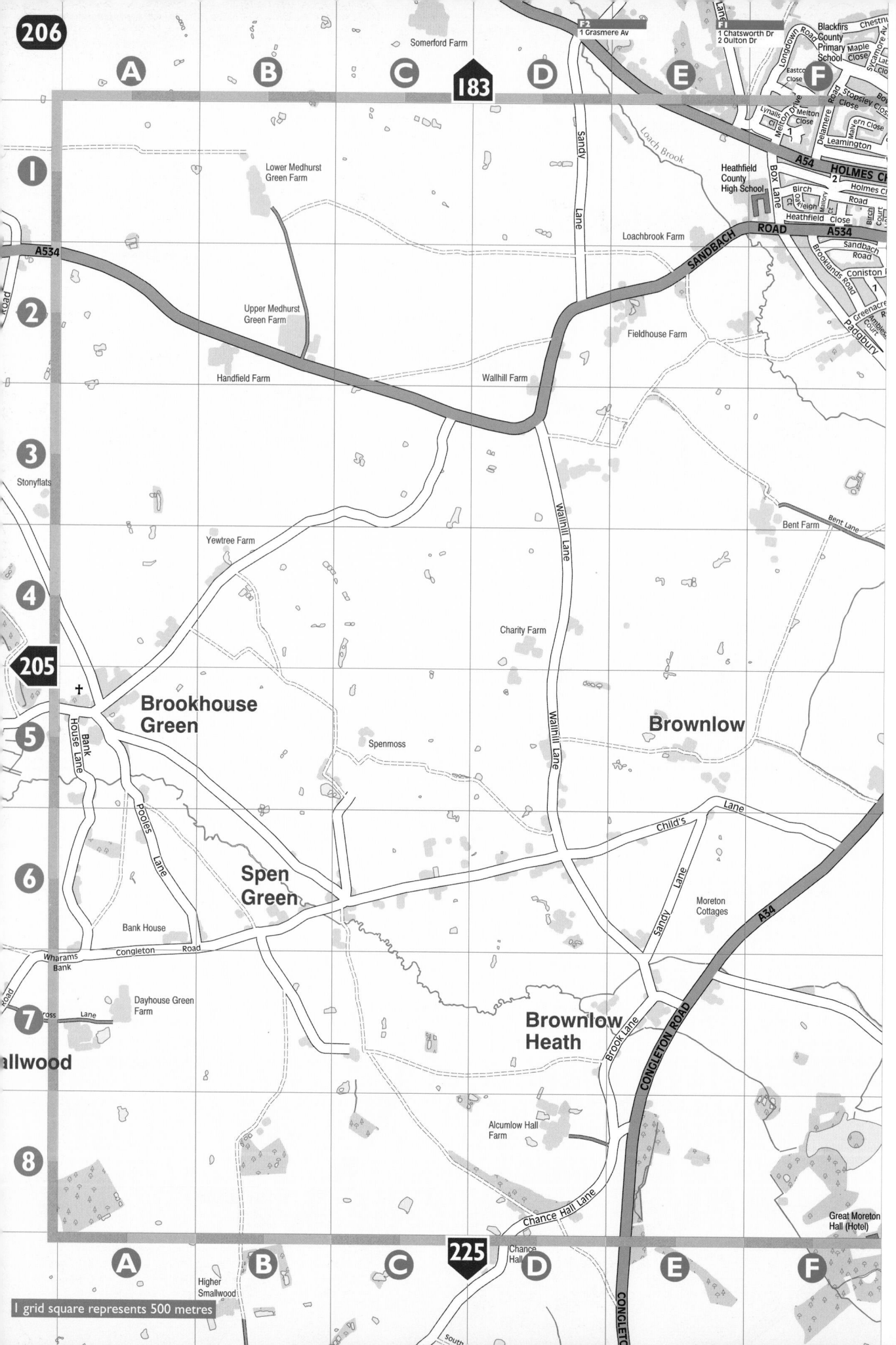

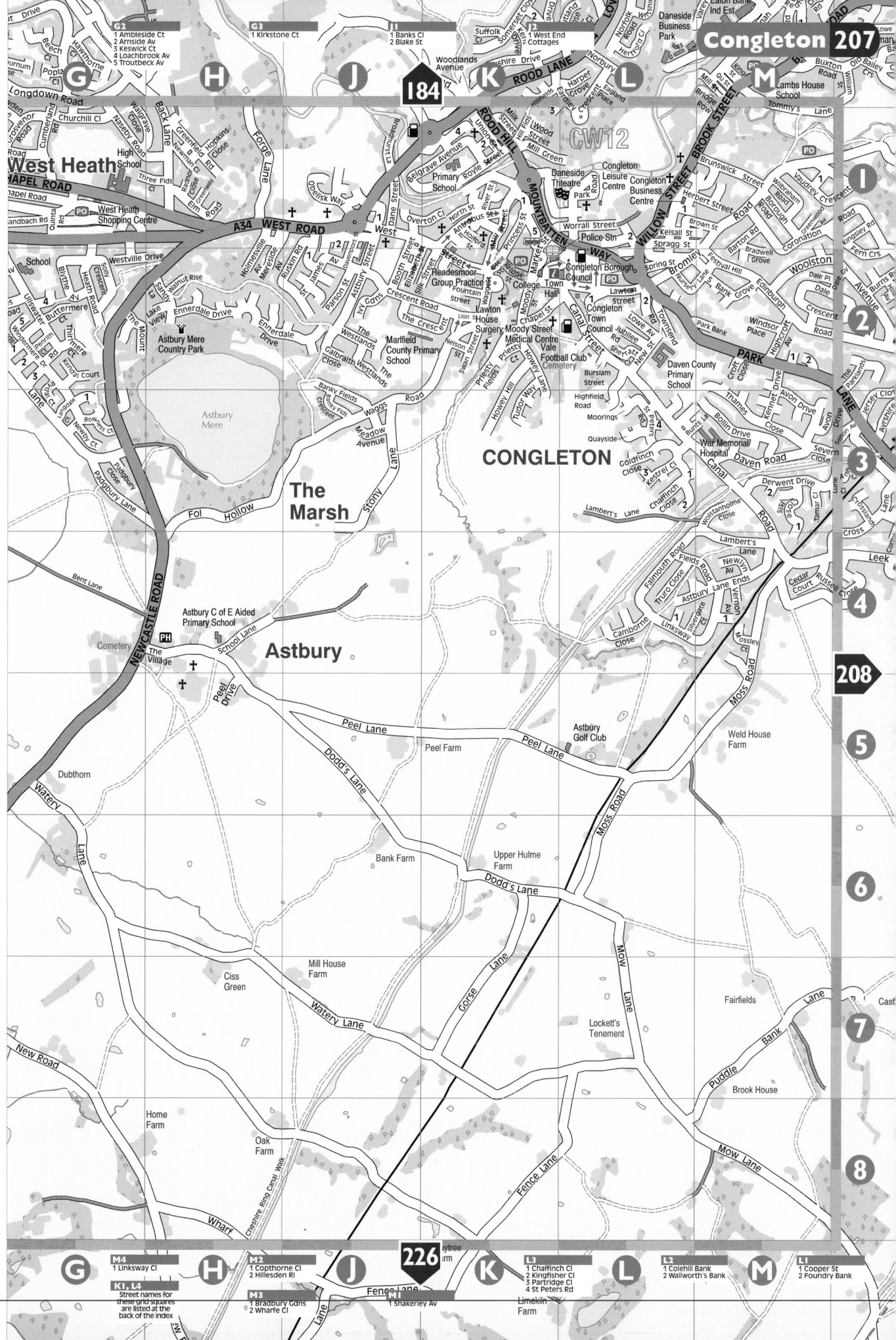

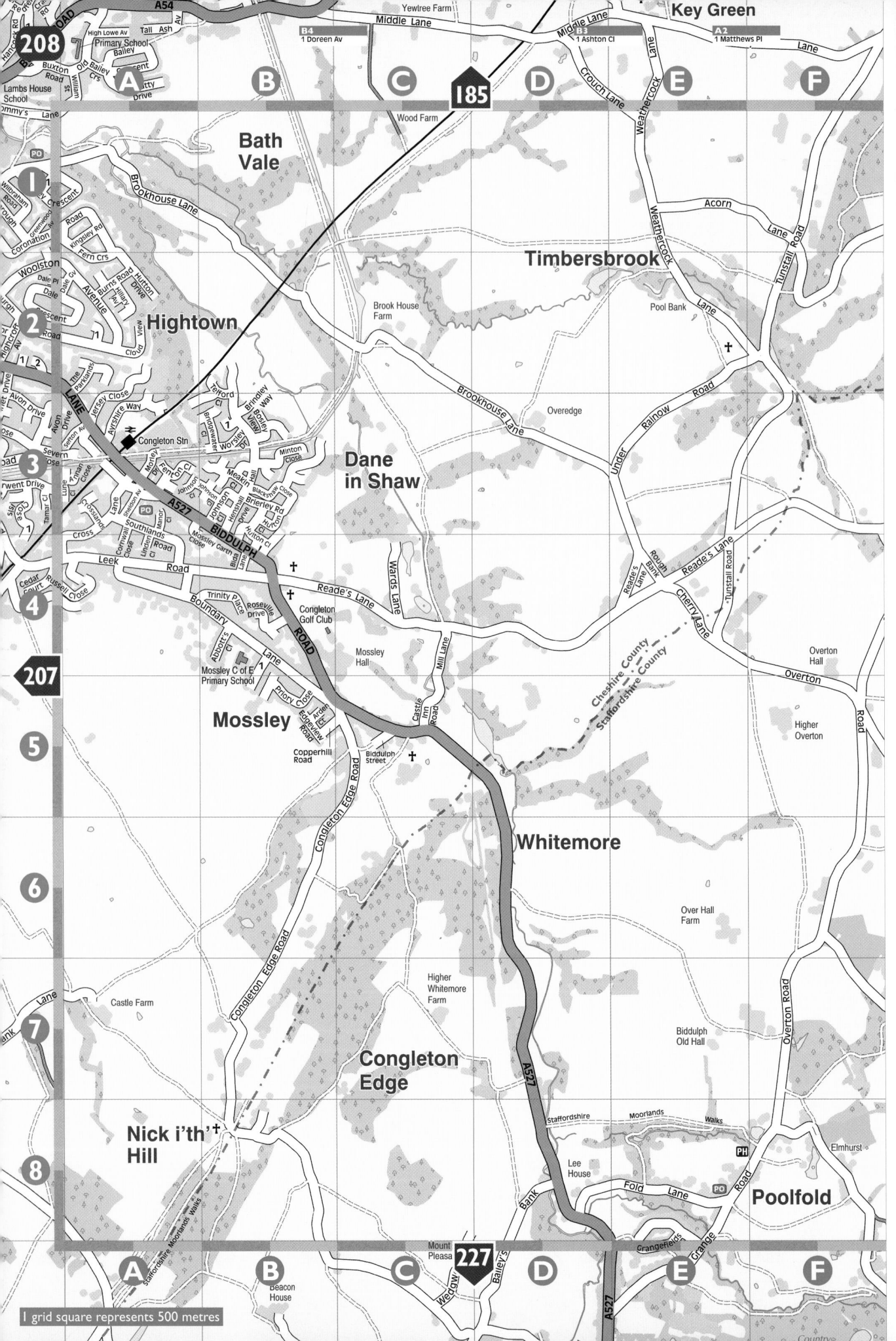

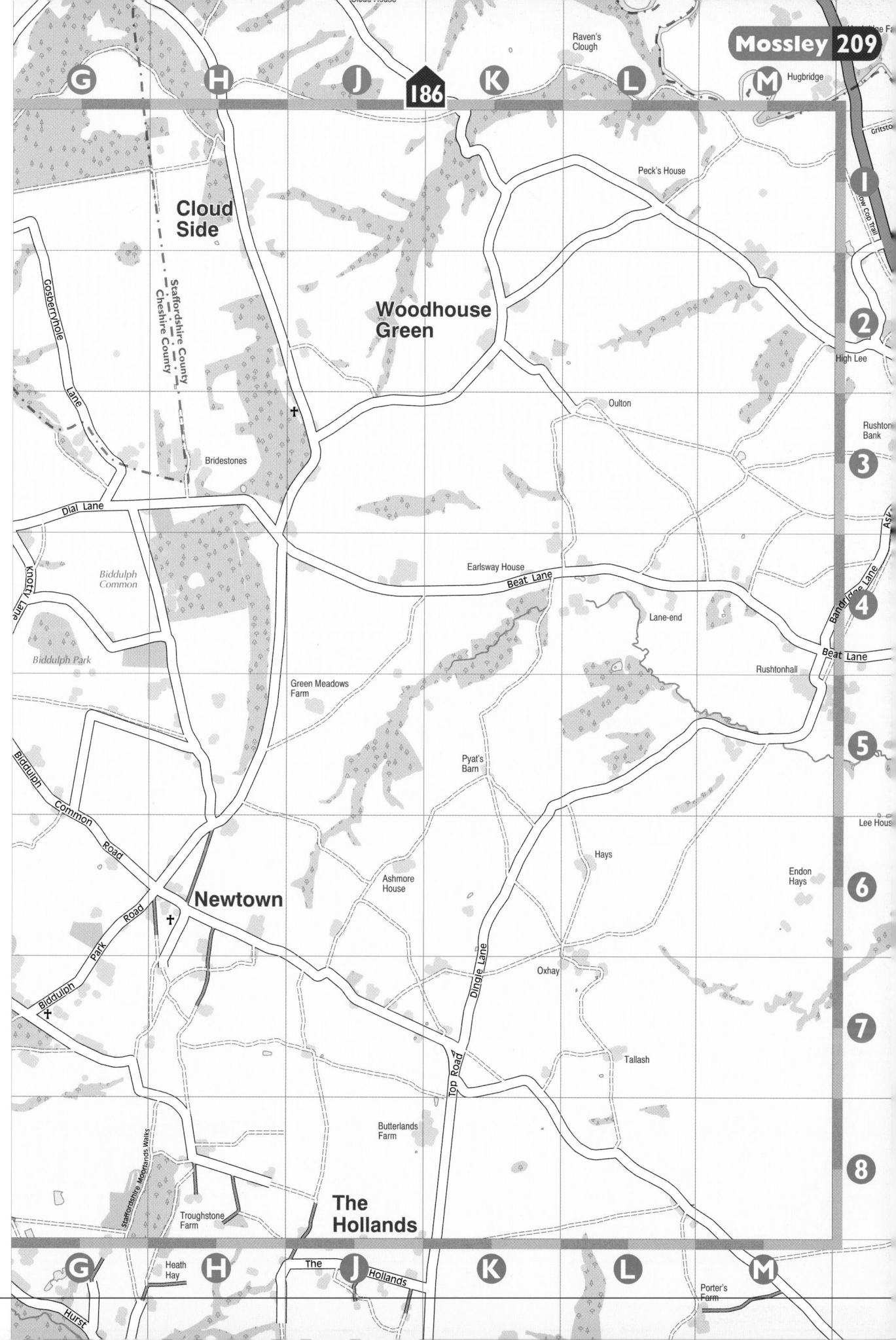

G H J K L M

186

Raven's Clough

Hugbridge

Gritsto

Peck's House

Cloud Side

Low Cop Trail

1

Gosberryhole Lane

Woodhouse Green

Staffordshire County
Cheshire County

High Lee

2

Oulton

Rushton Bank

Bridestones

3

Dial Lane

Earlsway House

Beat Lane

Bandridge Lane

Asf

Biddulph Common

Lane-end

4

Beat Lane

Knotty Lane

Biddulph Park

Rushtonhall

Green Meadows Farm

5

Pyat's Barn

Lee Hous

Biddulph

Common

Road

Hays

Endon Hays

6

Ashmore House

Newtown

Dingle Lane

Oxhay

7

Biddulph Park Road

Top Road

Tallash

Staffordshire Moorlands Walks

Butterlands Farm

8

Troughstone Farm

The Hollands

Heath Hay

The Hollands

Porter's Farm

G H J K L M

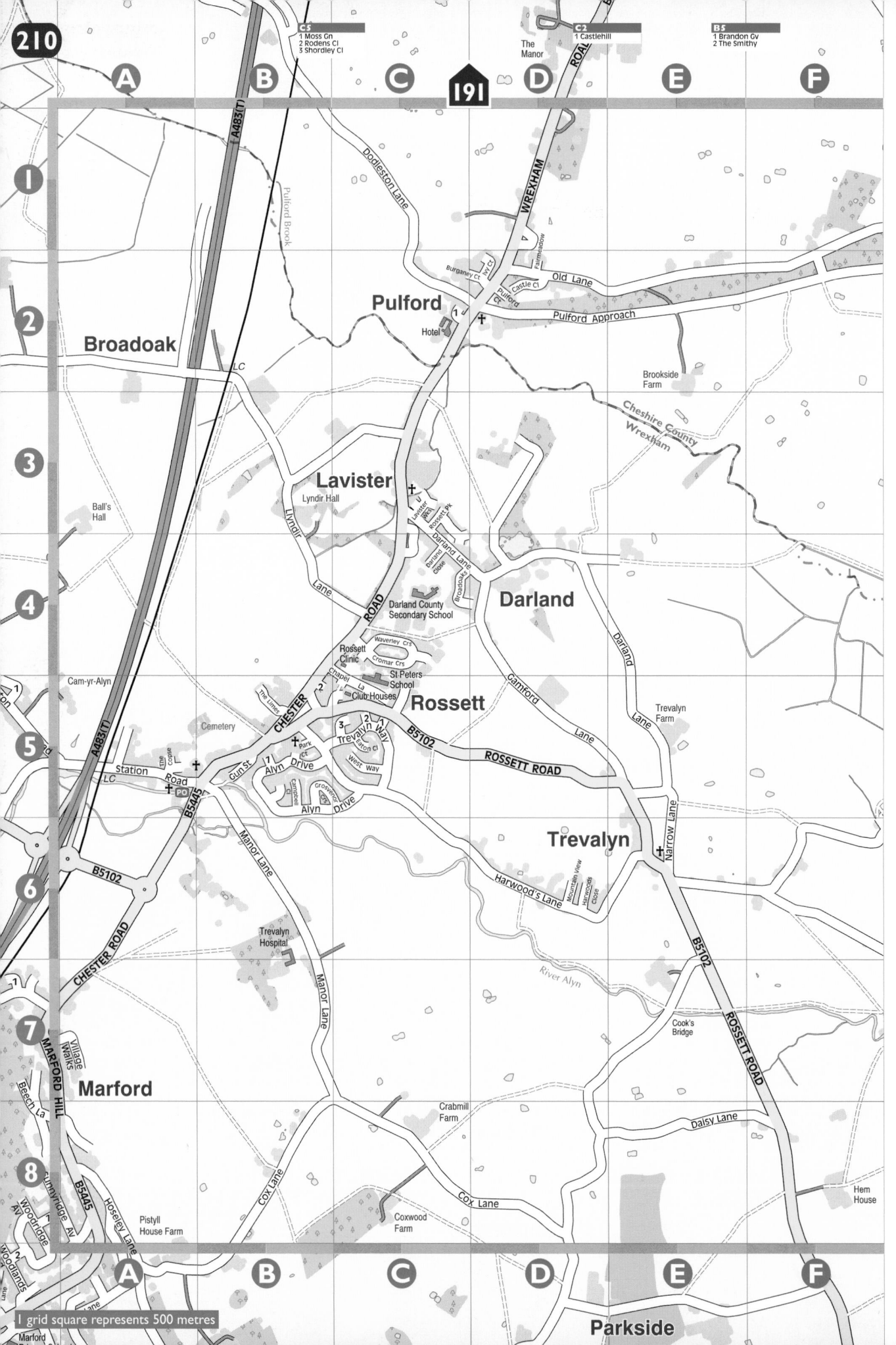

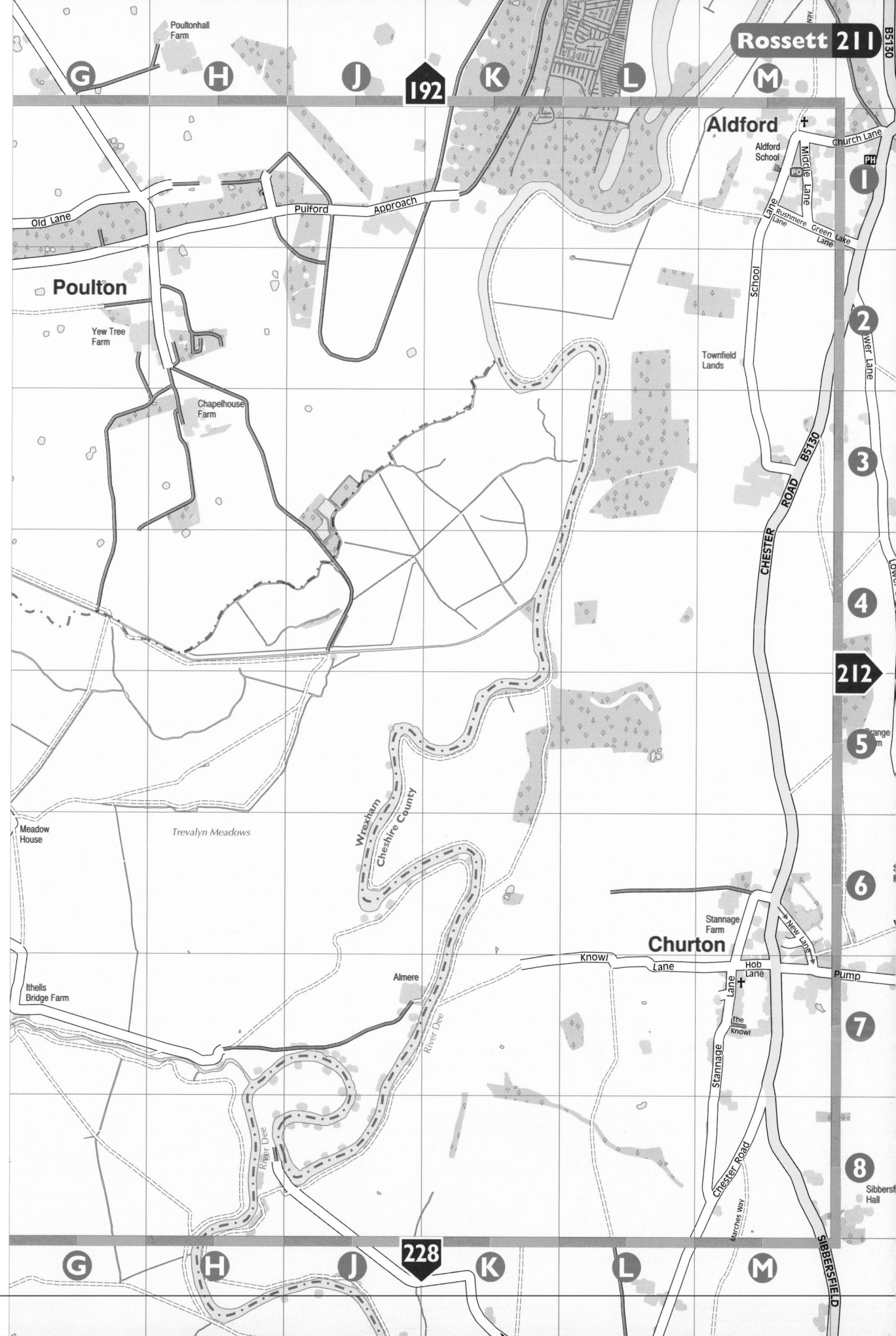

Poultonhall
Farm

G   H   J   **192**   K   L   M   I

Aldford

Old Lane

Pulford   Approach

Aldford
School

PO

Church Lane

Middle Lane

Rushmere Lane

Green Lane

Lake Lane

PH

Poulton

Yew Tree
Farm

Townfield
Lands

School Lane

Lower Lane

B5130

Chapelhouse
Farm

2

3

CHESTER ROAD

B5130

4

212

Wrexham

Cheshire County

5

Grange
Farm

Meadow
House

Trevalyn Meadows

6

Stannage
Farm

Churton

New Lane

Ithells
Bridge Farm

Almere

Know!   Lane

Hob
Lane

Pump

7

River Dee

Stannage Lane

The
Knowl

River Dee

Chester Road

Marches Way

8

Sibberst
Hall

G   H   J   **228**   K   L   M

SIBBERSFIELD

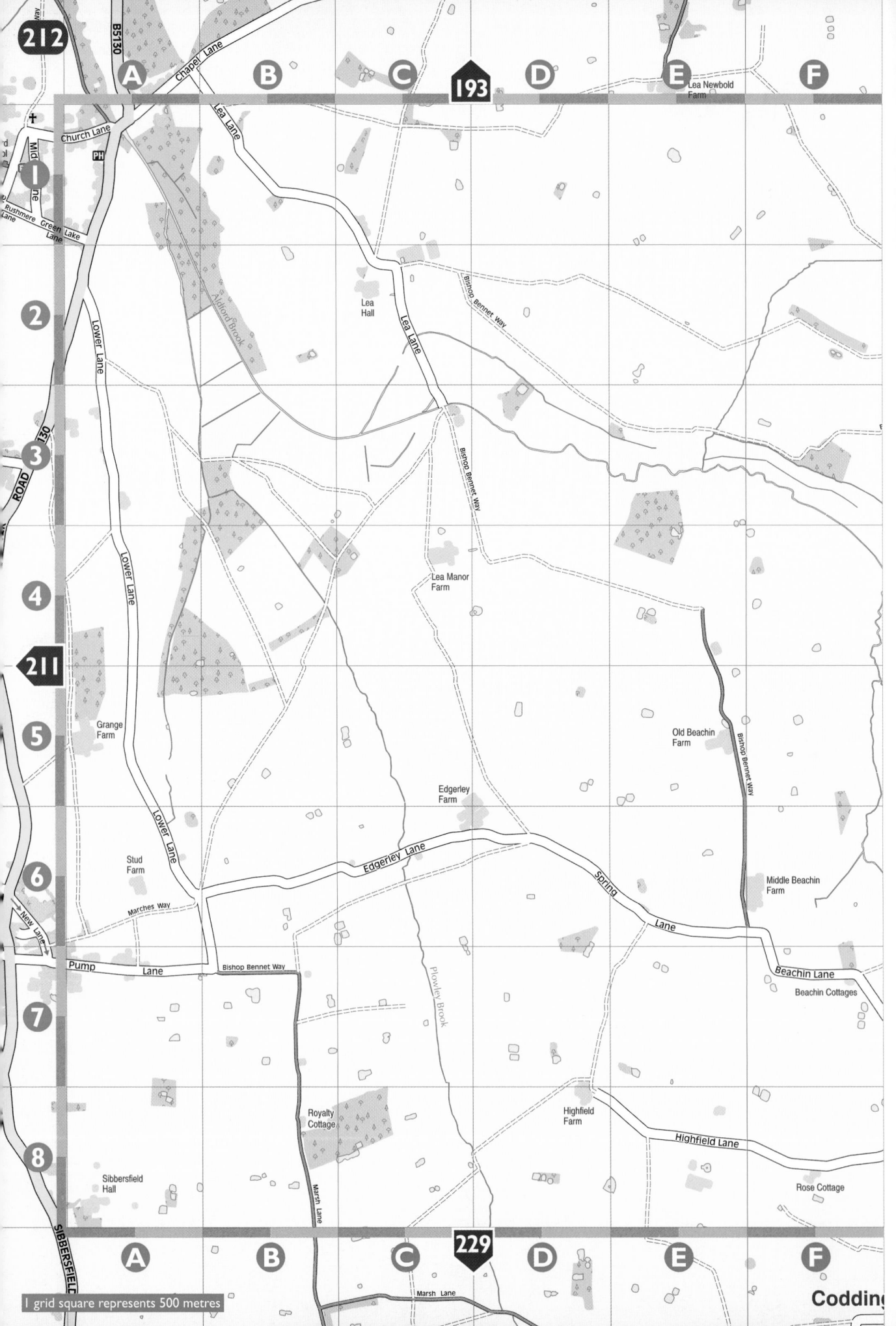

B5130

Chapel Lane

A

Church Lane

PH

Mid Ne

Rushmere Green Lake Lane

Lea Lane

B

C

D

E

Lea Newbold Farm

F

1

2

Lower Lane

Aldford Brook

Lea Hall

Lea Lane

Bishop Bennet Way

ROAD 130

3

Bishop Bennet Way

Lea Manor Farm

4

Lower Lane

5

Grange Farm

Old Beachin Farm

Bishop Bennet Way

Edgerley Farm

6

Stud Farm

Lower Lane

Edgerley Lane

Spring Lane

Middle Beachin Farm

Marches Way

New Lane

Pump Lane

Bishop Bennet Way

Plowley Brook

Beachin Lane

Beachin Cottages

7

8

Royalty Cottage

Highfield Farm

Highfield Lane

Sibbersfield Hall

Marsh Lane

Rose Cottage

A

B

C

D

E

F

Marsh Lane

Codding

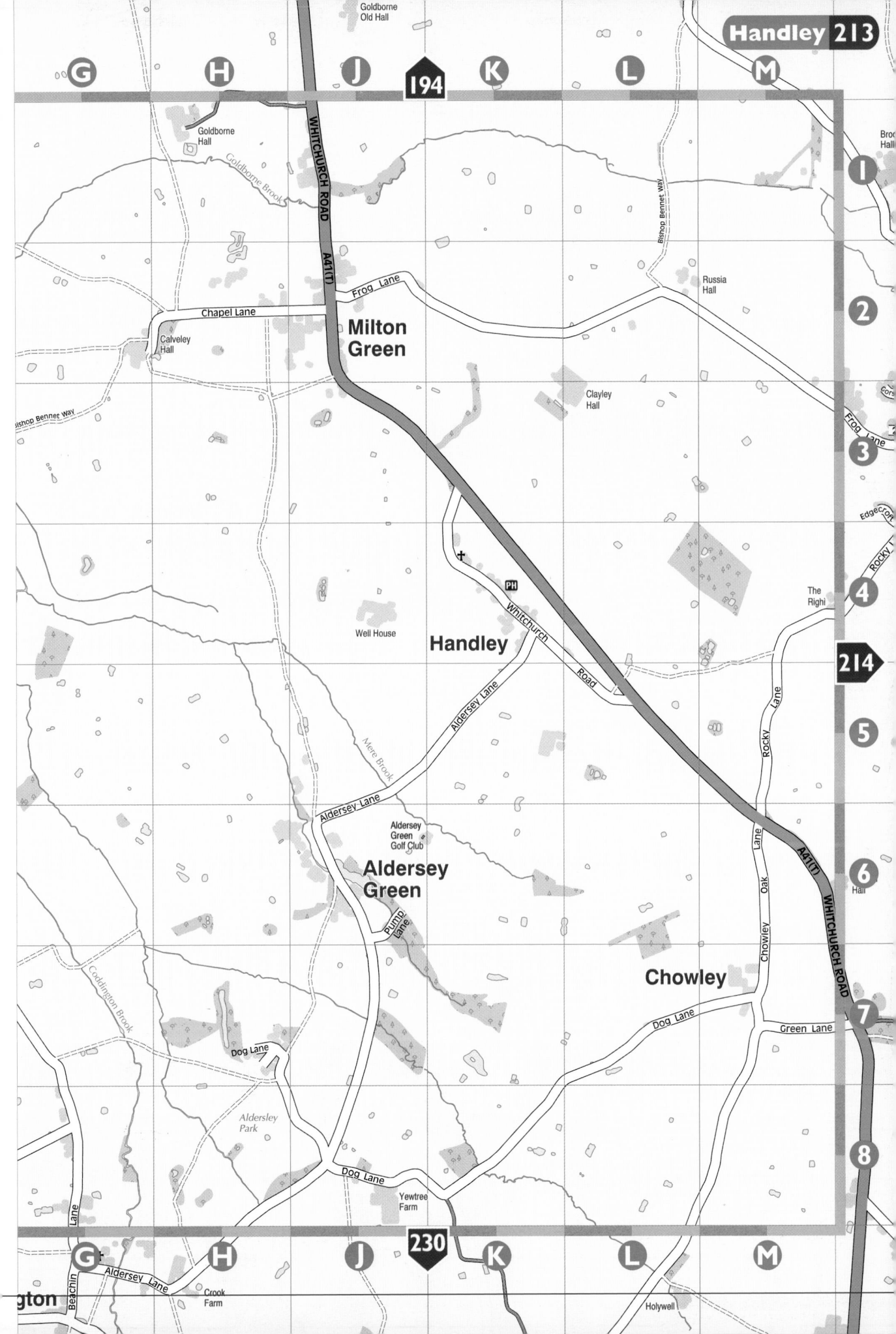

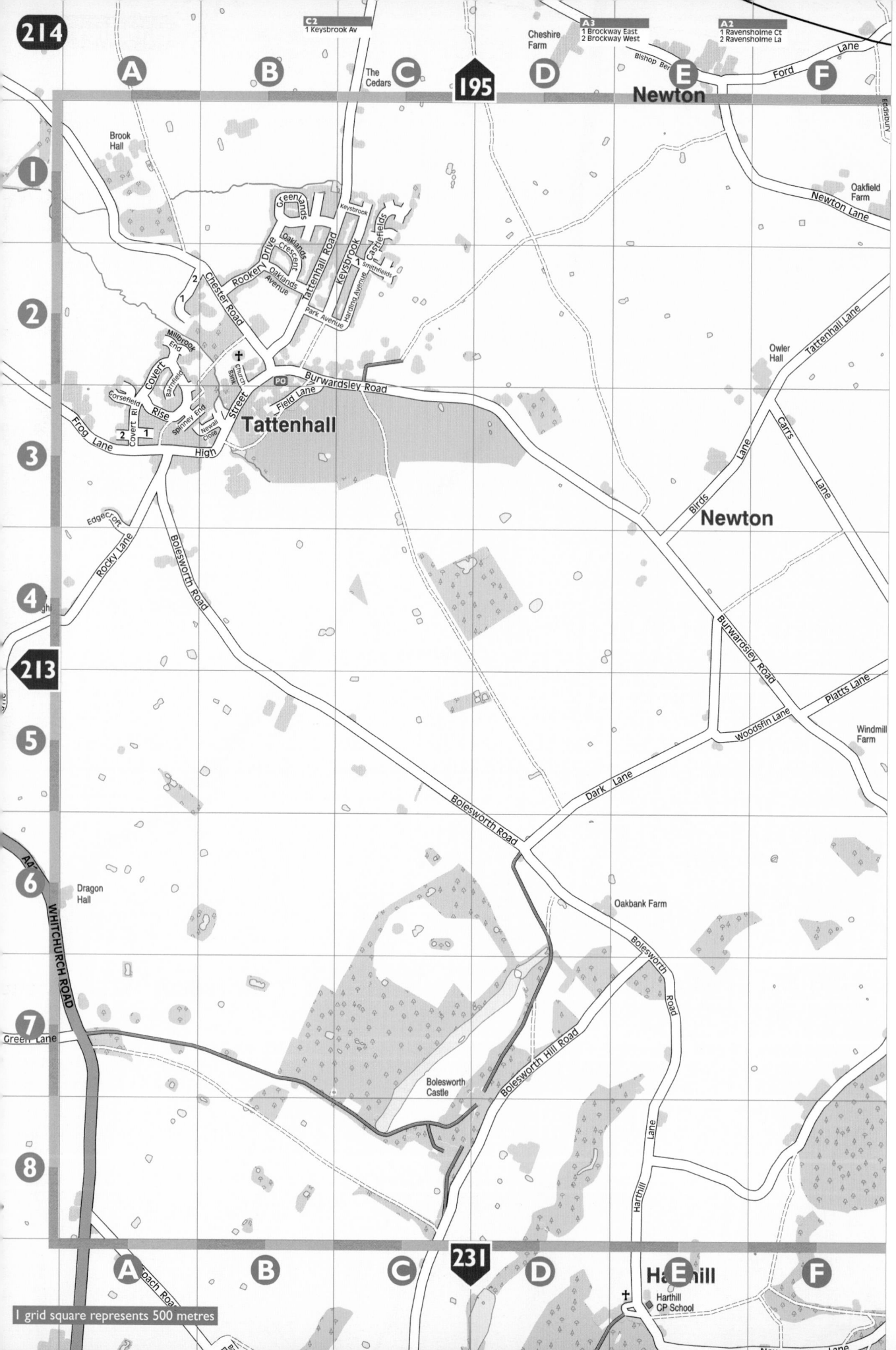

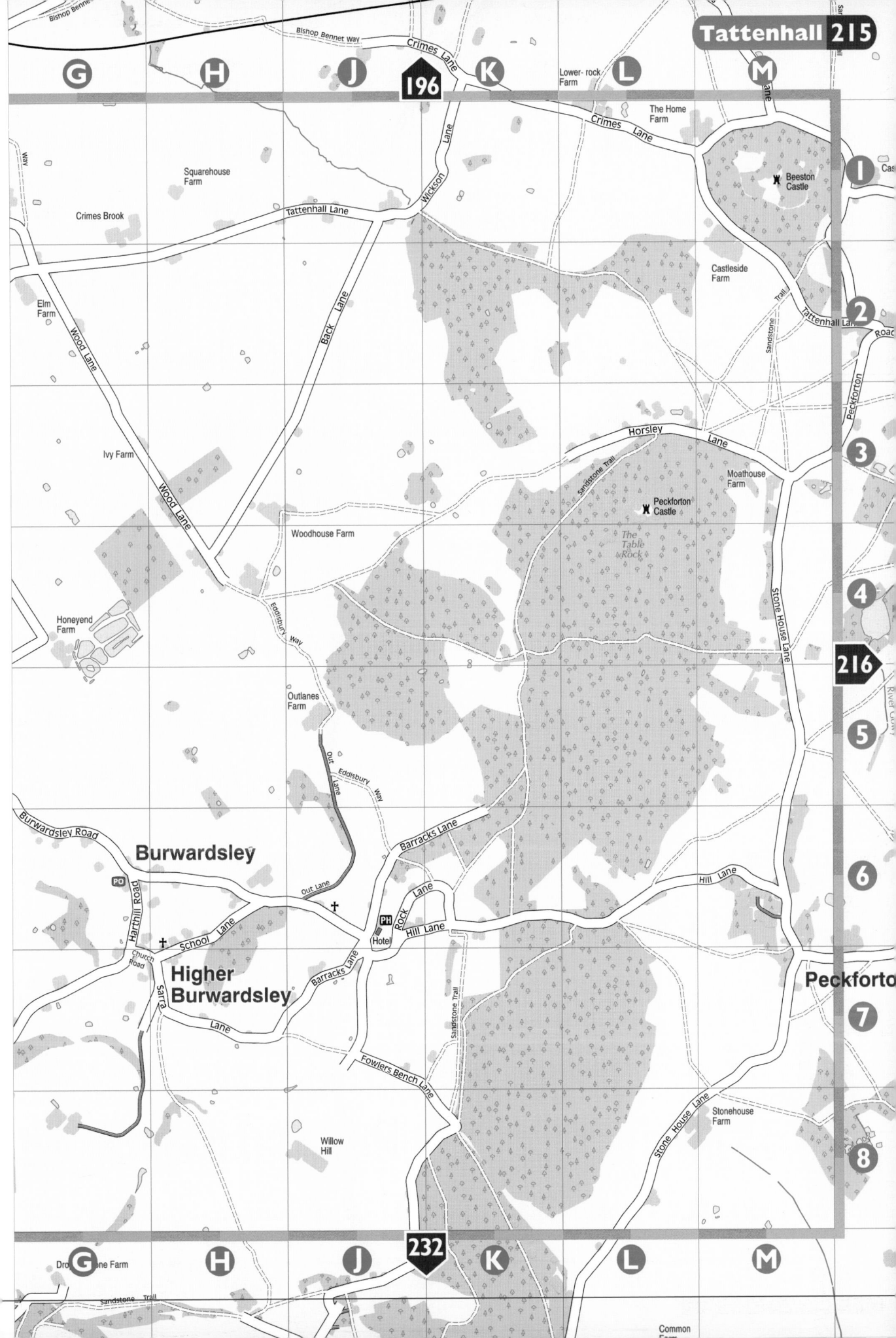

G   H   J   **196**   K   L   M

Bishop Bennet way

Bishop Bennet way

Crimes Lane

Lower- rock Farm

Crimes Lane

The Home Farm

1

Beeston Castle

Cas

Squarehouse Farm

Tattenhall Lane

Castleside Farm

2

Crimes Brook

Wickson Lane

Road

Elm Farm

Back Lane

Peckforton

Horsley Lane

3

Wood Lane

Sandstone Trail

Moathouse Farm

Ivy Farm

Peckforton Castle

4

Woodhouse Farm

The Table Rock

Stone House Lane

216

Honeyend Farm

Eddisbury Way

5

Outlanes Farm

Out Lane

Eddisbury Way

6

Burwardsley Road

Barracks Lane

Hill Lane

PO

Burwardsley

Rock Lane

Harthill Road

Out Lane

†

PH
Hotel

Hill Lane

Peckforto

School Lane

†

7

Church Road

Higher Burwardsley

Barracks Lane

Sarra Lane

Barracks Lane

Sandstone Trail

Fowlers Bench Lane

8

Willow Hill

Stone House Lane

Stonehouse Farm

G   H   J   **232**   K   L   M

Dro stone Farm

Sandstone Trail

Common Farm

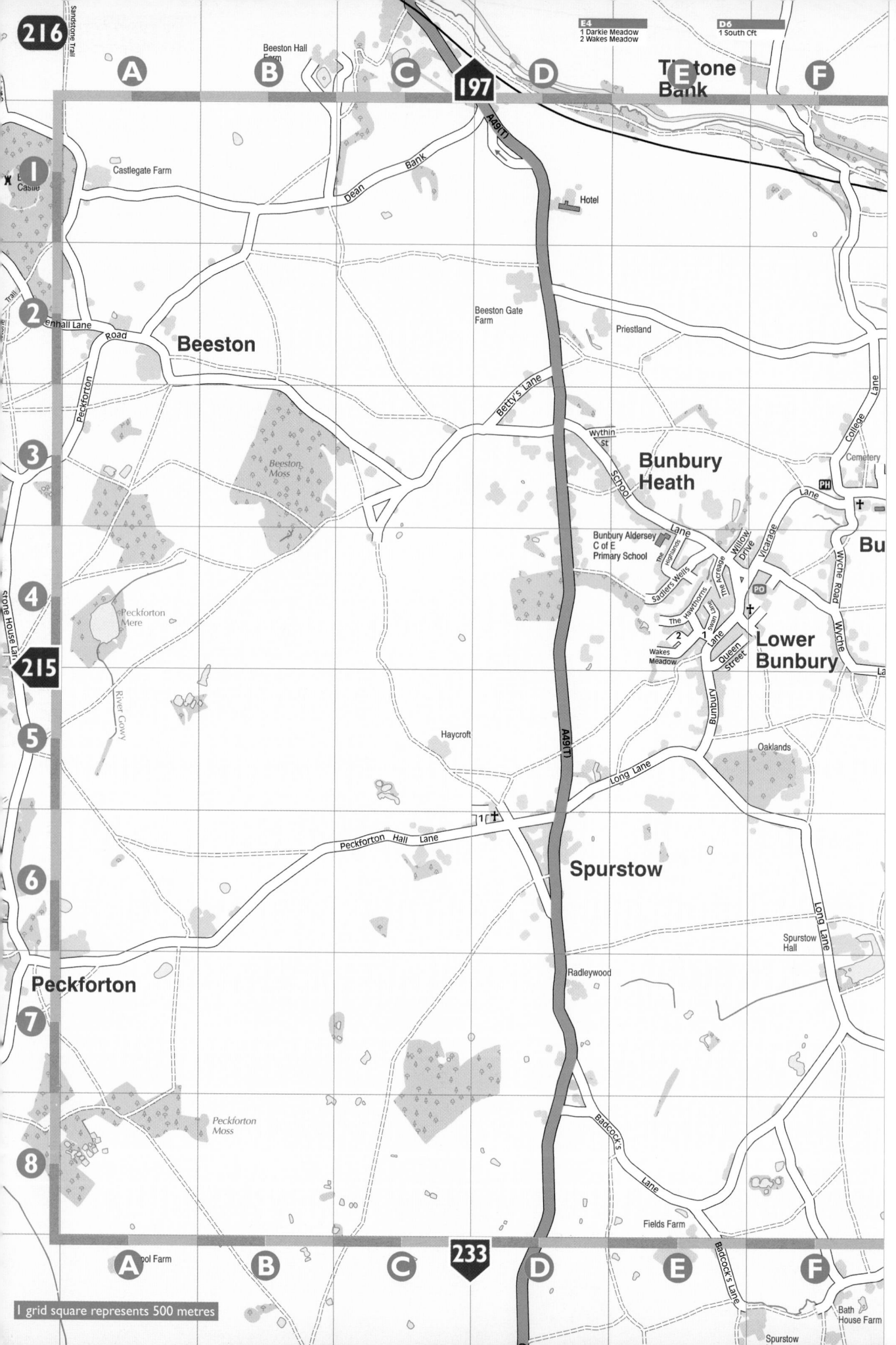

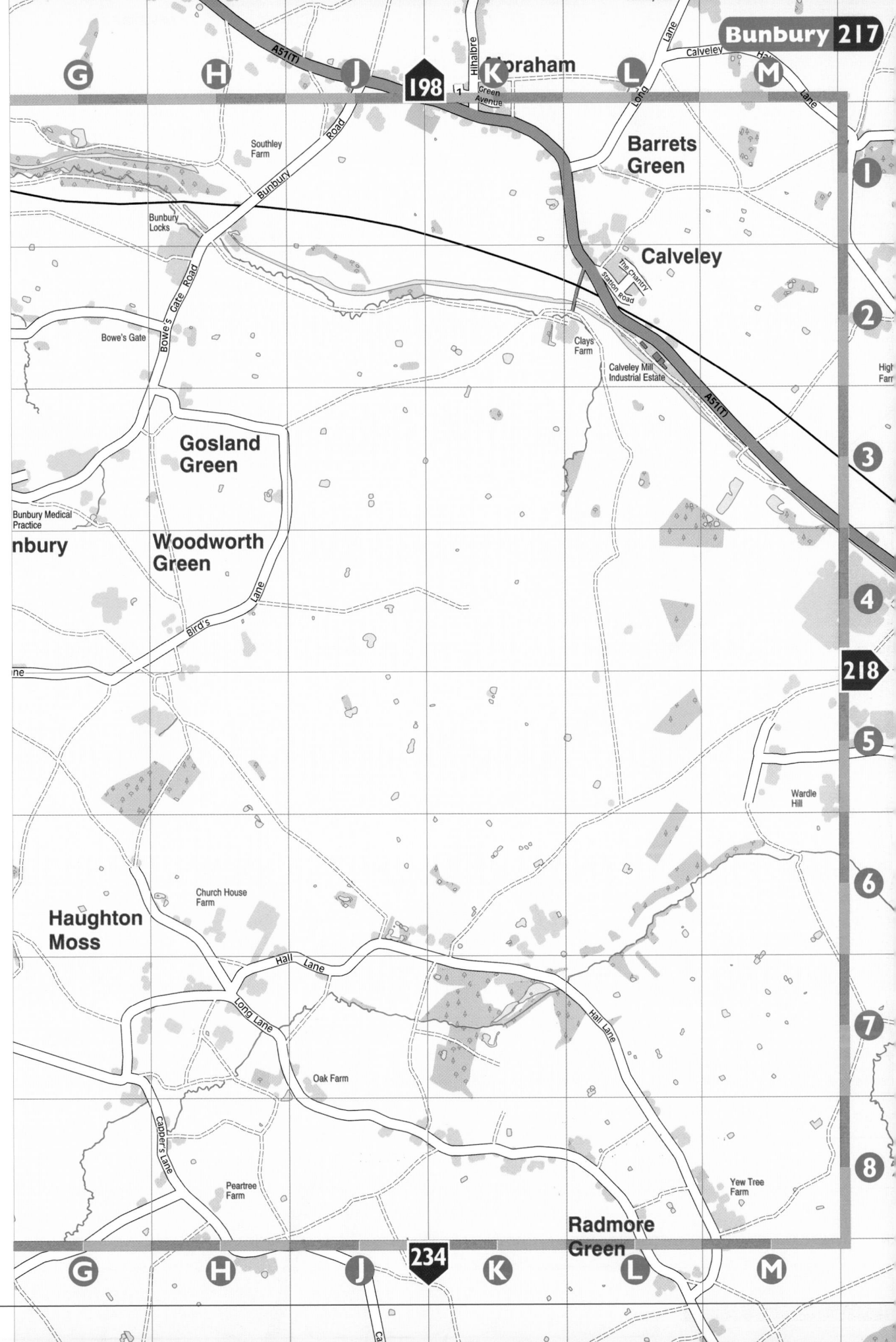

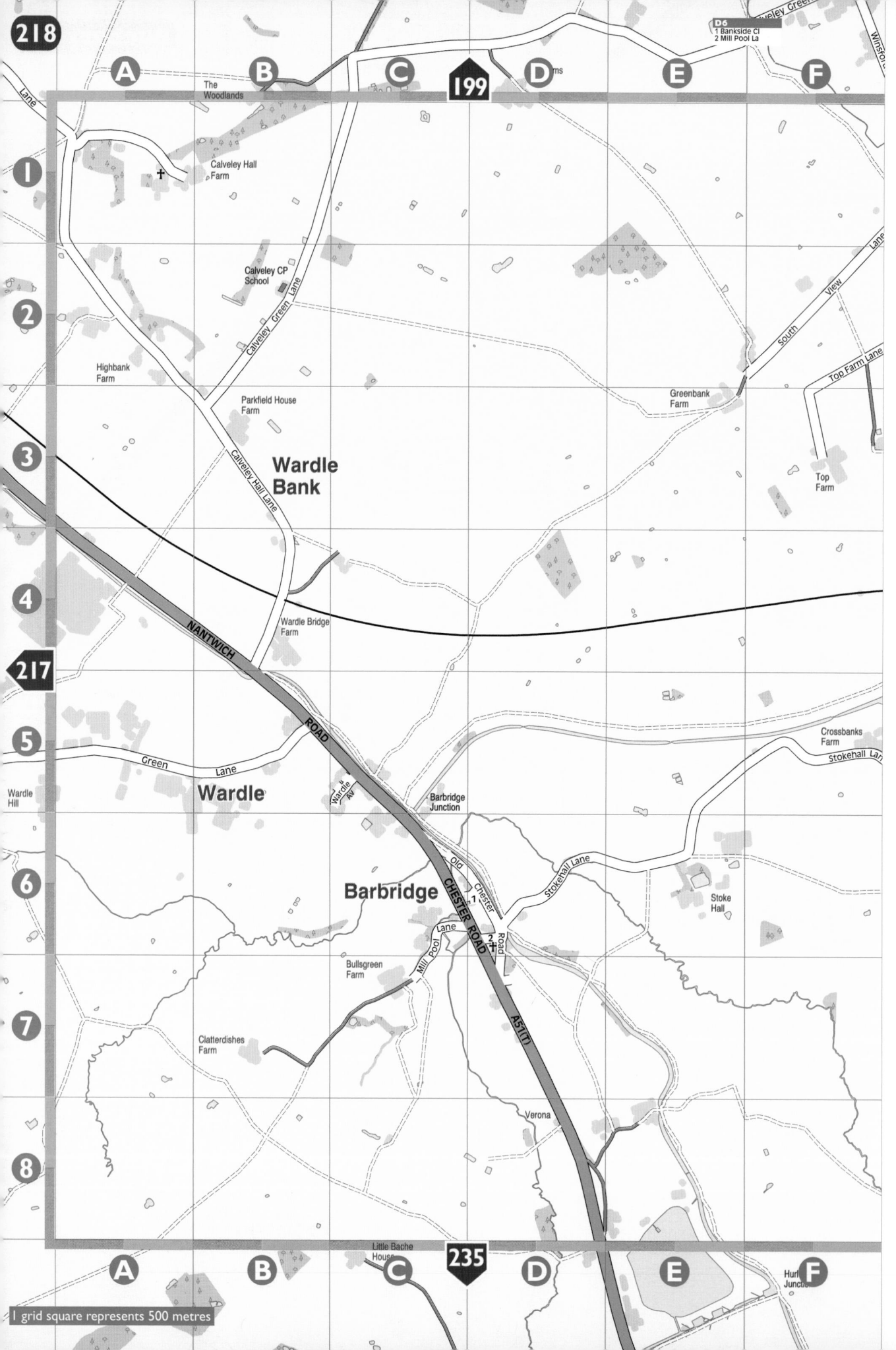

A B C **199** D E F

D6
1 Bankside Cl
2 Mill Pool La

The Woodlands

Calveley Hall
Farm

Calveley CP
School

Highbank
Farm

Parkfield House
Farm

**Wardle
Bank**

Calveley Green Lane

Calveley Hall Lane

Greenbank
Farm

South View

Top Farm Lane

Top
Farm

NANTWICH

ROAD

217

Green   Lane

Wardle

Wardle
Hill

Wardle AV

Barbridge
Junction

Crossbanks
Farm

Stokehall Lane

Stokehall Lane

Stoke
Hall

Barbridge

Old   Chester

Road

1

2

Lane

Mill Pool

Bullsgreen
Farm

CHESTER ROAD

A51(T)

Clatterdishes
Farm

Verona

A B C **235** D E F

Little Bache
House

Hurle
Junction

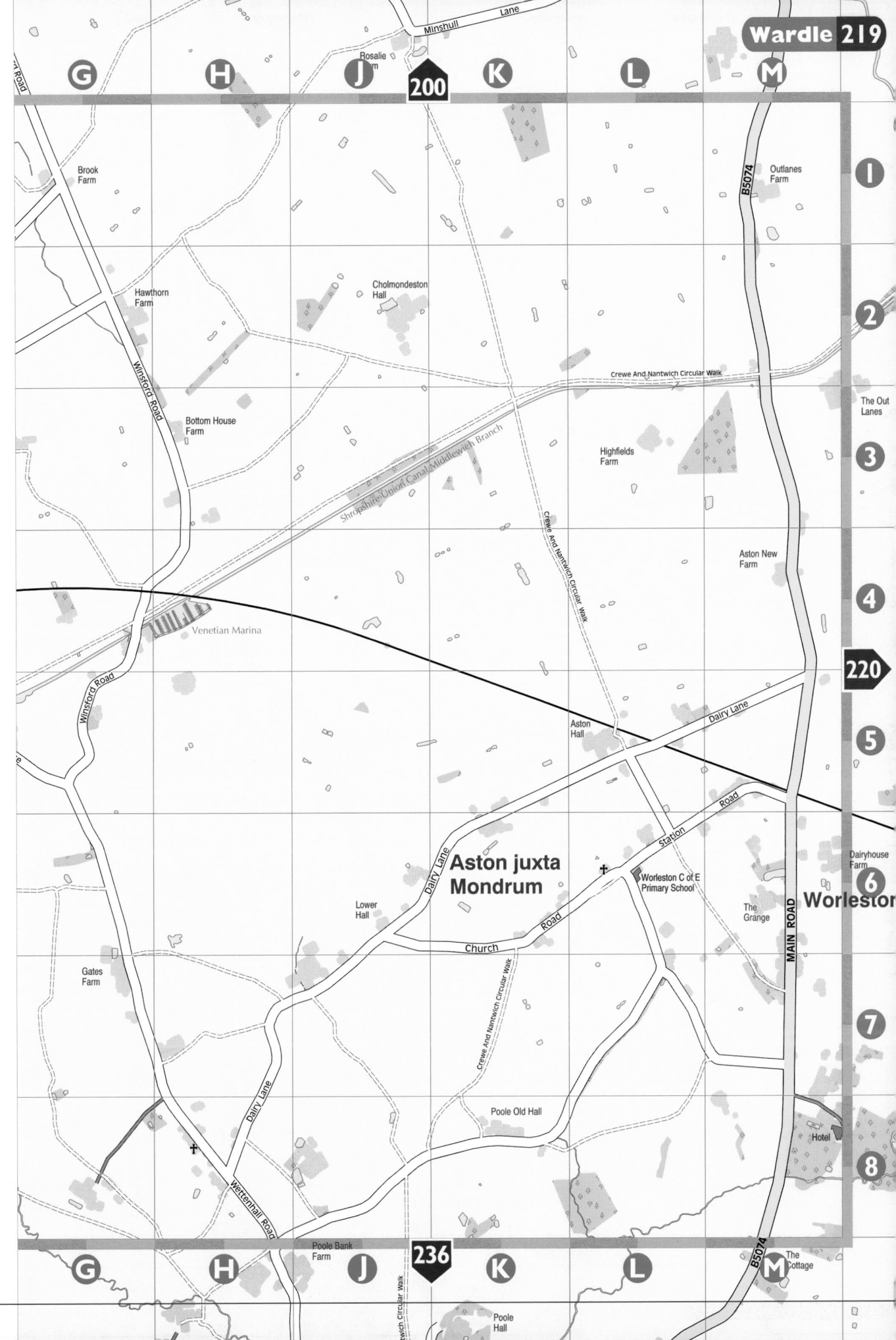

G H J K L M

200

220

236

I
2
3
4
5
6
7
8

Brook Farm

Winsford Road

Hawthorn Farm

Bottom House Farm

Rosalie Farm

Minshull Lane

Cholmondeston Hall

Shropshire Union Canal/Middlewich Branch

Venetian Marina

Winsford Road

Crewe And Nantwich Circular Walk

Highfields Farm

Crewe And Nantwich Circular Walk

Aston New Farm

Aston Hall

Dairy Lane

Aston juxta Mondrum

Dairy Lane

Lower Hall

Church Road

Station Road

Worleston C of E Primary School

Worleston

The Grange

MAIN ROAD

Dairyhouse Farm

Gates Farm

Crewe And Nantwich Circular Walk

Poole Old Hall

Dairy Lane

Wettenhall Road

Hotel

Poole Bank Farm

Poole Hall

Nantwich Circular Walk

Outlanes Farm

B5074

The Out Lanes

The Cottage

B5074

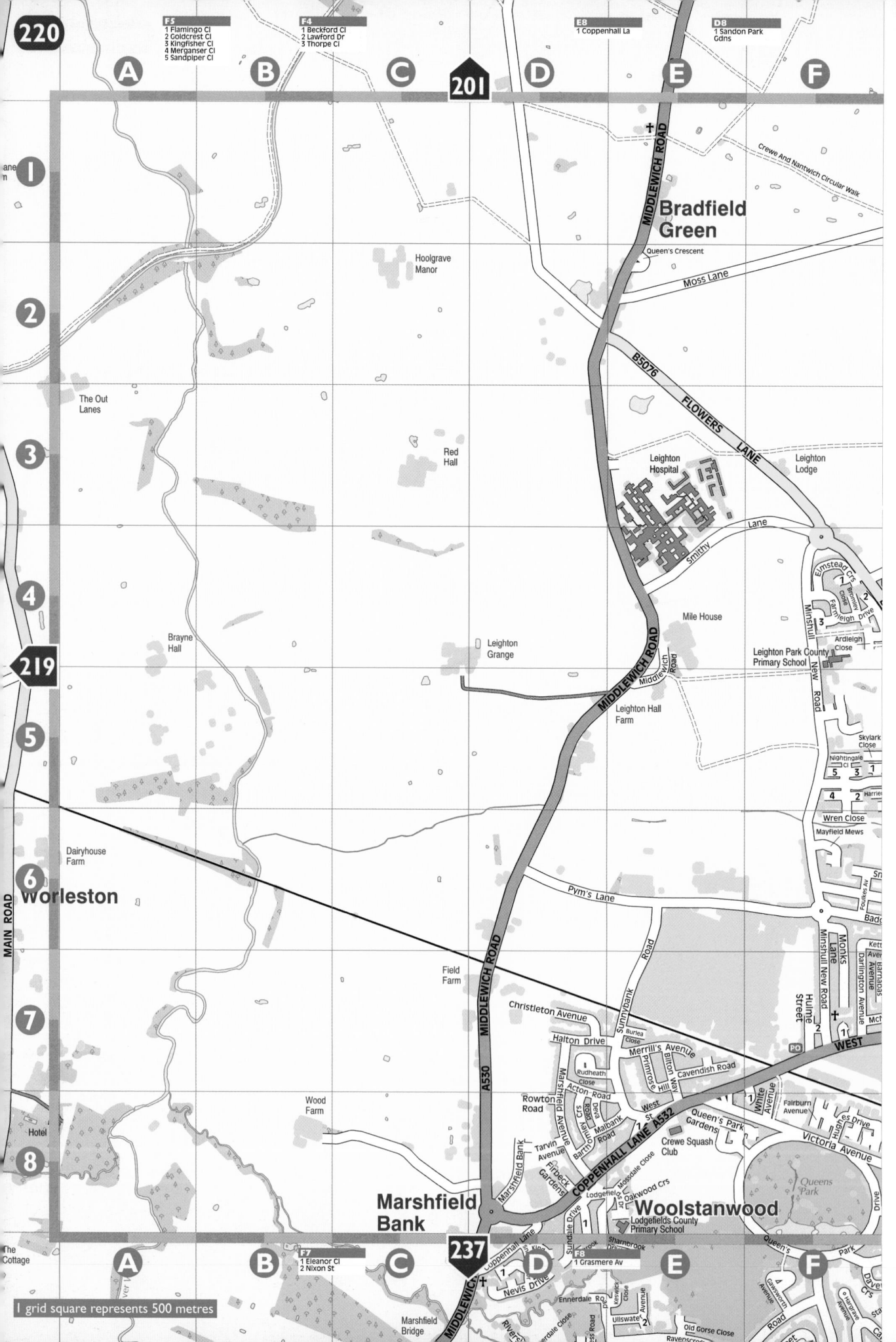

F5
1 Flamingo Cl
2 Goldcrest Cl
3 Kingfisher Cl
4 Merganser Cl
5 Sandpiper Cl

F4
1 Beckford Cl
2 Lawford Dr
3 Thorpe Cl

E8
1 Coppenhall La

D8
1 Sandon Park Gdns

A B C **201** D E F

1

Crewe And Nantwich Circular Walk

I

Bradfield Green

Queen's Crescent

Moss Lane

2

B5076

FLOWERS LANE

The Out
Lanes

Leighton Hospital

Leighton
Lodge

3

Red
Hall

Elmstead Crs

Bromley
Close

Farnleigh Drive

Lane

Smithy

Ardleigh
Close

4

MIDDLEWICH ROAD

Mile House

Leighton Park County
Primary School

New Road

Minshull

Brayne
Hall

Leighton
Grange

Skylark
Close

219

Middlewich
Road

Leighton Hall
Farm

Nightingale
Cl

5 4 3 2 1

Wren Close

Mayfield Mews

5

MIDDLEWICH ROAD

4 2 Harriet

Dairyhouse
Farm

Pym's Lane

Foxles Av

Bado

6

worleston

MAIN ROAD

Road

MONKS
LANE

Minshull New Road

Ketti
Aven

Barnabas
Avenue

Darlington Avenue

Mc

Field
Farm

Christleton Avenue

Hulme
Street

WEST

PO

7

A530

MIDDLEWICH ROAD

Sunnybank

Halton Drive

Merrill's Avenue

Burlea
Close

Primrose
Hill

Bilton Way

Cavendish Road

White
Avenue

Fairburn
Avenue

les Drive

Victoria Avenue

Rudheath
Close

Rowton
Road

Acton Road

WEST St

Malbank
Road

Queen's Park
Gardens

Wood
Farm

Hotel

8

Marshfield
Bank

Tarvin
Avenue

Finbeck
Gardens

Barth

Crs

Mossdale Close

Oakwood Crs

Crewe Squash
Club

Queens
Park

Drive

Lodgefields County
Primary School

Woolstanwood

Sundale Drive

Lodgefields

The
Cottage

A B C **237** D E F

7
1 Eleanor Cl
2 Nixon St

Nevis Drive

Coppenhall Lane A532

COPPENHALL LANE A532

7

Sharnbrook

E8
1 Grasmere Av

Ennerdale Rd

Keswick
Close

Ullswate

Queen's

Park

Dove

Gaxworth

Marshfield
Bridge

MIDDLEWICH

River

erdale Close

Rd

Old Gorse Close

Ravenscroft

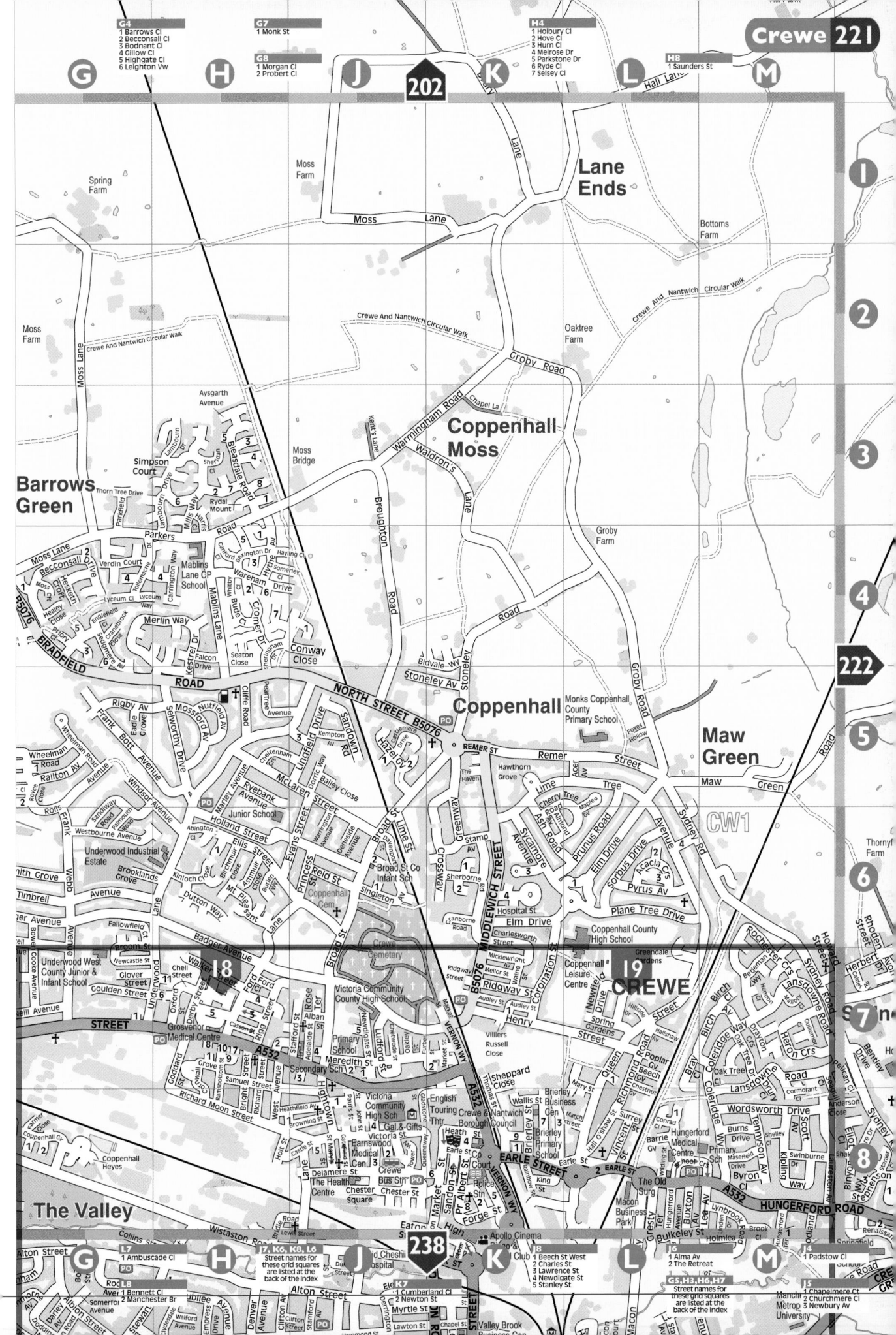

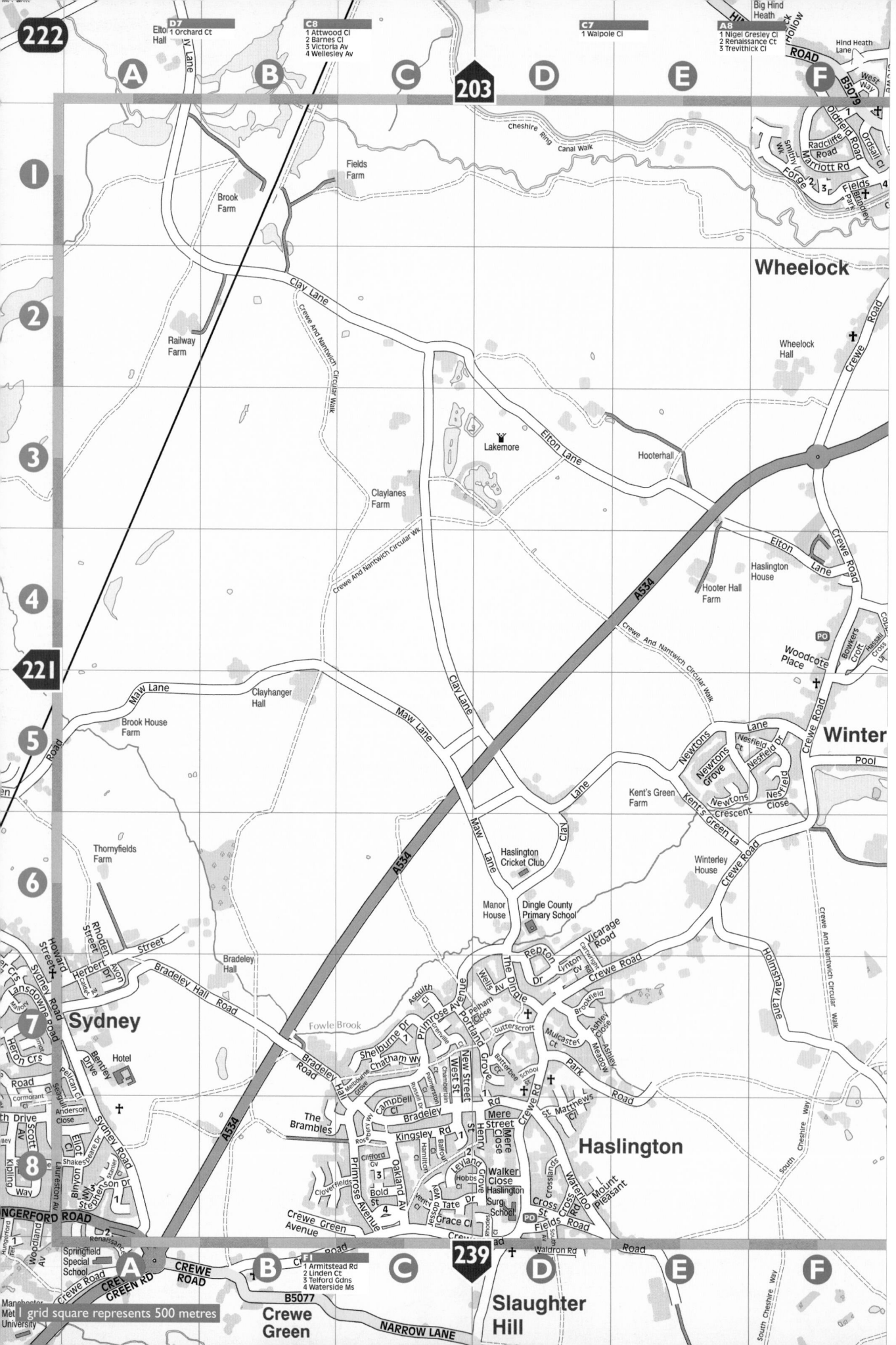

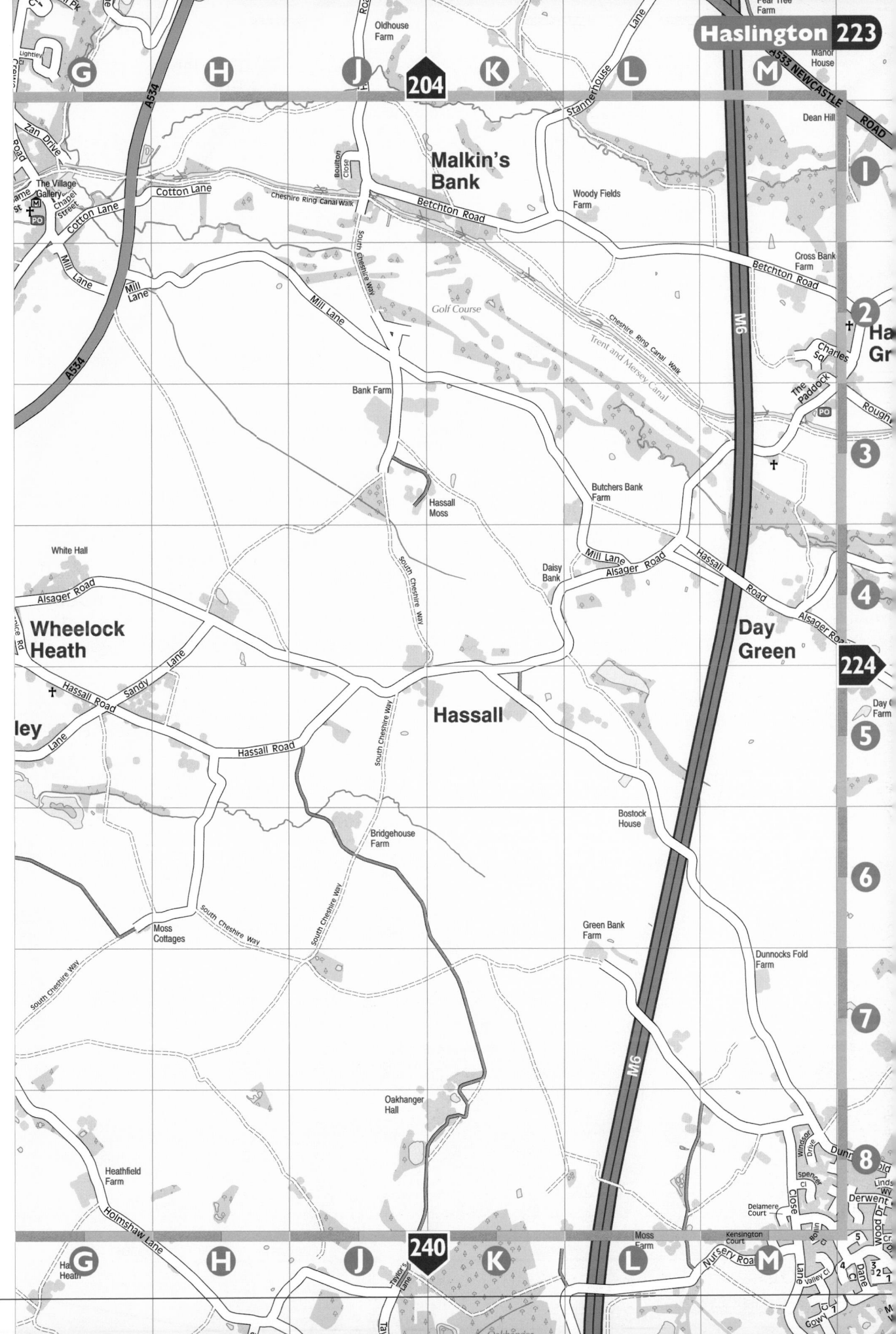

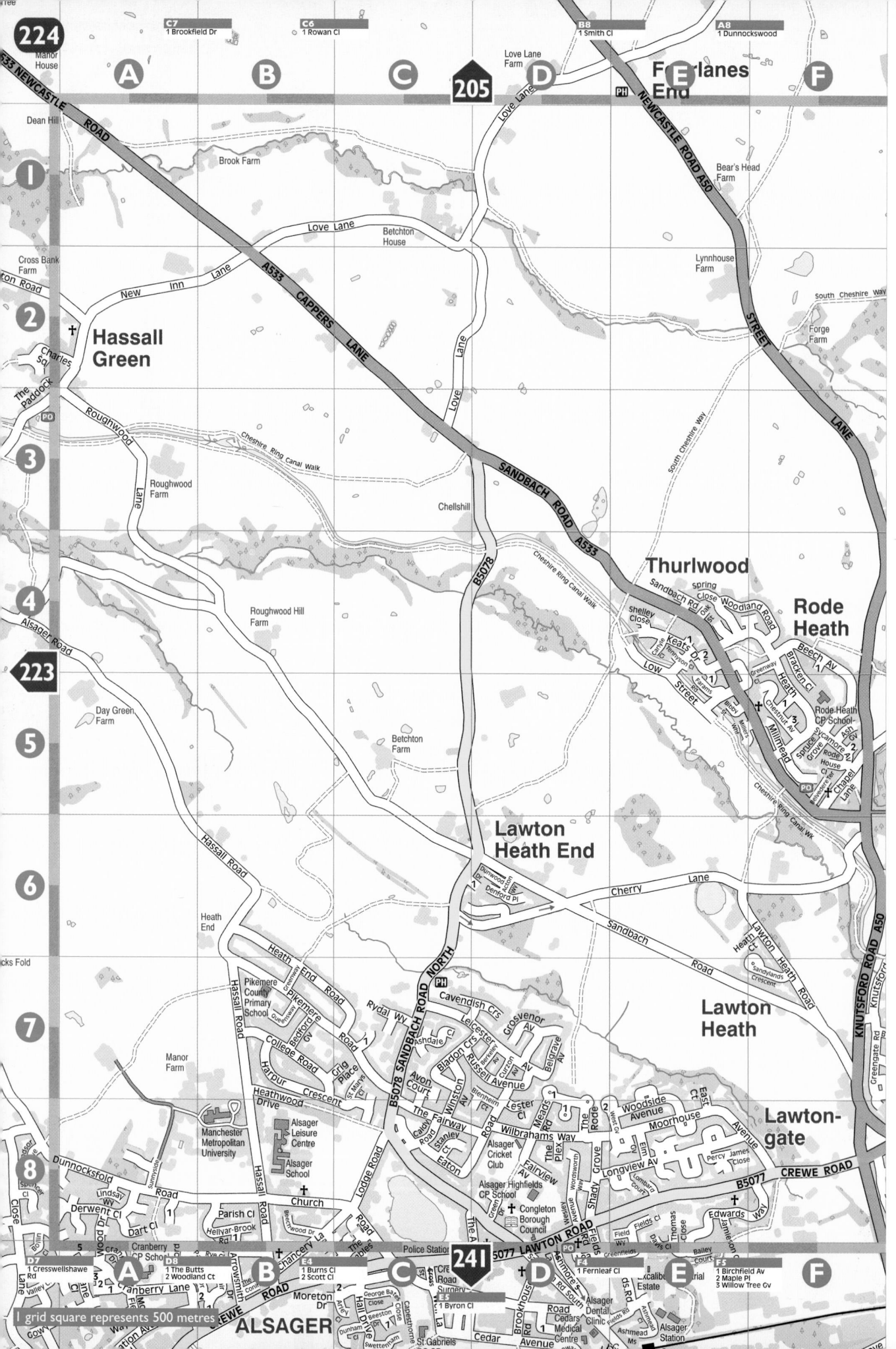

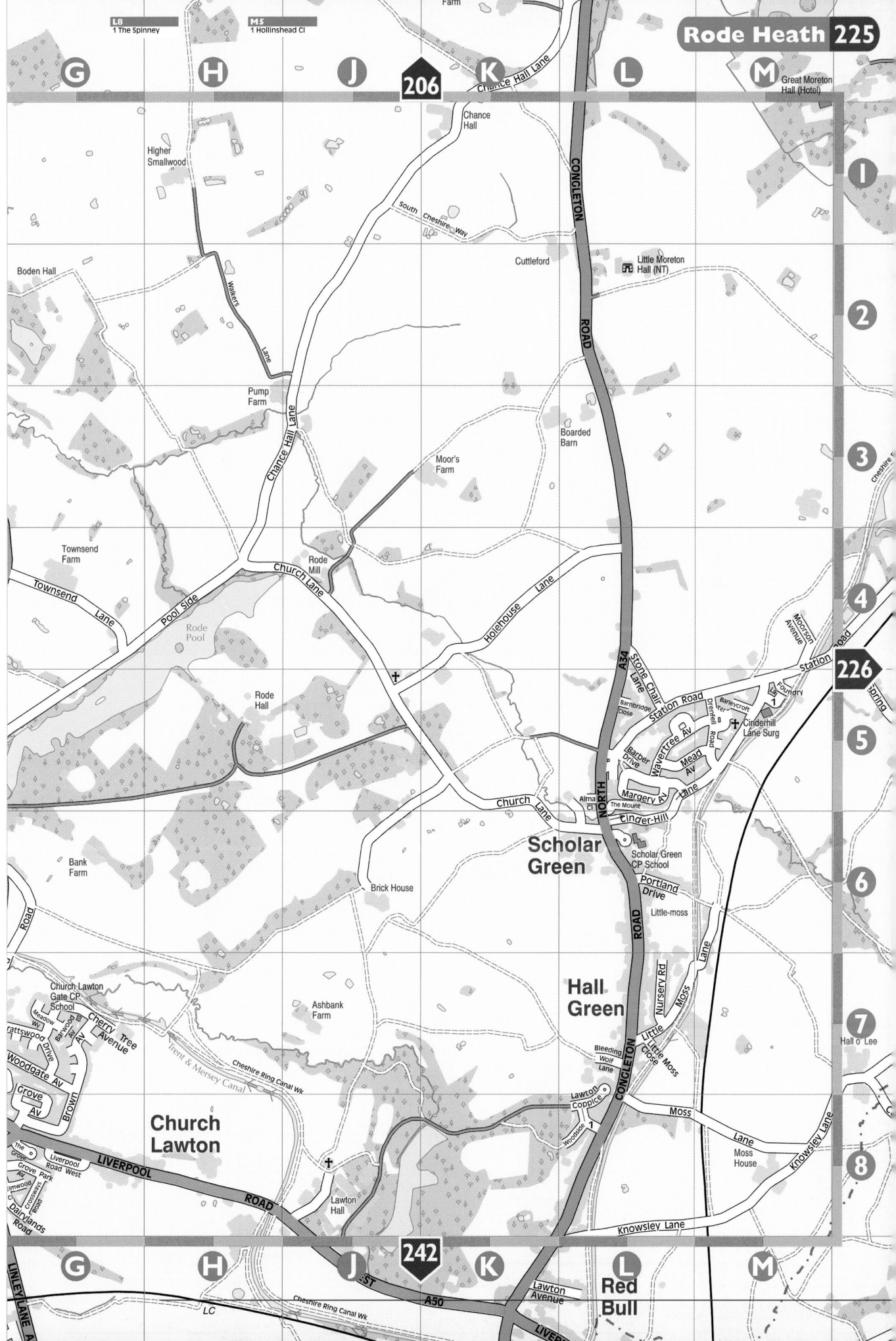

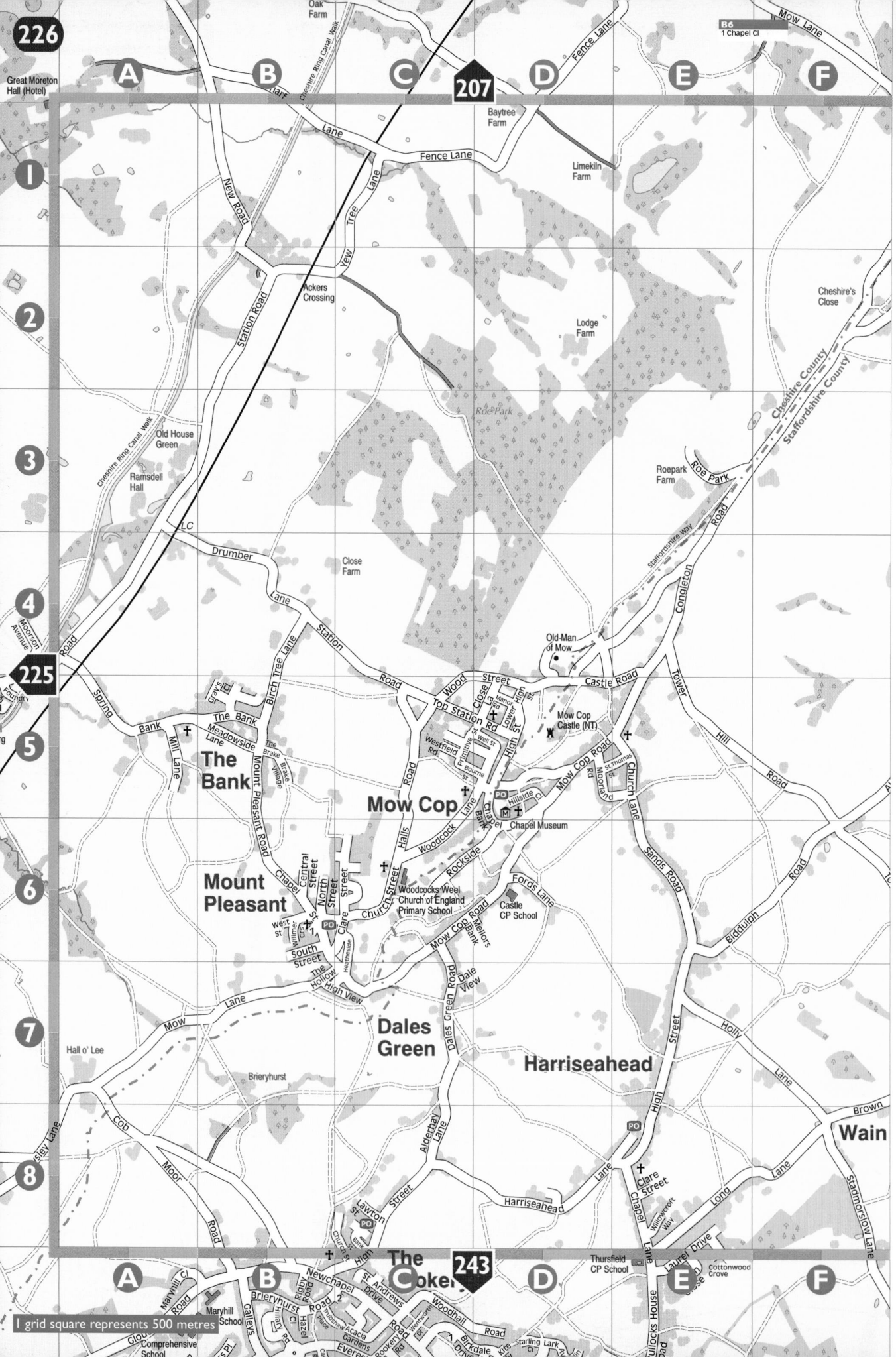

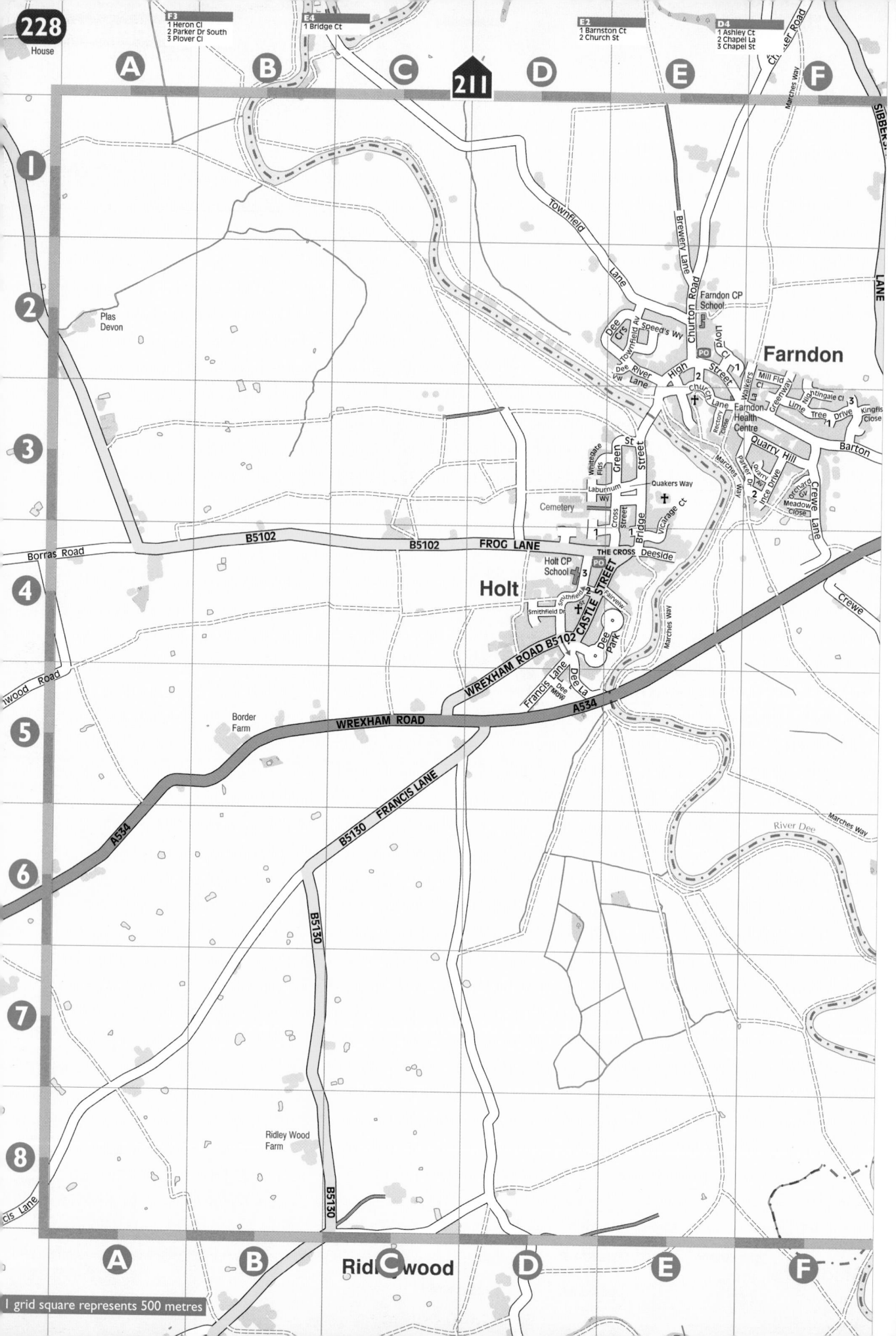

F3
1 Heron Cl
2 Parker Dr South
3 Plover Cl

E4
1 Bridge Ct

E2
1 Barnston Ct
2 Church St

D4
1 Ashley Ct
2 Chapel La
3 Chapel St

A B C D E F

1

2

Plas
Devon

Farndon

Farndon CP
School

Dee
Crs

Townfield Av

Speed's Wy

Churton Road

Brewery Lane

Dee
Vw

River
Lane

High
Street

PO

Walkers

Mill Fld

Greenfield

Nightingale Cl

Lime
Tree
Drive

Kingfisher
Close

3

Borras Road

B5102

B5102

FROG LANE

Whitegate
Flds

Green
Street

St
Street

Laburnum
Wy

Cross
Street

Bridge
Street

Quakers Way

Vicarage Ct

Marches Way

Parker Dr

Quarry
Av

Ince Drive

Orchard
Gv

Farndon
Health
Centre

Church Lane

Recon
Close

Quarry Hill

Crewe Lane

Meadow
Close

Barton

Cemetery

The Cross

Deeside

4

Holt CP
School

Holt

PO

Smithfield Dr

Smithfield La

CASTLE STREET

Fairview

Dee
Park

Dee La

Marches Way

Crewe

5

Border
Farm

WREXHAM ROAD

B5102

WREXHAM ROAD

Francis Lane

Dee
Mdw

A534

A534

River Dee

Marches Way

6

B5130

FRANCIS LANE

B5130

7

8

Ridley Wood
Farm

A534

wood Road

cis Lane

B5130

A B C D E F

1 grid square represents 500 metres

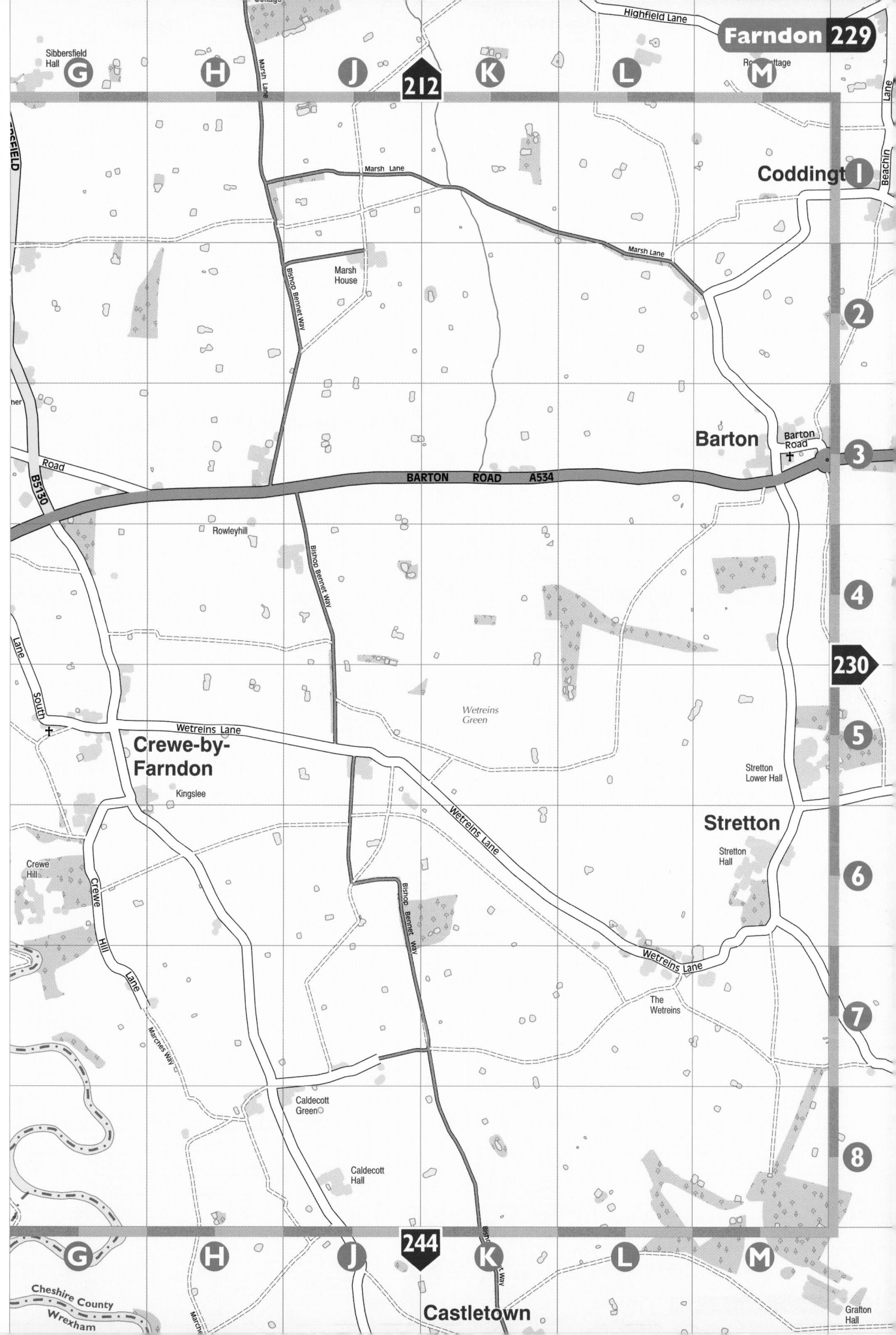

Highfield Lane

G H J K L M

212

Coddingt **1**

Beachin Lane

Marsh Lane

Marsh Lane

Bishop Bennet Way

Marsh House

2

Barton

Barton Road

3

BARTON ROAD A534

Road

B5130

Rowleyhill

Bishop Bennet Way

4

230

Wetreins Green

5

Stretton Lower Hall

Wetreins Lane

Crewe-by-Farndon

Kingslee

Stretton

Stretton Hall

Crewe Hill

6

Crewe Hill Lane

Wetreins Lane

Bishop Bennet Way

Wetreins Lane

The Wetreins

7

Marches Way

Caldecott Green

8

Caldecott Hall

Bishop Bennet Way

G H J K L M

244

Cheshire County

Wrexham

Castletown

Grafton Hall

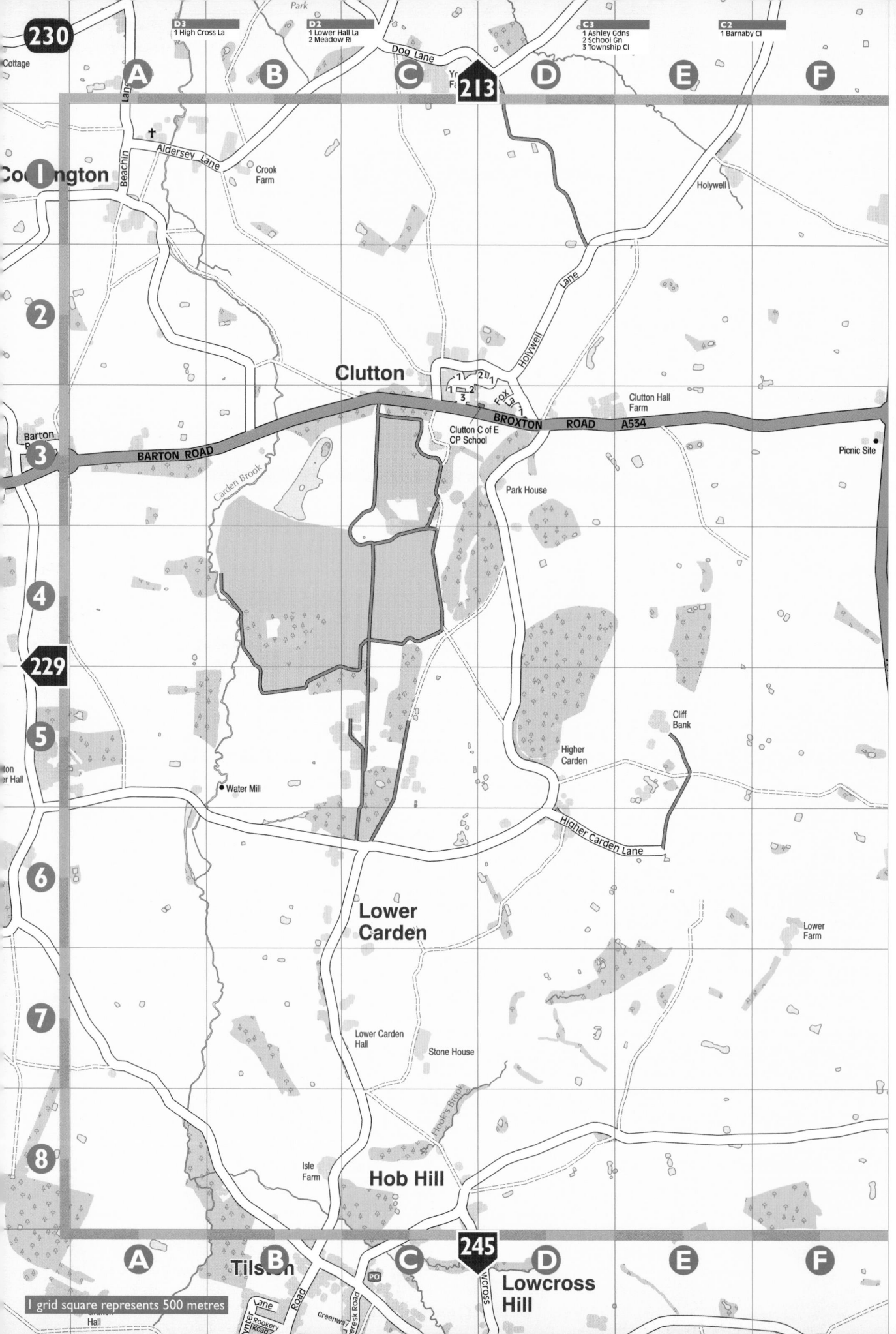

230

1 High Cross La D3

1 Lower Hall La D2
2 Meadow Ri

Dog Lane

C3 1 Ashley Gdns
2 School Gn
3 Township Cl

C2 1 Barnaby Cl

213

A

B

C

D

E

F

Cottage

†
Aldersey Lane

Co ington

1

Beachin

Crook Farm

Holywell

2

Clutton

3 Barton

BARTON ROAD

Carden Brook

1
1
3

2
2

1
1

FOX

BROXTON ROAD   A534

Clutton C of E
CP School

Clutton Hall
Farm

Picnic Site

Park House

229

4

5

Water Mill

Cliff
Bank

Higher
Carden

Higher Carden Lane

6

Lower
Carden

Lower
Farm

7

Lower Carden
Hall

Stone House

Hook's Brook

8

Isle
Farm

Hob Hill

A

B

C

245

D

E

F

Tils on

PO

Lowcross
Hill

Lane

Road

Greenway

eresk Road

Rookery
Road

Hall

1 grid square represents 500 metres

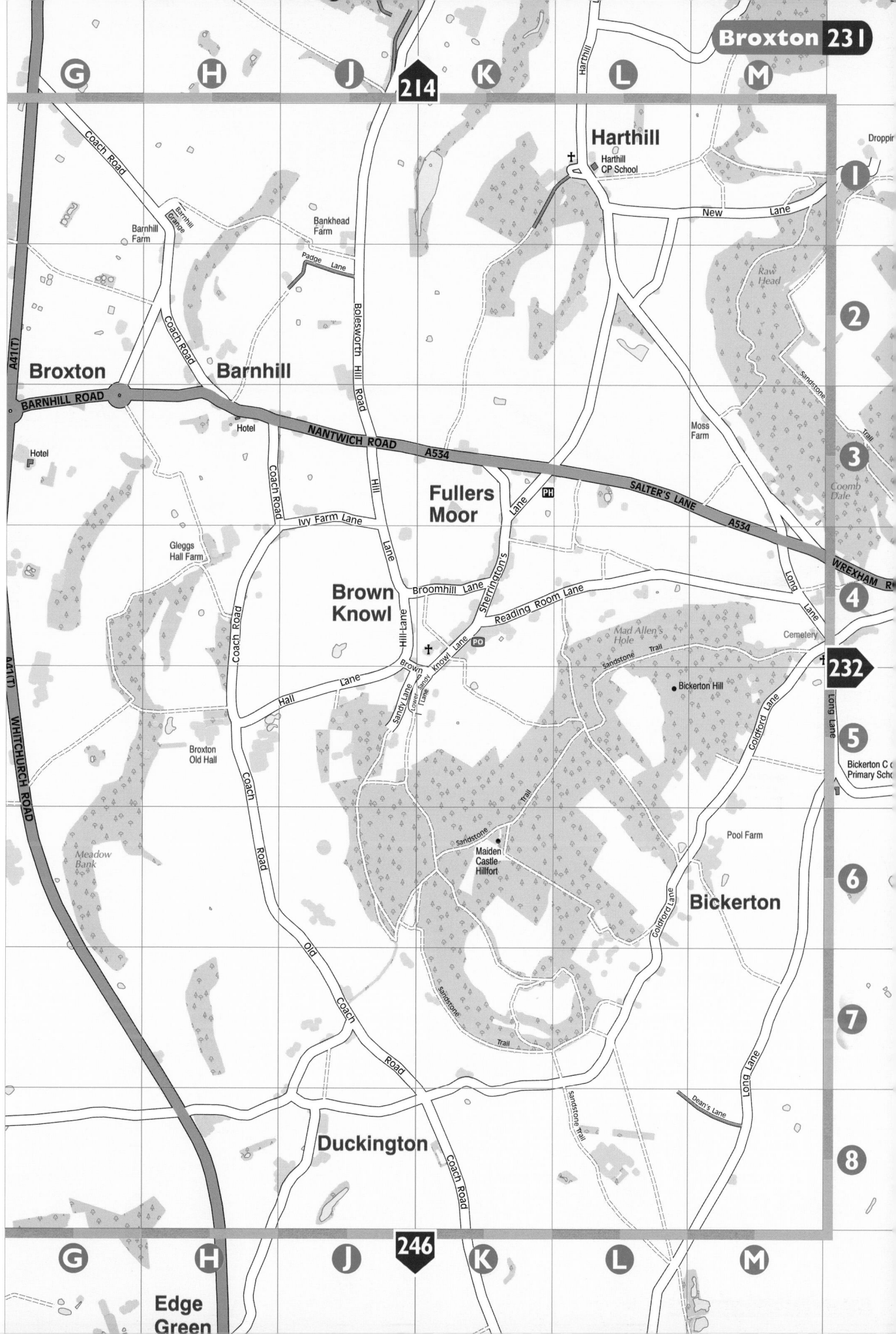

G H J K L M

214

231

Harthill

Harthill
CP School

Droppir

New Lane

1

Raw
Head

2

Sandstone

Coach Road

Barnhill
Grange

Bankhead
Farm

Barnhill
Farm

Padge Lane

Bolesworth Hill Road

Broxton

Barnhill

Moss
Farm

3

Coomb
Dale

Trail

A41(T)

BARNHILL ROAD

Hotel

NANTWICH ROAD A534

Hotel

Coach Road

Coach Road

Hill Lane

Fullers
Moor

Lane

PH

SALTER'S LANE A534

WREXHAM R

4

Ivy Farm Lane

Gleggs
Hall Farm

Brown
Knowl

Broomhill Lane

Sherrington's

Reading Room Lane

Mad Allen's
Hole

Sandstone Trail

Cemetery

Long Lane

232

Hill Lane

PO

Bickerton Hill

5

WHITCHURCH ROAD

Coach Road

Brown Lane

Hall Lane

Broxton
Old Hall

Lower Sandy Lane

Sandy Lane

Lane

Trail

Goldford Lane

Bickerton C
Primary Scho

Long Lane

A41(T)

Meadow
Bank

Sandstone

Maiden
Castle
Hillfort

Sandstone

Pool Farm

Bickerton

6

Goldford Lane

7

Old Coach Road

Trail

Sandstone Trail

Dean's Lane

Long Lane

8

Duckington

Coach Road

G H J K L M

246

Edge
Green

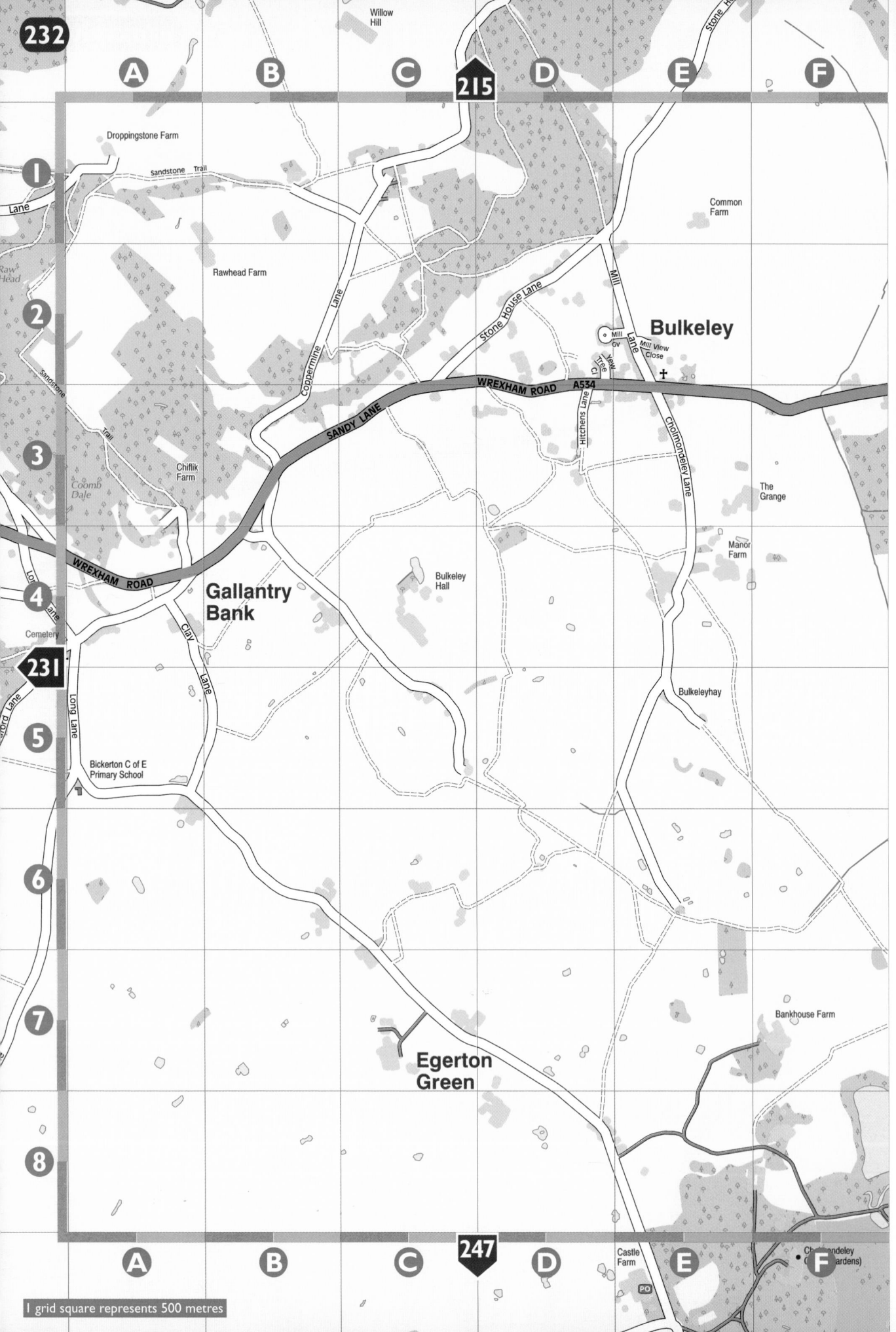

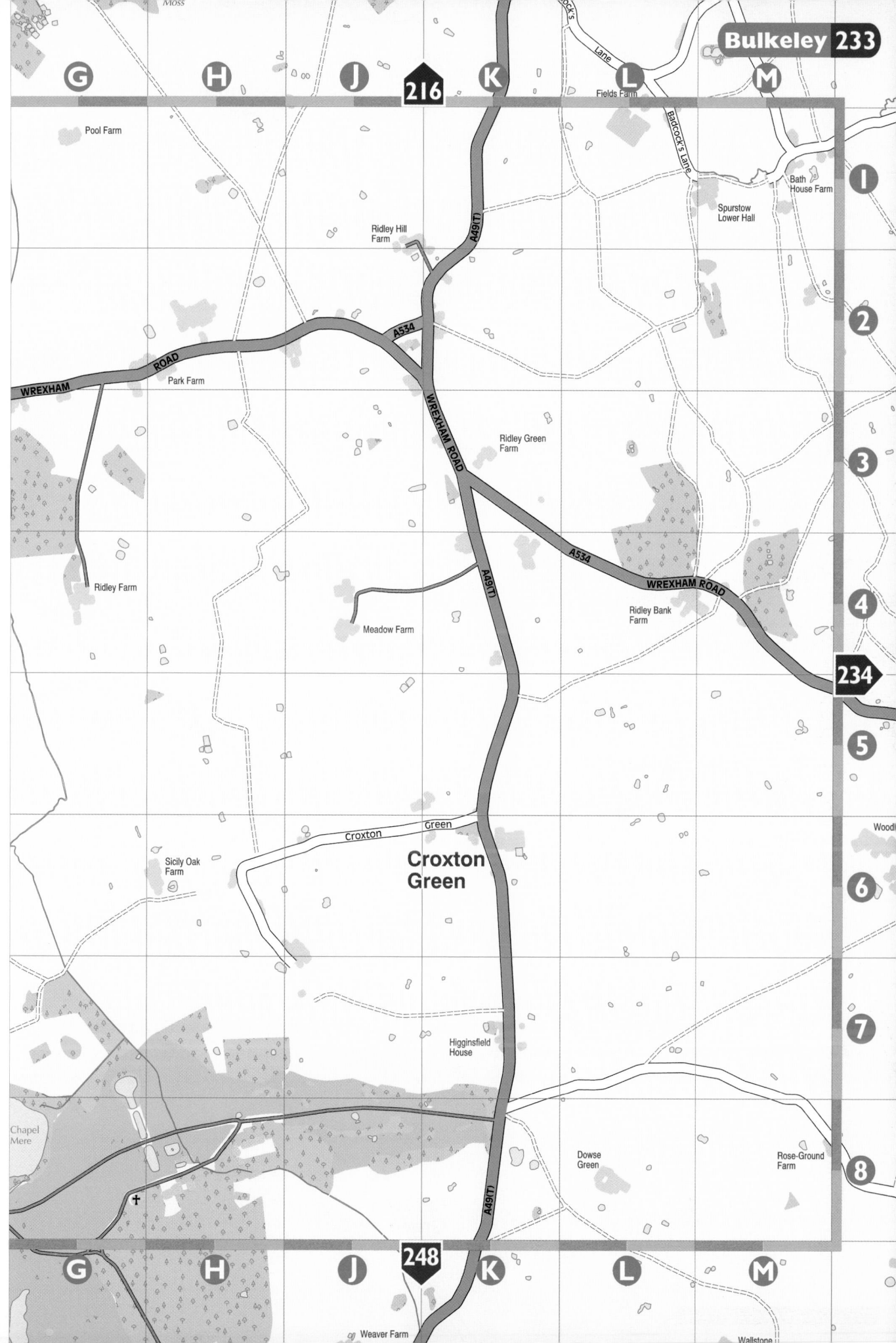

G   H   J   216   K   Fields Farm   L   M

Pool Farm

Bath House Farm

Spurstow Lower Hall

Ridley Hill Farm

A534

WREXHAM ROAD

Park Farm

A49(T)

WREXHAM ROAD

Ridley Green Farm

A534

Ridley Farm

WREXHAM ROAD

Meadow Farm

Ridley Bank Farm

234

Croxton Green

Croxton Green

Sicily Oak Farm

Wood

Higginsfield House

Chapel Mere

†

Dowse Green

Rose-Ground Farm

A49(T)

G   H   J   248   K   L   M

Weaver Farm

Wallstone

1
2
3
4
5
6
7
8

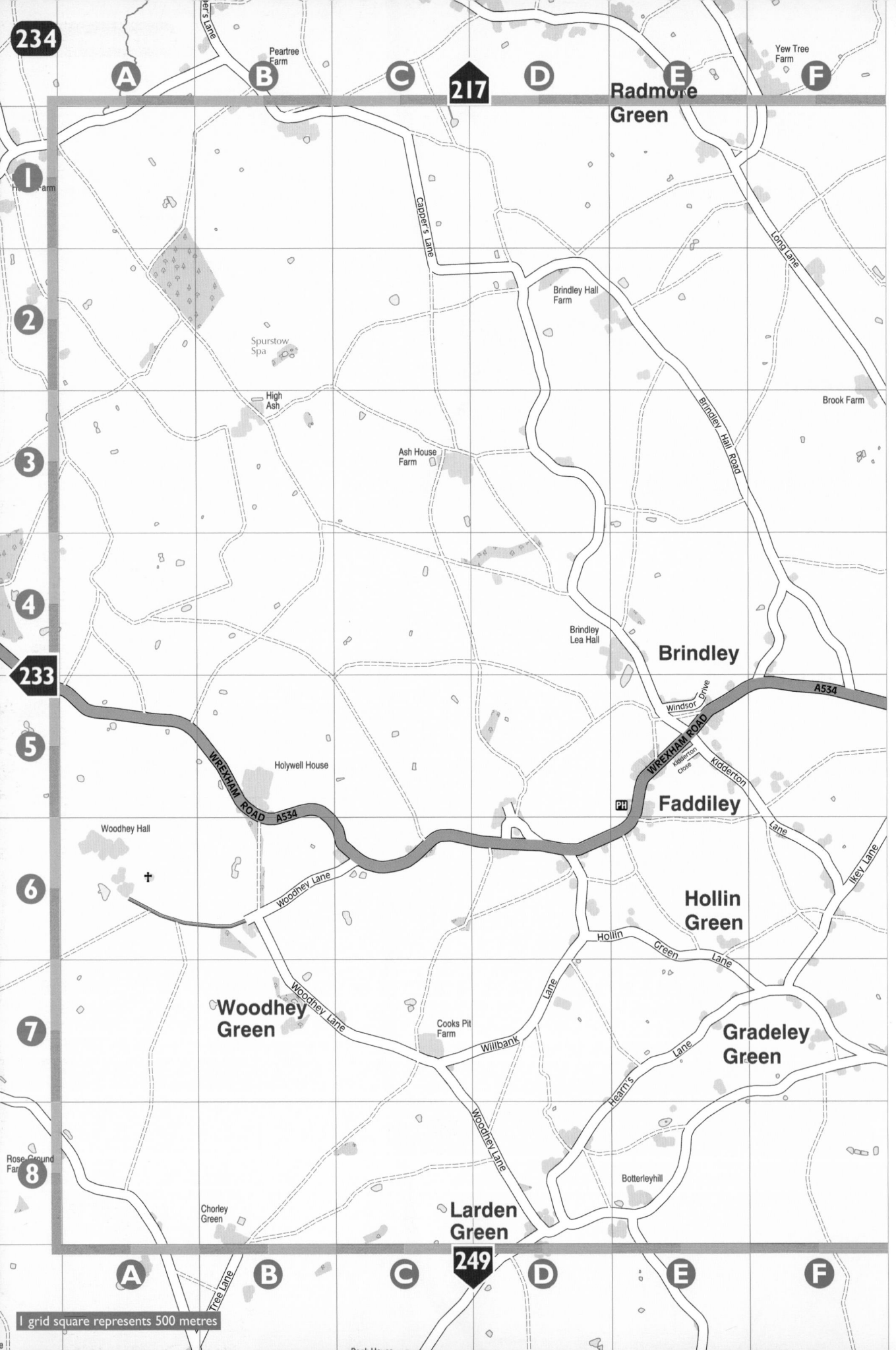

234

A B C **217** D E F

Radmore Green

Peartree Farm

Yew Tree Farm

1 Hill Farm

Cappers Lane

Long Lane

Brindley Hall Farm

2 Spurstow Spa

Brook Farm

High Ash

3 Ash House Farm

Brindley Hall Road

4 Brindley Lea Hall **Brindley**

233 A534

5 Holywell House WREXHAM ROAD Windsor Drive Kidderton Close Kidderton

Woodhey Hall WREXHAM ROAD A534 PH **Faddiley** Lane

Ikey Lane

6 † Woodhey Lane **Hollin Green**

Hollin Green Lane

7 **Woodhey Green** Woodhey Lane Cooks Pit Farm Willbank Hearn's Lane Lane **Gradeley Green**

8 Rose Ground Farm Chorley Green Woodhey Lane Botterleyhill **Larden Green**

A B C **249** D E F

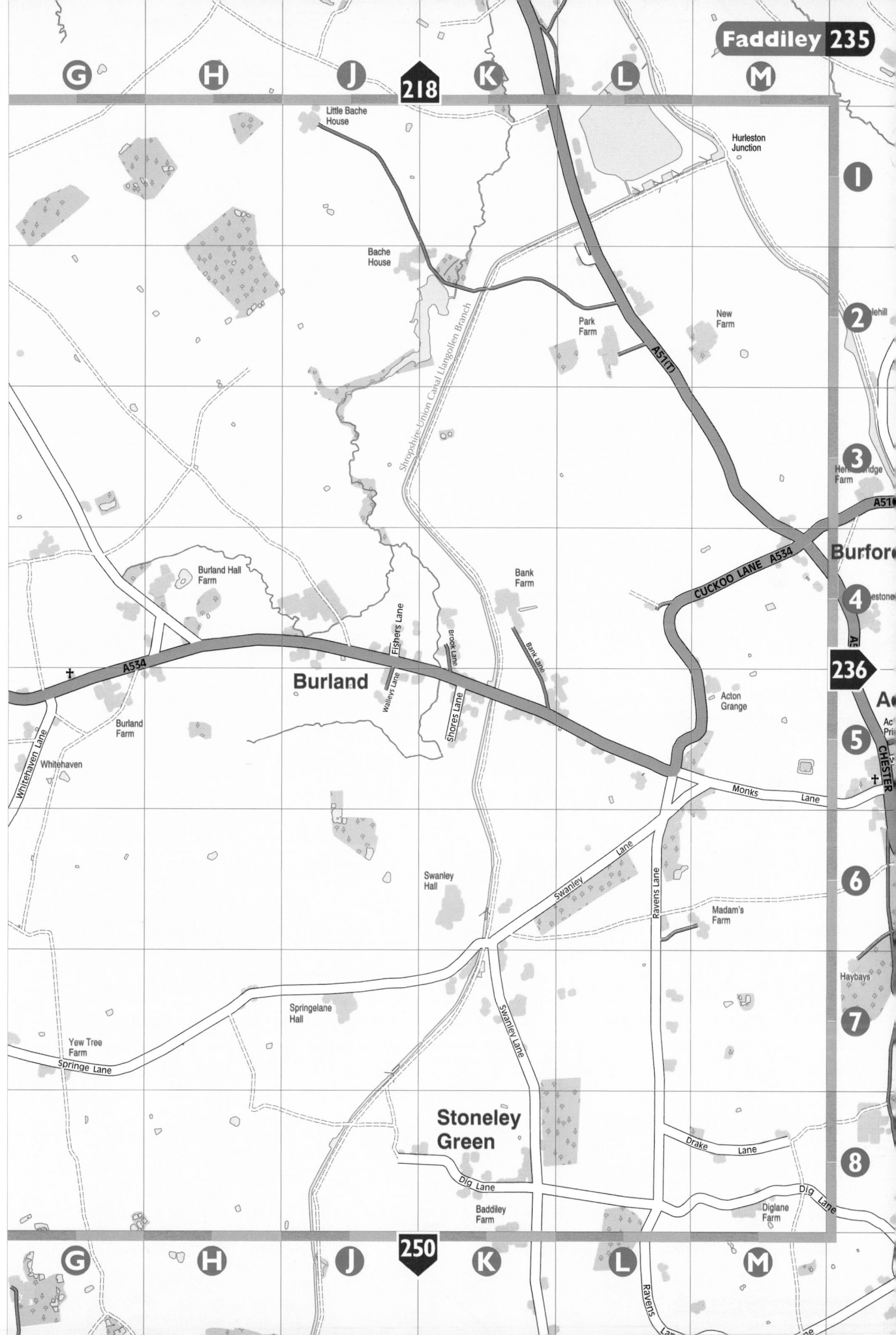

G H J 218 K L M

Little Bache House

Hurleston Junction

I

Bache House

2

Park Farm

New Farm

A51(T)

3

Hen?ridge Farm

A51

Burford

Burland Hall Farm

Bank Farm

CUCKOO LANE A534

4

Fishers Lane

Brook Lane

Bank Lane

Shropshire Union Canal Llangollen Branch

† A534

Burland

Walley's Lane

Shores Lane

Acton Grange

236

A?

Burland Farm

Whitehaven Lane

Whitehaven

5

Monks Lane

CHESTER

Swanley Hall

Swanley Lane

Ravens Lane

Madam's Farm

6

Haybays

Springelane Hall

Swanley Lane

7

Yew Tree Farm

Springe Lane

Stoneley Green

Drake Lane

8

Dig Lane

Baddiley Farm

Diglane Farm

Dig Lane

Ravens Lane

G H J 250 K L M

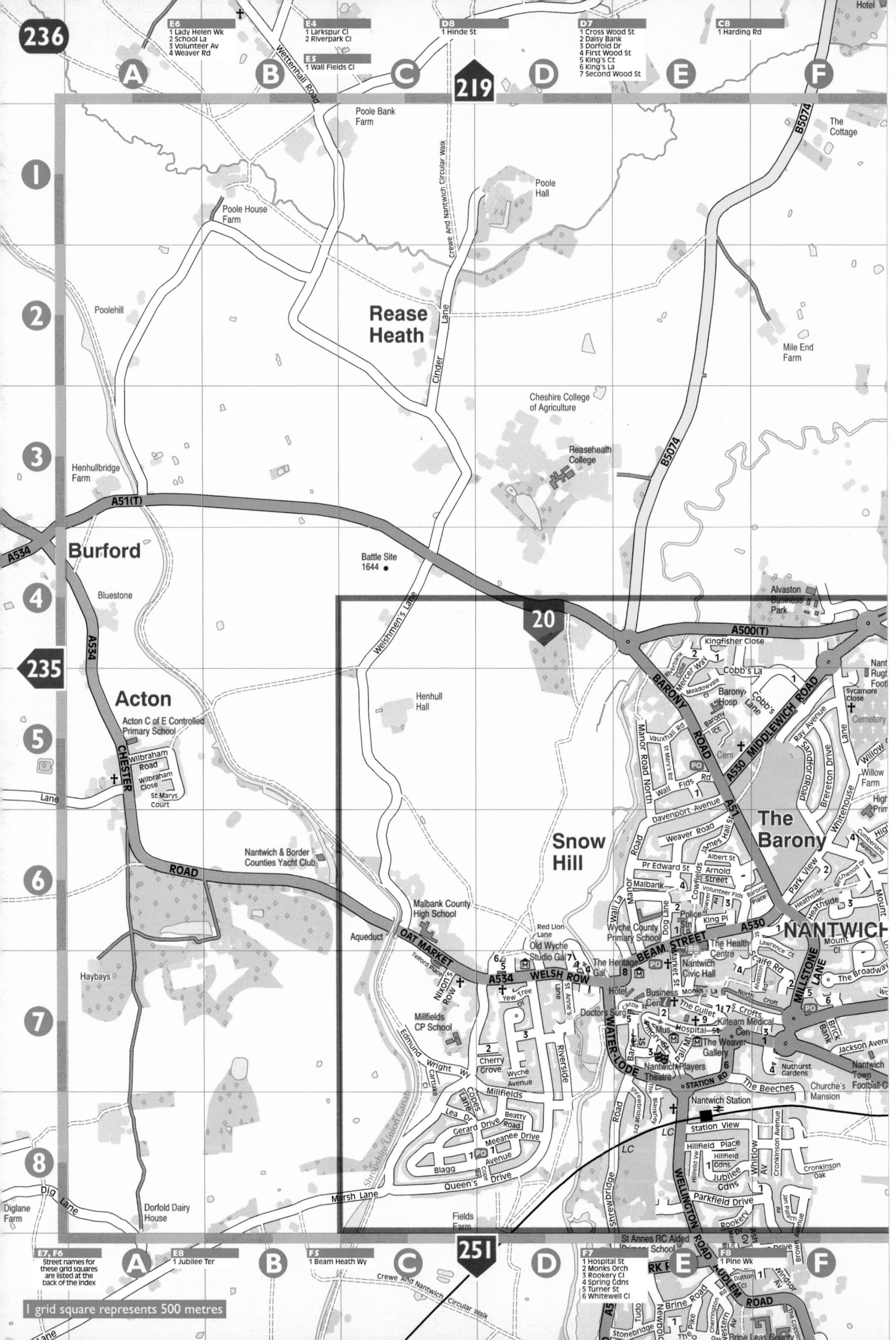

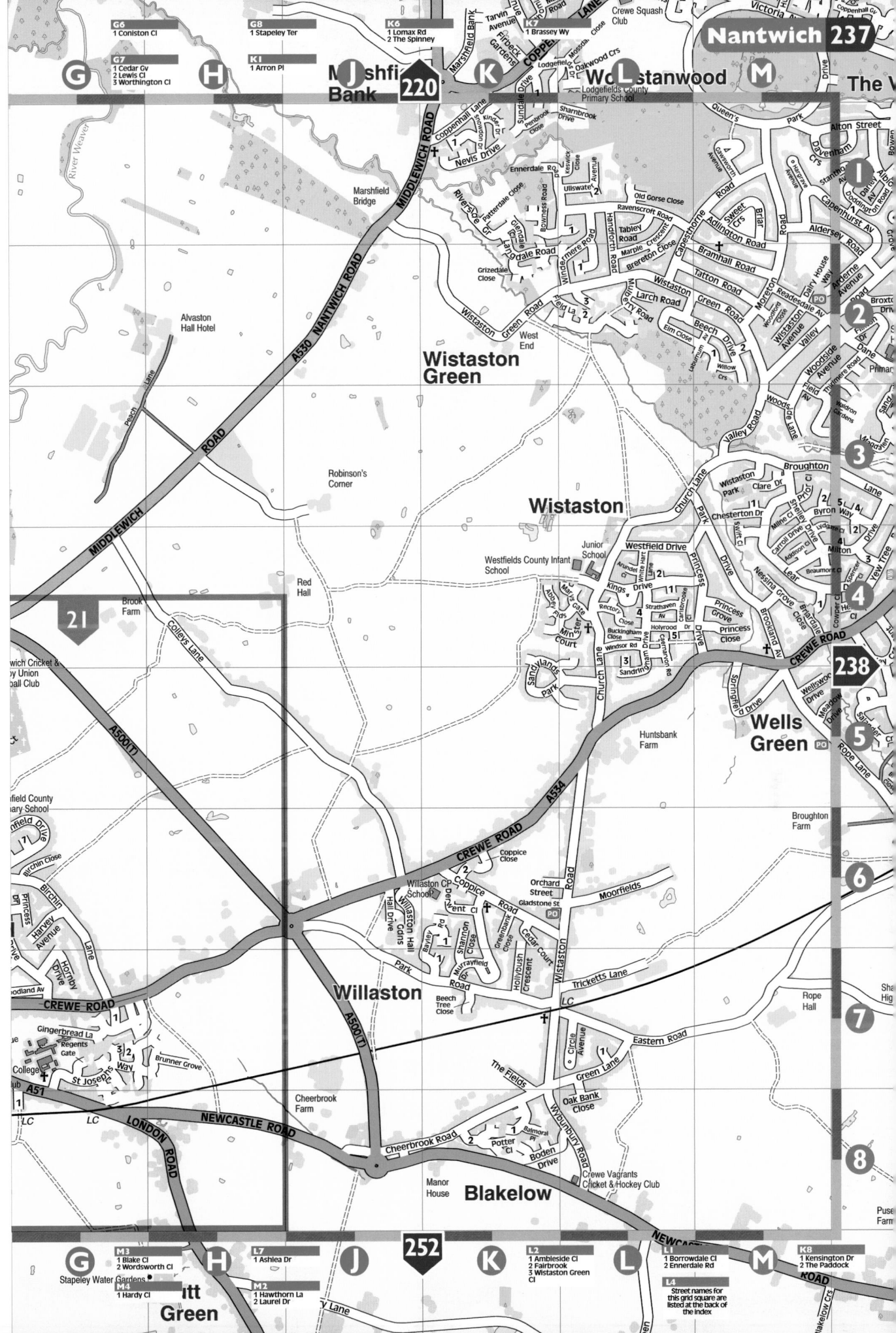

The W

G6
1 Coniston Cl

G8
1 Stapeley Ter

K6
1 Lomax Rd
2 The Spinney

G7
1 Cedar Gv
2 Lewis Cl
3 Worthington Cl

K1
1 Arron Pl

G H M J shfi Bank **220** K Wo L stanwood M

Crewe Squash Club

Lodgefields County Primary School

Marshfield Bank

Tarvin Avenue

COPPE

1 Brassey Wy

Firbeck Gardens

Lodgefield

Oakwood Crs

Mossdale

Queen's Park

Alton Street

I

Davenham Crs

Stantho

Albion

Dailey Av

Coddington

Capenhurst Av

Arderne Avenue

Broxto

Coppenhall G

Coppenhall

Victoria Avenue

Middlewich Road

Coppenhall Lane

Nevis Drive

Snowdon Dr

Pembrook

Kinder Dr

Sundale Drive

Sharnbrook Drive

Ennerdale Rd

Keswick Close

Ulliswate

Old Gorse Close

Ravenscroft Road

Capesthorne Road

Adlington Road

Sweet Crs

Briar

Moreton

Readesdale Av

Woodside

PO

Broxto Drive

Field Dane

Phman

Marshfield Bridge

Riverside Cr

Glendale

Langdale Road

Grizedale Close

Windermere Road

Bowness Road

Handforth Road

Tabley Road

Marple Crescent

Brereton Close

Bramhall Road

2

Valley

Waldron Gardens

Sandy

Alvaston Hall Hotel

Wistaston Green Road

West End

Wistaston Green Road

Larch Road

Wistaston Green Road

Beech Drive

Elm Close

Laburnum

Willow Crs

Mulberry Road

Woodside Avenue

Woodside Lane

Valley Road

3

Wistaston Green

Broughton Lane

Wistaston Park

Clare Dr

Prior

Milne Dr

Stapley

Carroll Drive

Addison Cl

Byron Way

Lidgate Cl

Milton

Yew Tree

Beech Road

Robinson's Corner

Wistaston

Church Lane

Chesterton Dr

Swift Cl

Princess Drive

Lear

Nessina Grove

Beaumont Cl

Westfield Drive

Arundel Cl

White Hart

Mary Gate

Kings Drive

Strathaven Av

Carisbrooke

Brookland Av

Princess Grove

Yew Tree Drive

Cowper Cl

4

Beardale Cl

Red Hall

Westfields County Infant School

Junior School

Rector's Close

Abbey Rds

Buckingham Close

Holyrood Dr

Princess Close

21

Brook Farm

Min ster court

Windsor Rd

Caernarvon Rd

Springfield Drive

CREWE ROAD

238

ch Cricket & y Union ball Club

Colleys Lane

Sandylands Park

Sandrin

Sandrin Rd

Wellswood Drive

Meadow Drive

Rope Lane

8

Middlewich Road

A500(T)

Huntsbank Farm

Wells Green

PO

Samber

5

field County ary School

Birchin Close

Birchin Lane

A534

Broughton Farm

6

7

Crewe Road

Coppice Close

Orchard Street

Gladstone St

PO

Moorfields

Willaston CP School

Coppice Derwent Cl

Bayley Rd

Shannon Close

Murrayfield Crescent

Greenbank Close

Hollybush Crescent

Cedar Court

Wistaston Road

Tricketts Lane

LC

Rope Hall

Sha Hig

7

Princess Drive

Harvey Avenue

Hornby Drive

Woodland Av

Hall Gdns

Willaston Hall

Park Road

Willaston

Beech Tree Close

Circle Avenue

Eastern Road

Green Lane

Crewe Road

St Joseph's

Gingerbread La

Regents Gate

Brunner Grove

Way

The Fields

Oak Bank Close

Wybunbury Road

CREWE ROAD

A51

LC

LC

London Road

Newcastle Road

Cheerbrook Farm

Cheerbrook Road

Manor House

Balmoral Pl

Potter Cl

Boden Drive

Crewe Vagrants Cricket & Hockey Club

Puse Farm

8

Blakelow

NEWCAST

Blakelow Crs

G **M3**
1 Blake Cl
2 Wordsworth Cl

M4
1 Hardy Cl

H **L7**
1 Ashlea Dr

J **252**

K **L2**
1 Ambleside Cl
2 Fairbrook
3 Wistaston Green Cl

L **L1**
1 Borrowdale Cl
2 Ennerdale Rd

M **K8**
1 Kensington Dr
2 The Paddock

Stapeley Water Gardens

M2
1 Hawthorn La
2 Laurel Dr

itt Green

L4
Street names for this grid square are listed at the back of the index

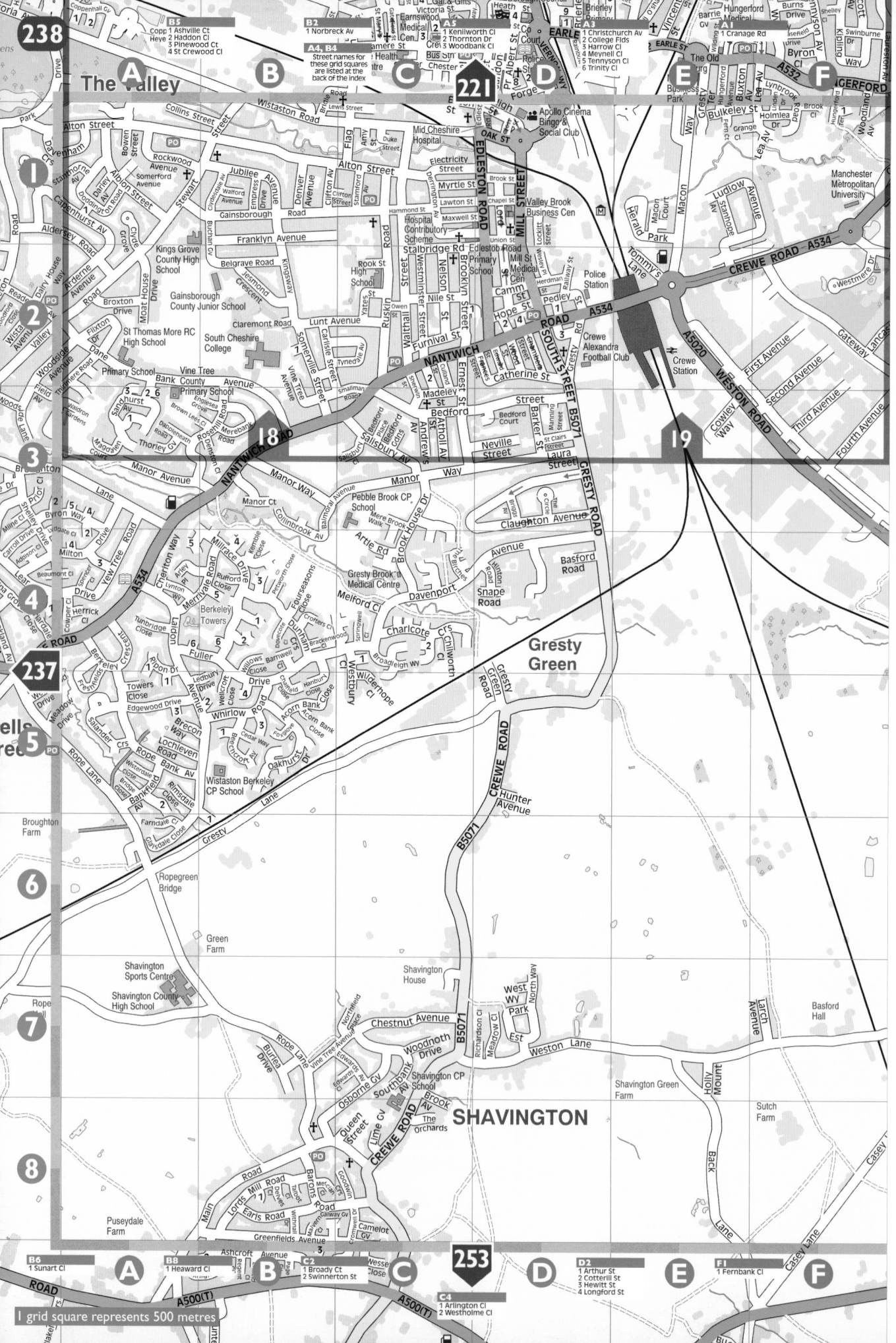

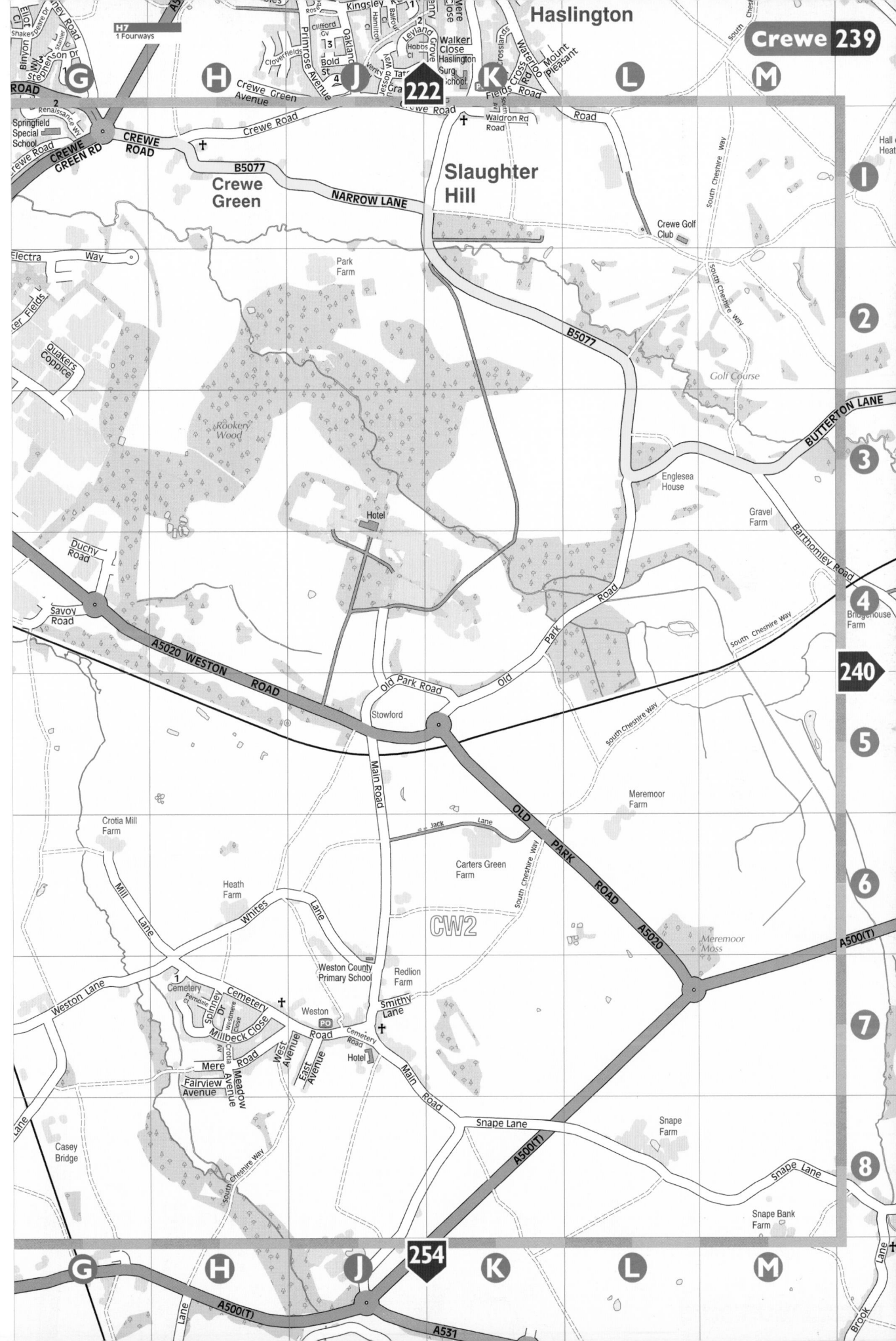

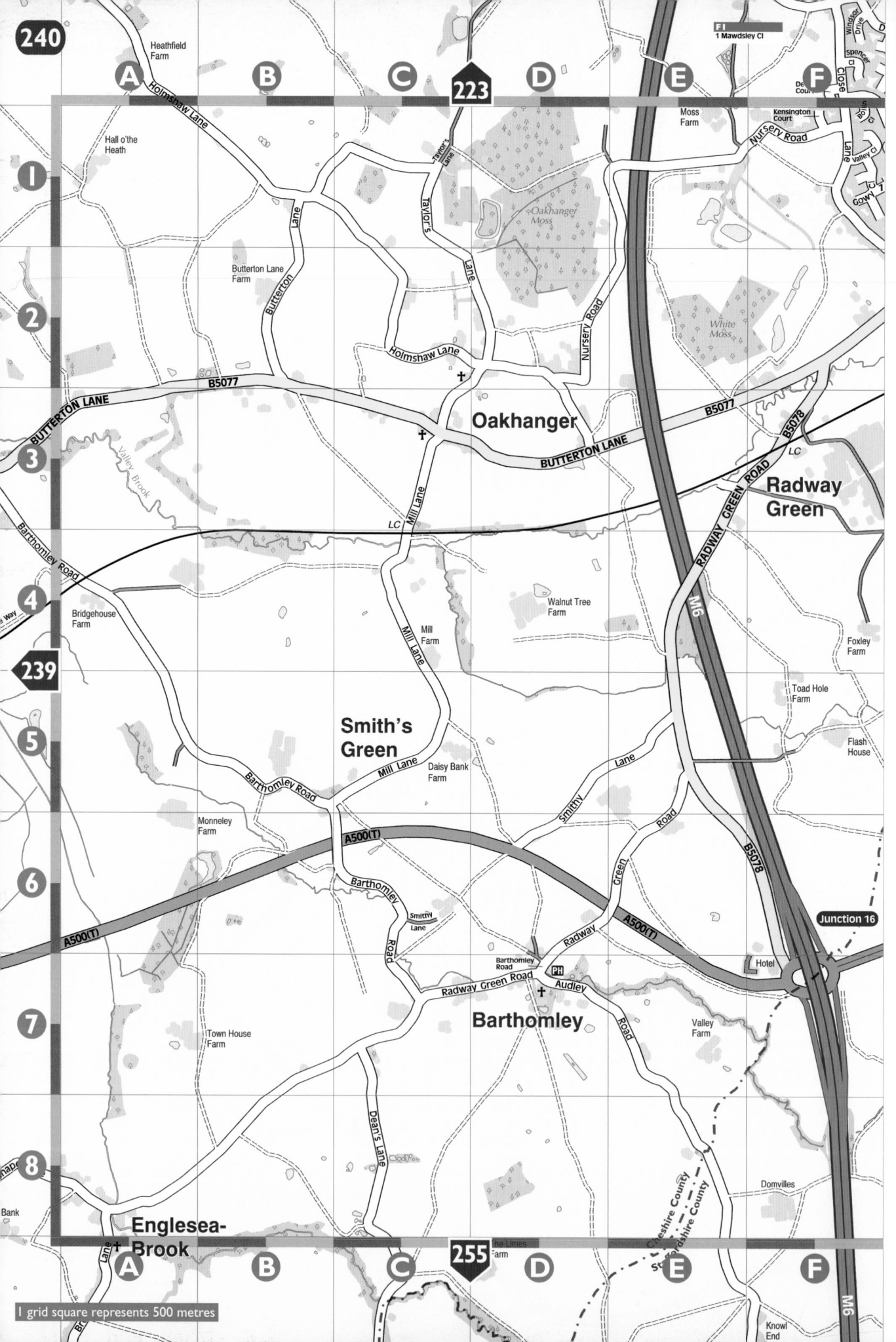

A   B   C   **223**   D   E   F

Heathfield Farm

Holmshaw Lane

Moss Farm

Nursery Road

Kensington Court

F1
1 Mawdsley Cl

Windsor Drive

Spencer Cl

De Court

Gowy Cl

1

Hall o'the Heath

Butterton Lane Farm

Butterton Lane

Taylor's Lane

Oakhanger Moss

White Moss

2

B5077

Holmshaw Lane

†

Oakhanger

B5077

B5078

BUTTERTON LANE

3

BUTTERTON LANE

Valley Brook

†

LC   Mill Lane

LC

Butterton Lane

RADWAY GREEN ROAD

Radway Green

LC

Barthomley Road

Walnut Tree Farm

M6

Foxley Farm

4

Bridgehouse Farm

Mill Farm

Way

Toad Hole Farm

Flash House

5

Smith's Green

Mill Lane

Daisy Bank Farm

Barthomley Road

Smithy Lane

Green Road

B5078

Monneley Farm

A500(T)

6

A500(T)

Barthomley

Smithy Lane

Radway Green Road

A500(T)

Junction 16

Hotel

Road

Barthomley Road

PH

Radway

Audley

7

Town House Farm

Dean's Lane

†

Barthomley

Road

Valley Farm

Cheshire County

Staffordshire County

Domvilles

8

Bank

Englesea-Brook

†

na Limes Farm

Knowl End

Lane

M6

A   B   C   **255**   D   E   F

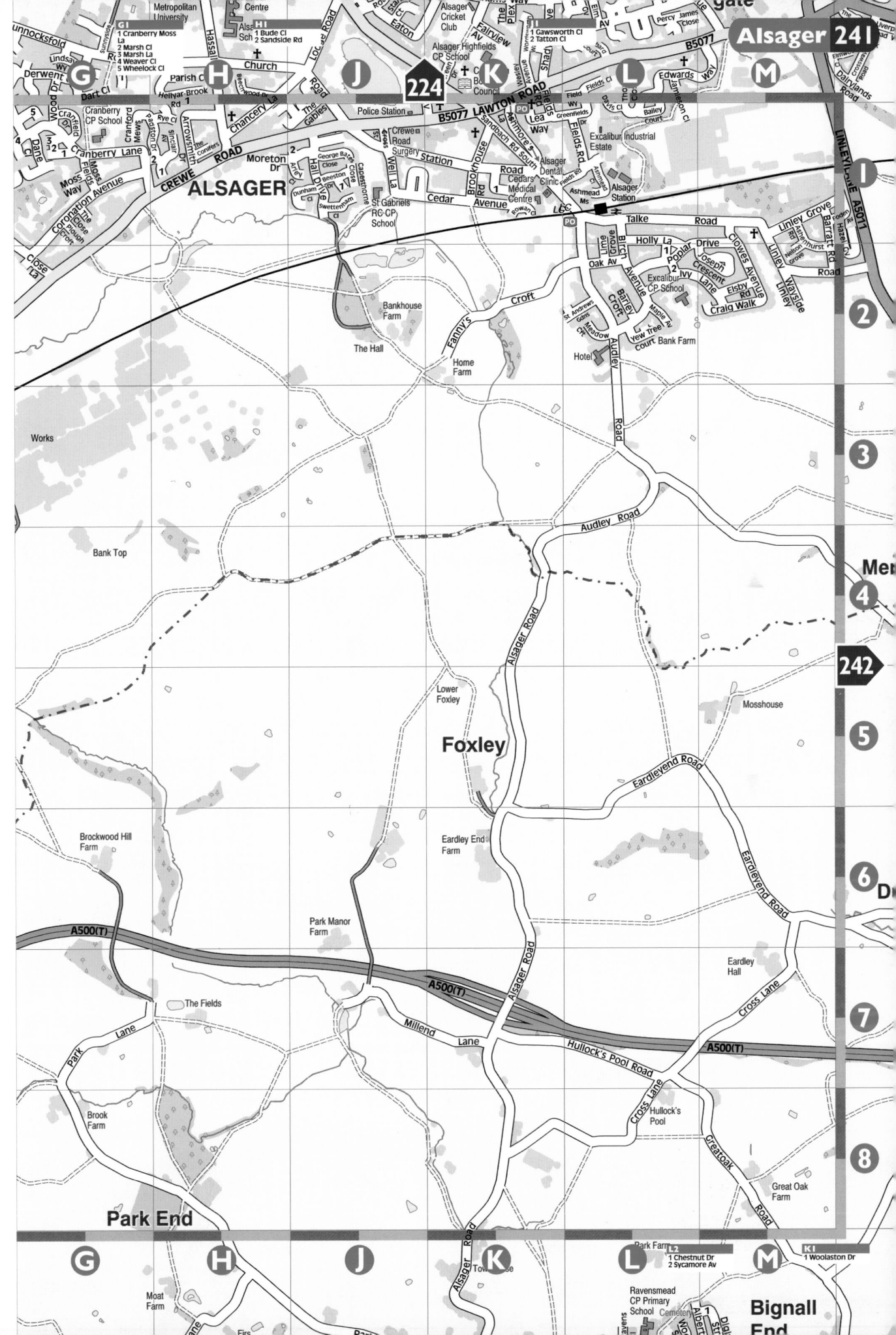

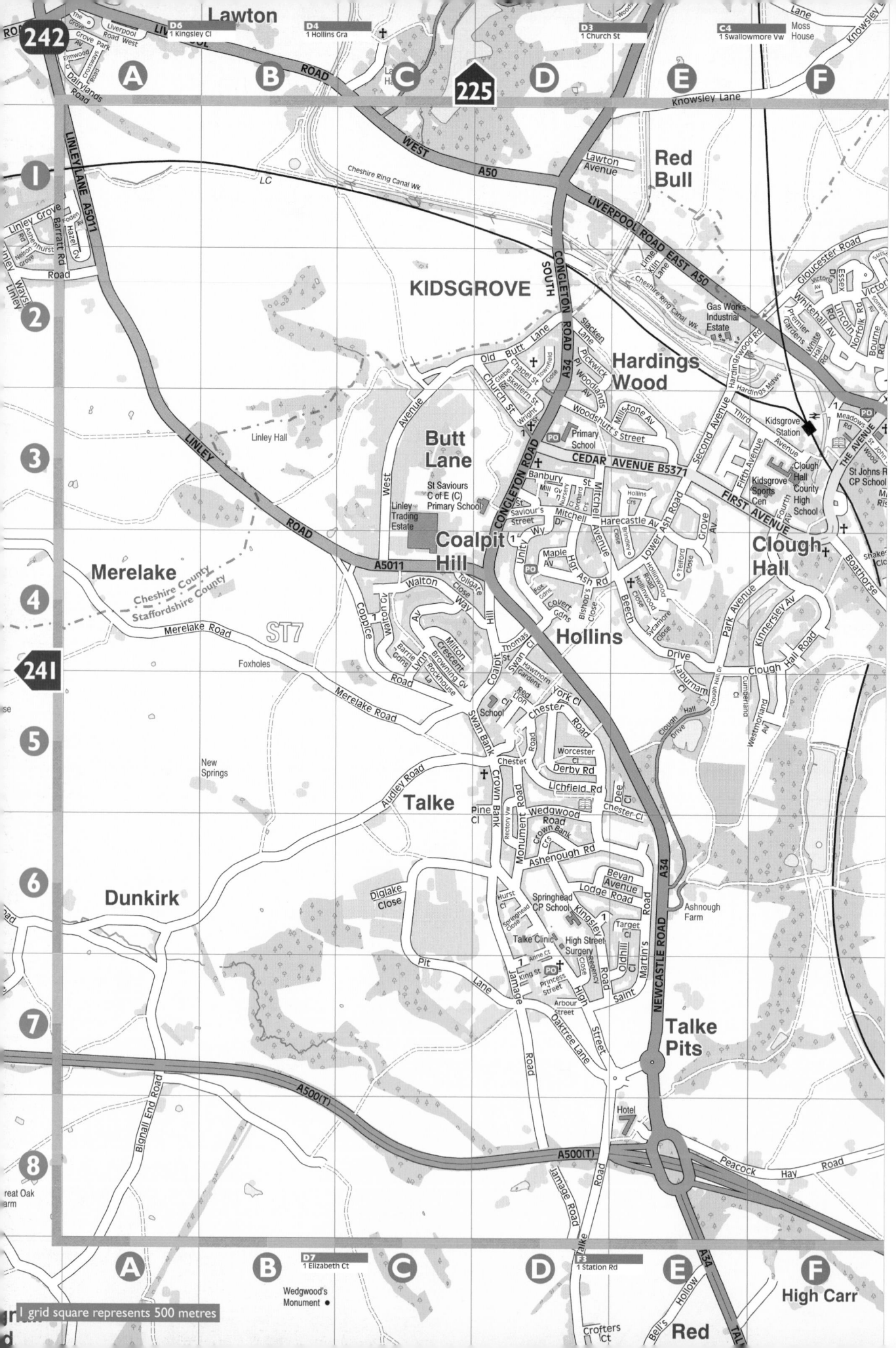

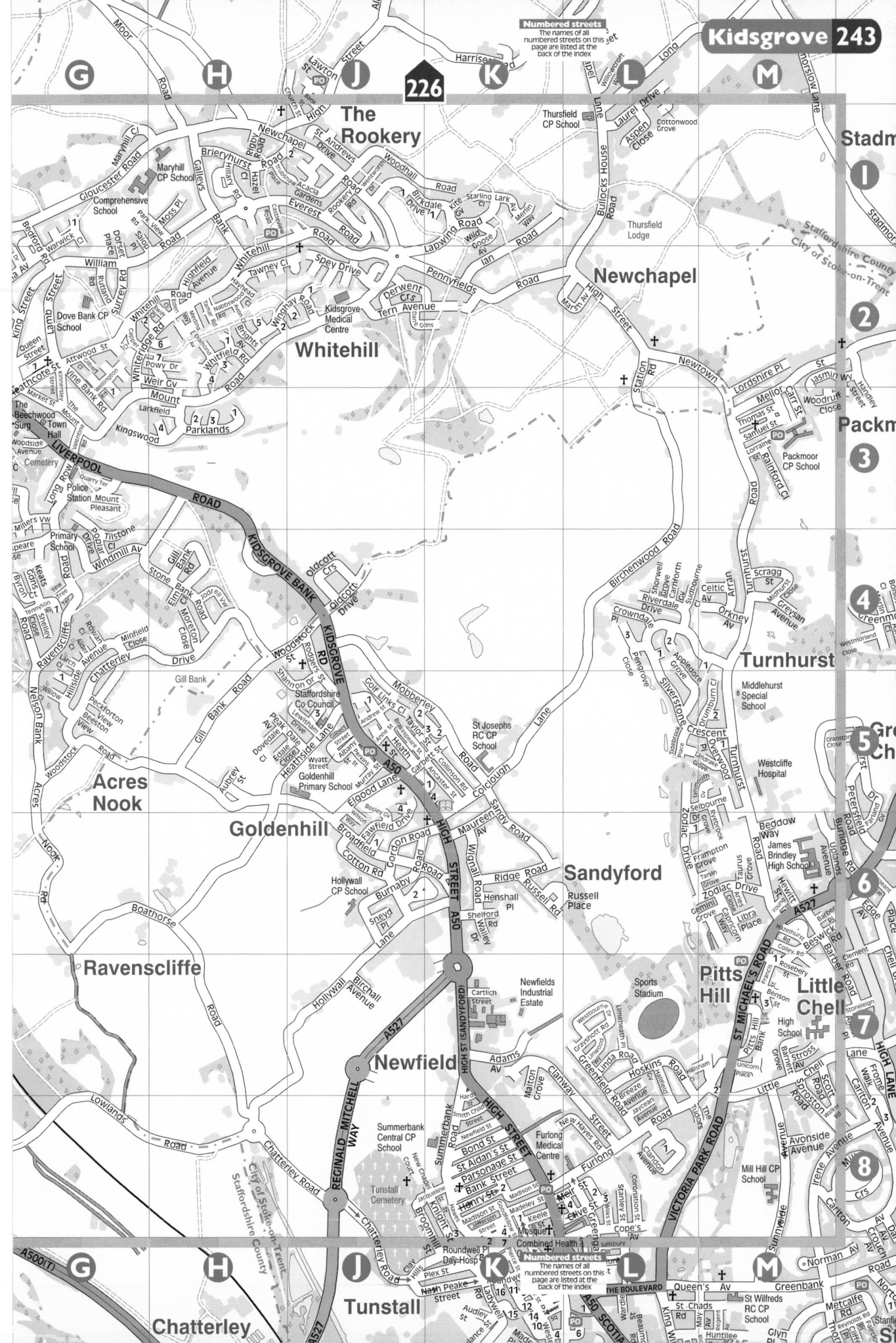

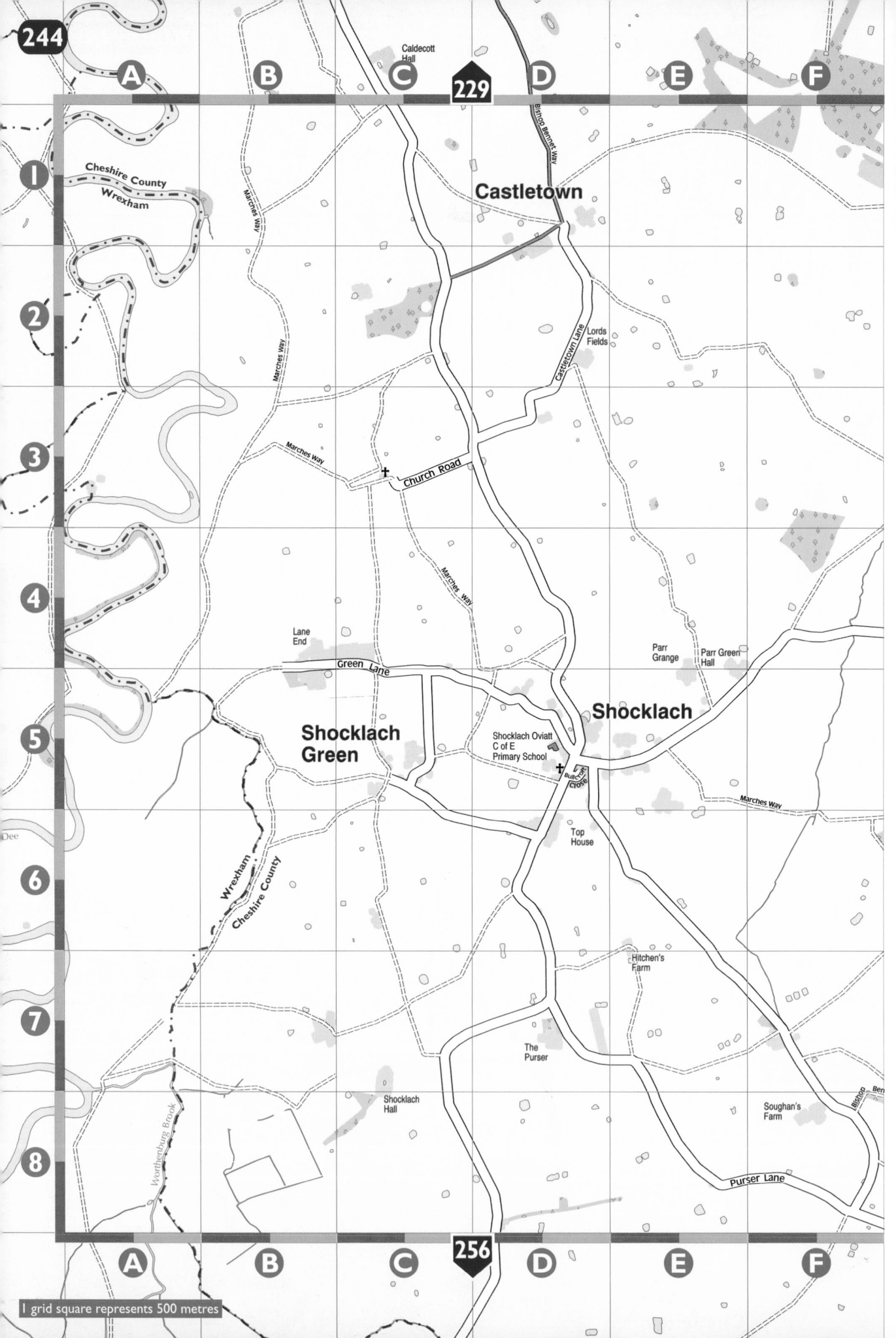

229

256

A B C D E F

1
2
3
4
5
6
7
8

Cheshire County
Wrexham

Marches Way

Caldecott
Hall

Castletown

Bishop Bennet Way

Castletown Lane

Lords
Fields

Marches Way

Church Road

Marches Way

Lane
End

Green Lane

Parr
Grange

Parr Green
Hall

**Shocklach
Green**

Shocklach Oviatt
C of E
Primary School

Shocklach

Bullcroft
Close

Top
House

Marches Way

Wrexham

Cheshire County

Dee

Hitchen's
Farm

The
Purser

Worthenbury Brook

Shocklach
Hall

Soughan's
Farm

Bishop Ben

Purser Lane

A B C D E F

1 grid square represents 500 metres

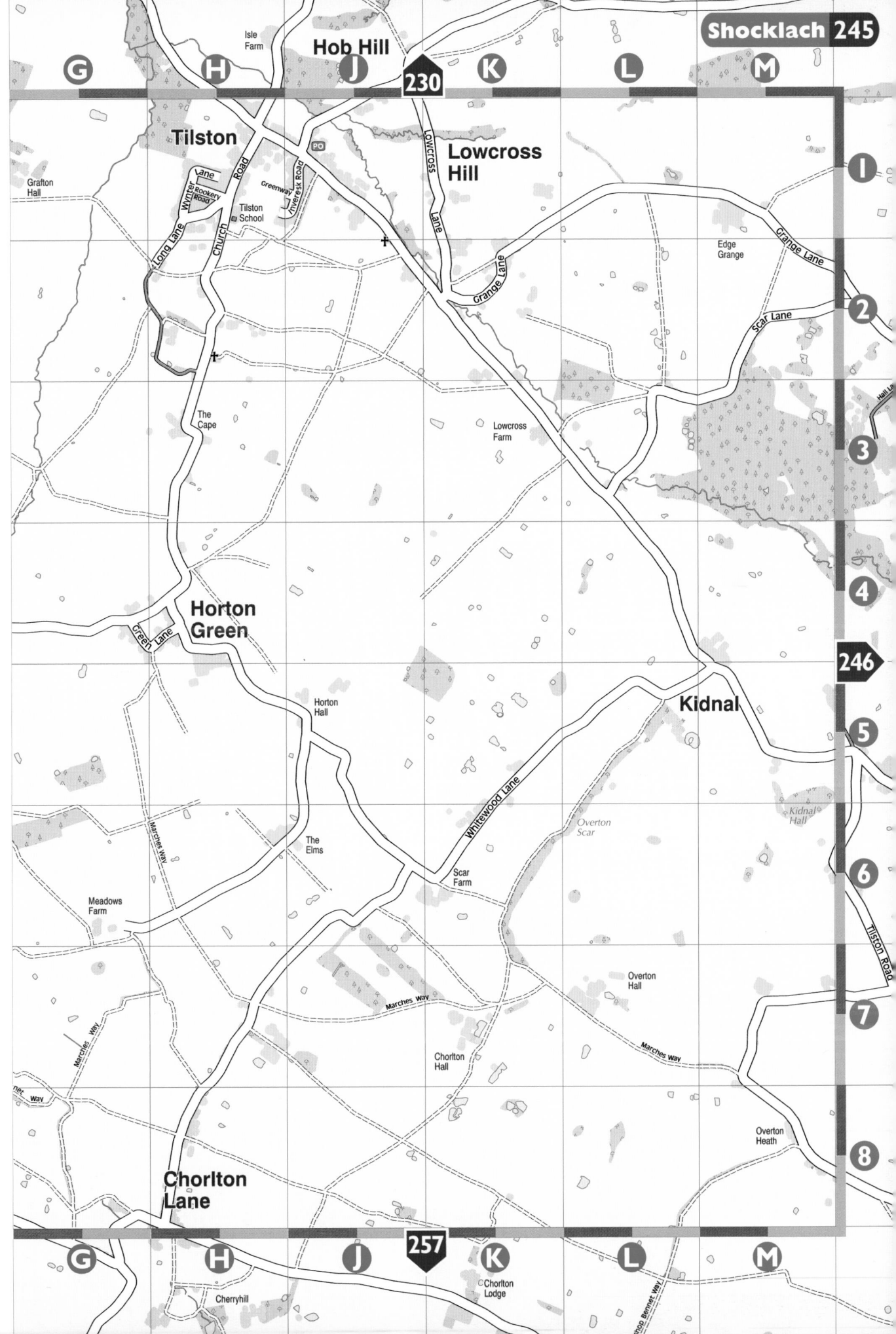

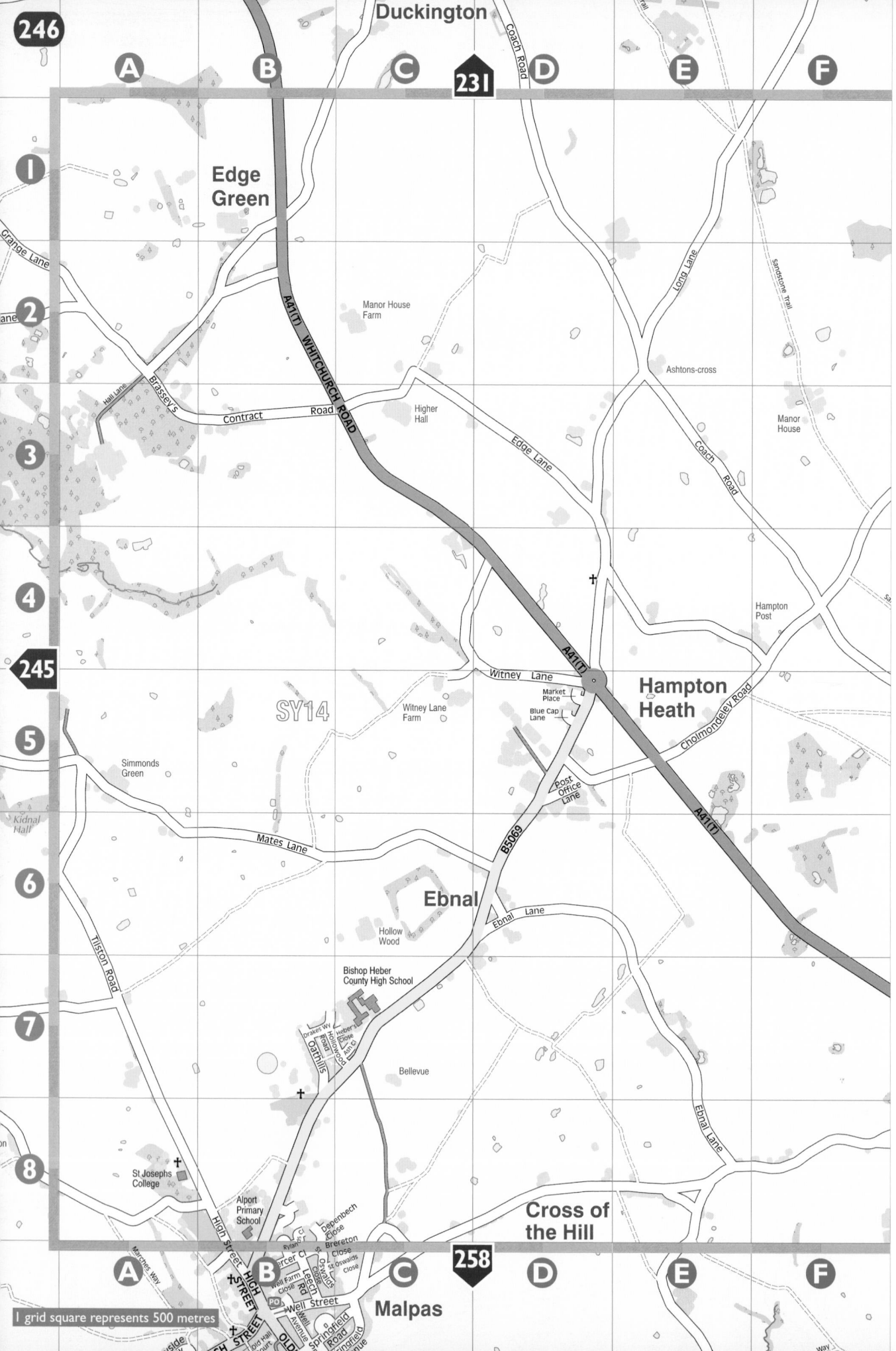

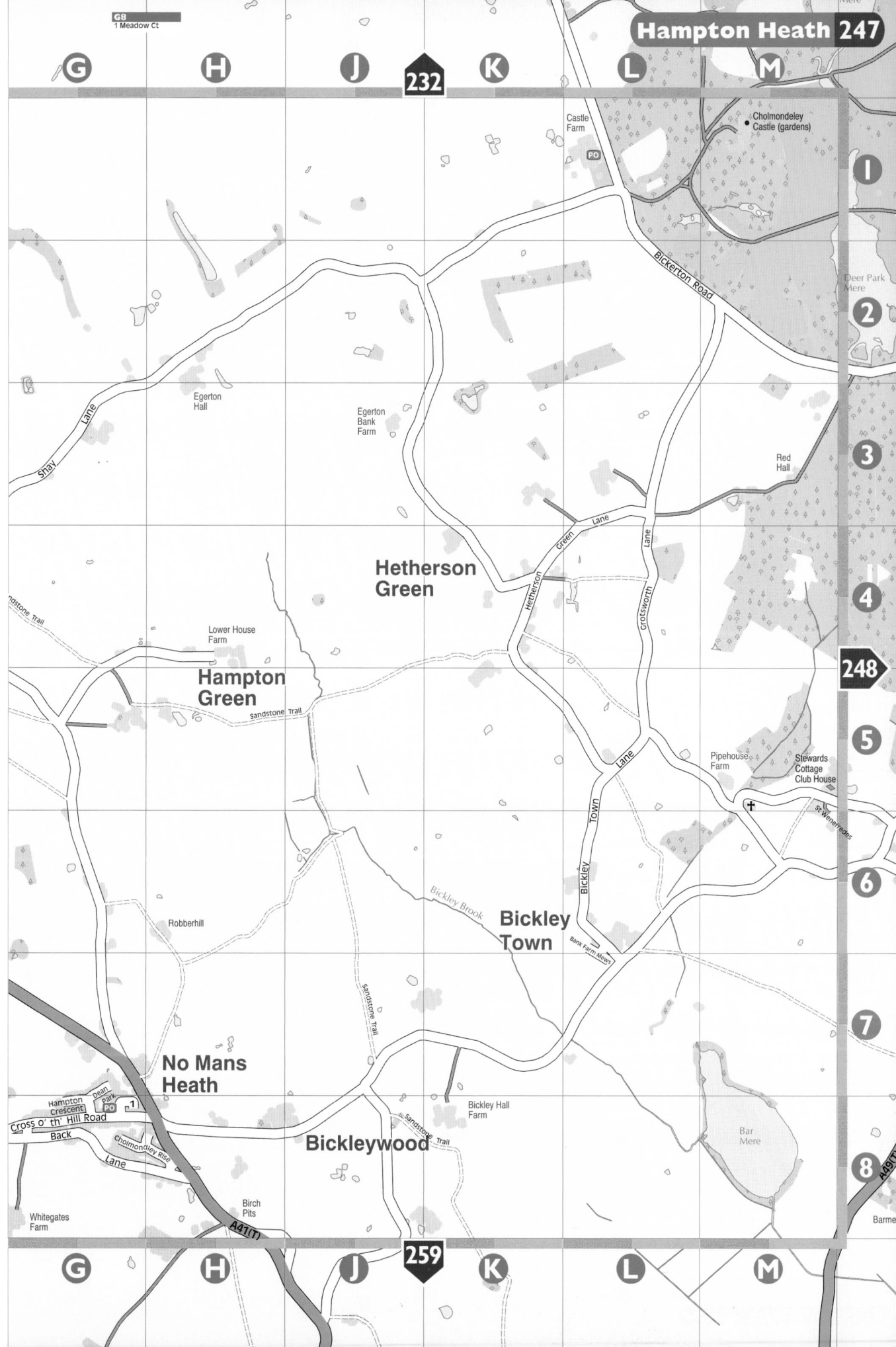

G8
1 Meadow Ct

G   H   J   232   K   L   M

I

2

3

248

4

5

6

7

8

Cholmondeley
Castle (gardens)

Castle
Farm

PO

Deer Park
Mere

Bickerton Road

Red
Hall

Mere

Egerton
Hall

Shav
Lane

Egerton
Bank
Farm

Hetherson
Green

Lane

Hetherson Green

Grotsworth Lane

Lower House
Farm

Sandstone Trail

Hampton
Green

Sandstone Trail

Lane

Pipehouse
Farm

Stewards
Cottage
Club House

St Wenerfredes

Bickley Brook

Bickley Town Lane

Bickley
Town

Bank Farm Mews

Robberhill

Sandstone Trail

No Mans
Heath

Hampton
Crescent

Dean
Park
PO   1

Cross o' th' Hill Road

Back

Cholmondley Rise

Lane

Bickleywood

Sandstone Trail

Bickley Hall
Farm

Bar
Mere

A49(T)

Barmer

Whitegates
Farm

Birch
Pits

A41(T)

G   H   J   259   K   L   M

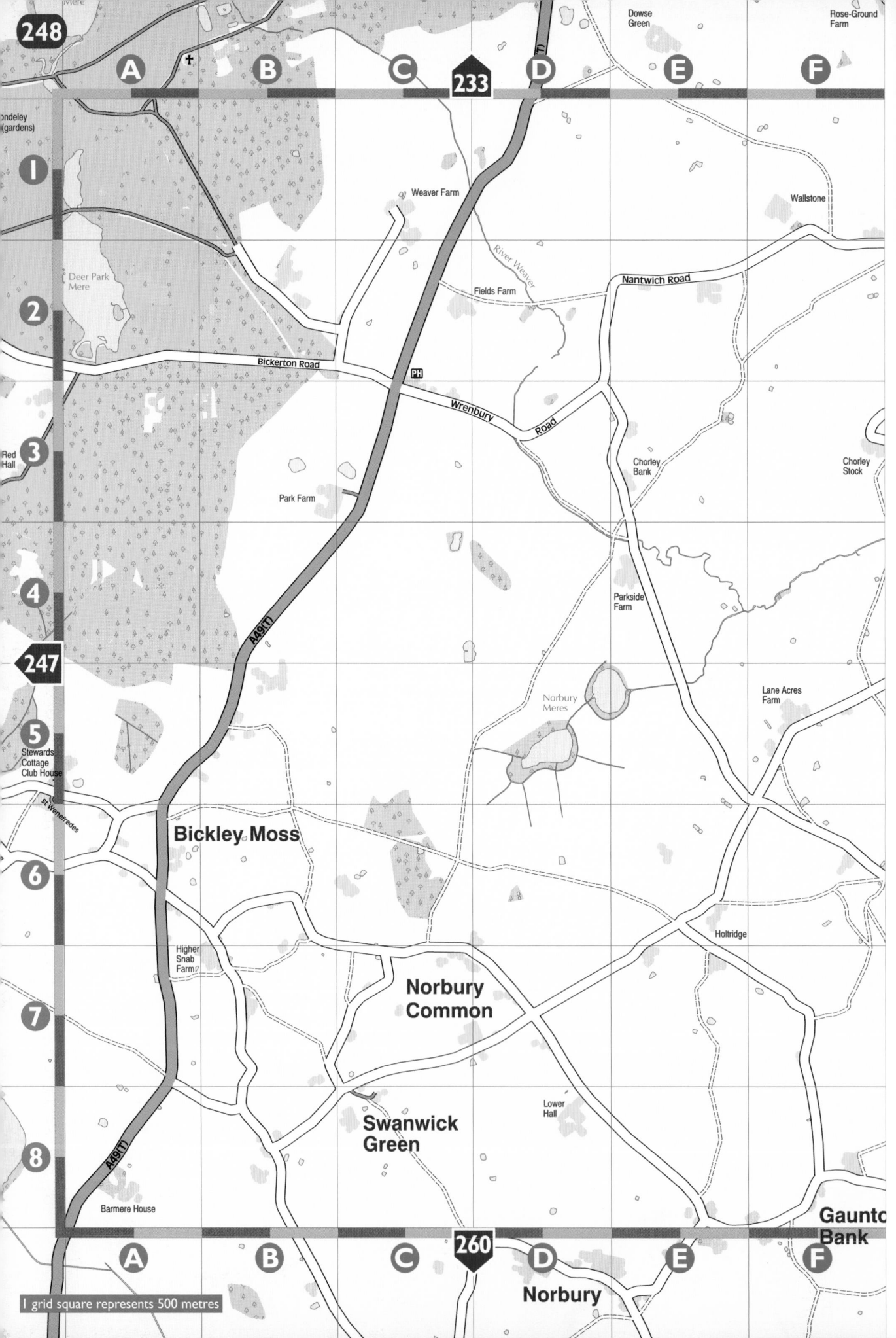

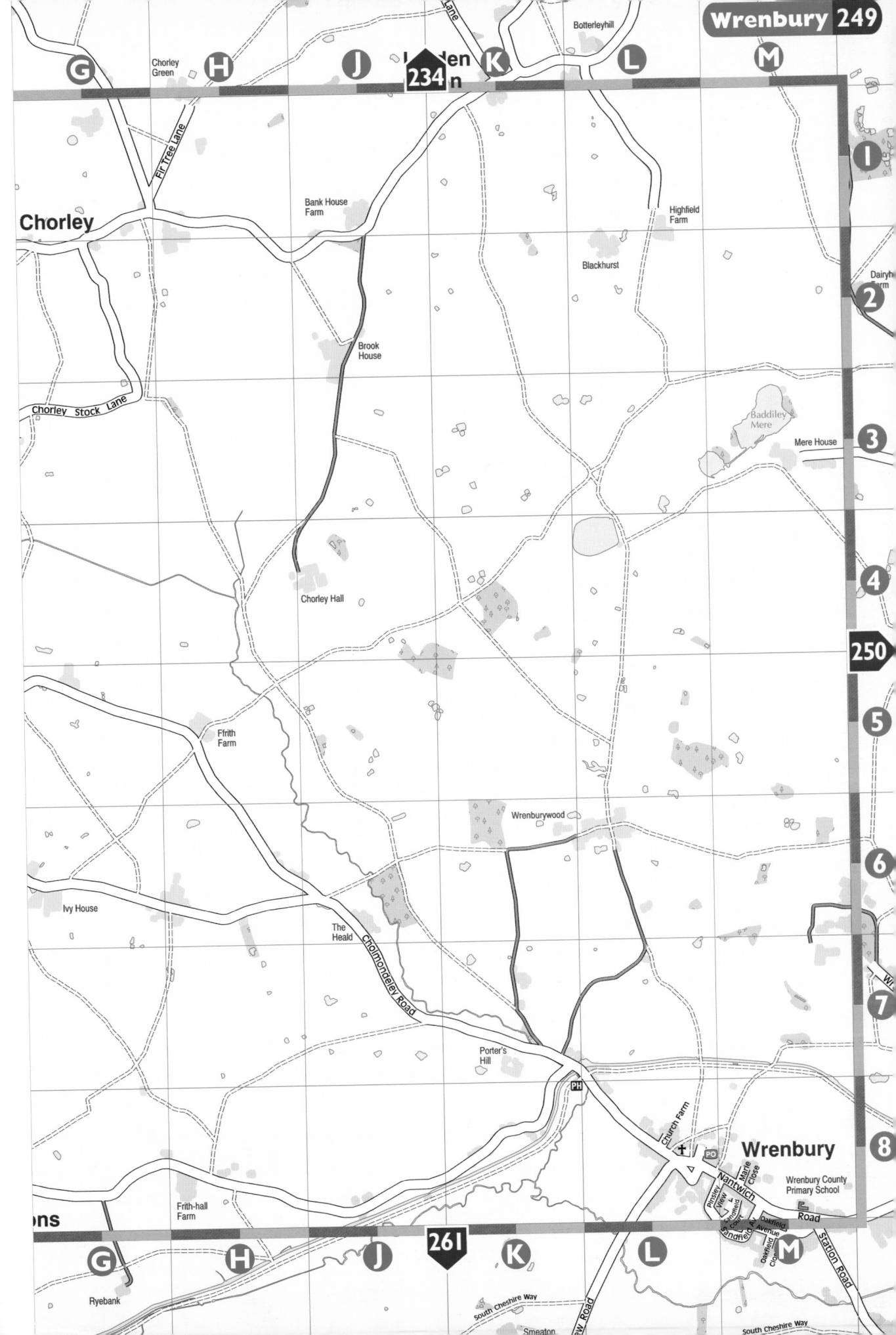

G H J 234 K L M

I

2

Botterleyhill

Chorley Green

Fir Tree Lane

Chorley

Bank House Farm

Highfield Farm

Blackhurst

Dairyh Farm

Baddiley Mere

Mere House

3

Chorley Stock Lane

Brook House

4

250

Chorley Hall

5

Ffrith Farm

Wrenburywood

6

Ivy House

The Heald

Cholmondeley Road

7

Porter's Hill

PH

Church Farm

Wrenbury

PO

Wrenbury County Primary School

8

Nantwich

Pinsley View

Marle Close

Oakfield Avenue

Sandfield Court

Oakfield Close

Road

Station Road

ons

Frith-hall Farm

G H J 261 K L M

Ryebank

South Cheshire Way

Smeaton

south Cheshire Way

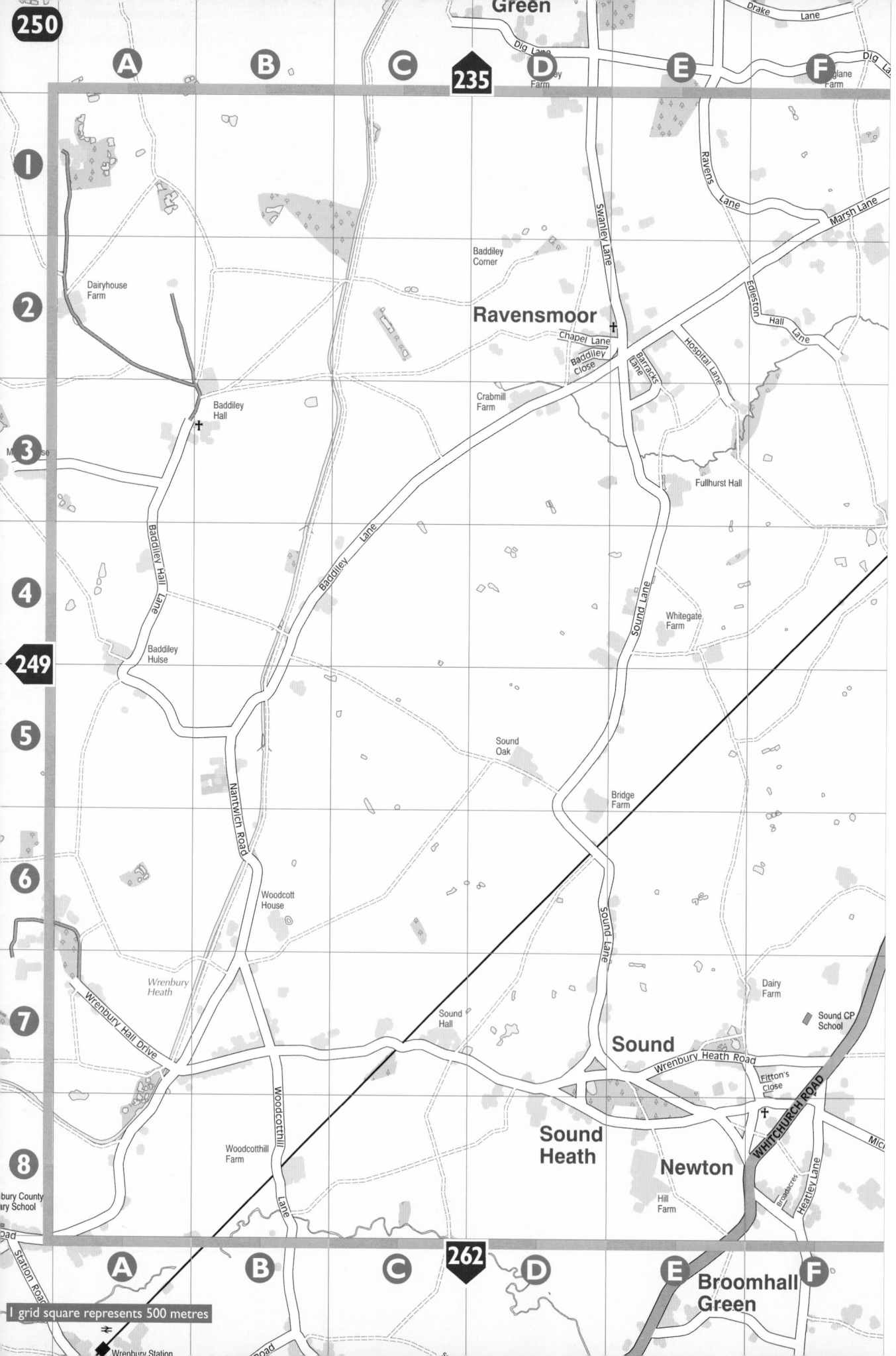

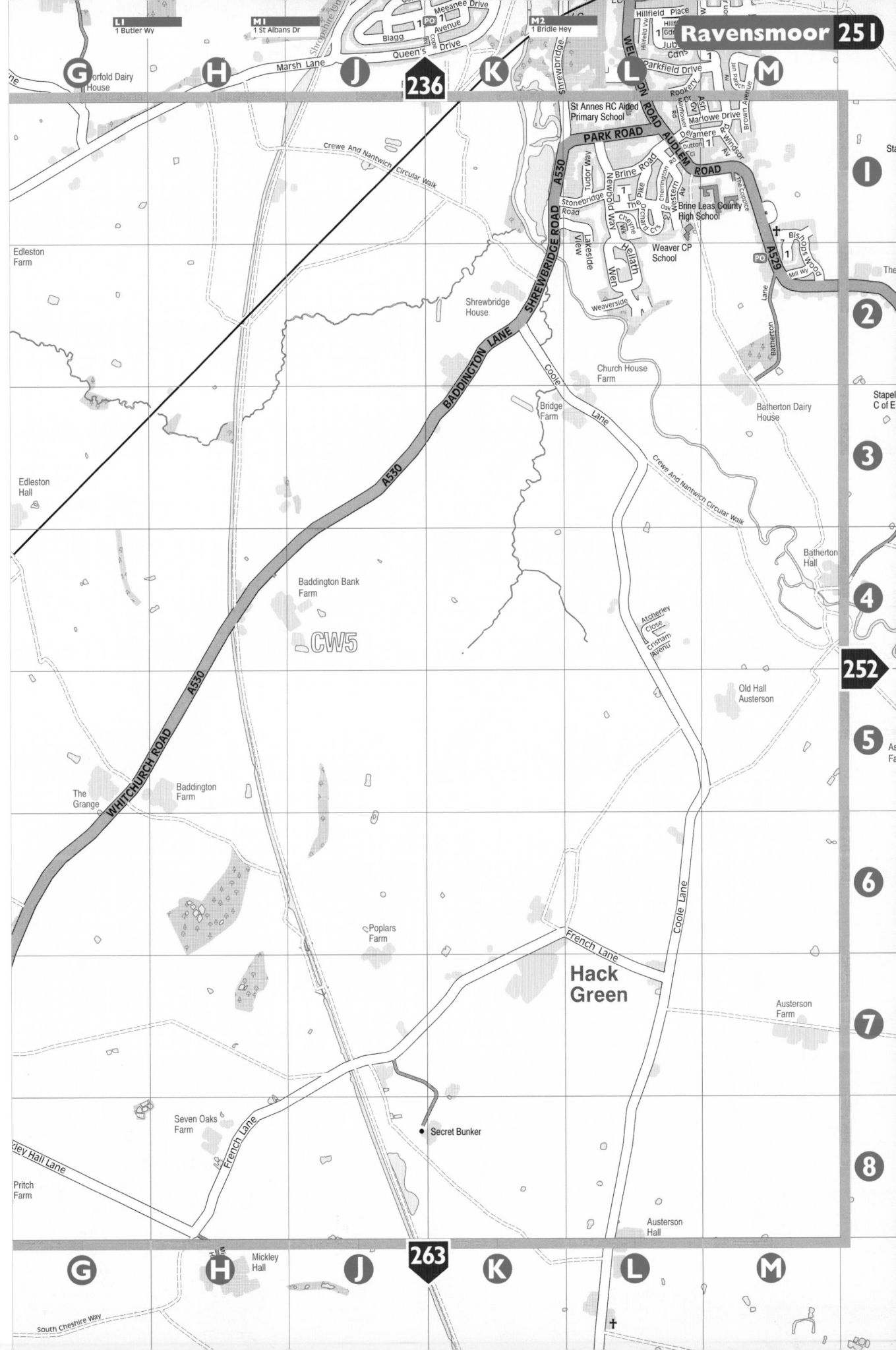

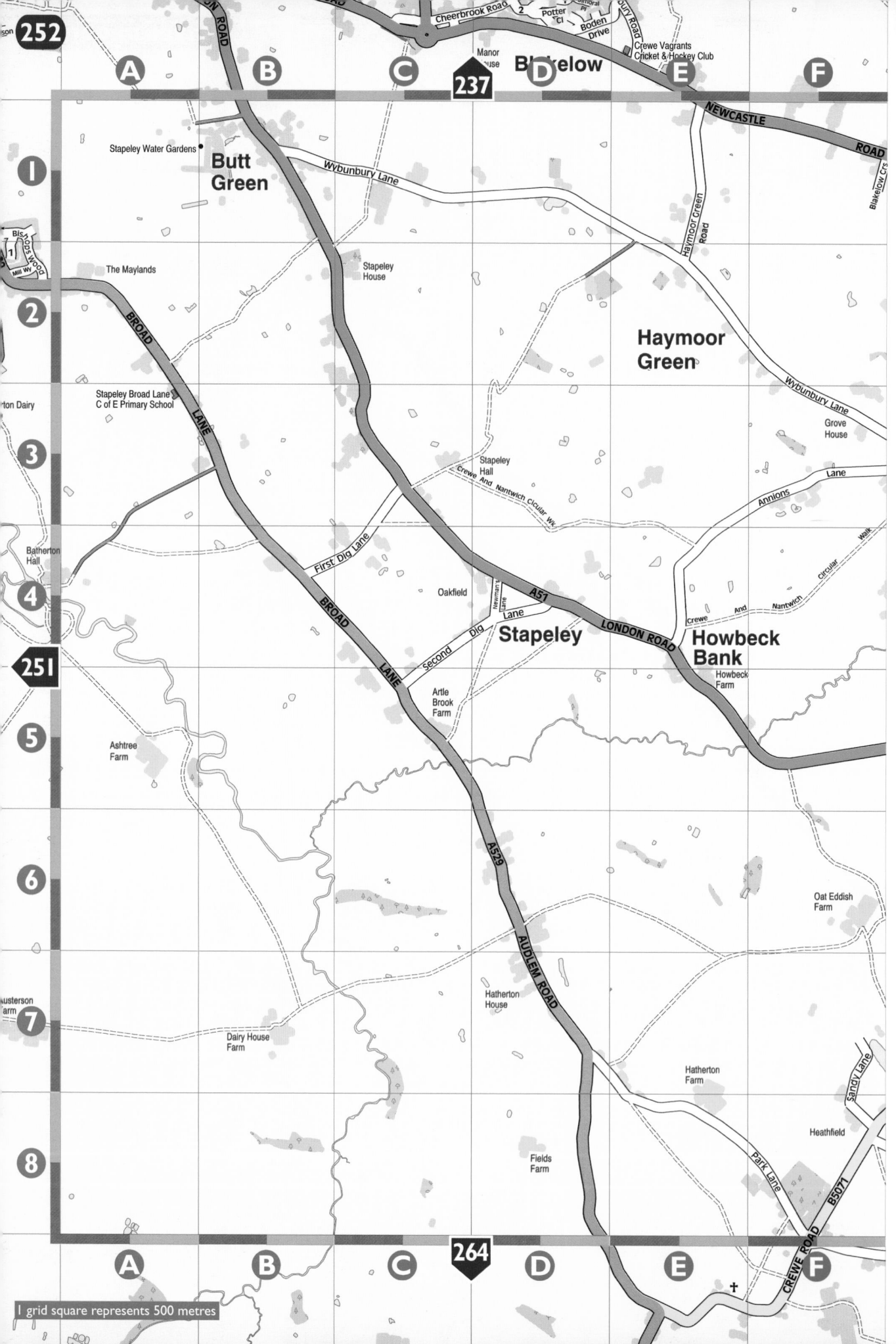

252

A   B   C   **237**   D   E   F

Cheerbrook Road

Potter
Cl
Boden
Drive

Crewe Vagrants
Cricket & Hockey Club

Blakelow

NEWCASTLE ROAD

1

Stapeley Water Gardens

**Butt
Green**

Wybunbury Lane

Blakelow Crs

Manor
House

The Maylands

Stapeley
House

Haymoor Green Road

2

BROAD LANE

**Haymoor
Green**

Wybunbury Lane

ton Dairy

Stapeley Broad Lane
C of E Primary School

Grove
House

3

Stapeley
Hall

Crewe And Nantwich Circular Wk.

Annions   Lane

Batherton
Hall

Circular   Walk

First Dig Lane

4

BROAD LANE

Oakfield

Newman's Lane

A57

LONDON ROAD

Crewe   And   Nantwich

Stapeley

**Howbeck
Bank**

251

Second   Dig   Lane

Artle
Brook
Farm

Howbeck
Farm

5

Ashtree
Farm

6

A529

Oat Eddish
Farm

AUDLEM ROAD

austerson
arm

7

Hatherton
House

Dairy House
Farm

Hatherton
Farm

Sandy Lane

Heathfield

8

Park Lane

Fields
Farm

B5071

CREWE ROAD

A   B   C   **264**   D   E   † F

1 grid square represents 500 metres

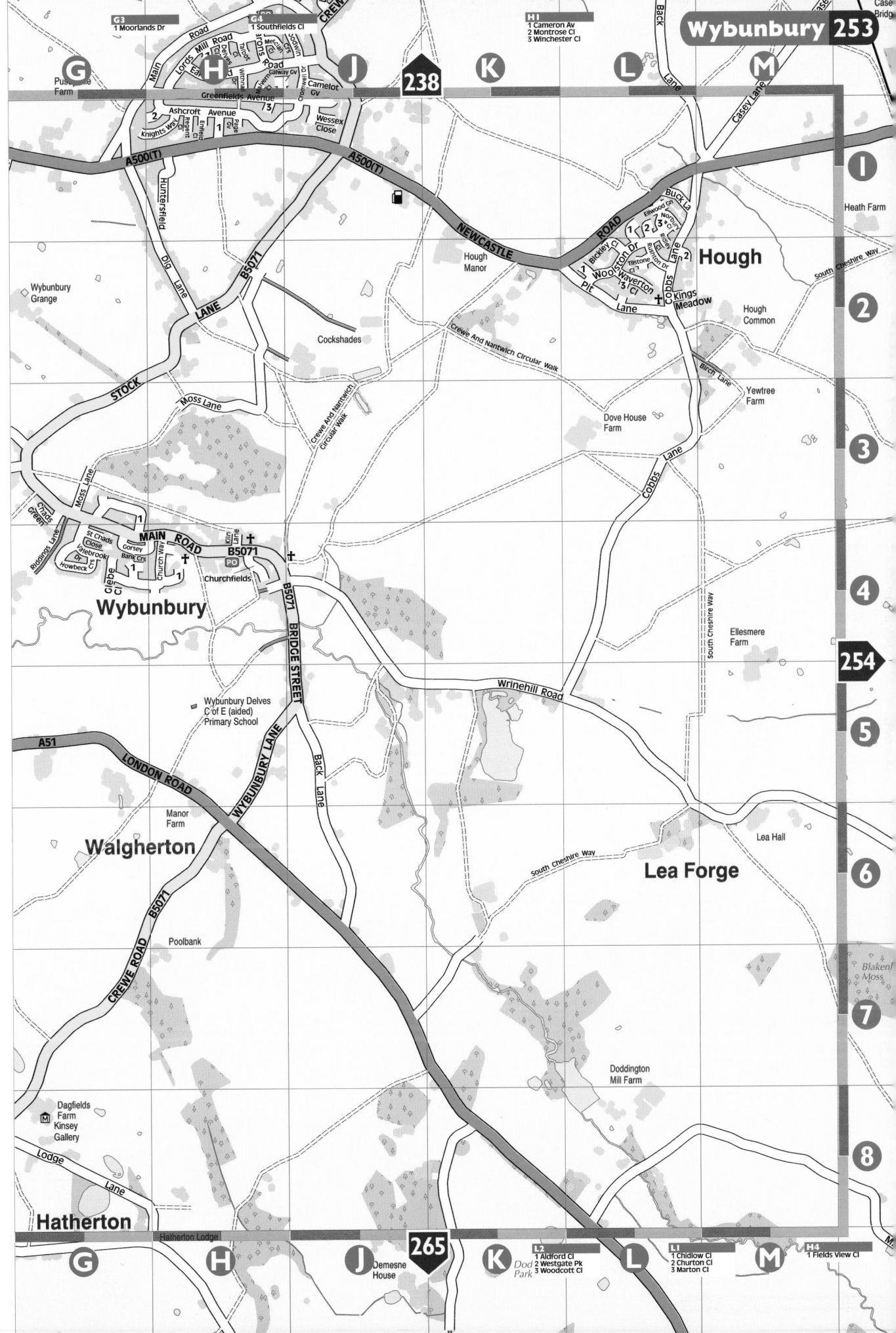

G3
1 Moorlands Dr

G4
1 Southfields Cl

H1
1 Cameron Av
2 Montrose Cl
3 Winchester Cl

G H J 238 K L M

Greenfields Avenue

Ashcroft Avenue

Knights Way

Wessex Close

A500(T) A500(T)

NEWCASTLE ROAD

BUCK La

Ellwood Gn

Woolston Dr

Bickley Cl

Waverton Cl

Tilstone Cl

Rushton Dr

Kings Meadow

Hough

Heath Farm

I

Pit Lane

Cobbs Lane

Hough Common

2

South Cheshire Way

Wybunbury Grange

Huntersfield

Dig Lane

B5071

LANE

Cockshades

Crewe And Nantwich Circular Walk

Birch Lane

Yewtree Farm

3

STOCK

Moss Lane

Crewe And Nantwich Circular Walk

Dove House Farm

Cobbs Lane

4

Chads Green

Ridding Lane

St Chads Close

Gorsey Bank Crs

Valebrook Dr

Howbeck Cr

Glebe Cl

Church Way

MAIN ROAD

B5071

PO

Churchfields

Kiln Lane

254

Ellesmere Farm

South Cheshire Way

Wybunbury

B5071 BRIDGE STREET

Wybunbury Delves C of E (aided) Primary School

Wrinehill Road

5

A51

LONDON ROAD

WYBUNBURY LANE

Back Lane

Lea Hall

6

Manor Farm

Walgherton

South Cheshire Way

Lea Forge

B5071

Poolbank

Blakenhall Moss

7

CREWE ROAD

Doddington Mill Farm

8

Dagfields Farm Kinsey Gallery

Lodge Lane

Hatherton

Hatherton Lodge

G H J 265 K L M

Demesne House

Dod Park

L2
1 Aldford Cl
2 Westgate Pk
3 Woodcott Cl

L1
1 Chidlow Cl
2 Churton Cl
3 Marton Cl

H4
1 Fields View Cl

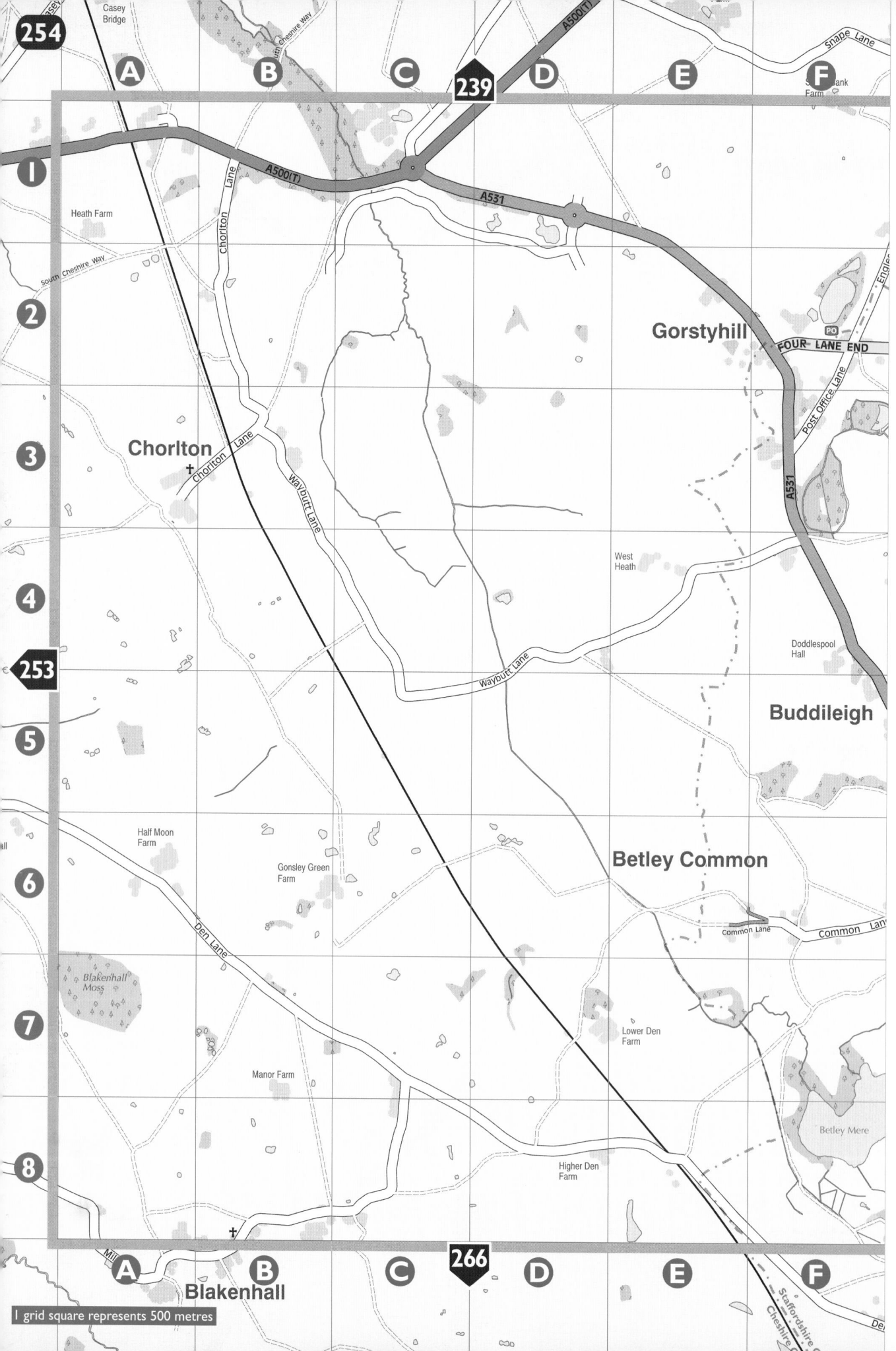

254

Ⓐ   Ⓑ   Ⓒ   **239**   Ⓓ   Ⓔ   Ⓕ

Casey Bridge

South Cheshire Way

A500(T)

A531

1

Heath Farm

South Cheshire Way

Chorlton Lane

2

Gorstyhill

FOUR LANE END

PO

Post Office Lane

A531

Snape Lane

Bank Farm

3

Chorlton

Chorlton Lane

Waybutt Lane

West Heath

253

4

Doddlespool Hall

Waybutt Lane

Buddileigh

5

Half Moon Farm

Gonsley Green Farm

Betley Common

6

Den Lane

Common Lane   Common Lane

Blakenhall Moss

7

Lower Den Farm

Manor Farm

Betley Mere

8

Higher Den Farm

Mill

Ⓐ   Ⓑ   Ⓒ   **266**   Ⓓ   Ⓔ   Ⓕ

Blakenhall

Staffordshire

Cheshire

Den

1 grid square represents 500 metres

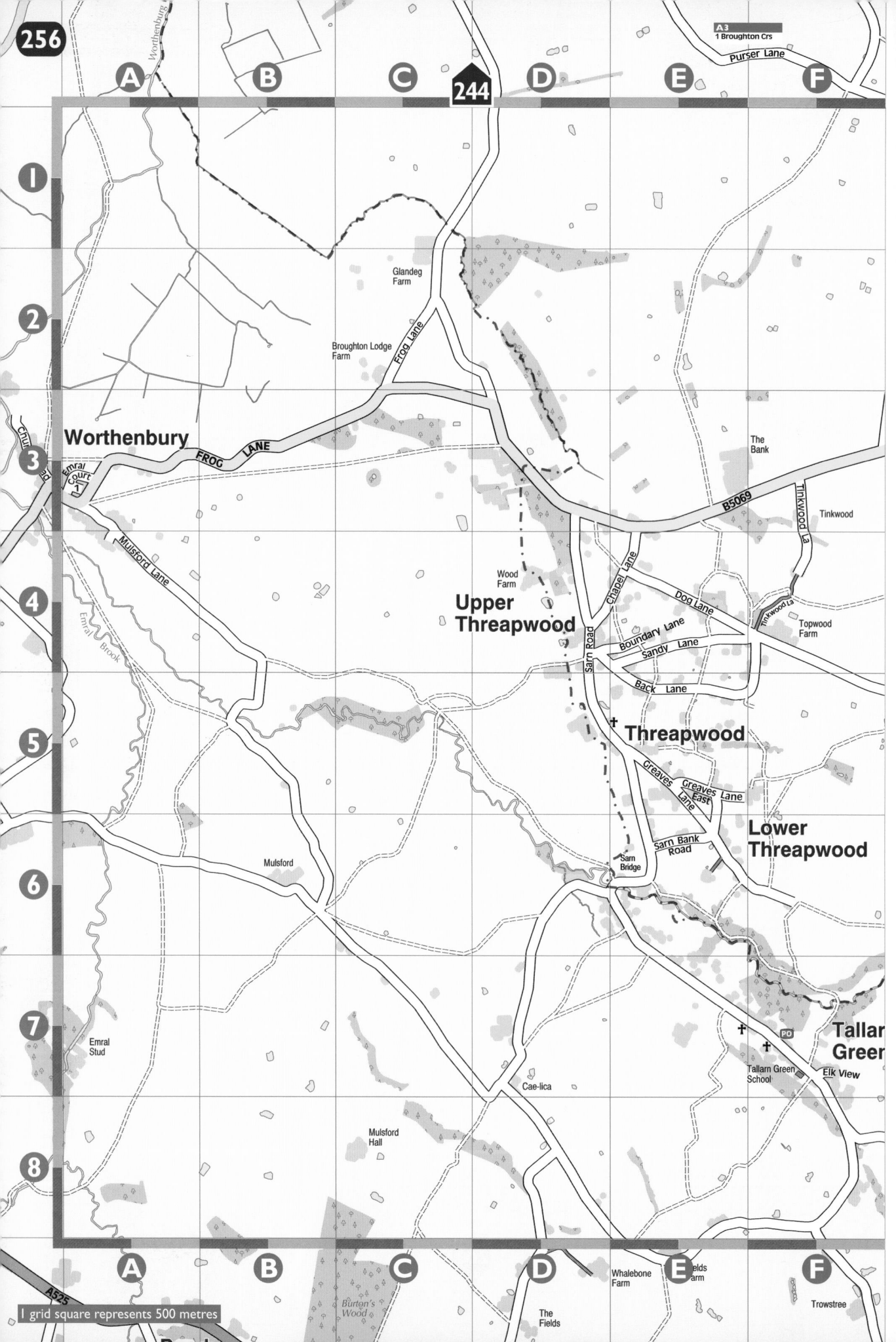

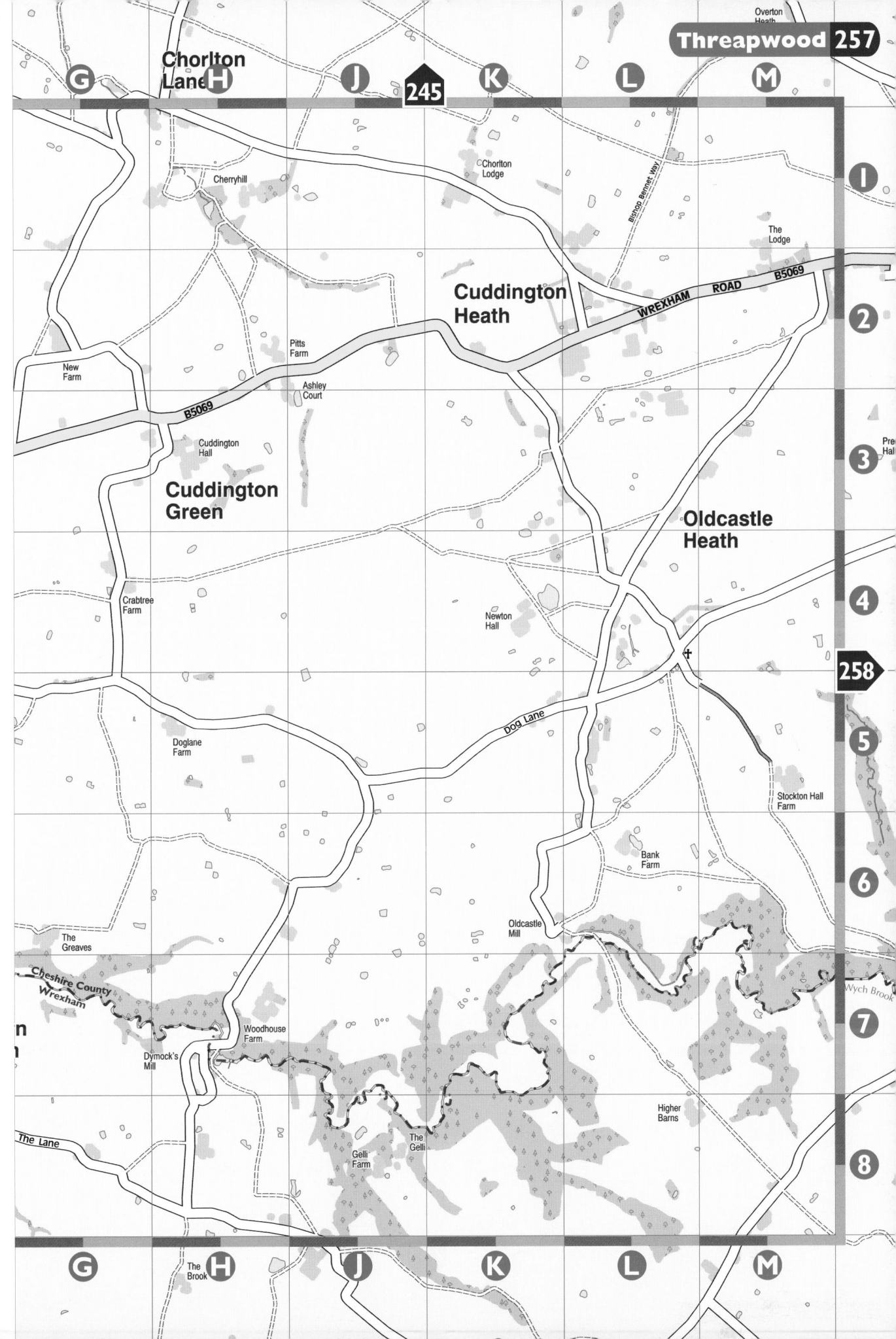

G   Chorlton
Lane H   J   **245**   K   L   M

Cherryhill

Chorlton
Lodge

I

Bishop Bennett Way

The
Lodge

**Cuddington
Heath**

WREXHAM   ROAD   **B5069**

2

Pitts
Farm

New
Farm

Pre
Hall

3

B5069

Ashley
Court

Cuddington
Hall

**Oldcastle
Heath**

**Cuddington
Green**

†

258

Crabtree
Farm

Newton
Hall

4

Dog Lane

5

Stockton Hall
Farm

Doglane
Farm

Bank
Farm

6

The
Greaves

Oldcastle
Mill

Cheshire County
Wrexham

Wych Brook

7

Woodhouse
Farm

Dymock's
Mill

Higher
Barns

The Lane

Gelli
Farm

The
Gelli

8

G   The
Brook H   J   K   L   M

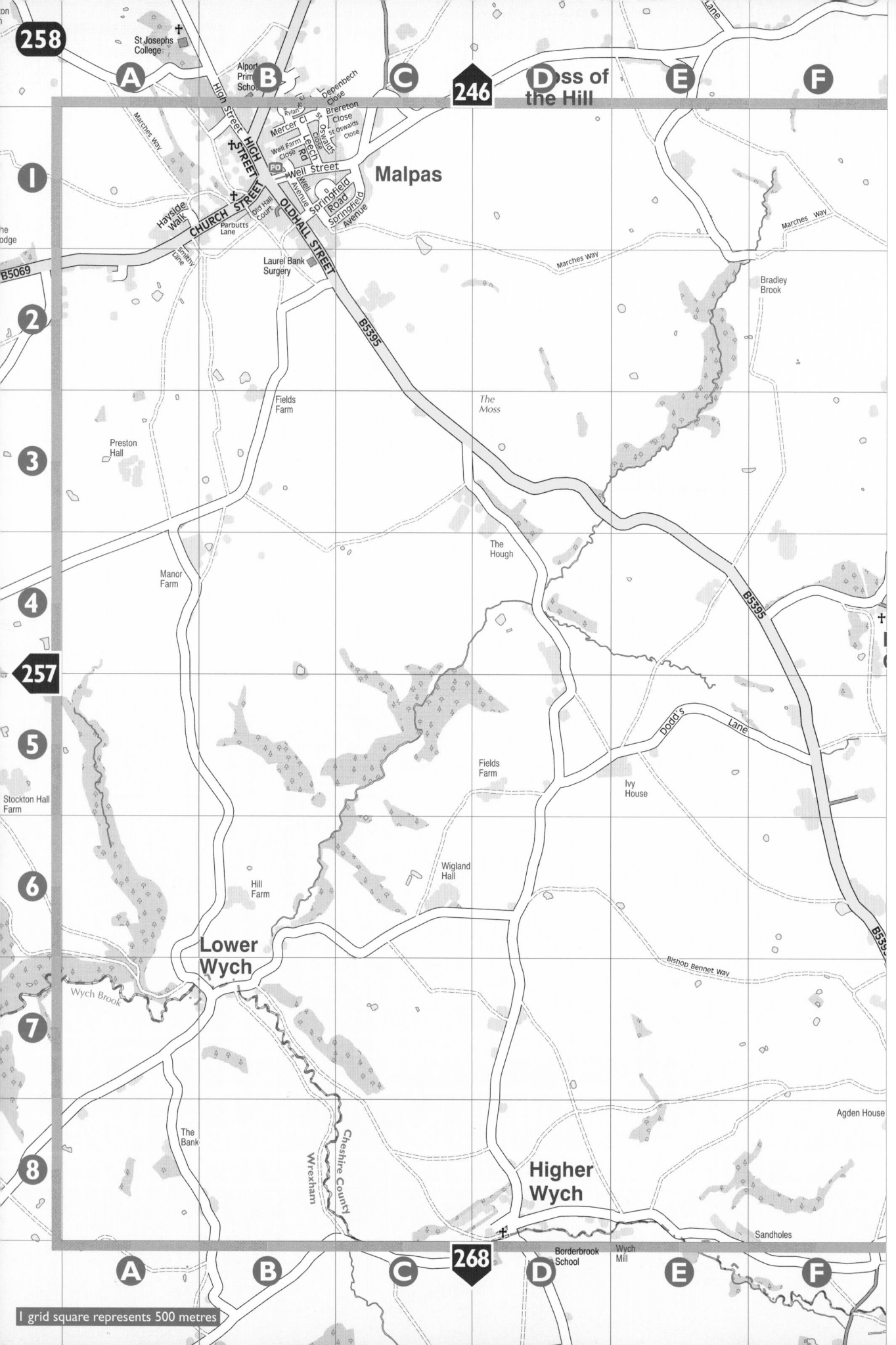

A **B** **C** 246 **D** oss of
the Hill **E** **F**

St Josephs
College

Alport
Primary
School

Depenbech
Close

Brereton
Close

Marches Way

Mercer Cl

Rylan's Cl

St Oswalds Close

Brereton Close

St Oswalds Close

HIGH STREET

Leech Rd

Well Farm
Close

I

Well Street

Malpas

Hayside Walk

PO

CHURCH STREET

Well
Avenue

Springfield
Road

Springfield
Avenue

Marches Way

B5069

Fenery
Lane

Parbutts
Lane

Old Hall
Court

OLD HALL STREET

Laurel Bank
Surgery

Bradley
Brook

2

B5395

Fields
Farm

The
Moss

3

Preston
Hall

Marches Way

4

Manor
Farm

The
Hough

B5395

257

Dodd's Lane

5

Stockton Hall
Farm

Fields
Farm

Ivy
House

6

Hill
Farm

Wigland
Hall

**Lower
Wych**

Bishop Bennet Way

Wych Brook

7

The
Bank

Wrexham

Cheshire County

Agden House

8

**Higher
Wych**

Sandholes

A **B** **C** 268 **D** **E** **F**

Borderbrook
School

Wych
Mill

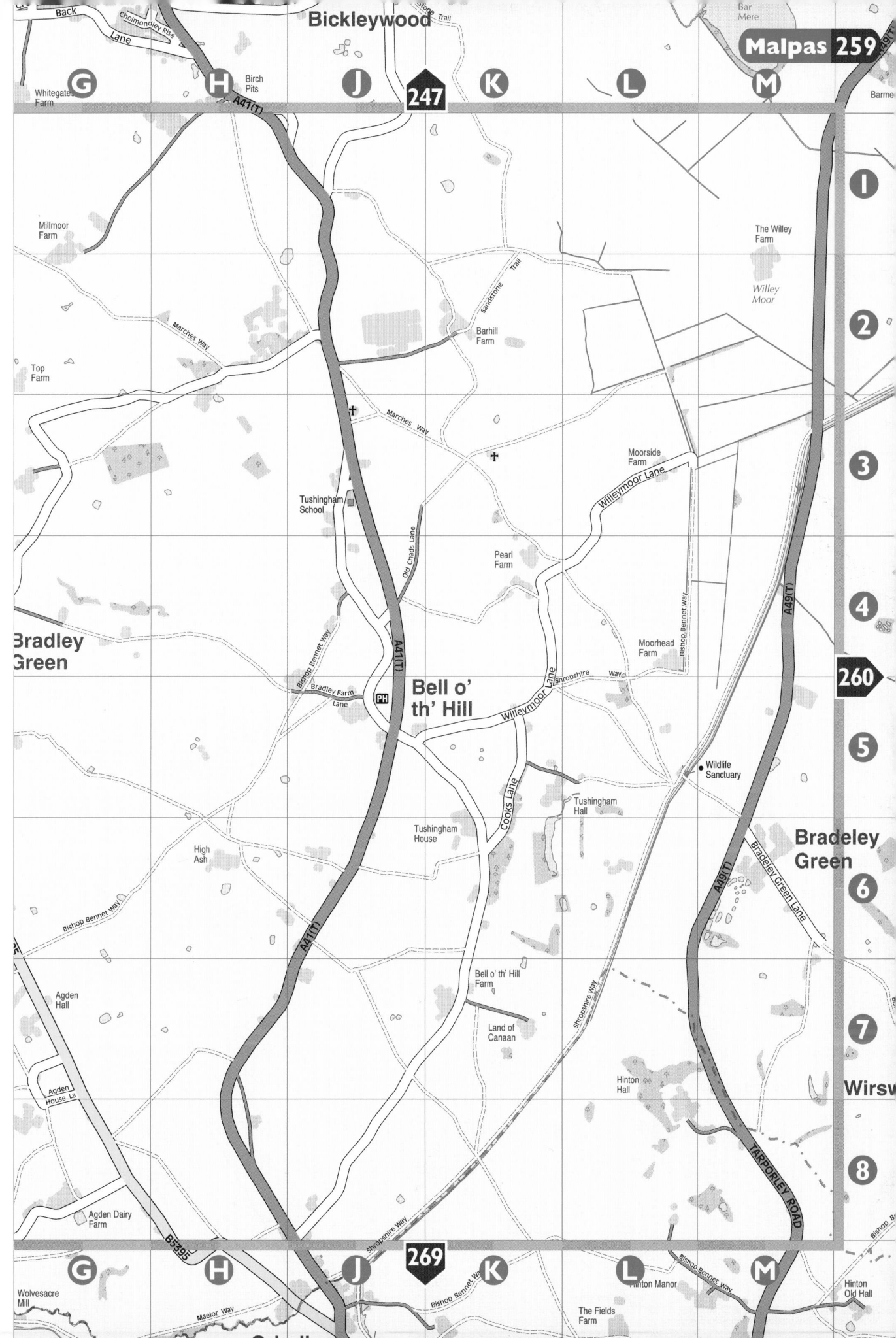

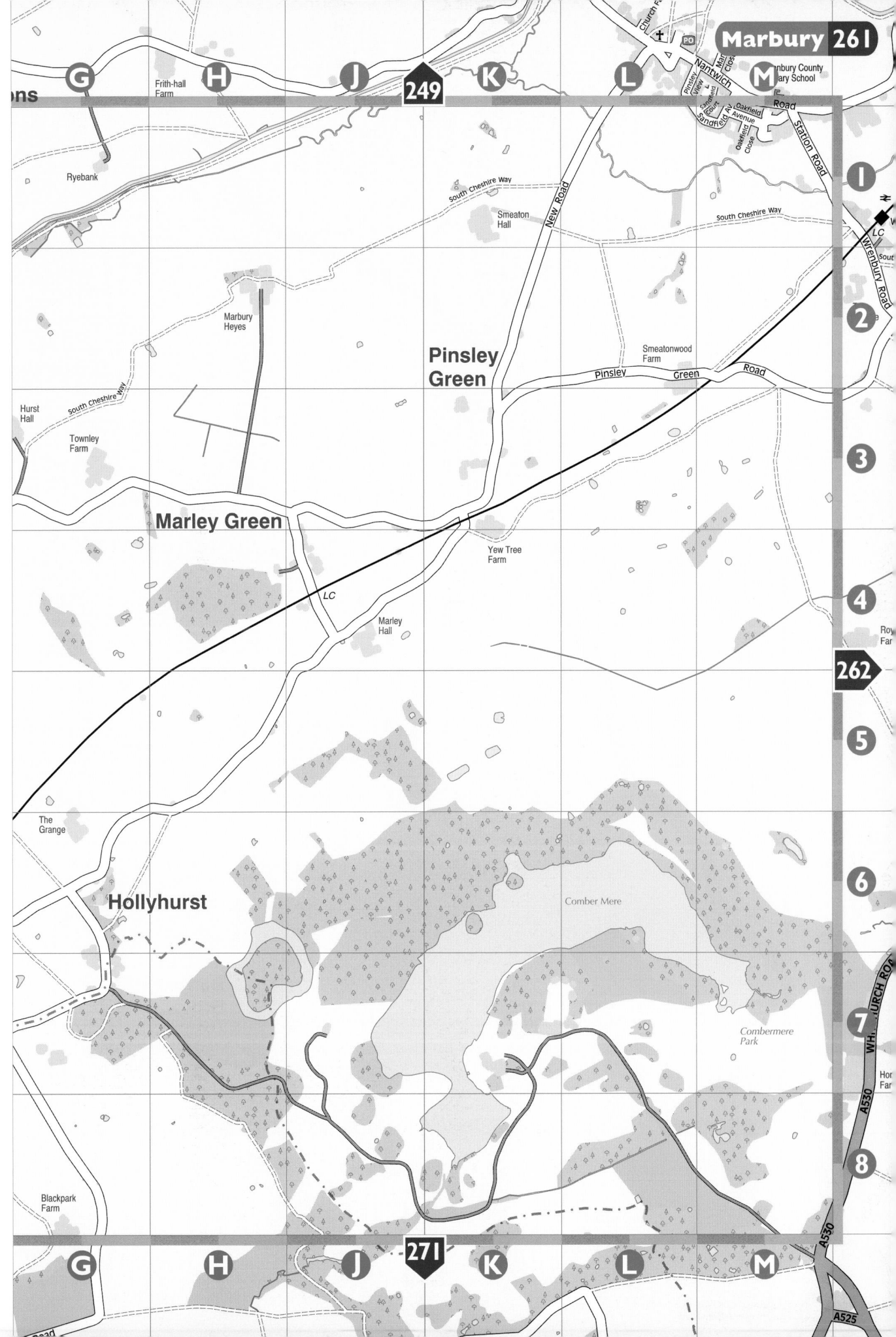

G
H
J
249
K
L
M

Church Fr
PO
View
Mall Clips
nbury County
ary School
Nantwich

Pinsley
Court
Sandfield Av
Oakfield
Avenue
Road

Sandfield
Oakfield
Close

Station Road

Frith-hall
Farm

I

Ryebank

LC
sout

Wrenbury Road

South Cheshire Way

South Cheshire Way

New Road

Smeaton
Hall

2

Marbury
Heyes

**Pinsley
Green**

Smeatonwood
Farm

Pinsley   Green   Road

3

Hurst
Hall

south Cheshire Way

Townley
Farm

Marley Green

4

Yew Tree
Farm

Roy
Far

262

LC

Marley
Hall

5

The
Grange

6

Hollyhurst

Comber Mere

Combermere
Park

7

WHI...CH ROA

A530

Hor
Far

8

Blackpark
Farm

A530

G
H
J
271
K
L
M

A525

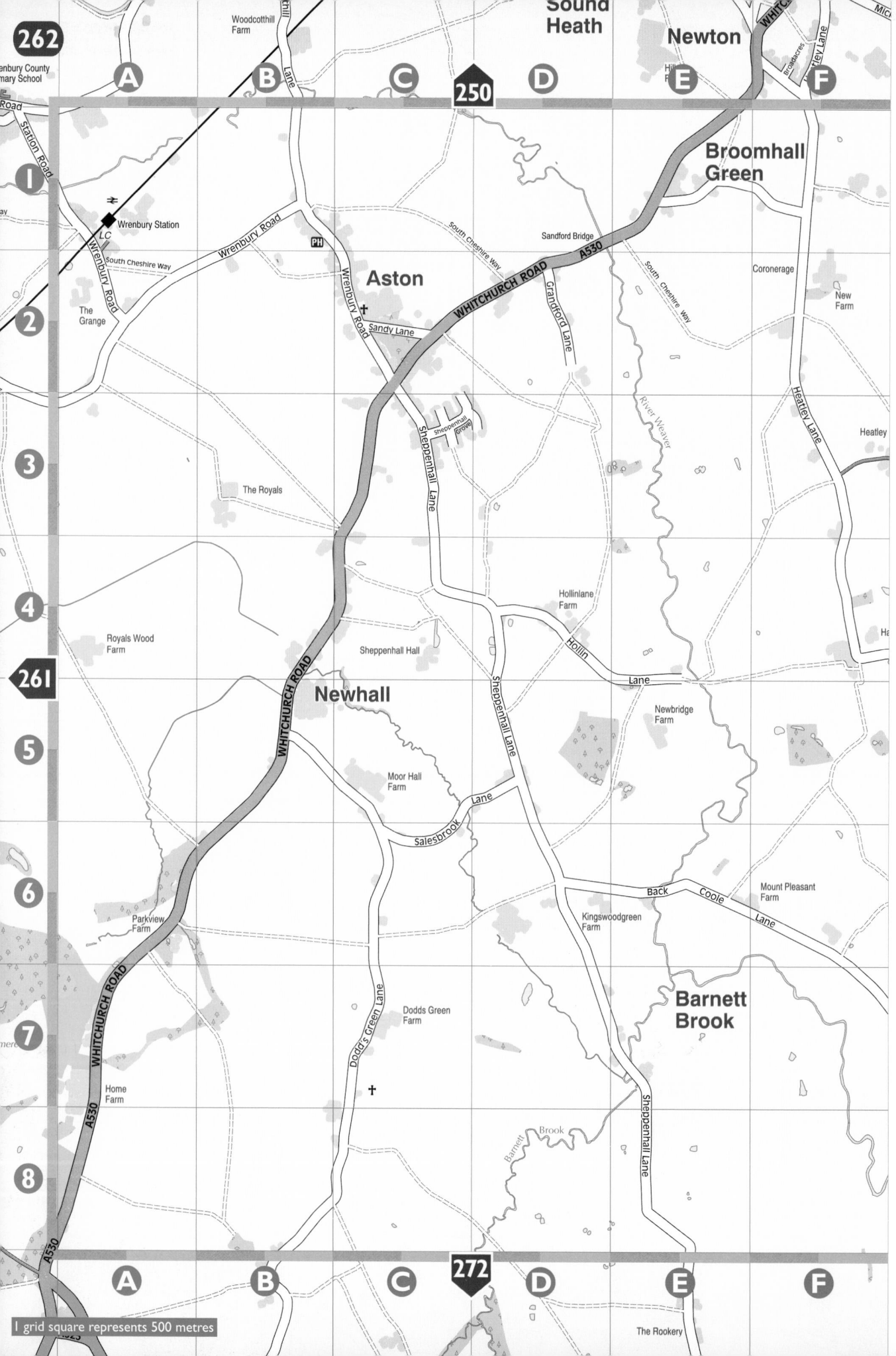

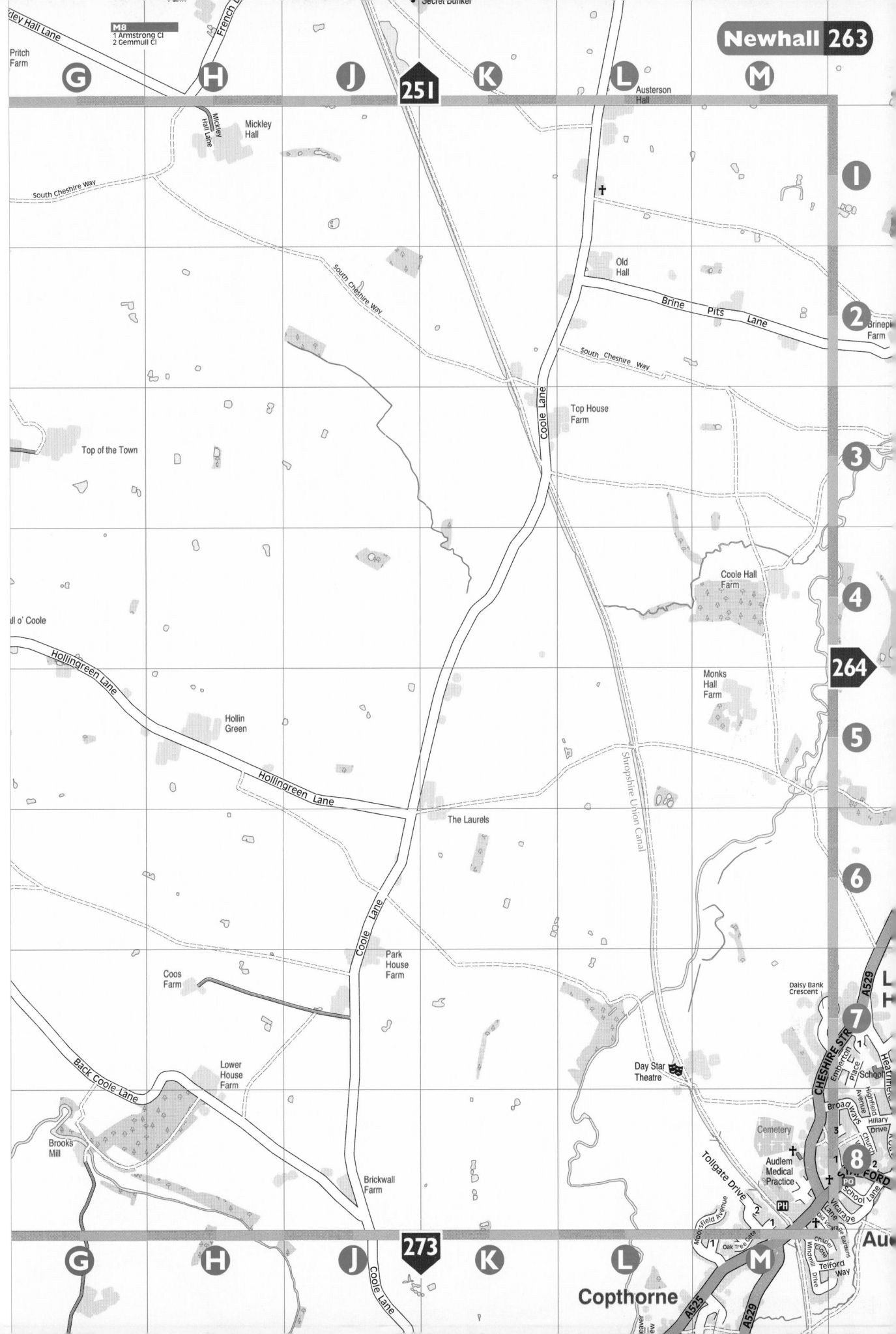

G   H   J   **251**   K   L   M

M8
1 Armstrong Cl
2 Gemmull Cl

Secret Bunker

Austerson
Hall

I

Mickley Hall Lane

Mickley
Hall

Mickley Hall Lane

South Cheshire Way

South Cheshire Way

Old
Hall

Brine   Pits   Lane

2

Brinepi
Farm

South Cheshire Way

Coole Lane

Top House
Farm

3

Top of the Town

Coole Hall
Farm

4

264

...ll o' Coole

Hollingreen Lane

Monks
Hall
Farm

5

Hollin
Green

Hollingreen Lane

Shropshire Union Canal

The Laurels

6

Coole Lane

Park House
Farm

Coos
Farm

Daisy Bank
Crescent

A529

L...
H...

7

Cheshire Str

Emberton
Place

...
School

Lower
House
Farm

Back Coole Lane

Day Star
Theatre

Broad...

Highfield
Avenue

Hillary
Drive

Heathfiel...

Church...

Brooks
Mill

Cemetery

Audlem
Medical
Practice

Tollgate Drive

School Lane

FORD

PO

8

...FORD

Vicarage
Lane

Brickwall
Farm

Moorsfield Avenue

PH

Telford
Way

Windmill Drive

Oak Tree ...

A525

A529

Au...

G   H   J   **273**   K   L   M

Copthorne

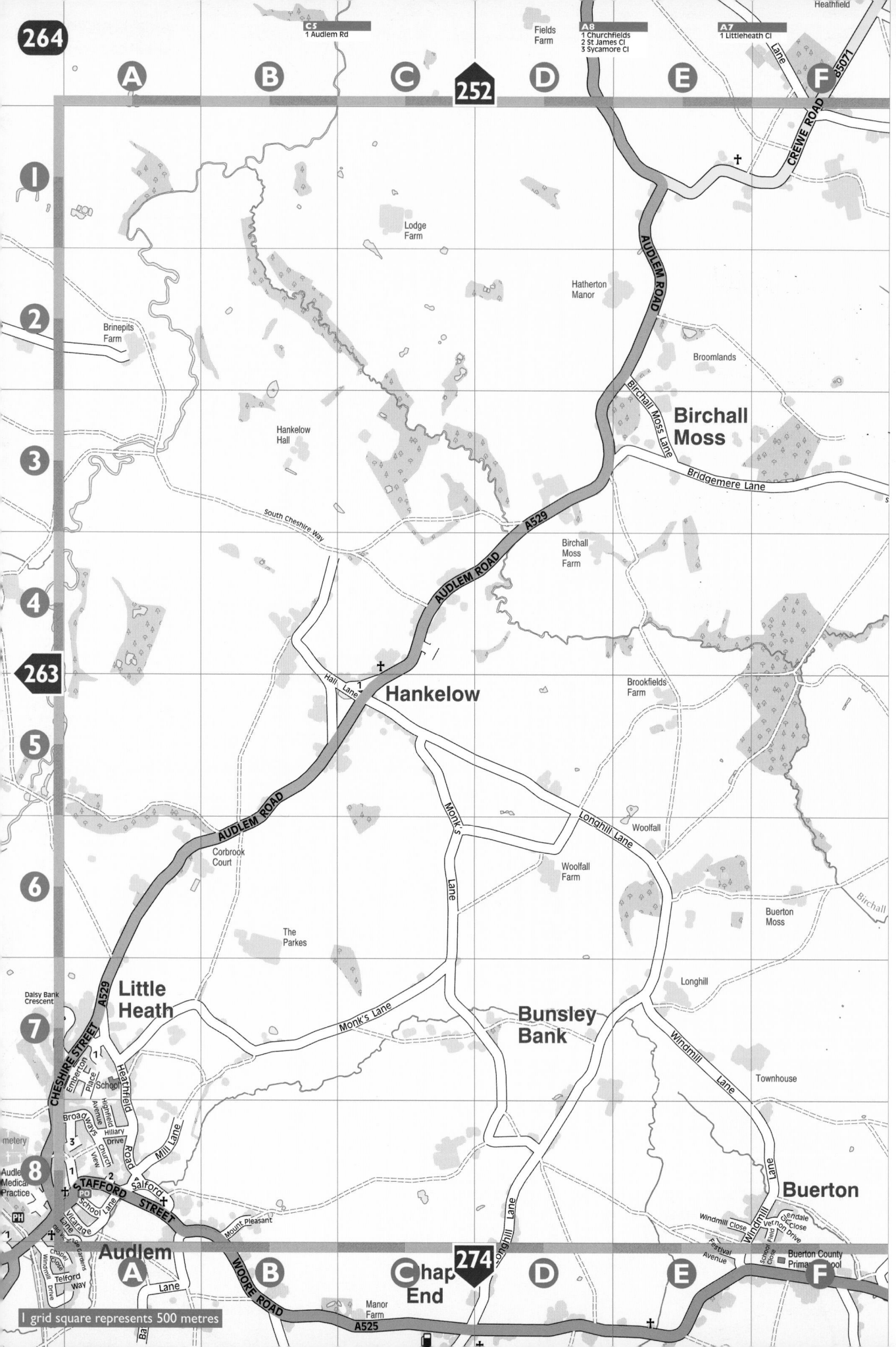

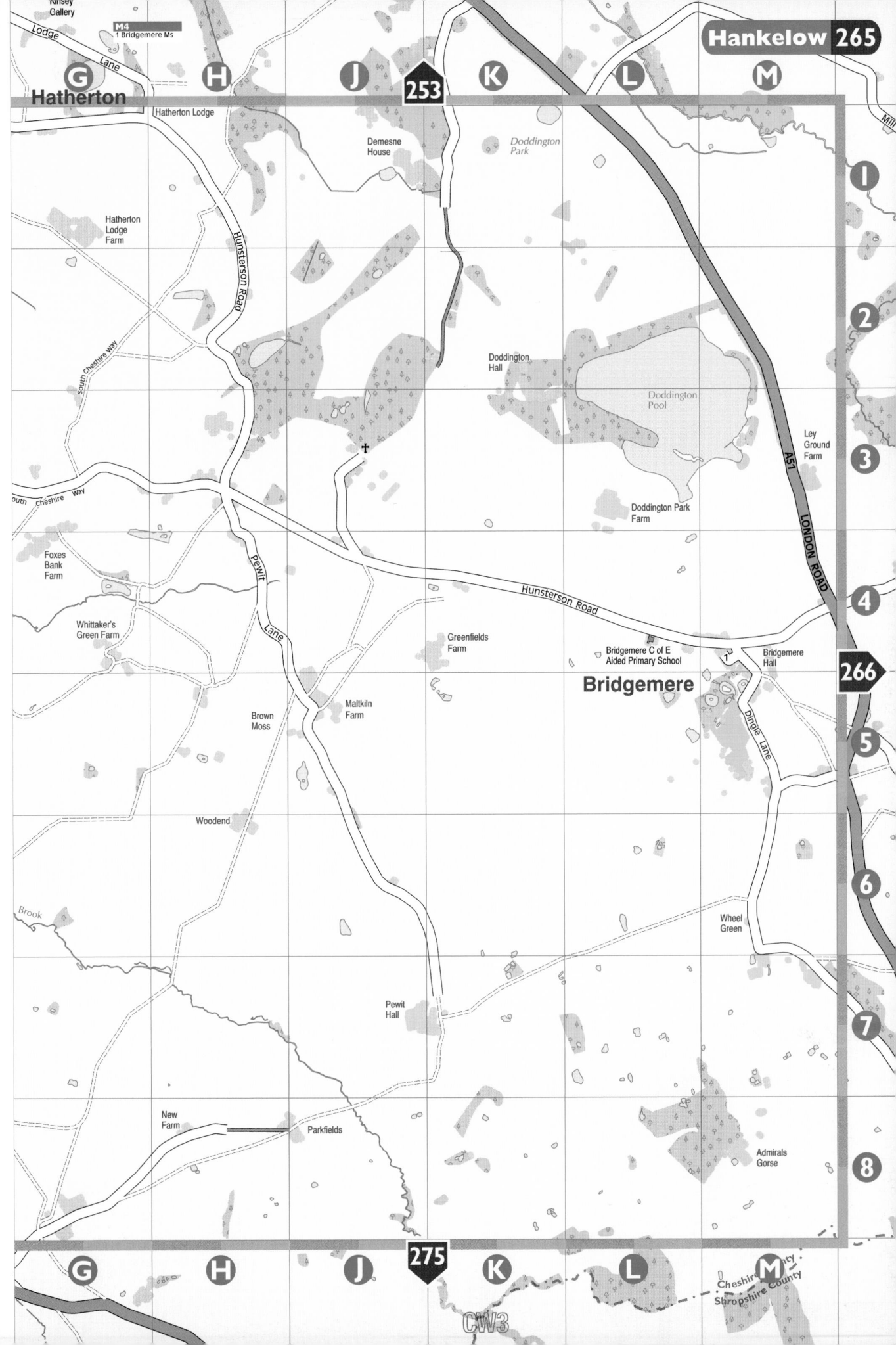

Kinsey Gallery

M4
1 Bridgemere Ms

Lodge Lane

G Hatherton

H

J

253

K

L

M

I

Hatherton Lodge

Demesne House

Doddington Park

Doddington Pool

2

Hatherton Lodge Farm

Doddington Hall

3

Ley Ground Farm

Hunterson Road

South Cheshire Way

South cheshire Way

Doddington Park Farm

LONDON ROAD

A51

Foxes Bank Farm

Pewit Lane

Hunsterson Road

4

Whittaker's Green Farm

Greenfields Farm

Bridgemere C of E Aided Primary School

Bridgemere Hall

266

Maltkiln Farm

Bridgemere

Brown Moss

Dingle Lane

5

Woodend

Wheel Green

6

Brook

Pewit Hall

7

New Farm

Parkfields

Admirals Gorse

8

G

H

J

275

K

L

M

Cheshire County
Shropshire County

CW3

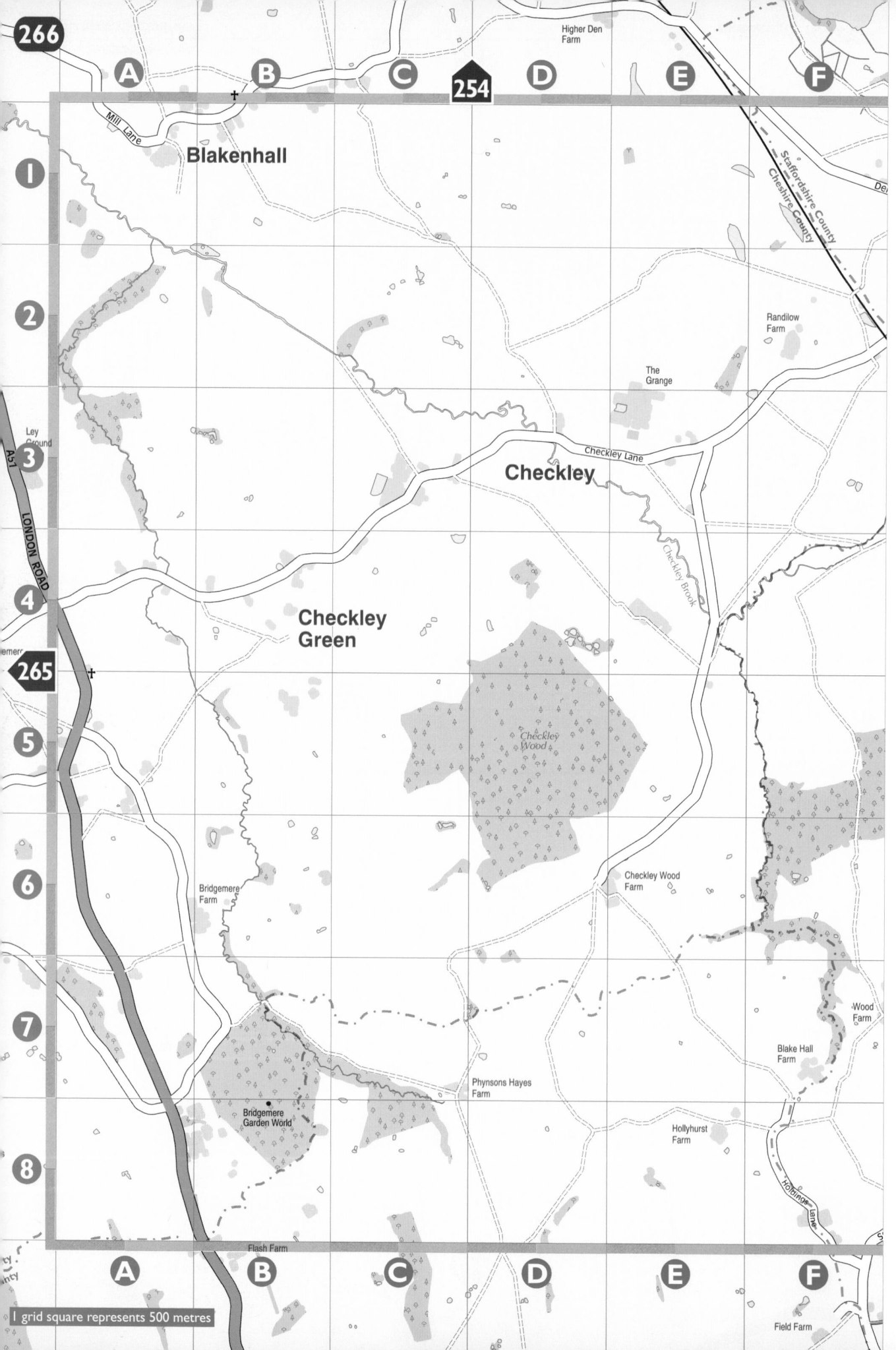

254

265

Mill Lane

Blakenhall

Ley Ground

A51

LONDON ROAD

Higher Den Farm

Staffordshire County
Cheshire County

De

Randilow Farm

The Grange

Checkley Lane

Checkley

Checkley Brook

Checkley Green

Checkley Wood

Bridgemere Farm

Checkley Wood Farm

Wood Farm

Blake Hall Farm

Phynsons Hayes Farm

Bridgemere Garden World

Hollyhurst Farm

Holdings Lane

Flash Farm

Field Farm

A B C D E F

1 2 3 4 5 6 7 8

I grid square represents 500 metres

Ravenshaw
K4 1 Fern Dene 2 Heather Gld
K6 1 Charles Cotton Dr
L4 1 Park Cl

Cracow Moss

G   H   J   255   K   L   M

I

Wrinehill

2

Bowseywood Farm

A531   MAIN ROAD   3

Lower Thornhill

Heighley Castle Way
Woodland Hills
Hidden Hills

Madeley Manor

KEELE ROAD

4

Wrinehill Hall

Higher Thornhill

College Close

Mea Cou Sch

Windy Arbour

New Road   Holm Oak Drive   Beck Road   Salisbury
Woodside
Arbour Close   Beech Green   Greenmeadows Road

A525 NEWCASTLE ROAD

Little Madeley   5

Police Station

Staffordshire County Council

PO   Mill Lane   Bevan Place

Middle Madeley

Wrinehill Wood

Apple Croft

Pear Tree Drive   Beresford Dale   Primrose Dell   Plover Field

The Bridle Path

Bower End

Moss Lane

Moss Lane Surgery

Cherry Green   Merlin Green

Madeley High School   Waterside Close

POOLSIDE A525

6

Hungerford La

Bower End Lane

Morningside   John Offley Road

Bramble Lea   Birch Dale

Moor Hall

The Holborn   Pastoral Close   Knightley   Netherset Hey Lane

Hungerford H Farm

7

Izaac Walton Way

Sir John Offley C of E Primary School

Madeley

Vicarage Lane   Castle Lane

Field House

Red Lane   Station Road

8

BAR HILL

Bar Hill House Farm

Mar Road

G   H   J   K   L   M

Onneley Golf Club

Hotel   PH

M5 1 Daltry Wy 2 Elkington Ri 3 Garners Wk 4 Heron Cl 5 Kingfisher Cl 6 Lindops La

L6 1 Grayling Willows 2 Laverock Gv 3 River Lea Ms

L5 1 Lynam Wy 2 Roseberry Dr 3 Thornhill Dr

Hey House

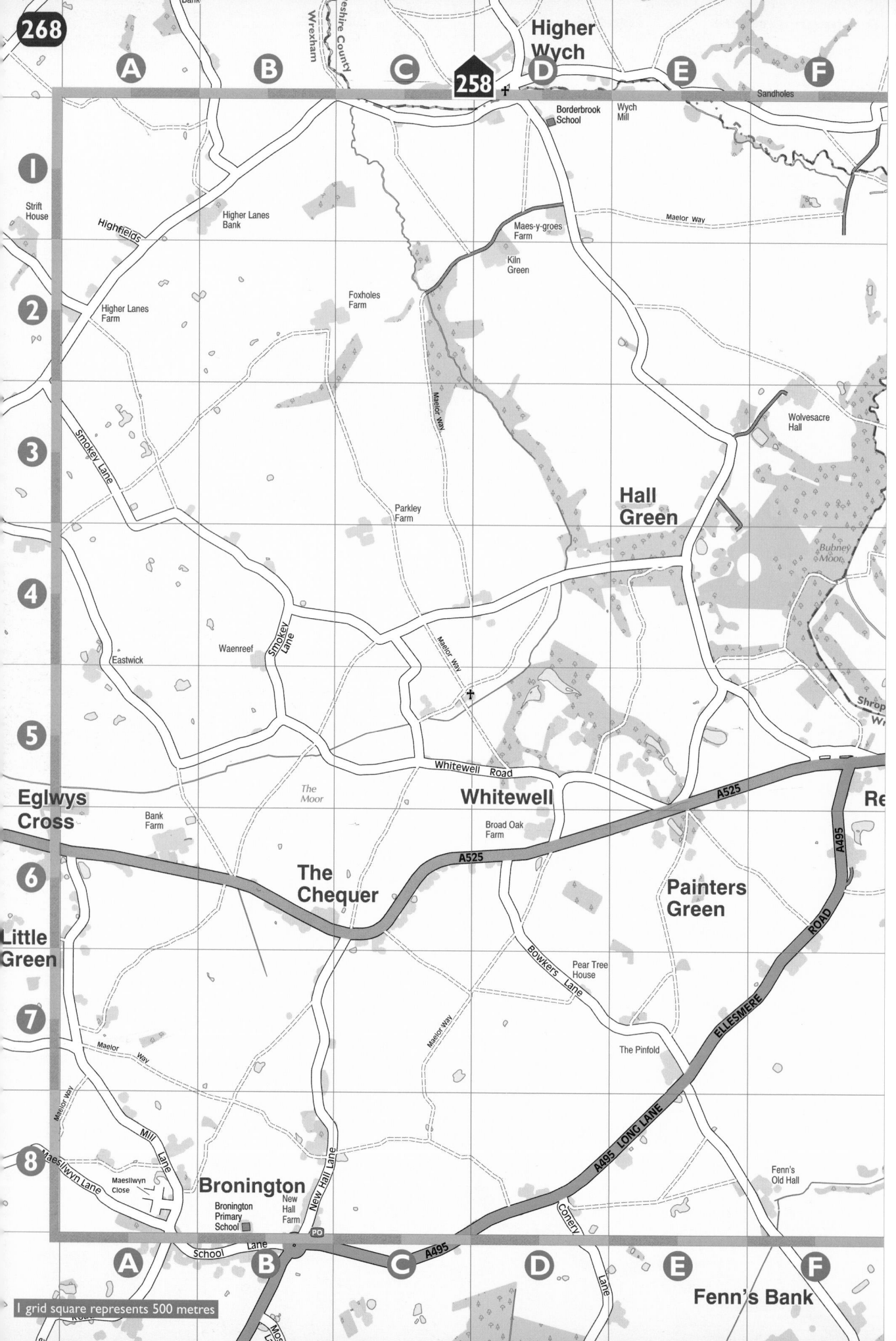

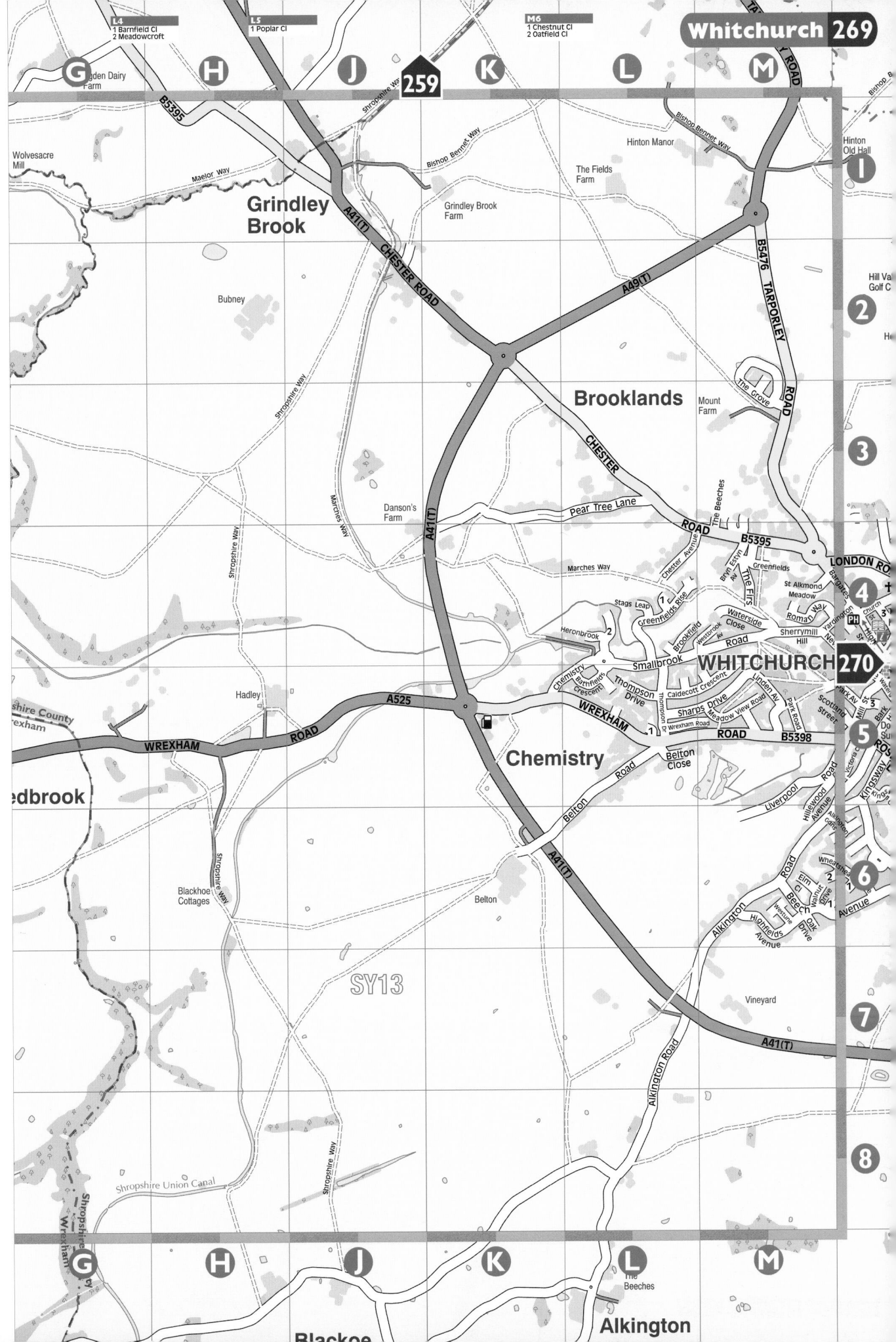

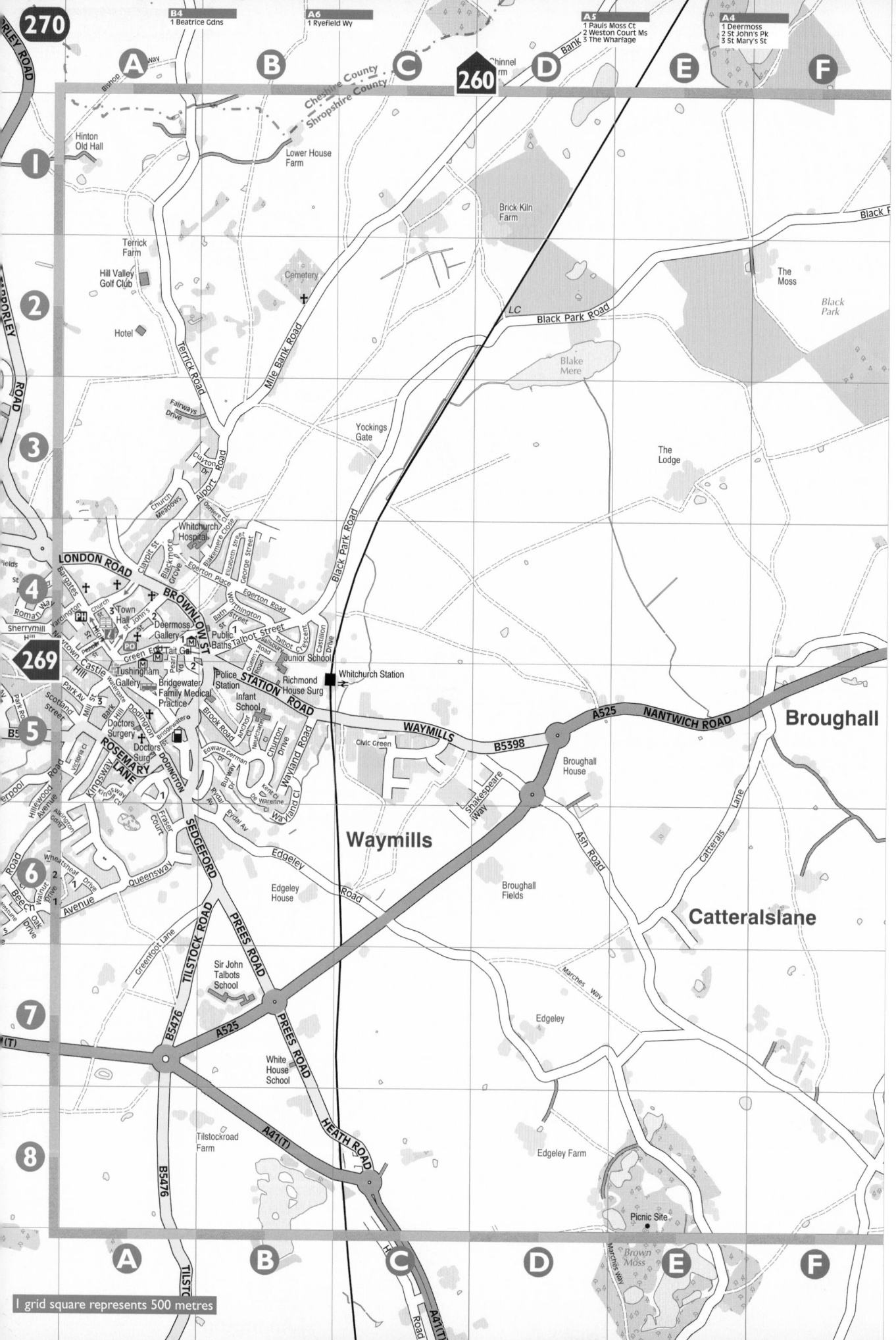

B4
1 Beatrice Gdns

A6
1 Ryefield Wy

A5
1 Pauls Moss Ct
2 Weston Court Ms
3 The Wharfage

A4
1 Deermoss
2 St John's Pk
3 St Mary's St

A B C D E F

I
2
3
4
5
6
7
8

Cheshire County
Shropshire County

Hinton
Old Hall

Lower House
Farm

Brick Kiln
Farm

The
Moss

Black
Park

Terrick
Farm

Cemetery

Hill Valley
Golf Club

Hotel

LC

Black Park Road

Blake
Mere

Fairways
Drive

Yockings
Gate

The
Lodge

Clayton Dr

Church
Meadows

Alport Road

Whitchurch
Hospital

Terrick Road

Mile Bank Road

Black Park Road

Clayton St

Blackmore
Grove

Blakemere Close

Elizabeth Street

George Street

Egerton place

Egerton Road

LONDON ROAD

BROWNLOW ST

Bargates

Deermoss
Gallery

Town
Hall

St John's St

Public
Baths

Talbot Street

Talbot Street

Bath
Street

Worthington

Talbot Crescent

Castillion
Road

Castillion
Drive

Roman Way

Sherrymill
Hill

Green End

Tait Gal

Junior School

Police
Station

Richmond
House Surg

Whitchurch Station

Whitchurch Station

Tushingham
Gallery

Bridgewater
Family Medical
Practice

STATION ROAD

Infant
School

Anchor

Brook Road

Chutton
Drive

Newcastle Rd

WAYMILLS

A525

NANTWICH ROAD

Broughall

Castle
Hill

Doctors
Surgery

Doctors
Surg

Park Av

Scotland
Street

ROSEMARY
LANE

DODINGTON

Edward German

Burway Rd

Kent Cl

De Warenne
Cl

Wayland Rd

Wayland Cl

Rydal Av

Civic Green

B5398

Broughall
House

Shakespeare
Way

Ash Road

Catteralls
Lane

Hillwood Avenue

Kingsway

Fraser
Court

SEDGEFORD

Edgeley
Road

Waymills

Broughall
Fields

Catteralslane

Wheatsheaf
Drive

Walnut
Drive

Queensway

Avenue

Beech

Oak
Drive

Edgeley
House

Greenfoot Lane

TILSTOCK ROAD

PREES ROAD

Sir John
Talbots
School

Marches Way

Edgeley

B5476

A525

PREES ROAD

White
House
School

Tilstockroad
Farm

A41(T)

HEATH ROAD

Edgeley Farm

B5476

Picnic Site

Brown
Moss

Marches Way

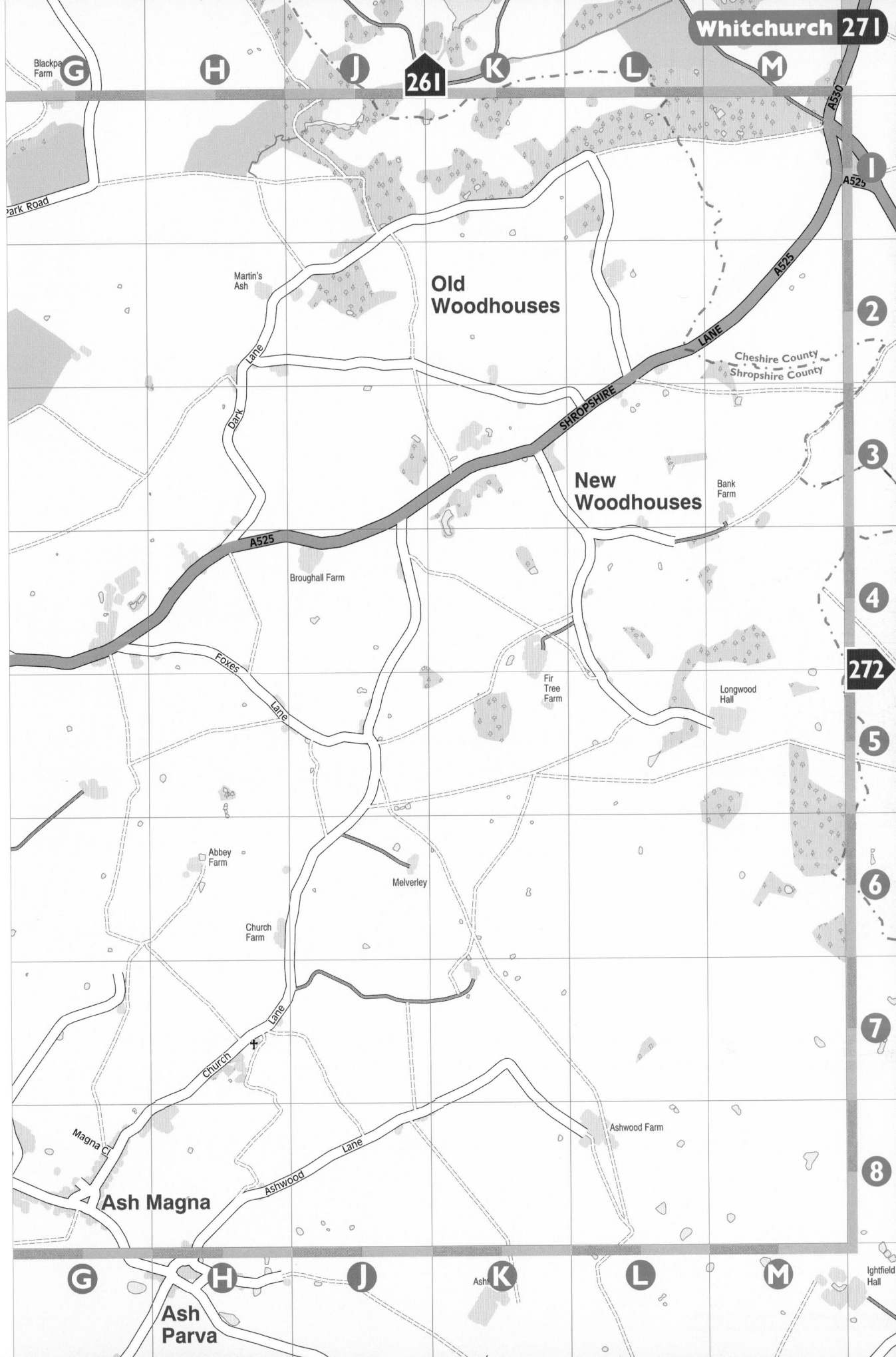

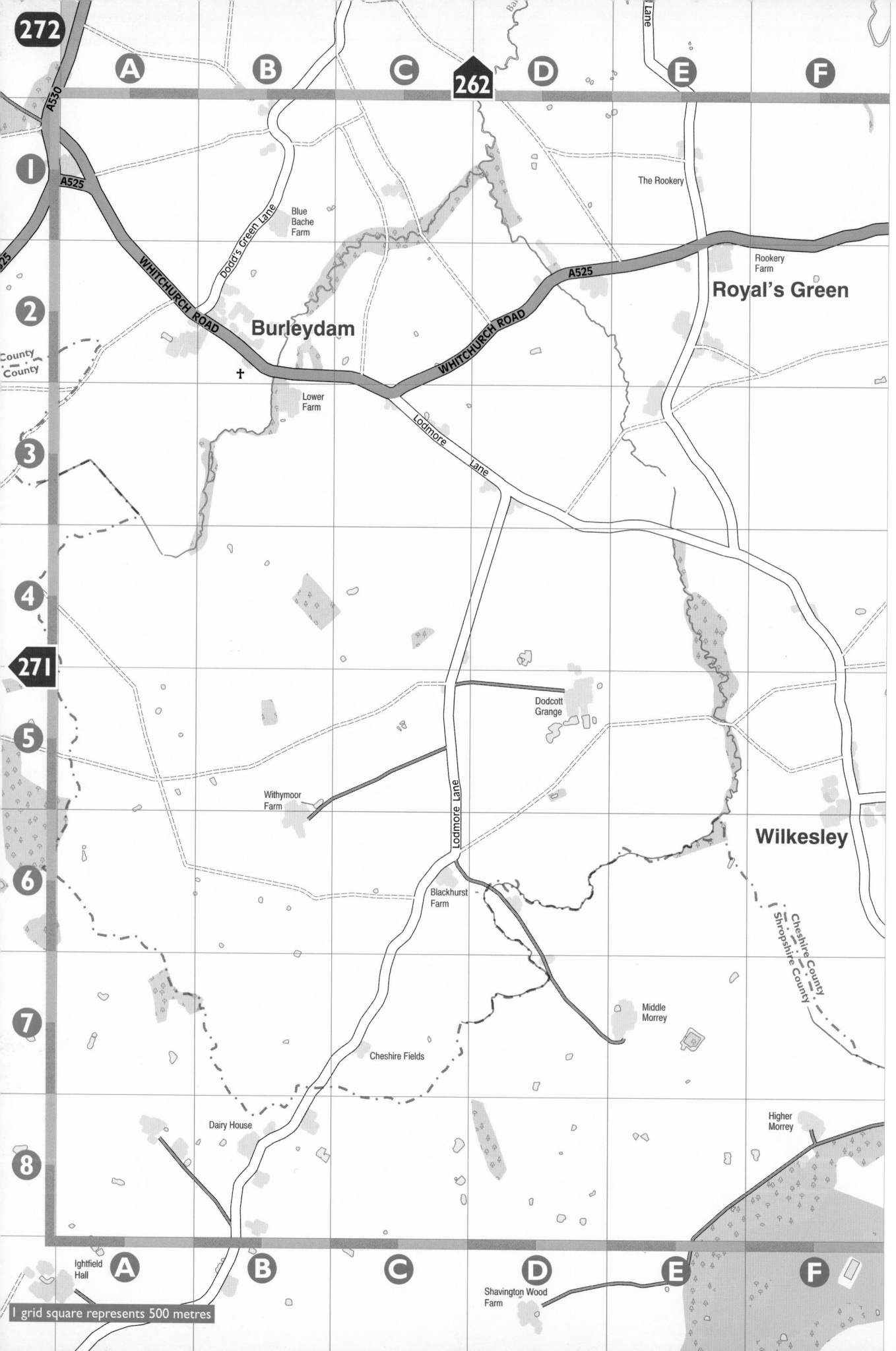

272

A   B   C   **262**   D   E   F

1

A530
A525

The Rookery

2

Blue
Bache
Farm

Dodd's Green Lane

WHITCHURCH ROAD

Burleydam

A525

WHITCHURCH ROAD

Rookery
Farm

Royal's Green

County
County

✝

Lower
Farm

Lodmore   Lane

3

4

271

Dodcott
Grange

5

Withymoor
Farm

Lodmore Lane

Wilkesley

6

Blackhurst
Farm

Cheshire County
Shropshire County

7

Cheshire Fields

Middle
Morrey

8

Dairy House

Higher
Morrey

Ightfield
Hall   A   B   C   D   Shavington Wood
Farm   E   F

I grid square represents 500 metres

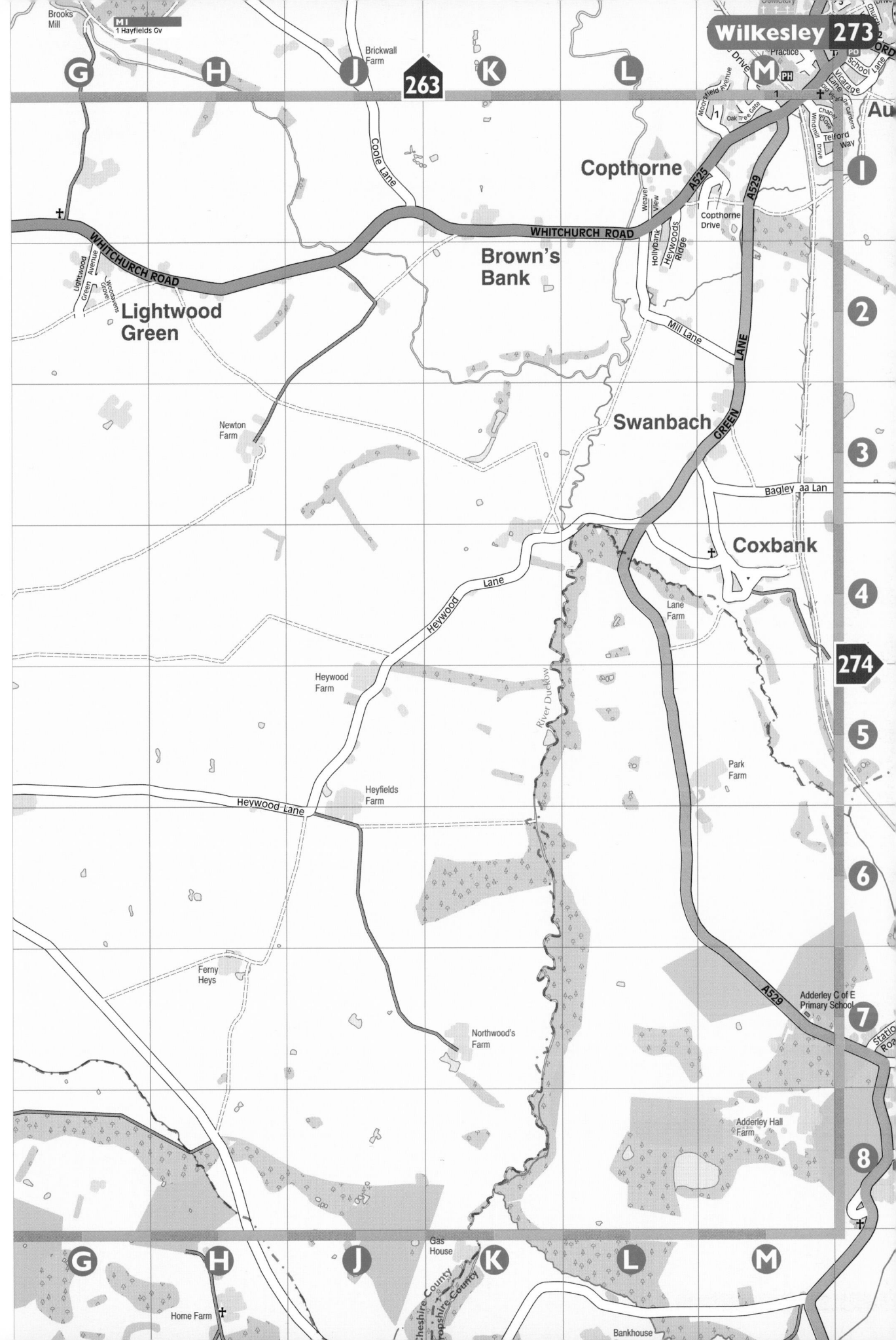

Brooks
Mill

M1
1 Hayfields Gv

Brickwall
Farm

263

Copthorne

Coole Lane

WHITCHURCH ROAD

Brown's
Bank

Weaver View

Hollybank

Heywoods Ridge

Copthorne
Drive

A525

A529

Moorfield Avenue

Oak Tree Gate

Vicarage Gardens

PH

Practice

PO

School

Lane

1

Telford Way

Chapel Close

Whitmill Drive

Au

Lightwood
Green

WHITCHURCH ROAD

Lightwood Green Avenue

Woodsavers
Grovers

Mill Lane

Swanbach

GREEN LANE

Bagley aa Lan

Coxbank

Newton
Farm

Lane
Farm

Heywood Lane

River Duckow

Heywood
Farm

Park
Farm

Heyfields
Farm

Heywood Lane

Ferny
Heys

Northwood's
Farm

A529

Adderley C of E
Primary School

Statio
Roa

Adderley Hall
Farm

Gas
House

Cheshire County

Shropshire County

Home Farm

Bankhouse

G H J K L M 1

274

2

3

4

5

6

7

8

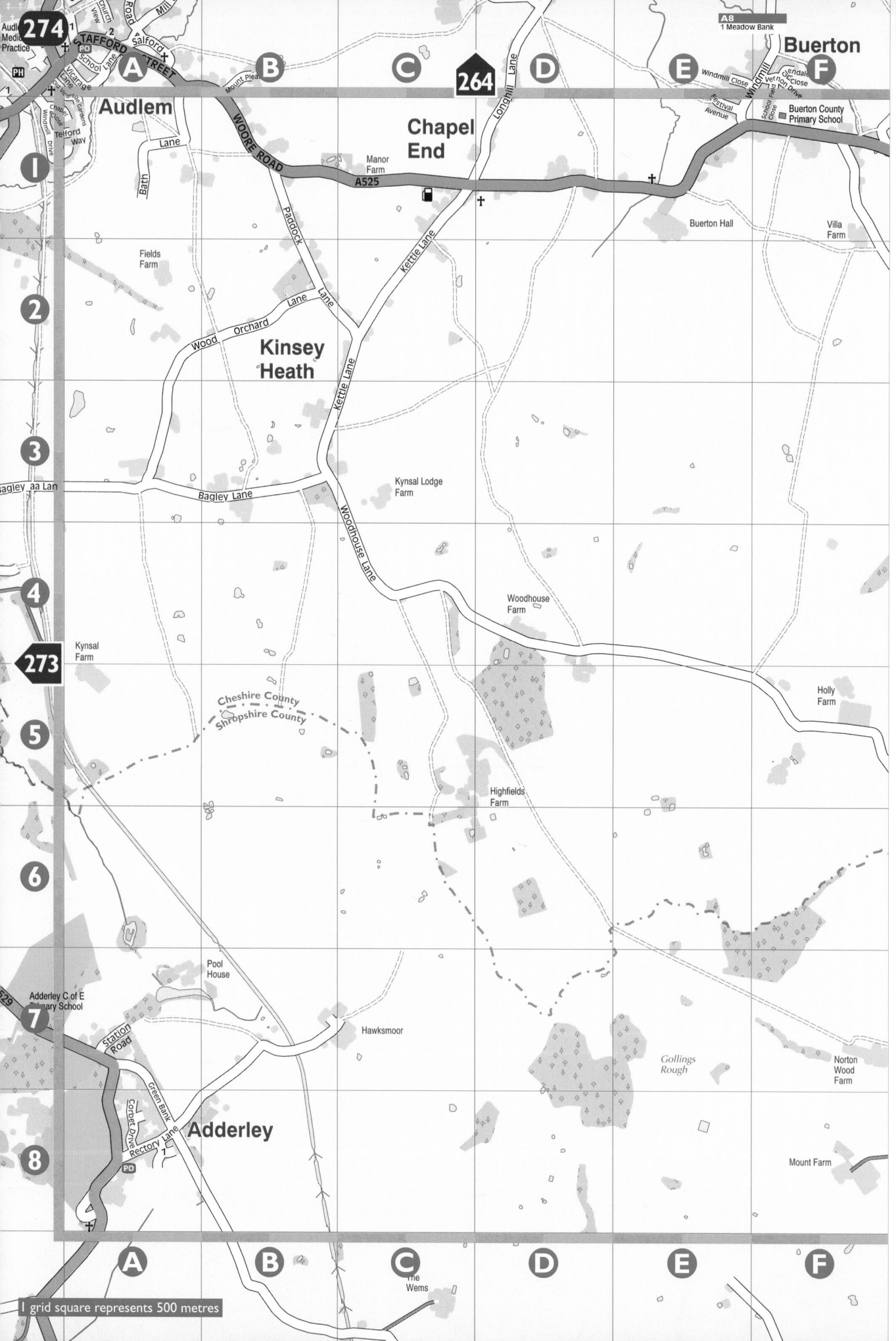

274

1 ·· 2

Audlem Medical Practice
PO
PH
Audlem
Stafford Street
Salford Lane
Vicarage
School Lane
Church Road
Mill Lane
Mount Pleasant
Woore Road
Bath Lane

A
B
C
D
E
F

264

Buerton
1 Meadow Bank
A8
Windmill Close
Vernon Drive
Windmill
Kendale Close
Buerton County Primary School

Chapel End

Manor Farm
A525
Kettle Lane
Longhill Lane

Festival Avenue
Schoolfield Close

Buerton Hall
Villa Farm

1

Fields Farm

Wood Orchard Lane
Paddock Lane
Kinsey Heath
Kettle Lane

2

3

Bagley aa Lan
Bagley Lane
Kynsal Lodge Farm
Woodhouse Lane

4

273
Kynsal Farm

Woodhouse Farm

Holly Farm

5

Cheshire County
Shropshire County

Highfields Farm

6

Pool House

Gollings Rough

Norton Wood Farm

529
Adderley C of E Primary School
7
Station Road
Hawksmoor

Green Bank
Corbet Drive
Rectory Lane
Adderley
PO
8

Mount Farm

A
B
C
The Wems
D
E
F

1 grid square represents 500 metres

G H J K L M

265

I

CW3

Cheshire County
Shropshire County

A525 WOORE ROAD

The
Grange

Fields
Farm

Gorsey Bank
Farm

2

Three
Wells

Woore
Hall

3

Canridden
Wood

College Fields

4

Hankins Heys Lane

Hankins Heys Lane

Hankins
Heys

5

Mere
Farm

Bellaport Home
Farm

6

Bellaport Road

Bellaport
Old Hall

Poplar Lane

7

The Grove

Bellaport Road

8

Bearstone

G H J K L M

Bearstone Road

Bellaport
Lodge

Abbot's Meads 145 H8
Acres Nook 243 G5
Acton 236 A5
Acton Bridge 127 L1
Adderley 274 A8
Adlington 86 B7
Adswood 46 D7
Alderley Edge 110 C2
Aldersey Green 213 J6
Aldford 211 M1
Allgreave 188 C2
Allostock 156 F1
Alpraham 198 D8
Alsager 241 H1
Altrincham 42 F7
Alvanley 124 C4
Anderton 103 J8
Antrobus 77 K8
Appleton 7 H1
Appleton Park 56 D7
Appleton Thorn 57 G8
Arclid 205 H3
Arclid Green 205 H4
Arley 78 B5
Arley Green 78 E6
Arthill 60 B4
Ashley 61 L7
Ashley Heath 61 K4
Ash Magna 271 G8
Ashton 148 F5
Ashton Heath 100 D2
Ashton-in-Makerfield 22 D1
Aspull Common 24 B3
Astbury 207 H4
Astle 135 K4
Astmoor 73 L1
Aston 100 D3
Aston 166 B1
Aston 262 C2
Aston juxta Mondrum 219 K6
Audlem 274 A1
Backford 121 H8
Backford Cross 120 F5
Balderton 191 K3
Ball o' Ditton 6 C2
Balterley 255 J3
Balterley Green 255 H2
Balterley Heath 255 G3
The Banks 49 K8
The Bank 226 B5
Barbridge 218 C6
Barnett Brook 262 E7
Barnhill 231 H2
Barnton 129 G1
The Barony 21 G4
Barrets Green 217 L1
Barrowmore Estate 147 L6
Barrow's Green 34 D8
Barrows Green 220 F3
Barthomley 240 D7
Barton 229 M3
Bate Heath 104 F1
Bath Vale 208 B1
Bearstone 275 M8
Beechwood 73 L7
Beeston 216 A2
Belgrave 191 L6
Bell o' th' Hill 259 J5
Benchill 44 C8
Betchton Heath 204 E7
Betley 255 G6
Betley Common 254 E6
Bewsey 4 B1
Bickerton 231 M6
Bickley Moss 248 A6
Bickley Town 247 K6
Bickleywood 247 J8
Biddulph 227 H5
Big Mancot 166 D2
Birchall Moss 264 E3
Birch Heath 197 H4
Birchwood 29 L8
Blackbrook 37 L2
Blackden Heath 158 B1
Blacon 144 F4
Blakelow 237 K8
Blakenhall 266 A1
Bold Heath 34 E5
Bollington 113 H5
Bollington Cross 112 D5
Booth Bank 60 B5
Booth Green 86 E5
Boothsdale 173 K1
Boots Green 133 G7
Bosley 186 D4
Bostock Green 154 C5
Bowdon 60 F3
Bowgreen 61 G2
Braddocks Hay 227 M4
Bradeley Green 259 M6
Bradfield Green 220 E1
Bradley 99 L5
Bradley Green 258 F4
Bradley Mount 112 B5
Bradwall Green 181 H8
Bramhall 65 M5
Bramhall Moor 66 B2
Bramhall Park 65 J3
Brassey Green 196 D6
Bredbury 47 M1
Bredbury Green 48 A2
Brereton Green 181 M7
Brereton Heath 182 E6
Bretton 167 L8
Brickhouses 204 E4
Bridgemere 265 L5
Bridgemont 89 L2
Bridge Trafford 147 G2
Brindley 234 E4
Broadheath 42 C5
Broadoak 210 A2
Broken Cross 130 F5
Broken Cross 137 K4
Bronington 268 B8
Brook Bottom 68 E3
Brookhouse 139 K1
Brookhouse Green 206 A5
Brooklands 43 H2

Brooklands 269 L3
Brookvale 74 B7
Broomedge 59 K3
Broomhall Green 262 E1
Broomhill 147 M4
Broughall 270 F5
Broughton 190 C1
Brownedge 181 M8
Brown Heath 171 H6
Brown Knowl 231 J4
Brown Lees 227 G7
Brownlow 206 E5
Brownlow Heath 206 D7
Brown's Bank 273 K2
Broxton 231 G2
Bruche 37 M5
Bruera 193 K6
Bryn 128 B6
Bucklow Hill 80 B1
Buckoak 124 F7
Buddileigh 254 F5
Budworth Heath 104 B3
Buerton 264 F8
Buglawton 185 H7
Bulkeley 232 E2
Bunbury 216 F4
Bunbury Heath 216 E3
Bunsley Bank 264 D7
Burford 236 A4
Burland 235 J5
Burleydam 272 B2
Burton 172 F8
Burton 118 D2
Burtonwood 27 G6
Burwardsley 215 G6
Butley Town 112 C4
Butt Green 252 B1
Butt Lane 242 C3
Byley 156 A5
Cadishead 31 J8
Cale Green 46 F6
Callands 36 D2
Calrofold 139 J2
Calveley 217 L2
Capenhurst 120 B4
Carr Green 40 F6
Carrington Moss 41 M1
Castlefields 73 M2
Castletown 244 D1
Catteralslane 270 E6
Chadkirk 48 B4
Chapel End 274 C1
Cheadle 45 L7
Cheadle Heath 46 A5
Cheadle Hulme 65 G4
Checkley 266 D3
Checkley Green 266 B4
Chelford 135 H1
Chemistry 269 K5
The Chequer 268 B6
Cherry Tree 48 F2
Chester 17 K6
Childer Thornton 94 B4
Cholmondeston 199 L8
Chorley 249 C1
Chorlton 254 A3
Chorlton Lane 245 H8
Chowley 213 L7
Christleton 170 E4
Church Lawton 225 H4
Church Minshull 201 H7
Churton 211 L6
Cinnamon Brow 29 G8
Clark Green 113 G1
Clifton 73 K8
Clive 178 E3
Clive Green 178 E6
Clock Face 34 D1
Clotton 173 K8
Clotton Common 173 K6
Cloud Side 209 H1
Clough Hall 242 F4
Clutton 230 B2
Coalpit Hill 242 C4
Cobbs 56 D4
Coddington 229 M1
Cold Moss Heath 204 C7
Collins Green 26 D3
Comberbach 103 K5
Commonside 126 C4
Common Side 175 K1
Compstall 49 G1
Congleton 207 K3
Congleton Edge 208 C7
Cooksongreen 126 F3
Coppenhall 221 K5
Coppenhall Moss 221 K3
Copthorne 273 C2
Cotebrook 174 F5
Coxbank 273 M4
Cracow Moss 255 H8
Cranage 157 G6
Crewe 19 K1
Crewe-by-Farndon 229 G5
Crewe Green 239 H1
Croft 29 H4
Cronton 33 H7
Cross Lane 201 K6
Cross o' th' Hill 246 D8
Cross Town 107 H2
Crowton 127 H3
Cross Wood 53 K2
Croxton Green 233 J6
Cuddington 127 L8
Cuddington Green 257 H3
Cuddington Heath 257 K2
Cuerdley Cross 54 A1
Culcheth 30 A1
Dale Brow 112 A7
Dales Green 226 C2
Dallam 36 F3
Danebank 68 E7
Danebridge 188 B5
Dane in Shaw 208 C3
Daresbury 75 H2
Darland 210 D4
Davenham 154 A2
Davenport 46 E8

Davenport 182 E5
Davenport Green 62 F2
Davenport Green 109 M1
Day Green 223 M4
Dean Row 84 F4
Deansgreen 59 H4
Delamere 150 D6
Didsbury 45 H1
Disley 68 B6
Ditton 52 B5
Dobs Hill 166 A3
Dodleston 191 G5
Doe Green 54 C1
Dones Green 102 B5
Duckington 231 J8
Duddon 173 G6
Duddon Common 173 J5
Dudlows Green 56 E7
Dunham Town 41 K8
Dunham Woodhouses 41 H8
Dunham-On-The-Hill 123 L6
Dunkirk 120 E5
Dunkirk 242 A6
Dutton 75 G8
Earlestown 26 F1
East Didsbury 45 K3
Eaton 185 G4
Eaton 198 A1
Ebnal 246 C6
Eccleston 192 E3
Edge Green 22 F1
Edge Green 246 B1
Edgeley 46 D5
Egerton Green 232 C7
Ellesmere Port 10 C6
Elton 97 G8
Elton Green 123 G2
Elworth 203 M6
Englesea-brook 240 A8
Ettiley Heath 203 K7
Faddiley 234 E5
Fanshowe 136 C8
Farnden 228 F2
Farnworth 53 G1
Fearnhead 38 A2
Feldy 79 G8
Fernilee 115 L3
Finney Green 84 C2
Fivecrosses 99 J7
Foggbrook 47 M5
Fourlanes End 205 L8
Fowley Common 25 J7
Foxley 241 K5
Foxwist Green 152 F6
Frandley 103 C1
Frodsham 99 K5
Fullers Moor 231 K3
Fulshaw Park 84 A7
Furness Vale 89 J1
Gallantry Bank 232 B4
Garden City 142 E5
Gateshath 194 F7
Gatley 45 G8
Gauntons Bank 248 F8
Gawsworth 161 L4
Gemini 36 D1
Gibb Hill 103 K3
Gillbent 64 F6
Gillow Heath 227 H2
Ginclough 113 L6
Glazebrook 31 G6
Glazebury 25 H6
Golborne 23 H5
Goldenhill 243 H6
Goostrey 157 K3
Gorse Covert 30 B6
Gorstage 128 B6
Gorstella 191 G3
Gorstyhill 254 E2
Gosland Green 217 H3
Gowhole 69 L8
Gradeley Green 234 E7
Grange 9 M8
Grappenhall 57 H2
Gravel 178 B4
Great Barrow 147 K6
Great Budworth 104 B5
Great Moor 47 J6
Great Sankey 36 B6
Great Sutton 94 D7
Great Warford 109 H5
Greenbank 12 B4
Greendale 111 J5
Greenlooms 171 M8
Gresty Green 238 D4
Grindley Brook 269 H1
Guilden Sutton 146 F7
Gurnett 138 F8
Hack Green 251 L7
Hague Bar 68 F4
Hale 61 M2
Hale 71 K2
Hale Bank 52 B8
Halebarns 62 D4
Halewood 50 F4
Hall Green 225 L7
Hall Lane 268 E3
Hallowsgate 149 H8
Halton 73 H4
Halton Brook 73 K3
Halton View 7 M3
Hampton Green 247 H5
Hampton Heath 246 E5
Handbridge 17 K9
Handforth 64 C8
Hand Green 197 H6
Handley 213 K4
Hankelow 264 C5
Hapsford 123 L3
Harden Park 110 B1
Hardings Wood 242 E2
Hargrave 195 G3
Harriseahead 226 D7
Hartford 128 E8
Hartfordbeach 129 H6
Harthill 231 L1
Haslington 222 D8

Hassall 223 K5
Hassall Green 224 A2
Hatchmere 126 D8
Hatherton 253 C8
Hatton 75 M3
Hatton Heath 194 A3
Haughton Moss 217 G6
Havannah 184 F4
Hawarden 166 D4
Hawk Green 67 L1
Haymoor Green 252 E2
Hazel Grove 67 J3
Heald Green 64 A3
Heath 9 G8
Heatley 40 D7
Heaton Mersey 45 L1
Heaton Norris 2 A3
Heaviley 47 G6
Hebden Green 176 F5
Helsby 98 C8
Henbury 137 H4
Hermitage Green 28 B4
Hetherson Green 247 J3
Higher Burwardsley 215 H7
Higher Disley 68 D7
Higherfence 139 G4
Higher Hurdsfield 138 F2
Higher Marston 104 C2
Higher Poynton 87 K2
Higher Runcorn 9 G5
Higher Shurlach 130 E7
Higher Walton 55 L5
Higher Whitley 76 E7
Higher Wincham 105 H7
Higher Wych 258 D8
High Lane 67 L5
Highlane 161 J5
High Legh 59 H7
Hightown 208 A2
Hillcliffe 56 C5
Hinderton 92 A3
Hob Hill 230 D8
Hockley 87 G1
Hodgehill 159 L4
The Hollands 209 J3
Hollinfare 40 A1
Hollin Green 234 E6
Hollins 242 D4
Hollins Green 40 C5
Hollinsgreen 180 C8
Hollowmoor Heath 148 A6
Hollyhurst 261 G6
Holmes Chapel 181 H3
Holt 228 D4
Hood Manor 36 C7
Hoofield 196 A2
Hoo Green 79 L2
Hoole 170 A1
Hoole Bank 146 C5
Hooton 93 M3
Hope Green 86 D3
Horton Green 245 H4
Horwich End 89 L7
Hough 110 D3
Hough 253 M2
Hough Green 52 A3
Houghton Green 28 E7
Howbeck Bank 252 E4
Howbeck Bank 252 E4
Howley 5 M7
Hulme 37 H1
Hulme Walfield 184 B5
Huntington 169 M6
Hunt's Cross 50 B6
Hurdsfield 15 L3
Huxley 196 A5
Huyton Quarry 32 B2
Illidge Green 205 H1
Ince 97 G6
Irlam 31 M3
Jodrell Bank 158 D3
Keckwick 54 F8
Kelsall 149 J8
Kenyon 24 A8
Kerridge 113 G6
Kerridge-end 139 J2
Kettleshulme 88 B3
Key Green 185 L8
Kidnal 245 L5
Kidsgrove 242 C2
Kingsley 126 D2
Kingsway 7 G4
Kingswood 36 A1
Kinnerton Green 190 A5
Kinsey Heath 274 B2
Kitt's Moss 65 K7
Knolls Green 82 E8
Knotbury 165 M7
Knowl Bank 255 L5
Knutsford 107 J3
Knypersley 227 L7
Lacey Green 84 B3
Lach Dennis 131 K7
Lache 168 E7
Lane Ends 49 K3
Lane Ends 68 E8
Lane Ends 221 L1
Lane Head 23 M6
Langley 163 J1
Larden Green 234 C8
Latchford 56 C1
Lately Common 25 J3
Lavister 210 B3
Lawton-gate 224 F8
Lawton Heath 224 C6
Lawton Heath End 224 D6
Lea by Backford 121 G8
Lea Forge 253 L6
Lea Green 201 G4
Ledsham 119 M2
Leftwich 13 G9
Ley Hey Park 48 E5
Lightwood Green 273 G2
Lindow End 109 G2
Lingley Green 35 J5
Lingley Mere 35 K4
Little Barrow 147 L3
Little Bollington 60 C2

Little Budworth 175 M5
Little Chell 243 M7
Little Heath 170 E4
Little Heath 264 A7
Little Leigh 102 C7
Little Madeley 267 M5
Little Mancot 166 C2
Little Moor 47 K4
Little Neston 91 K6
Littler 176 F2
Little Stanney 121 L3
Little Sutton 93 M6
Littleton 170 D3
Little Town 29 H2
Locking Stumps 29 H8
Longbarn 38 C3
Longford 37 H3
Long Green 147 M3
Longmoss 137 J4
Lostock Gralam 131 H2
Lostock Green 131 H4
Lowcross Hill 245 K1
Lower Bredbury 47 J3
Lower Bunbury 216 F4
Lower Carden 230 C6
Lower Heath 184 D6
Lower House 6 D5
Lowerhouse 112 E4
Lower Kinnerton 190 C3
Lower Peover 132 C3
Lower Pexhill 137 G8
Lower Stretton 76 E4
Lower Threapwood 256 F6
Lower Walton 56 A4
Lower Whitley 102 D1
Lower Withington 158 F4
Lower Wych 258 B6
Low Leighton 69 K4
Lowton 23 K4
Lowton Common 24 A4
Lowton Heath 23 J6
Lowton St Mary's 24 A5
Lugsdale 7 L6
Lunts Heath 34 A7
Lyme Green 162 C2
Lymm 58 E1
Macclesfield 15 J4
Macclesfield Forest 140 B7
Madeley 267 L6
Malkin's Bank 223 K1
Malpas 258 C1
Mancot Royal 166 F1
Manley 125 G8
Manley Common 125 J7
Manor Park 179 G4
Marbury 260 D4
Marford 210 A7
Marley Green 261 H3
Marple 48 E6
Marple Bridge 49 H5
Marpleridge 67 M2
Marshfield Bank 220 C8
Marsh Green 98 F4
Marsh Green 227 K2
The Marsh 207 J3
Marston 130 C1
Marthall 108 E8
Martinscroft 38 D5
Martin's Moss 205 M6
Marton 160 C8
Marton Green 152 D8
Maw Green 221 M5
Meadowbank 153 K7
Mellor 49 L6
Mere 80 B4
Mere Heath 153 M3
Merelake 242 A4
Mickle Trafford 146 E4
Middle Madeley 267 M5
Middlewich 179 K3
Middlewood 67 H7
Midway 86 D2
Mill Brow 49 L4
Milners Heath 194 C2
Milton Green 213 J2
Mobberley 81 L5
Mobberley 108 B1
Mollington 144 D3
Monk's Heath 136 B3
Moore 55 G6
Moorside 91 J5
The Moor 166 E3
Morley 83 J3
Morley Green 83 H3
Moss Bank 53 K4
Mossbrow 40 D5
Moss End 104 C2
Moss Houses 161 M2
Moss Lane 138 B3
Mossley 208 B5
Moss Nook 63 M4
Moston 145 K3
Moston Green 203 H5
Mottram St Andrew 111 G3
Mouldsworth 149 G1
Moulton 153 M5
Mount Pleasant 226 B6
Mow Cop 226 C5
Nantwich 21 H6
Ness 92 B7
Nessholt 91 L8
Neston 91 K5
Nether Alderley 110 A6
Netherton 98 F6
Newall Green 44 A8
Newchapel 243 L2
Newchurch Common 152 C5
Newfield 243 J7
Newhall 262 B5
New Horwich 89 M2
New Lane End 29 G2
New Mills 69 H4
New Pale 125 K6
Newpool 227 G6
Newsbank 183 L3
Newton 125 L2
Newton 145 L2
Newton 195 L8

Newton	214 E3	Poolfold	208 F8	Shaw Heath	2 E9

Newton 214 E3
Newton 250 E8
Newtonia 179 H4
Newton-Le-Willows 27 K1
Newton Park 27 M2
Newtown 69 H7
Newtown 99 K3
Newtown 209 H6
New Woodhouses 271 L3
Nick i'th' Hill 208 A8
No Mans Heath 247 H7
Noonsun 108 E3
Norbury 260 D1
Norbury Common 248 C7
Norbury Moor 66 E3
Norcott Brook 76 C6
Norley 126 F6
Northern Moor 43 M3
North Rode 185 L2
Northwich 13 J6
Norton 74 C3
Nova Scotia 152 C7
Oakgrove 162 C5
Oakhanger 240 D3
Oakmere 151 H5
Oakwood 29 M8
Occlestone Green 202 B2
Offerton 47 L5
Offerton Green 48 A6
Oglet 70 D4
Old Boston 22 B5
Oldcastle Heath 257 L3
Oldfield Brow 42 B7
Old Warren 166 E8
Old Woodhouses 271 K2
Ollerton 107 L6
Orford 37 K3
Oscroft 172 F2
Oughtrington 40 A8
Over 177 H4
Over Knutsford 107 J4
Over Peover 134 A4
Overpool 94 F5
Over Tabley 80 A7
Overton 99 H5
Paddington 38 A5
Paddockhill 83 C8
Padgate 37 M3
Painters Green 268 E6
Palacefields 73 M7
Park End 241 C8
Parkgate 91 J3
Parkgate 134 B4
Partington 40 F2
Peckforton 215 M7
Peel Hall 63 M2
Penketh 35 K8
Pennington 24 D1
Pentre 142 E7
Peover Heath 134 D5
Pewterspear 76 F1
Pickmere 104 F6
Picton 146 C1
Pinsley Green 261 K2
Piper's Ash 146 C8
Pitts Hill 243 M7
Plemstall 147 H3
Plumley 105 M8
Pocket Nook 24 C4

Poolfold 208 F8
Portwood 3 J1
Pott Shrigley 113 K1
Poulton 211 G2
Pownall Park 83 M4
Poynton 66 F8
Prestbury 112 A5
Preston Brook 74 F7
Preston on the Hill 75 G6
Puddinglake 156 A4
Puddington 118 E5
Pulford 210 C2
Quarrybank 174 C5
Queensferry 142 D6
Queen's Park 17 L7
Quoisley 260 B4
Radmore Green 217 L8
Radway Green 240 F3
Rainhill 33 K1
Rainhill Stoops 33 L2
Rainow 113 K7
Rainowlow 113 K5
Ravenscliffe 243 G7
Ravenshall 255 C8
Ravensmoor 250 D2
Rease Heath 236 C2
Redbrook 268 F5
Red Bull 242 E1
Reddish 40 A7
Rhuddall Heath 197 L3
Risley 29 L6
Rixton 39 M2
Rock End 227 M6
Rocksavage 73 H7
Rodeheath 185 H1
Rode Heath 224 F4
Romiley 48 D2
The Rookery 243 J1
Rosehill 61 J3
Rossett 210 C5
Rostherne 80 E1
Roundthorn 43 L7
Row-of-trees 109 J1
Rowton 170 F7
Rowton Moor 170 F6
Royal's Green 272 E2
Rudheath 130 D6
Rudheath Woods 156 D2
Ruloe 127 J5
Runcorn 9 K5
Rushgreen 39 M7
Rushton 175 K7
Saighton 193 M3
Sale 42 E1
Salterswall 177 G1
Saltney 168 C7
Sandbach 204 A6
Sandbach Heath 204 D6
Sandiway 152 B1
Sandlow Green 182 A3
Sandycroft 167 G2
Sandyford 243 L6
Sankey Bridges 36 C8
Saughall 144 B3
Scholar Green 225 K6
School Green 177 H7
Sealand 143 L6
Sharston 44 F7
Shavington 238 C8

Shaw Heath 2 E9
Shaw Heath 107 K1
Shell Green 53 L2
Shocklach 244 D5
Shocklach Green 244 B5
Shotton 142 B7
Shotwick 119 G8
Siddington 160 A1
Siddington Heath 159 M3
Simm's Cross 7 K5
Sinderland Green 41 K3
Skellorn Green 86 D4
Slaughter Hill 239 K1
Smallwood 205 M7
Smethwick Green 205 M1
Smiths Green 159 G2
Smith's Green 240 C5
Smithy Green 65 H4
Smithy Green 132 E2
Snow Hill 20 D5
Somerford 182 F5
Sound 250 E7
Sound Heath 250 D8
Southgate 73 L5
Speke 70 E1
Spen Green 206 B6
Sproston Green 180 D2
Spurstow 216 D6
Stamford Bridge 147 J8
Stanley Green 64 E7
Stanlow 96 B7
Stapeley 252 D4
Statham 39 K8
Stepping Hill 47 K8
Stoak 121 M5
Stockport 2 B3
Stockton Heath 56 C3
Stoneley Green 235 K8
Stretton 76 E2
Stretton 229 M6
Strines 68 C3
Stud Green 203 H3
Styal 63 M8
Sutton Green 120 B1
Sutton Lane Ends 162 F2
Sutton Manor 34 A2
Sutton Weaver 100 B1
Swanbach 273 L3
Swan Green 132 D5
Swanwick Green 248 C8
Swettenham 182 E1
Sworton Heath 58 F7
Sydney 222 A7
Tabley Hill 106 D1
Talke 242 C5
Talke Pits 242 E7
Tallarn Green 256 F7
Tarbock Green 32 C8
Tarporley 197 K2
Tarvin 172 C1
Tarvin Sands 172 C1
Tattenhall 214 B3
Tatton Dale 80 D3
Taxal 89 J8
Thelwall 57 L1
Thornsett 69 L2
Thorns Green 62 C7
Thornton-le-Moors 122 D3
Threapwood 256 E5

Thurlwood 224 E4
Tilston 245 H1
Tilstone Bank 197 L8
Tilstone Fearnall 197 L6
Timbersbrook 208 D2
Timperley 43 G5
Tirley Garth 174 B3
Tiverton 197 J7
Torkington 67 J2
Tower Hill 113 J8
Town End 33 J6
Town Fields 177 K5
Town of Lowton 23 G7
Town Park 74 B3
Trevalyn 210 D6
Turnhurst 243 M4
Twemlow Green 158 B7
Twiss Green 24 E7
Two Mills 119 L5
Tytherington 112 D8
Upper Threapwood 256 C4
Upton 52 B2
Upton 145 K6
Upton Heath 145 M4
Upton Rocks 52 E1
Utkinton 174 A5
Vicarscross 170 E1
Vulcan Village 27 J4
Wades Green 200 F7
Wain Lee 226 F8
Walgherton 253 G6
Walker Barn 139 M4
Walley's Green 201 M5
Warburton 40 A4
Warburton Green 62 C6
Wardle 218 B5
Wardle Bank 218 B3
Wardsend 87 G3
Wargrave 27 J3
Warmingham 202 E5
Warren 161 L3
Warrington 4 A4
Waterside 89 L1
Waverton 171 H8
Waymills 270 C6
Way's Green 177 L4
Weaverham 128 F4
Weetwood Common 173 J3
Well Green 62 D1
Wells Green 237 M5
Wervin 122 A8
West Bank 52 F7
Westbrook 36 A3
West Heath 206 F1
Weston 8 E9
Weston 72 F6
Weston 137 M5
Weston Point 8 A7
Westy 37 M7
Wettenhall 199 M5
Wettenhall Green 199 L6
Whaley Bridge 89 J5
Wharton 177 M1
Wharton Green 154 B8
Wheelock 222 F2
Wheelock Heath 223 G4
Whirley Grove 137 L1
Whisterfield 159 L1
Whiston 32 E1

Whiston Cross 32 D1
Whiston Lane Ends 32 C2
Whitby 121 H1
Whitbyheath 120 F3
Whitchurch 269 L5
Whitefield Lane End 32 B4
Whitegate 153 C5
Whitehill 243 J2
Whiteley Green 112 E2
Whitemore 208 D6
Whitewell 268 C5
Whitley Reed 77 J3
Widnes 6 E6
Wildboarclough 164 D6
Wilderspool 56 C2
Wilkesley 272 F6
Willaston 93 H4
Willaston 237 J7
Willington Corner 173 L2
Willow Green 102 B7
Wilmslow 84 B6
Wilmslow Park 84 D5
Wimbolds Trafford 122 F6
Wincham 130 D1
Wincle 187 M4
Windle Hill 92 C5
Windlehurst 67 L3
Windmill Hill 74 C2
Windy Arbor 32 D4
Windyharbour 159 J3
Winnington 12 C2
Winsford 177 K2
Winterley 222 F5
Winwick 28 B5
Winwick Quay 28 B8
Wirswall 260 A7
Wistaston 237 K3
Wistaston Green 237 K2
Withington Green 158 E1
Wolverham 95 J8
Woodbank 119 L6
Woodend 68 C4
Woodford 85 K2
Woodhey Green 234 B7
Woodhouse Green 209 J2
Woodhouse Park 63 J3
Woodhouses 42 B2
Woodhouses 98 E8
Wood Lanes 87 G4
Woodside 149 J3
Woodside 200 A6
Woods Moor 66 B1
Woodworth Green 217 H4
Woolstanwood 220 E8
Woolston 38 C5
Woolton 50 A3
Worleston 219 M6
Wornish Nook 184 A3
Worthenbury 256 A3
Wrenbury 249 M8
Wrights Green 57 G7
Wrinehill 267 G1
Wybunbury 253 G4
Wythenshawe 63 H1

USING THE STREET INDEX

Street names are listed alphabetically. Each street name is followed by its postal town or area locality, the Postcode District, the page number, and the reference to the square in which the name is found.

Example: Abbey Pl *CW/HAS* CW1...................... 221 K6 🔟

Some entries are followed by a number in a blue box. This number indicates the location of the street within the referenced grid square. The full street name is listed at the side of the map page.

GENERAL ABBREVIATIONS

ACC	ACCESS	CTYD	COURTYARD	HLS	HILLS	MWY	MOTORWAY	SE	SOUTH EAST
ALY	ALLEY	CUTT	CUTTINGS	HO	HOUSE	N	NORTH	SER	SERVICE AREA
AP	APPROACH	CV	COVE	HOL	HOLLOW	NE	NORTH EAST	SH	SHORE
AR	ARCADE	CYN	CANYON	HOSP	HOSPITAL	NW	NORTH WEST	SHOP	SHOPPING
ASS	ASSOCIATION	DEPT	DEPARTMENT	HRB	HARBOUR	O/P	OVERPASS	SKWY	SKYWAY
AV	AVENUE	DL	DALE	HTH	HEATH	OFF	OFFICE	SMT	SUMMIT
BCH	BEACH	DM	DAM	HTS	HEIGHTS	ORCH	ORCHARD	SOC	SOCIETY
BLDS	BUILDINGS	DR	DRIVE	HVN	HAVEN	OV	OVAL	SP	SPUR
BND	BEND	DRO	DROVE	HWY	HIGHWAY	PAL	PALACE	SPR	SPRING
BNK	BANK	DRY	DRIVEWAY	IMP	IMPERIAL	PAS	PASSAGE	SQ	SQUARE
BR	BRIDGE	DWGS	DWELLINGS	IN	INLET	PAV	PAVILION	ST	STREET
BRK	BROOK	E	EAST	IND EST	INDUSTRIAL ESTATE	PDE	PARADE	STN	STATION
BTM	BOTTOM	EMB	EMBANKMENT	INF	INFIRMARY	PH	PUBLIC HOUSE	STR	STREAM
BUS	BUSINESS	EMBY	EMBASSY	INFO	INFORMATION	PK	PARK	STRD	STRAND
BVD	BOULEVARD	ESP	ESPLANADE	INT	INTERCHANGE	PKWY	PARKWAY	SW	SOUTH WEST
BY	BYPASS	EST	ESTATE	IS	ISLAND	PL	PLACE	TDG	TRADING
CATH	CATHEDRAL	EX	EXCHANGE	JCT	JUNCTION	PLN	PLAIN	TER	TERRACE
CEM	CEMETERY	EXPY	EXPRESSWAY	JTY	JETTY	PLNS	PLAINS	THWY	THROUGHWAY
CEN	CENTRE	EXT	EXTENSION	KG	KING	PLZ	PLAZA	TNL	TUNNEL
CFT	CROFT	F/O	FLYOVER	KNL	KNOLL	POL	POLICE STATION	TOLL	TOLLWAY
CH	CHURCH	FC	FOOTBALL CLUB	L	LAKE	PR	PRINCE	TPK	TURNPIKE
CHA	CHASE	FK	FORK	LA	LANE	PREC	PRECINCT	TR	TRACK
CHYD	CHURCHYARD	FLD	FIELD	LDG	LODGE	PREP	PREPARATORY	TRL	TRAIL
CIR	CIRCLE	FLDS	FIELDS	LGT	LIGHT	PRIM	PRIMARY	TWR	TOWER
CIRC	CIRCUS	FLS	FALLS	LK	LOCK	PROM	PROMENADE	U/P	UNDERPASS
CL	CLOSE	FLS	FLATS	LKS	LAKES	PRS	PRINCESS	UNI	UNIVERSITY
CLFS	CLIFFS	FM	FARM	LNDG	LANDING	PRT	PORT	UPR	UPPER
CMP	CAMP	FT	FORT	LTL	LITTLE	PT	POINT	V	VALE
CNR	CORNER	FWY	FREEWAY	LWR	LOWER	PTH	PATH	VA	VALLEY
CO	COUNTY	FY	FERRY	MAG	MAGISTRATE	PZ	PIAZZA	VIAD	VIADUCT
COLL	COLLEGE	GA	GATE	MAN	MANSIONS	QD	QUADRANT	VIL	VILLA
COM	COMMON	GAL	GALLERY	MD	MEAD	QU	QUEEN	VIS	VISTA
COMM	COMMISSION	GDN	GARDEN	MDW	MEADOWS	QY	QUAY	VLG	VILLAGE
CON	CONVENT	GDNS	GARDENS	MEM	MEMORIAL	R	RIVER	VLS	VILLAS
COT	COTTAGE	GLD	GLADE	MKT	MARKET	RBT	ROUNDABOUT	VW	VIEW
COTS	COTTAGES	GLN	GLEN	MKTS	MARKETS	RD	ROAD	W	WEST
CP	CAPE	GN	GREEN	ML	MALL	RDG	RIDGE	WD	WOOD
CPS	COPSE	GND	GROUND	ML	MILL	REP	REPUBLIC	WHF	WHARF
CR	CREEK	GRA	GRANGE	MNR	MANOR	RES	RESERVOIR	WK	WALK
CREM	CREMATORIUM	GRG	GARAGE	MS	MEWS	RFC	RUGBY FOOTBALL CLUB	WKS	WALKS
CRS	CRESCENT	GT	GREAT	MSN	MISSION	RI	RISE	WLS	WELLS
CSWY	CAUSEWAY	GTWY	GATEWAY	MT	MOUNT	RP	RAMP	WY	WAY
CT	COURT	GV	GROVE	MTN	MOUNTAIN	ROW	ROW	YD	YARD
CTRL	CENTRAL	HGR	HIGHER	MTS	MOUNTAINS	S	SOUTH	YHA	YOUTH HOSTEL
CTS	COURTS	HL	HILL	MUS	MUSEUM	SCH	SCHOOL		

278

POSTCODE TOWNS AND AREA ABBREVIATIONS

AIMK .... Ashton-in-Makerfield
ALL/GAR .... Allerton/Garston
ALS/KID .... Alsager/Kidsgrove
ALT .... Altrincham
AUD/MAD/W .... Audlem/Madeley/Woore
BEB .... Bebington
BIDD .... Biddulph
BNG/LEV .... Burnage/Levenshulme
BRAM/HZG .... Bramhall/Hazel Grove
BURS/TUN .... Burslem/Tunstall
BUX .... Buxton
CCHDY .... Chorlton-cum-Hardy
CH/BCN .... Chester/Blacon
CHD/CHDH .... Cheadle (Gtr. Man)/Cheadle Hulme
CHF/WBR .... Chapel-en-le-Frith/Whaley Bridge
CHNE .... Chester northeast
CHSE .... Chester southeast
CHSW/BR .... Chester southwest/Broughton
CONG .... Congleton
CQ .... Connah's Quay
CW/HAS .... Crewe/Haslington
CW/SHV .... Crewe/Shavington
DID/WITH .... Didsbury/Withington
EDGY/DAV .... Edgeley/Davenport
END/WER .... Endon/Werrington
EP .... Ellesmere Port
FLINT .... Flint
FROD/HEL .... Frodsham/Helsby
GLSP .... Glossop
GOL/RIS/CUL .... Golborne/Risley/Culcheth
GTS/LS .... Great Sutton/Little Sutton
HALE/TIMP .... Hale/Timperley
HES .... Heswall
HLWD .... Halewood
HOLMCH .... Holmes Chapel
HTNM .... Heaton Moor
HUY .... Huyton
HYDE .... Hyde
IRL .... Irlam
KNUT .... Knutsford
LEEK .... Leek
LEIGH .... Leigh
LYMM .... Lymm
MALPAS .... Malpas
MANAIR .... Manchester Airport
MCFLDN .... Macclesfield north
MCFLDS .... Macclesfield south
MKTDR .... Market Drayton
MOLD/BUCK .... Mold/Buckley
MPL/ROM .... Marple/Romiley
MWCH .... Middlewich
NANT .... Nantwich
NEWLW .... Newton-le-Willows
NEWUL .... Newcastle-under-Lyme
NM/HAY .... New Mills/Hayfield
NSTN .... Neston
NTHLY .... Netherley
NTHM/RTH .... Northern Moor/Roundthorn
NWCHE .... Northwich east
NWCHW .... Northwich west
OFTN .... Offerton
PART .... Partington
POY/DIS .... Poynton/Disley
PS/BROM .... Port Sunlight/Bromborough
RAIN/WH .... Rainhill/Whiston
RDSH .... Reddish
RNFD/HAY .... Rainford/Haydock
RUNC .... Runcorn
SALE .... Sale
SBCH .... Sandbach
SPK/HALE .... Speke/Hale
STHEL .... St Helens
STKP .... Stockport
TPLY/KEL .... Tarporley/Kelsall
TYLD .... Tyldesley
WARR .... Warrington
WARRN/WOL .... Warrington north/Woolston
WARRS .... Warrington south
WARRW/BUR .... Warrington west/Burtonwood
WDN .... Widnes
WHITCH .... Whitchurch
WILM/AE .... Wilmslow/Alderley Edge
WLTN .... Woolton
WRX/GR/LL .... Wrexham/Gresford/Llay
WRXS/E .... Wrexham south & east
WSFD .... Winsford
WYTH/NTH .... Wythenshawe/Northenden

Abb - Anc

Index - streets

A

Abberley Rd WLTN L25 ..... 50 D5
Abbey Cl ALT WA14 ..... 61 G3
GOL/RIS/CU WA3 ..... 29 G4
NWCHW CW8 ..... 153 G5
WDN WA8 ..... 52 C4
WSFD CW7 ..... 177 K6
Abbey Ct WLTN L25 ..... 50 B2
Abbey Flds CW/SHV CW2 ..... 237 K4
Abbey Gn CH/BCN CH1 ..... 16 F4
Abbey Gv STKP SK1 ..... 3 L7
Abbey Hey RUNC WA7 ..... 74 C4
Abbey La NWCHW CW8 ..... 129 H7
NWCHW CW8 ..... 150 E7
Abbey Pl CW/HAS CW1 ..... 221 K6
Abbey Rd CHD/CHDH SK8 ..... 46 A7
GOL/RIS/CU WA3 ..... 24 C4
MCFLDN SK10 ..... 138 B2
SBCH CW11 ..... 203 L6
WDN WA8 ..... 52 B4
Abbey Sq CH/BCN CH1 ..... 16 F4
Abbey St CH/BCN CH1 ..... 17 G4
Abbey Wy NWCHW CW8 ..... 129 H8
Abbeyway North
RNFD/HAY WA11 ..... 22 A5
Abbeyway South
RNFD/HAY WA11 ..... 22 A6
Abbeywood Gv RAIN/WH L35 ..... 32 F2
Abbotsbury Cl CW/SHV CW2 ..... 238 B4
POY/DIS SK12 ..... 66 D7
Abbots Cl MCFLDN SK10 ..... 138 B2
Abbot's Dr CH/BCN CH1 ..... 145 J8
Abbotsfield Cl WARRS WA4 ..... 56 E6
Abbotsford Cl
GOL/RIS/CU WA3 ..... 23 K3
Abbotsford Gv ALT WA14 ..... 42 E4
Abbot's Gra CHNE CH2 ..... 16 E1
Abbots Hall Av STHEL WA9 ..... 34 D1
Abbots Knoll CH/BCN CH1 ..... 145 J8
Abbotsleigh Dr BRAM/HZG SK7 ..... 65 M2
Abbots Ms EP CH65 ..... 10 D5
Abbot's Nook CHNE CH2 ..... 16 F2
Abbots Pk CH/BCN CH1 ..... 145 J8
Abbots Wy NSTN CH64 ..... 91 K3
NWCHW CW8 ..... 129 H8
Abbott's Cl CONG CW12 ..... 208 B4
RUNC WA7 ..... 9 H7
Abbotts Rd CHSE CH3 ..... 171 H7
Abbotts Wy WSFD CW7 ..... 177 G2
Aber Av OFTN SK2 ..... 47 J8
Aberdare Cl WARRW/BUR WA5 ..... 36 E3
Aberdaron Dr CH/BCN CH1 ..... 168 E1
Aberdeen Crs EDGY/DAV SK3 ..... 2 C8
Aberdeen Gv EDGY/DAV SK3 ..... 2 D7
Aberfeldy Cl HOLMCH CW4 ..... 181 H2
Aberford Rd NTHM/RTH M23 ..... 44 A7
Abergele St OFTN SK2 ..... 46 F6
Aber Las FLINT CH6 ..... 116 B8
Aber Rd CHD/CHDH SK8 ..... 46 A6
Abingdon Av WARR WA1 ..... 38 E5
Abingdon Cl MCFLDN SK10 ..... 137 M4
Abingdon Crs CHSW/BR CH4 ..... 168 F6
Abingdon Gv HLWD L26 ..... 51 G3
Abingdon Rd BRAM/HZG SK7 ..... 65 L2
Abington Cl CW/HAS CW1 ..... 221 H6
Abington Rd SALE M33 ..... 43 J1
Abstone Cl WARR WA1 ..... 38 C5
Acacia Av CHD/CHDH SK8 ..... 65 G2
HALE/TIMP WA15 ..... 61 M1
KNUT WA16 ..... 106 E3
WARR WA1 ..... 38 D4
WDN WA8 ..... 53 H1
WILM/AE SK9 ..... 83 M7
Acacia Cl CHNE CH2 ..... 123 J1
Acacia Crs CW/HAS CW1 ..... 221 L6
Acacia Dr GTS/LS CH66 ..... 120 F3
HALE/TIMP WA15 ..... 61 M1
SBCH CW11 ..... 203 L5
Acacia Gdns ALS/KID ST7 ..... 243 J1
Acacia Gv RUNC WA7 ..... 9 M7
Academy St WARR WA1 ..... 5 H7
Academy Wy WARR WA1 ..... 5 G8
Acer Av CW/HAS CW1 ..... 221 L5
Achilles Av WARRN/WOL WA2 ..... 37 H2
Ackerley Cl WARRN/WOL WA2 ..... 37 M1
Ackers La WARRS WA4 ..... 56 E3
Ackers Rd WARRS WA4 ..... 56 E2
Ack La East BRAM/HZG SK7 ..... 65 J5
BRAM/HZG SK7 ..... 65 M3
Ack La West CHD/CHDH SK8 ..... 65 H5
Ackworth Dr NTHM/RTH M23 ..... 44 A6
Acorn Av CHD/CHDH SK8 ..... 45 L6
Acorn Bank Cl CW/SHV CW2 ..... 238 B5
Acorn Cl LEIGH WN7 ..... 24 F1
NWCHW CW8 ..... 151 M2
WSFD CW7 ..... 178 A4
Acorn Dr EP CH65 ..... 121 H3
Acorn La CONG CW12 ..... 208 E1
Acorn St NEWLW WA12 ..... 27 J1
A Ct AIMK WN4 ..... 22 B2
The Acreage HOLMCH CW4 ..... 157 L3
TPLY/KEL CW6 ..... 216 E4
Acrefield SALE M33 ..... 43 G1
Acrefield Pk WLTN L25 ..... 50 A1
Acrefield Rd WDN WA8 ..... 52 B3
WLTN L25 ..... 50 A1
Acre Gn HLWD L26 ..... 51 G6
Acre La CHD/CHDH SK8 ..... 65 H6
Acre Rd GTS/LS CH66 ..... 94 D7
Acres Ct WYTH/NTH M22 ..... 44 D8
Acres Crs FROD/HEL WA6 ..... 126 B2
Acresfield Rd HALE/TIMP WA15 ..... 43 G4
Acres La CHNE CH2 ..... 146 A4
Acres Nook Rd BURS/TUN ST6 ..... 243 G5
Acres Rd CHD/CHDH SK8 ..... 45 G7
Acre St MPL/ROM SK6 ..... 48 B2
Acreville Gv GOL/RIS/CU WA3 ..... 25 J5
Acton Av WARRS WA4 ..... 76 D1
Acton La NWCHW CW8 ..... 127 M1
Acton Rd CW/SHV CW2 ..... 220 D7
WARRW/BUR WA5 ..... 26 E6
Acton Wy ALS/KID ST7 ..... 224 D6
Adam Av GTS/LS CH66 ..... 94 C8
GTS/LS CH66 ..... 120 C1
Adam Cl CHD/CHDH SK8 ..... 46 B8
GTS/LS CH66 ..... 94 D8
Adams Av BURS/TUN ST6 ..... 243 K7
Adams Cl NEWLW WA12 ..... 27 K2
POY/DIS SK12 ..... 86 E2
Adams Hl KNUT WA16 ..... 107 G3
Adamson Ct WARRS WA4 ..... 57 H2
Adamson Gdns
DID/WITH M20 ..... 44 F1
Adamson St AIMK WN4 ..... 22 A1
WARRS WA4 ..... 56 B1
Adam St WARRN/WOL WA2 ..... 5 J2
Adcroft St STKP SK1 ..... 3 H9
Adder Hl CHSE CH3 ..... 170 B5
Addingham Av WDN WA8 ..... 52 C5
Addison Cl CW/SHV CW2 ..... 237 M4
Addison Rd HALE/TIMP WA15 ..... 61 L2
Addison Sq WDN WA8 ..... 6 F2
Adelaide Rd BRAM/HZG SK7 ..... 65 L6
CH/BCN CH1 ..... 144 D8
EDGY/DAV SK3 ..... 2 B8
Adelaide St CW/HAS CW1 ..... 18 E2
MCFLDN SK10 ..... 15 J3
Adela Rd RUNC WA7 ..... 8 E3
Adey Rd LYMM WA13 ..... 40 A7
Adfalent La NSTN CH64 ..... 93 G5
Adlington Cl HALE/TIMP WA15 ..... 43 K6
POY/DIS SK12 ..... 86 F2
Adlington Ct GOL/RIS/CU WA3 ..... 29 M6
GOL/RIS/CU WA3 ..... 29 M6
Adlington Dr NWCHE CW9 ..... 13 K9
SBCH CW11 ..... 204 C5
Adlington Pk MCFLDN SK10 ..... 86 C3
Adlington Rd CW/SHV CW2 ..... 237 M1
RUNC WA7 ..... 74 D2
WILM/AE SK9 ..... 84 E5
Adlington St MCFLDS SK11 ..... 14 E4
Admirals Rd GOL/RIS/CU WA3 ..... 38 E1
Adria Rd DID/WITH M20 ..... 45 J1
Adshall Rd CHD/CHDH SK8 ..... 46 A7
Adshead Cl WYTH/NTH M22 ..... 63 H1
Adshead Ct MCFLDN SK10 ..... 113 H4
Adswood Gv EDGY/DAV SK3 ..... 46 D6
Adswood La East OFTN SK2 ..... 46 F6
Adswood La West
EDGY/DAV SK3 ..... 46 E6
Adswood Old Hall Rd
CHD/CHDH SK8 ..... 46 D8
Adswood Rd CHD/CHDH SK8 ..... 46 C8
EDGY/DAV SK3 ..... 46 D7
Adswood Ter EDGY/DAV SK3 ..... 46 E6
Adwell Cl GOL/RIS/CU WA3 ..... 24 A4
Adwy Wynt FLINT CH6 ..... 116 B8
Aegean Rd ALT WA14 ..... 42 A6
Afton WDN WA8 ..... 52 A2
Agden Brow LYMM WA13 ..... 59 K4
Agden House La WHITCH SY13 ..... 259 G7
Agden La LYMM WA13 ..... 59 L5
Agecroft Rd MPL/ROM SK6 ..... 48 A3
NWCHE CW9 ..... 130 C5
Agnes St STHEL WA9 ..... 34 C1
Aimson Rd HALE/TIMP WA15 ..... 43 J5
Ainley Cl RUNC WA7 ..... 74 A7
Ainley Rd WYTH/NTH M22 ..... 63 K1
Ainscough Rd GOL/RIS/CU WA3 ..... 38 E1
Ainsdale Cl BRAM/HZG SK7 ..... 66 A5
WARRW/BUR WA5 ..... 35 M8
Ainsdale Dr CHD/CHDH SK8 ..... 64 B3
SALE M33 ..... 42 E2
Ainsworth La NWCHW CW8 ..... 101 G8
Ainsworth Rd NWCHW CW8 ..... 128 E3
Aintree Av SALE M33 ..... 42 C1
Aintree Cl BRAM/HZG SK7 ..... 66 F2
Aintree Gv EDGY/DAV SK3 ..... 46 E6
GTS/LS CH66 ..... 120 D1
Airdrie Cl PS/BROM CH62 ..... 93 K1
Aire WDN WA8 ..... 52 B2
Aire Cl EP CH65 ..... 10 A3
Airedale Cl CHD/CHDH SK8 ..... 45 J6
WARRW/BUR WA5 ..... 35 M5
Airedale Ct ALT WA14 ..... 42 E7
Airfield Vw CHSW/BR CH4 ..... 167 H6
Aitchison Rd NWCHE CW9 ..... 131 G2
Ajax Av WARRN/WOL WA2 ..... 37 H2
Akesmoor Dr OFTN SK2 ..... 47 J6
Akesmoor La BIDD ST8 ..... 226 F5
Alamein Crs WARRN/WOL WA2 ..... 5 H2
Alamein Dr MPL/ROM SK6 ..... 48 E2
WSFD CW7 ..... 177 K4
Alamein Rd NWCHW CW8 ..... 102 F8
Alan Dr HALE/TIMP WA15 ..... 62 A4
MPL/ROM SK6 ..... 48 E6
Alan Rd HTNM SK4 ..... 46 A1
Alan St NWCHE CW9 ..... 13 M3
Alban St CW/HAS CW1 ..... 18 E2
Albany Crs LYMM WA13 ..... 39 K8
Albany Gdns GTS/LS CH66 ..... 94 C5
Albany Gv LYMM WA13 ..... 39 J8
Albany Rd BRAM/HZG SK7 ..... 65 L8
LYMM WA13 ..... 58 C1
WILM/AE SK9 ..... 83 M7
Albany St BURS/TUN ST6 ..... 243 J5
Albany Ter RUNC WA7 ..... 9 G3
Alberta St STKP SK1 ..... 3 H7
Albert Av FLINT CH6 ..... 116 B7
Albert Cl CHD/CHDH SK8 ..... 65 G2
Albert Ct ALT WA14 ..... 42 D8
Albert Dr NSTN CH64 ..... 91 K4
WARRW/BUR WA5 ..... 35 K6
Albert Hill St DID/WITH M20 ..... 45 H1
Albert Pl ALT WA14 ..... 42 D7
NWCHE CW9 ..... 13 M2
Albert Rd CHD/CHDH SK8 ..... 65 G2
HALE/TIMP WA15 ..... 61 L1
HTNM SK4 ..... 46 B1
MCFLDN SK10 ..... 112 E4
WARRS WA4 ..... 57 G2
WDN WA8 ..... 7 L2
WILM/AE SK9 ..... 84 A6
Albert Rd East
HALE/TIMP WA15 ..... 61 L1
Albert Sq ALT WA14 ..... 61 K1
Albert St AIMK WN4 ..... 22 B1
BIDD ST8 ..... 227 K4
BRAM/HZG SK7 ..... 66 D1
CH/BCN CH1 ..... 17 J3
CW/HAS CW1 ..... 18 F2
EDGY/DAV SK3 ..... 2 D6
IRL M44 ..... 31 L6
KNUT WA16 ..... 106 F2
MCFLDS SK11 ..... 14 E5
NANT CW5 ..... 20 F4
RUNC WA7 ..... 9 G3
Albion Cl HTNM SK4 ..... 2 E1
Albion Pl BRAM/HZG SK7 ..... 66 D1
CH/BCN CH1 ..... 17 G7
Albion Rd NM/HAY SK22 ..... 69 J5
NWCHE CW9 ..... 13 K1
Albion St CH/BCN CH1 ..... 17 G6
CW/SHV CW2 ..... 18 A5
Albury Dr BNG/LEV M19 ..... 45 K2
Alcester Av EDGY/DAV SK3 ..... 45 M5
Alcester Rd CHD/CHDH SK8 ..... 45 H8
SALE M33 ..... 43 H2
Alcock St RUNC WA7 ..... 9 H1
Aldcliffe GOL/RIS/CU WA3 ..... 23 M5
Alder Av CQ CH5 ..... 166 A1
HUY L36 ..... 32 A4
POY/DIS SK12 ..... 86 F1
WDN WA8 ..... 53 G1
Alderbank Rd WARRW/BUR WA5 ..... 36 A6
Alder Cl ALS/KID ST7 ..... 243 G4
LEIGH WN7 ..... 24 F2
Alder Crs WARRN/WOL WA2 ..... 5 J1
Aldercroft Av WYTH/NTH M22 ..... 63 J2
Alderdale Dr MPL/ROM SK6 ..... 67 L5
Alderdale Gv WILM/AE SK9 ..... 83 L7
Alderdale Rd CHD/CHDH SK8 ..... 46 C8
Alder Dr GTS/LS CH66 ..... 120 F3
HALE/TIMP WA15 ..... 43 K7
Alderfield Dr SPK/HALE L24 ..... 71 G2
Alder Gv CHNE CH2 ..... 146 B8
EDGY/DAV SK3 ..... 2 A7
Alderhay La ALS/KID ST7 ..... 226 C8
Alder La FROD/HEL WA6 ..... 98 D1
WARRN/WOL WA2 ..... 37 H4
WARRW/BUR WA5 ..... 27 G5
WDN WA8 ..... 32 F8
Alderley Av GOL/RIS/CU WA3 ..... 23 K5
Alderley Cl BRAM/HZG SK7 ..... 66 F4
POY/DIS SK12 ..... 86 F2
SBCH CW11 ..... 204 D5
Alderley La LEIGH WN7 ..... 25 H2
Alderley Ldg WILM/AE SK9 ..... 84 A7
Alderley Pl CH/BCN CH1 ..... 144 E6
Alderley Rd MCFLDN SK10 ..... 110 F2
MCFLDN SK10 ..... 137 K1
MCFLDS SK11 ..... 135 H2
NWCHW CW8 ..... 12 D2
SALE M33 ..... 43 L2
WARRS WA4 ..... 38 D8
WILM/AE SK9 ..... 84 A8
Alderney Cl EP CH65 ..... 121 J3
MCFLDN SK10 ..... 137 M4
Alder Ri CHF/WBR SK23 ..... 89 K4
Alder Rd CHD/CHDH SK8 ..... 45 K7
GOL/RIS/CU WA3 ..... 23 M4
NWCHW CW8 ..... 128 D4
WARR WA1 ..... 38 D5
Alder Root La WARRN/WOL WA2 ..... 27 K5
Alders Av WYTH/NTH M22 ..... 44 C7
Aldersey Cl RUNC WA7 ..... 74 D3
Aldersey La CHSE CH3 ..... 230 A1
Aldersey Rd CW/SHV CW2 ..... 237 M1
Aldersgate NM/HAY SK22 ..... 69 H4
Aldersgate Av RUNC WA7 ..... 74 D5
Aldersgate Dr HLWD L26 ..... 51 G6
Aldersgate Rd CHD/CHDH SK8 ..... 65 J7
OFTN SK2 ..... 47 H6
Aldersgreen Av MPL/ROM SK6 ..... 67 M5
Alders Rd POY/DIS SK12 ..... 68 A5
WYTH/NTH M22 ..... 44 C7
Alder St NEWLW WA12 ..... 27 J1
Alders Wy MCFLDN SK10 ..... 111 L6
Alderton Dr AIMK WN4 ..... 22 A1
Alderton Gv WSFD CW7 ..... 153 M8
Alderue Av WYTH/NTH M22 ..... 44 D6
Alder Wood Av SPK/HALE L24 ..... 70 E1
Aldewood Cl GOL/RIS/CU WA3 ..... 30 A6
Aldfield Rd NTHM/RTH M23 ..... 43 L3
Aldford Cl CW/SHV CW2 ..... 253 L2
DID/WITH M20 ..... 45 J1
Aldford Pl WILM/AE SK9 ..... 109 M2
Aldford Rd CHNE CH2 ..... 145 M6
Aldgate EP CH65 ..... 10 B8
Aldington Dr MWCH CW10 ..... 179 K7
Aldridge Dr WARRW/BUR WA5 ..... 26 F5
Aldwick Av DID/WITH M20 ..... 45 J1
Aldwyn Crs BRAM/HZG SK7 ..... 66 C2
Aled Wy CHSW/BR CH4 ..... 168 D7
Alexander Dr HALE/TIMP WA15 ..... 43 G6
WDN WA8 ..... 6 A5
Alexander Gv RUNC WA7 ..... 9 L4
Alexandra Cl EDGY/DAV SK3 ..... 46 C6
Alexandra Gv IRL M44 ..... 31 M4
Alexandra Rd HTNM SK4 ..... 2 B2
MWCH CW10 ..... 179 K6
SALE M33 ..... 43 K1
WARRS WA4 ..... 56 F2
Alexandra St CQ CH5 ..... 142 B6
EP CH65 ..... 10 E4
WARR WA1 ..... 37 L5
WDN WA8 ..... 7 G7
WSFD CW7 ..... 177 J3
Alforde St WDN WA8 ..... 7 H7
Alfred Cl WDN WA8 ..... 7 J5
Alfred Rd GOL/RIS/CU WA3 ..... 24 A4
Alfred St IRL M44 ..... 31 L6
NEWLW WA12 ..... 27 L1
NWCHW CW8 ..... 12 E6
WDN WA8 ..... 7 J5
Alfreton Rd OFTN SK2 ..... 47 K6
Alfriston Dr NTHM/RTH M23 ..... 44 A2
Algernon St RUNC WA7 ..... 8 E1
WARR WA1 ..... 5 L4
WARRS WA4 ..... 56 C3
Algreave Rd EDGY/DAV SK3 ..... 46 A4
Alice Ct WDN WA8 ..... 53 G8
Alison Dr MCFLDN SK10 ..... 15 L3
Alkington Gdns WHITCH SY13 ..... 269 M6
Alkington Rd WHITCH SY13 ..... 269 L8
Allandale ALT WA14 ..... 42 B8
Allans Cl CQ CH5 ..... 142 C7
NSTN CH64 ..... 91 L6
Allansford Av CHSE CH3 ..... 171 G8
Allans Meadow NSTN CH64 ..... 91 L6
Allanson Rd WYTH/NTH M22 ..... 44 E3
Allcard St WARRW/BUR WA5 ..... 4 D2
Alldis St OFTN SK2 ..... 47 H7
Allen Av GOL/RIS/CU WA3 ..... 25 J8
Allenby Rd IRL M44 ..... 31 K8
Allendale RUNC WA7 ..... 74 B6
Allendale Av RAIN/WH L35 ..... 33 K1
Allen Dr NWCHE CW9 ..... 153 M2
Allen Rd RUNC WA7 ..... 8 B8
Allen St MCFLDS SK11 ..... 15 J7
WARRN/WOL WA2 ..... 4 F5
Allerby Wy GOL/RIS/CU WA3 ..... 23 L4
Allerdean Wk HTNM SK4 ..... 45 M1
Allerton Rd WDN WA8 ..... 7 K2
WLTN L25 ..... 50 A2
Allgreave Cl MWCH CW10 ..... 179 J6
SALE M33 ..... 43 K3
Allington La CHSW/BR CH4 ..... 17 J9
Allington Pl CHSW/BR CH4 ..... 17 J9
Allotment Rd IRL M44 ..... 31 K6
All Saints Dr WARRS WA4 ..... 57 L1
All Saints' Rd HTNM SK4 ..... 2 D1
SPK/HALE L24 ..... 70 C1
Allscott Wy AIMK WN4 ..... 22 C1
Allt Goch FLINT CH6 ..... 116 A6
Alma Av CW/HAS CW1 ..... 221 J6
Alma Cl ALS/KID ST7 ..... 225 L5
MCFLDS SK11 ..... 14 B6
Alma La WILM/AE SK9 ..... 84 A6
Alma Rd BRAM/HZG SK7 ..... 67 G4
SALE M33 ..... 42 E2
Alma St CHSE CH3 ..... 17 M4
NEWLW WA12 ..... 27 H1
Almeda Rd SPK/HALE L24 ..... 71 G2
Almer Dr WARRW/BUR WA5 ..... 36 C7
Almond Av CW/HAS CW1 ..... 221 K6
RUNC WA7 ..... 9 L7
Almond Cl EDGY/DAV SK3 ..... 2 A7
HLWD L26 ..... 50 E5
Almond Dr WARRW/BUR WA5 ..... 26 F6
Almond Gv WARR WA1 ..... 38 B5
Almond Tree Rd
CHD/CHDH SK8 ..... 65 G3
Alness Dr RAIN/WH L35 ..... 33 K2
Alnwick Dr EP CH65 ..... 121 K2
Alpine Rd STKP SK1 ..... 3 K5
Alpine St NEWLW WA12 ..... 27 G1
Alport Rd WHITCH SY13 ..... 270 A3
Alpraham Crs CHNE CH2 ..... 145 L6
Alsager Rd SBCH CW11 ..... 223 M4
Alsfeld Wy NM/HAY SK22 ..... 69 G4
Alstead Av HALE/TIMP WA15 ..... 62 A1
Alston Av SALE M33 ..... 42 F1
Alston Cl BRAM/HZG SK7 ..... 66 A3
Alstone Dr ALT WA14 ..... 42 A6
Alt WDN WA8 ..... 52 B2
Altair Av WYTH/NTH M22 ..... 63 K4
Altcar Wk WYTH/NTH M22 ..... 63 J2
Alton Dr MCFLDN SK10 ..... 15 L1
Alton Rd WILM/AE SK9 ..... 83 M4
Altrincham Rd NTHM/RTH M23 ..... 43 K5
WILM/AE SK9 ..... 63 J8
WILM/AE SK9 ..... 83 J2
WYTH/NTH M22 ..... 44 D6
Alt Wk WSFD CW7 ..... 178 A2
Alumbrook Av HOLMCH CW4 ..... 181 J1
Alum Ct HOLMCH CW4 ..... 181 J3
Alun Crs CHSW/BR CH4 ..... 169 G6
Alundale Rd WSFD CW7 ..... 177 J1
Alvanley Cl SALE M33 ..... 43 H3
Alvanley Crs EDGY/DAV SK3 ..... 46 C6
Alvanley Dr FROD/HEL WA6 ..... 124 C2
Alvanley Ri NWCHE CW9 ..... 13 J7
Alvanley Rd FROD/HEL WA6 ..... 124 C2
GTS/LS CH66 ..... 94 E8
Alvanley Vw CHNE CH2 ..... 123 H1
Alvaston Av HTNM SK4 ..... 46 B1
Alvaston Rd NANT CW5 ..... 21 G6
Alverstone Cl
WARRW/BUR WA5 ..... 35 J5
Alverton Cl WDN WA8 ..... 6 B5
Alveston Cl MCFLDN SK10 ..... 137 M3
Alveston Dr WILM/AE SK9 ..... 84 C4
Alvington Gv BRAM/HZG SK7 ..... 66 A3
Alvis Rd CQ CH5 ..... 167 H1
Alwain Gn SPK/HALE L24 ..... 70 F2
Alwinton Av HTNM SK4 ..... 45 L1
Alwyn Cl LEIGH WN7 ..... 24 F3
Alwyn Gdns CHNE CH2 ..... 145 L4
Alyndale Rd CHSW/BR CH4 ..... 168 D6
Alyn Dr WRX/GR/LL LL12 ..... 210 B5
Alyn Rd CHNE CH2 ..... 146 F3
Ambassador Dr HLWD L26 ..... 51 G3
Amberleigh Cl WARRS WA4 ..... 77 H1
Amberley Dr HALE/TIMP WA15 ..... 62 B4
NTHM/RTH M23 ..... 44 A7
Amberley Rd MCFLDS SK11 ..... 14 A8
Amberwood Dr NTHM/RTH M23 ..... 43 K6
Ambleside CHNE CH2 ..... 145 M6
Ambleside Av
HALE/TIMP WA15 ..... 43 J7
Ambleside Cl CW/SHV CW2 ..... 237 L2
MCFLDS SK11 ..... 137 M6
WSFD CW7 ..... 177 J1
Ambleside Ct CONG CW12 ..... 207 G2
Ambleside Crs
WARRN/WOL WA2 ..... 37 J1
Ambleside Rd EP CH65 ..... 121 J2
Ambrose Pl BURS/TUN ST6 ..... 243 M5
Ambuscade Cl CW/HAS CW1 ..... 19 J2
Amelia Cl WDN WA8 ..... 34 B8
Amelia St WARRN/WOL WA2 ..... 5 J2
Amersham Cl MCFLDN SK10 ..... 138 C1
Amis Gv GOL/RIS/CU WA3 ..... 23 L4
Amlwch Av OFTN SK2 ..... 47 K6
Amy St CW/SHV CW2 ..... 18 E5
Ancaster St BURS/TUN ST6 ..... 243 K5
The Anchorage CHSE CH3 ..... 171 G7
LYMM WA13 ..... 58 D1
NSTN CH64 ..... 91 J5
Anchor Cl RUNC WA7 ..... 74 D6
WHITCH SY13 ..... 270 B5

Ancoats Rd *KNUT* WA16 .... 108 E4
Anderson Cl *CW/HAS* CW1 .... 19 M5
  RAIN/WH L35 .... 33 K3
  WARRN/WOL WA2 .... 38 B2
Anderson St *OFTN* SK2 .... 14 E5
Andertons La *MCFLDS* SK11 .... 137 H4
Anderton Wy *WILM/AE* SK9 .... 84 D1
Andover Cl *WARRN/WOL* WA2 .... 37 L3
Andover Wy L25 .... 50 D4
Andrew Cl *WDN* WA8 .... 52 C4
Andrew Crs *CHSW/BR* CH4 .... 17 K8
Andrew Gv *NWCHW* SK10 .... 139 C5
Andrew La *MPL/ROM* SK6 .... 67 L3
Andrew's Cl *CHSE* CH3 .... 172 B2
Andrew St *BURS/TUN* ST6 .... 243 J5
  HTNM SK4 .... 2 E4
Anfield Rd *CHD/CHDH* SK8 .... 64 F2
Angel St *BRAM/HZG* SK7 .... 66 D1
Anglers Rest *IRL* M44 .... 31 L7
Anglesea Av *ALS/KID* ST7 .... 46 F6
Anglesey Cl *EP* CH65 .... 121 J3
Anglesey Dr *POY/DIS* SK12 .... 66 E6
Anglesey *CHD/CHDH* SK8 .... 45 M6
Anglesey Water *POY/DIS* SK12 .... 66 E6
Angus Gv *MWCH* CW10 .... 179 K2
Ankers Knowl La *MCFLDS* SK10 .... 140 D4
Ankers La *MCFLDS* SK11 .... 140 D5
Annable Rd *IRL* M44 .... 31 M4
  MPL/ROM SK6 .... 47 K1
Annan Cl *CONG* CW12 .... 208 A3
Ann Cl *GTS/LS* CH66 .... 94 D5
Anne Ct *ALS/KID* ST7 .... 242 F7
Anne St *BURS/TUN* ST6 .... 243 J5
  STHEL WA9 .... 34 D1
Anne's Wy *CHSW/BR* CH4 .... 17 K7
Annette Av *NEWLW* WA12 .... 22 A7
Annie St *WARRN/WOL* WA2 .... 5 J4
Annions La *NANT* CW5 .... 252 F3
Annis Cl *WILM/AE* SK9 .... 110 B2
Annis Rd *WILM/AE* SK9 .... 110 B2
Ann St *NWCHE* CW9 .... 130 D3
  RUNC WA7 .... 9 J1
Ann St West *WDN* WA8 .... 7 J7
Ansdell Rd *WDN* WA8 .... 7 K1
Ansley Gv *HTNM* SK4 .... 46 B1
Anson Cl *BRAM/HZG* SK7 .... 65 M7
  WARRN/WOL WA2 .... 37 L2
Anson Dr *POY/DIS* SK12 .... 87 H1
  WILM/AE SK9 .... 84 E3
Anthony Dr *NWCHW* CW9 .... 153 M5
Antons Cl *HLWD* L26 .... 50 F6
Antons Rd *HLWD* L26 .... 50 F6
Antony Rd *WARRS* WA4 .... 56 B3
Antrim Cl *BNG/LEV* M19 .... 45 K2
Antrim Dr *GTS/LS* CH66 .... 120 F2
Antrim Rd *WARRN/WOL* WA2 .... 37 G2
Antrobus St *CONG* CW12 .... 207 K1
Anvil Cl *CH/BCN* CH1 .... 144 A3
Appleby Av *HALE/TIMP* WA15 .... 43 J7
Appleby Cl *EDGY/DAV* SK3 .... 46 D7
  MCFLDS SK11 .... 137 M7
  WDN WA8 .... 52 C4
Appleby Dr *CQ* CH5 .... 166 C2
Appleby Rd *CHD/CHDH* SK8 .... 45 H8
  NTHLY L27 .... 32 A8
  WARRN/WOL WA2 .... 37 J1
Apple Cft *AUD/MAD/W* CW3 .... 267 L5
Applecross Cl
  GOL/RIS/CU WA3 .... 30 A6
Appledale Dr *GTS/LS* CH66 .... 121 F2
Apple Dell Av
  GOL/RIS/CU WA3 .... 23 J3
Appledore Cl *SPK/HALE* L24 .... 50 B8
Appledore Dr *NTHM/RTH* M23 .... 43 K5
Appledore Gv *ALS/KID* ST7 .... 243 L4
Applefield *NWCHW* CW8 .... 12 C5
Appleford Dr *WARRS* WA4 .... 56 E5
Apple Market St *NWCHE* CW9 .... 13 G2
Appleton Dr *EP* CH65 .... 120 F1
Appleton Gv *SALE* M33 .... 42 E2
Appleton Cl *CHNE* CH2 .... 145 L7
  HALE/TIMP WA15 .... 61 L3
  WDN WA8 .... 7 J2
Appleton St *NWCHW* CW8 .... 12 D2
  WDN WA8 .... 7 J8
Appleton Village *WDN* WA8 .... 7 H2
Apple Tree Gv *GTS/LS* CH66 .... 120 D1
Appletree Gv *WARRN/WOL* WA2 .... 37 M2
Apple Tree Rd *NM/HAY* SK22 .... 69 J2
Applewood Av *CQ* CH5 .... 142 F5
Appleyards La *CHSW/BR* CH4 .... 17 H9
  CHSW/BR CH4 .... 169 K5
April Ri *MCFLDS* SK10 .... 14 B3
Apsley Cl *ALT* WA14 .... 61 H1
Apsley Gv *ALT* WA14 .... 61 H1
Apsley St *STKP* SK1 .... 3 H5
Aragon Wy *MPL/ROM* SK6 .... 48 E6
Aran Cl *SPK/HALE* L24 .... 71 K2
Arbour Cl *AUD/MAD/W* CW3 .... 267 L5
  MCFLDS SK10 .... 138 D1
  NWCHE CW9 .... 130 C4
Arbour Crs *MCFLDS* SK10 .... 138 D1
Arbour Ms *MCFLDS* SK10 .... 138 D1
Arbour St *ALS/KID* ST7 .... 242 D7
Arbury Av *EDGY/DAV* SK3 .... 45 M3
Arbury La *WARRN/WOL* WA2 .... 28 C6
Arcadia Av *SALE* M33 .... 43 G3
Archer Av *WARRS* WA4 .... 56 E2
Archer Cl *MCFLDS* SK10 .... 112 C5
Archer St *LEIGH* WN7 .... 47 J7
  OFTN SK2 .... 47 J7
Archers *CH/BCN* CH1 .... 16 A3
  GTS/LS CH66 .... 120 E3
Arclid Cl *WILM/AE* SK9 .... 84 E2
Arden *WDN* WA8 .... 52 A2
Ardenbrook Ri *MCFLDS* SK10 .... 111 L6
Arden Cl *CHSE* CH3 .... 172 C1
  GOL/RIS/CU WA3 .... 30 B6
Arden Ct *BRAM/HZG* SK7 .... 65 K3
  CONG CW12 .... 208 B5
Arden Dr *NSTN* CH64 .... 91 L6
Ardenfield Dr *WYTH/NTH* M22 .... 63 L2
Arden Lodge Rd
  NTHM/RTH M23 .... 43 K5
Ardens Meadow *TPLY/KEL* CW6 .... 197 J4
Arden St *NM/HAY* SK22 .... 69 J5
Arderne Av *CW/SHV* CW2 .... 18 A7
Arderne Rd *HALE/TIMP* WA15 .... 43 G4

Ardern Gv *STKP* SK1 .... 3 H8
Ardern Lea *FROD/HEL* WA6 .... 124 D3
Ardleigh Cl *CW/HAS* CW1 .... 220 F4
Ardwick Rd *SPK/HALE* L24 .... 70 F1
Argosy Dr *MANAIR* M90 .... 62 F5
Argyle Cl *BRAM/HZG* SK7 .... 66 E2
Argyll Av *CHSW/BR* CH4 .... 16 B9
Argyll Cl *MCFLDS* SK10 .... 14 A3
Argyll Rd *CHD/CHDH* SK8 .... 45 M7
Aries Cl *BURS/TUN* ST6 .... 243 M6
Arkenshaw Rd *GOL/RIS/CU* WA3 .... 29 G5
Arkenstone Cl *WDN* WA8 .... 52 C2
Arkle Av *WILM/AE* SK9 .... 64 E8
Arklow Dr *SPK/HALE* L24 .... 71 K2
Arkwright Cl *RUNC* WA7 .... 73 M1
Arkwright Ct *WSFD* CW7 .... 177 G4
Arkwright Dr *MPL/ROM* SK6 .... 49 G6
Arkwright Rd *MPL/ROM* SK6 .... 49 G6
  RUNC WA7 .... 73 M1
Arley Av *WARRS* WA4 .... 56 D3
Arley Cl *ALS/KID* ST7 .... 241 J1
  ALT WA14 .... 42 D4
  CHNE CH2 .... 145 M6
  MCFLDS SK11 .... 14 A8
Arley Dr *SALE* M33 .... 43 G2
  WDN WA8 .... 52 B2
Arley End *KNUT* WA16 .... 59 J8
Arley Mere Cl *CHD/CHDH* SK8 .... 64 F1
Arley Mossend La *NWCHE* CW9 .... 104 D3
Arley Pl *CW/SHV* CW2 .... 238 A4
Arley Rd *NWCHE* CW9 .... 77 L4
  NWCHE CW9 .... 130 C4
  WARRS WA4 .... 57 J8
Arley Wk *SBCH* CW11 .... 203 K7
Arlington Cl *CW/SHV* CW2 .... 238 C4
Arlington Crs *WILM/AE* SK9 .... 83 L7
Arlington Dr *GOL/RIS/CU* WA3 .... 24 C4
  LEIGH WN7 .... 24 C4
  MCFLDS SK11 .... 14 A6
  OFTN SK2 .... 66 A1
  POY/DIS SK12 .... 86 D1
  WARRW/BUR WA5 .... 35 L8
Arlington Rd *CHD/CHDH* SK8 .... 45 J8
Arlington Wy *WILM/AE* SK9 .... 83 L7
Armadale Cl *EDGY/DAV* SK3 .... 46 E8
Armett St *MCFLDS* SK11 .... 14 F7
Armitstead Wy *HOLMCH* CW4 .... 157 G7
Armitage Rd *ALT* WA14 .... 61 K1
Armitstead Rd *SBCH* CW11 .... 222 F1
Armour Av *WARRN/WOL* WA2 .... 37 H2
Armoury Bank *AIMK* WN4 .... 22 B1
Armoury St *EDGY/DAV* SK3 .... 2 F7
Armscot Cl *WLTN* L25 .... 50 B5
Armscot Pl *WLTN* L25 .... 50 B5
Armstrong Cl
  AUD/MAD/W CW3 .... 263 M8
  GOL/RIS/CU WA3 .... 29 K8
Armthorpe Dr *GTS/LS* CH66 .... 94 B7
Arncliffe Dr *NTHM/RTH* M23 .... 63 G1
  WARRW/BUR WA5 .... 26 F6
Arncliffe Rd *WLTN* L25 .... 50 D3
Arndale *RUNC* WA7 .... 73 L7
Arne Cl *OFTN* SK2 .... 48 A7
Arnfield Rd *EDGY/DAV* SK3 .... 45 K8
Arnhem Crs *WARRN/WOL* WA2 .... 5 H2
Arnhem Wy *CHSE* CH3 .... 170 B7
Arnold Pl *WDN* WA8 .... 52 C5
Arnold's Crs *CHSW/BR* CH4 .... 190 A1
Arnold St *EDGY/DAV* SK3 .... 2 E9
  NANT CW5 .... 20 F4
Arnside Av *BRAM/HZG* SK7 .... 66 C2
  CONG CW12 .... 207 G2
Arnside Cl *CHD/CHDH* SK8 .... 45 H8
  MPL/ROM SK6 .... 67 L4
  WARRS WA4 .... 177 K2
Arnside Gv *WARRS* WA4 .... 56 B2
Arpley Rd *WARR* WA1 .... 5 C9
Arpley St *WARR* WA1 .... 4 E7
Arradon Ct *CHNE* CH2 .... 145 L7
Arran Av *EP* CH65 .... 121 J3
Arran Cl *HOLMCH* CW4 .... 181 J3
  WARRN/WOL WA2 .... 38 A2
Arran Dr *ALS/KID* ST7 .... 243 M4
  FROD/HEL WA6 .... 99 J5
Arrivals Wy *MANAIR* M90 .... 63 H5
Arron Pl *CW/SHV* CW2 .... 237 K1
Arrowcroft Rd *CHSE* CH3 .... 146 F7
Arrowsmith Dr *ALS/KID* ST7 .... 241 H1
Arrow St *LEIGH* WN7 .... 25 H1
Arthill La *ALT* WA14 .... 60 B3
Arthog Dr *HALE/TIMP* WA15 .... 61 M4
Arthog Rd *DID/WITH* M20 .... 45 J2
  HALE/TIMP WA15 .... 61 M4
Arthur Av *EP* CH65 .... 10 F8
Arthur St *BURS/TUN* ST6 .... 243 L8
  CH/BCN CH1 .... 16 B3
  CW/SHV CW2 .... 19 H7
  NWCHE CW9 .... 131 G2
  RUNC WA7 .... 8 F3
  WARRN/WOL WA2 .... 4 E5
Artists La *MCFLDS* SK10 .... 110 B6
Artle Rd *CW/SHV* CW2 .... 238 C4
Arundel Av *BRAM/HZG* SK7 .... 66 D4
Arundel Cl *CW/SHV* CW2 .... 237 L4
  HALE/TIMP WA15 .... 62 C3
  KNUT WA16 .... 107 G4
  MCFLDS SK10 .... 15 L1
Arundel Gv *OFTN* SK2 .... 47 H8
Arundel Rd *CHD/CHDH* SK8 .... 65 G6
Ascol Dr *NWCHE* CW9 .... 131 J1
Ascot Av *RUNC* WA7 .... 73 H6
  SALE M33 .... 42 C1
Ascot Cl *CONG* CW12 .... 184 D8
  MCFLDS SK10 .... 138 C1
  WARR WA1 .... 38 E5
  WARRS WA4 .... 57 J2
Ascot Dr *BRAM/HZG* SK7 .... 67 G2
  GTS/LS CH66 .... 120 D1
Ash Av *ALT* WA14 .... 42 A7
  CHD/CHDH SK8 .... 45 L7
  IRL M44 .... 31 K7
  NEWLW WA12 .... 27 J3
Ashbank *NWCHE* CW9 .... 130 D5
Ashberry Cl *WILM/AE* SK9 .... 84 D4
Ashberry Dr *WARRS* WA4 .... 57 H7
Ashbourne Av *CHD/CHDH* SK8 .... 45 M6

RUNC WA7 .... 73 H6
Ashbourne Cl *GTS/LS* CH66 .... 120 E4
Ashbourne Crs *SALE* M33 .... 43 K2
Ashbourne Dr *MPL/ROM* SK6 .... 67 L6
Ashbourne Ms
  MCFLDS SK10 .... 137 M4
Ashbourne Rd *BRAM/HZG* SK7 .... 66 F4
  WARRW/BUR WA5 .... 36 B7
Ashbrook Av *RUNC* WA7 .... 73 M8
  RUNC WA7 .... 99 M1
Ashbrook Cl *CHD/CHDH* SK8 .... 64 B3
Ashbrook Crs *WARRN/WOL* WA2 .... 37 K4
Ashbrook Dr *MCFLDS* SK10 .... 112 A6
Ashbrook Rd *MCFLDS* SK10 .... 110 F6
  MCFLDS SK10 .... 112 F5
Ashburn Gv *HTNM* SK4 .... 2 B2
Ashburn Rd *HTNM* SK4 .... 2 B2
Ashburton Rd *EDGY/DAV* SK3 .... 46 E8
Ashbury Cl *RUNC* WA7 .... 74 D2
Ashby Cl *SBCH* CW11 .... 203 J7
Ashby Pl *CHNE* CH2 .... 17 K1
  CHNE CH2 .... 145 L8
Ash Cl *GTS/LS* CH66 .... 120 F3
  HOLMCH CW4 .... 157 K8
  MALPAS SY14 .... 246 C7
  TPLY/KEL CW6 .... 197 K2
Ashcott Av *WYTH/NTH* M22 .... 44 D8
Ashcroft Av *CW/SHV* CW2 .... 253 H1
Ashcroft Rd *LYMM* WA13 .... 40 B8
Ashdale Cl *ALS/KID* ST7 .... 224 C7
Ashdale Dr *CHD/CHDH* SK8 .... 64 B2
Ashdene Rd *HTNM* SK4 .... 45 K2
  WILM/AE SK9 .... 83 M7
Ashdown Gv *HLWD* L26 .... 51 G3
Ashdown La *GOL/RIS/CU* WA3 .... 30 A7
Ashdown Rd *HTNM* SK4 .... 2 B2
  KNUT WA16 .... 107 M6
Ashenhurst Rd *ALS/KID* ST7 .... 241 M1
Ashenough Rd *ALS/KID* ST7 .... 242 D6
Ashfield *RAIN/WH* L35 .... 33 K1
  CHD/CHDH SK8 .... 45 K6
  CQ CH5 .... 166 D2
Ashfield Dr *MCFLDS* SK10 .... 14 B2
Ashfield Gv *EDGY/DAV* SK3 .... 46 E8
  IRL M44 .... 31 L6
  MPL/ROM SK6 .... 49 H3
Ashfield Rd *CHD/CHDH* SK8 .... 45 K6
  CQ CH5 .... 142 B6
  EDGY/DAV SK3 .... 46 F8
  HALE/TIMP WA15 .... 61 L1
Ashfield Rd North *EP* CH65 .... 10 E7
Ashfield St *MWCH* CW10 .... 179 K4
Ashford Cl *HLWD* L26 .... 50 E5
  WILM/AE SK9 .... 64 C8
Ashford Rd *WILM/AE* SK9 .... 84 A8
Ashgate La *NWCHE* CW9 .... 104 F7
Ashgate Wy *WYTH/NTH* M22 .... 44 E8
Ash Gv *ALS/KID* ST7 .... 224 F5
  ALT WA14 .... 61 J3
  CHD/CHDH SK8 .... 64 A6
  CHSW/BR CH4 .... 169 H7
  CQ CH5 .... 142 B6
  GTS/LS CH66 .... 94 C6
  HALE/TIMP WA15 .... 42 F5
  KNUT WA16 .... 107 K3
  MCFLDS SK11 .... 138 C7
  MPL/ROM SK6 .... 48 E7
  MWCH CW10 .... 179 K5
  NWCHW CW8 .... 128 E5
  RUNC WA7 .... 9 M7
  WARRN/WOL WA2 .... 56 D1
Ashgrove *WSFD* CW7 .... 177 K4
Ash Hay La *CHNE* CH2 .... 146 C3
Ash House La *NWCHW* CW8 .... 102 C5
Ashlands *FROD/HEL* WA6 .... 99 J3
Ashlands Rd *HALE/TIMP* WA15 .... 42 F3
Ash La *CQ* CH5 .... 166 D3
  HALE/TIMP WA15 .... 61 L3
  WARRS WA4 .... 56 A5
  WDN WA8 .... 51 M4
Ash Lawn Cl *CHNE* CH2 .... 145 J8
Ashlea Cl *CQ* CH5 .... 166 D2
Ashlea Dr *NANT* CW5 .... 237 L2
Ashleigh Cl *CHSW/BR* CH4 .... 168 E6
Ashleigh Rd *HALE/TIMP* WA15 .... 43 H4
Ashley Cl *CW/HAS* CW1 .... 222 D7
  RAIN/WH L35 .... 33 K2
  WARRS WA4 .... 57 J1
Ashley Ct *WRXS/E* L13 .... 228 D4
Ashley Dr *BRAM/HZG* SK7 .... 65 J6
  NWCHW CW8 .... 129 G6
  SALE M33 .... 42 E2
Ashley Gdns *MALPAS* SY14 .... 230 C3
  MPL/ROM SK6 .... 67 K4
Ashley Gra *NWCHW* CW9 .... 153 L1
Ashley Meadow *CW/HAS* CW1 .... 222 D7
Ashleymill La *ALT* WA14 .... 61 K4
Ashley Mill La North *ALT* WA14 .... 61 K4
Ashley Rd *ALT* WA14 .... 61 K1
  HALE/TIMP WA15 .... 61 L2
  KNUT WA16 .... 80 D4
  OFTN SK2 .... 47 J4
  RUNC WA7 .... 73 K2
  WILM/AE SK9 .... 84 B3
Ashley Wy *WDN* WA8 .... 7 H8
Ashley Wy West *WDN* WA8 .... 6 F7
Ashmead Cl *ALS/KID* ST7 .... 241 L1
Ashmeade *HALE/TIMP* WA15 .... 62 B3
Ashmead Ms *ALS/KID* ST7 .... 241 L1
Ashmoor Rd *WYTH/NTH* M22 .... 63 K3
Ashmore Av *EDGY/DAV* SK3 .... 45 M2
Ashmore Cl *GOL/RIS/CU* WA3 .... 39 G1
  MWCH CW10 .... 179 J6
Ashmore's La *ALS/KID* ST7 .... 241 K1
Ashmuir Cl *CH/BCN* CH1 .... 168 D1
Ash Priors *WDN* WA8 .... 52 D1
Ash Rd *CHNE* CH2 .... 123 J1
  CW/HAS CW1 .... 221 K6
  GOL/RIS/CU WA3 .... 40 A2
  LYMM WA13 .... 58 C1
  NWCHW CW8 .... 151 M2

PART M31 .... 40 D1
  POY/DIS SK12 .... 86 F1
  WARRN/WOL WA2 .... 28 B6
  WARRW/BUR WA5 .... 35 M8
  WHITCH SY13 .... 270 D6
Ashstead Rd *SALE* M33 .... 43 J3
Ash St *BRAM/HZG* SK7 .... 66 D1
  EDGY/DAV SK3 .... 46 B4
  GTS/LS CH66 .... 23 H2
  NWCHE CW9 .... 13 K1
Ash Ter *MCFLDS* SK11 .... 138 C8
Ashton Av *ALT* WA14 .... 42 E6
  MCFLDS SK11 .... 137 K3
  RAIN/WH L35 .... 33 J2
Ashton Cl *CONG* CW12 .... 208 B3
  FROD/HEL WA6 .... 99 J3
  MWCH CW10 .... 179 K7
  NWCHE CW9 .... 129 L8
  PS/BROM CH62 .... 93 J1
  RUNC WA7 .... 72 F6
Ashton Dr *FROD/HEL* WA6 .... 99 J3
  FROD/HEL WA6 .... 99 J2
  WLTN L25 .... 50 B5
Ashton Heath *AIMK* WN4 .... 22 C2
Ashton La *CHSE* CH3 .... 148 E6
Ashton Pl *BRAM/HZG* SK7 .... 66 F3
Ashton Rd *FROD/HEL* WA6 .... 149 K1
  GOL/RIS/CU WA3 .... 22 F2
  NEWLW WA12 .... 22 C6
  PART M31 .... 41 J1
Ashton St *WARRN/WOL* WA2 .... 5 C5
Ashtree Cl *MCFLDS* SK10 .... 112 C4
  NSTN CH64 .... 91 M5
Ashtree Cft *NSTN* CH64 .... 93 G5
Ashtree Dr *NSTN* CH64 .... 91 M5
Ashtree Farm Ct *NSTN* CH64 .... 93 G4
Ashurst Dr *EDGY/DAV* SK3 .... 46 B7
Ashurst Rd *WYTH/NTH* M22 .... 63 M1
Ash Vw *CO* CH5 .... 142 A8
Ashville Ct *CW/SHV* CW2 .... 238 B5
Ashville Rd *RUNC* WA7 .... 99 L1
Ashway Clough North
  OFTN SK2 .... 47 K7
Ashway Clough South
  OFTN SK2 .... 47 K7
Ashwell Av *GOL/RIS/CU* WA3 .... 23 K3
Ashwell Rd *NTHM/RTH* M23 .... 44 B5
Ashwood *ALT* WA14 .... 61 H4
Ashwood Av *AIMK* WN4 .... 22 A2
  GOL/RIS/CU WA3 .... 23 K4
  SALE M33 .... 42 E1
  WARR WA1 .... 38 A5
Ashwood Cl *GTS/LS* CH66 .... 120 D3
  NWCHW CW8 .... 103 H8
Ashwood Ct *CHNE* CH2 .... 170 A1
Ashwood Crs *MPL/ROM* SK6 .... 48 F5
  NWCHW CW8 .... 129 H1
Ashwood La *CHNE* CH2 .... 122 A7
  WHITCH SY13 .... 271 H8
Ashwood Rd *POY/DIS* SK12 .... 68 D6
Ashworth Cl *ALT* WA14 .... 61 H3
Ashworth Pk *KNUT* WA16 .... 106 F4
Askern Av *WYTH/NTH* M22 .... 63 K1
Askrigg Av *GTS/LS* CH66 .... 94 B7
Aspen Cl *ALS/KID* ST7 .... 243 L1
  GTS/LS CH66 .... 120 D3
  HALE/TIMP WA15 .... 43 L7
Aspen Gv *CH/BCN* CH1 .... 144 D5
  WARR WA1 .... 38 A5
The Aspens *NWCHW* CW8 .... 127 K7
Aspen Wy *CHNE* CH2 .... 146 B8
  MPL/ROM SK6 .... 68 A5
Aspenwood *AIMK* WN4 .... 22 A2
Aspenwood Cl *MPL/ROM* SK6 .... 48 E5
Aspinall Cl *WARRN/WOL* WA2 .... 38 A1
Aspull Cl *GOL/RIS/CU* WA3 .... 29 J8
Aspull Common *LEIGH* WN7 .... 24 C3
Asquith Cl *BIDD* ST8 .... 227 K4
  CW/HAS CW1 .... 222 C7
Assheton Wk *SPK/HALE* L24 .... 71 L2
Astbury Cl *ALS/KID* ST7 .... 243 J1
  GOL/RIS/CU WA3 .... 24 B4
  HALE/TIMP WA15 .... 42 E6
Astbury Crs *EDGY/DAV* SK3 .... 46 D6
Astbury Dr *NWCHW* CW8 .... 103 H8
Astbury Lane Ends *CONG* CW12 .... 207 L4
Astbury St *CONG* CW12 .... 207 J2
Aster Crs *RUNC* WA7 .... 73 M8
Astle Cl *MWCH* CW10 .... 179 J5
Astle Ct *MCFLDS* SK11 .... 135 G1
Astle La *MCFLDS* SK10 .... 135 L4
Astley Dr *KNUT* WA16 .... 107 J5
  WARRS WA4 .... 56 B1
  WDN WA8 .... 52 C1
Astley Ct *IRL* M44 .... 31 L4
Astley St *HTNM* SK4 .... 2 E5
Astmoor Bridge La *RUNC* WA7 .... 73 M2
Astmoor Rd *RUNC* WA7 .... 9 M1
  RUNC WA7 .... 73 M2
Aston Av *GOL/RIS/CU* WA3 .... 29 M7
  WSFD CW7 .... 177 H2
Aston Cl *EDGY/DAV* SK3 .... 46 C6
Aston Ct *WARR* WA1 .... 38 C3
Aston Fields Rd *RUNC* WA7 .... 74 E6
Aston Gn *RUNC* WA7 .... 74 E6
Aston Hl *CQ* CH5 .... 166 B1
Aston La *RUNC* WA7 .... 100 B1
Aston La North *RUNC* WA7 .... 74 E8
Aston La South *RUNC* WA7 .... 100 C5
Aston Md *CQ* CH5 .... 166 B1
Aston Park Rd *CQ* CH5 .... 142 B8
Aston Rd *CQ* CH5 .... 142 B8
Aston Wy *MWCH* CW10 .... 179 L5
Astor Dr *WARRS* WA4 .... 56 F4
Atcherley Cl *NANT* CW5 .... 251 M4
Athelbrae Cl *NWCHW* CW8 .... 12 F5
Athens St *STKP* SK1 .... 3 K6
Atherleigh Wy *LEIGH* WN7 .... 24 D1
Atherton La *IRL* M44 .... 31 L7
Atherton Rd *EP* CH65 .... 94 F4
Atherton St *EDGY/DAV* SK3 .... 2 C8
Athey St *MCFLDS* SK11 .... 14 E6
Athlone Av *CHD/CHDH* SK8 .... 46 C7
Athlone Rd *WARRN/WOL* WA2 .... 37 L3
Atholl Av *CW/SHV* CW2 .... 18 F9
Atholl Cl *MCFLDS* SK10 .... 14 A3
Athol Rd *BRAM/HZG* SK7 .... 65 K7
Athol St *HTNM* SK4 .... 2 D2

Atis Cft *FLINT* CH6 .... 116 C7
Atkinson St *OFTN* SK2 .... 3 K9
Atlanta Av *MANAIR* M90 .... 63 G4
Atlantic St *ALT* WA14 .... 42 A6
Atlow Dr *NTHM/RTH* M23 .... 44 B7
Attenbury's La *ALT* WA14 .... 42 E4
Atterbury Cl *WDN* WA8 .... 52 C2
Attlee Av *GOL/RIS/CU* WA3 .... 25 H8
Attlee Rd *HUY* L36 .... 32 A1
Attwood Cl *CW/HAS* CW1 .... 222 C8
Attwood St *HALE/TIMP* WA15 .... 43 H7
Attwood St *ALS/KID* ST7 .... 243 G2
Atwood Rd *DID/WITH* M20 .... 45 J1
Auburn Cl *WDN* WA8 .... 52 C1
Aubrey St *BURS/TUN* ST6 .... 243 H5
Auckery Av *GTS/LS* CH66 .... 120 D1
Auckland Rd *CH/BCN* CH1 .... 144 C8
Audie Murphy Rd
  WARRW/BUR WA5 .... 36 B6
Audlem Cl *RUNC* WA7 .... 73 M8
Audlem Dr *NWCHE* CW9 .... 13 K8
Audlem Rd *AUD/MAD/W* CW3 .... 264 B6
  AUD/MAD/W CW3 .... 264 C5
  NANT CW5 .... 251 L1
Audley Crs *CHSW/BR* CH4 .... 169 K6
Audley Rd *ALS/KID* ST7 .... 241 L4
  ALS/KID ST7 .... 242 C5
  CW/SHV CW2 .... 240 C7
Audley St *CW/HAS* CW1 .... 19 H1
Audley St West *CW/HAS* CW1 .... 19 G1
Audre Cl *WARRW/BUR* WA5 .... 35 K6
Aughton Wy *CHSW/BR* CH4 .... 167 K8
Augusta Dr *MCFLDS* SK10 .... 138 B1
Austell Rd *WYTH/NTH* M22 .... 63 K3
Austen Cl *WSFD* CW7 .... 203 K6
Austins Hl *CHSE* CH3 .... 172 C4
Austin St *NWCHE* CW9 .... 130 D2
Austral Av *WARR* WA1 .... 38 B5
Australia La *WARRS* WA4 .... 57 J3
Autumn Av *KNUT* WA16 .... 107 J2
Avalon Dr *DID/WITH* M20 .... 45 J4
Avebury Cl *GOL/RIS/CU* WA3 .... 23 L4
  WDN WA8 .... 53 L1
Avebury Rd *NTHM/RTH* M23 .... 44 A7
Aveley Cl *WARR* WA1 .... 38 B5
Avens Rd *PART* M31 .... 40 F1
Avenue St *STKP* SK1 .... 3 H3
The Avenue *ALS/KID* ST7 .... 224 B5
  ALS/KID ST7 .... 242 F3
  CHD/CHDH SK8 .... 64 A3
  CHSE CH3 .... 147 M5
  CQ CH5 .... 166 C4
  HALE/TIMP WA15 .... 61 M4
  HLWD L26 .... 50 E5
  KNUT WA16 .... 59 J7
  LYMM WA13 .... 58 C3
  MPL/ROM SK6 .... 47 K1
  NEWLW WA12 .... 22 C8
  NWCHE CW9 .... 103 K4
  NWCHE CW9 .... 130 B1
  SALE M33 .... 42 D1
  SBCH CW11 .... 203 L4
  TPLY/KEL CW6 .... 197 K3
  WARRS WA4 .... 59 K3
  WILM/AE SK9 .... 110 A3
Averham Cl *AIMK* WN4 .... 22 B2
Avery Cl *WARRN/WOL* WA2 .... 37 L2
Aviemore Dr *WARRN/WOL* WA2 .... 38 A1
Avocet Cl *NEWLW* WA12 .... 22 C8
  WARRN/WOL WA2 .... 37 L1
Avocet Dr *ALT* WA14 .... 42 B4
  WSFD CW7 .... 177 K6
Avon *WDN* WA8 .... 52 A2
Avon Av *WARRW/BUR* WA5 .... 35 L8
Avon Cl *ALS/KID* ST7 .... 243 H2
  MCFLDS SK10 .... 14 A1
  MPL/ROM SK6 .... 48 E7
Avon Ct *ALS/KID* ST7 .... 224 C7
Avondale *EP* CH65 .... 121 K7
Avondale Av *BRAM/HZG* SK7 .... 66 F2
Avondale Dr *WDN* WA8 .... 52 B3
Avondale Ri *WILM/AE* SK9 .... 84 D6
Avondale Rd *BRAM/HZG* SK7 .... 66 F2
  EDGY/DAV SK3 .... 2 B8
Avon Dr *CONG* CW12 .... 207 M3
  CW/HAS CW1 .... 222 A7
Avonlea Cl *CHSW/BR* CH4 .... 168 E8
Avonlea Rd *SALE* M33 .... 42 D3
Avon Rd *CHD/CHDH* SK8 .... 64 B5
  GOL/RIS/CU WA3 .... 30 A2
  HALE/TIMP WA15 .... 61 L4
Avonside Av *BURS/TUN* ST6 .... 243 M8
Avonside Wy *MCFLDS* SK11 .... 138 C7
Avon St *EDGY/DAV* SK3 .... 46 B5
Avro Wy *MANAIR* M90 .... 62 F5
Aylesbury Cl *GTS/LS* CH66 .... 120 C1
  MCFLDS SK10 .... 138 D1
Aylesby Cl *KNUT* WA16 .... 107 H3
Aylsham Cl *WDN* WA8 .... 52 C1
Aylwin Dr *SALE* M33 .... 43 H1
Ayr Cl *BRAM/HZG* SK7 .... 67 G2
Ayrshire Cl *MWCH* CW10 .... 179 K2
Ayrshire Wy *CONG* CW12 .... 208 A3
Aysgarth Av *CHD/CHDH* SK8 .... 45 J6
  CW/HAS CW1 .... 221 H3
Aysgarth Cl *SALE* M33 .... 43 H1
Ayshford Cl *ALT* WA14 .... 42 B6
Azalea Gv *HLWD* L26 .... 50 D2
  RUNC WA7 .... 73 M8

B

Babbacombe Rd *OFTN* SK2 .... 47 J6
  WARRW/BUR WA5 .... 35 L8
Babbage Rd *CQ* CH5 .... 143 G8
Bache Av *CHNE* CH2 .... 145 J7
Bache Dr *CHNE* CH2 .... 145 K7
Bachefield Av *CHSE* CH3 .... 169 M6
Bache Hall Ct *CHNE* CH2 .... 145 J7
Bachelor's La *CHSE* CH3 .... 170 A4
Back Adcroft St *STKP* SK1 .... 3 H9
Back Booth St *NEWLW* WA12 .... 27 L2
Back Bridge St *NEWLW* WA12 .... 27 H1
  NM/HAY SK22 .... 69 J3
Back Brook Pl *WARRS* WA4 .... 56 E1

Back Chapel St
 BRAM/HZG SK7 ...... 66 E1 🔢
Back Coole La NANT CW5 ...... 262 E6
Back Crosland Ter
 FROD/HEL WA6 ...... 124 B2
Back Cross La NEWLW WA12 ...... 22 B8 🔢
Back Eastford Rd
 WARRS WA4 ...... 56 A3 🔢
Back Eddisbury Rd
 MCFLDN SK10 ...... 139 H1
Backford CI RUNC WA7 ...... 74 C7 🔢
Backford Gdns GTS/LS CH66 ...... 120 F5 🔢
Back Forshaw St
 WARRN/WOL WA2 ...... 5 J3
Back Heathcote St
 ALS/KID ST7 ...... 243 G2 🔢
Back High St RUNC WA7 ...... 9 G2
Back La ALT WA14 ...... 41 H7
 AUD/MAD/W CW3 ...... 255 H4
 CHSE CH3 ...... 215 J2
 CONG CW12 ...... 183 L7
 CONG CW12 ...... 184 F2
 CW/SHV CW2 ...... 238 E8
 FROD/HEL WA6 ...... 124 C2
 HALE/TIMP WA15 ...... 61 M7
 KNUT WA16 ...... 59 M7
 KNUT WA16 ...... 132 B5
 MALPAS SY14 ...... 247 G8
 MALPAS SY14 ...... 256 E5
 NANT CW5 ...... 253 J5
 NWCHE CW9 ...... 78 D5
 SBCH CW11 ...... 181 H5
 SBCH CW11 ...... 205 K5
 TPLY/KEL CW6 ...... 173 G6
 WARRS WA4 ...... 76 D8
 WARRW/BUR WA5 ...... 26 D5
 WARRW/BUR WA5 ...... 54 A2
 TPLY/KEL CW6 ...... 197 H2
Back Lawrence St
 NEWLW WA12 ...... 27 C1 🔢
Back Legh St NEWLW WA12 ...... 27 C1 🔢
Back Market St
 NEWLW WA12 ...... 22 A8
Back Massie St
 CHD/CHDH SK8 ...... 45 K6 🔢
Back Paradise St
 MCFLDN SK11 ...... 14 F6 🔢
Back Queen St CH/BCN CH1 ...... 17 H4
Back Union St NM/HAY SK22 ...... 69 J5
Back Wallgate MCFLDS SK11 ...... 15 C5 🔢
Back Water St STKP SK1 ...... 3 H3 🔢
Badcock's La TPLY/KEL CW6 ...... 233 L1
Baddiley CI NANT CW5 ...... 250 D2
Baddiley Hall La NANT CW5 ...... 250 A4
Baddiley La NANT CW5 ...... 250 B4
Baddington La NANT CW5 ...... 251 K3
Badger Av CW/HAS CW1 ...... 220 F6
Badger Bait NSTN CH64 ...... 91 M6
Badger CI RUNC WA7 ...... 74 A6
 MCFLDN SK10 ...... 138 D2
Badgers CI CHSE CH3 ...... 170 E5
 GTS/LS CH66 ...... 120 F4 🔢
 WSFD CW7 ...... 177 G3 🔢
Badgers Pk NSTN CH64 ...... 91 M6
Badgersrake La GTS/LS CH66 ...... 93 K8
Badgers Set NWCHW CW8 ...... 127 K7
Badgers Wk CHNE CH2 ...... 145 L2
 WYTH/NTH M22 ...... 63 L3
Bag La NWCHW CW8 ...... 125 L1
Bagley La AUD/MAD/W CW3 ...... 273 M3
Bagmere CI SBCH CW11 ...... 181 M7
 SBCH CW11 ...... 203 M5 🔢
Bagmere La SBCH CW11 ...... 182 B7
Bagnall CI WARRW/BUR WA5 ...... 36 C7
Bagot Av WARRW/BUR WA5 ...... 4 D1
Bagstock Av POY/DIS SK12 ...... 86 E2
Baguley Av WDN WA8 ...... 52 A7
Baguley Crs EDGY/DAV SK3 ...... 46 D6
Baguley La SALE M33 ...... 43 L1 🔢
Bailey Av EP CH65 ...... 94 F6
Bailey CI CW/HAS CW1 ...... 221 J5
Bailey Ct ALS/KID ST7 ...... 241 L1 🔢
Bailey Crs CONG CW12 ...... 185 G8
 SBCH CW11 ...... 204 D6
Bailey La MANAIR M90 ...... 63 H3
 PART M31 ...... 31 M8
Bailey's Bank BIDD ST8 ...... 227 K1
Baileys CI WDN WA8 ...... 34 A7
Baileys La HLWD L26 ...... 51 G4
 SPK/HALE L24 ...... 71 G3
Bailey Wk ALT WA14 ...... 61 J4
Bainbridge Av GOL/RIS/CU WA3 ...... 31 M3
Baines Av IRL M44 ...... 31 M3
Baker Dr GTS/LS CH66 ...... 120 E1
Baker Rd RUNC WA7 ...... 8 B8
Baker's La KNUT WA16 ...... 132 C6
 WSFD CW7 ...... 177 L2
Baker St HALE/TIMP WA15 ...... 43 H5 🔢
 HTNM SK4 ...... 2 E1
 MCFLDS SK11 ...... 14 E7
Baker Wy CHSE CH3 ...... 148 E5
 CHSE CH3 ...... 170 E5
Bakestonedale Rd
 MCFLDN SK10 ...... 113 K1
Bakewell CI GTS/LS CH66 ...... 120 E4
Bakewell Rd BRAM/HZG SK7 ...... 66 E4
 WARRW/BUR WA5 ...... 27 C5
Bakewell St EDGY/DAV SK3 ...... 2 D8
Bala CI WARRW/BUR WA5 ...... 36 E2 🔢
Baldock CI WARRS WA4 ...... 57 J1
Baldock Rd DID/WITH M20 ...... 45 K1
Balfour CI CW/HAS CW1 ...... 222 C8
Balfour Gv BIDD ST8 ...... 227 L4 🔢
Balfour Rd ALT WA14 ...... 42 D5
Balfour St RUNC WA7 ...... 8 F4
Balham CI WDN WA8 ...... 34 A8
Ballantyne Wy
 GOL/RIS/CU WA3 ...... 23 L4 🔢
Ballater Crs CHSE CH3 ...... 170 B2
Ballater Dr WARRN/WOL WA2 ...... 28 E8
Balliol CI MCFLDS SK11 ...... 162 F1
Ball La FROD/HEL WA6 ...... 126 D1
 MCFLDN SK10 ...... 112 D7
Balmer Rd NTHM/RTH M23 ...... 44 A7
Balmoral Av CHD/CHDH SK8 ...... 65 C2
 CW/SHV CW2 ...... 238 B3

GOL/RIS/CU WA3 ...... 23 K3
 NWCHE CW9 ...... 13 J9
Balmoral CI KNUT WA16 ...... 107 H3
 WSFD CW7 ...... 177 J1
Balmoral Crs MCFLDN SK10 ...... 15 L1
Balmoral Dr ALT WA14 ...... 42 F4
 FROD/HEL WA6 ...... 98 B8
 HOLMCH WA4 ...... 181 H2
 MPL/ROM SK6 ...... 67 L5
 POY/DIS SK12 ...... 86 D1
Balmoral Gdns EP CH65 ...... 121 K1 🔢
Balmoral Gv BRAM/HZG SK7 ...... 66 F1
Balmoral Pk CH/BCN CH1 ...... 16 D1
 CH/BCN CH1 ...... 145 H8
Balmoral PI NANT CW5 ...... 237 K8
Balmoral Rd CHNE CH2 ...... 17 G1
 HTNM SK4 ...... 46 A1
 WARRS WA4 ...... 56 F2
 WDN WA8 ...... 34 A8
Balmoral Wy WILM/AE SK9 ...... 84 A6
Balniel St STHEL WA9 ...... 34 D1
Balsham CI WLTN L25 ...... 50 C5
Balshaw La IRL M44 ...... 31 M2
Baltic Rd ALT WA14 ...... 42 A6
Bamber Av SALE M33 ...... 43 L1
Bamford CI CHD/CHDH SK8 ...... 64 D4
 CHD/CHDH SK8 ...... 65 G8
 RUNC WA7 ...... 9 M9
 RUNC WA7 ...... 73 J6
Bamford Gdns
 HALE/TIMP WA15 ...... 43 K6 🔢
Bamford Gv DID/WITH M20 ...... 45 G1
Bamford St MCFLDN SK10 ...... 15 K3 🔢
 STKP SK1 ...... 3 G8
Bampton CI STKP SK1 ...... 47 H5 🔢
Bampton Rd WYTH/NTH M22 ...... 63 J3
Banastre Dr NEWLW WA12 ...... 27 M1
Banbury Av WLTN L25 ...... 50 C2
 MCFLDN SK10 ...... 138 E2
Banbury Dr ALT WA14 ...... 42 E4
 WARRW/BUR WA5 ...... 36 C8
Banbury Gv BIDD ST8 ...... 227 J4
Banbury Rd NTHM/RTH M23 ...... 43 M7
Banbury St ALS/KID ST7 ...... 242 D5
 STKP SK1 ...... 3 G6
Bancroft NWCHW CW8 ...... 101 L8
Bancroft Av CHD/CHDH SK8 ...... 65 C3
Bancroft CI MPL/ROM SK6 ...... 47 L1 🔢
 WLTN L25 ...... 50 C5
Bancroft Rd HALE/TIMP WA15 ...... 62 A1
 WDN WA8 ...... 53 K2
Bandon CI SPK/HALE L24 ...... 71 K2 🔢
Bangor CI GTS/LS CH66 ...... 120 F4 🔢
Bangor Rd CHD/CHDH SK8 ...... 45 M6
Bank CI CHNE CH2 ...... 145 L7
 MCFLDS SK11 ...... 15 K7 🔢
 NSTN CH64 ...... 92 A6
Bankes' La FROD/HEL WA6 ...... 72 E6
Bankfield CI CW/SHV CW2 ...... 238 A5
 HTNM SK4 ...... 2 B4
 IRL M44 ...... 31 K7 🔢
Bankfield Rd CHD/CHDH SK8 ...... 64 F3 🔢
 WDN WA8 ...... 52 B3
Bank Gdns WARRW/BUR WA5 ...... 35 L8 🔢
Bankhall La HALE/TIMP WA15 ...... 61 L4
Bankhall Rd HTNM SK4 ...... 46 A2
Bankhey NSTN CH64 ...... 91 M7
Bankhouse La FROD/HEL WA6 ...... 98 C8
 SBCH CW11 ...... 206 A5
Banklands CI IRL M44 ...... 31 K7 🔢
Bank La CONG CW12 ...... 185 H3
 MCFLDN SK10 ...... 114 C6
 NANT CW5 ...... 235 K4
Bank Mellor Rd NM/HAY SK22 ...... 69 J3 🔢
Bank Pas GOL/RIS/CU WA3 ...... 23 G3 🔢
Bank Rd MPL/ROM SK6 ...... 48 A1
Banks CI CONG CW12 ...... 207 J1 🔢
Banks Crs WARRS WA4 ...... 37 M8
Bankside HALE/TIMP WA15 ...... 62 B6
Bank Side NWCHW CW8 ...... 128 C3
Bankside RUNC WA7 ...... 74 E5
Bankside CI MPL/ROM SK6 ...... 49 J3 🔢
 NANT CW5 ...... 218 D6 🔢
 WILM/AE SK9 ...... 84 D2 🔢
Bankside Rd DID/WITH M20 ...... 45 H5
Banks La STKP SK1 ...... 3 M8
Banks Rd CO CH5 ...... 166 D5
Bank St ALS/KID ST7 ...... 226 C8
 BURS/TUN ST6 ...... 243 K8
 CHD/CHDH SK8 ...... 45 L6
 GOL/RIS/CU WA3 ...... 23 G3
 GOL/RIS/CU WA3 ...... 31 G7
 MCFLDS SK11 ...... 15 K7 🔢
 MCFLDS SK11 ...... 15 H7 🔢
 NEWLW WA12 ...... 26 F1 🔢
 WARR WA1 ...... 5 G7 🔢
 WDN WA8 ...... 53 G8
The Bank ALS/KID ST7 ...... 226 B5
Bank Vw HOLMCH CW4 ...... 157 L4
Banky Flds CONG CW12 ...... 207 J2
Banky Fields Crs CONG CW12 ...... 207 J3
Banner Hey RAIN/WH L35 ...... 32 D3
Bannister Dr CHD/CHDH SK8 ...... 64 F2
Bannister St OFTN SK2 ...... 3 H9
Bann St EDGY/DAV SK3 ...... 2 E7
Banstead Av WYTH/NTH M22 ...... 44 D5
Barbara St STHEL WA9 ...... 34 E1 🔢
Barbauld St WARR WA1 ...... 5 G7 🔢
Barber Dr ALS/KID ST7 ...... 225 L5
Barber PI BURS/TUN ST6 ...... 243 M6
Barber Rd BURS/TUN ST6 ...... 243 M6
Barberry CI ALT WA14 ...... 42 B4
Barber's La NWCHE CW9 ...... 77 J3
 NWCHE CW9 ...... 77 L4
 NWCHW CW8 ...... 12 F3
Barber St MCFLDS SK11 ...... 15 J8
Barbondale CI
 WARRW/BUR WA5 ...... 35 M5
Barcheston Rd CHD/CHDH SK8 ...... 64 C7
Barclay Rd POY/DIS SK12 ...... 86 E2
Bardale Gv AIMK WN4 ...... 22 A1
Bardell CI POY/DIS SK12 ...... 86 D2 🔢
Bardley Crs HUY L36 ...... 32 A5
Bardney Av GOL/RIS/CU WA3 ...... 22 F2

Bardon Rd NTHM/RTH M23 ...... 43 M6
Bardsea Av WYTH/NTH M22 ...... 63 K3
Bardsey CI EP CH65 ...... 121 J3 🔢
Bardsley Av WARRW/BUR WA5 ...... 36 F2
Bardsley St HTNM SK4 ...... 2 D1
Barfold CI OFTN SK2 ...... 48 A7
Barford CI WARRW/BUR WA5 ...... 36 B3
Barford Dr GOL/RIS/CU WA3 ...... 24 A4
 WILM/AE SK9 ...... 84 C3
Barford Gra NSTN CH64 ...... 93 H4
Barford Rd SPK/HALE L24 ...... 50 B6
Bargates St GOL/RIS/CU WA3 ...... 29 K8
Bar HI AUD/MAD/W CW3 ...... 267 J8
Barington Dr RUNC WA7 ...... 74 E5
Baristow CI CHNE CH2 ...... 17 G1
Barker Rd MPL/ROM SK6 ...... 47 M1
Barker's Hollow Rd WARRS WA4 ...... 75 G6
Barker St CW/SHV CW2 ...... 19 G9
 NANT CW5 ...... 20 E7
Bark HI WHITCH SY13 ...... 270 A5
Barkhill Rd CHSE CH3 ...... 170 B1
Barley Castle CI WARRS WA4 ...... 77 H1
Barleycastle La WARRS WA4 ...... 57 K7
Barleycorn CI SALE M33 ...... 44 A1 🔢
Barley Cft ALS/KID ST7 ...... 241 L2
 CHD/CHDH SK8 ...... 64 F4
 CHSE CH3 ...... 170 A5
Barleycroft Ter ALS/KID ST7 ...... 225 M5
Barley Dr BRAM/HZG SK7 ...... 65 L5
Barley Mow CI CH/BCN CH1 ...... 120 C2
Barley Rd WARRS WA4 ...... 57 J1
Barleywood CI CW/SHV CW2 ...... 238 B4 🔢
Barlow Crs MPL/ROM SK6 ...... 48 F8
Barlow Dr WSFD CW7 ...... 176 F4
Barlow Fold Rd MPL/ROM SK6 ...... 48 D1
Barlow Gv STHEL WA9 ...... 26 A2
Barlow HI MCFLDS SK11 ...... 187 M3
Barlow's La NWCHW CW8 ...... 153 M5
 WILM/AE SK9 ...... 84 B3
Barlow's La South
 BRAM/HZG SK7 ...... 66 C1
Barlow Wy SBCH CW11 ...... 204 A4
Barlow Wood Dr MPL/ROM SK6 ...... 68 B3
Barmouth CI WARRW/BUR WA5 ...... 36 E2
Barnabas Av CW/HAS CW1 ...... 220 F7
Barnaby CI MALPAS SY14 ...... 230 C2 🔢
Barnaby Rd POY/DIS SK12 ...... 86 D2
Barnack CI WARR WA1 ...... 38 A4
Barnacre Av NSTN CH64 ...... 91 H2
Barnard CI MCFLDS SK11 ...... 137 M6
Barnard St WARRW/BUR WA5 ...... 55 K1
Barnbridge CI ALS/KID ST7 ...... 225 L5
Barnbrook CI WSFD CW7 ...... 177 G3 🔢
 WYTH/NTH M22 ...... 63 K3 🔢
Barn Cft FROD/HEL WA6 ...... 98 C8
Barncroft RUNC WA7 ...... 74 D5
Barncroft Gdns
 WYTH/NTH M22 ...... 44 C7 🔢
Barn Croft Rd HLWD L26 ...... 51 G5
Barnes Av HTNM SK4 ...... 46 A2
 WARRN/WOL WA2 ...... 38 B2
Barnes CI CH/BCN CH1 ...... 144 F6 🔢
 CW/HAS CW1 ...... 222 C8 🔢
 WARRW/BUR WA5 ...... 36 A7
 WDN WA8 ...... 53 K2
Barneston Rd WDN WA8 ...... 53 J2
Barnett Av NEWLW WA12 ...... 26 E1
Barnett Gv BURS/TUN ST6 ...... 243 M7
Barnett St MCFLDS SK11 ...... 14 D6
Barnfield CHSE CH3 ...... 214 A3
Barnfield Av MPL/ROM SK6 ...... 48 D1
 RUNC WA7 ...... 74 D6
Barnfield CI GTS/LS CH66 ...... 120 C2
 WHITCH SY13 ...... 269 L4 🔢
Barnfield Rd MCFLDN SK10 ...... 112 F5
 WARR WA1 ...... 38 D6
Barnfield Rd East EDGY/DAV SK3 ...... 46 F8
Barnfield Rd West
 EDGY/DAV SK3 ...... 46 D8
Bargate CHD/CHDH SK8 ...... 45 G6
Barnham CI GOL/RIS/CU WA3 ...... 23 G4
 SPK/HALE L24 ...... 50 B8
Barnhill Gra CHSE CH3 ...... 231 H1
Barnhill Rd CHSE CH3 ...... 231 G3
Barnhouse La CHSE CH3 ...... 147 L5
 CHSE CH3 ...... 148 A3
Barn La GOL/RIS/CU WA3 ...... 22 F5
Barn Meadow NWCHW CW8 ...... 12 E1
Barn Rd CONG CW12 ...... 184 C8
Barnsfold Rd MPL/ROM SK6 ...... 67 M1
Barnside Wy MCFLDN SK10 ...... 138 C1 🔢
 NWCHE CW9 ...... 153 M4
Barns La LYMM WA13 ...... 41 G6
Barnsley St STKP SK1 ...... 3 K7
Barns PI HALE/TIMP WA15 ...... 62 C4
Barnstaple Wy
 WARRW/BUR WA5 ...... 35 L8
Barnston Ct CHSE CH3 ...... 228 E2 🔢
Barn St WDN WA8 ...... 7 G9
Barnswood CI WARRS WA4 ...... 57 J6
Barnton CI GOL/RIS/CU WA3 ...... 23 K5 🔢
Barn Wy NEWLW WA12 ...... 27 H1
Barnwell Av GOL/RIS/CU WA3 ...... 24 D8
Barnwell CI CW/SHV CW2 ...... 238 B4
Barnwood Rd NTHM/RTH M23 ...... 63 G1
The Barnyard CQ CH5 ...... 166 B1
Baron CI WARR WA1 ...... 38 C5
Baron Gn CHD/CHDH SK8 ...... 64 D5
Baronia PI NANT CW5 ...... 21 G5
Barons CI FLINT CH6 ...... 116 A6
 WDN WA8 ...... 52 C4
Barons Quay Rd NWCHE CW9 ...... 13 H1
Barons Rd CW/SHV CW2 ...... 238 B8
Barony Rd NANT CW5 ...... 20 F2
Barony Wy CHSW/BR CH4 ...... 168 C8
Barrack HI MPL/ROM SK6 ...... 48 A2
Barrack Hill CI MPL/ROM SK6 ...... 48 A1
Barracks La CHSE CH3 ...... 215 J7
 MCFLDN SK10 ...... 15 L6 🔢
 NANT CW5 ...... 250 E2
Barrastitch La NWCHW CW8 ...... 127 L6
Barratt Rd ALS/KID ST7 ...... 241 M1

Barrel Well HI CHSE CH3 ...... 17 M5
Barrie Gdns ALS/KID ST7 ...... 242 C4
Barrie Gv CW/HAS CW1 ...... 19 K3
Barrington Av CHD/CHDH SK8 ...... 65 C3
Barrington CI WARRW/BUR WA5 ...... 36 F2 🔢
Barrington Dr MWCH CW10 ...... 179 M5
Barrington Rd ALT WA14 ...... 42 D6
Barrow Av WARRN/WOL WA2 ...... 37 L2 🔢
Barrowdale Rd GOL/RIS/CU WA3 ...... 23 H4
Barrow Hall La
 WARRW/BUR WA5 ...... 35 L6
Barrow La CHSE CH3 ...... 147 K7
 CHSE CH3 ...... 148 B8
 GOL/RIS/CU WA3 ...... 28 C2
 HALE/TIMP WA15 ...... 62 B5
 NWCHE CW9 ...... 102 F2
Barrow Meadow
 CHD/CHDH SK8 ...... 64 E4
Barrows CI CW/HAS CW1 ...... 221 G4
Barrow's Brow WARR WA16 ...... 132 E3
Barrow's Green La WDN WA8 ...... 53 L2
Barrule Av BRAM/HZG SK7 ...... 66 E3
Barrule CI WARRS WA4 ...... 56 D5
Barrymore Av WARRS WA4 ...... 37 M8
Barrymore Crs NWCHE CW9 ...... 103 J4
Barrymore Rd NWCHW CW8 ...... 128 C3
 WARRS WA4 ...... 9 K9
Barsbank CI LYMM WA13 ...... 58 C1
Barsbank La LYMM WA13 ...... 58 C1
Barsbank Gdns WARRS WA4 ...... 76 L1
The Bars CH/BCN CH1 ...... 17 J5
Barston Av EP CH65 ...... 94 F7
Bartholomew CI RAIN/WH L35 ...... 33 L3
Bartholomew Wy
 CHSW/BR CH4 ...... 169 J6
Barthomley Crs CW/SHV CW2 ...... 220 D8
Barthomley Rd ALS/KID ST7 ...... 225 M5
 CW/HAS CW1 ...... 239 M3
 CW/HAS CW1 ...... 240 C6
Bartlegate RUNC WA7 ...... 74 B7 🔢
Bartlet CI CO CH5 ...... 142 F6 🔢
Bartley Rd WYTH/NTH M22 ...... 44 C4
Barton Av WARRS WA4 ...... 57 G2
 WILM/AE SK9 ...... 84 D2
Barton Ct WSFD CW7 ...... 177 M3
Barton Rd CHSE CH3 ...... 228 F3
 CONG CW12 ...... 207 M2
 HTNM SK4 ...... 45 L3
 MALPAS SY14 ...... 229 J3
Bartons PI NWCHW CW9 ...... 13 M1
Barton St GOL/RIS/CU WA3 ...... 23 C4
 MCFLDS SK11 ...... 14 F8
Barwood Av ALS/KID ST7 ...... 225 G7
Basford Rd CW/SHV CW2 ...... 238 D4
Basil St HTNM SK4 ...... 2 D2
Basle CI BRAM/HZG SK7 ...... 65 L1
Baslow Dr BRAM/HZG SK7 ...... 66 F4
 CHD/CHDH SK8 ...... 64 C4
Bateman Av BIDD ST8 ...... 227 H7
Batemans CI CW/SHV CW2 ...... 238 B4
Batemill CI MCFLDN SK10 ...... 137 M3 🔢
Batemill La MCFLDS SK11 ...... 134 D6
Bates La FROD/HEL WA6 ...... 98 D8
 FROD/HEL WA6 ...... 124 D1
Bate's Mill La TPLY/KEL CW6 ...... 196 E8
Bateson St STKP SK1 ...... 3 J4
Bath CI BRAM/HZG SK7 ...... 67 G2
Bath Crs CHD/CHDH SK8 ...... 65 H6
Batherton CI WDN WA8 ...... 7 J7
Batherton La NANT CW5 ...... 251 M2
Bathfields Crs WHITCH SY13 ...... 269 L5
Bath La AUD/MAD/W CW3 ...... 274 A1
Bath St ALT WA14 ...... 61 K2
 CH/BCN CH1 ...... 17 J5
 SBCH CW11 ...... 204 C6
 WARR WA1 ...... 4 F6
 WHITCH SY13 ...... 270 B4
Bathwood Dr NSTN CH64 ...... 91 L7 🔢
Batterbee Ct RUNC WA7 ...... 222 D7
Battersbay Gv BRAM/HZG SK7 ...... 66 E2
Battersby La WARRN/WOL WA2 ...... 5 J4
Battersea Ct WDN WA8 ...... 52 F1 🔢
Battersea Rd HTNM SK4 ...... 45 L3
Battery La WARR WA1 ...... 38 F6
Bawtry CI WARRN/WOL WA2 ...... 37 L3
Baxter CI RUNC WA7 ...... 74 D5 🔢
Baxter Gdns NTHM/RTH M23 ...... 44 A5
Baxter St WARRW/BUR WA5 ...... 4 B7
Baycliffe LYMM WA13 ...... 58 D2
Baycliffe CI RUNC WA7 ...... 75 K7
Baycroft Gv NTHM/RTH M23 ...... 44 A3
Bayley Rd NANT CW5 ...... 237 K7
Baytree CI GTS/LS CH66 ...... 120 F3
Bayvil CI RUNC WA7 ...... 74 E5 🔢
Bazley Rd WYTH/NTH M22 ...... 44 D3
Beach Gv NWCHW CW8 ...... 12 A7
Beach Rd NWCHW CW8 ...... 12 B6
 NWCHW CW8 ...... 129 H6
Beacomfold MPL/ROM SK6 ...... 49 H1
Beacon Rd NTHM/RTH M23 ...... 63 G2
Beacon Rd MPL/ROM SK6 ...... 48 A3
Beaconsfield Crs WDN WA8 ...... 34 A8
Beaconsfield Gv WDN WA8 ...... 34 B8
Beaconsfield Rd ALT WA14 ...... 42 D5
 CQ CH5 ...... 142 A6 🔢
 RUNC WA7 ...... 8 D6
 WDN WA8 ...... 53 H1
Beaconsfield St EP CH65 ...... 17 K5
Beacon Vw MPL/ROM SK6 ...... 48 A4
Beadnell Dr WARRW/BUR WA5 ...... 54 K4
Beaford Dr WYTH/NTH M22 ...... 63 K4
Beagle Point WSFD CW7 ...... 177 G3
Beal CI HTNM SK4 ...... 45 L3
Beam Heath Wy NANT CW5 ...... 21 G2
Beaminster CI HTNM SK4 ...... 45 M1
Beamish CI WARRS WA4 ...... 76 D1
Beamont St WDN WA8 ...... 53 C8 🔢

Beamsley Dr WYTH/NTH M22 ...... 63 H2
Beam St NANT CW5 ...... 20 E6
Bean Leach Av OFTN SK2 ...... 47 M6
Bean Leach Dr OFTN SK2 ...... 47 M6
Bean Leach Rd BRAM/HZG SK7 ...... 47 L8
Beard Crs NM/HAY SK22 ...... 69 K4
Beardsmore Dr
 GOL/RIS/CU WA3 ...... 23 L4
Bearhurst La MCFLDS SK11 ...... 136 F7
Beasley CI GTS/LS CH66 ...... 120 C1
Beathwaite Dr BRAM/HZG SK7 ...... 65 J3
Beat La MCFLDS SK11 ...... 209 K4
Beatrice Av CHD/CHDH SK8 ...... 64 C7
Beatrice Gdns WHITCH SY13 ...... 270 B4 🔢
Beatrice St WARRS WA4 ...... 56 D1 🔢
Beatty Av WARRN/WOL WA2 ...... 37 J3
Beatty CI CONG CW12 ...... 185 G3
Beatty Dr CONG CW12 ...... 185 G3
Beatty Rd NANT CW5 ...... 20 C8
Beaufort Av SALE M33 ...... 43 J1 🔢
Beaufort Cha WILM/AE SK9 ...... 84 F3
Beaufort CI RUNC WA7 ...... 9 J9
 WARRW/BUR WA5 ...... 36 A7
 WDN WA8 ...... 52 A4 🔢
 WILM/AE SK9 ...... 110 B2
Beaufort Rd OFTN SK2 ...... 47 K8
 SALE M33 ...... 43 J1
Beaufort St WARRW/BUR WA5 ...... 4 A8
Beaulieu Av WSFD CW7 ...... 177 M2
Beaumaris Crs BRAM/HZG SK7 ...... 66 C4
Beaumaris Dr EP CH65 ...... 121 K2
Beaumont CI BIDD ST8 ...... 227 K2
 CHSW/BR CH4 ...... 168 E6 🔢
 CW/SHV CW2 ...... 237 M4
Beauty Bank NWCHW CW8 ...... 152 E7
 WSFD CW7 ...... 200 A1
Beauvale CI OFTN SK2 ...... 47 J5
Beaverbrook Av
 GOL/RIS/CU WA3 ...... 25 H8
Beaver Rd DID/WITH M20 ...... 45 H1
Bebbington CI SALE M33 ...... 43 M2
Bebington Rd GTS/LS CH66 ...... 94 D8
Beccles Rd SALE M33 ...... 43 H3
Becconsall CI CW/HAS CW1 ...... 221 G4 🔢
Becconsall Dr CW/HAS CW1 ...... 221 G4
Bechers WDN WA8 ...... 52 B1
Beckenham Gv WSFD CW7 ...... 177 G3
Beckett Av WSFD CW7 ...... 178 D4
Beckett's La CHSE CH3 ...... 170 A4
Beckfield Rd NTHM/RTH M23 ...... 44 A7
Beckford CI CW/HAS CW1 ...... 220 F4
Beck La MCFLDN SK10 ...... 137 L2
Beck Rd AUD/MAD/W CW3 ...... 267 M5
Beckton Gdns WYTH/NTH M22 ...... 63 J1
Becontree Dr NTHM/RTH M23 ...... 43 K6
Beddow Wy BURS/TUN ST6 ...... 243 M6
Bedells La WILM/AE SK9 ...... 84 A6
Bedford Av EP CH65 ...... 121 G2
 SALE M33 ...... 43 K2
Bedford Av East EP CH65 ...... 121 H2
Bedford CI HUY L36 ...... 32 A1
Bedford Ct CW/SHV CW2 ...... 19 G9
Bedford Dr HALE/TIMP WA15 ...... 43 J6
Bedford Gdns CW/SHV CW2 ...... 19 G9
Bedford Gn IRL M44 ...... 31 J6
Bedford PI CW/SHV CW2 ...... 18 E9
Bedford Ri WSFD CW7 ...... 177 J6
Bedford Rd ALS/KID ST7 ...... 243 G1
 MCFLDS SK11 ...... 14 D7
Bedford St CW/SHV CW2 ...... 18 F9
 WARRS WA4 ...... 56 C4
Bedward Rw CH/BCN CH1 ...... 16 E5
Beech Av ALS/KID ST7 ...... 224 F4
 BRAM/HZG SK7 ...... 66 E2
 CHD/CHDH SK8 ...... 45 H7
 EDGY/DAV SK3 ...... 46 F6 🔢
 FROD/HEL WA6 ...... 99 J4
 GOL/RIS/CU WA3 ...... 23 M5
 GOL/RIS/CU WA3 ...... 30 A1
 KNUT WA16 ...... 81 L6
 MPL/ROM SK6 ...... 48 D6
 NM/HAY SK22 ...... 69 K3
 WARRS WA4 ...... 57 K1
 WARRW/BUR WA5 ...... 54 C1
 WHITCH SY13 ...... 269 M5
 WYTH/NTH M22 ...... 44 D4
Beech Bank MCFLDN SK10 ...... 15 G2
Beech CI CONG CW12 ...... 184 B8
 HOLMCH WA16 ...... 107 M6
 NEWLW WA12 ...... 27 J2
 NWCHW CW8 ...... 151 M2
 WILM/AE SK9 ...... 110 B1
Beech Cottages
 WILM/AE SK9 ...... 110 A4 🔢
Beech Crs LEIGH WN7 ...... 24 E1
 POY/DIS SK12 ...... 66 E8
Beech Cft AUD/MAD/W CW3 ...... 267 L5
Beechcroft Av CW/SHV CW2 ...... 238 B7
Beechcroft CI EP CH65 ...... 121 H1
Beech Dr ALS/KID ST7 ...... 242 E4
 CW/SHV CW2 ...... 237 L2
 KNUT WA16 ...... 107 H2
 LEIGH WN7 ...... 24 E2
The Beeches CHNE CH2 ...... 145 M6
 FROD/HEL WA6 ...... 98 C8
 NANT CW5 ...... 20 F7
 WHITCH SY13 ...... 269 M4
Beech Farm Dr MCFLDN SK10 ...... 15 G1
Beechfield Av WILM/AE SK9 ...... 83 L7
Beechfield Dr LEIGH WN7 ...... 24 F1
 MWCH CW10 ...... 179 H2
Beechfield Gdns NWCHW CW8 ...... 129 H6
Beechfield Rd CHD/CHDH SK8 ...... 65 H4
 EDGY/DAV SK3 ...... 46 F8
 EP CH65 ...... 10 D7
 WARRS WA4 ...... 57 G3
 WILM/AE SK9 ...... 110 B4
Beechfields WSFD CW7 ...... 178 A4 🔢
Beech Gv CHNE CH2 ...... 170 A1
 CW/HAS CW1 ...... 19 K2
 GTS/LS CH66 ...... 121 G4
 LEIGH WN7 ...... 24 E2
 WARR WA13 ...... 58 B2

MCFLDS SK11 .... 138 E7
NWCHW CW8 .... 128 D4
SBCH CW11 .... 204 D6
WARR CW1 .... 38 A5
WILM/AE SK9 .... 84 A6
WSFD CW7 .... 177 K5
Beech Hall Dr *MCFLDN* SK10 .... 138 C2
Beech Heyes Cl *NWCHW* CW8 .... 128 E4 🗓
Beech Heyes Dr
　NWCHW CW8 .... 128 E4 🗓
Beech Hey La *NSTN* CH64 .... 93 H3
Beechlands Av *CHSE* CH3 .... 170 A3 🗓
Beech La *FROD/HEL* WA6 .... 126 D5
　MCFLDN SK10 .... 15 C2
　MPL/ROM SK6 .... 48 C2
　NWCHW CW8 .... 129 C1
　TPLY/KEL CW6 .... 175 H6
　WILM/AE SK9 .... 84 A6
Beech Ms *OFTN* SK2 .... 47 G7
Beechmill Dr *GOL/RIS/CU* WA3 .... 29 K1
Beechmoore *WARRS* WA4 .... 55 H7
Beechpark Av *WYTH/NTH* M22 .... 44 C5
Beech Ri *CHF/WBR* SK23 .... 89 J7
　NWCHW CW8 .... 127 H2
Beech Rd *CHF/WBR* SK23 .... 89 L5
　CHF/WBR SK23 .... 89 L5
　CQ CH5 .... 166 A1
　EDGY/DAV SK3 .... 46 E6
　GOL/RIS/CU WA3 .... 23 G3
　HALE/TIMP WA15 .... 61 L1
　MPL/ROM SK6 .... 67 M5 🗓
　RUNC WA7 .... 9 M7
　RUNC WA7 .... 74 B8
　TPLY/KEL CW6 .... 175 K3
　WARRS WA4 .... 56 C4
　WILM/AE SK9 .... 110 B1
Beech St *MWCH* CW10 .... 179 J3
Beech St West *CW/HAS* CW1 .... 18 E3 🗓
Beech Tree Cl *NANT* CW5 .... 237 K7
Beechtree Farm Ct *WARR* WA16 .... 59 H5
Beechtree La *KNUT* WA16 .... 59 J5
Beechurst Rd *CHD/CHDH* SK8 .... 46 B7
Beech View Rd *FROD/HEL* WA6 .... 126 C3
Beech Wk *LEIGH* WN7 .... 24 E2
Beechway *CHNE* CH2 .... 145 J6 🗓
　MCFLDN SK10 .... 113 C5
　MPL/ROM SK6 .... 67 M5
　WILM/AE SK9 .... 83 M7
Beechways *WARRS* WA4 .... 56 D7
Beechways Dr *NSTN* CH64 .... 91 K4
Beechwood *ALT* WA14 .... 61 L8 🗓
　KNUT WA16 .... 107 L3
Beechwood Av *AIMK* WN4 .... 22 A2 🗓
　HLWD L26 .... 50 E5
　MPL/ROM SK6 .... 48 C2
　NEWLW WA12 .... 22 D8
　NWCHW CW8 .... 129 C6
　RUNC WA7 .... 73 M7
　RUNC WA7 .... 73 K7
　WARR WA1 .... 37 L4
　WARRW/BUR WA5 .... 35 M7 🗓
Beechwood Dr *ALS/KID* ST7 .... 224 B8
　CONG CW12 .... 184 F4
　GTS/LS CH66 .... 120 D3
　MPL/ROM SK6 .... 49 C6
　NWCHE CW9 .... 104 F6
　WILM/AE SK9 .... 84 E4 🗓
Beechwood Gv
　CHD/CHDH SK8 .... 65 C4 🗓
Beechwood La *GOL/RIS/CU* WA3 .... 24 D8
Beechwood Ms *MCFLDN* SK10 .... 14 F1
Beechwood Rd *CHSW/BR* CH4 .... 168 D7
Beecroft Cl *WARRW/BUR* WA5 .... 36 D5
Beenham Cl *SALE* M33 .... 42 C1
Beeston Av *HALE/TIMP* WA15 .... 42 F6
Beeston Brow *MPL/ROM* SK6 .... 113 H3
Beeston Cl *GOL/RIS/CU* WA3 .... 29 K8
　HOLMCH CW4 .... 181 C1
　MCFLDN SK10 .... 113 J5 🗓
　MWCH CW10 .... 179 K7
Beeston Dr *ALS/KID* ST7 .... 241 J1
　KNUT WA16 .... 107 G4
　WSFD CW7 .... 177 J3
Beeston Gn *GTS/LS* CH66 .... 94 E7 🗓
Beeston Gv *EDGY/DAV* SK3 .... 46 E7
Beeston Mt *MCFLDN* SK10 .... 113 H3
Beeston Rd *CHSW/BR* CH4 .... 190 B1
　WILM/AE SK9 .... 64 D7 🗓
Beeston St *NWCHW* CW8 .... 12 F4
Beeston Ter *MCFLDS* SK11 .... 137 L6
Beeston Vw *ALS/KID* ST7 .... 243 G5
　CHSW/BR CH4 .... 169 L5
Beggarman's La *KNUT* WA16 .... 107 G5
Begley Cl *MPL/ROM* SK6 .... 47 M3
Belfield Rd *DID/WITH* M20 .... 45 H1 🗓
Belfry Cl *WILM/AE* SK9 .... 84 D4
Belfry Dr *MCFLDN* SK10 .... 112 C8
Belgrave Av *ALS/KID* ST7 .... 224 D7
　CHSW/BR CH4 .... 168 E6
　CHSW/BR CH4 .... 191 M5
　CHSW/BR CH4 .... 192 C6
　CONG CW12 .... 207 J1
　MPL/ROM SK6 .... 48 F6 🗓
　WARR WA1 .... 37 M5
Belgrave Cl *CHSW/BR* CH4 .... 191 C6
　LEIGH WN7 .... 24 C4 🗓
　WDN WA8 .... 53 L1
Belgrave Crs *OFTN* SK2 .... 47 G8
Belgrave Dr *EP* CH65 .... 94 F7
Belgrave Pl *CHSW/BR* CH4 .... 17 H9
Belgrave Rd *ALT* WA14 .... 61 J1
　CHSE CH3 .... 170 B4
　CW/SHV CW2 .... 18 C7
　IRL M44 .... 31 J7
　MCFLDS SK11 .... 138 C8
　NWCHE CW9 .... 130 A4
Belgrave St *CH/BCN* CH1 .... 17 J3
Belgravia Gdns
　HALE/TIMP WA15 .... 61 L4
Bellaport Rd *MKTDR* TF9 .... 275 G8 🗓
Bellard Dr *CHNE* CH2 .... 146 A8
Bell Av *MCFLDS* SK11 .... 162 F1
Bellcroft *WYTH/NTH* M22 .... 44 E4 🗓
Belldale Cl *HTNM* SK4 .... 46 A2
Bellemonte Rd
　FROD/HEL WA6 .... 99 H6 🗓
Belleville Av *WYTH/NTH* M22 .... 63 L4 🗓

Bellevue La *CHSE* CH3 .... 146 D8
Belle Vue Ter *SBCH* CW11 .... 204 B6
Bellfield Av *CHD/CHDH* SK8 .... 65 H3 🗓
Bellhouse La *WARRS* WA4 .... 55 K5
　WARRS WA4 .... 57 J3
Bell House Rd *WDN* WA8 .... 7 M3
Bellingham Dr *RUNC* WA7 .... 9 H7
Bell La *RAIN/WH* L35 .... 34 A2
　WARRS WA4 .... 38 E8
　WARRS WA4 .... 57 L1
Bell Meadow Ct *TPLY/KEL* CW6 .... 197 J2
Bellringer Cl *BIDD* ST8 .... 227 J5
Belmont Av *GOL/RIS/CU* WA3 .... 23 J3
　MCFLDN SK10 .... 137 J3
　SBCH CW11 .... 203 M5
　WARRS WA4 .... 56 F1
Belmont Cl *HTNM* SK4 .... 2 E2
Belmont Crs *WARRW/BUR* WA5 .... 35 M6
Belmont Dr *CHSW/BR* CH4 .... 168 B6
　MPL/ROM SK6 .... 49 H3
Belmont Rd *BRAM/HZG* SK7 .... 65 L7
　CHD/CHDH SK8 .... 45 H6
　HALE/TIMP WA15 .... 61 L2
　NWCHE CW9 .... 103 M3
　NWCHE CW9 .... 130 C5
　WDN WA8 .... 53 K2
Belmont St *HTNM* SK4 .... 2 D2
Belmont Wy *HTNM* SK4 .... 2 E2
Belper Dr *NTHM/RTH* M23 .... 45 M3
Belsay Dr *NTHM/RTH* M23 .... 44 A8
Belstone Av *NTHM/RTH* M23 .... 63 C1
Belstone Cl *BRAM/HZG* SK7 .... 65 M2
Belton Cl *WHITCH* SY13 .... 269 L5
Belton Rd *WHITCH* SY13 .... 269 L6
Belvedere Cl *CQ* CH5 .... 142 D7 🗓
　FROD/HEL WA6 .... 99 J3
Belvedere Dr *CH/BCN* CH1 .... 144 E8
　MPL/ROM SK6 .... 47 J1
Belvedere Rd *AIMK* WN4 .... 22 C1
　NEWLW WA12 .... 22 B8
Belvedere Ter *ALS/KID* ST7 .... 224 F5
Belvoir Av *BRAM/HZG* SK7 .... 66 E4
Belvoir Rd *WARRS* WA4 .... 56 B4
　WDN WA8 .... 7 K2
Bembridge Cl *WARRW/BUR* WA5 .... 35 J5
　WDN WA8 .... 33 M8
Bembridge Dr *MWCH* CW10 .... 179 J4
Bempton Cl *OFTN* SK2 .... 48 A7 🗓
Bemrose Av *ALT* WA14 .... 42 C6
Benbrook Wy *MCFLDS* SK11 .... 161 L3
Benchill Court Rd
　WYTH/NTH M22 .... 44 E8
Benchill Dr *WYTH/NTH* M22 .... 44 D7
Benchill Rd *WYTH/NTH* M22 .... 44 C6
Bendee Av *NSTN* CH64 .... 92 A5
Bendee Rd *NSTN* CH64 .... 91 M5
Bengal St *EDGY/DAV* SK3 .... 2 E8
Bennet Cl *NSTN* CH64 .... 93 G4
Bennet Rd *NWCHE* CW9 .... 130 D6
Bennett Av *WARR* WA1 .... 37 M6
Bennett Cl *CW/HAS* CW1 .... 19 K3
　EDGY/DAV SK3 .... 2 A7
Bennett Randle Cl *SBCH* CW11 .... 203 L5
Bennett's La *CQ* CH5 .... 166 B2
　MCFLDS SK11 .... 186 E6
　WDN WA8 .... 53 L3
Bennett St *EDGY/DAV* SK3 .... 2 A7
　WARR WA1 .... 5 H7
Benson Rd *GOL/RIS/CU* WA3 .... 38 D2
Benson St *BURS/TUN* ST6 .... 243 M7
Bentham Av *WARRW/BUR* WA5 .... 37 J1
Bentham Rd *GOL/RIS/CU* WA3 .... 30 A2
Bentinck Rd *ALT* WA14 .... 42 C8
Bentinck St *RUNC* WA7 .... 8 E1
Bent La *CONG* CW12 .... 206 F3
　GOL/RIS/CU WA3 .... 30 A2
　LYMM WA13 .... 40 C6
　NWCHW CW8 .... 127 H3
Bentley Dr *CW/HAS* CW1 .... 222 A7
Bentley Gv *WSFD* CW7 .... 177 J6
Bentley's Farm La *WARRS* WA4 .... 76 E7
Benton Dr *CHNE* CH2 .... 145 J8 🗓
　MPL/ROM SK6 .... 49 J4
Bents Av *MPL/ROM* SK6 .... 47 M1
Bentside Rd *POY/DIS* SK12 .... 68 D7
Benty Heath La *NSTN* CH64 .... 93 G1
Beresford Dl *AUD/MAD/W* CW3 .... 267 K5
Beresford St *WARR* WA1 .... 37 L5 🗓
Berisford Cl *HALE/TIMP* WA15 .... 42 E5
Berkeley Av *ALS/KID* ST7 .... 224 D7
Berkeley Cl *LEIGH* WN7 .... 24 C4
　OFTN SK2 .... 47 J4
Berkeley Crs *CW/SHV* CW2 .... 238 A4
Berkeley Ri *WSFD* CW7 .... 177 G4
Berkeley Rd *BRAM/HZG* SK7 .... 66 F1
Berkley Dr *CHSW/BR* CH4 .... 169 K6
Berkshire Cl *MCFLDN* SK10 .... 137 L2 🗓
Berkshire Dr *CONG* CW12 .... 184 D8 🗓
　IRL M44 .... 31 J7
　WARR WA1 .... 38 D5
Berlin Rd *EDGY/DAV* SK3 .... 46 D6
Bernard Av *WARRS* WA4 .... 56 D4
Berne Cl *BRAM/HZG* SK7 .... 46 E8
Bernisdale Rd *KNUT* WA16 .... 81 M8
Bernsdale Cl *CQ* CH5 .... 166 F1
Berrington Av *MCFLDS* SK11 .... 162 A8
Berrington Gv *AIMK* WN4 .... 22 A1
Berristall Rd *MCFLDN* SK10 .... 113 K8
Berry Cl *GTS/LS* CH66 .... 120 C1
Berrycroft La *MPL/ROM* SK6 .... 48 A1
Berry Dr *GTS/LS* CH66 .... 94 C8
Berry Rd *WDN* WA8 .... 6 A3
Berrystead *NWCHW* CW8 .... 129 H8
Berrywood Dr *RAIN/WH* L35 .... 32 F2
Bertram St *NEWLW* WA12 .... 26 F1
Berwick Av *HTNM* SK4 .... 45 L2 🗓
Berwick Cl *MCFLDS* SK11 .... 137 M2
　WARR WA1 .... 38 E6 🗓
Berwick Ct *HOLMCH* CW4 .... 181 H2 🗓
Berwick Gdns *GTS/LS* CH66 .... 94 B5
Berwick Rd *GTS/LS* CH66 .... 94 B6
Berwick Rd *GTS/LS* CH66 .... 94 A6
Berwyn Cl *CHD/CHDH* SK8 .... 46 B7
Berwyn Dr *GTS/LS* CH66 .... 94 A6
Bessancourt *HOLMCH* CW4 .... 181 J1
Bessemer Rd *IRL* M44 .... 31 M6
Beswick Cl *CHSE* CH3 .... 146 A5
Beswick Dr *CW/HAS* CW1 .... 221 K1
Beswick Rd *BURS/TUN* ST6 .... 243 M6

Beswicks La *WILM/AE* SK9 .... 109 J1
Beswicks Rd *NWCHW* CW8 .... 12 F1
Beswick St *MCFLDS* SK11 .... 14 D5 🗓
Betchton Cl *SBCH* CW11 .... 204 C5
Betchton Rd *SBCH* CW11 .... 223 J1
Betchworth Crs *RUNC* WA7 .... 73 K6
Betchworth Wy *MCFLDN* SK10 .... 112 C8
Betjeman Cl *WARRS* WA4 .... 37 M8 🗓
Betley Cl *CW/HAS* CW1 .... 19 L1
Betley Rd *NWCHE* CW9 .... 13 K8
Betley Hall Gdns
　AUD/MAD/W CW3 .... 255 G6
Betlymere Rd
　CHD/CHDH SK8 .... 45 M8 🗓
Betnor Av *STKP* SK1 .... 3 M6
Betony Cl *HLWD* L26 .... 50 E3
Betsyfield Dr *GOL/RIS/CU* WA3 .... 29 C5
Bettison Av *LEIGH* WN7 .... 25 J1
Betty's La *TPLY/KEL* CW6 .... 216 D3
Bevan Av *ALS/KID* ST7 .... 242 D6
Bevan Cl *WARRW/BUR* WA5 .... 36 D6
Bevan Pl *AUD/MAD/W* CW3 .... 267 L6
Beverley Av *WARRS* WA4 .... 56 D4
Beverley Rd *OFTN* SK2 .... 47 J4
　WARRW/BUR WA5 .... 36 C6
Beverley Wy *GTS/LS* CH66 .... 94 B5
　MCFLDN SK10 .... 112 C8
Bevin Av *GOL/RIS/CU* WA3 .... 25 H8
Bevyl Rd *NSTN* CH64 .... 91 H2
Bewley Ct *CHSE* CH3 .... 170 A5
Bewsey Farm Cl
　WARRW/BUR WA5 .... 36 D5 🗓
Bewsey Park Cl
　WARRW/BUR WA5 .... 4 C2
Bewsey Rd *WARRW/BUR* WA5 .... 4 C3
Bewsey St *WARR* WA1 .... 5 G6
　WARRN/WOL WA2 .... 4 F5
Bexhill Av *HALE/TIMP* WA15 .... 42 F6 🗓
　WARRN/WOL WA2 .... 28 B8
Bexhill Cl *SPK/HALE* L24 .... 50 B8
Bexhill Rd *EDGY/DAV* SK3 .... 46 E8
Bexington Dr *CW/HAS* CW1 .... 221 H4
Bexton Cl *CW/HAS* CW1 .... 221 H4
Bexton La *KNUT* WA16 .... 106 F5
Bexton Rd *KNUT* WA16 .... 106 F4
Bibby Av *WARR* WA1 .... 37 L6
Bibby's La *MCFLDS* SK11 .... 139 G3
Bibby St *ALS/KID* ST7 .... 224 E5
Bibury Av *WYTH/NTH* M22 .... 63 H1
Bickerton Av *FROD/HEL* WA6 .... 99 K5
Bickerton Cl *GOL/RIS/CU* WA3 .... 29 K8
Bickerton Dr *BRAM/HZG* SK7 .... 66 A8
Bickerton Rd *ALT* WA14 .... 42 B7
　MALPAS SY14 .... 247 L2
Bickerton Wy *NWCHE* CW9 .... 129 L8
Bickley Cl *CW/SHV* CW2 .... 253 L2
　RUNC WA7 .... 9 L5
　WARRN/WOL WA2 .... 37 M1
Bickley Town La *MALPAS* SY14 .... 247 L6
Bicknell Cl *WARRW/BUR* WA5 .... 36 B4
Bida La *CONG* CW12 .... 208 B4
Biddall Dr *NTHM/RTH* M23 .... 44 B6
Biddulph Av *OFTN* SK2 .... 47 J7
Biddulph Common Rd
　BIDD ST8 .... 209 G5
Biddulph Park Rd *BIDD* ST8 .... 209 G6
Biddulph Rd *ALS/KID* ST7 .... 226 E6
　BIDD ST8 .... 208 D7
　CONG CW12 .... 208 B3
Bideford Dr *NTHM/RTH* M23 .... 43 M5
Bideford Rd *OFTN* SK2 .... 47 J3
　WARRN/WOL WA2 .... 35 L8
Bidston Cl *CHNE* CH2 .... 145 K7
Bidston Rd *WILM/AE* SK9 .... 84 E2 🗓
Bidston Wy *CW/SHV* CW2 .... 220 E7
Bidvale Wy *CW/HAS* CW1 .... 221 J4
Big Field La *TPLY/KEL* CW6 .... 174 B5
Biggin St *WARRN/WOL* WA2 .... 37 L3 🗓
Bignall End Rd *ALS/KID* ST7 .... 242 A8
Billington Av *NEWLW* WA12 .... 22 B6
Billington Cl
　WARRW/BUR WA5 .... 35 L4 🗓
Billington Rd *WDN* WA8 .... 33 H8 🗓
Bilson Dr *EDGY/DAV* SK3 .... 46 B5
Bilton Cl *WDN* WA8 .... 53 L2
Bilton Wy *CW/SHV* CW2 .... 220 E7
Bingham Dr *NTHM/RTH* M23 .... 43 M6
Bings Rd *CHF/WBR* SK23 .... 89 L5
Bingswood Rd *CHF/WBR* SK23 .... 89 L5
Binney Wy *CW/HAS* CW1 .... 13 L3
Binyon Wy *CW/HAS* CW1 .... 222 A8
Birchall Av *BURS/TUN* ST6 .... 243 J7
　GOL/RIS/CU WA3 .... 24 D8
Birchall Moss La *NANT* CW5 .... 264 E2
Birchall St *GOL/RIS/CU* WA3 .... 29 G5
Birch Av *ALS/KID* ST7 .... 241 L1
　BIDD ST8 .... 227 G6
　CW/HAS CW1 .... 19 L2
　IRL M44 .... 31 K7
　MCFLDN SK10 .... 14 B3
　MPL/ROM SK6 .... 48 D2
　SALE M33 .... 43 H1 🗓
　WARRN/WOL WA2 .... 28 A8
　WILM/AE SK9 .... 83 M6
　WSFD CW7 .... 178 A3
Birch Brook Rd *LYMM* WA13 .... 40 B7
Birch Cl *CW/HAS* CW1 .... 19 L1
　HOLMCH CW4 .... 181 K1
Birch Ct *CONG* CW12 .... 206 F1
Birchdale *ALT* WA14 .... 61 J2
Birch Dl *AUD/MAD/W* CW3 .... 267 L6
Birchdale Cl *CHD/CHDH* SK8 .... 64 B2
Birchdale Crs *WARRS* WA4 .... 56 C4
Birchdale Rd *WARR* WA1 .... 38 A5
　WARRS WA4 .... 56 C5
Birch Dr *BRAM/HZG* SK7 .... 66 C2
Birchen Rd *HLWD* L26 .... 51 G5
Birchenwood Rd
　BURS/TUN ST6 .... 243 L4
Birches Croft Dr *MCFLDN* SK10 .... 137 M3
Birches La *NWCHE* CW9 .... 131 G3
The Birches *CHSW/BR* CH4 .... 190 B1
　CW/SHV CW2 .... 238 C4
Birchfield Av *ALS/KID* ST7 .... 224 F5 🗓
　WDN WA8 .... 7 H1
Birchfield Crs *CQ* CH5 .... 166 B1 🗓
Birchfield Rd *EDGY/DAV* SK3 .... 46 A5

LYMM WA13 .... 40 B8
WARRW/BUR WA5 .... 36 B7
WDN WA8 .... 7 H2
WDN WA8 .... 34 A8
WDN WA8 .... 53 C1 🗓
Birch Heath La *CHSE* CH3 .... 170 E4
Birch Heath Rd *TPLY/KEL* CW6 .... 197 H4
Birch Hl *FROD/HEL* WA6 .... 125 J4
Birchin Cl *NANT* CW5 .... 21 J4
Birchin Cl *NANT* CW5 .... 21 H4
Birch La *CW/SHV* CW2 .... 253 M2
　MWCH CW10 .... 178 F2
Birchmuir *CH/BCN* CH1 .... 17 F1
Birch Ri *CHNE* CH2 .... 145 K6
　CQ CH5 .... 166 B3
Birch Rd *CHD/CHDH* SK8 .... 45 G7
　CHSW/BR CH4 .... 168 F7
　CONG CW12 .... 206 F1
　GOL/RIS/CU WA3 .... 40 D1
　PART M31 .... 40 D1
　PART M31 .... 41 M1
　POY/DIS SK12 .... 86 F2
　RUNC WA7 .... 9 K6
Birch Tree Av *BRAM/HZG* SK7 .... 67 G3
Birch Tree Cl *WYTH/NTH* M22 .... 63 K1 🗓
Birch Tree Dr *WYTH/NTH* M22 .... 63 K1 🗓
Birch Tree La *ALS/KID* ST7 .... 226 B5
　HOLMCH CW4 .... 157 J4
　WARRS WA4 .... 76 F6
Birch Tree Rd
　GOL/RIS/CU WA3 .... 23 M4 🗓
Birchvale Av *MPL/ROM* SK6 .... 48 D1
Birchway *BRAM/HZG* SK7 .... 65 K5
Birch Wy *MCFLDN* SK10 .... 111 L6
　MPL/ROM SK6 .... 67 M5
Birchyards *WARRS* WA4 .... 56 E7
Birchwood Bvd
　GOL/RIS/CU WA3 .... 38 D2
Birchwood Cl *CHNE* CH2 .... 123 J1 🗓
　GTS/LS CH66 .... 120 D3 🗓
　LEIGH WN7 .... 24 F1
Birchwood Dr *KNUT* WA16 .... 132 D5
　NANT CW5 .... 21 H5
　WILM/AE SK9 .... 84 D4
Birchwood Park Av
　GOL/RIS/CU WA3 .... 29 K7
　WARRW/WOL WA3 .... 37 L4
Bird Hall Av *CHD/CHDH* SK8 .... 46 C8
Bird Hall La *EDGY/DAV* SK3 .... 46 B5
Bird Hall Rd *CHD/CHDH* SK8 .... 46 B7
Birdlip Dr *NTHM/RTH* M23 .... 63 C1
Birds La *CHSE* CH3 .... 214 E3
　TPLY/KEL CW6 .... 217 H4
Birdwell Dr *WARRW/BUR* WA5 .... 36 A7
Birkdale Cl *BRAM/HZG* SK7 .... 66 A5
　MCFLDN SK10 .... 112 C8
Birkdale Ct *NWCHE* CW9 .... 13 L2
Birkdale Dr *ALS/KID* ST7 .... 243 J1
　SALE M33 .... 42 E2
Birkdale Gdns *WSFD* CW7 .... 177 G2 🗓
Birkdale Rd *WARRW/BUR* WA5 .... 35 M8
　WDN WA8 .... 34 B7
Birkenhead Rd *NSTN* CH64 .... 92 E3
Birkenhead St *NWCHE* CW9 .... 130 E4
Birkett Av *EP* CH65 .... 121 J2
Birkin Cl *KNUT* WA16 .... 81 K8 🗓
Birkinheath La *ALT* WA14 .... 61 H8
Birkworth Ct *OFTN* SK2 .... 47 K6 🗓
Birley Cl *HALE/TIMP* WA15 .... 42 F5
Birley Pk *DID/WITH* M20 .... 44 F1
Birley St *NEWLW* WA12 .... 22 B8
Birling Dr *NTHM/RTH* M23 .... 44 B8
Birnam Dr *RAIN/WH* L35 .... 33 K2
Birstall Ct *NANT* CW5 .... 73 K5
Birtles Cl *CHD/CHDH* SK8 .... 45 M7
　SBCH CW11 .... 204 C5
Birtles La *MCFLDN* SK10 .... 136 D3
Birtlespool Rd *CHD/CHDH* SK8 .... 45 M8
Birtles Rd *MCFLDN* SK10 .... 137 K3
　WARRN/WOL WA2 .... 37 J3
Birtwistle Rd *NWCHE* CW9 .... 130 D6
Bisham Pk *RUNC* WA7 .... 74 D2
Bishop Bennet Wy *CHSE* CH3 .... 195 L8
　CHSE CH3 .... 229 J2
　MALPAS SY14 .... 244 F8
　MALPAS SY14 .... 257 L1
　WHITCH SY13 .... 259 L4
　WHITCH SY13 .... 269 K1
Bishopdale Cl *WARRW/BUR* WA5 .... 35 M5
Bishopdale Dr *RAIN/WH* L35 .... 33 K2
Bishop Dr *WARRN/WOL* WA2 .... 32 D1
Bishopgates Dr *NWCHE* CW9 .... 129 L8 🗓
Bishop Rd *MCFLDN* SK10 .... 113 C5
　NWCHE CW9 .... 242 D4
Bishop's Cl *ALS/KID* ST7 .... 242 D4
　ALT WA14 .... 61 H3
　CHD/CHDH SK8 .... 46 A7
Bishops Ct *CHSW/BR* CH4 .... 167 J8
　WARRN/WOL WA2 .... 50 B2 🗓
　WLTN L25 .... 50 B2 🗓
Bishops Gdns *EP* CH65 .... 10 B7
Bishop St *CHNE* CH2 .... 17 L1
　STKP SK1 .... 3 J5
Bishops Wy *WDN* WA8 .... 53 K1
Bishops Wd *NANT* CW5 .... 251 M1
Bishopton Dr *MCFLDS* SK11 .... 137 M4
Bisley St *NTHM/RTH* M23 .... 43 M6
Bispham Rd
　WARRW/BUR WA5 .... 36 B8 🗓
Bittern Cl *POY/DIS* SK12 .... 86 A1
　RUNC WA7 .... 74 D4
　WARRN/WOL WA2 .... 37 K1 🗓
Bittern Gv *MCFLDN* SK10 .... 14 B2

Blackberry Gv *HLWD* L26 .... 50 D2
Blackbird Wy *BIDD* ST8 .... 227 L4
Blackboards La *GTS/LS* CH66 .... 94 A5
Blackbrook Av *CQ* CH5 .... 166 C2
　WARRN/WOL WA2 .... 37 M2
Blackbrook Rd *WDN* WA8 .... 52 C1
Blackburn Cl
　GOL/RIS/CU WA3 .... 23 M4 🗓
Blackburne Av *WDN* WA8 .... 52 B7
Blackburne Cl
　WARRN/WOL WA2 .... 38 C2 🗓
Blackburne Dr *WLTN* L25 .... 50 D5
Blackcarr Rd *NTHM/RTH* M23 .... 44 B7
Blackcroft Av *NWCHW* CW8 .... 129 C2
Blackden La *HOLMCH* CW4 .... 134 A8
　KNUT WA16 .... 134 A5
　MCFLDS SK11 .... 159 M4
Black Denton's Pl *WDN* WA8 .... 7 M3
Black Diamond St *CH/BCN* CH1 .... 17 H2
Blackdown Cl *GTS/LS* CH66 .... 94 A7 🗓
Blackeys La *NSTN* CH64 .... 91 L4
Black Firs La *CONG* CW12 .... 183 L7
Black Friars *CH/BCN* CH1 .... 16 F7
Blackheath La *RUNC* WA7 .... 54 E8
Blackhill La *KNUT* WA16 .... 106 F4
Blackhurst Brow *MCFLDN* SK10 .... 111 H1
Blackhurst St *WARR* WA1 .... 5 H7
Black La *MCFLDN* SK10 .... 15 J3
Blackledge Cl
　WARRN/WOL WA2 .... 38 A1 🗓
Blackley Cl *MCFLDN* SK10 .... 112 B8 🗓
　WARRS WA4 .... 56 D1
Black Lion La *GTS/LS* CH66 .... 94 B5
Blacklock Hall Rd *SPK/HALE* L24 .... 79 F2 🗓
Blackmore Gv *WHITCH* SY13 .... 270 A4
Black Moss Rd *ALT* WA14 .... 41 L5
Black Park Rd *WHITCH* SY13 .... 270 C4
Blackrod Av *SPK/HALE* L24 .... 70 C1
Blackshaw Cl *CONG* CW12 .... 208 B3
Blackshaw Dr *WARRW/BUR* WA5 .... 36 A5
Blackshaw La *WILM/AE* SK9 .... 109 M3
　EDGY/DAV SK3 .... 2 F7 🗓
　MCFLDS SK11 .... 14 F7
Blackstone Rd *OFTN* SK2 .... 47 K7
Blackthorn Cl *CHSE* CH3 .... 170 A7
　CHSW/BR CH4 .... 190 B1 🗓
Blackthorne Av *GTS/LS* CH66 .... 121 G4
Blackthorne Dr *SALE* M33 .... 42 C3
Blackwell La *MWCH* CW10 .... 179 K6 🗓
Blackwood Dr *NTHM/RTH* M23 .... 43 K4
Blacon Av *CH/BCN* CH1 .... 144 F7
Blacon Hall Rd *CH/BCN* CH1 .... 144 F7
Blacon Point Rd *CH/BCN* CH1 .... 168 D1
Bladen Cl *CHD/CHDH* SK8 .... 46 A8
Bladon Cl *NWCHE* CW9 .... 129 L8 🗓
Bladon Crs *ALS/KID* ST7 .... 224 C7
Blagg Av *NANT* CW5 .... 20 B9
Blair Cl *BRAM/HZG* SK7 .... 66 C4
　SALE M33 .... 42 C3
Blair Dr *WDN* WA8 .... 52 B1
Blairgowrie Dr *MCFLDN* SK10 .... 112 B8
Blakeacre Cl *HLWD* L26 .... 50 F6 🗓
Blakeacre Rd *HLWD* L26 .... 50 F6
Blake Cl *CH/BCN* CH1 .... 144 F6
　CW/SHV CW2 .... 237 M3 🗓
Blakeden La *WSFD* CW7 .... 176 D3
Blake Dr *OFTN* SK2 .... 47 L5
Blake La *WARRN/WOL* WA2 .... 152 A2
Blakeley La *KNUT* WA16 .... 82 E5
Blakelow Bank *MCFLDS* SK11 .... 15 M8
Blakelow Cl *MWCH* CW10 .... 179 H5
Blakelow Crs *NANT* CW5 .... 252 F1
Blakelow Rd *MCFLDS* SK11 .... 15 L8
Blakemere Av *SALE* M33 .... 43 L1 🗓
Blakemere Ct *GTS/LS* CH66 .... 10 E4
Blakemere La *FROD/HEL* WA6 .... 126 D4
Blakemere Wy *SBCH* CW11 .... 203 M4
Blake St *CONG* CW12 .... 207 J1 🗓
Blandford Dr *MCFLDN* SK10 .... 137 M4 🗓
　NWCHE CW9 .... 153 L1
Blandford Rd *HTNM* SK4 .... 46 B2
　WARRW/BUR WA5 .... 36 B7
The Blakeney *NANT* CW5 .... 20 E7
Blantern Rd *CHSW/BR* CH4 .... 190 A5
Blantyre St *RUNC* WA7 .... 72 F1
Blaven Cl *EDGY/DAV* SK3 .... 46 F7
Blay Cl *WLTN* L25 .... 50 D4
Blaze Hl *MCFLDN* SK10 .... 113 K4
Blazemoss Bank *OFTN* SK2 .... 47 K7
Bleak Hey Rd *WYTH/NTH* M22 .... 63 M2
Bleasdale Rd *CW/HAS* CW1 .... 221 H3
　NEWLW WA12 .... 22 B8
　WYTH/NTH M22 .... 63 C2
Bleatarn Rd *STKP* SK1 .... 47 H5
Bleeding Wolf La *ALS/KID* ST7 .... 225 L7
Blenheim Cl *ALT* WA14 .... 61 K2
　CQ CH5 .... 237 L4 🗓
　CW/SHV CW2 .... 237 L4 🗓
　MCFLDN SK10 .... 14 B3
　NWCHE CW9 .... 129 M8
　POY/DIS SK12 .... 66 F8 🗓
　WARRN/WOL WA2 .... 37 M2 🗓
　WILM/AE SK9 .... 84 D5
Blenheim Ct *ALS/KID* ST7 .... 224 C7
Blenheim Gdns *WSFD* CW7 .... 177 J5
Blenheim Rd *AIMK* WN4 .... 22 D2
　CHD/CHDH SK8 .... 65 H2
Blenheim Wy *SPK/HALE* L24 .... 70 B1
Bletchley Rd *HTNM* SK4 .... 45 L1
Bloomsbury Gv
　HALE/TIMP WA15 .... 43 G6
Bloomsbury La
　HALE/TIMP WA15 .... 43 G6
Bloomsbury Wy *WDN* WA8 .... 52 D1 🗓
Bloom St *EDGY/DAV* SK3 .... 2 B8
Blossom Hts *NWCHW* CW8 .... 12 C5
Blossom Rd *PART* M31 .... 40 E2
Blossoms Hey *CHD/CHDH* SK8 .... 64 E8
Blossoms La *BRAM/HZG* SK7 .... 85 G2
Blossoms St *OFTN* SK2 .... 46 F5 🗓
Bluebell Cl *BIDD* ST8 .... 227 L5
　CHSE CH3 .... 170 B6
　MCFLDN SK10 .... 138 D1 🗓
　NWCHW CW8 .... 129 L3
Bluebell Ct *RUNC* WA7 .... 73 M8 🗓
Bluebell Cl *CHD/CHDH* SK8 .... 45 K8 🗓

Bluebell La *MCFLDN* SK10 .... 138 C1
Bluebell Ms *MCFLDN* SK10 .... 138 D1 🅰
Bluebell Wy *WILM/AE* SK9 .... 84 C3
Blueberry Rd *ALT* WA14 .... 61 G2
Blue Cap La *MALPAS* SY14 ...... 246 D5
Bluecoat St *WARRN/WOL* WA2 .... 5 D3
Blue Hatch *FROD/HEL* WA6 .... 99 J4
Bluestone Dr *HTNM* SK4 .... 45 L1
Blundell's La *RAIN/WH* L35 .... 33 C3
Blyth Cl *HALE/TIMP* WA15 .... 43 K6
  MCFLDN SK10 .... 137 L3 🅰
  RUNC WA7 .... 74 D7
Blythe Av *BRAM/HZG* SK7 .... 65 J6
  CONG CW12 .... 207 C2
  WDN WA8 .... 13 H7
The Blythings *TPLY/KEL* CW6 .... 197 J1 🅰
Boathorse Rd *ALS/KID* ST7 ...... 242 F4
  BURS/TUN ST6 .... 243 C6
Boathouse La *NSTN* CH64 .... 91 H2
Boat La *WYTH/NTH* M22 .... 44 E3
Boat Stage *LYMM* WA13 .... 58 E1
Bob's La *IRL* M44 .... 31 K8
Boddens Hill Rd *HTNM* SK4 .... 46 A3
Bodden St *GOL/RIS/CU* WA3 ...... 24 A3
Boden Dr *NANT* CW5 .... 237 K8
Boden St *MCFLDN* SK11 .... 15 H5
Bodiam Cl *EP* CH65 .... 121 L2
Bodlondeb *FLINT* CH6 .... 116 B8 🅰
Bodmin Cl *MCFLDN* SK10 .... 137 L3 🅰
Bodmin Ct *RUNC* WA7 .... 74 B6 🅰
Bodmin Dr *BRAM/HZG* SK7 .... 65 L5
Bodmin Wy *HLWD* L26 .... 50 E4
Bognor Cl *SPK/HALE* L24 .... 50 B8 🅰
Bognor Rd *EDGY/DAV* SK3 .... 46 E8
Bohars *TPLY/KEL* CW6 .... 197 K4
Bolam Cl *NTHM/RTH* M23 .... 43 M3
Bolderstone Pl *WLTN* SK2 .... 47 L8
Bold La *WARRW/BUR* WA5 .... 26 C5
Bold Pl *CH/BCN* CH1 .... 17 H4
Bold Sq *CH/BCN* CH1 .... 17 J4
Bold St *ALT* WA14 .... 61 K1
  CW/HAS CW1 .... 222 C8
  RUNC WA7 .... 9 J1
  SBCH CW11 .... 204 B6
  WARR WA1 .... 4 F7
  WDN WA8 .... 7 G7
Bolesworth Hill Rd *CHSE* CH3 .... 214 D7
  CHSE CH3 .... 231 J2
Bolesworth Rd *CHNE* CH2 .... 145 M6
  CHSE CH3 .... 214 A4
Boleyn Cl *CH/BCN* CH1 .... 144 E6
Boleyn Ct *RUNC* WA7 .... 74 C1
Bollin Av *ALT* WA14 .... 61 H4
  WSFD CW7 .... 178 B2
Bollinbarn *MCFLDN* SK10 .... 14 C1
Bollinbarn Dr *MCFLDN* SK10 ...... 14 B1
  MCFLDN SK10 .... 138 A2
Bollinbrook Rd *MCFLDN* SK10 .... 14 C2
Bollin Cl *ALS/KID* ST7 .... 240 F1
  GOL/RIS/CU WA3 .... 30 A2
  LYMM WA13 .... 40 A8
  SBCH CW11 .... 203 L5
  WSFD CW7 .... 178 B2
Bollin Dr *ALT* WA14 .... 42 E4
  CONG CW12 .... 207 M3
  LYMM WA13 .... 39 M8
  SALE M33 .... 43 H2
Bollin Gv *BIDD* ST8 .... 227 L3
  MCFLDN SK10 .... 111 M5
Bollington Av *NWCHE* CW9 .... 13 L8
Bollington Rd *MCFLDN* SK10 ..... 135 M2
Bollington Rd *MCFLDN* SK10 ..... 112 D6
Bollinhead La *MCFLDS* SK11 ..... 163 K2
Bollin Hl *WILM/AE* SK9 .... 84 D5
Bollin Ms *MCFLDN* SK10 .... 112 A5 🅰
Bollin Sq *ALT* WA14 .... 61 H3 🅰
Bollinway *HALE/TIMP* WA15 ..... 62 A4
Bollin Wy *HALE/TIMP* WA15 ..... 112 A7
Bollinwood Cha *WILM/AE* SK9 .. 84 D5
Bolshaw Farm La
  CHD/CHDH SK8 .... 64 C6
Bolshaw Rd *CHD/CHDH* SK8 ..... 64 B6
Bolton Av *BNG/LEV* M19 .... 45 K2
  CHD/CHDH SK8 .... 65 H6
  WARRS WA4 .... 37 M8 🅰
Bolton Cl *GOL/RIS/CU* WA3 ..... 24 B4
  POY/DIS SK12 .... 66 D8
Bombay Rd *EDGY/DAV* SK3 ...... 46 C5
Bomish La *MCFLDS* SK11 .... 134 D8
Bonar Cl *EDGY/DAV* SK3 .... 2 A7
Bonar Rd *EDGY/DAV* SK3 .... 2 A8
Boncarn Dr *NTHM/RTH* M23 .... 44 A8
Bond Cl *WARRW/BUR* WA5 ...... 36 D8
Bond St *BURS/TUN* ST6 .... 243 K8
  MCFLDS SK11 .... 14 E7
  NWCHW CW8 .... 129 K3
Bongs Rd *OFTN* SK2 .... 47 M5
Bonington Ri *MPL/ROM* SK6 .... 49 H4
Bonis Crs *OFTN* SK2 .... 47 J8
Bonis Hall La *MCFLDN* SK10 .... 112 A2
Bonnywell Rd *LEIGH* WN7 ...... 24 F1
Bonville Cha *ALT* WA14 .... 42 A8
Bonville Rd *ALT* WA14 .... 42 A7
Booth Av *CHSE* CH3 .... 148 C5
  SBCH CW11 .... 204 D6
  TPLY/KEL CW6 .... 175 M5
Boothbank La *ALT* WA14 .... 60 A6
Booth Bed La *HOLMCH* CW4 .... 157 J3
  KNUT WA16 .... 133 H8
  KNUT WA16 .... 157 J1
Boothby St *MCFLDN* SK10 ...... 14 E4 🅰
  OFTN SK2 .... 47 J8
Boothfield Rd *WYTH/NTH* M22 .. 44 C6
Boothfields *KNUT* WA16 .... 107 J2
Booth La *MWCH* CW10 .... 179 K5
Booth Rd *ALT* WA14 .... 61 L2
  NWCHW CW8 .... 129 G8
  WILM/AE SK9 .... 84 A3
Boothsdale *TPLY/KEL* CW6 ..... 173 L1
Booths Hill Cl *LYMM* WA13 ..... 58 D2 🅰
Booth's Hill La *LYMM* WA13 .... 58 C1
Booth's Hill Rd *LYMM* WA13 .... 58 C1
Booth's La *LYMM* WA13 .... 58 B2 🅰
Boothsmere Cl *SBCH* CW11 .... 203 M4
Booth St *CONG* CW12 .... 207 J2

EDGY/DAV SK3 .... 2 F9
NEWLW WA12 .... 27 G1 🅰
WARRW/BUR WA5 .... 4 A9
Border Wy *CHSE* CH3 .... 170 C3
Bordley Wk *NTHM/RTH* M23 .... 43 L3
Bordon Rd *EDGY/DAV* SK3 ...... 46 B5
Borough Gv *FLINT* CH6 .... 116 B6
Borough Rd *CONG* CW12 .... 207 M1
  HALE/TIMP WA15 .... 42 E8
Borron Rd *NEWLW* WA12 .... 22 B7
Borron St *STKP* SK1 .... 3 K3
Borrowdale Av *CHD/CHDH* SK8 . 45 H8
  WARRN/WOL WA2 .... 37 H1
Borrowdale Cl *CW/SHV* CW2 ... 237 L1 🅰
  FROD/HEL WA6 .... 99 K4
Borrowdale Rd *OFTN* SK2 ...... 47 H5
  WDN WA8 .... 52 C4
Borth Av *OFTN* SK2 .... 47 J5
Boscombe Dr *BRAM/HZG* SK7 .. 66 C2
Bosden Av *BRAM/HZG* SK7 .... 66 E1
Bosden Cl *WILM/AE* SK9 .... 64 D7
Bosden Fold *STKP* SK1 .... 3 G7
Bosdenfold Rd *BRAM/HZG* SK7 . 66 E1 🅰
Bosden Hall Rd *BRAM/HZG* SK7 . 66 E1
Bosley Cl *MWCH* CW10 .... 179 J6
  WILM/AE SK9 .... 84 D2
Bosley Dr *POY/DIS* SK12 .... 87 G1 🅰
Bosley Gv *BURS/TUN* ST6 ...... 243 J5
Bosley Rd *EDGY/DAV* SK3 ...... 46 A4
Bosley Vw *CONG* CW12 .... 208 B3
Bossington Cl *OFTN* SK2 .... 47 J4
Bostock Gn *EP* CH65 .... 94 F7
Bostock Rd *MCFLDS* SK11 ...... 137 L5
  MWCH CW10 .... 154 D8
  WSFD CW7 .... 154 A8
Boston Av *RUNC* WA7 .... 9 K6
Boston Cl *BRAM/HZG* SK7 ..... 65 K5
  GOL/RIS/CU WA3 .... 24 B8
Boswell Av *WARRS* WA4 .... 56 B2
Botany Rd *SPK/HALE* L24 ...... 50 C8
Boteler Av *WARRW/BUR* WA5 .. 4 C3
Bottoms La *CHSW/BR* CH4 .... 17 K8
Boughton *CHSE* CH3 .... 17 L5
Boughton Hall Av *CHSE* CH3 ... 170 A3
Boughton Hall Dr *CHSE* CH3 ... 170 B3
Boulder Dr *NTHM/RTH* M23 .... 63 G2
The Boulevard
  BRAM/HZG SK7 .... 66 E2 🅰
  CHSW/BR CH4 .... 190 C1
  EP CH65 .... 94 F8
Boulting Av *WARRW/BUR* WA5 . 36 F2
Boulton Cl *SBCH* CW11 .... 223 J1
Boundary Dr *WLTN* L25 .... 50 D6
Boundary Farm Rd *HLWD* L26 . 50 D6
Boundary Gv *SALE* M33 .... 43 M2 🅰
Boundary La *CHSW/BR* CH4 ... 168 D7
  CONG CW12 .... 208 A4
  KNUT WA16 .... 134 D5
  MALPAS SY14 .... 256 E4
  MCFLDS SK11 .... 159 K5
Boundary La North
  NWCHW CW8 .... 151 M2
Boundary La South
  NWCHW CW8 .... 151 M2
Boundary Pk *NSTN* CH64 ...... 91 K4
Boundary Rd *CHD/CHDH* SK8 .. 45 M6
Boundary St *NWCHE* CW9 ...... 130 D2
Bourne Av *GOL/RIS/CU* WA3 .. 23 K4
Bourne Cl *NWCHW* CW8 .... 128 E5
Bournemouth Cl *RUNC* WA7 ... 74 D6 🅰
Bourne St *ALS/KID* ST7 .... 242 F2
Bourne St *ALS/KID* ST7 .... 226 C5
  WILM/AE SK9 .... 83 M6
Bourton Rd *WLTN* L25 .... 50 B6
Bouverie St *CH/BCN* CH1 ...... 16 E2
Bowden Cl *CONG* CW12 .... 183 M8
  GOL/RIS/CU WA3 .... 24 F8
  LEIGH WN7 .... 25 H2 🅰
Bowden Crs *NM/HAY* SK22 .... 69 K4
Bowden Dr *NWCHE* CW9 ...... 130 C4
Bowden La *MPL/ROM* SK6 ..... 48 E5
Bowden St *BRAM/HZG* SK7 ... 66 E1 🅰
Bowden View La *KNUT* WA16 .. 79 M2
Bowdon Cl *WARR* WA1 .... 37 M4 🅰
Bowdon Ri *ALT* WA14 .... 61 K2
Bowdon Rd *ALT* WA14 .... 61 J1
Bowen Cl *BRAM/HZG* SK7 ..... 65 M7 🅰
  WDN WA8 .... 33 K8 🅰
Bowen Cooke Av *CW/HAS* ... 18 A1
  CW/HAS CW1 .... 221 G6
Bowen St *CW/SHV* CW2 .... 18 A5
Bower Av *BRAM/HZG* SK7 ..... 66 D3
  HTNM SK4 .... 2 B2
Bower Crs *WARRS* WA4 .... 76 D2
Bower End La
  AUD/MAD/W CW3 .... 267 K6
Bowerfield Av *BRAM/HZG* SK7 . 66 E4
Bowerfield Crs *BRAM/HZG* SK7 . 66 E4
Bowerfold La *HTNM* SK4 ...... 2 B3
Bower Rd *HALE/TIMP* WA15 ... 61 L3
Bower St *WDN* WA8 .... 7 L2
Bowery Av *CHD/CHDH* SK8 .... 64 F6
Bowe's Gate Rd *TPLY/KEL* CW6 . 217 H2
Bowfell Cl *BEB* CH63 .... 93 K1 🅰
Bowfell Dr *MPL/ROM* SK6 ..... 67 L4
Bow Green Rd *ALT* WA14 ..... 61 G3
Bowhill La *AUD/MAD/W* CW3 . 255 J6
Bowkers Cl *SBCH* CW11 ...... 222 F4
Bowkers La *WHITCH* SY13 .... 268 D6
Bowland Av *GOL/RIS/CU* WA3 . 23 J3 🅰
  STHEL WA9 .... 34 A1
Bowland Cl *GOL/RIS/CU* WA3 . 30 B7 🅰
  OFTN SK2 .... 47 L7
  RUNC WA7 .... 73 L7
Bowland Cft *CW/HAS* CW1 ... 221 H3 🅰
Bowland Ri *WSFD* CW7 .... 177 H5
Bowland Rd *NTHM/RTH* M23 .. 43 M6
Bowler St *ALT* WA14 .... 61 G4
Bowley Av *WYTH/NTH* M22 ... 63 G4
Bowling Green Ct *NANT* CW5 . 20 F6 🅰
  NWCHW CW8 .... 12 F1
Bowman Av *WARRS* WA4 ..... 38 A7
Bramble Cl *CHSE* CH3 .... 170 A5
  MCFLDN SK10 .... 138 B2
  MWCH CW10 .... 179 L2
  WARRW/BUR WA5 .... 54 E1
Bowmont Cl *CHD/CHDH* SK8 .. 46 A8

Bowness Av *CHD/CHDH* SK8 .. 65 H3
  IRL M44 .... 31 K8
  WARRN/WOL WA2 .... 37 J2
  WSFD CW7 .... 177 K2
Bowness Cl *HOLMCH* CW4 .... 181 G1
Bowness Ct *CONG* CW12 ...... 207 C3
Bowness Rd *CW/SHV* CW2 .... 237 K1
Bowood Ct *WARRN/WOL* WA2 . 28 A8 🅰
Bowring Dr *NSTN* CH64 .... 91 H3
Bow St *LEIGH* WN7 .... 25 H1
Bowsey Wood Rd
  AUD/MAD/W CW3 .... 267 K3
Bow St *EDGY/DAV* SK3 .... 2 A7
Bowyer Av *NANT* CW5 .... 20 F5
Boxgrove Cl *WDN* WA8 .... 53 H1 🅰
Boxhill Dr *NTHM/RTH* M23 .... 44 A3 🅰
Box La *CONG* CW12 .... 206 F1
Boxmoor Cl *CHSW/BR* CH4 ... 169 G7
Box Tree Ms *MCFLDN* SK11 ... 14 A6
Boydell Av *WARRS* WA4 ...... 57 H2 🅰
Boydell Wy *CHSW/BR* CH4 ... 191 G5
Boyle Av *WARRN/WOL* WA2 ... 37 L3
Brabant Rd *CHD/CHDH* SK8 ... 65 H2
Brabyns Av *MPL/ROM* SK6 .... 48 D1
Brabyns Brow *MPL/ROM* SK6 . 49 C5
Bracadale Dr *EDGY/DAV* SK3 . 46 E7
Bracken Cl *ALS/KID* ST7 ...... 224 F4
  CHSW/BR CH4 .... 190 C1
  GOL/RIS/CU WA3 .... 29 J7
  MCFLDN SK10 .... 137 M3 🅰
  MPL/ROM SK6 .... 49 J5
Brackendale *CHNE* CH2 ...... 123 H1
  RUNC WA7 .... 75 K4
Brackendale Rd *CO* CH5 ...... 166 D1
Bracken Dr *NTHM/RTH* M23 .. 44 B7
Brackenfield Wy *WSFD* CW7 .. 177 G4
Brackenlea Pl *EDGY/DAV* SK3 . 46 D7 🅰
Bracken La *GTS/LS* CH66 ..... 94 E8
Bracken Wy *FROD/HEL* WA6 .. 99 J6
  KNUT WA16 .... 107 L4
  NWCHE CW9 .... 103 J5
  NWCHE CW9 .... 130 C1
  NWCHW CW8 .... 129 H1
Brackenwood Cl *CW/SHV* CW2 . 238 B4
Brackenwood Dr
  CHD/CHDH SK8 .... 45 K8 🅰
Brackenwood Gv
  RAIN/WH L35 .... 32 F1 🅰
Brackenwood Ms
  WILM/AE SK9 .... 84 E4 🅰
Brackley Av *IRL* M44 .... 31 K6
Brackley St *RUNC* WA7 .... 8 E1
  WARRS WA4 .... 56 E3
Bradburn Rd *IRL* M44 .... 31 L5
Bradburns La *NWCHW* CW8 .. 129 H6
Bradbury Av *ALT* WA14 .... 42 A7 🅰
Bradbury Gdns *CONG* CW12 .. 207 M3 🅰
Bradbury Rd *WSFD* CW7 ..... 178 A1
Bradda Mt *BRAM/HZG* SK7 ... 65 M2
Braddan Av *SALE* M33 .... 43 J1 🅰
Braddon Cl *NWCHE* CW9 ..... 129 M8
Bradeley Green La
  WHITCH SY13 .... 259 M6
Bradeley Hall Rd *CW/HAS* CW1 . 222 C8
Bradeley Rd *CW/HAS* CW1 ... 222 C8
Bradfield La *MCFLDN* SK10 ... 110 A6
Bradford La *WSFD* CW7 ...... 153 L5
Bradford St *CHSW/BR* CH4 ... 17 H9
Bradgate Av *CHD/CHDH* SK8 . 64 D3
Bradgate Cl *NTHM/RTH* M22 . 44 E4
Bradgate Rd *ALT* WA14 ...... 42 A7
  SALE M33 .... 43 H2 🅰
Bradlegh Rd *NEWLW* WA12 .. 27 L2
Bradley Bvd *WARRW/BUR* WA5 . 36 B6
Bradley Cl *HALE/TIMP* WA15 . 42 E5
  MWCH CW10 .... 179 H5
Bradley Farm La *WHITCH* SY13 . 259 J5
Bradley Fold *RAIN/WH* L35 ... 32 A4
Bradley La *FROD/HEL* WA6 ... 99 K6
  WARRW/BUR WA5 .... 26 F2
Bradley St *MCFLDS* SK11 .... 15 K8 🅰
Bradley Wy *WDN* WA8 .... 7 L3
Bradnor Rd *WYTH/NTH* M22 .. 44 D5
Bradshaw Av *CHSW/BR* CH4 . 168 B5
Bradshaw Crs *MPL/ROM* SK6 . 49 G5 🅰
Bradshaw Hall La
  CHD/CHDH SK8 .... 64 D4
Bradshaw La *LYMM* WA13 .... 59 K1
  WARRS WA4 .... 57 H1
Bradshaw Rd *MPL/ROM* SK6 . 48 F5
Bradshaw St *WDN* WA8 ...... 7 H1 🅰
Bradwall Rd *SBCH* CW11 .... 204 B5
Bradwall St *SBCH* CW11 ..... 204 B5
Bradwell Cl *EP* CH65 .... 95 G8
Bradwell Dr *CHD/CHDH* SK8 . 64 C5
Bradwell Gv *CONG* CW12 .... 207 M2
Bradwell Rd *BRAM/HZG* SK7 . 66 E4
  GOL/RIS/CU WA3 .... 23 L5
Braemar Av *NWCHE* CW9 .... 130 C5
Braemar Ct *CHSE* CH3 .... 170 C1
Braemar Cl *CW/SHV* CW2 .... 237 L4 🅰
  HOLMCH CW4 .... 181 J2
  RAIN/WH L35 .... 32 F1 🅰
  WARRN/WOL WA2 .... 38 A1 🅰
Braemar Dr *SALE* M33 .... 42 C2
Braemar Rd *BRAM/HZG* SK7 . 66 F1
Braeside Av *CO* CH5 .... 166 C2
Braeside Cl *GTS/LS* CH66 .... 94 C7 🅰
  MCFLDS SK11 .... 15 L8
  OFTN SK2 .... 47 M7
Braidwood Av *KNUT* WA16 ... 107 J1 🅰
Brains La *TPLY/KEL* CW6 ..... 198 A7
Braintree Rd *WYTH/NTH* M22 . 63 L4
Braithwaite Cl *RAIN/WH* L35 . 33 J1 🅰
  RUNC WA7 .... 73 K7 🅰
Braithwaite Rd *GOL/RIS/CU* WA3 . 23 K3
Brakeley La *NWCHW* CW8 ... 102 D8
Brakenwood Ms *WARRS* WA4 . 57 J3 🅰
Brakespeare St *BURS/TUN* ST6 . 243 J5
The Brake *ALS/KID* ST7 ...... 226 B5
Brake Village *ALS/KID* ST7 ... 226 B5
Bramall Cl *SBCH* CW11 ...... 204 C5

Bramble Lea *AUD/MAD/W* CW3 . 267 L6
The Brambles *CQ* CH5 .... 142 B6
  CW/HAS CW1 .... 222 B8
  NWCHE CW9 .... 130 C1
Bramble Wy *RUNC* WA7 ..... 73 L8 🅰
Brambling Cl *OFTN* SK2 ...... 48 A8
  RUNC WA7 .... 73 L7 🅰
Brambling Pk *HLWD* L26 ..... 50 E3
Brambling Wy
  GOL/RIS/CU WA3 .... 23 L4 🅰
Bramcote Av *NTHM/RTH* M23 . 44 B6 🅰
Bramhall Cl *HALE/TIMP* WA15 . 43 K6 🅰
  SALE M33 .... 43 L1
  SPK/HALE L24 .... 70 E2 🅰
  WSFD CW7 .... 177 H3
Bramhall Dr *HOLMCH* CW4 ... 181 G1
  PS/BROM CH62 .... 93 M1
Bramhall La South
  BRAM/HZG SK7 .... 66 E5
  OFTN SK2 .... 46 F6
Bramhall Moor La
  BRAM/HZG SK7 .... 66 B3
Bramhall Park Rd
  BRAM/HZG SK7 .... 65 J3
Bramhall Rd *CW/SHV* CW2 ... 237 M2
Bramhalls Pk *NWCHE* CW9 .. 129 J1
Bramhall St *WARRW/BUR* WA5 . 4 B7
Bramham Rd *MPL/ROM* SK6 . 48 F8
Bramley Cl *BRAM/HZG* SK7 .. 65 L6 🅰
  GTS/LS CH66 .... 120 F4 🅰
  WILM/AE SK9 .... 83 K8
Bramley Crs *HTNM* SK4 ...... 46 B3
Bramley Dr *BRAM/HZG* SK7 .. 65 L6
Brampton Av *MCFLDN* SK10 .. 14 A2 🅰
Brampton Rd *STHEL* WA9 .... 26 B1
Bramshaw Wy *BRAM/HZG* SK7 . 65 M2
Bramshill Cl *GOL/RIS/CU* WA3 . 30 A6
  NWCHE CW9 .... 130 C1
  NWCHW CW8 .... 129 G1
Bramway *BRAM/HZG* SK7 .... 65 L6
  MPL/ROM SK6 .... 67 M5
Brancaster Dr *GOL/RIS/CU* WA3 . 24 A5
Brancepeth Ct *EP* CH65 ..... 121 K1
Brandon *WDN* WA8 .... 52 A2
Brandon Av *CHD/CHDH* SK8 . 64 B3
  WYTH/NTH M22 .... 44 C4 🅰
Brandon Cl *WILM/AE* SK9 .... 84 D2 🅰
Brandon Gv *WRX/CR/LL* LL12 . 210 B5 🅰
Brandreth Cl *RAIN/WH* L35 .. 33 J1 🅰
Brandwood Av
  WARRN/WOL WA2 .... 37 H2 🅰
Branfield Cl *CHD/CHDH* SK8 .. 64 D3
Branksome Dr *CHD/CHDH* SK8 . 64 D3
Branksome Rd *HTNM* SK4 .... 46 B3
Bransdale Cl *WARRW/BUR* WA5 . 35 L5
Bransdale Wy *MCFLDS* SK11 . 137 M5
Bransford Cl *AIMK* WN4 ...... 22 C2
Branson Wk *HALE/TIMP* WA15 . 43 J6
Brantfield Ct
  WARRN/WOL WA2 .... 37 L2 🅰
Brantwood Rd
  CHD/CHDH SK8 .... 64 F3 🅰
Brassey's Contract Rd
  MALPAS SY14 .... 246 A2
Brassey St *CHSE* CH3 .... 17 M5
Brassey St *NANT* CW5 .... 237 K7 🅰
Brassington St
  AUD/MAD/W CW3 .... 255 G6 🅰
Brathay Cl *WARRN/WOL* WA2 . 37 J1
Brattswood Dr *ALS/KID* ST7 . 224 F7
Bray Cl *CHD/CHDH* SK8 ...... 64 E2
  CW/HAS CW1 .... 19 K2
  RUNC WA7 .... 73 K6
Braydon Cl *WLTN* L25 .... 50 C6 🅰
Brayford Rd *WYTH/NTH* M22 . 63 L6 🅰
Bray Rd *CHSW/BR* CH4 ...... 168 F6 🅰
  SPK/HALE L24 .... 50 C8
Braystan Gdns
  CHD/CHDH SK8 .... 45 H6 🅰
Braystones Cl *ALS/KID* ST7 .. 243 L5 🅰
Brayton Av *DID/WITH* M20 ... 45 J2
Breach House La *KNUT* WA16 . 81 M2
Bread St *MCFLDS* SK11 ...... 14 E7
Breaston Av *LEIGH* WN7 ..... 25 H1
Breck Rd *WDN* WA8 .... 7 K2
The Breck *GTS/LS* CH66 ..... 94 E5
Brecon Av *CHD/CHDH* SK8 .. 64 C3
Brecon Cl *POY/DIS* SK12 .... 66 F8 🅰
Brecon Dr *GTS/LS* CH66 ..... 120 E3
Brecon Wy *CW/SHV* CW2 .... 238 A5
  WSFD CW7 .... 177 H5
Bredbury Gn *MPL/ROM* SK6 . 48 A3
Bredon Cl *GTS/LS* CH66 ..... 94 A6
Breeze Av *BURS/TUN* ST6 ... 243 L8
Breezehill Cl *NSTN* CH64 .... 91 L4
Breezehill Pk *NSTN* CH64 .... 91 M4
Breezehill Rd *NSTN* CH64 .... 91 M4
Brenchley Dr *NTHM/RTH* M23 . 44 A2 🅰
Brencon Av *SALE* M33 .... 43 J3
Brendall Cl *OFTN* SK2 .... 48 A7
Brendon Av
  WARRN/WOL WA2 .... 37 G1 🅰
Brendor Rd *WLTN* L25 .... 50 B3
Brennus Pl *CH/BCN* CH1 ..... 16 E4
Brent Cl *POY/DIS* SK12 ...... 66 B8
Brent Dr *HTNM* SK4 .... 2 B5
Brentfield *WDN* WA8 .... 6 B1
Brent Moor Rd *BRAM/HZG* SK7 . 66 A1
Brentnall Cl
  WARRW/BUR WA5 .... 36 C7 🅰
Brentnall St *STKP* SK1 .... 3 G9
Brent Rd *HTNM* SK4 .... 2 B5
  NTHM/RTH M23 .... 44 A2
Brent Wy *HLWD* L26 .... 50 F6
Brentwood Av *ALT* WA14 .... 42 E5 🅰
  IRL M44 .... 31 K6
Brentwood Crs *ALT* WA14 ... 42 E6 🅰
Brentwood Dr *CHD/CHDH* SK8 . 45 H7
Brentwood Rd *CH/BCN* CH1 .. 144 E7
Brereton Cl *ALT* WA14 .... 61 J1
  CW/SHV CW2 .... 237 L2
  MALPAS SY14 .... 258 B1
  RUNC WA7 .... 74 A4 🅰
  SBCH CW11 .... 204 C5
Brereton Ct *CONG* CW12 .... 182 F6
Brereton Dr *NANT* CW5 ..... 21 H3

Brereton Gv *IRL* M44 .... 31 L6
Brereton Heath La *CONG* CW12 . 182 D6
Brereton La *HOLMCH* CW4 ... 180 C2
Brereton Rd *NWCHW* CW8 ... 129 G8
  WILM/AE SK9 .... 84 E1
Breton Cl *CHNE* CH2 .... 145 L7
Bretton Dr *CHSW/BR* CH4 ... 190 B1
Bretton La *CHSW/BR* CH4 ... 167 M7
Bretton Rd *CHSW/BR* CH4 ... 167 L8
Brett St *WYTH/NTH* M22 .... 44 E3 🅰
  WYTH/NTH M22 .... 44 E3 🅰
Brewer's Gn *BRAM/HZG* SK7 . 66 D1 🅰
Brewery Ct *CHSE* CH3 .... 228 E1
Brewery St *ALT* WA14 .... 42 D8
  STKP SK1 .... 3 H3
Brian Av *WARRN/WOL* WA2 .. 37 K4
  WARRS WA4 .... 56 E3
Briar Av *KNUT* WA16 .... 107 G1
  GOL/RIS/CU WA3 .... 40 B2
Briar Cl *KNUT* WA16 .... 107 G1
Briar Crs *WYTH/NTH* M22 .... 44 E7
Briardale Cl *CW/SHV* CW2 ... 237 M4
Briardale Gdns *GTS/LS* CH66 . 94 C6 🅰
Briardale Rd *GTS/LS* CH66 ... 94 C6
  NSTN CH64 .... 93 G4
Briardene Gdns
  WYTH/NTH M22 .... 44 E8 🅰
Briarfield Rd *CHD/CHDH* SK8 . 65 H1
  EP CH65 .... 10 D7
  HALE/TIMP WA15 .... 43 J6
Briarlands Av *SALE* M33 ..... 42 F2
Briarlands Cl *BRAM/HZG* SK7 . 65 K6 🅰
Briar La *NWCHW* CW8 .... 128 E5
Briar Rd *GOL/RIS/CU* WA3 ... 23 H4
Briars Cl *RAIN/WH* L35 ...... 33 K3
Briars Mt *HTNM* SK4 .... 46 A2
Briars Pk *CHD/CHDH* SK8 .... 65 J3
Briarstead Cl *BRAM/HZG* SK7 . 65 K5 🅰
Briarswood *ALS/KID* ST7 .... 243 H3 🅰
Briarswood Cl *RAIN/WH* L35 . 32 F2 🅰
Briarwood *RUNC* WA7 .... 74 B3
  WILM/AE SK9 .... 84 C5
Briarwood Av *MCFLDS* SK11 . 138 D7
  NTHM/RTH M23 .... 43 K4
  WARR WA1 .... 37 L5
Briarwood Crs *MPL/ROM* SK6 . 48 F8
Brick Bank *NANT* CW5 .... 21 H7
Brick Bank La *HOLMCH* CW4 . 157 H5
Brickbridge Rd *MPL/ROM* SK6 . 49 G7
Brickfields *HUY* L36 .... 32 A3
Brickhill La *HALE/TIMP* WA15 . 62 B8
Brickhurst Wy *WARR* WA1 ... 38 B4
Brickkiln La *ALT* WA14 .... 60 C1
Brick Kiln La *MWCH* CW10 ... 154 B5
Brickkiln Rw *ALT* WA14 ...... 61 J3
Brick St *NEWLW* WA12 ...... 26 F1
Bridge Av *WARRS* WA4 ...... 37 M8
Bridge Cl *CW/SHV* CW2 ..... 238 C5
  LYMM WA13 .... 59 H1 🅰
  PART M31 .... 41 G1
Bridge End Dr *NSTN* CH64 ... 91 L5 🅰
  WRXS/E LL13 .... 228 E4 🅰
Bridgedown *TPLY/KEL* CW6 .. 197 J3 🅰
Bridge Dr *CHD/CHDH* SK8 ... 45 K8
  CHSE CH3 .... 170 D5
  WILM/AE SK9 .... 84 D1
Bridge End Dr *MCFLDN* SK10 . 112 A5
Bridge End La *MCFLDN* SK10 . 112 A5
Bridgefield Av *WILM/AE* SK9 . 84 C3
Bridgefield St *STKP* SK1 ..... 2 F5
Bridge Gn *MCFLDN* SK10 .... 112 A5
Bridge Gv *HALE/TIMP* WA15 . 42 F5
Bridge La *BRAM/HZG* SK7 ... 65 M3
  FROD/HEL WA6 .... 99 J3
  NWCHW CW8 .... 151 M1
  WARR WA1 .... 38 C6
Bridgeman Rd *CH/BCN* CH1 .. 168 E1
Bridgeman St
  WARRW/BUR WA5 .... 36 D8 🅰
Bridge Meadow *GTS/LS* CH66 . 120 F2
Bridgemere Cl *SBCH* CW11 .. 203 M4 🅰
Bridgemere La *NANT* CW5 ... 264 E3
Bridgemere Ms *NANT* CW5 .. 265 M4 🅰
Bridgemere Wy *NWCHE* CW9 . 129 L8
  WDN WA8 .... 52 D1
Bridge Rd *HALE/TIMP* WA15 . 43 J5
  STHEL WA9 .... 34 D2
  WARR WA1 .... 38 C5
Bridge Rw *CONG* CW12 ...... 184 E8
Bridges Rd *EP* CH65 .... 11 L8
Bridge St *CH/BCN* CH1 ...... 17 G6
  CHF/WBR SK23 .... 89 L5
  CHSW/BR CH4 .... 168 D5
  CONG CW12 .... 207 K2
  CQ CH5 .... 142 F5
  GOL/RIS/CU WA3 .... 23 G5 🅰
  MCFLDS SK11 .... 14 F6
  NANT CW5 .... 253 J4
  NEWLW WA12 .... 23 G5
  NEWLW WA12 .... 27 H1
  NM/HAY SK22 .... 69 J3
  NSTN CH64 .... 91 L5
  NWCHE CW9 .... 130 D2
  RUNC WA7 .... 9 J2
  STKP SK1 .... 3 G9
  WARR WA1 .... 5 G7
  WRXS/E LL13 .... 228 E4
Bridge Vw *CQ* CH5 .... 142 F5
Bridge View *WDN* WA8 ...... 53 G8 🅰
Bridgewater Av *WARRS* WA4 . 37 M8
Bridgewater Cl *CONG* CW12 . 208 B3
Bridgewater Dr *CHSE* CH3 ... 170 C2
Bridgewater Ms *WARRS* WA4 . 56 C4 🅰
Bridgewater Pl *WSFD* CW7 ... 177 G3 🅰
Bridgewater Rd *ALT* WA14 ... 42 D5
Bridgewater St *LYMM* WA13 . 58 E1 🅰
  RUNC WA7 .... 9 G1
  WHITCH SY13 .... 270 A5
Bridgewater Wy *HUY* L36 .... 32 A4
Bridgeway East *RUNC* WA7 .. 74 C2
Bridgeway West *RUNC* WA7 . 74 B2
Bridgewood Dr *GTS/LS* CH66 . 120 C2
Bridgfield Cl *MPL/ROM* SK6 .. 67 L5 🅰
Bridle Hey *NANT* CW5 .... 251 M2 🅰

The Bridle Pth
AUD/MAD/W CW3 .... 267 K5
Bridle Rd BRAM/HZG SK7 .... 85 M1
CW/SHV CW2 .... 18 D5
Bridle Wy BRAM/HZG SK7 .... 85 M2
GTS/LS CW66 .... 120 D1
Brien Av ALT WA14 .... 42 D6
Brierley Dr WYTH/NTH M22 .... 63 H3 ▣
Brierley St CW/HAS CW1 .... 19 H3
WARRW/BUR WA5 .... 4 D5
Brierton Dr WYTH/NTH M22 .. 63 H3 ▣
Brieryhurst Rd ALS/KID ST7 .. 243 H1
Briggs Av CW/SHV CW2 ...... 238 D3
Briggs Cl SALE M33 .... 42 C3
Brighton Crs MCFLDS SK11 .. 163 H1 ▣
Brighton Rd HTNM SK4 .... 2 A5
HUY L36 .... 32 B1 ▣
Brighton St WARRW/BUR WA5 .. 4 B4
Brights Av ALS/KID ST7 ...... 243 H1
Bright St CW/HAS CW1 ...... 18 D3
Brightwell Cl
WARRW/BUR WA5 .... 35 L7 ▣
Brignall Gv GOL/RIS/CU WA3 .. 23 K3 ▣
Brimelow Crs
WARRW/BUR WA5 .... 54 E1 ▣
Brimelow St MPL/ROM SK6 .... 47 J1 ▣
Brimscombe Av
WYTH/NTH M22 .... 63 J2 ▣
WARRS WA4 .... 37 M8
WSFD CW7 .... 177 H2
Brindley Av MPL/ROM SK6 .... 48 F7
WARRS WA4 .... 37 M8
Brindley Cl ALS/KID ST7 .... 242 E3
Brindley Hall NANT CW5 .... 234 E3
Brindley La SBCH CW11 ...... 181 J8
Brindley Pk SBCH CW11 .... 222 F1
Brindley St RUNC WA7 .... 8 F1
Brindley Wy CONG CW12 .... 208 B3
MCFLDS SK11 .... 162 C1
Brinell Dr IRL M44 .... 31 M7
Brine Pits La NANT CW5 .... 263 L2
Brine Rd NANT CW5 .... 251 L1
Brinkburn Rd BRAM/HZG SK7 .. 67 G1
Brinkshaw Av WYTH/NTH M22 .. 63 L2
Brinksway EDGY/DAV SK3 ...... 2 A7
Brinnington Rd STKP SK1 ...... 3 L1
Brinton Cl WDN WA8 .... 6 B5
Briony Av HALE/TIMP WA15 .. 62 C2
Brisbane Cl BRAM/HZG SK7 .. 65 M7
Brisbane Rd CH/BCN CH1 .. 144 C8 ▣
Bristol Av RUNC WA7 .... 74 E6
Bristol Cl CH/BCN CH1 ...... 144 C8
Bristol Dr GTS/LS CW66 .... 120 E3
Bristow Cl WARRW/BUR WA5 .... 36 A4
Brittania Dr NWCHE CW9 .. 130 E5 ▣
Brittania Gdns FROD/HEL WA6 .. 124 B3
Brittania Rd FROD/HEL WA6 .. 124 B2
Brixham Av CHD/CHDH SK8 .. 64 F5
Brixham Wk BRAM/HZG SK7 .. 65 L5 ▣
Broadacre NWCHE CW9 ...... 103 K5
Broadacres NANT CW5 ...... 250 F8
Broadbent Av WARRS WA4 .... 37 M8
Broadcar Rd MCFLDS SK11 .. 139 J6
Broadfields RUNC WA7 .... 74 C4
Broadfield Rd BURS/TUN ST6 .. 243 J6
Broad Hey MPL/ROM SK6 .... 48 D1
Broad Hey Cl WLTN L25 ...... 50 B1
Broadheys La KNUT WA16 .... 58 D1
Broadhey Vw NM/HAY SK22 .. 69 H3
Broad Hill BRAM/HZG SK7 .... 66 A2
Broadhurst Av GOL/RIS/CU WA3 .. 29 M2
WARRW/BUR WA5 .... 36 D8 ▣
Broadhurst La CONG CW12 .. 207 J1
Broadhurst St EDGY/DAV SK3 .. 46 E5
Broadlake NSTN CH64 .... 92 F4
Broadland Gdns GTS/LS CW66 .. 120 F2
Broadland Rd GTS/LS CW66 .. 120 F2
Broad La HALE/TIMP WA15 .. 62 B4
HOLMCH CW4 .... 180 D4
NANT CW5 .... 252 B4
WARRS WA4 .... 57 J1
WARRW/BUR WA5 .... 26 D4
Broadleigh Wy CW/SHV CW2 .. 238 C4
Broadley Av GOL/RIS/CU WA3 .. 23 J5
WYTH/NTH M22 .... 44 D8 ▣
Broadmead CHSE CH3 ...... 170 C2
Broad Oak Av CHSW/BR CH4 .. 190 A1
WARRW/BUR WA5 .... 35 L8
Broadoak Av WYTH/NTH M22 .. 44 C7 ▣
Broadoak Dr WYTH/NTH M22 .. 44 D7 ▣
Broad Oak La DID/WITH M20 .. 45 J4
Broadoak La KNUT WA16 .... 59 K7
KNUT WA16 .... 81 J1
Broadoak Rd BRAM/HZG SK7 .. 65 M2
WYTH/NTH M22 .... 44 C8
Broadoaks WRX/GR/LL LL12 .. 210 C4
Broad St CW/HAS CW1 .... 18 E1
Broadwalk MCFLDN SK10 .... 112 A7
Broad Wk WILM/AE SK9 ...... 83 M4
Broadway BRAM/HZG SK7 .... 65 M2
CHD/CHDH SK8 .... 45 J8
HALE/TIMP WA15 .... 62 A3
NWCHE CW8 .... 129 H1
OFTN SK2 .... 47 J5
WDN WA8 .... 52 A3
WILM/AE SK9 .... 84 B6
Broadway Av CHD/CHDH SK8 .. 45 K7
Broadway East CHNE CH2 .. 145 L7
Broadways AUD/MAD/W CW3 .. 263 M8 ▣
The Broadway NANT CW5 .... 21 H6
Broadway West CHNE CH2 .. 145 K7
Broadwell Dr LEIGH WN7 .... 24 E3
Broadwood Cl MPL/ROM SK6 .. 67 M8
Broady Ct CW/SHV CW2 ...... 18 F7
Brock Cl CHD/CHDH SK8 .... 65 G4
Brock Hollow NSTN CH64 .. 203 M8
Brockhurst St NWCHE CW9 .. 13 J7
Brockhurst Wy NWCHE CW8 .. 12 F5
Brocklebank Dr NWCHW CW8 .. 12 F5
Brocklehurst Av MCFLDN SK10 .. 15 K2
Brocklehurst Dr MCFLDN SK10 .. 112 A6
Brocklehurst Wy MCFLDN SK10 .. 138 D1
Brock Rd GOL/RIS/CU WA3 .. 38 D1
Brock St MCFLDN SK10 ...... 15 G3
Brockway East CHSE CH3 .. 214 A3 ▣
Brockway West CHSE CH3 .. 214 A3 ▣
Brodie Cl CHNE CH2 .... 145 J3

Brogden Av GOL/RIS/CU WA3 .. 24 E8
Brogden Dr CHD/CHDH SK8 .. 45 H7 ▣
Brogden Gv SALE M33 .... 43 G1 ▣
Broken Banks MCFLDS SK11 .. 15 H1
Broken Cross MCFLDS SK11 .. 137 L4
Bromleigh Av CHD/CHDH SK8 .. 45 H6
Bromley Cl CW/HAS CW1 .... 220 F4
Bromley Dr HOLMCH CW4 .... 181 J2
Bromley Rd CONG CW12 .... 207 L2
MCFLDN SK10 .... 137 L4
SALE M33 .... 43 J2
Brompton Gdns
WARRW/BUR WA5 .... 4 A2
Brompton Rd HTNM SK4 .... 46 A2 ▣
Brompton Wy GTS/LS CW66 .. 120 E3
Bronington Cl WYTH/NTH M22 .. 44 E5
Bron Llwyn FLINT CH6 ...... 116 B8
Brookash Rd WYTH/NTH M22 .. 64 A4
Brook Av CW/SHV CW2 ...... 238 C7
HALE/TIMP WA15 .... 42 E6
WARRS WA4 .... 37 M7
WARRS WA4 .... 56 E3
WILM/AE SK9 .... 84 D1
Brook Bottom Rd NM/HAY SK22 .. 68 F3
Brook Cl CW/HAS CW1 ...... 19 L5
HALE/TIMP WA15 .... 42 E6
MALB WA16 .... 33 J6
Brookcot Rd NTHM/RTH M23 .. 43 M5
Brook Ct SBCH CW11 ...... 204 B6
Brookcroft Av
WYTH/NTH M22 .... 44 D7 ▣
Brookcroft Rd WYTH/NTH M22 .. 44 D7
Brookdale RAIN/WH L35 ...... 52 A1
Brookdale Av KNUT WA16 .. 107 J2 ▣
MPL/ROM SK6 .... 49 G8
Brookdale Cl CH/BCN CH1 .. 17 H4 ▣
Brookdale Ri CH/BCN CH1 .. 17 H4 ▣
Brookdale Rd BRAM/HZG SK7 .. 65 M3
CHD/CHDH SK8 .... 44 F7
Brookdale Wy CHSE CH3 .... 171 H7
Brook Dr MPL/ROM SK6 .... 48 F8
TPLY/KEL CW6 .... 149 K8
WARRW/BUR WA5 .... 36 A7
Brooke Av CHNE CH2 ...... 145 M4
Brooke Dr WILM/AE SK9 .... 64 B8 ▣
Brook End STHEL WA9 ...... 26 A3
Brookes Av CHSW/BR CH4 .. 190 B1
Brook Farm Cl PART M31 .... 40 E2 ▣
Brookfield Av HALE/TIMP WA15 .. 42 F5
POY/DIS SK12 .... 86 C1
RUNC WA7 .... 73 L2
STKP SK1 .... 3 K9
Brookfield Cl LYMM WA13 .... 58 D1
STKP SK1 .... 3 K9
TPLY/KEL CW6 .... 197 K4
Brookfield Crs CHD/CHDH SK8 .. 45 K7
HOLMCH CW4 .... 157 M3
Brookfield Dr ALS/KID ST7 .. 224 C7 ▣
HALE/TIMP WA15 .... 43 G5
HOLMCH CW4 .... 181 H1
Brookfield Gdns
WYTH/NTH M22 .... 44 C6 ▣
Brookfield La MCFLDS SK11 .. 15 L1 ▣
Brookfield Pk WYTH/NTH M22 .. 57 G1 ▣
Brookfield Rd CHD/CHDH SK8 .. 45 L7
GOL/RIS/CU WA3 .... 24 C8
LYMM WA13 .... 58 D1
NWCHE CW9 .... 103 K4
Brookfield St NEWLW WA12 .. 27 H1
Brook Furlong FROD/HEL WA6 .. 98 E2
Brook Gdns BIDD ST8 ...... 227 K2
Brook Gv CHD/CHDH SK8 .... 46 A7
Brook Hey NSTN CH64 ...... 91 H2
Brookhouse Cl
MCFLDN SK10 .... 137 M3 ▣
Brook House Dr CW/SHV CW2 .. 238 C4
Brookhouse La CONG CW12 .. 208 A1
CW/HAS CW1 .... 201 K6
TPLY/KEL CW6 .... 172 D6
WARRS WA4 .... 102 B2
Brookhouse Rd ALS/KID ST7 .. 241 K1
SBCH CW11 .... 204 B6
Brookland Av CW/SHV CW2 .. 237 M4
Brookland Dr SBCH CW11 .. 204 D6
Brookland La STHEL WA9 .... 26 A2
Brookland Rd
BURS/TUN ST6 .... 243 M7 ▣
Brooklands Av AIMK WN4 .. 22 D2 ▣
LEIGH WN7 .... 24 E1
MCFLDS SK11 .... 14 C7
Brooklands Cl IRL M44 ...... 31 M2
Brooklands Crs SALE M33 .. 43 H1
Brooklands Dr HOLMCH CW4 .. 157 L3
NWCHE CW8 .... 130 A3 ▣
Brooklands Gdns NSTN CH64 .. 91 J3
Brooklands Gv CW/HAS CW1 .. 221 G6
Brooklands Rd BRAM/HZG SK7 .. 66 E3
CONG CW12 .... 206 F1
NSTN CH64 .... 91 J3
SALE M33 .... 43 H1
Brooklands Station Ap
SALE M33 .... 43 G1 ▣
Brook La CHNE CH2 .... 17 G1
CHSW/BR CH4 .... 167 J4
CONG CW12 .... 206 E7
GOL/RIS/CU WA3 .... 39 G4
HALE/TIMP WA15 .... 42 E6
KNUT WA16 .... 107 H3
NANT CW5 .... 235 K4
NSTN CH64 .... 91 J2
NWCHE CW9 .... 130 D5
WILM/AE SK9 .... 109 M1
Brookledge La MCFLDN SK10 .. 86 C7
Brookleigh Av CQ CH5 ...... 166 D2 ▣
Brooklyn Crs CHD/CHDH SK8 .. 45 K7
Brooklyn Dr EP CH65 ...... 94 F7
LYMM WA13 .... 58 D1
Brook Lynn Av GOL/RIS/CU WA3 .. 23 M3
Brooklyn Rd CHD/CHDH SK8 .. 45 K7 ▣
OFTN SK2 .... 47 J6

Brooklyn St CW/SHV CW2 .... 18 F7
Brookmere Cl SBCH CW11 .. 203 L4 ▣
Brook Pl CH/BCN CH1 ...... 17 H3
WARRS WA4 .... 56 E1 ▣
Brook Rd CHD/CHDH SK8 .... 45 K6
CQ CH5 .... 142 A6
GTS/LS CW66 .... 94 D7
LYMM WA13 .... 39 K8
Brooks Av BRAM/HZG SK7 .. 66 D1
Brooks Dr HALE/TIMP WA15 .. 62 D4
NTHM/RTH M23 .... 43 K5
Brook Side CW/SHV CW8 .. 128 C3
Brookside CHSE CH3 ...... 148 E5
CHSE CH3 .... 170 A4
CQ CH5 .... 142 F5 ▣
FROD/HEL WA6 .... 126 C2
NWCHW CW8 .... 151 M1 ▣
Brookside Av LYMM WA13 .. 39 J8
MCFLDS SK11 .... 162 F1
OFTN SK2 .... 47 L6
POY/DIS SK12 .... 86 E1
WARRS WA4 .... 56 D3
WARRW/BUR WA5 .... 36 A7
Brookside Cl CHD/CHDH SK8 .. 45 K8
Brookside La MPL/ROM SK6 .. 67 L5
Brookside Rd CHD/CHDH SK8 .. 45 G6
CONG CW12 .... 207 K1 ▣
FROD/HEL WA6 .... 99 G4
SALE M33 .... 43 G2
Brookside Ter CHNE CH2 .. 145 K8
Brook Slack TPLY/KEL CW6 .. 175 K3
Brooks La MCFLDS SK11 .. 186 D2
MWCH CW10 .... 179 K4
Brooks St STKP SK1 .... 3 H9
Brook St AIMK WN4 .... 22 C2 ▣
BIDD ST8 .... 227 G7
BRAM/HZG SK7 .... 66 E2 ▣
CH/BCN CH1 .... 17 H3
CHD/CHDH SK8 .... 45 M6
CONG CW12 .... 207 M1
CW/SHV CW2 .... 19 G6
GOL/RIS/CU WA3 .... 23 G5
GOL/RIS/CU WA3 .... 24 A3
KNUT WA16 .... 107 C3
MCFLDS SK11 .... 15 J6
NSTN CH64 .... 91 L4
NWCHE CW9 .... 13 K1
NWCHE CW9 .... 130 E2
RUNC WA7 .... 9 G1 ▣
Brook Street Br CHNE CH2 .. 17 K2
Brookthorn Cl OFTN SK2 .. 47 M7 ▣
Brookvale Av North RUNC WA7 .. 74 B7
Brookvale Av South RUNC WA7 .. 74 B6
Brookway HALE/TIMP WA15 .. 42 F5
Brook Wy NWCHW CW8 .. 129 H8
WARRW/BUR WA5 .... 36 A7
Brookwood Av SALE M33 .. 42 E1
Brookwood Cl WARRS WA4 .. 56 B4
Broom Av WARRS WA4 ...... 56 E6
Broom Crs CHSE CH3 ...... 172 B3
Broome Ct RUNC WA7 ...... 74 B7 ▣
Broomehouse Av IRL M44 .. 31 L4
Bromfield Cl MCFLDS SK11 .. 135 C1
WILM/AE SK9 .... 84 A3 ▣
Broomfield Crs EDGY/DAV SK3 .. 47 G8
Broomfield La HALE/TIMP WA15 .. 61 L2
NWCHW CW8 .... 102 F8
Broomfields Rd WARRS WA4 .. 56 D5
Broomheath La CHSE CH3 .. 172 C5
Broomhill Dr BRAM/HZG SK7 .. 65 K3
Broomhill La CHSE CH3 .... 147 L4
CHSE CH3 .... 231 J4
Broom La BURS/TUN ST6 .. 243 J8
Broom La KNUT WA16 ...... 132 E2
Broom Rd HALE/TIMP WA15 .. 61 L1
PART M31 .... 40 F2 ▣
Broom's La TPLY/KEL CW6 .. 149 K7
Broom St CW/HAS CW1 .... 18 B1
Broom Wy HLWD L26 ...... 50 D5
Broomwood Rd
HALE/TIMP WA15 .... 43 J7
GOL/RIS/CU WA3 .... 24 D8
Broseley Av DID/WITH M20 .. 45 K1 ▣
Broseley La GOL/RIS/CU WA3 .. 24 D7
Brough St West MCFLDS SK11 .. 14 D7
Broughton Av GOL/RIS/CU WA3 .. 23 K5
Broughton Crs CW/SHV CW2 .. 237 M3
Broughton Hall Rd
CHSW/BR CH4 .... 190 C1
Broughton La CW/HAS CW1 .. 221 J3
Broughton Mills Rd
CHSW/BR CH4 .... 167 M6
Broughton Rd CW/HAS CW1 .. 221 J3
MCFLDN SK10 .... 86 C7
Broughville Dr DID/WITH M20 .. 45 J4
Brow La NWCHE CW9 ...... 77 K7
Browmere Dr GOL/RIS/CU WA3 .. 29 C5
Brown Av ALS/KID ST7 .... 225 C8
NANT CW5 .... 251 M1
Brown Heath Rd CHSE CH3 .. 171 G5
Brownhill Dr WARR WA1 .... 37 M4
Brownhills Rd TPLY/KEL CW6 .. 175 H6
Browning Av WDN WA8 .... 6 E5
Browning Cl CH/BCN CH1 .. 144 F6
SBCH CW11 .... 203 K7
Browning Dr EP CH65 ...... 94 F8
Browning Gv ALS/KID ST7 .. 242 C4
Browning St CW/HAS CW1 .. 18 E3
Browning Wy WSFD CW7 .. 176 F1
Brown Knowl La CHSE CH3 .. 231 J4
Brown La CHD/CHDH SK8 .. 64 A3
Brown Lees Cl CW/SHV CW2 .. 18 B9
Brown Lees Rd ALS/KID ST7 .. 226 F8
BIDD ST8 .... 227 H7
Brownley Court Rd
WYTH/NTH M22 .... 44 D7 ▣
Brownley Rd WYTH/NTH M22 .. 44 E7
WYTH/NTH M22 .... 63 L2
Brownlow Cl POY/DIS SK12 .. 86 E2
Brownlow St WHITCH SY13 .. 270 A4
Brown's La CHSW/BR CH4 .. 16 F9
Brown St ALT WA14 .... 61 K1
CONG CW12 .... 207 L1

MCFLDS SK11 .... 14 F7
STKP SK1 .... 2 F4 ▣
WDN WA8 .... 53 K5
WILM/AE SK9 .... 110 A3 ▣
Brownwood Av STKP SK1 .... 3 M5
Brownwood Cl SALE M33 .. 43 J3 ▣
Brows Av NTHM/RTH M23 .. 44 A3
The Brow FROD/HEL WA6 .. 126 C2
Broxton Cl WDN WA8 ...... 52 C1 ▣
Broxton Dr CW/SHV CW2 .. 18 A7
Broxton Rd GTS/LS CW66 .. 94 E7
NTHM/RTH M23 .... 43 K5
MALPAS SY14 .... 230 D3
Bruce Av WARRN/WOL WA2 .. 37 K3
Bruce Dr GTS/LS CW66 .... 94 D7
Bruche Av WARR WA1 ...... 37 M5
Bruche Dr WARR WA1 ...... 37 M4
The Bruen CHSE CH3 ...... 172 C1 ▣
Bruera Rd EP CH65 .... 94 F8
Brundage Rd WYTH/NTH M22 .. 63 K2
Brundrett St STKP SK1 ...... 3 K8
Brunel Rd MCFLDS SK11 .. 162 C1
Brunner Cv CW/SHV CW2 .. 21 K7
Brunner Pl WSFD CW7 .... 177 C4
Brunner Rd WDN WA8 ...... 7 G4
Brunstead Rd NTHM/RTH M23 .. 43 K6 ▣
Brunswick Crs GTS/LS CW66 .. 120 E1
Brunswick Dr ALT WA14 .... 42 D5
Brunswick St CONG CW12 .. 207 M1
MCFLDN SK10 .... 15 H4
STHEL WA9 .... 26 A1
Bruntleigh Av WARRS WA4 .. 57 G1 ▣
Bruntwood Av CHD/CHDH SK8 .. 64 A3
Bruntwood La CHD/CHDH SK8 .. 45 L8
CHD/CHDH SK8 .... 64 E3
Brussels Rd EDGY/DAV SK3 .. 46 D6
Bryant Av WARRS WA4 ...... 37 M8
Brydges Rd MPL/ROM SK6 .. 48 E7
Bryndale Gv SALE M33 .... 42 F3
Bryn Derw FLINT CH6 ...... 116 B8 ▣
Bryn Dr CQ CH5 .... 166 C2
Bryn Estyn Av WHITCH SY13 .. 269 M4
Bryn Gwyn FLINT CH6 ...... 116 B8
Bryn Helig FLINT CH6 ...... 116 B8 ▣
Brynlow Dr MWCH CW10 .. 179 H4
Brynmore Dr MCFLDS SK11 .. 15 L6
Brynn St WDN WA8 .... 7 J5
Bryn Onnen FLINT CH6 .... 116 B8
Bryn Rd FLINT CH6 .... 116 A7
Bryn Siriol FLINT CH6 ...... 116 B7
Bryn St AIMK WN4 .... 22 B1
Brynton Cl MCFLDN SK10 .. 14 F2
Brynton Rd MCFLDN SK10 .. 14 F2
Bryone Dr OFTN SK2 ...... 47 M7
Buchan Cl WARRW/BUR WA5 .. 36 B4 ▣
Buchan Gv CW/SHV CW2 .. 18 C6
Buckbean Wy HOLMCH CW4 .. 157 L3
Buckfast Cl CHD/CHDH SK8 .. 65 H5
HALE/TIMP WA15 .... 62 B2
MCFLDN SK10 .... 14 D1
POY/DIS SK12 .... 86 E1
WARRW/BUR WA5 .... 54 E1 ▣
Buckfast Ct RUNC WA7 .... 74 E1 ▣
Buckfast Wy MWCH CW10 .. 179 H3
Buckingham Av CHSE CH3 .. 170 A2
WDN WA8 .... 34 A8
Buckingham Cl CW/SHV CW2 .. 237 L4
Buckingham Dr KNUT WA16 .. 107 H3
NWCHE CW9 .... 129 L8
WARRW/BUR WA5 .... 36 A7
WSFD CW7 .... 177 J5 ▣
Buckingham Gdns EP CH65 .. 121 K2 ▣
Buckingham Rd ALT WA14 .. 42 F3
CHD/CHDH SK8 .... 64 F2
IRL M44 .... 31 J6
POY/DIS SK12 .... 66 D8
WILM/AE SK9 .... 83 M6
Buckingham St OFTN SK2 .. 47 G6 ▣
Buckingham Wy
HALE/TIMP WA15 .... 43 G6
Buckland Cl WDN WA8 ...... 6 A6
Buck La CW/SHV CW2 ...... 253 L1
Buckley Av MWCH CW10 .. 155 M5
Buckley Dr MPL/ROM SK6 .. 48 A3
Buckley St MCFLDS SK11 .. 14 F7
WARRN/WOL WA2 .... 4 F4
Bucklow Av KNUT WA16 .... 82 A8
PART M31 .... 31 M8
Bucklow Dr WYTH/NTH M22 .. 44 E4
Bucklow Gdns LYMM WA13 .. 40 A8
Bucklowhill La KNUT WA16 .. 80 A2
Bucklow Vw ALT WA14 .... 61 G1
Buckthorn Cl HALE/TIMP WA15 .. 43 L7
Buckton St WARR WA1 ...... 5 L3
Buckwood Cl BRAM/HZG SK7 .. 67 G1
Bude Cl ALS/KID ST7 ...... 241 H1 ▣
BRAM/HZG SK7 .... 65 M5
CW/HAS CW1 .... 221 M5
Bude Rd WDN WA8 .... 6 C1
Budworth Av RUNC WA7 .... 73 K5
SBCH CW11 .... 203 L7 ▣
Budworth Cl WLTN L25 .... 50 C2 ▣
Budworth Heath La
NWCHE CW9 .... 104 B3
Budworth La NWCHE CW9 .. 103 M5
Budworth Rd GTS/LS CW66 .. 120 E2
KNUT WA16 .... 105 K2
NWCHE CW9 .... 104 C3
SALE M33 .... 43 J1
Buerton Ap CHSE CH3 .... 193 M6
Buggen La NSTN CH64 .... 91 K4
Buildwas Rd NSTN CH64 .. 91 L2
Bulford La WYTH/NTH M22 .. 63 H2
Bulkeley Cl CHD/CHDH SK8 .. 45 L7
POY/DIS SK12 .... 86 E1
WILM/AE SK9 .... 84 C1
Bulkeley St CHSE CH3 ...... 170 A3
CW/HAS CW1 .... 19 L5
EDGY/DAV SK3 .... 46 F7
Bullcroft Cl MALPAS SY14 .. 244 D5
Bullfinch Ct HLWD L26 .... 50 E3 ▣
Bull Hi NSTN CH64 .... 91 M6
Bull Hill La MCFLDN SK10 .. 139 K2
Bull Hill La MCFLDN SK10 .. 139 K3

Bullocks House Rd ALS/KID ST7 .. 243 L1 ▣
Bullocks La MCFLDS SK11 .. 162 E1
Bullock St OFTN SK2 ...... 46 F5 ▣
Bumper's La CH/BCN CH1 .. 168 E4
Bunbury Cl CHNE CH2 ...... 122 A5
MWCH CW10 .... 179 J7
NWCHE CW9 .... 13 K8
Bunbury Dr RUNC WA7 .... 73 J6
Bunbury La TPLY/KEL CW6 .. 216 E5
Bunbury Rd TPLY/KEL CW6 .. 217 H1
Bunce La MCFLDS SK11 .... 184 A1
Bunkershill Rd MPL/ROM SK6 .. 48 B3
Bunting Cl GOL/RIS/CU WA3 .. 23 L4 ▣
Bunting Dr HLWD L26 ...... 50 D2
Buntingford Rd WARRS WA4 .. 57 J1 ▣
Bunts La CONG CW12 ...... 207 L3
Burbage Rd NTHM/RTH M23 .. 63 G2
Burdett Rd GTS/LS CW66 .. 120 E2
Burdon Av WYTH/NTH M22 .. 44 E8
Burfield Dr WARRS WA4 ...... 56 E3
Burford Av BRAM/HZG SK7 .. 65 J7
Burford Crs WILM/AE SK9 .. 83 L7
Burford Gv SALE M33 ...... 42 E3
Burford La LYMM WA13 .... 59 J2
Burgamot La NWCHE CW9 .. 103 J4
Burganey Ct CHSW/BR CH4 .. 210 C2
Burgess Av WARR WA1 .... 56 B1
Burgess La FROD/HEL WA6 .. 127 H7
Burgess St MCFLDN SK10 .. 15 L6
Burges St CHNE CH2 ...... 17 M1
Burjen Wy CW/HAS CW1 .. 221 H6
Burkhardt Dr NEWLW WA12 .. 27 L1 ▣
Burland Cl RUNC WA7 ...... 8 F4
Burlea Cl CW/SHV CW2 .... 220 E4
Burlea Dr CW/SHV CW2 .... 238 B7
Burleigh Cl BRAM/HZG SK7 .. 66 A3
Burlescombe Cl ALT WA14 .. 42 B6 ▣
Burley Av GOL/RIS/CU WA3 .. 23 K3
Burley Ct HTNM SK4 .... 2 A3 ▣
Burleyhurst La KNUT WA16 .. 82 E6
Burley La WARRS WA4 ...... 57 J8
Burlidge Rd BURS/TUN ST6 .. 243 M6
Burlington Cl HTNM SK4 .. 45 L2 ▣
Burlington Dr EDGY/DAV SK3 .. 46 F8
Burlington Gdns
EDGY/DAV SK3 .... 46 F8 ▣
Burlington Ms EDGY/DAV SK3 .. 46 F8
Burlington Rd ALT WA14 .... 42 D7
Burnaby Rd BURS/TUN ST6 .. 243 J6
Burnage Cl SPK/HALE L24 .. 70 F2
Burnage La HTNM SK4 .... 45 K2
Burnell Rd EP CH65 ...... 95 L8
Burnet Cl WARRN/WOL WA2 .. 38 C2
Burnfell GOL/RIS/CU WA3 .. 23 L5 ▣
Burnham Cl CHD/CHDH SK8 .. 64 F7 ▣
GOL/RIS/CU WA3 .... 24 E8 ▣
WARRW/BUR WA5 .... 35 M7
WILM/AE SK9 .... 84 C6
Burnham Rd CHSW/BR CH4 .. 168 F6
Burnsall Av GOL/RIS/CU WA3 .. 23 M4
Burnsall Dr WDN WA8 ...... 52 C1
Burns Av CHD/CHDH SK8 .. 45 M6 ▣
Burns Cl ALS/KID ST7 ...... 224 E4 ▣
ALS/KID ST7 .... 243 G4 ▣
GTS/LS CW66 .... 94 E8
RAIN/WH L35 .... 32 E1
WDN WA8 .... 6 F1
Burns Crs OFTN SK2 ...... 47 L5 ▣
WDN WA8 .... 6 F1
Burns Dr CW/HAS CW1 .... 19 L3
Burns Gv HUY L36 .... 32 K3
WARRN/WOL WA2 .... 37 J2
Burnside HALE/TIMP WA15 .. 62 D5
Burnside Av WARRS WA4 .. 56 D3
Burnside Rd CHD/CHDH SK8 .. 45 G7
STHEL WA9 .... 34 A1
Burns Rd CONG CW12 .... 208 A2
Burns Wy CH/BCN CH1 .. 144 E6
Burnt Acre MCFLDS SK11 .. 135 H1
Burnwood Gv ALS/KID ST7 .. 243 H2 ▣
Burran Rd WYTH/NTH M22 .. 63 K4
Burroughs Hl NWCHW CW8 .. 129 H5
Burrows La FROD/HEL WA6 .. 124 C3
The Burrows NWCHW CW8 .. 127 K7
Bursar Cl NEWLW WA12 .... 22 C7
Burslam St CONG CW12 .... 207 L2
Burton Av HALE/TIMP WA15 .. 43 G3
TPLY/KEL CW6 .... 197 J1
Burton Cl GOL/RIS/CU WA3 .. 29 M1
MWCH CW10 .... 179 J6
Burton Dr POY/DIS SK12 .. 66 D8
Burton Gn GTS/LS CW66 .. 94 D8 ▣
Burton Gv CW/HAS CW1 .. 221 H3 ▣
Burton La TPLY/KEL CW6 .. 172 F6
Burton Rd CH/BCN CH1 .. 144 E7
NSTN CH64 .... 91 L6
WARRN/WOL WA2 .... 37 K3
Burton St HTNM SK4 ...... 2 E1
Burtonwood Rd
WARRW/BUR WA5 .... 36 A4
Burwardsley Rd CHSE CH3 .. 214 B2
Burwardsley Wy NWCHE CW9 .. 129 L8
Burway Dr WHITCH SY13 .. 270 B5
Burwell Gv NTHM/RTH M23 .. 43 M5 ▣
Bury St RDSH SK5 .... 3 G1
Bushell Cl NSTN CH64 ...... 91 M5
Bushell Rd NSTN CH64 .... 91 M4
Bushel's Dr STHEL WA9 .... 34 D2
Bushey Dr NTHM/RTH M23 .. 44 A7
Bush Rd CHSE CH3 .... 170 E5
WDN WA8 .... 52 F7
Butcher La HTNM SK4 ...... 45 K5
Butler St CQ CH5 .... 142 D7
Butler Wy NANT CW5 ...... 251 L1 ▣
Butley Cl MCFLDN SK10 .... 138 D1
MWCH CW10 .... 179 J6
Butley La MCFLDN SK10 .. 111 M2
Butley St BRAM/HZG SK7 .. 47 L8
Butterbache Rd CHSE CH3 .. 170 A6
Butterbur Cl CHSE CH3 .... 170 A6
Buttercup Dr EDGY/DAV SK3 .. 46 D7 ▣
Butterfield Cl CHD/CHDH SK8 .. 65 H3 ▣
Buttermarket St WARR WA1 .. 5 H6 ▣
Buttermere Cl EP CH65 .... 121 J1 ▣
WARRN/WOL WA2 .... 37 J1

WYTH/NTH M22 .... 63 J2 ▣
Buttermere CI FROD/HEL WA6 .... 99 K4 ▣
Buttermere Ct CONG CW12 .... 207 G2
Buttermere Dr CW/HAS CW1 .... 221 H3 ▣
HALE/TIMP WA15 .... 62 C6
WILM/AE SK9 .... 108 F5
Butterton La CW/HAS CW1 .... 239 M3
Butteryhouse La
HALE/TIMP WA15 .... 62 E2
Button La NTHM/RTH M23 ...... 43 M2
Butts Av LEIGH WN7 .... 25 H1
Butts St LEIGH WN7 .... 25 G1
The Butts ALS/KID ST7 ...... 224 D8 ▣
AUD/MAD/W CW3 .... 255 G7
Buxton Av CW/HAS CW1 .... 19 K4
Buxton CI WARRW/BUR WA5 ...... 36 A4
Buxton Crs SALE M33 .... 43 K3
Buxton La MPL/ROM SK6 .... 48 E7
Buxton New Rd MCFLDN SK10 ... 139 J4
Buxton Old Rd CONG CW12 ... 184 F8
MCFLDS SK11 .... 139 G5
POY/DIS SK12 .... 68 D6
Buxton Rd BRAM/HZG SK7 ...... 66 F3
CHF/WBR SK23 .... 89 L3
CONG CW12 .... 184 F8
MCFLDN SK10 .... 15 K5
MCFLDS SK11 .... 15 H5 ▣
NM/HAY SK22 .... 69 H6
OFTN SK2 .... 47 J8 ▣
.... 47 G6
Buxton Rd West POY/DIS SK12 .. 68 A6
Buxton St BRAM/HZG SK7 ...... 66 D1 ▣
CHD/CHDH SK8 .... 45 G7 ▣
Byfield Rd WYTH/NTH M22 ...... 44 C8
Byland Av CHD/CHDH SK8 .... 65 H6
Byland CI WDN WA8 .... 34 C7
Bylands CI POY/DIS SK12 ..... 66 D8 ▣
Byley La MWCH CW10 .... 156 A8
MWCH CW10 .... 179 L2
Byng Av IRL M44 .... 31 J8
By-pass Rd CHSE CH3 .... 172 B1
Byre CI SALE M33 .... 44 A1
Byrom La GOL/RIS/CU WA3 ..... 23 M2
Byrom St ALT WA14 .... 61 K1
Byron Av RAIN/WH L35 .... 32 F1
Byron CI ALS/KID ST7 ...... 224 E5 ▣
CH/BCN CH1 .... 144 E6
CW/HAS CW1 .... 19 L4
MWCH CW10 .... 179 K7
SBCH CW11 .... 203 K6
Byron Ct ALS/KID ST7 ...... 243 G4
WARRN/WOL WA2 .... 37 J2 ▣
Byron Dr CHD/CHDH SK8 .... 45 M6 ▣
Byron's La MCFLDS SK11 .... 15 J9
MCFLDS SK11 .... 138 E7
Byrons St MCFLDS SK11 .... 15 H9
Byron St RUNC WA7 .... 8 F4
Byron Wy CW/SHV CW2 .... 237 M3
Bythom CI CHSE CH3 .... 170 E5 ▣

C

Cabot CI WARRW/BUR WA5 ...... 36 C3 ▣
Cadnam Dr WYTH/NTH M22 ...... 63 M1
Cadnant CI CH/BCN CH1 ...... 168 D1
Cadshaw CI GOL/RIS/CU WA3 .... 29 K7
Cae Bychan FLINT CH6 .... 116 B8
Cae Derw FLINT CH6 .... 116 B7
Cae Hir FLINT CH6 .... 116 B7
Caerleon Av WSFD CW7 ...... 177 H5
Caernarvon Av WSFD CW7 .... 177 H5 ▣
Caernarvon CI CQ CH5 .... 142 B7
Caernarvon Ct EP CH65 ...... 121 K2 ▣
Caernarvon Dr BRAM/HZG SK7 .. 66 C3
Caernarvon Rd CW/SHV CW2 .. 237 L4
Caesar Av FLINT CH6 .... 116 C7
Cairns Crs CH/BCN CH1 ...... 144 D8
Cairo St WARR WA1 .... 5 G7
Caister Wy WSFD CW7 .... 177 J5 ▣
Caistor St STKP SK1 .... 3 L2
Caithness CI NTHM/RTH M23 .. 44 A8 ▣
Calamine St MCFLDS SK11 ..... 15 J8
Calcutta Rd EDGY/DAV SK3 .... 46 C5
Caldbeck Av
WARRN/WOL WA2 .... 37 K2 ▣
Caldecott Crs WHITCH SY13 .. 269 L5
Caldecott Rd CW/HAS WA2 ... 222 A7
IRL M44 .... 31 M3
WYTH/NTH M22 .... 44 D4
Calderbrook Dr CHD/CHDH SK8 .. 46 A8
Calder CI MCFLDN SK10 ...... 112 F4
POY/DIS SK12 .... 86 D2
WDN WA8 .... 53 M1
Calderfield CI WARRS WA4 .... 56 B4
Calder Dr RAIN/WH L35 .... 33 H1
Caldey Rd NTHM/RTH M23 ..... 43 L7
Caldicott CI WSFD CW7 ...... 177 J5
Caldwell Av WARRW/BUR WA5 .. 36 F2
Caldwell Rd WDN WA8 .... 7 G6
Caldwell's Gate La NWCHE CW9 .. 78 A3
Caldy CI CHNE CH2 .... 145 K7
Caldy Dr GTS/LS CH66 .... 94 D8
Caldy Rd ALS/KID ST7 .... 224 C8
WILM/AE SK9 .... 84 D1
Caldy Valley Rd CHSE CH3 .... 170 B4
Caldy Wy WSFD CW7 .... 177 H3
Caldywood Dr RAIN/WH L35 .... 32 L1
Cale Gn EDGY/DAV SK3 .... 46 F6
Cale Rd NM/HAY SK22 .... 69 K4
Cale St OFTN SK2 .... 46 F5
California CI WARRW/BUR WA5 .. 36 C3
Callands Rd WARRW/BUR WA5 .. 36 D2

Calmington La RUNC WA7 ...... 54 F8
Calow Dr LEIGH WN7 .... 25 J1
Calrofold La MCFLDN SK10 .... 139 J3
Calstock CI WARRW/BUR WA5 .. 54 E1 ▣
Calve Croft Rd WYTH/NTH M22 .. 63 L3
Calveley Green La
TPLY/KEL CW6 .... 218 B2
Calveley Hall La TPLY/KEL ... 198 E8
TPLY/KEL CW6 .... 218 B3

Calveley Rd MCFLDN SK10 ... 137 M3 ▣
Calverhall Wy AIMK WN4 ...... 22 A1
Calverley Av ALS/KID SK9 .... 84 C4 ▣
Calverly CI RUNC WA7 .... 74 C7 ▣
Calverly Rd CHD/CHDH SK8 .... 46 A7 ▣
Calver Rd WARRN/WOL WA2 .... 27 M8
WARRN/WOL WA2 .... 37 G1
Camberley CI BRAM/HZG SK7 .. 66 A5
Camberley Dr WLTN L25 .... 50 C4
Camborne Av MCFLDN SK10 .... 137 L4
WLTN L25 .... 50 C4
Camborne CI CONG CW12 ..... 207 L4
RUNC WA7 .... 74 C6 ▣
Cambourne Rd
WARRW/BUR WA5 .... 26 F6
Cambo Wk HTNM SK4 .... 45 M1
Cambrai Av WARRS WA4 .... 56 C2
Cambrian Av CHSE CH3 ...... 170 B2
Cambrian Rd CH/BCN CH1 ..... 16 D3
EDGY/DAV SK3 .... 2 B8
Cambrian Wy CQ CH5 .... 166 A2
WLTN L25 .... 50 B1
WSFD CW7 .... 177 H4
Cambridge Av MCFLDS SK11 .... 14 D8
WILM/AE SK9 .... 83 M5
WSFD CW7 .... 177 G4
Cambridge Dr HLWD L26 .... 50 F4 ▣
Cambridge Gdns FROD/HEL WA6 .. 98 D8
WARRS WA4 .... 56 B5 ▣
Cambridge Rd CHD/CHDH SK8 .. 45 H6
CHNE CH2 .... 145 M7
EP CH65 .... 10 F8
HALE/TIMP WA15 .... 61 L2
MCFLDS SK11 .... 14 D8
Cambridge St OFTN SK2 ...... 47 G6
RUNC WA7 .... 9 L2
WDN WA8 .... 18 D1
Camden Ct RUNC WA7 .... 74 D3 ▣
Camden Rd EP CH65 .... 10 A7
Camden St CW/HAS CW1 .... 19 H3 ▣
Camelot Gv CW/SHV CW2 .... 238 C8
Cameron Av CW/HAS CW1 .... 19 L4
RUNC WA7 .... 8 D7
Cameron Ct WARRN/WOL WA2 .. 28 A8
Cameron Dr WDN WA8 .... 7 G5
Camm St CW/SHV CW2 .... 19 G7
Campbell Av RUNC WA7 .... 9 G7
Campbell CI CONG CW12 ..... 185 G8
CW/HAS CW1 .... 222 C8
WRX/GR/LL LL12 .... 210 B5
Campbell Crs WARRW/BUR WA5 .. 35 M6
Campbell Rd SALE M33 .... 42 F1
Campden Wy WILM/AE SK9 ..... 64 D8
Camphill Rd WLTN L25 .... 50 A5
Campion CI CHSE CH3 .... 170 A4
GOL/RIS/CU WA3 .... 29 J8 ▣
Camp Rd WLTN L25 .... 50 B3
Campsey Ash WDN WA8 .... 52 F1
Camrose CI RUNC WA7 .... 73 J6
Camsley La LYMM WA13 .... 58 B1
Cam St SK1 .... 50 A3 ▣
Canaan GOL/RIS/CU WA3 ...... 24 C4
Canada CI WARRN/WOL WA2 .... 38 A2
Canada St OFTN SK2 .... 47 G6
Canadian Av CHNE CH2 ...... 146 A8
Canal Reach RUNC WA7 .... 74 C2
Canal Rd ALT WA14 .... 42 E5
CONG CW12 .... 207 M3
Canal Side CH/BCN CH1 ...... 17 H4
Canalside EP CH65 .... 11 H5
Canal Side MCFLDS SK11 ..... 15 L7
NWCHW CW8 .... 129 H2
WARRS WA4 .... 55 J7
WARRS WA4 .... 57 J3
WARRS WA4 .... 74 F6
Canal St CH/BCN CH1 .... 16 E4
CHF/WBR SK23 .... 89 L5
CONG CW12 .... 207 L2
MCFLDN SK10 .... 15 L7
MPL/ROM SK6 .... 49 G6 ▣
NEWLW WA12 .... 26 F2
RUNC WA7 .... 9 K2
STKP SK1 .... 3 H7
Canal Ter MWCH CW10 .... 179 K4
Canal Wk MCFLDN SK10 ...... 112 F6
Canberra Rd BRAM/HZG SK7 ... 65 L7
Canberra Sq WARRN/WOL WA2 .. 37 K2
Canberra Wy CH/BCN CH1 .... 144 D8 ▣
Candelan Wy KNUT WA16 .... 59 J8
Candleford PI OFTN SK2 ...... 47 L8
Candleston Dr WARRW/BUR WA5 .. 35 G6
Canford CI CW/HAS CW1 ..... 221 H4
WARRW/BUR WA5 .... 36 C6
Canley CI STKP SK1 .... 3 H8
Cannell St RUNC WA7 .... 74 A6
Cannell St WARRW/BUR WA5 ... 36 B8 ▣
Canning St CH/BCN CH1 ...... 16 F4 ▣
HTNM SK4 .... 2 F3
Cann La NWCHE CW9 .... 104 F1
NWCHE CW9 .... 104 F1
WARRS WA4 .... 56 F8
Cannock St GTS/LS CH66 .... 120 E4
Cannon St EP CH65 .... 10 B7
STHEL WA9 .... 34 C1
Canon Dr ALT WA14 .... 61 H3
Canons Rd WARRS WA4 .... 36 D6
Canon St RUNC WA7 .... 8 F1
Canterbury Av
GOL/RIS/CU WA3 .... 23 K3 ▣
Canterbury CI GTS/LS CH66 .. 120 E4 ▣
Canterbury Pk DID/WITH M20 .. 44 F1 ▣
Canterbury Rd CH/BCN CH1 .... 37 M1
HALE/TIMP WA15 .... 62 C1
STKP SK1 .... 3 L6
WDN WA8 .... 52 C5
Canterbury St WARRS WA4 ..... 5 J9 ▣
Cantley CI RUNC WA7 .... 73 K6 ▣
Canton St MCFLDS SK11 ...... 15 H9
Canute PI KNUT WA16 .... 107 G2 ▣
Capeland CI CHSW/BR CH4 ... 168 E7 ▣
Capenhurst Av CW/SHV CW2 .. 237 M1
WARRN/WOL WA2 .... 38 A2
Capenhurst La NTHM/RTH M23 .. 43 M8
Capenhurst La CH/BCN CH1 .. 120 A5

EP CH65 .... 121 G1
Capesthorne CI ALS/KID ST7 . 241 J1
BRAM/HZG SK7 .... 66 F4 ▣
HOLMCH CW4 .... 181 H1 ▣
NWCHE CW9 .... 129 M8
SBCH CW11 .... 204 C5
.... 6 D4
Capesthorne Rd BRAM/HZG SK7 .. 66 F4
CHSE CH3 .... 171 H7
CW/SHV CW2 .... 237 L2
HALE/TIMP WA15 .... 43 K6
MPL/ROM SK6 .... 67 L5
WARRN/WOL WA2 .... 37 L2
WILM/AE SK9 .... 83 L7
Capesthorne Wy MCFLDS SK11 .. 15 L6
Capital CI ALS/KID ST7 .... 243 G2
Cappers La SBCH CW11 ...... 224 B2
TPLY/KEL CW6 .... 217 H8
Capricorn Wy BURS/TUN ST6 .. 243 M6
Captain's La AIMK WN4 ...... 22 C1 ▣
Capton CI BRAM/HZG SK7 ..... 66 A2
Carden Av WSFD CW7 .... 177 H3
Carden CI GOL/RIS/CU WA3 ... 29 K8 ▣
Cardeston CI RUNC WA7 .... 99 M1 ▣
Cardew Av WYTH/NTH M22 ..... 44 E8
Cardiff CI CW/SHV CW2 ..... 237 J4 ▣
Cardigan CI MCFLDS SK11 .... 14 B5
WARRW/BUR WA5 .... 36 D2
Carey St WDN WA8 .... 7 J3
Carisbrook Av MCFLDN SK10 ... 15 K2
Carisbrooke Av BRAM/HZG SK7 .. 66 D3
Carisbrooke CI CW/SHV CW2 .. 237 L4
Carkington Rd WLTN L25 ...... 50 C5
Carleton Rd POY/DIS SK12 .... 67 J8
Carlile St EDGY/DAV SK3 ...... 2 E8
Carlines Av CQ CH5 .... 166 A2
Carlin Ga HALE/TIMP WA15 ... 43 G6
Carling Dr WYTH/NTH M22 .... 63 L2
Carlingford CI EDGY/DAV SK3 . 46 E7 ▣
Carlingford Rd WARRS WA4 ... 56 B4
Carlisle CI KNUT WA16 .... 82 A6 ▣
MCFLDS SK11 .... 137 M7
MPL/ROM SK6 .... 48 A3
WSFD CW7 .... 177 G3
Carlisle Dr ALT WA14 .... 42 E4 ▣
Carlisle Rd CH/BCN CH1 .... 144 E7
Carlisle St CW/SHV CW2 ...... 18 D8
WARRS WA4 .... 56 C4 ▣
WILM/AE SK9 .... 110 A4
Carloon Dr NTHM/RTH M23 .... 44 B3
Carloon Rd NTHM/RTH M23 .... 44 B3
Carlow CI SPK/HALE L24 ...... 71 J2
Carlow Dr WYTH/NTH M22 ..... 63 L2
Carlton Av BRAM/HZG SK7 .... 65 K7 ▣
CHD/CHDH SK8 .... 64 F1
CHSW/BR CH4 .... 168 D6
MPL/ROM SK6 .... 48 D1
RUNC WA7 .... 73 K2
WILM/AE SK9 .... 84 C2
Carlton CI CHNE CH2 .... 146 E4
NSTN CH64 .... 91 J2
Carlton Ct HALE/TIMP WA15 .. 62 B3
Carlton Gn GTS/LS CH66 ..... 94 E4
STKP SK1 .... 3 K4
Carlton Rd GOL/RIS/CU WA3 .. 23 K3
HALE/TIMP WA15 .... 62 B2
HTNM SK4 .... 46 A2
LYMM WA13 .... 40 B7
NWCHE CW9 .... 13 K4
Carlton St WARRS WA4 .... 56 C4 ▣
WDN WA8 .... 7 H4
Carlton Wy GOL/RIS/CU WA3 .. 31 J7
Carlyle CI ALS/KID ST7 .... 224 E4
Carlyle Crs GTS/LS CH66 .... 94 E8
Carlyon Wy HLWD L26 .... 50 E4 ▣
Carmarthen CI
WARRW/BUR WA5 .... 36 D2
WSFD CW7 .... 177 J5 ▣
Carmel Av CH/BCN CH1 ...... 168 D1
Carmel CI WDN WA8 .... 34 B8 ▣
Carmel Ms WILM/AE SK9 ...... 84 B2
Carmenna Dr BRAM/HZG SK7 .. 65 M5
Carmichael CI PART M31 ..... 40 E5
Carmichael St EDGY/DAV SK3 .. 2 C9
Carnaby CI HUY L36 .... 32 A4 ▣
Carnarvon St STKP SK1 .... 3 K7
Carnegie CI MCFLDN SK10 .... 14 A2 ▣
SALE M33 .... 42 D1 ▣
Carnforth St SALE M33 ...... 43 G1 ▣
Carnforth Gv ALS/KID ST7 .. 243 L4
Carnforth Rd CHD/CHDH SK8 .. 46 B8
Carnoustie CI WILM/AE SK9 .. 84 D4 ▣
Carnoustie Dr CHD/CHDH SK8 . 64 C3
MCFLDN SK10 .... 112 C7
Caroline St EDGY/DAV SK3 .... 2 D9
IRL M44 .... 31 L4
WDN WA8 .... 7 J7 ▣
Carol St WARRS WA4 .... 56 D1
Carpenter Gv WARRN/WOL WA2 . 38 A3
Carr Brow MPL/ROM SK6 ...... 68 A5
Carr CI STKP SK1 .... 3 L7
Carrfield Av EDGY/DAV SK3 ... 47 G8
HALE/TIMP WA15 .... 43 K6
Carrgreen La LYMM WA13 ..... 40 F6
Carriage Dr BIDD ST8 ...... 227 L3
Carrick Dr EP CH65 .... 121 H2
Carrick Rd CHSW/BR CH4 ..... 16 B8
Carrington CI GOL/RIS/CU WA3 .. 29 J8
Carrington Field St OFTN SK2 . 46 F5
Carrington Rd STKP SK1 .... 3 L2
Carrington Wy CW/HAS CW1 .. 221 H4
Carr La GOL/RIS/CU WA3 ..... 24 A5
LEIGH WN7 .... 24 E4
SPK/HALE L24 .... 71 K2
WILM/AE SK9 .... 109 K2
Carr Mill Ms WILM/AE SK9 ... 84 B3 ▣
Carr Rd HALE/TIMP WA15 ..... 62 B2
Carrs Av CHD/CHDH SK8 ...... 45 M6
Carrs La CHSE CH3 .... 214 F3
Carrs Rd CHD/CHDH SK8 ...... 45 M6
Carr St ALS/KID ST7 .... 243 M3
Carrswood Rd NTHM/RTH M23 .. 43 J4

Carrwood HALE/TIMP WA15 .... 62 B5
KNUT WA16 .... 107 J3
Carr Wood Av BRAM/HZG SK7 .. 65 L4
Carrwood Rd BRAM/HZG SK7 ... 65 K3
Carrwood Rd WILM/AE SK9 .... 83 M4
Carsdale Rd WYTH/NTH M22 ... 63 J3
Carstairs Av CW/SHV SK3 ..... 47 G8
Cartbridge La HLWD L26 ...... 50 F3
Carter Av TPLY/KEL CW6 .... 149 K8 ▣
Carter La MCFLDS SK11 ..... 109 G8
Carter St CH/BCN CH1 .... 17 J3
Cartier CI WARRW/BUR WA5 ... 36 C3 ▣
Cartlake CI NANT CW5 .... 20 B7
Cartledge CI WARR WA8 ..... 152 A1 ▣
Cartlich St BURS/TUN ST6 ... 243 K7
Cartmel Av WARRN/WOL WA2 .. 37 J1 ▣
Cartmel CI BRAM/HZG SK7 .... 66 C1
CHD/CHDH SK8 .... 64 C1
HOLMCH CW4 .... 181 G1
MCFLDN SK10 .... 138 B2
WARRW/BUR WA5 .... 36 E2 ▣
Cartmel Dr GTS/LS CH66 .... 120 F2
HALE/TIMP WA15 .... 43 K6
Cartmell CI RUNC WA7 .... 73 H6
Cartridge CI WYTH/NTH M22 .. 63 M1 ▣
Cartridge La WARRS WA4 ..... 57 K6
Cartwright Rd CW/HAS CW1 .. 222 D6
Cartwright St RUNC WA7 .... 9 L3
WARRW/BUR WA5 .... 4 B5
Carver Av HOLMCH CW4 ...... 157 G6
Carver CI WSFD CW7 .... 154 A8 ▣
Carver Dr MPL/ROM SK6 ...... 48 E7
Carver Rd HALE/TIMP WA15 ... 61 L2
MPL/ROM SK6 .... 48 E7
Casey La CW/SHV CW2 .... 253 M1
Cashmere Rd EDGY/DAV SK3 .. 46 C5
Caspian Rd ALT WA14 .... 42 A6
Cassia Green La NWCHW CW8 . 152 B6
WSFD CW7 .... 152 D7
Cassley Rd SPK/HALE L24 .... 71 G1
Casson St CW/HAS CW1 .... 18 D2
Castillion Dr WHITCH SY13 .. 270 B4
Castle Bank CW/HAS CW1 ..... 12 F5
CHSW/BR CH4 .... 210 D2
TPLY/KEL CW6 .... 149 K8
Castle CI CHSW/BR CH4 ..... 167 H6
Castle Croft CHSW/BR CH4 .. 169 H7
Castle Dr CH/BCN CH1 .... 16 F8
EP CH65 .... 121 G1
Castle Dyke St FLINT CH6 ... 116 B5
Castle Edge Rd NM/HAY SK22 . 69 G2
Castle Farm La CW/SHV CW2 .. 47 J7 ▣
Castlefields Av South RUNC WA7 .. 73 M3
Castlefields CHSE CH3 ...... 214 C2
Castlefields Av East RUNC WA7 .. 74 A3
Castlefields Av North
RUNC WA7 .... 74 A2 ▣
Castlefields Av South
RUNC WA7 .... 74 A4 ▣
Castleford Dr MCFLDN SK10 . 111 L6
Castlegate MCFLDN SK10 .... 111 L6
Castlegate Ms MCFLDN SK10 . 111 M6 ▣
Castle Gn WARRS WA4 .... 56 A2
Castlehill CHSW/BR CH4 .... 210 C2 ▣
Castle HI MCFLDN SK10 ..... 111 L6
NEWLW WA12 .... 22 E8
WHITCH SY13 .... 270 A5
Castle Hill La CO CH5 ..... 142 B8 ▣
Castle Inn Rd CONG CW12 ... 208 C5
Castle La AUD/MAD/W CW3 .. 267 L7
Castlemead Wk NWCHE CW9 .. 129 L8
Castlemere Dr CW/HAS CW1 .. 221 J5
Castle Mill La HALE/TIMP WA15 .. 61 M6
HALE/TIMP WA15 .... 62 D8
HALE/TIMP WA15 .... 82 E1
Castle Ri CQ CH5 .... 166 D4
MCFLDN SK10 .... 111 M6
Castle Rd ALS/KID ST7 ..... 226 D5
FLINT CH6 .... 116 B5
RUNC WA7 .... 73 M4
Castle Shaw Rd OFTN SK2 .... 47 K7
Castle St CH/BCN CH1 .... 16 F7
CW/HAS CW1 .... 18 E3
EDGY/DAV SK3 .... 2 E8
FLINT CH6 .... 116 B5
MCFLDS SK11 .... 15 G5
NANT CW5 .... 20 E6
NWCHW CW8 .... 128 C4
WDN WA8 .... 53 K3
WRXS/E LL13 .... 228 D4
Castleton Dr MPL/ROM SK6 ... 67 M6
Castleton Rd BRAM/HZG SK7 .. 66 F6
Castleton St ALT WA14 ...... 42 C5 ▣
Castletown CI MCFLDN SK10 . 112 C8 ▣
Castletown La CHSE CH3 .... 244 D2
Castle Vw BIDD ST8 .... 227 J6
Castleview
BURS/TUN ST6 .... 243 M5 ▣
Castleview Rd ALS/KID ST7 . 243 H1
Castle Wy CHSW/BR CH4 ..... 191 G6
Castleway HALE/TIMP WA15 ... 62 B5
Castlewood Gdns OFTN SK2 ... 47 J7 ▣
Castner Av RUNC WA7 .... 8 C8
Catchpenny La MCFLDS SK11 . 158 E1
Catford CI WDN WA8 .... 52 C2
Catford Gn SPK/HALE L24 .... 70 F1
Catford Rd NTHM/RTH M23 .... 43 M7
Catfoss CI WARRN/WOL WA2 ... 37 L3
Catherine Dr CQ CH5 ...... 166 A2 ▣
Catherine Rd ALT WA14 ...... 61 J1
MPL/ROM SK6 .... 48 A4
Catherine St BRAM/HZG SK7 .. 47 L8
CH/BCN CH1 .... 16 D4
CW/SHV CW2 .... 19 G8
MCFLDS SK11 .... 14 F5
WARRW/BUR WA5 .... 36 C3
WDN WA8 .... 7 H8
Catherine Wy NEWLW WA12 .... 27 H2
Catkin Rd HLWD L26 .... 50 D2
Catterall Av WARRN/WOL WA2 . 37 K2 ▣
Catterals La WHITCH SY13 .. 270 E6
Catterick Av DID/WITH M20 .. 45 J1
SALE M33 .... 42 C2
Catterick CI HLWD L26 ...... 50 F4 ▣
Catterick Rd DID/WITH M20 .. 45 J1

Catterwood Dr
MPL/ROM SK6 .... 49 H2 ▣
Caughall Rd CHNE CH2 ...... 145 L4
Caunce Av GOL/RIS/CU WA3 ... 23 G5
Causeway Av WARRS WA4 ...... 56 C1 ▣
The Causeway ALT WA14 .... 42 D8
Cavalier Dr CH/BCN CH1 .... 144 E6
Cavan CI EDGY/DAV SK3 ...... 45 M5
Cavell CI WLTN L25 .... 50 A3
Cavell Dr EP CH65 .... 95 G8
Cavendish Av GOL/RIS/CU WA3 . 29 L7
Cavendish CI MCFLDN SK10 .. 138 D1 ▣
WARRW/BUR WA5 .... 36 D5
WSFD CW7 .... 177 G4
Cavendish Crs ALS/KID ST7 . 224 C7
Cavendish Farm Rd RUNC WA7 . 72 F7
Cavendish Gdns EP CH65 ..... 95 G8
Cavendish Ms WILM/AE SK9 ... 84 A7
Cavendish Rd ALT WA14 ...... 61 J1
BRAM/HZG SK7 .... 66 D3
CHSW/BR CH4 .... 169 H5
CW/SHV CW2 .... 220 E7
HTNM SK4 .... 45 M2
Cavendish St RUNC WA7 ...... 8 F3 ▣
Cavendish Wy HOLMCH CW4 .. 180 F2 ▣
Caversham CI WARRS WA4 ..... 56 D5
Cawdor Dr CHSE CH3 .... 170 A2
Cawdor PI HALE/TIMP WA15 .. 43 J6
Cawdor St RUNC WA7 .... 8 E1
WARRS WA4 .... 56 C4
Cawfield Av WDN WA8 .... 6 B3
Cawley Av GOL/RIS/CU WA3 ... 24 C8
Cawley La MCFLDN SK10 ...... 86 E5
Cawley St MCFLDS SK11 ...... 15 J6 ▣
.... 9 G5
Cawood CI GTS/LS CH66 ...... 94 B7
Cawthorne Av WARRS WA4 ..... 57 G2
Caxton CI WDN WA8 .... 52 C1 ▣
Caxton Rd RAIN/WH L35 ...... 33 L3
C' Ct AIMK WN4 .... 22 B2
The Ceal MPL/ROM SK6 .... 49 H2
Cecil Av SALE M33 .... 42 E1 ▣
Cecil Rigby CI SBCH CW11 .. 204 B6 ▣
Cecil Rd BIDD ST8 .... 227 J2
HALE/TIMP WA15 .... 61 L2
Cecil St CHSE CH3 .... 170 A3
Cedab Rd EP CH65 .... 10 F6
Cedar Av ALS/KID ST7 ...... 241 K1
ALS/KID ST7 .... 242 D3
ALT WA14 .... 42 C8
BRAM/HZG SK7 .... 66 E2
CQ CH5 .... 143 G5
GOL/RIS/CU WA3 .... 23 M5
GTS/LS CH66 .... 94 C6
RUNC WA7 .... 9 M8
RUNC WA7 .... 74 A8
WDN WA8 .... 53 H1
Cedar CI HOLMCH CW4 .... 157 K8
MWCH CW10 .... 179 L6
NWCHW CW9 .... 131 G1
POY/DIS SK12 .... 86 E1 ▣
SBCH CW11 .... 204 C7
Cedar Ct CONG CW12 .... 207 M4
GOL/RIS/CU WA3 .... 29 M2
NANT CW5 .... 237 K6
Cedar Crs NEWLW WA12 .... 27 K2
Cedardale Dr GTS/LS CH66 .. 120 F3
Cedardale Pk WDN WA8 .... 34 E8
Cedar Dr CHNE CH2 .... 146 B8
NWCHW CW8 .... 103 G8
Cedarfield Rd LYMM WA13 .... 40 B7
Cedar Gdns CQ CH5 .... 166 A1
Cedar Gv CHNE CH2 .... 146 B8
MCFLDS SK11 .... 138 D7
NANT CW5 .... 21 K6
NSTN CH64 .... 91 M4
WARR WA4 .... 38 A5
WARRS WA4 .... 56 B1
WSFD CW7 .... 178 A3
Cedar Ms CH/BCN CH1 .... 144 E8
Cedar Pk CHSE CH3 .... 170 C2
Cedar Rd CHD/CHDH SK8 ...... 45 G7
HALE/TIMP WA15 .... 61 L1
MPL/ROM SK6 .... 48 B8
NWCHW CW8 .... 128 C4
OFTN SK2 .... 47 H8
PART M31 .... 40 E1
RAIN/WH L35 .... 32 D1
WARRW/BUR WA5 .... 35 M6 ▣
Cedars Rd WYTH/NTH M22 ..... 63 K1
Cedar St NEWLW WA12 .... 27 J2 ▣
Cedar Wy CW/SHV CW2 .... 238 B5
Cedarway MCFLDN SK10 ..... 113 G4
Cedarways WARRS WA4 .... 56 D7 ▣
Cedarwood NWCHW CW8 ...... 127 K7
Cedarwood Av HTNM SK4 ...... 46 A3
Cedarwood Ct TPLY/KEL CW6 . 197 J1
Celandine CI CHSE CH3 ..... 170 A5
Celtic Av ALS/KID ST7 .... 243 H4
Celtic St CQ CH5 .... 3 K7
Celyn Crs CHSW/BR CH4 .... 168 D7
Cement PI CH/BCN CH1 ...... 17 H4 ▣
Cemetery Rd CW/SHV CW2 ... 239 H7
Cemlyn CI CH/BCN CH1 ...... 168 C1
Central Av EP CH65 .... 10 E9
LEIGH WN7 .... 25 J1 ▣
SALE M33 .... 42 D3
SPK/HALE L24 .... 70 D1
WARRN/WOL WA2 .... 5 J1
WARRS WA4 .... 56 B1
Central Dr BRAM/HZG SK7 .... 65 K2
CHD/CHDH SK8 .... 64 D4
CQ CH5 .... 142 B7
MPL/ROM SK6 .... 48 C1 ▣
NWCHW CW8 .... 129 G1
Central Expy RUNC WA7 ...... 73 K6 ▣
Central Gv NWCHE CW9 ..... 130 D6 ▣
Central Rd MANAIR M90 ...... 63 J6
NWCHE CW9 .... 130 D5
PART M31 .... 40 E1
WARRS WA4 .... 56 B1
Central St ALS/KID ST7 .... 226 B6
Central Wy ALT WA14 .... 42 D8
NEWLW WA12 .... 27 L2
SPK/HALE L24 .... 70 E2
WARRN/WOL WA2 .... 5 G5
Centre La LEIGH WN7 .... 24 F1

Centre Park Sq WARR WA1 ..... 4 F9
Centurion Cl GOL/RIS/CU WA3 .. 29 K8
Chadkirk Rd MPL/ROM SK6 ..... 48 B3
Chads Gn NANT CW5 .... 253 G3
Chadvil Rd OFTN SK2 .... 45 J7
Chadwell Rd OFTN SK2 .... 47 L5
Chadwick Av GOL/RIS/CU WA3 .. 29 H5
  WARRS WA4 .... 56 F3
Chadwick Cl WILM/AE SK9 ..... 84 C3
Chadwick Pl GOL/RIS/CU WA3 .. 29 L7
Chadwick Rd MWCH CW10 ...... 179 J6
  RUNC WA7 .... 73 L1
  STKP SK1 .... 3 G8
Chadwick Ter MCFLDN SK10 ... 15 K2
Chaffinch Cl CONG CW12 ..... 207 L3
  GOL/RIS/CU WA3 .... 38 F1
  WYTH/NTH M22 .... 44 F7
Chaffinch Dr BIDD ST8 ...... 227 L4
Chaffinch Gld HLWD L26 ..... 50 E3
Chaffinch Wy WSFD CW7 ...... 177 K6
Chain Maker's Rw
  CHSW/BR CH4 .... 168 E5
Chalfield Av GTS/LS CH66 .... 94 C7
Chalfield Cl CW/SHV CW2 .... 238 B5
  GTS/LS CH66 .... 94 C7
Chalfont Cl WARRS WA4 ...... 56 E6
Chalgrave Wd WDN WA8 .... 53 L1
Challinor St CHSE CH3 ...... 170 A3
Chamber Brook La
  FROD/HEL WA6 .... 126 C2
Chamberlain Ct CW/HAS CW1 . 222 C7
Chamberlain Wy BIDD ST8 ... 227 L4
Chambers St CW/SHV CW2 .... 19 G8
Chance Hall La ALS/KID ST7 . 225 H3
Chancel La WILM/AE SK9 ..... 84 B4
Chancellor Rd RUNC WA7 ..... 54 D7
Chancel Ms STKP SK1 .... 3 G8
Chancery La ALS/KID ST7 .... 241 H1
  MCFLDN SK10 .... 113 H5
Chandler Wy GOL/RIS/CU WA3 . 23 L4
Chandley St CHD/CHDH SK8 ... 45 K6
Chandos Ct CHSW/BR CH4 .... 169 L6
Change La NSTN CH64 .... 93 H4
Chantier Av WARRS WA4 ...... 37 L8
Chantry Av NWCHW CW8 ...... 129 H8
Chantry Cl POY/DIS SK12 .... 68 E7
Chantry Ct MCFLDS SK11 .... 138 D7
Chantry Fold POY/DIS SK12 .. 68 A8
Chantry Rd POY/DIS SK12 .... 68 D6
The Chantry TPLY/KEL CW6 .. 217 L2
Chapel Av FROD/HEL WA6 .... 126 C2
Chapel Bank ALS/KID ST7 ... 226 D5
Chapel Cl ALS/KID ST7 ..... 226 B6
  AUD/MAD/W CW3 .... 273 M1
  CH/BCN CH1 .... 144 A3
  CHSE CH3 .... 171 G7
  NWCHE CW9 .... 103 K5
  WSFD CW7 .... 199 M7
Chapel Ct ALT WA14 .... 42 D8
  NWCHE CW9 .... 13 H4
Chapel Cft MCFLDS SK11 .... 135 H1
Chapel Cross Rd
  WARRW/WOL WA2 .... 38 A2
Chapel Dr HALE/TIMP WA15 ... 62 C5
Chapelfields FROD/HEL WA6 .. 99 G4
Chapel House La NSTN CH64 . 119 C5
Chapel La ALS/KID ST7 ..... 228 F5
  ALS/KID ST7 .... 226 A8
  CHSE CH3 .... 170 A3
  CHSE CH3 .... 193 C8
  CHSE CH3 .... 193 K5
  CHSE CH3 .... 213 H2
  CW/HAS CW1 .... 221 K3
  FROD/HEL WA6 .... 126 C2
  FROD/HEL WA6 .... 126 C2
  GOL/RIS/CU WA3 .... 39 M3
  HALE/TIMP WA15............ 62 C5
  KNUT WA16 .... 80 B1
  KNUT WA16 .... 156 E1
  MALPAS SY14 .... 256 E4
  MCFLDN SK10 .... 113 L7
  MCFLDS SK11 .... 159 K3
  NANT CW5 .... 250 D2
  NWCHE CW9 .... 13 J2
  NWCHW CW8 .... 127 K1
  PART M31 .... 40 F1
  RAIN/WH L35 .... 33 M2
  TPLY/KEL CW6 .... 173 L2
  WARRS WA4 .... 56 C4
  WARRS WA4 .... 77 H1
  WARRS WA4 .... 102 A5
  WDN WA8 .... 33 J7
  WILM/AE SK9 .... 83 M6
  WRX/GR/LL LL12 .... 210 C5
  WRXS/E LL13 .... 228 D4
Chapelmere Cl SBCH CW11 ... 203 L5
Chapelmere Ct CW/HAS CW1 . 221 J5
Chapel Ms EP CH65 .... 10 C9
  EP CH65 .... 95 H8
Chapel Pl AIMK WN4 .... 22 B1
Chapel Rd CHF/WBR SK23 .... 89 M7
  KNUT WA16 .... 107 M6
  WARRW/WOL WA5 .... 54 E1
  WILM/AE SK9 .... 110 A3
  WSFD CW7 .... 177 M2
  WYTH/NTH M22 .... 44 D4
Chapel St AIMK WN4 .... 22 B1
  ALS/KID ST7 .... 226 B6
  ALS/KID ST7 .... 242 D2
  BRAM/HZG SK7 .... 66 E1
  CHD/CHDH SK8 .... 45 K7
  CHF/WBR SK23 .... 89 L4
  CHSE CH3 .... 17 K4
  CONG CW12 .... 207 K2
  CW/SHV CW2 .... 19 C6
  HTNM SK4 .... 45 K2
  MCFLDN SK10 .... 113 H4
  MCFLDS SK11 .... 15 H8
  NEWLW WA12 .... 27 H1
  NM/HAY SK22 .... 69 H6
  NWCHE CW9 .... 130 C1
  NWCHE CW9 .... 153 L4
  NWCHW CW8 .... 12 E4
  NWCHW CW8 .... 128 C3
  SBCH CW11 .... 204 B6

SBCH CW11 .... 223 G1
WDN WA8 .... 7 G7
WILM/AE SK9 .... 110 A3
WRXS/E LL13 .... 228 D4
Chapel Street (Lon Y Capel)
  FLINT CH6 .... 116 A6
Chapel Wks CHD/CHDH SK8 ... 65 H6
Chapman Cl WDN WA8 .... 33 K8
Charcoal Rd ALT WA14 ...... 60 E1
Charcoal Woods ALT WA14 ... 61 G1
Chard Dr WYTH/NTH M22 ..... 63 K3
Chardin Av MPL/ROM SK6 .... 49 J4
Charity La MCFLDS SK11 .... 139 M4
Charlcote Crs CW/SHV CW2 .. 238 C4
Charlecote Rd POY/DIS SK12 . 66 F8
Charles Av MPL/ROM SK6 .... 48 C5
  NWCHE CW9 .... 153 M2
  WARRW/BUR WA5 .... 35 M4
Charles Cotton Dr
  AUD/MAD/W CW3 .... 267 K6
Charles Crs CHSW/BR CH4 ... 17 K8
Charles Dr FLINT CH6 ...... 116 B7
Charles Rd CHNE CH2 .... 145 H4
Charles Sq SBCH CW11 ...... 223 M2
Charles St BIDD ST8 .... 227 J5
  BRAM/HZG SK7 .... 66 D1
  CH/BCN CH1 .... 17 H3
  CHNE CH2 .... 17 L2
  CW/HAS CW1 .... 18 F3
  GOL/RIS/CU WA3 .... 23 G3
  IRL M44 .... 31 L6
  STKP SK1 .... 3 J9
  WDN WA8 .... 7 G7
Charleston Cl GTS/LS CH66 . 120 D1
  SALE M33 .... 42 D2
Charlestown Rd East OFTN SK2 . 66 A1
Charlestown Rd West
  EDGY/DAV SK3 .... 65 M1
Charlesworth Ct SBCH CW11 . 204 C6
Charlesworth Crs
  CHF/WBR SK23 .... 89 K1
Charlesworth Rd CHF/WBR SK23.. 89 K1
Charlesworth St CW/HAS CW1 . 221 K6
  STKP SK1 .... 3 G9
Charlock Cl LEIGH WN7 ..... 24 F1
Charlock Sq ALT WA14 ...... 42 B4
Charlotte St BURS/TUN ST6 . 243 J5
  CH/BCN CH1 .... 16 D4
  CHD/CHDH SK8 .... 45 K7
  MCFLDS SK11 .... 15 H6
  STKP SK1 .... 3 L2
Charlotte St West
  MCFLDS SK11 .... 14 F5
Charlton Cl RUNC WA7 ...... 74 A5
Charlton St MCFLDS SK11 ... 14 D5
  WARRS WA4 .... 56 F1
Charminster Cl
  WARRW/BUR WA5 .... 36 B7
Charmouth Wk WYTH/NTH M22 . 63 M1
Charnock Av NEWLW WA12 .... 26 F1
Charnock Rd GOL/RIS/CU WA3. 29 M1
Charnville Rd CHD/CHDH SK8 . 44 F8
Charnwood ALS/KID ST7 ..... 243 H3
Charnwood Cl
  GOL/RIS/CU WA3 .... 30 B7
  MCFLDN SK10 .... 14 A3
Charnwood Crs
  BRAM/HZG SK7 .... 66 D4
Charter Av WARRW/BUR WA5 .. 37 G4
Charter Cl SALE M33......... 42 D1
Charter Crs GTS/LS CH66 ... 120 E1
Charterhall Dr CHNE CH2 ... 17 L4
Charterhouse Rd WLTN L25 .. 50 B3
Charter Rd HALE/TIMP WA15 . 42 E8
  MCFLDN SK10 .... 113 G5
Charter Wy MCFLDN SK10 .... 138 E1
Chartley Gv MWCH CW10 ..... 179 K2
Chartwell Dr NTHM/RTH M23 . 43 K5
Chartwell Gv HLWD L26 ..... 51 G3
Chartwell Pk SBCH CW11 .... 204 A8
Chase Briar Wd
  CHD/CHDH SK8 .... 65 H3
Chase Dr GTS/LS CH66 ...... 120 F3
Chasefield La ALT WA14 .... 61 G2
Chaser Ct CH/BCN CH1 ...... 168 F1
Chase Wy WILM/AE SK9 ...... 120 D2
Chatburn Av GOL/RIS/CU WA3. 23 J3
Chatburn Ct GOL/RIS/CU WA3. 29 M2
Chatcombe Rd WYTH/NTH M22.. 63 G2
Chatfield Dr GOL/RIS/CU WA3. 38 E1
Chatham St EDGY/DAV SK3 ... 2 C8
  MCFLDS SK11 .... 15 G5
Chatham Wy CW/HAS CW1 .... 222 C7
Chatsworth Av OFTN SK2 .... 46 F6
Chatswood Av GOL/RIS/CU WA3.. 46 F6
Chatsworth Cl
  MCFLDS SK11 .... 137 L6
Chatsworth Ct CW/SHV CW2 . 238 A4
  GTS/LS CH66 .... 94 C7
  HALE/TIMP WA15........... 43 J7
  NWCHE CW9 .... 13 J9
Chatsworth Dr CHNE CH2 .... 170 A1
  CONG CW12 .... 206 F1
  WDN WA8 .... 52 C1
Chatsworth Rd BRAM/HZG SK7. 66 F3
  MPL/ROM SK6 .... 67 M6
  WILM/AE SK9 .... 83 L8
Chatteris Pk RUNC WA7 ..... 74 E2
Chatterley Rd ALS/KID ST7 . 243 G5
Chatterley Rd BURS/TUN ST6. 243 J8
Chatterton Dr RUNC WA7 .... 74 E2
Chatwell Gdns WARRS WA4 ... 56 F7
Chaucer Cl CH/BCN CH1 ..... 144 E6
Chaucer Gv SBCH CW11 ...... 203 J7
Chaucer Ms STKP SK1 .... 3 L6
Chaucer Pl WARRS WA4 ...... 37 M8
Chaucer St RUNC WA7 .... 9 G4
Cheadle La KNUT WA16 ...... 132 A3
Cheadle Old Rd EDGY/DAV SK3. 46 D5
Cheadle Rd CHD/CHDH SK8 ... 45 L8
Cheadle Wd CHD/CHDH SK8 ... 64 E4
Cheam Rd HALE/TIMP WA15 ... 42 E7
Checkley Dr BIDD ST8 ...... 227 K3
Checkley La AUD/MAD/W CW3 . 265 B9
Cheddar Gv WARRW/BUR WA5 . 26 F5
Chedlee Dr CHD/CHDH SK8 ... 64 E3
Chedlin Dr NTHM/RTH M23... 44 A8
Chedworth Dr NTHM/RTH M23 . 44 B6
  WDN WA8 .... 33 J8

Cheerbrook Rd NANT CW5 .... 237 J8
Cheese Hill La NWCHW CW8 .. 127 H8
Chelford Av GOL/RIS/CU WA3. 23 K8
Chelford Cl CH/BCN CH1 .... 168 F2
  HALE/TIMP WA15........... 42 E6
Chelford Crs KNUT WA16 .... 134 C3
Chelford Rd CONG CW12 ..... 183 L8
  HOLMCH CW4 .... 158 B5
  KNUT WA16 .... 107 H4
  MCFLDN SK10 .... 109 J7
  MCFLDN SK10 .... 111 H7
  MCFLDS SK11 .... 135 J3
  SALE M33 .... 43 L2
  WILM/AE SK9 .... 64 D7
Chell St CW/HAS CW1 .... 18 C1
Chelmarsh Av AIMK WN4 ..... 22 C1
Chelmsford Rd EDGY/DAV SK3. 2 B8
Chelsea Cl BIDD ST8 .... 227 J3
Chelston Dr CHD/CHDH SK8 .. 64 C6
Cheltenham Cl MCFLDN SK10 . 112 C8
  WARRW/BUR WA5 .... 36 A4
Cheltenham Crs CW/HAS CW1. 221 H5
  RUNC WA7 .... 73 H6
Cheltenham Dr NEWLW WA12. 22 C7
Cheltenham Rd EDGY/DAV SK3. 46 B4
  EP CH65 .... 121 K1
Chemical St NEWLW WA12 .... 27 H1
Chemistry WHITCH SY13 ..... 269 K5
Chemistry La CO CH5 .... 142 E8
Chemistry Rd SPK/HALE L24 . 50 C7
Chepstow Av SALE M33 ...... 42 C1
Chepstow Cl BIDD ST8 ...... 227 J3
  MCFLDN SK10 .... 112 C8
  WARRW/BUR WA5 .... 36 E1
  WSFD CW7 .... 177 J5
Chepstow Dr WARR/HZG SK7. 67 G2
Cherington Cl
  NTHM/RTH M23 .... 44 B2
  WILM/AE SK9 .... 84 F1
Cherington Crs MCFLDS SK11. 14 C7
Cherington Rd CHD/CHDH SK8. 45 J8
Cheriton Cl HLWD L26 ...... 50 E4
Cheriton Ri OFTN SK2 ...... 48 A6
Cheriton Wy CW/SHV CW2 ... 238 A4
Cherrington Rd NANT CW5 .. 251 L1
Cherry Blossom Rd
  RUNC WA7 .... 73 M7
Cherry Cl NSTN CH64 .... 92 C4
Cherry Cnr LYMM WA13 ...... 58 A6
Cherry Crs WSFD CW7 .... 177 J4
Cherrycroft MPL/ROM SK6 ... 48 E3
Cherry Dale Rd CHSW/BR CH4. 190 A1
Cherryfields Rd MCFLDS SK11. 137 M5
Cherry Gv GTS/LS CH66 ..... 121 C3
  NANT CW5 .... 20 C7
Cherry Grove Rd CHSE CH3 .. 170 A3
Cherry Hl AUD/MAD/W CW3 ... 267 L6
Cherry La ALS/KID ST7 ..... 224 E6
  CONG CW12 .... 208 E4
  LYMM WA13 .... 58 B4
  NWCHW CW8 .... 128 D4
  NWCHW CW8 .... 151 M2
  SALE M33 .... 42 C2
Cherry Orchard Cl
  BRAM/HZG SK7 .... 65 K3
Cherry Orchard Rd CQ CH5... 166 D7
Cherry Rd CHSE CH3 .... 170 A3
Cherrysutton WDN WA8 ...... 52 B1
Cherry Tree Av ALS/KID ST7. 225 G7
  LYMM WA13 .... 58 D2
  NWCHW CW8 .... 103 G8
  POY/DIS SK12 .... 86 F1
  RUNC WA7 .... 9 L6
  WARRW/BUR WA5 .... 35 M8
Cherry Tree Cl OFTN SK2 ... 47 J8
Cherry Tree Ct OFTN SK2 ... 47 J8
Cherry Tree Dr BRAM/HZG SK7. 67 G2
  STHEL WA9 .... 26 A2
Cherry Tree La ALT WA14.... 60 E6
  MPL/ROM SK6 .... 48 E2
  OFTN SK2 .... 47 J7
Cherry Tree Rd CHD/CHDH SK8. 64 F3
  CW/HAS CW1 .... 221 K6
  GOL/RIS/CU WA3 .... 23 M4
  NTHM/RTH M23 .... 43 M3
Cherry V WLTN L25 .... 50 B1
Cherry Wk CHD/CHDH SK8 .... 65 J4
  KNUT WA16 .... 132 D5
Cherrywood Crs
  NWCHW CW8 .... 103 H8
  WARRN/WOL WA2 .... 37 K2
Cheryl Ct NWCHW CW8 .... 128 A8
Cheryl Dr WDN WA8 .... 53 K3
Chesham Av WYTH/NTH M22 .. 44 C8
Chesham Cl WILM/AE SK9 .... 83 M8
Chesham Pl ALT WA14 .... 61 J2
Chesham St CH/BCN CH1 ..... 17 J3
Cheshire Cl NEWLW WA12 .... 27 L1
Cheshire Ring Canal Wk
  ALS/KID ST7 .... 224 D4
  ALS/KID ST7 .... 226 A3
  ALS/KID ST7 .... 242 C2
  ALT WA14 .... 41 L7
  MCFLDN SK10 .... 87 H3
  MPL/ROM SK6 .... 48 F4
  MWCH CW10 .... 154 D4
  MWCH CW10 .... 179 J2
  NWCHW CW8 .... 129 J2
  SBCH CW11 .... 222 D1
  WARRS WA4 .... 55 J6
  WARRS WA4 .... 75 H2
  WARRS WA4 .... 101 K4
Cheshire Rd PART M31 ...... 40 D2
Cheshire St WARRS WA4 ..... 56 F5
Cheshyre Dr RUNC WA7 ...... 73 M1
Cheshyre's La RUNC WA7 .... 72 E6
  RUNC WA7 .... 72 E6
Chessington Cl WARRS WA4 .. 56 F5
Chester Ap CHSW/BR CH4 .... 192 D1
Chester Av GOL/RIS/CU WA3 . 23 K4
  HALE/TIMP WA15........... 61 M2

SALE M33 .... 42 B3
WHITCH SY13 .... 269 L4
Chester Cl ALS/KID ST7 .... 242 D5
  CQ CH5 .... 142 B7
  IRL M44 .... 31 K7
  WILM/AE SK9 .... 84 C2
Chester Dr AIMK WN4 .... 22 D2
Chesterfield Cl WSFD CW7 . 176 F3
Chestergate EDGY/DAV SK3 .. 2 D6
  MCFLDN SK10 .... 14 F4
  STKP SK1 .... 2 F5
Chester High Rd NSTN CH64 . 92 A2
Chester La WSFD CW7 .... 176 F2
Chester New Rd WARRS WA4 . 55 M5
Chester Rd ALS/KID ST7 .... 242 D5
  ALT WA14 .... 60 D6
  BRAM/HZG SK7 .... 66 D5
  BRAM/HZG SK7 .... 85 K2
  BRAM/HZG SK7 .... 85 M1
  CHSE CH3 .... 170 A6
  CHSE CH3 .... 194 E7
  CHSE CH3 .... 211 M8
  CHSE CH3 .... 214 B2
  CHSW/BR CH4 .... 167 C7
  CQ CH5 .... 166 B8
  EP CH65 .... 121 C1
  FLINT CH6 .... 116 D7
  FROD/HEL WA6 .... 98 F6
  FROD/HEL WA6 .... 124 B2
  GTS/LS CH66 .... 121 C3
  GTS/LS CH66 .... 121 C3
  HOLMCH CW4 .... 181 H2
  KNUT WA16 .... 80 B6
  KNUT WA16 .... 105 L7
  MCFLDS SK11 .... 14 D5
  MWCH CW10 .... 179 G2
  NANT CW5 .... 218 C6
  NANT CW5 .... 236 A5
  NSTN CH64 .... 91 L5
  NWCHW CW8 .... 12 E4
  NWCHW CW8 .... 128 E8
  NWCHW CW8 .... 151 K3
  POY/DIS SK12 .... 66 B8
  RUNC WA7 .... 74 E7
  TPLY/KEL CW6 .... 149 G7
  TPLY/KEL CW6 .... 149 M6
  WARRS WA4 .... 56 F3
  WARRS WA4 .... 56 A4
  WARRS WA4 .... 75 H2
  WHITCH SY13 .... 269 L4
  WRX/GR/LL LL12 .... 210 B5
  WSFD CW7 .... 176 F2
Chester Road (East) CQ CH5 . 142 D7
Chester Road Roman Rd
  KNUT WA16 .... 80 B6
Chester Road (West) CO CH5. 142 D7
Chester Sq CW/HAS CW1 ..... 18 E4
Chester St CHSW/BR CH4 .... 168 F5
  CW/HAS CW1 .... 18 F4
  EDGY/DAV SK3 .... 2 C6
  FLINT CH6 .... 116 B5
  WDN WA8 .... 18 D5
Chester Street (Heol Caer)
  FLINT CH6 .... 116 A5
Chesterton Cl MWCH CW10 .. 179 L7
Chesterton Dr CW/SHV CW2 . 237 M3
Chesterton Gv SBCH CW11 .. 203 K7
Chesterton Rd NTHM/RTH M23. 43 K4
Chester Wks MPL/ROM SK6 .. 48 A3
Chester Wy NWCHW CW9 ..... 13 G3
  NWCHE CW9 .... 13 J2
  NWCHE CW9 .... 130 C3
Chestnut Cl ALS/KID ST7 ... 224 F5
  CHD/CHDH SK8 .... 45 L7
  CW/SHV CW2 .... 238 C7
  GTS/LS CH66 .... 120 F3
  IRL M44 .... 31 K7
  LEIGH WN7 .... 24 F1
  MCFLDN SK10 .... 15 J1
  WARRW/BUR WA5 .... 35 M6
  WDN WA8 .... 53 H2
Chestnut Dr ALS/KID ST7 ... 241 L2
  CONG CW12 .... 183 M8
  HOLMCH CW4 .... 181 K1
  LEIGH WN7 .... 24 F1
  POY/DIS SK12 .... 86 F1
  SALE M33 .... 42 D3
Chestnut Dr South LEIGH WN7. 24 F2
Chestnut Gv CO CH5 .... 166 C2
  CW/HAS CW1 .... 19 J2
  GOL/RIS/CU WA3 .... 23 M3
  NWCHW CW8 .... 103 H8
  WSFD CW7 .... 177 J4
Chestnut La LEIGH WN7 ..... 24 F2
Cheswood Cl RAIN/WH L35 .. 32 E2
Chesworth Fold STKP SK1 ... 3 C8
Chetham Ct WARRN/WOL WA2. 37 G1
Chetton Dr RUNC WA7 .... 74 E5
Chetwode Av AIMK WN4 ..... 22 B2
Chetwode St CW/HAS CW1 ... 18 F2
Chetwood Dr WDN WA8 ...... 33 M8
Chevasse Wk WLTN L25 ..... 50 C1
Cheveley Cl MCFLDN SK10 .. 138 C2
Chevington Dr HTNM SK4 ... 45 K1
Cheviot Av CHD/CHDH SK8 .. 64 F2
  WARRN/WOL WA2 .... 37 G1
Cheviot Cl HTNM SK4 .... 2 D2
Cheviot Ct WSFD CW7 .... 177 H5
Cheviot Rd BRAM/HZG SK7 .. 66 B3
Chevithorne Cl ALT WA14 .. 42 B7
Chevoit Cl GTS/LS CH66 .... 94 A6
Chevron Cl RAIN/WH L35 ... 32 D5
Chevron Pl ALT WA14 .... 42 D5
Chevrons Rd CQ CH5 .... 142 B8
Chevrons Wy CO CH5 .... 142 B8
Cheyne Wk NANT CW5 .... 251 L1
Cheyney Rd CH/BCN CH1 .... 16 D2
Chicago Av MANAIR M90 .... 63 H5
Chichester Cl RUNC WA7 ... 74 D6
  SALE M33 .... 42 D1

Chichester Rd MPL/ROM SK6 . 48 C2
Chichester St CH/BCN CH1 .. 16 E3
Chidlow Cl CW/SHV CW2 .... 253 L1
  WDN WA8 .... 53 H7
Chidwall Rd WYTH/NTH M22 . 63 H2
Chigwell Cl WYTH/NTH M22 . 44 F7
Childer Crs GTS/LS CH66 ... 94 B5
Childer Gdns GTS/LS CH66 .. 94 B5
Child's La CONG CW12 ...... 206 E6
Childwall Rd GTS/LS CH66 .. 94 E4
Chilham Cl WSFD CW7 .... 177 J5
Chilham Pl MCFLDS SK11 ... 137 M6
Chillington Av WDN WA8 ... 6 C5
Chilmark Dr NTHM/RTH M23 . 44 A6
Chiltern Av MCFLDS SK11 .. 14 A7
  WARRN/WOL WA2 .... 37 G1
Chiltern Cl AIMK WN4 ...... 22 C2
  BRAM/HZG SK7 .... 66 B3
  CHSW/BR CH4 .... 169 H7
  NWCHW CW8 .... 152 A2
Chiltern Crs WARRN/WOL WA2. 37 C1
Chiltern Dr HALE/TIMP WA15. 61 M2
  OFTN SK2 .... 47 J8
Chiltern Gdns SALE M33 .... 43 J4
Chiltern Rd GOL/RIS/CU WA3. 24 E3
  STHEL WA9 .... 26 A1
  WARRN/WOL WA2 .... 37 G1
Chiltern Wy WSFD CW7 ..... 177 H5
Chilton Dr GTS/LS CH66 ... 120 F2
Chilwell Cl WDN WA8 .... 33 K8
Chilworth Cl CW/SHV CW2 .. 238 C4
China La WARRS WA4 .... 56 C2
The Chines NWCHW CW8 ..... 127 K7
Chinley Cl BRAM/HZG SK7 .. 65 L1
  HTNM SK4 .... 46 B1
  SALE M33 .... 43 K1
Chippenham Av OFTN SK2 ... 47 K5
Chippingdall Cl
  WARRW/BUR WA5 .... 36 C7
Chipstead Cl NWCHW CW8 .. 129 G8
Chirk Cl CHNE CH2 .... 145 M6
Chirk Pl WSFD CW7 .... 177 G3
Chiselden Av WYTH/NTH M22. 63 L2
Chiswick Cl RUNC WA7 ..... 74 D5
Chiswick Gdns WARRS WA4 .. 56 F6
Chiswick Rd DID/WITH M20 . 45 J1
Chisworth Cl BRAM/HZG SK7. 65 L1
Chokeberry Cl ALT WA14 ... 42 B4
Chollerton Cl KNUT WA16 .. 59 J8
Cholmondeley La MALPAS SY14.. 232 C1
Cholmondeley Rd EP CH65 .. 94 F8
  MALPAS SY14 .... 246 E5
  NANT CW5 .... 249 J6
  RUNC WA7 .... 73 K7
Cholmondeley St
  MCFLDS SK11 .... 15 G8
  WDN WA8 .... 53 G8
Cholmondley Ri MALPAS SY14. 247 G8
Chorley Hall Cl WILM/AE SK9. 109 M3
Chorley Hall La WILM/AE SK9. 109 M3
Chorley Rd SALE M33 .... 43 L2
Chorley's La WDN WA8 ...... 53 K1
Chorley Stock La NANT CW5. 249 G3
Chorley St WARRN/WOL WA2. 5 H4
Choriton Cl RUNC WA7 ..... 74 D5
Choriton Dr CHD/CHDH SK8 . 45 L6
Choriton La CW/SHV CW2 ... 254 A3
Chowley Oak La CHSE CH3 .. 213 M7
Chretien Rd WYTH/NTH M22 . 44 D2
Chrimes Dr NWCHW CW8 .... 150 F6
Christchurch Av CW/SHV CW2. 18 A4
Christie Cl GTS/LS CH66 ... 94 A3
Christie St STKP SK1 ...... 3 K3
  WDN WA8 .... 53 K3
Christleton Av CW/SHV CW2. 220 D7
  NWCHE CW9 .... 130 C3
Christleton Ct RUNC WA7 .. 54 C8
Christleton Dr GTS/LS CH66. 94 E6
Christleton Rd CHSE CH3 .. 170 A3
Chudleigh Cl ALT WA14 .... 42 B6
  BRAM/HZG SK7 .... 66 B3
  HLWD L26 .... 50 E3
Church Bank CHSE CH3 ...... 214 B2
Church Bk CHF/WBR SK23 ... 89 K1
Church Brow ALT WA14 ...... 61 H2
Church Cl BIDD ST8 .... 227 K6
  NWCHW CW8 .... 128 D5
Church College Cl CH/BCN CH1. 16 D1
Church Ct CHSE CH3 .... 148 F4
Church Cft CHSW/BR CH4 ... 191 C6
Church Dr NEWLW WA12 ..... 27 J3
  WARRN/WOL WA2 .... 38 A3
Church End SPK/HALE L24 .. 71 K3
Church Farm NANT CW5 ..... 249 L8
Churchfield Rd FROD/HEL WA6. 99 J3
Churchfields ALT WA14 ..... 61 H3
  AUD/MAD/W CW3 .... 264 A8
  FROD/HEL WA6 .... 98 C3
  GOL/RIS/CU WA3 .... 29 H5
  KNUT WA16 .... 107 J2
  NANT CW5 .... 253 H4
  NWCHW CW8 .... 129 H1
  NWCHW CW8 .... 152 B2
  WDN WA8 .... 34 B7
Churchgate STKP SK1 .... 3 G5
Church Gn LYMM WA13 .... 40 B4
Church Gv MPL/ROM SK6 .... 66 E2
Church Hall Cl CH/BCN CH1 . 144 E8
Church Hl KNUT WA16 ...... 107 G2
Church HI RUNC WA7 .... 54 D7
Churchill Av GOL/RIS/CU WA3. 25 H8
Churchill Cl CONG CW12 ... 207 G1
  CQ CH5 .... 166 A4
Churchill Crs MPL/ROM SK6 . 48 D5
Churchill Dr TPLY/KEL CW6 . 197 K5
Churchill Pkwy WSFD CW7 .. 177 K4
Churchill Rd ALT WA14 ..... 42 D5
Churchill St HTNM SK4 ..... 2 D1
Churchill Wy MCFLDS SK11 . 15 G5
  NSTN CH64 .... 91 L4
Church La ALS/KID ST7 ..... 225 H4
  ALS/KID ST7 .... 226 E5
  AUD/MAD/W CW3 .... 255 K7
  BRAM/HZG SK7 .... 85 J2
  CHNE CH2 .... 121 H8
  CHNE CH2 .... 121 J3
  CHNE CH2 .... 122 A5
  CHNE CH2 .... 145 K5

CHSE CH3 .... 146 F8
CHSE CH3 .... 211 M1
CHSE CH3 .... 228 E2
CONG CW12 .... 185 K3
CQ CH5 .... 166 D4
CW/SHV CW2 .... 237 L5
GOL/RIS/CU WA3 .... 23 K5
GOL/RIS/CU WA3 .... 29 M1
GTS/LS CH66 .... 94 D8
KNUT WA16 .... 82 B7
MCFLDN SK10 .... 113 L8
MCFLDS SK11 .... 137 H4
MCFLDS SK11 .... 161 K4
MCFLDS SK11 .... 162 F1
MPL/ROM SK6 .... 48 E6
MPL/ROM SK6 .... 48 C6
MPL/ROM SK6 .... 49 G7
NANT CW5 .... 20 E7
NM/HAY SK22 .... 69 J4
NSTN CH64 .... 91 L5
NWCHW CW8 .... 128 D3
SBCH CW11 .... 204 E6
SBCH CW11 .... 205 M7
WARRS WA4 .... 57 H3
WILM/AE SK9 .... 110 A2
Churchley Cl EDGY/DAV SK3 .... 46 A6
Churchley Rd EDGY/DAV SK3 .... 46 A5
Church Mdw NWCHW CW8 .... 102 D8
WHITCH SY13 .... 270 A3
Church Meadow Wk
WDN WA8 .... 52 B7
Churchmere Cl CW/HAS CW1 .... 221 J5
Church Ms KNUT WA16 .... 107 H2
MCFLDN SK10 .... 113 C4
NWCHE CW9 .... 104 E7
Church Pde EP CH65 .... 10 F5
Church Ri NWCHW CW8 .... 152 B2
Church Rd ALS/KID ST7 .... 224 B8
BIDD ST8 .... 227 K5
CH/BCN CH1 .... 144 A2
CHD/CHDH SK8 .... 45 G7
CHD/CHDH SK8 .... 65 H5
CHSE CH3 .... 148 F5
CHSE CH3 .... 215 C7
CHSE CH3 .... 244 C3
CHSW/BR CH4 .... 167 J8
CHSW/BR CH4 .... 192 E2
FROD/HEL WA6 .... 99 J5
HLWD L26 .... 50 F3
HTNM SK4 .... 2 D3
LYMM WA13 .... 58 D2
MALPAS SY14 .... 245 H2
MPL/ROM SK6 .... 49 G1
NANT CW5 .... 219 K6
NM/HAY SK22 .... 69 J5
NWCHE CW9 .... 13 K1
NWCHW CW8 .... 102 D8
NWCHW CW8 .... 129 H2
SPK/HALE L24 .... 71 L4
WILM/AE SK9 .... 83 L8
WILM/AE SK9 .... 84 D1
WLTN L25 .... 50 A1
WYTH/NTH M22 .... 44 D3
Church Rd South WLTN L25 .... 50 A2
Churchside MCFLDS SK11 .... 15 H5
Churchston Av BRAM/HZG SK7 .... 66 A2
Church St ALS/KID ST7 .... 226 B8
ALS/KID ST7 .... 226 C6
ALS/KID ST7 .... 242 D3
ALT WA14 .... 42 D7
CH/BCN CH1 .... 17 H2
CH/BCN CH1 .... 17 H2
CHD/CHDH SK8 .... 45 K6
CHSE CH3 .... 172 C2
CHSE CH3 .... 228 E2
EP CH65 .... 10 F5
FROD/HEL WA6 .... 99 H4
GOL/RIS/CU WA3 .... 23 H3
HTNM SK4 .... 2 E2
MALPAS SY14 .... 258 A1
MCFLDS SK11 .... 15 C5
MCFLDN SK10 .... 113 H4
MPL/ROM SK6 .... 48 F6
MPL/ROM SK6 .... 49 G7
NEWLW WA12 .... 22 E8
NWCHE CW9 .... 104 A4
NWCHE CW9 .... 104 E7
NWCHE CW9 .... 153 M1
NWCHW CW8 .... 128 C3
RUNC WA7 .... 9 G1
SBCH CW11 .... 204 B6
TPLY/KEL CW6 .... 149 J8
WARR WA1 .... 5 K6
WDN WA8 .... 53 C7
WHITCH SY13 .... 270 A4
WILM/AE SK9 .... 84 B5
WSFD CW7 .... 177 L3
Church Street (Heol-yr-eglwys)
FLINT CH6 .... 116 A6
Church St North TPLY/KEL CW6 .... 149 K7
Church St West MCFLDS SK11 .... 14 F5
Church Ter WILM/AE SK9 .... 64 D8
Church Vw AUD/MAD/W CW3 .... 264 A8
CQ CH5 .... 166 F1
FROD/HEL WA6 .... 126 B2
KNUT WA16 .... 107 G2
LYMM WA13 .... 40 B8
Church Wks CHSE CH3 .... 170 A4
Churchward CHNE CH2 .... 145 K8
Churchway MCFLDN SK10 .... 137 L2
Church Wy CH/BCN CH1 .... 144 B7
FROD/HEL WA6 .... 124 D3
NANT CW5 .... 253 H4
Churchwood Rd DID/WITH M20 .... 45 H1
Churchwood Vw LYMM WA13 .... 58 F1
Churton Av SALE M33 .... 42 E1
Churton Cl CW/SHV CW2 .... 253 L1
NWCHE CW9 .... 129 L8
Churton Dr WHITCH SY13 .... 270 B5
Churton Rd CHSE CH3 .... 228 E2
Churton St CHSE CH3 .... 170 A2

Cicely Mill La KNUT WA16 .... 80 C1
Cinder Cl CHSE CH3 .... 146 F7
Cinder La NWCHW CW8 .... 152 E6
Cinder-hill La ALS/KID ST7 .... 225 H1
Cinder La CHSE CH3 .... 146 F8
KNUT WA16 .... 134 C3
MCFLDS SK11 .... 134 E3
NANT CW5 .... 236 C2
NWCHE CW9 .... 131 G4
WARRS WA4 .... 57 M4
Cinnamon La WARRN/WOL WA2 .... 37 M1
Cinnamon La North
WARRN/WOL WA2 .... 28 F8
Circle Av NANT CW5 .... 237 L7
The Circle CW/SHV CW2 .... 238 D3
KNUT WA16 .... 80 C2
The Circuit CHD/CHDH SK8 .... 65 C5
EDGY/DAV SK3 .... 46 C6
WILM/AE SK9 .... 83 K7
WILM/AE SK9 .... 110 B1
Circular Dr CHSW/BR CH4 .... 168 E8
City Rd CH/BCN CH1 .... 17 J4
City Walls Rd CH/BCN CH1 .... 16 E5
Civic Gn WHITCH SY13 .... 270 C5
Civic Wy EP CH65 .... 10 D7
MWCH CW10 .... 179 J3
Clair Av CQ CH5 .... 167 G1
Clamhunger La KNUT WA16 .... 80 C5
Clandon Av BURS/TUN ST6 .... 243 L8
Clanfield Av WDN WA8 .... 52 C1
Clanway St BURS/TUN ST6 .... 243 K7
Clapgate MPL/ROM SK6 .... 48 A3
Clap Gate Crs WDN WA8 .... 52 B7
Clap Gates Crs WARRN/BUR WA5 .... 4 B3
Clap Gates Rd WARRN/BUR WA5 .... 4 B3
Clare Av CHNE CH2 .... 17 M1
WILM/AE SK9 .... 84 C1
Clare Dr CW/SHV CW2 .... 237 M3
EP CH65 .... 121 H3
MCFLDN SK10 .... 138 C1
Claremont Av ALT WA14 .... 42 D4
CQ CH5 .... 142 E6
MPL/ROM SK6 .... 48 C6
WDN WA8 .... 34 C8
Claremont Cl NWCHE CW9 .... 153 M1
WDN WA8 .... 34 B8
Claremont Gv DID/WITH M20 .... 45 G1
HALE/TIMP WA15 .... 61 L1
Claremont Rd CHD/CHDH SK8 .... 65 C4
CW/SHV CW2 .... 18 C8
GOL/RIS/CU WA3 .... 24 D8
OFTN SK2 .... 47 H8
RUNC WA7 .... 9 K3
Clarence Av CHSE CH3 .... 170 B2
WARRN/BUR WA5 .... 35 K6
WDN WA8 .... 34 A8
Clarence Cl WILM/AE SK9 .... 84 A6
WDN WA8 .... 34 B8
Clarence Gv CW/HAS CW1 .... 18 C2
Clarence Rd HALE/TIMP WA15 .... 61 M1
MCFLDN SK10 .... 113 G4
WARRS WA4 .... 57 H2
Clarence St CQ CH5 .... 142 B7
GOL/RIS/CU WA3 .... 23 G3
RUNC WA7 .... 8 F1
WARR WA1 .... 37 L5
Clarence Ter RUNC WA7 .... 9 G1
Clarendon Av HALE/TIMP WA15 .... 42 E7
HTNM SK4 .... 46 B1
Clarendon Cl CHSW/BR CH4 .... 169 L5
RUNC WA7 .... 74 D5
Clarendon Ct WARRN/WOL WA2 .... 27 M8
Clarendon Dr MCFLDN SK10 .... 139 C3
Clarendon Rd BRAM/HZG SK7 .... 66 F7
IRL M44 .... 31 L5
Clarendon St RDSH SK5 .... 3 G1
Clare Pl WSFD CW7 .... 177 J5
Clares Farm Cl WARR WA1 .... 38 F5
Clare St ALS/KID ST7 .... 226 C6
ALS/KID ST7 .... 226 E8
Clarke Av GOL/RIS/CU WA3 .... 24 F8
WARRS WA4 .... 56 D2
Clarke Crs HALE/TIMP WA15 .... 62 B1
Clarke La MCFLDN SK10 .... 112 F7
MCFLDS SK11 .... 139 J8
Clarke Ter MCFLDS SK11 .... 15 G9
Clary Meadow NWCHW CW8 .... 12 F1
NWCHW CW8 .... 129 L3
Claude St WARR WA1 .... 5 K4
Claughton Av CW/SHV CW2 .... 238 D3
Claverton Cl RUNC WA7 .... 73 H6
Claverton Rd NTHM/RTH M23 .... 43 L8
Claydon Ct HLWD L26 .... 51 G3
Claydon Gdns GOL/RIS/CU WA3 .... 39 M3
Clay Heyes MCFLDS SK11 .... 135 G1
Clayhill Cl NTHM/RTH M23 .... 43 M8
Clayhill Gn GTS/LS CH66 .... 94 C5
Clay La CQ CH5 .... 142 C8
CW/HAS CW1 .... 222 D6
HALE/TIMP WA15 .... 43 J8
KNUT WA16 .... 134 A4
MALPAS SY14 .... 232 A1
NTHM/RTH M23 .... 43 M8
SBCH CW11 .... 203 C8
WARRN/BUR WA5 .... 26 E6
WILM/AE SK9 .... 64 C7
WILM/AE SK9 .... 83 J8
WSFD CW7 .... 152 B8
Claypit Rd CHSW/BR CH4 .... 169 H7
Claypits La CHSE CH3 .... 170 F8
Claypit St WHITCH SY13 .... 270 A4
Clayton Av CONG CW12 .... 184 F7
DID/WITH M20 .... 45 H1
GOL/RIS/CU WA3 .... 23 L4
Clayton Crs RUNC WA7 .... 8 E4
WDN WA8 .... 6 F3
Clayton Dr WHITCH SY13 .... 270 A4
Clayton Rd GOL/RIS/CU WA3 .... 29 M6
Cleaver Ms MCFLDS SK11 .... 138 C8
Cleaver Rd CH/BCN CH1 .... 144 E8
Cledford Crs MWCH CW10 .... 179 K6
Cledford La MWCH CW10 .... 179 M5
Cleethorpes Rd RUNC WA7 .... 74 C5
Cleeve Rd NTHM/RTH M23 .... 44 A7
Cleeve Wy CHD/CHDH SK8 .... 65 H6
Clegg St WARRN/WOL WA2 .... 5 H3
Clegg St MPL/ROM SK6 .... 47 M1
Clelland St WARRS WA4 .... 56 C1

Clement Rd MPL/ROM SK6 .... 49 H5
Clement St HTNM SK4 .... 2 E2
Clemley Cl TPLY/KEL CW6 .... 149 K6
Clerewood Av CHD/CHDH SK8 .... 64 B5
Clevedon Cl MCFLDS SK11 .... 14 B7
Cleveland Dr GOL/RIS/CU WA3 .... 23 K4
GTS/LS CH66 .... 94 A6
Cleveland Gv CQ CH5 .... 142 E6
Cleveland Rd HALE/TIMP WA15 .... 61 M1
WARRN/WOL WA2 .... 37 H1
Cleveleys Av WSFD CW7 .... 177 H5
WDN WA8 .... 53 K1
Cleveleys Rd
WARRN/BUR WA5 .... 36 B8
Cleves Cl CH/BCN CH1 .... 144 D6
Clifden Dr WYTH/NTH M22 .... 63 L2
Cliffe Rd CW/HAS CW1 .... 221 H5
NSTN CH64 .... 91 M7
WARRS WA4 .... 56 C5
Cliffe St WARR WA1 .... 4 D6
WDN WA8 .... 7 L2
Cliff La LYMM WA13 .... 58 B6
MCFLDN SK10 .... 139 H2
NWCHW CW8 .... 101 J8
WARRS WA4 .... 57 M5
WARRS WA4 .... 57 K2
Cliffmere Cl CHD/CHDH SK8 .... 64 F1
Clifford Cl HALE/TIMP WA15 .... 43 G6
Clifford Dr CHSW/BR CH4 .... 168 F7
Clifford Gv CW/HAS CW1 .... 222 C8
Clifford Pl WSFD CW7 .... 177 J5
Clifford Rd MCFLDS SK11 .... 14 B6
POY/DIS SK12 .... 66 C8
NANT CW5 .... 46 A4
WILM/AE SK9 .... 83 M6
Cliff Rd NWCHW CW8 .... 101 K8
WARRS WA4 .... 84 A4
Cliff Side WILM/AE SK9 .... 84 B4
Clifton Av CHD/CHDH SK8 .... 64 A2
CW/SHV CW2 .... 18 D6
GOL/RIS/CU WA3 .... 29 K1
HALE/TIMP WA15 .... 42 E7
HLWD L26 .... 50 E3
PS/BROM CH62 .... 93 L1
Clifton Crs FROD/HEL WA6 .... 99 J3
Clifton Dr CH/BCN CH1 .... 168 E1
CHD/CHDH SK8 .... 44 F7
CHD/CHDH SK8 .... 64 A2
MPL/ROM SK6 .... 48 F5
NWCHE CW9 .... 13 J9
WILM/AE SK9 .... 83 L8
Clifton Gdns EP CH65 .... 121 J1
Clifton La RUNC WA7 .... 99 L1
Cliftonmill Mdw
GOL/RIS/CU WA3 .... 22 F4
Clifton Park Rd OFTN SK2 .... 47 G7
Clifton Rd LEIGH WN7 .... 24 C2
RUNC WA7 .... 9 H8
RUNC WA7 .... 73 J6
SALE M33 .... 43 H1
SBCH CW11 .... 203 K5
Clifton St CW/SHV CW2 .... 18 D6
WARRS WA4 .... 5 K9
WARRS WA4 .... 110 A3
Cliftonville Rd WARR WA1 .... 38 C6
Clincton Cl WDN WA8 .... 52 A4
Clincton Vw WDN WA8 .... 52 A4
Clitheroe Rd NWCHW CW8 .... 128 D3
Clive Av WARRN/WOL WA2 .... 37 J3
Clive Back La WSFD CW7 .... 178 C5
Cliveden Rd CHSW/BR CH4 .... 168 F7
Clivegreen La WSFD CW7 .... 178 C4
Clive La WSFD CW7 .... 178 C4
Clive St BURS/TUN ST6 .... 243 L8
Clock Face Rd WDN WA8 .... 34 E5
Cloister Rd HTNM SK4 .... 45 K2
The Cloisters CHD/CHDH SK8 .... 46 A7
Clos Coed CQ CH5 .... 142 E8
Close La ALS/KID ST7 .... 223 M8
ALS/KID ST7 .... 226 D5
ALS/KID ST7 .... 241 G2
The Close ALS/KID ST7 .... 241 G1
ALT WA14 .... 42 C7
CH/BCN CH1 .... 144 A3
CQ CH5 .... 166 B3
GOL/RIS/CU WA3 .... 49 G3
NWCHW CW8 .... 12 C6
Cloud Vw CONG CW12 .... 208 A2
Clough Av MPL/ROM SK6 .... 49 J6
SALE M33 .... 42 D3
WARRN/WOL WA2 .... 37 H2
WILM/AE SK9 .... 84 B2
Clough Bank MCFLDN SK10 .... 112 F5
Clough Hall Dr ALS/KID ST7 .... 242 E5
Clough Hall Rd ALS/KID ST7 .... 242 E5
Clough La NWCHW CW8 .... 12 C7
Clough Rd SPK/HALE L24 .... 50 D8
WSFD CW7 .... 177 L3
Clough Side MPL/ROM SK6 .... 49 J5
Cloughside POY/DIS SK12 .... 68 E6
The Clough RUNC WA7 .... 73 M3
Clovelly Av WARRN/BUR WA5 .... 35 L5
Clovelly Gv RUNC WA7 .... 74 B7
Clovelly Rd OFTN SK2 .... 47 J4
Clover Av EDGY/DAV SK3 .... 46 D7
Clover Cl WARRN/WOL WA2 .... 37 G1
HLWD L26 .... 50 D2
Clover Ct RUNC WA7 .... 74 B7
Clover Cft SALE M33 .... 43 K3
Cloverdale Dr AIMK WN4 .... 22 C2
Cloverdale Rd MCFLDS SK11 .... 138 B7
Clover Dr WSFD CW7 .... 177 K1
Cloverfield RUNC WA7 .... 10 B8
Cloverfield Gdns GTS/LS CH66 .... 94 D5
Cloverfields CW/HAS CW1 .... 222 B8
Clover La CHSW/BR CH4 .... 168 F7
Cloverley Dr HALE/TIMP WA15 .... 43 C8
Clover Pl CHSW/BR CH4 .... 168 F7
Clover Rd HALE/TIMP WA15 .... 43 G7
MPL/ROM SK6 .... 48 C1

CHD/CHDH SK8 .... 64 E3
Combermere Cl
CHD/CHDH SK8 .... 45 M8
Comboy Dr NWCHE CW9 .... 130 C6
Combs Cl NM/HAY SK22 .... 69 G4
Comfrey Gv HLWD L26 .... 50 E2
Commercial Av CHD/CHDH SK8 .... 64 E7
Commercial Rd BRAM/HZG SK7 .... 66 D1
MCFLDN SK10 .... 15 H4
Common Farm La
MCFLDS SK11 .... 134 E3
Commonhall St CH/BCN CH1 .... 16 F6
Common La AUD/MAD/W CW3 .... 254 C6
CHSE CH3 .... 171 G8
FROD/HEL WA6 .... 125 K3
GOL/RIS/CU WA3 .... 24 D8
MCFLDS SK11 .... 134 E3
NWCHE CW9 .... 131 L7
TPLY/KEL CW6 .... 173 J5
WARRS WA4 .... 56 J5
WARRS WA4 .... 76 E4
WSFD CW7 .... 152 C7
Common Rd NEWLW WA12 .... 26 E1
Commonside FROD/HEL WA6 .... 125 G3
Commons MI CW11 .... 204 B5
The Commons SBCH CW11 .... 204 B6
Common St NEWLW WA12 .... 26 E1
Commonwealth Cl
WSFD CW7 .... 177 J6
Company's Cl RUNC WA7 .... 72 F6
Compass Cl RUNC WA7 .... 74 D7
Compstall Rd MPL/ROM SK6 .... 48 D2
Compton Dr NTHM/RTH M23 .... 63 G2
Compton Pl CHSW/BR CH4 .... 169 G6
EP CH65 .... 10 D7
Compton Wy HLWD L26 .... 50 C2
Concorde Pl
WARRN/WOL WA2 .... 37 K2
Condliffe Cl SBCH CW11 .... 204 B7
Conery Cl FROD/HEL WA6 .... 98 C3
Conery La WHITCH SY13 .... 268 D8
Coney Gv NTHM/RTH M23 .... 44 A5
RUNC WA7 .... 74 B7
Congleton Cl WILM/AE SK9 .... 110 A4
Congleton Edge Rd
CONG CW12 .... 208 B7
Congleton La MCFLDS SK11 .... 135 H4
Congleton Rd ALS/KID ST7 .... 226 A2
ALS/KID ST7 .... 242 D3
BIDD ST8 .... 227 K3
CHSW/BR CH4 .... 167 J8
CONG CW12 .... 158 F7
CONG CW12 .... 184 D5
CONG CW12 .... 206 E7
CONG CW12 .... 225 L1
MCFLDN SK10 .... 110 A6
MCFLDS SK11 .... 138 A8
MCFLDS SK11 .... 160 C8
MCFLDS SK11 .... 161 K5
SBCH CW11 .... 204 B5
SBCH CW11 .... 204 F4
SBCH CW11 .... 205 M7
Congleton Rd North
ALS/KID ST7 .... 225 L8
Congleton Rd South
ALS/KID ST7 .... 242 D2
Conifer Cl GTS/LS CH66 .... 121 G4
Conifer Gv WARRW/BUR WA5 .... 35 M5
The Conifers ALS/KID ST7 .... 241 H1
Coniston Av CONG CW12 .... 206 F2
SALE M33 .... 43 J2
WARRW/BUR WA5 .... 35 K8
WSFD CW7 .... 177 J3
Coniston Cl GTS/LS CH66 .... 94 A3
NANT CW5 .... 21 J4
RUNC WA7 .... 73 K6
WILM/AE SK9 .... 109 G5
Coniston Dr FROD/HEL WA6 .... 99 K4
HOLMCH WA4 .... 180 F1
WILM/AE SK9 .... 64 C8
Coniston Rd CHD/CHDH SK8 .... 45 H6
CHNE CH2 .... 145 M7
MPL/ROM SK6 .... 67 K4
NSTN CH64 .... 91 L6
PART M31 .... 31 L8
Coniston Wk HALE/TIMP WA15 .... 43 K7
Coniston Wy MCFLDS SK11 .... 137 M7
Conleach Rd SPK/HALE L24 .... 70 E1
Connaught Av CQ CH5 .... 142 B6
WARR WA1 .... 37 L5
Connaught Cl WILM/AE SK9 .... 84 C4
Connaught Dr NEWLW WA12 .... 27 J2
Connell Rd NTHM/RTH M23 .... 44 A7
Connor Wy CHD/CHDH SK8 .... 44 F8
Conrad Cl CW/HAS CW1 .... 19 K3
Conroy Wy NEWLW WA12 .... 27 J3
Consett Av NTHM/RTH M23 .... 44 A6
Consort Cl MCFLDN SK10 .... 112 C6
Consort Pl ALT WA14 .... 61 H1
Constable Dr MPL/ROM SK6 .... 49 H4
WILM/AE SK9 .... 84 E4
Constables Cl RUNC WA7 .... 74 A3
Constance Rd PART M31 .... 40 F1
Constance Wy WDN WA8 .... 53 G7
Consul St WYTH/NTH M22 .... 44 E3
Convamore Rd
BRAM/HZG SK7 .... 65 K5
Conway Av IRL M44 .... 31 M4
WARRW/BUR WA5 .... 36 F2
WSFD CW7 .... 177 J5
Conway Cl CHSW/BR CH4 .... 168 D7
CW/HAS CW1 .... 221 J4
KNUT WA16 .... 107 G4
WARRW/BUR WA5 .... 35 M6
Conway Crs MCFLDN SK10 .... 15 L2
Conway Dr BRAM/HZG SK7 .... 66 C3
HALE/TIMP WA15 .... 43 J6
NEWLW WA12 .... 27 L1
Conway Rd BIDD ST8 .... 227 J6
CHD/CHDH SK8 .... 64 E2
SALE M33 .... 43 K1
Coogee Av WARRW/BUR WA5 .... 35 L5
Cooke's La NWCHE CW9 .... 130 F6
Cooke St BRAM/HZG SK7 .... 66 D1
Cook's Br WRX/GR/LL LL12 .... 210 F7
Cooks La WHITCH SY13 .... 259 K6
Cooksmere La SBCH CW11 .... 203 M3

Cook St *EDGY/DAV* SK3 .... 2 E6
 EP CH65 .... 10 F6
Coole La *AUD/MAD/W* CW3 ...... 263 J8
 AUD/MAD/W CW3 .... 273 J1
 NANT CW5 .... 251 K2
Coombe Dr *RUNC* WA7 .... 8 F7
Coombes Av *MPL/ROM* SK6 ..... 48 F7
Coombes St *OFTN* SK2 .... 47 H1
Co-operative St *BRAM/HZG* SK7 .. 66 E1
Cooper Av *NEWLW* WA12 .... 26 F1
 WARRN/WOL WA2 .... 37 M2
Coope Rd *MCFLDN* SK10 .... 112 E5
Coopers Cft *CHSE* CH3 .... 170 A5
Cooper St *BRAM/HZG* SK7 ...... 66 F1
 CONG CW12 .... 207 L1
 RUNC WA7 .... 9 G1
 STKP SK1 .... 3 H4
 WDN WA8 .... 7 J2
Coopers Wy *BIDD* ST8 .... 227 H4
Cope Av *NANT* CW5 .... 20 C9
Copeland Gv *RUNC* WA7 .... 73 L7
Copeland Rd *WARRS* WA4 .... 56 B2
Cope's Av *BURS/TUN* ST6 ...... 243 L8
Copes La *NANT* CW5 .... 20 B7
Copeswood Cl
 CHSW/BR CH4 .... 190 C1
Cop Meadow *MCFLDN* SK11 ... 162 F2
Coppenhall Gv *CW/SHV* CW2 ... 18 A3
Coppenhall Heyes *CW/SHV* CW2 .. 18 A3
Coppenhall La *CW/SHV* CW2 ... 220 E8
 CW/SHV CW2 .... 237 K1
Copper Beech Cl *CHSW/BR* CH4 .. 190 C1
Copperbeech Cl
 WYTH/NTH M22 .... 44 E3
Copperfield Cl
 GOL/RIS/CU WA3 .... 29 J7
Copperfield Rd *CHD/CHDH* SK8 .. 65 H7
 POY/DIS SK12 .... 86 D2
Copperfields *TPLY/KEL* CW6 ... 197 K2
 WILM/AE SK9 .... 84 C4
Copperhill La *CONG* CW12 ...... 208 B5
Coppermine La *MALPAS* SY14 .. 232 B3
Copper St *MCFLDS* SK11 .... 15 K8
Copper Wd *NWCHW* CW8 ...... 127 L1
Copperwood Dr *RAIN/WH* L35 .. 32 C2
Coppice Av *SALE* M33 .... 42 D2
Coppice Cl *BIDD* ST8 .... 227 K5
 NANT CW5 .... 237 K6
Coppice Dr *MWCH* CW10 .... 179 L6
 POY/DIS SK12 .... 68 A6
 WYTH/NTH M22 .... 44 D3
Coppice Gn *CHNE* CH2 .... 97 J8
 WARRN/BUR WA5 .... 36 B2
Coppice La *POY/DIS* SK12 .... 68 A6
 RAIN/WH L35 .... 32 B5
Coppice Ri *MCFLDS* SK11 ...... 138 D7
Coppice Rd *ALS/KID* ST7 .... 242 C4
 NANT CW5 .... 237 K6
 POY/DIS SK12 .... 87 H1
 SBCH CW11 .... 222 F4
The Coppice *CHF/WBR* SK23 ... 89 L7
 HALE/TIMP WA15 .... 62 B4
 NANT CW5 .... 251 M1
 NWCHW CW9 .... 130 C1
 NWCHW CW9 .... 127 J7
 SBCH CW11 .... 203 L5
Coppice Wy *WILM/AE* SK9 .... 84 E1
Coppins Cl *CHSE* CH3 .... 170 A2
 FROD/HEL WA6 .... 124 B1
The Coppins
 WARRN/WOL WA2 .... 37 J2
 WILM/AE SK9 .... 83 L8
Copse Av *WYTH/NTH* M22 ...... 63 L1
The Copse *HALE/TIMP* WA15 ... 62 D5
 MPL/ROM SK6 .... 49 J4
 NEWLW WA12 .... 22 B8
 RUNC WA7 .... 74 A6
 WRX/GR/LL LL12 .... 210 A5
Copthorne Cl *CONG* CW12 ..... 207 M2
Copthorne Dr
 AUD/MAD/W CW3 .... 273 M1
Coral Av *CHD/CHDH* SK8 .... 65 G3
Coral Rd *CHD/CHDH* SK8 .... 65 G3
Corbar Rd *OFTN* SK2 .... 47 G7
Corbet Av *WARRN/WOL* WA2 ... 5 J1
Corbet Dr *MKTDR* TF9 .... 274 A8
Corbet St *WARRN/WOL* WA2 ... 5 G1
Corcoran Dr *MPL/ROM* SK6 .... 48 F7
Corda Av *WYTH/NTH* M22 ...... 44 D4
Corfe Crs *BRAM/HZG* SK7 ...... 66 D3
Corfe Wy *WSFD* CW7 .... 177 J5
Corks La *POY/DIS* SK12 .... 68 E7
Corley Av *EDGY/DAV* SK3 ...... 45 M5
Cormorant Cl *CW/HAS* CW1 ... 19 M3
Cormorant Dr *RUNC* WA7 .... 8 D3
Cornbrook Rd *MCFLDS* SK11 .. 138 C8
Corner Cft *WILM/AE* SK9 .... 84 A8
Cornerhouse La *WDN* WA8 ..... 52 D1
The Corners *NWCHW* CW8 .... 128 E5
Cornfield *GTS/LS* CH66 .... 120 F3
 MCFLDN SK10 .... 138 C1
 SALE M33 .... 43 M1
Cornfield Rd *BIDD* ST8 .... 227 K5
 MPL/ROM SK6 .... 48 E1
Cornforth Wy *WDN* WA8 .... 52 F1
Corn Hey Rd *SALE* M33 .... 42 C2
Cornishway *WYTH/NTH* M22 ... 63 K4
Cornubia Rd *WDN* WA8 .... 7 M6
Cornwall Av *RUNC* WA7 .... 9 G3
Cornwall Cl *CONG* CW12 ...... 208 A4
 MCFLDN SK10 .... 137 L3
 MPL/ROM SK6 .... 67 L5
Cornwall Gv *CW/HAS* CW1 ..... 18 C2
Cornwall Rd *CHD/CHDH* SK8 .. 64 B4
 CHNE CH2 .... 145 L5
 CQ CH5 .... 142 B8
 IRL M44 .... 31 K7
 WDN WA8 .... 53 H1
Cornwall St *CH/BCN* CH1 ...... 17 G2
 WARR WA1 .... 37 L5
Cornwell Cl *WILM/AE* SK9 ...... 84 D4
Coronation Av *ALS/KID* ST7 ... 241 G1
 BIDD ST8 .... 227 H7
 GOL/RIS/CU WA3 .... 25 J3
 WARRS WA4 .... 57 J2
 WSFD CW7 .... 177 L3
Coronation Crs *CW/HAS* CW1 .. 221 L6

 SBCH CW11 .... 204 A7
Coronation Dr *FROD/HEL* WA6 .. 99 G3
 NEWLW WA12 .... 27 L3
 RAIN/WH L35 .... 32 C1
 RNFD/HAY WA11 .... 22 A3
 WARRW/BUR WA5 .... 35 M8
 WDN WA8 .... 52 B4
Coronation Gv *NWCHW* CW8 .. 102 F8
Coronation Rd
 CHSW/BR CH4 .... 190 B1
 CONG CW12 .... 207 M2
 EP CH65 .... 95 J8
 MWCH CW10 .... 179 K6
 RUNC WA7 .... 9 J4
 RUNC WA7 .... 74 F6
Coronation St *BURS/TUN* ST6.. 243 L7
 CHSW/BR CH4 .... 168 F5
 CW/HAS CW1 .... 19 H1
 MCFLDS SK11 .... 15 J9
Coroner's La *WDN* WA8 .... 34 A7
Coronet Av *NWCHW* CW9 ..... 129 M8
Coronet Wy *WDN* WA8 .... 52 B4
Corporation St *FLINT* CH6 ..... 116 A5
 STKP SK1 .... 3 G6
Correction Brow *POY/DIS* SK12.. 67 J6
Corridor Rd *EP* CH65 .... 96 B7
Corsham Rd *HLWD* L26 .... 50 E6
Corwen Cl *WARRW/BUR* WA5 .. 35 L6
Cosham Rd *WYTH/NTH* M22 ... 63 M1
Cossack Av *WARRN/WOL* WA2 .. 37 J3
Cotebrook Dr *CHNE* CH2 .... 145 L5
Cotebrook Rd *NWCHE* CW9 ... 130 C5
Cotefield Rd *MPL/ROM* SK6 .... 48 F7
Cotefield Rd *WYTH/NTH* M22 .. 63 H2
Cote Green La *MPL/ROM* SK6 .. 49 J3
Cote Green Rd *MPL/ROM* SK6 .. 49 H3
Cote Lea Ct *RUNC* WA7 .... 73 M6
Cotes Pl *CH/BCN* CH1 .... 168 E1
Cotgreaves Ct *CHSW/BR* CH4 .. 169 H7
Cotman Dr *MPL/ROM* SK6 ...... 49 J4
Cotswold Cl *CHNE* CH2 .... 145 M6
 MCFLDN SK10 .... 137 L3
 NWCHW CW8 .... 152 A2
Cotswold Gv *STHEL* WA9 .... 26 A1
Cotswold Rd *HTNM* SK4 .... 2 D1
 WARRN/WOL WA2 .... 37 H1
Cotswolds Cresent *HLWD* L26 .. 50 E5
Cotswold Wy *WSFD* CW7 ...... 177 H5
Cottage Cl *NSTN* CH64 .... 91 L5
Cottage Gdns *MPL/ROM* SK6 .. 47 K1
Cottage La *CQ* CH5 .... 166 D2
 MCFLDN SK10 .... 15 M6
Cottage Rd *CHSW/BR* CH4 .... 169 H7
Cottage St *MCFLDS* SK11 .... 14 D5
Cottam Crs *MPL/ROM* SK6 ..... 49 H5
Cottam Dr *WARRN/WOL* WA2 .. 37 J4
Cotterdale Dr *WARRW/BUR* WA5 .. 35 M5
Cotterill Cl *SALE* M33 .... 43 J3
Cotterill Dr *WARR* WA1 .... 38 C5
Cotterill St *CW/SHV* CW2 .... 19 G8
Cottesmore Gdns
 HALE/TIMP WA15 .... 62 C4
Cottesmore Wy
 GOL/RIS/CU WA3 .... 23 H3
Cotton La *CHSE* CH3 .... 171 J2
 RUNC WA7 .... 73 K4
 SBCH CW11 .... 223 H1
Cotton Rd *BURS/TUN* ST6 ..... 243 J6
Cotton Tree St *HTNM* SK4 .... 2 E5
Cottonwood Cl *ALS/KID* ST7 .. 243 L1
Cottrell Rd *HALE/TIMP* WA15 .. 62 D5
Coulton Rd *WDN* WA8 .... 53 L1
Council Av *AIMK* WN4 .... 22 B1
Councillor La *CHD/CHDH* SK8 .. 64 B8
 CHD/CHDH SK8 .... 46 B8
Countess Av *CHD/CHDH* SK8 .. 46 A7
Countess Ct *MCFLDS* SK11 ... 137 M5
Countess Rd *DID/WITH* M20 ... 45 H1
Countess St *OFTN* SK2 .... 47 G7
Countess Wy *CH/BCN* CH1 ... 145 J8
Counting House Rd
 POY/DIS SK12 .... 68 E7
Court Av *HLWD* L26 .... 51 G3
Courthill St *STKP* SK1 .... 3 K7
Courtland Dr *CQ* CH5 .... 166 A1
Courtney Gn *WILM/AE* SK9 ..... 84 D2
Courtney Pl *ALT* WA14 .... 61 G3
Courtney Rd *CHSW/BR* CH4 .. 168 E8
The Court *NSTN* CH64 .... 91 M6
Cousens Wy *CH/BCN* CH1 .... 145 H8
Covell Rd *POY/DIS* SK12 .... 66 D7
Covent Gdn *STKP* SK1 .... 3 G6
Coventry Av *EDGY/DAV* SK3 ... 45 M5
 GTS/LS CH66 .... 120 E4
Coverdale Av *RAIN/WH* L35 .... 33 K2
Coverdale Cl *WARRW/BUR* WA5 .. 35 M5
Coverdale Fold *SBCH* CW11 ... 203 K7
Covert Cl *WSFD* CW7 .... 177 H4
Covert Gdns *ALS/KID* ST7 ...... 242 D4
Covert Ri *CHSE* CH3 .... 214 A3
Covert Rd *WYTH/NTH* M22 ..... 44 E7
The Cove *HALE/TIMP* WA15 .... 61 M1
Covington Pl *WILM/AE* SK9 ..... 84 B6
Cowanway *WDN* WA8 .... 53 M8
Cowbrook La *MCFLDS* SK11 .. 162 B6
Cowburn Dr *NM/HAY* SK22 ..... 69 J3
Cowdell St *WARRN/WOL* WA2 .. 5 H2
Cowfields *NANT* CW5 .... 20 F5
Cowhey Cl *CHSW/BR* CH4 ..... 169 H7
Cow Hey La *RUNC* WA7 .... 73 G7
Cow La *BRAM/HZG* SK7 .... 47 K8
 CHSE CH3 .... 195 G2
 FROD/HEL WA6 .... 127 G7
 HALE/TIMP WA15 .... 61 M7
 MCFLDN SK10 .... 113 K8
 MCFLDS SK11 .... 15 H9
 WSFD CW7 .... 177 L4
Cowley Wy *CW/HAS* CW1 .... 19 K4
Cowlishaw Cl *SBCH* CW11 ..... 227 G7
Cown Edge Wy *MPL/ROM* SK6.. 49 J8
 MPL/ROM SK6 .... 49 L4
 OFTN SK2 .... 48 A8
Cowper Cl *CW/SHV* CW2 ...... 238 A4
Cowper Wy *HUY* L36 .... 32 A4
Cowthorne Dr *CHSE* CH3 ...... 171 G7

Cox La *WRX/GR/LL* LL12 .... 210 C8
Coxton La *WRX/GR/LL* LL12 ... 210 C8
Coylton Av *RAIN/WH* L35 .... 33 K2
Crab La *WARRN/WOL* WA2 .... 38 A1
Crabmill Dr *SBCH* CW11 .... 203 K5
Crabmill La *FROD/HEL* WA6 .. 126 E6
 SBCH CW11 .... 202 E4
Crabtree Av *BIDD* ST8 .... 62 D5
 HALE/TIMP WA15 .... 62 D5
 POY/DIS SK12 .... 68 E7
Crabtree Fold *RUNC* WA7 .... 74 C4
Crabtree Gn *CW/HAS* CW1 ... 221 L6
Crabtree La *KNUT* WA16 .... 59 G5
Crabwall Pl *CH/BCN* CH1 ..... 144 F7
Cracow Moss
 AUD/MAD/W CW3 .... 267 G1
Craddock Rd *SALE* M33 .... 43 J2
Cradley Wy *WILM/AE* SK9 ...... 84 C6
Cragside Av *WSFD* CW7 .... 177 M2
Craig Cl *HTNM* SK4 .... 46 B3
 MCFLDS SK11 .... 138 B7
Craig Dr *CHF/WBR* SK23 .... 89 L6
Craig Gdns *GTS/LS* CH66 .... 94 E5
Craig Rd *CONG* CW12 .... 184 F8
 HTNM SK4 .... 46 B3
 MCFLDS SK11 .... 138 B7
Craigside *BIDD* ST8 .... 227 J4
Craig Wk *ALS/KID* ST7 .... 241 M2
Craigwell Av *DID/WITH* M20 ... 45 J1
Craithie Rd *CHSE* CH3 .... 170 A2
Crampton Dr *HALE/TIMP* WA15 .. 62 C4
Cranage Cl *RUNC* WA7 .... 73 K5
Cranage La *NWCHE* CW9 ...... 130 D3
Cranage Rd *CW/SHV* CW2 ..... 18 A6
Cranberry Cl *ALT* WA14 .... 42 B4
Cranberry La *ALS/KID* ST7 .... 241 G1
Cranberry Moss La
 ALS/KID ST7 .... 241 G1
Cranborne Av *WARRS* WA4 .... 56 B3
Cranborne Rd *CW/HAS* CW1 ... 19 C1
 CW/HAS CW1 .... 221 K6
Cranbourne Av *CHD/CHDH* SK8 .. 65 H2
Cranbourne Rd *HALE/TIMP* WA15 .. 43 G6
Crandon Dr *DID/WITH* M20 .... 45 J4
Cranebrook Cl *WARRN/WOL* WA2 .. 221 L6
Cranesbill Cl *WYTH/NTH* M22 .. 63 J3
Cranfield Dr *ALS/KID* ST7 ...... 241 G1
Cranford Av *KNUT* WA16 .... 106 F3
 MCFLDS SK11 .... 15 M7
Cranford Ct *CHSW/BR* CH4 ... 169 G7
Cranford Dr *IRL* M44 .... 31 M1
Cranford Ms *ALS/KID* ST7 ..... 241 G1
Cranford Rd *WILM/AE* SK9 ..... 84 A3
Cranford Sq *KNUT* WA16 ...... 106 F3
Cranham Av *GOL/RIS/CU* WA3 .. 23 L5
Cranham Rd *WYTH/NTH* M22 .. 63 G2
Cranleigh Cl *WARRS* WA4 .... 56 B5
Cranleigh Dr *BRAM/HZG* SK7 .. 67 G4
 CHD/CHDH SK8 .... 45 M6
 SALE M33 .... 43 J3
Cranmere Cl *NWCHW* CW9 ... 130 A8
Cranmere Dr *SALE* M33 .... 42 D2
Cranshaw Av *STHEL* WA9 .... 34 D1
Cranshaw La *WDN* WA8 .... 34 B7
Cranston Dr *DID/WITH* M20 ... 45 H4
 SALE M33 .... 43 L1
Cranston Gv *CHD/CHDH* SK8 .. 44 F7
Cranswick Gn *GTS/LS* CH66 ... 94 C7
Crantock Cl *HLWD* L26 .... 50 F4
Crantock Dr *CHD/CHDH* SK8 .. 64 C4
Cranwell Rd *GOL/RIS/CU* WA3 .. 24 F8
Crauford Rd *CONG* CW12 ...... 184 F4
Craven Av *GOL/RIS/CU* WA3 ... 23 L5
Craven Ct *WARRN/WOL* WA2 ... 27 M8
Craven Dr *ALT* WA14 .... 42 C4
Craven Rd *ALT* WA14 .... 42 C5
 RAIN/WH L35 .... 33 J1
Cravenwood Rd *HLWD* L26 .... 50 F5
Crawford Av *WARRN/WOL* WA2 .. 37 G1
 WYTH/NTH M22 .... 63 K1
Crawford Cl *WLTN* L25 .... 50 D4
Crawford Pl *RUNC* WA7 .... 73 H6
Crawford's Wk *CHNE* CH2 ...... 17 G2
Crawley Av *WARRN/WOL* WA2.. 37 G1
 WYTH/NTH M22 .... 63 K1
Crawley Cl *WLTN* L25 .... 50 D4
Crawley Gv *OFTN* SK2 .... 47 H6
Crayford Rd *WYTH/NTH* M22 .. 63 L1
Creden Av *WYTH/NTH* M22 .... 63 L1
Crediton Cl *ALT* WA14 .... 42 B6
Cresanne St *MWCH* CW10 .... 179 K5
Crescent Cl *EDGY/DAV* SK3 ... 47 G7
Crescent Dr *CHF/WBR* SK23 ... 89 K2
 FROD/HEL WA6 .... 124 B1
Crescent Pk *HTNM* SK4 .... 2 A5
 HTNM SK4 .... 46 B3
Crescent Rd *ALT* WA14 .... 42 A6
 CHD/CHDH SK8 .... 45 J6
 CONG CW12 .... 207 J2
 EP CH65 .... 11 G6
 HALE/TIMP WA15 .... 61 L2
 HOLMCH CW4 .... 156 F6
 KNUT WA16 .... 80 B1
 STKP SK1 .... 3 L2
 WILM/AE SK9 .... 110 B2
The Crescent *ALT* WA14 .... 42 A7
 CHD/CHDH SK8 .... 45 K6
 CHNE CH2 .... 145 K6
 CONG CW12 .... 207 J2
 EDGY/DAV SK3 .... 47 G8
 EP CH65 .... 94 F7
 HALE/TIMP WA15 .... 42 F5
 HUY L36 .... 32 A2
 KNUT WA16 .... 80 B1
 LYMM WA13 .... 58 F2
 MCFLDN SK10 .... 111 G2
 MCFLDN SK10 .... 113 K8
 MCFLDS SK11 .... 15 H9
 MWCH CW10 .... 179 H3
 NANT CW5 .... 21 G5
 NM/HAY SK22 .... 69 J4
 NWCHW CW9 .... 13 H6
 NWCHW CW8 .... 128 D3
 NWCHW CW9 .... 129 G7
 TPLY/KEL CW6 .... 174 B5
Crescent Wy *EDGY/DAV* SK3 .. 47 G7
Cressbrook Rd *WARRS* WA4 ... 56 C4
Cresswell Av *NM/HAY* SK22 ... 69 J4

Cresswell Cl
 WARRW/BUR WA5 .... 36 D2
Cresswellshawe Rd
 ALS/KID ST7 .... 224 D7
Cresswell St *NM/HAY* SK22 .... 69 J4
Cresta Dr *RUNC* WA7 .... 72 F6
Crew Av *MCFLDN* SK10 .... 15 J3
Crewe and Nantwich
 Cicular Wk
 NANT CW5 .... 252 C3
Crewe and Nantwich
 Circular Wk *CW/HAS* CW1 .. 201 J6
Crewe and Nantwich
 Circular Wk *CW/HAS* CW1 .. 220 F1
 CW/HAS CW1 .... 221 L2
 CW/SHV CW2 .... 253 K2
Crewe and Nantwich
 Circular Wk *NANT* CW5 ...... 219 L2
 NANT CW5 .... 251 L3
Crewe And Nantwich
 Circular Wk *NANT* CW5 ...... 252 E4
 SBCH CW11 .... 222 B2
Crewe Green Av *CW/HAS* CW1 .. 222 B8
Crewe Green Rd *CW/HAS* CW1 .. 239 C5
Crewe Hill La *CHSE* CH3 .... 229 G6
Crewe La *CHSE* CH3 .... 228 F3
Crewe La South *CHSE* CH3 ... 228 F4
Crewe Rd *ALS/KID* ST7 .... 224 F8
 ALS/KID ST7 .... 241 H1
 CW/HAS CW1 .... 19 K7
 CW/HAS CW1 .... 239 H1
 CW/SHV CW2 .... 238 C8
 NANT CW5 .... 21 L6
 NANT CW5 .... 237 K6
 NANT CW5 .... 264 F1
 NTHM/RTH M23 .... 43 L4
 SBCH CW11 .... 204 B6
 SBCH CW11 .... 222 F2
Crewe St *CH/BCN* CH1 .... 17 J3
 CW/HAS CW1 .... 19 G4
Crewood Common Rd
 FROD/HEL WA6 .... 127 G1
Crib La *TPLY/KEL* CW6 .... 196 F5
Criccieth Ct *EP* CH65 .... 121 K2
Criccieth Rd *EDGY/DAV* SK3 .. 46 A5
Cricklewood Rd *WYTH/NTH* M22.. 63 J2
Criftin Cl *GTS/LS* CH66 .... 120 C2
Crimes La *CHSE* CH3 .... 196 C8
Cringle Dr *CHD/CHDH* SK8 ... 45 J8
Cringles Dr *RAIN/WH* L35 ...... 32 K5
Crisham Av *NANT* CW5 .... 251 L4
Crispin Rd *WYTH/NTH* M22 ... 63 L4
Croasdale Dr *RUNC* WA7 .... 73 L4
Crocus St *NWCHW* CW8 .... 129 H1
Croes Atti La *FLINT* CH6 .... 116 C7
Croesmere Dr *GTS/LS* CH66 .. 120 E2
Croft Av *GOL/RIS/CU* WA3 ...... 22 F2
Croft Cl *CHSE* CH3 .... 171 G7
 CONG CW12 .... 207 M2
 HALE/TIMP WA15 .... 62 C6
 TPLY/KEL CW6 .... 174 B5
Croft Gdns *WARRS* WA4 .... 57 G5
Croft Heath Gdns
 GOL/RIS/CU WA3 .... 29 C4
Croftlands Rd *WYTH/NTH* M22 .. 44 B8
Crofton Av *HALE/TIMP* WA15 .. 43 G4
 KNUT WA16 .... 107 H4
Crofton Cl *WARRS* WA4 .... 57 J7
Crofton Gdns
 GOL/RIS/CU WA3 .... 29 L1
Crofton Rd *RUNC* WA7 .... 8 C5
Croft Rd *CHD/CHDH* SK8 ...... 65 H1
 SALE M33 .... 43 L2
 WILM/AE SK9 .... 83 L8
Croftside *WARR* WA1 .... 38 F5
Croftside Wy *WILM/AE* SK9 .... 84 C6
Croft St *GOL/RIS/CU* WA3 ...... 23 G2
 WDN WA8 .... 7 H8
The Croft *CHNE* CH2 .... 145 K7
 RUNC WA7 .... 73 L3
Cromar Crs *WRX/GR/LL* LL12 .. 210 C4
Cromar Rd *BRAM/HZG* SK7 ... 66 F1
Crombie Av *WYTH/NTH* M22 .. 44 D4
Cromdale Av *BRAM/HZG* SK7 .. 66 F1
Cromdale Wy *WARRW/BUR* WA5 .. 35 L6
Cromer Dr *CW/HAS* CW1 ...... 221 H4
Cromer Rd *CHD/CHDH* SK8 ... 45 L6
 SALE M33 .... 43 J1
Cromer St *STKP* SK1 .... 3 K4
Cromer Wy *HLWD* L26 .... 50 F6
Cromford Ms *CHF/WBR* SK23 .. 89 L7
Cromley Rd *MPL/ROM* SK6 .... 66 A1
Crompton Cl *MPL/ROM* SK6 ... 48 F5
Crompton Rd *MCFLDS* SK11 ... 14 E8
Cromwell Av *CHD/CHDH* SK8 .. 45 G6
 MPL/ROM SK6 .... 48 C5
 WARRW/BUR WA5 .... 36 C4
Cromwell Av South
 WARRW/BUR WA5 .... 36 C8
Cromwell Dr *CW/SHV* CW2 ... 253 J1
Cromwell Rd *BRAM/HZG* SK7 .. 65 K6
 EP CH65 .... 10 F7
 IRL M44 .... 31 L5
 WDN WA8 .... 12 E3
Cromwell St *BIDD* ST8 .... 227 J3
 HTNM SK4 .... 2 C2
 RUNC WA7 .... 7 G9
Cronkinson Av *NANT* CW5 ..... 21 G9
Cronkinson Oak *NANT* CW5 ... 21 G9
Cronton La *RAIN/WH* L35 .... 33 H3
 WDN WA8 .... 33 M4
 WDN WA8 .... 33 M7
Cronton Park Cl *WDN* WA8 .... 33 J6

Cronton Rd *RAIN/WH* L35 ...... 32 B5
Cronulla Dr *WARRW/BUR* WA5 .. 35 K5
Crooked La *CHSE* CH3 .... 196 B1
Crookedyard Rd *MCFLDS* SK11 .. 139 L5
Crookenden Cl *CHNE* CH2 .... 145 J3
Crookenden Rd *CHNE* CH2 ... 145 J3
Crookilley Wy *STKP* SK1 .... 3 K2
Crook La *WSFD* CW7 .... 178 A2
Crook St *CH/BCN* CH1 .... 16 F5
Croppers Rd *WARRN/WOL* WA2 .. 37 M1
Crosby Av *WARRW/BUR* WA5 .. 37 G4
Crosby Gv *NSTN* CH64 .... 93 H3
Crosby St *OFTN* SK2 .... 46 F5
Crosfield St *WARR* WA1 .... 4 E6
Crossacres Rd *WYTH/NTH* M22 .. 44 F8
Crossall St *MCFLDS* SK11 ...... 15 G7
Crossefield Rd *CHD/CHDH* SK8 .. 65 G1
Crossfield Av *BIDD* ST8 .... 227 J6
 GOL/RIS/CU WA3 .... 29 M2
 LYMM WA13 .... 58 F1
 WSFD CW7 .... 177 K5
Crossfield Gv *MPL/ROM* SK6 .. 49 H3
 OFTN SK2 .... 47 H8
Crossfield Rd *HALE/TIMP* WA15 .. 62 B2
 MCFLDN SK10 .... 112 C6
 WILM/AE SK9 .... 64 D8
Crossfields *CHSE* CH3 .... 172 B2
Crossgate Av *WYTH/NTH* M22 .. 44 D6
Crossgate Ms *HTNM* SK4 .... 45 L2
Crossgates *WDN* WA8 .... 53 M1
Cross Gn *CHNE* CH2 .... 145 L6
Cross Gv *HALE/TIMP* WA15 ... 42 F4
Cross Hey *CHSW/BR* CH4 ...... 17 K8
Cross Hillocks La *RAIN/WH* L35 .. 51 L1
The Crossings *NEWLW* WA12 .. 27 L1
Crosslands *CONG* CW12 .... 208 A3
 CW/HAS CW1 .... 222 D8
Cross La *ALS/KID* ST7 .... 241 L8
 CONG CW12 .... 158 E8
 CONG CW12 .... 208 A4
 CW/HAS CW1 .... 201 J6
 GOL/RIS/CU WA3 .... 29 K5
 HOLMCH CW4 .... 158 C7
 MPL/ROM SK6 .... 48 E7
 MWCH CW10 .... 179 K6
 NANT CW5 .... 201 G7
 NEWLW WA12 .... 27 H1
 NSTN CH64 .... 91 L7
 SBCH CW11 .... 204 C7
 SBCH CW11 .... 205 M7
 WARRS WA4 .... 57 G2
 WARRS WA4 .... 84 F4
Cross La East *NEWLW* WA12 .. 27 L1
Cross La South *GOL/RIS/CU* WA3 .. 29 K6
Cross La West *PART* M31 .... 40 E2
Crossley Av *GTS/LS* CH66 ...... 94 E6
Crossley Crs *CHNE* CH2 .... 146 B7
Crossley St *WARR* WA1 .... 5 J5
Crossmoor Crs *MPL/ROM* SK6 .. 48 C2
Crossmoor Gv *MPL/ROM* SK6 .. 48 C2
Cross O' Th' Hill Rd
 MALPAS SY14 .... 247 G8
Cross Rd *CHD/CHDH* SK8 ...... 64 B5
 CW/HAS CW1 .... 222 D8
Cross St *ALS/KID* ST7 .... 241 J1
 BIDD ST8 .... 227 J4
 CHNE CH2 .... 17 L3
 CW/HAS CW1 .... 222 D8
 CW/SHV CW2 .... 19 G5
 GOL/RIS/CU WA3 .... 35 J5
 MCFLDS SK11 .... 15 H8
 NM/HAY SK22 .... 69 J4
 NSTN CH64 .... 91 L4
 NWCHE CW9 .... 130 C1
 NWCHW CW9 .... 129 H1
 RUNC WA7 .... 7 G9
 WARRN/WOL WA2 .... 5 H3
 WDN WA8 .... 7 K3
 WRXS/E LL13 .... 228 E3
The Cross *LYMM* WA13 .... 58 E1
 WRXS/E LL13 .... 228 D4
Crosstree La *CQ* CH5 .... 166 D3
Cross Tree Ri *CQ* CH5 .... 166 D4
Crosswaite La *OFTN* SK2 .... 47 K6
Crossway *BRAM/HZG* SK7 ...... 65 L7
 DID/WITH M20 .... 45 H1
 OFTN SK2 .... 47 G8
 OFTN SK2 .... 6 A4
Crossways *BIDD* ST8 .... 227 L3
 CQ CH5 .... 142 B7
Crossways Rd *ALS/KID* ST7 ... 225 G8
Cross Wood St *NANT* CW5 ...... 20 D6
Croston Cl *WDN* WA8 .... 33 J8
 WILM/AE SK9 .... 110 C3
Crotia Av *CW/SHV* CW2 .... 239 H7
Croton St *HTNM* SK4 .... 45 L2
Crouch La *CONG* CW12 .... 185 K8
Crouchley La *LYMM* WA13 ...... 58 F3
Croughton Rd *CHNE* CH2 ..... 121 M6
 CHNE CH2 .... 122 A5
 GTS/LS CH66 .... 94 F4
Crowborough Rd *BIDD* ST8 ... 227 M6
Crowder's La *NWCHE* CW9 ... 131 G8
Crowe Av *WARRN/WOL* WA2 .. 37 H1
Crowland Gdns
 CHD/CHDH SK8 .... 65 H6
Crowland Rd *NTHM/RTH* M23 .. 62 F1
Crow La East *NEWLW* WA12 ... 22 A8
Crow La West *NEWLW* WA12 ... 22 A8
Crowley La *NWCHE* CW9 .... 77 M1
Crowley Rd *HALE/TIMP* WA15 .. 43 H6
Crown Acres Rd *WLTN* L25 ..... 50 D4
Crown Av *WDN* WA8 .... 52 B4
Crown Bank *ALS/KID* ST7 ..... 242 D5
 SBCH CW11 .... 204 B6
Crown Bank Crs *ALS/KID* ST7 .. 242 D6
Crown Ct *BRAM/HZG* SK7 ..... 66 D1
Crowndale Pl *BURS/TUN* ST6 .. 243 L4
Crownest La *NWCHE* CW9 .... 103 K4
Crown Fields Cl *NEWLW* WA12 .. 22 B7
Crown Gdns *NEWLW* WA12 ... 22 B8
Crown Ga *RUNC* WA7 .... 73 M5
Crown Gn *LYMM* WA13 .... 59 H1
Crown La *KNUT* WA16 .... 132 D4
Crown Park Dr *NEWLW* WA12 .. 22 B8

Crown Passages
HALE/TIMP WA15 61 L2
Crown St MPL/ROM SK6 67 M1
NEWLW WA12 27 G1
NWCHE CW9 13 H1
WARR WA1 5 G6
Crown St West MCFLDS SK11 14 E6
Crowsdale Pl OFTN SK2 47 L8
Crowthorn Dr
NTHM/RTH M23 63 G2 3
Crowton Av SALE M33 42 D2 1
Crowton Vw FROD/HEL WA6 127 G6
Crow Wood La WDN WA8 53 K2
Crow Wood Pl WDN WA8 53 K1 1
Crow Wood Rd GOL/RIS/CU WA3 23 K3
Croxton Cl MPL/ROM SK6 48 E7
SALE M33 42 D2 2
Croxton Gn MALPAS SY14 233 J6
Croxton La MWCH CW10 155 G7
Croxton Wy NWCHW CW8 129 G8 2
Croyde Cl WYTH/NTH M22 63 M5
Croyde Rd SPK/HALE L24 71 G1
Crum Hl NWCHE CW9 13 J2
Crummock Rd CHD/CHDH SK8 64 B1 1
Cruttenden Rd OFTN SK2 47 J8
Cryers La CHNE CH2 122 F4
Cuckoo La NANT CW5 235 M4
NSTN CH64 92 B5
Cuckstoolpit Hl MCFLDN SK10 15 J5
Cuddington Crs EDGY/DAV SK3 46 D6
Cuddington La NWCHW CW8 151 J1
Cuerdley Gn WDN WA8 54 A2
Cuerdley Rd WARRW/BUR WA5 54 C1
Cuerdon Dr WARRS WA4 57 K3
Culbert Av DID/WITH M20 45 J1 5
Culbin Cl GOL/RIS/CU WA3 30 A6 2
Culcheth Av MPL/ROM SK6 48 F6 5
Culcheth Hall Dr
GOL/RIS/CU WA3 24 F8
Culcheth Rd ALT WA14 61 K1
Culford Cl RUNC WA7 74 D3 3
Culland St CW/SHV CW2 18 F8
Cullen Rd RUNC WA7 8 B8
Culmere Rd WYTH/NTH M22 63 K3
Culver Rd EDGY/DAV SK3 46 D7
Cumber Cl WILM/AE SK9 83 K8
Cumber Dr WILM/AE SK9 83 K8
Cumberland Av IRL M44 31 J7
NANT CW5 21 H4
Cumberland Cl ALS/KID ST7 242 E5
CW/HAS CW1 19 H1
Cumberland Dr ALT WA14 61 G4
MCFLDN SK10 113 H4 1
Cumberland Gv GTS/LS CH66 120 C1
Cumberland Rd CONG CW12 207 G1
PART M31 40 D2
SALE M33 43 J2
Cumberland St MCFLDN SK10 14 E4
MCFLDS SK11 14 D5
WARRS WA4 56 C1
Cumber La RAIN/WH L35 32 F1
WILM/AE SK9 83 K8
Cumbermere Dr SBCH CW11 203 L5
Cumbers Dr NSTN CH64 92 A7
Cumbers La NSTN CH64 92 A7
Cumbrae Dr EP CH65 121 J3
Cuncliffe Dr SALE M33 43 J1
Cundiff Cl MCFLDS SK11 15 K8 2
Cunliffe Av NEWLW WA12 22 B7
Cunliffe Cl RUNC WA7 74 A5
Cunliffe St EDGY/DAV SK3 2 B7
Cunningham Cl
WARRW/BUR WA5 35 M7 2
Cunningham Dr RUNC WA7 8 D6
WYTH/NTH M22 64 A4
Cunningham Rd WDN WA8 6 B5
Cuppin St CH/BCN CH1 16 F6
Curate St STKP SK1 3 K6
Curlender Wy SPK/HALE L24 71 L2
Curlew Cl GOL/RIS/CU WA3 23 K4 1
WSFD CW7 177 J7 1
Curlew Gv GOL/RIS/CU WA3 38 E1
Currans Rd WARRN/WOL WA2 37 G2 1
Curtis Rd HTNM SK4 46 A2
Curzon Av ALS/KID ST7 224 D7
Curzon Cl CHSW/BR CH4 16 B8
Curzon Dr HALE/TIMP WA15 43 H6
WARRS WA4 57 C5
Curzon Gn OFTN SK2 47 K4
Curzon Gv WSFD CW7 177 M3 1
Curzon Ms WILM/AE SK9 84 A6
Curzon Pk North CHSW/BR CH4 16 C8
Curzon Pk South
CHSW/BR CH4 169 G5
Curzon Rd CHD/CHDH SK8 64 B5
OFTN SK2 47 K5
POY/DIS SK12 86 E2
Curzon St CHSW/BR CH4 168 F5
RUNC WA7 8 F4
Cutgate Cl NTHM/RTH M23 43 L3 1
Cuthbert Rd CHD/CHDH SK8 45 L6
Cwm Eithion FLINT CH6 116 B8
Cwrt Onnen CQ CH5 166 E3 1
Cygnet Cl GTS/LS CH66 94 D8
Cygnet Ct WARR WA1 56 A1
Cyman Cl CH/BCN CH1 168 D1
Cymbal Ct RDSH SK5 3 G1
Cynthia Av WARR WA1 38 B5
Cynthia Dr MPL/ROM SK6 48 F7
Cynthia Rd RUNC WA7 8 E4
Cypress Av GTS/LS CH66 120 F3
WDN WA8 53 H1
Cypress Cl EDGY/DAV SK3 2 A7
WARR WA1 38 E5 1
Cypress Gv RUNC WA7 9 M9
Cypress Wy MPL/ROM SK6 68 A5
Cyril Bell Cl LYMM WA13 58 F1
Cyril St WARRN/WOL WA2 5 H3

D

Dacre's Bridge La RAIN/WH L35 32 D5
Daffodil Cl WDN WA8 34 E8
Dagnall Av WARRW/BUR WA5 36 F2
Daine Av NTHM/RTH M23 44 B3
Daintry St MCFLDS SK11 15 J6
Daintry Ter MCFLDN SK10 15 J6
Dairy Farm Cl LYMM WA13 58 F1
Dairyground Rd BRAM/HZG SK7 65 L5
Dairyhouse La ALT WA14 42 B5
Dairy House La BRAM/HZG SK7 85 H1
Dairy House Rd CHD/CHDH SK8 65 H7
Dairy House Wy CW/SHV CW2 237 M2
Dairylands Rd ALS/KID ST7 225 G8
Dairy La NANT CW5 219 H8
Daisy Av NEWLW WA12 27 J2
Daisy Bank NANT CW5 20 C7
Daisy Bank Crs
AUD/MAD/W CW3 263 M7
Daisybank Dr CONG CW12 184 D7
SBCH CW11 204 C6
Daisy Bank La NWCHW CW8 129 J1
WYTH/NTH M22 64 A3
Daisy Bank Rd LYMM WA13 58 C1
WARRW/BUR WA5 35 M8 1
Daisyfield Cl WYTH/NTH M22 63 J3 2
Daisy La WRX/GR/LL LL12 210 E8
Daisy Ms EDGY/DAV SK3 46 D8
Daisy Mill Bank Cl
GOL/RIS/CU WA3 29 L1
Daisy St OFTN SK2 46 F5 3
Daisy Wy MPL/ROM SK6 67 M5
Dakins Rd LEIGH WN7 25 H2
Dalby Cl GOL/RIS/CU WA3 30 B7
Dalby Gv STKP SK1 3 K5
Dale Av BRAM/HZG SK7 65 M4
GTS/LS CH66 94 C6
Dalebrook Rd SALE M33 43 J3
Dale Cl WARRW/BUR WA5 4 A9
WARRW/BUR WA5 36 D8
WDN WA8 52 A4
Dale Ct MWCH CW10 179 K5
Dale Crs CONG CW12 207 M2
Dalecroft FROD/HEL WA6 123 L3
Dale Dr CHNE CH2 145 K4
EP CH65 94 F7
Dalefords La NWCHW CW8 152 B4
Dale Gv CONG CW12 208 A2
HALE/TIMP WA15 42 F5
IRL M44 31 L6
Dale Head Rd MCFLDN SK10 111 M8
Dale Hey GTS/LS CH66 93 L2
Dale La WARRS WA4 56 E5
Dale Pl CONG CW12 207 M2
Dale Rd CQ CH5 142 A8
GOL/RIS/CU WA3 23 G5
MPL/ROM SK6 48 E5
NM/HAY SK22 69 J5
Dalesford Cl LEIGH WN7 24 C4
Dalesford Crs MCFLDS SK11 137 M4 5
Dales Green Rd ALS/KID ST7 226 C7
Daleside CHNE CH2 145 K4
Dales Rw HUY L36 32 B2
Dale St CHSE CH3 170 A3
EDGY/DAV SK3 46 D5
MCFLDN SK10 15 K5
RUNC WA7 9 G5
The Dale NSTN CH64 91 K6
TPLY/KEL CW6 197 J6
WARRW/BUR WA5 35 M7
Dale Vw ALS/KID ST7 226 C7
NEWLW WA12 22 E8
Dalewood Crs CHNE CH2 123 G1 1
Dalewood Gdns RAIN/WH L35 32 F2 5
Dallam La WARRN/WOL WA2 4 F5
Dallimore Rd NTHM/RTH M23 43 L6
Dalmahoy Cl WSFD CW7 177 J2 2
Dalston Dr BRAM/HZG SK7 65 J7
DID/WITH M20 45 J2 1
Dalton Av WARRW/BUR WA5 4 D2
Dalton Bank WARR WA1 5 K5
Dalton Cl CH/BCN CH1 168 E1
Dalton Ct RUNC WA7 73 L1
SBCH CW11 203 L5
Dalton St GOL/RIS/CU WA3 29 L6
RUNC WA7 73 K2
Dalton Wy MWCH CW10 179 K3
Daltry Wy AUD/MAD/W CW3 267 M5 1
Dalveen Dr HALE/TIMP WA15 42 F5 1
Dalwood Cl RUNC WA7 74 E5
Dame Hollow CHD/CHDH SK8 64 D5 1
Dameny Ct BRAM/HZG SK7 65 L4
Damery Rd BRAM/HZG SK7 65 L4
Dam Head La GOL/RIS/CU WA3 30 F8
Damhead La NSTN CH64 92 E5
Damian Dr NEWLW WA12 22 A7 1
Dam La GOL/RIS/CU WA3 22 F1
GOL/RIS/CU WA3 28 F5
GOL/RIS/CU WA3 31 G8
KNUT WA16 108 C1
WARR WA1 38 D5
Dams La KNUT WA16 132 D7
Damson La KNUT WA16 82 B8
Dam Wood Rd SPK/HALE L24 70 D2
Dan Bank MPL/ROM SK6 48 C6
Danby Cl RUNC WA7 73 K6 2
WARRW/BUR WA5 4 B2
Danby Fold RAIN/WH L35 33 H1 1
Dane Av EDGY/DAV SK3 46 A4 1
PART M31 31 M8
Dane Bank Av CONG CW12 184 E8
CW/SHV CW2 18 A8
Dane Bank Dr POY/DIS SK12 68 D6
Danebank Rd LYMM WA13 39 L8
Dane Bank Rd NWCHE CW9 13 L4
Danebank Rd East LYMM WA13 39 L8
Dane Cl ALS/KID ST7 241 G1
BRAM/HZG SK7 66 E2
CHSW/BR CH4 168 F7
SBCH CW11 203 L5
Dane Dr BIDD ST8 227 L3
WILM/AE SK9 84 D6
Danefield Ct CHD/CHDH SK8 64 D4 1
Danefield Rd HOLMCH CW4 157 J8
NWCHE CW9 153 M2
Dane Gdns ALS/KID ST7 243 J2
Dane Gv CHNE CH2 146 F4
Dane Hill Cl POY/DIS SK12 68 D7
Danesbury Ri CHD/CHDH SK8 45 K7 5
Danescroft WDN WA8 52 B1
Danes Sq MCFLDS SK11 138 D7 2
Dane St CONG CW12 207 J1
MWCH CW10 179 K2
NWCHE CW9 13 H3
Daneswell Rd SPK/HALE L24 71 G2 2
Dane Valley Wy HOLMCH CW4 156 C8
Daniel Adamson Av
PART M31 40 D1 1
Daniel Cl GOL/RIS/CU WA3 30 A8
Daniell Wy CHSE CH3 170 A5
Daniel's La STKP SK1 3 G4 1
Daniel St BRAM/HZG SK7 66 E2 5
Dans Rd WDN WA8 53 L2
Dappleheath Rd CW/SHV CW2 18 B9
Darby Cl NSTN CH64 91 L8
Darden Cl HTNM SK4 45 L1
Daresbury Cl EDGY/DAV SK3 46 D7 4
HOLMCH CW4 181 G1
SALE M33 43 M1 2
Daresbury Expy RUNC WA7 8 F2
WARRS WA4 75 G1
Daresbury La WARRS WA4 75 K2
Darian Av WYTH/NTH M22 63 K4
Daric Cl LEIGH WN7 24 C3
Dark Ark La CHSE CH3 149 J1
Darkie Meadow
TPLY/KEL CW6 216 E4 1
Dark La CHSE CH3 214 D5
FROD/HEL WA6 126 B3
MCFLDS SK11 137 G4
MCFLDS SK11 161 M1
NWCHE CW9 104 C5
WARRS WA4 76 D7
WHITCH SY13 271 H3
Darland Cl WRX/GR/LL LL12 210 C4
Darland La WRX/GR/LL LL12 210 C4
WRX/GR/LL LL12 210 E4
Darley Av CHD/CHDH SK8 45 H7
CW/SHV CW2 18 A6
WARRN/WOL WA2 37 L1
Darley Cl WDN WA8 52 B1
Darley Rd BRAM/HZG SK7 66 F5
Darlington Av CW/HAS CW1 220 F7
Darlington Crs CH/BCN CH1 144 A3
Darlington St MWCH CW10 179 J3
Darnaway Cl GOL/RIS/CU WA3 30 B6
Darnbrook Dr
WYTH/NTH M22 63 H3 2
Darnhall School La WSFD CW7 177 J7
Dart Cl ALS/KID ST7 224 A8
BIDD ST8 227 K3
Dartington Cl BRAM/HZG SK7 65 M1
NTHM/RTH M23 43 K6
Dartnall Cl POY/DIS SK12 68 A6
Darwick Dr HUY L36 32 A4
Darwin Gv BRAM/HZG SK7 65 L6
Darwin Rd CH/BCN CH1 144 C8
Darwin St NWCHW CW8 12 E5
Daten Av GOL/RIS/CU WA3 29 M6
Dauncey Cl CHNE CH2 145 J3 2
Davehall Av WILM/AE SK9 84 A5
Davenfield Gv DID/WITH M20 45 H1 3
Davenham Av WARR WA1 37 L4
Davenham Ct NWCHE CW9 154 A1
Davenham Crs CW/SHV CW2 237 M1
Davenham Rd NWCHE CW9 154 E1
WILM/AE SK9 64 D8 3
Davenham Wy MWCH CW10 179 K7
Davenport Av CW/SHV CW2 238 C4
NANT CW5 20 E4
WARRS WA4 37 M7
WILM/AE SK9 83 L8
Davenport Cl SBCH CW11 204 D4 1
Davenport La KNUT WA16 82 C6
MCFLDS SK11 160 A7
SBCH CW11 205 J2
Davenport Park La CONG CW12 182 D2
Davenport Park Rd OFTN SK2 47 G7
Davenport Rd BRAM/HZG SK7 66 D1
Davenport Rw RUNC WA7 73 K4 1
Davenport St CONG CW12 207 J2
CW/HAS CW1 221 J6
MCFLDN SK10 15 J5
Daven Rd CONG CW12 207 M3
Daveylands WILM/AE SK9 84 D6
Davey La WILM/AE SK9 110 A2
David Rd LYMM WA13 58 C1
David's Av WARRW/BUR WA5 36 B7
Davidson Av CONG CW12 185 G7
David St NWCHW CW8 12 F4
Davids Wk WLTN L25 50 C1 1
Davies Av CHD/CHDH SK8 64 B6
NEWLW WA12 22 C8
WARRS WA4 37 M8
Davies Cl WDN WA8 53 G8
Davies Rd MPL/ROM SK6 47 K1 1
PART M31 41 G1
Davies Wy LYMM WA13 58 D1
Davis Cl ALS/KID ST7 224 E8
Davy Av GOL/RIS/CU WA3 29 L7
Davy Rd RUNC WA7 73 L1
Dawley Cl AIMK WN4 22 A1
Dawlish Av CHD/CHDH SK8 64 F4
Dawlish Cl BRAM/HZG SK7 65 L5
GOL/RIS/CU WA3 40 B2 1
WLTN L25 50 C4
Dawn Cl NSTN CH64 91 M7
Dawn Gdns EP CH65 95 H8
Dawpool Cl CHNE CH2 145 K7
Dawson Dr CH/BCN CH1 16 F1
Dawson Rd ALT WA14 42 D5
CHD/CHDH SK8 64 D4
MCFLDN SK10 113 G5 1
MCFLDS SK11 137 M5
Dawson St STKP SK1 3 L2
Daylesford Cl CHD/CHDH SK8 45 J8
Daylesford Crs CHD/CHDH SK8 45 K8
Daylesford Rd CHD/CHDH SK8 45 K8
Deacon Cl ALT WA14 61 H3
GOL/RIS/CU WA3 29 G4
Deacon Ct WLTN L25 50 B2 2
Deacon Rd WDN WA8 7 J3
Deacons Cl STKP SK1 3 J5
Deakin's Rd WSFD CW7 153 M8
Dean Bank TPLY/KEL CW6 216 C1
Dean Cl MCFLDN SK10 113 G5
PART M31 31 M8
SBCH CW11 203 L4
WDN WA8 7 J4
WILM/AE SK9 84 C3
Dean Ct GOL/RIS/CU WA3 23 G5 2
Dean Crs WARRN/WOL WA2 37 H2 5
Dean Dr ALT WA14 61 H3
WILM/AE SK9 84 C3
Deane Av CHD/CHDH SK8 45 M7
HALE/TIMP WA15 43 G7
Deanery Cl CH/BCN CH1 145 J8
Deanery Wy STKP SK1 3 G4
Dean La BRAM/HZG SK7 66 E4
Dean Meadow NEWLW WA12 22 C8 1
Dean Moor Rd BRAM/HZG SK7 66 A2
Dean Pk MALPAS SY14 247 G8
Dean Rd GOL/RIS/CU WA3 23 G5
IRL M44 31 L6
WILM/AE SK9 84 E1
Dean Row Rd WILM/AE SK9 84 C3
Deans Cl CHNE CH2 145 K6 1
CHSE CH3 172 B3 1
Deansfield Wy CHNE CH2 123 G1
Deansgate EP CH65 10 B7
Deansgate La HALE/TIMP WA15 42 E5
Dean's La CW/SHV CW2 240 C8
CW/SHV CW2 255 J2
MALPAS SY14 231 M8
SBCH CW11 203 L6
WARRS WA4 57 M1
Deans Rd EP CH65 121 M1
Dean St MWCH CW10 179 J2
NWCHE CW9 130 C4
WDN WA8 7 J4
WSFD CW7 177 J3
Deans Wy CHSE CH3 172 B2
CHSW/BR CH4 190 A4
Deansway WDN WA8 52 C4
Deanwater Cl GOL/RIS/CU WA3 29 K8
Deanwater Ct CHD/CHDH SK8 64 D5 2
Dean Wy STHEL WA9 34 B1
Deanway WILM/AE SK9 84 C4
Dean Wood Cl RAIN/WH L35 32 F2 4
Debra Cl GTS/LS CH66 94 C8
Debra Rd GTS/LS CH66 120 C1
Dee Av HALE/TIMP WA15 43 K7
Dee Banks CHSE CH3 17 M9
Dee Cl ALS/KID ST7 242 E5
BIDD ST8 227 L3 1
SBCH CW11 203 L4
Dee Crs CHSE CH3 228 E2
Dee Fords Av CHSE CH3 170 A3
Dee Hills Pk CHSE CH3 17 K5
Dee La CHSE CH3 17 K5
WRXS/E LL13 228 D4
Dee Mdw WRXS/E LL13 228 D5
Dee Pk WRXS/E LL13 228 D4
Deepdale LEIGH WN7 25 J1 2
Deep Dl WARRW/BUR WA5 35 M6
Deepdale WDN WA8 52 C1
Deepdale Dr RAIN/WH L35 33 K1
Deepwood Gv RAIN/WH L35 32 E2 2
Deeracre Av OFTN SK2 47 J6
Deermoss WHITCH SY13 270 A4 1
Dee Rd CHNE CH2 146 F3
CQ CH5 142 F5
RAIN/WH L35 33 H1
Deer Park Ct RUNC WA7 73 M6 2
Deerwood Cl GTS/LS CH66 94 D5 1
MCFLDN SK10 137 M3 3
Deerwood Crs GTS/LS CH66 94 D5
Deeside EP CH65 121 H1
WRXS/E LL13 228 E4
Deeside Cl EP CH65 121 H2
Deeside Crs CH/BCN CH1 143 L7
Deeside La CH/BCN CH1 143 L7
Dee Vw CHSE CH3 228 E2
CQ CH5 142 C8
Dee Wy WSFD CW7 178 A2 2
Deiniol's Rd CQ CH5 166 E2
Deirdre Av WDN WA8 7 H3
De Lacy Rw RUNC WA7 74 A2
Delafield Cl WARRN/WOL WA2 37 M1
Delaford Cl EDGY/DAV SK3 46 E8 1
Delahays Dr HALE/TIMP WA15 62 A2
Delahays Rd HALE/TIMP WA15 62 B2
Delamere Av GOL/RIS/CU WA3 23 L6
GTS/LS CH66 94 E7 2
SALE M33 43 L1
STHEL WA9 34 A1
WDN WA8 52 C3
Delamere Cl BRAM/HZG SK7 67 G1
SBCH CW11 203 M4
Delamere Ct ALS/KID ST7 223 M8
Delamere Dr GTS/LS CH66 94 E8
MCFLDN SK10 15 M1
Delamere La CHSE CH3 149 J2
Delamere Park Wy East
NWCHW CW8 127 K7
Delamere Park Wy West
NWCHW CW8 127 K7
Delamere Ri WSFD CW7 177 H3 1
Delamere Rd BRAM/HZG SK7 67 G1
CHD/CHDH SK8 45 H7
CONG CW12 206 F1
FROD/HEL WA6 126 B6
NANT CW5 251 L1
OFTN SK2 47 H8
WILM/AE SK9 64 D8
Delamere St CH/BCN CH1 16 F3
CW/HAS CW1 18 E4
WARRW/BUR WA5 4 B6
WSFD CW7 177 G3
Delamere Wy FROD/HEL WA6 99 J7
FROD/HEL WA6 150 B1
WARRS WA4 76 A5
Delamer Rd ALT WA14 61 J1
Delamore's Acre NSTN CH64 93 G4
Delenty Dr GOL/RIS/CU WA3 29 K8
Delery Dr WARR WA1 37 L4
Delf La SPK/HALE L24 50 B7
Delfur Rd BRAM/HZG SK7 65 M5
Delhi Rd IRL M44 31 M4
Dell Dr WARRN/WOL WA2 38 A2
Dell Side MPL/ROM SK6 47 L1
The Dell CHSE CH3 146 F7 1
NWCHW CW8 127 J8
TPLY/KEL CW6 149 K8
Delmar Rd KNUT WA16 107 J3
Delphfields Rd WARRS WA4 56 C5
Delphfield RUNC WA7 74 D4
Delph La WARRN/WOL WA2 28 E6
WARRS WA4 75 G1
Delta Ct CHSW/BR CH4 168 B6 1
Delves Av WARRW/BUR WA5 4 C2
Delves Cl CW/SHV CW2 238 B8
Delves Wk CHSE CH3 170 B5
Delvine Dr CHNE CH2 145 K6
Delwood Gdns
WYTH/NTH M22 44 D8 3
Demage Dr GTS/LS CH66 120 D1
Demage La CH/BCN CH1 120 F8
CHNE CH2 145 K4
Demmings Rd CHD/CHDH SK8 45 M7
Denbigh Cl BIDD ST8 227 J6
BRAM/HZG SK7 66 C4
FROD/HEL WA6 124 A3
Denbigh Crs MWCH CW10 179 J5
Denbigh Dr WSFD CW7 177 H5
Denbigh Gdns EP CH65 121 J1 2
Denbigh St CH/BCN CH1 16 D2
HTNM SK4 2 D2
Denbury Av WARRS WA4 56 F2
Denbury Dr ALT WA14 42 B7 2
Denbury Gn BRAM/HZG SK7 66 A2
Dene Ct HTNM SK4 2 A3
Dene Dr WSFD CW7 177 K4
Denefield Cl MPL/ROM SK6 49 H3 1
Denehurst Cl
WARRW/BUR WA5 35 M8 2
Denehurst Park Wy
NWCHW CW8 127 K7
Dene Pk DID/WITH M20 45 G2
Dene Rd West DID/WITH M20 44 F1
Denesgate WSFD CW7 177 K4 1
Deneside Av CW/HAS CW1 221 J6
Deneside Crs BRAM/HZG SK7 66 F1
Denesway SALE M33 42 E1 1
Deneway BRAM/HZG SK7 65 J5
HTNM SK4 2 A3
MPL/ROM SK6 67 M5
Deneway Cl HTNM SK4 2 A3
Deneway Ms HTNM SK4 2 A3 2
Denford Cl CHSW/BR CH4 167 J8 1
Denford Pl ALS/KID ST7 224 D6
Denhall Cl CHNE CH2 145 L7
Denhall La NSTN CH64 118 A2
Denham Av WARRW/BUR WA5 36 B7
Denham Dr BRAM/HZG SK7 65 K5
Denholm Rd DID/WITH M20 45 J4 1
Denise Av WARRW/BUR WA5 35 L7
Denison Rd BRAM/HZG SK7 66 E4
Den La NANT CW5 254 A6
Denmark St HALE/TIMP WA15 42 D8
Dennett Cl WARR WA1 38 E6
Dennis Dr CHSW/BR CH4 169 H6
Dennison Rd CHD/CHDH SK8 65 G4
Dennis Rd WDN WA8 7 L6
Densham Av WARRN/WOL WA2 37 H2
Denshaw Cl BNG/LEV M19 45 L1
Denson Dr CQ CH5 166 A2
Denson Rd HALE/TIMP WA15 43 H4
Denston Cl CW/SHV CW2 18 C9
Denstone Av SALE M33 42 E1 2
Denstone Cl WLTN L25 50 B4 1
Denstone Dr CHSW/BR CH4 169 G8
Dentith Dr CH/BCN CH1 144 E7
Denton Cl WSFD CW7 177 J3 1
Denton Dr NWCHE CW9 130 C3
Denton St WDN WA8 7 L3
Denver Av CW/SHV CW2 18 D6
Denver Dr HALE/TIMP WA15 43 G7 1
Denver Rd WARRS WA4 57 G1 2
Denville Crs WYTH/NTH M22 63 L1
Depenbech Cl MALPAS SY14 246 B8
Depleach Rd CHD/CHDH SK8 45 K7 4
Depmore La FROD/HEL WA6 126 A2
Deptford Av NTHM/RTH M23 63 G1 1
De Quincey Rd ALT WA14 42 D3
Derby Cl IRL M44 31 J7
NEWLW WA12 27 H1 4
Derby Ct SALE M33 43 J1 3
Derby Dr WARR WA1 37 M5
Derby Pl CHNE CH2 17 K1
Derby Rd ALS/KID ST7 242 D5
GOL/RIS/CU WA3 23 J3
NM/HAY SK22 69 K3
WARRS WA4 56 C4
WDN WA8 34 D8
Derby Rw NEWLW WA12 27 K4
Derbyshire Hill Rd STHEL WA9 26 A1
Derbyshire Rd PART M31 40 E2 2
POY/DIS SK12 67 K7
Derbyshire Rd South SALE M33 43 K1
Derby St ALT WA14 42 E7
CONG CW12 207 K1 1
CW/HAS CW1 18 C1
EDGY/DAV SK3 2 D8
HUY L36 32 A2
MPL/ROM SK6 48 F7
NEWLW WA12 27 H1
Derek Av WARRN/WOL WA2 37 K3
Derrington Av CW/SHV CW2 18 F6
Derry Av WYTH/NTH M22 44 E8
Derwen Rd EDGY/DAV SK3 46 E5
Derwent Av GOL/RIS/CU WA3 23 J3 4
HALE/TIMP WA15 43 K7 1
WSFD CW7 178 B3
Derwent Cl ALS/KID ST7 224 A8
GOL/RIS/CU WA3 30 A2 1
HOLMCH CW4 181 G1
LEIGH WN7 24 E1 1
MCFLDS SK11 14 A9
NANT CW5 237 K6
PART M31 31 M8
RAIN/WH L35 33 H1
Derwent Crs ALS/KID ST7 243 J2
Derwent Dr BIDD ST8 227 L3 1
BRAM/HZG SK7 65 J7 1
CONG CW12 207 M3
GTS/LS CH66 94 B2
SALE M33 43 G2
WILM/AE SK9 64 C7
Derwent Rd CHNE CH2 145 M7
MPL/ROM SK6 67 L4
WARRS WA4 56 A2
WDN WA8 52 C3
Derwent St LEIGH WN7 24 E1 2
Derwent Wy NSTN CH64 91 M6
WILM/AE SK9 108 F5
Desilva St HUY L36 32 A2
Desmond Rd WYTH/NTH M22 44 E8

Desoto Rd WDN WA8 .... 52 E7
Desoto Rd East WDN WA8 .... 6 E9
Deva Av CHSW/BR CH4 .... 168 D6
Deva Cl BRAM/HZG SK7 .... 66 D3
　FLINT CH6 .... 116 C1
　POY/DIS SK12 .... 66 B8
Deva La CHNE CH2 .... 145 J6
Deva Link CH/BCN CH1 .... 16 A2
Deva Rd CW/SHV CW2 .... 220 D8
Devisdale Rd ALT WA14 .... 42 B8
Devon Cl MCFLDN SK10 ...... 137 M2
　MWCH CW10 .... 179 K2
Devon Gv BIDD ST8 .... 227 J3
Devon Pl CONG CW12 .... 184 E8
　WDN WA8 .... 53 G1
Devon Rd CHNE CH2 .... 145 M7
　IRL M44 .... 31 K7
　PART M31 .... 40 E2
Devonshire Dr WILM/AE SK9 . 110 B2
Devonshire Gdns NEWLW WA12 . 27 J2
Devonshire Park Rd OFTN SK2 . 47 G7
Devonshire Pl CHSW/BR CH4 . 17 J9
　RUNC WA7 .... 9 C1
Devonshire Rd ALT WA14 ..... 42 C6
　BRAM/HZG SK7 .... 66 F4
　CHSW/BR CH4 .... 167 J8
　HTNM SK4 .... 46 B2
　WARR WA1 .... 37 M4
Dewar St RUNC WA7 .... 73 L1
De Warenne Cl WHITCH SY13 . 270 B5
Dewar St GOL/RIS/CU WA3 ... 29 J7
Dewes St CW/HAS CW1 .... 18 D2
Dewhurst Rd GOL/RIS/CU WA3 . 38 D2
Dewint Av MPL/ROM SK6 ..... 49 H4
Dial Cl CW12 CONG 209 G3
Dial Park Rd OFTN SK2 .... 47 K8
Dial Rd HALE/TIMP WA15 ..... 62 C4
　OFTN SK2 .... 47 J7
Dialstone La OFTN SK2 .... 47 J5
Dial St WARR WA1 .... 5 H6
Diamond Av ALS/KID ST7 .... 243 H2
Diamond Cl BIDD ST8 .... 227 J4
Diamond Dr OFTN SK2 .... 47 C6
Diamond St MPL/ROM SK6 ... 67 M1
Dickens Cl CHD/CHDH SK8 ... 65 H7
　SBCH CW11 .... 203 K6
Dickens La POY/DIS SK12 .... 86 E1
Dickenson St WARRN/WOL WA2 . 5 J3
Dickson Cl WDN WA8 .... 7 J4
Dicksons Dr CHNE CH2 .... 145 K7
Dickson St WDN WA8 .... 7 H4
Didcot Cl WLTN L25 .... 50 D4
Didcot Rd WYTH/NTH M22 ... 63 J3
Didsbury Pk DID/WITH M20 .. 45 H2
Didsbury Rd HTNM SK4 .... 45 L2
Dierdens Ter MWCH CW10 ... 179 J3
Dierden St WSFD CW7 .... 178 B3
Diglake Cl ALS/KID ST7 ...... 242 C6
Diglands Av NM/HAY SK22 ... 69 K3
Dig La FROD/HEL WA6 .... 99 C5
　NANT CW5 .... 235 K8
　NANT CW5 .... 253 H2
　WARRN/WOL WA2 .... 29 G8
Diglee Rd CHF/WBR SK23 .... 89 J1
Dilworth Ct OFTN SK2 .... 47 L7
Dinas Cl CH/BCN CH1 .... 168 D1
Dingle Av NEWLW WA12 ...... 26 F2
　WILM/AE SK9 .... 109 K1
Dingle Bank CHSW/BR CH4 .. 16 E9
Dingle Bank Cl LYMM WA13 .. 58 E1
Dingle Bank Rd BRAM/HZG SK7 . 65 K2
Dingle Cl MCFLDN SK10 ...... 138 B1
　MPL/ROM SK6 .... 48 D2
Dingle Gv CHD/CHDH SK8 .... 44 F6
Dingle Rd BIDD ST8 .... 209 F6
　NANT CW5 .... 265 M5
　SBCH CW11 .... 204 C6
　TPLY/KEL CW6 .... 149 L6
　WARRS WA4 .... 56 F6
　WSFD CW7 .... 177 K2
The Dingle BRAM/HZG SK7 ... 65 J3
　CW/HAS CW1 .... 222 D7
　LYMM WA13 .... 58 E1
Dingle Wy NWCHW CW8 ..... 127 L7
Dingleway WARRS WA4 .... 56 D4
Dinmor Rd WYTH/NTH M22 .. 63 J4
Diploma Dr MWCH CW10 ..... 179 J2
Dirty Mile CO CW5 .... 166 A8
Distaff Rd POY/DIS SK12 ..... 66 B8
Ditchfield La KNUT WA16 .... 59 H8
Ditchfield Pl WDN WA8 .... 52 B4
Ditchfield Rd WARRW/BUR WA5 . 54 E1
　WDN WA8 .... 52 A4
Ditton Rd WDN WA8 .... 6 F8
Dixon Av NEWLW WA12 .... 22 C7
Dixon Cl RNFD/HAY WA11 .... 22 A4
　SALE M33 .... 43 K2
Dixon Dr MCFLDS SK11 .... 134 F1
Dixon Rd CONG CW12 .... 185 G7
Dixon St IRL M44 .... 31 L4
　WARR WA1 .... 4 E7
Dobb Hedge Cl
　HALE/TIMP WA15 .... 62 C6
Dobbinetts La HALE/TIMP WA15 . 62 D1
　NTHM/RTH M23 .... 43 L8
Dobell's Rd NWCHE CW9 .... 13 H7
Dobers La FROD/HEL WA6 ... 125 J1
Dock Rd CO CH5 .... 142 A4
　NWCHE CW9 .... 13 H4
　WDN WA8 .... 52 F7
　WDN WA8 .... 53 G7
Dock St EP CH65 .... 10 F4
　WDN WA8 .... 53 G7
Dock Yard Rd EP CH65 ...... 11 H6
Doctors Cl BIDD ST8 .... 227 J4
Doddington Cl SBCH CW11 .. 204 C4
Doddington Rd CW/HAS CW1 . 18 A6
Dodd's Green La WHITCH SY13 . 272 B3
Dodd's La CONG CW12 .... 207 J3
　MALPAS SY14 .... 258 E3
Doddswood Dr CONG CW12 . 184 F8
Dodge Fold OFTN SK2 .... 47 L6
Dodge Hl HTNM SK4 .... 2 F3
Dodgsley Dr FROD/HEL WA6 . 126 C3
Dodington WHITCH SY13 ..... 270 A5
Dodleston La CHSW/BR CH4.. 191 C7
Dog La CHSE CH3 .... 213 J8
　HOLMCH CW4 .... 181 L5

MALPAS SY14 .... 256 E4
NANT CW5 .... 20 E5
TPLY/KEL CW6 .... 149 H7
Dogmore La TPLY/KEL CW6 . 198 C1
Dolphin Crs GTS/LS CH66 ... 120 E2
Dombey Rd POY/DIS SK12 ... 86 D2
Domestic Ap MANAIR M90 ... 63 J6
Dominic St NTHM/RTH M23 .. 43 L3
Domville RAIN/WH L35 .... 32 E2
Domville Cl LYMM WA13 ..... 58 L1
Donagh Rd MCFLDN SK10 ... 137 M2
Dona St STKP SK1 .... 3 K7
Donkey La WILM/AE SK9 ..... 84 A7
Donne Ct CH/BCN CH1 .... 145 G6
Donnington Av CHD/CHDH SK8 . 45 M6
Donnington Cl LEIGH WN7 ... 24 D3
Donnington Wy
　CHSW/BR CH4 .... 168 F5
Dood's La WARRS WA4 .... 57 G7
Doodson Av IRL M44 .... 31 M2
Dooley La MPL/ROM SK6 ..... 48 B5
Dooley's Grig MCFLDS SK11 . 158 F3
Dooley's La WILM/AE SK9 ... 83 H2
Dorac Av CHD/CHDH SK8 .... 64 C6
Dorchester Cl ALS/KID ST7 . 243 C1
　HALE/TIMP WA15 .... 62 C1
　WILM/AE SK9 .... 84 D4
Dorchester Ct CHD/CHDH SK8 . 65 H3
　SALE M33 .... 43 H2
Dorchester Dr NTHM/RTH M23 . 43 L3
Dorchester Pk RUNC WA7 ... 74 D1
Dorchester Rd BRAM/HZG SK7 . 66 B3
　CHSW/BR CH4 .... 168 F7
　WARRW/BUR WA5 .... 36 B7
Dorchester Wy MCFLDN SK10 . 138 C1
　WARRW/BUR WA5 .... 26 F6
Doreen Av CONG CW12 ...... 208 B4
Dorfield Cl MPL/ROM SK6 ... 47 L1
Dorfold Cl SBCH CW11 .... 204 C5
Dorfold St NANT CW5 .... 20 C7
Dorfold Wy CHNE CH2 .... 145 L6
Doric Av FROD/HEL WA6 ..... 99 J5
　MPL/ROM SK6 .... 47 K1
Doris Rd EDGY/DAV SK3 ..... 2 A8
Dorking St STKP SK1 .... 3 M9
Dorland Gv OFTN SK2 .... 47 H5
Dormer Cl CHSE CH3 .... 56 E6
Dorney Ct WARRS WA4 ...... 56 F6
Dornoch Ct HOLMCH CW4 .. 181 H2
Dorothea St WARRN/WOL WA2 . 5 J2
Dorothy Rd BRAM/HZG SK7 . 66 F1
Dorric Wy CW/HAS CW1 ..... 221 C5
Dorrington Cl RUNC WA7 .... 74 D4
Dorrington Rd EDGY/DAV SK3 . 46 A5
Dorrit Cl POY/DIS SK12 ...... 86 E2
Dorset Av BRAM/HZG SK7 ... 65 K3
　CHD/CHDH SK8 .... 46 C8
Dorset Cl CONG CW12 .... 184 E8
Dorset Dr BIDD ST8 .... 227 J4
Dorset Pl ALS/KID ST7 .... 243 G1
　CHNE CH2 .... 146 A7
Dorset Rd ALT WA14 .... 42 B8
　CHNE CH2 .... 145 M5
　HUY L36 .... 32 A1
　IRL M44 .... 31 K6
Dorset Wy WARR WA1 .... 38 B4
Douglas Av BIDD ST8 .... 227 J5
　STHEL WA9 .... 26 B4
Douglas Cl NWCHW CW8 .... 12 B9
　WDN WA8 .... 53 M1
Douglas La WSFD CW7 .... 200 A6
Douglas Pl CHSW/BR CH4 .. 168 E6
Douglas Rd BRAM/HZG SK7 . 66 F1
　EDGY/DAV SK3 .... 46 E8
Dounrey Cl WARRN/WOL WA2 . 38 A2
Douthwaite Dr MPL/ROM SK6 . 48 E3
Dove Cl CHNE CH2 .... 97 J8
　EP CH65 .... 121 M1
　FROD/HEL WA6 .... 98 C7
　GOL/RIS/CU WA3 .... 29 M8
　SBCH CW11 .... 204 A4
Dovecote Cl CW/SHV CW2 .. 238 B4
Dovecote Gn
　WARRW/BUR WA5 .... 36 A3
Dove Ct WLTN L25 .... 50 B1
Dovedale Cl BURS/TUN ST6 . 243 H5
　CONG CW12 .... 185 C8
　MPL/ROM SK6 .... 67 L5
　WARRN/WOL WA2 .... 37 L1
Dovedale Rd OFTN SK2 ...... 47 K5
Dove Gv BIDD ST8 .... 227 K3
Dove Pl WSFD CW7 .... 178 B2
Dover Cl RUNC WA7 .... 74 E6
Dover Dr EP CH65 .... 121 K2
　WSFD CW7 .... 177 H6
Dover Rd CHSW/BR CH4 .... 169 G7
　MCFLDN SK10 .... 15 L1
　WARRS WA4 .... 57 G1
Dover St WDN WA8 .... 9 J1
Dove St GOL/RIS/CU WA3 ... 23 G3
Doward St WDN WA8 .... 7 L1
Dowland Cl NTHM/RTH M23 . 43 M2
Downes Cl MCFLDN SK10 ... 14 B2
Downesway WILM/AE SK9 ... 109 M3
Downham Av
　GOL/RIS/CU WA3 .... 29 M2
Downham Cha
　HALE/TIMP WA15 .... 43 H6
Downham Pl CH/BCN CH1 ... 144 E8
Downham Wk NTHM/RTH M23 . 43 K4
Downing Cl MCFLDS SK11 ... 162 F1
Downs Dr ALT WA14 .... 42 E4
Downs End KNUT WA16 ..... 107 J3
Downsfield Rd CHSW/BR CH4 . 168 F6
Downside WDN WA8 .... 52 B1
Downs Rd RUNC WA7 .... 9 H5
The Downs ALT WA14 .... 61 K1
　CHD/CHDH SK8 .... 64 D1
　NWCHW CW8 .... 127 K7
Downway La STHEL WA9 .... 26 A3
Doyle Av CHD/CHDH SK8 .... 47 K1
Dragon La RAIN/WH L35 ..... 32 D2
Dragon's La MWCH CW10 ... 202 B2
　SBCH CW11 .... 205 G3
Dragon Yd WDN WA8 .... 34 B8
Drake Av IRL M44 .... 31 L6
Drake Cl RAIN/WH L35 .... 32 E2
　WARRN/WOL WA2 .... 36 D3

Drake La NANT CW5 .... 235 L8
Drakelow La MWCH CW10 .. 155 L4
Drake Rd ALT WA14 .... 42 B4
　NSTN CH64 .... 91 L3
Drakes Wy MALPAS SY14 ... 246 B7
Drayford Cl NTHM/RTH M23 . 43 M2
Drayton Av CHD/CHDH SK8 . 64 B5
　SALE M33 .... 42 D3
Drayton Cl RUNC WA7 .... 8 E4
　SALE M33 .... 42 D3
　WILM/AE SK9 .... 84 D3
Drayton Crs CW/HAS CW1 .. 19 L2
Drayton Gv HALE/TIMP WA15 . 43 G8
Drenfield Rd ALS/KID ST7 ... 225 M5
Drill Field Rd NWCHE CW9 .. 13 H3
The Drive CHD/CHDH SK8 ... 46 C8
　DID/WITH M20 .... 45 J1
　HALE/TIMP WA15 .... 62 D4
　HOLMCH CW4 .... 181 J2
　LEIGH WN7 .... 24 F1
　LYMM WA13 .... 59 L3
　MPL/ROM SK6 .... 47 K1
　MPL/ROM SK6 .... 48 E6
　SALE M33 .... 42 E3
Drive Wy RAIN/WH L35 ...... 32 G2
Driveway RAIN/WH L35 ...... 32 F1
　RAIN/WH L35 .... 32 F2
Drome Rd CO CH5 .... 143 G3
Dronfield Rd WYTH/NTH M22 . 44 D4
Drovers Wy SBCH CW11 ..... 204 A7
Druid Cl AIMK WN4 .... 22 C2
Drumber La ALS/KID ST7 .... 226 B4
The Drumber WSFD CW7 .... 177 K5
Drumble Fld MCFLDS SK11 .. 135 G1
Drumburn Cl BURS/TUN ST6 . 243 M5
Drummond Av GTS/LS CH66 . 94 C8
Drummond Ct WDN WA8 .... 53 K2
Drummond St
　BURS/TUN ST6 .... 243 K5
Drummond Wy
　MCFLDN SK10 .... 137 L3
Druridge Dr WARRW/BUR WA5 . 35 M8
Drury Cl CW/HAS CW1 .... 19 L2
　CW/HAS CW1 .... 202 D8
　KNUT WA16 .... 107 G2
Dryden Av CHD/CHDH SK8 .. 45 L6
Dryden Cl CW/SHV CW2 ..... 238 A4
　RAIN/WH L35 .... 32 E1
Dryden Rd WARRN/WOL WA2 . 37 J2
Dryhurst Cl POY/DIS SK12 .. 68 D6
Dryhurst La POY/DIS SK12 .. 68 D6
Dublin Cft GTS/LS CH66 ..... 120 E3
Duchy Gv CW/HAS CW1 ..... 239 C4
Duchy St EDGY/DAV SK3 .... 2 D9
Duckers La CO CH5 .... 166 E2
Duck La CHSE CH3 .... 148 F5
Duckworth Gv
　WARRN/WOL WA2 .... 38 A3
Duddon Cl TPLY/KEL CW6 .. 173 G6
Duddon Hook La
　TPLY/KEL CW6 .... 172 F6
Duddon Rd TPLY/KEL CW6 . 173 H7
Dudleston Rd GTS/LS CH66 . 94 B6
Dudley Av RUNC WA7 .... 73 K2
Dudley Crs PS/BROM CH62 . 94 B1
Dudley Rd EP CH65 .... 10 D8
　HALE/TIMP WA15 .... 43 H5
　IRL M44 .... 31 K8
Dudley St WARRN/WOL WA2 . 5 H2
Dudlow Green Rd WARRS WA4 . 56 D7
Duke Av CHD/CHDH SK8 .... 64 F6
　GOL/RIS/CU WA3 .... 25 J5
Duke Cl RUNC WA7 .... 8 E2
Dukefield St WYTH/NTH M22 . 44 E4
Duke's Crs SBCH CW11 ...... 204 A4
Duke's La AIMK WN4 .... 22 C1
　BIDD ST8 .... 227 K5
　CH/BCN CH1 .... 17 C7
　CW/SHV CW2 .... 18 E5
　FLINT CH6 .... 116 A6
　GOL/RIS/CU WA3 .... 23 G3
　MCFLDS SK11 .... 15 G6
　NEWLW WA12 .... 27 H1
　STKP SK1 .... 2 F6
　WILM/AE SK9 .... 110 B2
Dukesway CHNE CH2 .... 145 L5
Dukes Whf RUNC WA7 ...... 74 F6
Dulas Ct CW/HAS CW1 ...... 145 L4
Dulverton Av CHSE CH3 ..... 170 C2
Dulwich Cl SALE M33 .... 42 D1
Dumbah La MCFLDN SK10 .. 112 C6
Dumbers MCFLDS SK11 ...... 187 G2
Dunacre Wy HLWD L26 ...... 50 F5
Dunbar Av NTHM/RTH M23 . 43 G1
Dunbar Cl GTS/LS CH66 ..... 94 C7
　HOLMCH CW4 .... 181 H2
Dunbeath Av RAIN/WH L35 . 33 K3
Dunbeath Cl RAIN/WH L35 .. 33 K3
Dunblane Av HTNM SK4 .... 2 C3
Duncan Av NEWLW WA12 ... 22 C7
　RUNC WA7 .... 9 L4
Duncansby Crs
　WARRW/BUR WA5 .... 35 L6
Duncan St WARRN/WOL WA2 . 5 K2
Duncombe Cl BRAM/HZG SK7 . 66 A1
Dundalk La WDN WA8 .... 6 B4
Dundas St CO CH5 .... 142 D7
Dundee Cl WARRN/WOL WA2 . 28 E8
Dundonald Av WARRS WA4 . 56 C3
Dundonald Rd CHD/CHDH SK8 . 65 G5
　DID/WITH M20 .... 45 J1
Dundrennan Cl POY/DIS SK12 . 66 D7
Dunelm Dr NTHM/RTH M23 . 43 K3
Dungeon La SPK/HALE L24 . 70 F3
Dunham Av GOL/RIS/CU WA3 . 22 F3
Dunham Cl ALS/KID ST7 ..... 241 J1
　SBCH CW11 .... 204 C6
Dunham Crs CW/SHV CW2 . 238 B4
Dunham Gv LEIGH WN7 ..... 25 J2
Dunham Lawn ALT WA14 ... 42 B8
Dunham Rd ALT WA14 ...... 42 C8
　LYMM WA13 .... 40 E5
　NWCHE CW9 .... 129 M8

PART M31 .... 41 K1
CW/SHV CW2 .... 239 J7
GOL/RIS/CU WA3 .... 23 J3
LEIGH WN7 .... 25 J2
MCFLDN SK10 .... 112 E5
NWCHE CW9 .... 130 D6
WARRN/WOL WA2 .... 5 J1
WARRS WA4 .... 56 D3
WARRW/BUR WA5 .... 36 A8
Eastbury Cl WDN WA8 .... 34 C7
Eastcott Cl CONG CW12 .... 183 M8
East Ct ALS/KID ST7 .... 224 E7
Eastdale Pl ALT WA14 .... 42 D5
Eastdale Rd WARR WA1 ..... 38 A5
East Dam Wood Rd
　SPK/HALE L24 .... 70 F2
East Downs Rd ALT WA14 .. 61 J2
　CHD/CHDH SK8 .... 64 F2
East Dr BIDD ST8 .... 227 K4
　MPL/ROM SK6 .... 67 M1
East Dudley St WSFD CW7 . 177 M3
Easter Ct WARRW/BUR WA5 . 36 B2
Eastern Av SPK/HALE L24 .. 70 F2
Eastern Pathway CHSW/BR CH4 . 17 J8
Eastern Rd NANT CW5 .... 237 L7
Eastfields Gv CH/BCN CH1 .. 144 A5
Eastford Rd WARRS WA4 ... 56 A3
East Front RAIN/WH L35 .... 32 E3
Eastgate Rd HOLMCH CW4 . 181 K1
　RUNC WA7 .... 54 E8
Eastgate St CH/BCN CH1 .... 17 G5
East Gn CO CH5 .... 143 G6
Eastham Gn SPK/HALE L24 . 50 E8
Eastham Rake GTS/LS CH66 . 93 J2
East Lancashire Rd
　GOL/RIS/CU WA3 .... 23 H6
East La NWCHW CW8 .... 152 A1
　RUNC WA7 .... 73 M5
East Lawns AUD/MAD/W CW3 . 255 G6
Eastleigh Crs LEIGH WN7 ... 25 H1
Eastleigh Rd CHD/CHDH SK8 . 64 B3
East Mains SPK/HALE L24 .. 71 G1
East Millwood Rd SPK/HALE L24 . 51 G8
Easton Dr CHD/CHDH SK8 .. 46 A7
East Over MPL/ROM SK6 .... 48 A4
East Park Rd MCFLDS SK11 . 138 B7
East Rd MANAIR M90 .... 63 J5
　MWCH CW10 .... 179 H3
　SPK/HALE L24 .... 51 H7
East St WDN WA8 .... 53 L8
East V MPL/ROM SK6 .... 49 G7
East Vw WARRS WA4 .... 57 H2
Eastward Av WA8 WLTN SK9 . 83 M6
Eastway GTS/LS CH66 .... 94 D5
　SALE M33 .... 42 F3
　WDN WA8 .... 6 A3
Eastwell Rd AIMK WN4 ...... 22 A1
Eastwood RUNC WA7 .... 74 C3
Eastwood Av NEWLW WA12 . 27 M1
Eastwood Rd WARRW/BUR WA5 . 26 F1
Eaton Av CHSW/BR CH4 .... 169 K5
Eaton Bank CONG CW12 .... 184 F7
Eaton Cl CHD/CHDH SK8 .... 64 F1
　CHSW/BR CH4 .... 167 J8
　POY/DIS SK12 .... 87 C1
　SBCH CW11 .... 204 C5
　WRX/GR/LL LL12 .... 210 C5
Eaton Crs NWCHE CW9 ..... 153 L2
Eaton Dr HALE/TIMP WA15 . 43 G4
　MWCH CW10 .... 179 H4
　WILM/AE SK9 .... 109 M2
Eaton Gv CHSW/BR CH4 .... 168 E7
Eaton La HOLMCH CW4 ..... 157 L3
　MCFLDS SK11 .... 138 D7
　NWCHE CW9 .... 153 K2
　TPLY/KEL CW6 .... 175 G6
　TPLY/KEL CW6 .... 197 L4
Eaton Ms CHSW/BR CH4 .... 169 K5
Eaton Rd ALS/KID ST7 .... 224 C8
　ALT WA14 .... 61 J3
　CHSW/BR CH4 .... 17 H9
　TPLY/KEL CW6 .... 197 K3
　WSFD CW7 .... 199 J5
Eaton St CW/SHV CW2 ...... 18 F4
　RUNC WA7 .... 9 G3
Eaton Vw NWCHE CW9 ..... 153 L4
Eaves Brow Rd GOL/RIS/CU WA3 . 29 H5
Eaves Knoll Rd NM/HAY SK22 . 69 G3
Ebbdale Cl STKP SK1 .... 3 J8
Ebnal La MALPAS SY14 ...... 246 D6
Ebor Rd WYTH/NTH M22 ... 44 E8
Ebury Pl CHSW/BR CH4 .... 17 G9
Ecclesbridge Rd MPL/ROM SK6 . 48 F8
Eccles Cl CHF/WBR SK23 ... 89 K4
Eccles Gv STHEL WA9 .... 34 E1
Eccles Rd CHF/WBR SK23 .. 89 M7
Eccleston Av CHSW/BR CH4 . 169 K6
　GTS/LS CH66 .... 94 B8
Eccleston Cl GOL/RIS/CU WA3 . 29 J7
Eccleston Dr RUNC WA7 .... 9 M5
Eccleston Rd CHSW/BR CH4 . 190 A5
　EDGY/DAV SK3 .... 46 E8
Eccups La WILM/AE SK9 .... 83 K4
Echo Cl CHSW/BR CH4 ..... 168 C1
Eckersley Ct NTHM/RTH M23 . 43 M6
Ecton Av MCFLDN SK10 ..... 139 G5
Ecton Cl WSFD CW7 .... 154 A8
Edale Cl ALT WA14 .... 61 J3
　BRAM/HZG SK7 .... 66 E3
　BURS/TUN ST6 .... 243 H5
　CHD/CHDH SK8 .... 64 D5
Edale Dr TPLY/KEL CW6 ..... 149 L6
Edale Gv SALE M33 .... 42 E2
Eddisbury Hl NWCHW CW8 . 150 C5
Eddisbury Rd GTS/LS CH66 . 120 F2
Eddisbury Ter MCFLDS SK11 . 15 L6
Eddisbury Wy CHSE CH3 .... 149 J1
　CHSE CH3 .... 195 M8
　CHSE CH3 .... 215 J5
　NWCHE CW9 .... 153 L1
Edelsten St WARRW/BUR WA5 . 4 C7
Eden Av GOL/RIS/CU WA3 .. 25 J8
　MPL/ROM SK6 .... 67 L5
　WSFD CW7 .... 177 M2
Edenbridge Gdns WARRS WA4 . 76 E1
Edenbridge Rd CHD/CHDH SK8 . 46 B8
Eden Cl ALS/KID ST7 .... 243 H2
　BIDD ST8 .... 227 L3
　GTS/LS CH66 .... 94 C7

RAIN/WH L35 33 H2
STKP SK1 3 J7
WILM/AE SK9 83 L7
Edendale WDN WA8 52 B2
Edendale Dr WYTH/NTH M22 63 K3
Eden Dr MCFLDN SK10 15 M3
Edenfield Cl KNUT WA16 108 A1
Edenfield Rd KNUT WA16 108 A1
Edenhall Cl HOLMCH CW4 181 G1
Edenhall Dr WLTN L25 50 D2 2
Edenhurst Dr HALE/TIMP WA15 43 H7
Edenhurst Rd OFTN SK2 47 H6
Eden Pl CHD/CHDH SK8 45 K6
Edensor Dr HALE/TIMP WA15 62 C1 2
Edgars Dr WARRN/WOL WA2 38 A2 1
Edgecroft CHSE CH3 214 A3
Edge Green La GOL/RIS/CU WA3 22 F2
Edge Green Rd GOL/RIS/CU WA3 22 F1
Edge Gv CHNE CH2 17 M4
Edgehill Cha WILM/AE SK9 84 E5
Edge La MALPAS SY14 246 D3
Edgeley Fold EDGY/DAV SK3 46 C5
Edgeley Rd BIDD ST8 227 K6
EDGY/DAV SK3 46 C5
WHITCH SY13 270 B6
Edgemoor ALT WA14 61 G2
Edgerley La CHSE CH3 212 C6
Edgerley Pl AIMK WN4 22 A1
Edgerton Rd GOL/RIS/CU WA3 23 L4
Edge View Ct BIDD ST8 227 J5
Edge View La KNUT WA16 109 H2
Edgeview Rd CONG CW12 208 B5
Edgeway MCFLDS SK11 137 J4
WILM/AE SK9 84 B7
Edgewell La TPLY/KEL CW6 198 A1
Edgewood Dr CW/SHV CW2 238 A5
Edgeworth Rd
GOL/RIS/CU WA3 22 F3 2
Edgworth St WARR WA1 4 F6
Edinburgh Cl CHD/CHDH SK8 45 M6 3
Edinburgh Dr HUY L36 32 A4
MCFLDN SK10 14 A3
Edinburgh Rd CONG CW12 207 M2
CW/SHV CW2 237 L4 3
WDN WA8 52 A4
Edinburgh Wy CHSW/BR CH4 17 K7
Edison Rd RUNC WA7 73 K1
Edith St RUNC WA7 8 F1
Edleston Hall La NANT CW5 250 E2
Edleston Rd CW/SHV CW2 19 G5
Edinburgh Cl SALE M33 42 D1 3
Edmonton Rd EDGY/DAV SK3 47 G8
Edmund Cl HTNM SK4 2 E1
Edmund Wright Wy NANT CW5 20 A7
Edna St CHNE CH2 17 L2
Edward Av MPL/ROM SK6 47 L1
Edward Gdns WARR WA1 38 F6
Edward German Dr
WHITCH SY13 270 B5
Edward Rd WARRW/BUR WA5 35 K6
Edwards Av CW/SHV CW2 238 C7
Edwards Cl CW/SHV CW2 238 B7
MPL/ROM SK6 48 E7 1
Edward's La SPK/HALE L24 50 B6
Edwards Rd CHSW/BR CH4 169 G6
Edward St CW/SHV CW2 19 G8
EP CH65 10 E4 2
MCFLDS SK11 14 D6 2
MPL/ROM SK6 49 G3
NWCHE CW9 130 C4
STKP SK1 3 G7
WDN WA8 53 K3 2
Edwards Wy ALS/KID ST7 224 E8
MPL/ROM SK6 48 E7
WDN WA8 52 C4
Edwin Dr FLINT CH6 116 B7
Edwin St STKP SK1 3 M7
WDN WA8 7 L2
Egdon Cl WDN WA8 53 L2 1
Egerton KNUT WA16 59 J7
Egerton Av LYMM WA13 40 C4
NWCHW CW8 129 G8
WARR WA1 37 L5
Egerton Dr CHNE CH2 145 K7
Egerton Moss
HALE/TIMP WA15 61 L7 1
Egerton Pl WHITCH SY13 270 A4
Egerton Rd CH/BCN CH1 144 D7
EDGY/DAV SK3 47 G8
HALE/TIMP WA15 62 A1
LYMM WA13 58 C2
WHITCH SY13 270 B4
WILM/AE SK9 84 B4
Egerton Sq KNUT WA16 107 G2 2
Egerton St CH/BCN CH1 17 J3
EP CH65 10 E5
RUNC WA7 8 F1
WARR WA1 5 K6
WARRS WA4 56 C3
Egerton Wk CHSW/BR CH4 191 G6
Eggbridge La CHSE CH3 171 G7
Eglington Av RAIN/WH L35 32 D2 1
Egremont Cl NTHLY L27 32 A8 1
Egremont Gv EDGY/DAV SK3 46 B4 1
Egremont Rd NTHLY L27 32 A8
Egypt St WARR WA1 4 F7
WDN WA8 6 F6
Eisenhower Cl
WARRW/BUR WA5 36 B7 2
Elaine Cl GTS/LS CH66 94 C8
WDN WA8 7 L2
Elaine St WARR WA1 5 M3
Elandor Rd SBCH CW11 203 K5
Elcho Rd ALT WA14 61 H1
Elcombe Av GOL/RIS/CU WA3 23 L5
Elderberry Wy WILM/AE SK9 84 E4
Elder Cl OFTN SK2 47 K4
Eldercroft Rd HALE/TIMP WA15 43 J7
Elder Dr CHSW/BR CH4 168 E7
Eldon Rd EDGY/DAV SK3 2 B9
MCFLDN SK10 137 M4 6
Eldon St WARR WA1 5 K6
Eldon Ter NSTN CH64 91 L5 2
Eleanor Cl CW/HAS CW1 220 F7 1
Eleanor St EP CH65 10 F5
WDN WA8 7 H7 1
Electricity St CW/SHV CW2 18 F5
Elf Mill Cl EDGY/DAV SK3 46 E6
Elgar Cl EP CH65 120 F1
Elgin Av DID/WITH M20 45 K1 3
HOLMCH CW4 181 H2
WARRS WA4 56 A2
Elgin Cl CHSE CH3 170 A1
Elgin Dr SALE M33 43 L1
Elgol Cl EDGY/DAV SK3 46 F7 1
Elgood La BURS/TUN ST6 243 M5
Eliot Cl CW/HAS CW1 222 A8
Elizabethan Wy NWCHE CW9 130 E6 1
Elizabeth Av POY/DIS SK12 68 D7
STKP SK1 3 H8
Elizabeth Cl TPLY/KEL CW6 149 K8
Elizabeth Ct ALS/KID ST7 242 D7 1
HTNM SK4 2 A3
WDN WA8 7 J7
Elizabeth Crs CHSW/BR CH4 17 K7
Elizabeth Dr WARR WA1 38 A4
Elizabeth Rd HUY L36 32 A4
PART M31 31 M8
Elizabeth St CONG CW12 207 J2
CW/HAS CW1 18 D1
LEIGH WN7 25 H1
MCFLDS SK11 15 G6 1
STHEL WA9 34 E1 2
WHITCH SY13 270 B4
Elkan Cl WDN WA8 53 L1
Elkan Rd WDN WA8 53 K1
Elkington Ri
AUD/MAD/W CW3 267 M5 2
Elkstone Cl BURS/TUN ST6 243 L8 1
Elk Vw MALPAS SY14 256 F7
Ella Gv KNUT WA16 107 H2
Elland Dr GTS/LS CH66 94 C7
Ellen Brook Rd WYTH/NTH M22 63 K4
Ellen St HTNM SK4 2 D1
WARRW/BUR WA5 4 D3
Ellerby Cl RUNC WA7 74 E5
Ellerton Av GTS/LS CH66 94 C7
Ellerton Cl WDN WA8 52 D1
Ellesmere Av CHNE CH2 145 K7
CHSW/BR CH4 167 K8 2
MPL/ROM SK6 48 F6 4
Ellesmere Cl SBCH CW11 203 L4
Ellesmere Dr CHD/CHDH SK8 46 A7
Ellesmere Rd ALT WA14 42 D6
EDGY/DAV SK3 46 A5
GOL/RIS/CU WA3 24 E8
NWCHE CW9 130 A8
WARRS WA4 56 B3
WHITCH SY13 268 E7
Ellesmere St RUNC WA7 9 J2
WARR WA1 5 J7
Ellesworth Cl WARRW/BUR WA5 36 C4
Ellingham Wy NWCHE CW9 153 L1
Elliot St WDN WA8 7 J4 1
Elliott Av GOL/RIS/CU WA3 23 H3
WARR WA1 37 L5
Ellis Ashton St HUY L36 32 A2
Ellis La FROD/HEL WA6 99 K3
Ellison St WARRS WA4 56 D3 1
Ellis St CW/HAS CW1 221 H6
WDN WA8 6 F7
Ellon Av RAIN/WH L35 33 K2
Elloway Rd SPK/HALE L24 71 G1
Ellwood Gn CW/SHV CW2 253 L1
Ellwood Rd STKP SK1 3 M6
Elm Av GOL/RIS/CU WA3 23 G3
WDN WA8 53 H2
Elm Beds Rd POY/DIS SK12 87 J2
Elm Cl ALS/KID ST7 243 H4
CW/SHV CW2 237 L2
POY/DIS SK12 86 F1
TPLY/KEL CW6 197 K2
WHITCH SY13 269 M6
Elm Crs WILM/AE SK9 110 B2
Elm Cft CQ CH5 166 E2
Elmdale Av CHD/CHDH SK8 64 B2 1
Elm Dr CW/HAS CW1 221 L6
HOLMCH CW4 157 K8
MCFLDN SK10 15 K1
Elmfield Av WYTH/NTH M22 44 E4
Elmfield Dr MPL/ROM SK6 48 E6
Elmfield Rd EDGY/DAV SK3 46 F7
WILM/AE SK9 110 B2
Elm Gv ALS/KID ST7 224 E8
CHSW/BR CH4 168 E7 2
DID/WITH M20 45 H1
GTS/LS CH66 121 G3
WARR WA1 37 M5
WDN WA8 7 J2
WILM/AE SK9 110 A2
WSFD CW7 178 A3
Elmley Cl OFTN SK2 48 A7
Elmore Cl HOLMCH CW4 181 H1 2
RUNC WA7 74 D3
Elmridge Dr HALE/TIMP WA15 62 C4
Elm Ri FROD/HEL WA6 99 J5
MCFLDN SK10 111 L6
Elm Rd CHD/CHDH SK8 45 G7
CONG CW12 207 H1
CQ CH5 166 A1
GOL/RIS/CU WA3 40 A2 2
HALE/TIMP WA15 61 L1
MPL/ROM SK6 67 M5
MWCH CW10 179 K5
NSTN CH64 92 F4
NWCHW CW8 128 D5
RUNC WA7 9 M6
WARRN/WOL WA2 28 B8
WARRW/BUR WA5 35 M8
Elm Rd South EDGY/DAV SK3 46 A5
Elmsett Cl WARRW/BUR WA5 35 L7
Elmsleigh Rd CHD/CHDH SK8 64 A2
Elmsmere Rd DID/WITH M20 45 K1
Elm Sq CHSW/BR CH4 168 F6 3
Elmstead Crs CW/HAS CW1 220 F4
Elmstead Rd MCFLDS SK11 135 G1
Elmsted Cl CHD/CHDH SK8 65 H1
The Elms GOL/RIS/CU WA3 23 M4
RUNC WA7 8 F5
Elm St EP CH65 10 E3 1
HUY L36 32 A2
LEIGH WN7 24 F1 3
NWCHE CW9 13 M1
Elmsway BRAM/HZG SK7 65 J5
HALE/TIMP WA15 62 B4
MCFLDN SK10 113 G5
MPL/ROM SK6 67 L6
Elmswood Av RAIN/WH L35 33 K2
Elm Tree Av LYMM WA13 58 D2
WARR WA1 37 M4
Elm Tree Ct TPLY/KEL CW6 198 A1
Elmtree Dr HTNM SK4 46 B2
Elm Tree Dr WYTH/NTH M22 63 K1
Elm Tree La SBCH CW11 203 K4
Elm Tree Rd GOL/RIS/CU WA3 23 M5 1
LYMM WA13 58 D2
MPL/ROM SK6 47 J1
Elmwood RUNC WA7 74 C3
Elmwood Av AIMK WN4 22 A2 4
CHNE CH2 145 M8
Elmwood Cl ALS/KID ST7 224 F8
CQ CH5 142 B8 2
Elmwood Gv WSFD CW7 177 M4 1
WSFD CW7 178 A4 2
Elmwood Rd NWCHW CW8 103 H8
Elnor Av CHF/WBR SK23 89 L7
Elnor La CHF/WBR SK23 89 M7
Elsby Rd ALS/KID ST7 241 M2
Elsinore Av IRL M44 31 M3
Elston Av NEWLW WA12 22 B7
Elstree Av CHSE CH3 170 B1
Elstree Gv EDGY/DAV SK3 2 C7
Elswick Av BRAM/HZG SK7 65 L5
Eltham Av OFTN SK2 47 J7 4
Eltham Cl AIMK WN4 22 D1 1
WDN WA8 53 L1
Elton Cl GOL/RIS/CU WA3 23 L5
GOL/RIS/CU WA3 29 J8
PS/BROM CH62 93 L1
WILM/AE SK9 84 E3
Elton Crossings Rd SBCH CW11 203 K6
Elton Dr BRAM/HZG SK7 66 D4
Elton La FROD/HEL WA6 97 L8
SBCH CW11 222 D3
Elton Lordship La
FROD/HEL WA6 98 A5
Elton Rd SALE M33 42 D2
SBCH CW11 203 J7
Elton Ter BURS/TUN ST6 243 J5 2
Elverston St WYTH/NTH M22 44 E3
Elvington Cl RUNC WA7 99 M1 2
Elway Rd AIMK WN4 22 C1
Elworth Av WDN WA8 34 A7
Elworth Rd SBCH CW11 203 K6
Elworth St SBCH CW11 204 A5
Elworthy Av HLWD L26 50 F3
Elwyn Av WYTH/NTH M22 44 D5 1
Elwyn Dr HLWD L26 50 F4
Ely Cl GTS/LS CH66 120 E4
Ely Pk RUNC WA7 74 E2
Embassy Cl CH/BCN CH1 144 C7
Emberton Pl AUD/MAD/W CW3 264 A7
Embleton Ct RUNC WA7 73 K7
Embridge Cswy BUX SK17 115 H7
Emerald Rd WYTH/NTH M22 63 M5 1
Emery Cl ALT WA14 42 D5
Emily St WDN WA8 7 H6
Emlyn Gv CHD/CHDH SK8 46 A6
Emmett St NWCHW CW8 129 H1
Empress Av MPL/ROM SK6 48 F7
Empress Dr CW/SHV CW2 18 C6
Emral Ct WRXS/E LL13 256 A3
Emslie Ct NSTN CH64 91 J4
Emsworth Dr SALE M33 43 J3
Enderby Rd CH/BCN CH1 16 E2
Endon Av MCFLDN SK10 113 G5
Endon Dr BIDD ST8 227 H7
Endsleigh Cl CHNE CH2 145 L4
Endsleigh Gdns CHNE CH2 145 L4 1
Enfield Cl CW/SHV CW2 253 H1
Enfield Park Rd
WARRN/WOL WA2 28 E8
Enfield Rd EP CH65 10 D7
Enford Av WYTH/NTH M22 63 G2 4
Englefield Av CHSW/BR CH4 168 D6
Englefield Cl CW/HAS CW1 221 G4
Englefield Dr FLINT CH6 116 C7
Englesa Brook La CW/SHV CW2 254 F2
Englesea Gv CW/SHV CW2 18 B9
Ennerdale CHNE CH2 145 M7 1
MCFLDS SK11 137 M7
Ennerdale Av WARRN/WOL WA2 37 H1
Ennerdale Cl WILM/AE SK9 108 F5
WSFD CW7 177 K1
Ennerdale Dr CONG CW12 207 H2
FROD/HEL WA6 99 J4
HALE/TIMP WA15 43 G4 1
Ennerdale Rd CHD/CHDH SK8 64 B1 2
CW/SHV CW2 237 L1 2
PART M31 40 E1
STKP SK1 3 L9
Ennis Cl NTHM/RTH M23 43 L7
SPK/HALE L24 71 K2
Ensor Wy NM/HAY SK22 69 J5
Enstone Rd WLTN L25 50 B6 1
Enticott Rd IRL M44 31 J7
Entwistle Gv LEIGH WN7 25 J1 3
Enville Rd ALT WA14 61 J1
Enville St WARRS WA4 5 J9
Epping Av STHEL WA9 34 B1
Epping Cl RAIN/WH L35 33 K2 3
Epping Dr WARR WA1 38 D4
Epsom Av CHD/CHDH SK8 64 E8
SALE M33 42 C2
WILM/AE SK9 64 E8
Epsom Cl BRAM/HZG SK7 66 F2
Epsom Gdns WARRS WA4 56 E5
Eric Av WARR WA1 37 L4
Eric Bullows Cl WYTH/NTH M22 63 J3
Eric St WDN WA8 7 J1
Erindale Crs FROD/HEL WA6 99 G6
Ermine Rd CHNE CH2 145 L8
Ernest St CHD/CHDH SK8 45 J6
CW/SHV CW2 18 F8
OFTN SK2 47 G6 4
Ernocroft La MPL/ROM SK6 49 L1
Ernocroft Rd MPL/ROM SK6 49 H3
Errington Cl OFTN SK2 47 L6 1
Errington Av EP CH65 10 E5 1
Errol Av WYTH/NTH M22 44 C8
Errwood Cl SPK/HALE L24 71 L2
Erskine Rd PART M31 40 F1
Erskine St MPL/ROM SK6 49 H2
Erwood St WARRN/WOL WA2 4 F4
Eryngo St STKP SK1 3 K6
Esher Dr SALE M33 43 H4
Eskdale CHD/CHDH SK8 45 J8
EP CH65 121 H1
Eskdale Av BRAM/HZG SK7 65 J7
Eskdale Cl RUNC WA7 73 K7
WSFD CW7 177 J2 3
Eskdale Dr HALE/TIMP WA15 43 J5
Esk Rd WSFD CW7 178 A2
Esonwood Rd RAIN/WH L35 32 D1
Essex Av EDGY/DAV SK3 46 B4
Essex Cl CONG CW12 184 E7
Essex Dr ALS/KID ST7 242 F2
BIDD ST8 227 K2
Essex Gdns IRL M44 31 J8
Essex Rd CHNE CH2 146 A7
Esthers La NWCHW CW8 128 D4
Esther St WDN WA8 7 K3 1
Estuary Vw CQ CH5 166 A2
Etchells Rd CHD/CHDH SK8 64 D3
Etchells St STKP SK1 3 G5
Ethelda Dr CHNE CH2 146 A7
Etherow Av MPL/ROM SK6 48 E2
Etherow Cl SBCH CW11 203 L5 3
Eton Rd EP CH65 95 K8
Eton St LEIGH WN7 24 F1
Ettiley Av SBCH CW11 203 J7
Ettrick Pk CHSE CH3 170 A2
Euclid Av WARRS WA4 57 H2
Europa Bvd WARRW/BUR WA5 36 B1
Europa Wy EDGY/DAV SK3 46 B6
EP CH65 10 F6
Eustace St WARRN/WOL WA2 4 E5
Evansleigh Dr CQ CH5 167 G1
Evans Pl WARRS WA4 56 D1
Evans Rd SPK/HALE L24 50 C7
Evans St CW/HAS CW1 221 J6
FLINT CH6 116 A5
Eva Rd EDGY/DAV SK3 46 A5
Eva St SBCH CW11 203 K4
Evelyn St WARRW/BUR WA5 36 D8
Everdon Cl WSFD CW7 177 M1
Everest Cl GTS/LS CH66 120 F1
Everest Rd ALS/KID ST7 243 J1
Everglade Cl MCFLDS SK11 138 B7
Everite Rd WDN WA8 52 B5
Eversley WDN WA8 52 B2
Eversley Cl FROD/HEL WA6 99 J6
WARRS WA4 56 F7 2
Eversley Ct CHNE CH2 145 J8 5
Eversley Pk CHNE CH2 145 J8
Eversley Rd DID/WITH M20 45 G1 1
Evesham Av HTNM SK4 46 B1 3
NTHM/RTH M23 43 K5
Evesham Cl LEIGH WN7 24 D3
MCFLDN SK10 112 E8 1
WARRS WA4 56 C4
Evesham Drive WILM/AE SK9 84 C2
Evesham Rd CHD/CHDH SK8 46 A8
Eveside Cl CHD/CHDH SK8 46 B8 1
Ewart St CHSW/BR CH4 168 B5
Ewloe Ct EP CH65 121 K2 4
Ewrin La MCFLDN SK10 114 C7
Exbourne Rd WYTH/NTH M22 63 J3
Excalibur Wy IRL M44 31 M5
Exchange Cl MCFLDS SK11 15 G5
Exchange Pl RAIN/WH L35 33 J1 3
Exchange St EDGY/DAV SK3 2 F6
MCFLDS SK11 15 G5
Exeley RAIN/WH L35 32 E2
Exeter Cl CHD/CHDH SK8 64 F4
Exeter Pl CH/BCN CH1 144 F7 2
Exeter Rd EP CH65 10 E7
Exit Rd West MANAIR M90 63 H5 2
Exmouth Crs RUNC WA7 74 E6
Exmouth Wy
WARRW/BUR WA5 26 F6 4
Exton Pk CH/BCN CH1 16 E1
Eyam Gv OFTN SK2 47 K8
Eyam Rd BRAM/HZG SK7 66 E4
Eyebrook Rd ALT WA14 61 G3

F

Factory La POY/DIS SK12 68 E5
WARR WA1 4 E8 1
WDN WA8 53 H1
Factory Rd CQ CH5 142 F8
Fairacre Dr MWCH CW10 179 K6
Fairacres Rd MPL/ROM SK6 67 L4 2
Fairbourne Av WILM/AE SK9 83 M8 2
Fairbourne Cl
WARRW/BUR WA5 36 E1 1
WILM/AE SK9 83 M8 3
Fairbourne Dr HALE/TIMP WA15 43 H3
WILM/AE SK9 83 M8
Fairbrook CW/SHV CW2 237 L2 2
Fairbrother Crs
WARRN/WOL WA2 37 K2
Fairburn Av CW/SHV CW2 220 F8
Fairburn Cl WDN WA8 53 L1 3
Fairclough Av WARR WA1 5 J8
Fairclough Rd RAIN/WH L35 33 H1
Fairclough St NEWLW WA12 27 H1
WARRW/BUR WA5 26 E6
Fairfax Av HALE/TIMP WA15 43 G6
Fairfax Cl MPL/ROM SK6 48 D5
Fairfax Dr RUNC WA7 73 K2
WILM/AE SK9 83 M8
Fairfield Av CHD/CHDH SK8 64 F2
EP CH65 121 G2
MCFLDN SK10 113 G5
SBCH CW11 204 A7
Fairfield Gdns WARRS WA4 56 E2
Fairfield Rd CHNE CH2 146 A8
CHSW/BR CH4 167 H8 1
CQ CH5 142 D7
HALE/TIMP WA15 43 J7
IRL M44 31 J7
LYMM WA13 58 F1
NWCHE CW9 130 A8
WARRS WA4 56 D2
WDN WA8 7 J2
Fairfield St WARR WA1 5 K4
Fairford Rd CHSW/BR CH4 168 F6 4
Fairford Wy WILM/AE SK9 84 D5
Fairhaven Cl BRAM/HZG SK7 65 M4
WARRW/BUR WA5 36 B8 3
Fairhaven Rd WDN WA8 53 J2
Fairholme Av NSTN CH64 91 K3 1
Fairholme Cl CH/BCN CH1 144 B3
Fairholme Rd HTNM SK4 2 B2
NWCHE CW9 154 A4
Fairlands Rd SALE M33 42 F2
Fairlawn HTNM SK4 2 C2
Fairlea Av DID/WITH M20 45 J2
Fairlie Dr HALE/TIMP WA15 43 H4
RAIN/WH L35 33 K2
Fair Md KNUT WA16 107 H4
Fairmeadow CHSW/BR CH4 210 D2
Fairmead Rd NTHM/RTH M23 44 C3
Fairmile Dr DID/WITH M20 45 J4
Fairoak Ct RUNC WA7 100 F1
Fairoak La RUNC WA7 100 F1
Fairveiw WRXS/E LL13 228 D4
Fairview Av ALS/KID ST7 224 D8
CW/SHV CW2 239 H7
Fairview Cl MPL/ROM SK6 48 F5 1
Fair View Cl NWCHW CW8 128 F1 1
Fairview Dr MPL/ROM SK6 48 F5
Fairview Rd GTS/LS CH66 121 G2
HALE/TIMP WA15 43 J7
MCFLDS SK11 14 B9
Fairway BRAM/HZG SK7 65 K6
CHD/CHDH SK8 45 H8 2
CQ CH5 167 G1
Fairway Av NTHM/RTH M23 43 K5
Fairway Dr SALE M33 42 E2
Fairways FROD/HEL WA6 99 K5
WARRS WA4 56 D7
Fairways Cl WLTN L25 50 B4
Fairways Dr GTS/LS CH66 94 D5
WHITCH SY13 270 A3
The Fairways WSFD CW7 177 G2
The Fairway ALS/KID ST7 224 C8
OFTN SK2 47 K5
Fairwood Rd NTHM/RTH M23 43 K5
Fairy La SALE M33 44 B1
Fairywell Cl WILM/AE SK9 84 D3 1
Fairywell Dr SALE M33 43 G3
Fairywell Rd HALE/TIMP WA15 43 H5
Falcon Cl MWCH CW10 179 K6
NM/HAY SK22 69 K4
WSFD CW7 177 K6
Falcondale Rd
WARRN/WOL WA2 28 B6
Falcon Dr CW/HAS CW1 221 H4
Falconers Gn WARRW/BUR WA5 36 B2
Falcon Rd GTS/LS CH66 120 F1
Falcons Wy RUNC WA7 73 L6
Fallibroome Cl MCFLDN SK10 137 L4 1
Fallibroome Rd MCFLDN SK10 137 L4
Fallowfield RUNC WA7 73 K3
Fallowfield Cl WSFD CW7 176 F3 2
Fallowfield Ct CW/HAS CW1 221 G6
Fallowfield Gv
WARRN/WOL WA2 38 B3
Fallows Wy RAIN/WH L35 32 C3
Falls Gv CHD/CHDH SK8 64 A1
Falmer Dr WYTH/NTH M22 63 K3 3
Falmouth Cl MCFLDN SK10 137 L4 2
Falmouth Dr WARRW/BUR WA5 54 E1
Falmouth Pl RUNC WA7 74 E6
Falmouth Rd CONG CW12 207 L4
CW/HAS CW1 221 G6
Falstone Cl GOL/RIS/CU WA3 30 B6
Falstone Dr RUNC WA7 74 E4
Falterley Rd NTHM/RTH M23 43 L4
Fancroft Rd WYTH/NTH M22 44 C7
Fanner's La KNUT WA16 58 C7
Fanny's Cft ALS/KID ST7 241 K2
Fanshawe La MCFLDS SK11 136 D8
Faraday Rd EP CH65 10 A9
Faraday St GOL/RIS/CU WA3 29 L7
Farams Rd ALS/KID ST7 224 E5
Farbailey Cl CHSW/BR CH4 169 H7
Farcroft Cl NTHM/RTH M23 43 M4 1
Farden Dr NTHM/RTH M23 43 K4
Farefield Av GOL/RIS/CU WA3 22 F2
Farfields Cl MCFLDS SK11 161 L3
Faringdon Cl WLTN L25 50 B6 2
Faringdon Rd WARRN/WOL WA2 28 B6
Farlands Dr DID/WITH M20 45 H5
Farley Cl MWCH CW10 179 H4 2
Farley Ct CHD/CHDH SK8 45 M8
Farley Rd SALE M33 43 J2
Farm Cl NWCHW CW8 128 D3
Farmdale Dr CHNE CH2 123 G1
Farmer Cl CW/SHV CW2 18 A3
Farmers Cl NTHM/RTH M23 44 A1 2
Farmers Heath GTS/LS CH66 120 D2
Farmer's La WARRW/BUR WA5 27 G6
Farmer St HTNM SK4 2 D1
Farmfield Cl CQ CH5 142 B7 3
Farmfield Dr MCFLDN SK10 138 B1
Farm La MCFLDS SK11 158 E3
POY/DIS SK12 68 A6
WARRS WA4 56 E4
Farmleigh Dr CW/HAS CW1 220 F4
Farmleigh Gdns
WARRW/BUR WA5 36 C6
Farm Rd CQ CH5 142 E5
NWCHE CW9 130 E5
NWCHW CW8 128 D3
NWCHW CW8 150 F4
STHEL WA9 34 D1
Farmside Cl WARRW/BUR WA5 4 B3
Farmstead Wy GTS/LS CH66 120 E3
Farm Wk ALT WA14 60 E2
Farm Wy NEWLW WA12 27 L3
Farnborough Gv HLWD L26 50 F3 1
Farndale WDN WA8 34 A7
Farndale Cl CW/SHV CW2 238 A6
WARRW/BUR WA5 35 M5
Farndale Gv AIMK WN4 22 C2
Farndon Av BRAM/HZG SK7 47 M8
Farndon Cl CHSW/BR CH4 167 J8 2
NWCHW CW8 152 A1
SALE M33 43 L1
Farndon Dr HALE/TIMP WA15 43 G6 2
Farndon Rd GTS/LS CH66 94 E6
Farne Cl EP CH65 121 J4 1
Farnham Av MCFLDS SK11 14 A8
Farnham Cl CHD/CHDH SK8 65 G5

WARRS WA4 56 E5
Farnham Dr BIDD ST8 227 H7
Farnhill Cl RUNC WA7 74 D4
Farnley Cl RUNC WA7 74 D3
Farnworth Cl BIDD ST8 227 H6
WDN WA8 34 B8 5
Farnworth Rd
WARRW/BUR WA5 35 K8
Farnworth St WDN WA8 34 B8
Farrant St WDN WA8 7 K4
Farrell Rd WARRS WA4 56 C4
Farrell St WARR WA1 5 L6
Far Ridings MPL/ROM SK6 48 D1
Farriers Wy WSFD CW7 177 G3 4
Farr St EDGY/DAV SK3 2 C7
Farthing Cl WLTN L25 50 A5
Farwood Cl MCFLDN SK10 137 M3
Faulkner Dr HALE/TIMP WA15 43 H8
MWCH CW10 179 L6
Faulkners Cl CHSW/BR CH4 190 A5
Faulkners La CHSE CH3 170 D5
KNUT WA16 108 E1
Faulkner St CHNE CH2 17 L1
Fawborough Rd
NTHM/RTH M23 43 M3
Fawfield Dr BURS/TUN ST6 243 J6
Fawley Gv WYTH/NTH M22 44 D8 1
Fawley Rd RAIN/WH L35 33 L3
Fawns Keep WILM/AE SK9 84 D5
Fawns Leap NWCHW CW8 127 L7
Faywood Dr MPL/ROM SK6 49 G6 2
Fearndown Wy MCFLDN SK10 112 C8
Fearnham Cl LEIGH WN7 24 E3 1
Fearnhead La WARRN/WOL WA2 38 C1
Feathers La CH/BCN CH1 16 F6 1
Feathers St FLINT CH6 116 A5 2
Feeny St STHEL WA9 34 B2 1
Feilden Ct CH/BCN CH1 144 F3
Feldom Rd NTHM/RTH M23 43 M2
Felix Rd NWCHW CW8 12 E3
Fellpark Rd NTHM/RTH M23 44 A2
Fellwood Gv RAIN/WH L35 32 E2
Felskirk Rd WYTH/NTH M22 63 J4
Felsted Av WLTN L25 50 C2 2
Felton Av WYTH/NTH M22 63 J1
Fence Av MCFLDN SK10 15 J4
Fence La CONG CW12 226 C1
Fence St OFTN SK2 47 K8 1
Fenham Dr WARRW/BUR WA5 35 L8
Fennel St WARR WA1 5 J6
Fenside Rd WYTH/NTH M22 44 E7
Fenton Av OFTN SK2 47 J8
Fenton Cl CONG CW12 208 A3
SPK/HALE L24 70 D1 1
WDN WA8 52 C1 6
Fenton Gn SPK/HALE L24 70 D2 1
Fenwick Dr HTNM SK4 45 L1
Fenwick La RUNC WA7 73 K6
Fenwick Rd GTS/LS CH66 120 E2
Ferguson Av GTS/LS CH66 94 E6
Ferguson Dr
WARRN/WOL WA2 37 K3 1
Ferma La CHSE CH3 147 K6
Fern Av NEWLW WA12 27 K2
Fernbank Cl CW/HAS CW1 19 M5
GOL/RIS/CU WA3 29 L8 1
WSFD CW7 178 B3 1
Fern Bank Dr NTHM/RTH M23 43 L4 1
Fernbank Ri MCFLDN SK10 113 H4
Fern Cl GOL/RIS/CU WA3 29 K8
MPL/ROM SK6 48 F6
Fern Ct CW/HAS CW1 19 K5
Fern Crs CONG CW12 208 A2
Ferndale Av CHNE CH2 123 G1
OFTN SK2 47 H8
Ferndale Cl CW/SHV CW2 239 H7
SBCH CW11 204 C7
WARR WA1 38 C5
WDN WA8 34 E5
Ferndale Crs MCFLDS SK11 137 L5 1
Ferndale Rd SALE M33 43 H2
Fern Dene AUD/MAD/W CW3 267 K5 1
Ferndown Av BRAM/HZG SK7 66 C3
Ferndown Rd NTHM/RTH M23 43 K4
Ferney Pl BURS/TUN ST6 243 J6 1
Fern Gv CQ CH5 166 A1
Fernhill MPL/ROM SK6 49 H6
Fernhill Rd CH/BCN CH1 144 E6
Fernhurst RUNC WA7 73 K4
Fernilee Cl NM/HAY SK22 69 J3 3
Fern Lea CHD/CHDH SK8 64 B3
Fernlea HALE/TIMP WA15 61 M3
Fern Lea Dr MCFLDS SK11 14 B4
Fernleaf Cl ALS/KID ST7 224 F4 1
Fernlea Rd NWCHE CW9 104 B6
Fernleigh NWCHW CW8 12 A5
Fernleigh Cl WSFD CW7 177 G3
Fernley Rd OFTN SK2 47 H6
Fernone WILM/AE SK9 84 D1
Fern Rd EP CH65 121 G2
Fernside Rd CQ CH5 142 A8 1
Fern Vw HALE/TIMP WA15 43 L7
Fern Wy NWCHW CW8 128 C3
Fernwood MPL/ROM SK6 49 J5
Fernwood Dr HLWD L26 50 F4 3
Fernwood Gv WILM/AE SK9 84 C4 3
Ferrous Wy IRL M44 31 M6 1
Ferry Cl CQ CH5 143 G6
Ferry La CH/BCN CH1 168 C3
WARRS WA4 38 E8
Festival Av AUD/MAD/W CW3 264 E8
WARRN/WOL WA2 37 K2
Festival Crs WARRN/WOL WA2 37 K2
Festival Dr MCFLDN SK10 110 F6
Festival Hl CONG CW12 207 M2
Festival Rd EP CH65 94 F7
Festival Wy RUNC WA7 9 L6
Ffordd Cledwen
(Cledwen Road)
CHSW/BR CH4 167 K7 1
Ffordd Glyndwr FLINT CH6 116 B7
Ffordd Y Fran FLINT CH6 116 B8
Fford Llewelyn FLINT CH6 116 B7
Fiddlers Ferry Rd WDN WA8 53 K4
Fiddlers La CH/BCN CH1 144 B2
Field Av CW/SHV CW2 237 M3
Fieldbank Rd MCFLDN SK10 14 C4
Field Cl BRAM/HZG SK7 65 K8
MCFLDN SK10 112 F5 1
MPL/ROM SK6 48 D7
NWCHW CW8 12 B5
Fieldfare WSFD CW7 178 A4
Fieldfare Cl GOL/RIS/CU WA3 23 K4
GOL/RIS/CU WA3 29 M8 1
Fieldgate WDN WA8 52 B6
Fieldhead Ms WILM/AE SK9 84 E4 5
Fieldhead Rd WILM/AE SK9 84 E4
Field Hey La NSTN CH64 93 H3
Field House La MPL/ROM SK6 49 G6
Fielding Av POY/DIS SK12 86 E2
Field La CHSE CH3 172 B2
CHSE CH3 214 B3
CW/SHV CW2 237 K2
WARRS WA4 56 C6
Field Rd STHEL WA9 34 D1
Fields Cl ALS/KID ST7 224 E8
Fields Dr SBCH CW11 204 A7
Fieldsend Dr LEIGH WN7 24 C4
Fieldside CQ CH5 166 C3
TPLY/KEL CW6 173 H6
Field Side Cl KNUT WA16 82 A8
Fields Rd ALS/KID ST7 241 K1
CONG CW12 207 L4
CW/HAS CW1 222 D8
The Fields NANT CW5 237 K7
Field St MPL/ROM SK6 47 M1
Fields View Cl NANT CW5 253 H4 1
Fieldsway RUNC WA7 73 G6
Fieldvale Rd SALE M33 42 E3
Field Vw BIDD ST8 227 K3
CQ CH5 166 E1
Field View Dr MCFLDS SK11 138 E7
Fieldview Dr WARRN/WOL WA2 37 J3
Field Wy ALS/KID ST7 224 E8
Fieldway CH/BCN CH1 144 A2
CHNE CH2 145 L8
FROD/HEL WA6 99 J5 1
GTS/LS CH66 94 B5
NWCHW CW8 128 C3
WDN WA8 53 L2
Fife Rd WARR WA1 37 L5
Fifth Av ALS/KID ST7 242 E3
FLINT CH6 116 A7
RUNC WA7 73 M5
Fildes Cl WARRW/BUR WA5 36 C7 3
Filey Rd OFTN SK2 47 J5
Filkin's La CHSE CH3 170 A3
Finchale Dr HALE/TIMP WA15 62 B3
Finch Cl STHEL WA9 34 D1
Finchdale Gdns
GOL/RIS/CU WA3 24 B4 2
Finchett Dr CH/BCN CH1 16 C2
Finch La HLWD L26 51 H6
Finchley Rd HALE/TIMP WA15 61 L1
Findlay Cl NEWLW WA12 27 J2 2
Findon Rd NTHM/RTH M23 44 A6
Finger House La WDN WA8 34 D3
Finger Post La FROD/HEL WA6 126 F7
Finland Rd EDGY/DAV SK3 46 D5
Finlan Rd WDN WA8 6 F7
Finlay Av WARRW/BUR WA5 54 E1 4
Finlow Hill La MCFLDN SK10 110 D6
Finney Cl WILM/AE SK9 84 C2
Finney Dr WILM/AE SK9 84 C2
Finney La CHD/CHDH SK8 64 C3
WYTH/NTH M22 64 A4
Finney's La MWCH CW10 179 H2
Finningley Ct
WARRN/WOL WA2 37 L3 4
Finsbury Pk WDN WA8 34 C7
Finsbury Wk WSFD CW7 177 G3
Fir Avenue HLWD L26 51 G4
Fir Av BRAM/HZG SK7 65 L4
Firbank CHNE CH2 123 J1
Firbank Cl RUNC WA7 74 D3
Firbank Rd NTHM/RTH M23 63 G1
Firbeck Cl CHSW/BR CH4 190 B1 4
Firbeck Gdns CW/SHV CW2 220 D8
Firbrook Av CQ CH5 166 C2
Fir Cl HLWD L26 51 G4
POY/DIS SK12 86 E1
TPLY/KEL CW6 197 K2
Firdale Rd NWCHW CW8 12 A5
Firemans Sq CH/BCN CH1 16 F4 2
Firethorne Rd HLWD L26 50 D2
Fir Gv MCFLDS SK11 138 C7
NWCHW CW8 128 E4 3
WARR WA1 37 M5
Fir La NWCHW CW8 152 A2
Firman Cl WARRW/BUR WA5 36 B4 3
Fir Rd BRAM/HZG SK7 65 L3
MPL/ROM SK6 48 E8
Firs Gv CHD/CHDH SK8 45 G8
Firs La WARRS WA4 56 B6
Firs Rd CHD/CHDH SK8 64 A1
First Av ALS/KID ST7 242 E3
CQ CH5 142 F3
CW/HAS CW1 19 K8
FLINT CH6 116 A7
MCFLDN SK10 86 D3
SBCH CW11 204 A7
First Dig La NANT CW5 252 B4
The Firs ALT WA14 61 H2
WHITCH SY13 269 M4
Fir St HTNM SK4 2 E4
IRL M44 31 J6
WDN WA8 7 L1
First Wood St NANT CW5 20 D5
Firs Wy SALE M33 42 C1
Firswood Mt CHD/CHDH SK8 45 G8
Firth Flds NWCHE CW9 153 M2
Firth Fields Cl NWCHE CW9 153 M2
Fir Tree Av CHSW/BR CH4 169 H7
GOL/RIS/CU WA3 23 M4
KNUT WA16 107 J4
Firtree Av WARR WA1 38 A4
Firtree Cl NWCHW CW8 103 H8 3
Fir Tree Cl WARRS WA4 76 D3
Firtree Gv GTS/LS CH66 121 G4
Fir Tree La CHSE CH3 170 E3
NANT CW5 249 H1
WARRW/BUR WA5 27 G6
Firvale Av CHD/CHDH SK8 64 B3
Firwood Cl OFTN SK2 47 J4 1
Firwood Rd BIDD ST8 227 L3
Fisher Av RAIN/WH L35 32 D2
WARRN/WOL WA2 37 H3
Fisherfield Dr GOL/RIS/CU WA3 30 A6
Fishermans Cl CW/HAS CW1 222 F5
Fisher Pl RAIN/WH L35 32 D2 2
Fisher Rd CH/BCN CH1 144 E8
Fishers Gn TPLY/KEL CW6 174 B7
Fishers La NANT CW5 235 J4
Fisher St RUNC WA7 9 K1
Fishpool Rd NWCHW CW8 174 F1
TPLY/KEL CW6 174 F2
Fistral Av CHD/CHDH SK8 64 C4
Fitton's Cl NANT CW5 250 F7
Fitton St NWCHE CW9 130 F2
Fitz Cl MCFLDN SK10 138 D1 4
Fitz Crs MCFLDN SK10 138 D1
Fitzherbert St WARRN/WOL WA2 5 H2
Fitzwalter Rd WARR WA1 38 D5
Fitzwilliam Av MCFLDS SK11 162 F1
Five Ashes Rd CHSW/BR CH4 169 H7
Flagcroft Dr NTHM/RTH M23 44 B7
Flagg Wood Av MPL/ROM SK6 48 D5
Flag La CW/SHV CW2 18 E5
NSTN CH64 91 M5
Flag La North CHNE CH2 145 L4
Flamingo Cl CW/HAS CW1 220 F5 1
Flamstead Av NTHM/RTH M23 43 L6 1
Flander Cl WDN WA8 52 C2
Flashes La NSTN CH64 92 B7
Flash La MCFLDN SK10 112 D5
NWCHE CW9 77 M7
Flat La SBCH CW11 204 B6
TPLY/KEL CW6 149 J8
Flatt La EP CH65 10 C7
Flatts La CHF/WBR SK23 88 F8
Flaxcroft Rd WYTH/NTH M22 63 H2
Flaxley Cl GOL/RIS/CU WA3 30 A7 1
Flaxmere Dr CHSE CH3 170 B4
Fleet La STHEL WA9 26 B2
Fleet St EP CH65 10 B7
Fleetwood Cl WARRW/BUR WA5 36 B8
Fleetwood Wk RUNC WA7 74 C5
Fleming Rd SPK/HALE L24 50 C6
WYTH/NTH M22 63 K2
Fleming St EP CH65 10 F5
Flers Av WARRS WA4 56 C1
Fletcher Dr ALT WA14 61 J3
POY/DIS SK12 67 M6
Fletcher Gv NWCHE CW9 130 C6
Fletchers La LYMM WA13 39 M8
Fletcher St CW/HAS CW1 18 D1
STKP SK1 3 G5
WARRS WA4 56 B1
Fletsand Rd WILM/AE SK9 84 C6
Flint Cl BRAM/HZG SK7 66 C3
NSTN CH64 91 K6
Flint Ct EP CH65 121 K2 5
Flint Dr NSTN CH64 91 L5
Flint Gv IRL M44 31 J6
Flint Meadow NSTN CH64 91 L5
Flint St EDGY/DAV SK3 2 F9
MCFLDN SK10 15 K5
Flittogate La KNUT WA16 105 K3
Flixton Dr CW/SHV CW2 18 A8
Floatshall Rd NTHM/RTH M23 43 M6
Floats Rd NTHM/RTH M23 43 L6
Flora St AIMK WN4 22 B2
Florence St HTNM SK4 2 F3
WARRS WA4 56 D1 4
Florida Cl WARRW/BUR WA5 36 C5
Florist St EDGY/DAV SK3 46 E5
Flowers La CW/HAS CW1 220 E3
Flower St NWCHW CW8 12 E5
Flowery Fld OFTN SK2 66 A1
Fluin La FROD/HEL WA6 99 J4
Foden Av ALS/KID ST7 241 M1
Foden La BRAM/HZG SK7 85 K1
WILM/AE SK9 109 J2
Foden St MCFLDN SK10 15 G3
Fogg's La WARRS WA4 77 G6
Fold La BIDD ST8 208 E8
MCFLDS SK11 186 D2
Fold Ms BRAM/HZG SK7 66 E1
Folds La CHF/WBR SK23 115 M2
Fold St GOL/RIS/CU WA3 23 G3
The Fold MCFLDN SK10 112 A4
Fol Hollow CONG CW12 207 H3
Folkestone Cl MCFLDN SK10 138 B2 1
Folkstone Wy RUNC WA7 74 C5
Folly La WARRW/BUR WA5 4 D2
Fonthill Gv SALE M33 42 F2
Forbes Cl GOL/RIS/CU WA3 29 L8
SALE M33 43 K2
STKP SK1 3 L7
Forbes Pk BRAM/HZG SK7 65 K5
Forbes Rd STKP SK1 3 L6
Fordbank Rd DID/WITH M20 45 G2
Ford Cl CW/HAS CW1 18 D1
Fordington Rd
WARRW/BUR WA5 36 B7
Fordland Cl GOL/RIS/CU WA3 23 L3 1
Ford La CHSE CH3 195 M8
CW/HAS CW1 18 D1
WYTH/NTH M22 44 E3
Ford Ldg DID/WITH M20 45 H2 1
Fords La ALS/KID ST7 226 D6
BRAM/HZG SK7 65 K6
Ford St EDGY/DAV SK3 2 C6
WARR WA1 5 L4
Foregate St CH/BCN CH1 17 H5
Foreland Cl WARRW/BUR WA5 35 J5
Forest Av HOLMCH CW4 157 J3
Forest Cl MCFLDN SK10 113 L7
NWCHW CW8 151 M1
Forest Dr CHSW/BR CH4 190 B1
HALE/TIMP WA15 42 F6 2
MCFLDS SK11 163 J1
SALE M33 42 E2
Forester Av KNUT WA16 107 J2
Foresters Cl FROD/HEL WA6 127 G6 1
Forest Gdns PART M31 40 D1
Forest Gate La TPLY/KEL CW6 149 L5
Forest La FROD/HEL WA6 126 C6
Forest Pl NWCHE CW9 13 K1
Forest Rd GTS/LS CH66 94 E5
MCFLDS SK11 139 L6
NWCHW CW8 151 M2
STHEL WA9 34 A1
TPLY/KEL CW6 197 K1
WSFD CW7 177 H4
Forest St CH/BCN CH1 17 J5
NWCHW CW8 128 C4
Forge Cl WDN WA8 33 J7
Forge Flds SBCH CW11 222 F1
Forge La CONG CW12 207 H1
Forge Rd CHF/WBR SK23 89 L5
GTS/LS CH66 94 C6
WARRW/BUR WA5 35 M7
Forge St CW/HAS CW1 19 G4
Forge Wy BIDD ST8 227 H8
CHSW/BR CH4 168 F8
Formby Cl WARRW/BUR WA5 35 M8
Formby Dr CHD/CHDH SK8 64 B4
Forrester Cl BIDD ST8 227 J4 2
Forrest Wy WARRW/BUR WA5 55 K1
Forshaw's La WARRW/BUR WA5 26 E4
Forshaw St WARRN/WOL WA2 5 J3
Forster Av NWCHW CW8 128 E4
Forster St GOL/RIS/CU WA3 23 G3
WARRN/WOL WA2 5 H3
Fortescue Rd OFTN SK2 47 K5
Fortyacre Dr MPL/ROM SK6 47 L1
Forty Acre La HOLMCH CW4 158 D7
Foscarn Dr NTHM/RTH M23 44 B7
Foster Rd CONG CW12 185 G7
Foster St WDN WA8 7 K2
Fothergill St WARR WA1 5 M3
Foulkes Av CW/HAS CW1 220 F6
Foundry Bank CONG CW12 207 L1 2
Foundry La ALS/KID ST7 225 M5
SBCH CW11 203 K5
WDN WA8 52 B7
Foundry St MCFLDN SK10 113 H4 2
NEWLW WA12 27 H1
WARRN/WOL WA2 5 G5
Fountain Av HALE/TIMP WA15 62 B1
Fountain Ct BIDD ST8 227 K3
Fountain La FROD/HEL WA6 99 G4
NWCHE CW9 153 M2
Fountains Cl MWCH CW10 179 G3
RUNC WA7 74 C7
Fountains Rd CHD/CHDH SK8 65 H6
Fountain St CONG CW12 207 K2
MCFLDN SK10 15 J5
Fountains Wk GOL/RIS/CU WA3 24 B4
Fouracres Rd NTHM/RTH M23 43 M7
Four Lanes End CW/SHV CW2 254 F2
Fourseasons Cl CW/SHV CW2 238 B4
Fourth Av ALS/KID ST7 242 F3
CQ CH5 142 E2
CW/HAS CW1 19 M9
FLINT CH6 116 A7
RUNC WA7 73 M5
Fourways CW/SHV CW2 239 H7 1
Fowey Cl MCFLDN SK10 137 K3
Fowler Rd CH/BCN CH1 144 D8
Fowlers-bench La CHSE CH3 215 J7
Fowler St MCFLDN SK10 15 G3
Fowley Common La
GOL/RIS/CU WA3 25 H7
Fownhope Av SALE M33 42 F1
Fownhope Rd SALE M33 42 F1
Foxall Wy GTS/LS CH66 120 D2
Fox Bench Cl CHD/CHDH SK8 65 J6
Fox Cl HALE/TIMP WA15 42 F6
Foxcote WDN WA8 52 B2
Foxcote Cl CH/BCN CH1 144 D7
Fox Cover CHSE CH3 146 F7 2
Fox Covert RUNC WA7 74 C5
Fox Covert La CHNE CH2 146 B4
Foxcovert La KNUT WA16 132 E5
Foxes Cl CQ CH5 166 E1
Foxes Fold NWCHW CW8 12 E1
Foxes Hey NWCHW CW8 127 K7
Foxes Hollow CW/HAS CW1 221 L5
Foxes La WHITCH SY13 271 H4
Foxes Wk CHSE CH3 170 A5
Foxfield Cl WARRN/WOL WA2 37 L1
Foxfield La WSFD CW7 176 F3 3
Foxfield Rd NTHM/RTH M23 63 G1
Fox Gdns ALS/KID ST7 242 D4
LYMM WA13 39 J8
Foxglove Av HLWD L26 50 E3
Foxglove Cl CHSE CH3 170 A6 3
CW/SHV CW2 238 D5
MCFLDN SK10 113 J4 1
Foxglove Ct FROD/HEL WA6 99 J4
Foxglove Dr ALT WA14 42 C4
Foxglove Wy NSTN CH64 91 L7
Fox Gv KNUT WA16 107 J3
Foxhall Rd HALE/TIMP WA15 42 E6
Foxhill ALT WA14 42 A7
Fox Hl TPLY/KEL CW6 149 K8
Foxhill Cha OFTN SK2 48 A7
Foxhill Ct TPLY/KEL CW6 197 K3
Foxhill Gv FROD/HEL WA6 98 D8
Foxhill La HLWD L26 50 F2
Foxhills Cl WARRS WA4 76 D1
Fox Hunter Cl CHSE CH3 148 F5
Foxlair Rd WYTH/NTH M22 63 H1
Foxland Rd CHD/CHDH SK8 45 H8
Fox La CHSE CH3 171 G7
MALPAS SY14 230 D3
Fox Lea CH/BCN CH1 144 A4
Foxlea NWCHE CW9 103 J5
Foxleigh HLWD L26 50 D3
Foxley Cl LYMM WA13 59 G2
Foxley Heath WDN WA8 6 E4
Fox's Bank La RAIN/WH L35 32 F5
WDN WA8 32 F5
Fox's Dr CQ CH5 142 F6
Foxshaw Cl RAIN/WH L35 32 D3
Fox St EDGY/DAV SK3 2 C8
RUNC WA7 9 G4
WARRW/BUR WA5 4 A6
Foxwist Cl CHNE CH2 17 G1
Foxwist Gn NWCHW CW8 152 E6
Foxwood Dr KNUT WA16 134 A4
Foy St AIMK WN4 22 B1 5
Framingham Rd SALE M33 43 H2
Frampton Gv BURS/TUN ST6 243 L6
Frances Av CHD/CHDH SK8 45 G6
Frances James Leech St
EDGY/DAV SK3 2 F7
Frances St CHD/CHDH SK8 45 L6
CW/SHV CW2 19 G8
IRL M44 31 L7
MCFLDS SK11 14 D5
Francis Cl WDN WA8 52 C4
Francis Ct CH/BCN CH1 17 J4
Francis La WRXS/E LL13 228 D5
Francis Rd FROD/HEL WA6 99 J3
IRL M44 31 M4
WARRS WA4 56 B3
Francis St BURS/TUN ST6 243 M7
CH/BCN CH1 17 J3
Frank Bott Av CW/HAS CW1 221 G5
Franklin Cl WARRW/BUR WA5 36 C4
Franklyn Av CW/SHV CW2 18 C6
Frank Perkins Wy IRL M44 31 M5
Frank St WDN WA8 7 M3
Frank Webb Av CW/HAS CW1 221 G6
Fraser Av SALE M33 43 L1
Fraser Ct CHSW/BR CH4 17 H9
WHITCH SY13 270 A6
Fraser Rd WARRW/BUR WA5 35 K6
Frawley Av NEWLW WA12 22 B7
Freckleton Cl
WARRW/BUR WA5 36 B8 3
Frederick St WARRS WA4 56 D1
WDN WA8 7 J3
Fredric Pl RUNC WA7 9 J1
Free Green La KNUT WA16 132 F3
Freemantle St EDGY/DAV SK3 2 B7
French La NANT CW5 251 H8
French St WDN WA8 53 K3
Frensham Wy WLTN L25 50 D4
Freshfield CHD/CHDH SK8 64 B4 1
Freshfield Cl MPL/ROM SK6 49 H3 2
Freshfield Dr MCFLDN SK10 138 C1
Freshfield Rd HTNM SK4 45 M2
Freshfields CW/SHV CW2 238 A5
KNUT WA16 106 E1
NWCHE CW9 103 J5
Freshfields Dr WARRN/WOL WA2 38 B3
Freshmeadow La
FROD/HEL WA6 124 A2
Freshpool Wy WYTH/NTH M22 44 E6
Freshwater WARRW/BUR WA5 35 K5
Freshwater Cl
WARRW/BUR WA5 35 K5 1
Frewland Av EDGY/DAV SK3 46 F8
Friars Av WARRW/BUR WA5 35 L7
Friars Cl ALT WA14 61 H3
MCFLDN SK10 113 K7
WILM/AE SK9 83 L4
Friars Ct CQ CH5 166 C4
Friars Ga WARR WA1 5 G8
Friars La WARR WA1 5 G8
Friars Wy MCFLDN SK10 137 L2 2
Frida Crs NWCHW CW8 12 E6
Friends La WARRW/BUR WA5 35 K6
Frieston Rd ALT WA14 42 F3 1
Frimley Gdns WYTH/NTH M22 63 K1
Frinton Cl SALE M33 42 F3
Frith Av NWCHW CW8 150 D4
Frith Ter MCFLDS SK11 138 D8 1
Frobisher Ct
WARRW/BUR WA5 36 D4 1
Frobisher Rd NSTN CH64 91 L4
Froda Av FROD/HEL WA6 99 H5
Frodsham Av HTNM SK4 2 A2
Frodsham Rd FROD/HEL WA6 124 D3
SALE M33 43 L2 2
Frodsham St CH/BCN CH1 17 G5
Froghall La KNUT WA16 59 L5
LYMM WA13 59 K4
WARR WA1 4 D5
WARRN/WOL WA2 4 E5
WARRW/BUR WA5 4 C6
Frog La CHSE CH3 213 J2
KNUT WA16 105 G3
MALPAS SY14 256 C2
WRXS/E LL13 228 D4
Frome Av OFTN SK2 47 J7 6
Frome Ct EP CH65 10 D3
Frome Wy WLTN L25 50 D3
Front St SBCH CW11 204 B6
Frosts Ms EP CH65 10 D5
Fryer Rd NWCHE CW9 131 G1
Fuchsia Cl GTS/LS CH66 120 F3
Fulbeck WDN WA8 52 C2
Fulbeck Cl CW/SHV CW2 238 B4 4
Fulbrook Dr CHD/CHDH SK8 65 G6 2
Fuller Dr CW/SHV CW2 238 A4
Fuller St BURS/TUN ST6 243 L8 2
Fullerton Rd HTNM SK4 46 B2
NWCHW CW8 129 G8
Fulmar Cl POY/DIS SK12 66 A8
Fulmar Dr OFTN SK2 47 M7
SALE M33 42 C2
Fulmards Cl WILM/AE SK9 84 C5
Fulshaw Av WILM/AE SK9 84 A6
Fulshaw Ct WILM/AE SK9 84 A7
Fulshaw Pk WILM/AE SK9 84 A8
Fulshaw Pk South WILM/AE SK9 83 M8
Fulstone Ms OFTN SK2 47 H6
Fulton Gv NWCHE CW9 153 M1
Fulwood Gdns GTS/LS CH66 94 C6
Fulwood Ms GTS/LS CH66 94 C6
Fulwood Rd GOL/RIS/CU WA3 23 L6
GTS/LS CH66 94 C6
Furber St CW/HAS CW1 18 F2
Furlong Rd BURS/TUN ST6 243 L8
WYTH/NTH M22 63 H1
Furnace La AUD/MAD/W CW3 267 K5
Furne Rd CH/BCN CH1 144 E8
Furness Cl HOLMCH CW4 181 G1
POY/DIS SK12 66 C8
WSFD CW7 177 H4
Furness Gv HTNM SK4 46 A3
Furness Lodge Cl
CHF/WBR SK23 69 K8
Furness Rd CHD/CHDH SK8 65 J6
Furnivall St SBCH CW11 204 B5
Furnival St CW/SHV CW2 18 F8
Furrocks Cl NSTN CH64 91 M7
Furrocks La NSTN CH64 91 M7
Furrocks Wy NSTN CH64 91 M7
The Furrows GTS/LS CH66 120 E4 2
Fylde Av CHD/CHDH SK8 64 C4
Fylde Rd HTNM SK4 46 A2
Fytton Cl MCFLDS SK11 161 K3

G

Gable Av WILM/AE SK9 84 A5
Gables Cl WARRN/WOL WA2 37 M1
The Gables ALS/KID ST7 241 J1
Gable St NEWLW WA12 27 G1
Gabriel Bank NWCHW CW8 127 G3
Gadbrook Pk NWCHE CW9 130 D7
Gadbrook Rd NWCHE CW9 130 D6
Gaddum Rd ALT WA14 61 G3
DID/WITH M20 45 J1
Gail Av HTNM SK4 2 C3
Gail Cl WILM/AE SK9 110 B2 2
Gainford Av CHD/CHDH SK8 45 H8
Gainford Cl WDN WA8 52 C1
Gainsborough Av
MPL/ROM SK6 49 H4 1
Gainsborough Cl
WILM/AE SK9 84 D4 5
Gainsborough Ct WDN WA8 52 B3 2
Gainsborough Dr
CHD/CHDH SK8 45 M6
Gainsborough Rd CW/SHV CW2 18 C6
WARRS WA4 56 B2
Gairloch Cl WARRN/WOL WA2 28 F8
Gaisgill Ct WDN WA8 52 C3 1
Gala Cl CHSW/BR CH4 190 C1
Galbraith Cl CONG CW12 207 J2
Galbraith Rd DID/WITH M20 45 J1
Gale Av WARRW/BUR WA5 36 F3
Galion Wy WDN WA8 33 M8
Galleys Bank ALS/KID ST7 243 H1
Galloway Cl HOLMCH CW4 181 J2
Gallowsclough La
FROD/HEL WA6 126 F8
NWCHW CW8 151 G1
Galston Av RAIN/WH L35 33 K2
Galway Gv CW/SHV CW2 238 B8
Game St SBCH CW11 222 F1
Gamford La WRX/GR/LL LL12 210 D5
Ganton Cl WDN WA8 34 B8
Ganworth Cl SPK/HALE L24 70 E2 2
Ganworth Rd SPK/HALE L24 70 E2
Garage Rd SPK/HALE L24 50 F7 1
Garbett St BURS/TUN ST6 243 J5
Garden Ct CH/BCN CH1 16 F4 5
Gardeners Cl BIDD ST8 227 G7
Garden La ALT WA14 42 D7
CH/BCN CH1 16 D2
Garden Rd KNUT WA16 106 F1
Garden St MCFLDN SK10 15 J3
MCFLDN SK10 112 F4
OFTN SK2 47 J7 6
WLTN L25 50 A2
Garden Wy CQ CH5 142 A6 2
Garfield St STKP SK1 3 J3 1
Garfit St MWCH CW10 179 J2
Garland Rd WYTH/NTH M22 63 L1
Garner Av HALE/TIMP WA15 43 G3
Garner Cl ALT WA14 61 K2
Garner's La EDGY/DAV SK3 46 F7
Garner St WARRN/WOL WA2 5 K2
Garners Wk
AUD/MAD/W CW3 267 M5 3
Garnett Av WARRS WA4 37 M8
Garnetts La WDN WA8 72 A1
Garnett St STKP SK1 3 G6
Garrett Fld GOL/RIS/CU WA3 29 K7
Garrett Wk EDGY/DAV SK3 2 A7
Garrick Gdns WYTH/NTH M22 44 D8
Garrigill Cl WDN WA8 34 B7
Garsdale Av RAIN/WH L35 33 K2
Garsdale Cl WARRW/BUR WA5 35 M5 1
Garside Av GOL/RIS/CU WA3 23 K5
Garston Cl HTNM SK4 2 A2
Garswood St AIMK WN4 22 B1
Garth Av HALE/TIMP WA15 42 E6
Garth Dr CHNE CH2 145 J7
Garth Ganol FLINT CH6 116 B8
Garthland Rd BRAM/HZG SK7 66 F1
Garthorp Rd NTHM/RTH M23 43 L3
Garth Rd MPL/ROM SK6 49 G6
OFTN SK2 47 J5
WYTH/NTH M22 44 D8
Garton Dr GOL/RIS/CU WA3 23 L3
Gartons La STHEL WA9 34 C1
Garven Pl WARR WA1 4 F7
Garway WLTN L25 50 C1
Garwood Cl WARRW/BUR WA5 36 B4
Gaskell Av KNUT WA16 106 F2
WARRS WA4 57 G1
Gaskell Rd ALT WA14 42 D6
Gaskell St WARRS WA4 56 C3
Gaskill Rd SPK/HALE L24 50 D8
Gas Rd MCFLDN SK10 15 H5
Gas St HTNM SK4 2 E5
Gateacre Vale Rd WLTN L25 50 B1
Gateacre Wk NTHM/RTH M23 43 L5
Gatefield St CW/HAS CW1 18 E3
Gatesheath Dr CHNE CH2 145 K5
Gatesheath La CHSE CH3 194 E7
Gate Warth St
WARRW/BUR WA5 36 D8 4
Gateway CW/HAS CW1 19 L7
Gathill Cl CHD/CHDH SK8 64 F3 3
Gatley Gn CHD/CHDH SK8 45 G7
Gatley Rd CHD/CHDH SK8 45 J7
SALE M33 43 L1
Gatwick Av NTHM/RTH M23 44 B6 2
Gaunts Wy RUNC WA7 73 L6
Gavin Rd WDN WA8 52 B5
Gawend La MCFLDS SK11 162 C2
Gawer Pk CH/BCN CH1 145 J8
Gawsworth Av CW/SHV CW2 237 M1
DID/WITH M20 45 J3 1
Gawsworth Cl ALS/KID ST7 241 J1 1
BRAM/HZG SK7 65 L7
EDGY/DAV SK3 46 D7 5
HALE/TIMP WA15 43 K6
HOLMCH CW4 181 H1
POY/DIS SK12 86 F2
Gawsworth Dr SBCH CW11 204 C4
Gawsworth Ms
CHD/CHDH SK8 45 H7 2
Gawsworth Rd GOL/RIS/CU WA3 22 F3
GTS/LS CH66 94 E8
MCFLDS SK11 137 K8
SALE M33 43 L2
Gayhurst Av
WARRN/WOL WA2 37 M2 2
Gaymoore Cl CHNE CH2 16 F2 1
Gayton Cl CHNE CH2 145 L7 1
Gee St EDGY/DAV SK3 2 D9
Gemini Gv BURS/TUN ST6 243 L6
Gemmull Cl
AUD/MAD/W CW3 263 M8 2
General St WARR WA1 5 J6
Geneva Rd BRAM/HZG SK7 65 K1
WSFD CW7 177 J3
George Bates Cl ALS/KID ST7 241 J1
George Mann Cl WYTH/NTH M22 63 J3
George Richards Wy ALT WA14 42 C5
George Rd WARRW/BUR WA5 36 C8 1
Georges Crs WARRS WA4 57 H2
George's La NWCHE CW9 104 D3
George's Rd HTNM SK4 2 D4
SALE M33 43 H1
George's Rd West POY/DIS SK12 86 D1
George St CH/BCN CH1 16 F4
CHF/WBR SK23 89 L5
EP CH65 10 E4
KNUT WA16 106 F2
MCFLDS SK11 15 H6
MPL/ROM SK6 49 L3
NEWLW WA12 22 A8 1
NWCHW CW8 129 H1
SBCH CW11 203 L4
STKP SK1 3 J5
WHITCH SY13 270 B4
WILM/AE SK9 110 A3 3
WSFD CW7 177 L3
George St East STKP SK1 3 M7
George St West MCFLDS SK11 14 F5
STKP SK1 3 L8
George VI Av MWCH CW10 179 J5
George VI Cl MWCH CW10 179 K6 3
Georgian Cl HLWD L26 50 F6 2
Gerard Dr NANT CW5 20 B8
Gerard St AIMK WN4 22 B1
Germander Cl HLWD L26 50 E3
Gerneth Cl SPK/HALE L24 50 C8
Gerneth Rd SPK/HALE L24 70 B1
Gerosa Av WARRN/WOL WA2 28 B4
Gerrard Av GTS/LS CH66 94 C8
HALE/TIMP WA15 43 G4
WARRW/BUR WA5 4 C2
Gerrard Dr NWCHW CW8 128 D3
Gerrard Rd GOL/RIS/CU WA3 29 G5
Gerrards Av CHSE CH3 170 A3
Gerrard's La HLWD L26 50 E2
Gerrard St WDN WA8 7 J5 1
Giantswood La CONG CW12 183 M3
Gibb Hl NWCHE CW9 103 K3
Gibb La MPL/ROM SK6 49 L7
Gibbon Av WYTH/NTH M22 63 K2 1
Gibbon Dr NWCHE CW9 131 G1
Gib La NTHM/RTH M23 44 C4
Gibsmere Cl HALE/TIMP WA15 43 K6 4
Gibson Crs SBCH CW11 203 K6
Gibson St WARR WA1 5 K7
WARRS WA4 56 D3 2
Gibson Wy ALT WA14 42 C4
Gibwood Rd WYTH/NTH M22 44 C4
Gigg La WARRS WA4 38 E8
WARRS WA4 55 H7
Gig La WARR WA1 38 D4
Gilbern Dr BIDD ST8 227 H7
Gilbert Cl ALS/KID ST7 243 G2
Gilbert Rd HALE/TIMP WA15 61 L3
Gilbert St BURS/TUN ST6 243 J5
Gilchrist Av MCFLDS SK11 137 L5
Gilchrist Rd IRL M44 31 L6
Gilderdale Cl GOL/RIS/CU WA3 30 B7
Gillan Cl RUNC WA7 74 C7
Gill Bank Rd ALS/KID ST7 243 H4
BURS/TUN ST6 243 H5
Gill Bent Rd CHD/CHDH SK8 65 G6
Gillbrook Rd DID/WITH M20 45 H1
Gillow Cl CW/HAS CW1 221 G4 4
Gill St STKP SK1 3 L1
Gillwood Dr MPL/ROM SK6 47 M3
Gilmore St EDGY/DAV SK3 2 F9
Giltbrook Cl WDN WA8 52 F1 3
Gilwell Cl WARRS WA4 57 J2
Gilwell Dr NTHM/RTH M23 43 M8 1
Gingerbread La NANT CW5 21 K6
Gipsy La CH/BCN CH1 144 F2
OFTN SK2 47 J6
Girton Cl EP CH65 11 G9
Girton Rd EP CH65 11 G9
Girvin Dr NSTN CH64 91 L6
Gisburn Av GOL/RIS/CU WA3 22 F2
Gladeside Rd WYTH/NTH M22 44 C8
The Glade HTNM SK4 46 A3
Gladewood Cl WILM/AE SK9 84 C4 4
Gladstone Av CH/BCN CH1 16 C4
Gladstone Gv BIDD ST8 227 K4
HTNM SK4 46 A1
Gladstone Rd ALT WA14 42 D6
CH/BCN CH1 16 D2
CHSW/BR CH4 190 B1
NSTN CH64 91 L4 1
Gladstone St CQ CH5 142 A6 3
CQ CH5 142 D7 4
CW/HAS CW1 18 F3
NANT CW5 237 K6
NWCHW CW8 12 E5
OFTN SK2 47 J8
WARRN/WOL WA2 4 E5
WDN WA8 7 J4
WSFD CW7 177 K5
Gladstone Ter CQ CH5 166 F1 1
Gladstone Wy CQ CH5 166 D2
Glaisdale Cl AIMK WN4 22 C1 2
CW/SHV CW2 238 A6
Glamis Cl CHSE CH3 170 A2
CW/SHV CW2 237 L4 4
Glan Aber Pk CHSW/BR CH4 169 G5
Glandon Dr CHD/CHDH SK8 65 J5
Glan Gors FLINT CH6 116 B8
Glanvor Rd EDGY/DAV SK3 2 A8
Glan Y Fferi (Ferry Bank)
CQ CH5 142 E6 2
Glastonbury Av CHD/CHDH SK8 65 J6
CHNE CH2 145 M5
GOL/RIS/CU WA3 24 B4
HALE/TIMP WA15 62 B2
Glastonbury Cl RUNC WA7 74 E1
Glastonbury Dr MWCH CW10 179 H3
POY/DIS SK12 66 D7
Glazebrook La GOL/RIS/CU WA3 31 G6
Glazebrook St WARR WA1 5 L5
Glazebury Dr NTHM/RTH M23 44 B7
Glaziers La GOL/RIS/CU WA3 29 K2
Gleadmere WDN WA8 52 C2
Gleave Av MCFLDN SK10 113 H4
Gleave Rd NWCHW CW8 128 D3
WARRW/BUR WA5 26 F6 5
Glebe Av AIMK WN4 22 B2
WARRS WA4 57 J3
Glebe Cl NANT CW5 253 G4
Glebecroft Av CHNE CH2 123 G1 2
Glebe Green Dr WSFD CW7 177 J6
Glebeland GOL/RIS/CU WA3 29 L1
Glebelands Rd KNUT WA16 107 G3
NTHM/RTH M23 43 M6
Glebe La WDN WA8 34 A7
Glebe Mdw CHNE CH2 146 F3
Glebe Rd NWCHW CW8 128 A8
Glebe St ALS/KID ST7 242 D2
STKP SK1 3 K6
The Glebe RUNC WA7 73 L3
Gleggs Cl CHSE CH3 170 B5
Glegg St MCFLDN SK10 15 J6
Glenathol Rd GTS/LS CH66 94 C8
Glenbourne Pk BRAM/HZG SK7 65 K7
Glenby Av WYTH/NTH M22 63 M1
Glen Cl GOL/RIS/CU WA3 40 B2
Glencoe Dr SALE M33 42 C2
Glencourse Rd WDN WA8 34 A7 1
Glendale Av CHNE CH2 123 G1 3
CQ CH5 166 F1
Glendale Cl AUD/MAD/W CW3 264 F8
CW/SHV CW2 237 K1
Glendene Av BRAM/HZG SK7 65 K7
Glendyke Rd GTS/LS CH66 94 C8
Gleneagles Cl BRAM/HZG SK7 66 A5
CHSE CH3 170 B1
WILM/AE SK9 84 D4 6
Gleneagles Dr HOLMCH CW4 181 H2
MCFLDN SK10 112 C8
WDN WA8 34 A7
WSFD CW7 177 J2 4
Gleneagles Rd CHD/CHDH SK8 64 C3
GTS/LS CH66 94 C8
Glenesk Ct CQ CH5 142 F6 2
Glenesk Rd GTS/LS CH66 94 C8
Glenfield ALT WA14 42 B8 2
Glenfield Dr POY/DIS SK12 86 D1
Glenholme Rd BRAM/HZG SK7 65 K5 3
Glenlea Dr DID/WITH M20 45 H4
Glenmaye Rd GTS/LS CH66 94 C8
Glenmere Rd DID/WITH M20 45 J4 2
Glenmoor Rd STKP SK1 3 J6
Glenn Pl WDN WA8 6 B3
Glenorchy Cl HOLMCH CW4 181 J2
Glen Ri HALE/TIMP WA15 43 G7 2
Glen Rd GTS/LS CH66 94 C8
Glenside Cl CH/BCN CH1 144 D7
Glenside Dr WILM/AE SK9 84 C6
The Glen CH/BCN CH1 144 E7
RUNC WA7 73 M6
Glenthorn Gv SALE M33 43 H1 1
Glenton Pk NSTN CH64 91 M6
Glenville Cl RUNC WA7 73 H6 3
WLTN L25 50 B1
Glenwood Cl GTS/LS CH66 94 C6 2
Glenwood Gdns GTS/LS CH66 94 C6 3
Glenwood Gv OFTN SK2 66 B1
Glenwood Rd GTS/LS CH66 94 C6
Gleyve KNUT WA16 59 J7
Glossop Rd MPL/ROM SK6 49 J3
Gloucester Av CQ CH5 142 B6 3
GOL/RIS/CU WA3 23 H3
MPL/ROM SK6 48 F6 5
Gloucester Cl GTS/LS CH66 120 F4 4
MCFLDN SK10 112 E8
WARR WA1 38 D5
Gloucester Rd ALS/KID ST7 242 F2
CHD/CHDH SK8 64 C5
HUY L36 32 A1
KNUT WA16 106 F4
POY/DIS SK12 66 D8
WDN WA8 53 H1
Gloucester St CH/BCN CH1 17 G2
EDGY/DAV SK3 2 D9
Glover Rd GOL/RIS/CU WA3 29 J7
Glovers Loom CHSE CH3 170 B5 1
Glover St CW/HAS CW1 18 B1
NEWLW WA12 27 J1 2
Glyn Av HALE/TIMP WA15 62 A2
Glynnedale Pk CQ CH5 166 A3
Glynne St CQ CH5 142 D7
Glynne Wy CQ CH5 166 D4
Goathland Wy MCFLDS SK11 15 H9
MCFLDS SK11 138 D7 3
Goddard Rd RUNC WA7 73 L1
Goddard St CW/HAS CW1 18 C2
Godfrey St WARRN/WOL WA2 5 L3
Godscroft La FROD/HEL WA6 98 E6
Godshill Cl WARRW/BUR WA5 35 K5
Godstow RUNC WA7 54 E8
Godward Rd NM/HAY SK22 69 H4
Golborne Dale Rd NEWLW WA12 23 G8
Golborne La KNUT WA16 78 F1
Golborne Rd GOL/RIS/CU WA3 23 J4
WARRN/WOL WA2 28 A5
Golborne St NEWLW WA12 22 E8
WARR WA1 4 F6
Goldcliffe Cl WARRW/BUR WA5 36 D2
Goldcrest Cl CW/HAS CW1 220 F5 2
RUNC WA7 73 M7
WSFD CW7 177 J7 2
WYTH/NTH M22 44 F7
Goldcrest Ms HLWD L26 50 E3 4
Goldcrest Wy BIDD ST8 227 L4 3
Goldfinch Cl CONG CW12 207 L3
HLWD L26 50 E3
Goldfinch Farm Rd
SPK/HALE L24 70 C1
Goldfinch La GOL/RIS/CU WA3 29 L8 2
Goldford La MALPAS SY14 231 L6
Goldie Av WYTH/NTH M22 63 M3
Goldsmith Dr SBCH CW11 203 K6
Goldsworth Fold
RAIN/WH L35 33 H1 2
Golf Links Cl BURS/TUN ST6 243 J5
Golf Rd HALE/TIMP WA15 61 M1
Gongar La CHSE CH3 148 E3
Gonsley Cl CHNE CH2 17 G1
Gonville Av MCFLDS SK11 162 F1
Gooch Dr NEWLW WA12 27 K2
Goodall St MCFLDS SK11 15 K7
Goodfellow St BURS/TUN ST6 243 K8
Goodlass Rd SPK/HALE L24 50 A7
Goodridge Av WYTH/NTH M22 63 J3 3
Goodrington Rd WILM/AE SK9 84 E2
Goodwin Crs CW/SHV CW2 238 C8
Goodwood Av NTHM/RTH M23 43 K4
Goodwood Cl CH/BCN CH1 16 B4
NWCHW CW8 129 H1 1
Goodwood Crs
HALE/TIMP WA15 43 J6
Goodwood Gv GTS/LS CH66 120 D1
Goodwood Ri MWCH CW10 179 G2
Goodwood Rd MPL/ROM SK6 48 E7
Gooseberry La RUNC WA7 74 D3 4
TPLY/KEL CW6 173 L1
Goosebrook Cl NWCHE CW9 103 J4
Goosebrook La NWCHE CW9 102 F2
Goose Gn ALT WA14 42 D8
Goose La WARRS WA4 76 A2
Goosetrey Cl WILM/AE SK9 84 E3 1
Goostrey La HOLMCH CW4 157 G5
HOLMCH CW4 158 A6
Gordale Cl CONG CW12 185 G7
WARRW/BUR WA5 35 M5
Gordon Av BRAM/HZG SK7 66 D1 3
WARR WA1 38 B5
Gordon La CHNE CH2 121 H7
Gordon Rd BURS/TUN ST6 243 J6
Gordon St HTNM SK4 2 F3
Gore La KNUT WA16 109 H1
Gorse Av MPL/ROM SK6 48 E6
Gorse Bank Rd HALE/TIMP WA15 62 C5
Gorse Cl FROD/HEL WA6 127 G6
Gorse Covert NWCHE CW9 130 C1
Gorse Covert Rd
GOL/RIS/CU WA3 30 A7
Gorsefield CHSE CH3 214 A3
Gorsefield Hey WILM/AE SK9 84 E4 7
Gorselands CHD/CHDH SK8 65 H7 2
Gorse La CONG CW12 207 K7
Gorse Sq PART M31 40 D1
Gorse Stacks CH/BCN CH1 17 G4
The Gorse ALT WA14 61 H4
Gorse Wy CHSE CH3 170 A7
Gorsewood Rd RUNC WA7 74 D6
Gorsey Av WYTH/NTH M22 44 C8
Gorsey Bank Crs NANT CW5 253 G4
Gorsey Bank Rd EDGY/DAV SK3 46 B4
Gorsey Brow MPL/ROM SK6 48 A2
STKP SK1 3 J6
Gorsey Dr WYTH/NTH M22 44 C8
Gorsey La ALT WA14 42 B7
LYMM WA13 41 G6
WARRN/WOL WA2 5 L2
WDN WA8 53 L4
Gorsey Mount St STKP SK1 3 H6
Gorsey Rd WILM/AE SK9 83 M5
WYTH/NTH M22 44 C8
Gorseywell La RUNC WA7 74 F6
Gorsley Cl MWCH CW10 179 J6
Gorstage La NWCHW CW8 128 B7
Gorstons La NSTN CH64 92 A6
Gorston Wk WYTH/NTH M22 63 J4
Gosberryhole La CONG CW12 209 G2
Gosforth Pl CHNE CH2 17 L1
Gosling Rd GOL/RIS/CU WA3 29 H5
Gosport Cl WARRN/WOL WA2 37 L3
Goss St CH/BCN CH1 16 F5 2
Gotherage Cl MPL/ROM SK6 48 E2
Gotherage La MPL/ROM SK6 48 E2
Gothic Cl MPL/ROM SK6 48 F2
Gough Av WARRN/WOL WA2 37 H2
Gough's La KNUT WA16 107 H5
Gough St EDGY/DAV SK3 2 D6
Goulden St CW/HAS CW1 18 B1
WARRW/BUR WA5 4 B5
Goulders Ct RUNC WA7 74 B7 5
Gourham Dr CHD/CHDH SK8 64 F3 4
Govan St WYTH/NTH M22 44 E3 4
Gower Av BRAM/HZG SK7 66 C1
Gowy Cl ALS/KID ST7 240 F1
SBCH CW11 203 L4
WILM/AE SK9 84 E3
Gowy Crs CHSE CH3 172 B3
Gowy Rd CHNE CH2 146 F3
Goyt Av MPL/ROM SK6 48 F8
Goyt Crs MPL/ROM SK6 47 M1
STKP SK1 3 L1
Goyt Pl CHF/WBR SK23 89 L5
Goyt Rd CHF/WBR SK23 89 L6
MPL/ROM SK6 48 F8 1
NM/HAY SK22 69 J6
POY/DIS SK12 68 D7
STKP SK1 3 L1
Goyt Valley Rd MPL/ROM SK6 47 M1
Goyt Vw NM/HAY SK22 69 H6
Goyt Wy MPL/ROM SK6 48 F3
MPL/ROM SK6 49 H7
NM/HAY SK22 69 J6
Grace Av WARRN/WOL WA2 37 H4
Grace Cl CW/HAS CW1 222 C8
Grace Rd EP CH65 10 E5
Gradwell St EDGY/DAV SK3 2 D7
Grafton Ms CHNE CH2 17 G2 1
Grafton Rd EP CH65 10 E4
Grafton St ALT WA14 42 D8 1
HTNM SK4 2 E1
NEWLW WA12 27 H1 5
WARRW/BUR WA5 4 B4
Graham Av GTS/LS CH66 94 D7
Graham Cl WDN WA8 52 C3 2
Graham Crs IRL M44 31 J8
Graham Dr HLWD L26 51 G4 1
POY/DIS SK12 68 C5
Graham Rd CH/BCN CH1 144 E8
STKP SK1 3 M7
WDN WA8 52 C4
Grainger's Rd NWCHE CW9 13 H9
Gralam Cl SALE M33 43 L3 3
Graley Cl HLWD L26 50 F6
Grammar School Rd
LYMM WA13 58 F2
WARRS WA4 56 F1
Grampian Wy GOL/RIS/CU WA3 23 K3
NSTN CH64 91 L7 3
WSFD CW7 177 G5
Granary Wy SALE M33 42 F2
Granby Cl RUNC WA7 74 C7 3
Granby Rd CHD/CHDH SK8 65 H4
HALE/TIMP WA15 43 G3
OFTN SK2 47 H7
WARRS WA4 56 B4
Grandford La NANT CW5 262 D2
Granford Cl ALT WA14 42 D5 3
Grange Av CHD/CHDH SK8 64 F1
HALE/TIMP WA15 43 H5
HALE/TIMP WA15 62 A2
NWCHW CW8 129 G1
WARRS WA4 37 L8
WLTN L25 50 D5
Grangebrook Dr WSFD CW7 177 J1 3
Grange Cl CW/HAS CW1 19 K5
GOL/RIS/CU WA3 23 J6
SBCH CW11 203 M5
Grange Ct BIDD ST8 227 K2
Grange Crs GTS/LS CH66 94 A3
Grange Dr NWCHW CW8 129 G6
WARRW/BUR WA5 36 A8
WDN WA8 6 B3
Grangefields BIDD ST8 227 L1
Grangelands MCFLDN SK10 137 M2 1
Grange La DID/WITH M20 45 H2
MALPAS SY14 245 K2
NWCHW CW8 128 B6
NWCHW CW8 153 G5
WSFD CW7 177 J2
Grange Lea MWCH CW10 179 H3
Grangemoor RUNC WA7 73 K5
Grange Park Av CHD/CHDH SK8 45 K7
RUNC WA7 9 L3
WILM/AE SK9 84 A4
Grange Park Rd CHD/CHDH SK8 45 K7
RUNC WA7 9 L3
Grange Pl IRL M44 31 K7
Grange Rd ALT WA14 61 J3
BIDD ST8 227 L1
BRAM/HZG SK7 65 M1
CHNE CH2 145 K8
CHSE CH3 149 G3
CHSE CH3 170 B2
CQ CH5 142 B8
EP CH65 10 E8
HALE/TIMP WA15 43 H5
MCFLDS SK11 14 F8
NWCHE CW9 130 D6
NWCHW CW8 129 G1
NWCHW CW8 151 M2 3
RUNC WA7 9 L3
Grangeside CHNE CH2 145 K5
Grange St LEIGH WN7 24 E1
The Grange NWCHW CW8 129 H7
Grangeway RUNC WA7 9 L8
Grange Wy SBCH CW11 203 M5
Grangeway WILM/AE SK9 64 D8
Grangewood Dr KNUT WA16 134 F1
Granston Cl WARRW/BUR WA5 36 E2 3
Granstone Cl BURS/TUN ST6 243 M5
Grant Cl WARRW/BUR WA5 36 D3
Grant Dr CQ CH5 166 A2
Grantham Av WARR WA1 37 L5
WARRS WA4 56 B4
Grantham Cl NWCHE CW9 130 C5
Grantham Rd HTNM SK4 2 B4
Grant Rd WARRW/BUR WA5 36 B6 2
Granville Dr GTS/LS CH66 94 B5
Granville Gdns DID/WITH M20 45 G2
Granville Rd CH/BCN CH1 16 C2
CHD/CHDH SK8 46 C7
HALE/TIMP WA15 43 J6
NWCHE CW9 13 J9
WILM/AE SK9 83 M7
Granville Sq WSFD CW7 177 K4 2
Granville St RUNC WA7 9 H1
WARR WA1 5 L4
WSFD CW7 177 L4
Grapes St MCFLDS SK11 15 H7 1
Grappenhall La WARRS WA4 57 K6
Grappenhall Rd EP CH65 120 F1
WARRS WA4 56 D3
Grasmere Av CONG CW12 206 F2 1
CW/SHV CW2 220 F8 1
WARRN/WOL WA2 37 K1
Grasmere Cl WSFD CW7 177 K2
Grasmere Crs BRAM/HZG SK7 65 L4
MPL/ROM SK6 67 L3
Grasmere Dr HOLMCH CW4 181 G1
RUNC WA7 73 K7
Grasmere Rd CHD/CHDH SK8 64 B1
CHNE CH2 145 M7
EP CH65 121 J2
FROD/HEL WA6 99 J4
HALE/TIMP WA15 43 J6
LYMM WA13 39 M8 1
NSTN CH64 91 L6
PART M31 40 E1
SALE M33 43 J2
WILM/AE SK9 110 A3
Grason Av WILM/AE SK9 84 C3
Grassfield Wy KNUT WA16 107 G5
Grassholme Dr OFTN SK2 48 A7
Grassington Crs WLTN L25 50 D2
Gratrix La SALE M33 43 M1
Gravel La WILM/AE SK9 83 L8
Grave Oak La GOL/RIS/CU WA3 25 H3
Graveyard La KNUT WA16 82 F7
Graylag Cl RUNC WA7 73 M7 2
Grayling Willows
AUD/MAD/W CW3 267 L6 1
Graymarsh Dr POY/DIS SK12 86 E2
Graysands Rd HALE/TIMP WA15 61 M1
Gray's Cl ALS/KID ST7 226 B5
Grayshott Rd BURS/TUN ST6 243 L7
Greasby Dr GTS/LS CH66 94 E8
Great Ashfield WDN WA8 52 D1
Great Egerton St STKP SK1 2 F4

Greatfield Rd WYTH/NTH M22 44 B8
Great King St MCFLDS SK11 14 E5
Great Moor St OFTN SK2 47 H7
Greatoak Rd ALS/KID ST7 241 M8
Great Portwood St STKP SK1 3 H3
Great Queen St MCFLDS SK11 14 E5
Great Riding RUNC WA7 74 C5
Great Underbank STKP SK1 2 F5
Greave Rd STKP SK1 47 J4
Greaves La MALPAS SY14 256 E5
Greaves La East MALPAS SY14 256 E5
Greaves Rd WILM/AE SK9 83 K5
Grebe Cl KNUT WA16 107 H1
POY/DIS SK12 66 B8
Greeba Av WARRS WA4 56 B1
Greeba Rd NTHM/RTH M23 43 L6
Greek St EDGY/DAV SK3 2 F8
RUNC WA7 8 F1
Green Acre Cl KNUT WA16 107 H4
Greenacre Cl WLTN L25 50 C4
Greenacre Rd CHSW/BR CH4 168 F8
WLTN L25 50 C4
Greenacres FROD/HEL WA6 99 J6
SBCH CW11 204 A5
TPLY/KEL CW6 173 G6
Greenacres Cl
GOL/RIS/CU WA3 24 B4 3
Greenacres Rd CONG CW12 206 F2
The Greenacres LYMM WA13 40 A8
Greenall Av WARRW/BUR WA5 35 K8 1
Greenall Rd NWCHE CW9 13 L2
Greenall's Av WARRS WA4 56 C3
Green Av NWCHE CW9 153 L1
NWCHW CW8 129 G1
TPLY/KEL CW6 198 D8
Greenbank CHSW/BR CH4 169 L7
Green Bank MKTDR TF9 274 A7
Greenbank Av CHD/CHDH SK8 45 G7 5
GTS/LS CH66 94 C5
HTNM SK4 45 L2 4
Greenbank Cl NANT CW5 237 K7
Greenbank Crs MPL/ROM SK6 48 F7
Greenbank Dr MCFLDN SK10 113 G4
Greenbank Gdns WARRS WA4 56 F2
Greenbank La NWCHW CW8 12 B6
Greenbank Rd CHD/CHDH SK8 45 G6 2
CHNE CH2 146 A8
CQ CH5 142 A7
MPL/ROM SK6 49 H3
WARRS WA4 56 F2
Greenbank St WARRS WA4 56 C2 1
Greenbeech Cl MPL/ROM SK6 48 E5 2
Green Bridge Cl RUNC WA7 74 A3 2
Greenbridge Rd RUNC WA7 74 B2
Greenbrow Rd NTHM/RTH M23 62 F1
Green Cl CHD/CHDH SK8 45 G6
Green Coppice RUNC WA7 74 C4
Green Ct GOL/RIS/CU WA3 24 B3
Green Cts ALT WA14 61 H1
Green Cft MPL/ROM SK6 48 D1
Greendale Dr MWCH CW10 179 H5
Greendale Gdns CW/HAS CW1 19 K1
Greendale La MCFLDN SK10 111 K4
Green Dr ALS/KID ST7 224 D8
HALE/TIMP WA15 43 G5
WILM/AE SK9 84 D2
Green End WHITCH SY13 270 A5
Greene's Rd RAIN/WH L35 32 D2
Greenfield BIDD ST8 227 K6 1
Greenfield Av CHSW/BR CH4 190 A5
Greenfield Cl EDGY/DAV SK3 46 E6 2
HALE/TIMP WA15 43 J6
NM/HAY SK22 69 G4
Greenfield Crs CHNE CH2 146 B7
CHSE CH3 171 H6
Greenfield Gdns CHNE CH2 123 H1
Greenfield La CHNE CH2 146 A7
FROD/HEL WA6 99 H3
Greenfield Rd BURS/TUN ST6 243 L7
CHSE CH3 171 H7
CHSW/BR CH4 167 J8
CONG CW12 207 H1
GTS/LS CH66 94 B5
MCFLDN SK10 113 G5
Greenfields CHNE CH2 145 M3
WHITCH SY13 269 M4
WSFD CW7 178 B3
Greenfields Av CW/SHV CW2 238 B8
WARRS WA4 56 D4
Greenfields Cl NEWLW WA12 22 C8 5
NSTN CH64 91 M7 1
WARR WA1 38 C5 2
Greenfields Cft NSTN CH64 91 L7
Greenfields Dr ALS/KID ST7 241 K1
NSTN CH64 91 L8
Greenfields La CHSE CH3 170 F7
Greenfields Ri WHITCH SY13 269 L4
Greenfield Wy NWCHW CW8 128 A8
Greenfinch Cl HLWD L26 50 E3 5
Greenfold Wy LEIGH WN7 25 H2
Greenfoot La WHITCH SY13 270 A7
Greenford Cl CHD/CHDH SK8 46 B8
Green Gables Cl
CHD/CHDH SK8 64 B3 5
Greengate HALE/TIMP WA15 62 D5
Greengate Rd ALS/KID ST7 224 F7
Greengates Crs NSTN CH64 91 L7
Greengates St BURS/TUN ST6 243 L8
Greenhalgh St HTNM SK4 2 F3
Green Hall Ms WILM/AE SK9 84 B6 2
Greenham Rd NTHM/RTH M23 43 M2
Greenhill Av CQ CH5 166 A3
Greenhill La WARRS WA4 76 A7
Greenhill Rd HALE/TIMP WA15 43 J6
Greenhills Cl MCFLDS SK11 15 K7
Green Hill St EDGY/DAV SK3 2 C9
Green Hill Ter EDGY/DAV SK3 2 C9
Greenhill Wk POY/DIS SK12 68 D6 5
Greenhouse Farm Rd
RUNC WA7 74 B6
Greenhythe Rd CHD/CHDH SK8 64 C6
Green Jones Brow
WARRW/BUR WA5 26 F6
Green Lake La CHSE CH3 211 M1
Greenland Cl TPLY/KEL CW6 197 K3
Greenlands CHSE CH3 214 B1
Green La AUD/MAD/W CW3 273 M3
BRAM/HZG SK7 66 D1
CH/BCN CH1 144 C6
CHNE CH2 146 C1
CHSE CH3 170 B2
CHSE CH3 213 M7
CHSW/BR CH4 168 E7
CHSW/BR CH4 190 A6
CQ CH5 142 B7
EP CH65 95 J8
GOL/RIS/CU WA3 24 A2
GTS/LS CH66 94 D8
HALE/TIMP WA15 43 H8
HALE/TIMP WA15 62 B1
HTNM SK4 2 B4
IRL M44 31 K7
KNUT WA16 80 D8
KNUT WA16 105 L6
KNUT WA16 134 D3
MALPAS SY14 244 C4
MALPAS SY14 245 G4
MCFLDN SK10 113 H3
MPL/ROM SK6 48 B3
NANT CW5 218 A5
NANT CW5 237 L7
NWCHE CW9 104 F8
NWCHE CW9 153 M1
POY/DIS SK12 67 J8
POY/DIS SK12 68 D7
SBCH CW11 203 G4
TPLY/KEL CW6 149 K8
WARR WA1 38 A4
WARRN/WOL WA2 28 A5
WARRS WA4 56 F7
WARRW/BUR WA5 26 E5
WDN WA8 6 C2
WILM/AE SK9 84 B5
WILM/AE SK9 109 M4
Green Lane Cl WARRN/WOL WA2 28 A5
Green La East CQ CH5 143 K5
Green La North
HALE/TIMP WA15 43 H8
Green Lane (West) CQ CH5 143 H1
Greenlaw Cl NWCHE CW9 13 K8
Green Lawns Dr
GTS/LS CH66 120 F4 5
Greenlea Cl EP CH65 121 H2
Green Mdw CQ CH5 166 A4 1
MPL/ROM SK6 48 F4
Green Meadows Dr
MPL/ROM SK6 48 F5
Greenmeadows Rd
AUD/MAD/W CW3 267 L5
Green Meadows Wk
WYTH/NTH M22 63 L3 1
Greenoak Dr SALE M33 43 J3
Green Oaks Pth WDN WA8 7 M4
Green Oaks Wy WDN WA8 7 L4
Greenore Dr SPK/HALE L24 71 K2 2
Green Pk NWCHW CW8 128 E5
Greenpark Rd WYTH/NTH M22 44 D3
Green Pastures HTNM SK4 45 L3
Green Rd PART M31 40 E1
Greensbridge La HLWD L26 51 H3
Greenshall La POY/DIS SK12 68 F6
Greenshank Cl NEWLW WA12 22 C8 4
Greenside Av FROD/HEL WA6 99 K5
Greenside Cl ALS/KID ST7 243 G5 1
Greenside Ct NWCHE CW9 131 K7
Greenside Dr ALT WA14 61 L3
IRL M44 31 M3
NWCHE CW9 131 G4
Green Strawberry EP CH65 121 G4
Green St EDGY/DAV SK3 46 F6
KNUT WA16 107 G2
MCFLDN SK10 15 J6
SBCH CW11 204 B5
WARRW/BUR WA5 4 C7
WILM/AE SK9 110 A3 4
WRXS/E LL13 228 E3
Greensway CHSW/BR CH4 16 A9
The Green CHD/CHDH SK8 64 F4
CHSE CH3 172 F2
CHSW/BR CH4 190 B5
EP CH65 121 H2
HTNM SK4 2 A3
MPL/ROM SK6 68 A1
MWCH CW10 179 K6
NSTN CH64 91 H6
NSTN CH64 91 M6
NWCHW CW8 129 H7
RUNC WA7 73 M3 2
WILM/AE SK9 84 E1
Green Tree Gdns MPL/ROM SK6 48 B2
Greenvale Dr CHD/CHDH SK8 45 J6
Green Vw LYMM WA13 40 B7
Greenview Dr DID/WITH M20 45 J4 3
Green Villa Pk WILM/AE SK9 83 L8
Greenville Rd NSTN CH64 91 M3 1
Green Wk ALT WA14 61 G1
CHD/CHDH SK8 45 G6
HALE/TIMP WA15 42 F5
NWCHW CW8 128 A8 1
Green Wy CH/BCN CH1 144 A3
Greenway ALS/KID ST7 224 B7
ALT WA14 42 A7
BRAM/HZG SK7 65 K6 2
CHSE CH3 228 F3
CONG CW12 207 H1
CW/HAS CW1 221 K6
MALPAS SY14 245 H1
MPL/ROM SK6 48 E3
WARR WA1 37 M5
WARRS WA4 56 D5
WARRW/BUR WA5 35 L5 3
WILM/AE SK9 84 A6
WYTH/NTH M22 44 E4
Greenway Cl ALS/KID ST7 224 F5
FROD/HEL WA6 124 B1 1
SALE M33 42 D1
Greenway Dr NWCHE CW9 130 C5
Greenway Rd BIDD ST8 227 L2
CHD/CHDH SK8 64 C6
HALE/TIMP WA15 42 F4
RUNC WA7 8 F5
SPK/HALE L24 71 G1
WDN WA8 7 J1
Greenway St CHSW/BR CH4 17 G8
Greenwood Av
CHSW/BR CH4 169 K5 2
CONG CW12 207 M1
OFTN SK2 47 J6
Greenwood Cl GOL/RIS/CU WA3 29 M2
HALE/TIMP WA15 43 K7
NWCHW CW8 128 D3 2
Greenwood Crs
WARRN/WOL WA2 37 K2 5
Greenwood Dr NEWLW WA12 27 K2
WILM/AE SK9 84 D4
Greenwood Rd LYMM WA13 58 E2
WYTH/NTH M22 44 B8
Greenwood St ALT WA14 42 D8
Greg Av MCFLDN SK10 112 E5
Greg Ms WILM/AE SK9 84 B2
Gregory Av MPL/ROM SK6 48 B3
Gregory Cl WARRW/BUR WA5 36 C5
Gregson Rd WDN WA8 7 M3
Grendale Av BRAM/HZG SK7 66 E3
STKP SK1 3 M6
Grenfell Cl NSTN CH64 91 J3
Grenfell Pk NSTN CH64 91 J3
Grenfell St WDN WA8 7 J5
Grenville Cl CW/HAS CW1 222 C7
Grenville Rd BRAM/HZG SK7 66 C1
Grenville St EDGY/DAV SK3 2 C7
Gresford Av CHNE CH2 17 J1
Gresford Cl RAIN/WH L35 32 F1 5
WARRW/BUR WA5 36 D2 2
Gresty Av WYTH/NTH M22 63 M3
Gresty Green Rd CW/SHV CW2 238 D4
Gresty La CW/SHV CW2 238 B6
Gresty Rd CW/SHV CW2 19 H8
Gresty Ter CW/HAS CW1 19 K5
Greta Av CHD/CHDH SK8 64 C6 2
Greville Dr WSFD CW7 178 A3
Grey Friars CH/BCN CH1 16 E6
Greyfriars Rd WYTH/NTH M22 63 H2
Greyhound Farm Rd
SPK/HALE L24 70 C1
Greyhound Park Rd
CH/BCN CH1 168 F1
Greyhound Rd MCFLDN SK10 111 H7
Greylands Rd DID/WITH M20 45 J4 2
Greymist Av WARR WA1 38 C5
Grey Rd ALT WA14 42 C7
Greysan Av ALS/KID ST7 243 M4
Greystoke Av HALE/TIMP WA15 43 K6
SALE M33 43 H1 4
Greystoke Dr WILM/AE SK9 110 A2 1
Greystoke Rd MCFLDN SK10 15 L1
Greystoke St STKP SK1 3 K6
Greystone Pk CW/HAS CW1 19 H3
Greystone Rd WARRW/BUR WA5 35 M8
Greystones GTS/LS CH66 94 D8
Greystones Rd CHSE CH3 170 C3
Grey St WARR WA1 5 J5
Grice St WARRS WA4 56 C3 2
Grid La MPL/ROM SK6 49 L3
Griffin Cl CH/BCN CH1 144 F7
NM/HAY SK22 69 J6
WARRW/BUR WA5 26 E6 1
Griffin Ms WDN WA8 53 H1 3
Griffith Av GOL/RIS/CU WA3 29 L7
Griffiths Ct CQ CH5 142 A7
Griffiths Dr NWCHE CW9 130 C6
Griffiths Rd NWCHE CW9 130 E4
Griffiths St WARRS WA4 37 M8
Grig Pl ALS/KID ST7 224 C7
Grimsditch La WARRS WA4 76 A6
Grimshaw Av MCFLDN SK10 113 G5 3
Grimshaw La MCFLDN SK10 113 G5 2
Grimshaw St GOL/RIS/CU WA3 23 G3
STKP SK1 3 K5
Grimstead Cl NTHM/RTH M23 43 L6 2
Grindley Bank CHNE CH2 146 F4
Grindley Gdns EP CH65 121 J2 1
Grisedale Av
WARRN/WOL WA2 37 H1 1
Grisedale Cl RUNC WA7 73 L7
Grisedale Wy MCFLDS SK11 138 A7 1
Gritstone Trail MCFLDS SK11 163 L3
MCFLDS SK11 187 J8
POY/DIS SK12 88 C5
Grizedale WDN WA8 52 B2
Grizedale Cl CW/SHV CW2 237 K2
Groarke Dr WARRW/BUR WA5 35 K7
Groby Rd ALT WA14 42 C8
CW/HAS CW1 221 K2
Groomscroft CQ CH5 166 B4
Groomsdale La CQ CH5 166 B4
Grosvenor Av ALS/KID ST7 224 D7
GOL/RIS/CU WA3 23 K4 2
NWCHW CW8 129 G8
WARR WA1 37 L5
Grosvenor Cl
WARRW/BUR WA5 36 C7 1
WILM/AE SK9 84 A8 1
Grosvenor Ct WSFD CW7 177 J5 1
Grosvenor Crs WRX/GR/LL LL12 210 B5
Grosvenor Dr POY/DIS SK12 86 C1 1
Grosvenor Gdns NEWLW WA12 27 H2
WYTH/NTH M22 44 E6
Grosvenor Park Rd
CH/BCN CH1 17 J5 1
Grosvenor Park Ter
CH/BCN CH1 17 J6
Grosvenor Pl BURS/TUN ST6 243 K8 2
CH/BCN CH1 17 G7
Grosvenor Rd ALT WA14 42 E6
CH/BCN CH1 16 F7
CHD/CHDH SK8 46 C8
CHSE CH3 172 A2
CHSW/BR CH4 16 E9
CONG CW12 207 G1
CQ CH5 142 B7
HTNM SK4 46 B1 1
HTNM SK4 46 A1 1
MPL/ROM SK6 48 F5
WDN WA8 34 B8
Grosvenor Rbt CH/BCN CH1 16 F7
Grosvenor St
BRAM/HZG SK7 66 D1 10
CH/BCN CH1 16 F7
CW/HAS CW1 18 C2
MCFLDN SK10 14 E4
RUNC WA7 9 K1
STKP SK1 3 G8 1
WSFD CW7 177 L4 1
Grotsworth La MALPAS SY14 247 L4
Grotto La KNUT WA16 134 A4
Grounds St WARRN/WOL WA2 5 H3
Grove Av ALS/KID ST7 225 G8
ALS/KID ST7 242 E4
CHSE CH3 170 B1
LYMM WA13 58 C1
NWCHE CW9 131 G1
WILM/AE SK9 84 A5
Grove Cl WSFD CW7 177 H4
Grove Gdns CHSE CH3 170 E2
Grove La CHD/CHDH SK8 65 H7
DID/WITH M20 45 H2 2
HALE/TIMP WA15 43 G6
HALE/TIMP WA15 62 A1
Grovemount NWCHE CW9 153 M2
Grove Pk KNUT WA16 107 G3
Grove Park Av ALS/KID ST7 225 G8
Grove Ri LYMM WA13 58 E1
Grove Rd CH/BCN CH1 120 E7
HALE/TIMP WA15 61 L1
The Groves CH/BCN CH1 17 H6
EP CH65 121 G4
Grove St BRAM/HZG SK7 66 E1 3
NM/HAY SK22 69 H5
RUNC WA7 8 F1
WARRS WA4 5 K9
WILM/AE SK9 84 B5 1
The Grove ALS/KID ST7 225 G8
CHD/CHDH SK8 65 G6
DID/WITH M20 45 H3
EDGY/DAV SK3 46 E5
GOL/RIS/CU WA3 23 K3
LYMM WA13 58 E1
SALE M33 43 H1
WARRW/BUR WA5 35 M8
WHITCH SY13 269 M3
Grove Wy WILM/AE SK9 84 B5
Grovewood Gdns RAIN/WH L35 32 E1
Grovewood Ms MCFLDS SK11 14 F8
Grub La TPLY/KEL CW6 149 J7
Grundey St BRAM/HZG SK7 66 E2 4
Grundy Cl WDN WA8 52 F1 5
Grundy St GOL/RIS/CU WA3 23 G5
HTNM SK4 45 L2
Guardian St WARRW/BUR WA5 4 D5
Guernsey Cl WARRS WA4 56 D4
Guernsey Dr EP CH65 121 J3
Guernsey Rd WDN WA8 53 L1
Guests Slack FROD/HEL WA6 126 B3
Guest St WDN WA8 7 G7 1
Guilden Gn CHSE CH3 146 E7
Guilden Sutton La CHSE CH3 146 C8
Guildford Av CHD/CHDH SK8 65 G6
Guildford Cl CHSW/BR CH4 168 F6 5
STKP SK1 3 M9 2
WARRN/WOL WA2 38 A3 2
Guillemot Cl CW/HAS CW1 19 M2
Guillemot Wy HLWD L26 50 E3
Gullane Cl MCFLDN SK10 112 B8
Gull Cl POY/DIS SK12 86 B1
The Gullet NANT CW5 20 F6
Gunco La MCFLDN SK10 112 C4
MCFLDS SK11 15 J9
Gunn Gv NSTN CH64 91 M4
Gunn St BIDD ST8 227 J4
Gun St WRX/GR/LL LL12 210 B5
Gutterscroft CW/HAS CW1 222 D7
Gutticar Rd WDN WA8 52 B4
Guy La CHSE CH3 171 H7
Guywood La MPL/ROM SK6 48 C1
Gwenbury Av STKP SK1 3 M6
Gwyn Av BIDD ST8 227 K6
Gwynedd Dr FLINT CH6 116 A6

H

Hackberry Cl ALT WA14 42 B4
Hacked Way La MCFLDS SK11 140 A6
Haddon Cl CW/SHV CW2 238 B5 2
HOLMCH CW4 181 H1
MCFLDS SK11 138 B7 2
MPL/ROM SK6 67 L6 1
WILM/AE SK9 109 M2
Haddon Dr WDN WA8 52 C1
Haddon Gv HALE/TIMP WA15 42 F5
SALE M33 43 G1
Haddon La NSTN CH64 92 B8
Haddon Rd BRAM/HZG SK7 66 E3
CHD/CHDH SK8 64 C5
GOL/RIS/CU WA3 23 K3
NSTN CH64 118 D2
Hadfield Gv WLTN L25 50 C1
Hadfield St NWCHE CW9 13 L1
Hadleigh Cl WARRW/BUR WA5 35 K7
Hadley Cl CHD/CHDH SK8 64 F3 5
Hadlow La NSTN CH64 92 F5
Hadlow Rd NSTN CH64 92 F6
Hadrian Dr CH/BCN CH1 144 E6
Hadrian Wy NWCHW CW8 152 B2
Hafod Cl CH/BCN CH1 168 D1
Hag Bank La POY/DIS SK12 68 D5
Haguebar Rd NM/HAY SK22 68 F4
Hague Bush Cl
GOL/RIS/CU WA3 23 L3 2
Hague Fold Rd NM/HAY SK22 68 F4
Haig Av IRL M44 31 J8
WARRW/BUR WA5 36 A8
Haig Rd KNUT WA16 81 J8
WDN WA8 7 G3
Haileybury Rd WLTN L25 50 B4
Hailsham Cl BURS/TUN ST6 243 L7
Hale Av POY/DIS SK12 86 D2
Hale Bank Rd WDN WA8 51 L7
Hale Cl LEIGH WN7 25 H2 2
Hale Dr SPK/HALE L24 70 F2
Hale Gate Rd WDN WA8 71 M1
Hale Gv WARRW/BUR WA5 36 A6 1
Hale Low Rd HALE/TIMP WA15 61 M1
Hale Rd HALE/TIMP WA15 61 L1
HTNM SK4 2 A2
SPK/HALE L24 70 C1
WDN WA8 6 A5
Hale St WARRN/WOL WA2 5 G3
Hale Vw RUNC WA7 8 D6
Hale View Rd FROD/HEL WA6 98 C8
HUY L36 32 A2
Halewood Av GOL/RIS/CU WA3 22 F3
Halewood Dr WLTN L25 50 B2
Halewood Pl WLTN L25 50 C1 2
Halewood Rd WLTN L25 50 B1
Halewood Wy WLTN L25 50 C2 5
Haley Rd North
WARRW/BUR WA5 26 E6
Haley Rd South
WARRW/BUR WA5 26 E6
Halfacre La WARRS WA4 57 L1
Halfacre Rd WYTH/NTH M22 44 C8
Half Moon La OFTN SK2 47 L6
Half St MCFLDS SK11 15 H9
Halifax Cl WARRN/WOL WA2 37 K2 5
Halkett Cl CHSW/BR CH4 168 E7 5
Halkyn Rd CHNE CH2 17 J1
Halkyn St FLINT CH6 116 A6
Hallam St OFTN SK2 47 G6
Hallas Gv NTHM/RTH M23 44 B3
Hallastone Rd FROD/HEL WA6 98 B8
Hall Av HALE/TIMP WA15 42 F5
WDN WA8 52 A3
Halla-way WARRS WA4 56 E1 2
Hall Cl MCFLDN SK10 112 D8
Hallcroft PART M31 31 M8
Hallcroft Pl WARRS WA4 57 G2
Hall Dr ALS/KID ST7 241 J1
NANT CW5 237 J6
NWCHE CW9 104 B6
WARRS WA4 56 D6
Hallefield Crs MCFLDN SK10 15 K6
Hallefield Dr MCFLDN SK10 15 J6
Hallefield Rd MCFLDS SK11 15 K6
Hallfield Dr CHNE CH2 123 H1
Hallfield Gv BURS/TUN ST6 243 L7
Hallfield Pk GTS/LS CH66 94 D8
Hallfields Rd CHSE CH3 172 C2
WARRN/WOL WA2 5 L1
Hallgate Dr CHD/CHDH SK8 64 A2 1
Hallgate Rd STKP SK1 3 M7
Hallgreen La CONG CW12 183 K4
Hall Gv MCFLDN SK10 138 D1 5
Hall Hl MCFLDN SK10 112 E5
Halliday Cl GOL/RIS/CU WA3 38 F1
Halliwell's Brow KNUT WA16 79 H1
Hall La AUD/MAD/W CW3 264 B5
CHSE CH3 231 J5
HUY L36 32 A2
KNUT WA16 82 C8
KNUT WA16 105 H3
MALPAS SY14 246 A3
MCFLDS SK11 162 F1
NTHM/RTH M23 44 B6
NWCHE CW9 102 F5
NWCHE CW9 104 E8
PART M31 31 M8
RAIN/WH L35 33 J3
SBCH CW11 202 E8
SBCH CW11 203 H7
STHEL WA9 26 A8
TPLY/KEL CW6 149 K6
TPLY/KEL CW6 174 C7
TPLY/KEL CW6 217 H7
WARRS WA4 57 H4
WARRS WA4 75 K2
WARRS WA4 76 D4
WARRW/BUR WA5 27 H4
WDN WA8 33 K6
WSFD CW7 199 M2
The Hall La TPLY/KEL CW6 198 B1
Hall Meadow CHD/CHDH SK8 64 E3
Hall Moss La BRAM/HZG SK7 65 H8
Hall Nook WARRW/BUR WA5 35 M8
Hall O'shaw St CW/HAS CW1 19 J3
Hallows Av WARRN/WOL WA2 37 K4
Hallows Cl TPLY/KEL CW6 149 J8
Hallows Dr TPLY/KEL CW6 149 J8
Hall Rd ALT WA14 61 J3
BRAM/HZG SK7 65 K3
WARR WA1 38 D5
WILM/AE SK9 84 E1
WILM/AE SK9 84 A5
Hallsgreen La CHNE CH2 122 F5
Hallshaw Av CW/HAS CW1 19 K2
Hallside Pk KNUT WA16 107 J3
Halls Rd ALS/KID ST7 226 C6
BIDD ST8 227 J3
Hall St CHD/CHDH SK8 45 K6
MCFLDS SK11 14 E5
NM/HAY SK22 69 H4
STHEL WA9 34 E1
STKP SK1 3 K6
WARR WA1 5 J7
Hall Ter WARRW/BUR WA5 35 L5 5
Hallwood Cl RUNC WA7 73 H6
Hallwood Dr GTS/LS CH66 93 J8
Hallwood Link Rd RUNC WA7 73 L6
Hallwood Park Av RUNC WA7 73 L6
Hallwood Rd NTHM/RTH M23 44 A6
WILM/AE SK9 84 E1
Hall Wood Rd WILM/AE SK9 84 D2
Hallworthy Cl LEIGH WN7 24 B3 2
Halsall Av WARRN/WOL WA2 37 K4
Halsall Cl RUNC WA7 74 C7 4
Halsnead Av RAIN/WH L35 32 C3
Halstead Gv CHD/CHDH SK8 44 F7
Halstone Av WILM/AE SK9 83 L8
Halton Brook Av RUNC WA7 73 K3
Halton Brow RUNC WA7 73 L3
Halton Ct RUNC WA7 73 K2
Halton Crs GTS/LS CH66 120 F2
Halton Dr CW/SHV CW2 220 D7
HALE/TIMP WA15 43 H3
Halton Hey RAIN/WH L35 32 D3
Halton Link Rd RUNC WA7 73 L4
Halton Lodge Av RUNC WA7 73 K5
Halton Rd CHNE CH2 145 M6
GTS/LS CH66 120 E3
RUNC WA7 9 K2
WARRW/BUR WA5 35 M6
Halton Station Rd RUNC WA7 99 M1
Halton View Rd WDN WA8 7 M2
Halton Wy GTS/LS CH66 120 E3
Hambledon Cl GTS/LS CH66 94 A6 1
Hamble Dr WARRW/BUR WA5 54 F1
Hambleton Cl WDN WA8 52 C1 2
Hambleton Dr NTHM/RTH M23 44 A8

Hambleton Pl *BIDD* ST8 .... 227 H7 □
Hambleton Rd *CHD/CHDH* SK8.... 64 C4
Hambleton Wy *WSFD* CW7 ...... 177 G5
Hambletts Hollow
　FROD/HEL WA6 .... 126 F6
Hamble Wy *MCFLDN* SK10 .... 137 L3
　IRL M44 .... 31 K8
Hamilton Cl *CW/HAS* CW1 .... 222 C8
　MCFLDN SK10 .... 139 G4 □
　NSTN CH64 .... 91 H2
Hamilton Crs *HTNM* SK4 .... 46 B3 □
Hamilton Pl *CH/BCN* CH1 .... 16 F5
Hamilton Sq *HTNM* SK4 .... 2 C7
Hamilton St *CHNE* CH2 .... 17 L1
Hammersley Av *STHEL* WA9 .... 34 C1
Hammersley St *STHEL* WA9 .... 34 C1 □
Hammond St *IRL* M44 .... 18 E6
Hamnett Ct *GOL/RIS/CU* WA3 .... 38 E1
Hamon Rd *HALE/TIMP* WA15 ..... 42 F4
Hampden Rd *SALE* M33 .... 43 G1 □
Hampshire Cl *CONG* CW12 .... 184 D8 □
Hampshire Rd *PART* M31 .... 40 D2
Hampson Av
　GOL/RIS/CU WA3 .... 29 M1 □
Hampson Cl *AIMK* WN4 .... 22 B2
Hampson Crs *WILM/AE* SK9 ...... 64 C8
Hampson St *STKP* SK1 .... 3 M8
Hampstead Dr *WSFD* CW7 .... 177 G4 □
Hampstead Dr *OFTN* SK2 .... 47 J7
Hampstead St *OFTN* SK2 .... 47 J7
Hampton Av *CO* CH5 .... 142 E8
Hampton Cl *NSTN* CH64 .... 91 L6 □
　WDN WA8 .... 53 L1 □
　NSTN CH64 .... 91 H2
Hampton Crs *MALPAS* SY14 ...... 247 C8
　WDN WA8 .... 33 J7
Hampton Dr *WARRW/BUR* WA5 ... 36 C8
　IRL M44 .... 31 K8
Hampton Gdns *EP* CH65 .... 10 A7
Hampton Gv *ALT* WA14 .... 42 E3
　CHD/CHDH SK8 .... 64 E2 □
Hampton Rd *CHSW/BR* CH4 ...... 168 F1
　IRL M44 .... 31 K8
Hams Cl *BIDD* ST8 .... 227 H7
Hamsterley Cl *GOL/RIS/CU* WA3 .. 30 B6
Hanbury Cl *CW/SHV* CW2 .... 238 B5
Hancock Rd *CONG* CW12 .... 184 F8
Handbridge *CHSW/BR* CH4 .... 17 G8
Handforth Cl *WARRS* WA4 .... 38 C8
Handforth La *RUNC* WA7 .... 73 K6 □
Handforth Rd *CW/SHV* CW2 ...... 237 L1
　WILM/AE SK9 .... 84 E3
Hand La *LEIGH* WN7 .... 24 E3
Handley Cl *EDGY/DAV* SK3 .... 46 C7
Handley Hl *WSFD* CW7 .... 177 H4
Handley Rd *BRAM/HZG* SK7 ...... 65 L1
Hand St *MCFLDS* SK11 .... 14 D5
Hangman's La *NWCHE* CW9 ...... 131 J5
　MWCH CW10 .... 179 J6
Hankelow Cl *CHNE* CH2 .... 17 G1
Hankey St *RUNC* WA7 .... 8 F2
Hankins Heys La
　AUD/MAD/W CW3 .... 275 G3
Hankinson Cl *PART* M31 .... 40 F2 □
　WDN WA8 .... 52 C3
Hanley Cl *POY/DIS* SK12 .... 68 D7
　WDN WA8 .... 52 C3
Hanley Rd *WDN* WA8 .... 52 C3
Hannesburg Gdns
　NTHM/RTH M23 .... 43 M8 □
Hannet Rd *WYTH/NTH* M22 ...... 63 K3
Hanns Hall Rd *NSTN* CH64 .... 92 C4
Hanover Dr *WSFD* CW7 .... 177 K6 □
Hanover Rd *ALT* WA14 .... 42 B5
Hanover St *WARR* WA1 .... 4 E8
Hanson Ms *STKP* SK1 .... 3 L4
Hanwell Cl *LEIGH* WN7 .... 24 D3
Hapsford Cl *GOL/RIS/CU* WA3 .... 29 J8
Hapsford La *CHNE* CH2 .... 97 K8
　FROD/HEL WA6 .... 123 L3
Hapton Pl *HTNM* SK4 .... 2 E2 □
Harbbour Cl *CHNE* CH2 .... 145 L5 □
Harbord St *WARR* WA1 .... 5 K8
Harbour Cl *MCFLDS* SK11 .... 161 J3
Harbury Crs *WYTH/NTH* M22 .... 44 C7 □
Harcourt Cl *GOL/RIS/CU* WA3 .... 38 E1
Harcourt Rd *ALT* WA14 .... 42 D6
Hardberry Pl *OFTN* SK2 .... 47 L6 □
Hardcastle Rd *EDGY/DAV* SK3.... 46 D5
Harden Pk *WILM/AE* SK9 .... 110 A1
Hardie Cl *STHEL* WA9 .... 34 A1 □
Hardie Rd *HUY* L36 .... 32 A1
Harding Av *CHSE* CH3 .... 214 C2
　WARRW/WOL WA2 .... 37 K3
Harding Rd *CHNE* CH2 .... 145 H4
　NANT CW5 .... 20 B8
Hardings Meadow *ALS/KID* ST7 .. 242 E2
Harding St *STKP* SK1 .... 3 M6
Hardingswood Rd *ALS/KID* ST7 .. 242 E2
Hardman Av *MPL/ROM* SK6 ...... 48 A3 □
Hardman St *EDGY/DAV* SK3 ...... 2 D7
Hardwick Cl *MPL/ROM* SK6....... 67 M6
Hardwick Dr *MCFLDN* SK11 ...... 138 B7
Hardwicke Rd *POY/DIS* SK12 ..... 66 F8
Hardwick Rd *PART* M31 .... 41 G1
　RUNC WA7 .... 73 K1
Hardy Cl *CW/SHV* CW2 .... 237 M4 □
　GTS/LS CH66 .... 120 F1
Hardy Dr *BRAM/HZG* SK7 .... 65 K5
　HALE/TIMP WA15 .... 42 F5
Hardy Rd *LYMM* WA13 .... 58 C2
Hardy St *BURS/TUN* ST6 .... 243 K8 □
　WARRW/WOL WA2 .... 5 H4
Harebell Cl *CHSE* CH3 .... 146 C8
Harecastle Av *ALS/KID* ST7 .... 242 D3
Harefield Dr *DID/WITH* M20 ...... 45 G2
Harefield Gn *SPK/HALE* L24 ...... 70 D1 □
Harefield Rd *SPK/HALE* L24 ...... 70 D1 □
　WILM/AE SK9 .... 64 E8 □
Hare La *CHSE* CH3 .... 146 C8
Hare's La *FROD/HEL* WA6 .... 98 E4
Harewood Av *GTS/LS* CH66 ...... 94 C8
Harewood Cl *WSFD* CW7 .... 177 G3
Harewood Wy *MCFLDS* SK11 .... 138 B7 □
Harfield Gdns *GTS/LS* CH66 ...... 94 C7
Harford Cl *BRAM/HZG* SK7 .... 66 A3 □
Hargate Dr *HALE/TIMP* WA15 .... 62 A3

Hargrave Av *CW/SHV* CW2 .... 237 M1
Hargrave Dr *GTS/LS* CH66 .... 94 E7
Hargreaves Ct *WDN* WA8 .... 53 K3 □
Hargreaves Rd
　HALE/TIMP WA15 .... 43 J6
　NWCHE CW9 .... 130 C4 □
Harington Cl *CHNE* CH2 .... 145 J3
Harington Rd *CHNE* CH2 .... 145 J4
Harland Dr *AIMK* WN4 .... 22 C1 □
Harland Gn *SPK/HALE* L24 .... 71 G1 □
Harlech Cl *WARRW/BUR* WA5 ... 36 E2
Harlech Dr *BIDD* ST8 .... 227 J6
　BRAM/HZG SK7 .... 66 C3
Harlech Wy *EP* CH65 .... 121 K1
Harleen Gv *OFTN* SK2 .... 47 K5
Harling Rd *WYTH/NTH* M22 ...... 44 D5
Harlow Cl *WARRS* WA4 .... 57 J1
Harlyn Av *BRAM/HZG* SK7 .... 65 M5
Harlyn Cl *HLWD* L26 .... 50 E6
Harlyn Gdns
　WARRW/BUR WA5 .... 54 D1 □
The Harn *GTS/LS* CH66 .... 120 C1 □
Harold St *STKP* SK1 .... 3 M8
Harper Cl *GTS/LS* CH66 .... 94 D8
Harper Gv *CONG* CW12 .... 184 E8
Harper Rd *WYTH/NTH* M22 ...... 44 E5
Harpers Rd *WARRN/WOL* WA2 ... 38 A3
Harper St *EDGY/DAV* SK3 .... 2 E9
Harptree Cl *RAIN/WH* L35 .... 32 E1
Harpur Cl *MCFLDS* SK11 .... 15 H8
Harpur Crs *ALS/KID* ST7 .... 224 B7
Harrier Cl *CW/HAS* CW1 .... 220 F5
Harrier Dr *HLWD* L26 .... 50 E3
Harriet St *IRL* M44 .... 31 L1
Harrington Dr *MCFLDS* SK11 .... 161 K3
Harrington Rd *ALT* WA14 .... 42 B7
Harris Cl *CW/HAS* CW1 .... 221 H3
Harriseahead La *ALS/KID* ST7 ... 226 D8
Harrison Dr *HOLMCH* CW4 ...... 157 H3
Harrison Gv *CO* CH5 .... 167 G1
Harrisons Pl *NWCHW* CW8 ...... 12 F3
Harrison St *WDN* WA8 .... 52 B6
Harrison Wy *NEWLW* WA12 ..... 22 C8
Harris Rd *NWCHE* CW9 .... 131 G2
Harris St *WDN* WA8 .... 7 M7
Harrogate St *WARRW/BUR* WA5 . 36 A4
Harrop La *MCFLDN* SK10 .... 86 E7
Harrop Rd *HALE/TIMP* WA15..... 61 M2
　MCFLDN SK10 .... 113 J4
　RUNC WA7 .... 9 J5
Harrop St *STKP* SK1 .... 3 J9
Harrow Cl *CW/SHV* CW2 .... 18 A9
　WARRS WA4 .... 56 E6
Harrow Dr *RUNC* WA7 .... 73 L2
　SALE M33 .... 43 G2
Harrow Rd *EP* CH65 .... 95 K8
　SALE M33 .... 43 G2
Harrow Wy *NWCHE* CW9 .... 153 L1 □
Harry Rowley Cl
　WYTH/NTH M22 .... 63 J2 □
Harrytown *MPL/ROM* SK6 .... 48 A2
Hart Av *SALE* M33 .... 43 M1 □
Hartford Av *WILM/AE* SK9 .... 83 M7 □
Hartford Br *NWCHE* CW9 .... 153 K1
Hartford Dr *EP* CH65 .... 94 F8
Hartford Gdns *HALE/TIMP* WA15 . 43 K7
Hartford Rd *NWCHE* CW9 .... 153 L2
　SALE M33 .... 43 G3
Hartford Wy *CH/BCN* CH1 .... 16 A4
Harthill Cl *CHSE* CH3 .... 214 E8
Harthill Rd *CH/BCN* CH1 .... 144 E6
　CHSE CH3 .... 215 G6
Hartington Dr *BRAM/HZG* SK7 .. 66 E4
Hartington Rd *ALT* WA14 .... 42 D5
　BRAM/HZG SK7 .... 65 L4
　CHD/CHDH SK8 .... 64 D4 □
　MPL/ROM SK6 .... 67 L6
　OFTN SK2 .... 47 K8
Hartland Cl *OFTN* SK2 .... 47 J4 □
　POY/DIS SK12 .... 66 D7 □
　WDN WA8 .... 34 A7
Hartley Cl *LYMM* WA13 .... 58 F1 □
Hartley Gn *MCFLDN* SK10 .... 112 F4 □
Hartley Rd *ALT* WA14 .... 42 C7
Hartley St *EDGY/DAV* SK3 .... 2 C8
Hart St *ALT* WA14 .... 42 D7
Hartswell Cl *GOL/RIS/CU* WA3 .. 23 C2 □
Hartswood Cl *WARRS* WA4 ...... 76 E1
Harvard Cl *RUNC* WA7 .... 74 D2 □
Harvard Ct *WARRN/WOL* WA2 ... 37 L1 □
Harvest Cl *NWCHE* CW9 .... 153 M4
　SALE M33 .... 44 A1 □
Harvest Rd *MCFLDN* SK10 .... 138 C1
Harvey Av *NANT* CW5 .... 21 J5
　NEWLW WA12 .... 26 F1 □
Harvey Ct *GOL/RIS/CU* WA3 ..... 24 B5 □
　WARRN/WOL WA2 .... 37 H1 □
Harvey La *GOL/RIS/CU* WA3 ..... 22 F3
Harvey Rd *CONG* CW12 .... 185 G7
Harvey St *STKP* SK1 .... 3 G5
Harwood Gdns *WARRS* WA4 ..... 57 G2
Harwood Rd *HTNM* SK4 .... 45 L2
Harwoods Cl *WRX/GR/LL* LL12 .. 210 D6
Harwood's La *WRX/GR/LL* LL12 .. 210 D6
Harwood St *HTNM* SK4 .... 2 E2 □
Haryngton Av *WARRW/BUR* WA5 .. 4 C2
Haselwell Cl *POY/DIS* SK12 ...... 66 E7
Haselhurst Wk
　NTHM/RTH M23 .... 43 M2 □
Haslam Rd *EDGY/DAV* SK3 .... 46 E6
Haslemere Av *HALE/TIMP* WA15 . 62 C6
Haslemere Dr *CHD/CHDH* SK8 .. 65 G3
　WARRW/BUR WA5 .... 35 K8
Haslemere Wy *CW/HAS* CW1 ... 221 K6 □
Haslin Crs *CHSE* CH3 .... 170 D5
Haslington Gv *HLWD* L26 .... 51 G6 □
Haslington Rd *WYTH/NTH* M22 .. 63 L2
Hassall Cross La *SBCH* CW11 .... 222 F4
Hassall Rd *ALS/KID* ST7 .... 224 D6
Hassals La *CHNE* CH2 .... 146 F1
Hastings Av *WARRN/WOL* WA2 .. 28 B8
Hastings Cl *CHD/CHDH* SK8 ..... 65 J3
　STKP SK1 .... 3 M9 □
　STKP SK1 .... 47 H5 □

Hastings Dr *HUY* L36 .... 32 A4
Hasty La *HALE/TIMP* WA15 .... 62 F5
　MANAIR M90 .... 62 F4
Hatchery La *WARRS* WA4 .... 57 H8
Hatchett Rd *WYTH/NTH* M22 .... 63 L3
Hatchmere Cl
　HALE/TIMP WA15 .... 43 K6 □
　SBCH CW11 .... 203 M5 □
　WARRW/BUR WA5 .... 4 B5
Hatchmere Dr *CHSE* CH3 .... 170 B4
Hatchmere Rd *CHD/CHDH* SK8.. 45 M8
Hatfield Ct *HOLMCH* CW4 .... 181 G1
Hatfield Gdns *WARRS* WA4 ...... 56 E8
Hathaway Dr *MCFLDS* SK11 ..... 138 C7
Hathaway Gdns *MPL/ROM* SK6 . 47 L1
Hatherlow *MPL/ROM* SK6 .... 48 A2
Hatherlow Ct *BRAM/HZG* SK7 ... 66 D2
Hatherlow La *NWCHE* CW9 ...... 129 M8 □
Hatherton Wy *CHNE* CH2 .... 16 F2
Hatley La *FROD/HEL* WA6 .... 98 F5
Hatton Av *PS/BROM* CH62 .... 93 L1
Hatton La *NWCHW* CW8 .... 12 C7
　WARRS WA4 .... 76 B3
Hatton Rd *CH/BCN* CH1 .... 144 E7
Hatton St *MCFLDS* SK11 .... 14 F7
　STKP SK1 .... 2 A7
Haughton Dr *WYTH/NTH* M22 .. 44 D3 □
Havannah La *CONG* CW12 .... 184 F6
　STHEL WA9 .... 26 B1
Havannah St *CONG* CW12 .... 184 F8
Haveley Rd *WYTH/NTH* M22 ..... 44 C7
Havelock Gv *BIDD* ST8 .... 227 J3
Haven Cl *BRAM/HZG* SK7 .... 66 B3
The Haven *CW/HAS* CW1 .... 221 K5
　HALE/TIMP WA15 .... 61 M1
Havergal St *RUNC* WA7 .... 8 F4
Haverston Dr *WYTH/NTH* M22 .. 63 H2 □
Havisham Cl *GOL/RIS/CU* WA3 .. 29 K7
Hawarden Br *CO* CH5 .... 142 C5
Hawarden Gdns *EP* CH65 .... 121 K2 □
Hawarden Rd *ALT* WA14 .... 42 D6
Hawes Cl *OFTN* SK2 .... 47 G6
Hawes Dr *BURS/TUN* ST6 .... 243 K6
Hawesdraw Gn *OFTN* SK2 .... 47 L6 □
Hawke Gn *HUY* L36 .... 32 A5
Hawkhurst Cl *BRAM/HZG* SK7 .. 167 J8
Hawke St *SBCH* CW11 .... 204 B6 □
Hawkeswick Dr *NTHM/RTH* M23 . 44 A1
Hawkins La *MCFLDN* SK10 ...... 139 K1
Hawkins Rd *NSTN* CH64 .... 91 M3
Hawkins Vw *CHSE* CH3 .... 147 L6
Hawkridge Dr *NTHM/RTH* M23 . 43 M2
Hawk Rd *NM/HAY* SK22 .... 69 K4
Hawks Ct *RUNC* WA7 .... 73 L6
Hawkshaw Cl *GOL/RIS/CU* WA3 . 29 J8
Hawkshead Cl *RUNC* WA7 .... 74 A7 □
Hawkshead Rd
　WARRW/BUR WA5 .... 26 E6
Hawkshead Wy *WSFD* CW7 ..... 177 K2
Hawkstone Gv
　FROD/HEL WA6 .... 98 C8 □
Hawley Dr *HALE/TIMP* WA15 .... 62 B4
Hawley La *HALE/TIMP* WA15 ..... 62 B4
Hawley's La *WARRN/WOL* WA2 .. 37 G3
Haworth Av *CONG* CW12 .... 184 F7
Haworth Cl *MCFLDS* SK11 .... 138 B7 □
　MPL/ROM SK6 .... 48 D6
　NEWLW WA12 .... 27 J1
　RUNC WA7 .... 9 H4
　WDN WA8 .... 53 H2 □
　WILM/AE SK9 .... 84 A5
Hawthorn Cl *CW/HAS* CW1 ...... 221 K5
　HALE/TIMP WA15 .... 42 F5
　HOLMCH CW4 .... 157 K8
　WSFD CW7 .... 177 J1 □
Hawthorn Dr *IRL* M44 .... 31 K7 □
Hawthorne Av *GOL/RIS/CU* WA3 . 50 E6
　HLWD L26 .... 50 E6
　WARR WA1 .... 38 B5
　WARRW/BUR WA5 .... 35 M6
Hawthorne Cl *CONG* CW12 ...... 184 A8
Hawthorne Dr *NSTN* CH64 ...... 93 H4
　SBCH CW11 .... 204 C6
Hawthorne Gv *POY/DIS* SK12 ... 67 J8
　WARR WA1 .... 37 M5 □
　WSFD CW7 .... 178 A3 □
Hawthorne Rd *FROD/HEL* WA6 .. 99 H3
　WARRS WA4 .... 56 C4 □
Hawthorne St *WARRW/BUR* WA5 . 4 E1
Hawthorn Gdns *ALS/KID* ST7 ... 242 D4 □
Hawthorn Gv *BRAM/HZG* SK7 .. 65 J6
　CW/HAS CW1 .... 221 K5
　HTNM SK4 .... 46 B1
　NWCHW CW8 .... 102 F8 □
　SALE M33 .... 56 D3 □
　WILM/AE SK9 .... 84 A5
Hawthorn La *CW/SHV* CW2 ..... 237 M2 □
　WILM/AE SK9 .... 84 A5
Hawthorn Pk *WILM/AE* SK9 ..... 84 A5
Hawthorn Ri *MCFLDN* SK10 ..... 111 L6
Hawthorn Rd *CHD/CHDH* SK8 .. 45 C7
　CHSE CH3 .... 170 E5
　CHSW/BR CH4 .... 168 F7
　GTS/LS CH66 .... 94 C6
　HALE/TIMP WA15 .... 61 L1
　HTNM SK4 .... 45 L2
　KNUT WA16 .... 131 M1 □
　LYMM WA13 .... 58 C3 □
　MCFLDN SK10 .... 112 F4
　NSTN CH64 .... 91 H4
　RUNC WA7 .... 9 G8
Hawthorns *CHSE* CH3 .... 170 A4
Hawthorn Vls *HOLMCH* CW4 .... 181 H1 □
Hawthorn Wk *NWCHE* CW9 .... 130 C1 □
　WILM/AE SK9 .... 84 A5 □

Hawthorn Wy *MCFLDN* SK10 .... 15 K1
Haybarn Rd *NTHM/RTH* M23 .... 44 B5
Hayburn Rd *OFTN* SK2 .... 47 J4
Haycastle Cl *WARRW/BUR* WA5 . 36 E3
Hay Cft *CHD/CHDH* SK8 .... 64 E4
Haycroft *GTS/LS* CH66 .... 120 D2
Haydock Av *SALE* M33 .... 42 B2
Haydock Cl *MCFLDN* SK10 ..... 138 C1 □
Haydock Dr *BRAM/HZG* SK7 .... 66 F2
　HALE/TIMP WA15 .... 43 H7
Haydock Park Gdns
　NEWLW WA12 .... 22 B3
Haydock St *AIMK* WN4 .... 22 B2 □
　NEWLW WA12 .... 22 A8
　WARRN/WOL WA2 .... 5 C5
Haydon Wy *CO* CH5 .... 142 F6 □
Hayes Crs *FROD/HEL* WA6 ...... 99 H3
Hayes Dr *NWCHW* CW8 .... 129 H1
Hayes Pk *CH/BCN* CH1 .... 16 E1
Haye's Rd *IRL* M44 .... 31 L7
Hayfield Cl *MCFLDN* SK10 ...... 138 B1 □
Hayfield Rd *NM/HAY* SK22 ..... 69 L3
　WARR WA1 .... 38 C4
Hayfields *KNUT* WA16 .... 107 J2
Hayfields Gv
　AUD/MAD/W CW3 .... 273 M1 □
Hayfield Wk *HALE/TIMP* WA15 .. 43 J6 □
Hayhead Cl *ALS/KID* ST7 .... 243 H2
Hayhurst Av *MWCH* CW10 ..... 179 J4
Hayhurst Cl *NWCHE* CW9 ...... 13 H3
Hayle Cl *MCFLDN* SK10 .... 137 K3 □
Hayling Cl *CW/HAS* CW1 .... 221 H4
Haymakers Cl *CH/BCN* CH1 .... 144 A4
Haymakers Wy *CH/BCN* CH1 ... 144 A4
Hayman Av *LEIGH* WN7 .... 24 D2
Haymoor Green Rd *NANT* CW5 . 252 E2
Hayside Wk *MALPAS* SY14 ..... 258 A1
Haythorp Av *WYTH/NTH* M22.. 63 L1
Hayton St *KNUT* WA16 .... 106 F3
Haywood Cl *GOL/RIS/CU* WA3 . 23 L3 □
Haywood Crs *RUNC* WA7 .... 74 D2 □
Hazel Av *CHD/CHDH* SK8 ...... 45 L7
　MCFLDN SK10 .... 138 A1 □
　MPL/ROM SK6 .... 48 D2
　RUNC WA7 .... 8 D7
　SALE M33 .... 43 H1 □
Hazelbadge Cl *POY/DIS* SK12 .. 66 C8 □
Hazelbadge Rd *POY/DIS* SK12 .. 66 C8
Hazelborough Cl
　GOL/RIS/CU WA3 .... 30 B6
Hazel Cl *ALS/KID* ST7 .... 243 H1
　GTS/LS CH66 .... 120 F3
　MPL/ROM SK6 .... 48 E8
Hazelcroft *WILM/AE* SK9 .... 110 A4
Hazel Dr *LYMM* WA13 .... 58 F2
　NWCHW CW8 .... 128 D5
　OFTN SK2 .... 47 K6
　POY/DIS SK12 .... 86 F1
　WSFD CW7 .... 177 J4
　WYTH/NTH M22 .... 64 A4
Hazel Gv *ALS/KID* ST7 .... 242 A1
　CW/HAS CW1 .... 221 J5
　GOL/RIS/CU WA3 .... 23 H4
　WARR WA1 .... 38 A4
Hazelhurst Dr *MCFLDN* SK10 .. 113 G4
Hazelhurst Rd *BURS/TUN* ST6 . 243 M6
Hazelmere Cl *NWCHW* CW8 ... 12 A8
Hazel Rd *ALT* WA14 .... 42 D7
　CHD/CHDH SK8 .... 65 H3
　CHSW/BR CH4 .... 168 F7
Hazelshaw La *SBCH* CW11 ..... 182 A8
Hazel St *BRAM/HZG* SK7 .... 66 E1 □
　WARR WA1 .... 5 M3
Hazelton Cl *LEIGH* WN7 .... 24 E3 □
Hazelwell *SALE* M33 .... 43 H1
Hazelwood Cl *STHEL* WA9 ..... 34 B1
Hazelwood Gv *HLWD* L26 ...... 50 D2 □
Hazelwood Ms *WARRS* WA4 ... 57 J3 □
Hazelwood Rd *BRAM/HZG* SK7 . 66 E1 □
　HALE/TIMP WA15 .... 61 L2
　NWCHW CW8 .... 103 H8
　OFTN SK2 .... 47 G8
　WILM/AE SK9 .... 84 D4
Hazlehurst Gv *AIMK* WN4 ...... 22 C1 □
Hazlehurst Rd *ALS/KID* ST7 .... 226 C7
Headland Cl *GOL/RIS/CU* WA3 . 23 L6
Headlands Rd *BRAM/HZG* SK7 . 65 M3
The Headlands *CH/BCN* CH1 ... 17 J5
Headworth Cl *NWCHE* CW9 ... 13 G9
Heald Cl *ALT* WA14 .... 61 J2
Heald Gv *CHD/CHDH* SK8 ..... 64 A3
Heald Rd *ALT* WA14 .... 61 J2
Heald St *NEWLW* WA12 .... 26 F1
　STKP SK1 .... 3 J5
Healey Av *BIDD* ST8 .... 227 H7
Healey Cl *CW/HAS* CW1 .... 221 G4
　NTHM/RTH M23 .... 43 M2
Health St *CO* CH5 .... 142 B6 □
Heapy St *MCFLDS* SK11 .... 15 J8
Hearn's La *NANT* CW5 .... 234 E8
Heath Av *ALS/KID* ST7 .... 224 F5
　GTS/LS CH66 .... 121 G3
　SBCH CW11 .... 204 E6
Heathbank Rd *CHD/CHDH* SK8.. 64 A4
　EDGY/DAV SK3 .... 46 B5
Heath Cl *CHSE* CH3 .... 170 B4
　CHSE CH3 .... 172 B3
Heathcote Gdns
　NWCHE CW9 .... 130 D5 □
Heathcote St *ALS/KID* ST7 ..... 242 F3
Heath Ct *ALS/KID* ST7 .... 224 E6
Heath Crs *EDGY/DAV* SK3 ...... 46 F7
Heath Dr *CHSE* CH3 .... 172 B3
　RUNC WA7 .... 9 G8
Heath End Rd *ALS/KID* ST7 .... 224 B6
Heather Av *IRL* M44 .... 31 K6
Heather Brae *NEWLW* WA12 ... 22 A8
Heather Cl *GOL/RIS/CU* WA3 .. 29 K7
　GTS/LS CH66 .... 120 C1
　MCFLDS SK11 .... 162 C1
　RUNC WA7 .... 73 L7
Heatherfield Ct *WILM/AE* SK9 .. 84 E4
Heathergate Pl
　CW/SHV CW2 .... 238 B4 □

Heather Gld
　AUD/MAD/W CW3 .... 267 K5 □
Heather Rd *ALT* WA14 .... 61 L3
Heatherside *ALS/KID* ST7 .... 226 C7
The Heathers *OFTN* SK2 .... 47 H8 □
Heather Wy *MPL/ROM* SK6 .... 48 E7
Heatherways *TPLY/KEL* CW6 ... 197 J1
Heath Farm La *PART* M31 ...... 41 G1
Heathfield *WILM/AE* SK9 .... 84 A7
Heathfield Av *CHD/CHDH* SK8 . 45 H7
　CW/HAS CW1 .... 18 D3
Heathfield Cl *CONG* CW12 ..... 206 F1
　NANT CW5 .... 21 H4
　SALE M33 .... 43 M1
Heathfield Pk *WARRS* WA4 .... 57 G2
　WDN WA8 .... 52 D1
Heathfield Rd
　AUD/MAD/W CW3 .... 264 A1
　EP CH65 .... 10 D7
　OFTN SK2 .... 46 F6
Heathfields Cl *CHNE* CH2 ...... 17 G1
Heathfield Sq *KNUT* WA16 ..... 106 F2 □
Heathgate Av *SPK/HALE* L24 ... 71 G2
Heath Gn *TPLY/KEL* CW6 ...... 174 C8
Heath Gv *GTS/LS* CH66 .... 94 B5
Heathlands Rd *GTS/LS* CH66 .. 94 B5
Heathland Ter *EDGY/DAV* SK3 . 46 C5
Heath La *CHNE* CH2 .... 121 L5
　CHSE CH3 .... 147 L6
　CHSE CH3 .... 170 A4
　GOL/RIS/CU WA3 .... 23 K6
　GOL/RIS/CU WA3 .... 29 G2
　GTS/LS CH66 .... 94 A5
　KNUT WA16 .... 58 D8
　KNUT WA16 .... 132 F5
　NSTN CH64 .... 93 J4
　NWCHE CW9 .... 102 B5
　NWCHE CW9 .... 104 A3
　WHITCH SY13 .... 260 E6
Heathmoor Av *GOL/RIS/CU* WA3 . 3 K6
Heath Park Gv *RUNC* WA7 ..... 8 F1
Heath Rd *AIMK* WN4 .... 22 B2
　ALT WA14 .... 61 K2
　CHNE CH2 .... 145 K5
　CONG CW12 .... 207 G2
　EDGY/DAV SK3 .... 46 F6
　HALE/TIMP WA15 .... 42 F4
　MCFLDN SK10 .... 112 C6
　NWCHW CW8 .... 128 E3
　RUNC WA7 .... 9 J7
　SBCH CW11 .... 204 D6
　WARRW/BUR WA5 .... 35 M7
　WDN WA8 .... 6 B1
　WHITCH SY13 .... 270 B8
Heath Road Crs *RUNC* WA7 ... 9 J5
Heath Rd South *RUNC* WA7 ... 9 G9
Heathside *NANT* CW5 .... 21 G5
Heathside La *BURS/TUN* ST6 ... 243 H5
Heathside Park Rd
　EDGY/DAV SK3 .... 45 M5
Heathside Rd *EDGY/DAV* SK3 .. 46 A5
Heaths La *TPLY/KEL* CW6 ...... 174 C2
Heath St *AIMK* WN4 .... 22 C2 □
　BIDD ST8 .... 227 J5
　BURS/TUN ST6 .... 243 J5
　CW/HAS CW1 .... 19 G3
　GOL/RIS/CU WA3 .... 23 G4
　WARRS WA4 .... 56 C4
Heathview Rd *WDN* WA8 ...... 52 A8
Heath Wy *TPLY/KEL* CW6 ...... 197 K4
Heathwood Dr *ALS/KID* ST7 ... 224 F7
Heathwood Gv *WARR* WA1 .... 38 B5
Heatley Cl *LYMM* WA13 .... 40 F3 □
Heatley La *NANT* CW5 .... 250 F8
Heaton Av *BRAM/HZG* SK7 .... 65 K1
Heaton Cl *MWCH* CW10 .... 179 J6
　SPK/HALE L24 .... 70 F1
Heaton Ct *GTS/LS* CH66 .... 94 C8
Heaton La *HTNM* SK4 .... 2 D5
Heaton Moor Rd *HTNM* SK4 ... 46 B1
Heaton Rd *HTNM* SK4 .... 2 B1
Heaton Sq *WSFD* CW7 .... 177 J4 □
Heaviley Gv *OFTN* SK2 .... 47 G6
Heaward Cl *CW/SHV* CW2 ..... 238 B8 □
Hebden Av *GOL/RIS/CU* WA3 .. 25 H8
Heber's Cl *MALPAS* SY14 ...... 246 C1
Heddon Cl *HTNM* SK4 .... 45 L1
Hedge Hey *RUNC* WA7 .... 74 A1
Hedge Rw *MCFLDN* SK10 ..... 113 K3
Hedgerow Dr *NWCHE* CW9 ... 130 C1 □
Hedingham Cl *HLWD* L26 ...... 51 G3
　MCFLDN SK10 .... 137 M4 □
Hefferston Grange Dr
　NWCHW CW8 .... 128 A5
Hefferston Ri *NWCHW* CW8 ... 128 A5
Heighley Castle Wy
　AUD/MAD/W CW3 .... 267 L3
Heighley La *AUD/MAD/W* CW3.. 267 L1
The Heights *FROD/HEL* WA6 ... 98 C8 □
Helena Cl *KNUT* WA16 .... 107 J2
Helen St *GOL/RIS/CU* WA3 ..... 22 F2
Hellath Wen *NANT* CW5 .... 251 J2
Hell Nook *GOL/RIS/CU* WA3 .. 22 E3
Hellyar-brook Rd *ALS/KID* ST7 . 224 B8
Helmsdale Cl *CW/HAS* CW1 ... 221 H6 □
Helmsdale La *WARRW/BUR* WA5 . 36 C6
Helmsley Cl *WARRW/BUR* WA5 . 4 B2
Helmsley Rd *HLWD* L26 .... 50 F5
Helsby Av *PS/BROM* CH62 .... 93 M1
Helsby Rd *FROD/HEL* WA6 ..... 124 C3
　SALE M33 .... 43 L2
Helsby St *WARR* WA1 .... 5 M4
Helston Av *HLWD* L26 .... 50 F3
Helston Cl *BRAM/HZG* SK7 .... 65 M5 □
　RUNC WA7 .... 74 B7
　WARRW/BUR WA5 .... 35 L7 □
Helston Gv *CHD/CHDH* SK8 ... 64 C4
Helton Cl *HOLMCH* CW4 ...... 181 G1
Hemingford Cl *GTS/LS* CH66 .. 120 D2 □
Hemlegh Vw *FROD/HEL* WA6 .. 124 B3
Hemmingshaw La *SBCH* CW11.. 205 H4
Hemming St *NWCHW* CW8 .... 129 K3 □
Hempcroft Rd *HALE/TIMP* WA15 . 43 J7
Hempshaw La *STKP* SK1 .... 3 K8
Hemsworth Av *GTS/LS* CH66 .. 94 C7
Henbury Cl *MWCH* CW10 ..... 179 J5
Henbury La *CHD/CHDH* SK8 .. 64 F6
Henbury Pl *RUNC* WA7 .... 73 H6

Henbury Ri MCFLDS SK11 137 J4
Henbury Rd WILM/AE SK9 64 D8 4
Henbury St OFTN SK2 47 J8
Henderson Cl WARRW/BUR WA5 35 K6
Henderson Rd HUY L36 32 A1
WDN WA8 6 F4
Henderson St MCFLDS SK11 14 F6
Hendham Cl BRAM/HZG SK7 66 A2 1
Hendham Dr ALT WA14 42 B6
Hendon Cl CW/HAS CW1 19 L1
Hendon Dr EDGY/DAV SK3 46 A5 2
Henley Av BIDD ST8 227 G6
CHD/CHDH SK8 64 F2
IRL M44 31 L6
Henley Cl NSTN CH64 91 L6
WARRS WA4 56 E6
Henley Ct RUNC WA7 73 K2 1
Henley Dr HALE/TIMP WA15 42 F5
WSFD CW7 177 M3 2
Henley Mnr GOL/RIS/CU WA3 24 D8
Henley Rd CHSW/BR CH4 168 F6
NSTN CH64 91 L6
Henrietta St CQ CH5 142 B6
Henry Pl CH/BCN CH1 17 G3
Henry St BURS/TUN ST6 243 K8
CW/HAS CW1 19 H2
CW/HAS CW1 222 D8
LEIGH WN7 25 G1
LYMM WA13 58 E1 3
STKP SK1 3 L7
TPLY/KEL CW6 197 J2 1
WARR WA1 4 E7
WDN WA8 7 M2 1
Henry Taylor St FLINT CH6 116 B5
Henry Wood Ct CHSW/BR CH4 168 E6
Henshall Av WARRS WA4 37 M8
Henshall Dr SBCH CW11 204 D4 2
Henshall Hall Dr CONG CW12 208 B3
Henshall La ALT WA14 41 J5
Henshall Pl BURS/TUN ST6 243 K6
Henshall Rd MCFLDN SK10 112 E5
Henshall St CH/BCN CH1 16 E2
Henshaw La MCFLDS SK11 160 E1
Henson Gv HALE/TIMP WA15 43 G8
Heol-y-bryn FLINT CH6 116 B8 4
Hepherd St WARRW/BUR WA5 36 D8 5
Hepley Rd POY/DIS SK12 87 G1
Hepple Cl HTNM SK4 45 M1 1
Hepworth Cl GOL/RIS/CU WA3 22 F2 2
Herald Pk CW/HAS CW1 19 J6
Heralds Cl WDN WA8 52 B4
Heralds Gn WARRW/BUR WA5 36 A2
Herbert St CONG CW12 207 L1
CW/HAS CW1 222 A7
EDGY/DAV SK3 2 D9
NWCHE CW9 131 G2
WARRW/BUR WA5 26 E6 2
Herdman St CW/SHV CW2 19 G7
Hereford Av GOL/RIS/CU WA3 23 H4 1
GTS/LS CH66 120 E4
Hereford Cl AIMK WN4 22 C2 5
WARR WA1 38 D5 1
Hereford Dr WILM/AE SK9 84 E1
Hereford Pl CH/BCN CH1 145 G8 1
Hereford Rd CHD/CHDH SK8 46 A8 1
Hereford Wy MWCH CW10 179 K2
Hereward Rd CHSE CH3 170 B3
Heritage Gdns DID/WITH M20 45 H2
Herle Dr WYTH/NTH M22 63 J3 4
Hermitage Av MPL/ROM SK6 48 F2
Hermitage Ct CH/BCN CH1 144 A4
Hermitage Dr HOLMCH CW4 157 K8
Hermitage Gdns
MPL/ROM SK6 48 F2 2
Hermitage Green La
WARRN/WOL WA2 28 A4
Hermitage La HOLMCH CW4 157 J4
Hermitage Rd CH/BCN CH1 144 A4
HALE/TIMP WA15 62 A1
Heronbrook WHITCH SY13 269 K4
Heron Cl AUD/MAD/W CW3 267 M5 4
CHSE CH3 228 F3 1
CHSW/BR CH4 167 H8
KNUT WA16 107 H1
RUNC WA7 74 D4 2
WSFD CW7 177 K7 1
Heron Ct HLWD L26 50 E3
NSTN CH64 91 J5
Heron Crs CW/HAS CW1 19 M2
Heron Dr POY/DIS SK12 86 A1
Heron Pl CHNE CH2 16 F2
Heron St EDGY/DAV SK3 2 D8
Herons Wy CHSW/BR CH4 192 B1
RUNC WA7 54 F8 1
Herrick Cl CW/SHV CW2 238 A4
Hertford Cl CONG CW12 184 E8
HLWD L26 50 F5
WARR WA1 38 E5
Hertford Gv IRL M44 31 J6
Hesketh Av DID/WITH M20 45 G1
Hesketh Cl WARRW/BUR WA5 35 M8
Hesketh Cft CW/HAS CW1 221 G4
Hesketh Dr NWCHE CW9 131 G1
Hesketh Meadow La
GOL/RIS/CU WA3 24 A4
Hesketh Rd SALE M33 42 F1 1
SPK/HALE L24 71 L2
Hesketh St North
WARRW/BUR WA5 36 D8 6
Hesketh St HTNM SK4 2 E2 3
WARRW/BUR WA5 36 D8 7
Heskin Cl RAIN/WH L35 33 H1
Hesnall Cl GOL/RIS/CU WA3 25 J4
Heswall Av GOL/RIS/CU WA3 29 L1
Heswall Rd GTS/LS CH66 94 D8 5
Hetherson Green La
MALPAS SY14 247 K4
Hever Dr HLWD L26 51 G3
Hewetson Crs MCFLDS SK11 137 L5
Hewitt Dr WSFD CW7 178 D4
Hewitt Gv NWCHE CW9 104 F7
Hewitt St BURS/TUN ST6 243 M6
CHNE CH2 17 M2
CW/SHV CW2 19 H8
NWCHE CW9 130 D2
WARRS WA4 56 C1
Hexham Cl OFTN SK2 47 L7 1
Hexham Wy MCFLDN SK10 112 C8
Heybridge La MCFLDN SK10 112 B5
Heybrook Rd NTHM/RTH M23 44 B7
Heyes Av HALE/TIMP WA15 43 H5 1
Heyes Dr HALE/TIMP WA15 43 H5
LYMM WA13 58 C2
Heyes Farm Rd MCFLDS SK11 137 L4 3
Heyes La HALE/TIMP WA15 43 H4
WARRS WA4 56 E4
WILM/AE SK9 110 B2
Heyes Mt RAIN/WH L35 33 J2
Heyes Pk NWCHW CW8 128 F8
Heyes Rd WDN WA8 52 C4
The Heyes WLTN L25 50 B2
Heyeswood La NWCHW CW8 129 G8
Heyfield Park Rd
GTS/LS CH66 94 B5 1
Heyland Rd NTHM/RTH M23 44 A6
Hey Lock Cl NEWLW WA12 27 J4 1
Heyridge Dr WYTH/NTH M22 44 D3
Heys Av MPL/ROM SK6 48 E1
NTHM/RTH M23 44 A3
Heysbank Rd POY/DIS SK12 68 D7
Heyscroft Rd HTNM SK4 46 A2
WLTN L25 50 B2
Heysham Cl RUNC WA7 74 C6
Heysham Rd NTHLY L27 32 A8 2
Hey Shoot La GOL/RIS/CU WA3 25 J7
Heys La MPL/ROM SK6 48 E1
Heysoms Av NWCHW CW8 12 C5
Heysoms Cl NWCHW CW8 12 C6 1
The Heys RUNC WA7 73 L3 1
Heywood Av GOL/RIS/CU WA3 23 H3
Hey Wood Cl NEWLW WA12 27 J4 2
Heywood Cl WILM/AE SK9 110 B2
Heywood Gdns RAIN/WH L35 32 E2
Heywood La AUD/MAD/W CW3 273 K4
WHITCH SY13 273 H5
Heywood Rd GTS/LS CH66 94 D7
SALE M33 43 H1
WILM/AE SK9 110 B2
Heywoods Rdg
AUD/MAD/W CW3 273 L2
The Heywoods CHNE CH2 145 J8
Heyworth Av MPL/ROM SK6 48 D1
Hibbert La MPL/ROM SK6 48 F7
Hibbert St NM/HAY SK22 69 H6 2
WDN WA8 7 J4
Hibel Rd MCFLDN SK10 15 G4
Hickhurst La TPLY/KEL CW6 198 B1
Hickmore Heys CHSE CH3 146 F8 1
Hickory Cl WARR WA1 38 E5
Hickson St NWCHW CW8 129 H1
Hickton Dr ALT WA14 42 B6
Hidcote Cl CW/SHV CW2 238 B4 6
Hidden Hills AUD/MAD/W CW3 267 L4
Hield Brow NWCHE CW9 104 C5
Hield Gv NWCHE CW9 104 C4
Hield La NWCHE CW9 104 C5
Higginbotham Gn
MCFLDS SK11 15 J9 2
Higham Av WARRW/BUR WA5 36 F3
High Bank ALT WA14 42 D7
High Bank Cl IRL M44 31 K6
Highbank Cl NWCHW CW8 129 H1
Highbank Dr DID/WITH M20 45 H4
Highbank Rd FROD/HEL WA6 126 C2
NWCHW CW8 12 D5
High Bank Side STKP SK1 3 G5
High Bent Av CHD/CHDH SK8 65 G6
Highcliffe Av CH/BCN CH1 145 H8
High Crest Av CHD/CHDH SK8 44 F7
Highcroft CQ CH5 142 A7
Highcroft Av CONG CW12 207 M2
Highcroft Rd MPL/ROM SK6 48 C1
High Cross La MALPAS SY14 230 D3 1
Highdales Rd NTHM/RTH M23 44 B7
High Elm Dr HALE/TIMP WA15 62 C4
High Elm Rd HALE/TIMP WA15 62 C4
High Elms CHD/CHDH SK8 65 H7
Higher Ash Rd ALS/KID ST7 242 D4
Higher Ashton WDN WA8 52 F1
Higher Barlow Rw STKP SK1 3 H7
Higher Bents La
MPL/ROM SK6 47 M1 4
Higher Bury St HTNM SK4 2 C4
Higher Carden La MALPAS SY14 230 D6
Higher Downs ALT WA14 61 J1
KNUT WA16 107 J3
Higher Fence Rd MCFLDN SK10 15 M2
Higher Heyes Dr
FROD/HEL WA6 126 B4
Higher Hillgate STKP SK1 3 H7
Higher La CHF/WBR SK23 114 D1
LYMM WA13 59 G3
LYMM WA13 59 J3
MCFLDN SK10 113 H6
POY/DIS SK12 88 E4
WARRS WA4 101 H1
Higher Rd HLWD L26 50 E5
SPK/HALE L24 51 H7
High Fld ALT WA14 60 B2
Highfield CHNE CH2 97 H8
CQ CH5 166 C4 1
MCFLDN SK10 112 A7
SALE M33 43 J1
Highfield Av ALS/KID ST7 243 H2
AUD/MAD/W CW3 264 A7
GOL/RIS/CU WA3 22 F4 2
LEIGH WN7 25 J1
MPL/ROM SK6 47 M2
NWCHE CW9 131 G1 1
WARRS WA4 56 D8
WARRW/BUR WA5 36 A7
Highfield Cl EDGY/DAV SK3 46 F8
NSTN CH64 91 L4
Highfield Crs WDN WA8 7 G1
WILM/AE SK9 84 C3
Highfield Dr LYMM WA13 58 C2
MCFLDN SK10 14 B2
NANT CW5 21 H4
Highfield Est WILM/AE SK9 84 C3
Highfield La CHSE CH3 212 E8
GOL/RIS/CU WA3 23 J7
WARRN/WOL WA2 28 C4
Highfield Pk HTNM SK4 45 M2
Highfield Pkwy BRAM/HZG SK7 65 K8
Highfield Rd BRAM/HZG SK7 65 M1
CH/BCN CH1 144 D7
CHD/CHDH SK8 64 F3
CONG CW12 207 L3
GTS/LS CH66 94 B6
HALE/TIMP WA15 43 H7
HALE/TIMP WA15 62 A2
LYMM WA13 58 C2
MCFLDN SK10 113 G4
MPL/ROM SK6 48 F6 5
NSTN CH64 91 L4
NWCHW CW8 13 G3
POY/DIS SK12 66 A8 1
WDN WA8 6 F2
Highfield Rd East BIDD ST8 227 K5
Highfield Rd North EP CH65 10 E7
Highfield Rd West BIDD ST8 227 K4
Highfields WHITCH SY13 268 A1
Highfields Av WHITCH SY13 269 M6
Highfield St EDGY/DAV SK3 2 A7
Highfield Ter NM/HAY SK22 69 K4
Highgate Cl CW/HAS CW1 221 G4 5
Highgate Rd ALT WA14 42 B8
High Gates Cl WARRW/BUR WA5 4 B3
High Grove Rd CHD/CHDH SK8 45 J7
High Hill Rd NM/HAY SK22 69 K3
Highland Av CQ CH5 166 A1
Highlands Dr OFTN SK2 47 M6
Highlands Rd OFTN SK2 47 M6
RUNC WA7 8 F8
The Highlands TPLY/KEL CW6 216 E4
Highland Wy KNUT WA16 107 G5
High Lea CHD/CHDH SK8 45 J7
High Lee Rd NM/HAY SK22 69 G4
High Legh Rd LYMM WA13 59 J4
High Lowe Av CONG CW12 185 G8
Highmarsh Crs NEWLW WA12 22 B7
High Meadow CHD/CHDH SK8 64 E4 1
High Mdw MPL/ROM SK6 48 C1
Highoaks Rd WLTN L25 50 B3
High Pk CQ CH5 166 C3
High St ALS/KID ST7 226 D5
ALS/KID ST7 242 D7
ALS/KID ST7 243 L2
ALT WA14 42 D8
BIDD ST8 227 J5
BRAM/HZG SK7 66 F2
BURS/TUN ST6 243 K8
BURS/TUN ST6 243 K6
CHD/CHDH SK8 45 K6
CHSE CH3 172 B2
CHSE CH3 214 A3
CHSE CH3 228 E2
CHSW/BR CH4 168 E6
CW/SHV CW2 19 G5
FROD/HEL WA6 99 H3
FROD/HEL WA6 126 F6
GOL/RIS/CU WA3 23 G4
MALPAS SY14 246 B8
MCFLDN SK10 113 H4
MCFLDS SK11 15 H9
NEWLW WA12 22 D8
NM/HAY SK22 69 J4
NSTN CH64 91 L5
NWCHE CW9 104 A5
NWCHW CW8 128 C3
RUNC WA7 8 F2
SBCH CW11 204 B6
SPK/HALE L24 71 K3
STKP SK1 3 G5
TPLY/KEL CW6 173 K8
TPLY/KEL CW6 197 J2
WARR WA1 5 J5
WHITCH SY13 270 A4
WLTN L25 50 A2
WSFD CW7 177 J3
High Street (Sandyford)
BURS/TUN ST6 243 K7
Hightown CW/HAS CW1 18 E2
MWCH CW10 179 J3
SBCH CW11 204 B6 4
Hightree Dr MCFLDS SK11 137 H4
High Vw ALS/KID ST7 226 B7
FROD/HEL WA6 98 C8
The Highway CQ CH5 166 A3
High Wood Fold MPL/ROM SK6 49 J4
Highwood Rd WARRS WA4 56 C5
Higifield Av SALE M33 43 J1
Hignett Av STHEL WA9 26 A2
Higson Av MPL/ROM SK6 47 M2
Hilary Av CHD/CHDH SK8 64 D4
GOL/RIS/CU WA3 23 K3
Hilary Cl CHSE CH3 170 B3
HTNM SK4 2 C3
WARRW/BUR WA5 35 K6
WDN WA8 53 L1
Hilary Rd WYTH/NTH M22 63 H3
Hilbre Bank TPLY/KEL CW6 198 D8
Hilbre Dr EP CH65 121 J3
Hilda Av CHD/CHDH SK8 45 L7
Hilden Rd WARRN/WOL WA2 37 L3
Hilditch Cl NTHM/RTH M23 44 B6 3
Hillary Av CONG CW12 208 A2
Hillary Dr AUD/MAD/W CW3 264 A8
Hillary Rd ALS/KID ST7 243 H1
Hillberry Crs WARRS WA4 56 B1
Hillbrook Rd BRAM/HZG SK7 65 K6
STKP SK1 47 J4 3
Hillbury Rd BRAM/HZG SK7 65 M3
Hill Cliffe Rd WARRS WA4 56 B4 1
Hill Cl NSTN CH64 92 A7
Hill Ct NSTN CH64 92 B7
Hill Court Ms MPL/ROM SK6 48 B2 2
Hillcourt Rd MPL/ROM SK6 67 L5
Hillcrest Av HOLMCH CW4 181 H1
Hill Crest Av HTNM SK4 46 A2
Hillcrest Av HUY L36 32 A2
Hillcrest Dr GTS/LS CH66 94 A6
Hillcrest Rd BRAM/HZG SK7 65 M3
GTS/LS CH66 94 B6
MCFLDN SK10 112 F5
MCFLDS SK11 138 A8 1
OFTN SK2 47 J6
TPLY/KEL CW6 149 L6
Hillcroft OFTN SK2 47 L6
Hillcroft Rd ALT WA14 42 A7
Hill Dr CHF/WBR SK23 89 K4
WILM/AE SK9 84 E1
Hillend Pl NTHM/RTH M23 44 A2 3
Hillend Rd NTHM/RTH M23 44 A2
Hillesden Ri CONG CW12 207 M2 2
Hillewood Av WHITCH SY13 269 M6
Hillfeild Vw NANT CW5 20 F9
Hillfield FROD/HEL WA6 99 H5
RUNC WA7 74 D4
Hillfield Gdns NANT CW5 20 F8
Hillfield Pl NANT CW5 20 F8
Hillfield Rd GTS/LS CH66 94 D5
Hill Flds CONG CW12 207 K1
Hillfields CONG CW12 207 K1
Hillfoot Av WLTN L25 50 B6
Hillfoot Crs WARRS WA4 56 B5
Hillfoot Gn WLTN L25 50 A5
Hillfoot La FROD/HEL WA6 125 L1
Hillfoot Rd WLTN L25 50 C6
Hillingden Av HLWD L26 50 F5
Hillington Rd EDGY/DAV SK3 2 A8
Hill La CHSE CH3 215 J6
CHSE CH3 231 J4
Hillock La WARR WA1 38 C4
Hill Ri ALT WA14 42 A7
MPL/ROM SK6 48 B2
Hill Rd CHSW/BR CH4 192 E3
Hill Rd North FROD/HEL WA6 124 D1
Hillsboro Av FROD/HEL WA6 99 J5
Hillsdown Wy GTS/LS CH66 120 C2
Hillside CQ CH5 166 C3
LYMM WA13 59 K3
NWCHW CW8 12 B5
Hillside Av ALS/KID ST7 243 G5
NEWLW WA12 26 F2
RUNC WA7 8 D7
Hillside Cl ALS/KID ST7 226 D5
BRAM/HZG SK7 66 A5 1
FROD/HEL WA6 98 D8 1
POY/DIS SK12 68 D6
Hillside Dr CW/HAS CW1 19 K1
GTS/LS CH66 94 E5
MCFLDN SK10 139 G3
WLTN L25 50 B1
Hillside Gv MPL/ROM SK6 49 H3
WARRW/BUR WA5 35 M7
Hillside La NWCHE CW9 153 L5 1
Hillside Rd CH/BCN CH1 144 E8
FROD/HEL WA6 99 J5
HALE/TIMP WA15 62 A1
KNUT WA16 107 G2
OFTN SK2 47 K5
TPLY/KEL CW6 149 K8
WARRS WA4 76 C1
Hillside Vw NM/HAY SK22 69 G4
Hill St CW/HAS CW1 19 G3
MCFLDS SK11 15 G8
MPL/ROM SK6 48 B2
RUNC WA7 9 H3
SBCH CW11 203 K5
WARR WA1 5 G6
WSFD CW7 177 M3
The Hill SBCH CW11 204 D7
Hill Top HALE/TIMP WA15 62 A3
MPL/ROM SK6 48 B1
NWCHW CW8 129 H1 1
Hilltop RUNC WA7 74 C5
Hill Top Av CHD/CHDH SK8 65 H3
WILM/AE SK9 84 B4
WSFD CW7 177 J3
Hill Top Ct CHD/CHDH SK8 65 H3 4
Hill Top Dr HALE/TIMP WA15 62 A2
Hilltop Dr MPL/ROM SK6 48 C6
Hill Top La NSTN CH64 92 B7
Hill Top Ri CHF/WBR SK23 89 J4
Hilltop Rd CHSE CH3 146 F7
LYMM WA13 58 C2
Hill Top Rd NWCHW CW8 127 M1
WARR WA1 38 C4
WARRS WA4 56 F2
WARRS WA4 101 J3
Hill Vw CHF/WBR SK23 89 J4
MCFLDN SK10 112 F5
WDN WA8 33 M7
Hill View Av FROD/HEL WA6 124 A3
Hillview Cl FROD/HEL WA6 99 J5
Hillview Ri NWCHW CW8 12 E1
Hilton Av WARRW/BUR WA5 36 B7 3
Hilton Cl MCFLDS SK11 137 M5 1
MWCH CW10 179 H4
Hilton Dr IRL M44 31 J7
Hilton Gv POY/DIS SK12 66 D8
Hilton Rd BRAM/HZG SK7 65 M2
POY/DIS SK12 67 J7
Hilton St AIMK WN4 22 B1
EDGY/DAV SK3 2 D7
Hinchley Cl NWCHW CW8 128 F8
Hinderton La NSTN CH64 92 A3
Hinderton Rd NSTN CH64 92 A4
Hinde St NANT CW5 20 C8
Hind Heath La SBCH CW11 203 M8
Hind Heath Rd SBCH CW11 203 L8
Hindle Av WARRW/BUR WA5 36 F3 1
Hindley Av WYTH/NTH M22 63 H2
Hindley Crs NWCHW CW8 129 G1
Hindley St STKP SK1 3 H8
Hindsford Cl NTHM/RTH M23 43 K3
Hinton Crs WARRS WA4 56 E4
Hinton Rd CW/SHV CW2 238 D4
RUNC WA7 9 H5
Hitchen's Cl RUNC WA7 74 D5 4
Hitchens La MALPAS SY14 232 D3
Hitch Lowes MCFLDS SK11 109 G8
Hobart Cl BRAM/HZG SK7 65 M7
Hobb La WARRS WA4 55 J7
Hobbs Cl CW/HAS CW1 222 C8
Hobbs Hill La KNUT WA16 78 E3
Hobby Ct RUNC WA7 73 L6 1
Hobcroft La KNUT WA16 81 M5
Hob Hey La GOL/RIS/CU WA3 24 D8
Hob La CHNE CH2 123 G5
CHSE CH3 211 M7
Hobson St MCFLDS SK11 15 G8
Hockenhull Av CHSE CH3 172 B3
Hockenhull Cl WYTH/NTH M22 63 L2 1
Hockenhull Crs CHSE CH3 172 B2
Hockenhull La CHSE CH3 172 B3
Hocker La MCFLDN SK10 110 B7
Hockerley Av CHF/WBR SK23 89 K4
Hockerley Cl CHF/WBR SK23 89 K4 1
Hockerley La CHF/WBR SK23 89 K4
Hockley Cl POY/DIS SK12 86 F1
Hockley Rd NTHM/RTH M23 43 M6
POY/DIS SK12 86 F1
Hodder Bank OFTN SK2 47 L7
Hodgehill La MCFLDS SK11 159 L8
Hodge La NWCHW CW8 128 D7
Hodgkinson Av
WARRW/BUR WA5 36 F3
Hodgson Dr HALE/TIMP WA15 43 G4 2
Hodnet Dr AIMK WN4 22 C1
Hogarth Rd MPL/ROM SK6 49 H4
Hoghton Rd SPK/HALE L24 71 L3
Hogshead La NWCHW CW8 151 J4
Holbein Cl CHSW/BR CH4 169 K6
Holborn Ct WDN WA8 52 F1
Holborn St STKP SK1 3 G6 1
The Holborn AUD/MAD/W CW3 267 L6
Holbrook Cl WARRW/BUR WA5 35 L7
Holbury Cl CW/HAS CW1 221 H4 1
Holcet Dr ALT WA14 42 B7 3
Holcombe Av GOL/RIS/CU WA3 23 J4
Holcombe Cl ALT WA14 42 B6 5
Holcombe Dr MCFLDN SK10 138 B1 2
Holcroft La GOL/RIS/CU WA3 30 C1
Holdings La AUD/MAD/W CW3 266 F8
Hole House Fold
MPL/ROM SK6 48 B2 3
Holehouse La ALS/KID ST7 225 K4
MCFLDN SK10 112 C2
MCFLDS SK11 139 J8
Hole House La NWCHW CW8 102 E8
Holes La WARR WA1 38 B5
Holford Av NWCHE CW9 131 G1
WARRW/BUR WA5 4 C1
Holford Crs KNUT WA16 107 G3
Holford St CONG CW12 207 K1
Holford Wy NEWLW WA12 27 M1
Holgrave Cl KNUT WA16 59 J8
Holiday La OFTN SK2 47 M6
Holker Cl POY/DIS SK12 66 F8
Holkham Cl WDN WA8 6 E3
Holland Cl SBCH CW11 204 C7
Holland Rd BRAM/HZG SK7 65 L5
HLWD L26 50 E6
SPK/HALE L24 70 E2
Hollands La TPLY/KEL CW6 149 J7
Hollands Pl MCFLDS SK11 15 L7 1
Hollands Rd NWCHE CW9 13 H5
Holland St CW/HAS CW1 221 H6
MCFLDS SK11 14 F7 2
Holland Wy HLWD L26 50 E6
Hollies Dr MPL/ROM SK6 49 G7
Hollies La WILM/AE SK9 84 F5
Hollies Rd HLWD L26 50 F5
The Hollies DID/WITH M20 44 F1
NWCHE CW9 153 L4 1
Holliney Av WYTH/NTH M22 63 M3
Holliney Rd WYTH/NTH M22 63 M3
Hollingford Pl KNUT WA16 106 F4
Hollin Green La NANT CW5 234 D6
Hollingreen La NANT CW5 263 G4
Hollingwood Cl AIMK WN4 22 A1 1
Hollingworth Dr MPL/ROM SK6 67 M1
Hollin La MCFLDS SK11 163 H4
NANT CW5 262 D4
WILM/AE SK9 63 M7
Hollin Rd MCFLDN SK10 113 G5
Hollins Crs ALS/KID ST7 242 E3
Hollinscroft Av
HALE/TIMP WA15 43 K7 2
Hollins Dr WARRN/WOL WA2 28 A6
Hollins Gra ALS/KID ST7 242 D4 1
Hollins Green Rd MPL/ROM SK6 48 F6
Hollinshead Cl ALS/KID ST7 225 M5 1
Hollins Hl TPLY/KEL CW6 174 E3
Hollins La MPL/ROM SK6 48 F6
NWCHE CW9 77 M8
WARRN/WOL WA2 27 L6
Hollins Mt MPL/ROM SK6 49 H4
Hollins Rd MCFLDS SK11 15 L9
Hollinwood Cl ALS/KID ST7 242 E4
Hollinwood La MPL/ROM SK6 68 B2
Hollinwood Rd ALS/KID ST7 242 E4
Holloway RUNC WA7 8 F4
Hollow Dr WARRS WA4 56 E3
Hollow La FROD/HEL WA6 126 A1
KNUT WA16 107 H3
Hollow Oak La NWCHW CW8 127 K8
Hollowood Rd MALPAS SY14 246 B7
The Hollows CHD/CHDH SK8 64 C3 1
The Hollow ALS/KID ST7 226 B7
Holly Av CHD/CHDH SK8 45 K7
NEWLW WA12 27 K1
Hollybank AUD/MAD/W CW3 273 L2
Holly Bank SALE M33 43 J1
Hollybank WARRS WA4 55 G7
Hollybank Rd RUNC WA7 73 M4
Holly Bank Rd WILM/AE SK9 84 B3
Hollybush Crs NANT CW5 237 K7
Holly Bush La GOL/RIS/CU WA3 39 J3
Hollybush Sq GOL/RIS/CU WA3 23 L3 1
Holly Cl CHNE CH2 146 F4
HALE/TIMP WA15 43 G6
SPK/HALE L24 71 K3
Holly Ct FROD/HEL WA6 98 C7
Hollycroft Av WYTH/NTH M22 44 D6 1
Holly Dr WSFD CW7 177 K4
Hollyfield Rd EP CH65 10 D7 1
Holly Gra ALT WA14 61 K2 1
BRAM/HZG SK7 65 M1
Holly Gv CQ CH5 166 B1
KNUT WA16 105 M1
WARR WA1 38 A5
Holly Heath Cl SBCH CW11 204 C7
Hollyhedge Court Rd
WYTH/NTH M22 44 E7
Holly Hedge La WARRS WA4 55 K6
Hollyhedge Rd NTHM/RTH M23 44 B7
WYTH/NTH M22 44 C7
Holly Hey RAIN/WH L35 32 D3
Hollyhey Dr NTHM/RTH M23 44 B6
Holly La ALS/KID ST7 226 E7
ALS/KID ST7 241 L1
WILM/AE SK9 63 L7
Holly Mt CW/SHV CW2 238 E7
Hollymount Av OFTN SK2 47 J7 2
Hollymount Dr OFTN SK2 47 J7
Hollymount Gdns OFTN SK2 47 K7
Hollymount Rd OFTN SK2 47 J7

Holly Rd *BRAM/HZG* SK7 .... 65 L7
  CHSW/BR CH4 .... 168 F7 🔢
  EP CH65 .... 10 F7
  GOL/RIS/CU WA3 .... 23 J4
  LYMM WA13 .... 40 B7 🔢
  MCFLDS SK11 .... 14 D6
  MPL/ROM SK6 .... 67 L5
  NWCHW CW8 .... 128 C4
  POY/DIS SK12 .... 86 E1
  WARRW/BUR WA5 .... 35 L7
Holly Rd North *WILM/AE* SK9 .... 84 A6
Holly Rd South *WILM/AE* SK9 .... 84 B7
Holly St *STKP* SK1 .... 3 K6
Holly Ter *WARRW/BUR* WA5 .... 35 M7
Hollythorn Av *CHD/CHDH* SK8 .... 65 J5 🔢
Holly Tree Dr *BIDD* ST8 .... 227 J2
  KNUT WA16 .... 132 D5
Hollytree Rd *KNUT* WA16 .... 131 M1
  WLTN L25 .... 50 B1
Holly Wk *NWCHW* CW8 .... 12 A5
Hollywall La *BURS/TUN* ST6 .... 243 J7
Hollyway *WYTH/NTH* M22 .... 44 E4
Hollywell Rd *FLINT* CH6 .... 116 A5
Hollywood Rd *MPL/ROM* SK6 .... 49 L4
Holmcrofts *NSTN* CH64 .... 91 L7
Holm Dr *CHNE* 123 J1
Holme Beech Gv *OFTN* SK2 .... 47 J4 🔢
Holme Cl *CHSE* CH3 .... 170 E5
Holme Rd *DID/WITH* M20 .... 44 F1
Holmes Chapel Rd *CONG* CW12 .... 183 C7
  HOLMCH CW4 .... 182 A3
  KNUT WA16 .... 107 H7
  MCFLDS SK11 .... 134 F7
  MWCH CW10 .... 179 M2
  NWCHE CW9 .... 131 M8
  SBCH CW11 .... 204 E4
Holmes Ct *GOL/RIS/CU* WA3 .... 29 J8 🔢
Holmes St *CHD/CHDH* SK8 .... 45 L6 🔢
  EDGY/DAV SK3 .... 2 F9
Holme St *CHSE* CH3 .... 171 L1
Holmesville Av *CONG* CW12 .... 207 H2
Holmfield Av *RUNC* WA7 .... 9 L3
Holmfield Cl *HTNM* SK4 .... 2 C1
Holmfield Dr *CHD/CHDH* SK8 .... 65 H4
  GTS/LS CH66 .... 120 D1
Holmlea Dr *CW/HAS* CW1 .... 19 L5
Holmlea Wy *MCFLDN* SK10 .... 113 H4 🔢
Holm Oak Dr *AUD/MAD/W* CW3 .... 267 L5
Holm Oak Wy *GTS/LS* CH66 .... 120 E4
Holmsfield Rd *WARR* WA1 .... 5 M7
Holmshaw La *CW/HAS* CW1 .... 222 F6
Holmwood Dr *EP* CH65 .... 121 H2 🔢
Holt Hey *NSTN* CH64 .... 92 A7
Holt La *RUNC* WA7 .... 73 M4
Holt's La *WILM/AE* SK9 .... 83 M1
Holt St *ALT* WA14 .... 42 C5
  CW/HAS CW1 .... 18 D3
  STKP SK1 .... 3 H8
Holtswell Cl *GOL/RIS/CU* WA3 .... 23 L3 🔢
Holwick Rd *NTHM/RTH* M23 .... 43 M2
Holyhead Cl *WARRW/BUR* WA5 .... 36 D1
Holyrood *WDN* WA8 .... 34 A8
Holyrood Dr *CW/SHV* CW2 .... 237 L4
Holyrood Wy *CHSE* CH3 .... 170 B1
Holywell Cl *NSTN* CH64 .... 91 H3
Holywell La *CHSE* CH3 .... 230 D2
Home Farm *MCFLDN* SK10 .... 137 M3 🔢
Homelands Cl *SALE* M33 .... 42 F2 🔢
Homelands Rd *SALE* M33 .... 42 F2
Home Pk *CH/BCN* CH1 .... 144 F3
Homer Dr *MPL/ROM* SK6 .... 49 H4
Homestead *HUY* L36 .... 32 A1 🔢
Homestead Crs *BNG/LEV* M19 .... 45 L1
Homestead Rd *POY/DIS* SK12 .... 68 C6
Homeway *FROD/HEL* WA6 .... 124 B2 🔢
Homewood Av
  WYTH/NTH M22 .... 44 D3 🔢
Homewood Crs *NWCHW* CW8 .... 129 H7
Honey Flds *TPLY/KEL* CW6 .... 197 L3
Honey Hall Rd *HLWD* L26 .... 50 E6
Honeysuckle Cl
  CHSW/BR CH4 .... 190 C1 🔢
  GTS/LS CH66 .... 120 F4
  HLWD L26 .... 50 D2 🔢
  NTHM/RTH M23 .... 43 K3
  WDN WA8 .... 34 B8 🔢
Honford Rd *WYTH/NTH* M22 .... 44 B8
Hong Kong Av *MANAIR* M90 .... 63 C4
Honister Av *WARRN/WOL* WA2 .... 37 J2
Honister Cl *NTHLY* L27 .... 51 C1
Honister Gv *RUNC* WA7 .... 73 L7
Honiton Wy *ALT* WA14 .... 42 A6
  WARRW/BUR WA5 .... 35 L8
Hood Gv *LEIGH* WN7 .... 25 L1
Hood La *WARRW/BUR* WA5 .... 36 C7
Hood La North
  WARRW/BUR WA5 .... 36 C6
Hood Rd *WDN* WA8 .... 6 F5
Hoofield La *CHSE* CH3 .... 196 A4
Hoogreen La *KNUT* WA16 .... 79 K3
Hooker St *NWCHW* CW8 .... 12 E5
Hookstone Dr *GTS/LS* CH66 .... 94 C6
Hoole Cl *CHD/CHDH* SK8 .... 46 A7
Hoole Gdns *CHNE* CH2 .... 170 B1
Hoole La *CHNE* CH2 .... 17 M4
  CHSE CH3 .... 17 L4
Hoole Rd *CHNE* CH2 .... 17 L1
Hoole Wy *CH/BCN* CH1 .... 17 H3
Hoole Way Rbt *CH/BCN* CH1 .... 17 H3
Hooleyhey La *MCFLDN* SK10 .... 140 D2
Hooley Range *HTNM* SK4 .... 46 B1
Hoolpool La *FROD/HEL* WA6 .... 97 M7
Hooper St *STKP* SK1 .... 2 F6
Hooten La *LEIGH* WN7 .... 25 J1
Hooton Gn *GTS/LS* CH66 .... 94 A2
Hooton La *GTS/LS* CH66 .... 94 B3
Hooton Rd *NSTN* CH64 .... 93 H3
  GTS/LS CH66 .... 93 M2
Hope Av *WILM/AE* SK9 .... 84 C1
Hope Carr La *LEIGH* WN7 .... 25 H2
Hope Carr Rd *LEIGH* WN7 .... 25 H1
Hope Carr Wy *LEIGH* WN7 .... 25 C1
Hope Cft *GTS/LS* CH66 .... 120 E2
Hope Farm Rd *GTS/LS* CH66 .... 120 E3
Hopefield Rd *LYMM* WA13 .... 40 B8 🔢
Hope Green Wy *POY/DIS* SK12 .... 86 D2 🔢
Hope La *GOL/RIS/CU* WA3 .... 25 L2

  MCFLDN SK10 .... 86 E3
Hope Rd *CHSW/BR* CH4 .... 190 B1
  SALE M33 .... 43 G1 🔢
Hopes Carr *STKP* SK1 .... 3 H6
Hope St *BRAM/HZG* SK7 .... 66 D2
  CHSW/BR CH4 .... 168 F6
  CW/SHV CW2 .... 19 G8
  HTNM SK4 .... 2 D5
  MCFLDN SK10 .... 15 J5
  NEWLW WA12 .... 27 H1
  NWCHW CW8 .... 12 F4
  SBCH CW11 .... 204 B6
Hope St West *MCFLDN* SK10 .... 14 E4
Hope Ter *EDGY/DAV* SK3 .... 2 F8 🔢
Hopkins Cl *CONG* CW12 .... 207 H1
Hopkins Fld *ALT* WA14 .... 61 H3
Hopton Av *WYTH/NTH* M22 .... 63 L1
Hopwood Cl *GOL/RIS/CU* WA3 .... 23 M4 🔢
Hopwood St *WARR* WA1 .... 5 J2
Horbury Gdns *GTS/LS* CH66 .... 94 C7
Hornbeam Av *GTS/LS* CH66 .... 120 F3
Hornbeam Cl
  HALE/TIMP WA15 .... 43 L7 🔢
  RUNC WA7 .... 74 C4
Hornbeam Crs *AIMK* WN4 .... 22 B1
Hornbeam Dr *NWCHW* CW8 .... 128 E8
Hornbeam Rd *HLWD* L26 .... 51 G5
Hornby Dr *NANT* CW5 .... 21 J6
Hornby La *WARRN/WOL* WA2 .... 28 A6
Horncastle Cl
  GOL/RIS/CU WA3 .... 23 M4 🔢
Hornsea Rd *OFTN* SK2 .... 48 A7
Horridge Av *NEWLW* WA12 .... 22 C7
Horrocks La *WARR* WA1 .... 5 G7
Horrocks Rd *CHNE* CH2 .... 145 L7
Horsemarket St *WARR* WA1 .... 5 H4
Horseshoe Cl *FROD/HEL* WA6 .... 126 B2 🔢
Horseshoe Crs
  WARRN/WOL WA2 .... 37 L1 🔢
Horseshoe Dr *MCFLDS* SK11 .... 14 D6
Horseshoe La *WILM/AE* SK9 .... 110 A2
Horsham Av *BRAM/HZG* SK7 .... 66 C3 🔢
Horsley La *TPLY/KEL* CW6 .... 215 L3
Horstone Crs *GTS/LS* CH66 .... 120 F2
Horstone Gdns *GTS/LS* CH66 .... 120 F2
Horstone Rd *GTS/LS* CH66 .... 120 F2
Horton St *OFTN* SK2 .... 46 F5
Hoseley La *WRX/GR/LL* LL12 .... 210 A8
Hoskins Rd *BURS/TUN* ST6 .... 243 L7
Hospital La *NANT* CW5 .... 250 L2
Hospital St *CW/HAS* CW1 .... 221 K6
  NANT CW5 .... 20 F7
Hospital Wy *RUNC* WA7 .... 73 M5
Hostock Rd *RAIN/WH* L35 .... 32 D2 🔢
Hotel Rd *MANAIR* M90 .... 63 J5
Hotel St *NEWLW* WA12 .... 27 H1
Hothershall Cl *CW/HAS* CW1 .... 221 H5 🔢
Hough Cl *MCFLDN* SK10 .... 113 K7
Hough Gn *CHSW/BR* CH4 .... 169 G6
  HALE/TIMP WA15 .... 61 L7
Hough Green Rd *WDN* WA8 .... 52 A2
Hough La *FROD/HEL* WA6 .... 126 F7
  NWCHW CW8 .... 103 G7
  WILM/AE SK9 .... 84 D7
Houghley Cl *MCFLDN* SK10 .... 138 C2
Hough's La *WARRS* WA4 .... 56 A6
Houghton Cl *CHNE* CH2 .... 17 M3
  NEWLW WA12 .... 27 H1 🔢
  WDN WA8 .... 7 M1
Houghton Cft *WDN* WA8 .... 33 J6
Houghton St *NEWLW* WA12 .... 27 H1 🔢
  RAIN/WH L35 .... 33 J1 🔢
  WARRN/WOL WA2 .... 5 G4
  WDN WA8 .... 53 K2
Houldsworth Av *ALT* WA14 .... 42 E5 🔢
Houndings La *SBCH* CW11 .... 204 B7
Housesteads Dr *CHNE* CH2 .... 17 M2
Housman Cl *CH/BCN* CH1 .... 145 C7
Hove Cl *CW/HAS* CW1 .... 221 H4 🔢
The Hove *RUNC* WA7 .... 74 D6
Howard Av *CHD/CHDH* SK8 .... 65 C3
  LYMM WA13 .... 40 A8
Howard Cl *MPL/ROM* SK6 .... 48 A2
Howard Ct *HALE/TIMP* WA15 .... 62 A3
Howard Rd *CHSW/BR* CH4 .... 168 D6
  GOL/RIS/CU WA3 .... 30 A2
  WYTH/NTH M22 .... 44 D3 🔢
Howard St *CW/HAS* CW1 .... 221 M6
  STKP SK1 .... 3 G3
Howards Wy *NSTN* CH64 .... 91 H6
Howarth Dr *IRL* M44 .... 31 M3 🔢
Howbeck Crs *NANT* CW5 .... 253 G4
Howden Rd *NM/HAY* SK22 .... 69 J3
Howells Av *GTS/LS* CH66 .... 120 C1
Howe Rd *CHSW/BR* CH4 .... 169 H5
Howe St *MCFLDN* SK10 .... 15 L2
Howey Hl *CONG* CW12 .... 207 H5
Howey La *CONG* CW12 .... 207 K2
  FROD/HEL WA6 .... 99 G5
Howey Ri *FROD/HEL* WA6 .... 99 G5
Howley La *WARR* WA1 .... 5 L7
Howson Rd *WARRN/WOL* WA2 .... 37 J2
Howty Cl *WILM/AE* SK9 .... 84 D3
Hoylake Cl *LEIGH* WN7 .... 24 D2
  RUNC WA7 .... 74 C6
Hoylake Rd *EDGY/DAV* SK3 .... 46 A4
  SALE M33 .... 43 M2
Hoyle St *WARRW/BUR* WA5 .... 4 D3
Hubert Dr *MWCH* CW10 .... 179 J4
Huccelote Av
  WYTH/NTH M22 .... 63 J2 🔢
Hucklow Av *NTHM/RTH* M23 .... 63 G2 🔢
Hudson Cl *WARRW/BUR* WA5 .... 36 D4
Hughes Av *CW/SHV* CW2 .... 220 F8
Hughes Pl *WARRN/WOL* WA2 .... 37 K2 🔢
Hughes St *WARR* WA1 .... 56 C1
Hugh St *CHSW/BR* CH4 .... 17 C9
Hulley Rd *MCFLDN* SK10 .... 138 E1
Hullock's Pool Rd *ALS/KID* ST7 .... 241 L7
Hulme Hall Av *CHD/CHDH* SK8 .... 65 G4
Hulme Hall Cl *CHD/CHDH* SK8 .... 65 C3 🔢
Hulme Hall Crs *CHD/CHDH* SK8 .... 65 G4
Hulme Hall La *KNUT* WA16 .... 132 B7
Hulme Hall Rd *CHD/CHDH* SK8 .... 65 C2
Hulme La *KNUT* WA16 .... 132 A5
Hulme Rd *SALE* M33 .... 43 K1
Hulme Sq *MCFLDS* SK11 .... 138 C7

Hulme St *CW/HAS* CW1 .... 220 F7
  STKP SK1 .... 3 L9
Hulseheath La *KNUT* WA16 .... 80 A1
Hulse La *NWCHE* CW9 .... 131 L6
Hulton Cl *CONG* CW12 .... 208 B3
Humber Cl *WDN* WA8 .... 53 M1
Humber Dr *BIDD* ST8 .... 227 L4
Humber Rd *GTS/LS* CH66 .... 120 F2
  WARRN/WOL WA2 .... 37 L2
Hume St *WARR* WA1 .... 5 L4
Humphrey's Cl *RUNC* WA7 .... 74 D5 🔢
Hungerford Av *CW/HAS* CW1 .... 19 K5
Hungerford La
  AUD/MAD/W CW3 .... 267 M3
Hungerford Pl *SBCH* CW11 .... 204 A7
Hungerford Rd *CW/HAS* CW1 .... 19 K4
Hungerford Ter *CW/HAS* CW1 .... 19 M5
Hunsterson Rd *NANT* CW5 .... 265 H1
Hunston Rd *SALE* M33 .... 42 F1
Hunt Cl *WARRW/BUR* WA5 .... 36 B4 🔢
Hunter Av *CW/SHV* CW2 .... 238 D5
  WARRN/WOL WA2 .... 37 H2
Hunters Cl *BIDD* ST8 .... 227 J4
  WILM/AE SK9 .... 84 F3 🔢
Hunters Ct *FROD/HEL* WA6 .... 98 D8
  RUNC WA7 .... 73 L6 🔢
Hunter's Crs *CHSE* CH3 .... 172 B3
Hunter's Dr *CHSE* CH3 .... 172 B3
Huntersfield *CW/SHV* CW2 .... 253 H1
Hunters Fld *NWCHW* CW8 .... 12 C4
Hunters Hl *FROD/HEL* WA6 .... 126 C3
  NWCHW CW8 .... 12 C4
Hunters Ms *WILM/AE* SK9 .... 84 C5
Hunters Ri *WSFD* CW7 .... 177 J3 🔢
Hunter St *CH/BCN* CH1 .... 16 F5
Hunters Wk *CH/BCN* CH1 .... 16 F5 🔢
Hunters Wy *NSTN* CH64 .... 91 J4
Huntley Rd *EDGY/DAV* SK3 .... 46 B5
Huntley St *WARRW/BUR* WA5 .... 36 C8
Huntly Cha *WILM/AE* SK9 .... 84 C6
Hunts Cl *CHSE* CH3 .... 170 B3
Hunts Cross Av *WLTN* L25 .... 50 B1
Huntsham Cl *ALT* WA14 .... 42 B6 🔢
Hunts La *WARRS* WA4 .... 56 F2
Huntsman Dr *IRL* M44 .... 31 M5
Hurdsfield Cl *MWCH* CW10 .... 179 J5 🔢
Hurdsfield Rd *MCFLDN* SK10 .... 15 K3
  OFTN SK2 .... 47 J8
Hurford Av *EP* CH65 .... 94 F8
Hurlbote Cl *WILM/AE* SK9 .... 64 D7 🔢
Hurlbutts Dr *CQ* CH5 .... 142 D6
Hurlestone Cl *CHNE* CH2 .... 146 F3 🔢
Hurley Cl *WARRW/BUR* WA5 .... 36 C7
Hurley Dr *CHD/CHDH* SK8 .... 64 E2 🔢
Hurn Cl *CW/HAS* CW1 .... 221 H4 🔢
Hurst Av *CHD/CHDH* SK8 .... 65 J6
  SALE M33 .... 42 C1
Hurst Fold *BNG/LEV* M19 .... 45 K1
Hursthead Rd *CHD/CHDH* SK8 .... 65 H5
Hurst La *GOL/RIS/CU* WA3 .... 25 H5
  MCFLDN SK10 .... 113 C4
Hurst Lea Rd *NM/HAY* SK22 .... 69 J5 🔢
Hurst Mill La *GOL/RIS/CU* WA3 .... 25 J4
Hurst Park Dr *HUY* L36 .... 32 A1
Hurst St *LEIGH* WN7 .... 25 H1
  WDN WA8 .... 53 C8 🔢
The Hurst *FROD/HEL* WA6 .... 126 C2
Hurstvale Av *CHD/CHDH* SK8 .... 64 B3 🔢
Hurstwood *CHSE* CH3 .... 171 C8
Hurstwood Rd *OFTN* SK2 .... 47 M6 🔢
Hutchins' Cl *MWCH* CW10 .... 179 L6 🔢
Hutchinson St *WDN* WA8 .... 7 C9
Huttfield Rd *SPK/HALE* L24 .... 51 C8 🔢
Hutton Dr *CONG* CW12 .... 208 A2
Huxley Cl *BRAM/HZG* SK7 .... 65 L5
  MCFLDN SK10 .... 14 B1
Huxley Dr *BRAM/HZG* SK7 .... 65 L5
Huxley La *CHSE* CH3 .... 196 A5
Huxley St *ALT* WA14 .... 42 D5
  NWCHW CW8 .... 12 E5
Huxton Gn *BRAM/HZG* SK7 .... 66 A2
Hyacinth Cl *EDGY/DAV* SK3 .... 46 D7 🔢
Hyde Bank Rd *NM/HAY* SK22 .... 69 J4
Hyde Cl *EP* CH65 .... 94 F8
  RUNC WA7 .... 73 K6 🔢
Hyldavale Av *CHD/CHDH* SK8 .... 45 H6
Hylton Cl *EP* CH65 .... 121 L2
Hylton Dr *CHD/CHDH* SK8 .... 65 J4
Hythe Av *CW/HAS* CW1 .... 221 H4
Hythe Rd *EDGY/DAV* SK3 .... 46 B4

I

Ian Rd *ALS/KID* ST7 .... 243 K2
Ikey La *NANT* CW5 .... 234 F6
Ilex Av *WARRN/WOL* WA2 .... 28 B6
Ilfracombe Rd *OFTN* SK2 .... 47 K4
Imperial Av *CH/BCN* CH1 .... 144 C8
Imperial Ms *EP* CH65 .... 10 D5
Ince Av *PS/BROM* CH62 .... 93 L1
Ince Cl *HTNM* SK4 .... 2 E2
Ince Dr *CHSE* CH3 .... 228 F3
Ince La *CHNE* CH2 .... 97 H8
  CHSE CH3 .... 122 F8
Ince Orchards *CHNE* CH2 .... 97 H8
Ince St *HTNM* SK4 .... 2 E2 🔢
Ingersley Rd *MCFLDN* SK10 .... 113 H4
Ingham Cl *CHSE* CH3 .... 170 A3
Ingham Rd *ALT* WA14 .... 42 D4
  WDN WA8 .... 33 M8
Ingle Dr *OFTN* SK2 .... 47 J5
Inglenook Rd
  WARRW/BUR WA5 .... 35 M8 🔢
Ingle Rd *CHD/CHDH* SK8 .... 46 A6
Inglesham Cl *LEIGH* WN7 .... 24 E5 🔢
  NTHM/RTH M23 .... 44 B6
Ingleton Cl *CHD/CHDH* SK8 .... 45 J6 🔢
  HOLMCH CW4 .... 181 C1
Ingleton Gv *RUNC* WA7 .... 73 K7
Ingleton Rd *EDGY/DAV* SK3 .... 2 A8
Inglewood Av *MWCH* CW10 .... 179 K7
Inglewood Cl
  GOL/RIS/CU WA3 .... 30 B6 🔢
Ingram Dr *HTNM* SK4 .... 45 L1

Inman Av *STHEL* WA9 .... 26 B2
Inner Central Rd *SPK/HALE* L24 .... 50 F7
Inner South Rd *SPK/HALE* L24 .... 50 E8
Inner West Rd *SPK/HALE* L24 .... 50 E8
Innisfree Ct *GTS/LS* CH66 .... 94 C7 🔢
Insall Rd *WARRN/WOL* WA2 .... 37 M2
Intack La *NWCHE* CW9 .... 78 A1
Intake Cl *NSTN* CH64 .... 93 G4 🔢
International Ap *MANAIR* M90 .... 63 J5 🔢
Inverness Rd *MALPAS* SY14 .... 245 J1
Ion Pth *WDN* WA8 .... 178 C3
Irby Cl *GTS/LS* CH66 .... 94 E8
Ireland Rd *SPK/HALE* L24 .... 71 L3
Ireland St *WARRN/WOL* WA2 .... 5 G1
  WDN WA8 .... 53 K2
Irene Av *BURS/TUN* ST6 .... 243 M8
Iris Cl *WDN* WA8 .... 52 C2
Ironbridge Dr *HOLMCH* CW4 .... 181 J2
Irons La *CHSE* CH3 .... 147 M5
Irvin Dr *WYTH/NTH* M22 .... 64 A4
Irving Cl *OFTN* SK2 .... 66 A1
Irving's Crs *CHSW/BR* CH4 .... 168 D6
Irwell La *RUNC* WA7 .... 9 K1
Irwell Ri *WILM/AE* SK9 .... 112 F5
Irwell Rd *WARRS* WA4 .... 56 B2
Irwell St *WDN* WA8 .... 53 G8
Irwin Dr *WILM/AE* SK9 .... 64 C7
Irwin Rd *ALT* WA14 .... 42 C4
Isabella Ct *CHSW/BR* CH4 .... 168 E6 🔢
Isherwood Cl *WARRN/WOL* WA2 .... 37 M1
Isherwood Dr *MPL/ROM* SK6 .... 48 D6
Isis Cl *CONG* CW12 .... 207 M5
Islay Cl *EP* CH65 .... 121 J4
Islington Dr *OFTN* SK2 .... 47 J8
Ivanhoe Av *GOL/RIS/CU* WA3 .... 23 K3
Iveagh Cl *RUNC* WA7 .... 74 A5 🔢
Iver Cl *WDN* WA8 .... 33 J6
Iver Rd *CHNE* CH2 .... 145 L5
Ivy Av *NEWLW* WA12 .... 27 J2
Ivychurch Ms *RUNC* WA7 .... 73 K2
Ivy Ct *CHSW/BR* CH4 .... 210 D2
Ivy Dr *NWCHW* CW8 .... 152 A2
Ivy Farm Dr *NSTN* CH64 .... 91 M6
Ivy Farm Gdns
  GOL/RIS/CU WA3 .... 24 D8 🔢
Ivy Farm La *CHSE* CH3 .... 231 J4
Ivy Gdns *CONG* CW12 .... 207 J2
Ivy House Rd *BIDD* ST8 .... 227 J2
  GOL/RIS/CU WA3 .... 23 K3 🔢
Ivy La *ALS/KID* ST7 .... 241 L2
  MCFLDS SK11 .... 14 A8
Ivy Meade Rd *MCFLDS* SK11 .... 137 M6
Ivy Ms *CHNE* CH2 .... 146 A7
Ivy Rd *GOL/RIS/CU* WA3 .... 23 H4
  MCFLDS SK11 .... 14 A7
  POY/DIS SK12 .... 86 E1
  WARR WA1 .... 38 E5
Ivy St *RUNC* WA7 .... 9 G4
Izaac Walton Wy
  AUD/MAD/W CW3 .... 267 L7

J

Jack Brady Cl *NTHM/RTH* M23 .... 43 L8
Jack La *CW/SHV* CW2 .... 239 K6
  MWCH CW10 .... 154 B7 🔢
Jackson Av *GOL/RIS/CU* WA3 .... 29 L1
  NANT CW5 .... 21 H7
  WARR WA1 .... 37 M5
Jackson Cl *RAIN/WH* L35 .... 33 K3
Jackson La *MCFLDN* SK10 .... 113 C5
Jackson Rd *CONG* CW12 .... 184 F2
Jacksons Edge Rd *POY/DIS* SK12 .... 68 A5 🔢
Jackson's La *BRAM/HZG* SK7 .... 66 B4
Jackson St *CHD/CHDH* SK8 .... 45 L6
  MCFLDS SK11 .... 15 H9
  WARRW/BUR WA5 .... 26 E6
Jacqueline St *BURS/TUN* ST6 .... 243 J8
Jamage Rd *ALS/KID* ST7 .... 242 D7
James Av *GTS/LS* CH66 .... 120 C1
James Cl *WDN* WA8 .... 53 C8
James Ct *WLTN* L25 .... 50 B2
James Hall St *NANT* CW5 .... 20 F4
James Rd *WLTN* L25 .... 50 B2
James St *CH/BCN* CH1 .... 17 H3
  EDGY/DAV SK3 .... 2 E9
  MCFLDS SK11 .... 15 G7
  NWCHE CW9 .... 130 C4
  STHEL WA9 .... 34 D1
  WARR WA1 .... 5 H6
James Wy *BIDD* ST8 .... 227 K5
Jamieson Cl *ALS/KID* ST7 .... 224 E8
  CHSE CH3 .... 170 A2 🔢
Jan Palach Av *NANT* CW5 .... 21 G9
Jarman St *MCFLDS* SK11 .... 138 F8
Jasmine Cl *NTHM/RTH* M23 .... 43 L3 🔢
Jasmin Wy *ALS/KID* ST7 .... 243 M2
Jaycean Av *BURS/TUN* ST6 .... 243 L8
Jay Cl *GOL/RIS/CU* WA3 .... 30 A8
Jayton Av *DID/WITH* M20 .... 45 H4
Jean Av *LEIGH* WN7 .... 24 E2
Jedburgh Av *GOL/RIS/CU* WA3 .... 94 A6
Jefferson St *BURS/TUN* ST6 .... 243 K8
Jellicoe Av *IRL* M44 .... 31 L6 🔢
Jennet's La *GOL/RIS/CU* WA3 .... 25 J3
Jennings Cl *EDGY/DAV* SK3 .... 46 D5
Jenny La *BRAM/HZG* SK7 .... 85 L1
Jepson St *OFTN* SK2 .... 47 G6
Jersey Av *EP* CH65 .... 121 J3
Jersey Cl *CONG* CW12 .... 208 A3
Jersey St *THEL* WA9 .... 34 C1
Jersey Wy *MWCH* CW10 .... 179 J2
Jervis Cl *WARRN/WOL* WA2 .... 38 A1
Jesmond Crs *CW/SHV* CW2 .... 18 C7
Jesmond Gv *CHD/CHDH* SK8 .... 65 H4 🔢
Jesmond Rd *CH/BCN* CH1 .... 16 C3
Jessop Dr *MPL/ROM* SK6 .... 48 A4
Jessop St *CW/HAS* CW1 .... 222 C8
Jeudwine Cl *WLTN* L25 .... 50 B4
Jockey St *WARRN/WOL* WA2 .... 5 C2
Jodrell Cl *HOLMCH* CW4 .... 181 C1
  MCFLDS SK11 .... 15 J7
Jodrell Meadow *CHF/WBR* SK23 .... 89 K4
Jodrell Rd *CHF/WBR* SK23 .... 89 K4
Jodrell St *MCFLDS* SK11 .... 15 J7

  NM/HAY SK22 .... 69 H5
Jodrell Vw *ALS/KID* ST7 .... 243 H4
Johannesburg Gdns
  NTHM/RTH M23 .... 43 M8 🔢
John Av *CHD/CHDH* SK8 .... 45 L7
John Brunner Crs *NWCHW* CW8 .... 12 E6
John Fryer Av *NWCHE* CW9 .... 105 G7
John Nicholas Crs *EP* CH65 .... 10 F6 🔢
  EP CH65 .... 11 G5 🔢
John Offley Rd
  AUD/MAD/W CW3 .... 267 K6
John Rd *LYMM* WA13 .... 58 C1
Johns Av *RUNC* WA7 .... 8 F5
Johns Cl *MCFLDN* SK10 .... 113 K7
Johnson Av *NEWLW* WA12 .... 22 B7
Johnson Cl *CONG* CW12 .... 208 B3
Johnsons La *WDN* WA8 .... 53 L4
Johnson St *CHF/WBR* SK23 .... 89 L4 🔢
  John's Pl *MPL/ROM* SK6 .... 48 C2 🔢
John Steet *MPL/ROM* SK6 .... 48 C2 🔢
John St *ALT* WA14 .... 42 D8 🔢
  BIDD ST8 .... 227 J5
  BRAM/HZG SK7 .... 66 D1 🔢
  CW/HAS CW1 .... 18 E2
  EP CH65 .... 10 D5
  GOL/RIS/CU WA3 .... 23 G4
  IRL M44 .... 31 L7
  MCFLDN SK10 .... 113 H4 🔢
  MCFLDS SK11 .... 15 H8
  MPL/ROM SK6 .... 49 H2
  MPL/ROM SK6 .... 49 H2
  STKP SK1 .... 3 G5
  TPLY/KEL CW6 .... 174 B5
  WARRN/WOL WA2 .... 5 G5
  WSFD CW7 .... 177 J3 🔢
Jonathan's Wy *CHSW/BR* CH4 .... 168 F7 🔢
Jones's La *MWCH* CW10 .... 180 D5
Jones Sq *STKP* SK1 .... 3 H9
Jonson Rd *NSTN* CH64 .... 91 L3
Jordangate *MCFLDN* SK10 .... 15 C4
Joseph Crs *ALS/KID* ST7 .... 241 L2
Joseph Johnson Ms
  WYTH/NTH M22 .... 44 E3 🔢
Joseph St *MPL/ROM* SK6 .... 49 C6 🔢
  WDN WA8 .... 7 L1
Joules Ct *STKP* SK1 .... 3 H6
Joule St *GOL/RIS/CU* WA3 .... 29 M7
Joyce Av *WSFD* CW7 .... 177 J2 🔢
Joy La *STHEL* WA9 .... 34 E2
  WARRW/BUR WA5 .... 26 D8
Jubilee Av *CW/SHV* CW2 .... 18 C5
  WARR WA1 .... 37 M4
  WARRW/BUR WA5 .... 35 L8 🔢
Jubilee Cl *BIDD* ST8 .... 227 K5
Jubilee Dr *RAIN/WH* L35 .... 32 D2
Jubilee Gdns *NANT* CW5 .... 20 F9
  NM/HAY SK22 .... 69 J5
Jubilee Gv *LYMM* WA13 .... 39 J8
Jubilee Rd *CONG* CW12 .... 207 L2
Jubilee St *CQ* CH5 .... 142 B6
  NM/HAY SK22 .... 69 J5
Jubilee Ter *NANT* CW5 .... 20 F8
Jubilee Wy *WDN* WA8 .... 6 C2
Jubits La *WDN* WA8 .... 34 A4
Judy La *MCFLDS* SK11 .... 163 G2
Julian Wy *WDN* WA8 .... 33 M8
Julius Cl *FLINT* CH6 .... 116 C7
Jumper La *MCFLDN* SK10 .... 113 L6
Junction La *NEWLW* WA12 .... 27 H1 🔢
Junction Rd *OFTN* SK2 .... 3 G9
  STKP SK1 .... 3 G9
June Av *HTNM* SK4 .... 46 B2 🔢
Juniper Dr *GTS/LS* CH66 .... 120 E3
Juniper Gv *GTS/LS* CH66 .... 120 F3
Juniper La *GOL/RIS/CU* WA3 .... 39 G4
Juniper Ri *MCFLDN* SK10 .... 137 L3 🔢
Jupiter Dr *CH/BCN* CH1 .... 168 E2
Jurby Ct *WARRN/WOL* WA2 .... 37 M3 🔢
  WARRN/WOL WA2 .... 37 L3 🔢
Justice St *MCFLDN* SK10 .... 15 C2

K

Kaleyards *CH/BCN* CH1 .... 17 G4
Kane Ct *GOL/RIS/CU* WA3 .... 24 A3
Karen Cl *WARRW/BUR* WA5 .... 26 F6
Karen Wy *GTS/LS* CH66 .... 120 D1
Katherine Rd *OFTN* SK2 .... 47 J1
Kay Av *MPL/ROM* SK6 .... 47 K1
Kaye Av *GOL/RIS/CU* WA3 .... 29 M1
Kay La *LYMM* WA13 .... 59 J4
Kay's Av *STKP* SK1 .... 3 L6
Kays Wood Rd *MPL/ROM* SK6 .... 48 D6
Kearsley Av *CQ* CH5 .... 166 A3
Keats Av *RAIN/WH* L35 .... 32 F1
Keats Cl *GTS/LS* CH66 .... 120 E4 🔢
  WDN WA8 .... 6 E4
Keats Dr *ALS/KID* ST7 .... 243 M2
  CW/SHV CW2 .... 238 A4 🔢
  MCFLDN SK10 .... 137 L3
Keats Gdns *ALS/KID* ST7 .... 243 M2
Keats Gv *WARRN/WOL* WA2 .... 37 J2
Keats La *NWCHE* CW9 .... 105 G7
Keble St *WDN* WA8 .... 7 J6
Keckwick La *RUNC* WA7 .... 54 F8
  WARRS WA4 .... 75 H2 🔢
Kedleston Gn *OFTN* SK2 .... 47 K5
Keele Crs *MCFLDS* SK11 .... 14 C8
Keele St *BURS/TUN* ST6 .... 243 K8
Keepers Cl *KNUT* WA16 .... 107 K1 🔢
Keepers La *NWCHE* CW9 .... 77 K8
  NWCHW CW8 .... 128 E4
Keith Av *WARRW/BUR* WA5 .... 35 L6
Keith Dr *EDGY/DAV* SK3 .... 46 B5
Kelbrook Ct *GTS/LS* CH66 .... 47 L7
Kelburn Ct *GOL/RIS/CU* WA3 .... 29 M6
Kelby Av *NTHM/RTH* M23 .... 44 B5
Kelfield Av *NTHM/RTH* M23 .... 44 A2
Kelmscott Cl *GTS/LS* CH66 .... 120 D2
Kelsall Av *PS/BROM* CH62 .... 93 L1
Kelsall Cl *GOL/RIS/CU* WA3 .... 38 C1
  PS/BROM CH62 .... 93 L1
  WDN WA8 .... 6 B1
Kelsall Crs *EDGY/DAV* SK3 .... 46 D6 🔢
Kelsall Rd *HALE/TIMP* WA15 .... 43 J6

Kelsall Rd CHD/CHDH SK8 ....46 A7
CHSE CH3 ....148 C8
Kelsall St CONG CW12 ....207 L1
Kelsborrow Cl NWCHE CW9 ....153 L1
Kelsborrow Wy TPLY/KEL CW6 ...149 K8
Kelso Wy MCFLDN SK10 ....112 C8
Kelvin Cl GOL/RIS/CU WA3 ....29 K6
Kelvindale Dr HALE/TIMP WA15 ...43 J5
Kelvin Gv CHE CW2 ....145 L8
Kelvin St GOL/RIS/CU WA3 ....29 L6
Kemberton Dr WARR WA1 ....34 A7
Kemble Av NTHM/RTH M23 ....44 C3
Kemble Cl CW/SHV CW2 ....238 B4
Kemmel Av WARRS WA4 ....56 C2
WYTH/NTH M22 ....44 E7
Kemp Rd MPL/ROM SK6 ....49 J4
Kempsell Wy HLWD L26 ....51 C5
Kempsford Cl NTHM/RTH M23 .....44 K6
Kempton Av CW/HAS CW1 ....221 J5
SALE M33 ....42 D1
Kempton Cl BRAM/HZG SK7 ....67 G2
CH/BCN CH1 ....16 C3
NEWLW WA12 ....22 D7
RUNC WA7 ....73 J6
Kempton Wy MCFLDN SK10 ......112 C8
Kendal Av SALE M33 ....43 J1
WARRN/WOL WA2 ....37 J2
Kendal Cl CHNE CH2 ....146 A6
GTS/LS CH66 ....120 D2
HALE/TIMP WA15 ....43 K7
Kendal Ct CONG CW12 ....207 G2
Kendal Dr BRAM/HZG SK7 ....65 J7
CHD/CHDH SK8 ....45 J8
GTS/LS CH66 ....120 D2
RAIN/WH L35 ....33 C1
Kendal Ri RUNC WA7 ....73 K7
Kendal Rd MCFLDS SK11 ....137 M6
WDN WA8 ....52 C3
Kendrick Cl NWCHW CW8 ....128 D3
Kendricks Fold RAIN/WH L35 ....33 H1
Kendrick St WARR WA1 ....4 F2
Kenilworth Av CHD/CHDH SK8 .....65 G1
KNUT WA16 ....107 J2
RUNC WA7 ....9 H7
WILM/AE SK9 ....84 D1
Kenilworth Cl CW/SHV CW2 ......238 A5
MCFLDS SK11 ....137 M6
MPL/ROM SK6 ....48 F4
Kenilworth Ct EP CH65 ....121 L2
Kenilworth Dr BRAM/HZG SK7 .....66 D4
WARR WA1 ....37 M4
Kenilworth Gdns NEWLW WA12 ....27 J2
Kenilworth Rd EDGY/DAV SK3 .....45 M5
GOL/RIS/CU WA3 ....23 L5
MCFLDS SK11 ....137 M7
NSTN CH64 ....91 L6
Kenley Av WDN WA8 ....33 K7
Kenmare Bank NWCHE CW9 ....13 K8
Kenmore Dr HALE/TIMP WA15 .....62 A1
Kenmore Gv IRL M44 ....31 K6
Kenmore Rd SALE M33 ....42 C3
WYTH/NTH M22 ....44 C5
Kennedy Av MCFLDN SK10 ....137 M3
Kennedy Cl CHNE CH2 ....146 A7
Kennedy Dr CO CH5 ....166 D2
Kennedy Wy HTNM SK4 ....2 B4
Kennel La NWCHW CW8 ....151 M5
Kennelwood Rd NWCHE CW9 ....103 J5
Kennerley Rd OFTN SK2 ....47 G7
Kennerley's La WILM/AE SK9 ......84 A5
Kennet Cl WILM/AE SK9 ....84 D2
Kennet Dr CONG CW12 ....207 M3
Kenneth Rd NTHM/RTH M23 ......63 G1
Kennett Rd MCFLDS SK11 ....137 M4
Kennet Wy MCFLDS SK11 ....137 M4
Kenninghall Rd WYTH/NTH M22 ...63 K1
Kennington Crs CO CH5 ....142 D8
Kensington Av WARRS WA4 ....57 J2
Kensington Ct ALS/KID ST7 ....240 F1
BURS/TUN ST6 ....243 L8
WILM/AE SK9 ....84 A6
WSFD CW7 ....177 J5
Kensington Dr NANT CW5 ....237 K8
Kensington Gdns
HALE/TIMP WA15 ....61 M3
Kensington Gn ALT WA14 ....42 E4
Kensington Rd EDGY/DAV SK3 ....46 B5
EP CH65 ....10 B8
Kensington Wy NWCHE CW9 ....153 L1
Kent Av CHD/CHDH SK8 ....46 C8
CO CH5 ....142 B7
MCFLDN SK10 ....112 E6
Kent Cl WHITCH SY13 ....270 B5
Kent Dr CONG CW12 ....184 D8
Kent Gv RUNC WA7 ....9 K4
Kentmere Av WSFD CW7 ....177 K2
Kentmere Cl CHD/CHDH SK8 ......64 B1
Kentmere Pl
WARRN/WOL WA2 ....37 G1
Kentmere Rd HALE/TIMP WA15 ...43 J6
Kentmore Cl HTNM SK4 ....45 L2
Kenton Rd HLWD L26 ....50 D5
Kentridge Dr GTS/LS CH66 ......120 D1
Kent Rd CHNE CH2 ....145 M1
EDGY/DAV SK3 ....46 B4
IRL M44 ....31 J7
PART M31 ....40 E2
WARRN/BUR WA5 ....36 C8
Kent's Green La CW/HAS CW1 ...222 C5
Kent's La CW/HAS CW1 ....221 J5
Kentstone Av HTNM SK4 ....45 K1
Kent St WARRS WA5 ....5 J9
WDN WA8 ....7 J5
Kentwell Dr MCFLDN SK10 ....138 C2
Kenview Cl WDN WA8 ....52 A8
Kenwick Cl GTS/LS CH66 ....120 C1
Kenwood Av BRAM/HZG SK7 .....65 K7
CHD/CHDH SK8 ....45 G6
HALE/TIMP WA15 ....62 A1
Kenworthy La WYTH/NTH M22 ...44 D2
Kenworthy St BURS/TUN ST6 ...243 L8
Kenyon Av SALE M33 ....43 L2
WARRN/BUR WA5 ....35 L7
Kenyon La WARRN/BUR WA5 ....23 M6
Kepwick Dr WYTH/NTH M22 ......63 L3
Kerfoot Cl WYTH/NTH M22 ....44 E4
Kerfoot St WARRN/WOL WA2 ......4 F2

Keristal Av CHSE CH3 ....170 A5
Kerne Gv NTHM/RTH M23 ....44 A3
Kerridge Cl MWCH CW10 ....179 H4
Kerridge Rd MCFLDN SK10 ......139 H1
Kerris Cl WYTH/NTH M22 ....63 L3
Kerry Cft GTS/LS CH66 ....120 E3
Kersal Dr HALE/TIMP WA15 ....43 J5
Kerscott Rd NTHM/RTH M23 ......43 M2
Kershaw Gv MCFLDS SK11 ....14 C5
Kershaw St BIDD ST8 ....43 K2
Kershaw Wy NEWLW WA12 ....22 C7
Kestral Gv HLWD L26 ....50 D3
Kestrel Av BIDD ST8 ....227 H6
CONG CW12 ....207 L3
MPL/ROM SK6 ....179 K7
MWCH CW10 ....177 J7
Kestrel Cl CW/HAS CW1 ....221 H5
Kestrel Dr CW/HAS CW1 ....221 H5
Kestrel La GOL/RIS/CU WA3 ......29 L8
Kestrel Rd NWCHW CW8 ....12 B5
Kestrels Wy RUNC WA7 ....73 M6
Keswick Av CHD/CHDH SK8 ......64 B1
CW/SHV CW2 ....237 L1
IRL M44 ....31 K8
MCFLDS SK11 ....137 M7
WARRN/WOL WA2 ....37 J2
WDN WA8 ....52 C3
WSFD CW7 ....177 K2
Keswick Cl CHNE CH2 ....146 A7
CW/SHV CW2 ....237 L1
IRL M44 ....31 K8
MCFLDS SK11 ....137 M7
WDN WA8 ....52 C3
Keswick Ct CONG CW12 ....207 G2
CW/SHV CW2 ....237 L1
IRL M44 ....31 K8
MCFLDS SK11 ....137 M7
WDN WA8 ....52 C3
WSFD CW7 ....177 K2
Keswick Crs WARRN/WOL WA2 ...37 J2
Keswick Dr BRAM/HZG SK7 ....65 J7
FROD/HEL WA6 ....99 K4
Keswick Rd HALE/TIMP WA15 .....43 K6
MPL/ROM SK6 ....67 L4
Ketland Cl CO CH5 ....142 C6
Ketland Pl CO CH5 ....142 C6
Kettell Av CW/HAS CW1 ....220 F6
Kettle La AUD/MAD/W CW3 ......274 C3
Kettleshulme Wy POY/DIS SK12 ...87 G2
Kew Dr CHD/CHDH SK8 ....64 E2
Keyes Cl GOL/RIS/CU WA3 ....29 M8
Keyes Gdns GOL/RIS/CU WA3 ....29 M8
Keysbrook CHSE CH3 ....214 C2
Keysbrook Av CHSE CH3 ....214 C2
Kidderton Cl NANT CW5 ....234 E5
Kidderton La NANT CW5 ....234 E5
Kidsgrove Bank ALS/KID ST7 .....243 H4
Kidsgrove Rd BURS/TUN ST6 ....243 J4
Kilbuck La RNFD/HAY WA11 ....22 A4
Kilburn Cl CHD/CHDH SK8 ....64 B5
Kilburn Rd EDGY/DAV SK3 ....2 B9
Kildare Cl SPK/HALE L24 ....71 K2
Kildonan Rd WARRS WA4 ....57 C2
Kilford Cl WARRN/BUR WA5 ....36 E2
Killingworth La
GOL/RIS/CU WA3 ....30 B7
Killins La CO CH5 ....142 A6
Kilmorey Pk CHNE CH2 ....17 L1
Kilmorey Park Av CHNE CH2 ......17 K1
Kilmorey Park Rd CHNE CH2 ......17 K1
Kilmory Av WLTN L25 ....50 C2
Kiln Cft MPL/ROM SK6 ....47 M3
Kilncroft RUNC WA7 ....74 B7
Kiln Croft La WILM/AE SK9 ....64 E8
Kiln La NANT CW5 ....253 H4
Kilsby Dr WDN WA8 ....53 L2
Kilshaw Rd WARRN/BUR WA5 ....26 F6
Kilsyth Cl WARRN/BUR WA5 ......28 F8
Kilworth Av SALE M33 ....42 F1
Kimberley Av MPL/ROM SK6 ......48 B2
Kimberley Dr WARRS WA4 ....56 C3
Kimberley Pl AIMK WN4 ....22 C1
Kimberley St EDGY/DAV SK3 ......46 E5
WARRW/BUR WA5 ....4 A6
Kinburn Rd BNG/LEV M19 ....45 K2
Kinder Dr CW/SHV CW2 ....237 K1
MPL/ROM SK6 ....49 G6
Kinder Gv MPL/ROM SK6 ....48 E2
Kinder St EDGY/DAV SK3 ....2 E9
Kinderton Cl KNUT WA16 ....59 J8
Kinderton St MWCH CW10 ....179 J3
King Edward Dr FLINT CH6 ....116 A7
King Edward Rd KNUT WA16 .....106 F2
MCFLDN SK10 ....14 F4
King Edward St CO CH5 ....142 B6
MCFLDN SK10 ....14 F4
MWCH CW10 ....179 J4
WARR WA1 ....37 L1
Kingfisher Cl
AUD/MAD/W CW3 ....267 M5
CHSE CH3 ....228 F3
CONG CW12 ....207 L3
CW/HAS CW1 ....220 F5
GOL/RIS/CU WA3 ....29 M8
NANT CW5 ....20 F1
RUNC WA7 ....73 M7
Kingfisher Gv NWCHE CW9 ......104 F7
Kingfisher Rd OFTN SK2 ....47 M8
King George Av NWCHE CW9 ....13 L4
King George Cl AIMK WN4 ....22 B1
King George Crs WARR WA1 ......37 L5
King George Rd
RNFD/HAY WA11 ....22 A5
King George St CO CH5 ....142 A6
Kingham Cl WLTN L25 ....50 C2
King James Ct RUNC WA7 ....73 L6
King Pl NANT CW5 ....20 C6
King's Acre ALT WA14 ....61 G3
Kings Av CHD/CHDH SK8 ....45 G8
FLINT CH6 ....116 B7
GOL/RIS/CU WA3 ....23 J8
Kingsbridge Cl MPL/ROM SK6 ....48 E5
Kingsbury Cl WARRS WA4 ....76 D1
King's Cl BRAM/HZG SK7 ....65 M2
CHSW/BR CH4 ....168 F7
WILM/AE SK9 ....84 A5
King's Ct NANT CW5 ....20 C6
RDSH SK5 ....3 G2
King's Crs MWCH CW10 ....179 J2
King's Crs East CHSE CH3 ....170 A3
King's Crs West CHSE CH3 ....170 A3
Kingsdale Av RAIN/WH L35 ....33 K1
Kingsdale Rd WARRN/BUR WA5 ..35 M5

Kingsdown Rd WYTH/NTH M22 ...63 J3
Kings Dr CHD/CHDH SK8 ....65 G1
CW/SHV CW2 ....237 L4
FROD/HEL WA6 ....124 B1
HTNM SK4 ....46 A1
MPL/ROM SK6 ....48 E5
WLTN L25 ....50 B2
Kingsfield Ct CHSW/BR CH4 .....192 B1
Kingsfield Crs BIDD ST8 ....227 K4
Kingsfield Dr DID/WITH M20 ......45 J2
Kingsfield Rd BIDD ST8 ....227 J5
Kingsgate Rd WYTH/NTH M22 ...63 J3
Kingshead Cl RUNC WA7 ....74 A2
Kingsholme Rd WYTH/NTH M22 ..63 J2
Kingsland Rd EDGY/DAV SK3 .....46 A5
King's La MWCH CW10 ....156 E5
NANT CW5 ....20 C6
TPLY/KEL CW6 ....175 K8
Kingsley Av PS/BROM CH62 ......93 L1
WILM/AE SK9 ....84 C2
Kingsley Cl ALS/KID ST7 ....242 D6
Kingsley Crs STKP SK1 ....9 H5
Kingsley Dr NWCHE CW9 ....13 J8
WARRS WA4 ....56 C5
Kingsley Gdns CHSE CH3 ....170 A4
Kingsley Rd ALS/KID ST7 ....242 D6
CHSE CH3 ....170 A4
CONG CW12 ....208 A1
CO CH5 ....142 F5
CW/HAS CW1 ....222 C8
EP CH65 ....10 F7
FROD/HEL WA6 ....99 K6
HALE/TIMP WA15 ....43 H5
NWCHW CW8 ....127 H3
RUNC WA7 ....9 H4
WYTH/NTH M22 ....44 D4
King's Lynn Cl DID/WITH M20 .....45 H1
Kingsmead CHNE CH2 ....145 L3
NWCHE CW9 ....154 A1
Kingsmead Ct
GOL/RIS/CU WA3 ....29 G4
Kingsmead Dr WLTN L25 ....50 B3
Kings Meadow CW/SHV CW2 ....253 L2
RUNC WA7 ....74 C4
Kingsnorth RAIN/WH L35 ....32 F2
Kings North BRAM/HZG SK7 ......66 E1
CHD/CHDH SK8 ....65 G1
GOL/RIS/CU WA3 ....23 G5
GTS/LS CH66 ....94 C5
IRL M44 ....31 L6
MPL/ROM SK6 ....48 A1
WARRN/WOL WA2 ....38 A2
WILM/AE SK9 ....83 L4
Kingsthorne Pk SPK/HALE L24 ...50 C6
Kingsthorne Rd WLTN L25 ....50 C6
Kingston Av DID/WITH M20 ....45 H5
MCFLDS SK11 ....15 M7
WARRN/BUR WA5 ....35 L6
Kingston Cl RUNC WA7 ....73 L2
SALE M33 ....42 D1
Kingston Hl CHD/CHDH SK8 ......45 K8
Kingston Pl BIDD ST8 ....227 L2
CHD/CHDH SK8 ....64 E2
Kingston Rd DID/WITH M20 ....45 H3
WILM/AE SK9 ....64 C8
Kingston St EDGY/DAV SK3 ....2 D6
King St ALS/KID ST7 ....242 D7
ALS/KID ST7 ....243 G2
BIDD ST8 ....227 J4
CH/BCN CH1 ....16 E4
CONG CW12 ....184 F8
CW/HAS CW1 ....19 H4
EP CH65 ....10 F5
KNUT WA16 ....107 G2
MCFLDN SK10 ....15 J4
MWCH CW10 ....179 J2
NEWLW WA12 ....27 H1
NWCHE CW9 ....130 E5
NWCHW CW8 ....129 H7
RUNC WA7 ....9 H1
STKP SK1 ....203 L4
King St East STKP SK1 ....3 G3
King St West EDGY/DAV SK3 ......2 E6
HTNM SK4 ....2 D5
Kingsway BRAM/HZG SK7 ....65 M2
CHD/CHDH SK8 ....45 J5
CHNE CH2 ....146 A7
CO CH5 ....142 A6
CW/SHV CW2 ....18 D7
DID/WITH M20 ....45 J4
FROD/HEL WA6 ....99 H5
HALE/TIMP WA15 ....42 E8
MCFLDN SK10 ....112 C6
MPL/ROM SK6 ....47 L1
NEWLW WA12 ....27 J2
NWCHE CW9 ....13 L2
STKP SK1 ....3 G4
WDN WA8 ....7 H4
WHITCH SY13 ....270 A5
WSFD CW7 ....177 M3
Kingsway North WARR WA1 ......37 L6
Kingsway South WARRS WA4 ....37 M8
Kingsway West CHNE CH2 ....145 L8
Kingswood ALS/KID ST7 ....243 G2
Kingswood Av CH/BCN CH1 ......144 C5
Kingswood Crs MWCH CW10 ....179 L7
Kingswood La CH/BCN CH1 ......144 C4
Kingswood Rd
WARRN/BUR WA5 ....36 A2
Kings Wood Wk
TPLY/KEL CW6 ....149 K7
Kinloch Cl CW/HAS CW1 ....221 H6
HLWD L26 ....51 C5
Kinnaird Crs STKP SK1 ....3 L1
Kinnerley Rd EP CH65 ....121 L1
Kinnersley Av ALS/KID ST7 ....242 F4
Kinnersley St ALS/KID ST7 ....243 G2
Kinnerton Cl CHSW/BR CH4 .....168 E7
Kinnerton Hts CHSW/BR CH4 ....190 A5
Kinnington Wy GTS/LS CH66 ....120 F5
Kinnock Pk WARRN/BUR WA5 ...26 E6
Kinross Cl OFTN SK2 ....66 A1
Kinross Ct WARRN/WOL WA2 ....28 F8
Kinsale Dr GOL/RIS/CU WA3 ......29 J3
Kinsey Av NTHM/RTH M23 ....43 M5
Kinsey Rd EP CH65 ....121 L3
Kinsey's La EP CH65 ....96 F4

Kintore Av BRAM/HZG SK7 ....66 F2
Kintore Cl WSFD CW7 ....178 A2
Kintore Dr WARRW/BUR WA5 ....35 K6
Kipling Av HUY L36 ....32 A3
WARRN/WOL WA2 ....37 J3
Kipling Cl OFTN SK2 ....47 M6
Kipling Gv STHEL WA9 ....34 A1
Kipling Rd CH/BCN CH1 ....144 F7
NWCHW CW8 ....19 M3
Kipling Wy CW/HAS CW1 ....221 H5
Kirby Cl CHNE CH2 ....145 K7
Kirby Dr SALE M33 ....43 K2
Kirkacre Av NEWLW WA12 ....27 J4
Kirkbeck LEIGH WN7 ....25 J1
Kirkbride Cl NTHLY L27 ....32 A8
Kirkby Av SALE M33 ....43 J2
Kirkby Dr SALE M33 ....43 K2
Kirkby Rd GOL/RIS/CU WA3 ....23 J8
Kirkcaldy Av WARRW/BUR WA5 ..35 K6
Kirkfell Dr MPL/ROM SK6 ....67 L4
Kirkham Av GOL/RIS/CU WA3 .....23 L6
Kirkham Rd CHD/CHDH SK8 ......64 C4
LEIGH WN7 ....24 D2
WDN WA8 ....53 J2
Kirklands SALE M33 ....43 G2
Kirkman Fold RAIN/WH L35 ....33 H1
Kirkstall Cl MCFLDN SK10 ....111 J8
POY/DIS SK12 ....66 D8
Kirkstead Rd CHD/CHDH SK8 ....65 J5
Kirkstone Av RUNC WA7 ....74 A8
Kirkstone Crs RUNC WA7 ....74 A8
Kirkwall Dr WARRW/BUR WA5 ....55 G1
Kirkwood Cl CHSE CH3 ....170 A2
Kishfield La CHF/WBR SK23 ....89 G7
Kitchener Av IRL M44 ....31 J8
Kitchen St CH/BCN CH1 ....16 D6
Kite Gv ALS/KID ST7 ....243 K1
Kitfield Av MWCH CW10 ....179 J5
Kitt's Moss La BRAM/HZG SK7 ...65 K6
Kiveton Dr AIMK WN4 ....22 C2
Knightley AUD/MAD/W CW3 .....267 M7
Knight Rd WARRW/BUR WA5 ....26 F6
Knightsbridge Av
NWCHE CW9 ....153 L1
WARRS WA4 ....57 J1
Knightsbridge Cl WILM/AE SK9 ..84 D3
Knight's Cl MCFLDS SK11 ....15 J7
Knights Gn FLINT CH6 ....116 A6
Knights La TPLY/KEL CW6 ....174 D3
Knights Meadow WSFD CW7 ....177 J1
Knight St BURS/TUN ST6 ....243 K8
DID/WITH M20 ....45 H2
MCFLDS SK11 ....15 J7
Knights Wy CW/SHV CW2 ....253 G1
Knightwake Rd NM/HAY SK22 ....69 G4
Knole Av POY/DIS SK12 ....66 F8
Knoll St NM/HAY SK22 ....69 H4
Knottingley Dr GTS/LS CH66 .....94 C7
Knotty La CONG CW12 ....209 G4
Knotty Ms WLTN L25 ....50 C5
Knowe Av WYTH/NTH M22 ....63 K3
The Knowe NSTN CH64 ....93 C4
Knowlbank Rd ALS/KID ST7 .....255 M6
Knowle Cl GTS/LS CH66 ....120 E1
Knowle Pk WILM/AE SK9 ....84 C1
Knowle Rd BIDD ST8 ....227 J5
MPL/ROM SK6 ....49 K6
Knowles St WDN WA8 ....7 L1
Knowl Hey Rd HLWD L26 ....51 C6
Knowl La CHSE CH3 ....211 L7
The Knowl CHSE CH3 ....211 M7
Knowsley Av GOL/RIS/CU WA3 ...23 H3
Knowsley Crs STKP SK1 ....3 M8
Knowsley Dr LEIGH WN7 ....24 D2
Knowsley Expy RAIN/WH L35 .....32 D6
WDN WA8 ....51 L4
Knowsley La ALS/KID ST7 ....225 L8
Knowsley Rd BRAM/HZG SK7 ....66 F4
CHNE CH2 ....146 A8
MCFLDS SK11 ....138 C7
RAIN/WH L35 ....33 K2
STKP SK1 ....3 M8
Knutsford Old Rd WARRS WA4 ...57 G2
Knutsford Rd ALS/KID ST7 ....224 F7
HOLMCH CW4 ....156 F5
KNUT WA16 ....107 K1
MCFLDS SK11 ....134 F1
NWCHE CW9 ....77 G7
WARRS WA4 ....5 H9
WILM/AE SK9 ....109 L1
Knutsford Wy CH/BCN CH1 ......168 F2
Knypersley Av OFTN SK2 ....47 J5
Knype Wy BIDD ST8 ....227 H6
Kohima Crs CHSE CH3 ....170 B7
Kronsbec Av GTS/LS CH66 ....94 D6
Kylemore Wy HLWD L26 ....36 D5
Kyle Rd BRAM/HZG SK7 ....66 F3
Kynaston Dr CHSW/BR CH4 .....168 C5

L

Laburnam Cl ALS/KID ST7 ....242 E4
Laburnum Av CW/SHV CW2 .....237 L2
WARR WA1 ....38 C5
Laburnum Cl CONG CW12 ....183 M8
HALE/TIMP WA15 ....43 H7
Laburnum Crs NWCHW CW8 ....129 H1
Laburnum Farm Cl
NSTN CH64 ....92 A7
Laburnum Gv CHSW/BR CH4 ....168 E6
CW/HAS CW1 ....221 K6
GTS/LS CH66 ....121 G4
NWCHW CW8 ....128 D4
RUNC WA7 ....9 K7
Laburnum La HALE/TIMP WA15 ...61 L4
WARRN/BUR WA5 ....35 J6
Laburnum Rd GOL/RIS/CU WA3 ..23 M8
IRL M44 ....31 K7
MCFLDS SK11 ....138 C7
NWCHE CW9 ....153 M1
Laburnum St AIMK WN4 ....22 B2
Laburnum Wy EDGY/DAV SK3 ....46 B4
WRXS/E LL13 ....228 D3
Lacey Av WILM/AE SK9 ....84 B4

Lacey Ct WDN WA8 ....7 J7
Lacey Gv WILM/AE SK9 ....84 B3
Lacey Gv WILM/AE SK9 ....84 C3
Lache Hall Crs CHSW/BR CH4 ...168 F8
Lache La CHSW/BR CH4 ....191 J3
Lache Park Av CHSW/BR CH4 ...169 G6
Lacy St STKP SK1 ....3 G7
Ladies Mile KNUT WA16 ....106 F2
Ladies Wk NSTN CH64 ....91 L4
Ladybarn Av GOL/RIS/CU WA3 ...22 F5
Ladybarn Crs BRAM/HZG SK7 ....65 M6
Ladybower CHD/CHDH SK8 ......65 J1
Ladybridge Ri CHD/CHDH SK8 ...65 J1
Ladybrook Av HALE/TIMP WA15 ..43 H5
Ladybrook Rd BRAM/HZG SK7 ...65 J5
Ladycroft WARR WA1 ....38 E5
Ladyfield St WILM/AE SK9 ....84 B5
Ladyfield Ter WILM/AE SK9 ....84 B5
Ladygates AUD/MAD/W CW3 ....255 G6
Lady Helen Wk NANT CW5 ....20 F5
Lady La GOL/RIS/CU WA3 ....29 J3
KNUT WA16 ....82 C5
Ladypit Rd CHF/WBR SK23 ....69 M8
Ladypool SPK/HALE L24 ....71 J3
Ladys Cl POY/DIS SK12 ....66 E8
Ladysmith Av AIMK WN4 ....22 C1
Ladysmith Rd DID/WITH M20 ....45 J2
Ladysmith St EDGY/DAV SK3 .....46 E5
Ladythorn Av MPL/ROM SK6 .....49 C7
Ladythorn Crs BRAM/HZG SK7 ...65 M6
Ladythorn Gv BRAM/HZG SK7 ...65 M6
Ladythorn Rd BRAM/HZG SK7 ...65 M6
Ladywell Cl BRAM/HZG SK7 ......66 A2
Ladywood Rd WARRW/BUR WA5 ..36 C3
Lagonda Cl BIDD ST8 ....227 H7
Lagos Gv WSFD CW7 ....177 L2
Laidon Av CW/SHV CW2 ....238 A4
Laira St WARRN/WOL WA2 ....5 J3
Laithwaite Cl STHEL WA9 ....34 B1
Lake House Ct NWCHW CW8 ....128 C3
Lakelands Cl MCFLDN SK10 ......15 L5
Lake La WARRS WA4 ....76 F7
Lakenheath Rd HLWD L26 ....50 E6
Lakeside AUD/MAD/W CW5 .....255 G6
CHSW/BR CH4 ....192 B2
MCFLDS SK11 ....186 D4
Lakeside Cl WDN WA8 ....52 A5
Lakeside Dr POY/DIS SK12 ....66 E7
WARR WA1 ....56 A1
Lakeside Gn OFTN SK2 ....47 J6
Lakeside Rd LYMM WA13 ....58 D3
Lakeside Vw NANT CW5 ....251 L1
Lakes Rd MPL/ROM SK6 ....49 G6
Lake St OFTN SK2 ....47 H7
Lake Vw CONG CW12 ....207 H2
RAIN/WH L35 ....32 E3
Lakewood CHSW/BR CH4 ....192 B2
Laleham Gn BRAM/HZG SK7 .....65 K1
Laleston Cl WDN WA8 ....6 C5
Lamberton Dr NTHM/RTH M23 ...43 L6
Lambert's La CONG CW12 ....207 M4
Lambert Wy NWCHW CW8 ......129 G8
Lamb La ALT WA14 ....61 K7
Lamborne Gv MWCH CW10 .....179 J3
Lambourn Av WDN WA8 ....33 J7
Lambourn Cl POY/DIS SK12 ......66 D8
Lambourn Dr CW/HAS CW1 ....221 H3
Lambourne Cl GTS/LS CH66 ....120 F4
WYTH/NTH M22 ....63 K3
Lambsickle Cl RUNC WA7 ....72 F6
Lambsickle La RUNC WA7 ....72 F6
Lambs La WARR WA1 ....38 A4
Lamb St ALS/KID ST7 ....243 C2
Lamerton Cl
WARRW/BUR WA5 ....35 K8
Lampeter Cl
WARRW/BUR WA5 ....36 E2
Lampits La CHSE CH3 ....147 G8
Lamport Cl WDN WA8 ....53 L1
Lampton Cl ALT WA14 ....42 D5
Lanark Av WYTH/NTH M22 ....44 D4
Lanark Cl BRAM/HZG SK7 ....67 G2
Lancashire HI RDSH SK5 ....2 F2
Lancashire La PART M31 ....40 E3
Lancaster Av GOL/RIS/CU WA3 ..23 J4
RAIN/WH L35 ....32 D1
RUNC WA7 ....8 D7
Lancaster Cl BRAM/HZG SK7 ....66 D4
MPL/ROM SK6 ....48 A3
WARRN/WOL WA2 ....37 M3
WSFD CW7 ....177 K6
Lancaster Dr CHSE CH3 ....170 B2
Lancaster Flds CW/HAS CW1 .....19 M8
Lancaster Pk CHSW/BR CH4 ....190 A1
Lancaster Rd DID/WITH M20 .....45 G1
IRL M44 ....31 J7
WDN WA8 ....53 G1
WILM/AE SK9 ....84 E3
Lancaster St STKP SK1 ....3 J3
WARRW/BUR WA5 ....4 B7
Lancelot Rd WYTH/NTH M22 ....63 M2
Lancelyn Dr WILM/AE SK9 ....84 D4
Lancer Ct RUNC WA7 ....73 L1
Lancers Cft GTS/LS CH66 ....120 E3
Lanchester Cl BIDD ST8 ....227 H6
Lancia Cl BIDD ST8 ....227 H7
Lancing Av DID/WITH M20 ....45 L1
WARRN/WOL WA2 ....28 A8
Lancing Cl WLTN L25 ....50 D3
Lancing Rd EP CH65 ....11 G9
WLTN L25 ....50 D3
Lancing Wy WLTN L25 ....50 D3
Land Cut La GOL/RIS/CU WA3 ....38 D1
Lander Cl WARRW/BUR WA5 ....36 D5
Landkey Rd NTHM/RTH M23 .....43 M2
Land La WILM/AE SK9 ....84 C6
Landor Cl GOL/RIS/CU WA3 ......23 L4
Landrake Gv BURS/TUN ST6 ....243 K8
Landscape Dene FROD/HEL WA6 .98 D8
Landseer Av NSTN CH64 ....91 M5
WARRS WA4 ....56 B3
Landseer Dr MCFLDN SK10 .....137 L4
MPL/ROM SK6 ....49 H5
Landside LEIGH WN7 ....24 F7
Landswood Pk NWCHW CW8 ....129 H8

Lane Ends MPL/ROM SK6 .... 48 D1
Lane Head Av GOL/RIS/CU WA3 .... 23 L4
Lanehead Rd CHF/WBR SK23 .... 89 J7
Laneside Dr BRAM/HZG SK7 .... 66 A3
Laneside Rd DID/WITH M20 .... 45 J4
NM/HAY SK22 .... 69 L5
The Lane MALPAS SY14 .... 257 C8
Langbar RAIN/WH L35 .... 32 E2
Langcliffe Av GOL/RIS/CU WA3 .... 29 L1 ☐
Langdale Av GOL/RIS/CU WA3 ...... 23 J3 ☐
LYMM WA13 .... 58 F1 ☐
Langdale Cl CHD/CHDH SK8 .... 64 C1
HALE/TIMP WA15 .... 42 E7
MCFLDN SK11 .... 137 M7
MPL/ROM SK6 .... 67 L4
WARRN/WOL WA2 .... 37 L1 ☐
WDN WA8 .... 52 C4
WSFD CW7 .... 177 K2 ☐
Langdale Ct CONG CW12 .... 207 G3
Langdale Rd BRAM/HZG SK7 .... 65 J7
CW/SHV CW2 .... 237 K1
PART M31 .... 40 E1
RUNC WA7 .... 9 J4
SALE M33 .... 42 E3
Langdale Wy FROD/HEL WA6 .... 99 J3
Langfield GOL/RIS/CU WA3 .... 23 L5
Langfoot SPK/HALE L24 .... 71 J5
Langford Ct CHSE CH3 .... 172 C2
Langford Dr LEIGH WN7 .... 24 E2
Langford Rd NWCHE CW9 .... 131 G1
Langford St MCFLDS SK11 .... 14 E5
Langford Wy WARRS WA4 .... 57 K8
Langham Gv HALE/TIMP WA15 ..... 43 H4
HTNM SK4 .... 46 B3
Langland Cl WARRW/BUR WA5 ..... 36 C2
Langley Av BRAM/HZG SK7 .... 66 B3
SBCH CW11 .... 204 C4
Langley Dr WILM/AE SK9 .... 84 E1
Langley Hall Cl MCFLDS SK11 ...... 139 H8
Langley Rd MCFLDS SK11 .... 163 H1
NWCHE CW9 .... 13 K7
Langport Dr CHSE CH3 .... 170 C2
Langston Gn BRAM/HZG SK7 .... 66 A3 ☐
Langton Cl NEWLW WA12 .... 22 A8 ☐
WDN WA8 .... 52 B1
Langton Gn WARR WA1 .... 38 D5
Langwell Cl GOL/RIS/CU WA3 .... 30 A7
Lanreath Cl MCFLDN SK10 .... 137 K3 ☐
Lansbury Rd HUY L36 .... 32 A2
Lansdown Cl BRAM/HZG SK7 .... 65 J5
Lansdowne FROD/HEL WA6 .... 99 K6
GOL/RIS/CU WA3 .... 29 L2
Lansdowne Av MPL/ROM SK6 .... 48 D2
Lansdowne Gv
CHSW/BR CH4 .... 169 G5 ☐
Lansdowne Rd ALT WA14 .... 42 D6
CHSE CH3 .... 171 K1
CW/HAS CW1 .... 19 L3
Lansdowne St MCFLDN SK10 .... 15 K3
Lansdown Rd CHSW/BR CH4 ..... 190 H1
Lantern Vw NM/HAY SK22 .... 69 H3
Lapwing Cl GOL/RIS/CU WA3 .... 23 K4
WSFD CW7 .... 177 J7
Lapwing Ct HLWD L26 .... 50 E3 ☐
Lapwing Gv RUNC WA7 .... 74 A6
Lapwing La MCFLDS SK11 .... 135 H5
WARRS WA4 .... 54 F5
Lapwing Rd ALS/KID ST7 .... 243 K2
Larch Av CHD/CHDH SK8 .... 65 G3 ☐
CO CH5 .... 142 B8
CW/SHV CW2 .... 238 F7
MCFLDS SK11 .... 138 A7
NEWLW WA12 .... 27 J2
WARRW/BUR WA5 .... 35 L7
WDN WA8 .... 53 H2 ☐
Larch Cl ALS/KID ST7 .... 243 G4
GOL/RIS/CU WA3 .... 23 M6
MPL/ROM SK6 .... 48 E7
NTHM/RTH M23 .... 43 J4
NWCHW CW8 .... 128 D5
POY/DIS SK12 .... 86 F1
RUNC WA7 .... 9 M8
Larchdale Cl GTS/LS CH66 .... 120 F4 ☐
Larchfields CH/BCN CH1 .... 144 A4
Larch Ri MCFLDN SK10 .... 111 K6
Larch Rd CW/SHV CW2 .... 237 L2
PART M31 .... 40 E2
RUNC WA7 .... 9 M9
Larchtree Cl NWCHW CW8 .... 103 H8 ☐
Larchway BRAM/HZG SK7 .... 65 J5
Larch Wy CHSW/BR CH4 .... 168 E6
Larchway MPL/ROM SK6 .... 67 M5
Larchways WARRS WA4 .... 56 D7
Larchwood Dr WILM/AE SK9 .... 84 E4
Lark Av ALS/KID ST7 .... 243 K1
Larkfield Av WARR WA1 .... 37 M5
Lark Hall Cl MCFLDN SK10 .... 139 G4
Lark Hall Crs MCFLDN SK10 .... 139 G5
Lark Hall Rd MCFLDN SK10 .... 139 G5
Larkhill Cl HALE/TIMP WA15 .... 43 H6
Larkhill Rd CHD/CHDH SK8 .... 46 C7
Lark Hill Rd EDGY/DAV SK3 .... 2 B7
Larkhill Vw EDGY/DAV SK3 .... 46 C7
Larkspur Cl CHSW/BR CH4 .... 168 F8
LEIGH WN7 .... 24 F1 ☐
NANT CW5 .... 20 F1
RUNC WA7 .... 73 M8 ☐
Larkstoke Cl WARRS WA4 .... 56 E6
Larkswood Dr OFTN SK2 .... 47 M7
Larne Av EDGY/DAV SK3 .... 46 B5
Larne Dr CHSW/BR CH4 .... 167 K8
Larwood Av HTNM SK4 .... 46 A3
Laskey La WARRS WA4 .... 38 F8
Latchford St WARRS WA4 .... 57 G1
Latebrook Cl BURS/TUN ST6 ...... 243 J5 ☐
Latham Av FROD/HEL WA6 .... 124 D8
NEWLW WA12 .... 22 C8
RUNC WA7 .... 9 L4
Latham Rd SBCH CW11 .... 204 A7
Latham St WSFD CW7 .... 177 J3 ☐
Lathom Av WARRN/WOL WA2 ...... 37 H4
Lathom Gv SALE M33 .... 43 G7
Lathom Rd IRL M44 .... 31 M4 ☐
Lathom Wy MCFLDN SK10 .... 15 L1
Launceston Cl RUNC WA7 .... 74 C6 ☐

WSFD CW7 .... 177 H5 ☐
Launceston Dr
BRAM/HZG SK7 .... 65 M5 ☐
WARRW/BUR WA5 .... 54 E1
Laura St CW/SHV CW2 .... 19 H9
Laurel Av CHD/CHDH SK8 .... 45 K7
NEWLW WA12 .... 27 K2
WARR WA1 .... 38 D5 ☐
Laurel Bank WARRS WA4 .... 57 J3
WDN WA8 .... 53 G1 ☐
WSFD CW7 .... 177 K4 ☐
Laurel Cl MWCH CW10 .... 179 H2
NWCHW CW8 .... 103 G8
SBCH CW11 .... 204 C7
Laurel Dr ALS/KID ST7 .... 243 L1
CW/SHV CW2 .... 237 M2 ☐
EP CH65 .... 121 H2
HALE/TIMP WA15 .... 43 H8
NSTN CH64 .... 93 H3
Laurel Gv CHNE CH2 .... 170 A1
GOL/RIS/CU WA3 .... 23 K4
Laurel Pk TPLY/KEL CW6 .... 173 C6
Laurels Farm Ct CHNE CH2 .... 123 H1 ☐
Laurel St HTNM SK4 .... 2 E4
Laurel Wk PART M31 .... 40 E2
Laurel Wy CHD/CHDH SK8 .... 65 J4
Laurelwood Dr GTS/LS CH66 ..... 120 E4
Laureston Av CW/HAS CW1 .... 19 M3
Lausanne Rd BRAM/HZG SK7 ...... 65 L1 ☐
GOL/RIS/CU WA3 .... 23 K4
Lavender Cl NTHM/RTH M23 .... 43 L3 ☐
RUNC WA7 .... 9 M5
Lavender Ct CO CH5 .... 142 B6 ☐
Lavender Rd NWCHE CW9 .... 130 E6
Lavenders Brow STKP SK1 .... 3 H5
Lavenham Ct BRAM/HZG SK7 ...... 66 A4 ☐
MCFLDN SK10 .... 138 C2
Laverock Gv
AUD/MAD/W CW3 .... 267 L6 ☐
Lavington Av CHD/CHDH SK8 .... 46 A6
Lavister Av BNG/LEV M19 .... 45 K1
Lavister Cl NWCHE CW9 .... 153 H8 ☐
Lavister Wks WRX/GR/LL LL12 ... 210 C3
Lawford Dr CW/HAS CW1 .... 220 F4 ☐
Lawn Av WARR WA1 .... 37 M4
Lawn Dr CHNE CH2 .... 145 K5
HALE/TIMP WA15 .... 42 E6
Lawnsdale NWCHW CW8 .... 127 K7
Lawnswood Gv CHNE CH2 .... 123 H1
Lawrence Av NWCHE CW9 .... 153 L4 ☐
Lawrence Av West
MWCH CW10 .... 179 J3 ☐
SBCH CW11 .... 203 K6 ☐
Lawrence Cl HOLMCH CW4 .... 157 G7
SBCH CW11 .... 203 K6 ☐
Lawrence Pl POY/DIS SK12 .... 86 D2
Lawrence Rd WARRS WA4 .... 42 C6
BRAM/HZG SK7 .... 66 E1
Lawrence St CO CH5 .... 167 G1 ☐
CW/HAS CW1 .... 18 F4
NEWLW WA12 .... 27 G1
STKP SK1 .... 2 F6
Laws Gdns CHSE CH3 .... 170 A4 ☐
Lawson Av CHD/CHDH SK8 .... 45 H7
WARRW/BUR WA5 .... 4 B6
Lawson Cl WARR WA1 .... 38 E5
Law St CHNE CH2 .... 17 L2
Lawton Av ALS/KID ST7 .... 242 D1
BRAM/HZG SK7 .... 65 L4 ☐
Lawton Cl GOL/RIS/CU WA3 .... 29 L1 ☐
MPL/ROM SK6 .... 47 M3 ☐
Lawton Coppice ALS/KID ST7 .... 225 L8
Lawton Crs BIDD ST8 .... 227 K4 ☐
Lawton Heath Rd ALS/KID ST7 ... 224 F6
Lawton Moor Rd
NTHM/RTH M23 .... 44 A3
Lawton Rd ALS/KID ST7 .... 241 K1
RAIN/WH L35 .... 33 K2
Lawton St ALS/KID ST7 .... 226 C8
BIDD ST8 .... 227 K4
CONG CW12 .... 207 L2
CW/SHV CW2 .... 18 F6
Lawton Wy SBCH CW11 .... 203 L5 ☐
Laxey Av WARR WA1 .... 38 D6 ☐
Laxton Cl GTS/LS CH66 .... 120 F4 ☐
Laxton Rd WLTN L25 .... 50 C6
Laxton Wy MWCH CW10 .... 179 J2 ☐
Layland Av CHD/CHDH SK8 .... 24 E8
Layton Cl GOL/RIS/CU WA3 .... 38 E1
STKP SK1 .... 3 J7
WLTN L25 .... 50 C2
Layton Dr MPL/ROM SK6 .... 48 C1
Layton Rd WLTN L25 .... 50 C2
Lea Av CW/HAS CW1 .... 19 L4
HOLMCH CW4 .... 157 J3
Lea Bank Cl MCFLDS SK11 .... 14 B5
Leaches La CO CH5 .... 166 E1
Lea Cl SBCH CW11 .... 204 C7
Leacroft Rd GOL/RIS/CU WA3 ...... 30 A6
Lea Cross Gv WDN WA8 .... 52 C1
Leadbeaters Rd MCFLDS SK11 ... 15 L1
Leadbrook Dr FLINT CH6 .... 116 D8
Leader Williams Rd IRL M44 .... 31 M3 ☐
Leadgate La CHSE CH3 .... 195 M2
Lea Dr MWCH CW10 .... 179 G8
NANT CW5 .... 20 B8
Leadsmithy St MWCH CW10 ...... 179 J3
Leadworks La CH/BCN CH1 .... 17 J4
Lea Farm Rd CHD/CHDH SK8 .... 64 F6 ☐
Leafield Rd POY/DIS SK12 .... 68 C6
WLTN L25 .... 50 D6
Leaf La WSFD CW7 .... 178 A2 ☐
Lea Hall Pk CH/BCN CH1 .... 145 G1
Leahurst Cl CHNE CH2 .... 145 M8
Lea La CHSE CH3 .... 212 B1
Leamington Av NEWLW WA12 ..... 27 J3 ☐
Leamington Cl NSTN CH64 .... 91 L6
WARRW/BUR WA5 .... 36 A4
Leamington Rd CONG CW12 ...... 206 F1 ☐
MCFLDN SK10 .... 137 H3 ☐
Lear Dr CW/SHV CW2 .... 237 M4
Lea Rd CHD/CHDH SK8 .... 64 B3
Leas Cl GTS/LS CH66 .... 94 C7 ☐
Leaside RUNC WA7 .... 75 K3
Leaside Rd CH/BCN CH1 .... 144 E6 ☐
Leaside Wy WILM/AE SK9 .... 84 B4
Lea's Pas MWCH CW10 .... 179 H3 ☐
The Leas HALE/TIMP WA15 .... 62 B1
Lea St NM/HAY SK22 .... 69 G4
Leatham Cl GOL/RIS/CU WA3 ...... 38 E1
Leather's La HLWD L26 .... 50 F5

Leaton Av NTHM/RTH M23 .... 44 A6
Lea Wy ALS/KID ST7 .... 241 K1
Leawood Cl WARRN/WOL WA2 .. 129 C6
Ledbury Dr CW/SHV CW2 .... 238 A5
Ledge Ley CHD/CHDH SK8 .... 64 E4
Ledley St MCFLDN SK10 .... 112 F5
Ledsham La CO CH5 .... 166 A6
GTS/LS CH66 .... 119 M1
Ledsham Park Dr
GTS/LS CH66 .... 94 A6 ☐
Ledsham Rd GTS/LS CH66 .... 94 A7
Ledston Cl NTHM/RTH M23 .... 43 M7
Ledston Cl RUNC WA7 .... 74 D3
Ledward La ALT WA14 .... 61 H2
Ledward St WSFD CW7 .... 178 A3
Ledyard Cl WARRW/BUR WA5 ...... 4 A2
Lee Av ALT WA14 .... 42 C5
Leech Rd MALPAS SY14 .... 258 B1
Lee Cl IRL M44 .... 31 M3
KNUT WA16 .... 106 F3
Lee Dr NWCHW CW8 .... 12 E5
Leek Old Rd MCFLDS SK11 .... 162 D5
Leek Rd CONG CW12 .... 208 A4
Leen La CH/BCN CH1 .... 17 C5
Lee Rd WARRW/BUR WA5 .... 36 B6 ☐
Leeside HTNM SK4 .... 46 A3
Lees La MCFLDN SK10 .... 85 H5
NSTN CH64 .... 92 B4
Lees Rd BRAM/HZG SK7 .... 65 K7
Leestone Rd WYTH/NTH M22 ...... 44 E6
Lee St CHSE CH3 .... 17 J4
STKP SK1 .... 3 C6
Legh Gdns KNUT WA16 .... 107 H3 ☐
Legh Rd KNUT WA16 .... 107 H4
MCFLDN SK10 .... 86 C7
POY/DIS SK12 .... 68 A6
SALE M33 .... 43 L1
Legh St AIMK WN4 .... 22 B2
GOL/RIS/CU WA3 .... 23 C4
LYMM WA13 .... 58 E1 ☐
NEWLW WA12 .... 27 G1
WARR WA1 .... 4 F6
Leicester Av ALS/KID ST7 .... 224 C7
HALE/TIMP WA15 .... 43 C4
Leicester Rd HALE/TIMP WA15 .... 61 L2
Leicester St NWCHE CW9 .... 11 K1
WARRW/BUR WA5 .... 4 B6
Leigh Av KNUT WA16 .... 107 J1
MPL/ROM SK6 .... 48 E6
WDN WA8 .... 7 G3
Leigh La NWCHW CW8 .... 102 C7
Leigh Rd CONG CW12 .... 185 H7
HALE/TIMP WA15 .... 61 L2
WILM/AE SK9 .... 83 K7
Leigh's Brow NWCHW CW8 .... 128 F1
Leighton Cha NSTN CH64 .... 91 K3
Leighton Dr LEIGH WN7 .... 24 B3
Leighton Pk NSTN CH64 .... 91 K4
Leighton Rd NSTN CH64 .... 91 J1
The Leightons NSTN CH64 .... 91 K4
Leighton St CW/HAS CW1 .... 18 C1
Leighton Vw CW/HAS CW1 .... 221 G4 ☐
Leighton Wy NWCHW CW8 .... 128 C3
Leinster St RUNC WA7 .... 8 E1
Lenham Wy SPK/HALE L24 .... 50 B8 ☐
Lenton Gdns WYTH/NTH M22 ...... 44 E7 ☐
Leominster Dr WYTH/NTH M22 .... 63 L1
Leonard St CH/BCN CH1 .... 16 D2
RUNC WA7 .... 8 B9
WARRN/WOL WA2 .... 5 J3
WARR WA1 .... 56 C3
Leon Cl WARRW/BUR WA5 .... 35 K5 ☐
Lerryn Dr BRAM/HZG SK7 .... 65 K3
Leslie Gv HALE/TIMP WA15 .... 43 G6
Leslie Rd WSFD CW7 .... 177 G5
Lessingham Rd WDN WA8 .... 52 F1
Lester Cl ALS/KID ST7 .... 224 D8
Leven Av WSFD CW7 .... 177 M2
Levens Cl CHD/CHDH SK8 .... 45 H8
Levens Rd BRAM/HZG SK7 .... 66 C2
Leven Wk EP CH65 .... 10 A2
Leveret Rd SPK/HALE L24 .... 71 G1
Leverett Cl ALT WA14 .... 42 A7 ☐
Lever St BRAM/HZG SK7 .... 66 A4
Levisham Gdns WARRW/BUR WA5.. 4 B2
Lewin St MWCH CW10 .... 179 J3
Lewis Av WARRW/BUR WA5 .... 36 F2
Lewis Cl NANT CW5 .... 21 K7
Lewis Crs WDN WA8 .... 7 G6
Lewis Gv WDN WA8 .... 6 B2 ☐
Lewisham Dr BURS/TUN ST6 ..... 243 J5
Lewis St CW/SHV CW2 .... 18 D5
Lexden St WARRW/BUR WA5 .... 4 B5
Leybrook Rd WYTH/NTH M22 ...... 63 J1
Leyburne St MPL/ROM SK6 .... 48 C2 ☐
Leyburn Rd SALE M33 .... 42 C3
Leycester Cl KNUT WA16 .... 107 H1
Leycester Dr WYTH/NTH M22 ...... 81 M5
Leycester Rd KNUT WA16 .... 107 H5
Leycett Dr NTHM/RTH M23 .... 44 A3
Leyfield Ct CHSW/BR CH4 .... 168 F7
Leygate Vw NM/HAY SK22 .... 69 H4
Ley Hey Av MPL/ROM SK6 .... 48 C2
Ley Hey Rd MPL/ROM SK6 .... 48 C2
Leyland Av CHD/CHDH SK8 .... 45 H6
DID/WITH M20 .... 45 K1
Leyland Dr CHSW/BR CH4 .... 168 B6
Leyland Gv CW/HAS CW1 .... 222 C8
Leyland St HTNM SK4 .... 2 E5
Ley La MPL/ROM SK6 .... 49 J4
Leys Rd ALT WA14 .... 42 E4
Leyton Cl RUNC WA7 .... 73 H6
Libra Pl BURS/TUN ST6 .... 243 M6
Libson Cl WARRW/BUR WA5 .... 38 A1
Lichfield Av GOL/RIS/CU WA3 ..... 23 K4 ☐
HALE/TIMP WA15 .... 62 C1
Lichfield Cl KNUT WA16 .... 107 K2 ☐
Lichfield Ct WSFD CW7 .... 177 K5
Lichfield Dr GTS/LS CH66 .... 120 E3
Lichfield Gv AIMK WN4 .... 22 C2 ☐
Lichfield Rd ALS/KID ST7 .... 242 D5

CH/BCN CH1 .... 144 F7
HLWD L26 .... 50 E6
Lichfield St MWCH CW10 .... 179 K2
Lichfield Wk MPL/ROM SK6 .... 48 A3 ☐
Lickers La RAIN/WH L35 .... 32 E2
Lidgetts La CHSE CH3 .... 113 J8
Liebig St WDN WA8 .... 7 H4
Liffey Av WYTH/NTH M22 .... 63 L1
Light Alders La POY/DIS SK12 ...... 68 A5
Lightburne Av LEIGH WN7 .... 24 E1
Lightburn St RUNC WA7 .... 8 E5
Lightfoot La TPLY/KEL CW6 .... 175 G8
Lightfoot St CHNE CH2 .... 17 K2
Lighthorne Av EDGY/DAV SK3 ..... 45 M5 ☐
Lighthorne Gv EDGY/DAV SK3 .... 45 M5 ☐
Lighthorne Rd EDGY/DAV SK3 .... 45 M5
Lighthouse Rd SPK/HALE L24 ...... 71 L5
Lightley Cl SBCH CW11 .... 204 A8
Light Oaks Rd GOL/RIS/CU WA3 ... 25 J3
Lightwood Green Av
AUD/MAD/W CW3 .... 273 G2
Lilac Av KNUT WA16 .... 106 E3
WARRW/BUR WA5 .... 36 A7
Lilac Cl MPL/ROM SK6 .... 47 K1 ☐
HALE/TIMP WA15 .... 62 A1
Lilac Crs RUNC WA7 .... 9 L6
Lilac Dr NWCHW CW8 .... 12 D5
Lilac Gv GTS/LS CH66 .... 121 G4
WARRS WA4 .... 56 E3
Lilac Rd GOL/RIS/CU WA3 .... 23 G3 ☐
HALE/TIMP WA15 .... 62 A1
Lilac St OFTN SK2 .... 46 F6
Liford Rd WARRW/BUR WA5 .... 4 C1
Liford St WARRW/BUR WA5 .... 35 M6 ☐
Liford Sq MCFLDS SK11 .... 138 D7 ☐
Liford St WARRW/BUR WA5 .... 4 D3
Lily Av NEWLW WA12 .... 27 J2
Lily Cl EDGY/DAV SK3 .... 46 D7
Lily La MWCH CW10 .... 156 A6
Lily Pl AIMK WN4 .... 22 C2
Limbrick Rd ALS/KID ST7 .... 255 M3
Lime Av FROD/HEL WA6 .... 99 J4
NM/HAY SK22 .... 69 K3
NWCHE CW9 .... 13 H8
NWCHW CW8 .... 128 D4
WDN WA8 .... 7 K1
Lime Cl GOL/RIS/CU WA3 .... 40 A2
MWCH CW10 .... 179 H2
SBCH CW11 .... 204 A5
TPLY/KEL CW6 .... 197 K2
Limefield Av LYMM WA13 .... 58 F2
Lime Gv ALS/KID ST7 .... 241 L2
CHD/CHDH SK8 .... 45 K6
CHNE CH2 .... 17 M1
CHNE CH2 .... 123 C1
CHSW/BR CH4 .... 168 D6
CW/SHV CW2 .... 238 C8
GOL/RIS/CU WA3 .... 23 K6
HALE/TIMP WA15 .... 43 H6
MCFLDN SK10 .... 15 K5
RUNC WA7 .... 9 L6
WSFD CW7 .... 178 A3
Limeheath Pl BURS/TUN ST6 ..... 243 L7
Lime Kiln La ALS/KID ST7 .... 242 E2
MPL/ROM SK6 .... 49 G7
Limekiln La WARRW/BUR WA5 .... 35 L1
Limes La WARRS WA4 .... 76 C5
The Limes GOL/RIS/CU WA3 .... 24 D8
WRX/GR/LL LL12 .... 210 B5
Lime St CW/HAS CW1 .... 221 J6
EP CH65 .... 10 E4
Lime Tree Av CW/HAS CW1 .... 221 K5
WARRS WA4 .... 56 E3
Lime Tree Cl GTS/LS CH66 .... 121 G4
Lime Tree Dr CHSE CH3 .... 228 F3
Limetree La KNUT WA16 .... 59 K6
Limeways WARRS WA4 .... 56 E3
Limewood Crs NWCHW CW8 ..... 103 H8
Limewood Gv NWCHW CW8 ..... 103 H8
Linbeck Gv GOL/RIS/CU WA3 ..... 23 L3
Lincoln Av CHD/CHDH SK8 .... 64 B5
GOL/RIS/CU WA3 .... 23 K3
IRL M44 .... 31 J8
Lincoln Cl GOL/RIS/CU WA3 ...... 24 C4 ☐
HUY L36 .... 32 B1
MCFLDN SK10 .... 113 K7
RUNC WA7 .... 75 K7
WARR WA1 .... 38 E6
Lincoln Dr AIMK WN4 .... 22 C2
CHNE CH2 .... 146 A7
HALE/TIMP WA15 .... 43 H7 ☐
Lincoln Ri MPL/ROM SK6 .... 48 A3
Lincoln Rd ALS/KID ST7 .... 242 F2
CH/BCN CH1 .... 144 F7
CO CH5 .... 166 A2
GTS/LS CH66 .... 120 D1
WILM/AE SK9 .... 84 E3
Lincoln Sq WDN WA8 .... 53 H2
Lincoln St CW/HAS CW1 .... 18 D2
Lincoln Wy RAIN/WH L35 .... 33 K3
Lincombe Hey MCFLDN SK10 .... 112 C5 ☐
Lincombe Rd WYTH/NTH M22 ..... 63 J4
Linda Dr BRAM/HZG SK7 .... 66 D3
Lindale Cl CONG CW12 .... 185 G7
Linda Rd BURS/TUN ST6 .... 243 L7
Lindbury Av OFTN SK2 .... 47 J5
Linden Av HALE/TIMP WA15 .... 42 E7
WHITCH SY13 .... 269 M5
Linden Cl CONG CW12 .... 208 A4
GTS/LS CH66 .... 120 F4
LYMM WA13 .... 39 M8
WARR WA1 .... 56 C3
Linden Ct SBCH CW11 .... 222 F1 ☐
WDN WA8 .... 33 M8 ☐
Linden Dr BIDD ST8 .... 227 J3
CHNE CH2 .... 146 F3
CW/HAS CW1 .... 19 L5
FROD/HEL WA6 .... 124 D3
Linden Gv BRAM/HZG SK7 .... 65 K8
CHNE CH2 .... 146 A2
CHSW/BR CH4 .... 168 D6
OFTN SK2 .... 47 H8
Linden Rd CHD/CHDH SK8 .... 65 C1 ☐
WDN WA8 .... 53 H1
Linden Wy MPL/ROM SK6 .... 48 A5
Lindfield Cl WARRS WA4 .... 55 H7 ☐
Lindfield Est North
WILM/AE SK9 .... 84 A6

Lindfield Est South
WILM/AE SK9 .... 83 M6
Lindi Av WARRS WA4 .... 57 H3
Lindisfarne Av EP CH65 .... 121 J3
GOL/RIS/CU WA3 .... 23 L4
Lindisfarne Cl MWCH CW10 .... 179 H3 ☐
SALE M33 .... 43 H3
Lindisfarne Dr POY/DIS SK12 ...... 86 D8
Lindley Av WARRS WA4 .... 37 M8
Lindop Cl KNUT WA16 .... 107 J2
Lindop Rd HALE/TIMP WA15 .... 61 M3
Lindops La
AUD/MAD/W CW3 .... 267 M5 ☐
Lindow Ct MPL/ROM SK6 .... 47 K1 ☐
Lindow Fold Dr WILM/AE SK9 ...... 83 K8
Lindow La WILM/AE SK9 .... 83 L6
Lindow St SALE M33 .... 43 M1 ☐
Lindrick Dr MCFLDN SK10 .... 112 C8
Lindrum Av CHD/CHDH SK8 .... 65 H3
Lindsay Av CHD/CHDH SK8 .... 34 E1
Lindsay St STHEL WA9 .... 34 A2
Lindsay Wk NWCHW CW8 .... 128 A8
Lindsay Wy ALS/KID ST7 .... 224 A8
Lindsell Rd ALT WA14 .... 42 C4
Lindsgate Dr
HALE/TIMP WA15 .... 43 H5 ☐
Lindsworth Cl
WARRW/BUR WA5 .... 36 C6 ☐
Lindwall Cl NTHM/RTH M23 .... 44 B2 ☐
Linear Vw NEWLW WA12 .... 27 J4
Linehan Cl HTNM SK4 .... 45 K2
Linen Hall Pl CH/BCN CH1 .... 16 F6 ☐
Lines Rd IRL M44 .... 31 M4
Lingard Rd WYTH/NTH M22 .... 44 D3
Lingdale Rd CHD/CHDH SK8 .... 64 F2
SALE M33 .... 42 B2
Lingfield Cl MCFLDN SK10 .... 112 C8 ☐
Lingfield Dr CW/HAS CW1 .... 221 J5
Lingfield Rd RUNC WA7 .... 8 D6
Lingley Green Av
WARRW/BUR WA5 .... 35 J6
Lingley Rd WARRW/BUR WA5 ...... 35 K6
Linglongs Av CHF/WBR SK23 ...... 89 J7
Linglongs Rd CHF/WBR SK23 ..... 89 J7
Lingmell Gdns HOLMCH CW4 ... 180 F1
Lings Wk WYTH/NTH M22 .... 63 L3
Lingwell Av WDN WA8 .... 52 D2
Lingwood Rd WARRW/BUR WA5 .. 35 L6
Linhope Cl HTNM SK4 .... 45 L1
Link Rd HUY L36 .... 32 B3
SALE M33 .... 42 D2
Links Av GTS/LS CH66 .... 94 C5
Linkside Av WARRN/WOL WA2 .... 28 B6
Linkside Wy GTS/LS CH66 .... 120 F4
Links Rd MPL/ROM SK6 .... 48 B8
MPL/ROM SK6 .... 48 D1
WILM/AE SK9 .... 109 L1
Linksway CHD/CHDH SK8 .... 45 G8
CHNE CH2 .... 145 J5
CONG CW12 .... 207 L4
The Link RUNC WA7 .... 9 L7
Linkway RUNC WA7 .... 9 L7
Linley Gv ALS/KID ST7 .... 241 M1
Linley Rd ALS/KID ST7 .... 241 M2
CHD/CHDH SK8 .... 65 H4
Linnards La NWCHE CW9 .... 104 F7
Linner Rd SPK/HALE L24 .... 70 D1
Linnet Cl NEWLW WA12 .... 27 J1
OFTN SK2 .... 47 M7
WARRN/WOL WA2 .... 37 L1
WSFD CW7 .... 178 A4 ☐
Linnet Gv GOL/RIS/CU WA3 .... 38 E1
MCFLDN SK10 .... 14 A2
Linnett Cl CW/HAS CW1 .... 221 J5 ☐
Linnet Wy BIDD ST8 .... 227 L4
Linney Rd BRAM/HZG SK7 .... 65 K2
Linton Av GOL/RIS/CU WA3 .... 22 F2
Linwood Cl RUNC WA7 .... 74 C7 ☐
Linwood Gv RAIN/WH L35 .... 32 E2
Linwood Wy BURS/TUN ST6 ...... 243 L7
Lion St CONG CW12 .... 207 K2
Lisburn Av SALE M33 .... 43 G1
Lisburne Av OFTN SK2 .... 47 K6
Lisburne Cl OFTN SK2 .... 47 K6 ☐
Lisburne La OFTN SK2 .... 47 J7
Liskeard Cl RUNC WA7 .... 74 B6
Liskeard Dr BRAM/HZG SK7 .... 65 M5
Lismore Av EDGY/DAV SK3 .... 46 B5
Lisson Gv HALE/TIMP WA15 .... 61 L2
Lister Cl MWCH CW10 .... 179 K6
Lister Rd WYTH/NTH M22 .... 63 L2
Litherland Av WYTH/NTH M22 ..... 63 L1
Litherland Rd SALE M33 .... 43 L1
Little Abbey Gtwy
CH/BCN CH1 .... 16 F4 ☐
Little Aston Cl MCFLDN SK10 .... 112 C8
Littlebrook Cl CHD/CHDH SK8 .... 46 C8 ☐
Little Brook Rd SALE M33 .... 42 C3
Little Chell La BURS/TUN ST6 ... 243 M7 ☐
Littlecote Gdns WARRS WA4 .... 76 D1
Littledale Rd WARRW/BUR WA5 .. 35 M5
Littledales La NWCHW CW8 ...... 128 D7
Little Egerton St STKP SK1 .... 2 F4
Littlegate RUNC WA7 .... 73 L4
Little Gn GTS/LS CH66 .... 120 D1
Littleheath Cl
AUD/MAD/W CW3 .... 264 A7 ☐
Little Heath La ALT WA14 .... 41 K7
Little Heath Rd CHSE CH3 .... 170 E3
SPK/HALE L24 .... 70 E2
Little La NSTN CH64 .... 91 H3
Little Meadow MCFLDN SK10 .... 112 D5 ☐
Little Meadow Rd ALT WA14 .... 61 L7
Little Moss Cl ALS/KID ST7 .... 225 L7
Little Moss La ALS/KID ST7 .... 225 L7
Littler La WSFD CW7 .... 176 F3
Little St John St CH/BCN CH1 ..... 17 H6 ☐
Little Stanney La CHNE CH2 ...... 121 L4
Littlestone Cl WDN WA8 .... 34 A8 ☐
Little St CONG CW12 .... 207 K2
MCFLDN SK10 .... 14 F4
Littleton Cl NWCHE CW9 .... 129 L8 ☐
WARRW/BUR WA5 .... 36 D8
Littleton La CHSE CH3 .... 170 D2

Little Underbank *STKP* SK1................ 3 C5
Little Wissage *GTS/LS* CH66 .... 120 F2 ▣
Littlewood Rd *WYTH/NTH* M22 ..... 44 C8
Littondale Av *RAIN/WH* L35 .... 33 K2 ▣
Littondale Cl *CONG* CW12 .... 184 F7
Liverpool Rd *ALS/KID* ST7 .... 243 F5
  CH/BCN CH1 .... 120 F5
  CHNE CH2 .... 16 F2
  IRL M44 .... 31 M4
  NSTN CH64 .... 91 M2
  WARRW/BUR WA5 .... 4 D7
  WDN WA8 .... 6 E3
  WHITCH SY13 .... 269 M6
Liverpool Rd East *ALS/KID* ST7 ... 242 D1
Liverpool Rd West *ALS/KID* ST7 ... 225 C8
Liverpool Rw *NEWLW* WA12 .... 27 K4
Liverpool St *NWCHE* CW9 .... 130 C4
Livingstone Cl *MCFLDN* SK10 .. 137 M4 ▣
  WARRW/BUR WA5 .... 36 D5
Livingstone Rd *EP* CH65 .... 10 L4
Livingstone Wy *MWCH* CW10 ... 179 K6 ▣
  RAIN/WH L35 .... 32 D2
Llanberis Rd *CHD/CHDH* SK8 ..... 64 E3
Llandaff Cl *GTS/LS* CH66 .... 120 E3
Llandovery Cl *WSFD* CW7 .... 177 H5 ▣
Llanfair Rd *EDGY/DAV* SK3 .... 2 B3
Llewellyn St *CQ* CW5 .... 142 A6
Lloyd Av *CHD/CHDH* SK8 .... 45 C6
Lloyd Cl *CHSE* CH3 .... 228 C2
Lloyd Crs *NEWLW* WA12 .... 26 F1
Lloyd Dr *EP* CH65 .... 121 K3
Lloyd Gdns *ALT* WA14 .... 61 K1 ▣
Lloyd Pl *CH/BCN* CH1 .... 144 B8
Lloyd Sq *ALT* WA14 .... 42 D8 ▣
Lloyd St *ALT* WA14 .... 42 D8
  FLINT CH6 .... 116 B5 ▣
  HTNM SK4 .... 2 D1
Llyndir La *WRX/GR/LL* LL12 ..... 210 B3
Llys Caer (Cadnant Court)
  CHSW/BR CH4 .... 167 K7 ▣
Llys Caer *CHSW/BR* CH4 .... 190 A1 ▣
Loachbrook Av *CONG* CW12 ...... 207 G2 ▣
Lobelia Gv *RUNC* WA7 .... 73 M8 ▣
Lochinvar St *GTS/LS* CH66 .... 93 M6
Lochleven Rd *CHD/CHDH* SK8 ... 238 A5
Lochmaben Cl *HOLMCH* CW4 ... 181 H3 ▣
Lochmaddy Cl *BRAM/HZG* SK7 .. 66 F3 ▣
Loch St *RUNC* WA7 .... 9 G1
Locker Av *WARRN/WOL* WA2 .... 37 H2
Lockerbie Cl *HOLMCH* CW4 .... 181 J2
  WARRN/WOL WA2 .... 28 E8
Lockett Rd *WDN* WA8 .... 53 G2
Lockett St *WARRS* WA4 .... 56 F1
Lockgate East *RUNC* WA7 .... 74 C2
Lockgate West *RUNC* WA7 .... 74 C2
Locking Stumps La
  WARRN/WOL WA2 .... 38 B1
Lockitt St *CW/SHV* CW2 .... 19 C6
Lock La *PART* M31 .... 40 D1
Lock Rd *ALT* WA14 .... 42 C6
  WARR WA1 .... 37 M5
Lockside *MPL/ROM* SK6 .... 49 C6
Locksley Cl *HTNM* SK4 .... 2 B3
Lockton La *WARRW/BUR* WA5 ..... 4 B2
Lodge Barn Rd *BIDD* ST8 .... 227 M6
Lodge Brow *MCFLDN* SK10 .... 113 C3
Lodge Cl *LYMM* WA13 .... 40 B8
Lodge Ct *HTNM* SK4 .... 45 M2
Lodge Dr *GOL/RIS/CU* WA3 ...... 29 M1
  NWCHE CW9 .... 153 M5 ▣
  WSFD CW7 .... 178 A3
Lodge Farm Cl *BRAM/HZG* SK7 .. 65 L2
Lodgefields Dr *CW/SHV* CW2 ... 220 D8
Lodge Hollow *FROD/HEL* WA6 .. 124 B1
Lodge La *CH/BCN* CH1 .... 144 A2
  MWCH CW10 .... 179 L2
  NANT CW5 .... 253 G8
  NEWLW WA12 .... 22 B3
  NWCHE CW9 .... 78 A6
  NWCHE CW9 .... 131 C2
  NWCHW CW8 .... 129 H8
  RUNC WA7 .... 73 L4
  WARRS WA4 .... 101 J4
  WARRW/BUR WA5 .... 4 B3
  WDN WA8 .... 33 H8
Lodge Rd *ALS/KID* ST7 .... 224 C8
  ALS/KID ST7 .... 242 D6
  KNUT WA16 .... 107 J1
  SBCH CW11 .... 203 L7
Lodmore La *WHITCH* SY13 .... 272 C6
Lofthouse Ga *WDN* WA8 .... 52 F1
Logwood Rd *HUY* L36 .... 32 A4
Lomas Cl *BNG/LEV* M19 .... 45 L1 ▣
Lomas Sq *MCFLDS* SK11 .... 138 D7 ▣
Lomas St *EDGY/DAV* SK3 .... 2 D9
Lomax Rd *NANT* CW5 .... 237 K6 ▣
Lombard St *ALS/KID* ST7 .... 224 E8
Lomond Av *HALE/TIMP* WA15 .... 62 A1
Lomond Cl *OFTN* SK2 .... 66 A1
Lomond Gv *EP* CH65 .... 120 F1
Lomond Rd *WYTH/NTH* M22 ..... 63 H1
London Pl *STKP* SK1 .... 3 G6
London Rd *FROD/HEL* WA6 ...... 99 H4
  KNUT WA16 .... 156 H1
  MCFLDN SK10 .... 86 C4
  MCFLDN SK10 .... 112 C5
  MCFLDS SK11 .... 162 D1
  NANT CW5 .... 21 J8
  NWCHE CW9 .... 13 H9
  OFTN SK2 .... 47 K8
  SBCH CW11 .... 203 K4
  WARRS WA4 .... 56 D8
  WHITCH SY13 .... 269 M4
  WILM/AE SK9 .... 110 A3
London Rd North *POY/DIS* SK12 .. 66 E8
London Rd South *POY/DIS* SK12 .. 86 D2
London Road Ter
  MCFLDS SK11 .... 138 D7 ▣
London Rw *NEWLW* WA12 .... 27 K4
London Sq *STKP* SK1 .... 3 G6
Loney St *MCFLDS* SK11 .... 14 E6
Long Acre *NWCHW* CW8 .... 127 K8
  NWCHW CW8 .... 128 C3
Longacres Rd *HALE/TIMP* WA15... 62 A5 ▣
Longacre St *MCFLDS* SK11 .... 15 E3
Longbarn Bvd *WARRN/WOL* WA2.. 38 C2
Long Barn La *WARR* WA1............ 38 D4
  WARRN/WOL WA2 .... 38 B2

Longburgh Cl *CHNE* CH2 .... 17 M2
Longbutt La *LYMM* WA13 .... 58 F2
Longbutts La *MCFLDS* SK11 ...... 15 L4
Longcroft Dr *ALT* WA14 .... 42 B8
Longcroft Rd *NTHM/RTH* M23 ... 44 A5
Long Croft La *CHD/CHDH* SK8 ... 64 E4
Longdale Dr *CH/BCN* CH1 .... 144 C7
Longden Cl *BRAM/HZG* SK7 ...... 66 F3
Longden St *MCFLDS* SK11 .... 15 K6
Longdin St *WARRS* WA4 .... 56 F1
Longdown Rd *CONG* CW12 .... 183 M8
Longfield Av *CHD/CHDH* SK8 ..... 64 C5
  CHNE CH2 .... 145 L5 ▣
  HALE/TIMP WA15............................ 43 J6
Longfield Rd *NTHM/RTH* M23 ... 43 M4
  WARRN/WOL WA2 .... 37 J3
Longford St *CW/SHV* CW2 .... 19 G8 ▣
  WARRN/WOL WA2 .... 5 G2
Long Grain Pl *OFTN* SK2 .... 47 K7
Longham Cl *BRAM/HZG* SK7 ..... 66 E5 ▣
Long Hey *HALE/TIMP* WA15 .... 62 A1
  RAIN/WH L35 .... 32 D2
Longhey Rd *WYTH/NTH* M22 ..... 44 D7
Long Hl *CHF/WBR* SK23 .... 115 M5
Longhope Rd *WYTH/NTH* M22 ... 63 H1
Longhorn Cl *MWCH* CW10 .... 179 K2 ▣
Longhurst La *MPL/ROM* SK6 ..... 49 H5
Longlands Dr *NM/HAY* SK22 ...... 69 H4
Longlands Rd *NM/HAY* SK22 ..... 69 H4
Long La *ALS/KID* ST7 .... 226 E8
  CH/BCN CH1 .... 144 B2
  CHNE CH2 .... 14 D8
  CHSE CH3 .... 194 C1
  CONG CW12 .... 159 G6
  KNUT WA16 .... 133 J3
  MALPAS SY14 .... 231 M4
  MALPAS SY14 .... 245 H2
  MALPAS SY14 .... 246 E2
  MCFLDN SK10 .... 113 H1
  MWCH CW10 .... 179 J4
  TPLY/KEL CW6 .... 199 G7
  TPLY/KEL CW6 .... 216 E5
  TPLY/KEL CW6 .... 217 L1
  WARRN/WOL WA2 .... 37 J5
  WHITCH SY13 .... 268 E8
Long La South *MWCH* CW10 .... 179 J5
Longlevens Rd *WYTH/NTH* M22 .. 63 J2
Longley Av *TPLY/KEL* CW6 .... 149 K6
Longley La *WYTH/NTH* M22 .... 44 D4
Longlooms Rd *EP* CH65 .... 121 K3
Long Marl Dr *WILM/AE* SK9 ...... 84 F8
Long Shoot Rd *MCFLDS* SK11 ... 158 E2
Longshut La *STKP* SK1 .... 3 G9
Longshut La West *OFTN* SK2 ...... 3 G9
Longsides Rd *HALE/TIMP* WA15.. 62 C5
Longsight La *CHD/CHDH* SK8 .... 64 F7
Longsight St *HTNM* SK4 .... 2 C4
Long Spinney *RUNC* WA7 .... 74 C4
Longster Trail *CHSE* CH3 .... 146 E8
  FROD/HEL WA6 .... 124 C1
Longstone La *TPLY/KEL* CW6 ... 151 K8
Longton Av *GOL/RIS/CU* WA3 .... 23 J4
Long Valley Rd *BIDD* ST8 .... 227 J2
Longview Av *ALS/KID* ST7 .... 224 D8
Longview Dr *HUY* L36 .... 32 A1
Longwood Av *OFTN* SK2 .... 47 H6 ▣
Longwood Cl *MPL/ROM* SK6 ..... 48 E1
  MWCH CW10 .... 179 J4
Longwood Rd *WARRS* WA4 .... 56 F2
  WYTH/NTH M22 .... 63 L1
Longworth Wy *WLTN* L25 .... 50 A1
Lon Odyn (Kiln Close)
  FLINT CH6 .... 116 A6 ▣
Lonsdale Av *LEIGH* WN7 .... 24 D2
Lonsdale Cl *WDN* WA8 .... 52 C4
Lonsdale Rd *HLWD* L26 .... 50 E6 ▣
Looe Cl *WDN* WA8 .... 52 D1
The Looms *NSTN* CH64 .... 91 H2
Loonies Ct *STKP* SK1 .... 3 G7 ▣
The Loont *WSFD* CW7 .... 177 J5
Lord Nelson St *WARR* WA1 .... 5 J7
Lordship La *FROD/HEL* WA6 ...... 97 M6
Lordshire Pl *ALS/KID* ST7 .... 243 M3 ▣
Lords La *GOL/RIS/CU* WA3 .... 29 J3
Lords Mill Rd *CW/SHV* CW2 .... 238 B3
Lord's St *IRL* M44 .... 31 J7
Lord St *BIDD* ST8 .... 227 K5
  CHSE CH3 .... 17 M5
  CW/SHV CW2 .... 19 G6
  GOL/RIS/CU WA3 .... 29 C4
  MCFLDN SK10 .... 113 H4
  MCFLDS SK11 .... 15 H8
  NEWLW WA12 .... 27 C1 ▣
  RUNC WA7 .... 8 F1
  STKP SK1 .... 3 G6
  WARRS WA4 .... 5 H9
Lorgill Cl *EDGY/DAV* SK3 .... 46 F8
Lorland Rd *EDGY/DAV* SK3 .... 46 B5
Lorna Gv *CHD/CHDH* SK8 .... 44 F6
Lorna Rd *CHD/CHDH* SK8 .... 65 H2
Lorraine Rd *HALE/TIMP* WA15 .... 43 G7
Lorraine St *ALS/KID* ST7 .... 243 M3 ▣
Lostock Av *BRAM/HZG* SK7 .... 66 B3
  POY/DIS SK12 .... 66 B8
Lostock Gn *NWCHE* CW9 .... 131 C3
Lostock Hall Rd *POY/DIS* SK12 .. 86 B1
Lostock Hollow *NWCHE* CW9 ... 131 C3
Lostock Rd *POY/DIS* SK12 .... 86 C2
Lostock Wy *WILM/AE* SK9 .... 64 D8
Lottery Rd *EDGY/DAV* SK3 .... 2 D6
Lotus Av *BIDD* ST8 .... 227 J5
Loughborough Cl *SALE* M33 .... 42 D1 ▣
Louise St *CH/BCN* CH1 .... 16 D3
Loushers La *WARRS* WA4 .... 56 D2
Lovage Cl *WARRN/WOL* WA2 .... 38 C3 ▣
Lovat Dr *KNUT* WA16 .... 107 H5

Love La *HTNM* SK4 .... 2 E3
  NANT CW5 .... 20 E7
  SBCH CW11 .... 224 B1
Lovel Rd *SPK/HALE* L24 .... 70 D2
Lovel Ter *WDN* WA8 .... 52 B7
Lovel Wy *SPK/HALE* L24 .... 70 D2
Lovely La *WARRW/BUR* WA5 .... 4 B5
Lowe St *CH/BCN* CH1 .... 17 H5
Lowcross La *MALPAS* SY14 ...... 245 K1
Lowe Av *CONG* CW12 .... 207 L2
  WARRS WA4 .... 37 M8
Lowe Crs *NWCHE* CW9 .... 77 J8
Lowe Dr *KNUT* WA16 .... 107 H2
Lower Appleton Rd *WDN* WA8 .. 7 K2 ▣
Lower Ash Rd *ALS/KID* ST7 ..... 242 E4
Lower Aston Hall La *CQ* CH5 .... 166 B1
Lower Bank St *MCFLDS* SK11 ... 15 J7 ▣
Lower Bridge St *CH/BCN* CH1 ... 17 G6
Lower Bury St *HTNM* SK4 .... 2 C4
Lower Carrs *STKP* SK1 .... 3 H6
Lower Church St *WDN* WA8 ...... 53 G7
Lower Cl *HLWD* L26 .... 51 G4
Lower Darwin St *NWCHW* CW8 . 12 F6
Lower Exchange St
  MCFLDS SK11 .... 15 G6
Lowerfield Dr *OFTN* SK2 .... 47 M7
Lower Field Rd *CHSW/BR* CH4 . 169 G7
Lowerfield Rd *MCFLDN* SK10 ... 15 J2
Lower Fold *MPL/ROM* SK6 .... 49 H5
Lower Greenshall La
  POY/DIS SK12 .... 68 C5
Lower Hague *NM/HAY* SK22 ...... 68 E4
Lower Haigh St *WSFD* CW7 ...... 177 J4
Lower Hall La *MALPAS* SY14 .... 230 D2 ▣
Lower Heath *CONG* CW12 .... 184 E8
Lower Heath Av *CONG* CW12 ... 184 E8
Lower High St *ALS/KID* ST7 .... 226 D5
Lower Hillgate *STKP* SK1 .... 3 H6
Lower House La *WDN* WA8 .... 6 F6
Lower La *CHSE* CH3 .... 212 A2
  TPLY/KEL CW6 .... 198 A1
Lowerlea *POY/DIS* SK12 .... 68 C6
Lower Macclesfield Rd
  CHF/WBR SK23 .... 89 K6
Lower Meadow Rd
  WILM/AE SK9 .... 64 E8
Lower Mersey St *EP* CH65 .... 10 F3
Lower Moat Cl *HTNM* SK4 .... 2 E1
Lower Mumforth St
  FLINT CH6 .... 116 B5 ▣
Lower Park Crs *POY/DIS* SK12 .. 66 B6
Lower Park Rd *CHSW/BR* CH4 ... 17 J7
  POY/DIS SK12 .... 66 B7
Lower Rake La *FROD/HEL* WA6 . 98 B8
Lower Rd *HLWD* L26 .... 51 H4
Lower Robin Hood La
  FROD/HEL WA6 .... 124 B1
Lower Sandy La *CHSE* CH3 ...... 231 J5
Lower Strines Rd *MPL/ROM* SK6 .. 49 G7
Lower Sydney St *FLINT* CH6 ... 116 B5 ▣
Lower Wash La *WARRS* WA4 ...... 56 E1
Lowes La *MCFLDS* SK11 .... 161 L3
The Lowes *ALT* WA14 .... 61 H3
Lowe St *GOL/RIS/CU* WA3 .... 23 C4
  MCFLDS SK11 .... 15 H7
  STKP SK1 .... 3 G6
Loweswater Cl
  WARRN/WOL WA2 .... 37 H1
Loweswater Dr
  CHD/CHDH SK8 .... 64 B1 ▣
Lowfield Gdns *GOL/RIS/CU* WA3 .. 25 J5
Lowfield Gv *RUNC* WA7 .... 74 F5
Lowfield Rd *EDGY/DAV* SK3 ...... 46 B5
Lowfields Av *PS/BROM* CH62 .... 93 L1 ▣
Lowfields Cl *PS/BROM* CH62 .... 93 L1 ▣
Low Hl *FROD/HEL* WA6 .... 123 K7
Lowick Cl *BRAM/HZG* SK7 .... 66 D2
Lowland Rd *OFTN* SK2 .... 47 H8
Lowlands Rd *BURS/TUN* ST6 ... 243 G8
  RUNC WA7 .... 8 F2
Lowland Wy *KNUT* WA16 .... 107 G5
Low Lea Rd *MPL/ROM* SK6 .... 49 H5
Low Leighton Rd *NM/HAY* SK22.. 69 K5
Low Meadow *CHF/WBR* SK23 .... 89 K4
Lowndes Cl *OFTN* SK2 .... 47 H5
Lowndes La *OFTN* SK2 .... 47 H5
Lownorth Rd *WYTH/NTH* M22 ... 63 L4
Lowry Cl *WARRW/BUR* WA5 .... 36 D5
Lowry Dr *MPL/ROM* SK6 .... 49 H4 ▣
Low St *ALS/KID* ST7 .... 224 E4
Lowther Av *GOL/RIS/CU* WA3 ... 24 F8
  HALE/TIMP WA15............................ 43 G6
Lowther Dr *RAIN/WH* L35 .... 33 H1
Lowther St *MCFLDN* SK10 .... 113 H4
Lowton Gdns *ALS/KID* ST7 .... 23 H7
Lowton Rd *GOL/RIS/CU* WA3 .... 23 H3
  SALE M33 .... 42 D2
Low Wood Rd *BRAM/HZG* SK7 .. 65 J3
Loxdale Dr *EP* CH65 .... 94 F8
Loxley Cl *WARRW/BUR* WA5 ...... 36 A4
Loyola Hey *RAIN/WH* L35 .... 33 L4
Lucerne Cl *CHSE* CH3 .... 170 B6
Lucerne Rd *BRAM/HZG* SK7 ..... 65 L1
Lucy St *EDGY/DAV* SK3 .... 2 E8
Ludford Gv *SALE* M33 .... 42 F2
Ludford St *CW/HAS* CW1 .... 18 F2
Ludlow Av *CW/HAS* CW1 .... 19 K6
Ludlow Cl *MCFLDN* SK10 .... 15 K1
  WSFD CW7 .... 177 H5
Ludlow Crs *RUNC* WA7 .... 9 J7
Ludlow Dr *EP* CH65 .... 121 L1
Ludlow Rd *CH/BCN* CH1 .... 145 G7
  STKP SK1 .... 47 J1
Ludwell Cl *CHSW/BR* CH4 .... 169 H7
Lugano Rd *BRAM/HZG* SK7 ...... 65 L1
Lugsdale Rd *WDN* WA8 .... 7 H6
Lullington Cl *WYTH/NTH* M22 .. 63 J3 ▣
Lulworth Cl *WSFD* CW7 .... 177 H5
Lulworth Gdns
  NTHM/RTH M23 .... 43 M4 ▣
Lulworth Gv *BURS/TUN* ST6 ... 243 L6 ▣
Lumb Brook Rd *WARRS* WA4 ..... 56 F4
Lumb Cl *BRAM/HZG* SK7 .... 65 L6
Lumber La *WARRW/BUR* WA5 .... 26 A4
Lumb La *BRAM/HZG* SK7 .... 65 L6
Lumley Pl *CH/BCN* CH1 .... 17 H6 ▣
Lumley Rd *CHNE* CH2 .... 145 J6 ▣
  MCFLDS SK11 .... 137 M5

Lundy Dr *EP* CH65 .... 121 J4
Lune Cl *CONG* CW12 .... 208 A3
Lunedale Gn *OFTN* SK2 .... 47 L6
Lunehurst *GOL/RIS/CU* WA3 .... 23 L4 ▣
Lunt Av *CW/SHV* CW2 .... 18 D8
  RAIN/WH L35 .... 32 E1
Lunt's Heath Rd *WDN* WA8 ...... 34 A7
Lupin Dr *CHSE* CH3 .... 170 B6
Lupus Wy *GTS/LS* CH66 .... 120 F1
Lurgan Av *SALE* M33 .... 43 J1 ▣
Luscombe Cl *HLWD* L26 .... 51 G4 ▣
Lutener St *ALT* WA14 .... 42 C4 ▣
Luther Gv *STHEL* WA9 .... 26 B2
Luton St *WDN* WA8 .... 7 H7
Lutyens Cl *MCFLDS* SK10 .... 137 M4 ▣
Lyceum Cl *CW/HAS* CW1 .... 221 G4
Lyceum Wy *CW/HAS* CW1 .... 221 G4
Lychgate *WARRS* WA4 .... 55 M5 ▣
Lycroft Cl *RUNC* WA7 .... 73 H6
Lydbury Cl *WARRW/BUR* WA5 ... 36 D2
Lydd Cl *SPK/HALE* L24 .... 50 B8
Lydden Rd *EP* CH65 .... 10 D4
Lydgate Cl *CW/SHV* CW2 .... 237 M4
Lydgate Rd *SALE* M33 .... 43 J2
Lydiate Ln *NSTN* CH64 .... 92 E4
  WARR WA1 .... 8 B9
  WLTN L25 .... 50 D2
Lydiat La *WILM/AE* SK9 .... 110 A4
Lydney Av *CHD/CHDH* SK8 .... 64 C5
Lydstep Cl *WARRW/BUR* WA5 ... 36 E2 ▣
Lydyett La *NWCHW* CW8 .... 129 H1
Lymcote Dr *NWCHW* CW8 ...... 129 G8 ▣
Lyme Av *MCFLDS* SK11 .... 138 D7
  WILM/AE SK9 .... 84 B3
Lyme Gv *ALT* WA14 .... 42 C8
  LYMM WA13 .... 58 C2
  MPL/ROM SK6 .... 48 F7
  MPL/ROM SK6 .... 48 D2
  OFTN SK2 .... 3 C9
Lyme Rd *BRAM/HZG* SK7 .... 66 E3
  POY/DIS SK12 .... 87 J1
Lyme St *BRAM/HZG* SK7 .... 66 D1 ▣
  HTNM SK4 .... 45 L2
Lyme Vw *MCFLDS* SK11 .... 162 D2
  POY/DIS SK12 .... 68 B6
Lymewood Dr *POY/DIS* SK12 .... 68 B6
  WILM/AE SK9 .... 84 B2
Lymington Dr *NTHM/RTH* M23 .. 43 K4
Lymm Av *LYMM* WA13 .... 58 C1
Lymmhay La *LYMM* WA13 .... 39 L8
Lymmington Av *LYMM* WA13 .... 58 C1
Lymm Rd *LYMM* WA13 .... 59 M3
  WARRS WA4 .... 57 M1
Lynalls Cl *CONG* CW12 .... 206 F1
Lynam Wy *AUD/MAD/W* CW3 .. 267 L5 ▣
Lynbrook Rd *CW/HAS* CW1 .... 19 L4
Lyncastle Rd *WARRS* WA4 .... 57 K8
Lyncombe Cl *CHD/CHDH* SK8 .. 65 H6 ▣
Lyndale Av *WARRN/WOL* WA2 ... 37 K4
Lyndale Ct *WSFD* CW7 .... 177 K6
Lyndene Gdns *CHD/CHDH* SK8 . 45 H6 ▣
Lyndene Rd *WYTH/NTH* M22 ..... 44 C7
Lyndhurst Av *BRAM/HZG* SK7 ... 66 C3
  SALE M33 .... 42 F1 ▣
Lyndhurst Rd *WILM/AE* SK9 ..... 83 K7 ▣
Lyndhurst Dr *BIDD* ST8 .... 227 G7
  HALE/TIMP WA15............................ 62 A2
Lyndon Gv *RUNC* WA7 .... 9 J6
Lyndon Rd *IRL* M44 .... 31 M3
Lyndor Cl *WLTN* L25 .... 50 B3
Lyndor Rd *WLTN* L25 .... 50 B3
Lyneal Av *GTS/LS* CH66 .... 120 C2
Lyneham Rd *RAIN/WH* L35 .... 32 F2
Lyneside Rd *BIDD* ST8 .... 227 H6
Lyngard Cl *WILM/AE* SK9 .... 84 D3
Lyngate Cl *STKP* SK1 .... 3 J7
Lynham Av *WARRW/BUR* WA5 ... 36 B1 ▣
Lynmouth Cl *BIDD* ST8 .... 227 H6
Lynmouth Gv *BURS/TUN* ST6 . 243 L5
Lynn Av *ALS/KID* ST7 .... 242 C4
Lynn Cl *RUNC* WA7 .... 9 J6
Lynndene *GTS/LS* CH66 .... 94 C5
Lynnwood Rd *BNG/LEV* M19 .... 45 K2
Lynthorpe Av *IRL* M44 .... 31 L6
Lynton Av *IRL* M44 .... 31 L6
Lynton Cl *CHSW/BR* CH4 .... 168 F6 ▣
  KNUT WA16 .... 107 J3
  WARRW/BUR WA5 .... 35 L8
Lynton Crs *WDN* WA8 .... 6 C1
Lynton Dr *MPL/ROM* SK6 .... 67 L4
Lynton Gdns *WARRS* WA4 .... 56 D8
Lynton Gv *CW/HAS* CW1 .... 222 D7 ▣
  HALE/TIMP WA15............................ 42 F7
Lynton La *WILM/AE* SK9 .... 110 A2
Lynton Ms *WILM/AE* SK9 .... 110 A2 ▣
Lynton Park Rd *CHD/CHDH* SK8 . 64 F4
Lynton Pl *CHSW/BR* CH4 .... 167 H8
Lynton Rd *CHD/CHDH* SK8 .... 45 J7
  HUY L36 .... 32 B1
Lyntonvale Av *CHD/CHDH* SK8 .. 45 G6
Lynton Wy *CW/SHV* CW2 .... 238 A4
Lynwood Av *GOL/RIS/CU* WA3 .. 23 L6
  WARRS WA4 .... 55 C5
Lynwood Rd *CH/BCN* CH1 .... 144 F7
Lyon's La *WARRS* WA4 .... 56 D6
Lyons Rd *WARRW/BUR* WA5 .... 35 M8
Lyon St *CH/BCN* CH1 .... 17 H3
  CW/HAS CW1 .... 19 H4
  MCFLDS SK11 .... 14 F6
  WARRS WA4 .... 5 H9
Lyster Cl *GOL/RIS/CU* WA3 .... 38 F1
Lytham Dr *BRAM/HZG* SK7 .... 66 E4
Lytham Rd *CHD/CHDH* SK8 .... 64 B3
  WDN WA8 .... 53 H2
Lytham St *EDGY/DAV* SK3 .... 46 F6 ▣
Lytherton Av *IRL* M44 .... 31 K8
Lythgoes La *WARRN/WOL* WA2 .. 5 H4

M

Mabledon Cl *CHD/CHDH* SK8 ..... 64 D4
Mablins La *CW/HAS* CW1 .... 221 H4
Macarthur Rd
  WARRW/BUR WA5 .... 36 B6 ▣

Macclesfield Rd *BRAM/HZG* SK7 . 66 F4
  CHF/WBR SK23 .... 89 J6
  CONG CW12 .... 184 F6
  HOLMCH CW4 .... 181 K1
  MCFLDN SK10 .... 112 A7
  MCFLDN SK10 .... 114 B5
  MCFLDN SK10 .... 137 M1
  WILM/AE SK9 .... 84 C6
Macdermott Rd *WDN* WA8 .... 52 F7
Macdonald Rd *IRL* M44 .... 31 L5
Mackets Cl *WLTN* L25 .... 50 C3
Macket's La *WLTN* L25 .... 50 C3
Macon Ct *CW/HAS* CW1 .... 19 J6
Macon Wy *CW/HAS* CW1 .... 19 J6
Maddocks Hl *FROD/HEL* WA6 .. 126 F7
Madeley Cl *ALT* WA14 .... 61 L4 ▣
  CHSW/BR CH4 .... 167 J3
Madeley St *BURS/TUN* ST6 ...... 243 K8
  CW/SHV CW2 .... 18 F9
Madeline Mckenna Ct
  WDN WA8 .... 52 C1 ▣
Madison Av *CHD/CHDH* SK8 ..... 65 G2
Madison St *BURS/TUN* ST6 ...... 243 K8
Madras St *EDGY/DAV* SK3 .... 46 C5 ▣
Madron Av *MCFLDN* SK10 .... 137 K3
Maelor Wy *WHITCH* SY13 .... 268 A7
Maes Alaw *FLINT* CH6 .... 116 B7
Maes Gwyn *FLINT* CH6 .... 116 C7
Maes-hyfryd *FLINT* CH6 .... 116 A7
Maesllwyn Cl *WHITCH* SY13 ... 268 A8
Maes Teg *FLINT* CH6 .... 116 A8
Maes-y-dre Av *FLINT* CH6 .... 116 B7
Mafeking Pl *AIMK* WN4 .... 22 C1 ▣
Magdala Pl *NWCHE* CW9 .... 130 C4
Magdalen Cl *CW/SHV* CW2 .... 18 A9
Magda Rd *OFTN* SK2 .... 47 J7
Magenta Av *IRL* M44 .... 31 L6
Mag La *LYMM* WA13 .... 58 F5
Magna Cl *WHITCH* SY13 .... 271 G8
Magnolia Cl *GTS/LS* CH66 ...... 120 F3
  HLWD L26 .... 50 D2 ▣
  WARR WA1 .... 38 E5 ▣
Magnolia Dr *RUNC* WA7 .... 73 M8 ▣
Magnolia Ri *MCFLDN* SK10 ..... 111 K6
Magpie Crs *ALS/KID* ST7 .... 243 H2 ▣
Mahood St *EDGY/DAV* SK3 .... 2 D9
Maidenhills *MWCH* CW10 .... 179 K4
Maidstone Cl *MCFLDN* SK10 ... 138 B2 ▣
Maidstone Rd *HTNM* SK4 .... 45 K1
Maidwell Cl *WSFD* CW7 .... 154 A8 ▣
Main Dr *RAIN/WH* L35 .... 32 E3
Main Front *RAIN/WH* L35 .... 32 E3
Main La *GOL/RIS/CU* WA3 .... 28 E1
Main Rd *AUD/MAD/W* CW3 ..... 255 G6
  CHSW/BR CH4 .... 238 B8
  CW/SHV CW2 .... 238 B8
  HOLMCH CW4 .... 157 J4
  MCFLDS SK11 .... 139 J8
  NANT CW5 .... 219 M7
  NANT CW5 .... 253 C4
  NWCHE CW9 .... 153 L4
Main St *CHSE* CH3 .... 147 K7
  FROD/HEL WA6 .... 99 C4
  RUNC WA7 .... 73 M4
Maintree Crs *SPK/HALE* L24 ..... 51 G8
Mainwaring Dr *CHSW/BR* CH4 . 168 C5
  WILM/AE SK9 .... 84 D4
Mainwaring Rd *KNUT* WA16 .... 134 A4
Mainwaring Ter
  NTHM/RTH M23 .... 44 A2 ▣
Mainwood Rd *HALE/TIMP* WA15 . 43 J7
Mairesfield Av *WARRS* WA4....... 57 H2
Maismore Rd *WYTH/NTH* M22 .. 63 G3
Maisterson Ct *NANT* CW5 .... 20 F6
Maitland St *STKP* SK1 .... 3 L9
Maitland Wy *CH/BCN* CH1 ...... 144 D8 ▣
Maitland-wood Cl *NWCHE* CW9 . 130 D5
Major Cross St *WDN* WA8 .... 7 H6 ▣
Makepeace Cl *CHSE* CH3 .... 170 C1 ▣
Makerfield Dr *NEWLW* WA12 ..... 22 A7
Malaga Av *MANAIR* M90 .... 63 H5 ▣
Malam Dr *NWCHE* CW9 .... 130 D6
Malbank *NANT* CW5 .... 20 E5
Malbank Rd *CW/SHV* CW2 .... 220 D8
Malcolm Av *WARRN/WOL* WA2 .. 37 K3
Malcolm St *RUNC* WA7 .... 9 K3
Malden Gv *NTHM/RTH* M23 ...... 44 A5 ▣
Maldon Cl *HLWD* L26 .... 50 F6
  OFTN SK2 .... 48 A7
Malgam Dr *DID/WITH* M20 .... 45 H4 ▣
Malham Ct *OFTN* SK2 .... 47 K6 ▣
Malhamdale Av *RAIN/WH* L35 .. 33 K2 ▣
Malhamdale Rd *CONG* CW12 .. 185 G7 ▣
Malin Cl *SPK/HALE* L24 .... 71 K2
Malinson Rd *WARRW/BUR* WA5 . 36 B7
Mallard Cl *HLWD* L26 .... 50 E3 ▣
  KNUT WA16 .... 107 H2 ▣
  OFTN SK2 .... 48 A7
  RUNC WA7 .... 73 M7 ▣
  WARRN/WOL WA2 .... 37 K1
Mallard Crs *POY/DIS* SK12 .... 66 A8
Mallard Gn *ALT* WA14 .... 42 B4 ▣
Mallard La *GOL/RIS/CU* WA3 .... 38 F1
Mallards Reach
  MPL/ROM SK6 .... 48 B2 ▣
Mallard Wy *WSFD* CW7 .... 177 K6
Malling Rd *NTHM/RTH* M23 ...... 44 A8
Mallory Cl *CW/HAS* CW1 .... 19 M1
Mallory Ct *CONG* CW12 .... 206 F1 ▣
Mallory Rd *EP* CH65 .... 10 B9
Mallory Wk *CHSW/BR* CH4 ..... 191 G5
Mallow Cl *CHSE* CH3 .... 170 A6 ▣
Mallowdale Rd *OFTN* SK2 .... 47 L7
Malmesbury Cl *MWCH* CW10 .. 179 H3 ▣
  POY/DIS SK12 .... 66 B8
Malmesbury Pk *RUNC* WA7 ...... 74 D1
Malpas Cl *CHD/CHDH* SK8 .... 46 A3 ▣
  NWCHE CW9 .... 13 M4
  WILM/AE SK9 .... 84 D3
Malpas Dr *ALT* WA14 .... 42 E4 ▣
  WARRW/BUR WA5 .... 36 C8
Malpas Rd *EP* CH65 .... 94 F8
  NWCHE CW9 .... 13 M4
  RUNC WA7 .... 9 K9
Malpas Wy *WARRW/BUR* WA5 .. 36 C8 ▣
Malsham Rd *NTHM/RTH* M23 ... 43 M2 ▣

Maltby Rd NTHM/RTH M23 .... 43 M6
Malt Kiln Rd KNUT WA16 .... 105 M8
Maltmans Rd LYMM WA13 .... 58 D1
Malton Av GOL/RIS/CU WA3 .... 23 L5
Malton Cl WDN WA8 .... 33 J7
Malton Dr ALT WA14 .... 42 A6
  BRAM/HZG SK7 .... 66 D5
Malton Gv BURS/TUN ST6 .... 243 K8
Malton Rd WLTN L25 .... 50 C3
Malt St KNUT WA16 .... 107 G2
Malvern Av CHD/CHDH SK8 .... 44 F7
  EP CH65 .... 121 J1
Malvern Cl CONG CW12 .... 206 F1
  CW/SHV CW2 .... 238 B8
  HTNM SK4 .... 2 D2
  WARRW/BUR WA5 .... 36 A4
Malvern Dr ALT WA14 .... 42 B7
  MCFLDN SK10 .... 112 E8
Malvern Rd CH/BCN CH1 .... 145 G8
  KNUT WA16 .... 106 F4
Malvern Ter LEIGH WN7 .... 24 F1
Malvern Wy WSFD CW7 .... 177 G4
Manchester Br CW/HAS CW1 .... 19 J4
Manchester New Rd PART M31 .... 40 F1
Manchester Rd ALT WA14 .... 42 D5
  CHD/CHDH SK8 .... 45 K4
  CONG CW12 .... 184 E7
  GOL/RIS/CU WA3 .... 39 L4
  KNUT WA16 .... 80 E8
  MCFLDN SK10 .... 112 C6
  NWCHE CW9 .... 13 M2
  PART M31 .... 31 M8
  WARR WA1 .... 5 L5
  WARR WA1 .... 39 G5
  WILM/AE SK9 .... 84 C4
Manchester Rw NEWLW WA12 .... 27 K4
Mancot La CQ CH5 .... 166 D1
Mancot Royal Cl CQ CH5 .... 166 D1
Mancot Wy CQ CH5 .... 166 D1
Mancroft Cl WARR WA1 .... 38 E5
Mandalay Gdns
  MPL/ROM SK6 .... 48 D5
Mandarin Gn ALT WA14 .... 42 B4
Manifold Cl SBCH CW11 .... 203 L4
Manifold Rd MPL/ROM SK6 .... 67 M6
Manley Av GOL/RIS/CU WA3 .... 22 F2
Manley Cl HOLMCH CW4 .... 181 G1
  NWCHE CW9 .... 13 J8
  NWCHE CW9 .... 77 J8
Manley Ct CQ CH5 .... 142 B5
Manley Gdns WARRW/BUR WA5 .... 4 C5
Manley Gv BRAM/HZG SK7 .... 65 L6
Manley La FROD/HEL WA6 .... 123 J7
Manley Rd FROD/HEL WA6 .... 124 D4
  HUY L36 .... 32 A4
  MCFLDS SK11 .... 138 A7
  SALE M33 .... 42 E3
Manley Vw CHNE CH2 .... 123 J1
Manna Dr CHNE CH2 .... 123 J1
Mannings La CHNE CH2 .... 146 B6
Mannings La South
  CHNE CH2 .... 146 A7
Manning St CW/SHV CW2 .... 19 H9
Manora Rd NWCHE CW9 .... 13 K3
Manor Av CW/SHV CW2 .... 238 A3
  GOL/RIS/CU WA3 .... 23 J4
  HOLMCH CW4 .... 157 M3
  NWCHE CW9 .... 104 B9
  RAIN/WH L35 .... 33 J2
  SALE M33 .... 42 D1
Manor Cl CHD/CHDH SK8 .... 65 J4
  CHSE CH3 .... 147 L6
  CHSW/BR CH4 .... 167 J5
  CONG CW12 .... 208 A3
  NSTN CH64 .... 91 J5
  WARR WA1 .... 38 D5
  WILM/AE SK9 .... 83 L4
Manor Ct CW/SHV CW2 .... 238 B3
  GOL/RIS/CU WA3 .... 23 J4
Manor Crs CHSW/BR CH4 .... 167 J4
  KNUT WA16 .... 107 H2
  MCFLDN SK10 .... 138 D1
  MWCH CW10 .... 179 J5
  WLTN L25 .... 50 B3
Manor Dr CHSE CH3 .... 170 B3
  NWCHE CW9 .... 130 C5
  NWCHW CW8 .... 129 H2
Manor Farm Cl CHNE CH2 .... 146 E4
Manor Farm Crs CH/BCN CH1 .... 120 B4
Manor Farm Rd RUNC WA7 .... 54 D8
Manor Fell RUNC WA7 .... 74 B5
Manorfield Cl CH/BCN CH1 .... 120 A4
Manor Flds MWCH CW10 .... 179 J5
Manor Gdns WILM/AE SK9 .... 84 D5
Manor Gv LEIGH WN7 .... 25 J1
  NWCHW CW8 .... 12 B7
Manor Hall Rd MPL/ROM SK6 .... 48 F5
Manorial Rd NSTN CH64 .... 91 J4
Manorial Rd South NSTN CH64 .... 91 J4
Manor La CHSW/BR CH4 .... 167 H5
  CQ CH5 .... 167 G6
  GTS/LS CH66 .... 120 D1
  HOLMCH CW4 .... 181 K2
  KNUT WA16 .... 107 L6
  MWCH CW10 .... 179 J4
  NWCHE CW9 .... 154 D2
  WRX/GR/LL LL12 .... 210 B6
Manor Pk CHSE CH3 .... 147 L6
Manor Park Av RUNC WA7 .... 54 C8
Manor Park Dr GTS/LS CH66 .... 120 D2
Manor Pk North KNUT WA16 .... 107 J2
Manor Park Rd CONG CW12 .... 185 K2
Manor Pk South KNUT WA16 .... 107 H3
Manor Rd ALS/KID ST7 .... 226 D5
  CHD/CHDH SK8 .... 65 J3
  CHF/WBR SK23 .... 89 L7
  CHSW/BR CH4 .... 169 H7
  CQ CH5 .... 143 G6
  FROD/HEL WA6 .... 99 J3
  HALE/TIMP WA15 .... 42 E8
  LYMM WA13 .... 58 E2
  MPL/ROM SK6 .... 48 F5
  NANT CW5 .... 20 E5
  NWCHW CW8 .... 151 M2
  RNFD/HAY WA11 .... 22 A5
  RUNC WA7 .... 73 K2
  SBCH CW11 .... 204 D6
  WDN WA8 .... 52 B3
  WILM/AE SK9 .... 83 L4
  WLTN L25 .... 50 B3
Manor Rd North NANT CW5 .... 20 F7
Manor Sq WSFD CW7 .... 177 G4
Manor St GOL/RIS/CU WA3 .... 23 H3
  NWCHW CW8 .... 12 C6
Manor Wy CW/SHV CW2 .... 238 B3
  SBCH CW11 .... 204 E6
Manse Cl CHNE CH2 .... 17 M3
Manse Field Rd FROD/HEL WA6 .... 126 B3
Manse Gdns NEWLW WA12 .... 22 D8
Mansell Cl WDN WA8 .... 34 C7
Mansell Dr HLWD L26 .... 50 E6
Mansfield Cl GOL/RIS/CU WA3 .... 30 A8
Mansfield Dr BIDD ST8 .... 227 G7
Mansfield Rd EP CH65 .... 121 G2
  GOL/RIS/CU WA3 .... 22 E3
Mansion Dr KNUT WA16 .... 107 H2
Manston Dr CHD/CHDH SK8 .... 65 G2
Manston Rd WARRW/BUR WA5 .... 54 F1
Manuel Perez Rd
  WARRW/BUR WA5 .... 36 B6
Manvers St HTNM SK4 .... 2 F1
Manx Rd WARRS WA4 .... 56 B1
Maori Dr FROD/HEL WA6 .... 99 G4
Maple Av ALS/KID ST7 .... 241 L2
  ALS/KID ST7 .... 242 D4
  CHD/CHDH SK8 .... 64 F2
  GOL/RIS/CU WA3 .... 23 M5
  GTS/LS CH66 .... 94 C6
  HALE/TIMP WA15 .... 43 L7
  MCFLDS SK11 .... 138 D7
  MPL/ROM SK6 .... 48 F8
  NEWLW WA12 .... 27 K2
  POY/DIS SK12 .... 69 G6
  POY/DIS SK12 .... 86 F1
  RUNC WA7 .... 9 M6
  WDN WA8 .... 7 K2
Maple Cl CONG CW12 .... 183 M8
  HOLMCH CW4 .... 157 K8
  OFTN SK2 .... 47 H6
  RAIN/WH L35 .... 32 E1
  SBCH CW11 .... 181 M7
  SBCH CW11 .... 204 C6
Maple Crs WARRW/BUR WA5 .... 35 M8
Maplecroft STKP SK1 .... 3 M8
Maple Gv CHNE CH2 .... 146 B8
  CHSW/BR CH4 .... 168 D7
  CW/HAS CW1 .... 221 L6
  GTS/LS CH66 .... 121 G3
  NWCHW CW8 .... 12 A5
  NWCHW CW8 .... 103 H8
  WARRS WA4 .... 56 D1
  WSFD CW7 .... 178 A3
Maple La NWCHW CW8 .... 151 M2
Maple Ms NTHM/RTH M23 .... 43 J4
Maple Pl ALS/KID ST7 .... 224 F5
  NTHM/RTH M23 .... 43 J4
  PART M31 .... 40 E1
  WARR WA1 .... 38 E5
  WARRN/WOL WA2 .... 28 B6
  WILM/AE SK9 .... 110 B2
Maple Rd BRAM/HZG SK7 .... 65 L7
  NTHM/RTH M23 .... 43 J4
  PART M31 .... 40 E1
  WARR WA1 .... 38 E5
  WARRN/WOL WA2 .... 28 B6
  WILM/AE SK9 .... 110 B2
Maple Rd West NTHM/RTH M23 .... 43 J4
The Maples WSFD CW7 .... 178 A1
Mapleton Dr RUNC WA7 .... 99 M1
Maplewood Gv CH/BCN CH1 .... 144 B4
Maplewood Rd WILM/AE SK9 .... 84 E4
Mapley Av WYTH/NTH M22 .... 44 D4
Maplin Dr OFTN SK2 .... 48 A7
Mapplewell Crs
  WARRW/BUR WA5 .... 36 A6
Marbury Gdns EP CH65 .... 94 F6
Marbury La NWCHE CW9 .... 103 L7
Marbury Rd CHSE CH3 .... 170 C2
  NWCHE CW9 .... 103 K6
  WILM/AE SK9 .... 84 B3
Marbury St WARRS WA4 .... 5 J9
March Av HTNM SK4 .... 46 B2
Marchbank Dr CHD/CHDH SK8 .... 45 J6
Marches Wy CH/BCN CH1 .... 17 G4
  CHSE CH3 .... 192 F8
  CHSE CH3 .... 244 B3
  MALPAS SY14 .... 244 B5
  WHITCH SY13 .... 269 J3
Marchien Wy WDN WA8 .... 52 F1
Marcliff Gv HTNM SK4 .... 46 B2
Marcross Cl WARRW/BUR WA5 .... 36 E3
Mardale Av WARRN/WOL WA2 .... 37 J1
  NTHLY L27 .... 51 G1
Mardale Ct HOLMCH CW4 .... 181 G2
Mardale Crs LYMM WA13 .... 58 F1
Mardale Dr CHD/CHDH SK8 .... 45 H6
Mardale Rd NTHLY L27 .... 51 G1
Marden Rd NTHM/RTH M23 .... 44 A7
Mardon Cl KNUT WA16 .... 81 K8
Marford Cft WYTH/NTH M22 .... 44 D6
Marford Crs SALE M33 .... 42 F2
Margaret Av WARR WA1 .... 38 B5
  WARR WA1 .... 8 J7
Margaret's La GTS/LS CH66 .... 94 A5
Margery Av ALS/KID ST7 .... 225 L5
Margery Av STHEL WA9 .... 34 E1
Maria Cl NANT CW5 .... 249 M8
Marian Av NEWLW WA12 .... 26 E1
Marian Dr CHSE CH3 .... 170 B4
  RAIN/WH L35 .... 33 H2
Marie Cl DR WARRS WA4 .... 57 K2
Marigold Cl MCFLDS SK11 .... 137 M5
Marina Av WARRW/BUR WA5 .... 36 B8
Marina Dr CHNE CH2 .... 145 L5
  CQ CH5 .... 166 B1
  EP CH65 .... 10 E8
  MPL/ROM SK6 .... 48 C5
  WARRN/WOL WA2 .... 37 J3
Marina Gv RUNC WA7 .... 9 K3
Marina La RUNC WA7 .... 74 E5
Marina Village RUNC WA7 .... 74 E5
Marine Av PART M31 .... 40 D1
Mariner Cl RUNC WA7 .... 74 D6
Marion Dr WARRS WA4 .... 72 F6
Maritime Cl NEWLW WA12 .... 22 C7
Mark Av CTS/LS CH66 .... 94 C8
Mark Ct CHNE CH2 .... 17 M3
Market Pl MALPAS SY14 .... 246 D5
  MCFLDN SK10 .... 15 G4
  MCFLDN SK10 .... 113 H4
  STKP SK1 .... 3 G4
  WSFD CW7 .... 177 M3
Market Sq CW/HAS CW1 .... 18 F4
Market St ALS/KID ST7 .... 243 G3
  ALT WA14 .... 42 D8
  CHF/WBR SK23 .... 89 L5
  CONG CW12 .... 207 K2
  CW/HAS CW1 .... 19 G1
  CW/HAS CW1 .... 19 G1
  EP CH65 .... 10 D9
  NANT CW5 .... 20 E6
  NEWLW WA12 .... 22 A8
  NM/HAY SK22 .... 69 H5
  NWCHE CW9 .... 13 H2
  POY/DIS SK12 .... 68 D6
  WDN WA8 .... 7 H6
Markfield Crs WLTN L25 .... 50 D3
Marland Av CHD/CHDH SK8 .... 65 H3
  CQ CH5 .... 166 A4
  WILM/AE SK9 .... 110 B2
  WSFD CW7 .... 177 J1
Marlborough Av CHD/CHDH SK8 .... 65 H3
  CQ CH5 .... 166 A4
  WILM/AE SK9 .... 110 B2
  WSFD CW7 .... 177 J1
Marlborough Cl
  CW/SHV CW2 .... 237 L4
  MCFLDN SK10 .... 112 D8
  MPL/ROM SK6 .... 48 D5
Marlborough Crs WARRS WA4 .... 56 F2
  WDN WA8 .... 34 A7
Marlborough Dr
  FROD/HEL WA6 .... 124 B2
  MCFLDN SK10 .... 112 D8
Marlborough Rd ALT WA14 .... 61 K2
  EP CH65 .... 121 K1
Marl Cft CHSE CH3 .... 170 B5
Marlcroft Av HTNM SK4 .... 46 B2
Marldon Pl BURS/TUN ST6 .... 243 J6
Marl Edge MCFLDN SK10 .... 112 A7
Marley Av CW/HAS CW1 .... 221 H6
Marley Cl HALE/TIMP WA15 .... 42 F5
  RAIN/WH L35 .... 33 L3
Marleyer Ri MPL/ROM SK6 .... 48 A4
Marley Rd POY/DIS SK12 .... 86 E2
Marley Wy CHSW/BR CH4 .... 168 E5
  WARRS WA4 .... 57 G2
Marl Heys CHNE CH2 .... 145 L5
Marlhill Cl OFTN SK2 .... 47 L7
Marling Cl FROD/HEL WA6 .... 99 K6
Marling Pk WDN WA8 .... 52 B3
Marlow Av CHNE CH2 .... 145 M5
Marlow Cl CHD/CHDH SK8 .... 64 F2
  GOL/RIS/CU WA3 .... 29 J7
Marlow Dr ALT WA14 .... 60 F2
  WILM/AE SK9 .... 64 C7
Marlowe Cl CH/BCN CH1 .... 145 G7
  CW/SHV CW2 .... 238 A4
  SBCH CW11 .... 203 K7
  WDN WA8 .... 6 E3
Marlowe Ct MCFLDS SK11 .... 138 C7
Marlowe Dr NANT CW5 .... 251 L1
Marlowe Rd NSTN CH64 .... 91 L4
  NWCHE CW9 .... 130 C5
Marlowe Wks MPL/ROM SK6 .... 47 L2
Marlston Av CHSW/BR CH4 .... 169 G6
Marlston Pl RUNC WA7 .... 73 H6
Marmion Cl GOL/RIS/CU WA3 .... 23 L3
Marmion Av WYTH/NTH M22 .... 44 E7
Marnel Dr CQ CH5 .... 142 E8
Maroon Rd WYTH/NTH M22 .... 63 M5
Marple Crs CW/SHV CW2 .... 237 L2
Marple Hall Dr MPL/ROM SK6 .... 48 D5
Marple Old Rd OFTN SK2 .... 48 A6
Marple Rd NWCHE CW9 .... 130 C5
  OFTN SK2 .... 47 K5
Marquis Dr CHD/CHDH SK8 .... 64 D5
Marrick Av CHD/CHDH SK8 .... 45 J7
Marriott Cl SBCH CW11 .... 222 F1
Marriott St STKP SK1 .... 3 H8
Marron Av WARRN/WOL WA2 .... 37 H2
Marsden Av WARRS WA4 .... 38 A8
Marsden Dr HALE/TIMP WA15 .... 43 J6
Marsden Rd HLWD L26 .... 50 F6
  MPL/ROM SK6 .... 48 C1
Marsden Ter MCFLDS SK11 .... 14 F6
Marshall Av WARRW/BUR WA5 .... 36 F2
Marshall La NWCHW CW8 .... 12 C6
Marshall Rd WARR WA1 .... 38 D5
Marshalls St NWCHW CW8 .... 12 C6
Marsham Dr MPL/ROM SK6 .... 49 G7
Marsham Rd BRAM/HZG SK7 .... 66 B8
Marsh Av ALS/KID ST7 .... 243 K2
Marsh Cl ALS/KID ST7 .... 241 G1
  EDGY/DAV SK3 .... 46 D6
Marshfield Av CW/SHV CW2 .... 220 D7
Marshfield Bank CW/SHV CW2 .... 220 D8
Marshfield La BIDD ST8 .... 227 G7
Marshfield Rd HALE/TIMP WA15 .... 43 J7
Marshgate WDN WA8 .... 52 B6
Marshgate Pl FROD/HEL WA6 .... 99 J2
Marsh Green Cl BIDD ST8 .... 227 K1
Marshgreen Rd BIDD ST8 .... 227 K1
Marsh Green Rd SBCH CW11 .... 203 K4
Marsh Gv BIDD ST8 .... 227 J1
Marsh Hall Rd WDN WA8 .... 34 B8
Marsh House La
  WARRN/WOL WA2 .... 5 K3
Marsh La ALS/KID ST7 .... 241 G1
  CHNE CH2 .... 97 G6
  CHNE CH2 .... 123 H1
  CHSE CH3 .... 212 B8
  FLINT CH6 .... 116 B5
  FROD/HEL WA6 .... 99 G4
  FROD/HEL WA6 .... 127 G6
  HOLMCH CW4 .... 181 L2
  KNUT WA16 .... 80 F1
  NANT CW5 .... 250 F1
  NM/HAY SK22 .... 69 K6
  RUNC WA7 .... 73 M1
  WARRS WA4 .... 101 K1
  WARRS WA4 .... 102 A3
  WARRW/BUR WA5 .... 54 C2
Marsh Rd WARRS WA4 .... 57 H8
Marsh St WARR WA1 .... 5 M3
  WDN WA8 .... 7 G9
Marsh Vw CQ CH5 .... 142 A5
Marsland Cl HALE/TIMP WA15 .... 43 H4
Marsland Rd HALE/TIMP WA15 .... 43 H6
  MPL/ROM SK6 .... 48 D5
  SALE M33 .... 43 K1
Marsland St BRAM/HZG SK7 .... 66 D2
  STKP SK1 .... 3 H2
Marsland Ter STKP SK1 .... 3 M8
Marson St WARRN/WOL WA2 .... 4 F5
Marston Cl PS/BROM CH62 .... 93 L1
Marston La NWCHE CW9 .... 104 C6
Martens Av IRL M44 .... 31 L7
Marthall Dr SALE M33 .... 43 L2
Marthall La KNUT WA16 .... 108 A6
Martham Cl WARRS WA4 .... 57 L1
Martham Dr OFTN SK2 .... 48 A6
Martin Av NEWLW WA12 .... 22 B7
  WARRN/WOL WA2 .... 37 K3
Martin Cl CHNE CH2 .... 145 J4
  OFTN SK2 .... 47 M7
  RUNC WA7 .... 74 A5
Martindale Gv RUNC WA7 .... 73 K7
Martin Rd CHNE CH2 .... 145 J4
  FROD/HEL WA6 .... 99 H4
Martinscroft Rd
  NTHM/RTH M23 .... 44 B7
Martinsfields NWCHW CW8 .... 101 M7
Martin's La CHSE CH3 .... 171 M3
Martland Av GOL/RIS/CU WA3 .... 23 K5
Martlet Av POY/DIS SK12 .... 68 C5
Martock Rd RAIN/WH L35 .... 32 F2
Martock Ri WYTH/NTH M22 .... 63 L1
Marton Av DID/WITH M20 .... 45 J2
Marton Cl CONG CW12 .... 184 E7
  CW/SHV CW2 .... 253 L1
  GOL/RIS/CU WA3 .... 24 E8
  SPK/HALE L24 .... 70 D2
Marton Gn EDGY/DAV SK3 .... 46 D7
  SPK/HALE L24 .... 70 D2
Marton Hall La MCFLDS SK11 .... 184 A1
Marton La MCFLDS SK11 .... 160 D5
  MCFLDS SK11 .... 184 F1
Marton Rd CHSW/BR CH4 .... 190 C1
Marwood Cl ALT WA14 .... 42 B6
Marwood Dr NTHM/RTH M23 .... 62 F1
Maryfield Cl GOL/RIS/CU WA3 .... 23 G5
Maryhill Cl ALS/KID ST7 .... 243 G1
Maryhill Rd RUNC WA7 .... 9 G7
Marylon Dr WYTH/NTH M22 .... 44 E4
Marys Ga CW/SHV CW2 .... 237 L4
Mary St CHD/CHDH SK8 .... 45 K6
  CW/HAS CW1 .... 19 H3
  STHEL WA9 .... 34 C1
  STKP SK1 .... 3 J4
  WDN WA8 .... 53 K5
Masefield Av WDN WA8 .... 6 F1
Masefield Dr CH/BCN CH1 .... 144 E6
  CW/HAS CW1 .... 19 L4
  HTNM SK4 .... 46 A2
Masefield Wy SBCH CW11 .... 203 K7
Maskery Pl CONG CW12 .... 207 K1
Mason Av WARR WA1 .... 37 L4
  WDN WA8 .... 34 A8
Mason Cl GTS/LS CH66 .... 120 D2
Mason Dr BIDD ST8 .... 227 H4
Masons La MCFLDN SK10 .... 15 L2
Mason St CHNE CH2 .... 16 F3
  RUNC WA7 .... 9 L1
  WARR WA1 .... 5 K7
  WLTN L25 .... 50 A2
Massey Av LYMM WA13 .... 58 A2
  NWCHW CW8 .... 129 G8
  WARRW/BUR WA5 .... 36 F2
  WSFD CW7 .... 177 M3
Massey Brook La LYMM WA13 .... 58 B2
Masseyfield Rd RUNC WA7 .... 74 A7
Massey Rd HALE/TIMP WA15 .... 42 E8
Massey St STKP SK1 .... 3 G6
  WILM/AE SK9 .... 110 A3
Massey Wk WYTH/NTH M22 .... 63 M3
Massie St CHD/CHDH SK8 .... 45 K6
Mates La MALPAS SY14 .... 246 B6
Mather Av GOL/RIS/CU WA3 .... 23 L6
  RUNC WA7 .... 8 B3
Mather Cl MWCH CW10 .... 179 J4
  NWCHE CW9 .... 103 J4
Mather Dr NWCHE CW9 .... 103 J4
  NWCHE CW9 .... 130 D5
Mathers Cl WARRN/WOL WA2 .... 29 G8
Mathieson Rd WDN WA8 .... 52 B1
Matlock Cl WARRW/BUR WA5 .... 36 A3
Matlock Dr BRAM/HZG SK7 .... 66 E4
Matlock Rd CHD/CHDH SK8 .... 64 C5
Matterdale Cl FROD/HEL WA6 .... 99 K5
Matthew Cl CHNE CH2 .... 17 M3
Matthews Pl CONG CW12 .... 208 A2
Matthews St WARR WA1 .... 5 L9
Matthew St MPL/ROM SK6 .... 49 G6
Matty's La FROD/HEL WA6 .... 99 G5
Mauldeth Cl HTNM SK4 .... 46 A1
Mauldeth Rd HTNM SK4 .... 46 A1
Maureen Av BURS/TUN ST6 .... 243 H6
Maveen Gv OFTN SK2 .... 47 G8
Mavor Cl CW/HAS CW1 .... 18 D3
Mawdsley Av WARR WA1 .... 38 E5
Mawdsley Cl ALS/KID ST7 .... 240 F1
Maw Green Cl CW/HAS CW1 .... 221 M5
Maw Green Rd CW/HAS CW1 .... 221 M5
Mawson Cl WARRW/BUR WA5 .... 36 D4
Maxfield Cl MCFLDS SK11 .... 137 M4
Maxwell Av CQ CH5 .... 166 D1
  OFTN SK2 .... 47 J7
Maxwell Cl EP CH65 .... 121 G2
Maxwell St CW/SHV CW2 .... 18 F6
  GOL/RIS/CU WA3 .... 29 L1
May Av CHD/CHDH SK8 .... 65 H6
  HTNM SK4 .... 2 A4
Mayberry Gv WARRN/WOL WA2 .... 38 C3
Maydor Av CHSW/BR CH4 .... 168 C5
Mayer St OFTN SK2 .... 47 J5
Mayfair Cl POY/DIS SK12 .... 66 E8
  WARRW/BUR WA5 .... 35 K5
Mayfair Dr NWCHE CW9 .... 153 L1
  SALE M33 .... 42 E2
Mayfair Gv WDN WA8 .... 6 B2
Mayfair Rd WYTH/NTH M22 .... 44 E8
Mayfield Av MCFLDS SK11 .... 138 C7
  WDN WA8 .... 52 B3
Mayfield Cl HALE/TIMP WA15 .... 43 H6
  HOLMCH CW4 .... 181 K1
Mayfield Dr GOL/RIS/CU WA3 .... 24 C4
  LEIGH WN7 .... 24 C4
  NWCHW CW8 .... 128 A8
Mayfield Gv NWCHW CW8 .... 128 A8
  WILM/AE SK9 .... 83 L7
Mayfield Ms CW/HAS CW1 .... 220 F6
Mayfield Rd BIDD ST8 .... 227 K6
  BRAM/HZG SK7 .... 65 L8
  CH/BCN CH1 .... 144 D7
  HALE/TIMP WA15 .... 43 H6
  KNUT WA16 .... 81 M8
  MPL/ROM SK6 .... 49 H3
  NWCHE CW9 .... 13 G8
  WARRS WA4 .... 57 G2
Mayfield St AIMK WN4 .... 22 A1
Mayfield Ter MCFLDS SK11 .... 138 C7
Mayfield Vw LYMM WA13 .... 58 E2
Mayflower Av SPK/HALE L24 .... 50 A6
Mayflower Rd NANT CW5 .... 20 F9
Mayhurst Av CCHDY M21 .... 44 D1
Mayor's Rd HALE/TIMP WA15 .... 42 E8
May St CHD/CHDH SK8 .... 65 C6
  GOL/RIS/CU WA3 .... 23 H7
Maythorn Av GOL/RIS/CU WA3 .... 29 G5
Maytree Av CHSE CH3 .... 170 B2
Maywood Av GOL/RIS/CU WA3 .... 39 G1
Mc Carthy Cl DID/WITH M20 .... 45 K4
Mc Clellan Pl WDN WA8 .... 7 H6
Mcgarva Wy EP CH65 .... 95 J8
Mcgough Cl STHEL WA9 .... 34 A1
Mckee Av WARRN/WOL WA2 .... 37 L2
Mc Kinley St BURS/TUN ST6 .... 243 K8
Mclaren St CW/HAS CW1 .... 221 H5
Mcminnis Av STHEL WA9 .... 26 A3
Mcneill Av CW/HAS CW1 .... 220 F7
Mead Av ALS/KID ST7 .... 225 L5
Mead Cl KNUT WA16 .... 106 F4
Meade Cl RAIN/WH L35 .... 33 K3
The Meade WILM/AE SK9 .... 84 B4
Meadow Av CONG CW12 .... 207 J3
  CW/SHV CW2 .... 239 H7
  HALE/TIMP WA15 .... 62 B1
  HOLMCH CW4 .... 157 J3
  STHEL WA9 .... 34 D1
Meadow Bank HALE/TIMP WA15 .... 43 G5
  HTNM SK4 .... 46 B2
  MKTDR TF9 .... 274 A8
  MPL/ROM SK6 .... 47 M1
  TPLY/KEL CW6 .... 149 K8
Meadowbank Gdns
  GOL/RIS/CU WA3 .... 25 J5
Meadow Brow WILM/AE SK9 .... 110 A2
Meadow Cl CHF/WBR SK23 .... 89 J4
  CHSE CH3 .... 172 B2
  CHSE CH3 .... 228 F3
  CW/SHV CW2 .... 238 D7
  FROD/HEL WA6 .... 124 B3
  HALE/TIMP WA15 .... 62 B1
  HOLMCH CW4 .... 157 L3
  LEIGH WN7 .... 24 C2
  MPL/ROM SK6 .... 67 M4
  NSTN CH64 .... 92 F4
  NWCHW CW8 .... 128 A8
  WDN WA8 .... 52 D1
  WILM/AE SK9 .... 83 L8
  WSFD CW7 .... 177 J1
Meadow Ct CH/BCN CH1 .... 144 F3
  MALPAS SY14 .... 247 G6
Meadow Cft ALS/KID ST7 .... 241 G2
  BRAM/HZG SK7 .... 66 E1
  CHSW/BR CH4 .... 190 A3
Meadow Cft NSTN CH64 .... 92 E4
Meadowcroft CH/BCN CH1 .... 144 A3
  CHSW/BR CH4 .... 190 A3
Meadowcroft WHITCH SY13 .... 269 L4
Meadowcroft CW/SHV CW2 .... 237 M5
  KNUT WA16 .... 106 F4
  MCFLDN SK10 .... 112 B5
  NWCHE CW9 .... 129 G1
Meadowfield CHF/WBR SK23 .... 89 J4
  TPLY/KEL CW6 .... 197 J3
Meadow Field Rd
  CHSW/BR CH4 .... 169 G7
Meadow Ga NWCHE CW9 .... 104 F7
Meadowgate Cl SBCH CW11 .... 203 K7
Meadow Gv NWCHE CW9 .... 13 L9
  WSFD CW7 .... 153 L7
Meadow Hey Cl WLTN L25 .... 50 B1
Meadow La CHSE CH3 .... 170 A7
  EP CH65 .... 11 G6
  NSTN CH64 .... 92 E3
  NWCHE CW9 .... 103 J5
  NWCHE CW9 .... 153 M5
  POY/DIS SK12 .... 68 D6
  WARRN/WOL WA2 .... 38 A2
Meadow Ri MALPAS SY14 .... 230 D2
  WSFD CW7 .... 177 G3
Meadow Rd CHSW/BR CH4 .... 167 H8
  NWCHW CW8 .... 128 K4
Meadows Gn GOL/RIS/CU WA3 .... 23 L7
Meadowside BIDD ST8 .... 227 H6
  BRAM/HZG SK7 .... 65 J2
  CHF/WBR SK23 .... 89 K4
  CQ CH5 .... 166 A3
  MCFLDN SK10 .... 87 H4
  NM/HAY SK22 .... 69 G5
  NWCHW CW8 .... 12 C4
Meadowside Av WYTH/NTH M22 .... 44 D7
Meadowside La WYTH/NTH M22 .... 226 B5
Meadows La CH/BCN CH1 .... 144 A4
  CHSW/BR CH4 .... 17 J9
Meadows Pl CHSW/BR CH4 .... 17 J8
  CHD/CHDH SK8 .... 64 F4
The Meadows CQ CH5 .... 142 B7
  FLINT CH6 .... 116 A6
  IRL M44 .... 31 K6
  NSTN CH64 .... 91 M6

RAIN/WH L35 .... 33 J2
Meadow St NM/HAY SK22 ...... 69 J4
NWCHE CW9 .... 13 J2
OFTN SK2 .... 47 J7
Meadowsway CHNE CH2 ..... 145 K4
Meadowsweet Rd
KNUT WA16 .... 107 M1
Meadowvale CI NANT CW5 .... 20 F2
Meadow Vw CHNE CH2 ...... 123 C1
CQ CH5 .... 143 C6
MWCH CW10 .... 179 H2
Meadow View Dr
FROD/HEL WA6 .... 99 G5
Meadow View Rd WHITCH SY13.. 269 M5
Meadow Wy ALS/KID ST7 .... 225 G7
HALE/TIMP WA15 .... 62 B1
MCFLDN SK10 .... 15 J2
WILM/AE SK9 .... 83 L8
Mead Rd WARR WA1 .... 38 A4
Meadscroft Dr WILM/AE SK9 .. 109 H3
Meads Rd ALS/KID ST7 ...... 224 D8
Meadway BRAM/HZG SK7 ..... 65 L7
GOL/RIS/CU WA3 .... 23 K4
GTS/LS CH66 .... 94 B5
MCFLDN SK10 .... 112 A7
MPL/ROM SK6 .... 66 B7
POY/DIS SK12 .... 73 K3
SALE M33 .... 42 E2
WDN WA8 .... 52 A3
Meadway Rd CHD/CHDH SK8 .. 65 H1
Meakin CI CONG CW12 ...... 208 B3
Mealhouse Brow STKP SK1 ... 3 G5
Meal St HTNM SK4 .... 2 E1
NM/HAY SK22 .... 69 J4
Mechanics' La CQ CH5 ...... 142 E6
Meddings CI WILM/AE SK9 ... 110 A4
Medina Av WSFD CW7 .... 177 M2
Medina CI CHD/CHDH SK8 ... 46 B8
Medina Wy ALS/KID ST7 ..... 243 H2
Medlar CI CHSW/BR CH4 .... 168 F7
Medway CI LEIGH WN7 ...... 24 C4
WARRN/WOL WA2 .... 37 L2
WILM/AE SK9 .... 84 D2
Medway Dr BIDD ST8 .... 227 K3
Medway Rd GOL/RIS/CU WA3.. 30 A2
Meeanee Dr NANT CW5 ..... 20 B8
Meerbrook Rd EDGY/DAV SK3 .. 46 A4
Mee St MCFLDS SK11 .... 138 E7
Meeting La WARRW/BUR WA5 .. 35 K7
Meg La MCFLDN SK10 .... 137 L4
MCFLDS SK10 .... 163 K2
Meir St BURS/TUN ST6 ...... 243 K8
Melbecks Wk NTHM/RTH M23 .. 43 M2
Melbourne Av MANAIR M90 .. 63 C4
Melbourne Gv CW/HAS CW1 .. 222 C7
Melbourne Rd BRAM/HZG SK7 .. 65 L6
CH/BCN CH1 .... 144 D8
Melbreck Av CQ CH5 .... 166 A3
Melbury Ct GOL/RIS/CU WA3.. 29 M6
Melbury Rd CHD/CHDH SK8 .. 65 H6
Melchett Crs NWCHE CW9 ... 130 D5
Melford CI CW/SHV CW2 .... 238 C4
Melford Dr MCFLDN SK10 ... 138 C2
RUNC WA7 .... 9 L5
Melford Rd BRAM/HZG SK7 .. 66 F3
Meliden Crs WYTH/NTH M22 .. 63 L2
Meliden Gv FROD/HEL WA6 .. 124 A3
Melkridge CI CHNE CH2 ..... 170 A1
Melksham CI MCFLDS SK11 .. 14 B7
Melling CI LEIGH WN7 ...... 24 F3
Mellington Av DID/WITH M20 .. 45 J4
Mellock CI NSTN CH64 ...... 91 M6
Mellock La NSTN CH64 ...... 91 M5
Mellor CI RAIN/WH L35 ..... 32 A5
RUNC WA7 .... 74 D4
Mellor Ct OFTN SK2 .... 47 L5
Mellor Crs WILM/AE SK9 .... 106 E3
Mellor Rd CHD/CHDH SK8 ... 65 H5
NM/HAY SK22 .... 69 J1
Mellors Bank ALS/KID ST7 .. 226 C6
Mellor St ALS/KID ST7 ..... 243 M3
CW/HAS CW1 .... 19 C1
Melrose Av CHSE CH3 ...... 170 B2
CQ CH5 .... 142 B8
DID/WITH M20 .... 45 J1
EDGY/DAV SK3 .... 45 M5
SALE M33 .... 43 H1
WARRS WA4 .... 56 D4
WARRW/BUR WA5 .... 26 F5
Melrose Crs EDGY/DAV SK3 .. 46 D8
HALE/TIMP WA15 .... 62 B3
POY/DIS SK12 .... 67 K7
Melrose Dr CW/HAS CW1 .... 221 H4
GTS/LS CH66 .... 120 F4
Melsomby Rd NTHM/RTH M23.. 44 A2
Meltham CI HTNM SK4 ...... 45 L3
Meltham Rd HTNM SK4 ...... 45 L3
Melton Av WARRS WA4 ...... 56 B4
Melton CI CONG CW12 ...... 206 F1
Melton Dr CONG CW12 ...... 206 F1
Melton Rd RUNC WA7 .... 73 H6
Melverly Dr CH/BCN CH1 ... 144 C3
Melville CI WARRN/WOL WA2 .. 5 C3
Melville Rd IRL M44 .... 31 J7
Melvin Wy WYTH/NTH M22 .. 44 E8
Menai Dr BIDD ST8 .... 227 K6
Menai Gv CHD/CHDH SK8 ... 46 A6
Menai Rd EDGY/DAV SK3 .... 46 E6
Mendip Av WARRN/WOL WA2 .. 37 H1
WYTH/NTH M22 .... 44 F8
Mendip CI CHD/CHDH SK8 .. 64 B5
GTS/LS CH66 .... 120 E1
HLWD L26 .... 50 E3
HTNM SK4 .... 2 E2
WSFD CW7 .... 177 H4
Menin Av WARRS WA4 ...... 56 C1
Menlow CI WARRS WA4 ..... 57 J3
Mentmore Gdns WARRS WA4 .. 56 F7
Mentone Av WYTH/NTH M22 .. 44 E8
Mentone Rd HTNM SK4 ..... 46 B1
Meols CI GTS/LS CH66 ...... 94 E8
Mercer CI MALPAS SY14 .... 258 B1
Mercer St NEWLW WA12 .... 22 D8
WARRW/BUR WA5 .... 26 E6
Mercer Wy CHSW/BR CH4 .. 168 F6

Merchants Crs GOL/RIS/CU WA3 .. 23 L3
Mercian CI CW/SHV CW2 .... 238 B8
Mercian Wy EDGY/DAV SK3.. 2 D9
Mercury Ct CH/BCN CH1 .... 168 E2
Merebank Rd NWCHE CW9 .. 154 A4
Merebrook Rd MCFLDS SK11 .. 137 M4
Mere Brook Wk CW/SHV CW2 .. 238 C3
Mere CI CW/HAS CW1 ...... 222 D8
GTS/LS CH66 .... 120 D2
KNUT WA16 .... 105 G5
SALE M33 .... 43 M1
Mere Crs NWCHW CW8 ..... 150 F6
Merecroft CHSE CH3 .... 170 A3
Meredith Av WARRS WA4 ... 57 H2
Meredith St CW/HAS CW1 .. 18 E2
Merefield Rd HALE/TIMP WA15 .. 43 J7
Merehaven CI KNUT WA16 .. 104 F5
Mereheath La KNUT WA16 .. 80 D5
Mereheath Pk KNUT WA16 .. 106 F1
Merelake Rd ALS/KID ST7 .. 242 A4
Mere La KNUT WA16 .... 104 F6
NWCHW CW8 .... 152 A2
Merepool CI MPL/ROM SK6 .. 48 D5
Mere Rd CW/SHV CW2 ..... 239 H7
NEWLW WA12 .... 22 F8
NWCHE CW9 .... 104 B6
WARRN/WOL WA2 .... 38 A2
Mereside Av CONG CW12 ... 159 G7
Mereside CI CHD/CHDH SK8 .. 45 M8
MCFLDN SK10 .... 14 A2
Mereside Gdns CHF/WBR SK23 .. 89 K6
Mereside Rd KNUT WA16 ... 80 C3
Mere St CW/HAS CW1 ..... 222 D8
The Mere CHD/CHDH SK8 .. 45 M8
Merevale CI RUNC WA7 .... 73 L6
Merewood Av WYTH/NTH M22 .. 44 D6
Merewood CI WARRN/WOL WA2 .. 37 K1
Mereworth Dr NWCHE CW9 .. 13 G9
Merganser CI CW/HAS CW1 .. 220 F5
Meriton Rd WILM/AE SK9 ... 64 C8
Merlin Av KNUT WA16 ...... 107 H1
Merlin CI OFTN SK2 .... 48 A6
RUNC WA7 .... 74 A4
WSFD CW7 .... 178 A4
Merlin Ct HLWD L26 .... 50 D3
Merlin Gn AUD/MAD/W CW3 .. 267 L6
Merlin Wy ALS/KID ST7 ..... 243 K1
CW/HAS CW1 .... 221 G4
Merrick Av WYTH/NTH M22 .. 44 E8
Merrick CI WARRN/WOL WA2 .. 37 L2
The Merridale HALE/TIMP WA15 .. 61 M4
Merriden Rd MCFLDN SK10 .. 14 D1
Merrill's Av CW/SHV CW2 .. 220 E7
Merriman Av KNUT WA16 .. 107 J1
Merrivale Rd CW/SHV CW2 .. 238 A4
WLTN L25 .... 55 C8
Merrybent CI OFTN SK2 .... 47 K8
Merrydale CI MCFLDN SK10 .. 137 M3
Merryman's La WILM/AE SK9 .. 109 H5
Mersey Crs DID/WITH M20 .. 44 D1
Mersey Mdw DID/WITH M20.. 44 F1
Mersey Rd DID/WITH M20... 44 F1
HTNM SK4 .... 45 M2
RUNC WA7 .... 9 G1
WDN WA8 .... 53 G8
Mersey Sq STKP SK1 .... 2 F5
Mersey St RUNC WA7 ...... 9 H1
STHEL WA9 .... 26 A1
STKP SK1 .... 3 K3
WARR WA1 .... 5 H8
Mersey View EP CH65 ..... 10 D2
Mersey View Rd WDN WA8.. 52 B8
Mersey View South Rd
RUNC WA7 .... 8 A8
Mersey Wk WARRS WA4 ... 37 M7
Mersey Wy WARRW/BUR WA5.. 36 C8
Mersham Rd WDN WA8 .... 33 M8
Merston Dr DID/WITH M20 .. 45 J5
Merstone CI HLWD L26 .... 51 G5
Merton Av BRAM/HZG SK7 .. 66 F4
Merton CI NSTN CH64 ...... 91 L7
Merton Dr CHSW/BR CH4 .. 169 G8
Merton Gv HALE/TIMP WA15 .. 43 H6
Merton Rd EDGY/DAV SK3 .. 46 B4
GTS/LS CH66 .... 120 E1
POY/DIS SK12 .... 66 B8
PS/BROM CH62 .... 94 B1
Mertoun Rd WARRS WA4 .. 56 B3
Mervyn Rd NWCHW CW8 ... 128 E3
Merwood Av CHD/CHDH SK8 .. 64 D4
Messuage La CONG CW12 .. 159 G8
Meteor Crs WARRN/WOL WA2.. 37 K2
Mevagissey Rd RUNC WA7.. 74 C7
Mevril Rd CHF/WBR SK23 .. 89 L7
The Mews CHD/CHDH SK8... 45 H7
NWCHW CW8 .... 129 H2
TPLY/KEL CW6 .... 197 J4
Meyer St EDGY/DAV SK3 ... 46 F6
Meynell CI CW/SHV CW2 ... 238 A3
Meynell Dr LEIGH WN7 ..... 24 F2
Meynell PI CH/BCN CH1 .... 145 G7
Micawber CI POY/DIS SK12 .. 86 E2
Micklegate CHNE CH2 ...... 146 E4
RUNC WA7 .... 74 D5
Micklehurst Gn OFTN SK2 .. 47 L7
Micklewright Av CW/HAS CW1.. 19 G1
Mickley Hall La NANT CW5 .. 263 H1
Middlecroft CHSE CH3 ...... 146 E7
Middlefields CHD/CHDH SK8 .. 46 B8
Middle Hillgate STKP SK1 .. 3 H6
Middlehills MCFLDS SK11 .. 139 G6
Middlehurst Av NWCHW CW8.. 128 C7
Middlehurst Rd WARRS WA4 .. 57 G2
Middle La CHSE CH3 .... 211 M1
CONG CW12 .... 185 J8
FROD/HEL WA6 .... 126 K2
Middle Rd SPK/HALE L24 .. 50 F7
Middle Wk FROD/HEL WA6 .. 99 H5
KNUT WA16 .... 107 L2
Middlewich Rd CW/HAS CW1.. 220 E5
CW/SHV CW2 .... 237 J1
HOLMCH CW4 .... 156 E6
KNUT WA16 .... 132 C8
MWCH CW10 .... 201 L4
NANT CW5 .... 21 G3
NWCHE CW9 .... 13 M2

SBCH CW11 .... 203 L6
WSFD CW7 .... 178 C3
Middlewich St CW/HAS CW1.. 19 G1
Middlewood
GOL/RIS/CU WA3 .... 23 M4
Middlewood Dr HTNM SK4 .. 46 A3
Middlewood Rd MPL/ROM SK6.. 67 K5
POY/DIS SK12 .... 67 G8
Middlewood Wy MCFLDN SK10.. 87 G6
Midfield CI BIDD ST8 ...... 227 J2
Midhurst CI ALS/KID ST7 .. 243 M4
CHD/CHDH SK8 .... 64 F4
Midland Rd BRAM/HZG SK7 .. 65 L1
Midland St WDN WA8 ..... 7 K3
Midland Ter NM/HAY SK22 .. 69 J5
Midland Wk BRAM/HZG SK7 .. 65 L1
Midland Wy WARR WA1 ... 4 E5
Midway CHD/CHDH SK8 ... 65 H7
Midwood St WDN WA8 .... 7 J5
Milborne CI CHNE CH2 ..... 145 L7
Milburn Av NTHM/RTH M23 .. 44 B2
Mile Bank Rd WHITCH SY13.. 260 D8
Mile End La OFTN SK2 ..... 47 H7
Miles CI GOL/RIS/CU WA3 .. 38 F1
Milford Gdns WARRS WA4 .. 56 D3
Milford Gv OFTN SK2 ...... 47 J5
Milk St CONG CW12 .... 207 K1
Millar Crs WDN WA8 ...... 7 G6
Mill Av WARRW/BUR WA5 .. 35 L5
Millbank LYMM WA13 ..... 58 E1
Mill Bank NSTN CH64 ...... 92 A7
Millbank CI MCFLDS SK11 .. 135 G1
Millbank Dr MCFLDN SK10 .. 137 M3
Millbeck CI CW/SHV CW2 .. 239 H7
Millbrook End CHSE CH3 .. 214 A2
Millbrook Rd NTHM/RTH M23.. 63 G1
Mill Brow MPL/ROM SK6 .. 49 K4
WDN WA8 .... 7 M2
Mill Brow Rd MPL/ROM SK6.. 49 L4
Millbuck Wy SBCH CW11 .. 203 J6
Mill CI CHNE CH2 .... 145 K6
EP CH65 .... 121 J3
KNUT WA16 .... 81 K8
WARRN/WOL WA2 .... 28 E3
Mill Cft FLINT CH6 .... 116 C7
Millcroft Rd WLTN L25 .... 50 C3
Milldale Rd LEIGH WN7 .... 24 B3
Millend La ALS/KID ST7 ... 241 J7
Millers CI CHSE CH3 ...... 171 G8
SALE M33 .... 44 A1
Millersdale Gv RUNC WA7 .. 73 K7
Millers La LYMM WA13 .... 40 F3
Millers Meadow MCFLDN SK10.. 113 L7
Miller St WARRS WA4 ..... 5 K9
Millers Vw ALS/KID ST7 .. 243 G4
Millers Whf ALS/KID ST7 .. 224 E5
Milley La KNUT WA16 ..... 105 J5
Mill Farm CI WARRN/WOL WA2.. 37 L1
Mill Field CI CHSE CH3 .. 228 F2
Millfield La CHSE CH3 .... 193 M3
Millfield Rd WDN WA8 .... 7 L1
Millfields NANT CW5 ..... 20 C7
Millgate STKP SK1 .... 3 G4
Millgate La DID/WITH M20.. 45 C4
Mill Gn CONG CW12 ...... 207 K1
NSTN CH64 .... 92 F4
Mill Green La WDN WA8 .. 34 D7
Mill Gv ALS/KID ST7 ..... 242 D3
MALPAS SY14 .... 232 D2
Mill Hey RAIN/WH L35 .... 33 L3
Mill Hill Av POY/DIS SK12 .. 66 D5
Mill Hill Dr SBCH CW11 .. 204 A8
Mill Hill Hollow POY/DIS SK12.. 66 D5
Mill Hill La SBCH CW11 .. 204 A8
Millhouse Av NTHM/RTH M23 .. 44 A8
WARRS WA4 .... 56 D3
Millhouse La GOL/RIS/CU WA3 .. 29 C6
Millington Av RUNC WA7 .. 73 M8
WDN WA8 .... 7 H7
Millington Hall La ALT WA14.. 60 B7
Millington La ALT WA14 .. 60 B6
NWCHW CW8 .... 128 A6
Mill La ALS/KID ST7 ...... 226 A5
AUD/MAD/W CW3 .... 264 A8
AUD/MAD/W CW3 .... 267 M5
AUD/MAD/W CW3 .... 273 L2
BRAM/HZG SK7 .... 65 K6
CHD/CHDH SK8 .... 45 K6
CHD/CHDH SK8 .... 46 A8
CHNE CH2 .... 145 K7
CHSE CH3 .... 147 L7
CHSE CH3 .... 171 K2
CHSE CH3 .... 172 C1
CHSE CH3 .... 195 J3
CONG CW12 .... 183 L3
CONG CW12 .... 208 C4
CQ CH5 .... 142 A6
CW/SHV CW2 .... 239 G6
CW/SHV CW2 .... 240 C5
FROD/HEL WA6 .... 99 L2
FROD/HEL WA6 .... 126 D1
GTS/LS CH66 .... 94 D8
HALE/TIMP WA15 .... 62 E8
HOLMCH CW4 .... 157 L3
HOLMCH CW4 .... 181 L3
HOLMCH CW4 .... 182 A4
KNUT WA16 .... 82 B8
KNUT WA16 .... 134 D3
LYMM WA13 .... 40 C7
MALPAS SY14 .... 232 D2
MCFLDN SK10 .... 85 L6
MCFLDN SK10 .... 85 M8
MCFLDN SK10 .... 113 J4
MCFLDS SK11 .... 15 H7
MCFLDS SK11 .... 135 L6
MWCH CW10 .... 179 H5
NANT CW5 .... 266 A1
NEWLW WA12 .... 27 L1
NSTN CH64 .... 92 C7
NSTN CH64 .... 118 C3
NWCHW CW8 .... 127 M7
RAIN/WH L35 .... 33 J3
SBCH CW11 .... 203 J3

SBCH CW11 .... 223 G2
TPLY/KEL CW6 .... 172 F5
TPLY/KEL CW6 .... 173 J3
TPLY/KEL CW6 .... 176 A4
TPLY/KEL CW6 .... 198 B2
WARRN/WOL WA2 .... 27 L7
WARRN/WOL WA2 .... 28 E8
WARRN/WOL WA2 .... 37 G1
WARRS WA4 .... 55 L5
WARRS WA4 .... 56 D3
WDN WA8 .... 33 K7
WDN WA8 .... 34 C8
WDN WA8 .... 34 D7
WHITCH SY13 .... 268 A8
WILM/AE SK9 .... 108 F6
WSFD CW7 .... 153 J6
WYTH/NTH M22 .... 44 E3
Millmead ALS/KID ST7 .... 224 F5
Mill Meadow NEWLW WA12.. 27 L1
Millom Av NTHM/RTH M23 .. 44 B3
Millom PI CHD/CHDH SK8 .. 64 B1
Mill Park Dr PS/BROM CH62.. 93 L1
Millrace Dr CH/SHV CW2 .. 238 B4
Mill Ri ALS/KID ST7 ...... 242 F3
Mill Rd MCFLDS SK11 ..... 15 J8
Millstone Av ALS/KID ST7 .. 242 E3
Millstone CI POY/DIS SK12.. 66 F7
Millstone La NANT CW5 ... 20 C7
Millstone Pas MCFLDS SK11.. 15 J8
Mill Stream CI HOLMCH CW4.. 157 K5
Mill St AIMK WN4 .... 22 C2
ALT WA14 .... 42 E7
BRAM/HZG SK7 .... 66 D1
CHSW/BR CH4 .... 17 H8
CONG CW12 .... 184 E8
CW/SHV CW2 .... 19 C5
GOL/RIS/CU WA3 .... 23 G4
MCFLDS SK11 .... 15 C5
NANT CW5 .... 20 E7
NSTN CH64 .... 91 L4
WHITCH SY13 .... 270 A5
WILM/AE SK9 .... 84 B5
WLTN L25 .... 50 A2
Mills Wy CW/HAS CW1 .... 221 H4
Mill View CI MALPAS SY14 .. 232 E2
Mill View Rd CQ CH5 ..... 142 A6
Millway CHSE CH3 .... 171 H7
HALE/TIMP WA15 .... 62 C5
Mill Wy NANT CW5 .... 251 M2
Millway Rd SPK/HALE L24 .. 51 G8
Millwood CI CHD/CHDH SK8.. 64 F4
Millwood Gdns RAIN/WH L35.. 32 F2
Millwood Rd SPK/HALE L24.. 70 E1
Milne CI CW/SHV CW2 .... 237 M4
Milner Av NWCHW CW8 ... 12 B6
Milner St WARRW/BUR WA5 .. 4 D7
Milnes Av LEIGH WN7 ..... 24 F2
Milnthorpe Rd
WARRW/BUR WA5 .... 26 E6
Milton Av IRL M44 .... 31 L6
NEWLW WA12 .... 27 H1
RAIN/WH L35 .... 32 E1
WDN WA8 .... 6 E5
Milton CI MPL/ROM SK6 .. 48 F8
MWCH CW10 .... 179 K7
NWCHE CW9 .... 105 C7
RAIN/WH L35 .... 32 E1
Milton Crs ALS/KID ST7 .. 242 D3
CHD/CHDH SK8 .... 45 J7
Milton Dr CW/SHV CW2 ... 237 M4
HALE/TIMP WA15 .... 43 G3
POY/DIS SK12 .... 66 D8
Milton Gv FROD/HEL WA6 .. 124 A3
WARRS WA4 .... 56 D2
Milton Rd CH/BCN CH1 ... 144 F6
EP CH65 .... 95 K8
GOL/RIS/CU WA3 .... 23 K5
WDN WA8 .... 7 G5
Milton Rough NWCHW CW8.. 127 L2
Milton St CH/BCN CH1 ... 17 H4
STHEL WA9 .... 34 A2
WDN WA8 .... 53 C7
Milton Wy SBCH CW11 ... 203 K6
Milvain Dr WARRN/WOL WA2.. 37 J3
Milverton Dr CHD/CHDH SK8.. 65 H7
Min Awel FLINT CH6 ..... 116 B8
Miners Wy SPK/HALE L24 .. 71 C1
WDN WA8 .... 7 H7
Minerva Av CW/HAS CW1 .. 168 D2
Minerva CI BIDD ST8 ..... 227 H7
WARRS WA4 .... 56 D2
Minfield CI ALS/KID ST7 .. 243 G4
Minn-end-lane MCFLDS SK11.. 187 G6
Minor Av MCFLDS SK11 .. 162 D2
Minshull La NANT CW5 ... 200 C8
Minshull New Rd CW/HAS CW1.. 220 F6
Minshull St KNUT WA16 .. 107 G2
Minster CI WSFD CW7 ... 177 K7
Minster Ct CW/SHV CW2 .. 237 L4
Minster Dr ALT WA14 .... 61 C4
CHD/CHDH SK8 .... 46 A7
Minton CI CONG CW12 ... 208 B3
Minton Wy WDN WA8 .... 34 B7
Mirfield Av HTNM SK4 ... 46 B3
Mirfield CI GOL/RIS/CU WA3.. 23 K5
HLWD L26 .... 50 F3
Mirion St CW/HAS CW1 ... 19 H3
Misty CI WDN WA8 ...... 52 C2
Mitchell Av ALS/KID ST7 .. 242 D3
WARRW/BUR WA5 .... 26 E7
Mitchell CI CHD/CHDH SK8.. 44 F6
Mitchell Rd ALS/KID ST7 .. 242 D3
Mitchell St AIMK WN4 ... 22 C2
GOL/RIS/CU WA3 .... 23 G4
WARRS WA4 .... 56 C4
Mithril CI WDN WA8 ..... 53 L1
Mitre CI RAIN/WH L35 ... 32 D3
Moat Av WYTH/NTH M22 .. 44 C8
Moat Gdns WYTH/NTH M22.. 44 C8
Moat House Dr CW/SHV CW2.. 18 B8
Moat La GOL/RIS/CU WA3 .. 39 L3
Moat Rd WYTH/NTH M22 .. 44 C8
Mobberley CI WARRS WA4 .. 57 K1
Mobberley Rd BURS/TUN ST6 .. 243 J6

KNUT WA16 .... 81 L2
KNUT WA16 .... 107 H2
WILM/AE SK9 .... 83 J3
Modbury CI BRAM/HZG SK7.. 66 A3
Moelfre Dr CHD/CHDH SK8 .. 65 J5
Moel Parc FLINT CH6 ..... 116 B8
Moggie La MCFLDN SK10 .. 86 F5
Mollington Ct CH/BCN CH1.. 144 E3
Mollington Rd WYTH/NTH M22.. 63 L4
Molly Pitcher Wy
WARRW/BUR WA5 .... 36 B7
Molly Potts CI KNUT WA16.. 107 H4
Molyneux Av WARRW/BUR WA5.. 4 D1
Mona Av CHD/CHDH SK8 .. 64 D3
Monaco Dr WYTH/NTH M22.. 44 D2
Monarch CI IRL M44 ..... 31 L6
Monarch Dr NWCHE CW9 .. 12 F8
Mond Av WDN WA8 ...... 7 G5
Mond St WDN WA8 ...... 129 H2
Money Ash Rd HALE/TIMP WA15.. 61 K1
Monfa Av EDGY/DAV SK3 .. 47 G8
Monica Dr WDN WA8 .... 34 A7
Monica Rd WLTN L25 .... 50 B8
Monica Ter AIMK WN4 ... 22 B2
Monks Gv EP CH65 ...... 10 D6
Monk's La AUD/MAD/W CW3.. 264 C7
CW/HAS CW1 .... 220 F6
NANT CW5 .... 20 F6
NANT CW5 .... 235 M5
Monks Orch NANT CW5 ... 21 G6
Monks St WARRW/BUR WA5.. 4 B5
Monk St CW/HAS CW1 ... 18 B2
Monks Wy NWCHW CW8 ... 129 H8
WLTN L25 .... 50 A2
Monkswood CI
WARRW/BUR WA5 .... 36 E2
Monmouth CI WARR WA1 .. 38 E5
Monmouth Crs AIMK WN4 .. 22 C2
Monmouth Rd CHD/CHDH SK8.. 65 H3
Monroe CI WARR WA1 .... 38 B5
Monsal Av OFTN SK2 .... 47 B5
Monsall CI MCFLDS SK11 .. 15 M6
Monsall St MCFLDS SK11 .. 15 M7
Montagu CI OFTN SK2 ... 47 K5
Montagu St MPL/ROM SK6.. 49 H2
Montclare Crs WARRS WA4 .. 56 E3
Montcliffe CI GOL/RIS/CU WA3.. 29 J7
Montgomery Rd WDN WA8 .. 6 A6
Montgomery Av CHSE CH3.. 170 A3
Montgomery Wy WSFD CW7.. 177 H5
Mont Morency Rd KNUT WA16.. 81 K8
Montpelier Av RUNC WA7 .. 72 F5
Montpellior Rd
WYTH/NTH M22 .... 63 K2
Montrose Av EDGY/DAV SK3.. 66 A1
Montrose CI CW/SHV CW2.. 253 H1
MCFLDN SK10 .... 14 A3
WARRN/WOL WA2 .... 28 F8
Montrose Ct HOLMCH CW4.. 181 H2
Monument Rd ALS/KID ST7.. 242 D6
Moody St CONG CW12 ... 207 K2
Moor CI BIDD ST8 .... 227 L3
Moorcroft KNUT WA16 ... 131 M1
Moorcroft CI CHSE CH3 .. 170 B3
Moorcroft Crs CHSE CH3 .. 146 C8
Moorcroft Rd NTHM/RTH M23.. 43 M3
Moordale Rd KNUT WA16 .. 107 H2
Moorditch La FROD/HEL WA6.. 98 B3
Moore Av STHEL WA9 .... 26 A1
WARRS WA4 .... 56 E3
Moore CI WDN WA8 ..... 53 K2
Moore Gv LYMM WA13 ... 40 B7
Moore La WARRS WA4 ... 55 H5
Moor End WYTH/NTH M22.. 44 D4
Mooreway RAIN/WH L35 .. 33 L3
Moorfield Av BIDD ST8 ... 227 K4
Moorfield Ct CQ CH5 .... 166 B3
Moorfield Crs GOL/RIS/CU WA3.. 24 A5
Moorfield Dr NSTN CH64 .. 91 J2
WILM/AE SK9 .... 83 L7
Moorfield Gv SALE M33 .. 43 K1
Moorfield Rd CQ CH5 .... 166 B2
WDN WA8 .... 34 D8
Moorfields NANT CW5 ... 237 L6
Moorhead La SBCH CW11 .. 205 J1
Moorhill Rd MCFLDS SK11.. 138 C8
Moorhouse Av ALS/KID ST7.. 224 E8
Moorhouse CI CHNE CW9 .. 74 D6
Mooring CI RUNC WA7 ... 74 D6
Moorings CONG CW12 ... 207 L3
Moorings CI NSTN CH64 .. 91 H3
The Moorings MWCH CW10.. 179 J5
POY/DIS SK12 .... 68 E6
Moorland Av SALE M33 .. 43 J1
Moorland Dr CHD/CHDH SK8.. 64 F4
RUNC WA7 .... 74 E5
Moorland Rd ALS/KID ST7.. 226 D5
BIDD ST8 .... 227 K4
DID/WITH M20 .... 45 H1
GTS/LS CH66 .... 94 E4
OFTN SK2 .... 47 C8
Moorlands Av LEIGH WN7 .. 24 F1
NWCHW CW8 .... 128 A8
Moorlands CI MCFLDN SK10.. 138 C1
Moorlands Dr NANT CW5 .. 253 C5
Moorlands Pk NWCHW CW8.. 128 A8
Moor La BRAM/HZG SK7 .. 85 K1
CHSE CH3 .... 171 G7
CHSW/BR CH4 .... 190 C6
CQ CH5 .... 166 E4
FROD/HEL WA6 .... 99 H4
FROD/HEL WA6 .... 123 L3
NTHM/RTH M23 .... 44 A2
WDN WA8 .... 6 F7
WILM/AE SK9 .... 83 J7
Moor La South WDN WA8 .. 6 F7
Moor Nook SALE M33 .... 43 K1
Moor Park Rd DID/WITH M20.. 45 J4
Moor-park Wy NWCHE CW9.. 129 M8
Moor Rd NTHM/RTH M23 .. 43 L4
Moorsfield Av
AUD/MAD/W CW3 .... 273 M1
Moorside KNUT WA16 .... 107 C2
Moorside Av NSTN CH64 .. 91 J4
Moorside Ct WDN WA8 ... 6 F6
Moorside La MCFLDN SK10.. 137 L4
NSTN CH64 .... 91 J5
Moorside Rd HTNM SK4 .. 46 A2

Moors La WSFD CW7 177 J7
Moorson Av ALS/KID ST7 225 M4
Moor Top Pl HTNM SK4 46 B1 5
Moorwood Dr SALE M33 42 E1
Moran Cl WILM/AE SK9 84 D2
Moran Crs MCFLDS SK11 14 D7
Moran Rd MCFLDS SK11 14 D7
Morcott La SPK/HALE L24 71 K2
Morden Av AIMK WN4 22 B1
Moresby Cl RUNC WA7 74 E5 2
Moresby Dr DID/WITH M20 45 H4 3
Moreton Av BRAM/HZG SK7 65 L7
SALE M33 42 F1 3
Moreton Cl ALS/KID ST7 243 H4
GOL/RIS/CU WA3 22 F3
Moreton Dr ALS/KID ST7 241 H1
HOLMCH CW4 181 H1
LEIGH WN7 24 E3 4
POY/DIS SK12 66 F8
SBCH CW11 204 C5
WILM/AE SK9 84 E1
Moreton La OFTN SK2 47 J5
Moreton Rd CW/SHV CW2 237 M2
Moreton St NWCHW CW8 12 D2
Moreville Cl NWCHE CW9 153 L1 3
Morgan Av WARRN/WOL WA2 37 J2
Morgan Cl CH/BCN CH1 144 F7
CW/SHV CW2 18 A3
Morland Av NSTN CH64 91 M5
Morley Br FROD/HEL WA6 123 J8
Morley Cl CHNE CH2 146 F4
Morley Dr CONG CW12 208 A3
Morley Green Rd WILM/AE SK9 83 J3
Morley Rd RUNC WA7 9 G5
WARRS WA4 56 A3
Morley's La TYLD M29 25 M1
Morley St WARR WA1 5 K5
Mornant Av NWCHW CW8 153 G1
Morningside AUD/MAD/W CW3 267 L6
Morningside Dr DID/WITH M20 45 J4
Mornington Av
CHD/CHDH SK8 45 K8 3
EP CH65 10 F8
Mornington Cl SBCH CW11 203 K5
Mornington Rd CHD/CHDH SK8 45 K8
Morphany La WARRS WA4 75 L6
Morrell Rd WYTH/NTH M22 44 D4
Morreys La TPLY/KEL CW6 149 M6
Morris Av WARRS WA4 37 M8
Morris Dr NWCHW CW8 128 D3
Morrison Cl WARRW/BUR WA5 36 A7 1
Morris Pk NWCHW CW8 129 H8
Mort Av WARRS WA4 38 A8
Mortimer Av WARRN/WOL WA2 5 H1
Mortimer Dr SBCH CW11 204 C7
Mortlake Cl WDN WA8 52 C1
Mortlake Crs CHSE CH3 170 A3 3
Morton Av FROD/HEL WA6 124 B3 1
Morton Cl WARRW/BUR WA5 36 C4
Morton Dr MCFLDS SK11 162 F1
Morton Rd CH/BCN CH1 144 E8
RUNC WA7 74 D4
Morval Crs RUNC WA7 9 M5
Morven Av BRAM/HZG SK7 66 F1
Morven Cl WARRN/WOL WA2 37 L1 5
Morven Dr NTHM/RTH M23 44 A7
Moscow Rd EDGY/DAV SK3 46 D5 3
Moscow Rd East EDGY/DAV SK3 46 D5
Mosedale Cl NTHM/RTH M23 43 L6
Mosedale Gv RUNC WA7 73 L7 3
Moseldene Rd OFTN SK2 47 K7
Moseley Av WARRS WA4 38 A8
Moseley Rd CHD/CHDH SK8 64 F1
Moseley St EDGY/DAV SK3 2 E8
Mosley Cl HALE/TIMP WA15 42 F5
Mosley Rd HALE/TIMP WA15 43 H6
Mossack Av WYTH/NTH M22 63 K3 3
Moss Bank CH/BCN CH1 16 E1
CHD/CHDH SK8 65 J7
WSFD CW7 177 H3
Moss Bank Rd WDN WA8 53 K5
Moss Bower Rd MCFLDS SK11 138 C8
Moss Brow MCFLDN SK10 112 E5
Moss Brow La KNUT WA16 58 D8
Moss Cl NSTN CH64 93 G4
WARRS WA4 56 E2
Moss Cft CW/HAS CW1 221 G4
Mossdale Cl CW/SHV CW2 220 E8
WARRW/BUR WA5 36 A5
Mossdale Dr RAIN/WH L35 33 K1
Mossdale Rd NTHM/RTH M23 43 M3
SALE M33 42 E3
Moss Dr MWCH CW10 179 K6
Mossfield Cl HTNM SK4 46 B2
Mossfield Crs ALS/KID ST7 243 H2 3
Mossfield Rd HALE/TIMP WA15 43 K6
Moss Flds ALS/KID ST7 241 G1
Mossford Av CW/HAS CW1 221 H5
Moss Ga GOL/RIS/CU WA3 30 A7
Moss Gn WRX/GR/LL LL12 210 C5 1
Moss Green Wy STHEL WA9 26 A3
Moss Gv CHSW/BR CH4 168 D6
LYMM WA13 40 B8
Mossgrove Rd HALE/TIMP WA15 42 F6
Mosshall La WARRS WA4 76 F3
Moss Hey Dr NTHM/RTH M23 44 B3
Mosslands Cl GTS/LS CH66 120 E2
Moss La ALS/KID ST7 225 L8
AUD/MAD/W CW3 267 K6
BRAM/HZG SK7 65 J7
CONG CW12 182 F7
CONG CW12 184 E6
CW/HAS CW1 220 E2
CW/HAS CW1 221 G4
CW/HAS CW1 221 J1
FROD/HEL WA6 124 F8
FROD/HEL WA6 127 G7
GOL/RIS/CU WA3 23 H7
GOL/RIS/CU WA3 25 K7
GOL/RIS/CU WA3 30 F7
HALE/TIMP WA15 42 F5
IRL M44 31 K7
KNUT WA16 59 L6
KNUT WA16 78 C1
KNUT WA16 80 D8
KNUT WA16 108 B8
KNUT WA16 108 F1
LYMM WA13 40 E3
LYMM WA13 41 H4
MCFLDN SK10 111 G2
MCFLDN SK10 112 E4
MCFLDS SK11 138 B7
MCFLDS SK11 159 K2
MWCH CW10 156 B5
NANT CW5 253 H3
NWCHE CW9 104 E6
NWCHE CW9 131 J5
NWCHW CW8 12 D4
NWCHW CW8 151 M1
PART M31 41 G1
SALE M33 42 D1
SBCH CW11 203 J5
STHEL WA9 26 A3
TPLY/KEL CW6 197 H2
WARRS WA4 55 G6
WILM/AE SK9 63 K7
WILM/AE SK9 110 B3
Mossley Ct CONG CW12 207 M4
CQ CH5 166 C4
Mossley Garth Cl CONG CW12 208 A3
Mossmere Rd CHD/CHDH SK8 46 A8 3
Moss Pl ALS/KID ST7 243 H1
Moss Rd CONG CW12 207 L6
IRL M44 31 H2
NWCHW CW8 12 D2
WARRS WA4 57 G1
WILM/AE SK9 110 C2
Moss Rose WILM/AE SK9 110 B2
Moss Side La GOL/RIS/CU WA3 39 L1
NWCHE CW9 77 J5
WARRS WA4 54 E5
Moss Side Rd IRL M44 31 K6
Moss Sq CW/HAS CW1 19 G4
MCFLDS SK11 138 D8 2
Moss St NWCHW CW8 128 D3 4
WDN WA8 53 K5
The Moss NWCHE CW9 103 K5 2
Mossvale GTS/LS CH66 94 D4
Moss View Rd MCFLDS SK11 138 A8 2
PART M31 41 G1
Moss Wy ALS/KID ST7 241 G1
Mosswood Pk DID/WITH M20 45 H4
Mosswood Rd WILM/AE SK9 84 E3 2
Moston Gv LYMM WA13 58 D1
Moston Rd CHNE CH2 145 K4
SBCH CW11 203 J7
Moston Wy GTS/LS CH66 120 F1 1
Mostyn Av CHD/CHDH SK8 64 E2 4
Mostyn Pl CH/BCN CH1 144 E6 3
Mostyn Rd BRAM/HZG SK7 66 C3
Mostyn St CQ CH5 142 A6
Motcombe Farm Rd
CHD/CHDH SK8 64 B3 5
Motcombe Gv CHD/CHDH SK8 64 A1
Motcombe Rd CHD/CHDH SK8 64 A2
Mottershead Rd WDN WA8 7 G5
WYTH/NTH M22 44 B8
Mottram Cl CHD/CHDH SK8 46 A7 3
WARRS WA4 57 H1
Mottram Dr HALE/TIMP WA15 43 G7 3
Mottram Fold STKP SK1 3 G7
Mottram Rd SALE M33 43 L1
WILM/AE SK9 110 B3
Mottram St STKP SK1 3 G7 2
Moughland La RUNC WA7 9 G6
Moulders La WARR WA1 5 H8
Mouldsworth Cl NWCHE CW9 129 L8 6
Moulton Cl KNUT WA16 107 J3 1
NWCHE CW9 129 L8 7
RUNC WA7 73 M8
Mountain Pl STKP SK1 3 K4
Mountain Vw CHSW/BR CH4 168 E6 4
FROD/HEL WA6 124 B1
WRX/GR/LL LL12 210 D6
Mountbatten Wy CONG CW12 207 K1
Mount Cl NANT CW5 21 H5
Mount Dr MPL/ROM SK6 48 F7
NANT CW5 21 H5
Mount Farm Wy GTS/LS CH66 120 C2
Mountfield Rd BRAM/HZG SK7 65 L7
CQ CH5 166 B1 3
EDGY/DAV SK3 46 C5
Mount Gv WYTH/NTH M22 44 F7
Mount Pk WLTN L25 50 A1
Mount Park Ct WLTN L25 50 A1
Mount Pl CHSE CH3 17 L4
Mount Pleasant ALS/KID ST7 243 G3
AUD/MAD/W CW3 264 B8
BRAM/HZG SK7 66 D1
CHNE CH2 97 G8
CW/HAS CW1 221 H6
CW/HAS CW1 222 D8
MCFLDN SK10 113 H3 1
WDN WA8 7 K1
WILM/AE SK9 84 B3
Mount Pleasant Av
FLINT CH6 116 A7 1
STHEL WA9 26 A1
Mount Pleasant Dr WSFD CW7 177 G5
Mount Pleasant Rd
ALS/KID ST7 226 B5
NWCHE CW9 153 M2
Mount Pleasent CHSW/BR CH4 168 F5
Mount Rd ALS/KID ST7 243 H3
HTNM SK4 2 B3
RUNC WA7 73 M4
Mount St WDN WA8 7 K1
WLTN L25 50 A2
Mount Ter MCFLDS SK11 15 L6
The Mount ALS/KID ST7 225 L5
ALS/KID ST7 243 G3
ALT WA14 42 D7
CHSE CH3 17 M5
CONG CW12 207 G2
HALE/TIMP WA15 62 C4
NWCHE CW9 130 A5
Mount Wy CHSE CH3 171 G8
Mourne Cl GTS/LS CH66 94 A6 3
Mowbray Av SALE M33 43 J1
Mowbray St STKP SK1 3 H7
Mow Cop Rd ALS/KID ST7 226 C6
Mowcroft La WARRW/BUR WA5 54 B1
Mow La ALS/KID ST7 226 A7
ALS/KID ST7 227 G2
CONG CW12 207 M8
Mowpen Brow KNUT WA16 59 H6
Moxon Av WARRS WA4 37 M7 1
Moyles Cl WDN WA8 52 D2 3
Mudhouse La NSTN CH64 118 F2
Mudhurst La POY/DIS SK12 88 E3
Muirfield Cl NWCHE CW9 13 K8
WARRN/WOL WA2 38 A1 3
WILM/AE SK9 84 D4 7
Muirfield Dr MCFLDN SK10 112 C8
WSFD CW7 177 J2 6
Muir Rd CH/BCN CH1 168 E1
Mulberry Av GOL/RIS/CU WA3 23 M5
Mulberry Cl CHD/CHDH SK8 64 C5
CHNE CH2 123 J1
WARR WA1 38 E6 2
Mulberry Gdns SBCH CW11 203 K5
Mulberry Ms HTNM SK4 2 E3
Mulberry Mount St
EDGY/DAV SK3 2 F8
Mulberry Ri NWCHW CW8 12 B5
Mulberry Rd CW/SHV CW2 237 L2
Mulcaster Ct CW/HAS CW1 222 D7
Mullacre Rd WYTH/NTH M22 44 D6
Mullein Cl GOL/RIS/CU WA3 23 K4
Mullins Av NEWLW WA12 22 C7 2
Mullion Cl HLWD L26 50 E4
RUNC WA7 74 B6 3
Mullion Dr HALE/TIMP WA15 42 E5
Mullion Gv WARRN/WOL WA2 38 A3 3
Mulsford La MALPAS SY14 256 A4
Munro Av WYTH/NTH M22 63 M2
Murdishaw Av RUNC WA7 74 C7
Muriel Cl WARRW/BUR WA5 35 K6
Murieston Rd HALE/TIMP WA15 61 L2
Murray Cl MCFLDN SK10 14 A2
Murrayfield MCFLDN SK10 112 A7
Murrayfield Dr NANT CW5 237 K7
Murray St BURS/TUN ST6 243 J5
Musbury Av CHD/CHDH SK8 65 H2
Museum St WARR WA1 4 E8
Musgrave Rd WYTH/NTH M22 63 K1
Mustard La GOL/RIS/CU WA3 29 H4
Muter Av WYTH/NTH M22 63 M2
Myddleton La WARRN/WOL WA2 28 B6
Myrica Gv CHNE CH2 170 B1
Myrtle Av CHSW/BR CH4 190 A5 1
NEWLW WA12 27 J2
Myrtle Gv CHNE CH2 170 A1
WARRS WA4 56 D1
Myrtle Rd PART M31 40 D2
Myrtle St CW/SHV CW2 18 F6
EDGY/DAV SK3 46 B4
EP CH65 10 E3
Mythorne Av IRL M44 40 C1 1

N

Nabbs Cl ALS/KID ST7 243 H2 4
Nabbswood Rd ALS/KID ST7 243 H2
Nab Cl MCFLDN SK10 113 J3
Nab La MCFLDN SK10 113 J3
Nairn Av HOLMCH CW4 181 H2
Nairn Cl WARRN/WOL WA2 38 A1
Nancy Vw MCFLDN SK10 113 H4 5
Nangreave Rd OFTN SK2 47 G6
Nan Nook Rd NTHM/RTH M23 43 M3
Nansen Cl WARRW/BUR WA5 36 D5
Nansen Rd CHD/CHDH SK8 45 G8
Nansmoss La WILM/AE SK9 83 K3
Nantwich Rd ALS/KID ST7 255 L3
CHSE CH3 231 J3
CW/SHV CW2 18 C9
GTS/LS CH66 120 F1
MALPAS SY14 248 E2
MWCH CW10 179 H3 4
MWCH CW10 201 M3
NANT CW5 218 A4
NANT CW5 237 J2
NANT CW5 249 L8
TPLY/KEL CW6 197 J4
WHITCH SY13 270 E5
Naomi Cl CH/BCN CH1 144 D7
Napier Rd CHNE CH2 145 J4
HTNM SK4 46 B1
Napier St BRAM/HZG SK7 66 D1
WARR WA1 5 J7
Naples Rd EDGY/DAV SK3 46 B6
Nares Cl WARRW/BUR WA5 36 C3
Narrow La CW/HAS CW1 239 J1
MCFLDN SK10 87 C3
WRX/GR/LL LL12 210 E6
The Narrows ALT WA14 42 C8 1
Naseby Rd CONG CW12 207 G1
Nathans Rd WYTH/NTH M22 44 C8
Nat La WSFD CW7 177 M2
Navigation Cl RUNC WA7 74 D6 2
Navigation Rd ALT WA14 42 D5
HALE/TIMP WA15 42 E6
NWCHW CW8 13 G4
Navigation St WARR WA1 5 L7
Naylor Av GOL/RIS/CU WA3 23 H4
Naylor Ct NWCHE CW9 13 H3
Naylor Rd WDN WA8 53 K3
Naylor St BURS/TUN ST6 243 M7 5
WARR WA1 5 H6
Neal Av CHD/CHDH SK8 64 A4
Nearbrook Rd WYTH/NTH M22 44 C8
Nearcroft Rd NTHM/RTH M23 44 A5
Nearmaker Av
WYTH/NTH M22 44 C8 1
Nearmaker Rd WYTH/NTH M22 44 C8
Neasham Cl HLWD L26 50 F4 5
Neath Av WYTH/NTH M22 44 D5
Neath Cl POY/DIS SK12 66 D7
Needham Cl RUNC WA7 73 K2 2
Needham Dr HOLMCH CW4 157 G7
NWCHW CW8 129 G8
Needhams Bank SBCH CW11 203 J6
Needhams Wharf Cl
MCFLDN SK10 15 M2 1
MCFLDN SK10 139 G3 1
Neills Rd STHEL WA9 26 B6
Neil St WDN WA8 7 K1
Nelson Av POY/DIS SK12 87 G1
RAIN/WH L35 32 E2
Nelson Bank ALS/KID ST7 243 G5
Nelson Cl POY/DIS SK12 87 G1 5
Nelson Dr IRL M44 31 L6
Nelson Gv ALS/KID ST7 241 M2
Nelson Pl RAIN/WH L35 32 E2 6
Nelson Rd EP CH65 10 E4
GOL/RIS/CU WA3 29 K8
Nelson St BRAM/HZG SK7 47 M8
CH/BCN CH1 17 J3
CONG CW12 207 K2
CQ CH5 142 B6
CW/SHV CW2 18 F7
MCFLDS SK11 15 G7
NEWLW WA12 27 G1
RUNC WA7 9 H2
WDN WA8 7 G9
Nemos Cl FROD/HEL WA6 124 C2 1
Neptune Cl RUNC WA7 74 D5 7
Nesfield Ct SBCH CW11 222 E5
Nesfield Dr CW/HAS CW1 222 F5
Nesfield Rd NTHM/RTH M23 43 M2
Nessina Gv CW/SHV CW2 237 M4
Neston Av SALE M33 43 L2 6
Neston Dr CHNE CH2 145 K7
Neston Gn GTS/LS CH66 94 D8
Neston Gv EDGY/DAV SK3 46 D7
Neston Rd NSTN CH64 91 M7
Neston Wy WILM/AE SK9 84 D1
Nethercote Av
NTHM/RTH M23 44 B6 4
Nethercroft Rd
HALE/TIMP WA15 43 J7
Netherfield WDN WA8 6 B4
Netherfields WILM/AE SK9 110 A4
Nether Fold MCFLDN SK10 112 A4
Nether Lea HOLMCH CW4 157 J4
Netherlea Ct HOLMCH CW4 157 J4
Netherley Rd RAIN/WH L35 32 C8
Netherpool Rd GTS/LS CH66 94 F4
Netherset Hey La
AUD/MAD/W CW3 267 M7
Netherton Dr FROD/HEL WA6 99 G5 2
Netherwood Rd WYTH/NTH M22 44 C5
Netley Rd NTHM/RTH M23 44 A8
Nettlebarn Rd WYTH/NTH M22 44 C7
Neufchatel Cl WHITCH SY13 270 B5
Neumann St NWCHE CW9 13 L2
Nevada Cl WARRW/BUR WA5 36 B4
Nevendon Dr NTHM/RTH M23 43 M8
Neville Av STHEL WA9 26 B2
WARRN/WOL WA2 37 K3
Neville Crs WARRW/BUR WA5 55 G1
Neville Dr CHSE CH3 170 B3 1
Neville Rd CHSE CH3 170 B3
Neville St BRAM/HZG SK7 66 D1
CW/SHV CW2 18 F9
NEWLW WA12 22 A8 3
Nevill Rd BRAM/HZG SK7 65 L2
Nevin Av BIDD ST8 227 K7
CHD/CHDH SK8 64 E3
Nevin Cl BRAM/HZG SK7 66 A5
Nevin Rd CH/BCN CH1 168 D1
Nevis Dr CW/SHV CW2 237 K1
Newall Cl CHSE CH3 214 B3
Newall Crs WSFD CW7 178 A3
Newall Rd NTHM/RTH M23 62 F1
Newark Gv BURS/TUN ST6 243 J5 4
New Bank Rd WDN WA8 52 B3
New Barn Av AIMK WN4 22 C1 6
New Barnet WDN WA8 33 M8 3
New Barn La LEIGH WN7 24 E2
New Beech Rd HTNM SK4 45 L2
Newberry Gv EDGY/DAV SK3 46 D7 2
Newbold Wy NANT CW5 251 L1
Newborough Cl
WARRW/BUR WA5 36 D2
Newboult Rd CHD/CHDH SK8 45 L6
Newbourne Cl
BRAM/HZG SK7 66 D1 13
Newbridge Cl RUNC WA7 74 C6 3
WARRW/BUR WA5 36 C2
New Bridge La STKP SK1 3 J5
New Bridge Rd EP CH65 95 M8
Newbridge Rd EP CH65 121 M1
Newbrook Av CCHDY M21 44 D1
Newburgh Cl RUNC WA7 74 D3
Newbury Av CW/HAS CW1 221 J5 3
WSFD CW7 177 G4 4
Newbury Cl CHD/CHDH SK8 65 G6 2
WDN WA8 52 F1
Newbury Rd CHD/CHDH SK8 64 C5
CHSW/BR CH4 168 F6 7
Newby Ct CONG CW12 207 G3
Newby Dr ALT WA14 42 D6 2
CHD/CHDH SK8 45 G7
SALE M33 43 K1
Newby Rd BRAM/HZG SK7 66 C2
HTNM SK4 2 A4
Newcastle Rd ALS/KID ST7 242 E7
AUD/MAD/W CW3 267 M5
CONG CW12 206 F6
CW/SHV CW2 253 K1
NANT CW5 21 L8
SBCH CW11 204 F1
Newcastle Rd North
SBCH CW11 181 L6
Newcastle Rd South
SBCH CW11 181 M7
Newcastle St CW/HAS CW1 18 B1
New Chapel Ct BURS/TUN ST6 243 J8
Newchapel Rd ALS/KID ST7 243 H1
New Chester Rd PS/BROM CH62 94 A1
Newchurch La GOL/RIS/CU WA3 29 M2
Newcombe Av
WARRN/WOL WA2 37 L4 2
New Crane Bank CH/BCN CH1 16 D5
New Crane St CH/BCN CH1 16 D4
Newcroft CH/BCN CH1 144 A2
Newcroft Dr EDGY/DAV SK3 46 D6 4
New Cut La WARR WA1 38 B6
Newdigate St CW/HAS CW1 18 F2
New Farm Ct CHSE CH3 147 L7
Newfield Ct LYMM WA13 40 A7 1
Newfield Dr CW/HAS CW1 19 J1
Newfield Rd LYMM WA13 58 D1
Newfield St BURS/TUN ST6 243 K8
SBCH CW11 204 D5
Newfield Ter FROD/HEL WA6 124 B2 3
New Forest Rd NTHM/RTH M23 43 J4
Newgate MCFLDS SK11 15 G6 2
Newgate Rd SALE M33 42 B3
WILM/AE SK9 83 K5
Newgate St CH/BCN CH1 17 G6
New Grosvenor Rd EP CH65 10 D4
Newhall Av SBCH CW11 204 A7
New Hall Av WYTH/NTH M22 64 B5
Newhall Ct CHNE CH2 145 L6
Newhall Dr NTHM/RTH M23 44 A2
New Hall La GOL/RIS/CU WA3 29 L3
WHITCH SY13 268 B8
Newhall Rd CHNE CH2 145 L6
New Hall Rd SALE M33 43 M1 5
New Hall St MCFLDN SK10 14 F3
Newham Cl MCFLDS SK11 162 F1 1
Newhaven Cl CHD/CHDH SK8 65 J2
Newhaven Rd WARRN/WOL WA2 28 B8
New Hayes Rd BURS/TUN ST6 243 K8
Newhey Av WYTH/NTH M22 44 D7
New Hey La NSTN CH64 93 G5
New Hey Rd CHD/CHDH SK8 45 L7
Newhey Rd WYTH/NTH M22 44 D8
New Horwich Rd CHF/WBR SK23 89 L5
New Hutte La HLWD L26 50 F6
Newington Ct ALT WA14 61 H1
New Inn La SBCH CW11 224 A2
New King St MWCH CW10 179 J2
Newland Cl WDN WA8 52 C1 9
Newlands Av BRAM/HZG SK7 65 L4
CHD/CHDH SK8 65 G5
IRL M44 31 M1
Newlands Cl CHD/CHDH SK8 65 G5
FROD/HEL WA6 99 J6
Newlands Dr DID/WITH M20 45 J4 6
GOL/RIS/CU WA3 23 J4
Newlands Rd CHD/CHDH SK8 45 K6
LEIGH WN7 24 F1 6
LEIGH WN7 24 F1 8
MCFLDN SK10 137 L5
NTHM/RTH M23 43 L4
WARRS WA4 56 F2
New La CHSE CH3 211 M6
CHSE CH3 231 M1
GOL/RIS/CU WA3 29 G5
WARRS WA4 57 H7
WSFD CW7 177 M8
Newlyn Av CONG CW12 207 M4
MCFLDN SK10 137 K3 3
Newlyn Cl BRAM/HZG SK7 66 D3
RUNC WA7 74 B6
Newlyn Dr AIMK WN4 22 B2
MPL/ROM SK6 48 A1
SALE M33 43 J3
Newlyn Gdns WARRW/BUR WA5 54 D1
New Manchester Rd WARR WA1 38 A5
Newman Cl CONG CW12 207 H1
New Manor Rd WARRS WA4 75 H6
Newman's La NANT CW5 252 D4
Newman St WARRS WA4 56 F1
Newmarket Cl ALT WA14 42 B2
MCFLDN SK10 112 C8 4
New Mill Stile WLTN L25 50 A1
Newmoore La RUNC WA7 54 F8
New Moor La BRAM/HZG SK7 66 D1
New Moss Rd IRL M44 31 K6
Newnham Dr EP CH65 95 J8
New Pale Rd FROD/HEL WA6 125 H4
New Park Rd CQ CH5 142 A8
New Platt La HOLMCH CW4 156 E3
Newpool Rd BIDD ST8 227 G6
Newpool Ter BIDD ST8 227 H7
Newquay Cl RUNC WA7 74 B6
Newquay Ct CONG CW12 207 L4 1
Newquay Dr BRAM/HZG SK7 65 M5
MCFLDN SK10 137 K4
New Rd AUD/MAD/W CW3 267 L5
CHF/WBR SK23 89 L6
CHF/WBR SK23 89 M3
CONG CW12 183 J3
CONG CW12 207 G7
CONG CW12 226 B1
CQ CH5 166 B8
GTS/LS CH66 94 A4
KNUT WA16 80 E1
LYMM WA13 58 E1
MCFLDN SK10 112 A5
NANT CW5 261 K1
NWCHE CW9 77 K3
NWCHE CW9 129 K1
SBCH CW11 205 M2
TPLY/KEL CW6 173 H6
WARRS WA4 5 J9
WSFD CW7 177 L2
New Roskell Sq FLINT CH6 116 B5
Newry Ct CHNE CH2 145 K8
Newry Pk CHNE CH2 145 K8
Newry Pk East CHNE CH2 145 K8
New School La GTS/LS CH66 94 B4
Newsham Cl WDN WA8 33 H8 3
Newsham Rd HUY L36 32 A4
Newsholme Cl
GOL/RIS/CU WA3 29 M1 2
Newstead Cl POY/DIS SK12 66 D7
Newstead Gv MPL/ROM SK6 47 L1
Newstead Ter HALE/TIMP WA15 42 F5
New St ALT WA14 42 C8
BIDD ST8 227 M6
CONG CW12 207 L2
CW/HAS CW1 222 C7
NM/HAY SK22 69 J5
NSTN CH64 91 L7
RUNC WA7 9 G3
SBCH CW11 203 K5
WILM/AE SK9 83 L7
Newton Av GOL/RIS/CU WA3 29 L7 1
Newton Bank MWCH CW10 179 H3
Newton Gv WARRN/WOL WA2 37 M1 2
Newton Hall Dr CHNE CH2 145 M7
Newton Hall La KNUT WA16 82 E6
Newton Hall Ms MWCH CW10 179 J4 2
Newton Heath MWCH CW10 179 H3
Newton Hollow
FROD/HEL WA6 125 H4
Newton La CHNE CH2 145 L7
CHSE CH3 195 G7
CHSE CH3 214 F1
NEWLW WA12 22 E6
WARRS WA4 75 J4
Newton Park Dr NEWLW WA12 27 M2

Newton Park Vw *CHNE* CH2 ...... 145 K7
Newton Rd *ALT* WA14 ...... 42 E5 🔲
  EP CH65 ...... 10 F7
  GOL/RIS/CU WA3 ...... 23 H7
  STHEL WA9 ...... 26 A1
  WARRN/WOL WA2 ...... 27 M4
  WILM/AE SK9 ...... 84 A3
Newtons Crs *CW/HAS* CW1 ...... 222 E5
Newtons Gv *CW/HAS* CW1 ...... 222 E5
Newtons La *CW/HAS* CW1 ...... 222 E5
Newton St *CW/HAS* CW1 ...... 19 G2
  EDGY/DAV SK3 ...... 2 E8
  MCFLDS SK11 ...... 14 F7
Newtown *ALS/KID* ST7 ...... 243 L2
  NSTN CH64 ...... 91 M6
  WHITCH SY13 ...... 269 M4
New Warrington Rd
  NWCHE CW9 ...... 130 B3
New Zealand Rd *STKP* SK1 ...... 3 K4
Niagara St *OFTN* SK2 ...... 47 G6
Nicholas Av *NWCHE* CW9 ...... 130 C6
Nicholas Ct *CH/BCN* CH1 ...... 16 E6
Nicholas Rd *WDN* WA8 ...... 52 C4
Nicholas St *CH/BCN* CH1 ...... 16 E5
Nicholas Street Ms *CH/BCN* CH1 .. 16 E6
Nicholls St *WARRS* WA4 ...... 57 H2
Nicholson Av *ALS/KID* ST7 ...... 243 L2
Nicholson Cl *MCFLDN* SK10 ...... 15 J2
Nicholson St *HTNM* SK4 ...... 2 F3
  WARR WA1 ...... 4 D6
Nickleby Rd *POY/DIS* SK12 ...... 86 E1
Nick Olson Cl *CHNE* CH2 ...... 146 F4 🔲
Nicol Av *GOL/RIS/CU* WA3 ...... 38 F3
Nidderdale Av *RAIN/WH* L35 ...... 33 L3 🔲
Nidderdale Cl *CONG* CW12 ...... 185 G2 🔲
Niddries Ct *NWCHE* CW9 ...... 153 M5
Niddries La *NWCHE* CW9 ...... 153 L5
Nield Ct *CHNE* CH2 ...... 145 K5
Nield's Brow *ALT* WA14 ...... 61 J2
Nields Wy *MPL/ROM* SK6 ...... 49 K8
Nigel Gresley Cl
  CW/HAS CW1 ...... 222 A8 🔲
Nightingale Cl *CHSE* CH3 ...... 228 F3
  CW/HAS CW1 ...... 220 F5
  GOL/RIS/CU WA3 ...... 29 M8 🔲
  MWCH CW10 ...... 179 K6 🔲
  RUNC WA7 ...... 73 L7
  WILM/AE SK9 ...... 84 B3
Nightingale Ct *WSFD* CW7 ...... 177 K6 🔲
Nightingale Gdns
  NTHM/RTH M23 ...... 44 A3 🔲
Nile St *CW/HAS* CW1 ...... 18 F7
Ninfield Rd *NTHM/RTH* M23 ...... 44 B8
Nisbet Av *WYTH/NTH* M22 ...... 63 L1
Nixon Dr *WSFD* CW7 ...... 177 J6 🔲
Nixon Rd *NWCHW* CW8 ...... 151 M1
Nixon's Rw *NANT* CW5 ...... 20 B6
Nixon St *CW/HAS* CW1 ...... 220 F7 🔲
  EDGY/DAV SK3 ...... 2 F8
  MCFLDS SK11 ...... 14 D4
Noahs Ark La *KNUT* WA16 ...... 108 E3
Noble Cl *GOL/RIS/CU* WA3 ...... 38 E1
Nook La *GOL/RIS/CU* WA3 ...... 23 H4
  NWCHE CW9 ...... 77 L6
  WARRN/WOL WA2 ...... 38 B2
  WARRS WA4 ...... 57 G1
The Nook *CHNE* CH2 ...... 145 L8
  CHSE CH3 ...... 146 C8
  CHSW/BR CH4 ...... 168 E6
  CQ CH5 ...... 166 D2
  WLTN L25 ...... 50 B1
Nora St *WARR* WA1 ...... 5 K7
Norbreck Av *CHD/CHDH* SK8 ...... 46 A6
  CW/SHV CW2 ...... 18 D8
Norbreck Cl *WARRW/BUR* WA5 .. 36 A8
Norbreck Crs *WARRW/BUR* WA5 .. 36 A8
Norbury Av *MPL/ROM* SK6 ...... 48 E6
  WARRN/WOL WA2 ...... 37 K4 🔲
Norbury Cl *CW/SHV* CW2 ...... 253 L1
  KNUT WA16 ...... 107 J1
Norbury Crs *BRAM/HZG* SK7 ...... 66 D2
Norbury Dr *CONG* CW12 ...... 184 E8
  MPL/ROM SK6 ...... 48 F6
  MWCH CW10 ...... 179 H4
Norbury Fold *RAIN/WH* L35 ...... 33 L3 🔲
Norbury Gv *BRAM/HZG* SK7 ...... 66 D2 🔲
Norbury Hollow Rd
  BRAM/HZG SK7 ...... 67 H4
Norbury St *MCFLDS* SK11 ...... 14 E7
  NWCHE CW9 ...... 13 M2
  STKP SK1 ...... 3 G6
Norcott Av *WARRS* WA4 ...... 56 D2
Norcott Dr *WARRW/BUR* WA5 .. 26 F6 🔲
Norcross Cl *OFTN* SK2 ...... 47 K7
Norden Cl *GOL/RIS/CU* WA3 ...... 29 J7
Norfolk Cl *IRL* M44 ...... 31 J7
Norfolk Dr *WARRW/BUR* WA5 .. 35 L6
Norfolk Gv *BIDD* ST8 ...... 227 J3
Norfolk Pl *WDN* WA8 ...... 52 C4
Norfolk Rd *ALS/KID* ST7 ...... 242 F2
  CHNE CH2 ...... 145 M8 🔲
  CONG CW12 ...... 184 E8
  EP CH65 ...... 10 E5
Norfolk St *RUNC* WA7 ...... 9 K1
Norgate St *DID/WITH* M20 ...... 45 H1 🔲
Norgrove Cl *RUNC* WA7 ...... 74 D4
Norland's La *RAIN/WH* L35 ...... 33 L4
  WDN WA8 ...... 53 K3 🔲
Norland St *WDN* WA8 ...... 53 L3 🔲
Norleane Crs *RUNC* WA7 ...... 9 J7
Norleigh Rd *WYTH/NTH* M22 ...... 44 D4
Norley Av *EP* CH65 ...... 94 F6
  PS/BROM CH62 ...... 93 L1
Norley Dr *CHSE* CH3 ...... 170 C3
  SALE M33 ...... 43 L1
Norley La *FROD/HEL* WA6 ...... 126 F6
Norley Pl *HLWD* L26 ...... 50 F6
Norley Rd *FROD/HEL* WA6 ...... 125 M2
  NWCHW CW8 ...... 152 A1
Norman Av *BRAM/HZG* SK7 ...... 66 C1 🔲
  NEWLW WA12 ...... 27 L1
  RNFD/HAY WA11 ...... 22 A5
Normanby Cha *ALT* WA14 ...... 42 B8
Norman Cl *GTS/LS* CH66 ...... 120 E4
Norman Dr *WSFD* CW7 ...... 177 J6 🔲
Normandy Av *WSFD* CW7 ...... 177 K4
Normandy Rd *CHNE* CH2 ...... 145 J3

RUNC WA7 ...... 9 G5
Norman's La *WARRS* WA4 ...... 76 F8
Norman's Pl *ALT* WA14 ...... 42 D8
Norman St *CQ* CH5 ...... 142 B8
  WARRN/WOL WA2 ...... 5 H4
Normanton Rd *EDGY/DAV* SK3 .. 46 A5
Norreys Av *WARRW/BUR* WA5 .. 4 D1
Norris Av *HTNM* SK4 ...... 2 A4
Norris Hill Dr *HTNM* SK4 ...... 2 A2
Norris Rd *CH/BCN* CH1 ...... 144 E7 🔲
  SALE M33 ...... 43 J2
Norris St *WARRN/WOL* WA2 ...... 5 K1
Norris Wy *SPK/HALE* L24 ...... 50 A6
  WARRN/WOL WA2 ...... 5 G1
North Brook Rd *TPLY/KEL* CW6 .. 174 B5
Northbury Rd *GTS/LS* CH66 ...... 120 E3
Northcliffe Rd *OFTN* SK2 ...... 47 J4
Northcombe Rd
  EDGY/DAV SK3 ...... 46 E7 🔲
Northcote Rd *BRAM/HZG* SK7 .. 65 M5
North Cft *NANT* CW5 ...... 20 F6
Northdale Rd *WARR* WA1 ...... 38 A4
North Downs *KNUT* WA16 ...... 107 J3
North Downs Rd *CHD/CHDH* SK8.. 64 F1
North Dr *KNUT* WA16 ...... 59 J8
  NWCHE CW9 ...... 130 E5
Northenden Rd *CHD/CHDH* SK8.... 45 G6
  SALE M33 ...... 43 L1
North End La *HLWD* L26 ...... 50 E1
North La *RAIN/WH* L35 ...... 52 A1
Northern Pathway
  CHSW/BR CH4 ...... 17 J8
Northern Ri *GTS/LS* CH66 ...... 94 E8
Northern Rd *SPK/HALE* L24 ...... 50 E8 🔲
Northfield Dr *BIDD* ST8 ...... 227 L3
  WILM/AE SK9 ...... 84 D4
Northfield Pl *CW/SHV* CW2 ...... 238 C7
Northfields *KNUT* WA16 ...... 107 J1
North Front *RAIN/WH* L35 ...... 32 E3
Northgate *TPLY/KEL* CW6 ...... 174 B5
Northgate Av *EDGY/DAV* SK3 .. 2 F4
  MCFLDN SK10 ...... 14 F3
North Gn *CQ* CH5 ...... 143 G6
North Harvey St *STKP* SK1 ...... 3 H5
North Linkside Rd *WLTN* L25 ...... 50 C3
North Manor Wy *WLTN* L25 ...... 50 C3
Northmead *MCFLDN* SK10 ...... 112 A7
Northolt Ct *WARRN/WOL* WA2 .. 37 L3 🔲
Northolt Rd *NTHM/RTH* M23 ...... 43 K2 🔲
North Pde *NSTN* CH64 ...... 91 G2
  SALE M33 ...... 43 K2 🔲
  SPK/HALE L24 ...... 70 E1
North Park Brook Rd
  WARRW/BUR WA5 ...... 36 E3
North Park Rd *BRAM/HZG* SK7 .. 65 L1 🔲
North Pl *STKP* SK1 ...... 3 G5
North Rd *EP* CH65 ...... 94 E1
  HALE/TIMP WA15 ...... 62 A4
  MANAIR M90 ...... 63 J6
  SPK/HALE L24 ...... 70 E1
North Stafford St *CW/HAS* CW1... 19 H3
North St *ALS/KID* ST7 ...... 226 B6
  CHSE CH3 ...... 170 A3
  CHSW/BR CH4 ...... 168 B5
  CONG CW12 ...... 207 K1
  CQ CH5 ...... 142 B7
  CQ CH5 ...... 167 G1
  CW/HAS CW1 ...... 221 J5
Northumberland Rd
  PART M31 ...... 40 E2 🔲
North Vale Rd *HALE/TIMP* WA15 .. 42 F2
North Vw *HUY* L36 ...... 32 A2
  WARRW/BUR WA5 ...... 35 L5
Northward Rd *CHSW/BR* CH4 ...... 16 B9
Northway *CHSW/BR* CH4 ...... 16 B9
North Wy *CW/SHV* CW2 ...... 238 D7
  HOLMCH CW4 ...... 181 J1
Northway *LYMM* WA13 ...... 39 K8 🔲
  NWCHW CW8 ...... 129 K3
  RUNC WA7 ...... 73 M4
  WARRN/WOL WA2 ...... 37 H2
  WDN WA8 ...... 6 A3
Northwich Rd *KNUT* WA16 ...... 106 B3
  KNUT WA16 ...... 156 D2
  NWCHE CW9 ...... 103 K2
  NWCHW CW8 ...... 128 D3 🔲
  RUNC WA7 ...... 74 C7
  WARRS WA4 ...... 76 F5
  WARRS WA4 ...... 101 K4
Northwood Av
  CHD/CHDH SK8 ...... 65 G1 🔲
  MWCH CW10 ...... 179 L7
  NEWLW WA12 ...... 27 M1 🔲
Northwood La *KNUT* WA16 ...... 78 F3
Northwood Rd *RUNC* WA7 ...... 73 L2
Norton Av *CHSW/BR* CH4 ...... 168 D6
  WARRW/BUR WA5 ...... 35 L7
Norton Ga *RUNC* WA7 ...... 74 C4
Norton Gv *HTNM* SK4 ...... 46 B3 🔲
Norton Hl *RUNC* WA7 ...... 74 C4
Norton La *RUNC* WA7 ...... 74 C4
Norton Rd *CHSE* CH3 ...... 170 C2
Norton's La *CHSE* CH3 ...... 148 B1
  TPLY/KEL CW6 ...... 149 M5
Norton Station Rd *RUNC* WA7 .. 74 D4
Norton Vw *RUNC* WA7 ...... 74 A4
Norton Village *RUNC* WA7 ...... 74 C4
Norton Wy *SBCH* CW11 ...... 203 K5
Nortonwood La *RUNC* WA7 ...... 74 C2
Norview Dr *DID/WITH* M20 ...... 45 H5
Norville *GTS/LS* CH66 ...... 94 E8
Norweb Wy *LEIGH* WN7 ...... 25 H1
Norwell Av *WYTH/NTH* M22 ...... 44 E7
Norwich Av *AIMK* WN4 ...... 22 D2
  GOL/RIS/CU WA3 ...... 23 K4
Norwood Av *BRAM/HZG* SK7 .. 65 K7 🔲
  GOL/RIS/CU WA3 ...... 23 L5
  MPL/ROM SK6 ...... 67 K5
Norwood Dr *CHSW/BR* CH4 ...... 169 H7
  HALE/TIMP WA15...
Norwood Rd *CHD/CHDH* SK8 .. 45 H6
  OFTN SK2 ...... 47 H8

Nottingham Cl *WARR* WA1 ...... 38 D6
Nuffield Rd *WYTH/NTH* M22 ...... 44 E8
Nun House Cl *WSFD* CW7 ...... 178 B3
Nun House Dr *WSFD* CW7 ...... 178 B3
Nunsmere Cl *WSFD* CW7 ...... 178 B3
Nun's Rd *CH/BCN* CH1 ...... 16 E6
Nursery Av *HALE/TIMP* WA15 ...... 61 L4
Nursery Cl *ALS/KID* ST7 ...... 242 D3
  OFTN SK2 ...... 47 K5
  WDN WA8 ...... 53 K1
  WLTN L25 ...... 50 D4
Nursery Dr *BIDD* ST8 ...... 227 J2
  POY/DIS SK12 ...... 66 D8
Nursery La *CONG* CW12 ...... 207 L2
  EDGY/DAV SK3 ...... 46 A5
  MCFLDN SK10 ...... 109 K7
  MCFLDS SK11 ...... 160 A1
  WILM/AE SK9 ...... 83 M6
Nursery Rd *ALS/KID* ST7 ...... 225 L7
  CHD/CHDH SK8 ...... 64 F3
  CW/HAS CW1 ...... 240 D2
  HTNM SK4 ...... 2 A3
  MCFLDN SK10 ...... 112 E5 🔲
  NWCHW CW8 ...... 129 H1
The Nursery *NWCHW* CW8 ...... 12 A6
Nutfield Av *CW/HAS* CW1 ...... 221 H5
Nuthurst Gdns *NANT* CW5 ...... 21 G7
Nuttall Ct *GOL/RIS/CU* WA3 ...... 29 J8
Nuttall St *IRL* M44 ...... 31 L6

O

Oak Av *ALS/KID* ST7 ...... 241 L2
  CHD/CHDH SK8 ...... 64 F7
  GOL/RIS/CU WA3 ...... 23 H4
  HTNM SK4 ...... 46 B2
  IRL M44 ...... 31 K7
  MCFLDS SK11 ...... 138 A7
  MPL/ROM SK6 ...... 48 C2
  NEWLW WA12 ...... 27 J1
  POY/DIS SK12 ...... 69 G6
  WILM/AE SK9 ...... 83 M7
  WSFD CW7 ...... 177 K5
Oak Bank Cl *NANT* CW5 ...... 237 L8
Oak Bank Dr *MCFLDN* SK10 ...... 113 H3
Oak Bank La *CHNE* CH2 ...... 146 C5
Oak Cl *RAIN/WH* L35 ...... 32 E1
  WILM/AE SK9 ...... 83 M6
Oakdale Av *FROD/HEL* WA6 ...... 99 K6
  WARRS WA4 ...... 56 D7
Oakdale Cl *CHSW/BR* CH4 ...... 190 B1 🔲
Oakdale Dr *CHD/CHDH* SK8 ...... 64 B2
  DID/WITH M20 ...... 45 J3
  GTS/LS CH66 ...... 94 C7
  WARR WA1 ...... 38 C5
Oakdene Av *MPL/ROM* SK6 ...... 48 F5
Oakdene Gdns *MPL/ROM* SK6 .. 48 F5
Oakdene Rd *HALE/TIMP* WA15 .. 43 H4
  MPL/ROM SK6 ...... 48 F5
Oakdene Wy *BIDD* ST8 ...... 227 K5
  TPLY/KEL CW6 ...... 197 K4
Oak Dr *BRAM/HZG* SK7 ...... 65 J5
  CHSW/BR CH4 ...... 190 A5
  MPL/ROM SK6 ...... 48 C2
  MWCH CW10 ...... 179 K5
  RUNC WA7 ...... 9 M8
  WHITCH SY13 ...... 269 M6
Oakenbank La *MCFLDN* SK10 .. 113 K4
Oakenclough Cl *WILM/AE* SK9 .. 84 D2 🔲
Oakfield Av *CHD/CHDH* SK8 ...... 45 L6
  CHNE CH2 ...... 145 L4
  GOL/RIS/CU WA3 ...... 22 F3
  KNUT WA16 ...... 107 J1
  NANT CW5 ...... 261 M1
Oakfield Cl *BRAM/HZG* SK7 ...... 65 L8
  NANT CW5 ...... 261 M1
  WILM/AE SK9 ...... 110 B1
Oakfield Dr *CHNE* CH2 ...... 145 L4
  WDN WA8 ...... 52 A4
Oakfield Ri *HOLMCH* CW4 ...... 181 H1
Oakfield Rd *CH/BCN* CH1 ...... 144 C8
  CQ CH5 ...... 166 A3
  EDGY/DAV SK3 ...... 46 F7
  GTS/LS CH66 ...... 93 L4
  HALE/TIMP WA15... ...... 42 E7
  KNUT WA16 ...... 131 M1
  POY/DIS SK12 ...... 66 F8
  WILM/AE SK9 ...... 110 B2
Oakfield St *HALE/TIMP* WA15 ...... 42 E7
Oak Gv *CHD/CHDH* SK8 ...... 45 L7
  EP CH65 ...... 121 G1
  NANT CW5 ...... 251 L1
  POY/DIS SK12 ...... 66 D8
Oakhead La *LEIGH* WN7 ...... 25 J1 🔲
Oakhill Cl *MCFLDN* SK10 ...... 112 B8 🔲
Oak House La *WSFD* CW7 ...... 177 H4 🔲
Oakhurst Cha *WILM/AE* SK9 ...... 110 A2
Oakhurst Dr *CHD/CHDH* SK8 ...... 46 B7
  CW/SHV CW2 ...... 238 B5
Oakland Av *CW/HAS* CW1 ...... 222 C8
  OFTN SK2 ...... 47 M6
Oaklands *CHSE* CH3 ...... 146 F7
  RAIN/WH L35 ...... 33 J1 🔲
Oaklands Av *CHD/CHDH* SK8.... 65 G2
  CHSE CH3 ...... 214 B2
  MPL/ROM SK6 ...... 49 J4 🔲
Oaklands Cl *WILM/AE* SK9 ...... 84 E3
Oaklands Crs *CHSE* CH3 ...... 214 B1
Oaklands Dr *BRAM/HZG* SK7 .. 66 E3
  LYMM WA13 ...... 58 D2
Oaklands Rd *GOL/RIS/CU* WA3 .. 23 M5
  KNUT WA16 ...... 107 M6
Oakland St *WARR* WA1 ...... 37 L5
  WDN WA8 ...... 53 G8
Oak La *MCFLDN* SK10 ...... 113 G6
  MCFLDS SK11 ...... 160 C7
  NWCHW CW8 ...... 151 M2
  WILM/AE SK9 ...... 83 M6
Oaklea Av *CHNE* CH2 ...... 145 M8
Oak Lea Av *WILM/AE* SK9.... ...... 84 A7
Oakleigh *KNUT* WA16 ...... 107 J5
Oakleigh Av *HALE/TIMP* WA15 .. 43 G5
Oakleigh Ct *CONG* CW12 ...... 206 F1 🔲
Oakleigh Ri *NWCHW* CW8 ...... 12 E1
Oakleigh Rd *CHD/CHDH* SK8 .. 64 E4

Oakley Cl *SBCH* CW11 ...... 204 A4
Oakley Rd *CQ* CH5 ...... 166 E2
Oak Leys *WARR* WA1 ...... 18 F2
Oak Meadow *NWCHW* CW8 ...... 128 C5
Oakmere Cl *SBCH* CW11 ...... 203 M5
  WYTH/NTH M22 ...... 44 D8 🔲
Oakmere Rd *CHD/CHDH* SK8 .. 45 M8 🔲
  WILM/AE SK9 ...... 64 D7 🔲
  WSFD CW7 ...... 176 F3 🔲
Oakmere St *RUNC* WA7 ...... 9 C3
Oak Ms *WILM/AE* SK9 ...... 84 C3
Oakmoor Rd *NTHM/RTH* M23 .. 44 A6
Oak Rd *CHD/CHDH* SK8 ...... 45 L6
  CHSW/BR CH4 ...... 168 F6
  GTS/LS CH66 ...... 93 L3
  HALE/TIMP WA15 ...... 61 L1
  LYMM WA13 ...... 58 C1
  MCFLDN SK10 ...... 111 H7
  MCFLDS SK11 ...... 135 C2
  PART M31 ...... 40 D2
  RAIN/WH L35 ...... 32 E1
  WARRW/BUR WA5 ...... 54 F1
Oaks Cl *STHEL* WA9 ...... 34 D1 🔲
The Oaks Dr *CHNE* CH2 ...... 145 J5
Oaks Pl *WDN* WA8 ...... 7 G6
The Oaks *CHD/CHDH* SK8 ...... 64 A2
Oakston Av *RAIN/WH* L35 ...... 33 K2 🔲
Oak St *ALS/KID* ST7 ...... 224 E4
  BRAM/HZG SK7 ...... 66 D1
  CW/SHV CW2 ...... 19 G5
  EDGY/DAV SK3 ...... 46 B4
  EP CH65 ...... 10 E3 🔲
  GOL/RIS/CU WA3 ...... 29 C5
  LEIGH WN7 ...... 24 F1
  NWCHE CW9 ...... 13 K1
  SBCH CW11 ...... 203 K4
Oak Tree Cl *NWCHW* CW8 ...... 103 H8 🔲
Oaktree Cl *OFTN* SK2 ...... 47 K4 🔲
Oaktree Cl *TPLY/KEL* CW6 ...... 197 K2
Oak Tree Ct *CHD/CHDH* SK8 .. 45 K6
Oaktree Ct *CHNE* CH2 ...... 170 A1 🔲
Oak Tree Dr *CW/HAS* CW1 ...... 19 L2
Oak Tree Ga *ADD/MAD/W* CW3 .. 273 M1 🔲
Oaktree La *ALS/KID* ST7 ...... 242 D7
Oak Tree La *MWCH* CW10 ...... 156 D5
Oak Vw *KNUT* WA16 ...... 107 J3
  MCFLDS SK11 ...... 160 C7
  SPK/HALE L24 ...... 71 C1
Oakway *DID/WITH* M20 ...... 45 J4 🔲
Oakways *WARRS* WA4 ...... 56 D7
Oakwood Av *AIMK* WN4 ...... 22 A2
  CHD/CHDH SK8 ...... 45 H7
  WARR WA1 ...... 5 M3
  WILM/AE SK9 ...... 83 L6
Oakwood Ct *ALT* WA14 ...... 61 G3 🔲
Oakwood Crs *CW/SHV* CW2 .. 220 E8
  SBCH CW11 ...... 204 E6
Oakwood Dr *LEIGH* WN7 ...... 24 E3
  MCFLDN SK10 ...... 112 C6
Oakwood Ga *ALT* WA14 ...... 61 G3 🔲
  NWCHW CW8 ...... 129 G2
  SBCH CW11 ...... 203 H4
Oakwood La *HLWD* L26 ...... 50 E5
Oak Wood Rd *KNUT* WA16... ...... 79 M7
Oakwood Rd *MPL/ROM* SK6 .. 48 C2
  POY/DIS SK12 ...... 68 D6 🔲
Oakworth Dr *HUY* L36 ...... 32 A5
Oatfield Cl *WHITCH* SY13 ...... 269 M6 🔲
Oathills Cl *TPLY/KEL* CW6 ...... 197 K3
Oathills La *MALPAS* SY14 ...... 246 B7
Oathills Dr *TPLY/KEL* CW6 ...... 197 K3
Oatlands *WILM/AE* SK9 ...... 110 B4
Oatlands Rd *WYTH/NTH* M22 .. 63 J2
Oat Market *NANT* CW5 ...... 20 D6
Oat St *STKP* SK1 ...... 3 J9
Oban Crs *EDGY/DAV* SK3 ...... 46 D8
Oban Dr *SALE* M33 ...... 43 L1
Oban Gv *WARRN/WOL* WA2 .. 38 A1
Obelisk Wy *CONG* CW12 ...... 207 J1
Occlestone Cl *SALE* M33 ...... 43 L3 🔲
Ocean St *ALT* WA14 ...... 42 B6
Offerton Dr *OFTN* SK2 ...... 47 K5
Offerton Fold *OFTN* SK2 ...... 47 J5 🔲
Offerton Gn *OFTN* SK2 ...... 47 M6
Offerton La *OFTN* SK2 ...... 47 J4
Offerton Rd *BRAM/HZG* SK7 .. 67 G1
  OFTN SK2 ...... 48 A8
Offerton St *STKP* SK1 ...... 3 L3
Offley Av *SBCH* CW11 ...... 204 B5
Offley Rd *SBCH* CW11 ...... 204 B5
Ogden Gv *CHD/CHDH* SK8 ...... 44 F8 🔲
Ogden Rd *BRAM/HZG* SK7 ...... 65 K7
Ogden St *DID/WITH* M20 ...... 45 H1 🔲
Oglet La *SPK/HALE* L24 ...... 70 C2
Oil Sites Rd *EP* CH65 ...... 11 C5
Okell Dr *HLWD* L26 ...... 50 E2 🔲
Okell St *RUNC* WA7 ...... 9 C3
Old Bank Cl *MPL/ROM* SK6 ...... 48 A1
Old Boston *RNFD/HAY* WA11 .. 22 A5
Oldbridge Rd *SPK/HALE* L24 .. 70 C1
Oldbrook Fold *HALE/TIMP* WA15.. 43 H8
Old Butt La *ALS/KID* ST7 ...... 242 D2
Old Chapel St *EDGY/DAV* SK3 .. 2 D9
Old Cherry La *LYMM* WA13 ...... 58 A6 🔲
Old Chester Rd *FROD/HEL* WA6.. 124 B1
  GTS/LS CH66 ...... 94 D7 🔲
  NANT CW5 ...... 218 C6
  WARRS WA4 ...... 55 M5
Old Church St *EP* CH65 ...... 10 F4 🔲
Old Coach Rd *MALPAS* SY14 .. 231 M3
  TPLY/KEL CW6 ...... 149 M7
Old Colliery Rd *RAIN/WH* L35 .. 32 D1
Oldcott Crs *ALS/KID* ST7 ...... 243 J4
Oldcott Dr *ALS/KID* ST7 ...... 243 J4
The Old Ctyd *WYTH/NTH* M22 .. 44 F7 🔲
Old Croft Ms *STKP* SK1 ......
Old Distillery Rd *SPK/HALE* L24 .. 50 E1 🔲
Old Farm Cl *NSTN* CH64 ...... 91 L4
Old Farm Dr *OFTN* SK2 ...... 47 M6 🔲
Oldfield Crs *CHSW/BR* CH4 ...... 168 F7
Oldfield Dr *CHSE* CH3 ...... 170 C2

  HALE/TIMP WA15 ...... 42 F6
  KNUT WA16 ...... 82 A8
Oldfield Rd *ALT* WA14 ...... 10 D8
  LYMM WA13 ...... 39 H8
  SBCH CW11 ...... 222 F1
Old Gardens St *STKP* SK1 ...... 3 H7
The Old Gdn *HALE/TIMP* WA15 .. 43 H5 🔲
Oldgate *WDN* WA8 ...... 52 C6
Old Gate Cl *MWCH* CW10 ...... 179 H5
Old Gorse Cl *CW/SHV* CW2... ...... 237 L1
Old Hall *RAIN/WH* L35 ...... 32 E4
Old Hall Av *CHF/WBR* SK23 ...... 89 L8
Old Hall Cl *WARRS* WA4 ...... 56 A4
Old Hall Ct *CHSE* CH3 ...... 148 F5
  MALPAS SY14 ...... 258 B1
Old Hall Crs *WILM/AE* SK9 ...... 84 E1 🔲
Old Hall Dr *AIMK* WN4 ...... 22 A2
  EP CH65 ...... 95 H8
  OFTN SK2 ...... 47 L6
Old Hall Gdns *CHNE* CH2 ...... 17 K1
Old Hall La *BRAM/HZG* SK7 .. 85 K3
  CHNE CH2 ...... 123 H1
  KNUT WA16 ...... 105 L1
  MPL/ROM SK6 ...... 49 J7
Old Hall Pk *CHSE* CH3 ...... 146 F7
Old Hall Pl *CH/BCN* CH1 ...... 16 F6 🔲
Old Hall Rd *CHD/CHDH* SK8 .. 45 G6
  CQ CH5 ...... 166 A3
  NWCHW CW8 ...... 13 J8
  WARRW/BUR WA5 ...... 54 F1
Oldhall St *MALPAS* SY14 ...... 258 B1
Old Hall St *MCFLDN* SK10 ...... 15 G2 🔲
Oldham St *HTNM* SK4 ...... 3 M6
Oldhams Hi *NWCHW* CW8 ...... 13 G1
Oldham Ct *MCFLDN* SK10 ...... 112 D8 🔲
Oldham St *MCFLDN* SK10 ...... 113 H4
  WARRS WA4 ...... 56 D1
Old Higher Rd *WDN* WA8 ...... 51 K7
Oldhill Cl *ALS/KID* ST7 ...... 242 F7
Old Hutte La *SPK/HALE* L24.. ...... 51 G7
Oldknow Rd *MPL/ROM* SK6 .. 49 G6
Old La *CHSW/BR* CH4 ...... 210 D2
  NWCHE CW9 ...... 103 J1
  NWCHW CW8 ...... 154 D2
  RAIN/WH L35 ...... 33 H2
Old Liverpool Rd
  WARRW/BUR WA5 ...... 4 C8
Old Market Pl *KNUT* WA16 ...... 107 G2 🔲
Old Meadow La
  HALE/TIMP WA15 ...... 62 B1
Old Mill La *BRAM/HZG* SK7 .. 67 G4
  MCFLDS SK11 ...... 15 J8
  WARRS WA4 ...... 102 F1
Old Mill Rd *SBCH* CW11 ...... 204 C6
Old Moss La *GOL/RIS/CU* WA3... 25 K6
Old Oak St *DID/WITH* M20 ...... 45 H1
Old Orch *NWCHE* CW9 ...... 77 J8
  RAIN/WH L35 ...... 33 J6
  WILM/AE SK9 ...... 84 A5
The Old Orch
  HALE/TIMP WA15 ...... 43 H4 🔲
The Old Paddock *HOLMCH* CW4.. 157 M4
Old Park Rd *CW/SHV* CW2 ...... 239 K5
  CW/SHV CW2 ...... 239 K5
Old Pearl La *CHSE* CH3 ...... 170 B3
The Old Quarry *WLTN* L25 ...... 50 A2 🔲
Old Quay Cl *NSTN* CH64 ...... 91 J5 🔲
Old Quay La *NSTN* CH64 ...... 91 K5
Old Quay St *RUNC* WA7 ...... 9 K1
Old Rectory Gdns
  CHD/CHDH SK8 ...... 45 K7 🔲
Old Rd *AUD/MAD/W* CW3 ...... 267 G1
  CHD/CHDH SK8 ...... 45 G6
  CHF/WBR SK23 ...... 89 L6
  HTNM SK4 ...... 2 E1
  NWCHE CW9 ...... 129 K1
  WARRS WA4 ...... 5 H9
  WILM/AE SK9 ...... 84 D1
Old School Cl *NSTN* CH64 ...... 91 M7
Old School House La
  WARRN/WOL WA2 ...... 28 A5
Old School Pl *AIMK* WN4 ...... 22 A1 🔲
Old Seals Wy *CH/BCN* CH1 ...... 16 B2
Old Smithy La *LYMM* WA13 ...... 58 C2
Old Stack Yd *CHSE* CH3 ...... 147 L7
Old Upton La *WDN* WA8 ...... 33 L8
Old Vicarage Gdns
  AUD/MAD/W CW3 ...... 263 M8
Old Vicarage Rd *NSTN* CH64 .. 93 G4
Old Wargrave Rd *NEWLW* WA12.. 27 H1
Old Warrington Rd
  NWCHE CW9 ...... 130 A2
Oldwood Rd *NTHM/RTH* M23 .. 43 K2
Old Wool La *CHD/CHDH* SK8 .. 45 M8
Old Wrexham Rd
  CHSW/BR CH4 ...... 169 J5
O'leary St *WARRN/WOL* WA2 .. 5 K2
Olive Dr *NSTN* CH64 ...... 91 L4
Oliver Cl *MCFLDN* SK10 ...... 112 F4 🔲
Oliver La *GTS/LS* CH66 ...... 94 D8
Olive Rd *HALE/TIMP* WA15 ...... 43 G4
  NSTN CH64 ...... 91 L4
Oliver St *EDGY/DAV* SK3 ...... 3 G8
  WARRN/WOL WA2 ...... 5 G4
Ollerbarrow Rd
  HALE/TIMP WA15 ...... 61 L2
Ollersett Av *NM/HAY* SK22 ...... 69 K4
Ollersett La *NM/HAY* SK22 ...... 69 K4
Ollershaw La *NWCHE* CW9 ...... 104 C8
Ollerton Cl *WARRS* WA4 ...... 57 H1
Ollerton Rd *WILM/AE* SK9 ...... 64 D7 🔲
Olney Av *WYTH/NTH* M22 ...... 44 D6
One Oak La *WILM/AE* SK9 ...... 84 F5
Onslow Rd *CH/BCN* CH1 ...... 144 D8 🔲
  EDGY/DAV SK3 ...... 2 A8
Onston La *NWCHW* CW8 ...... 127 L3
Openfields Cl *HLWD* L26 ...... 50 E2 🔲
Openshaw La *IRL* M44 ...... 31 L6 🔲
Orange Gv *WARRN/WOL* WA2 .. 37 L2
Orchard Av *CHF/WBR* SK23 ...... 89 K5
  LYMM WA13 ...... 58 F1
  NWCHW CW8 ...... 101 L8
  PART M31 ...... 31 M8
Orchard Brow *GOL/RIS/CU* WA3 .. 40 A2
Orchard Cl *CHD/CHDH* SK8 ...... 65 J5 🔲

CHNE CH2 .... 145 K7
CQ CH5 .... 166 D1 ⑥
FROD/HEL WA6 .... 99 C6
GTS/LS CH66 .... 120 F3
HOLMCH CW4 .... 157 L3
MCFLDS SK11 .... 14 D8
MWCH CW10 .... 179 J5
NWCHE CW9 .... 105 C6
NWCHW CW8 .... 128 D3
NWCHW CW8 .... 129 H1
POY/DIS SK12 .... 86 E1
RAIN/WH L35 .... 32 E3
WILM/AE SK9 .... 83 M7
WSFD CW7 .... 177 K5
Orchard Ct *CW/HAS* CW1 .... 222 D7 ⑨
OFTN SK2 .... 47 K6 ⑥
Orchard Crs *ALS/KID* ST7 .... 242 D3
MCFLDN SK10 .... 109 M6 ⑥
NANT CW5 .... 251 L1
Orchard Cft *CHSE* CH3 .... 146 E7
Orchard Dene *NWCHW* CW8 .... 127 K7
Orchard Dr *HALE/TIMP* WA15 .... 62 A1
NSTN CH64 .... 91 L7
NWCHW CW8 .... 102 D7
WILM/AE SK9 .... 84 E1
Orchard Gn *WILM/AE* SK9 .... 110 B3
Orchard Gv *CHSE* CH3 .... 228 F3
Orchard Hvn *GTS/LS* CH66 .... 120 E3
Orchard La *GTS/LS* CH66 .... 94 A4
Orchard Park La *CHNE* CH2 .... 97 H8
Orchard Pl *FROD/HEL* WA6 .... 98 C3 ⑥
HALE WA15 .... 43 H5
Orchard Ri *NWCHE* CW9 .... 153 L4
Orchard Rd *CHF/WBR* SK23 .... 89 K5
EP CH65 .... 121 G2
HALE/TIMP WA15 .... 42 E7
LYMM WA13 .... 40 B7
MPL/ROM SK6 .... 49 H2
Orchard Rd East
WYTH/NTH M22 .... 44 D2
Orchard Rd West
WYTH/NTH M22 .... 44 D2
The Orchards *CW/SHV* CW2 .... 238 C8
KNUT WA16 .... 104 F6
Orchard St *AIMK* WN4 .... 22 C1
CH/BCN CH1 .... 16 D3
CW/HAS CW1 .... 18 E2
NANT CW5 .... 237 K6
NWCHE CW9 .... 13 L2
STKP SK1 .... 3 H5
WARR WA1 .... 5 J6
WARRN/WOL WA2 .... 38 A2
WARRS WA4 .... 56 C4
The Orchard *FROD/HEL* WA6 .... 124 A2
Orchard V *EDGY/DAV* SK3 .... 46 C6
Orchard Wy *TPLY/KEL* CW6 .... 149 K7
WDN WA8 .... 52 A1 ⑥
Orchid Cl *CHSE* CH3 .... 170 A6
IRL M44 .... 31 L4
Orchil Cl *GTS/LS* CH66 .... 94 A6
Ordnance Av *GOL/RIS/CU* WA3 .... 29 M8
Ordsall *SBCH* CW11 .... 222 F1
Orford Av *POY/DIS* SK12 .... 68 D6
WARRN/WOL WA2 .... 5 J2
Orford Cl *MPL/ROM* SK6 .... 67 L5
Orford Gn *WARRN/WOL* WA2 .... 37 K3
Orford La *WARRN/WOL* WA2 .... 5 H3
Orford St *WARR* WA1 .... 5 H6
Oriel Cl *OFTN* SK2 .... 47 H6
Orient Dr *WLTN* L25 .... 50 B1
Orkney Av *ALS/KID* ST7 .... 243 M4
Orkney Cl *EP* CH65 .... 121 J3 ⑥
NTHM/RTH M23 .... 44 A8
WDN WA8 .... 53 L1
Orme Cl *MCFLDN* SK10 .... 112 A4
MCFLDN SK10 .... 138 D1 ⑥
Orme Crs *MCFLDN* SK10 .... 138 D1
Orme Rd *BIDD* ST8 .... 227 K7
Ormerod *MPL/ROM* SK6 .... 47 M3
SBCH CW11 .... 204 C7
Orme St *STKP* SK1 .... 3 L3
WILM/AE SK9 .... 110 A3
Ormonde Cl *CHNE* CH2 .... 145 J8
Ormonde St *CH/BCN* CH1 .... 17 J3
Ormsby Cl *EDGY/DAV* SK3 .... 46 E8 ⑥
Orms Gill Pl *OFTN* SK2 .... 47 L6 ⑥
Orphanage St *HTNM* SK4 .... 2 F1 ⑥
Orrell Cl *WARRN/WOL* WA5 .... 36 A6 ⑥
Orrishmere Rd *CHD/CHDH* SK8 .... 64 F1
Orton Av *NTHM/RTH* M23 .... 44 A3
Orton Cl *WSFD* CW7 .... 154 M8 ⑥
Orton Rd *NTHM/RTH* M23 .... 44 A3
Orwell Av *WYTH/NTH* M22 .... 44 D6
Orwell Cl *STHEL* WA9 .... 34 A1
WILM/AE SK9 .... 84 D2
Osborne Av *WARRN/WOL* WA2 .... 37 K3 ⑥
Osborne Cl *SBCH* CW11 .... 203 K7
Osborne Gv *CHD/CHDH* SK8 .... 64 A1
CW/SHV CW2 .... 238 C8
Osborne Rd *GOL/RIS/CU* WA3 .... 23 L5
HALE/TIMP WA15 .... 42 E7
OFTN SK2 .... 46 F5
WARRS WA4 .... 56 B3
Osborne St *MPL/ROM* SK6 .... 47 J1
Osbourne Pl *WILM/AE* SK9 .... 84 D6
Osbourne Pl *WA14* .... 42 D8 ⑥
Osier Cl *CHNE* CH2 .... 123 J1
Osmere Cl *WHITCH* SY13 .... 270 B3
Osprey Av *WSFD* CW7 .... 177 J7
Osprey Cl *MWCH* CW10 .... 179 K7
RUNC WA7 .... 73 M7
WARRN/WOL WA2 .... 37 L1
Osprey Dr *WILM/AE* SK9 .... 84 C4
Osprey Vw *ALS/KID* ST7 .... 243 K1 ⑥
Ossett Cl *RUNC* WA7 .... 74 D4 ⑥
Ossmere Cl *SBCH* CW11 .... 203 M4
Ostler's La *KNUT* WA16 .... 82 D4
Otley Gv *EDGY/DAV* SK3 .... 46 D8
Ottawa Cl *KNUT* WA16 .... 81 J8
Otterburn Pl *OFTN* SK2 .... 47 K6
Otters Bank *WSFD* CW7 .... 177 G3 ⑥
Otterspool Rd *MPL/ROM* SK6 .... 48 B5
Oughtrington Crs *LYMM* WA13 .... 59 H1
Oughtrington La *LYMM* WA13 .... 59 G2
Oughtrington Vw *LYMM* WA13 .... 40 B8
Oulton Av *CHNE* CH2 .... 145 L6
Oulton Dr *CONG* CW12 .... 206 F1 ⑥
Oulton Mill La *TPLY/KEL* CW6 .... 175 G5

Oulton Pl *CH/BCN* CH1 .... 17 G4
Oundle Pl *WLTN* L25 .... 50 B5
Ousel Nest *NWCHW* CW8 .... 127 K8 ⑥
Outer Central Rd *SPK/HALE* L24 .... 50 E7
Out La *CHSE* CH3 .... 215 J5
WLTN L25 .... 50 B2
Outram Cl *MPL/ROM* SK6 .... 48 F8 ⑨
Outwood Dr *CHD/CHDH* SK8 .... 64 A4
Outwood La *MANAIR* M90 .... 63 J4
Outwood La West
MANAIR M90 .... 63 H4 ⑥
Outwood Rd *CHD/CHDH* SK8 .... 64 B4
The Oval *CHD/CHDH* SK8 .... 64 B4
EP CH65 .... 121 J1
WYTH/NTH M22 .... 64 A4
Ovenhouse La *MCFLDN* SK10 .... 112 E6
Overdale Rd *NWCHW* CW8 .... 151 K3
Overdale Rd *MPL/ROM* SK6 .... 47 M3
NSTN CH64 .... 93 G3
POY/DIS SK12 .... 68 F6
WYTH/NTH M22 .... 44 D7
Overdene Rd *WSFD* CW7 .... 177 K4
Overfields *KNUT* WA16 .... 107 J1
Over Hall Dr *WSFD* CW7 .... 177 J5
Overhill Dr *WILM/AE* SK9 .... 84 E5 ⑥
Overhill La *WILM/AE* SK9 .... 84 E5
Overhill Rd *WILM/AE* SK9 .... 84 D5
Overlea Av *CQ* CH5 .... 166 C2
Overlea Dr *CQ* CH5 .... 166 C2 ⑥
Overleigh Ct *CHSW/BR* CH4 .... 17 G9
Overleigh Rd *CHSW/BR* CH4 .... 169 J3
Overpool Gdns *GTS/LS* CH66 .... 120 F1 ⑥
Overpool Rd *EP* CH65 .... 94 F7
GTS/LS CH66 .... 94 E6
Over Rd *NANT* CW5 .... 200 F4
Overton Av *WYTH/NTH* M22 .... 44 D7
Overton Cl *CONG* CW12 .... 207 J1
MWCH CW10 .... 179 H4 ⑥
SALE M33 .... 42 D2
Overton Dr *FROD/HEL* WA6 .... 99 J6
Overton Rd *BIDD* ST8 .... 208 F7
CONG CW12 .... 208 F5
WYTH/NTH M22 .... 44 D7
Overway *WSFD* CW7 .... 177 L3
Overwood Av *CH/BCN* CH1 .... 144 E4
Overwood La *CH/BCN* CH1 .... 144 C8
Overwood Pl *BURS/TUN* ST6 .... 243 M5
Ovington Cl *RUNC* WA7 .... 73 M8 ⑩
Owen Cl *CH/BCN* CH1 .... 144 E6
Owen Dr *SPK/HALE* L24 .... 70 B2
Owen Rd *RAIN/WH* L35 .... 33 J2
Owen St *CW/SHV* CW2 .... 18 E7
EDGY/DAV SK3 .... 2 D6
NWCHE CW9 .... 13 M2
WARRN/WOL WA2 .... 4 F3
Owley Wood Rd *NWCHW* CW8 .... 128 E3
Oxborough Cl *WDN* WA8 .... 33 M8 ⑨
Oxbridge Cl *SALE* M33 .... 42 D1 ⑦
Oxenham Rd *WARRN/WOL* WA2 .... 37 G1
Oxenhurst Gn *OFTN* SK2 .... 47 L7
Oxford Cl *GTS/LS* CH66 .... 120 E4
Oxford Dr *HLWD* L26 .... 50 F4
Oxford Gv *IRL* M44 .... 31 J6
Oxford Rd *ALT* WA14 .... 61 K1
CHSW/BR CH4 .... 168 F6
MCFLDS SK11 .... 14 D5
RUNC WA7 .... 9 G5
Oxford St *CW/HAS* CW1 .... 18 C2
NEWLW WA12 .... 27 H1 ⑪
WARRS WA4 .... 5 K9
WDN WA8 .... 7 J6
Oxford Wy *HTNM* SK4 .... 2 D2
Ox-hey Crs *BIDD* ST8 .... 227 K3
Ox-hey Dr *BIDD* ST8 .... 227 K3
Oxheys *RUNC* WA7 .... 74 C4
Ox La *RAIN/WH* L35 .... 32 C6
Oxmead Cl *WARRN/WOL* WA2 .... 38 B3
Oxmoor Cl *RUNC* WA7 .... 74 A7 ⑨
Oxney Cl *MCFLDN* SK10 .... 137 M4
Oxton Av *WYTH/NTH* M22 .... 44 C8
Oxton Cl *WDN* WA8 .... 33 J8
Oxton Gn *GTS/LS* CH66 .... 94 D8 ④

P

Packsaddle Pk *MCFLDN* SK10 .... 111 L7
Padarn Cl *CHSW/BR* CH4 .... 168 D7
Padden Brook *MPL/ROM* SK6 .... 48 B2
Paddington Bank *WARR* WA1 .... 37 M6
Paddock Brow *MCFLDN* SK10 .... 112 A7
Paddock Cha *POY/DIS* SK12 .... 66 F6
Paddock Cl *CHF/WBR* SK23 .... 88 F8
Paddock Dr *NSTN* CH64 .... 91 K2
Paddock Gv *STHEL* WA9 .... 34 D1
Paddock Hl *KNUT* WA16 .... 109 G1
Paddock La *AUD/MAD/W* CW3 .... 274 B1
CHF/WBR SK23 .... 88 F8
CHF/WBR SK23 .... 89 M7
LYMM WA13 .... 40 D5
LYMM WA13 .... 41 G7
Paddock Ri *RUNC* WA7 .... 73 L8
Paddock Rd *CHSW/BR* CH4 .... 192 E2
The Paddocks *EDGY/DAV* SK3 .... 47 G7
MCFLDN SK10 .... 112 A7
MCFLDS SK11 .... 152 B6
The Paddock *BRAM/HZG* SK7 .... 65 K3 ⑥
CHD/CHDH SK8 .... 47 L7
CHF/WBR SK23 .... 89 M6
CHNE CH2 .... 123 G1
CHSW/BR CH4 .... 16 C9
CQ CH5 .... 166 D2
FROD/HEL WA6 .... 99 J5
GTS/LS CH66 .... 120 D1
HALE/TIMP WA15 .... 43 H8 ⑥
LYMM WA13 .... 59 J1 ⑨
NANT CW5 .... 237 K8 ⑤
NWCHW CW8 .... 129 J8
SBCH CW11 .... 223 M3
TPLY/KEL CW6 .... 197 K3
Paddock Wk *NWCHW* CW8 .... 127 K7
Paddock Wy *CHSW/BR* CH4 .... 190 A5
Padgate La *WARR* WA1 .... 37 L5 ⑨

Padgbury Cl *CONG* CW12 .... 207 G3
Padgbury La *CONG* CW12 .... 206 F2
Padge La *CHSE* CH3 .... 231 J2
Padston Dr *ALS/KID* ST7 .... 241 G1
Padstow Cl *CW/HAS* CW1 .... 221 J4 ⑥
HLWD L26 .... 50 E3
MCFLDN SK10 .... 137 L4
WARRW/BUR WA5 .... 54 E1
Padstow Dr *BRAM/HZG* SK7 .... 65 M5
Padworth Pl *CW/HAS* CW1 .... 221 H3 ⑨
Page Gv *CW/SHV* CW2 .... 253 H1
Page La *WDN* WA8 .... 7 M3
Paignton Cl *HUY* L36 .... 32 B1 ⑧
Painswick Rd *GTS/LS* CH66 .... 120 E2
WYTH/NTH M22 .... 63 H3
Palace Ar *AIMK* WN4 .... 22 B1
Palace Fields Av *RUNC* WA7 .... 74 A5
Palace Hey *NSTN* CH64 .... 92 A7
Palatine Cl *CH/BCN* CH1 .... 144 D6
IRL M44 .... 31 M3
Palatine Rd *DID/WITH* M20 .... 44 F1
WYTH/NTH M22 .... 44 D3
Palgrave Cl *CH/BCN* CH1 .... 145 G7 ⑥
Palin Dr *WARRW/BUR* WA5 .... 35 M6 ⑥
Palliser Cl *GOL/RIS/CU* WA3 .... 39 G1
Pall Mall *RUNC* WA7 .... 20 E7
Palma Av *MANAIR* M90 .... 63 G4
Palmer Av *CHD/CHDH* SK8 .... 45 M6
Palmer Crs *WARRW/BUR* WA5 .... 36 D4
Palmer Rd *SBCH* CW11 .... 204 C7
Palmerston Cl *CH/BCN* CH1 .... 145 H8
Palmerston Rd *MCFLDS* SK11 .... 14 A6
Palmerston St *MCFLDN* SK10 .... 113 C4
Palmerston Wy *BIDD* ST8 .... 227 K4
Palm Gv *GTS/LS* CH66 .... 121 G3
WLTN L25 .... 50 B3
Palmwood Av *RAIN/WH* L35 .... 33 K2
Palmyra Sq North *WARR* WA1 .... 4 F7
Palmyra Sq South *WARR* WA1 .... 4 F8
Panfield Rd *WYTH/NTH* M22 .... 44 D3
Pangbourne Cl *EDGY/DAV* SK3 .... 46 C6
WARRS WA4 .... 56 E6
Panton Pl *CHNE* CH2 .... 17 M1
Panton Rd *CHNE* CH2 .... 17 M1
Parade Crs *SPK/HALE* L24 .... 70 E2
Parade Rd *MANAIR* M90 .... 63 J5
The Parade *CH/BCN* CH1 .... 144 E7
NSTN CH64 .... 91 H3
Paradise La *NANT* CW5 .... 200 D5
RAIN/WH L35 .... 32 D2
Paradise St *MCFLDS* SK11 .... 14 F6
Paragon Cl *WDN* WA8 .... 34 B7 ⑨
The Parchments *NEWLW* WA12 .... 22 D8
Parish Cl *ALS/KID* ST7 .... 224 B8
Park Av *ALS/KID* ST7 .... 242 E4
ALT WA14 .... 60 E4
BRAM/HZG SK7 .... 65 J7
CH/BCN CH1 .... 144 A2
CHD/CHDH SK8 .... 64 F3
CHF/WBR SK23 .... 89 K1
CHSE CH3 .... 214 B2
CHSW/BR CH4 .... 168 E6
CQ CH5 .... 142 C6
CQ CH5 .... 166 D2
EDGY/DAV SK3 .... 45 M5
FLINT CH6 .... 116 A6
GOL/RIS/CU WA3 .... 22 F2
HALE/TIMP WA15 .... 61 M3
LYMM WA13 .... 40 C4
LYMM WA13 .... 59 K4
MCFLDS SK11 .... 14 F8
MPL/ROM SK6 .... 48 C1
MWCH CW10 .... 179 J3
NANT CW5 .... 237 J7
NANT CW5 .... 251 L1
NEWLW WA12 .... 22 F5
NM/HAY SK22 .... 69 J5
NSTN CH64 .... 93 H4
NWCHW CW8 .... 129 K3
PART M31 .... 41 G1
POY/DIS SK12 .... 67 M6
RUNC WA7 .... 8 F7
TPLY/KEL CW6 .... 175 L4
TPLY/KEL CW6 .... 197 J2
WARRN/WOL WA2 .... 37 K3
WARRW/BUR WA5 .... 35 J5
WARRW/BUR WA5 .... 35 L6
WDN WA8 .... 7 K2
WHITCH SY13 .... 269 M5
WILM/AE SK9 .... 83 M5
Park Av North *NEWLW* WA12 .... 27 J2
Park Av South *NEWLW* WA12 .... 27 J2
Park Bank *CONG* CW12 .... 207 M2
Park Bvd *WARR* WA1 .... 5 G9
Park Brook Rd *MCFLDS* SK11 .... 14 A6
Parkbrook Rd *NTHM/RTH* M23 .... 44 B5
Park Cl *ALT* WA14 .... 42 F4
AUD/MAD/W CW3 .... 267 L4 ⑥
CHSE CH3 .... 172 B2
Park Ct *RUNC* WA7 .... 9 G7
WRX/GR/LL LL12 .... 210 B5
Park Crs *CHF/WBR* SK23 .... 89 K1
NWCHW CW8 .... 127 M8
WARRS WA4 .... 56 D6
WILM/AE SK9 .... 84 B3
Parkdale Rd *WARR* WA1 .... 38 A5
Park Dr *CHNE* CH2 .... 146 A8
CW/SHV CW2 .... 237 M3
EP CH65 .... 121 H1
HALE/TIMP WA15 .... 43 G5
HALE/TIMP WA15 .... 61 M3
HTNM SK4 .... 46 B2
Park Dr South *CHNE* CH2 .... 170 A1
Parkend Dr *LEIGH* WN7 .... 24 D2
Parkend Rd *NTHM/RTH* M23 .... 44 A7
Parker Av *NWCHW* CW8 .... 129 G6
Parker Dr *CHSE* CH3 .... 228 E3
Parker Dr South *CHSE* CH3 .... 228 F3 ⑥
Parkers Cl *RUNC* WA7 .... 73 L6
Parkers Rd *CW/HAS* CW1 .... 221 G4
Parker St *MCFLDS* SK11 .... 15 J6
RUNC WA7 .... 9 J1
WARR WA1 .... 4 E8
Park Est *CW/SHV* CW2 .... 238 D7
Parkett Heyes Rd
MCFLDS SK11 .... 137 L5
Park Farm Vw
BURS/TUN ST6 .... 243 K5 ⑨
Parkfield Cl *CW/HAS* CW1 .... 221 G4
Parkfield Av *MPL/ROM* SK6 .... 48 F6
WARRS WA4 .... 38 A8
Parkfield Dr *EP* CH65 .... 120 B1
FROD/HEL WA6 .... 124 B1
NANT CW5 .... 20 F9
Parkfield Rd *ALT* WA14 .... 42 C8
CHD/CHDH SK8 .... 64 F3
CHSW/BR CH4 .... 190 C1
KNUT WA16 .... 107 H4
NWCHE CW9 .... 13 M3

Parkfields La *WARRN/WOL* WA2 .... 37 M2
Parkgate *KNUT* WA16 .... 107 J1
Parkgate Av *KNUT* WA16 .... 134 A4
Parkgate Dr *OFTN* SK2 .... 47 M8
Parkgate La *KNUT* WA16 .... 81 J8
Parkgate Rd *CH/BCN* CH1 .... 16 F2 ⑥
CH/BCN CH1 .... 145 G2
GTS/LS CH66 .... 119 J2
MCFLDS SK11 .... 138 C8 ⑥
NSTN CH64 .... 91 J4
WARRS WA4 .... 56 D3
Park Gates Av *CHD/CHDH* SK8 .... 65 J3 ⑥
Park Gates Dr *CHD/CHDH* SK8 .... 65 J3
Parkgate Wy *RUNC* WA7 .... 74 C5
Park Gn *MCFLDS* SK11 .... 15 H7
Park Hill Rd *HALE/TIMP* WA15 .... 62 A3
Park House Dr *MCFLDN* SK10 .... 112 A4
SBCH CW11 .... 204 C4
Park House La *MCFLDN* SK10 .... 112 A4
Parkland Av *NM/HAY* SK22 .... 69 J3
Parkland Cl *WARRS* WA4 .... 57 H8
Parkland Dr *CHNE* CH2 .... 123 H1
Parklands *ALS/KID* ST7 .... 243 H3
GTS/LS CH66 .... 94 D7
WDN WA8 .... 52 C1
Parklands Dr *SALE* M33 .... 42 D2 ③
Parklands Gdns *GTS/LS* CH66 .... 94 D6
Parklands Rd *NTHM/RTH* M23 .... 43 M5
The Parklands *CONG* CW12 .... 208 A2
Parklands Vw *GTS/LS* CH66 .... 94 D6
Parklands Wy *POY/DIS* SK12 .... 66 E8
Park La *ALS/KID* ST7 .... 241 G7
ALT WA14 .... 60 B2
BIDD ST8 .... 227 J6
CHSE CH3 .... 195 L1
CONG CW12 .... 207 M2
FROD/HEL WA6 .... 99 H4
HALE/TIMP WA15 .... 62 A3
KNUT WA16 .... 104 E4
MCFLDS SK11 .... 14 E8
MCFLDS SK11 .... 15 H7
NANT CW5 .... 252 E8
NWCHE CW9 .... 153 M5
NWCHW CW8 .... 129 K3
POY/DIS SK12 .... 66 E8
SBCH CW11 .... 203 M6
STKP SK1 .... 3 M7
WARRS WA4 .... 55 M7
Parklea *GTS/LS* CH66 .... 94 D6
Park Lodge Cl *CHD/CHDH* SK8 .... 45 L8
Park Mount Cl *MCFLDS* SK11 .... 14 C9
Park Mount Dr *MCFLDS* SK11 .... 14 C9
Park Pl *HTNM* SK4 .... 45 M2 ⑥
Park Ri *MPL/ROM* SK6 .... 48 C1
Park Rd *ALT* WA14 .... 61 G2
CHD/CHDH SK8 .... 44 F6
CHD/CHDH SK8 .... 45 L6
CHF/WBR SK23 .... 89 K1
CHNE CH2 .... 122 E3
CONG CW12 .... 207 L1
CW/HAS CW1 .... 222 D7
EP CH65 .... 10 E9
EP CH65 .... 95 J8
HALE/TIMP WA15 .... 42 F4
HALE/TIMP WA15 .... 61 M3
LYMM WA13 .... 40 C4
LYMM WA13 .... 59 K4
MCFLDS SK11 .... 14 F8
MPL/ROM SK6 .... 48 C1
MWCH CW10 .... 179 J3
NANT CW5 .... 237 J7
NANT CW5 .... 251 L1
NEWLW WA12 .... 22 F5
NM/HAY SK22 .... 69 J5
NSTN CH64 .... 93 H4
NWCHW CW8 .... 129 K3
PART M31 .... 41 G1
POY/DIS SK12 .... 67 M6
RUNC WA7 .... 8 F7
TPLY/KEL CW6 .... 175 L4
TPLY/KEL CW6 .... 197 J2
WARRN/WOL WA2 .... 37 K3
WARRW/BUR WA5 .... 35 J5
WARRW/BUR WA5 .... 35 L6
WDN WA8 .... 7 K2
WHITCH SY13 .... 269 M5
WILM/AE SK9 .... 83 M5
Park Rd North *NEWLW* WA12 .... 27 K2
Park Rd South *NEWLW* WA12 .... 27 K2
Park Rd West *CHSW/BR* CH4 .... 16 A9
Park Rw *RUNC* WA7 .... 45 M3
Parkside Av *STHEL* WA9 .... 34 B1
Parkside Cl *MPL/ROM* SK6 .... 67 K4
Parkside La *MPL/ROM* SK6 .... 49 J6
Parkside Rd *NEWLW* WA12 .... 28 B3
SALE M33 .... 43 K1 ⑥
Parkside Wk *BRAM/HZG* SK7 .... 65 L1 ⑥
The Parks *RNFD/HAY* WA11 .... 22 B3
Parkstone Dr *CW/HAS* CW1 .... 221 H4 ⑥
Park St *CH/BCN* CH1 .... 17 G6
MCFLDS SK10 .... 113 H4
MCFLDS SK11 .... 15 H7
MPL/ROM SK6 .... 47 M1
NSTN CH64 .... 91 L4
NWCHW CW8 .... 12 E4
STKP SK1 .... 3 G4
Parksway *WARR* WA1 .... 38 D5
The Park *CHSE* CH3 .... 170 E4
WARRW/BUR WA5 .... 54 D1
Park Vale Rd *MCFLDS* SK11 .... 14 E8
Park Vw *AIMK* WN4 .... 22 B2
EDGY/DAV SK3 .... 45 M5
MCFLDN SK10 .... 15 J4
NANT CW5 .... 21 G5
STKP SK1 .... 3 L9
Park View Ri *NM/HAY* SK22 .... 69 J3
Park View Rd *ALS/KID* ST7 .... 243 G1
Park Wk *CHNE* CH2 .... 145 K8
Park Wy *CHNE* CH2 .... 144 A3
Parkway *BRAM/HZG* SK7 .... 65 J2
CQ CH5 .... 142 D2
EDGY/DAV SK3 .... 45 M5
HOLMCH CW4 .... 181 J1
NM/HAY SK22 .... 69 J3
WILM/AE SK9 .... 84 B6
Parkwood Cl *LYMM* WA13 .... 58 D2 ⑥

Parkwood Rd *NTHM/RTH* M23 .... 44 C5
RAIN/WH L35 .... 32 E2
Parliament St *NWCHW* CW8 .... 12 C4
Parliament Wy *GTS/LS* CH66 .... 120 F4
Parlington Cl *WDN* WA8 .... 52 C5
Parndon Dr *OFTN* SK2 .... 47 J5 ⑥
Parnell Av *WYTH/NTH* M22 .... 44 D4
Parren Av *RAIN/WH* L35 .... 32 C3
Parrs Mount Ms *HTNM* SK4 .... 45 M2 ⑥
Parr St *MCFLDS* SK11 .... 14 C6
WARR WA1 .... 5 H8
Parrs Wood Av *DID/WITH* M20 .... 45 J3
Parrs Wood La *DID/WITH* M20 .... 45 K3
Parrs Wood Rd *DID/WITH* M20 .... 45 H4
Parrs Wood View *WARRS* WA4 .... 57 G3
Parry Dr *WARRS* WA4 .... 57 L1
Parsonage Gdns *MPL/ROM* SK6 .... 49 G8
Parsonage St *BURS/TUN* ST6 .... 243 K8
HTNM SK4 .... 2 E4
MCFLDS SK11 .... 15 H7 ②
Parsonage Wy *CHD/CHDH* SK8 .... 36 A7
WARRW/BUR WA5 .... 36 A7
Parsons La *CHNE* CH2 .... 145 H5
Parson St *CONG* CW12 .... 207 J2
Partridge Av *NTHM/RTH* M23 .... 44 B6
Partridge Cl *CONG* CW12 .... 207 L3 ⑥
GOL/RIS/CU WA3 .... 29 G5
WSFD CW7 .... 177 K7
Partridge Wy *NWCHW* CW8 .... 104 F7 ②
Parvey La *MCFLDS* SK11 .... 162 E3
Paston Rd *WYTH/NTH* M22 .... 44 D5
Pastoral *AUD/MAD/W* CW3 .... 267 L7
Pasture Cl *MCFLDN* SK10 .... 138 C1 ⑥
TPLY/KEL CW6 .... 149 K8
WLTN L25 .... 50 B3
Pasture Dr *GOL/RIS/CU* WA3 .... 29 G5
Pasturefield Cl *SALE* M33 .... 43 M1 ⑥
Pasture Field Rd
WYTH/NTH M22 .... 63 M3
Pasture La *WARRN/WOL* WA2 .... 38 B3
Patch Croft Rd *WYTH/NTH* M22 .... 63 M3
Patch La *BRAM/HZG* SK7 .... 65 K7
Patmos La *KNUT* WA16 .... 131 M4
Patrivale Cl *WARR* WA1 .... 37 M5
Patten St *WARR* WA1 .... 5 G7 ⑨
Patterdale Av *WARRW/WOL* WA2 .... 37 J2
Patterdale Cl *CW/SHV* CW2 .... 237 K1
Patterdale Rd *OFTN* SK2 .... 47 H6
PART M31 .... 40 E1
WYTH/NTH M22 .... 44 E4
Patterson St *NEWLW* WA12 .... 22 B8
Paul Cl *WARRW/BUR* WA5 .... 35 K6
Paulden Av *NTHM/RTH* M23 .... 44 B6
Paulden Rd *NWCHE* CW9 .... 131 G2
Pauls Moss Ct *WHITCH* SY13 .... 270 A5 ⑥
Paul St *WARRN/WOL* WA2 .... 4 E5
Pavement La *KNUT* WA16 .... 81 L8
The Pavilions *NWCHE* CW9 .... 153 L2 ⑥
Paxford Pl *WILM/AE* SK9 .... 84 A7
Payne Cl *WARRN/BUR* WA5 .... 36 D6
Paythorne Cl
GOL/RIS/CU WA3 .... 29 M1 ⑥
Paythorne Gn *OFTN* SK2 .... 47 L7 ⑥
Peacefield *MPL/ROM* SK6 .... 48 E7
Peach Fld *CHSE* CH3 .... 170 B5
Peach La *NANT* CW5 .... 237 G3
Peacock Av *CHD/CHDH* SK8 .... 44 F6
WARR WA1 .... 37 L6
Peacock Dr *WSFD* CW7 .... 177 K5
Peacock Hay Rd *ALS/KID* ST7 .... 242 E8
Peacock La *KNUT* WA16 .... 59 J6
Peak Bank *MPL/ROM* SK6 .... 48 A2
Peak Dale Rd *BURS/TUN* ST6 .... 243 H5
Peakdale Av *CHD/CHDH* SK8 .... 64 A3
Peakdale Rd *MPL/ROM* SK6 .... 49 G8 ⑥
Peak Rd *NM/HAY* SK22 .... 69 K4
Peak St *STKP* SK1 .... 3 J4
Pearle St *MCFLDN* SK10 .... 15 G3
Pearl La *CHSE* CH3 .... 170 D3
Pearl St *BRAM/HZG* SK7 .... 47 L8
MCFLDS SK10 .... 112 A5 ⑥
Pearl Yd *WHITCH* SY13 .... 270 A5
Pearson Av *WARRS* WA4 .... 56 D2
Pearson St *PART* M31 .... 41 G1
Pearson St *MCFLDS* SK11 .... 15 K7
RDSH SK5 .... 3 G1
Pear Tree Av *CW/HAS* CW1 .... 221 H5
RUNC WA7 .... 9 M8
Pear Tree Cl *CQ* CH5 .... 142 A8 ②
Peartree Cl *FROD/HEL* WA6 .... 99 K3
Pear Tree Cl *MPL/ROM* SK6 .... 49 H4
Peartree Cl *SBCH* CW11 .... 204 E6
Pear Tree Dr *AUD/MAD/W* CW3 .... 267 K5
NWCHE CW9 .... 104 F6
Peartree Pl *WARRS* WA4 .... 5 J9
Pear Tree Wy *CHNE* CH2 .... 145 M7
GTS/LS CH66 .... 120 E3 ②
Pearwood Cl *TPLY/KEL* CW6 .... 197 K3
Peaslake Cl *MPL/ROM* SK6 .... 48 D2
Peasley Cl *WARRN/WOL* WA2 .... 38 B3
Peckfield Cl *RUNC* WA7 .... 74 A7 ⑥
Peckforton Cl *CHD/CHDH* SK8 .... 45 G7 ②
SBCH CW11 .... 203 L5 ⑥
Peckforton Dr *GTS/LS* CH66 .... 120 E3
RUNC WA7 .... 73 M8 ⑪
Peckforton Hall La
TPLY/KEL CW6 .... 216 C2
Peckforton Rd *TPLY/KEL* CW6 .... 216 A3
Peckforton Vw *ALS/KID* ST7 .... 243 G5
Peckforton Wy *CHNE* CH2 .... 145 L5
Peckmill Cl *WILM/AE* SK9 .... 84 E2 ②
Peck Mill La *FROD/HEL* WA6 .... 124 A5
Pedley Hl *MCFLDN* SK10 .... 113 L8
Pedley House La *KNUT* WA16 .... 108 L8
Pedley La *CONG* CW12 .... 185 L8
MCFLDS SK11 .... 108 C5
Pedley St *CW/SHV* CW2 .... 19 H7
Peebles Cl *GTS/LS* CH66 .... 93 M6 ①
Peel Av *ALT* WA14 .... 61 K2
Peel Cl *RAIN/WH* L35 .... 32 E1 ⑥
WARR WA1 .... 38 D6 ⑥

Peel Crs CHSE CH3 ... 148 E5
Peel Dr CONG CW12 ... 207 H5
Peelgate Dr CHD/CHDH SK8 ... 64 A2
Peel Hall La CHSE CH3 ... 148 E5
Peel Hall Rd NTHM/NTH M22 ... 63 H1
Peel House La WDN WA8 ... 53 H1
Peel La CONG CW12 ... 207 J5
Peel Rd HALE/TIMP WA15 ... 61 L1
Peel St CW/HAS CW1 ... 18 C2
  MCFLDS SK11 ... 15 G8
  NEWLW WA12 ... 27 C1
  OFTN SK2 ... 46 F6
  RUNC WA7 ... 8 F1
Peerswood CI NSTN CH64 ... 91 L7
Peewit CI WSFD CW7 ... 177 K7
Peggie's La MCFLDN SK10 ... 112 D1
Pelham CI CW/HAS CW1 ... 222 C7
Pelham Rd WARRS WA4 ... 57 J1
Pemberton CI NSTN CH64 ... 93 C4
Pemberton Rd CH/BCN CH1 ... 16 F4
Pembrey Wy WLTN L25 ... 50 D4
Pembroke CI CHSW/BR CH4 ... 169 L6
  CQ CH5 ... 142 B8
Pembroke Dr EP CH65 ... 121 C1
Pembroke Gdns WARRS WA4 ... 56 D8
Pembroke Gv IRL M44 ... 31 K6
Pembroke Rd MCFLDS SK11 ... 137 H5
Pembroke Wy WSFD CW7 ... 177 H5
Pembury CI WYTH/NTH M22 ... 63 J1
Penare Gorran Hvn
  RUNC WA7 ... 74 C6
Penarth Rd WYTH/NTH M22 ... 44 D4
Penbrook CI CW/SHV CW2 ... 237 K1
Pencarrow CI DID/WITH M20 ... 44 F1
Pendeen CI WYTH/NTH M22 ... 63 L3
Pendennis Rd HTNM SK4 ... 2 D1
Pendine CI WARRW/BUR WA5 ... 36 C2
Pendlebury Rd CHD/CHDH SK8 ... 45 C6
Pendle CI WARRS WA4 ... 56 F1
Pendle Gdns GOL/RIS/CU WA3 ... 29 L1
Pendle Rd GOL/RIS/CU WA3 ... 23 J3
Pendleton CI HLWD L26 ... 50 E5
Penfold CI CH/BCN CH1 ... 120 B4
Penfold Hey CHNE CH2 ... 145 K5
Penfolds RUNC WA7 ... 73 K3
Penfold Wy CHSW/BR CH4 ... 191 C5
Pengrove Ms BURS/TUN ST6 ... 243 L4
Penhale Ms HALE/TIMP WA15 ... 65 M5
Peniston Dr GTS/LS CH66 ... 94 B7
Penketh Av WARRW/BUR WA5 ... 4 C1
Penketh Rd WARRW/BUR WA5 ... 36 A8
Penketh's La RUNC WA7 ... 9 H1
Penkford La WARRW/BUR WA5 ... 26 D3
Penkmans La FROD/HEL WA6 ... 99 J6
Penlan Dr CQ CH5 ... 166 C2
Penlington Ct NANT CW5 ... 21 H5
Penmann CI HLWD L26 ... 50 F5
Penmann Crs HLWD L26 ... 50 F5
Penmark CI WARRW/BUR WA5 ... 36 C2
Penmere Gv SALE M33 ... 42 E3
Penmon Cha BRAM/HZG SK7 ... 66 B3
Pennant CI GOL/RIS/CU WA3 ... 39 C1
Penn Gn CHD/CHDH SK8 ... 65 H3
Penn House La BRAM/HZG SK7 ... 65 L5
Pennine Dr ALT WA14 ... 42 B7
Pennine La GOL/RIS/CU WA3 ... 23 J3
Pennine Rd BRAM/HZG SK7 ... 66 B3
  WARRW/WOL WA2 ... 37 L2
Pennine Wy BIDD ST8 ... 227 L2
  WSFD CW7 ... 177 H4
Pennington Av LEIGH WN7 ... 24 E1
Pennington Gdns LEIGH WN7 ... 24 E1
Pennington Gn GTS/LS CH66 ... 120 C1
Pennington La
  WARRW/BUR WA5 ... 26 C1
Pennington Rd LEIGH WN7 ... 24 F1
Penningtons La MCFLDS SK11 ... 137 L3
Penn La RUNC WA7 ... 8 E4
Penny Bank CI
  CHSW/BR CH4 ... 190 A1
Pennyfields Rd ALS/KID ST7 ... 243 K2
Penny La MCFLDN SK10 ... 139 K1
  RAIN/WH L35 ... 33 C5
  RDSH SK5 ... 3 G2
  RNFD/HAY WA11 ... 22 A5
  WARRW/BUR WA5 ... 26 D4
Pennymoor Dr ALT WA14 ... 42 B6
Pennypleck La NWCHE CW9 ... 78 A2
Penny's La NWCHE CW9 ... 130 E5
Penrhos Av CHD/CHDH SK8 ... 44 F8
Penrhyn Av CHD/CHDH SK8 ... 64 E3
  RUNC WA7 ... 9 J8
Penrhyn Crs BRAM/HZG SK7 ... 66 C4
Penrhyn Dr BRAM/HZG SK7 ... 66 C3
Penrhyn Rd EDGY/DAV SK3 ... 2 A8
  NWCHW CW8 ... 12 D3
Penrith Av MCFLDS SK11 ... 137 M7
  SALE M33 ... 43 J2
  WARRW/WOL WA2 ... 37 J2
Penrith CI FROD/HEL WA6 ... 99 K4
  PART M31 ... 31 L8
Penrith Ct CONG CW12 ... 207 G2
Penrose Gdns WARRW/BUR WA5 ... 54 D1
Penroy Av DID/WITH M20 ... 44 D1
Penry Av IRL M44 ... 31 L6
Penryn Av SALE M33 ... 43 J3
Penryn CI WARRW/BUR WA5 ... 35 L5
Pensarn Gdns
  WARRW/BUR WA5 ... 36 D2
Pensby Av CHNE CH2 ... 145 K7
Pensby Dr GTS/LS CH66 ... 94 D8
Pensford Rd NTHM/RTH M23 ... 62 F1
Penshaw Ct RUNC WA7 ... 73 L5
Pentland Av WARRW/WOL WA2 ... 37 H1
Pentland CI BRAM/HZG SK7 ... 66 B3
  CHSE CH3 ... 170 A2
  WSFD CW7 ... 177 H1
Pentland PI WARRW/WOL WA2 ... 37 H1
Pentre CI CHSE CH3 ... 148 F5
Pentre La CHSE CH3 ... 148 E5
Pentwyn Gv NTHM/RTH M23 ... 44 B5
Penzance CI MCFLDN SK10 ... 137 L4
Peover CI CONG CW12 ... 185 L5
  MCFLDS SK11 ... 134 F4
Peover Rd WILM/AE SK9 ... 64 E7
Pepler Av NTHM/RTH M23 ... 44 B2

Pepper Rd BRAM/HZG SK7 ... 66 B2
The Peppers LYMM WA13 ... 58 F1
Pepper St CH/BCN CH1 ... 17 C6
  CHSE CH3 ... 170 D4
  KNUT WA16 ... 81 M3
  LYMM WA13 ... 58 E1
  MCFLDS SK11 ... 134 E2
  MCFLDS SK11 ... 137 H4
  MWCH CW10 ... 179 J3
  SPK/HALE L24 ... 71 K3
  WARRS WA4 ... 77 C1
  WHITCH SY13 ... 270 A4
Percival CI CHNE CH2 ... 145 J4
Percival CI KNUT WA16 ... 134 B1
  RUNC WA7 ... 8 D2
Percival Rd CHNE CH2 ... 145 J4
  EP CH65 ... 10 D6
Percival St WARR WA1 ... 5 J7
Percy James CI ALS/KID ST7 ... 224 E8
Percy Rd CHSW/BR CH4 ... 17 H9
Percy St NWCHW CW9 ... 13 J2
  STKP SK1 ... 3 G4
  WARRW/BUR WA5 ... 4 B6
Peregrine CI WSFD CW7 ... 177 K7
Peregrine CI OFTN SK2 ... 47 M8
Perimeter Rd CHNE CH2 ... 97 J7
Perkins St BURS/TUN ST6 ... 243 J5
Perrey St RUNC WA7 ... 9 K2
Perrin Av RUNC WA7 ... 8 D4
Perrins Rd WARRW/BUR WA5 ... 26 F6
Perry Rd HALE/TIMP WA15 ... 43 H6
Perth CI BRAM/HZG SK7 ... 65 L7
  HOLMCH CW4 ... 181 H2
  WARRW/WOL WA2 ... 28 F8
Peterborough CI
  GTS/LS CH66 ... 120 F5
  MCFLDN SK10 ... 14 A1
Peter House La MCFLDS SK11 ... 162 F1
Peter Salem Dr
  WARRW/BUR WA5 ... 36 B6
Petersburg Rd EDGY/DAV SK3 ... 46 C6
Peters CI MCFLDN SK10 ... 112 A5
Petersfield Dr NTHM/RTH M23 ... 43 K5
Petersfield Gdns
  GOL/RIS/CU WA3 ... 24 E8
Petersgate RUNC WA7 ... 74 D5
Petersham Dr WARRS WA4 ... 56 E7
Peterstone CI
  WARRW/BUR WA5 ... 36 D2
Peter St ALTH WN4 ... 22 C1
  ALT WA14 ... 61 K1
  BRAM/HZG SK7 ... 66 D1
  GOL/RIS/CU WA3 ... 23 G4
  MCFLDS SK11 ... 14 E8
  NWCHE CW9 ... 13 M1
  STKP SK1 ... 3 J3
Peter St West MCFLDS SK11 ... 14 E6
Peterswood CI WYTH/NTH M22 ... 63 H1
Petheridge Dr
  WYTH/NTH M22 ... 63 H3
Petrel Av POY/DIS SK12 ... 66 A8
Petrel CI EDGY/DAV SK3 ... 46 D6
  WSFD CW7 ... 177 K7
Petunia CI MCFLDS SK11 ... 138 B7
Petworth Av WARRW/WOL WA2 ... 37 H1
Petworth CI CW/SHV CW2 ... 238 B4
  SPK/HALE L24 ... 50 B8
  WYTH/NTH M22 ... 44 E7
Pevensey Dr KNUT WA16 ... 107 G4
Peveril Av NM/HAY SK22 ... 69 J3
Peveril CI WARRS WA4 ... 56 D4
Peveril Dr BRAM/HZG SK7 ... 66 B1
Peveril Gdns POY/DIS SK12 ... 69 G6
Peveril Ms POY/DIS SK12 ... 69 G6
Peveril Rd ALT WA14 ... 42 C5
Pewit La NANT CW5 ... 265 H4
Pewsey Dr WYTH/NTH M22 ... 63 M1
Pewterspear Green Rd
  WARRS WA4 ... 76 D1
Pewterspear La WARRS WA4 ... 56 D8
Pexall Rd CONG CW12 ... 185 J1
Pexhill Dr MCFLDN SK10 ... 137 L5
Pexhill Rd MCFLDN SK10 ... 137 L4
  MCFLDS SK11 ... 160 C2
Pheasant CI NTHM/RTH M23 ... 29 M8
Pheasant CI NWCHE CW9 ... 104 F7
Pheasant Fld SPK/HALE L24 ... 71 J2
Pheasant Gv HLWD L26 ... 50 E3
Pheasant Ri ALT WA14 ... 61 K3
Pheasant Wk KNUT WA16 ... 59 J8
Pheasant Wy WSFD CW7 ... 177 K7
Philip Dr SALE M33 ... 43 H2
Philip Rd WDN WA8 ... 52 B4
Philips Dr WARRW/BUR WA5 ... 35 L6
Philips La GTS/LS CH66 ... 94 C8
Philip St CQ CH5 ... 167 G2
Phillips Rd CH/BCN CH1 ... 168 D1
Phillip St CHNE CH2 ... 17 K2
Phipps' La WARRW/BUR WA5 ... 26 E5
Phoenix Av WARRW/BUR WA5 ... 36 F2
Phoenix CI ALS/KID ST7 ... 243 J2
Phoenix St CQ CH5 ... 167 G2
Physics St SPK/HALE L24 ... 50 C7
Phythian Crs WARRW/BUR WA5 ... 35 M8
Piccadilly STKP SK1 ... 3 G6
Pichael Nook WARRS WA4 ... 38 A8
Pickenham CI MCFLDS SK11 ... 137 M6
Pickering CI HALE/TIMP WA15 ... 43 G5
Pickering Crs WARRS WA4 ... 57 K1
Pickering Rd WDN WA8 ... 52 B7
Pickerings CI RUNC WA7 ... 73 J6
Pickering's La WARRS WA4 ... 17 K1
Pickford's Brow STKP SK1 ... 3 G5
Pickford St MCFLDS SK11 ... 15 H6
Pickmere CI EDGY/DAV SK3 ... 46 C6
  SALE M33 ... 43 J2
  MCFLDS SK11 ... 203 M5
Pickmere Gdns
  CHD/CHDH SK8 ... 45 M7
Pickmere La KNUT WA16 ... 105 G6
Pickmere Rd WILM/AE SK9 ... 64 D7
Pickmere St WARRW/BUR WA5 ... 4 B7
Pickwick Rd POY/DIS SK12 ... 86 D1

Picow Farm Rd RUNC WA7 ... 8 B6
Picow St RUNC WA7 ... 8 F4
Picton Av EP CH65 ... 10 F8
  RUNC WA7 ... 9 K4
Picton CI GOL/RIS/CU WA3 ... 29 J8
  NWCHE CW9 ... 129 M8
  PS/BROM CH62 ... 93 K1
  WSFD CW7 ... 177 J4
Picton Dr WILM/AE SK9 ... 48 A6
Picton Gorse La CHNE CH2 ... 146 B4
Picton La CHNE CH2 ... 122 A5
Pierce St CQ CH5 ... 142 D7
  MCFLDS SK11 ... 14 E5
Pierpoint CI CH/BCN CH1 ... 16 F6
Pierpoint St NEWLW WA12 ... 23 G5
  WARRW/BUR WA5 ... 4 D3
Pigot PI WARRS WA4 ... 37 M7
Pike La FROD/HEL WA6 ... 126 A1
Pikemere Rd ALS/KID ST7 ... 224 B7
Pikenall La NWCHW CW8 ... 127 J1
Pike Rd MCFLDN SK10 ... 114 A6
Pike St WARRS WA4 ... 56 C3
The Pike NANT CW5 ... 251 L1
Pilgrim CI WARRN/WOL WA2 ... 28 A6
Pillar Box La SBCH CW11 ... 204 A1
Pillmoss La WARRS WA4 ... 76 A3
Pillory St NANT CW5 ... 20 E7
Pimblett St GOL/RIS/CU WA3 ... 23 G5
Pimlico Rd RUNC WA7 ... 8 D4
Pimmcroft Wy SALE M33 ... 43 M1
Pine Av NEWLW WA12 ... 27 J2
  WDN WA8 ... 7 K1
Pine CI ALS/KID ST7 ... 242 C5
  MCFLDS SK10 ... 15 M2
  MPL/ROM SK6 ... 48 E8
  RAIN/WH L35 ... 32 E1
Pinedale CI GTS/LS CH66 ... 120 F4
Pine Gdns CHNE CH2 ... 145 J6
Pine Gv CHNE CH2 ... 146 B8
  GOL/RIS/CU WA3 ... 23 J4
  GTS/LS CH66 ... 121 G3
  SBCH CW11 ... 204 C6
  WARR WA1 ... 38 A5
  WSFD CW7 ... 178 A3
Pinehey NSTN CH64 ... 91 K3
Pinehurst MCFLDN SK10 ... 111 L6
Pinellas RUNC WA7 ... 9 K1
Pine Rd BRAM/HZG SK7 ... 65 M4
  MCFLDS SK10 ... 15 M3
  POY/DIS SK12 ... 86 F1
  RUNC WA7 ... 9 M8
The Pines LEIGH WN7 ... 24 F1
Pine St EDGY/DAV SK3 ... 3 F8
Pine Tree CI CHSW/BR CH4 ... 190 B1
Pinetree CI NWCHW CW8 ... 103 H8
Pine Trees KNUT WA16 ... 81 M4
Pine Wk NANT CW5 ... 21 G9
Pineways WARRS WA4 ... 56 D7
Pinewood AIMK WN4 ... 22 A2
  ALT WA14 ... 61 G2
Pinewood Av WARR WA1 ... 37 L5
Pinewood CI CHNE CH2 ... 123 J1
Pinewood CI ALT WA14 ... 61 L3
  CW/SHV CW2 ... 238 B5
  HALE/TIMP WA15 ... 61 L3
Pinewood Rd WARRW/BUR WA5 ... 26 F5
  WILM/AE SK9 ... 84 E4
Pinfold CI HALE/TIMP WA15 ... 62 D5
Pinfold Ct CHSW/BR CH4 ... 169 L6
Pinfold Dr CHD/CHDH SK8 ... 65 G3
Pinfold La CHSW/BR CH4 ... 169 K6
  KNUT WA16 ... 108 D5
  KNUT WA16 ... 132 B1
  MWCH CW10 ... 179 H3
  TPLY/KEL CW6 ... 175 L5
Pinfold Rd WLTN L25 ... 50 C5
Pinfold St NWCHE CW9 ... 13 K4
Pinfold Wy NWCHW CW8 ... 128 D3
Pingard's La NWCHW CW8 ... 127 J6
Pingate Dr CHD/CHDH SK8 ... 65 G6
Pingate La CHD/CHDH SK8 ... 65 G6
Pingate La South
  CHD/CHDH SK8 ... 65 G6
Pingot Av NTHM/RTH M23 ... 44 B2
Pingot CI BRAM/HZG SK7 ... 170 B5
Pingot Rd NM/HAY SK22 ... 69 L4
Pinmill Brow FROD/HEL WA6 ... 99 H5
Pinmill CI FROD/HEL WA6 ... 99 H5
Pinners Brow WARRW/WOL WA2 ... 5 G4
Pinners Fold RUNC WA7 ... 74 B3
Pinnington Rd RAIN/WH L35 ... 32 E1
Pinsley Green Rd NANT CW5 ... 261 L2
Pinsley Vw NANT CW5 ... 249 L8
Pintail Av EDGY/DAV SK3 ... 46 D6
Pintail PI WSFD CW7 ... 177 K6
Pipe La WARR WA1 ... 38 B3
Piperhill Av WYTH/NTH M22 ... 44 D3
Pipers Ash WSFD CW7 ... 177 G3
Pipers La CHNE CH2 ... 146 B8
  NSTN CH64 ... 118 F4
The Pipers GOL/RIS/CU WA3 ... 23 M4
Pipit Av NEWLW WA12 ... 27 J1
Pipit La GOL/RIS/CU WA3 ... 38 L1
Pippin CI MWCH CW10 ... 179 J5
Pippins CI CQ CH5 ... 142 A7
Pippits Rw RUNC WA7 ... 73 L8
Pirie CI CONG CW12 ... 185 G7
Pirie Rd CONG CW12 ... 185 G7
Pitcheath La RUNC WA7 ... 74 D1
Pitchcombe Rd WYTH/NTH M22 ... 63 H2
Pitfield Gdns NTHM/RTH M23 ... 43 M5
Pit La ALS/KID ST7 ... 242 C7
  CW/SHV CW2 ... 253 L2
  NEWLW WA12 ... 27 K1
  NM/HAY SK22 ... 69 K3
  NWCHE CW9 ... 153 M4
  RUNC WA7 ... 9 M8
  WARRW/BUR WA5 ... 35 L4
  WILM/AE SK9 ... 83 M4
Pit PI WLTN L25 ... 50 A2
Pitt CI ALS/KID ST7 ... 159 H3
Pitts CI CHSE CH3 ... 172 C2
Pitts Heath La RUNC WA7 ... 74 D1
Pitts Hill Bank BURS/TUN ST6 ... 243 M7
Pitt St EDGY/DAV SK3 ... 15 H9
  MCFLDS SK11 ... 15 H9
  WARRW/BUR WA5 ... 4 D4
  WDN WA8 ... 53 G7
Place Rd ALT WA14 ... 42 C6
Plaistow Ct RUNC WA7 ... 73 L5
Plane Tree CI MPL/ROM SK6 ... 48 D7
Plane Tree Dr CW/HAS CW1 ... 221 L6

Plane Tree Gv
  RNFD/HAY WA11 ... 22 A5
Planetree Rd HALE/TIMP WA15 ... 62 A2
Plane Tree Rd PART M31 ... 40 D7
Plantagenet CI WSFD CW7 ... 177 K6
Plantation CI RUNC WA7 ... 74 A3
Plantation Dr GTS/LS CH66 ... 94 E5
Plant La SBCH CW11 ... 203 C5
Plant St SBCH CW11 ... 204 A5
Plas Newton La CHNE CH2 ... 145 M6
Platt Av SBCH CW11 ... 204 A5
Platts La CHNE CH2 ... 122 E2
  CHSE CH3 ... 193 L7
  CHSE CH3 ... 214 F5
Platt St CHD/CHDH SK8 ... 45 L6
Pleachway HTNM SK4 ... 45 M2
Pleasance Wy NEWLW WA12 ... 22 D8
Pleasant St MCFLDS SK11 ... 15 L3
  NWCHW CW8 ... 12 E4
Pleasant Wy CHD/CHDH SK8 ... 65 J6
Pleck Rd EP CH65 ... 121 G2
Plemstall CI CHNE CH2 ... 146 F4
Plemstall La CHNE CH2 ... 147 C3
Plemstall Wy CHNE CH2 ... 146 F3
The Plex ALS/KID ST7 ... 224 D8
Plinston Av WARRS WA4 ... 37 M8
Plough Cft ALS/KID ST7 ... 241 G1
Plough La CHSE CH3 ... 170 F5
  CQ CH5 ... 142 B8
Ploughmans Wy GTS/LS CH66 ... 120 E4
  MCFLDN SK10 ... 138 B1
Plover Av WSFD CW7 ... 177 K7
Plover CI CHSE CH3 ... 228 F3
  NEWLW WA12 ... 27 J1
Plover Dr ALT WA14 ... 42 B4
  BIDD ST8 ... 227 L4
  RUNC WA7 ... 74 D4
Plover Fld AUD/MAD/W CW3 ... 267 K6
Plovers La FROD/HEL WA6 ... 98 C7
Plover Wy GOL/RIS/CU WA3 ... 23 L4
Plowden Rd WYTH/NTH M22 ... 63 H2
Plowley CI DID/WITH M20 ... 45 H2
Pluckington Av HUY L36 ... 32 E2
Plucksbridge Rd MPL/ROM SK6 ... 68 A1
Plumley CI EDGY/DAV SK3 ... 46 F7
Plumley Gdns RAIN/WH L35 ... 52 A3
Plumley Moor Rd KNUT WA16 ... 105 L7
Plumley Rd WILM/AE SK9 ... 64 D7
Plumpstons La
  FROD/HEL WA6 ... 99 H3
Plumtre Av WARRW/BUR WA5 ... 4 D1
Plymouth CI RUNC WA7 ... 74 E6
Plymouth Dr BRAM/HZG SK7 ... 65 L5
Plymouth Gv EDGY/DAV SK3 ... 46 B5
Plymouth St CQ CH5 ... 142 A6
Poachers' La WARRS WA4 ... 56 F1
Pochard Av WSFD CW7 ... 177 K6
Pochard Dr ALT WA14 ... 42 B4
Pochard Ri RUNC WA7 ... 74 D4
Pochin Wy MWCH CW10 ... 179 L3
Pocket Nook La
  GOL/RIS/CU WA3 ... 24 A4
Pocklington Ct
  WARRN/WOL WA2 ... 37 H3
Pocklington Dr NTHM/RTH M23 ... 43 M5
Podsmead Rd WYTH/NTH M22 ... 63 H2
Poise Brook Dr OFTN SK2 ... 47 M7
Poise Brook Rd OFTN SK2 ... 47 M7
Poise CI BRAM/HZG SK7 ... 67 G1
Poleacre Dr WDN WA8 ... 52 D7
Pole La NWCHW CW8 ... 103 L3
Police St ALT WA14 ... 42 D7
Pollard Sq PART M31 ... 41 L1
Pollen CI SALE M33 ... 43 J2
Pollen Rd ALT WA14 ... 42 C6
Pollitt Cft MPL/ROM SK6 ... 47 M3
Pollitt Crs STHEL WA9 ... 34 C1
Polperro CI MCFLDN SK10 ... 137 L3
  WARRW/BUR WA5 ... 54 E1
Pond St GOL/RIS/CU WA3 ... 24 A4
Pond Wk STHEL WA9 ... 26 A3
Poolcroft SALE M33 ... 43 M1
Poole Av WARRW/WOL WA2 ... 37 H2
Poole CI BRAM/HZG SK7 ... 66 B3
Poole Crs WARRN/WOL WA2 ... 37 H2
Poole Hall La GTS/LS CH66 ... 94 E4
Poole Hall Rd EP CH65 ... 94 F4
Poole La CHNE CH2 ... 122 E2
Poole Old Hall La
  WARRN/WOL WA2 ... 37 H2
Pool End CI MCFLDN SK10 ... 112 D8
Pool End Rd MCFLDN SK10 ... 112 D8
Pooles La SBCH CW11 ... 206 A3
Poole St WSFD CW7 ... 177 L3
Poolford La NWCHE CW9 ... 77 L5
Pool House Rd POY/DIS SK12 ... 67 J7
Pool La CHNE CH2 ... 96 F7
  CHSE CH3 ... 148 C8
  LYMM WA13 ... 39 J8
  NWCHW CW8 ... 152 B2
  RUNC WA7 ... 9 J1
  SBCH CW11 ... 222 F5
  WARRS WA4 ... 56 A3
Pool Rd GOL/RIS/CU WA3 ... 40 A1
Pool Side ALS/KID ST7 ... 225 H4
Poolside Rd RUNC WA7 ... 9 J4
Pools Platt La NWCHE CW9 ... 77 L5
Pool St MCFLDS SK11 ... 15 J8
  WDN WA8 ... 7 K6
Pooltown Rd EP CH65 ... 94 F6
Poplar Av ALT WA14 ... 42 D6
  CQ CH5 ... 142 B8
  GOL/RIS/CU WA3 ... 29 J1
  NEWLW WA12 ... 27 K1
  NM/HAY SK22 ... 69 K3
  NWCHW CW9 ... 153 M4
  RUNC WA7 ... 9 M9
  WHITCH SY13 ... 269 L5
  WSFD CW7 ... 177 H4
Poplar CI CHD/CHDH SK8 ... 45 H7
  CONG CW12 ... 184 A8
  EP CH65 ... 95 H8
  NWCHW CW8 ... 152 A1
  RUNC WA7 ... 9 M9
  WARRW/BUR WA5 ... 35 L4
  WILM/AE SK9 ... 83 G7

MWCH CW10 ... 179 K5
Poplar Gv CHNE CH2 ... 123 G1
  CW/HAS CW1 ... 19 K2
  IRL M44 ... 31 K6
  MCFLDN SK10 ... 113 G4
  OFTN SK2 ... 47 J8
  SALE M33 ... 43 H1
Poplar La MKTDR TF9 ... 275 M6
Poplar Rd BNG/LEV M19 ... 45 K1
  CHSW/BR CH4 ... 168 F7
  MCFLDS SK11 ... 14 F8
  NWCHW CW8 ... 128 D4
Poplars Av WARRN/WOL WA2 ... 28 A8
The Poplars LEIGH WN7 ... 24 C4
  LYMM WA13 ... 39 K8
Poplar St GOL/RIS/CU WA3 ... 23 H3
  HTNM SK4 ... 45 L2
  LEIGH WN7 ... 24 F1
Poplar Wy MPL/ROM SK6 ... 68 A5
Poppy CI NTHM/RTH M23 ... 43 L3
Porlock CI STKP SK1 ... 47 J4
  WARRW/BUR WA5 ... 35 L8
Porlock Rd NTHM/RTH M23 ... 44 B6
Porter Av NEWLW WA12 ... 22 C7
  RAIN/WH L35 ... 33 K3
Porter Dr NWCHE CW9 ... 130 C6
Porters Cft CHSE CH3 ... 146 F7
Porter Rd RUNC WA7 ... 9 M2
Porter Wy NWCHE CW9 ... 130 C5
Portford CI MCFLDN SK10 ... 137 M3
Porthcawl CI WDN WA8 ... 52 C1
Porthleven Dr NTHM/RTH M23 ... 43 L6
Porthleven Rd RUNC WA7 ... 74 D7
Portland CI BRAM/HZG SK7 ... 66 B3
Portland Dr ALS/KID ST7 ... 225 L6
  BIDD ST8 ... 227 K2
Portland Gv CW/HAS CW1 ... 222 C7
Portland PI FROD/HEL WA6 ... 98 C8
Portland Rd ALT WA14 ... 61 J1
  NM/HAY SK22 ... 69 K5
Portland St RUNC WA7 ... 8 E1
Portloe Av HLWD L26 ... 50 F3
Portloe Rd CHD/CHDH SK8 ... 64 B5
Portmarnock CI
  MCFLDN SK10 ... 138 B1
Portola CI WARRS WA4 ... 57 J2
Portrea CI EDGY/DAV SK3 ... 46 E7
Portree Dr HOLMCH CW4 ... 181 H2
Portrush CI MCFLDN SK10 ... 112 C8
Portrush Rd NTHM/RTH M23 ... 63 L2
Portsmouth PI RUNC WA7 ... 74 E6
Port St STKP SK1 ... 2 E4
Portway RUNC WA7 ... 63 H2
Portwood PI RDSH SK5 ... 3 G3
Posnett St EDGY/DAV SK3 ... 2 A7
Post Office La CW/SHV CW2 ... 254 F3
  FROD/HEL WA6 ... 126 D7
  MALPAS SY14 ... 246 D5
  RUNC WA7 ... 8 A8
Post Office PI NWCHE CW9 ... 13 J1
Post Office St ALT WA14 ... 42 D7
Potter CI NANT CW5 ... 237 K8
Potters End BIDD ST8 ... 227 H3
Potters La WDN WA8 ... 51 M8
Pottery La RAIN/WH L35 ... 32 C1
Poulton CI HLWD L26 ... 50 D6
Poulton Crs WARR WA1 ... 38 D4
Poulton Dr WDN WA8 ... 6 A5
Pound Rd GTS/LS CH66 ... 94 C5
Poundswick La WYTH/NTH M22 ... 63 K1
Povey Rd WARRW/WOL WA2 ... 37 K3
Powderham CI
  BURS/TUN ST6 ... 243 L4
Powell Av GOL/RIS/CU WA3 ... 29 L8
Powell St WARRS WA4 ... 56 F1
Powell's Orch CHSW/BR CH4 ... 16 F9
Powey La CH/BCN CH1 ... 120 D1
Powicke Dr MPL/ROM SK6 ... 47 M3
Powicke Wk MPL/ROM SK6 ... 65 M6
Pownall Av WARRW/BUR WA5 ... 35 K6
Pownall Rd ALT WA14 ... 61 K1
  CHD/CHDH SK8 ... 65 G3
  WILM/AE SK9 ... 83 M4
Pownall Sq MCFLDS SK11 ... 14 E5
Pownall St BRAM/HZG SK7 ... 66 D1
  MCFLDN SK10 ... 15 C3
Powy Dr ALS/KID ST7 ... 243 G2
Powys CI CQ CH5 ... 142 D8
Powys St WARRW/BUR WA5 ... 4 C7
Poynings Dr WYTH/NTH M22 ... 63 J3
Poynton CI WARRS WA4 ... 57 H1
Poynton St MCFLDS SK11 ... 14 E5
Pratchitts Rw NANT CW5 ... 20 F7
Preece CI WDN WA8 ... 52 D1
Preece Ct CW/HAS CW1 ... 18 D2
Preesall Av CHD/CHDH SK8 ... 64 B4
Prees Rd WHITCH SY13 ... 270 B6
Premier Gdns ALS/KID ST7 ... 242 F2
Prenton Gn SPK/HALE L24 ... 70 E1
Prenton PI CHSW/BR CH4 ... 17 J9
Prescot Rd HALE/TIMP WA15 ... 61 M2
  WDN WA8 ... 6 B2
Prescot St CHNE CH2 ... 17 L2
Prescott Av GOL/RIS/CU WA3 ... 22 F2
Prescott Rd WILM/AE SK9 ... 84 B3
Prescott St GOL/RIS/CU WA3 ... 23 G3
Prestbury Av HALE/TIMP WA15 ... 42 E6
Prestbury CI NWCHE CW9 ... 129 M8
  OFTN SK2 ... 47 L8
Prestbury Dr MPL/ROM SK6 ... 47 L1
  WARRS WA4 ... 57 K1
Prestbury La MCFLDN SK10 ... 112 B5
Prestbury Rd MCFLDN SK10 ... 14 E4
  MCFLDN SK10 ... 110 F6
  WILM/AE SK9 ... 84 E7
Preston Av IRL M44 ... 31 M5
Preston on the HI WARRS WA4 ... 74 F6
Preston St STHEL WA9 ... 34 A2
Preston St West MCFLDS SK11 ... 14 D8
Prestwich Av GOL/RIS/CU WA3 ... 29 L1
Prestwick CI OFTN SK2 ... 3 M9
Prestwick CI MCFLDN SK10 ... 112 C7
  OFTN SK2 ... 177 J2
Pretoria St CHSW/BR CH4 ... 17 H9
Price Av SBCH CW11 ... 204 A7
Price Dr SBCH CW11 ... 204 A7

Price Gv STHEL WA9 26 A2
Priest Av CHD/CHDH SK8 45 G8
Priestfield Rd EP CH65 10 D7
Priest La MCFLDN SK10 111 H3
Priest St STKP SK1 46 F5
Priestway La NSTN CH64 118 E3
Priesty Ct CONG CW12 207 K2
Priesty Flds CONG CW12 207 K2
Primitive St ALS/KID ST7 226 C5
Primrose Av CW/HAS CW1 222 C7
MCFLDS SK11 14 C9
MPL/ROM SK6 48 E6
Primrose Bank ALT WA14 61 J3 1
Primrose Cha HOLMCH CW4 157 K4
Primrose Cl CHSE CH3 170 A6
RUNC WA7 74 A4
WARRN/WOL WA2 37 J3
WDN WA8 6 C3
Primrose Dell
AUD/MAD/W CW3 267 K6
Primrose Hl CW/SHV CW2 220 E7
NWCHW CW8 127 M8
TPLY/KEL CW6 149 L6
Primrose La FROD/HEL WA6 124 A3
Primrose Vw AIMK WN4 22 B2 5
Prince Albert St CW/HAS CW1 19 G4
Prince Edward St NANT CW5 20 E4
Prince of Wales Av FLINT CH6 116 A6
Prince Rd POY/DIS SK12 67 J7
Princes Av CH/BCN CH1 17 K4
MPL/ROM SK6 48 A1 4
NWCHE CW9 13 L2
Princes Dr FLINT CH6 116 B8
MPL/ROM SK6 48 D5
SALE M33 43 K1
Princes Pk NWCHW CW8 129 G2 1
Princes Pl WDN WA8 6 C2
Princes Rd ALT WA14 42 D6
EP CH65 94 F6
MPL/ROM SK6 48 A1
SALE M33 43 J1
Princess Av AIMK WN4 22 C1
CHD/CHDH SK8 65 G1
RNFD/HAY WA11 22 A5
WARR WA1 37 M6
WARRW/BUR WA5 35 L6
Princess Cl CW/SHV CW2 237 M4
Princess Crs MWCH CW10 179 K6
WARR WA1 37 M6 1
Princess Dr CW/SHV CW2 237 L4
MCFLDN SK10 112 E6
NANT CW5 21 H5
SBCH CW11 204 A5
Princess Gv CW/SHV CW2 237 M4
Princess Pkwy WYTH/NTH M22 44 C4
Princess Rd AIMK WN4 22 B1
DID/WITH M20 44 D1
KNUT WA16 156 E1
LYMM WA13 58 C1
WILM/AE SK9 83 M7
Princess St ALS/KID ST7 242 D7
ALT WA14 42 C4
BIDD ST8 227 K5
CH/BCN CH1 16 F5
CONG CW12 207 K2
CW/HAS CW1 221 J6
KNUT WA16 107 G2
MCFLDN SK10 112 F5
NWCHE CW9 130 E2
RUNC WA7 9 G1
WARRW/BUR WA5 36 D8 5
WSFD CW7 178 A3
Princes St FLINT CH6 116 B6 1
NEWLW WA12 27 H1 12
STKP SK1 2 F4
WDN WA8 7 H4
Princes Wy MCFLDS SK11 137 L5
Princeway FROD/HEL WA6 99 H4
Prince William Av CQ CH5 167 H1
Prince William Ct CQ CH5 166 A3
Prince William Gdns CQ CH5 166 E2 1
Prinknash Rd WYTH/NTH M22 63 K3
Prior Cl CW/SHV CW2 237 M3
Priors Cl CQ CH5 142 A8 4
WLTN L25 50 B2
Priorsfield Rd WLTN L25 50 B2
Priory Av NWCHE CW9 129 M8
Priory Cl CH/BCN CH1 145 J8 5
CONG CW12 208 B5
CW/HAS CW1 221 G4
RAIN/WH L35 32 C3
RUNC WA7 74 A3
WSFD CW7 177 J1 7
Priory Dr MCFLDN SK10 137 L2
Priory La MCFLDN SK10 137 L3
Priory Pl CH/BCN CH1 17 H5 1
Priory Rd ALT WA14 61 H4
CHD/CHDH SK8 46 A7
RUNC WA7 74 C2 1
WILM/AE SK9 83 L4
Priory St ALT WA14 61 J4
NWCHE CW9 13 J3
WARRS WA4 56 B1
The Priory NSTN CH64 91 K3
WARRN/WOL WA2 28 A5
Priory Wy NWCHW CW8 129 H8
WLTN L25 50 B2
Pritchard Dr NWCHE CW9 153 L2
Probert Cl CW/SHV CW2 18 A4
Proctors Cl WDN WA8 7 M1
Proctors La SBCH CW11 203 K7
Proffits La FROD/HEL WA6 98 E8
Promised Land La CHSE CH3 170 E7
Prospect Av IRL M44 31 L6
Prospect Cl CQ CH5 166 A2 1
Prospect Dr HALE/TIMP WA15 62 D5
NWCHE CW9 153 L2
Prospect La GOL/RIS/CU WA3 39 J1
Prospect Rd IRL M44 31 L6
Prospect V CHD/CHDH SK8 64 B3
Prosperity Wy MWCH CW10 179 K3
Prosser Rd CHNE CH2 145 J3
Provan Wy CH/BCN CH1 144 D7
Provident St STHEL WA9 26 A1
Provident Wy HALE/TIMP WA15 43 G5
Prunus Rd CW/HAS CW1 221 L6
The Pryors CHSE CH3 172 C1
Ptarmigan Pl WSFD CW7 177 K7 4
Public Hall St RUNC WA7 9 H1
Pudding La TPLY/KEL CW6 197 G5
Puddington La NSTN CH64 118 D4
Puddle Bank La CONG CW12 207 M7
Puffin Av POY/DIS SK12 86 A1
Pulford Ap CHSW/BR CH4 211 J1
Pulford Cl NWCHE CW9 129 L8
RUNC WA7 73 K6
Pulford Ct CHSW/BR CH4 210 D2
Pulford La CHSW/BR CH4 191 G6
Pulford Rd CH/BCN CH1 144 E7
EP CH65 94 F8
SALE M33 43 J2
WSFD CW7 177 J3
Pullman Dr NWCHE CW9 130 C4
Pump La CHSE CH3 212 A7
CHSE CH3 213 J6
RUNC WA7 73 M4
Pump Tree Ms MCFLDS SK11 137 L5 2
Purbeck Cl WYTH/NTH M22 63 J3 7
Purdy Cl WARRW/BUR WA5 36 D3
Purley Av NTHM/RTH M23 44 B3
Purley Dr IRL M44 31 J7
Purser La MALPAS SY14 244 E8
Putney Ct RUNC WA7 73 L5 2
Pye Cl RNFD/HAY WA11 22 B4
Pyecroft Cl WARRW/BUR WA5 35 K6
Pyecroft Rd WARRW/BUR WA5 35 K6
Pyecroft St CHSW/BR CH4 17 G9
Pymgate Dr CHD/CHDH SK8 64 A2
Pymgate La CHD/CHDH SK8 64 A2
Pym's La CW/HAS CW1 220 D6
Pyrus Av CW/HAS CW1 221 L6
Pyrus Gv FROD/HEL WA6 98 C8 6
Pytcheley Hollow
FROD/HEL WA6 126 F6

Q

Quadrant Cl RUNC WA7 74 D6 3
The Quadrant MPL/ROM SK6 48 A2
STKP SK1 3 L5
Quail Cl WARRN/WOL WA2 37 K1
Quakers Coppice CW/HAS CW1 239 G2
Quakers Wy WRXS/E LL13 228 E3
Quantock Cl GTS/LS CH66 94 A6 4
HTNM SK4 2 E3
WSFD CW7 177 G5 1
Quarry Av CHSE CH3 228 F3
Quarry Bank TPLY/KEL CW6 174 D2
Quarry Bank Rd WILM/AE SK9 83 M1
Quarry Cl CHSW/BR CH4 16 F9
RUNC WA7 73 K3
Quarry Hl CHSE CH3 228 F3
Quarry La CHSE CH3 170 D5
NSTN CH64 92 B3
TPLY/KEL CW6 149 K8
WARRS WA4 56 D6
Quarry Ri MPL/ROM SK6 48 B1
Quarry Rd MPL/ROM SK6 48 B2
NM/HAY SK22 69 M1
NSTN CH64 92 C3
Quarry St South WLTN L25 50 A2
Quarry Ter ALS/KID ST7 243 G3
Quay Fold WARRW/BUR WA5 4 B8
Quay Pl RUNC WA7 74 E5
Quayside CONG CW12 207 L3
Quay Side FROD/HEL WA6 99 K2
Quayside NSTN CH64 91 K7
Quayside Ms LYMM WA13 58 F1
Quayside Wy MCFLDS SK11 15 K7
The Quay FROD/HEL WA6 99 K2
Queastybirch La WARRS WA4 76 A4
Queenhill Rd WYTH/NTH M22 44 E3 5
Queen's Av CH/BCN CH1 17 K4
CQ CH5 167 G1 2
EP CH65 121 G1
FLINT CH6 116 B7
GOL/RIS/CU WA3 25 J5
MCFLDN SK10 15 J2
MPL/ROM SK6 48 A1
WARR WA1 37 L5
WDN WA8 52 B4
Queensbury Wy WDN WA8 52 D1
Queens Cl HTNM SK4 46 A2
MCFLDN SK10 112 E6
RUNC WA7 8 F5
Queens Crs CHNE CH2 145 L5
CW/HAS CW1 220 E2
WARR WA1 38 A4 1
Queen's Dr BIDD ST8 227 K6
CHD/CHDH SK8 65 G1
CHSW/BR CH4 17 K7
FROD/HEL WA6 124 B1
GOL/RIS/CU WA3 23 J4
HTNM SK4 46 A2
MWCH CW10 179 K6
NANT CW5 20 C6
NEWLW WA12 22 C7
SBCH CW11 204 A4
WARRS WA4 56 F2
Queens Gdns EP CH65 10 C7
Queensgate BRAM/HZG SK7 65 L7
NWCHW CW8 12 E3
Queen's Park Dr CW/SHV CW2 237 M1
Queen's Park Gdns
CW/SHV CW2 220 E8
Queen's Park Rd CHSW/BR CH4 17 H8
Queen's Park Vw CHSW/BR CH4 17 H8
Queens Pl CH/BCN CH1 17 H4
Queen's Rd BRAM/HZG SK7 66 E1
CH/BCN CH1 17 K3
CHD/CHDH SK8 45 M8
CHD/CHDH SK8 64 F1
CHSE CH3 170 B2
CQ CH5 142 F5
GTS/LS CH66 94 C5
HALE/TIMP WA15 62 B1
MPL/ROM SK6 48 A1
RNFD/HAY WA11 22 A5
RUNC WA7 8 F4
WHITCH SY13 270 B5
WILM/AE SK9 84 A6
Queen St ALS/KID ST7 243 G2
CH/BCN CH1 17 H4
CHD/CHDH SK8 45 L6
CONG CW12 184 F8
CQ CH5 142 D7
CW/HAS CW1 19 J3
CW/SHV CW2 238 C8
EP CH65 10 F4
FLINT CH6 116 B6 2
GOL/RIS/CU WA3 23 H4 2
KNUT WA16 106 F2
MCFLDN SK10 15 H4
MCFLDN SK10 113 H4
MPL/ROM SK6 48 F6 7
MWCH CW10 179 J3 3
NEWLW WA12 27 H1
NWCHE CW9 13 H4
RUNC WA7 9 G1
TPLY/KEL CW6 216 E4
Queen's Wy CHSW/BR CH4 167 H8 2
Queensway ALS/KID ST7 224 B7
BNG/LEV M19 45 K2
CHD/CHDH SK8 64 C4
CHNE CH2 145 M7
CQ CH5 142 A6
CW/HAS CW1 19 G4
FROD/HEL WA6 99 H5
IRL M44 31 M2
KNUT WA16 106 E1
POY/DIS SK12 86 D1
RUNC WA7 8 F1
WDN WA8 6 D7
WDN WA8 53 G7 4
WHITCH SY13 270 A6
WSFD CW7 177 K4
Queen Victoria St MCFLDS SK11 15 G5
The Quillet NSTN CH64 91 M5
Quinn St WDN WA8 7 J6
Quinta Rd CONG CW12 207 G1
Quintbridge Cl HLWD L26 50 E5

R

Raby Cl WDN WA8 53 K2
Raby Gdns NSTN CH64 91 L4
Raby Park Cl NSTN CH64 91 L4
Raby Park Rd NSTN CH64 91 L4
Racecourse La TPLY/KEL CW6 175 G2
Racecourse Pk WILM/AE SK9 83 M6 2
Racecourse Rd WILM/AE SK9 83 L6
Racefield Cl LYMM WA13 58 F1 4
Racefield Rd ALT WA14 42 C8
KNUT WA16 106 F3
The Race WILM/AE SK9 84 D2
Rackhouse Rd NTHM/RTH M23 44 B3
Radbroke Cl SBCH CW11 204 D4 3
Radcliffe Av GOL/RIS/CU WA3 29 L1
Radcliffe Rd MCFLDS SK11 162 D5
SBCH CW11 222 F1
Raddel La WARRS WA4 76 C7
Radford Cl CQ CH5 142 A5 1
OFTN SK2 47 K5
WDN WA8 52 C5
Radlet Dr HALE/TIMP WA15 43 G4
Radlett Cl WARRW/BUR WA5 54 E1
Radley Cl SALE M33 42 D1 3
Radley La WARRN/WOL WA2 37 K1
Radnor Cl CONG CW12 207 H1
CQ CH5 142 D8 2
HLWD L26 50 D6
SBCH CW11 203 L5
Radnor Dr CHSW/BR CH4 169 G7
WDN WA8 6 A2
Radnormere Dr CHD/CHDH SK8 45 M8
Radnor St WARRW/BUR WA5 4 B4
Radway Gn GTS/LS CH66 94 E7
Radway Green Rd
CW/SHV CW2 240 C7
Raeburn Av NSTN CH64 91 M5
Raeburn Dr MPL/ROM SK6 49 H4 3
Rae St EDGY/DAV SK3 2 B7
Raglan Ct GOL/RIS/CU WA3 29 M6
Raglan Dr ALT WA14 42 E4 4
Raglan Rd MCFLDN SK10 15 M1
SALE M33 42 F1
Ragley Cl POY/DIS SK12 66 F8 3
Railton Av CW/HAS CW1 221 G5
RAIN/WH L35 33 K2
Railton Cl RAIN/WH L35 33 K3 2
Railway Rd EDGY/DAV SK3 2 F7
GOL/RIS/CU WA3 23 H3 4
Railway St ALT WA14 42 D8
CW/SHV CW2 19 H7
HTNM SK4 2 D5
NEWLW WA12 27 H1
Rainbow Cl MWCH CW10 179 H5
WDN WA8 52 C1
Rainbow Dr HLWD L26 50 E4
Rainbow St CW/HAS CW1 19 H4
Rainford Av HALE/TIMP WA15 43 G7
Rainford Cl ALS/KID ST7 243 M3
Rainow Rd EDGY/DAV SK3 46 C6 2
MCFLDN SK10 139 G2
Rainow Vw MCFLDN SK10 113 J3 2
Rake La CHNE CH2 121 K7
CHSE CH3 171 G4
CHSW/BR CH4 192 A4
CQ CH5 166 F5
FROD/HEL WA6 98 B8
FROD/HEL WA6 123 K5
The Rake NSTN CH64 118 D3
Rake Wy CH/BCN CH1 144 A4
Raleigh Av RAIN/WH L35 32 D2
Raleigh Cl WARRW/BUR WA5 36 D3
Raleigh Rd NSTN CH64 91 L3
Ramillies Av CHD/CHDH SK8 65 H3
Ramp Rd East MANAIR M90 63 J5
Ramp Rd South MANAIR M90 63 H5
Ramp Rd West MANAIR M90 63 H5
Ramps Ga NWCHW CW8 152 A2 2
Ramsay Cl GOL/RIS/CU WA3 38 E1 2
Ramsbottom St CW/HAS CW1 18 D2 1
Ramsbrook Cl SPK/HALE L24 50 C8 1
Ramsbrook La SPK/HALE L24 71 J1
Ramsbrook Rd SPK/HALE L24 50 C8
Ramsdale Rd BRAM/HZG SK7 65 L4
Ramsden Ct CHSW/BR CH4 168 F8 2
Ramsey Cl AIMK WN4 22 B2 6
RAIN/WH L35 32 E1 2
WDN WA8 53 L1
Ramsey Rd EP CH65 121 J3
Ramsfield Rd SPK/HALE L24 51 G8
Ramsgill Cl NTHM/RTH M23 43 L3
Ramsons Cl HLWD L26 50 E3 7
Randle Meadow GTS/LS CH66 120 F2
Randolph Pl EDGY/DAV SK3 2 F9
Rangemoor Cl
GOL/RIS/CU WA3 30 A6 1
Rangemore Av WYTH/NTH M22 44 D4 1
Range Rd EDGY/DAV SK3 46 E6
Rannoch Cl GTS/LS CH66 120 F1
Ranulph Ct FROD/HEL WA6 99 J5
Ranworth Av HTNM SK4 45 M2
Ranworth Dr GOL/RIS/CU WA3 23 L5
Ranworth Rd
WARRW/BUR WA5 35 L6 4
Rappax Rd HALE/TIMP WA15 62 A4
Ratcliffe St STKP SK1 3 G8 2
Rathbone Pk TPLY/KEL CW6 197 K2 1
Rathlin Cl WDN WA8 53 L1
Rathmell Cl GOL/RIS/CU WA3 29 L1 4
Rathmel Rd NTHM/RTH M23 43 M2 3
Rathvale Dr WYTH/NTH M22 63 J4 1
Raven Cl SBCH CW11 204 A4
Ravenfield Cl HLWD L26 50 E4 3
Ravenfield Dr WDN WA8 52 C1
Ravenho La MCFLDN SK10 139 K1
Ravenhurst Ct GOL/RIS/CU WA3 29 M7
Ravenhurst Wy RAIN/WH L35 32 C3
Ravenna Av NTHM/RTH M23 43 K5 2
Ravenoak Park Rd
CHD/CHDH SK8 65 H4
Ravenoak Rd CHD/CHDH SK8 65 H3 5
CHD/CHDH SK8 65 J3 2
EDGY/DAV SK3 47 G8
Raven Rd HALE/TIMP WA15 43 H3
Ravenscar Crs WYTH/NTH M22 63 K4
Ravenscliffe Rd ALS/KID ST7 243 G4
Ravenscroft HOLMCH CW4 181 G1
Ravenscroft Cl SBCH CW11 204 C5
Ravenscroft Rd CW/SHV CW2 237 L1
Ravensdale Cl
WARRN/WOL WA2 37 K1 2
Ravensfield NWCHW CW8 127 K8 3
Ravensholme Ct CHSE CH3 214 A2 1
Ravensholme La CHSE CH3 214 A2 2
Ravens La NANT CW5 250 E1
Ravenswood NWCHW CW8 129 H8
Ravenswood Av HTNM SK4 46 A3 3
Ravenswood Dr
CHD/CHDH SK8 65 H4 2
Ravenswood Rd WILM/AE SK9 83 L8
Ravenwood Dr
HALE/TIMP WA15 62 D5
Rawcliffe Cl WDN WA8 33 M8 3
Rawdon Cl RUNC WA7 74 A5
Rawlings Cl GOL/RIS/CU WA3 38 F1
Rawlinson Crs HLWD L26 51 H4 1
Rawpool Gdns NTHM/RTH M23 44 A5
Rawson Rd CH/BCN CH1 168 E1
Ray Av NANT CW5 21 G2
Raydale Cl GOL/RIS/CU WA3 23 L3 6
Rayleigh Av NWCHE CW9 154 A4
Rayleigh Wy MCFLDN SK10 137 L3 7
Raymond Av WARRS WA4 56 D2
Raymond Rd NTHM/RTH M23 44 B2
Raymond St CH/BCN CH1 16 E4
Raymond Wy NSTN CH64 92 A5
Rayner St STKP SK1 3 L8
Raynham Av DID/WITH M20 45 H1
Readesdale Av CW/SHV CW2 237 M2
Reade's La CONG CW12 208 E4
CONG CW12 208 B4
Reading Room La CHSE CH3 231 K4
Reaper Cl WARRW/BUR WA5 36 D6
Reay St WDN WA8 7 L1
Rectors La CQ CH5 142 F8
Rectory Av GOL/RIS/CU WA3 23 J4
Rectory Cl CHSE CH3 228 E3
CW/SHV CW2 237 L4
FLINT CH6 116 A7
NANT CW5 20 F6
WARRN/WOL WA2 28 A6
Rectory Dr HLWD L26 50 F3
Rectory Flds STKP SK1 3 J5
Rectory Gn STKP SK1 3 J5
Rectory La CH/BCN CH1 119 M3
CQ CH5 166 D4
LYMM WA13 58 E2
MKTDR TF9 274 A8
WARRN/WOL WA2 28 A6
Rectory Vw ALS/KID ST7 242 D6
Redacre POY/DIS SK12 66 F6
Red Bank Av NEWLW WA12 27 M3
Redbourne Av HLWD L26 50 F6
Redbourne Dr WDN WA8 33 H8
Redbrook Rd HALE/TIMP WA15 43 K6
PART M31 40 E2
Redbrook Wy MCFLDN SK10 86 C7
Red Brow La WARRS WA4 74 F4
Redburn Rd NTHM/RTH M23 44 B5
Redcar Cl BRAM/HZG SK7 67 G3
Red Cow Yd KNUT WA16 107 G2 5
Reddish Av CHF/WBR SK23 89 J6
Reddish Crs LYMM WA13 39 M8
Reddish La CHF/WBR SK23 89 K6
LYMM WA13 39 M8
Reddish Rd CHF/WBR SK23 89 K6
Reddy La ALT WA14 60 B4
Redesdale Cl SBCH CW11 203 M5
WARRN/WOL WA2 37 L2 1
Redesmere Cl HALE/TIMP WA15 43 K6
NWCHE CW9 13 K8
Redesmere Dr CHD/CHDH SK8 45 M8
WILM/AE SK9 109 M3
Redesmere Rd MCFLDS SK11 160 B1
WILM/AE SK9 64 D7
Redfern Av CONG CW12 184 F8
SALE M33 43 L1
Redford Dr BRAM/HZG SK7 66 A2
Redgate NWCHW CW8 12 C5
Redhill Dr MPL/ROM SK6 47 K1
Redhill Rd CHSW/BR CH4 168 F6 8
TPLY/KEL CW6 149 J7
Redhills Ms EP CH65 10 D5
Red House La ALT WA14 41 J4
Redhouse La POY/DIS SK12 68 E6
Redland Cl CHSW/BR CH4 169 G5
Red La AUD/MAD/W CW3 267 K7
CHSE CH3 195 K6
FROD/HEL WA6 99 J4
POY/DIS SK12 68 B7
SBCH CW11 203 J6
WARRS WA4 56 C5
WARRS WA4 102 C3
Red Lion Cl ALS/KID ST7 242 D5
Red Lion La GTS/LS CH66 94 C5
NANT CW5 20 C5
Redmain Gv GOL/RIS/CU WA3 23 L4
Redmayne Cl NEWLW WA12 22 B8 3
Redmoor La NM/HAY SK22 69 H6
Red Pike GTS/LS CH66 94 D5
Redpoll Gv HLWD L26 50 E2
Redpoll La GOL/RIS/CU WA3 29 L8 4
Redruth Av MCFLDN SK10 137 L3 3
Redruth Cl RUNC WA7 74 C6
Redshank Av WSFD CW7 177 J7
Redshank Cl NEWLW WA12 22 C8 5
Redshank La GOL/RIS/CU WA3 29 M8
Redshaw Cl MWCH CW10 179 J6 1
Redstart Cl GOL/RIS/CU WA3 23 L4 7
Redstone Dr WSFD CW7 177 G3 3
Red Stone Hl FROD/HEL WA6 98 B8
Redstone Rd BNG/LEV M19 45 K1
Redvales Ct GOL/RIS/CU WA3 29 J8 3
Redvers Av GTS/LS CH66 94 A2
Redway La MCFLDN SK10 113 H5
Redwing Dr BIDD ST8 227 L4
Redwing Wy HLWD L26 50 D2
Redwood Cl CHSW/BR CH4 168 E6
NWCHW CW8 103 H8
WARR WA1 38 E6
Redwood Dr CHNE CH2 97 J8
GTS/LS CH66 120 F3
MPL/ROM SK6 47 M1 5
Reece Cl CHNE CH2 146 E4
Reedgate La NWCHE CW9 77 L3
Reed La NWCHE CW9 77 H7
Reedshaw Bank OFTN SK2 47 K7 3
Reedsmere Cl WARRS WA4 56 E2 1
Reedsmere Wk NWCHE CW9 103 K4
Rees Crs HOLMCH CW4 157 J8
Reeve Cl OFTN SK2 47 M7
Reeves Rd CHSE CH3 170 B4
Reeve St GOL/RIS/CU WA3 24 B4
Reevey Av BRAM/HZG SK7 66 C2
Regal Cl GTS/LS CH66 120 E1
NWCHE CW9 129 L8
Regency Cl ALS/KID ST7 242 D7
Regency Ct CHNE CH2 146 E4
Regency Pk WILM/AE SK9 83 M7 2
Regency Wy NWCHE CW9 129 L8
Regent Av MCFLDS SK11 14 D8
WARR WA1 38 A4
Regent Cl BRAM/HZG SK7 65 K8
CHD/CHDH SK8 46 C8
CW/SHV CW2 253 H1
WILM/AE SK9 83 M7
Regent Rd ALT WA14 42 D8 6
OFTN SK2 47 G6
WDN WA8 7 J2
Regents Cl CHSE CH3 170 B2
Regents Ga NANT CW5 21 J7
Regent St NEWLW WA12 27 G1
NWCHE CW9 153 M4
RUNC WA7 9 G1
WARR WA1 4 F7
Reginald Mitchell Wy
BURS/TUN ST6 243 J8
Reid Av WARRW/BUR WA5 36 F4 2
Reid Ct GTS/LS CH66 94 C5
Reid St CW/HAS CW1 221 J6
Reigate Cl WLTN L25 50 C2
Remer St CW/HAS CW1 221 K5
Rena Cl HTNM SK4 2 C2
Renaissance Ct
CW/HAS CW1 222 A8 2
Renaissance Wy CW/HAS CW1 239 G1
Rendel Cl NEWLW WA12 27 K2
Rendlesham Cl GOL/RIS/CU WA3 30 B6
Renfrew Cl MCFLDN SK10 137 M2
Renown Cl GOL/RIS/CU WA3 29 K8 5
Renown Wy SPK/HALE L24 50 A6
Renshaw St NWCHE CW9 130 D2
Rensherds Pl KNUT WA16 59 J7
Renton Av RUNC WA7 73 K2
Renton Rd WYTH/NTH M22 44 D8
Repton Cl KNUT WA16 59 J8
Repton Dr CW/HAS CW1 222 D7
Repton Rd EP CH65 95 K8
Reservoir Rd CHF/WBR SK23 89 K5
EDGY/DAV SK3 46 D5 3
EDGY/DAV SK3 46 D6 3
The Retreat CW/HAS CW1 221 J6 3
MPL/ROM SK6 48 B3
Revesby Cl WDN WA8 52 D2 4
Reveton Gn BRAM/HZG SK7 66 A2 2
Reynolds Av GOL/RIS/CU WA3 29 L7
STHEL WA9 26 B2
Reynolds Dr MPL/ROM SK6 49 H4 3
Reynold's La SBCH CW11 204 E5
Reynolds Ms WILM/AE SK9 84 E4 4
Reynolds St WARRS WA4 56 F1
Reynolds Wy WLTN L25 50 A2
Rhoden St CW/HAS CW1 222 A6
Rhodes Cl CW/HAS CW1 222 D8
Rhodes St WARRN/WOL WA2 5 J2
Rhona Dr WARRW/BUR WA5 35 L6 3
Rhos Av CHD/CHDH SK8 64 F3
Rhos Dr BRAM/HZG SK7 66 D3
Rhoswen FLINT CH6 116 B8 3
Rhuddlan Ct EP CH65 121 K2
Rhuddlan Rd CH/BCN CH1 144 D8
Rhum Cl EP CH65 121 J3
Rhyl St WDN WA8 6 F7 1
Ribble Av RAIN/WH L35 33 J1
WSFD CW7 178 B3
Ribble Cl GOL/RIS/CU WA3 29 M2
WDN WA8 53 M1
Ribble Dr BIDD ST8 227 L4
Ribble Pl WSFD CW7 178 B3 4
Ribble Rd WLTN L25 50 C1
Ribblesdale EP CH65 121 G1
Ribblesdale Av CONG CW12 185 G7

Ribchester Gdns
GOL/RIS/CU WA3 ...... 30 A1
Ribchester Wy RAIN/WH L35 ...... 32 A5
Richards Cft CHSE CH3 ...... 170 A5 🔲
SBCH CW11 ...... 203 K6 🔲
Richardson Cl CW/SHV CW2 ...... 238 D7
Richardson St STKP SK1 ...... 47 G5
WARRN/WOL WA2 ...... 5 K1
Richard St CW/HAS CW1 ...... 18 D3
NWCHE CW9 ...... 130 C5
STKP SK1 ...... 3 H3
Richbell Cl IRL M44 ...... 31 L1
Richmond Av RUNC WA7 ...... 73 L2
WARRS WA4 ...... 37 M8
WILM/AE SK9 ...... 64 D7
Richmond Cl GOL/RIS/CU WA3 ...... 24 D8
LYMM WA13 ...... 40 B8 🔲
SALE M33 ...... 43 M1 🔲
SBCH CW11 ...... 203 L5 🔲
Richmond Crs CHSE CH3 ...... 170 C5
Richmond Dr LYMM WA13 ...... 40 B8
NWCHE CW9 ...... 130 A4
Richmond Gdns NEWLW WA12 ...... 27 J2 🔲
Richmond Gn ALT WA14 ...... 61 H2
Richmond Gv CHD/CHDH SK8 ...... 64 F2
Richmond Hl KNUT WA16 ...... 107 H3 🔲
MCFLDS SK11 ...... 15 K8
Richmond Hill Rd
CHD/CHDH SK8 ...... 45 J1 🔲
Richmond Pl MCFLDS SK11 ...... 15 K9
Richmond Rd ALT WA14 ...... 42 D7
CW/HAS CW1 ...... 19 J3
HTNM SK4 ...... 45 M2 🔲
MPL/ROM SK6 ...... 48 C1
Richmond St WARRS WA4 ...... 57 C1
WDN WA8 ...... 7 L2 🔲
Richmond Wy HUY L36 ...... 32 A5
Ricroft Rd MPL/ROM SK6 ...... 47 K6
Ridding Av WYTH/NTH M22 ...... 63 L1 🔲
Ridding Cl OFTN SK2 ...... 47 K6
Ridding La RUNC WA7 ...... 74 B7
Riddings Ct HALE/TIMP WA15 ...... 42 F4
Riddings La NANT CW5 ...... 253 C4
NWCHW CW8 ...... 129 G8
HALE/TIMP WA15 ...... 61 M3
MPL/ROM SK6 ...... 49 G8
Ridge Av HALE/TIMP WA15 ...... 62 C6
MPL/ROM SK6 ...... 49 G8
Ridgeborne Cl
WARRW/BUR WA5 ...... 36 D2
Ridge Cl MPL/ROM SK6 ...... 48 C2
Ridge Crs MPL/ROM SK6 ...... 67 M1
Ridge End Fold MPL/ROM SK6 ...... 68 A3
Ridge Hl MCFLDS SK11 ...... 163 C5
TPLY/KEL CW6 ...... 174 B7
Ridgemont Av HTNM SK4 ...... 46 B2
Ridge Pk BRAM/HZG SK7 ...... 65 K6
Ridge Rd BURS/TUN ST6 ...... 243 K6
MPL/ROM SK6 ...... 49 G8
The Ridge NWCHW CW8 ...... 150 D5
Ridgetor Rd WLTN L25 ...... 50 A1
Ridge Vw MCFLDS SK11 ...... 138 C7
Ridgeway GOL/RIS/CU WA3 ...... 23 L5
WILM/AE SK9 ...... 84 F5
Ridgeway Cl GTS/LS CH66 ...... 120 C2
Ridgeway Gdns LYMM WA13 ...... 58 D1
Ridgeway Rd HALE/TIMP WA15 ...... 43 J7
The Ridgeway CHSE CH3 ...... 172 C1
CQ CH5 ...... 166 B2
FROD/HEL WA6 ...... 125 C2
POY/DIS SK12 ...... 68 C5
RUNC WA7 ...... 74 D6
WDN WA8 ...... 33 J6
WLTN L25 ...... 50 A1
Ridgewell Av
GOL/RIS/CU WA3 ...... 23 K4 🔲
Ridgmont Rd BRAM/HZG SK7 ...... 65 L8
Ridgway St CW/HAS CW1 ...... 19 G1
WARRN/WOL WA2 ...... 5 L2
The Ridgway MPL/ROM SK6 ...... 48 A3
Riding Fold HLWD L26 ...... 50 D2 🔲
The Ridings CHD/CHDH CH1 ...... 144 A3
Ridley Cl CW/SHV CW2 ...... 253 L1
Ridley Dr ALT WA14 ...... 42 E3 🔲
WARRW/BUR WA5 ...... 36 C8
Ridley Gv SALE M33 ...... 43 M1
Ridley Rd MCFLDS SK10 ...... 112 E4 🔲
Rigby Av CW/HAS CW1 ...... 221 C5 🔲
Rigby Rd ALS/KID ST7 ...... 243 H1
Rigbys La AIMK WN4 ...... 22 D1
Rigby St AIMK WN4 ...... 22 A1
ALT WA14 ...... 61 K1 🔲
GOL/RIS/CU WA3 ...... 23 G4 🔲
Rigg St CW/HAS CW1 ...... 18 D2
Riley Cl SALE M33 ...... 42 B3
SBCH CW11 ...... 203 K7
Riley Dr RUNC WA7 ...... 9 H6
Riley Wood MPL/ROM SK6 ...... 47 M3 🔲
Rilshaw La WSFD CW7 ...... 178 A4
Rilston Av GOL/RIS/CU WA3 ...... 29 K1
Rimington Av
GOL/RIS/CU WA3 ...... 23 J3 🔲
Rimington Cl GOL/RIS/CU WA3 ...... 29 L1 🔲
Rimsdale Cl CHD/CHDH SK8 ...... 64 A1
CW/SHV CW2 ...... 238 A5
Ringley Av GOL/RIS/CU WA3 ...... 22 F3
Ringmer Dr WYTH/NTH M22 ...... 63 J3 🔲
Ringmore Rd BRAM/HZG SK7 ...... 66 A2
Ring-o-bells La POY/DIS SK12 ...... 68 D6
Ring Rd CHNE CH2 ...... 146 B8
CHSE CH3 ...... 170 A2
Ringsfield Rd SPK/HALE L24 ...... 71 G1 🔲
Ringstead Cl WILM/AE SK9 ...... 84 D3 🔲
Ringstead Dr WILM/AE SK9 ...... 84 D3
Ringstone Wy CHF/WBR SK23 ...... 89 K4
Ringway CHSE CH3 ...... 171 H7
GTS/LS CH66 ...... 94 E8
NSTN CH64 ...... 91 M2
Ringway Gv SALE M33 ...... 43 L2
Ringway Rd MANAIR M90 ...... 63 J5
RUNC WA7 ...... 73 K2
WYTH/NTH M22 ...... 63 J4
Ringway Rd West MANAIR M90 ...... 63 J4
Ringwood Av BRAM/HZG SK7 ...... 66 B3
Ringwood Cl RUNC WA7 ...... 30 B7
Ripley Av CHD/CHDH SK8 ...... 65 H7
OFTN SK2 ...... 47 H8

Ripley Cl BRAM/HZG SK7 ...... 66 E4
Ripley St WARRW/BUR WA5 ...... 4 B4
Ripon Av GOL/RIS/CU WA3 ...... 23 K4
Ripon Cl HALE/TIMP WA15 ...... 62 C3
HUY L36 ...... 32 A1
MCFLDN SK10 ...... 138 C1
NEWLW WA12 ...... 22 C7 🔲
Ripon Dr AIMK WN4 ...... 22 D2
Rippleton Rd WYTH/NTH M22 ...... 44 E8
Rippon Av GTS/LS CH66 ...... 94 C7
Riseley St MCFLDN SK10 ...... 14 E4
The Rise CHF/WBR SK23 ...... 89 J7
Rishworth Cl OFTN SK2 ...... 47 K7 🔲
Rising Sun Rd MCFLDS SK11 ...... 138 A8
Risley Rd GOL/RIS/CU WA3 ...... 29 M6
Rissington Av NTHM/RTH M23 ...... 44 B6
Rivacre Brow GTS/LS CH66 ...... 94 C5
Rivacre Rd CH65 ...... 94 C5
GTS/LS CH66 ...... 94 C5
Riva Rd BNG/LEV M19 ...... 45 K2 🔲
Riverbank Cl MCFLDN SK10 ...... 112 F4
NANT CW5 ...... 20 E2
Riverdane Rd CONG CW12 ...... 184 F8
River La CHSE CH3 ...... 228 E2
CHSW/BR CH4 ...... 16 F9
PART M31 ...... 31 M8
River Lea Ms
AUD/MAD/W CW3 ...... 267 L6 🔲
Rivermead Av HALE/TIMP WA15 ...... 62 B6
Riverpark Cl NANT CW5 ...... 20 F1
River Rd WARRS WA4 ...... 56 C2
Riversdale FROD/HEL WA6 ...... 99 J3
WARR WA1 ...... 38 F5
Riversdale Rd CHD/CHDH SK8 ...... 45 J7 🔲
NWCHE CW9 ...... 13 K9
Riverside Cl WARR WA1 ...... 5 K8
Riverside St MCFLDS SK11 ...... 139 J8
Riverside Crs HOLMCH CW4 ...... 157 J8
Riverside Dr NWCHW CW8 ...... 12 C6
Riverside Gv CW/SHV CW2 ...... 237 K1
Riverside Pk CQ CH5 ...... 142 F6
Riverside Wk NSTN CH64 ...... 91 K7
Riversmead CHSE CH3 ...... 170 A7
Riverstone Dr NTHM/RTH M23 ...... 43 K5
River St CONG CW12 ...... 207 K1
MCFLDS SK11 ...... 15 J8
STKP SK1 ...... 3 L2
WILM/AE SK9 ...... 84 B4
Riverton Rd DID/WITH M20 ...... 45 H5
River Vw WSFD CW7 ...... 177 L3
Riverview Rd NSTN CH64 ...... 91 M7
Rivington Av GOL/RIS/CU WA3 ...... 23 J3
Rivington Gv IRL M44 ...... 31 K6
Rivington Rd EP CH65 ...... 10 D8
HALE/TIMP WA15 ...... 61 M2
RUNC WA7 ...... 100 F1
Rixton Av WARRW/BUR WA5 ...... 4 B1
The Roaches MCFLDS SK11 ...... 138 B7 🔲
Roachill Cl ALT WA14 ...... 42 B7
Road Beta MWCH CW10 ...... 179 K4
Road Five WSFD CW7 ...... 178 B2
Road Four WSFD CW7 ...... 178 B2
Road One WSFD CW7 ...... 154 B8
Roadside Ct GOL/RIS/CU WA3 ...... 23 J4
Road Three WSFD CW7 ...... 178 C3
Road Two WSFD CW7 ...... 178 B2
Roan Ct MCFLDS SK11 ...... 15 L6
Roan House Wy MCFLDS SK11 ...... 15 L6
Roan Ms MCFLDS SK11 ...... 15 L6
Roan Wy WILM/AE SK9 ...... 110 B4
Roaring Gate La
HALE/TIMP WA15 ...... 62 E1
Robert Moffat KNUT WA16 ...... 59 J7
Robert Owen Gdns
WYTH/NTH M22 ...... 44 D4 🔲
Robert Salt Ct ALT WA14 ...... 42 E6 🔲
Roberts Ct RUNC WA7 ...... 73 L6
Robertscroft Cl
WYTH/NTH M22 ...... 44 C8 🔲
Roberts Dr NWCHE CW9 ...... 130 C6
Roberts Rd NWCHE CW9 ...... 131 G2 🔲
Robert St BURS/TUN ST6 ...... 243 K8 🔲
NWCHW CW8 ...... 12 F6
RUNC WA7 ...... 9 L2
WARRW/BUR WA5 ...... 4 A5
WDN WA8 ...... 7 K3
Robeson Wy WYTH/NTH M22 ...... 44 F6
Robin Cl MCFLDN SK10 ...... 113 L7 🔲
RUNC WA7 ...... 74 D5
SBCH CW11 ...... 204 A4
Robin Crs MCFLDS SK11 ...... 162 D2
Robin Cft MPL/ROM SK6 ...... 47 K1
Robin Hood Av MCFLDS SK11 ...... 138 C7
Robin Hood La FROD/HEL WA6 ...... 124 B2
Robin La MCFLDS SK11 ...... 135 G1
MCFLDS SK11 ...... 162 D2
Robinsbay Rd WYTH/NTH M22 ...... 63 L5
Robins Cl BRAM/HZG SK7 ...... 65 L5
Robins Cft GTS/LS CH66 ...... 120 F2
Robin's La BRAM/HZG SK7 ...... 65 L5
GOL/RIS/CU WA3 ...... 29 K2
Robinsons Cft CHSE CH3 ...... 170 B5
Robinson St EDGY/DAV SK3 ...... 2 D9
Robinsway ALT WA14 ...... 61 J3
Robins Wy MCFLDN SK10 ...... 113 C5 🔲
Robinswood Rd WYTH/NTH M22 ...... 63 K5
Rob La NEWLW WA12 ...... 22 E8
Robson St WARR WA1 ...... 5 L4
Roby Gv WARRW/BUR WA5 ...... 36 A6 🔲
Roche Gdns CHD/CHDH SK8 ...... 64 F3
Rochester Cl GOL/RIS/CU WA3 ...... 23 G4 🔲
WARRW/BUR WA5 ...... 36 C7 🔲
Rochester Crs CW/HAS CW1 ...... 19 L1
Rochester Dr ALT WA14 ...... 42 E3 🔲
EP CH65 ...... 121 K1
Rochester Gv BRAM/HZG SK7 ...... 66 E1
Rochester Rd WYTH/NTH M22 ...... 63 K4
Rock Bank CHF/WBR SK23 ...... 89 K4
Rock Dr FROD/HEL WA6 ...... 99 J3
Rock Farm Cl NSTN CH64 ...... 92 A6
Rock Farm Dr NSTN CH64 ...... 92 A6
Rock Farm Gv NSTN CH64 ...... 92 A6 🔲

Rockfield Cl WDN WA8 ...... 52 D2
Rockfield Dr FROD/HEL WA6 ...... 124 C2
Rockford Ldg KNUT WA16 ...... 107 J3
Rockhill Rd WLTN L25 ...... 50 B3
Rockhouse La ALS/KID ST7 ...... 242 C4
Rockingham Cl GOL/RIS/CU WA3 ...... 30 B6
Rock La CHSE CH3 ...... 215 J6
WDN WA8 ...... 52 E1
Rocklee Gdns NSTN CH64 ...... 92 A6
Rocklynes MPL/ROM SK6 ...... 48 B2 🔲
Rocksavage Expy RUNC WA7 ...... 73 J7
Rockside ALS/KID ST7 ...... 226 C6
Rock St GOL/RIS/CU WA3 ...... 23 G2
NM/HAY SK22 ...... 69 J5 🔲
The Rock FROD/HEL WA6 ...... 124 B2
Rockwood Av CW/SHV CW2 ...... 238 A5
Rocky La CHSE CH3 ...... 213 M5
Rodborough Rd
NTHM/RTH M23 ...... 62 F1
Roddy La FROD/HEL WA6 ...... 126 D2
Rodeheath Cl WILM/AE SK9 ...... 84 D3 🔲
Rode House Cl ALS/KID ST7 ...... 224 F5
Rodens Cl WRX/GR/LL LL12 ...... 210 C5 🔲
Rodepool Cl WILM/AE SK9 ...... 84 D2 🔲
The Rode ALS/KID ST7 ...... 224 D8
Rodger Av AUD/MAD/W CW3 ...... 255 G6
Rodgers Cl FROD/HEL WA6 ...... 99 H3
Rodgers St BURS/TUN ST6 ...... 243 J4
Rodmill Dr CHD/CHDH SK8 ...... 64 E4
Rodney St MCFLDS SK11 ...... 15 G7
WARRN/WOL WA2 ...... 5 G2
Roebuck St CW/HAS CW1 ...... 18 E2
Roeburn Wy WARRW/BUR WA5 ...... 54 D1
Roedean Cl WLTN L25 ...... 50 B4 🔲
Roehampton Dr RUNC WA7 ...... 73 L5
Roehurst La WSFD CW7 ...... 177 J2
Roemarsh Ct RUNC WA7 ...... 73 L6
Roe Pk CONG CW12 ...... 226 E3
Roe St MCFLDS SK11 ...... 14 F6
Roewood La MCFLDN SK10 ...... 139 C3
Rogate Br NTHM/RTH M23 ...... 44 A7
Roger Av MCFLDS SK11 ...... 15 G6
Roger's Gn HLWD L26 ...... 50 E2 🔲
Rokeby Av GOL/RIS/CU WA3 ...... 23 J3
Rokeby Ct RUNC WA7 ...... 54 D7
Rokeden NEWLW WA12 ...... 22 D8 🔲
Roland Av RUNC WA7 ...... 8 B4
Rolleston St WARRN/WOL WA2 ...... 4 E5
Rollins La MPL/ROM SK6 ...... 49 G3
Rolls Av CW/HAS CW1 ...... 221 G6
Rolt Crs MWCH CW10 ...... 179 H4
Roman Cl NEWLW WA12 ...... 27 J2
RUNC WA7 ...... 73 L3
Roman Ct NSTN CH64 ...... 91 M5
Roman Dr CH/BCN CH1 ...... 144 D6
Romanes St NWCHW CW8 ...... 12 E5
Roman Rd HTNM SK4 ...... 2 F4
WARRS WA4 ...... 56 C3 🔲
Roman Wy SBCH CW11 ...... 203 L5
WHITCH SY13 ...... 269 M4
Romford Wy HLWD L26 ...... 50 F6 🔲
Romiley Gts GTS/LS CH66 ...... 94 E6
Romiley St STKP SK1 ...... 3 L3
Romney Cl WDN WA8 ...... 53 K2
Romney Wy NSTN CH64 ...... 91 M5
Romsey Dr CHD/CHDH SK8 ...... 65 H6
Ronald Dr WARRN/WOL WA2 ...... 4 B2
Ronaldshay WDN WA8 ...... 53 L2 🔲
Ronaldsway HLWD L26 ...... 51 G4
Ronan Rd WDN WA8 ...... 52 E7
Rood Hl CONG CW12 ...... 207 K1
Rood La CONG CW12 ...... 184 D8
Rookery Av AIMK WN4 ...... 22 B2
Rookery Cl NANT CW5 ...... 21 G7
SBCH CW11 ...... 203 J7
Rookery Dr CHSE CH3 ...... 214 B2
NANT CW5 ...... 20 F9
Rookerypool Cl WILM/AE SK9 ...... 84 D2 🔲
Rookery Ri WSFD CW7 ...... 178 A4
Rookery Rd ALS/KID ST7 ...... 243 J1
MALPAS SY14 ...... 245 H1
The Rookery CHSW/BR CH4 ...... 190 B1
NEWLW WA12 ...... 22 D8 🔲
Rook Rd WARRS WA4 ...... 37 L8
Rook St CW/SHV CW2 ...... 18 E7
Rookwood Av
NTHM/RTH M23 ...... 43 M5 🔲
Roome St WARRN/WOL WA2 ...... 5 J2
Rooth St HTNM SK4 ...... 2 C4
Rope Bank Av CW/SHV CW2 ...... 238 A5
Rope La CW/SHV CW2 ...... 238 A5
Ropers Bridge Cl WARR WA1 ...... 55 L2
The Ropewalk NSTN CH64 ...... 91 J4 🔲
Rosam Ct RUNC WA7 ...... 73 L6
Roscoe Av NEWLW WA12 ...... 27 L1 🔲
WARRN/WOL WA2 ...... 37 K4
Roscoe Crs RUNC WA7 ...... 8 C8
Roscoe St IRL M44 ...... 31 L3
Roscote Cl EDGY/DAV SK3 ...... 2 D7
Roseacre Dr CHD/CHDH SK8 ...... 64 C3
Rose Av IRL M44 ...... 31 M3
Rose Bank LYMM WA13 ...... 58 E1
MCFLDN SK10 ...... 112 F5 🔲
Rosebank Rd IRL M44 ...... 40 C1
Rosebery Dr
AUD/MAD/W CW3 ...... 267 L5 🔲
Rosebery Cl BIDD ST8 ...... 227 L4 🔲
Rosebery St BURS/TUN ST6 ...... 243 M7
OFTN SK2 ...... 47 K8
Rosebery Wy CW/HAS CW1 ...... 222 C8
Rose Cl RUNC WA7 ...... 74 D7
Rose Crs IRL M44 ...... 31 M3
WDN WA8 ...... 6 F6
Rosecroft Cl EDGY/DAV SK3 ...... 46 B8
Rosedale Av GOL/RIS/CU WA3 ...... 23 J5
WARR WA1 ...... 38 C5
Rosedene Cl CHNE CH2 ...... 145 L4
Rosefield Rd HLWD L26 ...... 50 F6
Roseheath Dr HLWD L26 ...... 50 F6
Rosehill Rd CW/SHV CW2 ...... 18 B9
Roselands Av SALE M33 ...... 42 F7
Rose La MPL/ROM SK6 ...... 48 E7
Rose Lea Cl WDN WA8 ...... 34 A8 🔲
Rosemary Av RUNC WA7 ...... 73 M7 🔲

WARRS WA4 ...... 56 E2
Rosemary Cl CHSW/BR CH4 ...... 190 C1 🔲
WARRW/BUR WA5 ...... 36 C6 🔲
Rosemary Dr NEWLW WA12 ...... 27 M1
Rosemary La STKP SK1 ...... 3 J6
WHITCH SY13 ...... 270 A5
Rosemere Dr GTS/LS CH66 ...... 120 F5
Rosemoor Gdns WARRS WA4 ...... 56 F7
Roseneath BRAM/HZG SK7 ...... 65 K3 🔲
Rose St RDSH SK5 ...... 3 C1
WDN WA8 ...... 6 F6
Rose Ter CW/HAS CW1 ...... 18 E1
Rose V CHD/CHDH SK8 ...... 64 B3
Rose View Av WDN WA8 ...... 53 G2
Roseville Dr CONG CW12 ...... 208 B4
Roseway BRAM/HZG SK7 ...... 65 M2
Rosewood Av CHNE CH2 ...... 145 K7
FROD/HEL WA6 ...... 99 K5 🔲
HTNM SK4 ...... 46 A3
WARR WA1 ...... 37 L5 🔲
Rosewood Cl CW/HAS CW1 ...... 221 L6 🔲
Rosewood Gdns
CHD/CHDH SK8 ...... 44 F6 🔲
Rosewood Gv CH/BCN CH1 ...... 144 B4 🔲
Rosgill Cl HTNM SK4 ...... 45 L2
Roskell Rd WLTN L25 ...... 50 C5
Roslyn Rd EDGY/DAV SK3 ...... 46 E7
Rossall Crs LEIGH WN7 ...... 25 C1
Rossall Dr BRAM/HZG SK7 ...... 65 M6
Rossall Gv GTS/LS CH66 ...... 94 D6
Rossall Rd WARRW/BUR WA5 ...... 36 B8
WDN WA8 ...... 53 K2
Ross Av EDGY/DAV SK3 ...... 46 E7
GTS/LS CH66 ...... 94 C7
Rossbank Rd EP CH65 ...... 10 A4
Rosscliffe Rd EP CH65 ...... 10 A4
Ross Cl WARRW/BUR WA5 ...... 36 D1
Ross Dr GTS/LS CH66 ...... 94 C7
Rossenclough Rd
WILM/AE SK9 ...... 84 D3 🔲
Rossendale Dr
GOL/RIS/CU WA3 ...... 30 A7 🔲
Rossendale Rd CHD/CHDH SK8 ...... 64 C4
Rosset Cl NWCHE CW9 ...... 129 L8
Rossett Av HALE/TIMP WA15 ...... 43 G4
WYTH/NTH M22 ...... 63 K3
Rossett Cl WARRW/BUR WA5 ...... 36 D8 🔲
WYTH/NTH M22 ...... 63 K3
Rossett Gv ALS/KID ST7 ...... 243 M4 🔲
Rossett Pk WRX/GR/LL LL12 ...... 210 C3
Rossett Rd WRX/GR/LL LL12 ...... 210 D5
Rossfield Rd EP CH65 ...... 10 A4
Rosslare Rd WYTH/NTH M22 ...... 63 L2
Rosslyn Cl CQ CH5 ...... 167 G2
Rosslyn Gv HALE/TIMP WA15 ...... 43 G6
Rosslyn La NWCHW CW8 ...... 152 A1
Rosslyn Rd CHD/CHDH SK8 ...... 64 D3
CHSE CH3 ...... 170 B1
Rossmill La HALE/TIMP WA15 ...... 62 C5
Rossmore Gdns GTS/LS CH66 ...... 94 D6
Rossmore Rd East GTS/LS CH66 ...... 94 D5
Rossmore Rd West GTS/LS CH66 ...... 94 D5
Rossmount Rd EP CH65 ...... 10 A5
Ross Rd EP CH65 ...... 10 B6
Ross St WDN WA8 ...... 7 K3
Rosswood Rd EP CH65 ...... 10 B5
Rostherne Av GOL/RIS/CU WA3 ...... 23 K4
GTS/LS CH66 ...... 94 E8
MPL/ROM SK6 ...... 67 L4
Rostherne Cl WARRW/BUR WA5 ...... 36 D8
Rostherne Crs WDN WA8 ...... 6 A1
Rostherne La ALT WA14 ...... 60 D7
Rostherne Rd EDGY/DAV SK3 ...... 46 M1
SALE M33 ...... 43 M1
WILM/AE SK9 ...... 83 L7
Rostherne Wy SBCH CW11 ...... 203 M5 🔲
Rosthernmere Rd
CHD/CHDH SK8 ...... 45 M8
Rostrevor Rd EDGY/DAV SK3 ...... 46 E7
Rothay Dr WARRW/BUR WA5 ...... 54 D1
Rothbury Cl RUNC WA7 ...... 73 L6 🔲
Rothbury Ct STHEL WA9 ...... 34 B2 🔲
Rotherby Rd WYTH/NTH M22 ...... 44 E8
Rotherdale Av HALE/TIMP WA15 ...... 43 K7
Rother Dr EP CH65 ...... 10 A3
Rotherwood Rd WILM/AE SK9 ...... 83 K7
Rothesay Crs SALE M33 ...... 42 C2
Rothesay Rd CHSW/BR CH4 ...... 16 B9
Rothley Av WYTH/NTH M22 ...... 44 D7
Rothwell Rd GOL/RIS/CU WA3 ...... 23 J3
Rottingdene Dr
WYTH/NTH M22 ...... 63 J3 🔲
Rough Bank CONG CW12 ...... 208 A4
Roughey Gdns WYTH/NTH M22 ...... 44 C8
Rough Heys La MCFLDS SK11 ...... 137 C4
Roughlea Av GOL/RIS/CU WA3 ...... 24 D8
Roughley Av WARRW/BUR WA5 ...... 36 D8 🔲
Roughlyn Crs CHSW/BR CH4 ...... 191 L3
Roughwood La SBCH CW11 ...... 224 A3
The Roundabout WDN WA8 ...... 33 K6
Roundcroft MPL/ROM SK6 ...... 48 D1
Round Gdns MCFLDN SK10 ...... 113 C4
Roundhey CHD/CHDH SK8 ...... 64 B4
Round Hill Meadow CHSE CH3 ...... 170 B5
Round Meadow MCFLDN SK10 ...... 113 K7
Round Thorn GOL/RIS/CU WA3 ...... 29 C5
Roundthorn Rd NTHM/RTH M23 ...... 43 M6
Roundthorn Wk
NTHM/RTH M23 ...... 43 M6 🔲
Roundway BRAM/HZG SK7 ...... 65 K6
Round Wy NM/HAY SK22 ...... 69 K4 🔲
Roundwood Av WYTH/NTH M22 ...... 44 D5
Roundy La MCFLDN SK10 ...... 86 F7
Rowan Av GOL/RIS/CU WA3 ...... 23 M5
SALE M33 ...... 43 J2
Rowan Cl ALS/KID ST7 ...... 224 C8 🔲
ALS/KID ST7 ...... 241 K1 🔲
ALS/KID ST7 ...... 243 G4
MWCH CW10 ...... 179 L6
RUNC WA7 ...... 9 L3
SBCH CW11 ...... 203 M6 🔲
WARRW/BUR WA5 ...... 35 M6
WSFD CW7 ...... 177 L1 🔲
Rowan Dr CHD/CHDH SK8 ...... 65 J4
Rowan Pk CHSE CH3 ...... 170 D5
Rowan Pl CHNE CH2 ...... 146 B8
Rowan Ri NWCHW CW8 ...... 129 G1
Rowan Rd CQ CH5 ...... 166 A1

NWCHW CW8 ...... 128 C4
Rowanside MCFLDN SK10 ...... 111 L6
Rowanside Dr WILM/AE SK9 ...... 84 E4 🔲
The Rowans CHSW/BR CH4 ...... 190 B1
Rowan Tree Dr SALE M33 ...... 43 H3
Rowan Wy MCFLDN SK10 ...... 15 J2
Rowden Crs CQ CH5 ...... 142 A6
Rowden St CQ CH5 ...... 142 A6
Rowfield Dr NTHM/RTH M23 ...... 62 F1 🔲
Rowland Cl WARRN/WOL WA2 ...... 38 A1
Rowlandsway WYTH/NTH M22 ...... 63 K2
Rowley Bank La KNUT WA16 ...... 79 J3
Rowley Rd BRAM/HZG SK7 ...... 66 E4 🔲
Rowley's Dr CQ CH5 ...... 142 C6
Rowley Wy KNUT WA16 ...... 107 H5
Rowson Dr IRL M44 ...... 31 K6
Rowthorn Cl WDN WA8 ...... 6 C5
Rowton Bridge Rd CHSE CH3 ...... 170 E5
Rowton Cl NWCHE CW9 ...... 129 M8
Rowton La CHSE CH3 ...... 170 F6
Rowton Rd CW/SHV CW2 ...... 220 D8
Roxborough Cl
WARRW/BUR WA5 ...... 27 G1 🔲
Roxborough Wk WLTN L25 ...... 50 C1
Roxburgh Cl MCFLDN SK10 ...... 14 A3
Roxburgh Rd GTS/LS CH66 ...... 93 M6
Roxby Wy KNUT WA16 ...... 107 G5
Roxholme Wk WYTH/NTH M22 ...... 63 J4
Royal Av WDN WA8 ...... 52 B4
Royal Gdns ALT WA14 ...... 60 F2
Royal Gv WYTH/NTH M22 ...... 153 L1
Royal George St EDGY/DAV SK3 ...... 2 F8
Royal La TPLY/KEL CW6 ...... 198 A1
Royal Mdw MCFLDN SK10 ...... 14 A3
Royal Oak Rd NTHM/RTH M23 ...... 44 B5
Royal Oak Yd STKP SK1 ...... 3 C5 🔲
Royal Rd POY/DIS SK12 ...... 68 D7
Royalthorn Dr
WYTH/NTH M22 ...... 44 C6 🔲
Royalthorn Rd WYTH/NTH M22 ...... 44 C6 🔲
HALE/TIMP WA15 ...... 42 E7
Royce Av BIDD ST8 ...... 227 H7
Royce Cl CW/HAS CW1 ...... 221 G5
Royden Av IRL M44 ...... 31 K4 🔲
RUNC WA7 ...... 8 F6
Royds Cl NWCHW CW8 ...... 129 H7
Roylance Dr MWCH CW10 ...... 179 J4
Royle Cl OFTN SK2 ...... 47 K7
Royleen Dr FROD/HEL WA6 ...... 99 K6
Royle Green Rd WYTH/NTH M22 ...... 44 E4
Royle's Pl NWCHW CW8 ...... 12 C6
Royle St CONG CW12 ...... 207 K1
NWCHE CW9 ...... 13 M3
OFTN SK2 ...... 3 H9
WSFD CW7 ...... 177 L3
Royon Dr EDGY/DAV SK3 ...... 46 B5
Royston Av WARR WA1 ...... 37 M5
Royston Cl GOL/RIS/CU WA3 ...... 23 L4 🔲
GTS/LS CH66 ...... 120 F2
Royton Av SALE M33 ...... 43 K2
Rozel Crs WARRW/BUR WA5 ...... 36 B8
Ruabon Rd DID/WITH M20 ...... 45 J2
Rubens Cl MPL/ROM SK6 ...... 49 J4
Rudd Av STHEL WA9 ...... 26 A2
Ruddpark Rd WYTH/NTH M22 ...... 63 K3
Rudgate RAIN/WH L35 ...... 32 E2
Rudheath La CW/SHV CW2 ...... 220 D7
Rudloe Ct WARRN/WOL WA2 ...... 37 M3
Rudstone Cl GTS/LS CH66 ...... 94 B7
Rudyard Cl MCFLDS SK11 ...... 14 C9
Rudyard Gv SALE M33 ...... 42 E2
Rufford Cl CW/SHV CW2 ...... 238 E5
WDN WA8 ...... 52 C2 🔲
Rugby Cl MCFLDN SK10 ...... 112 E8
Rugby Rd MCFLDN SK10 ...... 138 E1
SALE M33 ...... 43 G2
Rugby Rd EP CH65 ...... 121 J1
LEIGH WN7 ...... 24 F1
Ruislip Cl WLTN L25 ...... 50 C2
Ruislip Ct WARRN/WOL WA2 ...... 24 A2 🔲
Runcorn Docks Rd RUNC WA7 ...... 8 D3
Runcorn Rd NWCHW CW8 ...... 102 C6
WARRS WA4 ...... 55 C8
Runcorn Spur Rd RUNC WA7 ...... 9 K4
Runcorn-widnes Br WDN WA8 ...... 53 G8
Runger La MANAIR M90 ...... 62 F5
Runnymede WARR WA1 ...... 38 C5
Runnymede Cl EDGY/DAV SK3 ...... 46 C5
Rupert St BIDD ST8 ...... 227 J4
Ruscar Ct HLWD L26 ...... 50 E2 🔲
Ruscoe Av SBCH CW11 ...... 203 L6
Ruscolm Cl WARRW/BUR WA5 ...... 35 K5 🔲
Rushey Cl HALE/TIMP WA15 ...... 62 D5
Rushey Rd WYTH/NTH M22 ...... 44 C7
Rushfield Crs RUNC WA7 ...... 74 B7
Rushfield Rd CHD/CHDH SK8 ...... 65 G6
CHSW/BR CH4 ...... 169 H7
Rush Gdns LYMM WA13 ...... 40 A8
Rushgreen Rd LYMM WA13 ...... 39 M8
Rushmere Cl MCFLDN SK10 ...... 112 F2
Rushmere La CHSE CH3 ...... 211 M1
Rushmore Gv WARR WA1 ...... 38 A5
Rusholme Cl HLWD L26 ...... 51 G6 🔲
Rushside Rd CHD/CHDH SK8 ...... 64 F6
Rushton Av NEWLW WA12 ...... 22 B8
Rushton Cl MPL/ROM SK6 ...... 49 C7 🔲
NWCHE CW9 ...... 130 C5
WDN WA8 ...... 52 F1
Rushton Dr BRAM/HZG SK7 ...... 65 K1
CHNE CH2 ...... 145 L5
CW/SHV CW2 ...... 253 L2
MPL/ROM SK6 ...... 48 F8
MPL/ROM SK6 ...... 48 C1
MWCH CW10 ...... 179 J5
Rushton Fold MCFLDN SK10 ...... 111 G2
Rushton La TPLY/KEL CW6 ...... 175 J7
Rushton Rd CHD/CHDH SK8 ...... 65 C6 🔲
EDGY/DAV SK3 ...... 46 B5
Rushton St DID/WITH M20 ...... 45 H2 🔲
Rushyfield Crs MPL/ROM SK6 ...... 48 D1
Rushy Vw NEWLW WA12 ...... 22 A8
Ruskin Av NEWLW WA12 ...... 22 B8
WARRN/WOL WA2 ...... 37 J2 🔲
Ruskin Ct KNUT WA16 ...... 107 G2
Ruskin Dr EP CH65 ...... 121 K1

Ruskin Gdns *MPL/ROM* SK6 .... 48 A1 5
Ruskin Gv *MPL/ROM* SK6 .... 48 A1
Ruskin Rd *CONG* CW12.................. 207 J2
CW/SHV CW2 .... 18 E8
Ruskin Wy *KNUT* WA16 .... 107 G1
Russell Av *ALS/KID* ST7................ 224 C7
MPL/ROM SK6 .... 67 L5
Russell Cl *CONG* CW12 .... 207 M2
Russell Dr *CW/HAS* CW1 .... 222 C7
Russell Pl *BURS/TUN* ST6............ 243 L6
Russell Rd *BURS/TUN* ST6 .... 243 K6
HUY L36 .... 32 B2
PART M31 .... 41 G1
RUNC WA7 .... 8 C5
WSFD CW7 .... 177 J4
Russell St *OFTN* SK2 .... 47 G6
Russet Cl *MWCH* CW10 .... 179 H2
Russet Rd *NWCHW* CW8 .... 128 D4
Ruthin Av *CHD/CHDH* SK8........... 64 E2
Ruthin Cl *WARRW/BUR* WA5 ...... 36 E1 2
Rutland Av *GOL/RIS/CU* WA3 .... 23 K5
HLWD L26 .... 50 F4
WARRS WA4 .... 56 B4
Rutland Cl *CHD/CHDH* SK8 .... 45 H6
CONG CW12 .... 184 E8
SBCH CW11.................................. 203 J7
Rutland Dr *MWCH* CW10............... 179 J5
NWCHW CW8 .... 128 C3 4
Rutland Pl *CHNE* CH2 .... 146 A7 3
Rutland Rd *ALS/KID* ST7 .... 243 G2
ALT WA14 .... 42 D6
BRAM/HZG SK7 .... 66 E4
IRL M44 .... 31 K7
MCFLDS SK11 .... 138 C8
PART M31 .... 40 E2
Rutland St *RUNC* WA7 .... 8 F2
Rutter Av *WARRW/BUR* WA5 .... 36 F2
Rutter's La *BRAM/HZG* SK7 .... 66 C2
Ryburn Rd *MCFLDS* SK11............... 138 A7
Rycot Rd *SPK/HALE* L24................. 50 C8
Rydal Av *BRAM/HZG* SK7 .... 66 C1
MPL/ROM SK6 .... 67 L4
WARRS WA4 .... 56 A2
WHITCH SY13 .... 270 B6
Rydal Cl *CHD/CHDH* SK8 .... 45 H8 3
EP CH65 .... 121 J2
HOLMCH CW4............................... 181 H2
NSTN CH64 .... 91 M6
WSFD CW7 .... 177 K1
Rydal Ct *CONG* CW12 .... 207 G2
Rydal Dr *HALE/TIMP* WA15 .... 62 D4
Rydal Gv *CHSW/BR* CH4................ 169 G6
FROD/HEL WA6 .... 124 B3
RUNC WA7 .... 9 K7
Rydal Mt *CW/HAS* CW1 .... 221 H3
Rydal St *NEWLW* WA12.................... 27 J1
Rydal Wy *ALS/KID* ST7 .... 224 C7
WDN WA8 .... 52 C4
Ryde Av *HTNM* SK4......................... 46 B2
Ryde Cl *CW/HAS* CW1 .... 221 H4 5
Ryder Av *ALT* WA14 .... 42 E5 3
Ryder Gv *LEIGH* WN7 .... 25 J2 2
Ryder Rd *WARR* WA1 .... 38 C4
WDN WA8 .... 34 B8
Ryders St *NWCHW* CW8.................. 12 E3
Ryebank Av *CW/HAS* CW1........... 221 H5
Ryebank Wy *MCFLDN* SK10.......... 138 C1
Ryebrook Gv *BURS/TUN* ST6 ...... 243 M5
Ryeburn Av *WYTH/NTH* M22 ...... 63 K1 4
Rye Cl *ALS/KID* ST7 .... 241 H1
Ryecroft *CHNE* CH2 .... 123 H1
Ryecroft Av *GOL/RIS/CU* WA3......... 23 L3
Ryecroft Cl *MWCH* CW10 .... 179 H5 1
Ryecroft Gv *NTHM/RTH* M23 .... 44 A5
Ryecroft La *CHSE* CH3 .... 172 B6
KNUT WA16.................................... 81 L8
TPLY/KEL CW6 .... 172 E6
Ryedale Cl *HTNM* SK4..................... 46 B1
Ryefield Cl *HALE/TIMP* WA15 ...... 43 J7 2
Ryefield Rd *SALE* M33 .... 42 C2 2
Ryefield Wy *WHITCH* SY13 .... 270 A6 1
Ryeland St *CQ* CH5......................... 142 A5
Rylands Cl *MALPAS* SY14 .... 258 B1
Rylands St *WARR* WA1 .... 5 G7
WDN WA8 .... 7 J4 2
Ryles Cl *MCFLDS* SK11 .... 138 C7
Ryles Crs *MCFLDS* SK11 .... 138 C7
Ryle's Park Rd *MCFLDS* SK11 .... 138 C7
Ryle St *MCFLDS* SK11 .... 15 G8
Ryleys La *WILM/AE* SK9 .... 109 M3
Rylstone Av *CCHDY* M21 .... 44 D1

S

Sabre Cl *RUNC* WA7 .... 74 D5 8
Sack La *NWCHE* CW9 .... 78 F6
Saddleback Dr *MCFLDN* SK10 .... 111 M5
Saddlers Ri *RUNC* WA7 .... 74 C4 2
Saddlewood Av *BNG/LEV* M19...... 45 K2
Sadler Cl *WSFD* CW7 .... 177 K3 3
Sadler Rd *WSFD* CW7 .... 177 K3 4
Sadler's Cl *HOLMCH* CW4............. 181 H1
Sadlers La *TPLY/KEL* CW6 .... 175 G3
Sadler St *WDN* WA8 .... 7 L2
Sadlers Wls *TPLY/KEL* CW6 .... 216 E4
Saffron Cl *GOL/RIS/CU* WA3 .... 23 L4
WARRN/WOL WA2 .... 38 B3
Sagars Rd *WILM/AE* SK9 .... 64 C8
Sage Cl *WARRN/WOL* WA2 .... 38 C2
Saighton La *CHSE* CH3.................... 193 M2
St Aidan's St *BURS/TUN* ST6 .... 243 K8
St Alban Rd *WARRW/BUR* WA5....... 35 L7
St Albans Crs *ALT* WA14 .... 42 C4
St Albans Dr *NANT* CW5 .... 251 M1 1
St Albans Pl *NM/HAY* SK22 .... 69 J5 3
St Albans St *NM/HAY* SK22 .... 69 J4 5
St Aldates *MPL/ROM* SK6 .... 47 M2
St Alkmond Meadow
WHITCH SY13 .... 269 M4
St Ambrose Rd *WDN* WA8................. 7 M2
St Andrew's Av *CW/SHV* CW2.......... 18 F9
HALE/TIMP WA15............................. 42 E5
St Andrews Cl *ALT* WA14 .... 42 C3
Saint Andrew's Cl *MPL/ROM* SK6.. 48 B3
St Andrews Cl *NWCHE* CW9 .... 130 E5
WARRN/WOL WA2 .... 29 G8
St Andrews Dr *ALS/KID* ST7........... 243 J1
HOLMCH CW4............................... 181 H2
St Andrews Gdns *ALS/KID* ST7 .... 241 L2
St Andrews Rd *CHD/CHDH* SK8 .... 64 C3
EP CH65 .... 121 K1
MCFLDS SK11 .... 14 D7
St Anne's Av *MWCH* CW10............ 179 J4
WARRS WA4 .... 57 H2
St Annes Av East *WARRS* WA4 .... 57 H2
St Anne's La *NANT* CW5 .... 20 D6
St Anne's Rd *WDN* WA8 .... 53 H2
St Anne St *CH/BCN* CH1 .... 17 G3 1
St Ann's Rd *BRAM/HZG* SK7 .... 66 C3 2
MWCH CW10 .... 179 H3
St Ann's Rd North
CHD/CHDH SK8 .... 64 B3
St Ann's Rd South
CHD/CHDH SK8 .... 64 C3
St Ann's Sq *CHD/CHDH* SK8 .... 64 C4 1
St Anns St *SALE* M33 .... 43 M1 8
St Asaph Dr *WARRW/BUR* WA5..... 36 D2
St Asaph Rd *GTS/LS* CH66 .... 120 E4
St Augustine's Av
WARRS WA4 .... 37 M8 4
St Augustine's Rd
EDGY/DAV SK3 .... 46 B4 4
St Austel Cl *WARRW/BUR* WA5 ...... 54 E1
St Austell Av *MCFLDN* SK10.......... 137 K3
St Austell Cl *RUNC* WA7 .... 74 B6
St Austell Dr *CHD/CHDH* SK8.......... 64 B4
St Austins La *WARR* WA1 .... 4 F8
St Barnabas Ct *MCFLDS* SK11 ...... 15 H9 1
St Barnabas Pl *WARRW/BUR* WA5 .. 4 B5
St Bartholomews Ct *CQ* CH5 .... 143 L6
St Bede's Av *NWCHW* CW8 .... 128 D3
St Bees Cl *CHD/CHDH* SK8 .... 64 B1
St Benedicts Cl *WARRN/WOL* WA2 .. 5 H3
St Brannocks Rd *CHD/CHDH* SK8.. 65 H5
St Brides Cl *WARRW/BUR* WA5 .... 54 E1
St Bridget's Cl
WARRN/WOL WA2 .... 37 M1 3
St Catherine Dr *NWCHW* CW8....... 128 F8
St Catherine's Cl *FLINT* CH6 ..... 116 A6 5
St Chad's Av *MPL/ROM* SK6 .... 48 C2
St Chads Cl *NANT* CW5 .... 253 G4
St Chad's Flds *WSFD* CW7 .... 177 J7 3
St Chad's Gv *MPL/ROM* SK6 .... 48 C2
St Chad's Rd *CH/BCN* CH1.............. 144 F8
St Christophers Cl *CHNE* CH2 .... 145 J4
St Christopher's Dr
MPL/ROM SK6 .... 48 A2
St Clairs St *CW/SHV* CW2 .... 19 H9
St Crewood Cl *CW/SHV* CW2 .... 238 B5 4
St David's Av *MPL/ROM* SK6........... 48 B2
St Davids Cl *FLINT* CH6................... 116 B8
SALE M33 .... 43 G1 7
St David's Dr *CQ* CH5 .... 142 B6 7
GTS/LS CH66.................................. 120 F4
WARRW/BUR WA5 .... 36 E2
St David's Rd *BRAM/HZG* SK7 ..... 66 C3 3
St David's Ter *CHSW/BR* CH4 ...... 168 C5
St Elmo Av *OFTN* SK2 .... 47 K5
St Elmo Pk *POY/DIS* SK12 .... 67 J8
St Elphins Cl *WARR* WA1 .... 5 K6
St Ethelwold's St *CQ* CH5 .... 142 B8 3
St Gabriel's Av *HUY* L36................... 32 A2
St Georges Av *GTS/LS* CH66 ...... 120 F4 3
HALE/TIMP WA15 .... 43 G4 3
St George's Cl *KNUT* WA16 .... 107 J4
WARRS WA4 .... 76 E1 1
St George's Ct *ALT* WA14 .... 42 B5
St George's Crs *CHSE* CH3 .... 171 G7
CHSW/BR CH4 .... 17 J8
HALE/TIMP WA15............................. 43 G4
St George's Pl *MCFLDS* SK11 .... 15 H8
St Georges Rd *NM/HAY* SK22 .... 69 J4
WSFD CW7 .... 177 J4
St George's St *MCFLDS* SK11........... 15 H7
St Helens Cl *GOL/RIS/CU* WA3 .... 40 B1 1
St Helens Linkway *RAIN/WH* L35 .. 33 M3
St Helens Rd *LEIGH* WN7 .... 24 C3 1
NWCHE CW9 .... 13 K2
St Hilda's Dr *FROD/HEL* WA6 ...... 99 J3 2
St Hilda's Rd *WYTH/NTH* M22 .... 44 D3
St Hugh's Cl *ALT* WA14 .... 42 E4 5
St Ives Av *CHD/CHDH* SK8 .... 46 A6 1
St Ives Cl *MCFLDN* SK10 .... 137 L3 3
St Ives Crs *SALE* M33 .... 43 G3
St Ives Wy *CQ* CH5 .... 167 G1
HLWD L26 .... 50 F4
St James Av *CHNE* CH2 .... 145 M6
CONG CW12 .... 207 J2
MCFLDS SK11 .... 161 L2
St James Cl
AUD/MAD/W CW3 .... 264 A8 2
St James Ct *HALE/TIMP* WA15 .... 42 E8
St James Dr *SALE* M33 .... 43 G1
WILM/AE SK9 .... 84 A6 3
St James Mt *RAIN/WH* L35 .... 33 J2
Saint James Rd *RAIN/WH* L35.......... 33 J2
St James's Gv *ALT* WA14 .... 42 F3
St James St *CH/BCN* CH1.................. 17 H3
St James Ter *WSFD* CW7 .... 177 G4 5
St James' Wy *CHD/CHDH* SK8 .... 64 F6 2
St John Av *WARRS* WA4 .... 56 B2
St John's Av *KNUT* WA16 .... 106 F3
NWCHE CW9.................................. 130 F1
St John's Brow *RUNC* WA7 .... 9 J1
St John's Cl *MPL/ROM* SK6 .... 48 B2
NWCHE CW9 .... 130 D5
St Johns Dr *WSFD* CW7 .... 177 G4
St John's Pk *WHITCH* SY13 .... 270 A4 2
St Johns Pl *BIDD* ST8 .... 227 K5
St John's Rear Rd *CHSW/BR* CH4.. 17 J8
St John's Rd *ALT* WA14..................... 61 J1
BIDD ST8 .... 227 J6
BRAM/HZG SK7 .... 66 B3
CHSW/BR CH4 .... 17 J7
CONG CW12 .... 184 F7
HTNM SK4 .... 45 L2 6
HTNM SK4 .... 45 L2 8
KNUT WA16.................................... 106 F3
MCFLDS SK11 .... 14 F7
WILM/AE SK9 .... 109 L1
St John's St *RUNC* WA7 .... 9 J1
WHITCH SY13 .... 270 A4
St John St *CH/BCN* CH1 .... 17 G5
NEWLW WA12................................... 27 G1
St John's Wy *NWCHW* CW8 .... 152 A2
SBCH CW11................................... 204 E6
St John's Wd *ALS/KID* ST7 .... 242 F3
St Joseph's Cl
WARRW/BUR WA5 .... 35 L7 3
St Joseph St *BURS/TUN* ST6 ...... 243 K5 3
St Josephs Wy *NANT* CW5 .... 21 J7
St Katherines Wy *WARR* WA1 .... 5 L6
St Kilda Cl *EP* CH65.......................... 121 J3
St Lawrence Ct *NANT* CW5 .... 21 G5
St Lawrence Rd *FROD/HEL* WA6 .. 99 H5
St Leonards Dr *HALE/TIMP* WA15.. 42 F6
St Lesmo Rd *EDGY/DAV* SK3 .... 46 B4
St Luke's Av *GOL/RIS/CU* WA3 .... 23 K4 5
St Lukes Cl *HOLMCH* CW4 .... 181 K1
St Luke's Crs *WDN* WA8 .... 34 B8
St Luke's Wy *FROD/HEL* WA6 .... 99 H3
St Margaret's Av
WARRN/WOL WA2 .... 37 K3 4
St Margarets Ct
AUD/MAD/W CW3 .... 255 G6 3
St Margaret's Rd *ALT* WA14............ 42 C8
CHD/CHDH SK8 .... 46 A6 2
St Mark's Av *ALT* WA14.................... 42 A7
St Marks Crs *GTS/LS* CH66 .... 120 F5 4
St Marks Rd *CHSW/BR* CH4............ 168 F6
St Martin's Av *HTNM* SK4.................. 2 A4
St Martins Dr *GTS/LS* CH66 .... 120 D2
St Martins La *RUNC* WA7 .... 74 D5
St Martin's Rd *ALS/KID* ST7 .... 242 E7
MPL/ROM SK6 .... 49 G6
St Martin's Wy *CH/BCN* CH1 .... 16 E4
St Mary's Av *NWCHW* CW8 ...... 128 D3 7
St Marys Cl *ALS/KID* ST7................ 224 C7
STKP SK1 .... 3 J5
WARRS WA4 .... 56 C6
St Marys Ct *NANT* CW5................... 236 A5
WLTN L25 .... 50 A2
St Mary's Dr *CHD/CHDH* SK8 ..... 45 M6 4
NWCHW CW8 .... 153 G4
St Mary's Hl *CH/BCN* CH1 .... 17 G7
St Mary's Pl *WLTN* L25 .... 50 A2 3
St Mary's Rd *ALT* WA14 .... 61 H2
CHSW/BR CH4 .... 191 G5
NANT CW5...................................... 20 E3
NM/HAY SK22................................... 69 H4
POY/DIS SK12.................................. 68 D7
RUNC WA7 .... 73 M3
WARRW/BUR WA5 .... 35 M7
WDN WA8 .... 53 G8
St Mary's St *CW/HAS* CW1............... 18 E3
WHITCH SY13 .... 270 A4 3
St Mary's Wy *CHSW/BR* CH4 .... 167 J7
STKP SK1 .... 3 J8
St Matthews Cl *CW/HAS* CW1....... 222 D8
WARRS WA4 .... 56 D5
St Matthew's Rd *EDGY/DAV* SK3 .... 2 D8
St Mawes Cl *WDN* WA8 .... 6 C1
St Mawgan Ct
WARRN/WOL WA2 .... 37 M2 4
St Michael's Av *BRAM/HZG* SK7 .... 65 L5
St Michaels Cl *NWCHW* CW8 .... 102 D7
WDN WA8 .... 52 C5
St Michael's Rd *BURS/TUN* ST6.... 243 M7
STHEL WA9 .... 34 A1
WDN WA8 .... 52 C5
St Michael's Wy *MWCH* CW10....... 179 J3
St Monicas Cl *WARRS* WA4 .... 56 D5
St Nicholas Rd *GOL/RIS/CU* WA3 .. 24 A3
RAIN/WH L35 .... 32 C3
St Olave St *CH/BCN* CH1 .... 17 G7
St Oswalds Cl *MALPAS* SY14 .... 258 B1
WARRN/WOL WA2 .... 28 B6 1
St Oswald's Crs *SBCH* CW11 .... 181 M7
St Oswalds Rd *AIMK* WN4 .... 22 A2
St Oswalds Wy *CH/BCN* CH1............ 17 G3
St Paul's Cl *CW/HAS* CW1................ 18 E3
St Pauls Gdns *GTS/LS* CH66............. 94 B5
St Paul's Rd *MCFLDN* SK10 .... 15 J6
WDN WA8 .... 7 H6
St Paul's St *CW/HAS* CW1 .... 18 E3
STKP SK1 .... 3 K2
St Peter's Av *KNUT* WA16 .... 106 F3
St Peter's Cl *LYMM* WA13 .... 40 A8 3
St Peter's Dr *TPLY/KEL* CW6 .... 175 M5
St Petersgate *STKP* SK1...................... 3 G5
St Peter's Ri *SBCH* CW11 .... 203 L5
St Peters Rd *CONG* CW12 .... 207 L3 4
St Peter's Sq *STKP* SK1 .... 2 F5 1
St Peters Wy *CHNE* CH2 .... 146 F4
WARRN/WOL WA2 .... 5 H4
St Saviour's Rd *OFTN* SK2 .... 47 J7
St Saviour's St *ALS/KID* ST7............ 242 D3
Saintsbridge Rd
WYTH/NTH M22 .... 63 J2 6
St Simons Cl *OFTN* SK2.................... 47 J4
St Stephen Rd
WARRW/BUR WA5 .... 35 M7
St Stephen's Av
WARRN/WOL WA2 .... 37 H1
St Stephens Ct *SBCH* CW11........... 203 K5
St Thomas Ct *WDN* WA8 .... 6 C2 1
St Thomas's Pl *STKP* SK1.................... 3 G8
St Thomas St *ALS/KID* ST7 .... 226 D5
St Thomas' Vw *EP* CH65 .... 95 H8
St Vincent Dr *NWCHW* CW8 .... 128 F8
St Vincent Rd
WARRW/BUR WA5 .... 35 M7 5
St Vincent St *HALE/TIMP* WA15 .... 42 D8
St Wenefredes *MALPAS* SY14 .... 247 M5
St Werburgh St *CH/BCN* CH1 .... 17 G5
St Wilfrid's Dr *WARRS* WA4 .... 57 J3
Salander Crs *CW/SHV* CW2 .... 238 A5
Salcombe Dr *WLTN* L25 .... 50 B5
Salcombe Rd *OFTN* SK2 .... 47 J4
Sale Heys Rd *SALE* M33 .... 42 F1
Sale Rd *NTHM/RTH* M23 .... 44 A2
Salesbrook La *NANT* CW5 .... 262 C6
Salford *AUD/MAD/W* CW3.............. 264 A8
Salisbury Av *CHSW/BR* CH4 .... 168 D6
CW/SHV CW2 .... 18 E9
Salisbury Cl *AUD/MAD/W* CW3 .... 267 M5
CW/SHV CW2 .... 238 C3
GTS/LS CH66 .... 120 F4 10
Salisbury Pl *MCFLDN* SK10 .... 112 E8 2
Salisbury Rd *ALT* WA14 .... 42 D5
WHITCH SY13 .... 270 B4
Salisbury St *CH/BCN* CH1 .... 16 D1
CQ CH5 .... 142 B6 5
GOL/RIS/CU WA3 .... 23 G4
RUNC WA7 .... 9 G4
WARR WA1 .... 5 L5
WDN WA8 .... 7 J4
Salkeld St *NWCHE* CW9 .... 13 M3
Salop Pl *ALS/KID* ST7 .... 243 G1
Saltash Cl *HLWD* L26........................ 50 E4
RUNC WA7 .... 74 B6
WYTH/NTH M22 .... 63 K3
Saltdene Rd *WYTH/NTH* M22 .... 63 J3 10
Saltersgate *GTS/LS* CH66................ 120 F2
Salter's La *CHNE* CH2 .... 146 C4
CHSE CH3 .... 231 L3
MCFLDS SK11 .... 159 H4
Salthill Dr *WYTH/NTH* M22 .... 63 L2
Salt Line Wy *SBCH* CW11 .... 203 K6
Saltney Ferry Rd
CHSW/BR CH4 .... 168 B5
Salton Gdns *WARRW/BUR* WA5 .... 4 B2
Saltrush Rd *WYTH/NTH* M22............ 63 K2
Saltwood Dr *RUNC* WA7 .... 74 C7
Saltworks Cl *FROD/HEL* WA6 .... 99 K2
Salusbury St *FLINT* CH6 .... 116 B5 4
Salvin Cl *AIMK* WN4 .... 22 D1
Samlesbury Cl *DID/WITH* M20 ..... 44 F1 5
Samuel St *ALS/KID* ST7................... 243 M3
CH/BCN CH1 .... 17 J3
CW/HAS CW1 .... 18 D2
HTNM SK4 .... 2 D1
MCFLDS SK11 .... 15 G6
WARRW/BUR WA5 .... 4 A8
Sanbec Gdns *WDN* WA8 .... 33 K7 1
Sandacre Rd *NTHM/RTH* M23........... 44 B5
Sandalwood *RUNC* WA7 .... 74 C3 1
Sandalwood Cl
WARRN/WOL WA2 .... 37 K2 3
Sandbach Rd *ALS/KID* ST7........... 224 E4
CONG CW12 .... 206 F1
SALE M33 .... 43 M1 9
SBCH CW11 .... 224 D3
Sandbach Rd North
ALS/KID ST7 .... 224 C7
Sandbach Rd South
ALS/KID ST7 .... 241 K1
Sandby Dr *MPL/ROM* SK6 .... 49 H4
Sanderling Rd *OFTN* SK2 .... 48 A7
Sanders Hey Cl *RUNC* WA7 .... 74 A7
Sanderson Cl
WARRW/BUR WA5 .... 35 K6 4
Sanders Sq *MCFLDS* SK11 .... 138 D7 2
Sandfield Av *NANT* CW5 .... 261 M1
Sandfield Cl *GOL/RIS/CU* WA3 .. 23 M4 7
Sandfield Ct *FROD/HEL* WA6 ...... 99 H4 1
NANT CW5...................................... 261 M1
Sandfield Crs *GOL/RIS/CU* WA3 ..... 25 J5
Sandfield La *NWCHW* CW8 .... 127 L3
NWCHW CW8 .... 129 J8
Sandfields *FROD/HEL* WA6 .... 99 H4 2
Sandford Br *NANT* CW5.................. 262 D1
Sandford Rd *NANT* CW5 .... 21 G3
SALE M33 .... 43 M1 10
Sandgate Cl *SPK/HALE* L24 .... 50 B8
Sandgate Rd *MCFLDN* SK10 .... 138 F2
Sandham Rd *SPK/HALE* L24 .... 71 G1
Sandheys *NSTN* CH64 .... 91 J3 1
Sandhill La *MPL/ROM* SK6................ 49 L3
Sandhill Wk *WYTH/NTH* M22 .... 63 H2
Sandhole La *KNUT* WA16 .... 134 D1
NWCHW CW8 .... 127 H5
Sandhurst Av *CW/SHV* CW2 .... 18 A9
Sandhurst Dr *WILM/AE* SK9 .... 84 C3
Sandhurst Rd *DID/WITH* M20 .... 45 H2
HLWD L26 .... 51 G6
OFTN SK2 .... 47 H7
Sandhurst St *WARRS* WA4 .... 56 F1 1
Sandicroft Cl *GOL/RIS/CU* WA3....... 29 J7
Sandiford Rd *HOLMCH* CW4 .... 181 J1
Sandilands Rd *NTHM/RTH* M23 .... 43 K4
Sandileigh *CHNE* CH2 .... 145 L8
Sandileigh Av *CHD/CHDH* SK8 .... 46 A6
HALE/TIMP WA15.............................. 61 M1
KNUT WA16..................................... 106 F2
Sandileigh Dr *HALE/TIMP* WA15.... 61 M1
Sandiway *BRAM/HZG* SK7 .... 65 L2
KNUT WA16..................................... 107 H2
MPL/ROM SK6 .... 47 M1
RAIN/WH L35 .... 32 D2
Sandiway Av *WDN* WA8.................... 52 A3
Sandiway Cl *MPL/ROM* SK6 .... 48 F4
NWCHW CW8 .... 152 A2
Sandiway Dr *DID/WITH* M20............. 45 G1
Sandiway La *NWCHE* CW9.............. 103 G2
Sandiway Pk *NWCHW* CW8............ 128 E8
Sandiway Pl *ALT* WA14 .... 42 D7 2
Sandiway Rd *ALT* WA14 .... 42 D6
CW/HAS CW1 .... 221 G6
WILM/AE SK9 .... 64 D7
Sand La *MCFLDN* SK10 .... 109 M7
Sandle Bridge La *KNUT* WA16 .... 108 E7
Sandle Bridge Ri *WILM/AE* SK9.... 108 F5
Sandon Crs *NSTN* CH64 .... 91 L7
Sandon Park Gdns
CW/SHV CW2 .... 220 D8 1
Sandon Pl *WDN* WA8 .... 53 K3
Sandon Rd *CHNE* CH2 .... 145 K8
Sandon St *CW/HAS* CW1 .... 19 G4
Sandown Cl *GOL/RIS/CU* WA3 .... 24 F8 1
MWCH CW10 .... 179 J4
RUNC WA7 .... 73 J6
WILM/AE SK9 .... 84 D4 8
Sandown Crs *NWCHW* CW8 .... 152 A2
Sandown Dr *HALE/TIMP* WA15 .... 62 D6
SALE M33 .... 42 E1
Sandown Pl *MCFLDS* SK11 ...... 137 M5 3
Sandown Rd *BRAM/HZG* SK7 .... 67 G3
CQ CH5 .... 142 A8
CW/HAS CW1 .... 221 J5
EDGY/DAV SK3 .... 46 B4
Sandpiper Cl *CW/HAS* CW1 ...... 220 F5 3
NEWLW WA12 .... 22 C8 6
Sandpiper Ct *CHSW/BR* CH4 .... 192 B2
Sandpiper Dr *EDGY/DAV* SK3 .... 46 D6
Sandpiper Gv *HLWD* L26 .... 50 E3 8
Sandra Dr *NEWLW* WA12 .... 27 K1
Sandringham Av *CHSE* CH3 .... 170 A2
FROD/HEL WA6 .... 124 B1
Sandringham Cl *ALT* WA14 .... 60 F3 1
NWCHE CW9 .... 129 L8 3
WSFD CW7 .... 177 J1
Sandringham Dr *CW/SHV* CW2 .. 237 L5
HTNM SK4 .... 46 A3
POY/DIS SK12 .... 86 D1
WARRW/BUR WA5 .... 36 C8
Sandringham Gdns *EP* CH65 .... 121 K2 7
Sandringham Rd
BRAM/HZG SK7 .... 66 F2
CHD/CHDH SK8 .... 65 G1
MCFLDN SK10 .... 15 L3
MPL/ROM SK6 .... 47 J1
WDN WA8 .... 33 M8
Sandringham Wy
WILM/AE SK9 .... 84 A6 3
Sandrock Rd *CHSE* CH3 .... 170 E5
Sandsdown Cl *BIDD* ST8 .... 227 J3
Sandside Rd *ALS/KID* ST7 .... 241 H1 2
Sands Rd *ALS/KID* ST7 .... 226 E6
Sandstone Cl *RAIN/WH* L35............ 33 J3
Sandstone Trail *FROD/HEL* WA6.. 124 F2
MALPAS SY14 .... 231 K6
MALPAS SY14 .... 246 F4
NWCHW CW8 .... 150 A3
TPLY/KEL CW6 .... 197 G8
TPLY/KEL CW6 .... 215 M2
Sandwich Dr *MCFLDN* SK10 .... 138 C1
Sandwood Av *CHSW/BR* CH4 .. 190 B1 6
Sandy Brow La *GOL/RIS/CU* WA3.. 28 E2
Sandy Cl *MCFLDN* SK10 .... 112 F5
Sandyhill Pl *WSFD* CW7 .... 177 K6 1
Sandyhill Rd *WSFD* CW7 .... 177 K5 1
Sandylands Crs *ALS/KID* ST7 .... 224 F7
Sandylands Pk *CW/SHV* CW2 .... 237 K5
Sandy La *CHSE* CH3 .... 170 A4
CHSE CH3 .... 172 C1
CHSE CH3 .... 193 J1
CHSE CH3 .... 231 J5
CHSW/BR CH4 .... 168 D6
CHSW/BR CH4 .... 190 A6
CONG CW12 .... 182 E1
CONG CW12 .... 206 E6
CONG CW12 .... 206 D1
CONG CW12 .... 207 H2
CQ CH5 .... 142 F5
FROD/HEL WA6 .... 124 B2
GOL/RIS/CU WA3 .... 24 A2
GOL/RIS/CU WA3 .... 29 G3
HOLMCH CW4................................. 157 J3
KNUT WA16.................................... 132 E6
KNUT WA16.................................... 133 J1
LYMM WA13 .... 40 B7
MALPAS SY14 .... 232 B3
MALPAS SY14 .... 256 E4
MCFLDN SK10................................. 137 J2
MPL/ROM SK6 .... 48 C1
NANT CW5....................................... 252 F8
NANT CW5....................................... 262 C2
NEWLW WA12 .... 22 F4
NSTN CH64 .... 92 A6
NTHM/RTH M23 .... 43 K5
NWCHW CW8 .... 128 B1
NWCHW CW8 .... 152 C6
RDSH SK5 .... 2 F1
RUNC WA7 .... 8 B8
RUNC WA7 .... 74 E6
SBCH CW11.................................... 203 K7
SBCH CW11.................................... 223 G5
WARRN/WOL WA2 .... 37 H1
WARRS WA4 .... 56 D4
WARRW/BUR WA5 .... 36 A8
WDN WA8 .... 33 L8
WDN WA8 .... 35 H6
WILM/AE SK9 .... 83 K4
Sandy La West
WARRN/WOL WA2 .... 37 G1
Sandy Moor La *RUNC* WA7 .... 74 D1
Sandymoor La *RUNC* WA7................ 74 D1
Sandy Rd *BIDD* ST8......................... 227 J2
BURS/TUN ST6 .... 243 K5
Sandy Wy *CQ* CH5........................... 166 A3
Sankey La *WARRS* WA4 .... 75 M4
Sankey St *GOL/RIS/CU* WA3 ...... 23 G4 6
NEWLW WA12 .... 27 G1
WARR WA1 .... 4 E7
WDN WA8 .... 7 G9
Sankey Wy *WARRW/BUR* WA5 .... 4 A7
Santon Dr *GOL/RIS/CU* WA3 ...... 23 L4 5
Sapling Gv *SALE* M33 .... 42 D2
Sapling La *TPLY/KEL* CW6 .... 197 L1
Sargent Rd *MPL/ROM* SK6 .... 47 K2
Sarn Av *WYTH/NTH* M22 .... 44 D8
Sarn Bank Rd *MALPAS* SY14 .... 256 E6
Sarn Br *MALPAS* SY14...................... 256 E6
Sarn Rd *MALPAS* SY14 .... 256 D4
Sarra La *CHSE* CH3......................... 215 H7
Sarsfield Av *GOL/RIS/CU* WA3......... 23 K4
Saughall Cl *NWCHE* CW9 .... 129 L8
Saughall Hey *CH/BCN* CH1 .... 144 A3
Saughall Rd *CH/BCN* CH1 .... 16 C1
Saundersfoot Cl
WARRW/BUR WA5 .... 36 E2
Saunders St *CW/HAS* CW1............... 18 D3
Saville Av *WARRW/BUR* WA5............. 4 D2
Saville Rd *CHD/CHDH* SK8 .... 45 H6
Saville St *MCFLDS* SK11 .... 15 K8
Savoy Rd *CW/HAS* CW1 .... 239 G4
Sawley Av *GOL/RIS/CU* WA3 .... 23 K3
Sawley Cl *GOL/RIS/CU* WA3............. 30 A2
RUNC WA7 .... 74 E5
Sawley Dr *CHD/CHDH* SK8............... 65 H6
Sawpit St *LYMM* WA13...................... 41 G5
Sawyer Dr *BIDD* ST8......................... 227 J3
Saxfield Dr *NTHM/RTH* M23 .... 44 C6
Saxon Crossway *WSFD* CW7........... 177 H3
Saxon Rd *RUNC* WA7 .... 9 L3
Saxons La *NWCHW* CW8 .... 12 E6
Saxon Ter *WDN* WA8 .... 7 K3
Saxon Wy *CH/BCN* CH1 .... 144 E6
GTS/LS CH66................................... 120 F4
Sayce St *WDN* WA8............................ 7 J3
Scafell Av *WARRN/WOL* WA2 ...... 37 J1 3
Scafell Cl *BEB* CH63 .... 93 K1 2
MPL/ROM SK6 .... 67 L4
NTHLY L27... 51 G1
Scaife Rd *NANT* CW5 .... 21 G6
Scaliot Cl *NM/HAY* SK22 .... 69 H4 2
Scarisbrick Av *DID/WITH* M20 .... 45 K1 5

Scar La MALPAS SY14 ..... 245 M2
Sceptre Cl NEWLW WA12 ..... 27 G1[7]
Schofield Gdns LEIGH WN7 ..... 24 E1[5]
Schofield St LEIGH WN7 ..... 24 E1
Scholars Green La LYMM WA13 ..... 58 F1
School Av NSTN CH64 ..... 91 M6
School Bank FROD/HEL WA6 ..... 127 G6[2]
School Brow MPL/ROM SK6 ..... 48 A2
  WARR WA1 ..... 5 J6
School Cl KNUT WA16 ..... 106 E1
  POY/DIS SK12 ..... 86 F1
  WHITCH SY13 ..... 260 E4
School Ct EDGY/DAV SK3 ..... 46 F6[8]
School Crs CW/HAS CW1 ..... 19 K4
School Dr NWCHW CW8 ..... 129 G1
School Field Cl
  AUD/MAD/W CW3 ..... 274 F1
School Gn MALPAS SY14 ..... 230 C3[2]
School La ALT WA14 ..... 41 K8
  AUD/MAD/W CW3 ..... 264 A8
  AUD/MAD/W CW3 ..... 266 F8
  CHD/CHDH SK8 ..... 65 G4[2]
  CHNE CH2 ..... 123 G1
  CHNE CH2 ..... 146 E4
  CHSE CH3 ..... 146 E7
  CHSE CH3 ..... 211 M2
  CHSE CH3 ..... 215 H7
  CONG CW12 ..... 184 D4
  CONG CW12 ..... 207 H4
  DID/WITH M20 ..... 45 J1
  FROD/HEL WA6 ..... 99 J5[2]
  FROD/HEL WA6 ..... 125 G7
  FROD/HEL WA6 ..... 126 D7
  GOL/RIS/CU WA3 ..... 30 C7
  GOL/RIS/CU WA3 ..... 40 A2
  GTS/LS CH66 ..... 93 M3
  HUY L36 ..... 32 A2
  IRL M44 ..... 31 K7
  IRL M44 ..... 31 M2
  KNUT WA16 ..... 105 J2
  KNUT WA16 ..... 134 A1
  MCFLDN SK10 ..... 110 F6
  MCFLDS SK11 ..... 136 F6
  MCFLDS SK11 ..... 160 C7
  MPL/ROM SK6 ..... 49 H1
  NANT CW5 ..... 20 E5
  NSTN CH64 ..... 91 H3
  NSTN CH64 ..... 91 M6
  NSTN CH64 ..... 92 B2
  NWCHE CW9 ..... 103 H1
  NWCHE CW9 ..... 104 B4
  NWCHE CW9 ..... 131 C2
  NWCHE CW9 ..... 153 L4
  NWCHW CW8 ..... 129 J8
  NWCHW CW8 ..... 152 A2
  POY/DIS SK12 ..... 66 F8[4]
  POY/DIS SK12 ..... 86 F1
  RAIN/WH L35 ..... 33 M3
  RUNC WA7 ..... 73 H4
  SBCH CW11 ..... 181 M7
  SBCH CW11 ..... 202 D5
  SBCH CW11 ..... 203 K5
  SBCH CW11 ..... 204 E6
  SBCH CW11 ..... 205 M7
  TPLY/KEL CW6 ..... 216 D3
  WARRS WA4 ..... 76 E6
  WDN WA8 ..... 34 E5
  WHITCH SY13 ..... 260 E4
  WLTN L25 ..... 50 A3
School Rd EP CH65 ..... 10 C7
  HALE/TIMP WA15 ..... 61 M1
  NWCHE CW9 ..... 130 D6
  WARRN/WOL WA2 ..... 37 J3
  WILM/AE SK9 ..... 64 D8
  WSFD CW7 ..... 153 K7
  WSFD CW7 ..... 178 A2
School Rd North NWCHE CW9 ..... 130 E6
School Rd South NWCHE CW9 ..... 130 E6
Schools Hl CHD/CHDH SK8 ..... 64 D1
School St BRAM/HZG SK7 ..... 66 E2
  CHNE CH2 ..... 17 K1
  CW/HAS CW1 ..... 222 D7
  GOL/RIS/CU WA3 ..... 23 G4
  NEWLW WA12 ..... 27 H1
  WARRS WA4 ..... 5 H9
School Wy NWCHE CW9 ..... 13 J2
  SPK/HALE L24 ..... 70 B1
  WDN WA8 ..... 53 K1
Schooner Cl RUNC WA7 ..... 74 D6[4]
Science Rd SPK/HALE L24 ..... 50 C8
Scilly Cl EP CH65 ..... 121 J3
Scotch Hall La NWCHE CW9 ..... 102 F1
Scotland Rd WARR WA1 ..... 5 C6
Scotland St WHITCH SY13 ..... 269 M5
Scots Rd CQ CH5 ..... 166 D2
Scott Av CW/HAS CW1 ..... 19 M3
  HUY L36 ..... 32 A4
  RAIN/WH L35 ..... 32 F1
  WDN WA8 ..... 6 E4
Scott Cl ALS/KID ST7 ..... 224 E4[8]
  MCFLDN SK10 ..... 139 G5[6]
  SBCH CW11 ..... 203 K6
Scott Dr MPL/ROM SK6 ..... 49 H4
Scotthorpe Cl MCFLDS SK11 ..... 137 M6[8]
Scotton Av GTS/LS CH66 ..... 94 B7
Scott Rd BURS/TUN ST6 ..... 243 M7[7]
  GOL/RIS/CU WA3 ..... 23 K3
  MCFLDN SK10 ..... 112 A5
Scotts Av STHEL WA9 ..... 34 A1
Scott St WARRN/WOL WA2 ..... 5 H4
Scout Dr NTHM/RTH M23 ..... 43 M8
Scragg St ALS/KID ST7 ..... 243 M4
Scroggins La PART M31 ..... 31 L8
Sea Bank MWCH CW10 ..... 179 K3
Seabury St WARRS WA4 ..... 57 G1
Seacombe Cl GTS/LS CH66 ..... 120 E1
Seacombe Gv EDGY/DAV SK3 ..... 46 B4
Seaford Cl RUNC WA7 ..... 74 D3
Seaford Pl WARRN/WOL WA2 ..... 28 A8
Seagull Cl CW/HAS CW1 ..... 19 M2
Seahill Rd CH/BCN CH1 ..... 143 M4
Sealand Av CQ CH5 ..... 142 F5
Sealand Cl SALE M33 ..... 43 L2
  WARRN/WOL WA2 ..... 37 L5[2]
Sealand Rd CH/BCN CH1 ..... 16 A3
  CQ CH5 ..... 143 H5
  NTHM/RTH M23 ..... 43 M2
Sea La RUNC WA7 ..... 73 K2

Seal Rd BRAM/HZG SK7 ..... 65 M4
Seamon's Dr ALT WA14 ..... 42 A6[2]
Seamon's Rd ALT WA14 ..... 42 A6
Seathwaite Grove Cl RUNC WA7 ..... 73 L7
Seaton Cl BRAM/HZG SK7 ..... 66 D3
  CW/HAS CW1 ..... 221 H4
Seaton Pk RUNC WA7 ..... 74 E1
Seaton St WSFD CW7 ..... 178 D3
Sea Vw NSTN CH64 ..... 91 L8
Seaville St CHSE CH3 ..... 17 K4
Secker Av WARRS WA4 ..... 56 D2
Secker Cl WARRS WA4 ..... 56 D2
Second Av ALS/KID ST7 ..... 242 E5
  CQ CH5 ..... 142 F1
  CW/HAS CW1 ..... 19 L9
  FLINT CH6 ..... 112 A7
  MCFLDN SK10 ..... 86 D3
  RUNC WA7 ..... 73 M4
  SBCH CW11 ..... 204 A7
Second Dig La NANT CW5 ..... 252 C5
Second Wood St NANT CW5 ..... 20 D5
Sedbergh Cl HOLMCH CW4 ..... 181 G1
Sedbergh Gv RUNC WA7 ..... 73 L7
Sedburgh Cl SALE M33 ..... 42 D1[5]
Sedbury Cl NTHM/RTH M23 ..... 43 M3[5]
Seddon Av WA14 ..... 61 K2
Seddon St MWCH CW10 ..... 179 J2
Sedgefield Cl MCFLDN SK10 ..... 112 C8
Sedgefield Rd CH/BCN CH1 ..... 16 C5
Sedgeford WHITCH SY13 ..... 270 A6
Sedgemoor Cl WILM/AE SK9 ..... 83 H2[6]
Sedgewick Crs
  WARRW/BUR WA5 ..... 26 E6[3]
Sedgmere Av CW/HAS CW1 ..... 221 G4
Sedum Cl CHSE CH3 ..... 170 A6
Sefton Av CONG CW12 ..... 208 A3
  WDN WA8 ..... 53 G1[4]
Sefton Dr WILM/AE SK9 ..... 84 C2
Sefton Rd CHNE CH2 ..... 146 A8
Sefton St NEWLW WA12 ..... 26 F1
Selborne RAIN/WH L35 ..... 32 F2
Selbourne Dr BURS/TUN ST6 ..... 243 L5
Selby Cl POY/DIS SK12 ..... 66 D7[8]
  RUNC WA7 ..... 54 E8
Selby Gdns CHD/CHDH SK8 ..... 65 J6
Selby Gn GTS/LS CH66 ..... 94 B7
Selby St WARRW/BUR WA5 ..... 4 A7
Selkirk Av WARRS WA4 ..... 57 L1[5]
Selkirk Cl GTS/LS CH66 ..... 93 M7[2]
  MCFLDN SK10 ..... 137 M2
Selkirk Dr CHSW/BR CH4 ..... 169 G5
  HOLMCH 181 H1
Selkirk Rd CHSW/BR CH4 ..... 16 B9
Seller St CH/BCN CH1 ..... 17 J4
Selsdon Cl CW/HAS CW1 ..... 169 J5[8]
Selsey Av EDGY/DAV SK3 ..... 45 M5
  SALE M33 ..... 42 F1
Selsey Cl CW/HAS CW1 ..... 221 H4[2]
Selsey Dr DID/WITH M20 ..... 45 J4
Selside Rd NTHLY L27 ..... 51 C1
Selstead Rd WYTH/NTH M22 ..... 63 J3
Selworth Cl HALE/TIMP WA15 ..... 42 E6[8]
Selworthy Dr CW/HAS CW1 ..... 221 H5
  WARRS WA4 ..... 57 K1
Selwyn Cl WDN WA8 ..... 53 K1[7]
Selwyn Dr CHD/CHDH SK8 ..... 65 J5
  MCFLDS SK11 ..... 162 F1[9]
Semer Cl CONG CW12 ..... 185 G8
Seneschal Ct RUNC WA7 ..... 73 L6[4]
Senna La NWCHE CW9 ..... 103 H4
Sennen Cl RUNC WA7 ..... 74 B7
Sens Cl CH/BCN CH1 ..... 16 E4
Sephton Av GOL/RIS/CU WA3 ..... 29 L1
Serenity La CQ CH5 ..... 166 B8
Sergeant York Loop
  WARRW/BUR WA5 ..... 36 B7[8]
Serin Cl NEWLW WA12 ..... 27 J1
  OFTN SK2 ..... 47 M8
The Serpentine CHSW/BR CH4 ..... 16 C9
Service St HTNM SK4 ..... 46 B4
Service Cl EP CH65 ..... 94 F6
Sett Valley Trail NM/HAY SK22 ..... 69 M2
Sevenoaks Cl MCFLDN SK10 ..... 14 C1
Sevenoaks Rd CHD/CHDH SK8 ..... 45 H6
Seven Sisters La KNUT WA16 ..... 107 J8
Seven Stiles Dr MPL/ROM SK6 ..... 48 E5
Severn Cl ALT WA14 ..... 42 C6
  BIDD ST8 ..... 227 L4
  CONG CW12 ..... 207 M3
  WARRN/WOL WA2 ..... 37 L2[8]
  WDN WA8 ..... 53 M1
Severn Dr BRAM/HZG SK7 ..... 65 J6
Severn Rd GOL/RIS/CU WA3 ..... 29 M2
  RAIN/WH L35 ..... 33 H1
Severnvale EP CH65 ..... 121 G1
Sewell St RUNC WA7 ..... 9 K3
Sextant Cl RUNC WA7 ..... 74 D6
Sexton Av STHEL WA9 ..... 26 B2
Seymore Cha KNUT WA16 ..... 107 G4
Seymour Dr GTS/LS CH66 ..... 94 E6
  WARR WA1 ..... 38 A5
Seymour La HALE/TIMP WA15 ..... 43 G7
  MPL/ROM SK6 ..... 48 E6
Seymour Rd CHD/CHDH SK8 ..... 65 G4
  OFTN SK2 ..... 47 H6

Shakespeare Dr CHD/CHDH SK8 ..... 45 M6
  CW/HAS CW1 ..... 222 A8
Shakespeare Gv
  WARRN/WOL WA2 ..... 37 H2
Shakespeare Rd MPL/ROM SK6 ..... 47 L1
  NSTN CH64 ..... 91 L3
  STHEL WA9 ..... 34 A2
  WDN WA8 ..... 7 G1[8]
Shakespeare Wy WHITCH SY13 ..... 270 C6
Shalcombe Cl HLWD L26 ..... 51 G5
Shalford Dr WYTH/NTH M22 ..... 63 K4
Shallacres EP CH65 ..... 94 F5
Shallcross Av CHF/WBR SK23 ..... 89 L8
  CHF/WBR SK23 ..... 89 L7
Shallcross Mill Rd
  CHF/WBR SK23 ..... 89 L7
Shallcross Rd CHF/WBR SK23 ..... 89 L8
Shandon Av WYTH/NTH M22 ..... 44 D3
Shanklin Cl WARRW/BUR WA5 ..... 35 J6
Shannon Cl CHSW/BR CH4 ..... 168 E7[8]
  NANT CW5 ..... 237 K7
Shannon Dr BURS/TUN ST6 ..... 243 H5
Shannon Rd WYTH/NTH M22 ..... 63 L1
Shap Av HALE/TIMP WA15 ..... 43 K7[8]
Shargate Cl WILM/AE SK9 ..... 84 C3[8]
Sharnbrook Dr CW/SHV CW2 ..... 237 L1
Sharon Park Cl WARRS WA4 ..... 57 J3
Sharples St HTNM SK4 ..... 2 E1
Sharpley St MCFLDN SK10 ..... 14 E4[8]
Sharps Dr WHITCH SY13 ..... 269 L5
Sharp St WARRN/WOL WA2 ..... 5 H3
  WDN WA8 ..... 7 H4
Sharrington Dr NTHM/RTH M23 ..... 43 L6
Sharston Crs KNUT WA16 ..... 107 H3
Sharston Rd WYTH/NTH M22 ..... 44 E5
Shavington Av CHNE CH2 ..... 145 M8
Shavington Wy NWCHE CW9 ..... 129 L8
Shawbury Av SALE M33 ..... 42 F2[8]
Shawbury Rd NTHM/RTH M23 ..... 44 B8
Shaw Cl GTS/LS CH66 ..... 94 E8
Shawcross Av WYTH/NTH M22 ..... 44 F4
Shawcross St STKP SK1 ..... 3 H8
Shawdene Rd WYTH/NTH M22 ..... 44 C4
Shaw Dr KNUT WA16 ..... 107 J1
Shawell Ct WDN WA8 ..... 53 L2[8]
Shaw Entry WDN WA8 ..... 33 G5
Shaw Heath EDGY/DAV SK3 ..... 2 F8
Shaw Rd SPK/HALE L24 ..... 50 D7
Shaw Rd South
  EDGY/DAV SK3 ..... 46 F5[11]
Shaw's Av WARRN/WOL WA2 ..... 5 H1
Shaws La MCFLDN SK10 ..... 111 J4
  WSFD CW7 ..... 153 M8
Shaw's Rd ALT WA14 ..... 42 D8
Shaw St BIDD ST8 ..... 227 J5
  GOL/RIS/CU WA3 ..... 30 A1
  MCFLDS SK11 ..... 14 F5
  RUNC WA7 ..... 8 F3
  WARRN/WOL WA2 ..... 5 G4
Shay Av HALE/TIMP WA15 ..... 62 E3
Shayfield Av WYTH/NTH M22 ..... 44 D7[8]
Shayfield Dr WYTH/NTH M22 ..... 44 D7
Shayfield Rd WYTH/NTH M22 ..... 44 D7
Shay La CHSE CH3 ..... 172 E1
  HALE/TIMP WA15 ..... 62 D3
  MALPAS SY14 ..... 247 G3
Shay's La TPLY/KEL CW6 ..... 151 L8
Sheaf Cl CHSE CH3 ..... 172 C2
Shearbrook La HOLMCH CW4 ..... 157 K3
Sheardhall Av CHF/WBR SK23 ..... 68 E7
Shearwater Rd OFTN SK2 ..... 47 M7
Sheath St NWCHE CW9 ..... 13 H2
Shed La CHSE CH3 ..... 170 A2
Sheepfield Cl GTS/LS CH66 ..... 94 C5[8]
Sheerwater Cl WARR WA1 ..... 37 M5
Sheffield Cl WARRW/BUR WA5 ..... 36 C7[8]
Sheffield St WARRW/BUR WA5 ..... 2 F2
Sheiling Ct ALT WA14 ..... 42 C8
The Sheilings
  GOL/RIS/CU WA3 ..... 23 M4[8]
Shelagh Av WDN WA8 ..... 7 H3
Shelbourne Ms MCFLDN SK10 ..... 137 M4[8]
Shelburne Dr CW/HAS CW1 ..... 222 C7
Sheldon Av CHSE CH3 ..... 170 B2
  CONG CW12 ..... 170 A5
Sheldon Cl PART M31 ..... 40 F1[8]
Sheldon Rd BRAM/HZG SK7 ..... 66 E5
  POY/DIS SK12 ..... 87 J2
Sheldrake Cl NSTN CH64 ..... 91 L7
Sheldrake Rd ALT WA14 ..... 42 B4
Sheldwich Cl LEIGH WN7 ..... 24 F1[8]
  LEIGH WN7 ..... 24 F1[8]
Shelford Rd BURS/TUN ST6 ..... 243 K6
Shelley Av NWCHE CW9 ..... 104 F7
Shelley Cl ALS/KID ST7 ..... 224 E4
  ALS/KID ST7 ..... 243 G4
  CW/HAS CW1 ..... 19 L3
  MWCH CW10 ..... 179 L7[8]
Shelley Ct CHD/CHDH SK8 ..... 65 G3
  SBCH CW11 ..... 203 K6[8]
Shelley Dr CW/SHV CW2 ..... 237 M3[8]
Shelley Gv WARRS WA4 ..... 37 M8[8]
Shelley Pl RAIN/WH L35 ..... 32 F1[8]
Shelley Rd CH/BCN CH1 ..... 144 F7
  WDN WA8 ..... 7 G2
Shelley St STHEL WA9 ..... 34 B2
Shellow La MCFLDS SK11 ..... 161 J7[8]
Shelton Cl WDN WA8 ..... 53 M1[8]
Shenhurst Cl WILM/AE SK9 ..... 83 L8[2]
Shentonfield Rd
  WYTH/NTH M22 ..... 44 E6
Shenton Park La SALE M33 ..... 42 C5[8]
Shepcroft La WARRS WA4 ..... 76 C2
Shepherds Fold Dr WSFD CW7 ..... 177 J1
Shepherd's La CHNE CH2 ..... 145 K7
Shepherd St BIDD ST8 ..... 227 J5
Shepley Cl BRAM/HZG SK7 ..... 66 D3
Shepley La MPL/ROM SK6 ..... 48 F8
Sheppard Cl CW/HAS CW1 ..... 19 M3
Sheppenhall Gv NANT CW5 ..... 262 C3
Sheppenhall La NANT CW5 ..... 262 C3
Shepperton Ct WARRS WA4 ..... 56 D6
Shepsides Cl GTS/LS CH66 ..... 120 C1
Shepton Dr NTHM/RTH M23 ..... 63 G2[8]
Shepton Rd GTS/LS CH66 ..... 120 E2
  NTHM/RTH M23 ..... 43 M1[8]
Sheraton Rd CHSE CH3 ..... 171 H7

Sherborne Av WLTN L25 ..... 50 D4
Sherborne Cl RUNC WA7 ..... 74 F1
  CW/HAS CW1 ..... 221 K6
  EDGY/DAV SK3 ..... 46 A5
Sherbourne Av CHSW/BR CH4 ..... 169 H7
Sherbourne Cl CHD/CHDH SK8 ..... 65 H6
Sherbourne Rd EP CH65 ..... 121 K3[8]
  MCFLDS SK11 ..... 137 M5[8]
Sherbourne Wy
  WARRW/BUR WA5 ..... 26 F6[7]
Sherbrook Cl SALE M33 ..... 42 F1[8]
Sherbrooke Rd POY/DIS SK12 ..... 68 D5
Sherbrook Ri WILM/AE SK9 ..... 84 C6
Sherford Cl BRAM/HZG SK7 ..... 66 A2
Sheridan Av GOL/RIS/CU WA3 ..... 23 K5[8]
Sheridan Cl CW/HAS CW1 ..... 221 H5
Sheri Dr NEWLW WA12 ..... 27 K2
Sheringham
  CHSW/BR CH4 ..... 168 E7[8]
Sheringham Dr CW/HAS CW1 ..... 221 H5
Sheringham Rd
  WARRW/BUR WA5 ..... 35 L6[8]
Sherman Dr RAIN/WH L35 ..... 33 K3
Sherratt Cl CONG CW12 ..... 207 L2
Sherrington's La CHSE CH3 ..... 231 K4
Sherrymill Hl WHITCH SY13 ..... 269 M4
Sherway Dr HALE/TIMP WA15 ..... 43 J6
Sherwin St CW/SHV CW2 ..... 18 F8
Sherwood Av HTNM SK4 ..... 46 A3
Sherwood Cl MPL/ROM SK6 ..... 48 F8[8]
  WDN WA8 ..... 52 C3
Sherwood Crs
  WARRW/BUR WA5 ..... 26 E6[4]
  LEIGH WN7 ..... 25 H2[8]
Sherwood Gv FROD/HEL WA6 ..... 124 A1
Sherwood Rd CH/BCN CH1 ..... 144 E7
Shetland Cl WARRN/WOL WA2 ..... 28 E8[8]
  WDN WA8 ..... 53 L1[8]
Shetland Dr EP CH65 ..... 121 J3
Shevington Cl WDN WA8 ..... 53 L1[7]
Shevington Gdns
  NTHM/RTH M23 ..... 44 B3[8]
Shield St EDGY/DAV SK3 ..... 2 E7
Shiers Dr CHD/CHDH SK8 ..... 45 L8
Shiggins Cl WARRW/BUR WA5 ..... 26 F4
Shillingford Cl WARRS WA4 ..... 56 F7
Shilton Cl MWCH CW10 ..... 179 L6[8]
Shipbrook Rd CHNE CH2 ..... 145 M6[8]
Shipgate St CH/BCN CH1 ..... 17 G7
Ship St FROD/HEL WA6 ..... 99 J2
Shipton Cl WARRW/BUR WA5 ..... 36 B4
  WDN WA8 ..... 52 D1[8]
Shiredale Cl CHD/CHDH SK8 ..... 46 B8
Shirley Av CHD/CHDH SK8 ..... 64 C6
  MPL/ROM SK6 ..... 48 E6[8]
Shirley Cl BRAM/HZG SK7 ..... 66 C2[8]
Shirley Dr WARRS WA4 ..... 57 C2
Shirley Gv EDGY/DAV SK3 ..... 46 E7
Shirley Cl MCFLDN SK10 ..... 112 A6
Shirleys Dr MCFLDN SK10 ..... 112 A6
Shocklach Rd CHNE CH2 ..... 145 M6[8]
Shone Av WYTH/NTH M22 ..... 63 M2[8]
Shones Cft NSTN CH64 ..... 92 A7
Shop La TPLY/KEL CW6 ..... 175 M2
Shordley Cl WRX/GR/LL L12 ..... 33 C5[8]
Shoreham Dr WARRW/BUR WA5 ..... 55 C1
Shores Green Dr NWCHE CW9 ..... 104 F7
Shores La NANT CW5 ..... 235 K5
Short Cl NEWLW WA12 ..... 26 E1
Shortland Crs BNG/LEV M19 ..... 45 K1
Short St BRAM/HZG SK7 ..... 66 D1
  GOL/RIS/CU WA3 ..... 23 H3[8]
  HTNM SK4 ..... 2 E2
  NEWLW WA12 ..... 26 E1
  WDN WA8 ..... 53 G7[8]
Short St East HTNM SK4 ..... 2 F2
Shorwell Cl WARRW/BUR WA5 ..... 35 J5
Shotwick La CH/BCN CH1 ..... 119 H8
Shotwick Rd EP CH65 ..... 118 E8
Shrewbridge Crs NANT CW5 ..... 20 E7
Shrewbridge Rd NANT CW5 ..... 20 D9
Shrewsbury Gdns
  CHD/CHDH SK8 ..... 65 J6[8]
Shrewsbury Rd SALE M33 ..... 43 C2[8]
Shrewsbury St WARRS WA4 ..... 56 D1
Shrewsbury Wy
  CHSW/BR CH4 ..... 168 F6[8]
Shrigley Cl WILM/AE SK9 ..... 84 D3
Shrigley Ri MCFLDN SK10 ..... 113 J3[8]
Shrigley Rd MCFLDN SK10 ..... 87 H8
  POY/DIS SK12 ..... 87 J2
Shropshire Cl MWCH CW10 ..... 179 J4
  WARR WA1 ..... 38 E5
Shropshire Rd EP CH65 ..... 121 J3
Shropshire Wy WHITCH SY13 ..... 259 K5
  WHITCH SY13 ..... 269 J8
Shuldham Cl KNUT WA16 ..... 59 J8
Shurlach Rd NWCHE CW9 ..... 130 D7
Shutley La NWCHW CW8 ..... 102 D7
Sibbersfield La CHSE CH3 ..... 211 M8
Sibell St CH/BCN CH1 ..... 17 J3
Sidcup Rd NTHM/RTH M23 ..... 43 M7
Siddall St NWCHE CW9 ..... 13 M2
Siddeley Cl CHSW/BR CH4 ..... 167 J8
Siddeley Dr NEWLW WA12 ..... 26 F1
Siddington Av EDGY/DAV SK3 ..... 46 C6
Siddington Bank MCFLDS SK11 ..... 159 M1
Siddington Rd POY/DIS SK12 ..... 86 F2
  WILM/AE SK9 ..... 64 D7[8]
Siddorn St WSFD CW7 ..... 177 J3[8]
Siddow Common LEIGH WN7 ..... 25 C1
Side Av ALT WA14 ..... 61 J3[8]
Side End La CHF/WBR SK23 ..... 114 F1
Side La TPLY/KEL CW6 ..... 172 E6
Sidlaw Cl GTS/LS CH66 ..... 94 A6
Sidmouth Cl WARRW/BUR WA5 ..... 35 L2[8]
Sidmouth Cl CHD/CHDH SK8 ..... 64 F6[8]
Sidney Rd NSTN CH64 ..... 91 M3
Siemens Rd IRL M44 ..... 31 L7
Sienna Cl IRL M44 ..... 31 L6[8]
Silcock St GOL/RIS/CU WA3 ..... 23 G4
Silk Hl CHF/WBR SK23 ..... 89 M4

Silk Mill St KNUT WA16 ..... 107 G2
The Silk Rd MCFLDN SK10 ..... 15 H4
  MCFLDN SK10 ..... 112 C6
  MCFLDN SK11 ..... 15 H5
Silkstone Crs RUNC WA7 ..... 74 B5[8]
Silk St CONG CW12 ..... 207 J2
Silsden Av GOL/RIS/CU WA3 ..... 24 B4
Silverbirch Cl SALE M33 ..... 42 D2[8]
Silverbirch Cft
  CHSW/BR CH4 ..... 190 B1[7]
Silverbirch Wy GTS/LS CH66 ..... 120 F4
Silverdale NWCHW CW8 ..... 12 D4
Silverdale Av FROD/HEL WA6 ..... 99 J5
  MPL/ROM SK6 ..... 67 L4
Silverdale Cl WILM/AE SK9 ..... 84 A8
  NEWLW WA12 ..... 56 B2
Silverdale Rd CHD/CHDH SK8 ..... 45 H8
  NEWLW WA12 ..... 56 B2
  WARRS WA4 ..... 56 B2
Silvergate Ct CONG CW12 ..... 207 L4
Silver La GOL/RIS/CU WA3 ..... 30 A5
Silvermine Cl ALS/KID ST7 ..... 243 H2[8]
Silverne Dr EP CH65 ..... 121 G2
Silverstone Crs BURS/TUN ST6 ..... 243 L1
Silver St MCFLDN SK10 ..... 113 H4[8]
  WARRN/WOL WA2 ..... 5 G4
Silverwood ALS/KID ST7 ..... 243 H3[8]
Simkin Av WARRS WA4 ..... 37 M8
Simons Cl RAIN/WH L35 ..... 32 C4
  SALE M33 ..... 43 G1[8]
Simonside WDN WA8 ..... 52 C3
Simons La FROD/HEL WA6 ..... 99 H6
Simonstone Rd CHSW/BR CH4 ..... 167 K8
Simonsway NTHM/RTH M23 ..... 63 G1
  WYTH/NTH M22 ..... 63 H1
Simonswood Cl
  MWCH CW10 ..... 179 H4[8]
Simpson Ct CW/HAS CW1 ..... 221 G3
Simpson La MCFLDN SK10 ..... 87 K5
Simpson Rd CHNE CH2 ..... 145 J4
Simpson St EDGY/DAV SK3 ..... 2 F8[8]
  WILM/AE SK9 ..... 83 M6[8]
Simpsons Wy CHSW/BR CH4 ..... 190 B1
Sinclair Av ALS/KID ST7 ..... 241 H1
  WARRN/WOL WA2 ..... 37 H2
Sinderland La ALT WA14 ..... 41 J3
  LYMM WA13 ..... 41 J3
Sinderland Rd ALT WA14 ..... 41 J3
  PART M31 ..... 41 J3
Singapore Av MANAIR M90 ..... 63 G4
Singleton Av CW/HAS CW1 ..... 221 J6
Singleton Rd EP CH65 ..... 94 F8
Siskin Cl NEWLW WA12 ..... 27 J1
Siskin Rd NM/HAY SK22 ..... 69 M1
Sitch La NM/HAY SK22 ..... 69 J4
Six Acre Gdns WARRS WA4 ..... 55 G7
Six Acre La RUNC WA7 ..... 55 G7
Sixth Av CQ CH5 ..... 142 E3
  FLINT CH6 ..... 116 A7
Skeath Cl SBCH CW11 ..... 204 D6
Skeffington Gv RAIN/WH L35 ..... 32 E2
Skellern St ALS/KID ST7 ..... 243 G1
Skellorn Green La MCFLDN SK10 ..... 86 F4
Skelton Rd ALT WA14 ..... 42 A8
Skiddaw Cl RUNC WA7 ..... 74 A8[8]
Skip's La CHSE CH3 ..... 170 E5
Skipton Cl BRAM/HZG SK7 ..... 66 C4
Skipton Dr GTS/LS CH66 ..... 94 C8
Skipton Rd HUY L36 ..... 32 B1[8]
Skye Cl EP CH65 ..... 121 J3
  WDN WA8 ..... 53 L1
Skylark Cl ALS/KID ST7 ..... 220 F5
Slacken La ALS/KID ST7 ..... 242 D2
Slack La CQ CH5 ..... 166 B7
Slack St MCFLDS SK11 ..... 15 J9[8]
  MCFLDS SK11 ..... 138 F7[8]
Slade La KNUT WA16 ..... 81 M5
Slade St NWCHE CW9 ..... 13 M2
Slag La GOL/RIS/CU WA3 ..... 23 M2
Slaidburn Crs
  GOL/RIS/CU WA3 ..... 22 F2[8]
Slater St BIDD ST8 ..... 227 J5
  MCFLDS SK11 ..... 14 E8
  WARRS WA4 ..... 5 K9
Sleddale Cl OFTN SK2 ..... 47 K7
Sledmoor Rd NTHM/RTH M23 ..... 43 M3
Sleeper's Wy MCFLDS SK11 ..... 139 L5
Simmonds Cl NWCHE CW9 ..... 153 L1
Slutchers La WARR WA1 ..... 4 F9
Small Av WARRN/WOL WA2 ..... 37 J2
Smallbrook La WHITCH SY13 ..... 269 L5
Small Crs WARRN/WOL WA2 ..... 37 J2
Small La KNUT WA16 ..... 81 M4
Smallman Rd CW/SHV CW2 ..... 18 D9
Smallshaw La AIMK WN4 ..... 22 A2[8]
Smethwick La SBCH CW11 ..... 182 E8
Smith Child St BURS/TUN ST6 ..... 243 K8
Smith Cl ALS/KID ST7 ..... 224 B8[8]
Smith Crs WARRN/WOL WA2 ..... 37 K4
Smith Dr WARRN/WOL WA2 ..... 37 K4
Smithfield Dr WRXS/E LL13 ..... 228 D4
Smithfield La SBCH CW11 ..... 204 C6
Smithfields CHSE CH3 ..... 214 C2
Smithfields St WRXS/E LL13 ..... 228 D4
Smith Gv CW/HAS CW1 ..... 221 J8
Smithills Cl GOL/RIS/CU WA3 ..... 29 K7[8]
Smith La KNUT WA16 ..... 114 A7
  MCFLDN SK10 ..... 114 A7
Smith Rd WDN WA8 ..... 6 F6
Smiths Lawn WILM/AE SK9 ..... 84 A7
Smith St CHD/CHDH SK8 ..... 45 M6[8]
  MCFLDS SK11 ..... 15 H9
  WARR WA1 ..... 5 H7
Smithy Bank WSFD CW7 ..... 200 A1
Smithy Brow GOL/RIS/CU WA3 ..... 28 F5
  MCFLDN SK10 ..... 113 J4
Smithy Cl CH/BCN CH1 ..... 144 A3
  NSTN CH64 ..... 92 A8[8]
  WDN WA8 ..... 33 J6
Smithy La ALT WA14 ..... 60 D1
  BIDD ST8 ..... 227 K2
  CHSE CH3 ..... 148 F2
  CONG CW12 ..... 184 B5
  CW/HAS CW1 ..... 220 E4

CW/SHV CW2 .... 239 J7
CW/SHV CW2 .... 240 D6
FROD/HEL WA6 .... 98 C7
FROD/HEL WA6 .... 126 B2
GOL/RIS/CU WA3 .... 29 C5
GTS/LS CH66 .... 94 C6
MALPAS SY14 .... 258 A2
MCFLDN SK10 .... 111 J2
MCFLDN SK10 .... 113 L7
MCFLDS SK11 .... 186 E6
MPL/ROM SK6 .... 49 M3
NSTN CH64 .... 93 C4
NWCHE CW9 .... 104 A4
NWCHE CW9 .... 131 G2
NWCHW CW8 .... 102 B6
NWCHW CW8 .... 128 A7
PART M31 .... 40 F1
TPLY/KEL CW6 .... 174 B6
WDN WA8 .... 33 J7
Smithy Pathway
CHSW/BR CH4 .... 168 F8
Smithy St BRAM/HZG SK7 .... 66 D1
The Smithy WRX/GR/LL LL12 .... 210 B5
Smithy Wk SBCH CW11 .... 222 F1
Smokehall La NWCHE CW9 .... 153 M6
Smokey La WHITCH SY13 .... 268 B4
Smokies Wy BIDD ST8 .... 227 J3
Smyth Rd WDN WA8 .... 53 K2
Snab La NSTN CH64 .... 91 M8
Snabwood Cl NSTN CH64 .... 91 L7
Snaefell Ri WARRS WA4 .... 56 C5
Snape La CW/SHV CW2 .... 239 K8
Snape Rd CW/SHV CW2 .... 238 D4
MCFLDN SK10 .... 138 E2
Snelson La KNUT WA16 .... 134 D1
KNUT WA16 .... 134 C5
Sneyd Pl BURS/TUN ST6 .... 243 J6
Snipe Cl POY/DIS SK12 .... 86 A1
Snowberry Cl WDN WA8 .... 34 E8
Snowdon Cl GTS/LS CH66 .... 94 A6
WARRW/BUR WA5 .... 35 L6
Snowdon Cresent
CHSW/BR CH4 .... 169 G7
Snowdon Dr CW/SHV CW2 .... 237 K1
Snowdonia Wy WSFD CW7 .... 177 H5
Snowdon St NWCHW CW8 .... 128 F1
Snowdrop Cl RUNC WA7 .... 73 M8
Snow Hl MCFLDS SK11 .... 15 J8
Soane Cl AIMK WN4 .... 22 D1
Solly Crs CONG CW12 .... 207 G2
Solvay Rd NWCHW CW8 .... 129 K2
Solway Cl WARRN/WOL WA2 .... 28 F8
Solway Gv RUNC WA7 .... 73 K7
Solway Rd WYTH/NTH M22 .... 44 E8
Somerby Dr WYTH/NTH M22 .... 63 J1
Somerford Av CW/SHV CW2 .... 18 A6
Somerford Cl SBCH CW11 .... 204 C4
Somerford Cl CHSW/BR CH4 .... 167 J8
Somerley Cl CW/HAS CW1 .... 221 H4
Somerset Av ALS/KID ST7 .... 242 F2
Somerset Cl CONG CW12 .... 184 D8
IRL M44 .... 31 K6
Somerset Rd ALT WA14 .... 42 D6
CHNE CH2 .... 145 M7
Somerset St CHNE CH2 .... 17 G2
Somerset Wy WARR WA1 .... 38 B4
Somerton Av SALE M33 .... 43 J1
WYTH/NTH M22 .... 63 J1
Somerton Rd MCFLDS SK11 .... 137 M6
NSTN CH64 .... 91 L7
Somerville Cl KNUT WA16 .... 59 J8
NSTN CH64 .... 91 L7
Somerville Crs EP CH65 .... 95 J8
Somerville Gdns
HALE/TIMP WA15 .... 42 F5
Somerville Rd WDN WA8 .... 6 B5
Somerville St CW/SHV CW2 .... 18 D8
Soot Hl NWCHW CW8 .... 129 J1
Sorbus Cl CHNE CH2 .... 123 J1
Sorbus Dr CW/HAS CW1 .... 221 L6
Sorrel Cl CHSE CH3 .... 170 A6
WARRN/WOL WA2 .... 38 C2
Sossmoss La MCFLDN SK10 .... 109 K6
Soudan Rd OFTN SK2 .... 47 G6
Sound La NANT CW5 .... 250 D6
Souter's La CH/BCN CH1 .... 17 H6
South Acre Ct MCFLDS SK11 .... 139 C5
WILM/AE SK9 .... 84 D1
Southampton Wy RUNC WA7 .... 74 E6
South Av CHNE CH2 .... 17 J2
CW/HAS CW1 .... 222 D8
LEIGH WN7 .... 25 J1
WARRN/WOL WA2 .... 5 H2
WARRS WA4 .... 56 C3
South Bank CH/BCN CH1 .... 145 J8
CQ CH5 .... 142 B8
Southbank NWCHE CW9 .... 104 A5
Southbank Av CW/SHV CW2 .... 238 C7
South Bank Cl WILM/AE SK9 .... 110 B2
South Bank Gv CONG CW12 .... 207 M2
South Bank Ter RUNC WA7 .... 72 C1
South Cheshire Wy
ALS/KID ST7 .... 224 E5
CW/SHV CW2 .... 253 M2
NANT CW5 .... 253 K6
NANT CW5 .... 262 A2
WHITCH SY13 .... 260 D5
South Cl TPLY/KEL CW6 .... 197 J2
WILM/AE SK9 .... 83 M6
South Crescent Rd
CHSW/BR CH4 .... 17 J7
South Cft TPLY/KEL CW6 .... 216 D6
South Crofts NANT CW5 .... 20 F6
South Dl WARRW/BUR WA5 .... 35 M7
Southdale Rd WARR WA1 .... 38 A5
Southdown Cl HTNM SK4 .... 2 D3
Southdown Crs CHD/CHDH SK8 .... 64 F4
South Downs KNUT WA16 .... 107 J3
South Downs Dr ALT WA14 .... 61 K4
South Downs Rd ALT WA14 .... 61 J3
South Dr CHD/CHDH SK8 .... 45 G8
HALE/TIMP WA15 .... 43 G5
KNUT WA16 .... 132 A1
NWCHE CW9 .... 130 D6
Southern Cl BRAM/HZG SK7 .... 65 M2
Southern Crs BRAM/HZG SK7 .... 65 M3
Southern Rd SPK/HALE L24 .... 70 E2
Southern St WARRS WA4 .... 56 C3
Southey Cl SBCH CW11 .... 203 K7

WDN WA8 .... 6 E4
Southfield MCFLDN SK10 .... 112 A8
Southfield Rd GTS/LS CH66 .... 94 C6
Southfields Cl KNUT WA16 .... 107 J1
Southfields Av
WARRW/BUR WA5 .... 35 M6
Southfields Cl NANT CW5 .... 253 G4
Southfields Dr
HALE/TIMP WA15 .... 43 H5
South Front RAIN/WH L35 .... 32 E4
South Gn CO CH5 .... 143 G6
South Gv SALE M33 .... 43 H1
WILM/AE SK9 .... 110 A3
South Hill Rd FROD/HEL WA6 .... 124 C1
Southlands HOLMCH CW4 .... 181 J2
Southlands Av
WARRW/BUR WA5 .... 54 F1
Southlands Ms RUNC WA7 .... 8 F6
Southlands Rd CONG CW12 .... 208 A3
Southlands Vw HOLMCH CW4 .... 157 L3
South La WDN WA8 .... 34 E7
South Md WLTN L25 .... 50 C3
South Md POY/DIS SK12 .... 66 B7
South Meade HALE/TIMP WA15 .... 43 G5
South Meadway MPL/ROM SK6 .... 67 M5
Southmoor Rd NTHM/RTH M23 .... 44 B5
South Oak La WILM/AE SK9 .... 83 M6
South Pde BRAM/HZG SK7 .... 65 M2
RUNC WA7 .... 8 A8
SPK/HALE L24 .... 70 E2
South Park Dr POY/DIS SK12 .... 66 E8
South Park Rd CHD/CHDH SK8 .... 45 H6
MCFLDS SK11 .... 14 F7
South Pier Rd EP CH65 .... 11 G3
Southpool Cl BRAM/HZG SK7 .... 66 A2
Southport St STHEL WA9 .... 26 A1
South Rd ALT WA14 .... 61 J2
EP CH65 .... 121 J1
SPK/HALE L24 .... 51 G8
South St ALS/KID ST7 .... 226 B6
CHSE CH3 .... 170 A3
CW/SHV CW2 .... 19 H8
WDN WA8 .... 7 J4
WILM/AE SK9 .... 110 A3
South Vale Crs HALE/TIMP WA15 .... 42 F7
South Vw BIDD ST8 .... 227 J4
HUY L36 .... 32 B2
South View Av MCFLDS SK11 .... 161 K2
South View Gdns
CHD/CHDH SK8 .... 64 C1
South View La WSFD CW7 .... 218 F2
South View Rd CH/BCN CH1 .... 16 D4
Southward Rd RNFD/HAY WA11 .... 22 A5
Southwark Pl WSFD CW7 .... 177 G4
South Wy CH/BCN CH1 .... 144 E8
Southway ALT WA14 .... 42 E6
RUNC WA7 .... 73 L5
WDN WA8 .... 6 A4
Southway Av WARRS WA4 .... 56 D5
Southwell Cl GOL/RIS/CU WA3 .... 23 J4
MPL/ROM SK6 .... 48 A5
South West Av MCFLDN SK10 .... 112 F5
Southwick Rd NTHM/RTH M23 .... 44 B5
Southwood Av RUNC WA7 .... 74 C2
Southwood Av OFTN SK2 .... 47 H8
Southworth Av
WARRW/BUR WA5 .... 36 F4
Southworth La
WARRN/WOL WA2 .... 28 D5
Southworth Rd NEWLW WA12 .... 22 F3
Sovereign Cl GOL/RIS/CU WA3 .... 23 L5
NWCHE CW9 .... 130 E6
RUNC WA7 .... 74 D5
Sovereign Ct GOL/RIS/CU WA3 .... 29 J8
Spalding Dr NTHM/RTH M23 .... 63 C2
Sparkford Av NTHM/RTH M23 .... 43 K3
Spark Hall Cl WARRS WA4 .... 76 E2
Spark La RUNC WA7 .... 73 M3
SBCH CW11 .... 205 J3
Spark Rd NTHM/RTH M23 .... 43 M5
Sparks Cl CHSE CH3 .... 170 B5
Sparrowbutts Gv
ALS/KID ST7 .... 243 J2
Sparrowhawk Cl HLWD L26 .... 50 E5
RUNC WA7 .... 74 A5
Sparrow La KNUT WA16 .... 107 H3
Sparthfield Rd HTNM SK4 .... 2 C2
Sparth La HTNM SK4 .... 2 C2
Spath La WILM/AE SK9 .... 64 D7
Spath La East CHD/CHDH SK8 .... 65 H7
Spath Rd DID/WITH M20 .... 45 G1
Spath Wk CHD/CHDH SK8 .... 65 H7
Spawell Cl GOL/RIS/CU WA3 .... 23 L3
Speakman Av NEWLW WA12 .... 22 B7
Speakman St RUNC WA7 .... 8 F1
Spedding Wy BIDD ST8 .... 227 L4
Speed's Wy CHSE CH3 .... 228 E2
Speedwell Cl CHSE CH3 .... 170 A4
GOL/RIS/CU WA3 .... 23 L4
Speke Bvd SPK/HALE L24 .... 70 B1
Speke Church Rd SPK/HALE L24 .... 70 B1
Speke Hall Av SPK/HALE L24 .... 50 B8
Speke Hall Rd SPK/HALE L24 .... 50 B7
WLTN L25 .... 50 B6
Speke Rd HLWD L26 .... 51 H6
WDN WA8 .... 51 M5
WLTN L25 .... 50 B3
Speke Town La SPK/HALE L24 .... 50 B8
Spencer Brook MCFLDN SK10 .... 111 M6
Spencer Cl ALS/KID ST7 .... 223 M8
CW/SHV CW2 .... 238 A4
WDN WA8 .... 6 E5
Spencer St NWCHW CW8 .... 12 F5
Spenlow LEIGH WN7 .... 25 J1
Spenlow Cl MCFLDN SK10 .... 86 E3
Spennymoor Ct RUNC WA7 .... 73 L5
Spenser Rd NSTN CH64 .... 91 H3
Spey Cl ALT WA14 .... 42 C6
WSFD CW7 .... 177 M2
Spey Dr ALS/KID ST7 .... 243 J2
Spink La KNUT WA16 .... 105 G6
Spinnaker Cl RUNC WA7 .... 74 D6
Spinnerbottom NM/HAY SK22 .... 69 M2
Spinner Crs NWCHE CW9 .... 103 K5
Spinners La POY/DIS SK12 .... 66 B8
Spinners Wy MCFLDN SK10 .... 112 F5

Spinney Av HOLMCH CW4 .... 157 M3
WDN WA8 .... 52 A3
Spinney Cl WSFD CW7 .... 178 A4
Spinney Dr CW/SHV CW2 .... 239 H7
GTS/LS CH66 .... 120 D2
SALE M33 .... 42 D1
Spinney End CHSE CH3 .... 214 A3
Spinney Gdns WARRS WA4 .... 57 H8
Spinney La NANT CW5 .... 106 E2
Spinney Md MCFLDN SK10 .... 15 K1
Spinney Rd NTHM/RTH M23 .... 44 B5
The Spinney ALS/KID ST7 .... 225 L8
CHD/CHDH SK8 .... 64 E1
FROD/HEL WA6 .... 126 E7
NANT CW5 .... 237 K6
NSTN CH64 .... 91 K4
NWCHW CW8 .... 127 K7
SBCH CW11 .... 204 C6
Spion Kop AIMK WN4 .... 22 A1
Spirewood Gdns
MPL/ROM SK6 .... 48 A3
Spital Wk CHSE CH3 .... 17 M5
Spodegreen La ALT WA14 .... 60 C4
Spout La KNUT WA16 .... 82 B8
Spragg St CONG CW12 .... 207 L1
Spring Av GTS/LS CH66 .... 94 C6
Spring Bank ALS/KID ST7
BRAM/HZG SK7 .... 66 D1
Springbank MCFLDN SK10 .... 112 E5
Springbank Cl RUNC WA7 .... 73 H5
Springbank Crs WSFD CW7 .... 177 J4
Spring Bank Pl EDGY/DAV SK3 .... 2 F7
Spring Bank Rd NM/HAY SK22 .... 69 J4
Springbourne FROD/HEL WA6 .... 99 K6
Spring Cl ALS/KID ST7 .... 224 E4
Springcroft NSTN CH64 .... 91 J5
Springdale Gdns DID/WITH M20 .... 45 G1
Springe La NANT CW5 .... 235 C7
Springfield Av
BRAM/HZG SK7 .... 66 D1
FROD/HEL WA6 .... 124 B1
GOL/RIS/CU WA3 .... 22 F4
LYMM WA13 .... 40 B7
MALPAS SY14 .... 258 B1
MPL/ROM SK6 .... 48 F6
WARR WA1 .... 37 M4
WARRS WA4 .... 57 H1
Springfield Cl NWCHW CW8 .... 129 C1
Springfield Crs NWCHW CW8 .... 129 C1
Springfield Dr CHNE CH2 .... 145 L8
CW/SHV CW2 .... 237 M5
WILM/AE SK9 .... 83 K7
Springfield Gv BIDD ST8 .... 227 K5
Springfield La IRL M44 .... 31 M2
Springfield Rd ALT WA14 .... 42 D7
BIDD ST8 .... 227 K5
CHD/CHDH SK8 .... 45 H7
KNUT WA16 .... 81 M8
MALPAS SY14 .... 258 B1
MCFLDS SK11 .... 137 M4
WDN WA8 .... 52 A4
Springfields CHNE CH2 .... 146 E4
KNUT WA16 .... 107 J1
MCFLDN SK10 .... 112 A5
NWCHW CW8 .... 127 K8
Springfields Dr CONG CW12 .... 207 K1
Springfield St WARR WA1 .... 4 F7
Spring Gdns BRAM/HZG SK7 .... 66 D1
CW/HAS CW1 .... 19 J2
GTS/LS CH66 .... 94 C6
HALE/TIMP WA15 .... 43 J7
MCFLDN SK10 .... 15 G2
NANT CW5 .... 21 G7
STKP SK1 .... 3 J6
Springhead Cl ALS/KID ST7 .... 242 D6
Springhill MCFLDN SK10 .... 139 G3
Spring Hl TPLY/KEL CW6 .... 197 J4
Springholm Dr WARRS WA4 .... 76 D1
Spring La CHSE CH3 .... 212 D6
GOL/RIS/CU WA3 .... 29 H6
LYMM WA13 .... 59 L1
Spring Meadow NWCHW CW8 .... 12 E1
Springmount
GOL/RIS/CU WA3 .... 23 L5
Spring Mt NM/HAY SK22 .... 69 J4
Spring Rd ALT WA14 .... 61 K2
POY/DIS SK12 .... 86 F2
The Springs ALT WA14 .... 61 H2
Spring St CONG CW12 .... 207 L2
CQ CH5 .... 142 A5
WDN WA8 .... 7 H8
WILM/AE SK9 .... 84 A5
Spring V BRAM/HZG SK7 .... 66 E2
Springwell Cl CW/SHV CW2 .... 238 C4
Springwood Av NANT CW5 .... 107 J1
Springwood Cl CH/BCN CH1 .... 144 C8
Springwood Crs MPL/ROM SK6 .... 48 E2
Springwood La MPL/ROM SK6 .... 48 F2
Springwood Wy MCFLDN SK10 .... 112 D7
Sprink La CONG CW12 .... 185 K7
Sproston Rd BURS/TUN ST6 .... 243 M7
Sproston Wy NWCHE CW9 .... 129 L8
Spruce Cl GOL/RIS/CU WA3 .... 23 M5
WARR WA1 .... 38 C5
Spruce Gv ALS/KID ST7 .... 224 F5
Spuley La MCFLDN SK10 .... 113 K1
Spunhill Av GTS/LS CH66 .... 120 C1
Spurling Rd WARRW/BUR WA5 .... 26 F6
Spurston Cl KNUT WA16 .... 59 J8
Square St MCFLDS SK11 .... 15 J9
The Square CHSE CH3 .... 170 E4
HTNM SK4 .... 2 A2
NSTN CH64 .... 91 H3
Squires Av WDN WA8 .... 7 G4
Squirrel Av NWCHW CW8 .... 12 B5
Squirrel Dr ALT WA14 .... 42 C4
Squirrel Hayes Av BIDD ST8 .... 227 L6
Squirrels Cha MCFLDN SK10 .... 111 M7
Squirrel's Jump WILM/AE SK9 .... 110 B3
Stable La CHSE CH3 .... 149 G1
TPLY/KEL CW6 .... 174 F3
The Stablings WILM/AE SK9 .... 84 A7
Stadium Wy CH/BCN CH1 .... 16 B3
Stadmorslow La ALS/KID ST7 .... 226 F8
Stafford Cl MCFLDN SK10 .... 137 M2
Stafford Rd CQ CH5 .... 142 F5
WARRS WA4 .... 56 C2

Staffordshire Moorlands Wks
BIDD ST8 .... 208 D8
CONG CW12 .... 227 G1
Staffordshire Wy ALS/KID ST7 .... 226 E4
Stafford St AUD/MAD/W CW3 .... 264 A8
CW/HAS CW1 .... 18 E2
NM/HAY SK22 .... 69 J3
Stage La LYMM WA13 .... 40 C8
Stags Leap WHITCH SY13 .... 269 L4
Stainburne Rd OFTN SK2 .... 47 J6
Staines Cl WARRS WA4 .... 56 A8
Stainmoor Ct OFTN SK2 .... 47 K6
Stainmore Cl GOL/RIS/CU WA3 .... 30 B6
Stainton Cl HLWD L26 .... 50 E4
Staithes Rd WYTH/NTH M22 .... 63 K4
Stalbridge Rd CW/SHV CW2 .... 18 F7
Stallard Wy MWCH CW10 .... 179 J4
Stalmine Av CHD/CHDH SK8 .... 64 B2
Stamford Av ALT WA14 .... 42 A6
CW/SHV CW2 .... 18 E6
Stamford Cl MCFLDS SK11 .... 138 C8
NWCHE CW9 .... 12 F9
Stamford Ct LYMM WA13 .... 58 F1
Stamford La CHSE CH3 .... 171 H2
Stamford New Rd ALT WA14 .... 42 D8
Stamford Park Rd
HALE/TIMP WA15 .... 61 L1
Stamford Rd ALT WA14 .... 60 B2
ALT WA14 .... 61 H2
CH/BCN CH1 .... 144 E6
MCFLDS SK11 .... 138 C7
WILM/AE SK9 .... 84 A3
WILM/AE SK9 .... 110 A3
Stamford St ALT WA14 .... 42 D7
EP CH65 .... 10 A7
Stamford Wy ALT WA14 .... 42 D7
Stamp Av CW/SHV CW2 .... 221 K6
Stancliffe Rd WYTH/NTH M22 .... 44 E7
Stancross Rd NTHM/RTH M23 .... 43 J3
Standford Dr NWCHE CW9 .... 13 J9
Stanford Crs WLTN L25 .... 50 D4
Stanhope Av CW/HAS CW1 .... 19 K6
Stanhope Cl WILM/AE SK9 .... 84 D4
Stanhope Rd ALT WA14 .... 61 G2
Stanier Cl CW/HAS CW1 .... 222 A8
Stanlaw Rd EP CH65 .... 10 F9
Stanley Av BRAM/HZG SK7 .... 66 D1
MPL/ROM SK6 .... 48 D5
WARRS WA4 .... 56 F2
WARRW/BUR WA5 .... 35 K5
Stanley Cl NWCHW CW8 .... 129 G8
WDN WA8 .... 7 L1
Stanley Ct ALS/KID ST7 .... 224 C8
Stanley Dr CHD/CHDH SK8 .... 64 D6
HALE/TIMP WA15 .... 43 G7
Stanley Gv NWCHE CW9 .... 130 E2
Stanley Hall La POY/DIS SK12 .... 68 C5
Stanley Mt SALE M33 .... 43 G1
Stanley Park Ct
CHSW/BR CH4 .... 168 E7
Stanley Park Dr CHSW/BR CH4 .... 168 E7
Stanley Pl CH/BCN CH1 .... 16 E5
CQ CH5 .... 142 A7
WARRS WA4 .... 56 F2
Stanley Place Ms CH/BCN CH1 .... 16 E6
Stanley Rd BIDD ST8 .... 227 J2
CHD/CHDH SK8 .... 64 D6
EP CH65 .... 10 E3
KNUT WA16 .... 106 F2
Stanley St BIDD ST8 .... 227 J4
BURS/TUN ST6 .... 243 L8
CH/BCN CH1 .... 16 E5
CW/HAS CW1 .... 19 J4
NEWLW WA12 .... 27 G1
NWCHE CW9 .... 130 C4
RUNC WA7 .... 9 J1
STKP SK1 .... 3 J4
WARR WA1 .... 5 G8
Stannage La CHSE CH3 .... 211 M7
Stanner Cl WARRW/BUR WA5 .... 36 D3
Stannerhouse La SBCH CW11 .... 223 L1
Stanneybrook Cl
FROD/HEL WA6 .... 127 G6
Stanney Cl PS/BROM CH62 .... 93 L1
Stanneylands Cl WILM/AE SK9 .... 84 C2
Stanneylands Dr WILM/AE SK9 .... 84 B2
Stanneylands Rd WILM/AE SK9 .... 64 B8
Stanney La EP CH65 .... 121 J1
Stanney Mill La CHNE CH2 .... 121 M3
Stanney Mill Rd EP CH65 .... 121 M2
Stanney Woods Av EP CH65 .... 121 J3
Stansbury Pl OFTN SK2 .... 47 L6
Stansfield Av WARR WA1 .... 37 M8
Stansfield Cl LEIGH WN7 .... 25 J2
Stanstead Dr
WARRW/BUR WA5 .... 54 F1
Stanthorne Av CW/SHV CW2 .... 237 M1
Stanton Cl NSTN CH64 .... 91 M4
Stanton Dr CHNE CH2 .... 145 K7
Stanton Rd WARRS WA4 .... 57 K1
Stanway Dr HALE/TIMP WA15 .... 61 M1
Stanwood Gdns RAIN/WH L35 .... 32 L1
Stapeley Bdns HLWD L26 .... 51 C6
Stapeley Ter NANT CW5 .... 21 J7
Stapleford Cl NTHM/RTH M23 .... 43 M8
Stapleton Av SPK/HALE L24 .... 70 D1
Stapleton Rd MCFLDN SK10 .... 138 B2
Stapley Cl RUNC WA7 .... 8 E4
Starbeck Dr GTS/LS CH66 .... 94 B6
Starkey Gv WARRS WA4 .... 37 M8
Star La LYMM WA13 .... 39 J8
MCFLDS SK11 .... 138 D8
Starling Cl ALS/KID ST7 .... 243 K1
RUNC WA7 .... 74 D5
Start La CHF/WBR SK23 .... 89 J5
Stash Gv NTHM/RTH M23 .... 44 B5
Statham Av WARRS WA4 .... 58 C1
WARRN/WOL WA2 .... 37 J2
Statham Cl LYMM WA13 .... 58 D1
Statham Dr LYMM WA13 .... 58 D1
Statham La LYMM WA13 .... 39 H7
Statham St MCFLDS SK11 .... 14 F7
Station Approach
GTS/LS CH66 .... 98 C6
Station Cl NSTN CH64 .... 91 M5
Station Gn GTS/LS CH66 .... 94 C5
Station Hl NWCHW CW8 .... 127 M2
Station La CHNE CH2 .... 146 F4

CQ CH5 .... 166 C4
Station Rd ALS/KID ST7
ALS/KID ST7 .... 225 L5
ALS/KID ST7 .... 226 B4
ALS/KID ST7 .... 241 J1
ALS/KID ST7 .... 242 F3
ALS/KID ST7 .... 243 L3
ALT WA14 .... 41 H7
AUD/MAD/W CW3 .... 267 J2
BIDD ST8 .... 227 J3
CH/BCN CH1 .... 17 J2
CH/BCN CH1 .... 145 H1
CHD/CHDH SK8 .... 65 H2
CHF/WBR SK23 .... 69 K8
CHNE CH2 .... 97 G7
CHSE CH3 .... 149 G1
CONG CW12 .... 186 A2
CQ CH5 .... 142 D7
CQ CH5 .... 166 C4
CQ CH5 .... 167 G2
EDGY/DAV SK3 .... 2 E7
EP CH65 .... 10 E3
GTS/LS CH66 .... 94 C6
HOLMCH CW4 .... 158 A4
HOLMCH CW4 .... 181 J2
HTNM SK4 .... 45 L3
IRL M44 .... 31 L5
KNUT WA16 .... 81 M5
MCFLDS SK11 .... 135 G2
MKTDR TF9 .... 274 A7
MPL/ROM SK6 .... 48 F6
MPL/ROM SK6 .... 48 F5
NANT CW5 .... 20 F7
NANT CW5 .... 219 L6
NANT CW5 .... 261 M1
NM/HAY SK22 .... 69 H5
NSTN CH64 .... 91 L5
NSTN CH64 .... 91 J4
NSTN CH64 .... 118 A2
NWCHE CW9 .... 13 L1
NWCHW CW8 .... 131 G2
NWCHW CW8 .... 94 C7
NWCHW CW8 .... 128 A3
NWCHW CW8 .... 150 D4
RAIN/WH L35 .... 33 J1
RUNC WA7 .... 8 F2
SBCH CW11 .... 203 K5
TPLY/KEL CW6 .... 217 L2
WARRS WA4 .... 56 F2
WARRW/BUR WA5 .... 35 M7
WARRW/BUR WA5 .... 54 D1
WHITCH SY13 .... 270 B5
WILM/AE SK9 .... 84 A1
WILM/AE SK9 .... 84 A3
WRX/GR/LL LL12 .... 210 A5
WSFD CW7 .... 178 B3
Station Rd North
WARRN/WOL WA2 .... 38 A2
Station Rd South
WARRN/WOL WA2 .... 38 A3
Station St BRAM/HZG SK7 .... 66 D2
MCFLDN SK10 .... 15 G3
RAIN/WH L35 .... 33 J1
Station Vw CHNE CH2 .... 17 L4
WARRS WA4 .... 20 F8
Staveley Dr WSFD CW7 .... 177 K2
Stavesacre LEIGH WN7 .... 24 F1
Staveton Cl BRAM/HZG SK7 .... 65 M1
Steadings Ri KNUT WA16 .... 80 D6
Steam Mill St CHSE CH3 .... 17 K4
Stearns Cl CH/BCN CH1 .... 145 G7
Steele Rd MWCH CW10 .... 179 K7
Steele St CH/BCN CH1 .... 17 G6
Steel St WARR WA1 .... 5 M4
Steeple Ct NSTN CH64 .... 91 L5
Steeple St MCFLDN SK10 .... 15 J3
Steer Br WHITCH SY13 .... 260 C3
Stein Av GOL/RIS/CU WA3 .... 23 L4
Stelfox Av HALE/TIMP WA15 .... 43 G7
Stenhills Crs RUNC WA7 .... 9 K3
Stephenson Dr CW/HAS CW1 .... 222 A8
Stephenson Rd NEWLW WA12 .... 27 J2
Stephenson Wy WSFD CW7 .... 177 G4
Stephens Ter GTS/LS CH66 .... 94 B6
Stephen St STKP SK1 .... 3 L7
WARR WA1 .... 5 M4
Stephens Cl WSFD CW7 .... 178 A1
Sterndale Rd EDGY/DAV SK3 .... 46 E7
MPL/ROM SK6 .... 48 B3
Sterne Cl SBCH CW11 .... 203 K6
Stetchworth Rd WARRS WA4 .... 56 C3
Stevenage Cl MCFLDS SK11 .... 14 D7
Stevenage Dr MCFLDS SK11 .... 14 D7
Stevens St WILM/AE SK9 .... 110 A3
Steventon Cl RUNC WA7 .... 54 E8
Steward's Wy WDN WA8 .... 6 E4
Stewart St CW/SHV CW2 .... 18 B6
Stewerton Cl
GOL/RIS/CU WA3 .... 22 F2
Stile Cl BIDD ST8 .... 227 H7
Stile End CHNE CH2 .... 146 F4
Stiles Av MPL/ROM SK6 .... 48 E5
The Stiles NWCHW CW8 .... 127 L7
Stirling Av BRAM/HZG SK7 .... 66 D3
MPL/ROM SK6 .... 48 B5
Stirling Cl CHSE CH3 .... 170 A2
EDGY/DAV SK3 .... 46 C6
MCFLDN SK10 .... 137 M2
WARR WA1 .... 38 C5
Stirling Rd SPK/HALE L24 .... 70 B1
Stirrup Cl WARRN/WOL WA2 .... 38 A1
Stitch La HTNM SK4 .... 2 D2
Stockdale Av EDGY/DAV SK3 .... 46 F7
Stockham Cl RUNC WA7 .... 74 A4
Stockham La RUNC WA7 .... 74 C7
Stockholm Rd EDGY/DAV SK3 .... 46 D6
Stock La NANT CW5 .... 253 G3
Stockley La WARRS WA4 .... 76 C3
Stockport Rd EDGY/DAV SK3 .... 46 A5
HALE/TIMP WA15 .... 42 F7
MPL/ROM SK6 .... 48 F6
WARRS WA4 .... 57 L1
Stockport Rd West
MPL/ROM SK6 .... 47 J1
STKP SK1 .... 3 M3
Stocks Av CHSE CH3 .... 170 A4
Stocks Hl WSFD CW7 .... 177 L5

Stocks La *CHSE* CH3 .... 170 A3
  KNUT WA16 .... 133 K2
  MCFLDN SK10 .... 113 L7
  WARRW/BUR WA5 .... 35 K7
Stockswell Rd *RAIN/WH* L35 .... 32 F8
Stockton Av *EDGY/DAV* SK3 .... 46 B4
Stockton La *WARRS* WA4 .... 56 E3
Stockton Rd *WILM/AE* SK9 .... 83 M8
Stockton Wood Rd
  SPK/HALE L24 .... 70 C1
Stoke Abbott Cl *BRAM/HZG* SK7 .. 65 L5
Stoke Cl *PS/BROM* CH62 .... 93 L1
Stoke Gdns *EP* CH65 .... 95 J8
Stokehall La *NANT* CW5 .... 218 D6
Stokes St *GOL/RIS/CU* WA3 .... 29 L7
Stokoe Av *ALT* WA14 .... 42 A6
Stoneacre Gdns *WARRS* WA4 .... 56 D8
Stoneacre Rd *WYTH/NTH* M22 .... 63 J2
Stonebank Dr *NSTN* CH64 .... 92 A6
Stone Bank Rd *ALS/KID* ST7 .... 243 G4
Stone Barn La *RUNC* WA7 .... 73 M6
Stonebridge *NANT* CW5 .... 251 L1
Stone Chair La *ALS/KID* ST7 .... 225 L4
Stonechat Cl *CW/HAS* CW1 .... 221 C5 3
  GOL/RIS/CU WA3 .... 23 L4 1
  RUNC WA7 .... 73 L7 1
Stone Cft *CHSE* CH3 .... 170 B4
Stonecrop Cl *GOL/RIS/CU* WA3 .... 29 J8
  RUNC WA7 .... 73 M8 2
Stonecross Dr *RAIN/WH* L35 .... 33 K3
Stone Cross La North
  GOL/RIS/CU WA3 .... 23 J5 2
Stone Cross La South
  GOL/RIS/CU WA3 .... 23 J6
Stonehaven Dr
  WARRN/WOL WA2 .... 38 A1
Stone Hay *RAIN/WH* L35 .... 32 D1
Stoneheads Ri *CHF/WBR* SK23 .... 89 K4
Stone Heyes La *NWCHW* CW8 .... 102 F7
Stonehill Cl *WARRS* WA4 .... 56 D8
Stonehills La *RUNC* WA7 .... 9 M3
Stonehouse Gn *CONG* CW12 .... 207 K1 6
  MCFLDN SK10 .... 14 E1
Stoneleigh Cl *CQ* CH5 .... 142 F6 1
  MCFLDN SK10 .... 14 E1
Stoneleigh Gdns *WARRS* WA4 .... 55 K3
Stoneley Av *CW/HAS* CW1 .... 221 J5
Stoneley Rd *CW/HAS* CW1 .... 221 K5
Stone Md *MPL/ROM* SK6 .... 48 E1
Stone Mead Av
  HALE/TIMP WA15 .... 62 C5
Stonepail Cl *CHD/CHDH* SK8 .... 44 F7
Stonepail Rd *CHD/CHDH* SK8 .... 45 G7 2
Stone Pit Cl *GOL/RIS/CU* WA3 .... 23 L3
Stone Pit La *GOL/RIS/CU* WA3 .... 28 F2
Stone Pl *CHNE* CH2 .... 17 L1
Stone Rw *MPL/ROM* SK6 .... 49 G6
Stones Manor La *NWCHW* CW8 .... 12 A9
Stoneyfold La *MCFLDS* SK10 .... 139 G6
Stoney Holt *RUNC* WA7 .... 74 C4 8
Stoneyland Dr *NM/HAY* SK22 .... 69 G4
Stoney La *TPLY/KEL* CW6 .... 150 C6
  WILM/AE SK9 .... 83 M7
Stonyhurst Rd *WLTN* L25 .... 50 B3
Stony La *CONG* CW12 .... 207 J3
Stopford St *EDGY/DAV* SK3 .... 2 D8
Stopsley Cl *CONG* CW12 .... 183 M8
Store St *MCFLDN* SK10 .... 113 H4 7
  OFTN SK2 .... 47 J8
Storeton Cl *WYTH/NTH* M22 .... 63 L2 2
Stortford Dr *NTHM/RTH* M23 .... 44 B2
Stour Av *RAIN/WH* L35 .... 33 J1
Stour Cl *ALT* WA14 .... 42 C6
Stour Ct *EP* CH65 .... 10 D4
Stourport Cl *MPL/ROM* SK6 .... 48 A3 2
Stourvale Rd *HLWD* L26 .... 50 F5 3
Stowe Cl *WLTN* L25 .... 50 B5
Stradbroke Cl *GOL/RIS/CU* WA3 .... 24 A5
Straight Length *FROD/HEL* WA6 .. 98 E5
Straight Mile *CHSW/BR* CH4 .... 191 M7
Straker Av *EP* CH65 .... 94 F6
Stratfield Ms *NTHM/RTH* M23 .... 43 K3
Stratfield Gdns *MPL/ROM* SK6 .... 47 M1
Stratford Rd *CH/BCN* CH1 .... 144 E8
  NSTN CH64 .... 91 K6
Stratford Wy *MCFLDS* SK11 .... 138 C7 1
Strathaven Av *CW/SHV* CW2 .... 237 L4
Strathmore Cl *HOLMCH* CW4 .... 181 H2
Stratton Cl *RUNC* WA7 .... 74 B6
Stratton Pk *WDN* WA8 .... 33 M7
Stratton Rd *OFTN* SK2 .... 47 J4 3
  WARRW/BUR WA5 .... 36 B7
Strawberry Cl *ALT* WA14 .... 42 B5 1
  GOL/RIS/CU WA3 .... 29 J8
Strawberry Dr *EP* CH65 .... 121 G4
Strawberry Flds *CHSE* CH3 .... 170 B5
Strawberry La *CH/BCN* CH1 .... 120 C7
  NWCHW CW8 .... 127 M1
  WILM/AE SK9 .... 84 D4
Streamside Cl *HALE/TIMP* WA15 .. 43 H8
Stream Ter *STKP* SK1 .... 3 J3
Street Hey La *NSTN* CH64 .... 93 H2
Street La *MCFLDN* SK10 .... 86 D4
  SBCH CW11 .... 224 E2
  WARRS WA4 .... 102 C1
The Street *BUX* SK17 .... 115 L8
  CHNE CH2 .... 146 C5
  CHNE CH2 .... 146 E3
  MCFLDN SK10 .... 115 H6
Stretton Av *DID/WITH* M20 .... 45 J1
  GOL/RIS/CU WA3 .... 23 L5 4
Stretton Cl *PS/BROM* CH62 .... 93 L1 1
Stretton Rd *WARRS* WA4 .... 76 F2
Stretton Wk *NWCHW* CW8 .... 129 M8 6
Stretton Wy *RAIN/WH* L35 .... 32 B4
Strickland St *CQ* CH5 .... 142 B7
Strines Rd *MPL/ROM* SK6 .... 49 G2
Stringer St *SBCH* CW11 .... 204 C6
Stringer Crs *WARRS* WA4 .... 37 L8
Stringer's La *TPLY/KEL* CW6 .... 190 B7
Stringer St *STKP* SK1 .... 3 K4
Stromness Cl
  WARRN/WOL WA2 .... 38 B1 1
Stross Av *BURS/TUN* ST6 .... 243 M7

Stuart Av *IRL* M44 .... 31 M2
  WLTN L25 .... 50 C5
Stuart Cl *CHSE* CH3 .... 170 C1
  WSFD CW7 .... 177 K6 6
  WSFD CW7 .... 177 J7 8
Stuart Dr *MPL/ROM* SK6 .... 48 C5
  WARRS WA4 .... 56 F2
Stuart Pl *CH/BCN* CH1 .... 17 H3
Stuart Rd *RUNC* WA7 .... 54 B8
Stubbins Cl *NTHM/RTH* M23 .... 43 L3
Stubbs La *KNUT* WA16 .... 82 D8
  NWCHE CW9 .... 131 H2 1
Stubbs Pl *CH/BCN* CH1 .... 168 C1 5
Stubbs Ter *MCFLDS* SK11 .... 15 J7 2
Stubby La *MCFLDN* SK10 .... 135 L3
Studland Rd *WYTH/NTH* M22 .... 63 M1
Sturgess St *NEWLW* WA12 .... 26 F1
Styal Av *CHD/CHDH* SK8 .... 64 A1
Styal Rd *WILM/AE* SK9 .... 84 A3
Styal Vw *WILM/AE* SK9 .... 84 B2 1
Styperson Wy *POY/DIS* SK12 .. 86 E1 2
Sudbourne Cl *ALS/KID* ST7 .... 243 L4
Sudbrook Cl
  GOL/RIS/CU WA3 .... 23 L4 12
Sudbury Cl *WLTN* L25 .... 50 D2
Sudbury Dr *CHD/CHDH* SK8 .... 64 C5
Sudbury Rd *BRAM/HZG* SK7 .... 66 E4
Sudbury Wy *SPK/HALE* L24 .... 50 B8 8
Sudlow La *KNUT* WA16 .... 106 B7
Suez St *NEWLW* WA12 .... 27 C1
  WARR WA1 .... 4 F7
Suffolk Av *EP* CH65 .... 94 F7
Suffolk Cl *CONG* CW12 .... 184 D8
  MCFLDN SK10 .... 137 M3
  WARR WA1 .... 38 D6
Suffolk Dr *WILM/AE* SK9 .... 84 B3
Suffolk Pl *WDN* WA8 .... 52 C5
Suffolk St *ALT* WA14 .... 42 B8
  RUNC WA7 .... 8 E1
Sugar La *FROD/HEL* WA6 .... 124 E7
  MCFLDN SK10 .... 86 F8
  MCFLDN SK10 .... 113 K7
Sugar Pit La *KNUT* WA16 .... 106 E1
Sulby Av *WARRS* WA4 .... 56 B1
Sulgrave Av *POY/DIS* SK12 .... 66 F8
Summerbank Rd
  BURS/TUN ST6 .... 243 K8
Summerdale Rd *CQ* CH5 .... 142 A8
Summerfield *ALS/KID* ST7 .... 243 H3 6
Summerfield Av
  WARRW/BUR WA5 .... 36 F2
Summerfield Cl
  CHSW/BR CH4 .... 190 A1 6
Summerfield Pl *WILM/AE* SK9 .... 84 A6
Summerfield Rd *CHSE* CH3 .... 146 F7 2
  KNUT WA16 .... 81 M8
  WYTH/NTH M22 .... 63 J2
Summerfields *KNUT* WA16 .... 107 J1 8
Summerhill Rd *MCFLDN* SK10 .... 111 L8
Summer La *RUNC* WA7 .... 73 M3
  WARRS WA4 .... 75 H6
  WARRS WA4 .... 76 A4
Summerlea *CHD/CHDH* SK8 .... 65 H4 8
Summers Wy *KNUT* WA16 .... 107 G5
Summertrees Rd *GTS/LS* CH66 .... 120 F5
Summerville Gdns *WARRS* WA4 .... 56 F3
Summit Cl *WARRS* WA4 .... 76 E3
  WILM/AE SK9 .... 84 B5
Sumner Cl *RAIN/WH* L35 .... 33 K3
Sumner Rd *CH/BCN* CH1 .... 144 E8
Sumpter Pathway *CHNE* CH2 .... 17 H1
Sunart Cl *CW/SHV* CW2 .... 238 B6 6
Sunbank La *HALE/TIMP* WA15 .... 62 D6
  HALE/TIMP WA15 .... 62 F6
Sunbeam St *NEWLW* WA12 .... 27 J1 3
Sunbury Cl *WILM/AE* SK9 .... 84 E2
Sunbury Crs *CHSW/BR* CH4 .. 168 F6 10
Sunbury Gdns *WARRS* WA4 .... 56 E5
Suncroft Cl *WARR* WA1 .... 38 E5
Sundale Dr *CW/SHV* CW2 .... 237 K1
Sunderland St *MCFLDS* SK11 .... 15 H6
Sundial Rd *OFTN* SK2 .... 47 K6
Sundown Cl *NM/HAY* SK22 .... 69 G4
Sunfield *MPL/ROM* SK6 .... 48 A8
Sunfield Ct *GTS/LS* CH66 .... 120 D1 8
Sunningdale Av *SALE* M33 .... 43 L1
  WDN WA8 .... 52 B3
Sunningdale Cl *NWCHE* CW9 .. 130 E5 2
  WARRW/BUR WA5 .... 26 F6
  WSFD CW7 .... 177 G2
Sunningdale Dr *BRAM/HZG* SK7 .. 66 A5
  IRL M44 .... 31 M1
Sunningdale Rd *CHD/CHDH* SK8 .. 65 G5
  MCFLDN SK11 .... 14 B8
Sunningdale Wy *NSTN* CH64 .... 91 L8
Sunny Bank *WILM/AE* SK9 .... 83 K8
Sunnybank Cl *MCFLDS* SK11 .... 138 D7
Sunny Bank Rd *ALT* WA14 .... 61 J4
Sunnybank Rd *CW/SHV* CW2 .... 220 E7
Sunnydale *RAIN/WH* L35 .... 33 K1
Sunnyfield Rd *HTNM* SK4 .... 45 M1
Sunnyside *ALS/KID* ST7 .... 243 H2
  CQ CH5 .... 166 D2
  WARRW/BUR WA5 .... 35 L6 8
Sunnyside La *RUNC* WA7 .... 54 E8
Sunset Av *WYTH/NTH* M22 .... 44 D2
Sunwell Ter *MPL/ROM* SK6 .... 48 F8 8
Surrey Dr *CONG* CW12 .... 184 B8
Surrey Rd *ALS/KID* ST7 .... 243 G2
  CHNE CH2 .... 146 A7
  MCFLDS SK11 .... 138 A8
Surrey St *CW/HAS* CW1 .... 19 J3
  RUNC WA7 .... 9 G3
  WARRS WA4 .... 56 D1
Surridge *KNUT* WA16 .... 59 J7
Surtees Rd *NTHM/RTH* M23 .... 44 A2
Susan Dr *WARRW/BUR* WA5 .... 35 K7
Susan St *WDN* WA8 .... 7 J4
Suspension Br *CHSW/BR* CH4 .. 17 J6
Sussex Av *MCFLDS* SK11 .... 138 A7 3
Sussex Dr *ALS/KID* ST7 .... 242 F2
Sussex Rd *CHNE* CH2 .... 145 M8
  EDGY/DAV SK3 .... 46 B4
  IRL M44 .... 31 J6
  PART M31 .... 40 C2 3
Sussex Wk *WDN* WA8 .... 53 K3 3

Sutherland Dr *MCFLDN* SK10 .... 14 A2
Sutherland Wy *CHSE* CH3 .... 170 B1
Sutton Av *GOL/RIS/CU* WA3 .... 24 E8
  NSTN CH64 .... 91 L6
Sutton Cswy *FROD/HEL* WA6 .... 99 L2
Sutton Dr *CHNE* CH2 .... 146 F4 8
  MCFLDN SK11 .... 138 D7
  NWCHE CW9 .... 104 F6 8
  PS/BROM CH62 .... 93 L1
Sutton Fld *NWCHW* CW8 .... 152 F5
Sutton Hall Dr *GTS/LS* CH66 .... 94 A6
Sutton Hall Gdns *GTS/LS* CH66 .. 94 A6
Sutton La *MWCH* CW10 .... 179 J5
Sutton Rd *HTNM* SK4 .... 2 B1
  POY/DIS SK12 .... 86 F2
  WILM/AE SK9 .... 109 M3
Suttons La *MPL/ROM* SK6 .... 49 G7
  WDN WA8 .... 7 J7
Sutton St *RUNC* WA7 .... 9 K3
  WARR WA1 .... 5 J8
Sutton Wy *EP* CH65 .... 10 B9 1
  EP CH65 .... 10 B9
  GTS/LS CH66 .... 94 A6
Sutton Wood Rd *SPK/HALE* L24 .. 70 C1
Swaine St *EDGY/DAV* SK3 .... 2 E6
Swale Av *RAIN/WH* L35 .... 33 J1
Swalecliff Av *NTHM/RTH* M23 .... 43 K3
Swale Cl *WILM/AE* SK9 .... 84 E2
Swaledale Av *CONG* CW12 .... 185 G7
  RAIN/WH L35 .... 33 K1
Swaledale Cl *WARRW/BUR* WA5 .. 35 M5
Swale Dr *ALT* WA14 .... 42 C6
Swale Rd *EP* CH65 .... 10 A3
Swallow Cl *ALS/KID* ST7 .... 243 G2 2
  GOL/RIS/CU WA3 .... 29 M8 2
  MCFLDN SK10 .... 139 G5 7
Swallow Ct *WSFD* CW7 .... 177 K1
Swallow Dr *SBCH* CW11 .... 204 A4
Swallowfield Cl
  CW/SHV CW2 .... 238 A4 8
Swallowmore Vw
  ALS/KID ST7 .... 242 C4 1
Swallow St *STKP* SK1 .... 3 H9
Swallow Wk *BIDD* ST8 .... 227 K5
Swanage Av *NTHM/RTH* M23 .... 43 K3
  OFTN SK2 .... 47 K6
Swanage Cl *WARRS* WA4 .... 56 D2
Swanage Ct *WSFD* CW7 .... 177 K7 8
Swan Av *STHEL* WA9 .... 26 A2
Swan Bank *ALS/KID* ST7 .... 242 C5
Swan Cl *ALS/KID* ST7 .... 242 D4
  GTS/LS CH66 .... 120 C2
  POY/DIS SK12 .... 66 B8
Swan Ct *NWCHW* CW8 .... 127 L5
Swan Gv *KNUT* WA16 .... 132 D5
Swan La *TPLY/KEL* CW6 .... 216 E4
Swanley La *NANT* CW5 .... 235 L6
Swanlow Av *WSFD* CW7 .... 177 K7
Swanlow Dr *WSFD* CW7 .... 177 K6
Swanlow La *WSFD* CW7 .... 177 J5
Swann Gv *CHD/CHDH* SK8 .... 65 H4
Swann La *CHD/CHDH* SK8 .... 65 H3
Swan Rd *HALE/TIMP* WA15 .... 43 G3
Swanscoe Av *MCFLDN* SK10 .... 113 G5
Swanscoe Cl *MWCH* CW10 .... 179 L4 6
Swanscoe La *MCFLDN* SK10 .... 139 H1
Swan St *CONG* CW12 .... 207 K2
  WILM/AE SK9 .... 84 B5
Swanwick Cl *HOLMCH* CW4 .... 157 J3
Swaylands Dr *SALE* M33 .... 43 H3
Sweet Briar Crs *CW/SHV* CW2 .. 237 M1
Sweet Brier Cl *NWCHW* CW8 .. 103 H8 7
Sweetfield Gdns *GTS/LS* CH66 .. 94 C5
Sweetfield Rd *GTS/LS* CH66 .... 94 D5
Sweettooth La *SBCH* CW11 .... 204 A5
Swettenham Cl *ALS/KID* ST7 .... 241 J1
  SBCH CW11 .... 204 C5
Swettenham Rd *CONG* CW12 .... 182 F1
  WILM/AE SK9 .... 64 D7 8
Swettenham St *MCFLDS* SK11 .... 15 K8 8
Swift Cl *ALS/KID* ST7 .... 243 H2 2
  CW/SHV CW2 .... 237 M3
  WARRN/WOL WA2 .... 37 L1 8
Swift Dr *BIDD* ST8 .... 227 L4
Swinburne Dr *CW/HAS* CW1 .... 19 M3
Swinchiard La *FLINT* CH6 .... 116 A6
Swinchiard Wk *FLINT* CH6 .... 116 A6
Swindale Av
  WARRN/WOL WA2 .... 37 H1 8
Swinden Cl *RUNC* WA7 .... 74 D2 8
Swine Market *NANT* CW5 .... 20 E6
Swineyard La *NWCHW* CW9 .... 57 M8
Swinford Dr *WDN* WA8 .... 53 L2 6
Swinley Cha *WILM/AE* SK9 .... 84 E5
Swinleys Hey *CHSE* CH3 .... 170 A5 6
Swinnerton St *CW/SHV* CW2 .... 18 F8
Swinton Sq *KNUT* WA16 .... 107 G2 6
Swireford Rd *FROD/HEL* WA6 .... 124 B2
Swiss Hl *WILM/AE* SK9 .... 110 B3
Swithin Rd *WYTH/NTH* M22 .... 63 L4
Swn-y-gwynt *FLINT* CH6 .... 116 B8 6
Swynnerton Wy *WDN* WA8 .... 34 B7 8
Swythamley Cl *EDGY/DAV* SK3 .. 46 A4 6
Swythamley Rd *EDGY/DAV* SK3 .. 46 A4
Sycamore Av *ALS/KID* ST7 .... 224 F5
  ALS/KID ST7 .... 241 L2 8
  ALT WA14 .... 42 A7 8
  CONG CW12 .... 183 M8
  CW/HAS CW1 .... 221 K6
  GOL/RIS/CU WA3 .... 23 G3
  HLWD L26 .... 50 E6
  NEWLW WA12 .... 27 L1 7
  WDN WA8 .... 7 J1
  WSFD CW7 .... 177 J4
Sycamore Crs
  GOL/RIS/CU WA3 .... 40 B2 8
  GOL/RIS/CU WA3 .... 40 B2 8
  MCFLDS SK11 .... 14 B8
  NWCHW CW8 .... 103 H8
Sycamore Dr *CHSW/BR* CH4 .. 168 F8

  GTS/LS CH66 .... 120 F3
  LYMM WA13 .... 39 K8
  NWCHW CW10 .... 179 K7
  RUNC WA7 .... 74 A8
Sycamore Farm Cl
  .... 14 A1 1
Sycamore Gv *CHSW/BR* CH4 .. 190 B1 3
  SBCH CW11 .... 204 A4
Sycamore La
  WARRW/BUR WA5 .... 36 B6 8
Sycamore Ri *MCFLDS* SK11 .... 14 B8
Sycamore Rd *NM/HAY* SK22 .... 69 L2
  PART M31 .... 40 D1
  RUNC WA7 .... 9 M6
Sycamore St *EDGY/DAV* SK3 .... 46 B4 8
  WARRW/BUR WA5 .... 36 B6 8
Sycamore Wk *CHD/CHDH* SK8 .. 45 K6 1
Syddal Cl *BRAM/HZG* SK7 .... 65 K7
Syddal Crs *BRAM/HZG* SK7 .... 65 K8
Syddal Gn *BRAM/HZG* SK7 .... 65 K7
Syddal Av *CHD/CHDH* SK8 .... 64 D4
Syddall Rd *BRAM/HZG* SK7 .... 65 K7
Sydney Av *LEIGH* WN7 .... 24 D2
Sydney Rd *BRAM/HZG* SK7 .... 65 M7
  CH/BCN CH1 .... 16 D2
  CW/HAS CW1 .... 221 L6
Sydney St *NWCHW* CW8 .... 12 B5
  OFTN SK2 .... 47 J5
  RUNC WA7 .... 8 B9
Sydney Wk *FLINT* CH6 .... 116 A5 8
Syers Ct *WARR* WA1 .... 37 L4
Sykes Meadow *EDGY/DAV* SK3 .. 46 C6
Sylvan Av *HALE/TIMP* WA15 .... 43 J1
  SALE M33 .... 43 J1
  WILM/AE SK9 .... 83 M7
Sylvan Cl *NWCHW* CW8 .... 12 A6
Sylvan Ct *WLTN* L25 .... 50 A3
Sylvan Gv *ALT* WA14 .... 42 D7
Sylvester Av *STKP* SK1 .... 47 H6
Sylvia Crs *WARRN/WOL* WA2 .. 37 K3 3
Symondley Rd *MCFLDS* SK11 .. 162 F2
Synge St *WARRN/WOL* WA2 .... 5 J1
Sytch Cft *NSTN* CH64 .... 91 L4

T

Tabley Av *WDN* WA8 .... 6 A1
Tabley Cl *KNUT* WA16 .... 106 E1
  SBCH CW11 .... 203 L5
Tabley Gdns *MPL/ROM* SK6 .... 49 C8
Tabley Gv *HALE/TIMP* WA15 .... 43 C4
  KNUT WA16 .... 106 E2
Tabley Hill La *KNUT* WA16 .... 106 B1
Tabley Mere Gdns
  CHD/CHDH SK8 .... 64 F1
Tabley Rd *CW/SHV* CW2 .... 237 L1
  KNUT WA16 .... 106 D1
  SALE M33 .... 43 L2 8
  WILM/AE SK9 .... 64 D7
Tabley St *NWCHE* CW9 .... 13 J1
Tabor St *MCFLDS* SK11 .... 15 K8 8
Tadgers La *FROD/HEL* WA6 .... 98 D3
Tadman Gv *ALT* WA14 .... 42 A6
Talbot Av *NSTN* CH64 .... 91 M6
Talbot Cl *CW/SHV* CW2 .... 238 B8
  GOL/RIS/CU WA3 .... 38 E1
  NSTN CH64 .... 91 M6
Talbot Crs *WHITCH* SY13 .... 270 B4
Talbot Gdns *NSTN* CH64 .... 91 M6
Talbot Rd *ALT* WA14 .... 61 H2
  FROD/HEL WA6 .... 123 L5
  WILM/AE SK9 .... 110 B3
Talbot St *BRAM/HZG* SK7 .... 47 K8
  CH/BCN CH1 .... 17 H2
  GOL/RIS/CU WA3 .... 23 G4
  WHITCH SY13 .... 270 B4
Taliesin Av *CQ* CH5 .... 142 A6
Talisman Cl *RUNC* WA7 .... 74 E5 8
Talke Rd *ALS/KID* ST7 .... 241 L1
Talland Cl *HLWD* L26 .... 50 E3
Tall Ash Av *CONG* CW12 .... 185 G8
Tall Trees Cl *NWCHW* CW8 .... 12 A6
Tall Trees Pl *OFTN* SK2 .... 47 J6
Talman Dr *AIMK* WN4 .... 22 D1
Tamar Cl *CONG* CW12 .... 207 M3
  MCFLDN SK10 .... 137 L1 10
Tamar Dr *NTHM/RTH* M23 .... 44 A8 3
Tamar Rd *ALS/KID* ST7 .... 243 H2
Tamar Wk *WSFD* CW7 .... 178 A2 3
Tame Cl *BIDD* ST8 .... 227 K3
  SBCH CW11 .... 203 L4
Tamworth Cl *BRAM/HZG* SK7 .. 66 D4 8
Tamworth St *STKP* SK1 .... 3 L3
Tanfield Rd *DID/WITH* M20 .... 45 H5
Tanhill Cl *OFTN* SK2 .... 47 L6
Tan House La *WARRW/BUR* WA5 .. 27 C8
  WDN WA8 .... 7 M4
Tankersley Gv *WARRW/BUR* WA5.. 36 A7
Tanner's La *GOL/RIS/CU* WA3 .... 23 H4
  WARRN/WOL WA2 .... 4 F5
Tannery La *NSTN* CH64 .... 91 L4
Tannery Wy *ALT* WA14 .... 42 E5 8
Tannock St *WARRW/BUR* WA5 .. 56 C8
Tanyard Dr *HALE/TIMP* WA15 .. 62 C6
Tanyard La *HALE/TIMP* WA15 .. 61 M7
Tapley Av *POY/DIS* SK12 .... 86 E2
Taplow Cl *WARRS* WA4 .... 56 E6
Taplow Gv *CHD/CHDH* SK8 .... 64 C3
Tarbock Rd *SPK/HALE* L24 .... 50 D8
Tarbolton Crs *HALE/TIMP* WA15.. 62 C1
Target Cl *ALS/KID* ST7 .... 242 E6
Tarleton Cl *HLWD* L26 .... 50 E4 8
Tarnbeck *RUNC* WA7 .... 74 C5
Tarn Cl *WSFD* CW7 .... 177 J1
Tarn Ct *WARR* WA1 .... 38 F5
Tarn Mt *MCFLDS* SK11 .... 138 A7
Tarnside *OFTN* SK2 .... 47 M6
The Tarns *CHD/CHDH* SK8 .... 64 B1
Tarnway *GOL/RIS/CU* WA3 .... 23 M5
Tarporley Cl *EDGY/DAV* SK3 .. 46 C7 1
Tarporley Rd *CHSE* CH3 .... 172 C5
  GTS/LS CH66 .... 94 E8
  NWCHW CW8 .... 151 L4
  TPLY/KEL CW6 .... 172 E5

  WARRS WA4 .... 76 D4
  WARRS WA4 .... 102 C3
  WHITCH SY13 .... 259 M8
Tarran Pl *ALT* WA14 .... 42 E6
Tarrant Ct *CH/BCN* CH1 .... 144 E3
Tarvin Av *CW/SHV* CW2 .... 220 D8
Tarvin Cl *EP* CH65 .... 95 J8 2
  GOL/RIS/CU WA3 .... 23 L5
  MCFLDS SK11 .... 138 E7
  MWCH CW10 .... 179 K7
  RUNC WA7 .... 73 J6
Tarvin Gv *BURS/TUN* ST6 .... 243 M6
Tarvin Rd *CHD/CHDH* SK8 .... 46 A8
  CHSE CH3 .... 170 A3
  FROD/HEL WA6 .... 124 D2
Tasman Cl *WARRW/BUR* WA5 .. 36 C4
Tate Cl *WDN* WA8 .... 52 D2 8
Tate Dr *CW/HAS* CW1 .... 222 C8
Tatland Dr *WYTH/NTH* M22 .... 63 M1 8
Tattenhall La *CHSE* CH3 .... 214 F2
  TPLY/KEL CW6 .... 215 M2
Tattenhall Rd *CHSE* CH3 .... 195 J7
Tatton Cl *ALS/KID* ST7 .... 241 J1 8
  BRAM/HZG SK7 .... 47 M8
  CHD/CHDH SK8 .... 46 A8
  CHSW/BR CH4 .... 168 E7 3
  NWCHE CW9 .... 129 M8 8
  WSFD CW7 .... 177 H3
Tatton Dr *SBCH* CW11 .... 204 C5
Tattonmere Gdns
  CHD/CHDH SK8 .... 46 A8
Tatton Rd *CW/SHV* CW2 .... 237 L2
  WILM/AE SK9 .... 64 E7
Tatton Stile *KNUT* WA16 .... 82 A8 8
Tatton St *KNUT* WA16 .... 107 G2
  STKP SK1 .... 3 G5
Taunton Cl *BRAM/HZG* SK7 .... 67 G2
Taunton Rd *HUY* L36 .... 32 B2 8
Taurus Gv *BURS/TUN* ST6 .... 243 K6
Tavistock Rd *WARRW/BUR* WA5.. 35 L8
Tavlin Av *WARRW/BUR* WA5 .... 36 F3
Tawney Cl *ALS/KID* ST7 .... 243 H2
Tawny Ct *RUNC* WA7 .... 73 L5
Taxal Moor Rd *CHF/WBR* SK23 .. 89 J8
Taxi Rd *MANAIR* M90 .... 63 H5
Taxmere Cl *SBCH* CW11 .... 203 M5
Tay Cl *BIDD* ST8 .... 227 L3
Tayfield Rd *WYTH/NTH* M22 .... 63 J2
Taylor Rd *ALT* WA14 .... 42 A7
Taylor's La *CW/HAS* CW1 .... 240 C1
  WARRW/BUR WA5 .... 54 A2 8
Taylors Rw *RUNC* WA7 .... 9 M3
Taylor St *BURS/TUN* ST6 .... 243 J5
  WARRS WA4 .... 56 D1
  WDN WA8 .... 7 L2
Taylors Vw *CQ* CH5 .... 142 M8 3
Teal Av *KNUT* WA16 .... 107 H2
  POY/DIS SK12 .... 86 E1
Teal Cl *ALT* WA14 .... 42 B4
  OFTN SK2 .... 47 M7
  WARRN/WOL WA2 .... 37 L1
  WSFD CW7 .... 177 K7
Teal Gv *GOL/RIS/CU* WA3 .... 38 F1
  HLWD L26 .... 50 E3
Tedder Dr *WYTH/NTH* M22 .... 63 M5
Tedder Sq *WDN* WA8 .... 6 A5
Teddington Cl *WARRS* WA4 .... 56 E7
Tees Ct *EP* CH65 .... 10 A3
Teesdale Cl *OFTN* SK2 .... 47 L6 8
Tefler Ct *MWCH* CW10 .... 179 L6
Teggsnose La *MCFLDS* SK11 .. 139 J8 8
Tegid Wy *CHSW/BR* CH4 .... 168 D7
Tegsnose Mt *MCFLDS* SK11 .. 139 J8 8
Telford Cl *ALS/KID* ST7 .... 242 F4
  CONG CW12 .... 208 B2
  WDN WA8 .... 33 K8
Telford Gdns *SBCH* CW11 .... 222 F1 8
Telford Pl *NANT* CW5 .... 20 B6
Telford Rd *EP* CH65 .... 95 L8
  MPL/ROM SK6 .... 49 G8
Telford Wy *AUD/MAD/W* CW3 .. 273 M1
  CHSW/BR CH4 .... 168 F6 11
  MWCH CW10 .... 179 L3
Tempest Rd *WILM/AE* SK9 .... 110 C3
Temple Ct *GOL/RIS/CU* WA3 .... 29 L6
Templeton Cl *ALT* WA14 .... 42 E6
Tenby Cl *WARRW/BUR* WA5 .... 36 F2
Tenby Dr *CHD/CHDH* SK8 .... 65 H3
  RUNC WA7 .... 73 K2 8
Tenby Rd *EDGY/DAV* SK3 .... 46 B5
  MCFLDS SK11 .... 137 L6
Tenement La *CHD/CHDH* SK8 .. 65 J1
Tennyson Av *ALS/KID* ST7 .... 243 C4
  CW/HAS CW1 .... 19 L3
Tennyson Cl *ALS/KID* ST7 .... 224 F4
  CW/SHV CW2 .... 238 A3 8
  HTNM SK4 .... 46 A3
  MCFLDS SK11 .... 137 L5
  NWCHE CW9 .... 130 C5 2
Tennyson Dr *WARRN/WOL* WA2 .. 37 J2
Tennyson Rd *CHD/CHDH* SK8 .. 45 K6 8
  EP CH65 .... 10 B9
  HUY L36 .... 32 A4
  WDN WA8 .... 7 G2
Tennyson St *STHEL* WA9 .... 34 A2
Tennyson Wk *CH/BCN* CH1 .... 145 G7 8
Tensing Cl *WARRW/BUR* WA5 .. 36 B4
Terence Av *WARR* WA1 .... 37 M5
Terminal Rd East
  MANAIR M90 .... 63 H5 3
Terminal Rd North *MANAIR* M90 .. 63 H5
Terminal Rd South
  MANAIR M90 .... 63 H5 8
Tern Av *ALS/KID* ST7 .... 243 J2 2
Tern Cl *ALT* WA14 .... 42 B4
  BIDD ST8 .... 227 L4
  WDN WA8 .... 34 B8 8
Tern Dr *POY/DIS* SK12 .... 66 B8
Terrace Rd *WDN* WA8 .... 53 G7
Terrick Rd *WHITCH* SY13 .... 270 A2
Terrig St *CQ* CH5 .... 142 B8
Tetbury Cl *WYTH/NTH* M22 .... 63 H3
Tetchill Cl *GTS/LS* CH66 .... 120 D2
  RUNC WA7 .... 74 D4
Tetton La *MWCH* CW10 .... 202 E2
Teviot Wy *RDSH* SK5 .... 3 G1
Tewit Hall Cl *SPK/HALE* L24 .... 70 C1
Tewit Hall Rd *SPK/HALE* L24 .. 70 C1

Tewkesbury Av HALE/TIMP WA15.. 62 C1
Tewkesbury Cl CHD/CHDH SK8........ 65 H6
CHNE CH2 .... 145 M5
GTS/LS CH66 .... 120 E5
MWCH CW10 .... 179 H3
POY/DIS SK12 .... 66 D8
WLTN L25 .... 50 C2
Tewkesbury Dr
MCFLDN SK10 .... 112 E8
Tewkesbury Rd
EDGY/DAV SK3 .... 46 B6
GOL/RIS/CU WA3 .... 23 H4
Thackeray Dr CHSE CH3 .... 170 C2
Thackery Ct SBCH CW11 .... 203 K6
Thames Av LEIGH WN7 .... 24 F3
Thames Cl CONG CW12 .... 207 M3
Thamesdale EP CH65 .... 121 H1
Thames Dr BIDD ST8 .... 227 K3
Thames Gdns EP CH65 .... 121 G1
Thames Rd GOL/RIS/CU WA3 .... 29 M2
Thames Side EP CH65 .... 121 H1
Thatcher Cl ALT WA14 .... 61 J4
Thatcher Gv BIDD ST8 .... 227 H4
Thaxted Dr OFTN SK2 .... 48 A7
Theatre Ct NWCHE CW9 .... 13 H3
Thelwall Cl HALE/TIMP WA15 ..... 42 E6
Thelwall La WARRS WA4 .... 56 F1
Thelwall New Rd WARRS WA4 .... 57 H1
Thelwall Rd GTS/LS CH66 .... 94 E8
SALE M33 .... 43 L1
Theobald Rd ALT WA14 .... 61 K3
Thetford Cl MCFLDN SK10 .... 138 C1
Thetford Rd WARRW/BUR WA5 .... 35 L6
Thewlis St WARRW/BUR WA5 .... 4 B7
Third Av ALS/KID ST7 .... 242 E3
CW/HAS CW1 .... 19 L9
FLINT CH6 .... 116 A7
POY/DIS SK12 .... 86 D3
RUNC WA7 .... 73 M5
SBCH CW11 .... 204 A7
Thirlby Dr WYTH/NTH M22 .... 63 K3
Thirlemere Rd STKP SK1 .... 3 L9
Thirlmere MCFLDS SK11 .... 137 M7
Thirlmere Av
WARRN/WOL WA2 .... 37 J1
Thirlmere Cl FROD/HEL WA6 .... 99 K4
HOLMCH CW4 .... 181 G1
WILM/AE SK9 .... 109 M3
Thirlmere Ct CONG CW12 .... 207 G2
Thirlmere Dr LYMM WA13 .... 58 F1
Thirlmere Rd CHNE CH2 .... 146 A7
CW/SHV CW2 .... 237 M3
EP CH65 .... 121 J2
GOL/RIS/CU WA3 .... 23 J3
NSTN CH64 .... 91 L6
PART M31 .... 31 L8
WYTH/NTH M22 .... 63 H2
Thirsk Av SALE M33 .... 42 C1
Thirsk Cl RUNC WA7 .... 73 J6
Thirsk Wy MCFLDN SK10 .... 138 C1
Thistle Sq PART M31 .... 40 E2
Thistleton Cl MCFLDS SK11 .... 15 G9
Thistlewood Dr WILM/AE SK9 .... 84 D5
Thomas Brassey Cl CHNE CH2 .... 17 K2
Thomas Cl ALS/KID ST7 .... 224 E8
CH/BCN CH1 .... 144 F6
CHNE CH2 .... 146 F4
EP CH65 .... 121 H2
Thomas Ct RUNC WA7 .... 73 M5
Thomasons Bridge La
WARRS WA4 .... 55 L6
Thomas St ALS/KID ST7 .... 242 D4
ALS/KID ST7 .... 243 M3
BIDD ST8 .... 227 J3
CW/HAS CW1 .... 19 G2
FLINT CH6 .... 116 B5
GOL/RIS/CU WA3 .... 23 G4
HALE/TIMP WA15 .... 42 E8
MPL/ROM SK6 .... 48 A1
MPL/ROM SK6 .... 49 H2
RUNC WA7 .... 9 J1
STKP SK1 .... 3 G9
WDN WA8 .... 7 G7
Thomas St West OFTN SK2 .... 3 H9
Thompson Av GOL/RIS/CU WA3 .... 29 L1
Thompson Dr WHITCH SY13 .... 269 L5
Thompson St GOL/RIS/CU WA3 .... 29 L7
Thomson St EDGY/DAV SK3 .... 2 F8
Thoresway Rd WILM/AE SK9 .... 83 M7
Thoriby Rd GOL/RIS/CU WA3 .... 29 M1
Thorley Dr HALE/TIMP WA15 .... 43 H7
Thorley Gv CW/SHV CW2 .... 18 B9
Thorley La HALE/TIMP WA15 .... 43 H6
HALE/TIMP WA15 .... 62 B1
HALE/TIMP WA15 .... 62 F3
Thorley Ms BRAM/HZG SK7 .... 65 M5
Thornberry Cl CH/BCN CH1 .... 144 B4
Thornbrook Wy SBCH CW11 .... 203 K7
Thornbury Av
GOL/RIS/CU WA3 .... 23 L5
Thornbury Cl CHD/CHDH SK8 .... 65 J3
Thornbush Cl GOL/RIS/CU WA3 .... 23 L5
Thorn Cl WARRW/BUR WA5 .... 54 F1
Thorndale Gv HALE/TIMP WA15 .... 43 G7
Thorn Dr WYTH/NTH M22 .... 64 A4
Thorndyke Cl RAIN/WH L35 .... 33 L3
Thorne Cl MCFLDN SK10 .... 112 A7
Thorne Dr GTS/LS CH66 .... 94 B8
Thorneycroft Rd
HALE/TIMP WA15 .... 43 H7
Thorney Dr BRAM/HZG SK7 .... 65 J6
Thorneyholme Dr KNUT WA16 .... 107 H3
Thornfield Cl GOL/RIS/CU WA3 .... 23 J4
Thornfield Gv CHD/CHDH SK8 .... 65 G2
Thornfield Hey WILM/AE SK9 .... 84 E4
Thornfield Rd HTNM SK4 .... 46 A1
Thornfields CQ CH5 .... 142 A8
Thorn Gv CHD/CHDH SK8 .... 65 H5
HALE/TIMP WA15 .... 61 L1
Thorngrove Av NTHM/RTH M23 .... 43 K5
Thorngrove Dr WILM/AE SK9 .... 84 C6
Thorngrove Hl WILM/AE SK9 .... 84 C6
Thorngrove Rd WILM/AE SK9 .... 84 C6
Thornham Rd SALE M33 .... 42 E2
Thornhill Dr
AUD/MAD/W CW3 .... 267 L5
Thornholme Rd MPL/ROM SK6 .... 48 F8
Thorn La NWCHW CW8 .... 12 A9
Thornleigh Av PS/BROM CH62 .... 93 M1
Thornleigh Dr GTS/LS CH66 .... 94 E6
Thornley Rd LYMM WA13 .... 58 C1
Thorn Rd BRAM/HZG SK7 .... 65 K7
RUNC WA7 .... 9 M8
WARR WA1 .... 38 A4
Thornsett NM/HAY SK22 .... 69 K2
Thornsgreen Rd
WYTH/NTH M22 .... 63 K4
Thornton WDN WA8 .... 6 C5
Thornton Av MCFLDS SK11 .... 138 A7
Thornton Bank
TPLY/KEL CW6 .... 198 D8
Thornton Cl LEIGH WN7 .... 24 F3
Thorntondale Dr
WARRW/BUR WA5 .... 35 M5
Thornton Dr CHNE CH2 .... 145 K7
CW/SHV CW2 .... 238 A5
WILM/AE SK9 .... 84 D1
Thornton Ga CHD/CHDH SK8 .... 45 G6
Thornton Green La CHNE CH2 .... 122 E3
Thornton Rd CHD/CHDH SK8 .... 64 C3
EP CH65 .... 95 L8
WARRW/BUR WA5 .... 36 B8
Thorn Tree Dr CW/HAS CW1 .... 221 G3
Thorntree Gn WARRS WA4 .... 57 H7
Thornway BRAM/HZG SK7 .... 65 J4
MCFLDN SK10 .... 113 G5
MPL/ROM SK6 .... 67 M5
Thornwythe Gv GTS/LS CH66 .... 94 E8
Thornycroft WSFD CW7 .... 177 G3
Thornycroft Cl MCFLDS SK11 .... 161 L3
Thornycroft St MCFLDS SK11 .... 15 J6
Thorpe Cl CW/HAS CW1 .... 220 F4
Thorp St MCFLDN SK10 .... 15 H4
Thorsby Rd HALE/TIMP WA15 .... 42 E7
Thowler La ALT WA14 .... 59 M6
Threaphurst La BRAM/HZG SK7 .... 67 J2
Threapwood Rd
WYTH/NTH M22 .... 63 L3
Three Fields Cl CONG CW12 .... 207 G1
Threeways NWCHW CW8 .... 127 K8
Thresher Cl SALE M33 .... 43 M1
Threshfield Dr HALE/TIMP WA15 .... 43 J5
Throstle Gv MPL/ROM SK6 .... 48 E7
Thurlestone Dr BRAM/HZG SK7 .... 66 B2
Thurlestone Rd ALT WA14 .... 42 B6
Thurlow GOL/RIS/CU WA3 .... 23 L5
Thursfield Av ALS/KID ST7 .... 243 J1
Thurston Cl WARRW/BUR WA5 .... 36 D6
Thurston Gn WILM/AE SK9 .... 110 A3
Thurston Rd CHSW/BR CH4 .... 168 E7
Thynne St WARR WA1 .... 4 E8
Tibbs Cross La WDN WA8 .... 34 D3
Tidal La WARRN/WOL WA2 .... 37 M4
Tidebrook Pl BURS/TUN ST6 .... 243 L5
Tideswell Cl CHD/CHDH SK8 .... 64 D4
Tideswell Rd BRAM/HZG SK7 .... 66 E4
Tidnock Av CONG CW12 .... 184 D7
Tiffield Ct WSFD CW7 .... 154 A8
Tilbury Pl RUNC WA7 .... 74 E6
Tildsley Crs RUNC WA7 .... 72 F6
Tilewright Cl ALS/KID ST7 .... 243 H2
Tillard Av EDGY/DAV SK3 .... 46 B4
Tilley St WARR WA1 .... 5 J5
Tillhey Rd WYTH/NTH M22 .... 63 K2
Tilman Cl WARRW/BUR WA5 .... 36 B4
Tilson Rd NTHM/RTH M23 .... 43 M7
Tilstock Rd WHITCH SY13 .... 270 A7
Tilston Av WARRS WA4 .... 38 A8
Tilstone Cl ALS/KID ST7 .... 243 G4
CW/SHV CW2 .... 253 L2
NWCHE CW9 .... 13 K9
Tilston Rd MALPAS SY14 .... 246 A6
Timberfields Rd CH/BCN CH1 .... 144 A4
Timber La NWCHE CW9 .... 13 H1
Timberscombe Gdns WARR WA1 .... 38 E6
Timber St MCFLDN SK10 .... 15 L2
Timbrell Av CW/HAS CW1 .... 221 G6
Timmis Cl WARRN/WOL WA2 .... 38 A1
Timmis Crs WDN WA8 .... 7 G3
Timperley Av WARRS WA4 .... 38 A8
Timperley La LEIGH WN7 .... 25 H2
Timperley St WDN WA8 .... 7 J5
Timpson Rd NTHM/RTH M23 .... 43 L5
Tinkwood La MALPAS SY14 .... 256 F4
Tinsley St WARRS WA4 .... 56 F1
Tintagel Cl MCFLDN SK10 .... 137 L4
RUNC WA7 .... 74 C6
Tintern Av AIMK WN4 .... 22 D1
CHNE CH2 .... 145 M6
Tintern Cl POY/DIS SK12 .... 66 D7
WARRW/BUR WA5 .... 36 E2
Tintern Dr HALE/TIMP WA15 .... 62 C2
Tintern Gv STKP SK1 .... 3 L6
Tintern Rd CHD/CHDH SK8 .... 65 H6
Tipping St ALT WA14 .... 61 K1
HALE/TIMP WA15 .... 61 K1
Tipton Cl CHD/CHDH SK8 .... 46 B8
Tipton Dr NTHM/RTH M23 .... 44 A2
Tiree Cl BRAM/HZG SK7 .... 66 F3
Tirley La TPLY/KEL CW6 .... 173 M1
Tithebarn Dr NSTN CH64 .... 91 H2
Tithebarn Rd HALE/TIMP WA15 .... 62 C4
The Tithings RUNC WA7 .... 73 L3
Tiverton Av SALE M33 .... 42 F1
Tiverton Cl CHNE CH2 .... 145 L7
HUY L36 .... 32 B2
SBCH CW11 .... 204 C5
WDN WA8 .... 52 C1
Tiverton Dr SALE M33 .... 42 F1
Tiverton Rd HLWD L26 .... 50 E6
Tiverton Sq WARRW/BUR WA5 .... 35 L8
Tiviot Dl STKP SK1 .... 3 G4
Tiviot Wy STKP SK1 .... 3 J1
Tobermory Rd CHD/CHDH SK8 .... 64 C2
Todbrook Cl CHF/WBR SK23 .... 89 J6
Toft Cl CHSW/BR CH4 .... 168 E7
WDN WA8 .... 6 E3
Toft Rd KNUT WA16 .... 107 G3
Toftwood Av RAIN/WH L35 .... 33 L3
Tolland La HALE/TIMP WA15 .... 61 M4
Tollard Cl CHD/CHDH SK8 .... 65 H5
Toll Bar Av MCFLDS SK11 .... 15 L6
Toll Bar Rd CHSE CH3 .... 170 C3
MCFLDS SK11 .... 137 M4
WARRN/WOL WA2 .... 37 G1
Tollbar St STKP SK1 .... 3 H7
Tollemache Dr CW/HAS CW1 .... 221 G4
Tollgate Cl ALS/KID ST7 .... 242 C4
Tollgate Dr AUD/MAD/W CW3 .... 263 M8
Tomkinson St CHNE CH2 .... 17 K2
Tom La ALT WA14 .... 60 E6
Tomlinson Av WARRN/WOL WA2 .... 37 K4
Tommy's La CONG CW12 .... 184 F8
CW/HAS CW1 .... 19 J7
Tonbridge Cl MCFLDN SK10 .... 138 B2
SPK/HALE L24 .... 50 B8
Toogood Cl CHNE CH2 .... 146 F4
Topcroft Cl WYTH/NTH M22 .... 44 E4
Top Farm La WSFD CW7 .... 218 F2
Topfield Rd WYTH/NTH M22 .... 63 J1
Topping Ct GOL/RIS/CU WA3 .... 29 H8
The Toppings MPL/ROM SK6 .... 48 A1
Top Rd BIDD ST8 .... 209 K7
FROD/HEL WA6 .... 99 K7
FROD/HEL WA6 .... 126 B3
Top Station Rd ALS/KID ST7 .... 226 C5
Torbay Dr OFTN SK2 .... 3 M9
Torcross Wy HLWD L26 .... 50 E4
Torkington La BRAM/HZG SK7 .... 67 K1
Torkington Rd BRAM/HZG SK7 .... 66 F2
CHD/CHDH SK8 .... 45 H7
WILM/AE SK9 .... 84 C6
Torkington St EDGY/DAV SK3 .... 2 C9
Toronto Av MANAIR M90 .... 63 H5
Toronto Rd OFTN SK2 .... 47 G6
Torquay Gv OFTN SK2 .... 47 H8
Torridon Gv GTS/LS CH66 .... 120 F1
Torrin Cl EDGY/DAV SK3 .... 46 F7
Torrington Dr HLWD L26 .... 50 E6
Torrise TPLY/KEL CW6 .... 197 K3
Torr Rd MCFLDS SK11 .... 138 C8
Torrs Va NM/HAY SK22 .... 69 J5
Torr Top St NM/HAY SK22 .... 69 J5
Torrvale Rd NM/HAY SK22 .... 69 H5
Torville Dr BIDD ST8 .... 227 L4
Totland Cl WARRW/BUR WA5 .... 35 J5
Totland Gv CHNE CH2 .... 145 L8
Totnes Av BRAM/HZG SK7 .... 66 A2
HLWD L26 .... 50 F3
Totridge Cl OFTN SK2 .... 47 K7
Tottenham Dr NTHM/RTH M23 .... 43 K5
Tourney Gn WARRW/BUR WA5 .... 36 A2
Tours Av NTHM/RTH M23 .... 44 A2
Tower Cl BIDD ST8 .... 227 G6
Tower Hl MCFLDN SK10 .... 113 K8
Tower Hill Rd ALS/KID ST7 .... 226 E4
BIDD ST8 .... 226 F6
Tower La LYMM WA13 .... 58 F2
NWCHW CW8 .... 128 B3
RUNC WA7 .... 74 C5
Tower Rd CH/BCN CH1 .... 16 D4
Towers Cl CW/SHV CW2 .... 238 A5
POY/DIS SK12 .... 66 F7
Towers La FROD/HEL WA6 .... 124 B5
Towers Rd POY/DIS SK12 .... 66 F6
Tower Wy CW/HAS CW1 .... 18 F4
WLTN L25 .... 50 A1
Towneley Ct WDN WA8 .... 7 G3
Town Farm La FROD/HEL WA6 .... 126 E6
Townfield Av AIMK WN4 .... 22 B2
CHSE CH3 .... 228 E2
Townfield Cl ALS/KID ST7 .... 242 D2
Townfield Ct NWCHW CW8 .... 129 H1
Townfield Gdns ALT WA14 .... 42 D7
Townfield La CH/BCN CH1 .... 120 D8
CHSE CH3 .... 172 A2
CHSE CH3 .... 228 D1
FROD/HEL WA6 .... 99 J5
KNUT WA16 .... 132 F7
LYMM WA13 .... 40 B5
NWCHW CW8 .... 103 G8
TPLY/KEL CW6 .... 197 J6
Townfield Rd ALT WA14 .... 42 D7
KNUT WA16 .... 108 A1
RUNC WA7 .... 74 C2
Townfields AIMK WN4 .... 22 A1
KNUT WA16 .... 107 J2
Town Flds SBCH CW11 .... 204 A7
Townfields Crs WSFD CW7 .... 177 K5
Townfields Dr WSFD CW7 .... 177 J6
Townfields Gdns WSFD CW7 .... 177 K5
Townfields Rd WSFD CW7 .... 177 K5
Townfield Vw RUNC WA7 .... 74 C2
Town Fold MPL/ROM SK6 .... 49 H5
Town Hl WARR WA1 .... 4 E5
Town La KNUT WA16 .... 81 M8
NSTN CH64 .... 91 M6
SPK/HALE L24 .... 71 K3
Townley Pl MCFLDS SK11 .... 15 H6
Townley St MCFLDS SK11 .... 15 H6
Townscliffe La MPL/ROM SK6 .... 49 H6
Townsend La ALS/KID ST7 .... 225 G4
Townsend Rd CONG CW12 .... 207 L2
Townsfield Dr TPLY/KEL CW6 .... 175 M5
Townshend Rd NWCHE CW9 .... 131 G1
Township Cl MALPAS SY14 .... 230 C3
Townson Dr LEIGH WN7 .... 24 F3
Town St MPL/ROM SK6 .... 49 H5
Town Well FROD/HEL WA6 .... 126 C2
Tracy Dr NEWLW WA12 .... 27 L1
Trafalgar Av POY/DIS SK12 .... 87 G1
Trafalgar Cl NWCHE CW9 .... 153 L1
POY/DIS SK12 .... 87 G1
Trafford Av WARRW/BUR WA5 .... 4 B2
Trafford Crs RUNC WA7 .... 73 J6
Trafford Dr HALE/TIMP WA15 .... 43 H4
Trafford Rd WILM/AE SK9 .... 84 A3
WILM/AE SK9 .... 110 A3
Trafford St CH/BCN CH1 .... 17 G2
Tragan Cl OFTN SK2 .... 47 K6
Tragan Dr OFTN SK2 .... 47 K6
WARRW/BUR WA5 .... 54 D1
Tramway Rd IRL M44 .... 31 M5
Tranby Cl WYTH/NTH M22 .... 44 F8
Tranmere Dr WILM/AE SK9 .... 84 E1
Tranmere Rd EDGY/DAV SK3 .... 46 B4
Trans Pennine Trail
WARRW/BUR WA5 .... 54 D3
WDN WA8 .... 53 G7
Trap Rd CONG CW12 .... 159 J8
Trap St MCFLDS SK11 .... 159 G5
Travers' Entry STHEL WA9 .... 26 A6
Travis Brow HTNM SK4 .... 2 C5
Travis St WDN WA8 .... 7 J4
Trawden Gn OFTN SK2 .... 47 K8
Treborth Rd CH/BCN CH1 .... 168 D1
Tree Bank Cl RUNC WA7 .... 9 G6
Treen Cl MCFLDN SK10 .... 137 K3
Tree Tops NSTN CH64 .... 91 L7
Treetops Cl WARR WA1 .... 37 M5
Tree Wy KNUT WA16 .... 107 G5
Trefoil Cl CHSE CH3 .... 170 B6
GOL/RIS/CU WA3 .... 29 J7
Tregele Cl CH/BCN CH1 .... 168 D1
Trelawny Av FLINT CH6 .... 116 B6
Trelawny Sq FLINT CH6 .... 116 A5
Trenance Cl RUNC WA7 .... 74 B7
Trenchard Dr WYTH/NTH M22 .... 63 M5
Trent Av WSFD CW7 .... 178 B3
Trent Cl BRAM/HZG SK7 .... 65 J6
RAIN/WH L35 .... 33 H1
WDN WA8 .... 34 B8
WSFD CW7 .... 178 B3
Trentdale EP CH65 .... 121 H1
Trent Gv BIDD ST8 .... 227 K6
Trentham Av HTNM SK4 .... 45 M1
Trentham Cl WDN WA8 .... 34 B8
Trentham St RUNC WA7 .... 8 E1
Trent Rd RAIN/WH L35 .... 33 H1
Tressel Dr STHEL WA9 .... 34 A1
Trevalyn Wy WRX/GR/LL LL12 .... 210 C5
Trevithick Cl CW/HAS CW1 .... 222 A8
Trevone Cl KNUT WA16 .... 107 G3
Trevor Av SALE M33 .... 42 F2
Trevor Gv STKP SK1 .... 3 K7
The Triangle HALE/TIMP WA15 .... 43 H5
Tribune Av ALT WA14 .... 42 B5
Trickett La NWCHW CW8 .... 152 A1
Tricketts La NANT CW5 .... 237 L7
Trinity Cl CW/SHV CW2 .... 18 B9
Trinity Ct GOL/RIS/CU WA3 .... 29 M7
Trinity Gdns EDGY/DAV SK3 .... 65 M1
Trinity La MCFLDS SK11 .... 162 F1
Trinity Pl CONG CW12 .... 208 B4
WDN WA8 .... 7 J6
Trinity Sq MCFLDN SK10 .... 15 L3
Trinity St CH/BCN CH1 .... 16 F5
MPL/ROM SK6 .... 48 F7
Trispen Cl HLWD L26 .... 50 E4
Troon Cl BRAM/HZG SK7 .... 66 A5
HOLMCH CW4 .... 181 H2
Troon Dr CHD/CHDH SK8 .... 64 C3
Troon Rd NTHM/RTH M23 .... 43 M6
Trossach Cl WARRN/WOL WA2 .... 37 L2
Troutbeck Av CONG CW12 .... 207 G2
WARRW/BUR WA5 .... 4 C2
Troutbeck Cl RUNC WA7 .... 74 A7
Troutbeck Gv WSFD CW7 .... 177 K2
Troutbeck Rd CHD/CHDH SK8 .... 64 B1
HALE/TIMP WA15 .... 43 K7
Trouthall La KNUT WA16 .... 131 M1
Trubshaw Pl ALS/KID ST7 .... 243 H1
Trueman's Ct CQ CH5 .... 166 C4
Trueman's Wy CQ CH5 .... 166 C3
Trumans La GTS/LS CH66 .... 94 C5
Truro Cl BRAM/HZG SK7 .... 65 M5
CONG CW12 .... 207 L4
GTS/LS CH66 .... 120 F4
MCFLDN SK10 .... 137 L3
RUNC WA7 .... 74 C6
WARR WA1 .... 38 B4
Tudor Av FLINT CH6 .... 116 A8
Tudor Cl CQ CH5 .... 142 B7
GTS/LS CH66 .... 120 F4
NWCHE CW9 .... 130 E6
WARRS WA4 .... 57 G2
WSFD CW7 .... 177 K6
Tudor Dr MCFLDN SK10 .... 111 K5
Tudor Gn WILM/AE SK9 .... 84 E3
Tudor Rd ALT WA14 .... 42 B5
RUNC WA7 .... 74 B1
WILM/AE SK9 .... 84 E3
WLTN L25 .... 50 C5
The Tudors BURS/TUN ST6 .... 243 M8
Tudor Wy CHSE CH3 .... 170 A5
CONG CW12 .... 207 K3
NANT CW5 .... 251 L1
Tue La WDN WA8 .... 33 K5
Tuffley Rd NTHM/RTH M23 .... 44 A8
Tulip Cl EDGY/DAV SK3 .... 46 D7
Tulip Dr HALE/TIMP WA15 .... 43 K6
Tulip Rd PART M31 .... 40 E2
Tully Av NEWLW WA12 .... 26 E1
Tulworth Rd POY/DIS SK12 .... 66 D8
Tumblewood Dr
CHD/CHDH SK8 .... 45 L8
Tunbridge Cl CW/SHV CW2 .... 238 A4
WARRW/BUR WA5 .... 36 A4
Tunnel Rd NWCHW CW8 .... 129 H2
Tunnicliffe Rd MCFLDS SK11 .... 162 F1
Tunnicliffe St MCFLDN SK10 .... 15 G4
Tunshill Rd NTHM/RTH M23 .... 43 L3
Tunstall Rd BIDD ST8 .... 227 J7
CONG CW12 .... 186 A8
Tunstall St HTNM SK4 .... 2 F2
Turf La MCFLDS SK11 .... 162 C1
Turf Lea Rd MPL/ROM SK6 .... 68 B3
Turnall Rd WDN WA8 .... 52 B5
Turnberry Cl LYMM WA13 .... 39 J8
MCFLDN SK10 .... 112 C8
NWCHE CW9 .... 130 E5
WSFD CW7 .... 177 J2
Turnberry Dr WILM/AE SK9 .... 84 D4
Turnberry Rd CHD/CHDH SK8 .... 64 C3
Turnbury Rd WYTH/NTH M22 .... 44 E7
Turncliff Crs MPL/ROM SK6 .... 48 D5
Turncroft La STKP SK1 .... 3 K6
Turner Cl WDN WA8 .... 52 D1
Turner Rd MPL/ROM SK6 .... 48 F6
Turner St MCFLDN SK10 .... 113 H4
NANT CW5 .... 21 G6
Turnfield Rd CHD/CHDH SK8 .... 64 C1
Turnhurst Rd BURS/TUN ST6 .... 243 M5
Turnill Dr AIMK WN4 .... 22 B2
Turnlea Cl BIDD ST8 .... 227 H6
Turnock St MCFLDS SK11 .... 15 J7
The Turnpike MPL/ROM SK6 .... 48 D5
Turnstone Av NEWLW WA12 .... 22 C8
Turnstone Dr HLWD L26 .... 50 E3
Turnstone Rd OFTN SK2 .... 48 A7
Turret Hall Dr
GOL/RIS/CU WA3 .... 23 L4
Turrocks Cl NSTN CH64 .... 91 L7
Turrocks Cft NSTN CH64 .... 91 L7
Turton Cl GOL/RIS/CU WA3 .... 29 J7
Turton St GOL/RIS/CU WA3 .... 23 G4
Turves Rd CHD/CHDH SK8 .... 64 E3
Tuscan Cl WDN WA8 .... 34 B7
Tuscan Rd DID/WITH M20 .... 45 H4
Tushingham Cl CHSE CH3 .... 170 B5
Tuson Dr WDN WA8 .... 33 M8
Tutor Bank NEWLW WA12 .... 27 K1
Tweed Cl ALT WA14 .... 42 C6
Tweedsmuir Cl
WARRN/WOL WA2 .... 29 G8
Tweenbrook Av NTHM/RTH M23 .... 63 G1
Twemlow Av SBCH CW11 .... 204 B4
Twemlow La HOLMCH CW4 .... 157 H6
Twenty Acre Rd
WARRW/BUR WA5 .... 36 C4
Twigworth Rd
WYTH/NTH M22 .... 63 J2
Twining Brook Rd
CHD/CHDH SK8 .... 65 H1
Twinnies Rd WILM/AE SK9 .... 84 B3
Twiss Green Dr GOL/RIS/CU WA3 .... 24 E8
Twiss Green La GOL/RIS/CU WA3 .... 24 D8
Twist Av GOL/RIS/CU WA3 .... 23 J4
Twoacre Av WYTH/NTH M22 .... 44 C7
Two Acre Gv GTS/LS CH66 .... 120 F3
Twyford Cl DID/WITH M20 .... 44 F1
WDN WA8 .... 34 B8
Twyford La WDN WA8 .... 34 D6
Tyberton Pl SPK/HALE L24 .... 50 C6
Tyler St WILM/AE SK9 .... 110 A3
Tyne Cl WARRN/WOL WA2 .... 37 L2
Tynedale Av CW/SHV CW2 .... 18 D8
Tynedale Cl MCFLDS SK11 .... 14 E5
Tynemouth Rd RUNC WA7 .... 74 C6
Tynesdale EP CH65 .... 121 H1
Tynwald Crs WDN WA8 .... 33 M7
Tynwald Dr WARRS WA4 .... 56 C5
Tyrer Rd NEWLW WA12 .... 27 J3
Tyrone Cl NTHM/RTH M23 .... 43 K4
Tytherington Cl MWCH CW10 .... 179 J6
Tytherington Dr MCFLDN SK10 .... 112 D8
Tytherington La MCFLDN SK10 .... 112 D7
Tytherington Park Rd
MCFLDN SK10 .... 138 D2

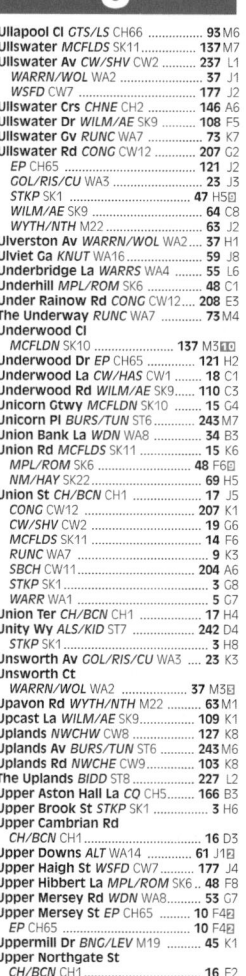

U

Ullapool Cl GTS/LS CH66 .... 93 M6
Ullswater MCFLDS SK11 .... 137 M7
Ullswater Av CW/SHV CW2 .... 237 L1
WARRN/WOL WA2 .... 37 J1
WSFD CW7 .... 177 J2
Ullswater Crs CHNE CH2 .... 146 A6
Ullswater Dr WILM/AE SK9 .... 108 F5
Ullswater Gv RUNC WA7 .... 73 K7
Ullswater Rd CONG CW12 .... 207 G2
EP CH65 .... 121 J2
GOL/RIS/CU WA3 .... 23 J3
STKP SK1 .... 47 H5
WILM/AE SK9 .... 64 C8
WYTH/NTH M22 .... 63 J2
Ulverston Av WARRN/WOL WA2 .... 37 H1
Ulviet Ga KNUT WA16 .... 59 J8
Underbridge La WARRS WA4 .... 55 L6
Underhill MPL/ROM SK6 .... 48 C1
Under Rainow Rd CONG CW12 .... 208 E3
The Underway RUNC WA7 .... 73 M4
Underwood Cl
MCFLDN SK10 .... 137 M3
Underwood Dr EP CH65 .... 121 H2
Underwood La CW/HAS CW1 .... 18 C1
Underwood Rd WILM/AE SK9 .... 110 C3
Unicorn Gtwy MCFLDN SK10 .... 15 G4
Unicorn Pl BURS/TUN ST6 .... 243 M7
Union Bank La WDN WA8 .... 34 B3
Union Rd MCFLDS SK11 .... 15 K6
MPL/ROM SK6 .... 48 F6
NM/HAY SK22 .... 69 H5
Union St CH/BCN CH1 .... 17 J5
CONG CW12 .... 207 K1
CW/SHV CW2 .... 19 G6
MCFLDS SK11 .... 14 F6
RUNC WA7 .... 9 K3
SBCH CW11 .... 204 A6
STKP SK1 .... 3 G8
WARR WA1 .... 5 G7
Union Ter CH/BCN CH1 .... 17 H4
Unity Wy ALS/KID ST7 .... 242 D4
STKP SK1 .... 3 H8
Unsworth Av GOL/RIS/CU WA3 .... 23 K3
Unsworth Ct
WARRN/WOL WA2 .... 37 M3
Upavon Rd WYTH/NTH M22 .... 63 M1
Upcast La WILM/AE SK9 .... 109 K1
Uplands NWCHW CW8 .... 127 K8
Uplands Av BURS/TUN ST6 .... 243 M6
Uplands Rd NWCHE CW9 .... 103 K8
The Uplands BIDD ST8 .... 227 L2
Upper Aston Hall La CQ CH5 .... 166 B3
Upper Brook St STKP SK1 .... 3 H6
Upper Cambrian Rd
CH/BCN CH1 .... 16 D3
Upper Downs ALT WA14 .... 61 J1
Upper Haigh St WSFD CW7 .... 177 J4
Upper Hibbert La MPL/ROM SK6 .... 48 F8
Upper Mersey Rd WDN WA8 .... 53 G7
Upper Mersey St EP CH65 .... 10 F4
EP CH65 .... 10 F4
Uppermill Dr BNG/LEV M19 .... 45 K1
Upper Northgate St
CH/BCN CH1 .... 16 F2
Upper Raby Rd NSTN CH64 .... 92 A2
Upton Av CHD/CHDH SK8 .... 65 G4
Upton Bridle Pth WDN WA8 .... 33 M8
Upton Cl GOL/RIS/CU WA3 .... 23 K4
SPK/HALE L24 .... 70 E1
WSFD CW7 .... 153 M8
Upton Dr ALT WA14 .... 42 E4
CHNE CH2 .... 145 J6
WARRW/BUR WA5 .... 35 M7
Upton Gra WDN WA8 .... 33 K8
Upton Gn SPK/HALE L24 .... 70 E1
Upton La CHNE CH2 .... 145 J5

Upton Pk CHNE CH2 .... 145 K6
Upton Rd GTS/LS CH66 .... 94 D8
Upwood Rd GOL/RIS/CU WA3 ... 23 K5
Urban Dr HALE/TIMP WA15 ..... 42 E8
Urban Rd HALE/TIMP WA15 ..... 42 E8
Ure Ct EP CH65 .... 10 A3
Urmston Av NEWLW WA12 ..... 22 B7
Urwick Rd MPL/ROM SK6 ..... 48 B3
Utkinton La TPLY/KEL WA6 .... 174 D6
Utkinton Rd TPLY/KEL CW6 .... 197 J1

V

Vahler Ter RUNC WA7 .... 9 L2
Vale Av WARRN/WOL WA2 ..... 5 H1
Valebrook Dr NANT CW5 ..... 253 C4
Vale Cl BRAM/HZG SK7 .... 47 L8
  CHSW/BR CH4 .... 190 C1
  HTNM SK4 .... 45 M2
  MPL/ROM SK6 .... 48 F2
Vale Ct WARRS WA4 .... 101 C1
Vale Cresent CHD/CHDH SK8 ... 64 F2
Vale Gdns EP CH65 .... 95 H8
  FROD/HEL WA6 .... 98 B8
Vale Head WILM/AE SK9 ..... 84 D2
Valentine Rd ALS/KID ST7 ..... 243 C4
  NEWLW WA12 .... 26 F1
Vale Owen Rd
  WARRN/WOL WA2 .... 37 K3
Vale Rd ALT WA14 .... 61 H3
  EP CH65 .... 95 H8
  HALE/TIMP WA15 .... 43 C7
  HTNM SK4 .... 45 M3
  MPL/ROM SK6 .... 48 B4
  NWCHE CW9 .... 104 B6
  NWCHW CW8 .... 129 J8
  TPLY/KEL CW6 .... 198 A8
  WILM/AE SK9 .... 83 L4
Vale Royal Dr NWCHW CW8 ... 153 C5
Vale Vw NWCHW CW9 .... 130 D3
Valewood Av HTNM SK4 ..... 46 A3
Valiant Cl WARRN/WOL WA2 .... 37 M2
Valley Cl ALS/KID ST7 .... 240 F1
  CHD/CHDH SK8 .... 64 E1
  KNUT WA16 .... 107 C5
Valley Ct WARRN/WOL WA2 ..... 37 M3
Valley Dr CHNE CH2 .... 145 J7
  GTS/LS CH66 .... 94 D7
  WILM/AE SK9 .... 84 C1
Valley La NWCHW CW8 ..... 151 M1
Valley Rd BRAM/HZG SK7 ..... 65 M3
  CHD/CHDH SK8 .... 64 E1
  CW/SHV CW2 .... 237 M3
  MCFLDS SK11 .... 138 A7
  NWCHW CW8 .... 128 C3
Valley Vw GTS/LS CH66 ..... 94 D7
  NEWLW WA12 .... 27 H3
  NWCHE CW9 .... 130 C5
Valley Wy KNUT WA16 ..... 107 C5
Vanguard Ct GOL/RIS/CU WA3 .. 29 K8
Varden Gv EDGY/DAV SK3 ..... 46 D7
Varden Rd POY/DIS SK12 ..... 86 E1
Vardon Dr WILM/AE SK9 ..... 84 D6
Varey Rd CONG CW12 ..... 184 F8
Vaudrey Crs CONG CW12 ..... 207 M1
Vaudrey Dr BRAM/HZG SK7 ..... 66 E2
  CHD/CHDH SK8 .... 65 G1
  HALE/TIMP WA15 .... 43 G4
  WARR WA1 .... 38 D5
Vaughan Rd CHF/WBR SK23 ..... 89 L7
  HTNM SK4 .... 2 C1
Vaughans La CHSE CH3 ..... 170 A4
Vauxhall Cl WARRW/BUR WA5 .. 35 M8
Vauxhall Rd NANT CW5 ..... 20 E3
Vauxhall Wy WSFD CW7 ..... 177 J6
Vawdrey Dr NTHM/RTH M23 .... 43 M2
Venable's Ct CH/BCN CH1 .... 144 F8
  NWCHE CW9 .... 13 J1
Venables Wy KNUT WA16 ..... 59 J8
  MWCH CW10 .... 179 L7
Venlow Gdns CHD/CHDH SK8 ... 65 H3
Venns Rd WARRN/WOL WA2 ..... 5 L3
Ventnor Cl MWCH CW10 ..... 179 J4
  WARRW/BUR WA5 .... 35 K5
Ventnor Rd DID/WITH M20 ..... 45 J1
  HTNM SK4 .... 46 A2
Verbena Cl PART M31 .... 40 F1
  RUNC WA7 .... 73 M8
Verdin Av NWCHW CW9 ..... 12 F1
Verdin Av NWCHW CW9 ..... 153 M5
  WSFD CW7 .... 177 J2
Verdin Ct CW/HAS CW1 ..... 221 G4
Verdin St NWCHE CW9 ..... 130 C4
Verdure Av SALE M33 .... 43 J3
Vere St WARR WA1 .... 18 E2
Verity Cl CW/HAS CW1 ..... 222 C4
Vermont Cl WARRW/BUR WA5 .. 36 C5
Vernon Av CONG CW12 ..... 207 M4
  GTS/LS CH66 .... 94 A3
  STKP SK1 .... 3 L4
Vernon Cl CH/BCN CH1 ..... 144 A4
  CHD/CHDH SK8 .... 64 E3
  POY/DIS SK12 .... 86 D2
Vernon Dr AUD/MAD/W CW3 ... 264 F8
  MPL/ROM SK6 .... 48 C5
Vernon Gv SALE M33 .... 43 L1
Vernon Pk HALE/TIMP WA15 ... 43 G4
Vernon Rd CH/BCN CH1 ..... 16 D4
  MPL/ROM SK6 .... 47 L1
  POY/DIS SK12 .... 86 E2
Vernon St BRAM/HZG SK7 ..... 66 D1
  CW/HAS CW1 .... 18 C1
  MCFLDN SK10 .... 15 L5
  STKP SK1 .... 3 G4
  WARR WA1 .... 5 H8
Vernon Wy CW/HAS CW1 ..... 19 G2
  CW/SHV CW2 .... 19 G5
Veronica Cl DID/WITH M20 ..... 45 J1
Veronica Wy GTS/LS CH66 ..... 94 D5
Verrill Av NTHM/RTH M23 ..... 44 C3
Veryan Cl HLWD L26 .... 50 F3
Vetch Cl GOL/RIS/CU WA3 ..... 31 H7
The Vetches CHSE CH3 ..... 146 F7
Viaduct Rd ALT WA14 .... 42 D5
Viaduct St EDGY/DAV SK3 ..... 2 E6

NEWLW WA12 .... 27 G1
Vicarage Av CHD/CHDH SK8 ... 65 H4
Vicarage Cl CHSE CH3 ..... 146 F7
  SPK/HALE L24 .... 71 L3
Vicarage Gdns WRXS/E LL13 .. 228 E4
Vicarage Gdns SBCH CW11 ... 203 K4
Vicarage Gv WSFD CW7 ..... 177 K7
Vicarage Hl FROD/HEL WA6 ... 98 C8
Vicarage La ALT WA14 .... 61 J3
  AUD/MAD/W CW3 .... 264 A8
  AUD/MAD/W CW3 .... 267 L7
  FROD/HEL WA6 .... 98 C8
  FROD/HEL WA6 .... 99 J5
  NSTN CH64 .... 118 D2
  POY/DIS SK12 .... 66 E7
  SBCH CW11 .... 203 L4
  TPLY/KEL CW6 .... 175 M5
  TPLY/KEL CW6 .... 216 F4
Vicarage Rd AIMK WN4 ..... 22 B2
  CHNE CH2 .... 17 M1
  CW/HAS CW1 .... 222 D6
  EDGY/DAV SK3 .... 46 E6
  NWCHE CW9 .... 13 L3
  WDN WA8 .... 7 H6
Vicarage Wk NWCHE CW9 ..... 13 L4
Vicarage Wy MCFLDS SK11 ... 137 M5
Vicars Cl CHSE CH3 .... 148 F5
Vicars Cross Rd CHSE CH3 ... 170 B2
Vicar's La CH/BCN CH1 ..... 17 H6
Vickers Cl CQ CH5 .... 166 C1
Vickers Rd WDN WA8 .... 52 E8
Vickers Wy NWCHE CW9 ..... 13 J4
Victoria Av ALS/KID ST7 ..... 242 F2
  BRAM/HZG SK7 .... 66 E1
  CHD/CHDH SK8 .... 65 G2
  CW/HAS CW1 .... 222 C8
  CW/SHV CW2 .... 220 F8
  DID/WITH M20 .... 45 L1
  HALE/TIMP WA15 .... 42 E5
  HOLMCH CW4 .... 181 J2
  MPL/ROM SK6 .... 47 M1
  WARRS WA4 .... 57 G2
  WARRW/BUR WA5 .... 35 K6
  WDN WA8 .... 53 G2
Victoria Cl BRAM/HZG SK7 ..... 65 K6
  EDGY/DAV SK3 .... 2 F9
  WHITCH SY13 .... 270 A5
Victoria Crs CHNE CH2 ..... 16 F1
Victoria Crs CHNE CH2 ..... 16 F1
  CHSW/BR CH4 .... 17 J7
  CQ CH5 .... 142 A6
Victoria Dr SALE M33 .... 43 K1
Victoria Gv WDN WA8 .... 53 C1
Victoria Pk NWCHW CW8 ..... 12 F1
Victoria Park Rd
  BURS/TUN ST6 .... 243 L8
Victoria Pl RAIN/WH L35 ..... 33 J1
  WARRS WA4 .... 56 C3
Victoria Rd CH/BCN CH1 ..... 17 G3
  CHNE CH2 .... 16 F1
  CHSW/BR CH4 .... 168 D6
  CQ CH5 .... 142 A6
  EP CH65 .... 10 D7
  HALE/TIMP WA15 .... 43 G6
  HALE/TIMP WA15 .... 61 L2
  IRL M44 .... 31 M3
  MCFLDN SK10 .... 137 M3
  NEWLW WA12 .... 22 C8
  NSTN CH64 .... 92 A6
  NWCHE CW9 .... 13 L3
  RUNC WA7 .... 9 J2
  SALE M33 .... 43 K1
  STKP SK1 .... 3 L5
  WARRS WA4 .... 56 D3
  WARRW/BUR WA5 .... 35 L8
  WDN WA8 .... 7 H6
  WILM/AE SK9 .... 84 A6
  WYTH/NTH M22 .... 44 D4
Victoria Rw BIDD ST8 ..... 227 J8
Victoria Sq WSFD CW7 ..... 177 G4
Victoria St ALT WA14 .... 42 D7
  CW/HAS CW1 .... 18 F3
  KNUT WA16 .... 106 F2
  NM/HAY SK22 .... 69 H6
  NWCHE CW9 .... 130 E2
  RAIN/WH L35 .... 33 J1
  SBCH CW11 .... 204 A5
  WARR WA1 .... 5 J6
  WDN WA8 .... 7 J6
Victoria Ter RAIN/WH L35 ..... 33 J1
Victoria Wk MCFLDN SK10 ..... 15 J4
Victoria Wy BRAM/HZG SK7 ... 65 K6
Victory Rd IRL M44 .... 31 J8
Vienna Rd EDGY/DAV SK3 ..... 46 D6
Vienna Rd East EDGY/DAV SK3 .. 46 D6
Viewlands Dr WILM/AE SK9 ... 84 D2
View Rd RAIN/WH L35 .... 33 J2
Villa Cl BIDD ST8 .... 227 J6
Villa Farm SBCH CW11 ..... 205 H3
Village Cl NWCHE CW9 ..... 131 G4
  RUNC WA7 .... 74 A9
  WARRS WA4 .... 38 E8
Village La WARRS WA4 ..... 102 D1
Village Rd CHSE CH3 .... 147 L1
  CHSE CH3 .... 170 F4
  CHSE CH3 .... 171 H8
Village St RUNC WA7 .... 74 E2
The Village CONG CW12 ..... 207 H4
  MCFLDN SK10 .... 112 A6
  NSTN CH64 .... 118 D4
Village Wks WRX/GR/LL LL12 .. 210 A7
Village Wy WILM/AE SK9 ..... 84 D3
Villa Rd CQ CH5 .... 143 H6
Villars St WARR WA1 .... 5 K7
Villdale Av OFTN SK2 .... 47 J5
Villiers Russell Cl CW/HAS CW1 .. 19 G2
Vincent Cl WARRW/BUR WA5 .. 36 B4
Vincent Dr CHSW/BR CH4 ..... 169 H6
Vincent St CW/HAS CW1 ..... 19 G2
  MCFLDS SK11 .... 15 G7
Vine Bank Rd ALS/KID ST7 ... 243 G2
Vine Cl MCFLDS SK11 ..... 138 A7
Vine Crs WARRW/BUR WA5 ... 35 L6
Vine Gv OFTN SK2 .... 47 J6
Vine Rd GTS/LS CH66 .... 94 D7
Vine St BRAM/HZG SK7 ..... 66 E1
  MCFLDN SK10 .... 113 H4
  RUNC WA7 .... 9 G3

WDN WA8 .... 7 H6
Vine Tree Cl CW/SHV CW2 ..... 18 D8
Violet Cl GOL/RIS/CU WA3 ..... 29 J8
Violet St AIMK WN4 .... 22 B2
  OFTN SK2 .... 46 F6
  WDN WA8 .... 7 G7
Virginia Cha NTHM/RTH M23 ... 43 K5
Virginia Dr CH/BCN CH1 ..... 144 C7
Viscount Dr CHD/CHDH SK8 ... 64 D5
  MANAIR M90 .... 62 F5
Vista Av NEWLW WA12 ..... 22 A8
Vista Rd NEWLW WA12 ..... 22 A8
  WARR WA1 .... 9 H6
The Vista IRL M44 .... 31 J8
Vista Wy NEWLW WA12 ..... 22 A8
Volunteer Av NANT CW5 ..... 20 F5
Volunteer Flds NANT CW5 ..... 20 F5
Volunteer St CH/BCN CH1 ..... 17 G6
  FROD/HEL WA6 .... 99 J3
Vose Cl WARRW/BUR WA5 ..... 36 D6
Vulcan Cl NEWLW WA12 ..... 27 J3
  WARRN/WOL WA2 .... 37 M2
Vyrnwy Rd CHSW/BR CH4 ..... 168 D6

W

Waddington Cl
  GOL/RIS/CU WA3 .... 23 M4
  WARRN/WOL WA2 .... 37 M3
Wadebridge Av NTHM/RTH M23 .. 43 K5
Wade Crs NWCHW CW8 ..... 102 F8
Wades La WSFD CW7 ..... 177 K1
Wadeson Wy GOL/RIS/CU WA3 .. 29 H5
Wade St NWCHE CW9 .... 13 M1
Wadham Wy HALE/TIMP WA15 .. 61 M3
Wadsworth Dr HALE/TIMP WA15 .. 62 D6
Waggs Rd CONG CW12 ..... 207 J3
Wagg St CONG CW12 ..... 207 K2
Waine St CW/HAS CW1 ..... 19 H1
Wainwright Cl OFTN SK2 ..... 47 G5
Wainwright Rd ALT WA14 ..... 42 B7
Wakefield Crs MPL/ROM SK6 ... 48 A3
Wakefield Rd GTS/LS CH66 ... 120 E3
Wakefield Rd GOL/RIS/CU WA3 .. 23 G5
Wakeham Cha MCFLDS SK11 ... 137 M5
Wakes Meadow
  TPLY/KEL CW6 .... 216 E4
Walden Cl WARRS WA4 ..... 57 K1
Walden Crs BRAM/HZG SK7 ..... 66 C1
Walden Dr CHD/CHDH SK8 ..... 45 K7
Waldon Av CONG CW12 ..... 184 D7
Waldon Rd MCFLDS SK11 ..... 138 A7
Waldron Rd CW/HAS CW1 ..... 239 K1
Waldron's La CW/HAS CW1 ..... 221 J3
Walfield Av CONG CW12 ..... 184 D7
Walford Av CW/SHV CW2 ..... 18 C6
Walford Rd AIMK WN4 .... 22 C1
Walgrave Cl CONG CW12 ..... 184 A8
Walker Av STHEL WA9 ..... 34 B1
Walker Cl CW/HAS CW1 ..... 222 D8
Walker Dr MWCH CW10 ..... 179 J4
Walker La MCFLDS SK11 ..... 162 E2
Walker Rd BURS/TUN ST6 ..... 243 M8
  IRL M44 .... 31 M3
Walkers La ALS/KID ST7 ..... 225 H2
  CHSE CH3 .... 228 F3
  GTS/LS CH66 .... 94 D3
  STHEL WA9 .... 34 A1
  TPLY/KEL CW6 .... 197 K3
  WARRW/BUR WA5 .... 54 L1
Walker St CHNE CH2 .... 17 K2
  CW/HAS CW1 .... 18 C1
  MCFLDN SK10 .... 14 E4
  STKP SK1 .... 2 F5
  WARRN/WOL WA2 .... 4 E5
The Walk SPK/HALE L24 ..... 70 A2
Wallace St NWCHW CW8 ..... 12 E5
  WDN WA8 .... 7 H4
Wallbank Rd BRAM/HZG SK7 ... 66 A3
Wallcroft NSTN CH64 .... 93 G5
Wallerscote Cl NWCHW CW8 ... 128 E4
Wallerscote Rd NWCHW CW8 ... 128 D3
Wallet St MCFLDS SK11 ..... 15 J8
Walley Dr BURS/TUN ST6 ..... 243 K6
Walleys La NANT CW5 ..... 235 J5
Walley St BIDD ST8 .... 227 J4
Wall Fields Cl NANT CW5 ..... 20 F3
Wall Fields Rd NANT CW5 ..... 20 E3
Wallhill La CONG CW12 ..... 206 D3
Wall Hill Wy NWCHW CW8 ... 127 M1
Wallingford Rd WILM/AE SK9 ... 64 C7
Wallis St CW/HAS CW1 ..... 19 H3
  WARRS WA4 .... 56 B1
Wall La NANT CW5 .... 20 E6
Walls Av CH/BCN CH1 .... 16 D5
Wallsend Ct WDN WA8 .... 52 F1
Wallworth's Bank
  CONG CW12 .... 207 L2
Walmer Dr BRAM/HZG SK7 ..... 66 A3
Walmer Pl WSFD CW7 ..... 177 J6
Walmsley St NEWLW WA12 ..... 22 D8
  RDSH SK5 .... 2 F1
  WDN WA8 .... 7 M4
Walney Rd WYTH/NTH M22 ..... 44 D8
Walnut Av NWCHW CW8 ..... 102 F8
Walnut Cl CHNE CH2 ..... 145 K5
  WARR WA1 .... 38 E5
  WILM/AE SK9 .... 84 E4
Walnut Dr WHITCH SY13 ..... 269 M6
  WSFD CW7 .... 178 A3
Walnut Gv GTS/LS CH66 ..... 120 F3
Walnut La NWCHW CW8 ..... 129 G7
Walnut Ri CONG CW12 ..... 207 H2
Walnut Rd PART M31 .... 40 D1
Walnut Tree La SBCH CW11 ... 204 A1
Walnut Tree Rd EDGY/DAV SK3 .. 46 A5
Walpole Av CQ CH5 .... 166 A4
  RAIN/WH L35 .... 32 F1
Walpole Cl CW/HAS CW1 ..... 222 C7
Walpole Gv WARRN/WOL WA2 .. 37 J2
Walpole Rd RUNC WA7 ..... 73 H6
Walpole St CH/BCN CH1 ..... 16 E2
Walsh Cl NEWLW WA12 ..... 22 C1
Walsingham Dr RUNC WA7 ..... 74 D2

Walsingham Rd
  WARRW/BUR WA5 .... 35 M7
Walters Green Crs
  GOL/RIS/CU WA3 .... 23 G2
Walter St CH/BCN CH1 ..... 17 H2
  WARR WA1 .... 37 L5
  WDN WA8 .... 53 K3
Waltham Av GOL/RIS/CU WA3 .. 25 J5
Waltham Ct RUNC WA7 ..... 54 B8
Waltham Dr CHD/CHDH SK8 ... 65 H6
Waltham Pl CHSW/BR CH4 ..... 169 G6
Walton Av WARRW/BUR WA5 .. 35 L7
Walton Dr MPL/ROM SK6 ..... 48 D5
Walton Gv ALS/KID ST7 ..... 242 C4
Walton Heath Dr MCFLDN SK10 .. 112 B8
Walton Heath Rd WARRS WA4 .. 56 B3
Walton Lea Rd WARRS WA4 ... 55 M5
Walton New Rd WARRS WA4 ... 56 B4
Walton Pl CH/BCN CH1 ..... 144 E8
Walton Rd ALT WA14 .... 42 B7
  GOL/RIS/CU WA3 .... 29 M1
  GOL/RIS/CU WA3 .... 29 L7
  SALE M33 .... 42 F3
  WARRS WA4 .... 56 C4
The Waltons CHSW/BR CH4 ..... 169 L6
Walton St RUNC WA7 ..... 9 H3
  STKP SK1 .... 3 H9
Walton Wy ALS/KID ST7 ..... 242 C4
Wandsworth Wy WDN WA8 ..... 6 F9
Wansfell Pl WARRN/WOL WA2 .. 37 L1
Warbler Cl HLWD L26 .... 50 D2
Warbreck Gv SALE M33 ..... 43 K1
Warburton Bridge Rd
  GOL/RIS/CU WA3 .... 40 A3
Warburton Cl HALE/TIMP WA15 .. 62 D6
  LYMM WA13 .... 40 A8
  MPL/ROM SK6 .... 48 A3
Warburton Dr HALE/TIMP WA15 .. 62 D6
Warburton La LYMM WA13 ..... 40 A7
  PART M31 .... 40 F1
Warburton Rd WILM/AE SK9 ... 64 D8
Warburton St DID/WITH M20 ... 45 H1
  WARRS WA4 .... 56 D3
Warburton Vw
  GOL/RIS/CU WA3 .... 40 A2
Ward Av MCFLDN SK10 ..... 113 G4
Ward Cl WARRW/BUR WA5 ..... 36 B3
Ward La POY/DIS SK12 ..... 68 E8
Wardle Av NANT CW5 ..... 218 C5
Wardle Crs MCFLDS SK11 ..... 161 K3
Wardle Ms MWCH CW10 ..... 179 J4
Wardle Rd SALE M33 .... 43 H1
Wardle St MCFLDS SK11 ..... 137 M5
Wardour Cl CW/HAS CW1 ..... 222 C7
Wardour St WARRW/BUR WA5 .. 4 B4
Wards La CONG CW12 ..... 208 C4
  SBCH CW11 .... 181 J7
Ward St MPL/ROM SK6 ..... 47 M1
  STKP SK1 .... 3 J9
Wareham Cl WARR WA1 ..... 38 C4
Wareham Dr CW/HAS CW1 ..... 221 H4
Warford Av POY/DIS SK12 ..... 87 C2
Warford Crs WILM/AE SK9 ..... 109 H5
Warford Hall Dr WILM/AE SK9 .. 109 G4
Warford La WILM/AE SK9 ..... 109 G4
Wargrave Ms NEWLW WA12 ..... 27 J3
Wargrave Rd NEWLW WA12 ..... 27 J1
Warham St ALS/KID ST7 ..... 84 B5
Waring Av STHEL WA9 ..... 26 B2
  WARRS WA4 .... 37 M7
Warkick Rd CH/BCN CH1 ..... 144 F7
Warkworth Cl WDN WA8 ..... 52 C1
Warley Cl CHD/CHDH SK8 ..... 45 L6
Warmingham La MWCH CW10 ... 179 K6
  SBCH CW11 .... 203 H4
Warmingham Rd CW/HAS CW1 .. 221 J3
  SBCH CW11 .... 202 D6
Warmley Rd NTHM/RTH M23 ... 43 K4
Warnley Cl WDN WA8 .... 52 D1
Warren Av CHD/CHDH SK8 ..... 45 K7
  KNUT WA16 .... 106 E2
  NWCHE CW9 .... 131 G2
Warren Cl BRAM/HZG SK7 ..... 66 A3
  KNUT WA16 .... 106 F2
  NWCHE CW9 .... 179 H5
  POY/DIS SK12 .... 66 B8
Warren Ct FROD/HEL WA6 ..... 99 K6
  GTS/LS CH66 .... 120 D1
Warren Cft RUNC WA7 ..... 74 C5
Warren Dr CHSW/BR CH4 ..... 190 A1
  GTS/LS CH66 .... 94 B3
  HALE/TIMP WA15 .... 62 D5
  MCFLDS SK11 .... 161 K3
  NEWLW WA12 .... 22 F8
  WARRS WA4 .... 56 C4
Warrener St SALE M33 ..... 43 K1
Warren Gv MCFLDS SK11 ..... 161 K3
Warren Hey WILM/AE SK9 ..... 84 E4
Warren La NWCHW CW8 ..... 129 G8
  WARR WA1 .... 38 D4
Warren Lea MPL/ROM SK6 ..... 49 H2
  POY/DIS SK12 .... 66 E7
Warren Rd CHD/CHDH SK8 ..... 65 H2
  EDGY/DAV SK3 .... 46 E6
  WARRN/WOL WA2 .... 37 K3
  WARRS WA4 .... 56 C4
Warren St STKP SK1 .... 3 G4
The Warren NWCHW CW8 ..... 127 K7
Warren Wy TPLY/KEL CW6 ..... 197 K3
Warrington Av CW/HAS CW1 ... 221 J6
  EP CH65 .... 121 H2
Warrington La LYMM WA13 ..... 59 K1
Warrington Rd AIMK WN4 ..... 22 C3
  CHNE CH2 .... 146 D5
  GOL/RIS/CU WA3 .... 28 B1
  KNUT WA16 .... 80 B5
  LYMM WA13 .... 39 H8
  NEWLW WA12 .... 23 C6
  NWCHE CW9 .... 103 K5
  NWCHW CW8 .... 128 A4
  RAIN/WH L35 .... 33 M4
  RUNC WA7 .... 54 D8
  RUNC WA7 .... 73 J2
  WARRS WA4 .... 55 M6
  WARRW/BUR WA5 .... 35 K8
  WDN WA8 .... 7 L3

Warslow Dr SALE M33 ..... 43 L3
Warsop Av WYTH/NTH M22 ..... 44 E7
Warton Cl BRAM/HZG SK7 ..... 66 A5
  WARRW/BUR WA5 .... 55 G1
  WLTN L25 .... 50 C2
Warton Dr NTHM/RTH M23 ..... 44 A7
Warwick Av AIMK WN4 ..... 22 D2
  NEWLW WA12 .... 27 K3
  WARRW/BUR WA5 .... 35 K2
  WDN WA8 .... 35 K5
Warwick Cl ALS/KID ST7 ..... 243 G2
  CHD/CHDH SK8 .... 46 A8
  HUY L36 .... 32 A1
  KNUT WA16 .... 107 J3
  MCFLDS SK11 .... 137 M6
  NSTN CH64 .... 91 L7
Warwick Ct EP CH65 .... 121 L1
Warwick Dr BRAM/HZG SK7 ..... 66 D4
  HALE/TIMP WA15 .... 61 L3
  HTNM SK4 .... 2 A2
Warwick Pl WSFD CW7 ..... 177 J6
Warwick Rd HALE/TIMP WA15 ... 61 L3
  HTNM SK4 .... 2 A2
  HUY L36 .... 32 A1
  IRL M44 .... 31 M3
  MCFLDS SK11 .... 137 L6
  MPL/ROM SK6 .... 48 A2
Warwick St BIDD ST8 ..... 227 J5
  LEIGH WN7 .... 25 K1
Wasdale Dr CHD/CHDH SK8 ..... 64 B1
Wasdale Gv CW/HAS CW1 ..... 221 H5
Washbrook Dr NTHM/RTH M23 .. 43 K4
Washington Cl BIDD ST8 ..... 227 J2
Washington Dr CQ CH5 ..... 166 A2
  WARRW/BUR WA5 .... 36 B6
Wash La KNUT WA16 ..... 132 D8
  WARRS WA4 .... 56 E1
Washway Rd ALT WA14 ..... 42 E3
Wasley Cl WARRN/WOL WA2 ... 37 M1
Wastdale Rd NTHM/RTH M23 ... 43 K4
Waste La NWCHW CW8 ..... 150 F6
  WDN WA8 .... 151 L1
  TPLY/KEL CW6 .... 149 L7
Watburn Rd NM/HAY SK22 ..... 69 K3
Watch La SBCH CW11 ..... 203 G6
Waterbank Rw NWCHE CW9 ..... 13 H4
Waterbridge Ct WARRS WA4 ... 56 D4
Waterfoot La CHF/WBR SK23 ... 89 K6
Waterford Av DID/WITH M20 ... 44 E1
  MPL/ROM SK6 .... 48 E2
Waterford Dr NSTN CH64 ..... 92 A5
Waterford Wy RUNC WA7 ..... 74 C6
Watergate MCFLDN SK10 ..... 137 J2
Watergate La WLTN L25 ..... 50 B2
Watergate Sq CH/BCN CH1 ..... 16 F6
Watergate Wy WLTN L25 ..... 50 B2
Waterhouse Av
  MCFLDN SK10 .... 112 F4
Water La RAIN/WH L35 ..... 32 D4
  WILM/AE SK9 .... 84 A5
Water-lode NANT CW5 ..... 20 D6
Waterloo Gv ALS/KID ST7 ..... 243 G5
Waterloo La FROD/HEL WA6 ... 125 J3
Waterloo Rd BRAM/HZG SK7 ... 65 M3
  CHNE CH2 .... 145 J8
  CW/HAS CW1 .... 222 D8
  MPL/ROM SK6 .... 48 E2
  NWCHW CW8 .... 12 F4
  POY/DIS SK12 .... 66 B8
  RUNC WA7 .... 8 F2
  STKP SK1 .... 3 H6
  WDN WA8 .... 53 G7
Waterloo St West MCFLDS SK11 .. 15 J4
Watermead EDGY/DAV SK3 ..... 46 E8
Watermeetings La
  MPL/ROM SK6 .... 48 E2
Watermill Dr MCFLDS SK11 ..... 15 L6
Watersedge FROD/HEL WA6 ..... 99 K2
Waters Edge MPL/ROM SK6 ..... 49 G4
  NWCHE CW9 .... 129 K1
Watersedge Cl
  CHD/CHDH SK8 .... 65 H1
Watersfield Cl CHD/CHDH SK8 .. 64 F4
Waters Gn MCFLDS SK11 ..... 15 J7
  MPL/ROM SK6 .... 48 F7
  WARRS WA4 .... 56 D4
Waterside Av MPL/ROM SK6 ... 48 F7
Waterside Cl AUD/MAD/W CW3 .. 267 L6
  WHITCH SY13 .... 269 M6
Waterside Ms WARRS CW11 ... 222 F1
Waterside Rd NM/HAY SK22 ... 68 E5
Waterside Vw NWCHE CW9 ..... 130 E5
Waterside Wy MWCH CW10 ... 179 H2
Waters Reach POY/DIS SK12 ... 66 F7
Waters Reams CHSE CH3 ..... 170 B4
Water St MCFLDN SK10 ..... 113 G4
  MCFLDS SK11 .... 14 F6
  NEWLW WA12 .... 22 C8
  NWCHE CW9 .... 13 H4
  RUNC WA7 .... 9 H1
  STKP SK1 .... 3 H2
  WDN WA8 .... 7 G9
Water Tower Rd NSTN CH64 ... 91 L2
Water Tower St CH/BCN CH1 ... 16 F4
Watertower Vw CHNE CH2 ..... 17 M4
Waterway CHSE CH3 .... 171 H7
Waterways WARRW/BUR WA5 .. 36 D6
Waterworks Dr NEWLW WA12 ... 22 F8
Waterworks La GTS/LS CH66 ... 93 L3
  WARRN/WOL WA2 .... 28 B5
Watery La CONG CW12 ..... 207 G5
  FROD/HEL WA6 .... 99 L7
  WARRN/WOL WA2 .... 27 L6
Watford Bridge Rd
  NM/HAY SK22 .... 69 K3
Watford La NM/HAY SK22 ..... 69 J3
Watford Rd NM/HAY SK22 ..... 69 J2
Watkins Av NEWLW WA12 ..... 26 F1
Watkinson Wy WDN WA8 ..... 7 L4
Watkin St CQ CH5 .... 167 G1
  WARRN/WOL WA2 .... 4 C2
Watling Crs CHSW/BR CH4 ..... 169 L5
Watling Rd TPLY/KEL CW6 ..... 150 C6
Watling St NWCHE CW9 ..... 13 H2
  NWCHW CW8 .... 13 G2
Watson Av AIMK WN4 .... 22 C1

GOL/RIS/CU WA3 .... 22 F3
Watson's Cl CHSW/BR CH4 .... 190 C1
Watson Sq STKP SK1 .... 3 H6
Watton Cl WARRS WA4 .... 57 J1
Wavell Av WDN WA8 .... 52 C4
Wavell Rd WYTH/NTH M22 .... 63 K2
Wavells Wy CHSE CH3 .... 170 B7
Waveney Dr ALT WA14 .... 42 C6
WILM/AE SK9 .... 84 D2
Waveney Rd WYTH/NTH M22 .... 44 E8
Waverley Av WARRS WA4 .... 56 C4
Waverley Cl MCFLDN SK10 .... 139 G4
Waverley Crs WRX/CR/LL LL12 .... 210 C4
Waverley Dr CHD/CHDH SK8 .... 65 H6
Waverley Rd EDGY/DAV SK3 .... 2 B9
GOL/RIS/CU WA3 .... 23 K3
Waverley Ter CHNE CH2 .... 145 L8
Waverton Ap CHSE CH3 .... 193 K6
Waverton Cl CW/SHV CW2 .... 253 L2
NWCHE CW9 .... 129 L8
Waverton Mill Quays
CHSE CH3 .... 171 H7
Waverton Rd GTS/LS CH66 .... 94 F3
Wavertree Av ALS/KID ST7 .... 225 L5
WDN WA8 .... 7 G4
Wavertree Dr MWCH CW10 .... 179 H5
Wavertree Rd CH/BCN CH1 .... 144 C7
Waybutt La CW/SHV CW2 .... 254 D5
Wayfarers Dr NEWLW WA12 .... 27 L3
Wayford Cl FROD/HEL WA6 .... 99 H3
Wayland Cl WHITCH SY13 .... 270 B6
Wayland Rd WHITCH SY13 .... 270 B5
Waylands Dr WLTN L25 .... 50 B5
Waymills WHITCH SY13 .... 270 C5
Way's Gn WSFD CW7 .... 177 L4
Wayside Ct CHNE CH2 .... 146 F4
Wayside Dr POY/DIS SK12 .... 66 C8
Wayside Gdns BRAM/HZG SK7 .... 67 G2
Wayside Linley ALS/KID ST7 .... 241 M2
Wayside Rd MCFLDN SK10 .... 15 M6
Waywell La WARRN/WOL WA2 .... 37 M1
Weald Dr GTS/LS CH66 .... 94 A6
Wealstone Ct CHNE CH2 .... 145 L1
Weal Stone La CHNE CH2 .... 145 L6
Wearhead Cl GOL/RIS/CU WA3 .... 23 G5
Weaste La WARRS WA4 .... 57 K2
Weates Cl WDN WA8 .... 53 L1
Weathercock La CONG CW12 .... 208 E1
Weatherley Dr MPL/ROM SK6 .... 48 D6
Weaver Av RAIN/WH L35 .... 33 H1
Weaver Av ALS/KID ST7 .... 241 G1
ALT WA14 .... 61 J3
BIDD ST8 .... 227 K3
SBCH CW11 .... 203 L5
Weaver Ct MCFLDS SK11 .... 14 E6
Weaver Crs FROD/HEL WA6 .... 99 K3
Weaver Gra NWCHE CW9 .... 153 L4
Weaver Gv CHNE CH2 .... 146 F3
STHEL WA9 .... 26 A1
Weaverhall La WSFD CW7 .... 178 B7
Weaverham Rd NWCHW CW8 .... 152 A2
Weaver La FROD/HEL WA6 .... 99 H2
Weaver Rd EP CH65 .... 121 J1
FROD/HEL WA6 .... 99 K3
GOL/RIS/CU WA3 .... 30 A2
NANT CW5 .... 20 E5
NWCHE CW9 .... 153 L5
NWCHW CW8 .... 12 F4
RUNC WA7 .... 73 G6
Weaverside NANT CW5 .... 251 L2
Weaverside Av RUNC WA7 .... 73 M8
Weavers La BRAM/HZG SK7 .... 65 K6
Weaver St CH/BCN CH1 .... 16 F5
WSFD CW7 .... 177 L4
Weaver Valley Rd WSFD CW7 .... 177 M1
Weaver Vw NANT CW5 .... 201 G6
NWCHW CW8 .... 128 D3
Weaver Wy NWCHE CW9 .... 13 G2
Webb Dr WARRW/BUR WA5 .... 26 F6
Webb La STKP SK1 .... 3 K6
Webb's La MWCH CW10 .... 179 J2
Webster Cl CHSW/BR CH4 .... 190 C1
Websters La GTS/LS CH66 .... 120 F2
Weddell Cl WARRW/BUR WA5 .... 36 D5
Wedgwood Dr WDN WA8 .... 34 B8
Wedgwood La BIDD ST8 .... 227 J3
Wedgwood Rd ALS/KID ST7 .... 242 D6
CQ CH5 .... 166 E3
Wednesbury Dr
WARRW/BUR WA5 .... 35 M6
Weedon Av NEWLW WA12 .... 22 B7
Weighbridge Rd CQ CH5 .... 118 B7
Weir Gv ALS/KID ST7 .... 243 G2
Weir La WARR WA1 .... 38 E6
Weir St NWCHE CW9 .... 13 H5
WARRS WA4 .... 56 A3
Welbeck Av NEWLW WA12 .... 27 K2
Welbeck Cl MWCH CW10 .... 179 G3
Welburn Av WYTH/NTH M22 .... 63 J1
Welbury Rd NTHM/RTH M23 .... 43 M3
Welcroft St STKP SK1 .... 3 H7
Weldon Av CW/SHV CW2 .... 238 B5
Weldon Rd ALT WA14 .... 42 C6
Welford Av GOL/RIS/CU WA3 .... 23 J2
Welford Cl WILM/AE SK9 .... 84 E4
Welkin Rd MPL/ROM SK6 .... 47 J1
Welland Dr HLWD L26 .... 50 E7
SBCH CW11 .... 203 J7
Welland Rd WILM/AE SK9 .... 84 D2
Well Av MALPAS SY14 .... 258 B1
Well Bank SBCH CW11 .... 204 B6
Wellbank Dr HLWD L26 .... 51 G3
Well Bank La KNUT WA16 .... 134 C5
Wellbrook Cl RUNC WA7 .... 74 C7
SPK/HALE L24 .... 50 C8
Wellbrooke Cl AIMK WN4 .... 22 C1
Wellbrook Gn SPK/HALE L24 .... 70 D1
Well Cl NSTN CH64 .... 92 A8
Wellcroft Cl CW/SHV CW2 .... 238 B5
Weller Av POY/DIS SK12 .... 86 D2
Weller Cl POY/DIS SK12 .... 86 D2
Wellesbourne Cl
MCFLDN SK10 .... 137 M3
Wellesbourne Dr
NTHM/RTH M23 .... 43 M5
Wellesley Av CW/HAS CW1 .... 222 C8
EP CH65 .... 10 F8

Wellesley Cl NEWLW WA12 .... 22 B7
Welles St SBCH CW11 .... 204 B5
Well Farm Cl MALPAS SY14 .... 258 B3
Wellfield RUNC WA7 .... 74 E7
WDN WA8 .... 34 A8
WSFD CW7 .... 177 M2
Wellfield Cl KNUT WA16 .... 105 G5
Wellfield La GOL/RIS/CU WA3 .... 24 E8
NTHM/RTH M23 .... 44 A5
OFTN SK2 .... 47 J6
Wellfield St WARRW/BUR WA5 .... 4 B6
Wellgreen Cl HALE/TIMP WA15 .... 62 C1
Wellington Cl EP CH65 .... 10 F7
WARRN/WOL WA2 .... 37 M2
Wellington Ga SPK/HALE L24 .... 71 L2
Wellington Gv OFTN SK2 .... 46 F5
Wellington Pl ALT WA14 .... 61 K1
Wellington Rd ALS/KID ST7 .... 243 G3
BRAM/HZG SK7 .... 67 H4
CHSW/BR CH4 .... 190 B1
EP CH65 .... 10 D9
MCFLDN SK10 .... 112 F4
NANT CW5 .... 20 E9
Wellington Rd North EP CH65 .... 10 F8
Wellington Rd South
EDGY/DAV SK3 .... 2 F6
STKP SK1 .... 3 G8
Wellington St BRAM/HZG SK7 .... 66 F1
CQ CH5 .... 142 B6
MCFLDS SK11 .... 15 C6
NEWLW WA12 .... 27 G1
NWCHW CW8 .... 12 F4
RUNC WA7 .... 9 G1
STKP SK1 .... 3 G6
WARR WA1 .... 5 J7
WDN WA8 .... 7 G9
Well La ALS/KID ST7 .... 241 J1
BIDD ST8 .... 227 J2
CH/BCN CH1 .... 144 F3
CHNE CH2 .... 145 L7
FROD/HEL WA6 .... 126 C2
FROD/HEL WA6 .... 148 F1
MCFLDN SK10 .... 112 B5
MCFLDN SK10 .... 139 H2
NSTN CH64 .... 91 M7
NWCHE CW9 .... 77 G8
NWCHW CW8 .... 128 C2
TPLY/KEL CW6 .... 175 M5
WARRS WA4 .... 76 E4
WARRW/BUR WA5 .... 54 E1
Well Ml MPL/ROM SK6 .... 47 L1
Wells Av CW/HAS CW1 .... 222 D7
Wells Cl BIDD ST8 .... 227 K4
CHD/CHDH SK8 .... 64 C5
CHNE CH2 .... 146 F4
GTS/LS CH66 .... 120 E4
WARR WA1 .... 38 D4
Wells Dr HTNM SK4 .... 45 L2
Well St ALS/KID ST7 .... 226 D5
BIDD ST8 .... 227 J5
MALPAS SY14 .... 258 B1
NM/HAY SK22 .... 69 H4
WSFD CW7 .... 177 J3
Wellswood Dr CW/SHV CW2 .... 237 M5
Wellswood Rd GTS/LS CH66 .... 94 E5
Welsby Cl WARRN/WOL WA2 .... 37 M1
Welshampton Cl GTS/LS CH66 .... 120 D2
Welsh La WSFD CW7 .... 177 K6
Welshmen's La NANT CW5 .... 20 A1
Welshpool Cl NTHM/RTH M23 .... 44 B2
WARRW/BUR WA5 .... 36 D1
Welsh Rd CH/BCN CH1 .... 119 J6
CQ CH5 .... 142 E6
GTS/LS CH66 .... 94 A3
Welsh Rw MCFLDN SK10 .... 110 A6
Welton Av DID/WITH M20 .... 45 J2
Welton Cl SPK/HALE L24 .... 70 D1
WILM/AE SK9 .... 83 L8
Welton Dr WILM/AE SK9 .... 83 L8
Welton Gn SPK/HALE L24 .... 70 D1
Welton Gv WILM/AE SK9 .... 83 L8
Welwyn Cl WARRS WA4 .... 57 J1
Wemyss Av CH/BCN CH1 .... 144 D8
Wendlebury Cl LEIGH WN7 .... 24 E3
Wendon Rd NTHM/RTH M23 .... 44 B7
Wendover Rd NTHM/RTH M23 .... 43 J5
Wenger Rd WDN WA8 .... 34 B7
Wenlock Cl MCFLDN SK10 .... 14 D1
OFTN SK2 .... 48 A6
WARR WA1 .... 38 A4
Wenlock Crs CQ CH5 .... 166 E1
Wenlock Dr HLWD L26 .... 50 E5
Wenlock Gdns GTS/LS CH66 .... 120 F2
Wenlock La GTS/LS CH66 .... 120 F2
Wenlock Rd LEIGH WN7 .... 24 E2
RUNC WA7 .... 74 A8
SALE M33 .... 43 H5
Wenlock Wy CHSW/BR CH4 .... 168 F6
Wensley Av HLWD L26 .... 50 E5
Wensleydale Av
CHD/CHDH SK8 .... 45 J6
CONG CW12 .... 185 G7
RAIN/WH L35 .... 33 K1
Wensleydale Cl
NTHM/RTH M23 .... 62 F1
WARRW/BUR WA5 .... 35 M4
Wensley Dr BRAM/HZG SK7 .... 66 D5
Wensley Rd CHD/CHDH SK8 .... 45 J6
GOL/RIS/CU WA3 .... 23 L5
Wentworth Av HALE/TIMP WA15.. 43 G6
MCFLDN SK10 .... 137 M6
WARR WA1 .... 38 B5
Wentworth Cl MPL/ROM SK6 .... 48 F4
NWCHE CW9 .... 130 E5
WDN WA8 .... 34 A7
Wentworth Dr ALS/KID ST7 .... 243 J1
BRAM/HZG SK7 .... 66 A5
Wentworth Gv WSFD CW7 .... 177 G2
Wepre Dr CQ CH5 .... 142 A5
Werneth Cl BRAM/HZG SK7 .... 47 L8
Werneth St STKP SK1 .... 3 M2
Wervin Rd CHNE CH2 .... 145 M3
Wesley Av ALS/KID ST7 .... 224 D8
SBCH CW11 .... 204 B6
Wesley Cl NANT CW5 .... 20 F7
NSTN CH64 .... 91 K5

Wesley Pl CW/SHV CW2 .... 19 G7
NWCHE CW9 .... 13 K2
Wesley Rd BRAM/HZG SK7 .... 66 E1
STKP SK1 .... 3 H6
Wessenden Bank East
OFTN SK2 .... 47 K7
Wessenden Bank West
OFTN SK2 .... 47 K7
Wessex Cl CW/SHV CW2 .... 253 J1
WARR WA1 .... 38 E5
Wessex Dr NWCHE CW9 .... 130 C6
Westage Gdns NTHM/RTH M23 .... 44 A5
Westage La NWCHE CW9 .... 104 B4
West Av ALS/KID ST7 .... 242 C3
ALT WA14 .... 42 A7
CHD/CHDH SK8 .... 64 C3
CW/HAS CW1 .... 18 D3
CW/SHV CW2 .... 239 H7
GOL/RIS/CU WA3 .... 23 H3
LEIGH WN7 .... 25 J1
MWCH CW10 .... 179 J2
NWCHE CW9 .... 130 C6
WARRN/WOL WA2 .... 5 H1
WARRS WA4 .... 56 C3
West Bank CH/BCN CH1 .... 145 J8
WILM/AE SK9 .... 110 A4
West Bank Rd MCFLDN SK10 .... 14 C3
West Bank St WDN WA8 .... 53 G7
West Bond St MCFLDS SK11 .... 14 E6
Westbourne Av CW/HAS CW1 .... 221 G6
Westbourne Dr BURS/TUN ST6 .... 243 L7
Westbourne Rd CH/BCN CH1 .... 145 G8
WARRS WA4 .... 56 B5
Westbrook Av WARRS WA4 .... 56 D2
WHITCH SY13 .... 269 M4
Westbrook Centre
WARRW/BUR WA5 .... 36 C3
Westbrook Crs
WARRW/BUR WA5 .... 36 C3
Westbrook Dr MCFLDN SK10 .... 14 E2
Westbrook Rd FROD/HEL WA6 .... 126 B2
Westbrook Wy
WARRW/BUR WA5 .... 36 A3
Westbury Av SALE M33 .... 42 C3
Westbury Cl CW/SHV CW2 .... 238 C4
MWCH CW10 .... 179 J4
WARR WA1 .... 38 A4
Westbury Dr MCFLDS SK11 .... 14 B6
MPL/ROM SK6 .... 48 E6
Westbury Wy
CHSW/BR CH4 .... 168 F6
West Dr BRAM/HZG SK7 .... 66 A5
Westcliffe Gdns WARRS WA4 .... 76 E1
West Cl MCFLDN SK10 .... 112 C5
Westdale Rd WARR WA1 .... 38 A5
West Downs Rd CHD/CHDH SK8 .. 64 F1
West Dr CHD/CHDH SK8 .... 45 G8
NSTN CH64 .... 91 K6
WARRW/BUR WA5 .... 36 B8
WSFD CW7 .... 177 M2
West Dudley St WSFD CW7 .... 177 M3
West End CHSE CH3 .... 148 E5
West End Av CHD/CHDH SK8 .... 45 G6
West End Cottages
CONG CW12 .... 207 J2
Westenra Av EP CH65 .... 94 F7
Westerham Cl MCFLDN SK10 .... 14 C5
Western Ap CHNE CH2 .... 145 L8
Western Av CH/BCN CH1 .... 168 D1
MCFLDS SK11 .... 138 C7
NANT CW5 .... 251 L1
SPK/HALE L24 .... 70 C1
Western Ct CHNE CH2 .... 145 L8
Western Dr MCFLDS SK11 .... 138 C7
Westfield CW/SHV CW2 .... 237 L4
KNUT WA16 .... 106 E3
OFTN SK2 .... 47 H8
Westfield Dr CW/SHV CW2 .... 237 L4
CHD/CHDH SK8 .... 64 F4
NWCHE CW9 .... 13 L4
RUNC WA7 .... 8 E4
Westfield Ms RUNC WA7 .... 8 E4
Westfields HALE/TIMP WA15 .... 61 M4
Westfield Rd ALS/KID ST7 .... 226 C5

CHSW/BR CH4 .... 190 B1
EP CH65 .... 10 E5
HALE/TIMP WA15 .... 62 A1
MCFLDN SK10 .... 14 F2
Westminster St CW/SHV CW2 .... 19 G7
Westmoreland Cl ALT WA14 .... 61 H4
WDN WA8 .... 7 J2
Westmorland Av ALS/KID ST7 .... 242 F5
Westmorland Cl
MCFLDN SK10 .... 137 M2
Westmorland Rd DID/WITH M20 .. 45 G2
PART M31 .... 40 E2
SALE M33 .... 43 J2
Westmorland Ter
HOLMCH WA4 .... 181 H1
Weston Cl CQ CH5 .... 142 F6
MWCH CW10 .... 179 H3
Weston Court Ms
WHITCH SY13 .... 270 A5
Weston Crs RUNC WA7 .... 72 F6
Weston Dr CHD/CHDH SK8 .... 46 D8
Weston Gv CHNE CH2 .... 145 L6
WYTH/NTH M22 .... 44 B3
Weston La CW/SHV CW2 .... 238 D7
Weston Point Expy RUNC WA7 .... 8 C4
Weston Rd CW/HAS CW1 .... 19 K8
RUNC WA7 .... 8 D9
WILM/AE SK9 .... 84 D6
West Over MPL/ROM SK6 .... 48 A4
Westover Rd WARR WA1 .... 37 M5
West Park Av POY/DIS SK12 .... 66 C4
West Park Dr GTS/LS CH66 .... 120 F4
West Park Rd BRAM/HZG SK7 .... 65 K2
STKP SK1 .... 3 L3
West Quay Rd WARRN/WOL WA2.. 36 F1
Westrees NWCHW CW8 .... 127 K7
West Rd ALT WA14 .... 61 J2
CONG CW12 .... 207 H1
EP CH65 .... 121 J1
NWCHW CW8 .... 128 B4
RUNC WA7 .... 8 A8
SPK/HALE L24 .... 50 D7
West St ALS/KID ST7 .... 226 B6
BIDD ST8 .... 227 J5
CHNE CH2 .... 17 J1
CONG CW12 .... 207 J1
CW/HAS CW1 .... 18 D2
CW/HAS CW1 .... 222 C7
CW/SHV CW2 .... 220 E8
EDGY/DAV SK3 .... 2 C6
MCFLDS SK11 .... 14 D5
MWCH CW10 .... 179 J3
WARRN/WOL WA2 .... 5 H2
WILM/AE SK9 .... 110 A3
Westune WHITCH SY13 .... 269 M6
West V NSTN CH64 .... 91 L6
West Vale Rd HALE/TIMP WA15 .... 42 F7
West Vw HUY L36 .... 32 B2
WARRN/WOL WA2 .... 38 A3
West View Av HUY L36 .... 32 B2
West View Rd FROD/HEL WA6 .... 127 G6
WYTH/NTH M22 .... 44 E4
Westville Dr CONG CW12 .... 207 G2
Westward Rd CHSE CH3 .... 170 A4
WILM/AE SK9 .... 83 M6
Westway CQ CH5 .... 166 E2
West Wy CW/SHV CW2 .... 238 D7
HOLMCH WA4 .... 181 H1
SBCH CW11 .... 203 M8
WRX/GR/LL LL12 .... 210 C5
Westwood RUNC WA7 .... 74 C3
Westwood Av HALE/TIMP WA15 .. 42 F5
Westwood Ct NSTN CH64 .... 91 L2
Westwood Dr SALE M33 .... 43 H2
Westwood Rd CHD/CHDH SK8 .... 64 B4
OFTN SK2 .... 47 H8
Westy La WARRS WA4 .... 37 L8
Wet Gate La LYMM WA13 .... 40 D8
Wetheral Rd MCFLDN SK10 .... 138 E3
Wetherby Cl CH/BCN CH1 .... 16 C3
NEWLW WA12 .... 22 C7
Wetherby Dr BRAM/HZG SK7 .... 67 G2
Wetherby Wy GTS/LS CH66 .... 94 B7
Wetreins La CHSE CH3 .... 229 H5
Wettenhall Rd NANT CW5 .... 219 H8
Wetton La NWCHW CW8 .... 101 L7
Wexford Av SPK/HALE L24 .... 71 K2
Wexwood Gv RAIN/WH L35 .... 32 F2
Weybourne Cl CHSW/BR CH4 .... 168 E7
Weybridge Cl WARRS WA4 .... 56 E5
Weybridge Dr MCFLDN SK10 .... 138 B1
Wey Gates Dr HALE/TIMP WA15... 62 C6
Weyhill Rd NTHM/RTH M23 .... 44 A8
Weyman Av RAIN/WH L35 .... 32 E1
Weymouth Cl RUNC WA7 .... 74 E6
Weymouth Rd
WARRW/BUR WA5 .... 26 F6
Whaddon Dr CHSW/BR CH4 .... 168 F8
Whaley Rd CHF/WBR SK23 .... 89 J3
Whalley Av GOL/RIS/CU WA3 .... 25 J5
Whalley Cl HALE/TIMP WA15 .... 42 F4
Whalley Gv WDN WA8 .... 53 L1
Whalley Hayes MCFLDS SK11 .... 14 F4
Whalley Rd HALE/TIMP WA15 .... 62 A2
NWCHE CW9 .... 13 J5
OFTN SK2 .... 47 J5
Whalley St WARR WA1 .... 5 K8
Wharams Bank SBCH CW11 .... 205 M7
The Wharfage WHITCH SY13 .... 270 A5
Wharf Cl CHF/WBR SK23 .... 89 L5
Wharfdale Cl CW/HAS CW1 .... 221 H3
Wharfdale Cl
WARRW/BUR WA5 .... 36 A5
Wharfe Cl CONG CW12 .... 207 M3
Wharfedale RUNC WA7 .... 74 B6
Wharfedale Av RAIN/WH L35 .... 33 K1
Wharfedale Rd CONG CW12 .... 185 G7
Wharfe La EP CH65 .... 10 A3
Wharf La CONG CW12 .... 207 H8
Wharford La RUNC WA7 .... 74 E1
Wharf Rd ALT WA14 .... 42 D5
BIDD ST8 .... 227 K3
CHF/WBR SK23 .... 89 L5
NEWLW WA12 .... 26 E2
Wharf St HTNM SK4 .... 2 F2
WARR WA1 .... 5 K8

Wharton Park Rd WSFD CW7 .... 177 M2
Wharton Rd WSFD CW7 .... 177 M3
Whatcroft Cl RUNC WA7 .... 73 K6
Whatcroft La NWCHE CW9 .... 154 E3
Wheat Cft EDGY/DAV SK3 .... 46 F7
WARRW/BUR WA5 .... 36 C6
Wheatfield Cl GTS/LS CH66 .... 120 C1
NWCHW CW8 .... 129 L3
Wheatfield Rd WDN WA8 .... 33 J7
Wheatlands RUNC WA7 .... 73 L3
Wheatley Av NEWLW WA12 .... 22 C7
Wheatley Rd CW/HAS CW1 .... 221 L6
Wheat Moss MCFLDS SK11 .... 135 G3
Wheatsheaf Cl WHITCH SY13 .... 269 M6
Wheatsheaf La NWCHE CW9 .... 77 H8
Wheatsheaf Rd
CHF/WBR SK23 .... 89 L6
Wheelman Rd CW/HAS CW1 .... 221 G5
Wheelock Cl ALS/KID ST7 .... 241 G1
WILM/AE SK9 .... 84 D3
Wheelock Dr WSFD CW7 .... 178 B3
Wheelock St MWCH CW10 .... 179 J3
Wheelock Wy ALS/KID ST7 .... 243 H2
Wheelwright Cl
MPL/ROM SK6 .... 48 F4
Wheldon Cl CHNE CH2 .... 145 L4
Wheldrake Cl GTS/LS CH66 .... 94 B7
Whernside WDN WA8 .... 52 C2
Whernside Cl HTNM SK4 .... 2 F3
Whetmorhurst Rd
MPL/ROM SK6 .... 49 L8
Whetstone Hey GTS/LS CH66 .... 94 D7
Whetstone Rd BIDD ST8 .... 227 J2
Whickham Cl WDN WA8 .... 52 F1
Whimbrel Av NEWLW WA12 .... 27 J1
Whimbrel Cl RUNC WA7 .... 73 M7
Whimbrel Pk HLWD L26 .... 50 E3
Whimbrel Rd OFTN SK2 .... 48 A7
Whinberry Rd ALT WA14 .... 42 B5
Whinchat Av NEWLW WA12 .... 22 C3
Whinchat Cl OFTN SK2 .... 48 A8
Whinchat Dr GOL/RIS/CU WA3 .... 38 F1
Whinfell Gv RUNC WA7 .... 73 L7
Whipcord La CH/BCN CH1 .... 16 C3
Whirley Cl MWCH CW10 .... 179 J5
Whirley La MCFLDN SK10 .... 136 F3
Whirley Rd MCFLDN SK10 .... 137 H2
Whirlow Rd CW/SHV CW2 .... 238 B5
Whisterfield La MCFLDS SK11 .... 159 K1
Whiston Cl WSFD CW7 .... 154 A8
Whiston St MCFLDS SK11 .... 14 E6
Whitbarrow Rd LYMM WA13 .... 39 J8
Whitbread Dr BIDD ST8 .... 227 L4
Whitburn Rd NTHM/RTH M23 .... 44 A8
Whitby Av CHNE CH2 .... 145 K7
WARRN/WOL WA2 .... 37 K2
Whitby Cl CHD/CHDH SK8 .... 45 J6
CW/HAS CW1 .... 221 H4
POY/DIS SK12 .... 66 C7
Whitby La CH/BCN CH1 .... 121 G5
Whitby Rd EP CH65 .... 10 F7
RUNC WA7 .... 9 H5
Whitby's La WSFD CW7 .... 177 H3
Whitchurch Cl WARR WA1 .... 38 A4
Whitchurch Rd
AUD/MAD/W WA3 .... 273 G1
CHSE CH3 .... 170 B3
CHSE CH3 .... 171 G8
CHSE CH3 .... 213 K4
CHSE CH3 .... 231 G2
MALPAS SY14 .... 246 D4
WHITCH SY13 .... 262 A7
Whitchurch Wy RUNC WA7 .... 73 K6
White Av CW/SHV CW2 .... 220 E8
Whitebarn Rd WILM/AE SK9 .... 110 B4
Whitebeam Cl GTS/LS CH66 .... 120 E3
Whitebeam Cl HALE/TIMP WA15 .. 43 L7
RUNC WA7 .... 74 C3
White Broom LYMM WA13 .... 40 B8
Whitecarr La HALE/TIMP WA15 .... 62 D1
Whitechapel St DID/WITH M20 .... 45 H1
Whitecroft Av
GOL/RIS/CU WA3 .... 23 L3
Whitecroft Heath Rd
MCFLDS SK11 .... 159 H1
Whitecroft Rd GTS/LS CH66 .... 120 E2
MPL/ROM SK6 .... 68 C2
Whitecross Rd WARRW/BUR WA5 .. 4 B6
Whitefield HTNM SK4 .... 2 C1
Whitefield Cl LYMM WA13 .... 40 A8
Whitefield Gv LYMM WA13 .... 40 A8
Whitefield La RAIN/WH L35 .... 32 A6
Whitefield Rd WARRS WA4 .... 56 B4
Whitefields CHNE CH2 .... 123 H1
White Friars CH/BCN CH1 .... 2 D3
Whitegate Av GOL/RIS/CU WA3 .... 29 M2
Whitegate Cl MWCH CW10 .... 179 J6
Whitegate Flds WRXS/E LL13 .... 228 D3
Whitegate La CHSE CH3 .... 148 E5
Whitegate Rd WSFD CW7 .... 152 F8
Whitegates Cl HALE/TIMP WA15 .. 43 H7
NSTN CH64 .... 92 A3
Whitegates Crs NSTN CH64 .... 92 A4
Whitegates Rd CHD/CHDH SK8 .... 45 K7
Whitehall Av ALS/KID ST7 .... 242 F7
Whitehall Cl NWCHW CW8 .... 103 G8
WILM/AE SK9 .... 84 A7
Whitehall Dr NWCHW CW8 .... 129 J8
White Hall La SBCH CW11 .... 202 E3
Whitehall La TPLY/KEL CW6 .... 175 K4
Whitehall Pl FROD/HEL WA6 .... 99 H4
FROD/HEL WA6 .... 99 J4
Whitehall Rd ALS/KID ST7 .... 242 F7
White Hart Gdns NWCHW CW8 .. 128 F8
Whitehall Rd DID/WITH M20 .... 45 J2
SALE M33 .... 43 H2
White Hart La CW/SHV CW2 .... 237 L4
Whitehaven Gdns
DID/WITH M20 .... 45 G2
Whitehaven La NANT CW5 .... 235 G5
Whitehaven Rd BRAM/HZG SK7 .. 65 J2
Whitehill Rd ALS/KID ST7 .... 243 G1
Whitehouse Dr
HALE/TIMP WA15... 62 B4
NTHM/RTH M23 .... 62 F1
White House Dr WARR WA1 .... 38 E5
Whitehouse Expy RUNC WA7 .... 73 M7
Whitehouse La ALT WA14 .... 41 K5

KNUT WA16 .... 105 L7
NANT CW5 .... 21 H3
Whitehouse Rd *KNUT* WA16 .... 80 B1
White La *CHSE* CH3 .... 170 D4
Whitelea Dr *EDGY/DAV* SK3 .... 46 D7
Whiteleas Rd *CHF/WBR* SK23 .. 115 K2
Whiteley Pl *ALT* WA14 .... 42 D6
White Lodge Ms *NWCHW* CW8 .. 152 A1
Whitemere Ct *EP* CH65 .... 10 E4 5
Whitemore Rd *MWCH* CW10 .... 179 J6
Whiteoak Cl *MPL/ROM* SK6 .... 48 E5
White Park Cl *MWCH* CW10 .... 179 K2
Whiteridge Rd *ALS/KID* ST7 ... 243 G2
White Rd *NM/HAY* SK22 .... 69 J3
Whitesands Rd *LYMM* WA13 .... 39 J8
Whites La *CW/SHV* CW2 .... 239 H6
Whitesmead Rd *POY/DIS* SK12 .. 68 D7 1
Whites Meadow *CHSE* CH3 ..... 170 A5
White St *MCFLDS* SK11 .... 15 H9
 WARR WA1 .... 4 E7
 WARRS WA4 .... 56 C3
 WDN WA8 .... 53 G7 8
Whitethorn Av
 WARRW/BUR WA5 .... 35 M7
Whitethorn Cl *MPL/ROM* SK6 .. 48 E5 1
White Way Gv *CO* CH5 .... 142 F6 2
Whitewell Rd *WHITCH* SY13 ... 268 C5
Whitewood La *MALPAS* SY14 ... 245 K6
Whitfield Av *WARR* WA1 .... 37 M5
Whitfield Rd *ALS/KID* ST7 .... 243 H2
The Whitfields *MCFLDN* SK10 .. 14 A3
Whitle Rd *NM/HAY* SK22 .... 69 J3
Whitley Av *NWCHW* CW8 ..... 129 C1 1
 WARRS WA4 .... 38 A8
Whitley Cl *MWCH* CW10 .... 179 H5
 RUNC WA7 .... 8 F6
Whitley Dr *NWCHW* CW8 ..... 129 G8 1
Whitley Gdns *HALE/TIMP* WA15 .. 45 H5
Whitley La *KNUT* WA16 .... 79 C5
Whitley Pl *HALE/TIMP* WA15 ... 45 H5
Whitley Pl *HTNM* SK4 .... 46 B1
Whitlow Av *ALT* WA14 .... 42 B4
 GOL/RIS/CU WA3 .... 22 F3
 NANT CW5 .... 21 G9
Whitlow La *NWCHE* CW9 .... 153 M4
Whitmoor Cl *RAIN/WH* L35 ..... 33 L3 2
Whitneys Rd *NM/HAY* SK22 .... 69 H2
Whitney Pl *WLTN* L25 .... 50 C2 2
Whitney Rd *WLTN* L25 .... 50 C1
Whitsand Rd *WYTH/NTH* M22 .. 44 E7
Whitson Cl *KNUT* WA16 .... 59 J8
Whitstable Pk *WDN* WA8 ...... 33 L8
Whittaker Av
 WARRN/WOL WA2 .... 37 K2 6
Whittington Gdns *NWCHE* CW9.. 153 M3
Whittle Av *WARRW/BUR* WA5 .. 36 A5
Whittlebank Rd *NM/HAY* SK22 ... 69 H2
Whittle Cl *CO* CH5 .... 167 G1 3
Whittle Hall La
 WARRW/BUR WA5 .... 35 M6
Whittlewood Cl
 GOL/RIS/CU WA3 .... 30 A7 4
Whitton Dr *CHNE* CH2 .... 145 L7
Whitwell Cl *WARRW/BUR* WA5 .. 35 K5
Whitworth Cl *GOL/RIS/CU* WA3 .. 38 E1
Wicken St *OFTN* SK2 .... 47 J5
Wicker La *CHSE* CH3 .... 147 G8
 HALE/TIMP WA15 .... 62 B4
Wicklow Av *EDGY/DAV* SK3 .... 46 B5 1
Wicklow Cl *GTS/LS* CH66 ...... 94 A6
Wicklow Dr *WYTH/NTH* M22 .... 63 L2
Wickson La *CHSE* CH3 .... 215 K1
Wicksten Dr *RUNC* WA7 .... 9 L3
Widdale Av *RAIN/WH* L35 ...... 33 K1 2
Widdale Dr *WARRW/BUR* WA5 ... 35 M5
Widgeon Cl *POY/DIS* SK12 ..... 66 B8 1
Widgeon Rd *ALT* WA14 .... 42 B4
Widnes Rd *WARRW/BUR* WA5 ... 54 A2
 WDN WA8 .... 7 J5
The Wiend *CHNE* CH2 .... 145 K8
Wigan Rd *AIMK* WN4 .... 22 B1
 GOL/RIS/CU WA3 .... 23 H1
The Wigdale *CO* CH5 .... 166 C4 2
Wight Cl *EP* CH65 .... 121 J3
Wightman Av
 WARRN/WOL WA2 .... 22 C7 8
Wigmore Cl *GOL/RIS/CU* WA3 ... 30 A7 5
Wignall Rd *BURS/TUN* ST6 .... 243 K6
Wigsey La *LYMM* WA13 .... 40 D3
Wigshaw Cl *LEIGH* WN7 .... 24 F3
Wigshaw La *GOL/RIS/CU* WA3 .. 29 L1
Wigwam Cl *POY/DIS* SK12 ..... 66 C8
Wilbraham Cl *NANT* CW5 ...... 236 A5
Wilbraham Rd *CONG* CW12 .... 207 M1
 NANT CW5 .... 236 A5
 NWCHW CW8 .... 128 C3
Wilbraham St *STHEL* WA9 ..... 34 E1
Wilbrahams Wy *ALS/KID* ST7 .. 224 D8
Wilcock Rd *RNFD/HAY* WA11 ... 22 A4
Wilcote Cl *WDN* WA8 .... 34 C8
Wilcott Dr *WILM/AE* SK9 ...... 83 M1
Wilcott Rd *CHD/CHDH* SK8 .... 45 G7
Wild Arum Cl
 GOL/RIS/CU WA3 .... 23 L4 14
Wilderhope Cl *CW/SHV* CW2 ... 238 C5
Wilderspool Cswy *WARRS* WA4 .. 5 G9
Wilderspool Crs *WARRS* WA4 .. 56 B3
Wild Goose Av *ALS/KID* ST7 ... 243 K1
Wilding Av *RUNC* WA7 .... 9 K2
Wildings Old La
 GOL/RIS/CU WA3 .... 29 G4
Wilding St *CW/HAS* CW1 ...... 19 K4
Wildmoor La *CHSE* CH3 ...... 147 K3
Wild St *BRAM/HZG* SK7 .... 66 D2 3
 MPL/ROM SK6 .... 47 M2
Wildwood Gv *WARR* WA1 ...... 38 B5
Wilford Av *SALE* M33 .... 43 G2
Wilkin Cft *CHD/CHDH* SK8 .... 64 E3
Wilkins La *WILM/AE* SK9 ...... 63 L7
Wilkinson Av *WARR* WA1 ...... 37 M6
Wilkinson Cl *WDN* WA8 .... 53 G7 7
Wilkinson Rd *HTNM* SK4 ...... 46 A4
Wilkinson St *WARRN/WOL* WA2 ... 5 K4
Wilkinson St North *EP* CH65 ... 10 E5
Wilks Av *WYTH/NTH* M22 ..... 63 M2
Wilks St *BURS/TUN* ST6 ...... 243 L8
Willan Rd *CH/BCN* CH1 ...... 144 D8

Willard St *BRAM/HZG* SK7 .... 66 D1 19
Willaston Dr *HLWD* L26 .... 51 G6
Willaston Hall Gdns *NANT* CW5 .. 237 J6
Willaston Rd *NSTN* CH64 ...... 92 D2
Willbank La *NANT* CW5 .... 234 D7
Willdor Gv *EDGY/DAV* SK3 .... 46 B6 8
Willenhall Rd *NTHM/RTH* M23 .. 44 C2
Willeymoor La *WHITCH* SY13 .. 259 K5
William Av *BIDD* ST8 .... 227 K5
William Penn Cl
 WARRW/BUR WA5 .... 35 L8 8
Williams Av *NEWLW* WA12 .... 22 C7
Williams Cl *CHNE* CH2 .... 145 J8 7
Williamson Crs *CHF/WBR* SK23 .. 89 K4
Williamson Rd *CHF/WBR* SK23 .. 89 K4
William St *CHNE* CH2 .... 17 L2
 CONG CW12 .... 185 G8
 DID/WITH M20 .... 45 H1
 MCFLDN SK10 .... 15 L5
 NWCHE CW9 .... 13 M2
 STKP SK1 .... 3 L9 11
 WDN WA8 .... 7 L1
 WSFD CW7 .... 177 L3
Williams Wy *MCFLDS* SK11 ... 137 J4
Willington Av *PS/BROM* CH62 ... 93 L1
Willington La *TPLY/KEL* CW6 .. 149 K8
Willington Rd *CHSE* CH3 ..... 172 F2
 TPLY/KEL CW6 .... 173 K1
Willis Cl *RAIN/WH* L35 .... 32 D2
Willis La *RAIN/WH* L35 .... 32 D2
Willis Rd *EDGY/DAV* SK3 ...... 46 E6
Willis St *WARR* WA1 .... 5 L4
Willmer Crs *ALS/KID* ST7 .... 226 B6
Willoughby Cl *WARRW/BUR* WA5.. 36 C3
Willoughby St
 BURS/TUN ST6 .... 243 K5 8
Willow Av *CHD/CHDH* SK8 .... 64 F2
 NEWLW WA12 .... 22 D8
 RAIN/WH L35 .... 32 D1
 WDN WA8 .... 53 H2
Willoway Rd *CHSE* CH3 ...... 170 B2 8
Willow Bank *CHD/CHDH* SK8 .. 65 G6
 FROD/HEL WA6 .... 124 E2
 NANT CW5 .... 21 H4
Willowbank Dr *MCFLDN* SK10 .. 113 J3
Willow Bank Est *NEWLW* WA12 .. 27 M1
Willowbrow Rd *BEB* CH63 .... 92 D1
Willow Cl *ALS/KID* ST7 .... 243 G5
 CHNE CH2 .... 145 K4
 LYMM WA13 .... 39 L8
 POY/DIS SK12 .... 86 E1
 RUNC WA7 .... 9 K8
 WSFD CW7 .... 177 K1
Willow Ct *CHSW/BR* CH4 ..... 190 A5 8
 MPL/ROM SK6 .... 48 F7 8
 MWCH CW10 .... 179 J2
 NANT CW5 .... 21 H3
Willow Crs *CHNE* CH2 .... 146 A8
 CW/SHV CW2 .... 237 M2
 WARR WA1 .... 38 B4
Willowcroft Wy *ALS/KID* ST7 .. 226 E8
Willowdale *NEWLW* WA12 .... 27 L1
Willowdale Av *CHD/CHDH* SK8 .. 64 B2 8
Willowdale Wy *GTS/LS* CH66 .. 120 F4
Willow Dr *CH/BCN* CH1 ...... 144 D7
 SALE M33 .... 42 E2
 SBCH CW11 .... 204 E5
 TPLY/KEL CW6 .... 216 D1
 WARRS WA4 .... 56 D3 4
 WILM/AE SK9 .... 84 D1
Willowfield Gv *AIMK* WN4 .... 22 A2
Willow Gn *KNUT* WA16 .... 106 F1
 NWCHW CW8 .... 128 D4
Willowgreen La *NWCHW* CW8 .. 102 B7
Willow Gv *CHNE* CH2 .... 123 C2
 CHNE CH2 .... 146 B8
 GOL/RIS/CU WA3 .... 23 G3
 GTS/LS CH66 .... 121 G3
 MPL/ROM SK6 .... 48 F7
 NWCHW CW8 .... 103 H8
Willow Hayes *CHSE* CH3 ..... 148 F5
Willowherb Cl *CHSE* CH3 .... 170 B6 1
Willow La *BEB* CH63 .... 92 D1
 CQ CH5 .... 142 E8
 HOLMCH CW4 .... 157 L3
 WARRS WA4 .... 56 D8
Willow Lea *CH/BCN* CH1 ..... 144 F2
Willowmead Dr *MCFLDN* SK10 .. 112 A7
Willow Rd *CHSW/BR* CH4 ..... 168 F6
 MPL/ROM SK6 .... 67 M5
 NEWLW WA12 .... 22 E8
 PART M31 .... 40 E2
Willows Cl *CW/SHV* CW2 ..... 238 B5
Willow Sq *WSFD* CW7 .... 178 A2 8
The Willows *FROD/HEL* WA6... 99 J4
 NWCHW CW8 .... 104 F7
 PART M31 .... 40 F1
Willow St *CONG* CW12 .... 207 L1
Willow Tree Gv *ALS/KID* ST7 .. 224 F5 8
Willow Tree Ms
 CHD/CHDH SK8 .... 64 B3 8
Willow Tree Rd *ALT* WA14 .... 61 K2
Willow Wy *BRAM/HZG* SK7 .... 65 J5
 CHSW/BR CH4 .... 190 B1
 DID/WITH M20 .... 45 J1
 MCFLDN SK10 .... 112 A7
Wilmere La *WDN* WA8 .... 34 A6
Wilmot Av *WARRW/BUR* WA5 ... 35 M6
Wilmot Dr *GOL/RIS/CU* WA3 ... 22 F5
Wilmslow Crs *WARRS* WA4 .... 38 D8
Wilmslow Gr *GTS/LS* CH66 .... 94 E7
Wilmslow Old Rd
 HALE/TIMP WA15 .... 62 F6
 MCFLDN SK10 .... 84 C5
Wilmslow Park Rd *WILM/AE* SK9.. 84 C5
Wilmslow Rd *BRAM/HZG* SK7 .. 85 H3
 CHD/CHDH SK8 .... 45 K7
 CHD/CHDH SK8 .... 64 D3
 DID/WITH M20 .... 45 J3
 HALE/TIMP WA15 .... 62 F6
 MCFLDN SK10 .... 85 G8
 MCFLDN SK10 .... 111 J3
 WILM/AE SK9 .... 84 D1 1
 WILM/AE SK9 .... 110 A2
Wilsden Rd *WDN* WA8 .... 52 B3 8
Wilsford Cl *GOL/RIS/CU* WA3 .. 23 H3 1

Wilson Cl *WARRS* WA4 .... 57 K1
Wilson Crs *NWCHE* CW9 ..... 131 H1
Wilson Dr *NWCHE* CW9 ...... 153 M5
Wilson La *GOL/RIS/CU* WA3 ... 29 L7
Wilson Patten St *WARR* WA1 ... 4 E8
Wilson Rd *HUY* L36 .... 32 B4
 RAIN/WH L35 .... 32 D1
Wilson St *WARRW/BUR* WA5 ... 4 E1
Wilson Wy *BURS/TUN* ST6 .... 243 J6
Wilton Av *CHD/CHDH* SK8 .... 64 C5
Wilton Cl *NWCHW* CW8 .... 129 L8
Wilton Crs *MCFLDS* SK11 .... 137 L6
 WILM/AE SK9 .... 109 M2
Wilton Dr *HALE/TIMP* WA15 ... 62 C4
Wilton La *GOL/RIS/CU* WA3 ... 24 A7
Wilton Rd *CO* CH5 .... 166 D2
Wiltshire Cl *MCFLDS* SK10 .... 137 L2
 WARR WA1 .... 38 D6
Wiltshire Dr *CONG* CW12 .... 184 E8
Wiltshire Rd *PART* M31 ...... 40 E2 8
Wilwick La *MCFLDS* SK11 .... 137 M5
Wimbledon Dr *EDGY/DAV* SK3 .. 46 C6 8
Wimbledon Lawns *ALT* WA14 .. 61 J1
Wimborne Cl *CHD/CHDH* SK8 .. 46 C8 8
Winbolt St *OFTN* SK2 .... 47 J8 8
Wincanton Av *NTHM/RTH* M23 .. 43 K4
Wincham Av *NWCHE* CW9 .... 130 F1
Wincham La *NWCHE* CW9 .... 130 D1
Wincham Rd *SALE* M33 ...... 42 E2
Winchcombe Cl *LEIGH* WN7 .. 24 E3 8
Winchester Av *AIMK* WN4 .... 22 A1
 EP CH65 .... 121 K1
 WARR/BUR WA5 .... 36 C7
Winchester Cl *CW/SHV* CW2 .. 253 H1 8
 WILM/AE SK9 .... 83 L7 8
 WLTN L25 .... 50 B5
Winchester Dr *HTNM* SK4 .... 46 B2
Winchester Pk *DID/WITH* M20 .. 44 F1
Winchester Pl *WDN* WA8 ..... 52 C4 2
Winchester Rd *HALE/TIMP* WA15.. 62 C3
Winchester Sq *CHSW/BR* CH4 .. 168 F8
Wincle Av *POY/DIS* SK12 ..... 86 F2 8
Windermere Av *CHNE* CH2 ... 146 A6
 SALE M33 .... 43 K2 8
 WARRN/WOL WA2 .... 18 A4
 WDN WA8 .... 34 B8 10
Windermere Dr *CONG* CW12 .. 207 G2
 WILM/AE SK9 .... 109 M3
Windermere Rd *CW/SHV* CW2 .. 237 L2
 EP CH65 .... 121 J2
 MPL/ROM SK6 .... 67 K3
 STKP SK1 .... 3 L9
 WSFD CW7 .... 177 J2
Windermere St *WDN* WA8 .... 34 B8
Windfield Gdns *GTS/LS* CH66 .. 94 D5
Windfields Cl *CHD/CHDH* SK8 .. 65 H1 8
The Windings *MWCH* CW10 ... 179 H2
Windle Cl *GOL/RIS/CU* WA3 ... 29 J8 8
 NSTN CH64 .... 91 L2
 OFTN SK2 .... 47 L7
Windlehurst Old Rd
 MPL/ROM SK6 .... 67 M2
Windlehurst Rd *MPL/ROM* SK6 .. 67 K4
Windmill Av *ALS/KID* ST7 .... 243 G4
Windmill Cl *AUD/MAD/W* CW3 .. 264 E8
 WARRS WA4 .... 56 C6
Windmill Dr *AUD/MAD/W* CW3 .. 273 M1
Windmill Hill Av *RUNC* WA7... 74 D2
Windmill Hill Av East *RUNC* WA7 .. 74 D4
Windmill Hill Av North
 RUNC WA7 .... 74 C3
Windmill Hill Av South
 RUNC WA7 .... 74 D3
Windmill Hill Av West *RUNC* WA7.. 74 C2
Windmill La *AUD/MAD/W* CW3 .. 264 E7
 MCFLDN SK10 .... 113 H6
 WARRS WA4 .... 56 C6
 WARRS WA4 .... 75 G5
 WARRW/BUR WA5 .... 35 L7
Windmill Ri *CHNE* CH2 ...... 145 K5
Windmill Rd *SALE* M33 ...... 43 M1 12
Windmill St *MCFLDS* SK11 ... 15 J8
 RUNC WA7 .... 9 K2
Windscale Rd *WARRN/WOL* WA2.. 38 A2
Windsor Av *CHD/CHDH* SK8 .. 44 F7
 CO CH5 .... 142 B6 8
 CW/HAS CW1 .... 221 G5
 HTNM SK4 .... 46 A1 2
 NANT CW5 .... 251 M1
 NEWLW WA12 .... 27 K2
 TPLY/KEL CW6 .... 197 K3 8
 WILM/AE SK9 .... 83 M6
Windsor Cl *MCFLDN* SK10 .... 112 E6
 NWCHW CW8 .... 127 M8
 POY/DIS SK12 .... 66 D8
Windsor Dr *ALS/KID* ST7 ..... 223 M8
 ALT WA14 .... 42 F4
 CHSW/BR CH4 .... 190 A1
 EP CH65 .... 121 G1
 MPL/ROM SK6 .... 48 E7 8
 NANT CW5 .... 234 E5
 RNFD/HAY WA11 .... 22 A5
 WARRS WA4 .... 57 H1
 WSFD CW7 .... 177 J7 8
Windsor Gv *CHD/CHDH* SK8 .. 64 F4
 MPL/ROM SK6 .... 48 E2 8
 RUNC WA7 .... 9 K1
Windsor Pl *CONG* CW12 ..... 207 M2
Windsor Rd *AIMK* WN4 .... 22 B2
 BRAM/HZG SK7 .... 66 F2
 CHSW/BR CH4 .... 168 F6
 CW/SHV CW2 .... 237 L4
 GOL/RIS/CU WA3 .... 23 J4
 MPL/ROM SK6 .... 47 J1
 WDN WA8 .... 34 A8
Windsor Sq *MCFLDS* SK11 ... 138 D8
Windsor St *OFTN* SK2 .... 47 G6 8
 WARRW/BUR WA5 .... 4 B5
Windsor Wy *KNUT* WA16 ..... 106 F2
Windways *GTS/LS* CH66 ...... 94 D5
Windy Arbor Cl *RAIN/WH* L35 .. 32 D3
Windy Arbor Rd *RAIN/WH* L35 .. 32 C4
Windy Bank Av
 GOL/RIS/CU WA3 .... 23 L4 15
Winfield Gv *MPL/ROM* SK6 .... 49 H3 8
Winfield St *WDN* WA8 .... 7 K4

Winfrith Rd *WARRN/WOL* WA2 .. 38 A3
Wingate Dr *DID/WITH* M20 ... 45 J2
 HALE/TIMP WA15 .... 43 C7
Wingfield Dr *WILM/AE* SK9 ... 83 L6
Wingfield Pl *WSFD* CW7 ..... 177 H6
Winghay Rd *ALS/KID* ST7 .... 243 H2
Winhill Rd *NM/HAY* SK22 ..... 69 J3 7
Winifred Rd *DID/WITH* M20 .. 45 H1
 OFTN SK2 .... 47 G7
Winkle St *CW/SHV* CW2 .... 5 J3
Winkwell Dr *CHSW/BR* CH4 ... 169 C7
Winmarith Dr *HALE/TIMP* WA15.. 62 D5
Winmarleigh Gdns *LEIGH* WN7 .. 24 E1
Winmarleigh St *WARR* WA1 .... 4 E7
Winnington Av *NWCHW* CW8 .. 12 A4
Winnington Gn *OFTN* SK2 .... 47 K7
Winnington La *NWCHW* CW8 .. 129 J3
Winnington Rd *MPL/ROM* SK6 .. 48 F4
 NWCHW CW8 .... 12 F1
 WSFD CW7 .... 177 J3
The Winnows *RUNC* WA7 ..... 73 K5 8
Winscombe Dr *CHSE* CH3 .... 170 C2
Winsfield Rd *BRAM/HZG* SK7 .. 66 D4
Winsford Dr *WARRW/BUR* WA5 .. 26 E5
Winsford Gv *GTS/LS* CH66 ... 120 C1
Winsford Rd *WSFD* CW7 ..... 199 K2
Winsford Wy *CH/BCN* CH1 ... 168 F2
Winsham Cl *BRAM/HZG* SK7 .. 66 A2 8
Winsham Rd *SALE* M33 ...... 42 E2
Winsley Rd *NTHM/RTH* M23 .. 43 K2
Winslow Cl *RUNC* WA7 .... 74 D4
Winstanley Cl
 WARRW/BUR WA5 .... 36 C7 7
Winstanley Rd *NSTN* CH64 ... 91 L7
Winster Dr *NTHLY* L27 .... 51 G1
Winster Gv *OFTN* SK2 .... 47 G6
Winston Av *ALS/KID* ST7 .... 224 C8
 NEWLW WA12 .... 26 B2
 STHEL WA9 .... 26 B2
Winston Cl *MPL/ROM* SK6 .... 48 D5
Winterbottom La *KNUT* WA16 .. 79 K5
Winterburn Gn *OFTN* SK2 .... 47 L5
Winterely Dr *HLWD* L26 ..... 51 H6
Winterford La *TPLY/KEL* CW6 .. 198 B1
Winter Gv *STHEL* WA9 .... 26 B1
Winterslow Av *NTHM/RTH* M23 .. 43 K3
Winterton Wy *MCFLDS* SK11 .. 162 C1
Winton Gv *RUNC* WA7 .... 74 D3 8
 GOL/RIS/CU WA3 .... 23 L7
Winton Rd *ALT* WA14 .... 61 J2
Winwick La *GOL/RIS/CU* WA3 .. 23 L8
Winwick Link Rd
 WARRN/WOL WA2 .... 28 B6
 NEWLW WA12 .... 27 L2
 WARRN/WOL WA2 .... 5 G5
Winwick Rd *NEWLW* WA12 .... 5 G5
Winwick Vw *WARRW/BUR* WA5 .. 26 D3
Winwood Rd *DID/WITH* M20 .. 45 J4
Wirksmoor Rd *NM/HAY* SK22 .. 69 H5
Wirral Cl *GOL/RIS/CU* WA3 ... 29 L1
Wirral Crs *EDGY/DAV* SK3 .... 46 A4
 NSTN CH64 .... 91 M7
Wirral Vw *CO* CH5 .... 166 A3
Wirral Wy *NSTN* CH64 .... 91 C1
Wirswall Rd *WHITCH* SY13 ... 266 C3
Wisbech Dr *NTHM/RTH* M23 .. 43 M3 8
Wisenholme Cl *RUNC* WA7 ... 73 L8
Wistaston Av *CW/SHV* CW2 ... 237 M2
Wistaston Green Cl
 CW/SHV CW2 .... 237 L2 8
Wistaston Green Rd
 CW/SHV CW2 .... 237 K2
Wistaston Pk *CW/SHV* CW2 .. 237 M3
Wistaston Rd *CW/SHV* CW2 .. 18 D5
 NANT CW5 .... 237 L7
Wisterdale Cl *CW/SHV* CW2 .. 238 A4
Witham Av *WYTH/NTH* M22 .. 44 E7 8
Witham Cl *CW/SHV* CW2 ..... 238 A4 8
Witham Wy *BIDD* ST8 .... 227 L3
Withenfield Rd *NTHM/RTH* M23 .. 43 M4
Withens Cl *NWCHW* CW8 .... 128 D4 8
Withens Gn *OFTN* SK2 .... 47 L6
Withenshaw La *MCFLDS* SK11 .. 163 K7
Withen's La *NWCHW* CW8 .... 128 D4
Withers Av *WARRN/WOL* WA2 .. 5 L1
Wither's La *KNUT* WA16 ..... 58 B8
Withington Av *GOL/RIS/CU* WA3.. 25 C8
Withington Cl *NWCHE* CW9 .. 13 J7
 SBCH CW11 .... 204 C5
Withington Rd *SPK/HALE* L24.. 70 F1
Withinlee Rd *MCFLDN* SK10 .. 111 J6
Withins Rd *GOL/RIS/CU* WA3 .. 29 M1
Within Wy *SPK/HALE* L24 .... 71 L3
Withnall Dr *CW/SHV* CW2 .... 238 B8
Withnell Rd *DID/WITH* M20 .. 45 K1
Withy Cl *FROD/HEL* WA6 ..... 99 J4
Withycombe Dr
 WARRW/BUR WA5 .... 35 L8
Withy Cft *CHSE* CH3 .... 170 B5
Withyfold Dr *MCFLDN* SK10 .. 15 J2
Withypool Dr *OFTN* SK2 ...... 47 H7
Witney Gdns *WARRS* WA4 .... 56 F6
Witney La *MALPAS* SY14 ..... 246 D5
Wittenbury Rd *HTNM* SK4 ... 46 B2
Witton St *NWCHE* CW9 ...... 13 J1
Witt Rd *WDN* WA8 .... 7 G7
Wivern Pl *RUNC* WA7 .... 9 K1
Woburn Av *NEWLW* WA12 .... 27 K2
Woburn Cl *MCFLDN* SK10 .... 14 E1
 NWCHE CW9 .... 12 E9
Woburn Dr *CHNE* CH2 .... 145 M5 8
 HALE/TIMP WA15 .... 62 B2
 WDN WA8 .... 33 K7
Woburn Rd *WARRN/WOL* WA2 .. 28 A8
Woking Rd *CHD/CHDH* SK8 .. 65 G6
Wold Ct *CO* CH5 .... 166 C4
Wolsey Dr *ALT* WA14 .... 61 G3
Wolstanholme Cl *CONG* CW12 .. 207 M3
Wolverham Rd *EP* CH65 ...... 121 J1
Wolverton Dr *RUNC* WA7 .... 74 D3
Wolvesey Pl *WSFD* CW7 ..... 177 H6 1
Woodacre Rd *GTS/LS* CH66 .. 94 F4
Woodacres Ct *WILM/AE* SK9 .. 83 M6 8
Woodale Cl *WARRW/BUR* WA5 .. 35 L5
Woodall Dr *RUNC* WA7 .... 9 J5

Woodavens Gv
 AUD/MAD/W CW3 .... 273 G2
Woodbank Av *MPL/ROM* SK6 .. 47 L1
 STKP SK1 .... 3 M7
 STKP SK1 .... 47 J4 8
Woodbank Cl *CW/BCN* CW2 .. 238 A5 8
Woodbank La *CW/BCN* CH1 .. 119 K7
Woodbank Rd *EP* CH65 ...... 121 H2
 WARRW/BUR WA5 .... 36 A8
Woodbine Av *IRL* M44 .... 31 K8 8
Woodbine Crs *OFTN* SK2 .... 46 F5 14
Woodbine Rd *LYMM* WA13 ... 40 B8
Woodbourne Rd *NM/HAY* SK22 .. 69 C7
 SALE M33 .... 43 G2
Woodbridge Av *HLWD* L26 ... 50 D2
Woodbridge Cl *WARRS* WA4 .. 56 F8
Woodbridge Gv
 NTHM/RTH M23 .... 44 A3 8
Woodbrook Cl *CHF/WBR* SK23.. 89 L5
Woodbrook Rd *WILM/AE* SK9.. 110 B3
Woodburn Dr *WYTH/NTH* M22 .. 44 D4
Woodbury Rd *EDGY/DAV* SK3 .. 46 B5 8
Woodchurch *GTS/LS* CH66 ... 94 E7
Woodclose *GTS/LS* CH66 ..... 94 A3
Woodcock La *ALS/KID* ST7 ... 226 C6
 EP CH65 .... 121 H2 8
Woodcote Av *BRAM/HZG* SK7 .. 65 J3
Woodcote Cl
 WARRN/WOL WA2 .... 37 K3 7
Woodcote Pl *SBCH* CW11 .... 222 F4
Woodcote Rd *ALT* WA14 ..... 42 D3
Woodcote Vw *WILM/AE* SK9 .. 84 F3
Woodcott Cl *CW/SHV* CW2 ... 253 L2 8
Woodcotthill La *NANT* CW5 .. 250 B7
Woodcroft *OFTN* SK2 .... 47 K6
Wood Dr *ALS/KID* ST7 .... 241 C1
Woodedge *AIMK* WN4 .... 22 A1
Woodend Av *SPK/HALE* L24 .. 50 C2
Woodend Cl *MWCH* CW10 ... 179 J6 8
Woodend La *GOL/RIS/CU* WA3 .. 39 K2
 KNUT WA16 .... 82 E4
Wood End La *NSTN* CH64 .... 92 E8
Woodend La *SPK/HALE* L24 .. 50 C8
Woodend Rd *EDGY/DAV* SK3 .. 46 F8
 EP CH65 .... 94 F6
 WYTH/NTH M22 .... 44 D8
Woodfall Cl *NSTN* CH64 ...... 92 A6
Woodfall Gv *NSTN* CH64 ..... 92 A6
Woodfall La *NSTN* CH64 ..... 91 M6
Woodfield *WYTH/NTH* M22 ... 63 K1
Woodfield Av *FLINT* CH6 ..... 116 B7
Woodfield Cl *CHSW/BR* CH4 .. 190 A1 8
Woodfield Crs *AIMK* WN4 .... 22 A2 8
 MPL/ROM SK6 .... 47 M2 8
Woodfield Gv *CHNE* CH2 .... 146 B7
 ALT WA14 .... 42 C6
 CHD/CHDH SK8 .... 65 H5
Woodfield Rd North *EP* CH65 .. 10 E7
Woodfin Cft *MCFLDS* SK11 ... 135 C1
Woodford Av *GOL/RIS/CU* WA3 .. 23 K5
Woodford Cl *CW/SHV* CW2 ... 237 M2
 FROD/HEL WA6 .... 124 D2 8
 RUNC WA7 .... 73 H6 8
 WARRS WA4 .... 57 J1
Woodford Gdns *DID/WITH* M20.. 45 C2
Woodford La *MCFLDN* SK10 .. 85 J6
 WSFD CW7 .... 177 G5
Woodford La West *WSFD* CW7.. 177 G5
Woodford Rd *BRAM/HZG* SK7 .. 65 L7
 POY/DIS SK12 .... 66 B7
 WILM/AE SK9 .... 85 G4
Woodgate Av *ALS/KID* ST7 ... 224 F7
Woodgate Cl *MPL/ROM* SK6 .. 47 M1 8
Woodgate La *NANT* CW5 ..... 200 C2
Woodhall Dr *BRAM/HZG* SK7 .. 85 K1
 WARRW/BUR WA5 .... 36 A4
Woodhall Av *ALS/KID* ST7 ... 243 J1
Woodham Cl *NWCHW* CW8 ... 12 B9
Woodham Gv *NSTN* CH64 .... 91 M7 8
Woodham Rd *NTHM/RTH* M23.. 43 M3
Woodhatch Rd *RUNC* WA7 ... 74 F2
Woodhead Dr *HALE/TIMP* WA15.. 61 J8
Woodhead Rd *HALE/TIMP* WA15.. 61 K4
Woodhey La *NANT* CW5 ...... 234 E2
Woodheys *HTNM* SK4 .... 45 M1
Woodheys Dr *SALE* M33 ..... 42 D3
Woodhouse Cl *GOL/RIS/CU* WA3.. 38 F1
Woodhouse End Rd
 MCFLDS SK11 .... 161 L3
Woodhouse La *ALT* WA14 .... 41 H8
 ALT WA14 .... 42 B3
 AUD/MAD/W CW3 .... 274 C3
 BIDD ST8 .... 227 L2
 MCFLDS SK11 .... 161 K3
 SALE M33 .... 42 C2
 WYTH/NTH M22 .... 44 D7
 WYTH/NTH M22 .... 63 J4
Woodhouse La East
 HALE/TIMP WA15 .... 43 H3 8
Woodhouse Rd *WYTH/NTH* M22 .. 63 K4
Woodland Av *BRAM/HZG* SK7 .. 66 E3
 CW/HAS CW1 .... 19 M5
 LYMM WA13 .... 59 G2
 NANT CW5 .... 21 J6
 NEWLW WA12 .... 27 M1 8
 WDN WA8 .... 6 F2
Woodland Bank *CHNE* CH2 .. 146 F3 8
Woodland Cl *MCFLDS* SK11 .. 135 C1
Woodland Ct *ALS/KID* ST7 ... 224 D8 8
Woodland Crs *CO* CH5 ...... 142 A6 8
Woodland Dr *LYMM* WA13 ... 58 F2 8
Woodland End *MCFLDS* SK11 .. 135 C1 8
Woodland Gdns
 CW/HAS CW1 .... 221 K6 8
Woodland Hills
 AUD/MAD/W CW3 .... 267 C3
Woodland Rd *ALS/KID* ST7 ... 224 E4
 EP CH65 .... 121 H2
 HLWD L26 .... 50 E5
Woodlands Av *ALS/KID* ST7 .. 242 D2
 CHD/CHDH SK8 .... 65 G2
 CONG CW12 .... 184 D8
 LEIGH WN7 .... 24 F1
 NSTN CH64 .... 91 K4
 TPLY/KEL CW6 .... 175 G4

Woodlands Ct CQ CH5 .... 166 C4
Woodlands Crs KNUT WA16 ..... 59 J8
Woodlands Dr CHNE CH2 .... 145 L8
  HOLMCH CW4 .... 157 L3
  KNUT WA16 .... 107 H2
  OFTN SK2 .... 47 J4
  SALE M33 .... 43 J3
  WARRS WA4 .... 57 K1
Woodlands Gv NWCHW CW8 ... 128 F1
Woodlands La CHSE CH3 .... 170 A2
  HALE/TIMP WA15 .... 42 E7
Woodlands Park Rd OFTN SK2 ... 47 K4
Woodlands Pkwy
  HALE/TIMP WA15 .... 42 E7
Woodlands Rd ALT WA14 .... 42 E7
  CHSE CH3 .... 170 A6
  CHSW/BR CH4 .... 169 G5
  HTNM SK4 .... 45 K2
  MCFLDS SK11 .... 14 E8
  NM/HAY SK22 .... 69 G4
  NSTN CH64 .... 91 K4
  NWCHW CW8 .... 12 A9
  POY/DIS SK12 .... 68 A6
  WILM/AE SK9 .... 84 E1
Woodlands Rd East
  NWCHW CW8 .... 12 A8
The Woodlands NWCHE CW9 ... 105 G6
  NWCHW CW8 .... 12 E1
Woodland St BIDD ST8 .... 227 K5
  CQ CH5 .... 142 A6
Woodlands Wy TPLY/KEL CW6 ... 197 K1
Woodland Vw GTS/LS CH66 ...... 94 B4
Wood La CHSE CH3 .... 215 G2
  CHSW/BR CH4 .... 167 H8
  HALE/TIMP WA15 .... 43 G7
  HOLMCH CW4 .... 157 J3
  HUY L36 .... 32 B2
  KNUT WA16 .... 82 B3
  MPL/ROM SK6 .... 48 D7
  MWCH CW10 .... 180 D8
  NSTN CH64 .... 91 J2
  NSTN CH64 .... 118 C2
  NWCHW CW8 .... 128 E4
  PART M31 .... 40 E1
  RUNC WA7 .... 73 M8
  RUNC WA7 .... 74 C6
  TPLY/KEL CW6 .... 173 K5
  WARRS WA4 .... 56 E4
Wood La East MCFLDN SK10 .. 87 H4
Wood La North MCFLDN SK10 .. 87 H4
Wood La South MCFLDN SK10 ... 87 G5
Wood La West MCFLDN SK10 .... 87 G4
Woodlark Cl WSFD CW7 .... 178 A4
Woodlea Av CHNE CH2 .... 145 M5
Woodlea Ct NWCHW CW8 .... 12 C4
Woodlea Dr MCFLDN SK10 ..... 112 E4
Woodley Cl OFTN SK2 .... 47 K5
Woodley Fold
  WARRW/BUR WA5 .... 35 M8
Woodman St STKP SK1 .... 2 F4
Wood Mt HALE/TIMP WA15 ..... 43 H7
Woodmount Cl MPL/ROM SK6 ... 48 E2
Woodnoth Dr CW/SHV CW2 .... 238 C7
Wood Orchard La
  AUD/MAD/W CW3 .... 274 D2
Woodpecker Cl GOL/RIS/CU WA3.. 29 M8
Woodpecker Dr HLWD L26 ...... 50 E2
  NWCHE CW9 .... 129 M8
Woodridge RUNC WA7 .... 74 C3
Wood Rd HALE/TIMP WA15 ..... 43 G3
  HLWD L26 .... 50 E5
  SALE M33 .... 43 H3
Woodrock Rd WLTN L25 .... 50 B2
Woodrow Wy IRL M44 .... 31 M4
Woodroyd Cl BRAM/HZG SK7 ... 65 K3
Woodruff Cl ALS/KID ST7 ...... 243 M3
Woodruffe Gdns MPL/ROM SK6 .. 48 A4
Wood's Cl WLTN L25 .... 50 A1
Woodsfin La CHSE CH3 .... 214 E5
Woods Gv FROD/HEL WA6 .... 65 H5
Woodshutt's St ALS/KID ST7 ... 242 D3
Woodside ALS/KID ST7 .... 225 L8
  AUD/MAD/W CW3 .... 267 L5
  KNUT WA16 .... 107 H2

MCFLDS SK11 .... 160 A1
Woodside Av ALS/KID ST7 ..... 224 E8
  ALS/KID ST7 .... 242 F3
  CW/SHV CW2 .... 237 M2
  FROD/HEL WA6 .... 99 K5
Woodside Cl CQ CH5 .... 166 A3
Woodside Dr MPL/ROM SK6 .... 67 L5
  SBCH CW11 .... 204 C6
Woodside La CW/SHV CW2 ..... 237 M3
  POY/DIS SK12 .... 66 B3
Woodside Rd CH/BCN CW10 .... 144 C7
  LYMM WA13 .... 59 H3
  WARRW/BUR WA5 .... 35 M6
Woodside St NM/HAY SK22 ..... 69 H6
Woods La CHD/CHDH SK8 ...... 65 H5
  NWCHW CW8 .... 12 E1
Woods Moor La EDGY/DAV SK3 .. 47 G8
Woodsome Dr EP CH65 .... 121 H3
Wood Sorrel Wy
  GOL/RIS/CU WA3 .... 23 L4
Woods Rd IRL M44 .... 31 M4
The Woods ALT WA14 .... 42 E6
Woodstock Av CHD/CHDH SK8 .. 65 G5
  NEWLW WA12 .... 27 K2
Woodstock Cl LEIGH WN7 .... 24 E3
Woodstock Dr MWCH CW10 .... 179 L7
Woodstock Gdns WARRS WA4 ... 56 F6
Woodstock Gv WDN WA8 .... 52 D2
Woodstock Rd ALT WA14 ...... 42 C4
  BURS/TUN ST6 .... 243 G5
Wood St ALS/KID ST7 .... 226 C5
  ALT WA14 .... 42 D8
  CHD/CHDH SK8 .... 45 K6
  CONG CW12 .... 207 K1
  CQ CH5 .... 167 G2
  CW/SHV CW2 .... 19 G8
  EDGY/DAV SK3 .... 2 C7
  EDGY/DAV SK3 .... 2 E6
  GOL/RIS/CU WA3 .... 23 H4
  MCFLDS SK11 .... 15 H6
  NM/HAY SK22 .... 69 H5
  WARR WA1 .... 5 M5
  WDN WA8 .... 7 L3
Woodthorn Cl RUNC WA7 .... 54 F8
Woodthorpe Dr
  CHD/CHDH SK8 .... 65 G2
Woodvale ALT WA14 .... 61 J2
Woodvale Cl
  WARRN/WOL WA2 .... 37 L3
Woodvale Dr GOL/RIS/CU WA3 ... 23 L3
Woodvale Rd GTS/LS CH66 ...... 94 D3
  KNUT WA16 .... 107 G4
  WLTN L25 .... 50 B2
Wood Vw WYTH/NTH M22 ...... 44 D3
Woodview Crs WDN WA8 ...... 52 A4
Woodview Rd WDN WA8 .... 52 A4
Wood Ville CQ CH5 .... 166 D2
Woodville Dr MPL/ROM SK6 .... 48 E8
Woodville Pl WDN WA8 .... 6 A2
Woodville Rd ALT WA14 .... 42 C8
Woodward St NWCHW CW8 .... 128 D3
Woodward Wk CHSE CH3 ...... 172 C1
Woodwise La NTHM/RTH M23 ... 43 L3
Woolacombe Cl WARRS WA4 ... 56 D1
Woolaston Dr ALS/KID ST7 .... 241 K1
Woollen Rd IRL M44 .... 31 C5
Woolley Av POY/DIS SK12 ...... 86 D1
Woolley Cl FROD/HEL WA6 ..... 99 K2
Woolmer Cl GOL/RIS/CU WA3 ... 30 B6
Woolston Av CONG CW12 ..... 207 M2
Woolston Dr CW/SHV CW2 ..... 253 L2
Woolston Grange Av WARR WA1.. 38 E4
  WARRN/WOL WA2 .... 38 C2
Woolton Bvd WLTN L25 .... 50 B2
Woolton Mt WLTN L25 .... 50 A1
Woolton Pk WLTN L25 .... 50 A1
Woolton Park Cl WLTN L25 ..... 50 A1
Woolton St WLTN L25 .... 50 B2
Woore Rd AUD/MAD/W CW3 .... 274 B1
Worcester Av
  GOL/RIS/CU WA3 .... 23 H4
Worcester Cl ALS/KID ST7 ..... 242 D3

MPL/ROM SK6 .... 48 A3
  WARRW/BUR WA5 .... 36 B7
Worcester Pl CH/BCN CW1 .... 145 G7
Worcester Rd CHD/CHDH SK8 ... 46 A8
  SALE M33 .... 42 D1
Worcester St EP CH65 .... 10 F5
Worcester Wk EP CH65 .... 10 F5
Wordsworth Av STHEL WA9 .... 34 A1
  WARRS WA4 .... 56 B1
  WDN WA8 .... 6 E4
Wordsworth Cl
  CW/SHV CW2 .... 237 M3
  SBCH CW11 .... 203 M4
Wordsworth Crs CH/BCN CH1 .. 145 G7
Wordsworth Dr CW/HAS CW1 ... 19 L3
Wordsworth Ms
  CH/BCN CH1 .... 145 G7
Wordsworth Sq CH/BCN CH1 ... 145 G7
Wordsworth Wy ALS/KID ST7 .. 224 D8
  GTS/LS CH66 .... 120 E3
Works La NWCHE CW9 .... 130 E3
World Wy MANAIR M90 .... 63 H4
Worleston Cl MWCH CW10 .... 179 J6
Worrall St CONG CW12 .... 207 L1
  EDGY/DAV SK3 .... 2 E9
Worsborough Av
  WARRW/BUR WA5 .... 36 B7
Worsley Av CH/BCN CH1 ..... 144 A4
  WARRS WA4 .... 37 M8
Worsley Crs OFTN SK2 .... 47 H5
Worsley Dr CONG CW12 ...... 208 B3
Worsley Rd WARRS WA4 ...... 56 B3
Worsley St GOL/RIS/CU WA3 ... 23 C4
  WARRW/BUR WA5 .... 4 D2
Worthing Cl OFTN SK2 .... 47 K6
Worthing St NWCHE CW9 ..... 130 C4
Worthington Av PART M31 ..... 40 F1
Worthington Cl MCFLDS SK11 .. 137 H4
  NANT CW5 .... 21 K7
  RUNC WA7 .... 74 A5
Wotton Dr AIMK WN4 .... 22 D1
Wrekin Av NTHM/RTH M23 .... 63 C1
Wrekin Cl WLTN L25 .... 50 B4
Wrekin Wy CHSW/BR CH4 ..... 168 F6
Wrenbury Cl EDGY/DAV SK3 ... 46 C6
Wrenbury Dr CHD/CHDH SK8 ... 45 L6
Wrenbury Hall Dr NANT CW5 ... 250 A7
Wrenbury Heath Rd NANT CW5.. 250 E7
Wrenbury Rd MALPAS SY14 ... 248 C3
  NANT CW5 .... 262 A1
Wren Cl BIDD ST8 .... 227 L4
  CW/HAS CW1 .... 220 F6
  GOL/RIS/CU WA3 .... 29 M8
  MCFLDN SK10 .... 14 A2
  OFTN SK2 .... 47 M7
  RUNC WA7 .... 74 A6
Wren Gv HLWD L26 .... 50 E3
Wrenmere Cl SBCH CW11 ..... 203 L4
Wrenshot La KNUT WA16 .... 59 J7
Wrexham Cl BIDD ST8 .... 227 K3
  WARRW/BUR WA5 .... 36 E2
Wrexham Rd CHSW/BR CH4 ... 169 J6
  MALPAS SY14 .... 257 L2
  NANT CW5 .... 234 F5
  TPLY/KEL CW6 .... 233 G3
  WHITCH SY13 .... 269 L5
  WRXS/E LL13 .... 228 D5
Wright Av NWCHE CW9 ...... 130 C6
Wright Crs WDN WA8 .... 53 G8
Wrights Bank North OFTN SK2 ... 47 K7
Wrights Bank South OFTN SK2 .. 47 L7
Wright's La SBCH CW11 ...... 204 D6
  WARRW/BUR WA5 .... 35 L1
  WDN WA8 .... 53 M2
Wright St ALS/KID ST7 ...... 242 D3
Wrigley La MCFLDN SK10 ..... 111 H8
Wrinehill Rd NANT CW5 .... 253 K5
Wroxham Cl CHNE CH2 .... 17 G2
  FROD/HEL WA6 .... 98 B8
Wroxham Rd WARRW/BUR WA5 .. 35 L6
Wyatt Av WARRN/WOL WA2 .... 22 D1
Wyatt St BURS/TUN ST6 ...... 243 J5
  HTNM SK4 .... 2 E4

Wybersley Rd MPL/ROM SK6 ... 68 A3
  NANT CW5 .... 253 H6
Wybunbury La NANT CW5 ..... 252 B1
  NANT CW5 .... 253 H6
Wybunbury Rd NANT CW5 .... 237 K8
Wyche Av NANT CW5 .... 20 C7
Wyche Cl NWCHW CW9 .... 130 E6
Wyche La TPLY/KEL CW6 ..... 216 F4
Wychelm Rd PART M31 .... 40 F1
Wyche Rd TPLY/KEL CW6 ..... 216 F4
Wych La MCFLDN SK10 .... 86 C7
Wych-house La MWCH CW10 .. 179 J3
Wychwood ALT WA14 .... 61 H3
Wychwood Av LYMM WA13 ..... 58 C1
Wycliffe Av WILM/AE SK9 ...... 84 A6
Wycliffe Rd GTS/LS CH66 ..... 120 F1
Wycliffe St HTNM SK4 .... 2 D4
Wyedale EP CH65 .... 121 H1
Wynchgate Rd BRAM/HZG SK7.. 67 G1
Wyncroft Cl EP CH65 .... 121 G1
  WDN WA8 .... 52 C5
Wyncroft Rd WDN WA8 .... 52 C5
Wyndham Cl BRAM/HZG SK7 ... 65 L5
Wyndham Crs GTS/LS CH66 ... 120 E2
Wyndham Rd CH/BCN CH1 .... 144 C8
The Wynd TPLY/KEL CW6 ..... 149 J8
Wyne Cl BRAM/HZG SK7 .... 67 G1
Wynfield Av WYTH/NTH M22 ... 63 M5
Wyngate Rd CHD/CHDH SK8 ... 64 F3
  HALE/TIMP WA15 .... 61 M4
Wynnstay Rd CHSW/BR CH4 ... 167 J8
Wynter La MALPAS SY14 ..... 245 H1
Wynton Cl LEIGH WN7 .... 24 E2
Wynyard Cl SALE M33 .... 43 K2
Wynyard Rd WYTH/NTH M22 ... 63 J1
Wyrevale Gv AIMK WN4 .... 22 C1
Wyswall Cl HLWD L26 .... 50 E3
Wythburn Gv RUNC WA7 ...... 73 L7
Wythburn St STKP SK1 .... 47 H5
Wythenshawe Rd
  NTHM/RTH M23 .... 43 L4
Wythens Rd CHD/CHDH SK8 ... 64 B4
Wythin St TPLY/KEL CW6 ..... 216 D3
Wyville Cl BRAM/HZG SK7 ..... 67 G2

Y

Yarcombe Cl HLWD L26 .... 50 F3
Yardington WHITCH SY13 .... 269 M4
Yardley Av WARRW/BUR WA5 ... 4 D1
Yarmouth Dr NTHM/RTH M23 ... 44 B3
Yarmouth Rd WARRW/BUR WA5.. 35 L6
Yarrow Cl CHSW/BR CH4 ..... 190 C1
Yarwood Av NTHM/RTH M23 .. 43 M5
Yarwood Cl NWCHW CW8 ...... 13 G5
Yarwood Av NTHM/RTH M23 ... 60 E4
Yarwood St ALT WA14 .... 61 K1
Yatehouse La MWCH CW10 ... 155 J7
Yates Cl WARRW/BUR WA5 ..... 36 C7
Yates Rd CHNE CH2 .... 122 E3
  NM/HAY SK22 .... 69 J3
Yates St CW/SHV CW2 .... 18 E7
  STKP SK1 .... 3 L2
Yattendon Av
  NTHM/RTH M23 .... 43 K4
Yealand Av HTNM SK4 .... 2 C2
Yeald Brow LYMM WA13 ...... 58 B1
Yeardsley Av CHF/WBR SK23 ... 89 K1
Yeardsley Cl BRAM/HZG SK7 .. 65 L1
Yeardsley Gn CHF/WBR SK23 .. 89 K4
Yeardsley La CHF/WBR SK23 .. 89 K1
Yearsleys La FROD/HEL WA6 .. 127 G7
Yeld La TPLY/KEL CW6 .... 149 L6
Yelverton Cl HLWD L26 .... 50 F3
Yeoford Dr ALT WA14 .... 42 B6
Yeoman Cl BRAM/HZG SK7 .... 66 D1
Yeoman Wy GTS/LS CH66 ..... 120 E3
Yeovil Cl WARR WA1 .... 38 C4
Yerburgh St CHNE CH2 ...... 145 K8
Yewdale Dr GTS/LS CH66 ..... 120 F3
Yewdale Rd OFTN SK2 .... 47 H6
Yewlands NWCHW CW8 .... 127 K7
Yewlands Dr KNUT WA16 ..... 107 J2

Yew St HTNM SK4 .... 46 B4
Yew Tree Av BRAM/HZG SK7 ... 66 F4
  NEWLW WA12 .... 22 A8
  WYTH/NTH M22 .... 44 D3
Yew Tree Cl CHNE CH2 ...... 122 E3
  CHSW/BR CH4 .... 190 C1
  LYMM WA13 .... 39 L8
  MALPAS SY14 .... 232 D2
  MCFLDN SK10 .... 112 B5
  MCFLDS SK11 .... 14 B9
  MPL/ROM SK6 .... 48 C7
  MWCH CW10 .... 179 H2
  TPLY/KEL CW6 .... 175 M5
  WILM/AE SK9 .... 84 D5
Yew Tree Ct ALS/KID ST7 ..... 241 L2
Yew Tree Dr MPL/ROM SK6 .... 47 K1
  NANT CW5 .... 20 C6
  NWCHW CW8 .... 103 H8
  WYTH/NTH M22 .... 44 D3
Yew Tree Gv CHD/CHDH SK8 ... 64 A1
Yewtree La NTHM/RTH M23 ... 44 B2
  POY/DIS SK12 .... 86 F2
  WYTH/NTH M22 .... 44 D3
Yew Tree La CONG CW12 ..... 226 C2
  WARRS WA4 .... 57 J7
Yew Tree Park Rd
  CHD/CHDH SK8 .... 65 H6
Yewtree Rd KNUT WA16 ...... 131 M1
Yew Tree Rd CW/SHV CW2 .... 238 A4
  EDGY/DAV SK3 .... 65 M1
  MCFLDN SK10 .... 87 H3
  WLTN L25 .... 50 C4
Yew Tree Ter ALS/KID ST7 ... 243 G4
Yew Tree Wy GOL/RIS/CU WA3.. 23 H5
  MCFLDN SK10 .... 112 B6
The Yonne CH/BCN CH1 .... 16 E5
York Av CQ CH5 .... 142 B7
  GOL/RIS/CU WA3 .... 29 M2
  WARRW/BUR WA5 .... 35 L5
York Cl ALS/KID ST7 .... 242 D5
  BIDD ST8 .... 227 K2
  CHD/CHDH SK8 .... 46 A7
York Crs WILM/AE SK9 .... 84 D5
York Dr ALT WA14 .... 61 K3
  BRAM/HZG SK7 .... 67 G2
  CHNE CH2 .... 146 F4
  MANAIR M90 .... 62 F5
  WARRS WA4 .... 57 G2
  WSFD CW7 .... 177 K6
York Pl RUNC WA7 .... 9 H3
York Rd AIMK WN4 .... 22 C2
  ALT WA14 .... 61 J3
  EP CH65 .... 10 E8
  HUY L36 .... 32 K1
  IRL M44 .... 31 K7
  WARRS WA4 .... 57 G2
  WDN WA8 .... 52 C4
York Rd South AIMK WN4 ..... 22 C4
Yorkshire Rd PART M31 ...... 40 E2
York St CH/BCN CH1 .... 17 H4
  DID/WITH M20 .... 45 H1
  EDGY/DAV SK3 .... 23 G3
  GOL/RIS/CU WA3 .... 23 G3
  HALE/TIMP WA15 .... 61 L1
  MCFLDN SK10 .... 15 J5
  RUNC WA7 .... 9 G4
  WARRS WA4 .... 5 J9
Young St BURS/TUN ST6 ..... 243 M6
Yule St EDGY/DAV SK3 .... 2 C7

Z

Zan Dr SBCH CW11 .... 223 G1
Zinnia Dr IRL M44 .... 31 L4
Zion St NWCHW CW8 .... 12 E4
Zodiac Dr BURS/TUN ST6 ..... 243 M6
Zurich Gdns BRAM/HZG SK7 ... 65 L1

Index - featured places

Abbey Gate College
  CHSE CH3 .... 193 L4
Abbey Gate School
  CHNE CH2 .... 16 F3
The Accord Clinic
  MWCH CW10 .... 179 J3
Acorn Business Park
  EDGY/DAV SK3 .... 2 D5
Acorns Surgery
  MWCH CW10 .... 179 J3
Acton C of E Controlled
Primary School
  NANT CW5 .... 236 A5
Adderley C of E Primary
School
  MKTDR TF9 .... 273 M7
Adelaide Street County
Secondary School
  CW/HAS CW1 .... 18 D2
Adlington CP School
  MCFLDS SK10 .... 86 E7
Adswood Clinic
  EDGY/DAV SK3 .... 46 E7
Adswood Primary School
  EDGY/DAV SK3 .... 46 D7
A & E Wythenshawe Hospital
  NTHM/RTH M23 .... 43 M7
Aircraft Factory
  CHSW/BR CH4 .... 167 K6
Alban Retail Park
  WARRN/WOL WA2 .... 37 G2
Albert Road Medical Centre
  WDN WA8 .... 7 K2
Alderley Edge CP School
  WILM/AE SK9 .... 110 A2

Alderley Edge Cricket Club
  WILM/AE SK9 .... 110 B3
Alderley Edge Golf Club
  WILM/AE SK9 .... 109 L1
Alderley Edge School for Girls
  WILM/AE SK9 .... 109 M2
Aldersley Green Golf Club
  CHSE CH3 .... 213 J6
Alderwood CP School
  SPK/HALE L24 .... 70 E1
Aldford School
  CHSE CH3 .... 211 M1
The Alexandra Hospital
  CHD/CHDH SK8 .... 45 K6
Alexandra Industrial Estate
  WDN WA8 .... 6 F7
Alexandra Park Junior
& Infant School
  EDGY/DAV SK3 .... 46 C5
All Hallows RC High School
  MCFLDS SK11 .... 14 C6
All Saints C of E Junior School
  WDN WA8 .... 52 B1
All Saints C of E Primary School
  MPL/ROM SK6 .... 49 G7
Alport Primary School
  MALPAS SY14 .... 246 B8
Alsager Cricket Club
  ALS/KID ST7 .... 224 D8
Alsager Dental Clinic
  ALS/KID ST7 .... 241 L1
Alsager Highfields CP School
  ALS/KID ST7 .... 224 D8
Alsager Leisure Centre
  ALS/KID ST7 .... 224 B8

Alsager School
  ALS/KID ST7 .... 224 B8
Altrincham & Broadheath
CP School
  ALT WA14 .... 42 C4
Altrincham C of E Primary
School
  ALT WA14 .... 42 C7
Altrincham General Hospital
  ALT WA14 .... 42 C8
Altrincham Grammar School
for Boys
  ALT WA14 .... 61 K2
Altrincham Grammar School
for Girls
  ALT WA14 .... 61 J1
Altrincham Ice Rink
  ALT WA14 .... 42 D6
Altrincham Industrial Centre
  ALT WA14 .... 42 A6
Altrincham Rugby Football Club
  HALE/TIMP WA15 .... 43 J5
Altrincham Leisure Centre
  HALE/TIMP WA15 .... 42 E7
Altrincham Preparatory School
  ALT WA14 .... 61 J2
Altrincham Priory Hospital
  HALE/TIMP WA15 .... 62 A4
Alvanley Primary School
  FROD/HEL WA6 .... 124 D3
Alvaston Business Park
  NANT CW5 .... 21 G1
Amalgamated Sports Club
  POY/DIS SK12 .... 68 B6

Ambulance Station
  CHNE CH2 .... 17 G2
Amphitheatre
  CH/BCN CH1 .... 17 H6
Annandale Medical Centre
  KNUT WA16 .... 107 J1
Antrobus C of E
Controlled School
  NWCHE CW9 .... 77 J8
Apollo Cinema Bingo
& Social Club
  CW/HAS CW1 .... 19 G4
Appleton Thorn Community
Primary School
  WARRS WA4 .... 57 J8
Aquinas Sixth Form College
  OFTN SK2 .... 47 H6
The Archways Surgery
  MPL/ROM SK6 .... 48 B2
Arclid Industrial Estate
  SBCH CW11 .... 205 G4
Arden Primary School
  MPL/ROM SK6 .... 47 K1
Arley House
  NWCHE CW9 .... 78 D6
Arley Primary School
  RUNC WA7 .... 73 M2
Art Gallery
  NSTN CH64 .... 91 M2
Art Theatre
  NM/HAY SK22 .... 69 H5
Ash Grove CP School
  MCFLDS SK11 .... 138 C8
Ashley C of E Primary School
  HALE/TIMP WA15 .... 61 M7

Ashley Retail Park
  WDN WA8 .... 7 K6
Ashley School
  WDN WA8 .... 6 B1
Ashmount Industrial Centre
  FLINT CH6 .... 116 B4
Ashton Hayes County
Primary School
  CHSE CH3 .... 148 E4
Astbury C of E Aided
Primary School
  CONG CW12 .... 207 H4
Astbury Golf Club
  CONG CW12 .... 207 L5
Astmoor County
Primary School
  RUNC WA7 .... 73 M2
Aston CP School
  RUNC WA7 .... 100 C3
Atherton County Infant School
  EP CH65 .... 94 F7
Atlantic Business Centre
  ALT WA14 .... 42 C5
Audlem Medical Practice
  AUD/MAD/W CW3 ...... 263 H2
Austin Rawlinson Sports Centre
  SPK/HALE L24 .... 70 C1
Avondale Industrial Estate
  EDGY/DAV SK3 .... 46 B4
Avondale Recreation Centre
  EDGY/DAV SK3 .... 46 B5
Avondale Secondary School
  EDGY/DAV SK3 .... 2 A1
Baguley Hall Primary School
  NTHM/RTH M23 .... 44 A6

Baileys Business Park
MCFLDN SK10 .... 112 F5
Bankfield High School
WDN WA8 .... 6 A2
Bank Quay Trading Estate
WARRW/BUR WA5 .... 4 D9
Banks Lane Primary School
STKP SK1 .... 3 L8
Barlow Medical Centre
DID/WITH M20 .... 45 H1
The Barlow RC High School
DID/WITH M20 .... 45 J2
Barnton County
Primary School
NWCHW CW8 .... 103 G8
Barony Hospital
NANT CW5 .... 20 F2
Barrack Hill Primary School
MPL/ROM SK6 .... 48 A2
Barrington Medical Centre
ALT WA14 .... 42 D6
Barrow C of E County
Primary School
CHSE CH3 .... 147 K6
Barrow Hall Community
Primary School
WARRW/BUR WA5 .... 35 K5
Beach Tennis Club
NWCHW CW8 .... 129 H6
Beamont Community
Junior School
WARRN/WOL WA2 .... 5 K2
Beaver Road Junior
& Infant School
DID/WITH M20 .... 45 H1
Bedford Methodist
Primary School
LEIGH WN7 .... 25 H1
Beech House Group Practice
BRAM/HZG SK7 .... 66 E2
Beechwood County
Primary School
CW/HAS CW1 .... 18 E2
Beechwood County
Primary School
RUNC WA7 .... 73 K7
The Beechwood Surgery
ALS/KID ST7 .... 243 G3
Beeston Castle
TPLY/KEL CW6 .... 215 H1
Belgrave County
Infant School
CHSW/BR CH4 .... 169 H7
Bell Tower
CH/BCN CH1 .... 17 G5
Benchill Junior & Infant School
WYTH/NTH M22 .... 44 C6
Benchill Medical Practice
WYTH/NTH M22 .... 44 D8
The Berrisford Gallery
WILM/AE SK9 .... 109 L1
Bethesda School
CHD/CHDH SK8 .... 64 D1
Betley C of E Primary School
AUD/MAD/W CW3 .... 255 H6
Bewsey Lodge Community
Primary School
WARRW/BUR WA5 .... 4 C3
Bewsey Old School
WARRW/BUR WA5 .... 4 B3
Bexton CP School
KNUT WA16 .... 106 D7
Bickerton C of E
Primary School
MALPAS SY14 .... 232 A5
Biddulph Community
Health Centre
BIDD ST8 .... 227 K6
Biddulph High School
BIDD ST8 .... 227 K7
Biddulph Medical Centre
BIDD ST8 .... 227 K5
Biddulph Valley Leisure Centre
BIDD ST8 .... 227 K3
Birchwood C of E Primary
School
COL/RIS/CU WA3 .... 38 F1
Birchwood Community
High School
GOL/RIS/CU WA3 .... 38 D1
Birchwood Medical Centre
GOL/RIS/CU WA3 .... 38 E1
Bishop Heber County
High School
MALPAS SY14 .... 246 C7
Bishop Martin C of E
Primary School
WLTN L25 .... 50 A2
Bishops C of E High School
CHSE CH3 .... 170 A4
Bishop Wilson C of E
Primary School
NSTN CH64 .... 118 D3
B & J Leisure Centre
WILM/AE SK9 .... 84 A5
Black Cat Industrial Estate
WDN WA8 .... 7 G8
Blackfirs County
Primary School
CONG CW12 .... 183 M8
Blacksheep Gallery
CQ CH5 .... 166 E4
Blacon Clinic
CH/BCN CH1 .... 144 E7
Blacon County High School
CH/BCN CH1 .... 144 D8
Blacon County Infant School
CH/BCN CH1 .... 144 E7
Blacon Hall County
Junior School
CH/BCN CH1 .... 144 E7
Blue Chip Business Park
ALT WA14 .... 42 B5
Blue Planet Aquarium
EP CH65 .... 121 K3
Boat Museum
EP CH65 .... 11 G4

Bold Industrial Estate
WDN WA8 .... 34 C7
Bold Street Medical Centre
WARR WA1 .... 4 F8
Bollinbrook C of E
Primary School
MCFLDN SK10 .... 14 D1
Bollin CP School
ALT WA14 .... 61 H3
Bollington Cross
C of E Primary School
MCFLDN SK10 .... 112 E5
Bollington Leisure Centre
MCFLDN SK10 .... 112 E6
Bollington Medical Centre
MCFLDN SK10 .... 112 F4
Bolshaw Primary School
CHD/CHDH SK8 .... 64 B5
Bolton County Junior
& Infant School
WARRS WA4 .... 56 F1
Borderbrook School
MALPAS SY14 .... 268 D1
Borron Road Industrial Estate
NEWLW WA12 .... 22 C8
Boughton Health Centre
CHSE CH3 .... 17 L4
Boughton Heath CP School
CHSE CH3 .... 170 A4
Boughton St Pauls
County Infant School
CHSE CH3 .... 17 K4
Bowdon Cricket Club
ALT WA14 .... 61 J3
Bowdon Rugby Union
Football Club
HALE/TIMP WA15 .... 43 J8
Bowdon Vale Cricket Club
ALT WA14 .... 61 J4
Bowers Business Park
WDN WA8 .... 7 K6
Brabyns School
MPL/ROM SK6 .... 49 G5
Bradshaw Community
Primary School
WARRS WA4 .... 57 H2
Bradshaw Hall Infant
& Junior School
CHD/CHDH SK8 .... 64 E3
Bramhall Hall
BRAM/HZG SK7 .... 65 L3
Bramhall Health Centre
BRAM/HZG SK7 .... 65 L6
Bramhall High School
BRAM/HZG SK7 .... 65 M4
Bramhall Park Medical Centre
BRAM/HZG SK7 .... 65 L2
Braunhall Park Golf Course
BRAM/HZG SK7 .... 65 K4
Bredbury Green
Primary School
MPL/ROM SK6 .... 47 M3
Brentwood Gallery
& Framing Centre
WARRS WA4 .... 56 C3
Brentwood School
ALT WA14 .... 42 E5
Brereton C of E Aided School
SBCH CW11 .... 181 M7
Briars Hey School
RAIN/WH L35 .... 33 K3
Brickfield Business Centre
NWCHE CW9 .... 130 D3
Bridge College
OFTN SK2 .... 47 K4
Bridge Hall Primary School
EDGY/DAV SK3 .... 46 D6
Bridge House Medical Centre
CHD/CHDH SK8 .... 65 H1
Bridge Industrial Estate
SPK/HALE L24 .... 50 B7
Bridgemere C of E
Aided Primary School
NANT CW5 .... 265 L4
Bridgewater Community
High School
WARRS WA4 .... 56 D6
Bridgewater Community
High School
WARRS WA4 .... 56 D5
Bridgewater Family
Medical Practice
WHITCH SY13 .... 270 A5
Brierley Business Centre
CW/HAS CW1 .... 19 H3
Brierley County Primary
School
CW/HAS CW1 .... 19 H3
Brine Leas County High
School
NANT CW5 .... 251 L1
Broad Oak Community
Primary School
STHEL WA9 .... 26 A1
Broadoak High School
PART M31 .... 40 E2
Broad Oak Primary School
DID/WITH M20 .... 45 H4
Broad Street County
Infant School
CW/HAS CW1 .... 221 J6
Broken Cross County
Primary School
MCFLDS SK11 .... 137 L5
Broken Cross Surgery
MCFLDN SK10 .... 137 L4
Bronington Primary School
WHITCH SY13 .... 268 B8
Brook Acre Community
Primary School
WARRN/WOL WA2 .... 37 L3
Brook Dean CP School
WILM/AE SK9 .... 64 D7
Brook Farm Residential
Special School
TPLY/KEL CW6 .... 197 K4
The Brookfield School
WDN WA8 .... 53 K2

Brookfield Surgery
LYMM WA13 .... 58 E1
Brookhead Junior School
CHD/CHDH SK8 .... 45 M7
Brookside Infant School
GTS/LS CH66 .... 94 D8
Brookside Primary School
MPL/ROM SK6 .... 67 L6
Brookvale County
Comprehensive School
RUNC WA7 .... 74 C7
Brookvale County
Junior School
RUNC WA7 .... 74 B7
Brookvale Recreation Centre
RUNC WA7 .... 74 C6
Brookway High School
NTHM/RTH M23 .... 43 L4
Broomfields Community
Junior School
WARRS WA4 .... 56 E5
Broomwood CP School
HALE/TIMP WA15 .... 43 K7
Broughton Industrial Estate
CHSW/BR CH4 .... 167 M6
Broughton Junior
& Infant School
CHSW/BR CH4 .... 167 J8
Brow CP School
RUNC WA7 .... 73 M3
Brownhall Moor
Industrial Estate
BRAM/HZG SK7 .... 66 B2
Brown Lees Road
Industrial Estate
BIDD ST8 .... 227 H8
Bruche Community
Junior & Infant School
WARR WA1 .... 38 A5
Bruntwood Primary School
CHD/CHDH SK8 .... 64 C2
Brymau Five Trading Estate
CHSW/BR CH4 .... 168 C5
Brymau Four Trading Estate
CHSW/BR CH4 .... 168 D5
Brymau One Trading Estate
CHSW/BR CH4 .... 168 E5
Brymau Three Trading Estate
CHSW/BR CH4 .... 168 E5
Brymau Two Trading Estate
CHSW/BR CH4 .... 168 E5
Budworth Sailing Club
NWCHE CW9 .... 104 A5
Buerton County
Primary School
AUD/MAD/W CW3 .... 274 F1
Buglawton County
Primary School
CONG CW12 .... 185 G3
Buglawton Hall School
CONG CW12 .... 185 J7
Bunbury Aldersey
C of E Primary School
TPLY/KEL CW6 .... 216 D4
Bunbury Medical Practice
TPLY/KEL CW6 .... 217 G3
Burnage Rugby Club
HTNM SK4 .... 45 L3
Burton Manor College
NSTN CH64 .... 118 D3
Burtonwood Community
Primary School
WARRW/BUR WA5 .... 26 E5
Burtonwood Industrial Centre
WARRW/BUR WA5 .... 26 E5
Business Centre
NANT CW5 .... 20 E6
Business Centre
WARR WA1 .... 5 G6
Business Centre
WARRW/BUR WA5 .... 4 D4
Button Lane Primary School
NTHM/RTH M23 .... 43 M2
Byley CP School
MWCH CW10 .... 156 A5
Byrchall High School
AIMK WN4 .... 22 B3
Cadishead Junior School
IRL M44 .... 31 K6
Cadishead Recreation Centre
IRL M44 .... 31 K7
Calderbank Surgery
EDGY/DAV SK3 .... 46 E5
Cale Green Primary School
EDGY/DAV SK3 .... 46 E5
Cale Green Surgery
EDGY/DAV SK3 .... 46 F6
Callands Community
Primary School
WARRW/BUR WA5 .... 36 E2
Calveley CP School
TPLY/KEL CW6 .... 218 B2
Calveley Mill Industrial Estate
TPLY/KEL CW6 .... 217 L2
Camberley Medical Centre
WLTN L25 .... 50 C4
Cambridge Road CP School
EP CH65 .... 10 F8
Canalside Industrial Estate
EP CH65 .... 11 H4
Cannon Drew Junior School
CQ CH5 .... 166 D4
Capenhurst Grange School
GTS/LS CH66 .... 120 E2
Capenhurst Primary School
CH/BCN CH1 .... 120 B4
Capesthorne Hall
MCFLDS SK11 .... 136 A3
Capital Business Centre
BRAM/HZG SK7 .... 65 K6
Carver Theatre
MPL/ROM SK6 .... 48 F7
Castle CP School
ALS/KID ST7 .... 226 D6
Castlefields Health Centre
RUNC WA7 .... 74 A2
Castle Surgery
NWCHW CW8 .... 12 E4

Castle Tennis & Bowling Club
NWCHW CW8 .... 12 F5
The Castle
CH/BCN CH1 .... 16 F8
Castle View CP School
RUNC WA7 .... 73 K4
Catalyst Museum
WDN WA8 .... 53 G7
Causeway Medical Centre
WARRS WA4 .... 56 B1
Cavendish School
RUNC WA7 .... 73 H7
Cedar Cross Medical Centre
RAIN/WH L35 .... 32 D1
Cedars Medical Centre
ALS/KID ST7 .... 241 K1
Chaigley School
WARRS WA4 .... 38 E8
Chantry Court
CH/BCN CH1 .... 168 E2
Chapelfield Clinic
WDN WA8 .... 52 B3
Chapel Museum
ALS/KID ST7 .... 226 D6
Chapel Street Clinic
WDN WA8 .... 7 H7
Chatfield Community
Primary School
GOL/RIS/CU WA3 .... 38 C1
Cheadle Cricket Club
CHD/CHDH SK8 .... 45 J7
Cheadle Golf Course
CHD/CHDH SK8 .... 45 L8
Cheadle Heath Clinic
EDGY/DAV SK3 .... 46 A4
Cheadle Heath Junior
& Infant School
EDGY/DAV SK3 .... 46 A5
Cheadle Heath Sports Centre
CHD/CHDH SK8 .... 46 A6
Cheadle Hulme College
CHD/CHDH SK8 .... 65 H5
Cheadle Hulme Medical Centre
CHD/CHDH SK8 .... 65 G4
Cheadle Hulme School
CHD/CHDH SK8 .... 65 G4
Cheadle Medical Practice
CHD/CHDH SK8 .... 45 K6
Cheadle Primary School
CHD/CHDH SK8 .... 45 K6
Cheadle RC Junior
& Infants School
CHD/CHDH SK8 .... 64 E2
Cheadle Royal Hospital
CHD/CHDH SK8 .... 64 C2
Cheadle Royel Shopping Centre
CHD/CHDH SK8 .... 64 D2
Cheadle Swimming
& Recreation Centre
CHD/CHDH SK8 .... 45 L8
Cheadle Town Football Club
CHD/CHDH SK8 .... 45 L7
Chelford C of E Primary School
MCFLDS SK11 .... 134 F1
Cherry Grove County
Primary School
CHSE CH3 .... 170 A3
Cherry Manor Primary School
SALE M33 .... 42 C2
Cherry Tree Community
Primary School
LYMM WA13 .... 58 C2
Cherry Tree Hospital
OFTN SK2 .... 47 J7
Cheshire County Council
CH/BCN CH1 .... 16 F4
Cheshire County Council
CH/BCN CH1 .... 17 H6
Cheshire County Council
CH/BCN CH1 .... 143 L1
Cheshire County Council
CHNE CW2 .... 17 M1
Cheshire County Council
CHNE CW2 .... 121 H8
Cheshire County Council
CHSW/BR CH4 .... 192 B1
Cheshire County Council
GTS/LS CH66 .... 120 F2
Cheshire County Council
RUNC WA7 .... 74 F7
Cheshire County Council
WILM/AE SK9 .... 84 D1
Cheshire County Council
WILM/AE SK9 .... 84 A6
Cheshire County Officers
Sports Club
CHNE CW2 .... 146 A6
Cheshire Health Clinic
SBCH CW11 .... 204 B5
Cheshire Magistrates Court
MCFLDN SK10 .... 15 G3
Cheshire Museums
NWCHE CW9 .... 13 G5
Chesire County Council
WDN WA8 .... 7 J5
Chesnut Lodge Special School
WDN WA8 .... 6 C3
Chesterbank Business Park
CHSW/BR CH4 .... 168 D5
Chester Boughton Hall
Cricket Club
CHSE CH3 .... 170 B3
Chester Business Centre
CH/BCN CH1 .... 17 H5
Chester Business Park
CHSW/BR CH4 .... 192 C1
Chester Cathedral
CH/BCN CH1 .... 17 G5
Chester Catholic
Aided High School
CHSW/BR CH4 .... 169 K6
Chester City Council
CH/BCN CH1 .... 16 A3
Chester City Council
CH/BCN CH1 .... 17 J5
Chester City Council
CH/BCN CH1 .... 145 G7

Chester City Council
CH/BCN CH1 .... 168 F3
Chester City Football Club
CH/BCN CH1 .... 168 E3
Chester County Court
CH/BCN CH1 .... 16 F5
Chester Figure Clinic
CH/BCN CH1 .... 17 C5
The Chestergate Clinic
MCFLDN SK10 .... 14 F4
Chester Golf Course
CHSW/BR CH4 .... 16 C7
Chester Rugby Union
Football Club
CHSE CH3 .... 170 D2
Chester Swimming Association
CH/BCN CH1 .... 17 J5
Chester Toy Museum
CH/BCN CH1 .... 17 G6
Chester Visitors Centre
CH/BCN CH1 .... 17 H5
Childer Thornton CP School
GTS/LS CH66 .... 94 B4
Cholmondeley Castle
MALPAS SY14 .... 247 M1
Christie Street
Industrial Estate
STKP SK1 .... 3 K9
Christleton County
Primary School
CHSE CH3 .... 170 D4
Christleton High School
CHSE CH3 .... 170 E5
Christleton Sports Centre
CHSE CH3 .... 170 F5
Christleton Sports Club
CHSE CH3 .... 170 F3
Church Coppenhall
County Junior School
CW/HAS CW1 .... 221 H6
Church Hill Gallery
KNUT WA16 .... 107 G2
Church Lawton Gate
CP School
ALS/KID ST7 .... 225 G7
Church Street Industrial Estate
WARR WA1 .... 5 J7
Cinderhill Lane Surgery
ALS/KID ST7 .... 225 M5
Cinnamon Brow C of E
Primary School
WARRN/WOL WA2 .... 37 M1
City College Manchester
NTHM/RTH M23 .... 43 M4
City College Manchester
NTHM/RTH M23 .... 43 K4
City College Manchester
NTHM/RTH M23 .... 44 C3
City Walls Medical Centre
CH/BCN CH1 .... 16 E5
Civic Centre
CQ CH5 .... 142 A5
Civic Hall
BRAM/HZG SK7 .... 66 E2
Civic Hall
WSFD CW7 .... 177 K3
The Civic Hall
MCFLDN SK10 .... 113 G4
Cledford County Junior School
MWCH CW10 .... 179 J5
The Clinic Centre
MCFLDS SK11 .... 138 D7
Clinic for the Handicapped
WARRN/WOL WA2 .... 4 F5
The Clinic
CQ CH5 .... 166 A3
Clinic & Welfare Centre
WARR WA1 .... 38 B5
Clough Hall County
High School
ALS/KID ST7 .... 242 F3
Cloughwood School
NWCHW CW8 .... 12 C9
Club House
MCFLDN SK10 .... 112 C7
Club Houses
WRX/GR/LL LL12 .... 210 C5
Club Theatre
ALT WA14 .... 42 D8
Clutton C of E CP School
MALPAS SY14 .... 230 C3
Clwydian Community
Care NHS Trust
CQ CH5 .... 142 A5
The Cobbs Community
Infant School
WARRS WA4 .... 56 E4
College
NANT CW5 .... 21 J7
College of Law Christleton Hall
CHSE CH3 .... 170 D4
Comberbach CP School
NWCHE CW9 .... 103 J4
Commercial Business Centre
RAIN/WH L35 .... 33 J1
The Commons Surgery
SBCH CW11 .... 204 B6
Community Care for Health
WDN WA8 .... 7 H6
Concord Business Park
WYTH/NTH M22 .... 63 J3
Concord Business Park
WYTH/NTH M22 .... 63 L3
Congleton Borough Council
ALS/KID ST7 .... 224 D8
Congleton Borough Council
CONG CW12 .... 207 L2
Congleton Business Centre
CONG CW12 .... 207 L1
Congleton Golf Club
CONG CW12 .... 208 B4
Congleton Leisure Centre
CONG CW12 .... 207 L1
Congleton Town Council
CONG CW12 .... 207 L2
Constance Industrial Estate
WDN WA8 .... 7 H9

Coppenhall County
High School
CW/HAS CW1 .... **221** L6
Coppenhall Leisure Centre
CW/HAS CW1 .... **19** J1
Cottage Crafts & Gallery
GOL/RIS/CU WA3 .... **29** G4
Council Offices
KNUT WA16 .... **107** G3
Council Offices
NWCHE CW9 .... **13** H2
Countess of Chester Hospital
CHNE CH2 .... **145** J6
County Galleries
ALT WA14 .... **42** D8
County Hall
CH/BCN CH1 .... **17** G7
County Primary School
FLINT CH6 .... **116** C6
County Secondary School
FLINT CH6 .... **116** A8
Courtyard Studio Gallery
MCFLDN SK10 .... **136** B3
Cranberry CP School
ALS/KID ST7 .... **241** G1
Cranford Lodge Hospital
KNUT WA16 .... **106** F3
Cransley School
NWCHE CW9 .... **103** L3
Crewe Alexandra
Football Club
CW/SHV CW2 .... **19** H8
Crewe Golf Club
CW/HAS CW1 .... **239** L1
Crewe & Nantwich
Borough Council
CW/HAS CW1 .... **19** G3
Crewe Road Surgery
ALS/KID ST7 .... **241** J1
Crewe Squash Club
CW/SHV CW2 .... **220** E8
Crewe Vagrants Cricket
& Hockey Club
NANT CW5 .... **237** L8
Croft Community
Primary School
GOL/RIS/CU WA3 .... **29** H4
Cromdale Way Community
Hall & Health Centre
WARRW/BUR WA5 .... **35** L6
Cronton C of E School
WDN WA8 .... **33** J6
Crossacres Junior
& Infant School
WYTH/NTH M22 .... **44** F8
Cross Clinic
LYMM WA13 .... **58** E1
Crown Courts
CH/BCN CH1 .... **16** F7
Crown Industrial Estate
ALT WA14 .... **42** E5
Crown Royal Industrial Park
STKP SK1 .... **3** J7
Crowton Christ Church
C of E Primary School
NWCHW CW8 .... **127** H3
Cuddington CP School
NWCHW CW8 .... **151** M2
Culcheth Clinic
GOL/RIS/CU WA3 .... **29** L1
Culcheth Community
Primary School
GOL/RIS/CU WA3 .... **25** G8
Culcheth Hall School
ALT WA14 .... **61** J1
Culcheth High School
GOL/RIS/CU WA3 .... **30** A1
Culcheth Sports Club
GOL/RIS/CU WA3 .... **29** M1
The Dale Primary School
MPL/ROM SK6 .... **48** D5
Dallam Community
Primary School
WARRW/BUR WA5 .... **36** F3
Danebridge Medical Centre
NWCHE CW9 .... **13** H3
Daneside Business Park
CONG CW12 .... **184** E8
Daneside Theatre
CONG CW12 .... **207** K1
Dane Valley County High
School
CONG CW12 .... **184** F7
Daresbury CP School
WARRS WA4 .... **75** H2
Darland County Secondary
School
WRX/GR/LL LL12 .... **210** C4
Darwin Street CP School
NWCHW CW8 .... **12** E4
Daven County Primary School
CONG CW12 .... **207** L2
Davenham C of E
Aided Primary School
NWCHW CW9 .... **153** M2
Davenham Cricket Club
NWCHW CW9 .... **153** M2
David Lewis Centre
WILM/AE SK9 .... **109** G6
Day Star Theatre
AUD/MAD/W CW3 .... **263** L7
Deacon Trading Estate
NEWLW WA12 .... **27** G2
Dean Lane Medical Centre
BRAM/HZG SK7 .... **66** D4
Dean Row County
Junior School
WILM/AE SK9 .... **84** E3
Dean Valley CP School
MCFLDN SK10 .... **112** E4
Dee Banks School
CHSE CH3 .... **170** A5
Dee Point CP School
CH/BCN CH1 .... **168** D1
Deermoss Gallery
WHITCH SY13 .... **270** A4
Deeside College
CQ CH5 .... **142** F3

Deeside Community Hospital
CQ CH5 .... **142** A8
Deeside Industrial Estate
CQ CH5 .... **143** G3
Delamere School
NWCHW CW8 .... **150** C6
Delamere Forest Golf Club
NWCHW CW8 .... **150** A6
Delamere Forest School
FROD/HEL WA6 .... **126** C8
Demmings Infant School
CHD/CHDH SK8 .... **45** M7
Derwen School
CHSW/BR CH4 .... **190** A5
Deva Business Park
CQ CH5 .... **143** G4
Deva Industrial Park
CQ CH5 .... **167** G1
Dial Park Primary School
OFTN SK2 .... **47** K8
Didsbury C of E Primary
School
DID/WITH M20 .... **45** H1
Didsbury Cricket Club
DID/WITH M20 .... **45** J3
Didsbury Road Primary School
HTNM SK4 .... **45** M2
Dingle County Primary School
CW/HAS CW1 .... **222** D6
Disley CP School
POY/DIS SK12 .... **68** D6
District C E Primary School
NEWLW WA12 .... **22** A8
Ditton C of E Primary School
WDN WA8 .... **52** A3
Ditton CP School
WDN WA8 .... **6** A3
Ditton Hall St Michaels
RC Primary School
WDN WA8 .... **52** C5
Ditton Medical Centre
WDN WA8 .... **6** A4
Dodleston C of E
County Primary School
CHSW/BR CH4 .... **191** H7
Dorin Park School
CHNE CH2 .... **145** K6
Dove Bank CP School
ALS/KID ST7 .... **243** G2
Drug Dependency Clinic
WDN WA8 .... **7** H7
Duddon St Peters
C of E Primary School
TPLY/KEL CW6 .... **173** H6
Dunham on Hill CP School
FROD/HEL WA6 .... **123** L6
Dunkirk Trading Estate
CH/BCN CH1 .... **120** D7
Duttons Business Centre
NWCHE CW9 .... **13** G4
Eagle Sports Club
WARRW/BUR WA5 .... **36** B8
Earnswood Medical Centre
CW/HAS CW1 .... **18** E3
Eaton Bank Industrial Estate
CONG CW12 .... **184** F8
Eaton CP School
TPLY/KEL CW6 .... **198** B1
Eaton Golf Club
CHSE CH3 .... **171** J7
Ebbe Fonte Galleria
WILM/AE SK9 .... **84** B5
Eccleston C of E
Aided Primary School
CHSW/BR CH4 .... **192** E2
Edgeley Medical Practice
EDGY/DAV SK3 .... **2** B8
Edleston Road County
Primary School
CW/SHV CW2 .... **18** F7
Egerton CP School
KNUT WA16 .... **106** F2
Ellesmere Port
Business Centre
EP CH65 .... **10** D8
Ellesmere Port Catholic
High School
EP CH65 .... **121** G1
Ellesmere Port Clinic
EP CH65 .... **95** H8
Ellesmere Port Hospital
EP CH65 .... **121** G2
Ellesmere Port Stadium
EP CH65 .... **121** L1
Elmridge Primary School
HALE/TIMP WA15 .... **62** C4
Elms Medical Centre
CHNE CH2 .... **17** K1
Elton County Primary School
CHNE CH2 .... **97** G8
Elworth C of E Primary School
SBCH CW11 .... **203** L5
Elworth Hall County
Primary School
SBCH CW11 .... **203** L5
Elworth Mount Pleasant
Cricket Club
SBCH CW11 .... **203** K4
English Martyrs RC
Primary School
BIDD ST8 .... **227** K5
English Touring Theatre
CW/HAS CW1 .... **19** G3
Ensor Trading Estate
NM/HAY SK22 .... **69** J6
Epic Leisure Centre
EP CH65 .... **95** J8
Eric Moore Health Centre
WARRN/WOL WA2 .... **4** F5
Etchells Primary School
CHD/CHDH SK8 .... **64** C3
Europa Business Park
EDGY/DAV SK3 .... **46** B6
Evelyn Street Community
Primary School
WARRW/BUR WA5 .... **4** A8
Everite Road Industrial Estate
WDN WA8 .... **52** B5

Excalibur CP School
ALS/KID ST7 .... **241** L2
Excalibur Industrial Estate
ALS/KID ST7 .... **241** L1
Express Industrial Estate
WDN WA8 .... **52** A5
Expressway Business Park
CQ CH5 .... **142** E7
Eyton Place Practice
FLINT CH6 .... **116** A6
Fairfield C of E School
WARR WA1 .... **5** K4
Fairfield County High School
WARR WA1 .... **53** J1
Fairfield County
Junior & Infant School
WDN WA8 .... **7** K1
Fairhill Industrial Estate
IRL M44 .... **31** M5
Fairway Primary School
OFTN SK2 .... **47** L5
Fairway Trading Estate
WDN WA8 .... **6** D8
Fallibroome High School
MCFLDN SK10 .... **137** L2
Farndon CP School
CHSE CH3 .... **228** E2
Farndon Health Centre
CHSE CH3 .... **228** E3
Farnworth C of E
Junior & Infant School
WDN WA8 .... **34** A8
Fearnhead Cross
Medical Centre
WARRN/WOL WA2 .... **37** M2
Fire Station
CH/BCN CH1 .... **17** G3
Firs School
CHNE CH2 .... **145** L7
Fleming Industrial Estate
WARR WA1 .... **5** J6
Flint Child Health Clinic
FLINT CH6 .... **116** B6
Flint Football Club
FLINT CH6 .... **116** B5
Flint Leisure Centre
FLINT CH6 .... **116** A5
Flintshire County Council
FLINT CH6 .... **116** A6
Flowcrete Business Park
SBCH CW11 .... **203** J3
Flower Gallery
WARRS WA4 .... **57** K1
Fordton Leisure Centre
WARRN/WOL WA2 .... **37** G1
Forest School
HALE/TIMP WA15 .... **42** F6
The Forge Shopping Centre
WARRS WA4 .... **56** C3
Forum Leisure Centre
WYTH/NTH M22 .... **63** J1
The Forum Shopping Centre
CH/BCN CH1 .... **16** F5
The Framing Studio & Gallery
EDGY/DAV SK3 .... **2** F6
Frodsham C of E
Primary School
FROD/HEL WA6 .... **99** J5
Frodsham County High School
FROD/HEL WA6 .... **99** H4
Frodsham Golf Club
FROD/HEL WA6 .... **99** H7
Frodsham Town Council
FROD/HEL WA6 .... **99** G4
Frodsham Weaver Vale
CP School
FROD/HEL WA6 .... **99** J2
Fulshaw C of E CP School
WILM/AE SK9 .... **83** M6
Furlong Medical Centre
BURS/TUN ST6 .... **243** K8
Furness Vale Industrial Estate
CHF/WBR SK23 .... **69** K8
Furness Vale Primary School
CHF/WBR SK23 .... **89** K1
Gainsborough County
Junior School
CW/SHV CW2 .... **18** C7
Gainsborough Galleries
MPL/ROM SK6 .... **48** C2
Gainsbourgh Galleries
MPL/ROM SK6 .... **48** F6
The Gallery Furnishings
OFTN SK2 .... **47** H7
The Gallery
ALT WA14 .... **61** K1
The Gallery
IRL M44 .... **31** L7
Garden City Industrial Estate
CQ CH5 .... **142** F4
Garden Lane Medical Centre
CH/BCN CH1 .... **16** E3
Garrick Theatre
EDGY/DAV SK3 .... **2** F6
Garven Place Clinic
WARR WA1 .... **4** E7
Gas Works Industrial Estate
ALS/KID ST7 .... **242** E2
Gateway Theatre
CH/BCN CH1 .... **16** E5
Gateworth Industrial Estate
WARRW/BUR WA5 .... **55** K1
Gatley Health Centre
CHD/CHDH SK8 .... **45** G6
Gatley Primary School
CHD/CHDH SK8 .... **45** G7
Gawsworth CP School
MCFLDS SK11 .... **161** M2
Geldart Gallery
MCFLDS SK11 .... **137** H4
Gemini Business Park
WARRW/BUR WA5 .... **36** F1
Gilded Hollins School
LEIGH WN7 .... **24** C3
Glazebury C of E
Primary School
GOL/RIS/CU WA3 .... **25** H5

Golborne All Saints RC School
GOL/RIS/CU WA3 .... **23** H4
Golborne Clinic
GOL/RIS/CU WA3 .... **23** H3
Golborne CP School
GOL/RIS/CU WA3 .... **23** G4
Golborne High School
GOL/RIS/CU WA3 .... **23** J3
Goldenhill Primary School
BURS/TUN ST6 .... **243** J5
Golden Triangle
Industrial Estate
WDN WA8 .... **52** C6
Goostrey Business Park
HOLMCH CW4 .... **156** F3
Goostrey County
Primary School
HOLMCH CW4 .... **157** M4
Gorse Covert Primary School
GOL/RIS/CU WA3 .... **30** B6
Gorsewood CP School
RUNC WA7 .... **74** E5
Gorsey Bank CP School
WILM/AE SK9 .... **83** M5
Gorsthills CP School
GTS/LS CH66 .... **120** C1
Goyt Valley Industrial Estate
CHF/WBR SK23 .... **69** K8
Goyt Valley Medical Practice
CHF/WBR SK23 .... **89** L4
Grandstands
CH/BCN CH1 .... **16** D6
Grange CP School
WSFD CW7 .... **177** H3
Grange Junior School
NWCHW CW8 .... **129** G6
Grange Road C of E
Primary School
ALT WA14 .... **61** J3
Grange School
NWCHW CW8 .... **129** H7
Grappenhall Clinic
WARRS WA4 .... **57** H2
Grappenhall Cricket Club
WARRS WA4 .... **57** G3
Grappenhall Hall School
WARRS WA4 .... **57** H3
Grappenhall Sports Club
WARRS WA4 .... **56** F3
Great Budworth C of E Primary
School
NWCHE CW9 .... **104** B4
Great Moor Clinic
OFTN SK2 .... **47** J7
Great Moor Primary School
OFTN SK2 .... **47** H8
Great Sankey Community
High School
WARRW/BUR WA5 .... **35** K4
Great Sankey Community
Primary School
WARRW/BUR WA5 .... **36** A7
Great Sutton Health Centre
GTS/LS CH66 .... **94** D8
Greenbank Residential School
NWCHW CW8 .... **12** D7
Greenbank School
CHD/CHDH SK8 .... **65** G3
Greenbank Surgery
NSTN CH64 .... **92** F4
Greencourts Business Park
WYTH/NTH M22 .... **64** A5
Greenfields CP School
WSFD CW7 .... **177** G3
Green Lane High School
HALE/TIMP WA15 .... **62** A1
Green Lane School
WARR WA1 .... **38** B4
Greenoaks Farm Industrial
Estate
WDN WA8 .... **7** M4
Gresty Brook Medical Centre
CW/SHV CW2 .... **238** C4
Grosvenor Medical Centre
CH/BCN CH1 .... **18** C2
Grosvenor Museum
CH/BCN CH1 .... **16** F7
Grosvenor Nuffield Hospital
CHSW/BR CH4 .... **169** J6
Grosvenor Shopping Centre
CH/BCN CH1 .... **17** G6
Grove House Practice
RUNC WA7 .... **9** H2
Guardian Medical Centre
WARRW/BUR WA5 .... **4** C5
Guardian Street Industrial
Estate
WARRW/BUR WA5 .... **4** D5
Guilden Sutton C of E CP School
CHSE CH3 .... **146** F7
Gwynedd CP Junior School
FLINT CH6 .... **116** A6
Hague Bar Primary School
NM/HAY SK22 .... **68** E4
Halebank C of E
Controlled Primary School
WDN WA8 .... **52** A8
Hale Barns Cricket Club
HALE/TIMP WA15 .... **62** E4
Halebarns Cricket Club
HALE/TIMP WA15 .... **62** D6
Hale C of E School
SPK/HALE L24 .... **71** L3
Hale Preparatory School
HALE/TIMP WA15 .... **61** L1
Hale Primary School
SPK/HALE L24 .... **71** K3
Halewood C of E
Primary School
HLWD L26 .... **51** G3
Halewood Community
Comprehensive School
HLWD L25 .... **50** D5
Halewood Health Centre
HLWD L26 .... **50** F5
Halewood Sports Centre
HLWD L26 .... **51** G5

Hallwood Health Centre
RUNC WA7 .... **73** M5
Hallwood Park CP School
RUNC WA7 .... **73** L6
Halton Borough Council
RUNC WA7 .... **73** M4
Halton Borough Council
WDN WA8 .... **6** E7
Halton Borough Council
WDN WA8 .... **7** J5
Halton Borough Council
WDN WA8 .... **7** G7
Halton Borough Council
WDN WA8 .... **52** B4
Halton College
WDN WA8 .... **7** H6
Halton College of Further
Education
WDN WA8 .... **7** G5
Halton General Hospital
NHS Trust
RUNC WA7 .... **73** M6
Halton Health Authority
WDN WA8 .... **53** K2
Halton Lodge County
Junior & Infant School
RUNC WA7 .... **9** M7
Halton Magistrates Court
RUNC WA7 .... **73** M4
Halton St Marys C of E
Primary School
RUNC WA7 .... **74** A4
Hammond School
CHNE CH2 .... **146** C5
Handbridge Medical Centre
CHSW/BR CH4 .... **17** G8
Handforth Health Centre
WILM/AE SK9 .... **84** D1
Handley Hill CP School
WSFD CW7 .... **177** J4
Happy Feet Health Centre
FLINT CH6 .... **116** A5
The Harlequin Theatre
NWCHE CW9 .... **13** G3
Harrytown RC High School
MPL/ROM SK6 .... **48** A2
Hartford Business Centre
NWCHW CW8 .... **128** F8
Hartford CP School
NWCHW CW8 .... **129** H8
Hartford High School
NWCHW CW8 .... **12** A7
Hartford Manor CP School
NWCHW CW8 .... **12** B8
Harthill CP School
CHSE CH3 .... **231** L1
Haslington CP School
CW/HAS CW1 .... **222** D8
Haslington Cricket Club
CW/HAS CW1 .... **222** D6
Haslington Surgery
CW/HAS CW1 .... **222** D8
Havannah County
Primary School
CONG CW12 .... **184** F6
Haveley Hey Junior
& Infant School
WYTH/NTH M22 .... **44** C8
Hawarden Castle
CQ CH5 .... **166** E5
Hawarden CP Infants School
CQ CH5 .... **166** D4
Hawarden Health Centre
CQ CH5 .... **166** D4
Hawarden High School
CQ CH5 .... **166** B3
Hawarden Industrial Park
CHSW/BR CH4 .... **167** H6
Hawthorne Business Park
WARRW/BUR WA5 .... **4** E1
Hazel Grove Clinic
BRAM/HZG SK7 .... **66** E1
Hazel Grove High School
BRAM/HZG SK7 .... **66** C3
Hazel Grove Primary
& Infant School
BRAM/HZG SK7 .... **66** E1
Heald Green Medical Centre
CHD/CHDH SK8 .... **64** B4
Health Authority
SPK/HALE L24 .... **70** E1
The Health Centre Surgery
HLWD L26 .... **50** F5
The Health Centre
ALT WA14 .... **42** D7
The Health Centre
CW/HAS CW1 .... **18** E4
The Health Centre
NANT CW5 .... **20** E5
The Heath County
Comprehensive School
RUNC WA7 .... **9** K9
Heathfield County High School
CONG CW12 .... **206** E1
Heath Lane Medical Centre
CHSE CH3 .... **170** A3
Heath Road Medical Centre
RUNC WA7 .... **9** J6
Heaton Moor Rugby
Union Football Club
HTNM SK4 .... **46** B1
Heaton Norris Health Centre
HTNM SK4 .... **2** D2
Hebden Green Special School
WSFD CW7 .... **177** K4
Helsby County High School
FROD/HEL WA6 .... **98** E7
Helsby Health Centre
FROD/HEL WA6 .... **124** B1
Hempshaw Business Centre
STKP SK1 .... **3** M9
Henbury High School
MCFLDN SK10 .... **137** L4
Heritage Centre
CH/BCN CH1 .... **17** G6
The Heritage Gallery
NANT CW5 .... **20** E6

Hermitage County
Primary School
HOLMCH CW4 .... 181 K1
Heyes Lane Junior
& Infant School
HALE/TIMP WA15 .... 43 H4
Higher Side Community
Comprehensive School
RAIN/WH L35 .... 33 G1
Highfield County Junior
& Infant School
CH/BCN CH1 .... 144 F8
Highfield County
Primary School
NANT CW5 .... 21 H3
Highfield School
HLWD L26 .... 51 G5
High Lane Medical Centre
MPL/ROM SK6 .... 67 L5
High Lane Primary School
MPL/ROM SK6 .... 67 L4
High Legh CP School
KNUT WA16 .... 59 J7
High Street CP School
WSFD CW7 .... 177 K3
High Street Surgery
ALS/KID ST7 .... 242 D6
Hillcrest Grammar School
EDGY/DAV SK3 .... 46 F6
Hillgate Business Centre
STKP SK1 .... 3 H8
Hillside CP School
FROD/HEL WA6 .... 98 D8
Hill Top CP School
ALS/KID ST7 .... 242 D5
Hill Valley Golf Club
WHITCH SY13 .... 270 A2
Hill View CP School
RUNC WA7 .... 73 L8
Hinderton School
EP CH65 .... 121 G1
Historic House
MCFLDS SK11 .... 161 L4
HM Remand Centre
GOL/RIS/CU WA3 .... 29 L4
Holcroft Clinic
GOL/RIS/CU WA3 .... 29 L1
Hollinhey CP School
MCFLDS SK11 .... 162 H1
Holly House Estate
MWCH CW10 .... 156 C5
Hollywall CP School
BURS/TUN ST6 .... 243 J6
Holmes Chapel County
Comprehensive School
HOLMCH CW4 .... 181 G2
Holmes Chapel
County Primary School
HOLMCH CW4 .... 181 H1
Holmes Chapel Health Centre
HOLMCH CW4 .... 181 J1
Holt CP School
WRXS/E LL13 .... 228 D4
Holy Family Primary School
WLTN L25 .... 50 D3
Holy Family RC
Primary School
WDN WA8 .... 33 K6
Holy Spirit School
RUNC WA7 .... 73 L4
Hong Sing Chinese
Medical Centre
BRAM/HZG SK7 .... 66 D1
Hood Manor Community
Primary School
WARRN/BUR WA5 .... 36 C6
Hood Manor Medical Centre
WARRN/BUR WA5 .... 36 C7
Hoole All Saints C of E
County Infant School
CHNE CH2 .... 170 A1
Horns Mill CP School
FROD/HEL WA6 .... 124 A3
Hospital Contributory Scheme
CW/SHV CW2 .... 18 F6
Howley Quay Industrial Estate
WARR WA1 .... 5 L7
Hulme Hall School
CHD/CHDH SK8 .... 65 G3
Hungerford County
Primary School
CW/HAS CW1 .... 19 L3
Hungerford Medical Centre
CW/HAS CW1 .... 19 K3
Huntington CP School
CHSE CH3 .... 170 A7
Hunts Cross CP School
WLTN L25 .... 50 C6
Hunts Cross Group Practice
WLTN L25 .... 50 B5
Hurdsfield CP School
MCFLDN SK10 .... 15 H4
Hurdsfield Industrial Estate
MCFLDN SK10 .... 138 F2
Hurdsfield Junior School
MCFLDN SK10 .... 15 L1
Hursthead Infant
& Primary School
CHD/CHDH SK8 .... 65 J6
Huxley C of E CP School
CHSE CH3 .... 196 A5
The Instructor College
STKP SK1 .... 3 G6
Interchange Motorway
Industrial Estate
HUY L36 .... 32 A3
Irlam & Cadishead
Community High School
IRL M44 .... 31 H4
Irlam County Primary School
IRL M44 .... 31 H4
Irlam Industrial Estate
IRL M44 .... 31 L5
Ivy Bank CP School
MCFLDS SK11 .... 138 L4
Ivy Bank Trading Estate
KNUT WA16 .... 82 A8

Ivy Farm Court Doctors
Surgery
SPK/HALE L24 .... 71 K3
Jacksons Lane Recreation
Centre
BRAM/HZG SK7 .... 66 A3
James Brindley High School
BURS/TUN ST6 .... 243 M6
Jeff Joseph Sale
Moor Technology College
SALE M33 .... 43 K2
J H Godwin CP School
CH/BCN CH1 .... 144 D8
John Arnold Galleries
BIDD ST8 .... 227 J4
John Street CP School
EP CH65 .... 10 E5
John Street Medical Centre
GOL/RIS/CU WA3 .... 23 G4
John Summers High School
CQ CH5 .... 142 C7
Kelsall CP School
TPLY/KEL CW6 .... 149 J8
Kelsall Medical Centre
TPLY/KEL CW6 .... 149 K7
Kelsborrow Castle
TPLY/KEL CW6 .... 149 L8
Kenmore Medical Centre
WILM/AE SK9 .... 84 A6
Kerfoot Business Park
WARRN/WOL WA2 .... 4 F1
Kidsgrove Medical Centre
ALS/KID ST7 .... 243 J2
Kidsgrove Sports Centre
ALS/KID ST7 .... 242 F3
Kiltearn Medical Centre
NANT CW5 .... 20 E6
King School
MCFLDN SK10 .... 15 K4
Kingsfield Co First
& Secondary Schoo;
BIDD ST8 .... 227 K4
Kings Grove County
High School
CW/SHV CW2 .... 18 B7
Kingsley CP School
FROD/HEL WA6 .... 125 M2
Kings School
CHSW/BR CH4 .... 169 H8
Kings School
MCFLDN SK10 .... 14 F4
Kingsway County High School
CHNE CH2 .... 145 M7
Kingsway School
CHD/CHDH SK8 .... 45 J8
Kingsway Secondary School
CHD/CHDH SK8 .... 45 J7
Kinsey Gallery
NANT CW5 .... 253 G8
The Knoll Surgery Partnership
FROD/HEL WA6 .... 99 H3
Knowles Industrial Estate
CHF/WBR SK23 .... 89 J1
Knowsley Metropolitan
Borough Council
HLWD L26 .... 50 F5
Knutsford Civic Centre
KNUT WA16 .... 107 G3
Knutsford County
High School
KNUT WA16 .... 106 F3
Knutsford Crown Courts
KNUT WA16 .... 107 G3
Knutsford Cty High School
KNUT WA16 .... 106 E3
Knutsford Football Club
KNUT WA16 .... 106 F1
Knutsford Golf Club House
KNUT WA16 .... 107 G1
Knutsford Leisure Centre
KNUT WA16 .... 106 F3
Knutsford Sports Club
KNUT WA16 .... 106 F1
Knutsford Squash
Racquets Club
KNUT WA16 .... 107 H3
Knypersley First School
BIDD ST8 .... 227 H6
Knypersley Sports Club
BIDD ST8 .... 227 J7
Kus Industrial Estate
CQ CH5 .... 167 G6
Lacey Green CP School
WILM/AE SK9 .... 84 A3
Lache County Junior
& Infant School
CHSW/BR CH4 .... 169 G7
Lache Health Centre
CHSW/BR CH4 .... 169 G7
Lady Barn House School
CHD/CHDH SK8 .... 64 D1
Ladybridge CP School
CHD/CHDH SK8 .... 46 B7
Ladybrook Primary School
BRAM/HZG SK7 .... 65 M5
Lakeside Surgery
LYMM WA13 .... 58 D2
Lambs House School
CONG CW12 .... 184 F8
Lane End Primary School
CHD/CHDH SK8 .... 65 J2
Langley Road
Industrial Estate
WARRS WA4 .... 77 K2
Larkhill Junior & Infant School
EDGY/DAV SK3 .... 2 B7
Latchford Medical Centre
WARRS WA4 .... 56 E1
Laurel Bank Surgery
MALPAS SY14 .... 258 B2
Lawnhurst Trading Estate
CHD/CHDH SK8 .... 46 B7
Lawton House Surgery
CONG CW12 .... 207 K2
Leaf Lane Infant School
WSFD CW7 .... 178 A2
Leftwich County High School
NWCHE CW9 .... 130 A8

Leftwich CP School
NWCHE CW9 .... 130 A8
Leigh Cricket Club
LEIGH WN7 .... 24 F2
Leigh Rugby Union
Football Club
LEIGH WN7 .... 24 E3
Leighton Hospital
CW/HAS CW1 .... 220 E3
Leighton Park County
Primary School
CW/HAS CW1 .... 220 F4
Lime Tree Primary School
SALE M33 .... 43 L1
Lindow CP School
WILM/AE SK9 .... 109 K1
Linley Trading Estate
ALS/KID ST7 .... 242 C3
Lisburne School
OFTN SK2 .... 47 L6
Little Bollington C of E
Primary School
ALT WA14 .... 60 B2
Little Leigh CP School
NWCHW CW8 .... 102 F3
Little Moreton Hall
CONG CW12 .... 225 L2
Little Theatre
KNUT WA16 .... 106 F1
The Little Theatre
CH/BCN CH1 .... 17 G3
Liverpool Airport
SPK/HALE L24 .... 70 C2
Liverpool University
NSTN CH64 .... 92 D5
L & M Business Park
ALT WA14 .... 42 B6
Locking Stumps
Community Primary School
GOL/RIS/CU WA3 .... 29 J7
Lodgefields County
Primary School
CW/SHV CW2 .... 220 E8
The Lodge Victoria Infirmary
NWCHW CW8 .... 12 F2
Longbarn Community
Primary School
WARRN/WOL WA2 .... 38 B3
Longford Street Surgery
WARRN/WOL WA2 .... 5 G2
Long Lane Community
Primary School
WARRN/WOL WA2 .... 37 H3
Longton Medical Centre
RAIN/WH L35 .... 33 H1
Loreto Convent
Grammar School
ALT WA14 .... 42 C7
Lostock Gralam C of E
CP School
NWCHE CW9 .... 131 G2
Lostock Gralam Football Club
NWCHE CW9 .... 130 F2
Lostock Hall CP School
POY/DIS SK12 .... 86 B1
Lostock Social & Sports Club
NWCHE CW9 .... 130 E3
Loushers Lane Special School
WARRS WA4 .... 56 D2
Lower Park CP School
POY/DIS SK12 .... 66 C8
Lower Peover C of E
Primary School
KNUT WA16 .... 132 E3
Lowton High School
GOL/RIS/CU WA3 .... 24 B4
Lowton Junior & Infant School
GOL/RIS/CU WA3 .... 24 A5
Lowton St Marys C of E School
GOL/RIS/CU WA3 .... 24 B4
Lowton West Primary School
GOL/RIS/CU WA3 .... 23 J4
Ludworth Primary School
MPL/ROM SK6 .... 49 G4
Lum Head Primary School
CHD/CHDH SK8 .... 64 B1
Lunts Heath CP School
WDN WA8 .... 34 B7
Lyme Park
POY/DIS SK12 .... 88 B3
Lymm High School
LYMM WA13 .... 59 H1
Lymm Rugby Football Club
LYMM WA13 .... 58 E3
Lyon Industrial Estate
ALT WA14 .... 42 B5
Mablins Lane CP School
CW/HAS CW1 .... 221 H4
Macclesfield Borough Council
POY/DIS SK12 .... 66 B8
Macclesfield College
MCFLDS SK11 .... 14 D9
Macclesfield District
General Hospital
MCFLDN SK10 .... 14 C4
Macclesfield Golf Club
MCFLDS SK11 .... 15 L9
Macclesfield Leisure Centre
MCFLDN SK10 .... 137 L2
Macclesfield Silk Museum
MCFLDS SK11 .... 15 G6
Macclesfield Town
Football Club
MCFLDS SK11 .... 138 D8
Macclesfield West
Park Museum
MCFLDN SK10 .... 14 E3
Macdonald Road
Medical Centre
IRL M44 .... 31 L4
Mackenzie Industrial Estate
CHD/CHDH SK8 .... 46 B6
Mackets Primary School
WLTN L25 .... 50 C3
Macon Business Park
CW/HAS CW1 .... 19 J4
Madeley High School
AUD/MAD/W CW3 .... 267 L6

Mads Little Theatre
MCFLDS SK11 .... 15 H7
Magda House Medical Centre
OFTN SK2 .... 47 K8
Malbank County High School
NANT CW5 .... 20 B5
Manchester City Council
NTHM/RTH M23 .... 44 B6
Manchester City Council
NTHM/RTH M23 .... 44 B2
Manchester City Council
SALE M33 .... 42 C2
Manchester City Council
WYTH/NTH M22 .... 44 D7
Manchester Medical Centre
KNUT WA16 .... 106 F2
Manchester Metropolitan
University
ALS/KID ST7 .... 224 B8
Manchester Metropolitan
University
CW/HAS CW1 .... 19 M6
Manchester Metropolitan
University
DID/WITH M20 .... 44 F1
Manchester Metropolitan
University
DID/WITH M20 .... 45 H1
Manchester Port Health
Authority
RUNC WA7 .... 9 G1
Mancot Clinic
CQ CH5 .... 166 D2
Mancunian Community
Health NHS Trust
WYTH/NTH M22 .... 44 C4
Manley Village School
FROD/HEL WA6 .... 125 G6
Manor House CP School
FROD/HEL WA6 .... 99 J3
Manor Industrial Estate
WARRS WA4 .... 37 L8
Manor Park County
Primary School
KNUT WA16 .... 107 J2
Mansfield CP School
EP CH65 .... 120 F1
Manway Business Park
ALT WA14 .... 42 E5
The Maples Medical Centre
NTHM/RTH M23 .... 43 M8
Marcliffe Industrial Estate
BRAM/HZG SK7 .... 66 F3
The Margaret Thompson
Medical Centre
SPK/HALE L24 .... 51 G8
Market Hall
CH/BCN CH1 .... 16 F5
Market Hall
EP CH65 .... 10 E9
Marlborough CP School
MCFLDN SK10 .... 112 D8
Marlfield County
Primary School
CONG CW12 .... 207 J2
Marple Clinic
MPL/ROM SK6 .... 48 F6
The Marple Cottage Surgery
MPL/ROM SK6 .... 48 F7
Marple Gallery
MPL/ROM SK6 .... 48 F6
Marple Hall School
MPL/ROM SK6 .... 48 C5
Marsh Lane Trading Estate
KNUT WA16 .... 69 K5
Marton & District
C of E Primary School
MCFLDS SK11 .... 160 C2
Marton Meadows Golf Club
MCFLDS SK11 .... 160 C7
Maryhill CP School
ALS/KID ST7 .... 243 H1
Massey Hall Special School
WARRS WA4 .... 57 M2
Mcilvride Medical Practice
POY/DIS SK12 .... 66 D8
Meadow County
Junior School
GTS/LS CH66 .... 120 E2
Meadows Special School
BIDD ST8 .... 227 J5
Meadway Health Centre
SALE M33 .... 42 E2
Megabowl
CH/BCN CH1 .... 168 F1
Mellor CP School
MPL/ROM SK6 .... 49 L6
Mellor Primary School
MPL/ROM SK6 .... 49 L6
Mellor Sports Club
MPL/ROM SK6 .... 49 K6
Melodys Antiques Galleries
CH/BCN CH1 .... 17 J4
Menorah Synagogue
WYTH/NTH M22 .... 44 F1
Mere Golf & Country Club
KNUT WA16 .... 80 C4
Mersey Regional
Health Authority
RUNC WA7 .... 9 M1
Mersey Vale Primary School
HTNM SK4 .... 46 A3
Merton House School
CH/BCN CH1 .... 145 J8
Mickle Trafford
County Primary School
CHNE CH2 .... 146 A4
Mid Cheshire College
NWCHE CW9 .... 13 H6
Mid Cheshire College
NWCHW CW8 .... 12 B7
Mid Cheshire College
WSFD CW7 .... 177 K3
Mid Cheshire Hospital
CW/HAS CW1 .... 19 G4
Middlehurst Special School
ALS/KID ST7 .... 243 M5

Middlewich Athletic
& Supporters Club
MWCH CW10 .... 179 H2
Middlewich County
High School
MWCH CW10 .... 179 J4
Middlewich County
Junior & Infant School
MWCH CW10 .... 179 H3
Middlewich Cricket Club
MWCH CW10 .... 179 H2
Middlewich Leisure Centre
MWCH CW10 .... 179 J4
Middlewich Medical Centre
MWCH CW10 .... 179 J3
Middlewich Town Council
MWCH CW10 .... 179 J3
Military Museum
CH/BCN CH1 .... 16 F7
Millbank Business Centre
NWCHE CW9 .... 13 L2
Millbrook Business Centre
NTHM/RTH M23 .... 43 L6
Millbrook Industrial Estate
NTHM/RTH M23 .... 43 L6
Millfields CP School
NANT CW5 .... 20 B7
Mill Green Special School
NEWLW WA12 .... 27 L1
Mill Hill CP School
BURS/TUN ST6 .... 243 M8
Millingford Industrial Estate
GOL/RIS/CU WA3 .... 23 H4
Mill Lane Industrial Estate
EP CH65 .... 121 M1
Mill Street Medical Centre
CW/SHV CW2 .... 19 G7
Millwood CP School
SPK/HALE L24 .... 70 F2
Millwood Road
Doctors Surgery
SPK/HALE L24 .... 50 F8
Moat House School
HTNM SK4 .... 2 E1
Mobberley C of E
Primary School
KNUT WA16 .... 82 C7
Mollington Church of England
Controlled Primary School
CH/BCN CH1 .... 144 E2
Monks Coppenhall
County Primary School
CW/HAS CW1 .... 221 L5
Moody Street Medical Centre
CONG CW12 .... 207 K2
Moore CP School
WARRS WA4 .... 55 G7
Moore Rugby Union
Football Club
WARRS WA4 .... 55 H6
Moorfield CP School
WDN WA8 .... 53 K1
Moorfield Junior
& Infant School
BRAM/HZG SK7 .... 66 C3
Moor Lane Business Centre
WDN WA8 .... 7 G7
Mosque
BURS/TUN ST6 .... 243 K8
Mosscroft Primary School
HUY L36 .... 32 A1
Moss Hey Primary School
BRAM/HZG SK7 .... 65 J7
Moss Industrial Estate
LEIGH WN7 .... 24 B3
Moss Lane Business Centre
SBCH CW11 .... 203 K6
Moss Lane Surgery
AUD/MAD/W CW3 .... 267 K6
Mossley C of E Primary School
CONG CW12 .... 208 B4
Moss View Primary School
PART M31 .... 41 G1
Mostyn House School
NSTN CH64 .... 91 J4
Mottram St Andrew
Grant Maintained
Primary School
MCFLDN SK10 .... 111 H2
Moulton CP School
NWCHE CW9 .... 153 M4
Mow Cap Castle
ALS/KID ST7 .... 226 D5
Murdishaw Health Centre
RUNC WA7 .... 74 D5
Murdishaw West CP School
RUNC WA7 .... 74 D6
Museum & Art Gallery
WARR WA1 .... 4 F8
Nantwich & Border
Counties Yacht Club
NANT CW5 .... 236 B6
Nantwich Civic Hall
NANT CW5 .... 20 F6
Nantwich Cricket
& Rugby Union Football Club
NANT CW5 .... 21 H2
Nantwich Museum
NANT CW5 .... 20 E7
Nantwich Players Theatre
NANT CW5 .... 20 E7
Nantwich Town Football Club
NANT CW5 .... 21 H7
National Trading Estate
BRAM/HZG SK7 .... 66 C1
Navigation Primary School
ALT WA14 .... 42 D6
Neston County High School
NSTN CH64 .... 91 M3
Neston CP School
NSTN CH64 .... 91 L5
Neston Cricket Club
NSTN CH64 .... 91 J4
Neston Medical Centre
NSTN CH64 .... 91 L4
Neston Recreation Centre
NSTN CH64 .... 91 M3

Neston St Marys
C of E Primary School
NSTN CH64 .... 91 M3
Neston Surgery
NSTN CH64 .... 91 M5
Nether Alderley CP School
MCFLDN SK10 .... 110 B8
Nether Alderley CP School
MCFLDN SK10 .... 110 A6
Netherpool County
Infant School
GTS/LS CH66 .... 94 E5
Network Clinic
MCFLDN SK10 .... 112 F5
Nevill Road Junior
and Infant School
BRAM/HZG SK7 .... 65 L2
Newall Green High School
NTHM/RTH M23 .... 43 M8
Newall Green Primary School
NTHM/RTH M23 .... 44 B8
Newby Road Industrial Estate
BRAM/HZG SK7 .... 66 D2
Newchurch Community
Primary School
GOL/RIS/CU WA3 .... 29 L2
Newfields Industrial Estate
BURS/TUN ST6 .... 243 K7
New Hutte Junior School
HLWD L26 .... 50 E6
Newman RC High School
WARRS WA4 .... 37 M7
New Mills CP School
NM/HAY SK22 .... 69 H4
New Mills Football Club
NM/HAY SK22 .... 69 K4
New Mills School
& Sixth Form Centre
NM/HAY SK22 .... 69 J5
New Mills Swimming Pool
NM/HAY SK22 .... 69 J4
New Mills Town Council
NM/HAY SK22 .... 69 H5
News Gallery
NSTN CH64 .... 91 L5
Newton Bank
Preparatory School
NEWLW WA12 .... 22 E8
Newton Community Hospital
NEWLW WA12 .... 27 H3
Newton CP School
CHNE CH2 .... 145 L8
Newton Health Clinic
NEWLW WA12 .... 22 B8
Newton Le Willows CP School
NEWLW WA12 .... 27 J1
Newton-le-willows Sports Club
NEWLW WA12 .... 22 C8
Newtown CP School
NM/HAY SK22 .... 69 H6
New Wellington School
HALE/TIMP WA15 .... 42 F6
Norbury Hall Primary School
BRAM/HZG SK7 .... 66 E3
Norfolk House
Preparatory School
SBCH CW11 .... 204 B5
Norley C of E CP School
FROD/HEL WA6 .... 127 G7
Norris Bank Medical Centre
HTNM SK4 .... 2 A5
Norris Bank Primary School
HTNM SK4 .... 46 B1
North Cheshire
Health Authority
RUNC WA7 .... 9 L1
North Cheshire Jewish
Primary School
CHD/CHDH SK8 .... 64 B2
Northenden Primary School
WYTH/NTH M22 .... 44 D3
Northern Moor Clinic
NTHM/RTH M23 .... 43 M3
Northgate Area
CHNE CH2 .... 17 G3
Northgate Medical Centre
CH/BCN CH1 .... 16 F3
Northgate Village Surgery
CHNE CH2 .... 16 F2
Northwich Rowing Club
NWCHE CW9 .... 13 G6
Northwich Sailing Club
WSFD CW7 .... 178 A6
Northwich Victoria
Football Club
NWCHE CW9 .... 13 J3
Norton Priory County
High School
RUNC WA7 .... 74 B3
Norton Priory
Recreation Centre
RUNC WA7 .... 74 B2
Oakdene Primary School
RAIN/WH L35 .... 33 J2
Oakenclough CP School
WILM/AE SK9 .... 84 D3
Oakfield County Junior
& Infant School
WDN WA8 .... 52 A4
Oaklands County Infant School
WILM/AE SK9 .... 84 E3
Oaklands Golf & Country Club
TPLY/KEL CW6 .... 174 D8
Oaklands Special Day School
WSFD CW7 .... 177 G5
Oakwood Avenue Community
Primary & Infant School
WARR WA1 .... 5 M2
Oakwood Medical Centre
NWCHW CW8 .... 129 G2
Oakwood Primary School
PART M31 .... 40 D1
Odeon Theatre
CH/BCN CH1 .... 16 F4
Offerton Green Clinic
OFTN SK2 .... 47 M7
Offerton Health Centre
STKP SK1 .... 3 M8

Offerton High School
OFTN SK2 .... 47 L5
Offley County Junior
& Infant School
SBCH CW11 .... 204 B5
The Old Bank Surgery
TPLY/KEL CW6 .... 149 K7
Oldfield CP School
CHSE CH3 .... 170 C1
Old Foundry Estate
WDN WA8 .... 7 K7
Old Hall Clinic
CHD/CHDH SK8 .... 45 H6
Old Hall Community
Primary School
WARRW/BUR WA5 .... 36 D4
Old Hall Surgery
EP CH65 .... 10 D9
The Old Surgery
CW/HAS CW1 .... 19 K4
Oldwood Primary School
WYTH/NTH M22 .... 63 H2
Old Wyche Studio Gallery
NANT CW5 .... 20 C6
Oriel Bank High School
EDGY/DAV SK3 .... 46 F7
Orrishmere Primary School
CHD/CHDH SK8 .... 65 G1
Ortenbrook School
PART M31 .... 40 E2
The Osteopathic Health Centre
CH/BCN CH1 .... 16 C1
Our Lady of Lourdes
RC Primary School
PART M31 .... 40 D1
Our Lady of Perpetual
Succour Junior School
WDN WA8 .... 51 M4
Our Lady of Perpetual
Succour RC Infant School
WDN WA8 .... 52 B3
Our Ladys Catholic
Primary School
WARRS WA4 .... 56 E1
Our Ladys RC Infant School
EP CH65 .... 121 G1
Our Ladys RC Junior School
EP CH65 .... 121 G1
Our Ladys RC Primary School
EDGY/DAV SK3 .... 2 D8
Our Ladys RC Primary School
RUNC WA7 .... 74 A6
Outlet Village
EP CH65 .... 121 L2
Outwood Primary School
CHD/CHDH SK8 .... 64 C5
Overdale Primary School
MPL/ROM SK6 .... 47 M3
Over Hall CP School
WSFD CW7 .... 177 H5
Overleigh St Marys C of E
County Primary School
CHSW/BR CH4 .... 169 K5
Over St Johns C of E County
Primary School
WSFD CW7 .... 177 H3
Owl Halt Industrial Estate
CQ CH5 .... 143 H6
Oxhey First School
BIDD ST8 .... 227 L3
Packmoor CP School
ALS/KID ST7 .... 243 M3
Padgate Business Centre
WARR WA1 .... 38 B4
Padgate Business Centre
WARR WA1 .... 38 A4
Padgate C of E Primary School
WARRN/WOL WA2 .... 38 A3
Padgate Community
High School
WARRN/WOL WA2 .... 37 M2
Padgate Medical Centre
WARRN/WOL WA2 .... 38 A3
Palacefields County
Infant School
RUNC WA7 .... 74 A6
Palace Theatre
WARR WA1 .... 5 G7
Palatine Industrial Estate
WARRS WA4 .... 56 C1
Paradise Silk Mill Museum
MCFLDS SK11 .... 15 H7
Park County Middle School
BIDD ST8 .... 227 J6
The Park CP School
RUNC WA7 .... 74 A3
Parkdale Industrial Estate
WARR WA1 .... 5 K8
Parkgate CP School
NSTN CH64 .... 91 J3
Park Green Surgery
MCFLDS SK11 .... 15 H6
Parklands CP Infant School
GTS/LS CH66 .... 94 C6
Parklands High School
WYTH/NTH M22 .... 63 J1
Park Lane Special School
MCFLDS SK11 .... 14 D9
Park Lane Surgery
MCFLDS SK11 .... 14 F8
Parkl Lane Gallery
POY/DIS SK12 .... 86 F1
Park Medical Centre
CHNE CH2 .... 145 M8
Park Medical Practice
HALE/TIMP WA15 .... 43 G4
Park Road Community Primary
School
WARRW/BUR WA5 .... 35 L6
Parkroyal CP School
MCFLDS SK11 .... 14 E6
Park School
NTHM/RTH M23 .... 43 M4
Parkside Hospital
MCFLDN SK10 .... 137 K8
Parkway Business Centre
CQ CH5 .... 142 E2

Parr Flat Community
Infant School
STHEL WA9 .... 26 A1
Parrs Wood High School
DID/WITH M20 .... 45 K3
Partington CP School
PART M31 .... 40 F1
Partington Health Centre
PART M31 .... 40 F1
Partington Shopping Centre
PART M31 .... 40 F1
Partington Sports Centre
PART M31 .... 40 F2
Patterdale Lodge
Group Practice
NEWLW WA12 .... 22 D8
Patterdale Lodge
Medical Centre
NEWLW WA12 .... 27 G1
Peacefield Primary School
MPL/ROM SK6 .... 48 E7
Pear Mill Industrial Estate
MPL/ROM SK6 .... 47 J2
Pebble Brook CP School
CW/SHV CW2 .... 238 C3
Peckforton Castle
TPLY/KEL CW6 .... 215 L3
The Peel Centre
STKP SK1 .... 3 H4
Peel Hall Primary School
WYTH/NTH M22 .... 63 M1
Peelhouse Lane Surgery
WDN WA8 .... 7 L2
Peerglow Industrial Estate
ALT WA14 .... 42 E4
Penarlag CP School
CQ CH5 .... 166 A2
Penketh Business Park
WARRW/BUR WA5 .... 36 B8
Penketh Community
High School
WARRW/BUR WA5 .... 36 A7
Penketh Community
Primary School
WARRW/BUR WA5 .... 35 K8
Penketh Health Clinic
WARRW/BUR WA5 .... 35 L8
Penketh South Community
Primary School
WARRW/BUR WA5 .... 54 F1
Penketh Swimming Baths
WARRW/BUR WA5 .... 35 L7
Penkford Technology School
NEWLW WA12 .... 26 E2
Pentre Industrial Estate
CQ CH5 .... 142 F8
Peover Superior
Endowed Primary School
KNUT WA16 .... 134 B4
Pewithall CP School
RUNC WA7 .... 9 J8
Phil Hughes Practice
CHD/CHDH SK8 .... 65 G1
Phoenix Medical Centre
STKP SK1 .... 3 H7
Pikemere County
Primary School
ALS/KID ST7 .... 224 B7
Pine Surgery
WARRS WA4 .... 76 D2
Pinnacle Business Centre
HTNM SK4 .... 2 F2
Piper Hill School
NTHM/RTH M23 .... 44 B2
Pius Xii RC School
GTS/LS CH66 .... 94 D6
Plantation Primary School
HLWD L26 .... 50 F4
Police Hq
CH/BCN CH1 .... 16 F7
Pooltown CP School
EP CH65 .... 94 F7
Portal Golf & Country Club
TPLY/KEL CW6 .... 197 K1
Portrait Gallery
WDN WA8 .... 7 H1
PO Sorting Office
CH/BCN CH1 .... 17 H2
Pott Shrigley C of E
Primary School
MCFLDN SK10 .... 113 K1
Poundswick Primary School
WYTH/NTH M22 .... 63 J2
Power Wash Trading Estate
BIDD ST8 .... 227 J4
Pownall Green Primary School
BRAM/HZG SK7 .... 65 L5
Pownall Hall School
WILM/AE SK9 .... 83 M4
Poynton Clinic
POY/DIS SK12 .... 66 E8
Poynton County High School
POY/DIS SK12 .... 86 F1
Poynton Leisure Centre
POY/DIS SK12 .... 86 F2
Poynton Parish Council
POY/DIS SK12 .... 66 E8
Poynton Sports Club
POY/DIS SK12 .... 66 E8
Prestbury C of E
Primary School
MCFLDN SK10 .... 111 M5
Prestbury Golf Club
MCFLDN SK10 .... 111 M8
Prestbury Village
Lawn Tennis Club
MCFLDN SK10 .... 111 M5
Priestley Business Centre
WARRW/BUR WA5 .... 4 C6
Priestley College
WARRS WA4 .... 56 C1
Priestnall School
HTNM SK4 .... 45 M1
Priorslegh Medical Centre
POY/DIS SK12 .... 66 E8
Prospect Vale Primary School
CHD/CHDH SK8 .... 64 B3

Pryors Hayes Golf Club
CHSE CH3 .... 173 G3
Public Baths
WHITCH SY13 .... 270 B4
Puss Bank County
Junior & Infant School
MCFLDS SK10 .... 15 L5
Quay Business Centre
WARRN/WOL WA2 .... 37 G1
Queensferry Industrial Estate
CQ CH5 .... 142 E8
Queensgate Primary School
BRAM/HZG SK7 .... 65 L8
Queens Park County
High School
CHSW/BR CH4 .... 17 H8
Queens Preparatory School
CH/BCN CH1 .... 145 J8
Queens Road Primary School
CHD/CHDH SK8 .... 65 G1
The Queen's School
CH/BCN CH1 .... 16 E5
Queensway Business Centre
WDN WA8 .... 52 F7
Quinta CP School
CONG SK12 .... 207 G2
Rackhouse Primary School
NTHM/RTH M23 .... 44 A3
Rainhill Clinic
RAIN/WH L35 .... 33 J1
Rainhill High School
RAIN/WH L35 .... 33 K2
Rainhill Village Surgery
RAIN/WH L35 .... 33 J1
Rainow CP School
MCFLDN SK10 .... 113 K8
Ramillies Hall School
CHD/CHDH SK8 .... 65 J2
Ravenbank Community
Primary School
LYMM WA13 .... 58 F1
Readesmoor Group Practice
CONG CW12 .... 207 K2
Reaseheath College
NANT CW5 .... 236 D3
Record Business Park
WARRN/WOL WA2 .... 4 F1
Recreation Centre
CHD/CHDH SK8 .... 65 H5
Red Bank School
NEWLW WA12 .... 27 L3
The Reginald Mitchell
County Primary School
ALS/KID ST7 .... 242 D3
Register Office
CH/BCN CH1 .... 16 F5
Richmond House Surgery
WHITCH SY13 .... 270 B5
The Ridge College
MPL/ROM SK6 .... 48 E7
Ridge Danyers College
CHD/CHDH SK8 .... 64 F1
Ridge Danyers College
MPL/ROM SK6 .... 48 F7
The Ridings County
Infant School
CH/BCN CH1 .... 144 B3
Ringstones Industrial Estate
CHF/WBR SK23 .... 89 K2
Rivacre Valley CP School
GTS/LS CH66 .... 94 E5
Riverside Trading Estate
NWCHW CW8 .... 13 G4
R L Hughes County
Junior & Infant School
AIMK WN4 .... 22 A1
The Roaches School
BIDD ST8 .... 227 H6
Robson Street Clinic
WARR WA1 .... 5 L5
Rock Surgery
FROD/HEL WA6 .... 99 H3
Rode Heath CP School
ALS/KID ST7 .... 224 F5
Romiley CP School
MPL/ROM SK6 .... 48 D2
Romiley Health Centre
MPL/ROM SK6 .... 48 C2
Rose Bank Special School
NWCHW CW8 .... 103 G8
Rose Cottage Surgery
WARRW/BUR WA5 .... 35 L8
Roseheath Primary School
HLWD L26 .... 50 F5
Rose Hill Primary School
MPL/ROM SK6 .... 48 E6
Rossett Clinic
WRX/GR/LL LL12 .... 210 C4
Rossmore CP School
GTS/LS CH66 .... 94 C5
Rother Drive Business Park
EP CH65 .... 10 B3
Roundwood Upper School
WYTH/NTH M22 .... 44 C5
Rowing Club
CH/BCN CH1 .... 17 J6
Royal Oak Industrial Estate
STKP SK1 .... 3 H8
Royal Oak Primary School
NTHM/RTH M23 .... 44 A5
Rudheath County High School
NWCHE CW9 .... 130 D5
Rudheath CP School
NWCHE CW9 .... 130 D6
Rudheath Dental
Health Centre
NWCHE CW9 .... 130 E5
Rudheath Leisure Centre
NWCHE CW9 .... 130 D5
Rugby Union Football Club
FLINT CH6 .... 116 B5
Runcorn All Saints
C of E Primary School
RUNC WA7 .... 9 G1
Runcorn County Court
RUNC WA7 .... 73 M4
Runcorn Football Club
RUNC WA7 .... 9 K1

Runcorn Rowing Club
RUNC WA7 .... 73 K8
Ruskin County High School
CW/SHV CW2 .... 18 E7
Rycroft Park Sports Club
CHD/CHDH SK8 .... 64 F3
Ryles Park County High School
MCFLDS SK11 .... 14 E9
Ryleys Preparatory School
WILM/AE SK9 .... 109 M3
Sacred Heart RC
Primary School
NTHM/RTH M23 .... 43 L6
Sacred Heart RC
Primary School
WARRW/BUR WA5 .... 4 A7
Saighton C of E Primary
School
CHSE CH3 .... 193 L3
St Aelreds RC High School
NEWLW WA12 .... 22 D8
St Aidan RC Primary School
NTHM/RTH M23 .... 44 B3
St Aidans C of E Community
Primary School
STHEL WA9 .... 34 E1
St Albans Catholic
Primary School
WARRW/BUR WA5 .... 4 D4
St Albans RC Primary School
MCFLDN SK10 .... 137 L3
St Ambrose College
HALE/TIMP WA15 .... 62 B3
St Ambrose Primary School
SPK/HALE L24 .... 71 G1
St Ambrose RC Primary School
EDGY/DAV SK3 .... 46 D7
St Andrews Ce Primary School
WARRN/WOL WA2 .... 37 J1
St Andrews School
CHSW/BR CH4 .... 17 G9
St Annes Ear Nose
& Throat Hospital
ALT WA14 .... 61 J1
St Annes RC Aided
Primary School
NANT CW5 .... 251 L1
St Anns C of E Primary School
RAIN/WH L35 .... 33 J1
St Anns C of E Primary School
WARRN/WOL WA2 .... 5 H1
St Anthonys RC Junior School
WYTH/NTH M22 .... 63 K3
St Anthonys RC School
CHSW/BR CH4 .... 168 E6
St Augustines Catholic
Primary School
WARRS WA4 .... 37 L8
St Augustines RC
Primary School
RUNC WA7 .... 74 A2
St Barnabas C E Aided
Primary School
WARRW/BUR WA5 .... 4 C6
St Barnabas C of E
Primary School
MCFLDS SK11 .... 15 H9
St Bartholomews RC
Primary School
RAIN/WH L35 .... 33 J1
St Basils RC Primary School
RAIN/WH L35 .... 52 K2
St Bedes RC Junior
& Infant School
WDN WA8 .... 7 H2
St Bedes RC Primary School
NWCHW CW8 .... 128 F5
St Benedicts Catholic
Primary School
WARRN/WOL WA2 .... 5 L1
St Benedicts RC Primary School
CHD/CHDH SK8 .... 64 E8
St Benedicts RC Primary School
WILM/AE SK9 .... 84 E1
St Bertelines Primary School
RUNC WA7 .... 74 C4
St Brides Preparatory School
MCFLDN SK10 .... 14 E4
St Bridgets Catholic
Primary School
WARRN/WOL WA2 .... 37 M1
St Catherines
Preparatory School
MPL/ROM SK6 .... 49 H5
St Catherines RC
Primary School
GOL/RIS/CU WA3 .... 23 L5
St Chads C of E
Primary School
WSFD CW7 .... 177 L4
St Chads RC School
RUNC WA7 .... 73 K5
St Christophers Infant School
SPK/HALE L24 .... 50 D8
St Christophers Junior School
SPK/HALE L24 .... 50 D8
St Christophers RC
Primary School
MPL/ROM SK6 .... 48 A2
St Clements RC Primary School
RUNC WA7 .... 9 G6
St Davids High School
CHSW/BR CH4 .... 168 E4
St Davids Trading Estate
CHSW/BR CH4 .... 168 D5
St Edmund Arrowsmith
RC High School
AIMK WN4 .... 22 B2
St Edwards RC Primary School
MCFLDS SK11 .... 138 C7
St Edwards RC Primary School
RUNC WA7 .... 9 K1
St Elizabeth RC Primary School
WYTH/NTH M22 .... 63 L2
St Ethelwolds School
CQ CH5 .... 142 B8

St Gabriels C of E
Primary School
HUY L36 .... 32 A2
St Gabriels RC CP School
ALS/KID ST7 .... 241 J1
St Georges C of E
Infant School
OFTN SK2 .... 46 F6
St Georges C of E
Junior School
OFTN SK2 .... 46 F6
St Georges C of E School
NM/HAY SK22 .... 69 J4
St Gregorys Catholic
High School
WARRW/BUR WA5 .... 36 D7
St Gregorys RC Primary School
MCFLDN SK10 .... 112 F4
St Helens C of E Primary
School
GOL/RIS/CU WA3 .... 40 B1
St Helens College
NEWLW WA12 .... 22 B8
St Helens Metropolitan
Borough Council
NEWLW WA12 .... 27 G1
St Hilarys School
WILM/AE SK9 .... 110 A3
St Hughs RC School
HALE/TIMP WA15 .... 42 F5
St James C of E Junior School
CHNE CH2 .... 170 A1
St James C of E Primary School
AUD/MAD/W CW3 .... 264 A7
St James C of E Primary School
WARRS WA4 .... 5 H9
St James RC High School
CHD/CHDH SK8 .... 64 F5
St John Fisher Junior
& Infant School
WDN WA8 .... 53 K3
St Johns C of E Primary School
FROD/HEL WA6 .... 126 C2
St Johns C of E Primary School
HTNM SK4 .... 45 L2
St Johns C of E Primary School
MCFLDN SK10 .... 113 G5
St Johns C of E Primary School
SBCH CW11 .... 204 E6
St Johns Medical Centre
ALT WA14 .... 61 J1
St Johns Primary School
MCFLDS SK11 .... 14 A7
St Johns RC CP School
ALS/KID ST7 .... 242 F3
St Johns RC Primary School
WYTH/NTH M22 .... 44 D8
St John's Wood School
KNUT WA16 .... 107 K2
St John Vianney School
HTNM SK4 .... 46 B2
St Josephs Catholic
Primary School
WARRW/BUR WA5 .... 35 L7
St Josephs College
MALPAS SY14 .... 246 A8
St Josephs RC CP School
BURS/TUN ST6 .... 243 K5
St Josephs RC Primary School
STKP SK1 .... 3 G5
St Josephs RC Primary School
WSFD CW7 .... 177 H3
St Julies High School
WLTN L25 .... 50 B3
St Leos Primary School
RAIN/WH L35 .... 32 E2
St Lewis's Catholic
Primary School
GOL/RIS/CU WA3 .... 29 H3
St Lukes C of E School
GOL/RIS/CU WA3 .... 23 L5
St Lukes RC Primary School
FROD/HEL WA6 .... 99 J4
St Margarets Ce Junior School
WARRN/WOL WA2 .... 37 J3
St Margarets C of E
Controlled Infant School
WARRN/WOL WA2 .... 37 J2
St Margarets Ward RC
Primary School
SALE M33 .... 42 E7
St Margaret Ward RC
High School
BURS/TUN ST6 .... 243 M7
St Marks R C Primary School
HLWD L26 .... 51 G4
St Martins Clinic
CH/BCN CH1 .... 16 F1
St Martins RC Primary School
RUNC WA7 .... 74 E5
St Mary's Centre
CH/BCN CH1 .... 17 G7
St Mary's C of E Primary School
IRL M44 .... 31 J6
St Marys C of E Primary School
MCFLDS SK11 .... 186 D4
St Marys RC Infant School
NEWLW WA12 .... 22 B8
St Marys RC Junior School
NEWLW WA12 .... 27 L1
St Marys RC Primary School
CONG CW12 .... 207 K1
St Marys RC Primary School
CW/SHV CW2 .... 18 A8
St Marys RC Primary School
MPL/ROM SK6 .... 49 H5
St Marys RC Primary School
MWCH CW10 .... 179 J4
St Marys RC Primary School
NM/HAY SK22 .... 69 H4
St Marys RC School
HTNM SK4 .... 2 F3
St Marys School
FLINT CH6 .... 116 B7
St Matthews C of E
Primary School
WARRS WA4 .... 76 E2

St Monicas Catholic
Primary School
WARRS WA4 .... 56 D5
St Nichols RC Aided High School
NWCHW CW8 .... 12 D7
St Oswalds Catholic
Primary School
WARR WA1 .... 37 M4
St Oswalds Primary School
AIMK WN4 .... 22 A1
St Paul of the Cross Catholic
Primary School
WARRW/BUR WA5 .... 26 E6
St Pauls RC High School
NTHM/RTH M23 .... 44 B8
St Pauls RC Primary School
POY/DIS SK12 .... 86 E2
St Peter & St. Paul High School
WDN WA8 .... 6 F1
St Peters Catholic Primary
School
WARR WA1 .... 38 C5
St Peters C of E Primary School
NEWLW WA12 .... 22 B8
St Peters Primary School
NTHM/RTH M23 .... 63 H1
St Peters RC Primary School
BRAM/HZG SK7 .... 66 D3
St Peters School
WRX/GR/LL LL12 .... 210 C5
St Philips Church & Community
Primary School
WARRW/BUR WA5 .... 36 B3
St Philips RC Primary School
OFTN SK2 .... 47 K6
St Richard Gwyn High School
FLINT CH6 .... 116 B7
St Saviours C of E
Primary School
ALS/KID ST7 .... 242 C3
St Saviours RC Aided School
GTS/LS CH66 .... 120 E1
St Simons RC Primary School
BRAM/HZG SK7 .... 66 E1
St Stephens C of E
Primary School
BRAM/HZG SK7 .... 47 M8
St Stephen's Primary School
WARRN/WOL WA2 .... 37 H1
St Teresas RC School
IRL M44 .... 31 L4
St Theresa Primary School
CH/BCN CH1 .... 144 F7
St Theresas RC Primary School
STHEL WA9 .... 34 C1
St Thomas Becket RC
High School
HUY L36 .... 32 A1
St Thomas Ce Primary School
WARRS WA4 .... 56 D3
St Thomas C of E Junior
& Infant School
GOL/RIS/CU WA3 .... 23 G3
St Thomas C of E
Primary School
STKP SK1 .... 3 H7
St Thomas C of E School
AIMK WN4 .... 22 C1
St Thomas Hospital
EDGY/DAV SK3 .... 2 F9
St Thomas More RC High School
CW/SHV CW2 .... 18 B8
St Thomas of Canterbury
C of E Junior School
CH/BCN CH1 .... 16 E2
St Thomas's C of E
Primary School
ALS/KID ST7 .... 243 G4
St Vincent RC Infant School
HALE/TIMP WA15 .... 42 E7
St Vincents Catholic
Primary School
WARRW/BUR WA5 .... 54 E1
St Vincents RC Primary School
KNUT WA16 .... 107 J2
St Weburgh C of E
Primary School
WARRS WA4 .... 56 B2
St Werburgh & St. Columba RC
Primary School
CHNE CH2 .... 17 M2
St Wilfreds C of E
Primary School
WARRS WA4 .... 57 H3
St Wilfreds RC Primary School
NWCHW CW8 .... 12 D8
St Wilfrids C of E
Primary School
WYTH/NTH M22 .... 44 E4
St Winefrides R C
Aided Primary School
NSTN CH64 .... 91 M5
St Winifreds RC Primary School
HTNM SK4 .... 46 A2
Sale Football Club
SALE M33 .... 43 H1
Sale Grammar School
SALE M33 .... 43 J1
Salford City Council
IRL M44 .... 31 K7
Salford City Council
IRL M44 .... 31 M4
Saltney Clinic
CHSW/BR CH4 .... 168 C6
Sandbach County High
School for Girls
SBCH CW11 .... 203 M5
Sandbach CP School
SBCH CW11 .... 204 A6
Sandbach Cricket Club
SBCH CW11 .... 204 B5
Sandbach R U F C
SBCH CW11 .... 204 B4
Sandbach School Foundation
SBCH CW11 .... 204 A6
Sandbach Town Hall
SBCH CW11 .... 204 B6

Sandilands Primary School
NTHM/RTH M23 .... 43 J4
Sandiway CP School
NWCHW CW8 .... 152 A1
Sandiway Golf Club
NWCHW CW8 .... 152 D2
Sandiway Surgery
NWCHW CW8 .... 152 A2
Sandycroft County
Primary School
CQ CH5 .... 166 E1
Sankey Bridge
Industrial Estate
WARRW/BUR WA5 .... 36 C8
Sankey Medical Centre
WARRW/BUR WA5 .... 35 L5
Sankey Valley Industrial Estate -
NEWLW WA12 .... 27 H2
Saughall Village Surgery
CH/BCN CH1 .... 143 M3
Scholar Green CP School
ALS/KID ST7 .... 225 L6
The Schoolhouse Surgery
POY/DIS SK12 .... 68 C6
School Lane Farm
MPL/ROM SK6 .... 49 H1
Sealand Child Health Centre
CQ CH5 .... 142 F5
Sealand CP School
CQ CH5 .... 142 E6
Sett Valley Medical Centre
NM/HAY SK22 .... 69 J4
Shavington County
High School
CW/SHV CW2 .... 238 A7
Shavington CP School
CW/SHV CW2 .... 238 C7
Shavington Sports Centre
CW/SHV CW2 .... 238 A7
Shaw Heath Health Centre
EDGY/DAV SK3 .... 2 F9
Shay Lane Medical Centre
HALE/TIMP WA15 .... 62 C3
Shocklach Oviatt C of E
Primary School
MALPAS SY14 .... 244 D5
Shotton CP School
CQ CH5 .... 142 B6
Shotton Town Council Office
CQ CH5 .... 142 B6
Shrigley Hall Hotel Golf
& Country Club
MCFLDN SK10 .... 87 J8
Simms Cross County
Primary School
WDN WA8 .... 7 G5
Sir John Deanes College
NWCHE CW9 .... 13 H6
Sir John Offley C of E
Primary School
AUD/MAD/W CW3 .... 267 L7
Sir John Talbots School
WHITCH SY13 .... 270 B7
Sir Thomas Boteler
High School
WARRS WA4 .... 56 E1
Smallwood C of E
Primary School
SBCH CW11 .... 205 M7
Sound CP School
NANT CW5 .... 250 F7
South Cheshire College
CONG CW12 .... 207 K2
South Cheshire College
CW/SHV CW2 .... 18 C8
Southfields School
SALE M33 .... 42 F1
South Manchester High School
WYTH/NTH M22 .... 63 K1
South Manchester University
Hospitals NHS Trust
NTHM/RTH M23 .... 43 M8
Southmead Junior
& Infant School
RAIN/WH L35 .... 32 E2
Southmoor Business Park
NTHM/RTH M23 .... 43 L5
South Park Court
Business Centre
MCFLDS SK11 .... 15 G8
South Trafford College
ALT WA14 .... 42 D4
Speke Community
Comprehensive School
SPK/HALE L24 .... 70 D2
Speke Comprehensive School
SPK/HALE L24 .... 70 D1
Speke Family Health Clinic
SPK/HALE L24 .... 70 E1
Sports Centre
MPL/ROM SK6 .... 49 G5
Sports Stadium
BURS/TUN ST6 .... 243 L7
Springfield Special School
CW/HAS CW1 .... 239 G1
Springfield Surgery
BRAM/HZG SK7 .... 66 D1
Springhead CP School
ALS/KID ST7 .... 242 D6
Springwood Primary School
MPL/ROM SK6 .... 48 E1
Squirrel Hayes County
First School
BIDD ST8 .... 227 K5
Staffordshire County Council
AUD/MAD/W CW3 .... 267 L5
Staffordshire County Council
BURS/TUN ST6 .... 243 J5
Stag Industrial Estate
ALT WA14 .... 42 B6
Stamford Park Junior
& Infant School
HALE/TIMP WA15 .... 61 L1
Stanlaw Abbey CP School
EP CH65 .... 121 K2
Stanney Grange CP School
EP CH65 .... 121 J2

Stanney High School
EP CH65 .... 121 J2
Stanney Mill Industrial Estate
CHNE CH2 .... 121 M3
Stanney Mill Industrial Estate
CHNE CH2 .... 121 M1
Stapeley Broad Lane
C of E Primary School
NANT CW5 .... 252 A3
Statham Community
Primary School
LYMM WA13 .... 39 J8
Stella Maris School
HTNM SK4 .... 45 L2
Stepping Hill Hospital
OFTN SK2 .... 47 H8
Stepping Stones
Montessori School
MCFLDN SK10 .... 14 E4
Stewards Cottage Club House
MALPAS SY14 .... 247 M5
Stockport Acute Services
NHS Trust
OFTN SK2 .... 47 J8
Stockport College of Further
& Higher Education
EDGY/DAV SK3 .... 3 G8
Stockport County Court
STKP SK1 .... 2 F6
Stockport County Football Club
EDGY/DAV SK3 .... 46 D5
Stockport Cricket Club
EDGY/DAV SK3 .... 46 E6
Stockport Grammar School
OFTN SK2 .... 47 H7
Stockport Metropolitan
Borough Council
CHD/CHDH SK8 .... 65 G2
Stockport Metropolitan
Borough Council
EDGY/DAV SK3 .... 2 F7
Stockport Metropolitan
Borough Council
MPL/ROM SK6 .... 49 G6
Stockport Metropolitan
Borough Council
MPL/ROM SK6 .... 49 G2
Stockport Metropolitan
Borough Council
OFTN SK2 .... 47 K6
Stockport Road Medical
Practice
MPL/ROM SK6 .... 48 F6
Stockport Rugby Union
Football Club
BRAM/HZG SK7 .... 65 M3
Stockport School
OFTN SK2 .... 47 H7
Stockport Super Bowl
EDGY/DAV SK3 .... 2 F7
Stockport Trading Estate
HTNM SK4 .... 46 B4
Stockton Heath
Community Primary School
WARRS WA4 .... 56 C3
Stockton Heath Medical Centre
WARRS WA4 .... 56 C3
Stockton Wood JMI School
SPK/HALE L24 .... 70 C1
Styal Primary School
WILM/AE SK9 .... 63 L8
Summerbank Central
CP School
BURS/TUN ST6 .... 243 J8
Sutton County High School
GTS/LS CH66 .... 94 E7
Sutton Green CP School
GTS/LS CH66 .... 94 B7
Sutton Hall Golf Club
RUNC WA7 .... 100 A1
Sutton Manor Community
Primary School
STHEL WA9 .... 34 A2
Sutton Way County
Junior School
GTS/LS CH66 .... 94 E8
Swanlow Medical Centre
WSFD CW7 .... 177 J4
Sycamore Lane
Community Primary School
WARRW/BUR WA5 .... 36 B7
Syddal Park School
BRAM/HZG SK7 .... 65 K7
Tait Gallery
WHITCH SY13 .... 270 A4
Taliesin Junior School
CQ CH5 .... 142 A7
Talke Clinic
ALS/KID ST7 .... 242 D6
Tallarn Green School
MALPAS SY14 .... 256 E5
Tarporley Business Centre
TPLY/KEL CW6 .... 197 J3
Tarporley C of E
Primary School
TPLY/KEL CW6 .... 197 K3
Tarporley County High School
TPLY/KEL CW6 .... 197 K4
Tarporley War
Memorial Hospital
TPLY/KEL CW6 .... 197 J2
Tarvin CP School
CHSE CH3 .... 172 B3
Tarvin Road Medical Centre
CHSE CH3 .... 17 M5
Taxal Lodge School
CHF/WBR SK23 .... 89 K7
Tennis Club
WILM/AE SK9 .... 83 K8
Terra Nova Preparatory School
HOLMCH CW4 .... 158 D3
Thames Trading Centre
IRL M44 .... 31 M5
Thelwall Community
Infant School
WARRS WA4 .... 57 J1

Thelwall Community
Junior School
WARRS WA4 .... 57 K1
Thelwall New Road Surgery
WARRS WA4 .... 57 H1
Thomas Wedge School
CH/BCN CH1 .... 144 A3
Thornfield School
HTNM SK4 .... 45 M1
Thorn Grove Primary School
CHD/CHDH SK8 .... 65 G6
Thornsett CP School
NM/HAY SK22 .... 69 L1
Thursfield CP School
ALS/KID ST7 .... 243 K1
Tilston School
MALPAS SY14 .... 245 H1
Timperley Health Centre
HALE/TIMP WA15 .... 43 G5
Timperley Park Road
CP School
ALT WA14 .... 42 E4
Tone Up & Tan Health Centre
BRAM/HZG SK7 .... 66 D1
Torkington Primary School
BRAM/HZG SK7 .... 67 C3
Towers Business Park
DID/WITH M20 .... 45 H3
Town Hall & Mayors Parlour
FLINT CH6 .... 116 A5
Town House Practice
WDN WA8 .... 7 K3
Trafford Health Authority
HALE/TIMP WA15 .... 61 J3
Trafford Healthcare NHS Trust
SALE M33 .... 43 K1
Trafford Metropolitan Borough
Council
ALT WA14 .... 42 C8
Trafford Metropolitan Borough
Council
PART M31 .... 40 F1
Tregenna Health Centre
& Dental Surgery
WYTH/NTH M22 .... 63 L3
Tregenna Surgery
WYTH/NTH M22 .... 63 K4
Trevalyn Hospital
WRX/GR/LL LL12 .... 210 F4
Trident Industrial Estate
GOL/RIS/CU WA3 .... 29 L5
Tushingham Gallery
WHITCH SY13 .... 270 A1
Tushingham School
MALPAS SY14 .... 259 J3
Twiss Green Community
Primary School
GOL/RIS/CU WA3 .... 24 E8
Tyntesfield CP School
SALE M33 .... 42 E9
Tytherington County
High School
MCFLDN SK10 .... 138 D2
Tytherington Shopping Centre
MCFLDN SK10 .... 138 D1
Underwood Industrial Estate
CW/HAS CW1 .... 221 G6
The Unicorn Gallery
WILM/AE SK9 .... 84 B5
University College Chester
CH/BCN CH1 .... 16 E1
University of Liverpool
NSTN CH64 .... 92 B4
University of Liverpool
NSTN CH64 .... 92 D5
University of Manchester
MCFLDS SK11 .... 158 D2
Upton Acresfield CP School
CHNE CH2 .... 145 M4
Upton by Chester County
High School
CHNE CH2 .... 145 M4
Upton County Infants School
WDN WA8 .... 52 B1
Upton Medical Centre
WDN WA8 .... 52 B1
Upton Mill View CP School
CHNE CH2 .... 145 L6
Upton Priory County Junior
& Infant School
MCFLDN SK10 .... 137 M2
Upton St Marys C of E
Infant School
CHNE CH2 .... 145 L5
Upton Village Surgery
CHNE CH2 .... 145 K6
Upton Westlea CP School
CHNE CH2 .... 145 L6
Uri Jacobi Oriental
Carpet Gallery
CH/BCN CH1 .... 16 E1
Utkinton C of E Controlled
Primary School
TPLY/KEL CW6 .... 174 B4
Vale Football Club
CONG CW12 .... 207 K2
Vale Royal Abbey Golf Club
NWCHW CW8 .... 153 H4
Valley Brook Business Centre
CW/SHV CW2 .... 19 G3
Valley School
BRAM/HZG SK7 .... 65 J9
Verdin County High School
WSFD CW7 .... 177 J2
Vernon County Infant School
POY/DIS SK12 .... 86 E3
Vernon County Junior School
POY/DIS SK12 .... 86 E3
Vernon Industrial Estate
STKP SK1 .... 3 H1
Vernon Park Primary School
STKP SK1 .... 3 G1
Vicars Cross Golf Club
CHSE CH3 .... 171 G2
Victoria Community County
High School
CW/HAS CW1 .... 18 E1

Victoria Community
High School
CW/HAS CW1 .... 18 F3
Victoria County Infant School
CH/BCN CH1.......................... 16 E2
Victoria Gallery & Gifts
CW/HAS CW1 .... 18 F3
Victoria Road CP School
NWCHE CW9........................... 13 L2
Victoria Road CP School
RUNC WA7 .... 9 G4
Victoria Trading Estate
RAIN/WH L35 .... 33 J1
The Village Gallery
SBCH CW11 .... 223 G1
Village Medical Centre
WLTN L25 .... 50 A2
The Village Surgery
BRAM/HZG SK7 .... 65 L6
Vine Tree County Primary
School
CW/SHV CW2 .... 18 B8
Virgin Cinemas
CH/BCN CH1............................ 168 F1
Virgin Cinemas
EDGY/DAV SK3......................... 2 F7
Wade Deacon High School
WDN WA8............................... 7 G1
Wallerscote County
Primary School
NWCHW CW8 .... 128 E4
Walray Pictures Gallery
NSTN CH64 .... 91 J5
Walton Hall
WARRS WA4 .... 56 A6
Walton Park Leisure Centre
SALE M33 .... 43 G2
Warford Hall Hospital
MCFLDN SK10.......................... 109 J6
Warford Hall Hospital
WILM/AE SK9 .... 109 H6
Wargrave C of E Primary
School
NEWLW WA12 .... 27 J3
Wargrave House School
NEWLW WA12 .... 27 J3
War Memorial Hospital
CONG CW12 .... 207 M3
Warmingham C of E
Primary School
SBCH CW11 .... 202 E4
Warren Wood Primary School
OFTN SK2 .... 48 A6
Warrington Borough Council
GOL/RIS/CU WA3...................... 29 M1
Warrington Borough Council
WARR WA1 .... 4 F7
Warrington Borough Council
WARR WA1 .... 5 L5
Warrington Borough Council
WARR WA1 .... 38 B5
Warrington Borough Council
WARR WA1 .... 38 F5
Warrington Borough Council
WARRN/WOL WA2 .... 37 H2
Warrington Borough Council
WARRN/WOL WA2 .... 37 M2
Warrington Borough Council
WARRS WA4 .... 37 M8
Warrington Borough Council
WARRS WA4 .... 56 E5
Warrington Borough Council
WARRW/BUR WA5..................... 36 F2
Warrington Business Park
WARRN/WOL WA2 .... 37 J3
Warrington Central
Trading Estate
WARRN/WOL WA2 .... 4 E4

Warrington Community
Health Care NHS Trust
WARRN/WOL WA2 .... 27 M6
Warrington Hospital NHS Trust
WARRW/BUR WA5.................... 4 B5
Warrington New Town
Cricket Club
WARRW/BUR WA5.................... 36 D7
Warrington Rugby
League Football Club
WARRS WA4 .... 56 B1
Warrington Sports Club
WARRS WA4 .... 56 A5
Warrington Town A F C
WARRS WA4 .... 56 E2
Warwick County
Primary School
MCFLDS SK11.......................... 137 M6
Watergate School
WLTN L25 .... 50 B2
Waterloo Industrial Park
STKP SK1................................ 3 H6
Waters Green Clinic
MCFLDS SK11.......................... 15 H5
Waterside Hotel
& Galleon Leisure Centre
DID/WITH M20 .... 45 J4
Water Street School
MCFLDN SK10.......................... 113 H4
Waverton CP School
CHSE CH3 .... 171 G7
Weatherstone Business Centre
NSTN CH64 .... 92 C4
Weaver CP School
NANT CW5 .... 251 L2
The Weaver Gallery
NANT CW5 .... 20 F7
The Weaver Gallery
NWCHW CW8 .... 12 F3
Weaverham County
High School
NWCHW CW8 .... 128 C4
Weaverham Forest CP School
NWCHW CW8 .... 128 C3
Weaverham Special School
NWCHW CW8 .... 128 E4
Weaverham Surgery
NWCHW CW8 .... 128 D3
Weaver Park Industrial Estate
FROD/HEL WA6 .... 99 K2
Well Green Primary School
HALE/TIMP WA15 .... 62 B2
Werneth School
MPL/ROM SK6 .... 47 M2
West Bank County
rimary School
WDN WA8............................... 52 F8
West Bank Medical Centre
WDN WA8............................... 53 G7
Westbrook Medical Centre
WARRW/BUR WA5.................... 36 B3
West Cheshire College
CH/BCN CH1............................ 145 G7
West Cheshire College
EP CH65 .... 10 C8
Westcliffe Hospital
BURS/TUN ST6........................ 243 M5
Western Avenue
Medical Centre
CH/BCN CH1............................ 144 D8
Westfields County
Infant School
CW/SHV CW2 .... 237 K4
West Heath Shopping Centre
CONG CW12 .... 207 G1

Westlands County High School
CONG CW12 .... 207 G1
Westminster Industrial Park
EP CH65 .... 94 F6
Westminster Surgery
EP CH65 .... 10 E4
Weston County Primary School
CW/SHV CW2 .... 239 J7
Weston Point County
Primary School
RUNC WA7 .... 8 D8
Weston Primary School
RUNC WA7 .... 73 G6
Whaley Bridge Primary School
CHF/WBR SK23 .... 89 K5
Wharton C of E Controlled
Junior School
WSFD CW7 .... 177 M3
Wharton Health Centre
WSFD CW7 .... 177 M3
Wharton Retail Park
WSFD CW7 .... 177 M1
Whirley County Primary
School
MCFLDN SK10.......................... 137 J3
Whiston Health Centre
RAIN/WH L35 .... 32 D1
Whitby County High School
GTS/LS CH66 .... 121 G3
Whitby Heath County
Primary School
EP CH65 .... 121 H1
Whitchurch C of E
Junior School
WHITCH SY13 .... 270 B4
Whitchurch C of E
Infant School
WHITCH SY13 .... 270 B5
Whitchurch Hospital
WHITCH SY13 .... 270 A4
Whitegate C of E
Primary School
NWCHW CW8 .... 152 F5
White House School
WHITCH SY13 .... 270 B7
Whitley County Primary School
WARRS WA4 .... 76 D8
Widnes Community
Midwifery & Ante Natal
WDN WA8............................... 7 G1
Widnes Cricket Club
WDN WA8............................... 34 B8
Widnes Public Baths
WDN WA8............................... 7 H5
Widnes Rugby Football Club
WDN WA8............................... 6 F5
Widnes Sixth Form College
WDN WA8............................... 33 L7
Wigan & Leigh College
LEIGH WN7............................. 24 D1
Wigan Metropolitan
Borough Council
GOL/RIS/CU WA3...................... 23 H4
Wigan Metropolitan
Borough Council
GOL/RIS/CU WA3...................... 24 A4
Willaston C of E Primary School
NSTN CH64 .... 92 F4
Willaston CP School
NANT CW5 .... 237 J6
William Beaumont
Community High School
WARRN/WOL WA2 .... 37 H3

William Stockton CP School
EP CH65 .... 10 C7
The Willows Primary School
HALE/TIMP WA15 .... 42 F6
Willow Wood County
Infant & Junior School
WSFD CW7 .... 178 A2
Wilmslow Albion
Football Club
WILM/AE SK9 .... 84 A1
Wilmslow Golf Club
KNUT WA16 .... 109 H3
Wilmslow Grange
County Primary School
WILM/AE SK9 .... 64 C8
Wilmslow Health Centre
WILM/AE SK9 .... 84 A6
Wilmslow High School
WILM/AE SK9 .... 84 B6
Wilmslow Leisure Centre
WILM/AE SK9 .... 84 B6
Wilmslow Preparatory School
WILM/AE SK9 .... 84 B5
Wilmslow Road Medical Centre
WILM/AE SK9 .... 64 D8
Wilmslow Rugby Club
WILM/AE SK9 .... 83 M3
Wimboldsley CP School
MWCH CW10 .... 178 F8
Wincham CP School
NWCHE CW9........................... 104 F7
Wincle C of E Primary School
MCFLDS SK11.......................... 187 M3
Windmill Hill County
Primary School
RUNC WA7 .... 74 C2
Winnington Park CP School
NWCHW CW8 .... 12 C4
Winnington Park Rugby Club
NWCHW CW8 .... 12 A5
Winsford Darnall County
Primary School
WSFD CW7 .... 177 K6
Winsford Industrial Estate
WSFD CW7 .... 178 C2
Winsford Police Station
WSFD CW7 .... 177 L3
Winstanley Industrial Estate
WARRN/WOL WA2 .... 37 H3
Winwick C of E Primary School
WARRN/WOL WA2 .... 28 B6
Winwick Parish Leisure Centre
WARRN/WOL WA2 .... 28 B6
Wistaston Berkeley CP School
CW/SHV CW2 .... 238 B5
Wistaston County
Junior School
CW/SHV CW2 .... 237 L4
Witton Albion Football Club
NWCHE CW9........................... 130 D2
Witton Churchwalk C of E
Primary School
NWCHE CW9........................... 13 K3
Witton Street Surgery
NWCHE CW9........................... 13 K1
Woodcocks Weel C of E Primary
School
ALS/KID ST7 .... 226 C6
Woodend Industrial Estate
SPK/HALE L24 .... 50 D7
Woodfall County Junior
& Infant School
NSTN CH64 .... 92 A6

Woodfield County Junior
& Infant School
CHNE CH2............................... 146 A7
Woodford Aerodrome
MCFLDN SK10.......................... 86 B2
Woodford Cricket Club
BRAM/HZG SK7 .... 85 L1
Woodford Lodge County
High School
WSFD CW7 .... 177 G5
Woodford Preparatory School
BRAM/HZG SK7 .... 85 K2
Woodheys Primary School
SALE M33 .... 42 E2
Woodhouse Park
Primary School
WYTH/NTH M22....................... 63 K4
Woodlands County
Infant School
GTS/LS CH66 .... 120 F2
Woodlands County
Junior School
GTS/LS CH66 .... 120 F3
Woodlands Industrial Estate
NEWLW WA12 .... 22 C6
Wood Memorial CP School
CHSW/BR CH4 .... 168 E6
Woodside County
Primary School
RUNC WA7 .... 73 L5
Woodside School
WYTH/NTH M22....................... 44 F8
Woolston C of E
Primary School
WARR WA1 .... 38 C4
Woolston Community
High School
WARR WA1 .... 38 B4
Woolston Community
Primary School
WARR WA1 .... 38 C5
Woolston Surgery
WARR WA1 .... 38 D5
Woolton County Infant School
WLTN L25 .... 50 B1
Woolton House Medical Centre
WLTN L25 .... 50 A2
Woolton Surgery
WLTN L25 .... 50 A2
Woolton Swimming Pool
WLTN L25 .... 50 A2
Worleston C of E
Primary School
NANT CW5 .... 219 L6
Worth County Primary School
POY/DIS SK12.......................... 86 F1
Wrenbury County
Primary School
NANT CW5 .... 249 M8
Wybunbury Delves
C of E Primary School
NANT CW5 .... 253 H5
Wyche County Primary School
NANT CW5 .... 20 E5
Wythenshawe Hall
NTHM/RTH M23....................... 44 B4
York Road Group Practice
EP CH65 .... 10 E8
Yorston Lodge School
KNUT WA16 .... 106 F3

Page 7
H6 1 Major Cross St

Page 15
G7 1 Wardle St

Page 17
H4 1 Brookdale Pl, 2 Cement Pl

Page 22
A2 1 Ashwood Av, 2 Aspenwood, 3 Beechwood Av, 4 Elmwood Av, 5 Smallshaw Cl, 6 Woodfield Crs
B1 1 Albert St, 2 Armoury Bank, 3 Chapel Pl, 4 Council Av, 5 Foy St, 6 King George Cl, 7 Millingford Gv
B7 1 Wellesley Cl
C1 1 Captain's La, 2 Glaisdale Cl, 3 Harland Cr, 4 Kimberley Pl, 5 Mafeking Pl, 6 New Barn Av, 7 Watson Av, 8 Wellbrooke Cl, 9 Wyrevale Gv
C7 1 Maritime Cl, 2 Mullins Av, 3 Ripon Cl, 4 Wetherby Cl, 5 Wightman Av
1 Dean Meadow, 2 Dunlin Av, 3 Greenfields Cl, 4 Greenshank Cl, 5 Redshank Cl, 6 Sandpiper Cl, 7 Sunnybank Cl, 8 Water St
F2 1 Croft Av, 2 Hepworth Cl, 3 Prescott Av, 4 Slaidburn Crs, 5 Stewerton Cl, 6 Croft Av, 7 Hepworth Cl, 8 Prescott Av, 9 Slaidburn Crs, 10 Stewerton Cl, 11 Croft Av, 12 Hepworth Cl
F3 1 Dunham Av, 2 Edgeworth Rd
F4 1 Cliftonmill Mdw, 2 Highfield Av, 3 Springfield Av
F5 1 Ladybarn La
1 Waterworks Dr

Page 23
G3 1 Bank Pas, 2 Lilac Rd, 3 Prescott St
G5 1 Bridge St, 2 Dean Cl, 3 Maryfield Cl, 4 Pimblett St, 5 Wakefield St, 6 Wearhead Cl
J3 1 Apple Dell Av, 2 Bowland Av, 3 Chatburn Av, 4 Derwent Av, 5 Langdale Av, 6 Rimington Av, 7 Thirlmere Rd
1 Curlew Cl, 2 Grosvenor Av, 3 Lichfield Av, 4 Ridgewell Av, 5 St Luke's Av
L3 1 Fordland Cl, 2 Hague Bush Cl, 3 Haywood Cl, 4 Hollybush Sq, 5 Holtswell Cl, 6 Raydale Cl, 7 Whitecroft Av
L4 1 Avebury Cl, 2 Ballantyne Wy, 3 Brambling Wy, 4 Bunting Cl, 5 Landor Cl, 6 Lunehurst, 7 Redstart Cl, 8 Royston Cl, 9 Santon Dr, 10 Speedwell Cl, 11 Stonechat Cl, 12 Sudbrook Cl, 13 Turret Hall Dr, 14 Wild Arum Cl, 15 Windy Bank Av
L5 1 Burnfell, 2 Sovereign Cl, 3 Springmount, 4 Stretton Av, 5 Thornbury Av, 6 Thurlow
M4 1 Birch Tree Rd, 2 Blackburn Cl, 3 Chestnut Gv, 4 Hopwood Cl, 5 Horncastle Cl, 6 Middlewood, 7 Sandfield Cl, 8 The Sheilings, 9 Waddington Cl

Page 24
E3 1 Fearnham Cl, 2 Hazelton Cl, 3 Inglesham Cl, 4 Moreton Dr, 5 Wendlebury Cl, 6 Winchcombe Cl, 7 Woodstock Cl
F1 1 Acorn Cl, 2 The Drive, 3 Elm St, 4 Larkspur Ct, 5 Malvern Ter, 6 Newlands Cl, 7 The Pines, 8 Poplar St, 9 Sheldwich Cl
C6 1 Lindsworth Cl, 2 Rosemary Cl, 3 Wheat Cft
C7 1 Brentnall St, 2 Chippingdall Cl, 3 Fildes Cl, 4 Grosvenor Ct, 5 Rochester Cl, 6 Sheffield Cl, 7 Winstanley Cl, 8 Yates Cl
H1 1 Alma St, 2 Back Bridge St, 3 Chemical St, 4 Derby Cl, 5 Duke St, 6 Grafton St, 7 Hotel St, 8 Houghton Cl, 9 Junction La, 10 Oxford St, 11 Princes St

Page 27
G1 1 Alpine St, 2 Back Booth St, 3 Back Lawrence St, 4 Back Leigh St, 5 Booth St, 6 Lord St, 7 Sceptre Cl, 8 Stanley St

Page 29
J8 1 Aspull Cl, 2 Campion Cl, 3 Holmes Ct, 4 Redvales Ct, 5 Sovereign Ct, 6 Windle Ct
M1 1 Hampson Av, 2 Newsholme Cl, 3 Paythorne Cl, 4 Warrington Rd
M8 1 Fieldfare Cl, 2 Keyes Gdns, 3 Nightingale Cl, 4 Swallow Cl, 5 Wren Cl
C3 1 Cabot Cl, 2 Cartier Cl
C8 1 George Rd, 2 Malpas Wy
D2 1 Cresswell Cl, 2 Cresford Cl, 3 Pensarn Gdns, 4 Peterstone Cl, 5 Stanner Cl
D3 1 Drake Cl
D4 1 Frobisher Ct
D5 1 Bewsey Farm Cl
1 Shiggins Cl
D8 1 Bridgeman St, 2 Broadhurst Av, 3 Cannell St, 4 Gate Warth St, 5 Hepherst St, 6 Hesketh St North, 7 Hesketh St, 8 Princess St, 9 Roughley Av
E1 1 Fairbourne Cl, 2 Ruthin Cl
E2 1 Bala Cl, 2 Cartmel Cl, 3 Cranston Cl, 4 Lampeter Cl, 5 Lydstep Ct, 6 Monkswood Cl, 7 Rossett Cl, 8 Tintern Cl, 9 Wrexham Cl
E6 1 Brompton Gdns, 2 Danby Cl, 3 Farnside Cl, 4 Lewisham Gdns

Page 32
E1 1 Peel Cl, 2 Ramsey Cl
E2 1 Cheswood Cl, 2 Deepwood Gv, 3 Drake Cl, 4 Earlwood Gdns, 5 Linwood Gv, 6 Nelson Pl

Page 33
J1 1 Braithwaite St, 2 Brandreth Cl, 3 Exchange Pl, 4 Houghton St, 5 Oaklands, 6 Station St, 7 Victoria St

Page 34
A7 1 Glencourse Rd, 2 Kemberton Dr, 3 Marlborough Crs, 4 Wentworth Cl
B8 1 Amelia Cl, 2 Barrow's Rw, 3 Beaconsfield Gv, 4 Carmel Ct, 5 Dragon Yd, 6 Farnworth Cl, 7 Honeysuckle Cl, 8 Tern Cl, 9 Trentham Cl, 10 Windermere Cl
D1 1 Anne St, 2 Meadow Av, 3 Northfield Cl, 4 Oaks Cl

Page 35
K6 1 Albert Dr, 2 Clarence Av, 3 Kintore Dr, 4 Sanderson Cl, 5 Victoria Av
L5 1 Clovelly Av, 2 Coogee Av, 3 Greenway, 4 Hall Ter
M5 1 Garsdale Cl
M6 1 Cedar Rd, 2 Conway Cl, 3 Lilford Dr, 4 Palin Dr, 5 Southfields Av, 6 Woodside Rd

Page 36
A3 1 Dovecote Gn, 2 Matlock Cl
A4 1 Cheltenham Cl
A5 1 Wharfdale Cl
A6 1 Hale Gv, 2 Orrell Cl, 3 Roby Gv
A7 1 Morrison Cl, 2 Parsonage Wy
B4 1 Bicknell Cl, 2 Buchan Cl, 3 Firman Cl, 4 Hunt Cl, 5 Tilman Cl
B6 1 Audie Murphy Rd, 2 Grant Rd, 3 Macarthur Rd, 4 Manuel Perez Rd, 5 Sycamore La
B7 1 Charminster Cl, 2 Eisenhower Cl, 3 Hilton Av, 4 Lynham Av, 5 Sergeant York Loop
B8 1 Bispham Rd, 2 Cleveleys Rd, 3 Fairhaven Cl, 4 Freckleton St

Page 37
A7 1 Brendon Av, 2 Chiltern Av, 3 Chiltern Crs, 4 Crawley Av, 5 Harvard Ct, 6 Kentmere Pl, 7 Wansfell Pl
G2 1 Currans Rd
G6 1 Edgworth St, 2 Marson St, 3 Paul St
G7 1 Cliffe St, 2 Egypt St, 3 Garven Pl, 4 Henry St, 5 Suez St
G8 1 Winmarleigh St
H1 1 Grisedale Cl, 2 Harvey Ct, 3 Pentland Pl, 4 Swindale Cl
H2 1 Achilles Av, 2 Armour Av, 3 Brandwood Av, 4 Clough Av, 5 Dean Crs, 6 Poole Av, 7 Poole Crs
H4 1 Corbet St
H5 1 St Benedicts Cl
H6 1 Ashton St, 2 Chorley St, 3 Erwood St, 4 Hardy St, 5 Rodney St, 6 St Peter's Wy, 7 Silver St
H7 1 Bank St, 2 Bennett St, 3 Bewsey St, 4 Blackhurst St, 5 James St, 6 Naylor St, 7 Patten La, 8 Rylands St, 9 Town Hl, 10 Union St, 11 Westminster Pl

Page 38
A3 1 Church Dr, 2 Guildford Cl, 3 Mullion Cl, 4 West Vw
E6 1 Berwick Cl, 2 Mulberry Cl, 3 Shropshire Cl

Page 40
A8 1 Dyers Cl, 2 Heatley St, 3 St Peter's St, 4 Warburton St
H8 1 Barbauld St, 2 Bridge St, 3 Friars Ga, 4 Friars La, 5 School St, 6 Stanley St, 7 Wilson Patten St
J1 1 Ambleside Crs, 2 Cartmel Av, 3 Scafell Av, 4 Tweenbrow Av
J2 1 Byron Ct, 2 The Coppins, 3 Keswick Av, 4 Penrith Av, 5 Ruskin Av
J3 1 Cossack Av, 2 Kipling Av
J4 1 Richardson St
J5 1 Adam St, 2 Alamein Crs, 3 Arnhem Crs, 4 Garner St, 5 Synge St
J6 1 Chester St, 2 Hopwood St, 3 Morley St
J7 1 Cockhedge La, 2 Crossley St, 3 Dutton St, 4 High St, 5 Parr St, 6 Percival St
J8 1 Canterbury St, 2 Enville St, 3 Peartree Pl, 4 Sutton St, 5 York St
K1 1 Bittern Cl, 2 Ravensdale St
K2 1 Caldbeck Av, 2 Catterall Av, 3 Cherwell Cl, 4 Concorde St, 5 Greenwood Crs, 6 Halifax Cl, 7 Hughes Pl, 8 Sandalwood Cl, 9 Whittaker Av
K3 1 Ferguson Dr, 2 Osborne Av, 3 Powey Rd, 4 St Margaret's Av, 5 Sylvia Crs, 6 Vale Owen Rd, 7 Woodcote Cl
K4 1 Norbury Av
K5 1 Matthews St
L1 1 Dovedale Cl, 2 Durnock Cl, 3 Horseshoe Crs, 4 Langdale Cl, 5 Morven Cl, 6 Swift Cl
L2 1 Barrow Av, 2 Brantfield Ct, 3 Medway Cl, 4 Redesdale Cl, 5 Severn Cl, 6 Tyne Cl
L3 1 Andover Cl, 2 Biggin Ct, 3 Duxford Ct, 4 Finningley Ct, 5 Jurby Ct, 6 Northolt Cl, 7 Sealand Cl, 8 Woodvale Cl
L4 1 Bridlemere Cl, 2 Newcombe Av
L5 1 Beresford St, 2 Brookland St, 3 Padgate La, 4 Pinewood Av, 5 Rosewood Av, 6 Walter St
M1 1 Briers Cl, 2 Newton Av, 3 St Bridget's Cl
M2 1 Blenheim Cl, 2 Gayhurst Av, 3 Lancaster Cl, 4 St Mawgan Ct, 5 Vulcan Cl, 6 Wellington St
M3 1 Jurby Cl, 2 Pocklington Ct, 3 Unsworth Ct
M4 1 Bowdon Cl
M5 1 Hawthorne Cl
M6 1 Princess Av, 2 Stansfield St
M7 1 Moxon Av, 2 Pigot Pl
M8 1 Betjeman Cl, 2 Bolton Av, 3 Chaucer Pl, 4 St Augustine's Av, 5 Shelley Gv, 6 Starkey Gv

Page 42
E2 1 Brook Farm Cl, 2 Derbyshire Rd, 3 Devon Rd, 4 Northumberland Rd, 5 Sussex Rd, 6 Thistle Sq, 7 Westmorland Rd, 8 Wiltshire Rd, 9 Yorkshire Rd
A6 1 Alstone Dr, 2 Seamon's Dr
A7 1 Bradbury Av, 2 Leverett Cl, 3 Sycamore Av
B4 1 Avocet Dr, 2 Blackberry Cl, 3 Charlock Sq, 4 Chokeberry Cl, 5 Cranberry Cl, 6 Mallard Cn, 7 Mandarin Cn, 8 Plover Dr
B5 1 Strawberry Cl, 2 Tribune Av
B6 1 Ayshford Cl, 2 Burlescombe Cl, 3 Chudleigh Cl, 4 Crediton Cl, 5 Holcombe Cl, 6 Huntsham Cl, 7 Marwood Cl
B7 1 Chevithorne Cl, 2 Denbury Dr, 3 Holcot St
B8 1 Dunham Lawn, 2 Glenfield
C2 1 Beenham Cl
C3 1 Corn Hey Rd, 2 Ryefield Rd
C4 1 Shenton Park Av
C5 1 Lutener St
C6 1 Place Rd, 2 Spey Cl
D1 1 The Narrows
D2 1 Cambridge Cl, 2 Carnegie Cl, 3 Edinburgh Cl, 4 Kempton Av, 5 Kingston Cl, 6 Loughborough Cl, 7 Oxbridge Cl, 8 Radley Cl, 9 Sedburgh Cl, 10 Worcester Rd
D5 1 Chevron Pl, 2 Eastdale Pl, 3 Granford Cl
E1 1 Barrington Cl, 2 Newby Dr, 3 Somerset Rd
E3 1 Ridley Dr, 2 Rochester Cl, 3 Washway Rd
E4 1 Carlisle Dr, 2 Cholmondeley Av, 3 Malpas Dr, 4 Raglan Rd, 5 Wellington St
M3 1 Houldsworth Cl, 2 Newton Rd, 3 Ryder Av, 4 Tannery Wy
F1 1 Astbury Cl, 2 Brentwood Crs, 3 Chofford Cl, 4 Robert Salt Ct, 5 Selworth Cl, 6 Southway, 7 Thelwall Av
M7 1 Airedale Ct, 2 Thorsby Rd, 3 Woodlands La
M8 1 Massey Rd, 2 Thomas St
F1 1 Hesketh Rd, 2 Lyndhurst Av, 3 Moreton Av, 4 Sherbrook Av
F2 1 Beechfield, 2 Homelands Cl, 3 Shawbury Gv
F3 1 Frieston Rd
F5 1 Dalveen Dr, 2 Somerville Gdns
F6 1 Bexhill Av, 2 Forest Dr

Page 43
G1 1 Acrefield, 2 Brogden Gv, 3 Brooklands Station Ap, 4 Carnforth Dr, 5 Hampden Rd, 6 Hope Rd, 7 St Davids Cl, 8 Simons Cl
G3 1 Milton Dr
G4 1 Ennerdale Av, 2 Hodgson Dr, 3 St George's Av
G6 1 Colville Gv, 2 Farndon Dr
G7 1 Denver Dr, 2 Glen Rl, 3 Mottram Dr
H1 1 Birch Av, 2 Clifton Rd, 3 Glenthorn Gv, 4 Greystoke Av, 5 Hazel Av
H2 1 Bradgate Rd, 2 Westwood Dr
H3 1 Woodhouse La East
H4 1 The Old Orch
H5 1 Baker St, 2 Heyes Av, 3 Lindsgate Dr, 4 The Old Gdn, 5 Southfields Dr
H6 1 Downham Cha
H7 1 Cherry Tree Cl, 2 Lincoln Dr
H8 1 The Paddock
J1 1 Beaufort St, 2 Braddan Av, 3 Derby Ct, 4 Lurgan Av, 5 Moorland Av, 6 Somerton Av
J3 1 Brownwood Cl
J6 1 Conway Dr, 2 Hayfield Wk
J7 1 Ambleside Av, 2 Ryefield Cl
K1 1 Alexandra Rd, 2 Marsland Rd, 3 Moorfield Gv, 4 Moor Nook, 5 Parkside Rd
K2 1 North Pde, 2 Windermere Av, 3 Wynyard Cl
K4 1 Yattendon Av
K5 1 Appledore Cl, 2 Ravenna Av
K6 1 Bamford Gdns, 2 Bramhall Cl, 3 Brunstead Cl, 4 Gibsmere Cl, 5 Hatchmere Cl
K7 1 Derwent Av, 2 Hollinscroft Av, 3 Shap Av, 4 Troutbeck Rd
L1 1 Baguley La, 2 Blakemere Av
L2 1 Croft Rd, 2 Frodsham Rd, 3 Neston Av, 4 Tabley Rd
L3 1 Cutgate Cl, 2 Dominic Cl, 3 Gralam Cl, 4 Jasmine Cl, 5 Lavender Cl, 6 Occlestone Cl, 7 Poppy Cl, 8 Woodwise La
L4 1 Fern Bank Dr
L6 1 Flamstead Av, 2 Grimstead Cl
L7 1 Aspen Cl, 2 Hornbeam Cl
M1 1 Cornfield Cl, 2 Daresbury Cl, 3 Hart Av, 4 Lindow St, 5 New Hall Av, 6 Pasturefield Cl, 7 Richmond Cl, 8 St Anns St, 9 Sandbach Rd, 10 Sandford Rd, 11 Thresher Cl, 12 Windmill Rd
M2 1 Bebbington Cl, 2 Boundary Gv, 3 Drafford Cl, 4 Haselhurst Wk, 5 Landkey Cl, 6 Malsham Rd, 7 Rathmel Rd, 8 Vawdrey Dr
M7 1 Shepton Rd

Page 44
A1 1 Barleycorn Wy, 2 Farmers Cl, 3 Harvest Cl
A5 1 Boxhill Dr, 2 Nightingale Gdns, 3 Woodbridge Gv
A6 1 Chilmark Dr, 2 Connell Rd
A7 1 Whitehouse Dr
A8 1 Caithness Cl, 2 Luton Dr, 3 Millhouse Av, 4 Tamar Dr
B2 1 Cherington Cl, 2 Lindwall Cl, 3 Milburn Av, 4 Welshpool Cl
B5 1 Pentwyn Dr
B6 1 Bramcote Av, 2 Gatwick Av, 3 Hilditch Cl, 4 Nethercote Av
B7 1 Martinscroft Rd
C5 1 Kemble Av, 2 Verrill Av
C6 1 Brookfield Rd, 2 Royalthorn Dr
C7 1 Barncroft Gdns, 2 Broadoak Av, 3 Harbury Crs, 4 Old Rectory Gdns
D1 1 Brooklyn Rd, 2 Chapel St, 3 Danesbury Ri, 4 Depleach Rd, 5 Holmfield Cl, 6 Malvern Cl, 7 Oxford Wy, 8 Rena Cl, 9 Vaughan Rd, 10 Yealand Av
D2 1 Andrew St, 2 Green La, 3 Hilary Cl, 4 Longsight St
D3 1 Chester St, 2 Heaton La, 3 Hope St
D5 1 Brett St, 2 Consul St, 3 Copperbeech Cl, 4 Govan St, 5 Joseph Johnson Ms, 6 Queenhill Rd
E4 1 Bellcroft, 2 Dukefield St, 3 Marylon Dr
E6 1 Carrsfield Rd
E7 1 Chigwell Cl, 2 Kemmel Av, 3 Lemton Gdns, 4 Warsop Av, 5 Witham Av
E8 1 Ashgate Av, 2 Briardene Gdns, 3 Ebor Rd
F1 1 Brompton Rd, 2 Masefield Dr, 3 Ventnor Rd
F6 1 Mitchell Cl, 2 Rosewood Gdns
F7 1 Chaffinch Cl, 2 The Old Ctyd
F8 1 Ogden Gv
G4 1 Alfriston Dr, 2 Brenchley Cl, 3 Hillend Rd, 4 Mainwaring Ter, 5 Tours Av
H2 1 Clarendon Cr, 2 Grove La, 3 Knight St, 4 Rushton St
H3 1 Kingston Av
H4 1 Cranston Dr, 2 Malgam Dr, 3 Moresby Dr
H7 1 Brogden Dr, 2 Gawsworth Ms, 3 Poplar St
H8 1 Arnside Cl, 2 Fairway, 3 Rydal Cl
J1 1 Alford Cl, 2 Chiswick St, 3 Culbert Av, 4 Ventnor Rd
J2 1 Dalston Dr
J3 1 Gawsworth Av
J4 1 Denholm Cl, 2 Giemmere Rd, 3 Greenview Dr, 4 Greylands Rd, 5 Moor Park Rd, 6 Newlands Cl, 7 Winchester Dr
J6 1 Ingleton Cl, 2 Wensleydale Av, 3 Whitby Cl
J7 1 Riversdale Rd
K1 1 Beal Cl, 2 Broseley Av, 3 Elgin Av, 4 Lancing Av, 5 Scarisbrick Av
K5 1 Kilburn Rd, 2 Madras Rd
K6 1 Back Massie St, 2 Chandley St, 3 Church St, 4 Sycamore Wk
C7 1 Tarporley Cl
C8 1 Littlebrook Cl, 2 Wimborne Cl
L6 1 Holmes St, 2 Wrenbury Dr
L8 1 Tumblewood Dr
M1 1 Hepple Cl, 2 Trentham Av
M7 1 Park Pl, 2 Parrs Mount Ms, 3 Richmond Rd
D5 1 Brett St, 2 Consul St, 3 Copperbeech Cl, 4 Govan St, 5 Joseph Johnson Ms, 6 Queenhill Rd
E4 1 Bellcroft, 2 Dukefield St, 3 Marylon Dr
E6 1 Carrsfield Rd
E7 1 Chigwell Cl, 2 Kemmel Av, 3 Lemton Gdns, 4 Warsop Av, 5 Witham Av
E8 1 Ashgate Av, 2 Briardene Gdns, 3 Ebor Rd
F1 1 Brompton Rd, 2 Masefield Dr, 3 Ventnor Rd
F6 1 Mitchell Cl, 2 Rosewood Gdns
F7 1 Chaffinch Cl, 2 The Old Ctyd
F8 1 Ogden Gv
B2 1 Bramley Crs, 2 June Av, 3 March Av, 4 Marlcroft Av, 5 Meadow Bank
H3 1 Hamilton Crs, 2 Norton Gv
H4 1 Egremont Gv, 2 Laburnum Wy, 3 Merton Rd, 4 St Augustine's Rd, 5 Stockton Av, 6 Sycamore St, 7 Tranmere Rd
H8 1 Braystan Gdns, 2 Lyndene Gdns
J1 1 Malden Gv
C1 1 Albury Dr, 2 Antrim Cl, 3 Chapel St, 4 Riva Rd
C7 1 Brooklyn Rd, 2 Chapel St, 3 Danesbury Ri, 4 Depleach Rd, 5 Old Rectory Gdns
C8 1 Littlebrook Cl, 2 Wimborne Cl
D1 1 Bluebell Cl, 2 Brackenwood Gv, 3 Mornington Av
D2 1 Coppice Dr, 2 Haughton Dr, 3 Homewood Av, 4 Howard Rd
D4 1 Rangemore Av, 2 Robert Owen Gdns
E1 1 Elwyn Av
L6 1 Hollycroft Av, 2 Marford Cl
D7 1 Broadoak Rd, 2 Brookcroft Av, 3 Brownley Court Rd, 4 Shayfield Av
L2 1 Alcester Av, 2 Ashmore Av, 3 Lighthorne Av, 4 Lighthorne Gv, 5 Melrose Av
L6 1 Berwick Av, 2 Burlington Cl, 3 Croton St, 4 Greenbank Av, 5 Kentmore Cl, 6 St John's Rd, 7 Wells Dr
D8 1 Ashcott Av, 2 Broadley Av, 3 Delwood Gdns, 4 Fawley Gv, 5 Oakmere Cl
E7 1 Betleymere Rd, 2 Combermere Cl, 3 Mereside Cl, 4 Newberry Cl
E8 1 Adswood Old Hall Rd

Page 46
A1 1 Grosvenor Av, 2 Windsor Av
F1 1 Adamson Gdns, 2 Canterbury Pk, 3 Samlesbury Cl, 4 Twyford Cl
A3 1 Cedarwood Av, 2 Middlewood Dr, 3 Ravenswood Av
F6 1 Dane Av, 2 Meerbrook Rd, 3 Swythamley Rd
F7 1 Churchley Cl, 2 Hendon Dr, 3 Kingsland Rd
F8 1 Ogden Gv

Page 45
G1 1 Eversley Rd
G6 1 Carlton Dr, 2 Greenbank Rd, 3 Kenwood Av, 4 Thornton La
G7 1 Acres Rd, 2 Buxton St, 3 Greenbank Av, 4 Peckforton Cl, 5 Stonepail Rd
H1 1 Albert Hill St, 2 Belfield Rd, 3 Davenfield Gv, 4 King's Lynn Cl, 5 Norgate St, 6 Ogden St, 7 Warburton St
A5 1 Grosvenor Rd, 2 Windsor Av
A8 1 Calverly Rd, 2 The Cloisters, 3 Mottram Cl
B1 1 Albert Rd, 2 Evesham Cl, 3 Grosvenor Rd, 4 Moor Top Pl
1 Hereford Cl, 2 Malpas Cl, 3 Mossmere Rd
E8 1 St Ives Av, 2 St Margaret's Rd

(continued)
B2 1 Hamilton Crs, 2 Norton Gv
E4 1 Armoury St, 2 Blackshaw St, 3 Bowdon St, 4 Bulkeley St, 5 Castle St, 6 Hope Ter, 7 Lucy St, 8 Moseley St, 9 Newton St, 10 Nixon St, 11 Simpson St, 12 Spring Bank Pl
E5 1 Arnold St, 2 Booth St, 3 Gilmore St, 4 Harper St, 5 Holmes St, 6 Kinder St, 7 Victoria Cl, 8 Worrall St
B5 1 Lismore Av, 2 Plymouth Gv, 3 Wicklow Av, 4 Woodbury Rd
B6 1 Tewkesbury Rd, 2 Willdor Gv
B8 1 Eveside Cl, 2 Middlefields
C1 1 Colchester Pl, 2 Garston Cl
F1 1 Burley Ct, 2 Dene Ct, 3 Deneway Ms, 4 Elizabeth Ct, 5 The Green, 6 May Av, 7 Newby Rd, 8 Norris Hill Dr, 9 Winchester Dr
F2 1 Avenue St, 2 Back Water St, 3 Brewery St, 4 Corporation St, 5 Daniel's La, 6 Deanery Wy, 7 King St East, 8 Little Egerton St, 9 Millgate, 10 Park St, 11 Percy St, 12 Portwood Pl
F3 1 Banbury St, 2 Covent Gdn, 3 Etchells St, 4 Harvey St, 5 High Bank Side, 6 Holborn St, 7 Lavenders Brow, 8 Little Underbank, 9 London Pl, 10 London Sq, 11 Lord St, 12 Lower Carrs, 13 Lower Hillgate, 14 Lowe St, 15 Massey St, 16 Meadow Brow, 17 Middle Hillgate, 18 Norbury St, 19 North Harvey St, 20 North Pl, 21 Orchard St, 22 Pickford's Brow, 23 Royal Oak Yd, 24 St Peter's Sq, 25 Tatton St, 26 Watson Rd, 27 Wesley St
C5 1 Alexandra St, 2 Rainow Rd, 3 Stirling Cl, 4 Wimbledon Dr
D1 1 Aberdeen Gv, 2 Atherton St, 3 Elstree Gv, 4 Hartley St, 5 Heron St, 6 Roscoe St, 7 Stopford St
F5 1 Back Adcroft St, 2 Bannister St, 3 Blossoms St, 4 Brentnall St, 5 Brooks St, 6 Bullock St, 7 Charlesworth St, 8 Daisy St, 9 Harrison St, 10 Royle St, 11 Shaw Rd South, 12 Thomas St West, 13 Walton St, 14 Woodbine Crs
D6 1 Kelsall Rd, 2 Lynn Cl, 3 Marsh Cl, 4 Newcroft Dr, 5 Reservoir Rd
E1 1 Belmont Rd, 2 Church St, 3 Clement St, 4 Edmund Cl, 5 Hamilton Sq, 6 Hapton Pl, 7 Harwood Cl, 8 Hesketh St, 9 Ince St, 10 Orphanage St, 11 Short St East
E3 1 Canning St, 2 Florence St, 3 Greenhalgh St, 4 Hatton St, 5 Laurel St, 6 Mulberry Ms, 7 Nicholson St, 8 Railway St, 9 Roman Rd, 10 Tunstall St
E5 1 Astley St, 2 Brown St, 3 Chestergate, 4 Cook St, 5 Cotton Tree St, 6 Gas St, 7 Hooper St, 8 Lawrence St, 9 Leyland St, 10 Mersey Sq, 11 Port St, 12 St Petersgate, 13 St Peter's Sq, 14 Swaine St, 15 Warren St, 16 Woodman St

Page 47
G1 1 St Paul's St
G2 1 Bateson St, 2 Brady St, 3 Carlton Crs, 4 Emperor St, 5 Garfield St, 6 Marsland St, 7 Mountain St, 8 Peter St, 9 Queen St, 10 St Mary's Wy, 11 Stanley St
G3 1 Alpine Rd, 2 Athens St, 3 Eryngo St, 4 George St, 5 Glebe St, 6 Gorsey Brow, 7 Rectory Cn, 8 Rosemary La, 9 Stourport St, 10 Upper Brook St
G4 1 Dona St, 2 Layton Cl
G6 1 Buckingham St, 2 College St, 3 Colonial Rd, 4 Peter St, 5 Toronto Rd, 6 Windsor St
G7 1 Crescent Cl, 2 Crescent Wy
G8 1 Crossway
H1 1 Dawson St
H2 1 Offerton St, 2 Orme St, 3 Werneth St
H3 1 Chaucer Ms, 2 Crimshaw St, 3 Westland Av
H4 1 George St East, 2 Hampson St, 3 Knowsley Crs, 4 Maplecroft, 5 Stephen St
H5 1 Bampton Cl, 2 Dorking Cl, 3 Dorland Gv, 4 Guildford Cl, 5 Hastings Cl, 6 Old Croft Ms, 7 Prestwich Cl, 8 Thirlemere Rd, 9 Ullswater Rd, 10 William St
H6 1 Longwood Av
H8 1 Arundel Gv, 2 The Heathers
J1 1 Brimelow St
J2 1 Firwood Cl, 2 Hartland Cl, 3 Hillbrook Rd, 4 Holme Beech Gv, 5 Stratton Rd, 6 Woodbank Av
J5 1 Mayer St, 2 Offerton Fold, 3 Parndon Dr
J7 1 Archer St, 2 Castle Farm La, 3 Castlewood Gdns, 4 Eltham Av, 5 Frome Av, 6 Garden St, 7 Hollymount Av, 8 Meadow St
J8 1 Buxton Rd, 2 Cherry Tree Cl, 3 Winbolt St
K2 1 Davies Rd, 2 Lindow Ct
K4 1 Oak Tree Cl
K5 1 Chippenham Av, 2 Woodley Cl
K6 1 Amlwch Av, 2 Birkworth Ct, 3 Lindworth Ct, 4 Malham Ct, 5 Orchard Ct, 6 Stainmoor Ct, 7 Tragan Cl, 8 Worthing Cl
K8 1 Ashway Clough North, 2 Ashway Clough South, 3 Reedshaw Bank, 4 Rishworth Cl, 5 Wessenden Bank East
K9 1 Fence St, 2 Merrybent Cl, 3 Trawden Gn
L1 1 Bancroft Cl, 2 Dorfield Cl
L5 1 Burns Crs, 2 Mellor Ct
L6 1 Errington Cl, 2 Hardberry Pl, 3 Hawdraw Gn, 4 Orms Gill Pl, 5 Stansbury Pl, 6 Teesdale Cl
L7 1 Hexham Cl, 2 Paythorne Gn, 3 Wrights Bank South
L8 1 Werneth Cl
M1 1 Brookdale Cl, 2 Burnside Cl, 3 Clegg St, 4 Higher Bents La, 5 Meadow Bank, 6 Redwood Dr
M2 1 Woodfield Crs
M3 1 Kiln Cft, 2 Lawton Cl, 3 Riley Wood Cl
M6 1 Bean Leach Av, 2 Hurstwood Rd, 3 Kipling Cl, 4 Old Farm Dr
M7 1 Brookthorn Cl, 2 Poise Brook Dr

Page 48
A3 1 Clapgate, 2 Durham Cl, 3 George St, 4 Lancaster Cl, 5 Lichfield Wk, 6 Southwell Cl, 7 Spirewood Gdns, 8 Stourport Cl, 9 Warburton Cl, 10 Worcester Cl
C2 1 Chichester Rd, 2 Crossmoor Av, 3 John's Pl, 4 Leyburn Cv
D6 1 Oak Dr
D8 1 Shirley Av

F6
1 Belgrave Av 2 Church St 3 Culchetch Av 4 Ellesmere Av 5 Gloucester Av 6 Highfield Rd 7 Queen St 8 Springfield Av 9 Union Rd

F7
1 Chadwick St 2 Cotefield Cl 3 Trinity St 4 Waterside Av 5 Willow Cl

F8
1 Coyt Rd 2 Outram St 3 Sherwood Cl 4 Sunwell Ter

Page 50

A1 1 Woolton Park Cl
A2 1 Berrington Av 2 The Old Quarry 3 St Mary's Pl
A3 1 Cam St
B1 1 Dove Ct 2 Meadow Hey Cl
B2 1 Bishops Ct 2 Deacon Ct
B4 1 Denstone Cl 2 Roedean Cl
B6 1 Enstone Rd 2 Faringdon Cl
B8 1 Bognor Cl 2 Lenham Wy 3 Sudbury Wy
C1 1 Davids Wk 2 Halewood Pl 3 Knotty Ms
C2 1 Budworth Dr 2 Felsted Av 3 Halewood Wy 4 Kingham Cl 5 Warton Cl 6 Whitney Pl
C4 1 Dunmow Wy
C6 1 Braydon Cl
C8 1 Ramsbrook Cl
D2 1 Blackberry Gv 2 Edenhall Dr 3 Hazelwood Av 4 Honeysuckle Cl 5 Magnolia Cl 6 Riding Fold
D3 1 Lancing Rd
D4 1 Pembrey Wy
D8 1 Wellbrook Cl
E2 1 Comfrey Gv 2 Okell St 3 Openfields Cl 4 Pipit Cl 5 Rogerson's Gn 6 Ruscar Cl
E3 1 Bullfinch Ct 2 Chaffinch Gld 3 Chudleigh Cl 4 Goldcrest Ms 5 Greenfinch Cl 6 Lapwing Cl 7 Ramsons Cl 8 Sandpiper Cl 9 Sparrowhawk Cl 10 Wren Gv
E4 1 Carlyon Wy 2 Cheriton Cl 3 Ravenfield Cl 4 Stainton Cl 5 Tarleton Cl
E5 1 Cotswolds Cresent 2 Mendip Cl
E6 1 Lonsdale Rd 2 Tiverton Rd
F2 1 Eastham Gn 2 Northern Rd 3 Penketh Gn
F3 1 Farnborough Gv 2 Yarcombe Cl
F4 1 Cambridge Dr 2 Catterick Cl 3 Fernwood Dr 4 Neasham Cl
F5 1 Penmann Cl 2 Stourvale Rd
F6 1 Blakeacre Cl 2 Georgian Cl 3 Romford Wy
F7 1 Garage Rd

Page 52

A1 1 Orchard Wy
A4 1 Beaufort Cl 2 Woodview Cres
A7 1 Acrefield Rd 2 Gainsborough Ct 3 Wilsden Rd
B4 1 Westminster Cl
B7 1 Church Meadow Wk 2 Cock Lane Ends
C1 1 Auburn Cl 2 Broxton Cl 3 Burnham Cl 4 Caxton Cl 5 Chatsworth Dr 6 Fenton Cl 7 Hambleton Cl 8 Madeline Mckenna Ct 9 Newland Cl 10 Warkworth Cl
C2 1 Rufford Cl
C3 1 Gaisgill Cl 2 Graham Cl 3 Kendal Rd 4 Sherwood Cl
C4 1 Kenneth Rd 2 Winchester Pl
C7 1 Bloomsbury Wy 2 Shipton Cl 3 Turner Cl 4 Warnley Cl
D2 1 Brentfield 2 Lingwell Av 3 Moyles Cl 4 Revesby Cl 5 Tate Cl
D4 1 Alverton Cl 2 Poulton Dr
E2 1 Jubilee Wy 2 St Thomas Ct
E4 1 Rowthorn Cl 2 Thornton
F3 1 Battersea Cl 2 Burton Cl 3 Gillbrook Cl 4 Grundy Cl 5 Whickham Cl
F3 1 Clayton Crs 2 Holkham Cl 3 Marlowe Cl
F4 1 Millington Cl 2 Wordsworth Av
F5 1 Moorside Cl 2 Rhyl St
1 Desoto Rd East 2 Desoto Rd West

Page 53

G1 1 Birchfield Rd 2 Devon Pl 3 Laurel Bank 4 Sefton Av 5 Victoria Gv
G2 1 Birchfield Av 2 Bradshaw St
G3 1 Shelley Rd 2 Timmis Crs 3 Towneley St
G4 1 Mond Av 2 Wallace St
G5 1 Alexandra St 2 Alforde St 3 Bold St 4 Chapel St 5 Darlington Cl 6 Eleanor St 7 Ellis St 8 Emily St 9 Finlan Rd 10 Guest St 11 Lewis Crs 12 Luton St 13 Major Cross St 14 Market St 15 Millar Crs 16 Miners Wy 17 St Paul's Rd 18 Thomas St 19 Vicarage Rd 20 Victoria Rd 21 Violet St 22 Witt Rd
G6 1 Hutchinson St 2 Marsh St
G7 1 Chidlow Cl 2 Constance Wy 3 Dock Rd 4 Queensway 5 Short St 6 White St 7 Wilkinson Cl

2 Doward St 3 Stanley Cl 4 Susan St

J5 1 Bell House Rd 2 Black Denton's Pl 3 Cliffe St 4 Edwin St 5 Esther St 6 Harris St 7 Henry St 8 Parr St 9 Richmond St 10 Sadler St 11 Taylor St
K1 1 Crow Wood Pl 2 Selwyn Cl
K1 1 Barnes Cl 2 Drummond Ct 3 Moore Cl
K2 1 East St 2 Edward St 3 Hargreaves Cl 4 Norland St 5 Sussex St 6 Walter St
K3 1 Belfield Av 2 Butterfield Cl 3 Blue Briar Wd 4 Hill Top Cl 5 Ravenoak Rd
H4 1 Jesmond Gv 2 Ravenswood Dr 3 Summerlea
H6 1 Chapel Wks 2 Crowland Gdns 3 Lyncombe Cl 4 Melbury Rd
H7 1 Dickens Cl 2 Gorselands
M1 1 Shelton Cl

Page 56

B2 1 Bridgewater Ms 2 Carlisle St 3 Carlton St 4 Hawthorne Rd
F2 1 Stanley Pl
F6 1 Woodstock Gdns
F7 1 Chatwell Gdns 2 Eversley Cl

Page 63

G2 1 Beacon Dr 2 Compton Dr 3 Crowthorn Dr 4 Enford Av 5 Shepton Dr 6 Spalding Dr
H5 1 Chicago Av 2 Exit Rd West 3 Malaga Av 4 Terminal Rd East 5 Terminal Rd South
G4 1 Aldercroft Av 2 Brimscombe Av 3 Buttermere Av 4 Harry Rowley Cl 5 Hucclecote Av 6 Saintsbridge Rd 7 Twigworth Rd
J3 1 Cranesbill Cl 2 Daisyfield Cl 3 Goodridge Av 4 Hertle Dr 5 Lullington Cl 6 Poynings Dr 7 Purbeck Cl 8 Ringmer Dr 9 Rottingdene Dr 10 Saltdene Rd 11 Somerby Dr
K1 1 Birch Tree Dr 2 Crawley Av 3 Longmere Av 4 Ryeburn Av
K3 1 Bardsea Av 2 Brayford Rd 3 Falmer Dr 4 Knowe Av 5 Mossack Av
M5 1 Emerald Rd

Page 64

B1 1 Crummock Rd 2 Ennerdale Rd 3 Loweswater Rd 4 Wasdale Dr
H1 1 Ainsdale Dr 2 Ashbrook Cl 3 Green Gables Cl 4 Hurstvale Av 5 Motcombe Farm Rd 6 Willow Tree Ms
H2 1 Hawthorn Av 2 Larch Av 3 Lime Av 4 Mount Pleasant 5 Pine Av
H3 1 Bradley Wy 2 Cross St 3 Lower Appleton Rd 4 Maple Av 5 Mount St 6 Robert St 7 Routledge St 8 Saxon Ter 9 Westmorland Av
H4 1 Alfred Cl 2 Elliot St 3 Gerrard St 4 Grenfell St 5 Hibbert St 6 Liebig St 7 Lugsdale Rd 8 Midwood St 9 Rylands St 10 Salisbury St 11 Timperley St 12 Travis St
H5 1 Batherton Cl 2 Caroline St 3 Elizabeth Cl 4 Lacey Ct 5 Margaret Ct 6 Pool St 7 Sutton's La 8 Trinity Pl

Page 65

G1 1 Kenilworth Av 2 Linden Rd 3 Northwood Av

G2 1 Woodthorpe Dr
D1 1 Almond Tree Rd 2 Hulme Hall Cl 3 Larch Av 4 Pinfold Dr
G4 1 Beechwood Gv 2 School La 3 Upton Av
G4 1 Fulbrook Dr 2 Newbury Cl 3 Rushton Rd
H1 1 Watersedge Cl 2 Windfields Cl
H2 1 Sedgemoor Cl 2 Station Rd 3 Warren Rd
H3 1 East St 2 Edward St 3 Hargreaves Cl 4 Norland St 5 Sussex St 6 Walter St
H4 1 Jesmond Gv 2 Ravenswood Dr 3 Summerlea
H6 1 Chapel Wks 2 Crowland Gdns 3 Lyncombe Cl 4 Melbury Rd
H7 1 Dickens Cl 2 Gorselands
M1 1 Ladybridge Ri
J3 1 Meadowside
J5 1 Park Cates Av 2 Ravenoak Rd
J5 1 Hollython Av 2 Orchard Cl
F6 1 Shrewsbury Gdns 2 Thorney Dr
J7 1 Derwent Dr
K3 1 Arden Cl 2 Cherry Orchard Cl 3 The Paddock 4 Roseneath
K5 1 Briarstead Cl 2 Convamore Rd 3 Glenholme Rd
H5 1 Briarlands Cl 2 Greenway 3 Victoria Cl
L4 1 Carlton Av 2 Kenwood Av 3 Norwood Av
J2 1 Chisworth Cl 2 Lausanne Rd 3 Midland Wk 4 North Park Rd 5 Parkside Wk 6 Zurich Gdns
L4 1 Lawton Gn
L5 1 Barley St 2 Brixham Wk
L6 1 Bramley Cl 2 Bramley Dr 3 Manley Gv
M5 1 Helston Cl 2 Launceston Cl 3 Penhale Ms 4 Thorley Ms
M7 1 Bowen Cl

Page 66

A1 1 Duncombe Cl
A2 1 Hendham Cl 2 Reveton Gn 3 Winslade Cl
A3 1 Alston Cl 2 Harford Cl 3 Langston Gn 4 Modbury Cl
A5 1 Hillside Cl 2 Troon Cl
A6 1 Highfield Rd
B8 1 Widgeon Cl
C1 1 Norman Av 2 Walden Crs
C2 1 Shirley Cl
C5 1 Horsham Av 2 St Ann's Rd 3 St David's Rd
C8 1 Hazelbadge Cl
D1 1 Albert St 2 Albion St 3 Ash St 4 Brewer's Gn 5 Buxton St 6 Charles St 7 Crown Ct 8 Gordon Av 9 Grosvenor St 10 John St 11 Lyme St 12 Newborne Cl 13 Powell St 14 Smithy St 15 Springfield Av 16 Station Vw 17 Willard St 18 Yeoman Cl
D2 1 Marsland St 2 Norbury Gv 3 Wild St
D4 1 Charnwood Crs 2 Tamworth St
D7 1 Abbotsbury Cl 2 Covell Rd 3 Dundrennan Cl 4 Hartland Cl 5 Selby Cl
D8 1 Bylands Cl 2 Lambourn Cl 3 Tewkesbury Cl
E1 1 Back Chapel St 2 Bowden St 3 Grove St 4 Hazel St 5 Victoria Av 6 Vine St 7 Wesley St
E2 1 The Boulevard 2 Brook St 3 Daniel St 4 Grundey St 5 Spring V
E3 1 Barrule Av
E4 1 Lavenham Cl 2 Rowley Rd
E8 1 Mayfair Cl
F1 1 Cromdale Av 2 Wellington St
F2 1 Avondale Rd
F3 1 Carlton Pl 2 Kyle Rd 3 Lochmaddy Cl
F4 1 Capesthorne Cl
F8 1 Blenheim Cl 2 Mallard Cl 3 Ragley Cl 4 School La

Page 72

A2 1 Castlefields Av North
A3 1 Constables Cl 2 Green Bridge Cl
A4 1 Brereton Cl 2 Castlefields Av South 3 Village Cl
A5 1 Iveagh Cl
A7 1 Hawkshead Cl 2 Oxmoor Cl 3 Peckfield Cl
A8 1 Skiddaw Cl
B5 1 Silkstone Crs
B6 1 Allendale 2 Bodmin Cl 3 Mullion Cl 4 Wharfedale
B7 1 Bartlegate 2 Broome Ct 3 Clover Ct 4 Coney Gv 5 Goulders Ct 6 Killncroft
E4 1 Priory Rd 2 Southwood Av 3 Townfield Rd
C5 1 Sandalwood
C4 1 Kings Meadow 2 Saddlers Rd 3 Stoney Holt
E5 1 Cloverfield
C6 1 Camborne Cl 2 Launceston Cl 3 Newbridge Cl 4 Penare Gorran Hvn 5 Tintagel Cl 6 Truro Cl
C7 1 Backford Cl 2 Calverly Cl 3 Granby Cl 4 Halsall Cl 5 Linwood Cl 6 Wellbrook Cl
D2 1 Adlington Rd 2 Ashbury Cl 3 Harvard Cl 4 Haywood Crs 5 Swinden Cl
D3 1 Camden Cl 2 Chorlton Cl 3 Culford Cl 4 Gooseberry La 5 Winton Gv
D4 1 Dorrington Cl 2 Heron Cl 3 Mellor Cl 4 Ossett Cl
D5 1 Barton Cl 2 Baxter Cl 3 Chiswick Cl 4 Hitchen's Cl 5 Humphrey's Cl 6 Micklegate 7 Neptune Cl 8 Sabre Cl 9 Sovereign Cl
D6 1 Bournemouth Cl 2 Navigation Cl 3 Quadrant Cl 4 Schooner Cl

Page 73

G1 1 Alcock St 2 Bridgewater St 3 Canon St 4 Clarence Ter 5 Cooper St 6 Egerton St 7 Granville St 8 Loch St 9 Penketh's La 10 Princess St 11 Public Hall St 12 Wellington St
H1 1 Ann St 2 Fredric St 3 Grosvenor St 4 Pinellas 5 St John's Brow 6 St John's St
H2 1 Malcolm St 2 Sewell St 3 Sutton St 4 Wilding Av 5 Windmill St
H3 1 Marina Gv
H4 1 Heath Road Cres
H6 1 Cheltenham Crs 2 Claverton Cl 3 Glenville Cl 4 Woodford Cl
J2 1 Cambridge St 2 Cartwright St 3 Grange Park Av 4 Stenhills Crs 5 Vahler Ter
J5 1 Bickley Cl 2 Lavender Cl
J6 1 Laburnum Gv
J6 1 Kempton Cl 2 Thirsk Cl
K2 1 Henley Cl 2 Needham Cl 3 Tenby Dr
K3 1 The Winnows
K4 1 Davenport Rw

Page 74

A2 1 Brackley St 2 Clarence St 3 Edith St 4 Egerton St 5 Greek St 6 Grove St 7 Handley St 8 Lord St 9 Speakman St
A3 1 Burland Cl 2 Curzon St 3 Drayton Cl 4 The Elms 5 Havergal St 6 Lightburn St 7 Queen's Cl 8 Southlands Ms 9 Stapley Cl 10 Westfield Ms
A4 1 Cawley St 2 Chaucer St 3 Hawthorn Av 4 Salisbury St
A5 1 Albert St 2 Arthur St 3 Back High St 4 Brook St 5 Devonshire Pl 6 Eaton St 7 Greenway Rd 8 High St 9 Nelson St 10 New St 11 Oakmere St 12 Queensway 13 Surrey St 14 Vine St 15 Walton St
B5 1 Priory Rd 2 Southwood Av 3 Townfield Rd
C4 1 Kings Meadow 2 Saddlers Rd 3 Stoney Holt
C5 1 Sandalwood
C6 1 Camborne Cl 2 Launceston Cl 3 Newbridge Cl 4 Penare Gorran Hvn 5 Tintagel Cl 6 Truro Cl

Page 84

A5 1 Hawthorn Pk 2 Hawthorn Vw 3 Hawthorn Wk 4 Kings Cl
A6 1 Earls Wy 2 Putney Cl 3 Spennymoor St
A7 1 Kensington Ct 2 St James' Dr 3 Sandringham Wy
B2 1 Alderley Lodge 2 Grosvenor Cl 3 Westminster Dr
B2 1 Styal Vw
B3 1 Carr Mill Ms 2 Marbury Rd
B3 1 Grove St 2 Warham St
B6 1 Covington Pl 2 Green Hall Ms
C2 1 Stanneylands Cl
C2 1 Chadwick Cl 2 Shargate Cl
C4 1 Calverley Cl 2 Connaught Cl 3 Fernwood Cl 4 Gladewood Cl
C7 1 Croftside Wy
D1 1 Anderton Wy 2 The Link 3 Thornton Dr 4 Wilmslow Rd
D2 1 Bankside Cl 2 Brandon Cl 3 Oakenclough Cl 4 Roctepool Cl 5 Rookerypool Cl 6 Viewlands Dr
D4 1 Fairywell Cl 2 Ringstead Cl 3 Rossenclough Rd 4 Sedgeford Cl
D5 1 Manor Gdns 2 Rodeheath Cl 3 Yew Tree Cl
D6 1 Avondale Ri
E1 1 Old Hall Cl 2 Wadsworth Cl
E2 1 Bidston Dr 2 Peckmill Cl
E6 1 Goosetrey Cl 2 Mosswood Rd
E4 1 Beechwood Dr 2 Brackenwood Ms 3 Broomfield Cl 4 Cherry Tree Cl 5 Chestnut Cl 6 Fieldhead Ms 7 Corsefield Hey 8 Lymewood Dr 9 Reynolds Ms 10 Rowanside Dr 11 Thornfield Hey 12 Warren Hey
E5 1 Overhill Dr
E5 1 Hunters Cl
E6 1 Braeside Cl 2 Calder Wy 3 Chadwell Cl 4 Eden Cl 5 Innisfree Cl 6 Leas Cl

Page 94

E7 1 Bidston Gn 2 Burton Gn 3 Heswall Rd 4 Oxton Gn

Page 120

E4 1 Canterbury Cl 2 The Furrows 3 Keats Cl 4 Wells Cl
A2 1 Peterborough Cl 2 Woodstock Cl
A3 1 Badgers Gn 2 Bangor Cl 3 Bramley Cl 4 Gloucester Cl 5 Green Lawns Dr 6 Lambourne Cl 7 Larchdale Cl 8 Laxton Cl 9 St Georges Gn 10 Salisbury Cl 11 Truro Cl 12 West Park Dr
A4 1 Lea Bank Cl
A6 1 Park Mount Cl 2 Shadewood Rd
A7 1 Grisedale Wy 2 Manley Rd 3 Sussex Av
A8 1 Hillcrest Rd 2 Moss View Rd
E2 1 Elm Dr 2 Meadow Wy

Page 121

K2 1 Buckingham Gdns 2 Caernarvon Ct 3 Criccieth Ct 4 Ewloe Ct 5 Flint Ct 6 Hawarden Gdns 7 Sandringham Gdns
J1 1 Acacia Cl 2 Birchwood Cl 3 Manna Dr 4 Sorbus Cl
H1 1 Goodwood Cl 2 Hill Top 3 Laburnum Crs 4 Townfield Cl
J5 1 Cloverdale 2 The Hawthorns 3 Kestrel Rd 4 Mulberry Ri 5 Sylvan Cl
J6 1 Milner Rd
J7 1 Kingsley Cl 2 Marshalls Ct 3 Thorn La 4 Woodlands Rd East
K6 1 Manor St
C1 1 Barnside Wy 2 Haydock Cl 3 Moorlands Cl 4 Pasture Cl 5 Thetford Cl 6 Thirsk Wy
C2 1 Beechwood Ms 2 Cheveley Cl 3 Stoneleigh Cl 4 Woburn Cl
C6 1 Adlington St 2 Albert St 3 Anderson St 4 Boothby St 5 Charlton St 6 Cumberland St 7 George St West 8 Great Queen St 9 Grosvenor St 10 Hall St 11 Hope St West 12 King Edward St 13 Langford St 14 Pierce St 15 Pinfold St 16 Pownall Sq 17 Poynton St 18 Sharpley St 19 Tynedale Cl 20 Walker St 21 Waterloo St West 22 Westminster St 23 Whalley Mews
C5 1 Back Paradise St 2 Blackshaw St 3 Crossall St 4 Crown St West 5 Hatton St 6 Henderson St 7 Holland St 8 Marsden Ter 9 Norbury St 10 Peter St West 11 St John's Rd 12 Water St 13 Whiston St
C6 1 Barton St 2 Grange Rd
K5 1 Walnut Cl
M6 1 Ambleside 2 Dunham Wy 3 Shipbrook Rd 4 Shocklach Rd

Page 123

B1 1 Hayfield Cl 2 Holcombe Dr 3 Portmarnock Cl 4 Weybridge St
B2 1 Folkestone Cl 2 Kirkstall Cl 3 Maidstone Cl 4 Merriden Cl 5 Sevenoaks Cl 6 Wetheral Rd
B5 1 Cherington Cl 2 Edward St 3 Honeshow Cl 4 Stevenage Cl
B6 1 Cambridge Av 2 Cherington Cl 3 Rudyard Cl 4 Sycamore Ri
B7 1 Cloverdale Rd 2 Haddon Cl 3 Harewood Wy 4 Haworth Cl 5 The Roaches
E5 1 Allen St 2 Bank St 3 Cawley St 4 Dainty St 5 Dainty Ter 6 Goodall St 7 Green St 8 Hallefield Crs 9 Hallefield Dr 10 Hallefield Rd 11 Jodrell Cl 12 Knight's Ct 13 Leigh St 14 Lower Bank St 15 Parker St 16 Pearson St 17 Quayside Vw 18 Stubbs Ter
E6 1 Bradley St 2 Byrons St 3 Coronation St 4 Cuncliff Cl 5 Higginbotham Gn 6 Richmond Pl 7 Rose St 8 Square St 9 Tabor Strret
E7 1 Mee St 2 Slack St
F2 1 Arundel Cl 2 Lathom Wy
F3 1 Delamere Av 2 Howe St 3 Pleasant St 4 Timber St
F4 1 Wayside Rd 2 William St
F5 1 Capesthorne Wy 2 Eddisbury Ter 3 Hollands Pl 4 Roan Ms 5 Toll Bar Av 6 Watermill Cl

Page 129

B1 1 Brennus Pl 2 Cambrian Rd 3 Canal St 4 Canning St 5 Delamere St 6 Enderby Rd 7 Garden Ct 8 Hunter St 9 King St 10 Little Abbey Gateway 11 Mason St 12 Raymond St 13 The Yonne
J3 1 Bedward Rw 2 Crook St 3 Grey Friars 4 Hamilton Pl 5 Hunters Wk 6 Linen Hall Pl 7 Nicholas Street Ms 8 Old Hall Pl 9 Pierpoint Ct 10 Princess St 11 Sens Cl 12 Stanley Place Ms 13 Trinity St 14 Watergate St 15 White Friars
J4 1 Bunce St
J5 1 Powell's Orch 2 Selsdon Ct
K1 1 Church St 2 Eardswick Cl 3 Gloucester St 4 Gonsley Cl 5 Hornby St 6 Stafford St 7 Trafford St 8 Wroxham Cl
K2 1 Back Queen St 2 Brook Pl 3 George St 4 Henry Pl 5 James St 6 Kaleyards 7 Oulton Pl 8 Queens Pl 9 St Anne St 10 Samuel St 11 Victoria Rd
K3 1 Bridge St 2 Leen La 3 Lumley Pl 4 Newgate St 5 Priory Pl 6 St Werburgh St 7 Souter's La

Page 130

K3 1 Albion Pl 2 Lower Bridge St 3 Mary's Hl 4 St Olave St 5 Steele St
K2 1 Belgrave Pl 2 Greenwood Av 3 Hugh St 4 Overleigh St 5 Pretoria St
L1 1 Gresford Av 2 Pickering St
L3 1 Albert St 2 Bold Sq 3 Francis St 4 Lee St 5 Seaville St 6 Seller St 7 Steam Mill St
L3 1 Bath St 2 Forest St
L4 1 Eastern Pathway 2 St John's Rear Rd 3 South Crescent Rd
L5 1 Allington La
L4 1 Bishop St 2 Burges St 3 Gosforth Pl 4 Kilmorey Park Rd 5 Law St 6 Longburgh Cl 7 Prescot St 8 Stone Pl 9 Sumpter Pathway 10 Tomkinson St
M2 1 Matthew Cl
M3 1 The Mount

Page 137

B1 1 Marlowe Ct 2 Mayfield Ter 3 Stamford Rd 4 Stratford Wy
C8 1 Ash Ter 2 Cleaver Ms 3 Cornbrook Rd 4 Parkgate Rd 5 Torr Rd
D1 1 The Coppice 2 Hawthorn Ms 3 Hedgerow Dr
D2 1 Tennyson Cl
E1 1 Buckfast Ct
E5 1 Marina Village 2 Moresby Cl 3 Talisman Cl
K6 1 Aston Gn 2 Portsmouth Pl 3 Southampton Wy 4 Weymouth Cl
L2 1 Kingston Cl 2 Warrington Rd
L3 1 The Heys
L5 1 Earls Wy 2 Putney Cl 3 Spennymoor St
L6 1 Hobby Ct 2 Hunters Cl 3 Rothbury Cl 4 Seneschal Cl
L7 1 Bowland Cl 2 Brambling Cl 3 Mosedale Cv 4 Stonechat Cl 5 Whinfell Gv
L8 1 Bramble Wy 2 Dunngall Gv 3 Pippits Rw
M1 1 Marsh La
M3 1 Cheshyre Dr 2 The Green
M5 1 Thomas Ct
M6 1 Cote Lea Ct 2 Deer Park Ct
M7 1 Cherry Blossom Rd 2 Graylag Cl 3 Kingfisher Cl 4 Mallard Ri 5 Rosemary Av
M8 1 Ashbrook Av 2 Aster Crs 3 Audlem Cl 4 Azalea Gv 5 Bluebell Cl 6 Larkspur Cl 7 Lobelia Gv 8 Magnolia Dr 9 Millington Cl 10 Ovington Cl 11 Peckforton Dr 12 Stonecrop Cl 13 Verbena Cl 14 Weaverside Av

Page 138

A2 1 Peterborough Cl 2 Woodstock Cl
A3 1 Argyll Cl 2 Atholl Cl 3 Blenheim Cl 4 Montrose Cl 5 Murray Cl 6 Roxburgh Cl
A4 1 Lea Bank Cl
A6 1 Park Mount Cl 2 Shadewood Rd
A7 1 Grisedale Wy 2 Manley Rd 3 Sussex Av
A8 1 Hillcrest Rd 2 Moss View Rd

Page 142

B6 1 Ashfield Rd 2 Connaught Av 3 Gloucester Av 4 Health St 5 King Edward St 6 Lavender Ct 7 St David's Ct 8 Salisbury St 9 Windsor Av
B8 1 Castle Hill St 2 Elmwood Cl 3 St Ethelwold's St 4 South Bank
D8 1 Pembroke Cl 2 Radnor Cl
G8 1 Hereford Pl
C7 1 Bank St 2 Broken Banks 3 Crossall St 4 Eden Cl 5 Hobson St 6 Lower Exchange St 7 Mill St 8 Nelson St 9 Newgate 10 Paradise St 11 Park Gn 12 Parsonage St 13 Roe St 14 Sunderland St 15 Townley Pl 16 Townley St 17 Wardle St 18 Wellington St
C7 1 Canton St 2 Cholmondeley St 3 Coronation St 4 Hall St 5 Harpur Cl 6 Jackson St 7 St Barnabas St 8 St George's Pl 9 Smith St 10 Thistleton Cl
D7 1 Chantry Cl 2 Danes St 3 Coathland Wy 4 Hall St 5 Lomas Sq 6 London Road Ter 7 Sanders Sq 8 Sherwood Rd
D8 1 Frith Ter 2 Moss Sq

Page 145

C5 1 Landsowne Gv 2 Rothesay Rd
D6 1 Compton Pl 2 Waltham Rd

Page 166

B1 1 Birchfield Crs 2 Moorfield Cl 3 Mountfield Rd 4 Wedgwood Rd

Page 168

E6 1 Beaumont Cl 2 Isabella Cl 3 Laburnum Gv 4 Mountain Vw
E7 1 Capeland Cl 2 Elm Gv 3 Halkett St 4 Kinnerton Cl 5 Shannon Cl 6 Sheringham Cl 7 Stanley Park Ct 8 Tatton Cl 9 Weybourne Cl
F6 1 Abingdon Crs 2 Bray Rd 3 Eaton St 4 Fairford Rd 5 Guildford Cl 6 Lynton Cl 7 Newbury Rd 8 Redhill Rd 9 Shrewsbury Dr 10 Sunbury Crs 11 Telford Wy 12 Wenlock Wy 13 Westbury Wy 14 Wrekin Wy

Page 169

C5 1 Landsowne Gv 2 Rothesay Rd
D6 1 Meadow Field Rd 2 Snowdon Crescent
H2 1 Cambrian Rd 2 Charlotte St 3 Goodwood Cl 4 Jesmond Rd 5 Kempton Cl
H7 1 Chiltern Cl 2 Johnsons Cl
J1 1 Abbot's Nook 2 Gaymoore Cl 3 Henshall Rd

Page 170

A1 1 Coppins Cl 2 Jamieson Cl 3 Stirling Cl 4 Woodlands La
A7 1 Blackthorn Cl

Page 177

G2 1 Ferndale Gdns 2 Wentworth Dr
G3 1 Badgers Cl 2 Beckenham Av 3 Bridgewater Pl 4 Farriers Wy 5 Meadow Ri 6 Otters Bank 7 Pipers Ash 8 Redstone Dr 9 Thornycroft
G4 1 Brackenhale Wy 2 Hampstead Ct 3 Manor Sq 4 Newbury Av 5 St James Wy 6 Southwark Pl 7 Victoria Sq
G5 1 Quantock Cl
H2 1 Aston Av
H3 1 Delamere Ri
H4 1 Oak House La 2 Pentland Cl
H4 1 Caernarvon Cl 2 Cheviot Cl 3 Launceston Cl 4 Llandovery Cl 5 Pembroke Cl 6 Snowdonia Av

Notes

Notes

Notes

Notes

Notes